Handbook of
U.S. Labor Statistics

Employment, Earnings, Prices, Productivity, and Other Labor Data

13th Edition
2010

HANDBOOK OF U.S. LABOR STATISTICS

Employment, Earnings, Prices, Productivity, and Other Labor Data

13th Edition
2010

Edited by Mary Meghan Ryan

Lanham, MD

Published in the United States of America
by Bernan Press, a wholly owned subsidiary of
The Rowman & Littlefield Publishing Group, Inc.
4501 Forbes Boulevard, Suite 200
Lanham, Maryland 20706

Bernan Press
800-865-3457
info@bernan.com
www.bernan.com

ISBN-13: 978-1-59888-404-3
eISBN-13: 978-1-59888-405-0

ISSN: 1526-2553

♾™ The paper used in this publication meets the minimum requirements of American National Standard for Information Sciences—Permanence of Paper for Printed Library Materials, ANSI/NISO Z39.48-1992.
Manufactured in the United States of America.

CONTENTS

LIST OF TABLES

CHAPTER 1: POPULATION, LABOR FORCE, AND EMPLOYMENT STATUS

POPULATION, LABOR FORCE, AND EMPLOYMENT STATUS

CHAPTER 2: EMPLOYMENT, HOURS, AND EARNINGS

EMPLOYMENT AND HOURS

EARNINGS

CHAPTER 3: OCCUPATIONAL EMPLOYMENT AND WAGES

CHAPTER 4: LABOR FORCE AND EMPLOYMENT PROJECTIONS BY INDUSTRY AND OCCUPATION

CHAPTER 5: PRODUCTIVITY AND COSTS

CHAPTER 6: COMPENSATION OF EMPLOYEES

EMPLOYER COSTS FOR EMPLOYEE COMPENSATION (ECEC)

EMPLOYEE BENEFITS SURVEY

OCCUPATIONAL EARNINGS

CHAPTER 7: RECENT TRENDS IN THE LABOR MARKET

MASS LAYOFFS

JOB OPENINGS, HIRES, AND SEPARATIONS

CHAPTER 8: LABOR-MANAGEMENT RELATIONS

CHAPTER 9: PRICES

PRODUCER PRICE INDEX

CONSUMER PRICE INDEX

EXPORT AND IMPORT PRICE INDEXES

CHAPTER 10: INTERNATIONAL LABOR COMPARISONS

CHAPTER 11: CONSUMER EXPENDITURES

CHAPTER 12: AMERICAN TIME USE SURVEY

CHAPTER 13: INCOME DATA IN THE UNITED STATES (CENSUS BUREAU)

CHAPTER 14: OCCUPATIONAL SAFETY AND HEALTH

LIST OF FIGURES

PREFACE

Bernan Press is pleased to present a compilation of Bureau of Labor Statistics (BLS) data in this 13th edition of its award-winning *Handbook of U.S Labor Statistics: Employment, Earnings, Prices, Productivity, and Other Labor Data*. BLS provides a treasure trove of historical information about all aspects of labor and employment in the United States. The current edition maintains the content of previous editions and updates the text with additional data and new features. The data in this *Handbook* are excellent sources of information for analysts in both government and the private sector.

The *Handbook* addresses many of the issues that are being discussed across the United States, such as high unemployment and the recession that began in December 2007, the rapidly increasing costs of health care services and prescription drugs, the decline in real median household income, and the dramatic aging of the labor force. In addition, this publication provides an abundance of data on topics such as prices, productivity, consumer expenditures, occupational safety and health, international labor comparisons, and much more.

The comprehensive and historical data presented in the *Handbook* allow the user to understand the background of current events and compare today's economy with previous years. Select data in this publication go back to 1913 and several tables have data going back to the 1940s.

FEATURES OF THIS PUBLICATION

- Over 200 tables that present authoritative data on labor market statistics, including employment and unemployment, mass layoffs, prices, productivity, and data from the American Time Use Survey (ATUS).

- Each section is preceded by a figure that calls attention to noteworthy trends in the data.

- In addition to the figures, the introductory material for to each chapter also contains highlights of other salient data. For example, the highlights in Chapter 1 showcase the increase in unemployment and in Chapter 4, the highlights call attention to employment projections from 2008 to 2018.

- The tables in each section are also preceded by notes and definitions, which contain concise descriptions of the data sources, concepts, definitions, and methodology from which the data are derived.

- The introductory notes also include references to more comprehensive reports. These reports provide additional data and more extensive descriptions of estimation methods, sampling, and reliability measures.

- The 13th edition of the *Handbook* also includes an article titled "U.S. Labor Market in 2008: Economy in Recession" from the March 2009 edition of the *Monthly Labor Review*, a BLS publication. The article examines the weaknesses in the labor market that began during the second half of 2007 and worsened during 2008 as the U.S. economy entered a recession; unemployment rose sharply, both employment and the employment-population ratio declined, and median weekly earnings grew at about the same rate as inflation in 2008.

NEW IN THIS EDITION

Several changes have taken place in this edition. Most notably, Chapter 10 "International Labor Comparisons" (formerly titled Foreign Labor Price Statistics) and Chapter 13 "Income Data in the United States (Census Bureau)" have been expanded to include additional tables. The new tables in Chapter 10 compare unemployment rates by sex and age, women's share of the labor force, and employment in agriculture, industry, and manufacturing in 10 different countries. The new tables in Chapter 13 include data on the change in real median household income during recessions as well as median household and family income by state.

In addition, there are new tables in Chapter 6 "Compensation of Employees" on employee benefits, as well as several new figures throughout the book on a variety of topics, including the Consumer Price Index (CPI), median income by state, and occupational safety and health.

SOURCES OF ADDITIONAL INFORMATION

BLS data are primarily derived from surveys conducted by the federal government or through federal-state cooperative arrangements. The comparability of data over time can be affected by changes in the surveys, which are essential for keeping pace with the current structure of economic institutions and for taking advantage of improved survey techniques. Revisions of current data are also periodically made as a result of the availability of new information. In addition, some tables in this *Handbook* were dropped due to the data being from a one-time survey that is now outdated or due to the survey being entirely restructured. Introductory notes to each chapter summarize specific factors that may affect the data. In the tables, the ellipsis character ("…") indicates that data are not available.

More extensive methodological information, including further discussion of the sampling and estimation procedures used for each BLS program, is contained in the *BLS Handbook of Methods*. This publication is in the process of being updated, and completed chapters are available on the BLS Web site at <http://www.bls.gov>. Other sources of current data and analytical include the *Monthly Labor Review* and a daily Internet publication, *The Editor's Desk* (TED). All of these publications can be found on the BLS Web site as well. Other relevant publications, including those from the Census Bureau, are noted in the notes and definitions in each chapter.

OTHER PUBLICATIONS BY BERNAN PRESS

The *Handbook of U.S. Labor Statistics Handbook of U.S Labor Statistics: Employment, Earnings, Prices, Productivity, and Other Labor Data* is just one of a number of publications in Bernan Press's award-winning U.S. DataBook Series. Other titles include *The Almanac of American Education*; *Business Statistics of the United States: Patterns of Economic Change*; *Crime in the United State*; *State Profiles: The Population and Economy of Each U.S. State*; *United States Foreign Trade Highlights: Trends in the Global Market*; and *Vital Statistics of the United States: Births, Life Expectancy, Deaths, and Selected Health Data*. In addition, Bernan Press publishes *Employment, Hours, and Earnings: States and Areas* as a special edition of this *Handbook*. Each of these titles provides the public with statistical information from official government sources.

If you have any questions or suggestions as to how we could make future editions even more useful, please contact us by e-mail at info@bernan.com or by letter at Bernan Press, 4051 Forbes Boulevard, Suite 200, Lanham, MD 20706. Please visit our Web site at <http://www.bernan.com>.

ARTICLE

U.S. LABOR MARKET IN 2008: ECONOMY IN RECESSION

The following article, written by James Marschall Borbely, is excerpted from the March 2009 edition of the Monthly Labor Review, *a Bureau of Labor Statistics (BLS) publication. The full article can be found on the BLS Web site at <http://www.bls.gov/opub/mlr/2009/03/contents.htm>. James Marschall Borbely is an economist in the Division of Labor Force Statistics at BLS. For more information on the Current Population Survey (CPS), please see Chapter 1 of this* Handbook.

CPS data show that the labor market weakness that began during the second half of 2007 worsened during 2008 as the U.S. economy entered a recession; unemployment rose sharply, both employment and the employment-population ratio declined, and median weekly earnings grew at about the same rate as inflation in 2008.

Turmoil in the housing, credit, and financial markets plagued the U.S. economy in 2008, and the National Bureau of Economic Research (NBER) identified December 2007 as the beginning of a recession.[1] The labor market started to slide during the second half of 2007 and continued sliding throughout 2008. In the fourth quarter of 2008, the unemployment rate rose to 6.9 percent and the unemployment level reached 10.6 million, an increase of 2.1 percentage points and 3.3 million persons, respectively, over the fourth quarter of 2007. The current recession has hit the labor market particularly hard. The increase in the unemployment rate in 2008 was larger than that experienced during the 2001 recession and was the largest fourth-quarter-to-fourth-quarter increase since 1982.

The number of employed persons aged 16 years and older, as measured by the Current Population Survey (CPS), was 144.0 million in the fourth quarter of 2008, 2.2 million lower than a year earlier.[2] This over-the-year decrease more than offset the 654,000 increase in 2007. The last time employment declined over the year was in 2001, also a recessionary period. Reflecting the employment decline in 2008, the employment-population ratio also fell during the year, from 62.8 percent in the fourth quarter of 2007 to a fourth-quarter 2008 figure of 61.3 percent, the lowest ratio since the first quarter of 1987, when it was 61.1 percent. The 1.5-percentage-point over-the-year decline was the largest fourth-quarter-to-fourth-quarter decline in the history of the series, which dates back to 1948.

While unemployment increased and employment contracted in 2008, the labor force participation rate was essentially unchanged, indicating that much of the downturn in the labor market resulted from individuals losing jobs.

In 2008, individuals in the prime working age group (25 to 54 years) experienced sharp increases in unemployment; men in the age group experienced greater increases in

unemployment, and larger declines in employment, than did women. In the fourth quarter of 2008, the unemployment rate for persons of prime working age (25 to 54 years) was 5.9 percent, the highest rate since the second quarter of 1993 and up from 3.9 percent in the fourth quarter of 2007.

The number of unemployed persons aged 25 to 54 years, 6.1 million in the fourth quarter of 2008, increased by 2.1 million over the year. The unemployment rate for prime-working-age men rose by 2.4 percentage points, to 6.2 percent, in the fourth quarter of 2008, while the unemployment rate for women aged 25 to 54 years increased from 4.0 percent to 5.5 percent that same quarter.

During 2008, the overall employment level for individuals aged 25 to 54 years fell by 2.2 million, to 98.3 million, in the fourth quarter. The significant increase in the number of unemployed men in this age group coincided with a large decrease in the number of such employed men and a decline in their employment-population ratio. Employment among men in the 25-to-54-year-old age group decreased by 1.6 million, accounting for about three-quarters of the decline in employment of prime-working-age individuals in 2008, and the men's employment-population ratio fell by 2.6 percentage points, to 84.6 percent. By comparison, the number of employed prime-working-age women was down by 528,000 in the fourth quarter of 2008, and their employment-population ratio fell by 0.7 percentage point, to 71.7 percent. (See Table 1.) One reason men made up the majority of the employment decline in 2008 is that employment in historically male-dominated occupations, such as construction and extraction, fell sharply over the year.

In 2008, young workers were affected by poor labor market conditions more than workers aged 55 years and older were. In general, age helps explain variations in the labor market success of individuals, because, as older workers gain more experience and accumulate more skills, their marketability rises, resulting in longer job tenure and, ultimately, lower unemployment rates than those of young workers. In 2008, labor force participation and employment continued to trend upward for workers aged 55 years and older, but labor market conditions weakened for workers aged 16 to 19 years, as the group's unemployment rose sharply and labor force participation and employment declined.

In the fourth quarter of 2008, the labor force participation rate for teenagers 16 to 19 years was 38.7 percent, 2.4 percentage points lower than a year earlier. This group's rate has been on a downward trend since its most recent high of 52.6 percent in the second quarter of 2000 and is currently the lowest rate in the history of the series, which began in 1948. Teenagers may be participating in the labor force at a lower rate in recent years for a number of reasons; for example, they may be facing greater pressure to do well in school, and they are attending college at higher rates.[3] By contrast, the participation rate for adults age 55 years and older continued to trend upward in 2008, increasing by 1.0 percentage point, to 39.8 percent. The participation rate for older adults has been climbing since the second quarter of 1995. Several factors may have contributed to this rise, including a gradual increase in the usual retirement age for receiving Social Security benefits, a decline in the number of individuals covered by defined-benefit plans, and the decreased availability of employer-provided retiree health benefits.[4]

The jobless rate among teenagers (16 to 19 years) was 20.7 percent in the fourth quarter of 2008, 4.4 percentage points higher than a year earlier and the highest rate since the second quarter of 1992. The unemployment rate for young adults (20 to 24 years) also rose during 2008, increasing by 2.7 percentage points, to 11.3 percent. The unemployment rate for individuals aged 55 years and older increased by 1.7 percentage points, to 4.8 percent, in the fourth quarter of 2008.

Employment among teens dropped again in 2008, falling by 606,000, after declining by 322,000 in 2007. The teen employment-population ratio continued to trend downward and stood at 30.7 percent in the fourth quarter, 3.7 percentage points lower than a year earlier. Young adults' (20 to 24 years) employment also declined in 2008, falling by 404,000, and their employment-population ratio fell by 2.0 percentage points, to 65.7 percent. In contrast, employment among workers aged 55 years and older increased by 937,000 in the fourth quarter of 2008. The employment-population ratio for older workers rose to 37.9 percent from the 37.6-percent rate posted a year earlier. (See Table 1.)

The major racial and ethnic groups were also adversely affected by weakness in the labor market. In 2008, unemployment rates were higher over the year for the major racial and ethnic groups. The percentage-point increase was greatest for Blacks and Hispanics, whose unemployment rates rose by 2.9 and 3.1 percentage points, to 11.5 percent and 8.9 percent, respectively, in the fourth quarter. The unemployment rate for Whites increased by 2.1 percentage points over the year, to 6.3 percent. The unemployment rate for Asians, 4.6 percent (not seasonally adjusted), was 0.9 percentage point higher than a year earlier.

In 2008, employment among the major racial and ethnic groups was lower than a year earlier. In the fourth quarter, the number of employed Whites was 118.1 million, 1.9 million lower than in the fourth quarter of 2007. The employment decline in 2008 followed a year of slowing employment growth. In 2007, employment among Whites grew by only 349,000, after increasing by 2.1 million in 2006. During 2008, employment among Hispanics or Latinos fell by 389,000, to 20.2 million, in contrast to an increase of 583,000 in 2007 and nearly 1.0 million in 2006. After experiencing virtually no employment growth in 2007 and a gain of about a half million in 2006, employment among Blacks fell by 294,000 in 2008, to 15.7 million. Employment among Asians stood at 6.8 million (not seasonally adjusted) in the fourth quarter of 2008, practically unchanged from the 6.9 million figure posted a year earlier.

Reflecting the declines in employment among the racial and ethnic groups, the employment-population ratios for these groups fell sharply during 2008. The Hispanic or Latino employment-population ratio declined by 2.7 percentage points, to 61.9 percent, in the fourth quarter of 2008. The ratio for Blacks fell by 1.8 percentage points, to 56.1 percent, and the ratio for Whites declined by 1.4 percentage points, to 62.1 percent. The employment-population ratio for Asians was 63.2 percent (not seasonally adjusted) in the fourth quarter of 2008, 1.1 percentage points lower than a year earlier. (See Table 1.)

During 2008, labor force participation for the major racial and ethnic groups remained relatively flat or edged lower. The participation rates for both Blacks and Whites were about unchanged, at 63.4 percent and 66.2 percent, respectively, in the fourth quarter of 2008. The rate for Hispanics or Latinos fell by 0.6 percentage point, to 68.0 percent. The labor force participation rate for Asians was 66.2 percent (not seasonally adjusted).

Individuals at each level of educational attainment were affected by the weak labor market in 2008, but those with less education experienced greater percentage-point increases in their unemployment rates. Education is a major determinant of success and activity in the labor market. Individuals with more education tend to have lower unemployment rates. Indeed, in 2008, individuals with less education experienced greater percentage-point increases in their unemployment rates than their more educated counterparts did. The unemployment rate for individuals 25 years and older with less than a high school diploma increased from 7.5 percent to 10.6 percent in the fourth quarter of 2008. The jobless rate for high school graduates with no college rose by 2.4 percentage points, to 7.0 percent, the highest quarterly rate since the series began in 1992. The unemployment rate for those with some college or an associate's degree increased by 2.0 percentage points, to 5.5 percent. Among college graduates, the unemployment rate increased by 1.2 percentage points, to 3.3 percent, equal to the previous peak in the fourth quarter of 1992. (See figure on page xxii.)

In 2008, the employment-population ratio decreased for all levels of educational attainment. The ratio for individuals with less than a high school diploma fell by 1.0 percentage point, to 42.3 percent. For high school graduates with no college, the ratio fell by 1.6 percentage points, to 58.1 percent. At 67.8 percent, the employment-population ratio for individuals with some college or an associate's degree was 1.5 percentage points lower than a year earlier. Finally, in the fourth quarter of 2008, the ratio for college graduates decreased by 0.9 percentage point, to 75.2 percent.

Table 1. Employment Status of the Civilian Noninstitutional Population, 16 Years and Older by Age and Selected Characteristics, Quarterly Averages, Seasonally Adjusted, 2007–2008

(Number in thousands, percent.)

Characteristic	Quarter IV, 2007	2008				Change from: quarter IV (2007) to quarter IV (2008)
		Quarter I	Quarter II	Quarter III	Quarter IV	
Total, 16 Years and Over						
Civilian labor force	153 625	153 738	154 281	154 650	154 648	1 023
Participation rate	66.0	66.0	66.1	66.1	65.9	-0.1
Employed	146 276	146 138	145 989	145 299	144 046	-2 230
Employment-population ratio	62.8	62.8	62.5	62.1	61.0	-1.5
Unemployed	7 349	7 599	8 291	9 350	10 602	3 253
Unemployment rate	4.8	4.9	5.4	6.0	6.9	2.1
Both Sexes, 16 to 19 Years						
Civilian labor force	7 012	6 867	7 049	6 880	6 629	-383
Participation rate	41.1	40.3	41.3	40.3	38.7	-2.4
Employed	5 866	5 720	5 801	5 524	5 260	-606
Employment-population ratio	34.4	33.6	34.0	32.3	30.7	-3.7
Unemployed	1 146	1 147	1 249	1 356	1 369	223
Unemployment rate	16.3	16.7	17.7	19.7	20.7	4.4
Both Sexes, 20 to 24 Years						
Civilian labor force	15 158	15 056	15 213	15 278	15 161	3
Participation rate	74.1	74.0	74.6	74.8	74.1	0.0
Employed	13 852	1 695	1 718	1 657	13 448	-404
Employment-population ratio	67.7	67.3	67.3	66.8	65.7	-2.0
Unemployed	1 306	1 361	1 494	1 621	1 713	407
Unemployment rate	8.6	9.0	9.8	10.6	11.3	2.7
Both Sexes, 25 to 54 Years						
Civilian labor force	104 503	104 265	104 430	104 603	104 407	-96
Participation rate	83.0	83.1	83.2	83.2	83.0	0.0
Employed	100 453	100 070	99 814	99 314	98 276	-2 177
Employment-population ratio	79.7	79.8	79.5	79.0	78.1	-1.6
Unemployed	4 050	4 195	4 616	5 288	6 131	2 081
Unemployment rate	3.9	4.0	4.4	5.1	5.9	2.0
Men, 25 to 54 Years						
Civilian labor force	56 451	56 219	56 156	56	561	-304
Participation rate	90.7	90.7	90.6	90.8	90.2	-0.5
Employed	54 302	5 959	53 634	53 370	52 653	-1 649
Employment-population ratio	87.2	87.1	86.5	85.9	84.6	-2.6
Unemployed	2 149	2 260	2 523	3 032	3 494	1 345
Unemployment rate	3.8	4.0	4.5	5.4	6.2	2.4
Women, 25 to 54 Years						
Civilian labor force	48 052	48 046	48 274	48 201	48 260	208
Participation rate	75.4	75.7	76.0	75.8	75.8	0.4
Employed	46 151	46 111	46 181	45 945	45 623	-528
Employment-population ratio	72.4	72.6	72.7	72.2	71.7	-0.7
Unemployed	1 901	1 935	2 093	2 256	2 637	736
Unemployment rate	4.0	4.0	4.3	4.7	5.5	1.5
Both Sexes, 55 Years and Over						
Civilian labor force	26 948	27 452	27 563	28 021	28 408	1 460
Participation rate	8.8	9.2	9.2	9.6	9.8	1.0
Employed	26 121	26 553	26 662	26 891	27 058	937
Employment-population ratio	37.6	37.9	37.9	38.0	37.9	0.3
Unemployed	826	899	901	1 130	1 350	524
Unemployment rate	3.1	3.3	3.3	4.0	0.8	1.7
White						
Civilian labor force	125 292	125 206	125 556	125 937	125 987	695
Participation rate	66.3	66.3	66.3	66.4	66.2	-0.1
Employed	119 977	119 692	119 557	119 160	118 101	-1 876
Employment-population ratio	63.5	63.4	63.2	62.8	62.1	-1.4
Unemployed	5 315	5 514	5 999	6 777	7 885	2 570
Unemployment rate	4.2	4.4	4.8	5.4	6.3	2.1
Black						
Civilian labor force	17 513	17 683	17 733	17 809	17 757	244
Participation rate	63.3	63.9	63.8	63.8	63.4	0.1
Employed	16 007	16 116	16 083	15 908	15 713	-294
Employment-population ratio	57.9	58.2	57.9	57.0	56.1	-1.8
Unemployed	1 506	1 566	1 650	1 901	2 044	538
Unemployment rate	8.6	8.9	9.0	10.7	11.5	2.9
Asian[1]						
Civilian labor force	7 172	7 170	7 202	7 269	7 166	-6
Participation rate	66.7	67.2	67.0	67.2	66.2	-0.5
Employed	6 908	6 935	6 923	6 971	6 893	-69
Employment-population ratio	64.3	65.0	64.8	64.4	63.2	-1.1
Unemployed	264	235	279	298	326	62
Unemployment rate	3.7	3.3	3.9	4.1	4.6	0.9
Hispanic[2]						
Civilian labor force	21 829	21 761	22 049	22 174	22 132	303
Participation rate	68.6	68.6	68.9	68.7	68.0	-0.6
Employed	20 554	20 333	20 450	20 436	20 165	-89
Employment-population ratio	64.6	64.1	63.9	63.3	61.9	-2.7
Unemployed	1 274	1 428	1 599	1 738	1 967	69
Unemployment rate	5.8	6.6	7.3	7.8	8.9	3.1

[1]Not seasonally adjusted.
[2]May be of any race.

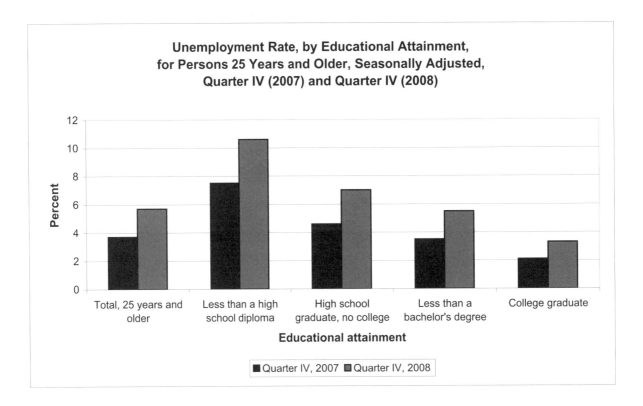

Unemployment Rate, by Educational Attainment, for Persons 25 Years and Older, Seasonally Adjusted, Quarter IV (2007) and Quarter IV (2008)

During 2008, the number of persons who were unemployed due to job loss rose sharply, as did the number of long-term unemployed. Most of the increase in total unemployment in 2008 was among job losers, as opposed to individuals leaving their jobs voluntarily or those entering or reentering the labor force. Unemployed job losers are those who lost their jobs involuntarily; they include persons on temporary layoff (awaiting recall) and those not on layoff: permanent job losers and persons who completed temporary jobs. Over the year, the number of persons who were unemployed due to job loss rose by about 2.4 million, to 6.1 million, in the fourth quarter of 2008; persons who did not expect to be recalled to work accounted for most of the increase in job losers. Since the fourth quarter of 2006, the number of unemployed job losers has been on an upward trend, increasing by nearly 3.0 million. During 2008, the number of unemployed reentrants to the labor force also trended upward, increasing by 511,000, to 2.7 million, in the fourth quarter of 2008. The number of job leavers (persons who quit or otherwise terminated their employment voluntarily and immediately began looking for work) rose by 178,000, to 964,000, and the number of unemployed new entrants to the labor force increased by 115,000, to 805,000. (See Table 2.)

About 2.4 million unemployed persons had been jobless for at least 27 weeks at the end of 2008, an increase of approximately 1.0 million from a year earlier. (See Table 2.) These long-term unemployed individuals made up a larger proportion of the total unemployed than they did the previous year: 22.2 percent in the fourth quarter of 2008, up from 18.1 percent a year earlier and well above a recent low of 10.7 percent in the second quarter of 2001. At the

end of 2008, the number of unemployed persons who had been looking for work for less than 5 weeks was 3.2 million, up by 599,000 from the fourth quarter of 2007. The average (mean) duration of unemployment in the fourth quarter of 2008, 19.5 weeks, was higher than a year earlier, as was the median duration, 10.4 weeks.

The number of persons employed part time for economic reasons rose dramatically during 2008. Those employed part time for economic reasons, also referred to as involuntary part-time workers, are persons who would have preferred to work full time, but could not because of slack work or because they were unable to find full-time work. The number of persons who were employed part time for economic reasons rose by 2.9 million over the year, to 7.4 million in the fourth quarter of 2008. Involuntary part-time employment was on an increasingly upward trend during 2008, rising by 487,000 in the second quarter, 653,000 in the third quarter, and 1.4 million in the fourth quarter. As is typical during labor market downturns, nearly all of the increase occurred among those who cited slack work or business conditions as their reason for working part time. A rise in economic part-time employment due to slack work generally occurs before a rise in unemployment, because, faced with a decline in demand for their goods and services, many employers tend to reduce workers' hours rather than lay off workers.[5]

Both the number of persons who wanted a job but were not in the labor force and the subset of persons who were marginally attached to the labor force increased in 2008. The category "not in the labor force" consists of persons who are neither employed nor unemployed. In the fourth quarter of 2008, there were 80.2 million persons who were

Table 2. Unemployed persons, by Reason and Duration of Unemployment, Quarterly Averages, Seasonally Adjusted, 2007–2008

(Numbers in thousands except for average and median duration, percent.)

Reason and duration	Quarter IV, 2007	2008				Change from: quarter IV (2007) to quarter IV (2008)
		Quarter I	Quarter II	Quarter III	Quarter IV	
Reason for Unemployment						
Job losers and persons who completed temporary jobs	3 697	3 939	4 275	4 979	6 146	2 449
On temporary layoff	1 008	1 028	1 110	1 239	1 435	427
Not on temporary layoff	2 689	2 912	3 165	3 740	4 711	2 022
Job leavers	786	800	863	952	964	178
Reentrants	2 183	2 135	2 409	2 644	2 694	511
New entrants	690	675	739	823	805	115
Percent distribution						
Job losers and persons who completed temporary jobs	50.3	52.2	51.6	5.0	57.9	7.6
On temporary layoff	13.7	13.6	13.4	13.2	13.5	-0.2
Not on temporary layoff	36.6	38.6	38.2	39.8	44.4	7.8
Job leavers	10.7	10.6	10.4	10.1	9.1	-1.6
Reentrants	29.7	28.3	29.1	28.1	25.4	-4.3
New entrants	9.4	8.9	8.9	8.8	7.6	-1.8
Duration of Unemployment						
Less than 5 weeks	2 611	2 704	2 829	2 997	3 210	599
5 to 1 weeks	2 325	2 449	2 673	2 937	3 198	873
15 weeks or more	2 406	2 440	2 809	3 425	4 197	1 791
15 to 26 weeks	1 078	1 120	1 287	1 546	1 839	761
27 weeks or more	1 328	1 320	1 522	1 879	2 358	1 030
Average (mean) duration, in weeks	16.9	16.8	17.1	17.9	19.5	2.6
Median duration, in weeks	8.5	8.4	9.2	9.8	10.0	1.9
Percent distribution						
Less than 5 weeks	35.6	35.6	34.0	32.0	30.3	-5.3
5 to 1 weeks	31.7	32.3	32.2	31.4	30.2	-1.5
15 weeks or more	32.8	32.1	33.8	36.6	39.6	6.8
15 to 26 weeks	14.7	14.8	15.5	16.5	17.3	2.6
27 weeks or more	18.1	17.4	18.3	20.1	22.2	4.1

not in the labor force (not seasonally adjusted). Of those who were not in the labor force, slightly more than half were 55 years and older.

The number of persons who were not in the labor force and wanted a job was 5.0 million in the fourth quarter of 2008 (not seasonally adjusted), an increase of 730,000 from a year earlier. Among this group, some had looked for a job sometime during the previous year and would have been available to work had they been offered a job. These individuals who were "marginally attached to the labor force" numbered 1.8 million in the fourth quarter of 2008, up by 474,000 from a year earlier. Some persons who were marginally attached to the labor force were not currently looking for a job because they felt that no jobs were available to them; such "discouraged workers" numbered 578,000 in the fourth quarter of 2008, or 234,000 more than a year earlier. (See Table 3.)

Paralleling the unemployment rate, the five alternative measures of labor underutilization increased in 2008. Alternative measures of labor underutilization are constructed by the Bureau of Labor Statistics (BLS) with the use of CPS data. Labeled U–1 through U–6 (U–3 is the official unemployment rate), the measures—which tend to show similar cyclical patterns—provide additional insight into the degree to which labor resources are underutilized.[6]

U–4 through U–6 include the following broader groups in addition to the unemployed persons in U–3: discouraged workers (U–4); all marginally attached workers (U–5); and the marginally attached plus persons employed part time for economic reasons (U–6). In 2008, U–4 rose to 7.2 percent and U–5 to 7.9 percent. U–6 increased by 4.2 percentage points, to 12.7 percent. Most of the rise in U–6 was due to the increase in overall unemployment and in those employed part time for economic reasons, rather than a rise in those marginally attached to the labor force.[7] (See Table 4.)

In 2008, employment rose in management, professional, and related occupations and in service occupations, while it fell sharply in construction occupations. Employment also declined in sales and office occupations, production occupations, and transportation occupations. During 2008, the number of people employed in management, professional, and related occupations rose by 836,000, after increasing by 608,000 in 2007. (The data presented in this section are not seasonally adjusted.) Service occupations, which include health care support, protective service, and food preparation and serving related occupations, experienced another year of employment growth, rising by 723,000 in the fourth quarter of 2008 after a smaller increase in 2007.

In the fourth quarter of 2008, employment in construction and extraction occupations declined by 1.2 million, after

Table 3. Persons Not in the Labor Force, Quarterly Averages, Not Seasonally Adjusted, 2007–2008

(Number in thousands.)

Category	Quarter IV, 2007	2008				Change from: quarter IV (2007) to quarter IV (2008)
		Quarter I	Quarter II	Quarter III	Quarter IV	
Total not in the labor force	79 185	79 985	79 146	78 711	80 164	979
Persons who currently want a job	4 289	4 719	5 148	5 044	5 019	730
Marginally attached to the labor force[1]	1 357	1 555	1 463	1 606	1 831	474
Reasons for not looking:						
Discouragement over job prospects[2]	344	421	411	436	578	234
Reasons other than discouragement[3]	1 013	1 134	1 052	1 170	1 253	240

[1]Persons who have searched for work during the previous 12 months and who were available to take a job during the reference week.
[2]Reasons for discouragement include "thinks no work available," "could not find work," "lacks schooling or training," "employer thinks person is too young or too old," and other types of discrimination.
[3]Includes those respondents who did not actively look for work in the previous weeks for such reasons as childcare and transportation problems, as well as a small number for which reason for nonparticipation was not determined.

Table 4. Alternative Measures of Labor Underutilization, Quarterly Averages, Seasonally Adjusted, 2007–2008

(Percent.)

Measure	Quarter IV, 2007	2008				Change from: quarter IV (2007) to quarter IV (2008)
		Quarter I	Quarter II	Quarter III	Quarter IV	
U–1 Persons unemployed 15 weeks or longer, as a percent of the civilian labor force	1.6	1.6	1.8	2.2	2.7	1.1
U–2 Job losers and persons who completed temporary jobs, as a percent of the civilian labor force	2.4	2.6	2.8	3.2	4.0	1.6
U–3 Total unemployed, as a percent of the civilian labor force (official unemployment rate)	4.8	4.9	5.4	6.0	6.9	2.1
U–4 Total unemployed plus discouraged workers, as a percent of the civilian labor force plus discouraged workers ..	5.0	5.2	5.6	6.3	7.2	2.2
U–5 Total unemployed, plus discouraged workers, plus all other marginally attached workers, as a percent of the civilian labor force plus all marginally attached workers	5.6	5.9	6.3	7.0	7.9	2.3
U–6 Total unemployed, plus all marginally attached workers, plus total employed part time for economic reasons, as a percent of the civilian labor force plus all marginally attached workers	8.5	9.0	9.7	10.8	12.7	4.2

Note: Marginally attached workers are persons who currently are neither working nor looking for work, but who indicate that they want and are available for a job and have looked for work sometime in the past 12 months. Discouraged workers, a subset of the marginally attached, have given a job-market-related reason for not currently looking for a job. Persons employed part time for economic reasons are those who want and are available for full-time work, but have had to settle for a part-time schedule.

remaining about unchanged in 2007 and following an increase of 1.5 million over the 4-year period from the fourth quarter of 2002 to the fourth quarter of 2006. During 2008, sales and office occupations employment fell by about 1.1 million, after a decline of 300,000 in 2007. Office and administrative support occupations accounted for nearly the entire decline in sales and office occupations in 2008. Production occupations saw no job growth in 2007, and employment fell by 939,000 in 2008. Employment in transportation and material moving occupations declined by 446,000 in the fourth quarter of 2008. (See Table 5.)

Employment gains among men and women in management, business, and related occupations were about equal in 2008. Men made up approximately 98 percent of construction and extraction occupation employment in 2008 and accounted for a proportionate share of the job loss in those occupations. Women accounted for the majority of the employment increase in service occupations

and for nearly the entire decline in office occupations and administrative support occupations.

Median weekly earnings for full-time wage and salary workers increased in 2008 at about the same rate as inflation, as measured by the Consumer Price Index (CPI-U). Median usual weekly earnings rose to $722 in 2008, an increase of 3.9 percent, about the same as the increase in the Consumer Price Index (CPI-U). (See Table 6.) Workers with usual weekly earnings in the tenth decile (top 10 percent of workers) experienced an increase of 5.7 percent, to $1,693, in 2008, while workers with earnings in the first decile (bottom 10 percent of workers) experienced an increase of 4.8 percent, to $346. In 2008, median weekly earnings for both men and women grew at about the same rate (4.2 percent and 3.9 percent, respectively.) The ratio of women's earnings to men's was 79.9 percent. Over time, the earnings gap between the sexes has narrowed considerably: in 1979, women's earnings were 62.5 percent of men's.[8]

Table 5. Employment, by Major Occupation and Sex, Quarterly Averages, Not Seasonally Adjusted, 2007–2008

(Number in thousands.)

Occupation	Total			Men			Women		
	Quarter IV, 2007	Quarter IV, 2008	Change from: quarter IV (2007) to quarter IV (2008)	Quarter IV, 2007	Quarter IV, 2008	Change from: quarter IV (2007) to quarter IV (2008)	Quarter IV, 2007	Quarter IV, 2008	Change from: quarter IV (2007) to quarter IV (2008)
Total, 16 Years and Older	146 731	144 500	-2 231	784	76 555	-1 854	68 322	67 945	-377
Management, professional, and related occupations	52 266	53 102	836	25 520	25 899	379	26 746	27 203	457
Management, business, and financial operations occupations	21 690	22 180	490	12 428	12 742	314	9 262	9 438	176
Professional and related occupations	30 576	30 922	346	13 092	13 157	65	17 485	17 766	281
Service occupations	23 831	24 554	723	10 298	10 242	126	13 533	14 131	598
Health care support occupations	3 087	3 312	225	331	364	33	2 757	2 948	191
Protective service occupations	2 981	3 104	123	2 316	2 366	50	665	738	73
Food preparation and serving related occupations	7 719	7 882	163	3 391	3 477	86	4 327	4 405	78
Building and grounds cleaning and maintenance occupations	5 354	5 431	77	3 305	3 240	-65	2 049	2 191	142
Personal care and service occupations	4 690	4 826	136	955	977	22	3 734	3 849	115
Sales and office occupations	36 253	5 187	-1 066	13 195	12 995	-200	23 059	22 192	-867
Sales and related occupations	16 511	16	-156	8 267	8 070	-197	8 245	8 284	39
Office and administrative support occupations	19 742	18 833	-909	4 928	4 925	-3	14 814	13 908	-906
Natural resources, construction, and maintenance occupations	15 854	14 514	-1 340	15 153	13 901	-1 252	701	613	-88
Farming, fishing, and forestry occupations	934	932	-2	744	713	-31	190	219	29
Construction and extraction occupations	9 561	8 349	-1 212	9 269	8 143	-1 126	292	206	-86
Installation, maintenance, and repair occupations	5 359	5 234	-125	5 140	5 046	-94	219	188	-31
Production, transportation, and material moving occupations	18 527	17 143	-1 384	14 244	13 336	-908	4 283	3 806	-477
Production occupations	9 520	8 581	-9	6 608	607	-5	2 911	2 507	-404
Transportation and material moving occupations	9 007	8 561	-446	7 636	7 262	-374	1 372	1 299	-73

Among the major racial and ethnic groups, Hispanics saw the largest percent increase in median earnings in 2008: 5.2 percent. The earnings increases for Asians (3.7 percent), Whites (3.6 percent), and Blacks (3.5 percent) were about the same.

Among the major occupation groups, workers in farming, fishing, and forestry occupations saw the largest over-the-year percent increase in earnings; although earnings for this occupation group remained the lowest overall, they were up 12.9 percent, to $420 per week. The earnings increases for workers in sales and related occupations and in production occupations were the lowest among the major occupation groups, at 2.0 percent and 2.4 percent, respectively, in 2008. Median weekly earnings for management, business, and financial operations occupations remained the highest among the major occupation groups, increasing to $1,128.

Educational attainment is a major determinant of earnings. Workers 25 years and older with at least a bachelor's degree continued to have the highest median weekly earnings among the major education groups: $1,115 in 2008, with an over-the-year percentage increase of 4.0 percent. Workers with some college or an associate's degree earned $722, and high school graduates with no college earned $618 in 2008, both up slightly from a year earlier. Earnings of workers with less than a high school diploma remained the lowest among the major education groups, $453 in 2008, but this group experienced the largest over-the-year percentage increase, 5.8 percent. (See Table 6.)

The overall increase in unemployment—most notably, the rise in the number of job losers—reflects the changes in labor force status flow data. Each month, millions of individuals move between employment and unemployment, and millions of others enter or leave the labor market. In addition, people move into and out of the survey universe of the civilian noninstitutional population aged 16 years and older. The flow of individuals between labor force states illustrates the fluid nature of the U.S. labor market and can be used to analyze changes in employment and unemployment.[9]

As stated earlier, from the fourth quarter of 2007 to the fourth quarter of 2008, the number of unemployed persons aged 16 years and older increased by 3.3 million and the number of unemployed job losers increased by 2.4 million. The rise in the number of job losers corresponds with the sharp increase in the number of employed persons who became unemployed from the fourth quarter of 2007 to the fourth quarter of 2008. In addition, the share of individuals from outside the labor force who became unemployed increased sharply, contributing to the rise in unemployment. Thus, the flow data show that the likelihood of employed persons becoming unemployed and the likelihood of new and returning entrants becoming unemployed both grew substantially over the period.

A greater understanding of the rise in unemployment in 2008 also can be gleaned by examining the flows from unemployment. The data indicate that, from the fourth quarter of 2007 to the fourth quarter of 2008, unemployed individuals became less likely to find employment and

Table 6. Median Usual Weekly Earnings of Full-Time Wage and Salary Workers, by Selected Characteristics, Annual Averages, 2007–2008

(Dollars, percent.)

Characteristic	2007	2008	Percent change (2007–2008)
Total, 16 Years and Older	695	722	3.9
CPI-U (1982–1984 = 100)	207	215	3.8
Men	766	798	4.2
Women	614	638	3.9
White	716	742	3.6
Men	788	825	4.7
Women	626	65	4.5
Black	569	589	3.5
Men	600	620	3.3
Women	533	554	3.9
Asian	830	861	3.7
Men	936	966	3.2
Women	731	753	3.0
Hispanic[1]	503	529	5.2
Men	520	559	7.5
Women	473	501	5.9
Management, business, and financial operations occupations	1 080	1 128	4.4
Professional and related occupations	951	980	3.0
Service occupations	454	475	4.6
Sales and related occupations	643	656	2.0
Office and administrative support occupations	581	601	3.4
Farming, fishing, and forestry occupations	372	420	12.9
Construction and extraction occupations	646	688	6.5
Installation, maintenance, and repair occupations	749	774	3.3
Production occupations	581	595	2.4
Transportation and material moving occupations	570	593	4.0
Total, 25 years and older	738	761	3.1
Less than a high school diploma	428	453	5.8
High school graduate, no college	604	618	2.3
Some college or associate's degree	704	722	2.6
Bachelor's degree or higher, total	1 072	1 115	4.0

[1]May be of any race.

much more likely to remain unemployed. In fact, the likelihood that an unemployed person would find employment was at a series low in the fourth quarter of 2008, dating back to February 1990. The percentage of unemployed individuals who remained unemployed rose from 51 percent in the fourth quarter of 2007 to 58 percent in the fourth quarter of 2008. Historically, the unemployed remain unemployed far longer during periods of labor market weakness.[10]

New CPS data on the employment status of persons with a disability were collected in 2008. In June 2008, questions were added to the CPS to identify persons with a disability in the civilian noninstitutional population aged 16 years and older. The collection of these data is sponsored by the Department of Labor's Office of Disability Employment Policy. The new questions allowed the BLS to begin releasing monthly CPS labor force data on persons with a disability. In the fourth quarter of 2008, these individuals had a labor force participation rate of 23.1 percent, compared with a rate of 71.4 percent for persons with no disabilities. The unemployment rate for persons with a disability was 11.5 percent in the fourth quarter of 2008, while the rate for persons with no disability was 6.4 percent. There also was a large difference in the employment-population ratios between persons with a disability and those with no disability in the fourth quarter of 2008, at 20.4 percent and 66.9 percent, respectively.[11]

In sum, data from the household survey indicate that the labor market continued to deteriorate in 2008, reflecting the onset of a recession. Unemployment rates increased gradually in the beginning of the year and accelerated after the first quarter of 2008. Employment declined for nearly all major worker groups, with men accounting for a much larger proportion of the decline than women. The employment-population ratio fell over the year, but labor force participation remained relatively flat. Also, more individuals were unemployed due to job loss, a greater number were unemployed for 27 weeks or longer, and the number of persons employed part time for economic reasons increased dramatically. Median weekly earnings for full-time wage and salary workers increased at about the same rate as inflation.

NOTES

1. NBER is generally recognized as the official arbiter of recessions in the United States. The organization determined that the recession prior to the current one lasted from March 2001 to November 2001. The NBER has not yet determined an end point for the recession that began in December 2007.

2. The data in this article are based on information collected in the CPS, also called the household survey, a sample survey of about 60,000 households nationwide sponsored jointly by the Bureau of Labor Statistics and the Census

Bureau. Although the CPS is a monthly survey, the data analyzed throughout this article are seasonally adjusted quarterly averages, unless otherwise noted. All over-the-year changes are comparisons of fourth-quarter data from 2007 to 2008.

3. For further information on teen school enrollment and employment, see Teresa L. Morisi, "Youth enrollment and employment during the school year," *Monthly Labor Review*, February 2008, pp. 51–63; on the Internet at <http://www.bls.gov/opub/mlr/2008/02/art3full.pdf>. (visited Mar. 9, 2009).

4. For additional information on trends in labor force participation, see Abraham Mosisa and Steven Hipple, "Trends in labor force participation in the United States," *Monthly Labor Review*, October 2006, pp. 35–57; on the Internet at <http://www.bls.gov/opub/mlr/2006/10/art3full.pdf>. (visited Mar. 9, 2009).

5. For additional information on persons working part time for economic reasons, see Emy Sok, "Involuntary part-time work on the rise," *Issues in Labor Statistics*, December 2008; on the Internet at <http://www.bls.gov/opub/ils/pdf/opbils71.pdf>. (visited Mar. 9, 2009).

6. For further information about the alternative measures of unemployment, see John E. Bregger and Steven E. Haugen, "BLS introduces new range of alternative unemployment measures," *Monthly Labor Review*, October 1995, pp. 19–26;

on the Internet at <http://www.bls.gov/opub/mlr/1995/10/art3full.pdf>. (visited Mar. 9, 2009).

7. For an additional analysis of labor force underutilization, see Sharon Cohany, "The Unemployment Rate and Beyond: Alternative Measures of Labor Underutilization," *Issues in Labor Statistics*, June 2008; on the Internet at <http://www.bls.gov/opub/ils/pdf/opbils67.pdf>. (visited Mar. 9, 2009).

8. The CPS first began collecting weekly earnings data each month in 1979.

9. For further background information about labor force status flows, see Randy Ilg, "Analyzing CPS data using gross flows," *Monthly Labor Review*, September 2005, pp. 10–18; on the Internet at <http://www.bls.gov/opub/mlr/2005/09/art2full.pdf >. (visited Mar. 9, 2009).

10. For an additional analysis of labor force status flows, see Randy Ilg, "Why Has Unemployment Risen? Insights From Labor Force Flows," *Issues in Labor Statistics*, June 2008; on the Internet at <http://www.bls.gov/opub/ils/pdf/opbils66.pdf >. (visited Mar. 9, 2009).

11. For additional information on monthly disability data, see "New monthly data series on the employment status of people with a disability," *Labor Force Statistics from the Current Population Survey* (Bureau of Labor Statistics, Feb. 6, 2009), on the Internet at <http://www.bls.gov/cps/cpsdisability.htm>. (visited Mar. 9, 2009).

Chapter One

POPULATION, LABOR FORCE, AND EMPLOYMENT STATUS

POPULATION, LABOR FORCE, AND EMPLOYMENT STATUS

HIGHLIGHTS

This chapter presents the detailed historical information collected in the Current Population Survey (CPS), a monthly survey of households that gathers data on the employment status of the population. Basic data on labor force, employment, and unemployment are shown for various characteristics of the population, including age, sex, race, Hispanic origin, and marital status.

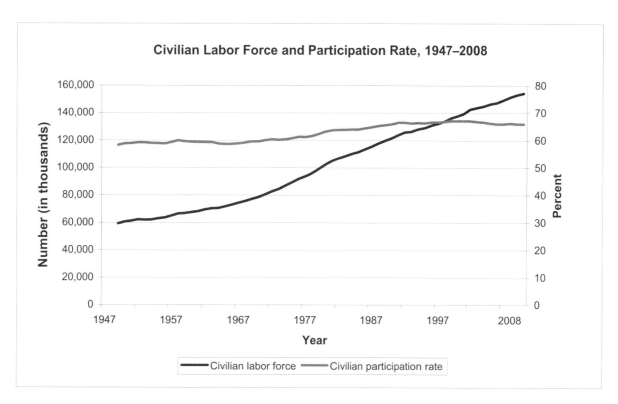

In 2008, there were over 154 million people in the labor force, a slight increase of 0.8 percent from the year before. In comparison, there were only 59.3 million people in the labor force in 1947. While the labor force has grown considerably, the labor force participation rate has grown much slower, increasing from 58.3 percent in 1947 to 66.0 percent in 2008. (See Table 1-1.)

OTHER HIGHLIGHTS

- While the civilian labor force participation rate remained stable at 66.0 percent in 2008, the labor force participation rate of those 65 years and over increased, as it has every since 1999. In 2008, the labor force participation rate of those 65 years and over was 16.8 percent—the highest it has been since 1970, when it was 17.0 percent. (See Table 1-8.)

- From 1988 to 2008, employment has increased from 114.9 million to 145.3 million, an increase of 26.4 percent. However, employment in agriculture has decreased sharply during the same period, declining from nearly 3.2 million in 1988 to less than 2.2 million in 2008. (See Table 1-3.)

- From 1972 through 1986, the number of Black men exceeded the number of Black women in the labor force. Since 1987, the number of Black women has exceeded the number of Black men in the labor force. (See Table 1-7.)

NOTES AND DEFINITIONS

CURRENT POPULATION SURVEY OF HOUSEHOLDS

Collection and Coverage

The Current Population Survey (CPS) is a monthly survey that analyzes and publishes statistics on the labor force, employment, and unemployment, classified by a variety of demographic, social, and economic characteristics. This survey is conducted by the Census Bureau for the Bureau of Labor Statistics (BLS). The information is collected from a probability sample of approximately 60,000 households. Respondents are interviewed to obtain information about the employment status of each household member age 16 years and over. Persons under 16 years of age are excluded from the official estimates because child labor laws, compulsory school attendance, and general social custom in the United States severely limit the types and amount of work that these children can do.

The inquiry relates to the household member's employment status during the calendar week, Sunday through Saturday, that includes the 12th day of the month. This is known as the "reference week." Actual field interviewing is conducted during the following week (the week that contains the 19th day of the month).

Concepts and Definitions

The concepts and definitions underlying the labor force data have been modified—but not substantially altered—since the inception of the survey in 1940 when it began as a Work Projects Administration program. Current definitions of some of the major concepts used in the CPS are described below.

The *civilian noninstitutional population* includes persons 16 years of age and over who reside in the 50 states and the District of Columbia who are not inmates of institutions (such as penal and mental facilities and homes for the aged) and who are not on active duty in the armed forces.

An *employed person* is any person who, during the reference week: (1) did any work at all (at least one hour) as a paid employees in their own business, profession, or on their own farm, or who worked 15 hours or more as an unpaid worker in an enterprise operated by a member of the family; and (2) any person who was not working but who had a job or business from which he or she was temporarily absent due to vacation, illness, bad weather, childcare problems, maternity or paternity leave, labor-management disputes, job training, or other family or personal reasons, despite whether the employee was being paid for the time off or was seeking other jobs.

Each employed person is counted only once, even if he or she holds more than one job. For purposes of occupation and industry classification, multiple jobholders are counted as being in the job at which they worked the greatest number of hours during the reference week.

Included in the total are employed citizens of foreign countries who were temporarily in the United States but not living on the premises of an embassy. Excluded are persons whose only activity during the reference week consisted of work around their own house (painting, repairing, or own home housework) or volunteer work for religious, charitable, and similar organizations.

Unemployed persons are all persons who had no employment during the reference week, but who were available for work (except for temporary illness) and had made specific efforts to find employment some time during the four-week period ending with the reference week. Persons who were waiting to be recalled to a job from which they had been laid off need not have been looking for work to be classified as unemployed.

Reasons for unemployment are divided into four major groups: (1) job losers, defined as (a) persons on temporary layoff, who have been given a date to return to work or who expect to return to work within six months; (b) permanent job losers, whose employment ended involuntarily and who began looking for work; and (c) persons who completed a temporary job and began looking for work after the job ended; (2) job leavers, defined as persons who quit or otherwise terminated their employment voluntarily and immediately began looking for work; (3) reentrants, defined as persons who previously worked but were out of the labor force prior to beginning their job search; and (4) new entrants, defined as persons who had never worked but were currently searching for work.

Duration of unemployment represents the length of time (through the current reference week) that persons classified as unemployed had been looking for work. For persons on layoff, duration of unemployment represents the number of full weeks they had been on layoff. Mean duration of unemployment is the arithmetic average computed from single weeks of unemployment; median duration of unemployment is the midpoint of a distribution of weeks of unemployment.

A *spell of unemployment* is a continuous period of unemployment of at least one week's duration and is terminated by either employment or withdrawal from the labor force.

Extent of unemployment refers to the number of workers and proportion of the labor force that were unemployed at some time during the year. The number of weeks unemployed is the total number of weeks accumulated during the entire calendar year.

The *unemployment rate* is the number of unemployed persons as a percentage of the civilian labor force.

The *civilian labor force* comprises all civilians classified as employed or unemployed.

The *participation rate* represents the proportion of the civilian noninstitutional population currently in the labor force.

The *employment-population ratio* represents the proportion of the population that is currently employed.

Persons not in the labor force are all persons in the civilian noninstitutional population who are neither employed nor unemployed. Information is collected about their desire for and availability to take a job at the time of the CPS interview, job search activity during the prior year, and reason for not looking for work during the four-week period ending with the reference week. Persons not in the labor force who want and are available for a job and who have looked for work within the past 12 months (or since the end of their last job, if they had held one within the past 12 months), but who are not currently looking, are designated as *marginally attached to the labor force.* The marginally attached are divided into those not currently looking because they believe their search would be futile—so-called *discouraged workers*—and those not currently looking for other reasons, such as family responsibilities, ill health, or lack of transportation.

Discouraged workers are defined as persons not in the labor force who want and are available for a job and who have looked for work sometime in the past 12 months (or since the end of their last job, if they held one within the past 12 months), but who are not currently looking because they believe that there are no jobs available or there are none for which they would qualify. The reasons for not currently looking for work include a person's belief that no work is available in his or her line of work or area; he or she could not find any work; he or she lacks necessary schooling, training, skills, or experience; employers would think he or she is too young or too old; or he or she would encounter hiring discrimination.

Usual full- or part-time status refers to hours usually worked per week. Full-time workers are those who usually work 35 hours or more (at all jobs). This group includes some individuals who worked less than 35 hours during the reference week for economic or noneconomic reasons. Part-time workers are those who usually work less than 35 hours per week (at all jobs), regardless of the number of hours worked during the reference week. These concepts are used to differentiate a person's normal schedule from his or her specific activity during the reference week. Unemployed persons who are looking for full-time work or who are on layoff from full-time jobs are counted as part of the full-time labor force; unemployed persons who are seeking part-time work or who are on layoff from part-time jobs are counted as part of the part-time labor force.

Year-round, full-time workers are workers who primarily worked at full-time jobs for 50 weeks or more during the preceding calendar year. Part-year workers worked either full- or part-time for 1 to 49 weeks.

At work part-time for economic reasons, sometimes called involuntary part-time, refers to individuals who gave an economic reason for working 1 to 34 hours during the reference week. Economic reasons include slack work or unfavorable business conditions, inability to find full-time work, and seasonal declines in demand. Those who usually work part-time must also indicate that they want and are available to work full-time to be classified as working part-time for economic reasons.

At work part-time for noneconomic reasons refers to persons who usually work part-time and were at work 1 to 34 hours during the reference week for a noneconomic reason. Noneconomic reasons include illness or other medical limitations, childcare problems or other family or personal obligations, school or training, retirement or Social Security limits on earnings, and being in a job where full-time work is less than 35 hours. This also includes workers who gave an economic reason for usually working 1 to 34 hours but said they do not want to work full-time or were unavailable for full-time work.

Absences are defined as instances in which persons who usually work 35 or more hours a week worked less than that during the reference period for reasons of illness or family obligations. Excluded are situations in which work was missed for vacation, holidays, or other reasons. The estimates are based on one-fourth of the sample only.

Earnings are all money income of $1 or more from wages and salaries and all net money income of $1 or more from farm and nonfarm self-employment.

Usual weekly earnings for wage and salary workers include any overtime pay, commissions, or tips usually received (at the main job in the case of multiple jobholders). Earnings reported on a basis other than weekly (such as annual, monthly, or hourly) are converted to weekly. The term "usual" is as perceived by the respondent. If the respondent asks for a definition of usual, interviewers are instructed to define the term as more than half the weeks worked during the past 4 or 5 months.

Minimum wage refers to the prevailing federal minimum wage which was $5.85 per hour from January 2008 to July 23, 2008. Beginning July 24, 2008, the prevailing federal minimum wage increased to $6.55 per hour. Data are for wage and salary workers who were paid hourly rates and refer to a person's earnings at the sole or principal job.

A *multiple jobholder* is an employed person who, during the reference week, had two or more jobs as a wage and salary worker, was self-employed and also held a wage and salary job, or worked as an unpaid family worker and also held a wage and salary job. Self-employed persons with multiple businesses and persons with multiple jobs as unpaid family workers are excluded.

Occupation, industry, and class of worker for members of the employed population are determined by the job held during the reference week. Persons with two or more jobs are classified as being in the job at which they worked the greatest number of hours. The unemployed are classified according to their last job. Beginning with data published in 2003, the systems used to classify occupational and industry data changed. They are currently based on the Standard Occupational Classification (SOC) system and the North American Industry Classification System (NAICS). (See the following section on historical comparability for a discussion of previous classification systems used in the CPS.) The class-of-worker breakdown assigns workers to one of the following categories: private and government wage and salary workers, self-employed workers, and unpaid family workers. Wage and salary workers receive wages, salaries, commissions, tips, or pay in kind from a private employer or from a government unit. Self-employed workers are those who work for profit or fees in their own businesses, professions, trades, or on their own farms. Only the unincorporated self-employed are included in the self-employed category in the class-of-worker typology. Self-employed workers who respond that their businesses are incorporated are included among wage and salary workers, because they are technically paid employees of a corporation. An unpaid family worker is a person working without pay for 15 hours or more per week on a farm or in a business operated by a member of the household to whom he or she is related by birth or marriage.

Educational attainment refers to years of school completed in regular schools, which include graded public, private, and parochial elementary, and high schools, whether day or night school. Colleges, universities, and professional schools are also included.

Tenure refers to length of time a worker has been continuously employed by his or her current employer. These data are collected through a supplement to the CPS. All employed persons were asked how long they had been working continuously for their present employer and, if the length of time was one or two years, a follow-up question was asked about the exact number of months. The follow-up question was included for the first time in the February 1996 supplement to the CPS. CPS supplements that obtained information on tenure in the January of 1983, 1987, and 1991 did not include the follow-up question. Prior to 1983, the question on tenure was asked differently. Data prior to 1983 are thus not strictly comparable to data for subsequent years.

White, Black, and Asian are terms used to describe the race of persons. Persons in these categories are those who selected that race only. Persons in the remaining race categories—American Indian or Alaskan Native, Native Hawaiian or Other Pacific Islander, and persons who selected more than one race category—are included in the estimates of total employment and unemployment but are not shown separately because the number of survey respondents is too small to develop estimates of sufficient quality for monthly publication.

Hispanic origin refers to persons who identified themselves in the enumeration process as being Spanish, Hispanic, or Latino. Persons of Hispanic or Latino origin may be of any race.

Single, never married; married, spouse present; and other marital status are the terms used to define the marital status of individuals at the time of the CPS interview. Married, spouse present, applies to a husband and wife if both were living in the same household, even though one may be temporarily absent on business, vacation, in a hospital, etc. Other marital status applies to persons who are married, spouse absent; widowed; or divorced. Married, spouse absent relates to persons who are separated due to marital problems, as well as husbands and wives living apart because one was employed elsewhere, on duty with the armed forces, or any other reason.

A *household* consists of all persons—related family members and all unrelated persons—who occupy a housing unit and have no other usual address. A house, an apartment, a group of rooms, or a single room is regarded as a housing unit when occupied or intended for occupancy as separate living quarters.

A *householder* is the person (or one of the persons) in whose name the housing unit is owned or rented. The term is not applied to either husbands or wives in married-couple families; it refers only to persons in families maintained by either men or women without a spouse.

A *family* is defined as a group of two or more persons residing together who are related by birth, marriage, or adoption. All such persons are considered as members of one family. Families are classified as either married-couple families or families maintained by women or men without spouses.

Children refer to "own" children of the husband, wife, or person maintaining the family, including sons and daughters, stepchildren, and adopted children. Excluded are other related children, such as grandchildren, nieces, nephews, cousins, and unrelated children.

Historical Comparability

While the concepts and methods are very similar to those used for the inaugural survey in 1940, a number of changes have been made over the years to improve the accuracy and usefulness of the data. Only recent major changes are described here.

Major changes to the CPS, such as the complete redesign of the questionnaire and the use of computer-assisted interviewing for the entire survey, were introduced in 1994. In addition, there were revisions to some of the labor force concepts and definitions, including the implementation of changes recommended in 1979 by the National Commission on Employment and Unemployment Statistics (NCEUS, also known as the Levitan Commission). Some of the major changes to the survey at this time were:

1) The introduction of a redesigned and automated questionnaire. The CPS questionnaire was totally redesigned in order to obtain more accurate, comprehensive, and relevant information, and to take advantage of state-of-the-art computer interviewing techniques. Computer-assisted interviewing has important benefits, most notably that it facilitates the use of a relatively complex questionnaire that incorporates complicated skip patterns and standardized follow-up questions. Additionally, certain questions are automatically tailored to the individual's situation to make them more understandable.

2) Official labor force measures were defined more precisely. While the labor force status of most people is straightforward, some persons are more difficult to classify correctly, especially if they are engaged in activities that are relatively informal or intermittent. Many of the changes to the questionnaire were made to deal with such cases. This was accomplished by rewording and adding questions to conform more precisely to the official definitions, making the questions easier to understand and answer, minimizing reliance on volunteered responses, revising response categories, and taking advantage of the benefits of an automated interview.

3) The amount of data available was expanded. The questionnaire redesign also made it possible to collect several types of data on topics such as multiple job holding and usual hours regularly for the first time.

4) Several labor definitions were modified. The most important definitional changes concerned discouraged workers. The Levitan Commission had criticized the former definition because it was based on a subjective desire for work and on somewhat arbitrary assumptions about an individual's availability to take a job. As a result of the redesign, two requirements were added: For persons to qualify as discouraged, they must have engaged in some job search within the past year (or since they last worked, if they worked within the past year), and they must be currently available to take a job. (Formerly, availability was inferred from responses to other questions; now, there is a direct question.) Also, beginning in January 1994, questions on this subject are asked of the full CPS sample, permitting estimates of the number of discouraged workers to be published monthly (rather than quarterly).

Beginning in January 2003, several other changes were introduced into the CPS. These changes included the following:

1) Population controls that reflected the results of the 2000 census were introduced into the monthly CPS estimation process. The new controls increased the size of the civilian noninstitutional population by about 3.5 million in May 2002. As a result, they also increased the estimated numbers of people unemployed and employed. Because the increases were roughly proportional, however, the overall unemployment rate did not change significantly. Data from January 2000 through December 2002 were revised to reflect these new controls. Over and above these revisions, the U.S. Census Bureau introduced another large upward adjustment to the controls as part of its annual update of population estimates for 2003. These updated population estimates were not available in time to incorporate them into the revised population controls for January 2000 to December 2002. Thus, the data on employment and unemployment levels for January 2003 (and beyond) are not strictly comparable with those for earlier months. The unemployment rate and other ratios, however, were not substantially affected by the 2003 population control revisions.

2) Questions on race and Hispanic origin were modified to comply with the new standards for maintaining, collecting, and presenting federal data on race and ethnicity for federal statistical agencies. The questions were reworded to indicate that individuals could select more than once race category and to convey more clearly that individuals should report their own perception of what race is. These changes had no impact on the overall civilian noninstitutional population and civilian labor force. However, they did reduce the population and labor force levels of Whites, Blacks, and Asians beginning in January 2003.

3) Improvements were introduced to both the second stage and composite weighting procedures. These changes adapted the weighting procedures to the new race/ethnic classification system and enhanced the stability over time for demographic groups. The second-stage weighting procedure substantially reduced the variability of estimates and corrected, to some extent, for CPS underreporting.

Changes in the Occupational and Industrial Classification System

In January 2003, the CPS adopted the 2002 census industry and occupational classification systems, which were derived, respectively, from the 2002 North American Industry Classification System (NAICS) and the 2000 Standard Occupational Classification (SOC) system. The 1990 Census occupational and industry classifications were replaced. The introduction of the new industry and occupational classification systems in 2003 created a complete break in comparability at all levels of industry and occupation aggregation. The composition of detailed occupations and industries changed substantially in the 2002 systems compared with the 1990 systems, as did the structure for aggregating them into major groups. Therefore, any comparisons of data on the different classifications are not possible without major adjustments.

Historical employment series on the 2002 Census classifications are available at broad levels of occupational and industry aggregation back to 1983. However, historical employment series at the detailed occupational and industry levels on the 2002 classifications are available back to 2000 only.

Beginning with industry data in 2009, BLS began using the 2007 Census industry classification system, which was derived from the 2007 NAICS series. Several industry titles were revised with no change to the industry definitions. The differences between the 2002 and 2007 classifications are relatively insignificant. BLS did not make any revisions to historical data with the introduction of 2007 NAICS series.

Sources of Additional Information

A complete description of sampling and estimation procedures and further information on the impact of historical changes in the surveys can be found in the updated version of Chapter 1 of the *BLS Handbook of Methods*. This can be found on the BLS Web site at <http://www.bls.gov/opub/hom/>.

Table 1-1. Employment Status of the Civilian Noninstitutional Population, 1947–2008

(Thousands of people, percent.)

Year	Civilian noninstitutional population	Civilian labor force								Not in labor force
		Total	Participation rate	Employed				Unemployed		
				Total	Percent of population	Agriculture	Nonagricultural industries	Number	Unemployment rate	
1947	101 827	59 350	58.3	57 038	56.0	7 890	49 148	2 311	3.9	42 477
1948	103 068	60 621	58.8	58 343	56.6	7 629	50 714	2 276	3.8	42 447
1949	103 994	61 286	58.9	57 651	55.4	7 658	49 993	3 637	5.9	42 708
1950	104 995	62 208	59.2	58 918	56.1	7 160	51 758	3 288	5.3	42 787
1951	104 621	62 017	59.2	59 961	57.3	6 726	53 235	2 055	3.3	42 604
1952	105 231	62 138	59.0	60 250	57.3	6 500	53 749	1 883	3.0	43 093
1953[1]	107 056	63 015	58.9	61 179	57.1	6 260	54 919	1 834	2.9	44 041
1954	108 321	63 643	58.8	60 109	55.5	6 205	53 904	3 532	5.5	44 678
1955	109 683	65 023	59.3	62 170	56.7	6 450	55 722	2 852	4.4	44 660
1956	110 954	66 552	60.0	63 799	57.5	6 283	57 514	2 750	4.1	44 402
1957	112 265	66 929	59.6	64 071	57.1	5 947	58 123	2 859	4.3	45 336
1958	113 727	67 639	59.5	63 036	55.4	5 586	57 450	4 602	6.8	46 088
1959	115 329	68 369	59.3	64 630	56.0	5 565	59 065	3 740	5.5	46 960
1960[1]	117 245	69 628	59.4	65 778	56.1	5 458	60 318	3 852	5.5	47 617
1961	118 771	70 459	59.3	65 746	55.4	5 200	60 546	4 714	6.7	48 312
1962[1]	120 153	70 614	58.8	66 702	55.5	4 944	61 759	3 911	5.5	49 539
1963	122 416	71 833	58.7	67 762	55.4	4 687	63 076	4 070	5.7	50 583
1964	124 485	73 091	58.7	69 305	55.7	4 523	64 782	3 786	5.2	51 394
1965	126 513	74 455	58.9	71 088	56.2	4 361	66 726	3 366	4.5	52 058
1966	128 058	75 770	59.2	72 895	56.9	3 979	68 915	2 875	3.8	52 288
1967	129 874	77 347	59.6	74 372	57.3	3 844	70 527	2 975	3.8	52 527
1968	132 028	78 737	59.6	75 920	57.5	3 817	72 103	2 817	3.6	53 291
1969	134 335	80 734	60.1	77 902	58.0	3 606	74 296	2 832	3.5	53 602
1970	137 085	82 771	60.4	78 678	57.4	3 463	75 215	4 093	4.9	54 315
1971	140 216	84 382	60.2	79 367	56.6	3 394	75 972	5 016	5.9	55 834
1972[1]	144 126	87 034	60.4	82 153	57.0	3 484	78 669	4 882	5.6	57 091
1973[1]	147 096	89 429	60.8	85 064	57.8	3 470	81 594	4 365	4.9	57 667
1974	150 120	91 949	61.3	86 794	57.8	3 515	83 279	5 156	5.6	58 171
1975	153 153	93 774	61.2	85 846	56.1	3 408	82 438	7 929	8.5	59 377
1976	156 150	96 158	61.6	88 752	56.8	3 331	85 421	7 406	7.7	59 991
1977	159 033	99 008	62.3	92 017	57.9	3 283	88 734	6 991	7.1	60 025
1978[1]	161 910	102 250	63.2	96 048	59.3	3 387	92 661	6 202	6.1	59 659
1979	164 863	104 962	63.7	98 824	59.9	3 347	95 477	6 137	5.8	59 900
1980	167 745	106 940	63.8	99 302	59.2	3 364	95 938	7 637	7.1	60 806
1981	170 130	108 670	63.9	100 397	59.0	3 368	97 030	8 273	7.6	61 460
1982	172 271	110 204	64.0	99 526	57.8	3 401	96 125	10 678	9.7	62 067
1983	174 215	111 550	64.0	100 834	57.9	3 383	97 450	10 717	9.6	62 665
1984	176 383	113 544	64.4	105 005	59.5	3 321	101 685	8 539	7.5	62 839
1985	178 206	115 461	64.8	107 150	60.1	3 179	103 971	8 312	7.2	62 744
1986[1]	180 587	117 834	65.3	109 597	60.7	3 163	106 434	8 237	7.0	62 752
1987	182 753	119 865	65.6	112 440	61.5	3 208	109 232	7 425	6.2	62 888
1988	184 613	121 669	65.9	114 968	62.3	3 169	111 800	6 701	5.5	62 944
1989	186 393	123 869	66.5	117 342	63.0	3 199	114 142	6 528	5.3	62 523
1990[1]	189 164	125 840	66.5	118 793	62.8	3 223	115 570	7 047	5.6	63 324
1991	190 925	126 346	66.2	117 718	61.7	3 269	114 449	8 628	6.8	64 578
1992	192 805	128 105	66.4	118 492	61.5	3 247	115 245	9 613	7.5	64 700
1993	194 838	129 200	66.3	120 259	61.7	3 115	117 144	8 940	6.9	65 638
1994[1]	196 814	131 056	66.6	123 060	62.5	3 409	119 651	7 996	6.1	65 758
1995	198 584	132 304	66.6	124 900	62.9	3 440	121 460	7 404	5.6	66 280
1996	200 591	133 943	66.8	126 708	63.2	3 443	123 264	7 236	5.4	66 647
1997[1]	203 133	136 297	67.1	129 558	63.8	3 399	126 159	6 739	4.9	66 836
1998[1]	205 220	137 673	67.1	131 463	64.1	3 378	128 085	6 210	4.5	67 547
1999[1]	207 753	139 368	67.1	133 488	64.3	3 281	130 207	5 880	4.2	68 385
2000[1]	212 577	142 583	67.1	136 891	64.4	2 464	134 427	5 692	4.0	69 994
2001	215 092	143 734	66.8	136 933	63.7	2 299	134 635	6 801	4.7	71 359
2002	217 570	144 863	66.6	136 485	62.7	2 311	134 174	8 378	5.8	72 707
2003[1]	221 168	146 510	66.2	137 736	62.3	2 275	135 461	8 774	6.0	74 658
2004[1]	223 357	147 401	66.0	139 252	62.3	2 232	137 020	8 149	5.5	75 956
2005	226 082	149 320	66.0	141 730	62.7	2 197	139 532	7 591	5.1	76 762
2006[1]	228 815	151 428	66.2	144 427	63.1	2 206	142 221	7 001	4.6	77 387
2007[1]	231 867	153 124	66.0	146 047	63.0	2 095	143 952	7 078	4.6	78 743
2008[1]	233 788	154 287	66.0	145 362	62.2	2 168	143 194	8 924	5.8	79 501

[1]Not strictly comparable with data for prior years. See notes and definitions for information on historical comparability.

Table 1-2. Employment Status of the Civilian Noninstitutional Population, by Sex, 1970–2008

(Thousands of people, percent.)

Sex and year	Civilian noninstitutional population	Civilian labor force		Employed				Unemployed		Not in labor force
		Total	Participation rate	Total	Percent of population	Agriculture	Non-agricultural industries	Number	Unemployment rate	
Men										
1970	64 304	51 228	79.7	48 990	76.2	2 862	46 128	2 238	4.4	13 076
1971	65 942	52 180	79.1	49 390	74.9	2 795	46 595	2 789	5.3	13 762
1972[1]	67 835	53 555	78.9	50 896	75.0	2 849	48 047	2 659	5.0	14 280
1973[1]	69 292	54 624	78.8	52 349	75.5	2 847	49 502	2 275	4.2	14 667
1974	70 808	55 739	78.7	53 024	74.9	2 919	50 105	2 714	4.9	15 069
1975	72 291	56 299	77.9	51 857	71.7	2 824	49 032	4 442	7.9	15 993
1976	73 759	57 174	77.5	53 138	72.0	2 744	50 394	4 036	7.1	16 585
1977	75 193	58 396	77.7	54 728	72.8	2 671	52 057	3 667	6.3	16 797
1978[1]	76 576	59 620	77.9	56 479	73.8	2 718	53 761	3 142	5.3	16 956
1979	78 020	60 726	77.8	57 607	73.8	2 686	54 921	3 120	5.1	17 293
1980	79 398	61 453	77.4	57 186	72.0	2 709	54 477	4 267	6.9	17 945
1981	80 511	61 974	77.0	57 397	71.3	2 700	54 697	4 577	7.4	18 537
1982	81 523	62 450	76.6	56 271	69.0	2 736	53 534	6 179	9.9	19 073
1983	82 531	63 047	76.4	56 787	68.8	2 704	54 083	6 260	9.9	19 484
1984	83 605	63 835	76.4	59 091	70.7	2 668	56 423	4 744	7.4	19 771
1985	84 469	64 411	76.3	59 891	70.9	2 535	57 356	4 521	7.0	20 058
1986[1]	85 798	65 422	76.3	60 892	71.0	2 511	58 381	4 530	6.9	20 376
1987	86 899	66 207	76.2	62 107	71.5	2 543	59 564	4 101	6.2	20 692
1988	87 857	66 927	76.2	63 273	72.0	2 493	60 780	3 655	5.5	20 930
1989	88 762	67 840	76.4	64 315	72.5	2 513	61 802	3 525	5.2	20 923
1990[1]	90 377	69 011	76.4	65 104	72.0	2 546	62 559	3 906	5.7	21 367
1991	91 278	69 168	75.8	64 223	70.4	2 589	61 634	4 946	7.2	22 110
1992	92 270	69 964	75.8	64 440	69.8	2 575	61 866	5 523	7.9	22 306
1993	93 332	70 404	75.4	65 349	70.0	2 478	62 871	5 055	7.2	22 927
1994[1]	94 354	70 817	75.1	66 450	70.4	2 554	63 896	4 367	6.2	23 538
1995	95 178	71 360	75.0	67 377	70.8	2 559	64 818	3 983	5.6	23 818
1996	96 206	72 086	74.9	68 207	70.9	2 573	65 634	3 880	5.4	24 119
1997[1]	97 715	73 261	75.0	69 685	71.3	2 552	67 133	3 577	4.9	24 454
1998[1]	98 758	73 959	74.9	70 693	71.6	2 553	68 140	3 266	4.4	24 799
1999[1]	99 722	74 512	74.7	71 446	71.6	2 432	69 014	3 066	4.1	25 210
2000[1]	101 964	76 280	74.8	73 305	71.9	1 861	71 444	2 975	3.9	25 684
2001	103 282	76 886	74.4	73 196	70.9	1 708	71 488	3 690	4.8	26 396
2002	104 585	77 500	74.1	72 903	69.7	1 724	71 179	4 597	5.9	27 085
2003[1]	106 435	78 238	73.5	73 332	68.9	1 695	71 636	4 906	6.3	28 197
2004[1]	107 710	78 980	73.3	74 524	69.2	1 687	72 838	4 456	5.6	28 730
2005[1]	109 151	80 033	73.3	75 973	69.6	1 654	74 319	4 059	5.1	29 119
2006[1]	110 605	81 255	73.5	77 502	70.1	1 663	75 838	3 753	4.6	29 350
2007[1]	112 173	82 136	73.2	78 254	69.8	1 604	76 650	3 882	4.7	30 036
2008[1]	113 113	82 520	73.0	77 486	68.5	1 650	75 836	5 033	6.1	30 593
Women										
1970	72 782	31 543	43.3	29 688	40.8	601	29 087	1 855	5.9	41 239
1971	74 274	32 202	43.4	29 976	40.4	599	29 377	2 227	6.9	42 072
1972[1]	76 290	33 479	43.9	31 257	41.0	635	30 622	2 222	6.6	42 811
1973[1]	77 804	34 804	44.7	32 715	42.0	622	32 093	2 089	6.0	43 000
1974	79 312	36 211	45.7	33 769	42.6	596	33 173	2 441	6.7	43 101
1975	80 860	37 475	46.3	33 989	42.0	584	33 404	3 486	9.3	43 386
1976	82 390	38 983	47.3	35 615	43.2	588	35 027	3 369	8.6	43 406
1977	83 840	40 613	48.4	37 289	44.5	612	36 677	3 324	8.2	43 227
1978[1]	85 334	42 631	50.0	39 569	46.4	669	38 900	3 061	7.2	42 703
1979	86 843	44 235	50.9	41 217	47.5	661	40 556	3 018	6.8	42 608
1980	88 348	45 487	51.5	42 117	47.7	656	41 461	3 370	7.4	42 861
1981	89 618	46 696	52.1	43 000	48.0	667	42 333	3 696	7.9	42 922
1982	90 748	47 755	52.6	43 256	47.7	665	42 591	4 499	9.4	42 993
1983	91 684	48 503	52.9	44 047	48.0	680	43 367	4 457	9.2	43 181
1984	92 778	49 709	53.6	45 915	49.5	653	45 262	3 794	7.6	43 068
1985	93 736	51 050	54.5	47 259	50.4	644	46 615	3 791	7.4	42 686
1986[1]	94 789	52 413	55.3	48 706	51.4	652	48 054	3 707	7.1	42 376
1987	95 853	53 658	56.0	50 334	52.5	666	49 668	3 324	6.2	42 195
1988	96 756	54 742	56.6	51 696	53.4	676	51 020	3 046	5.6	42 014
1989	97 630	56 030	57.4	53 027	54.3	687	52 341	3 003	5.4	41 601
1990[1]	98 787	56 829	57.5	53 689	54.3	678	53 011	3 140	5.5	41 957
1991	99 646	57 178	57.4	53 496	53.7	680	52 815	3 683	6.4	42 468
1992	100 535	58 141	57.8	54 052	53.8	672	53 380	4 090	7.0	42 394
1993	101 506	58 795	57.9	54 910	54.1	637	54 273	3 885	6.6	42 711
1994[1]	102 460	60 239	58.8	56 610	55.3	855	55 755	3 629	6.0	42 221
1995	103 406	60 944	58.9	57 523	55.6	881	56 642	3 421	5.6	42 462
1996	104 385	61 857	59.3	58 501	56.0	871	57 630	3 356	5.4	42 528
1997[1]	105 418	63 036	59.8	59 873	56.8	847	59 026	3 162	5.0	42 382
1998[1]	106 462	63 714	59.8	60 771	57.1	825	59 945	2 944	4.6	42 748
1999[1]	108 031	64 855	60.0	62 042	57.4	849	61 193	2 814	4.3	43 175
2000[1]	110 613	66 303	59.9	63 586	57.5	602	62 983	2 717	4.1	44 310
2001	111 811	66 848	59.8	63 737	57.0	591	63 147	3 111	4.7	44 962
2002	112 985	67 363	59.6	63 582	56.3	587	62 995	3 781	5.6	45 621
2003[1]	114 733	68 272	59.5	64 404	56.1	580	63 824	3 868	5.7	46 461
2004[1]	115 647	68 421	59.2	64 728	56.0	546	64 182	3 694	5.4	47 225
2005[1]	116 931	69 288	59.3	65 757	56.2	544	65 213	3 531	5.1	47 643
2006[1]	118 210	70 173	59.4	66 925	56.6	543	66 382	3 247	4.6	48 037
2007[1]	119 694	70 988	59.3	67 792	56.6	490	67 302	3 196	4.5	48 707
2008[1]	120 675	71 767	59.5	67 876	56.2	518	67 358	3 891	5.4	48 908

[1]Not strictly comparable with data for prior years. See notes and definitions for information on historical comparability.

Table 1-3. Employment Status of the Civilian Noninstitutional Population, by Sex, Age, Race, and Hispanic Origin, 1988–2008

(Thousands of people.)

Characteristic	1988	1989	1990	1991	1992	1993	1994	1995	1996	1997	1998
ALL RACES											
Both Sexes											
Civilian noninstitutional population	184 613	186 393	189 164	190 925	192 805	194 838	196 814	198 584	200 591	203 133	205 220
Civilian labor force	121 669	123 869	125 840	126 346	128 105	129 200	131 056	132 304	133 943	136 297	137 673
Employed	114 968	117 342	118 793	117 718	118 492	120 259	123 060	124 900	126 708	129 558	131 463
Agriculture	3 169	3 199	3 223	3 269	3 247	3 115	3 409	3 440	3 443	3 399	3 378
Nonagricultural industries	111 800	114 142	115 570	114 449	115 245	117 144	119 651	121 460	123 264	126 159	128 085
Unemployed	6 701	6 528	7 047	8 628	9 613	8 940	7 996	7 404	7 236	6 739	6 210
Not in labor force	62 944	62 523	63 324	64 578	64 700	65 638	65 758	66 280	66 647	66 837	67 547
Men, 16 Years and Over											
Civilian noninstitutional population	87 857	88 762	90 377	91 278	92 270	93 332	94 355	95 178	96 206	97 715	98 758
Civilian labor force	66 927	67 840	69 011	69 168	69 964	70 404	70 817	71 360	72 087	73 261	73 959
Employed	63 273	64 315	65 104	64 223	64 440	65 349	66 450	67 377	68 207	69 685	70 693
Agriculture	2 493	2 513	2 546	2 589	2 575	2 478	2 554	2 559	2 573	2 552	2 553
Nonagricultural industries	60 780	61 802	62 559	61 634	61 866	62 871	63 896	64 818	65 634	67 133	68 140
Unemployed	3 655	3 525	3 906	4 946	5 523	5 055	4 367	3 983	3 880	3 577	3 266
Not in labor force	20 930	20 923	21 367	22 110	22 306	22 927	23 538	23 818	24 119	24 454	24 799
Men, 20 Years and Over											
Civilian noninstitutional population	80 553	81 619	83 030	84 144	85 247	86 256	87 151	87 811	88 606	89 879	90 790
Civilian labor force	62 768	63 704	64 916	65 374	66 213	66 642	66 921	67 324	68 044	69 166	69 715
Employed	59 781	60 837	61 678	61 178	61 496	62 355	63 294	64 085	64 897	66 284	67 135
Agriculture	2 271	2 307	2 329	2 383	2 385	2 293	2 351	2 356	2 356	2 356	2 350
Nonagricultural industries	57 510	58 530	59 349	58 795	59 111	60 063	60 943	61 750	62 541	63 927	64 785
Unemployed	2 987	2 867	3 239	4 195	4 717	4 287	3 627	3 239	3 146	2 882	2 580
Not in labor force	17 785	17 915	18 114	18 770	19 034	19 613	20 230	20 487	20 563	20 713	21 075
Women, 16 Years and Over											
Civilian noninstitutional population	96 756	97 630	98 787	99 646	100 535	101 506	102 460	103 406	104 385	105 418	106 462
Civilian labor force	54 742	56 030	56 829	57 178	58 141	58 795	60 239	60 944	61 857	63 036	63 714
Employed	51 696	53 027	53 689	53 496	54 052	54 910	56 610	57 523	58 501	59 873	60 771
Agriculture	676	687	678	680	672	637	855	881	871	847	825
Nonagricultural industries	51 020	52 341	53 011	52 815	53 380	54 273	55 755	56 642	57 630	59 026	59 945
Unemployed	3 046	3 003	3 140	3 683	4 090	3 885	3 629	3 421	3 356	3 162	2 944
Not in labor force	42 014	41 601	41 957	42 468	42 394	42 711	42 221	42 462	42 528	42 382	42 748
Women, 20 Years and Over											
Civilian noninstitutional population	89 532	90 550	91 614	92 708	93 718	94 647	95 467	96 262	97 050	97 889	98 786
Civilian labor force	50 870	52 212	53 131	53 708	54 796	55 388	56 655	57 215	58 094	59 198	59 702
Employed	48 383	49 745	50 535	50 634	51 328	52 099	53 606	54 396	55 311	56 613	57 278
Agriculture	625	642	631	639	625	598	809	830	827	798	768
Nonagricultural industries	47 757	49 103	49 904	49 995	50 702	51 501	52 796	53 566	54 484	55 815	56 510
Unemployed	2 487	2 467	2 596	3 074	3 469	3 288	3 049	2 819	2 783	2 585	2 424
Not in labor force	38 662	38 339	38 483	39 000	38 922	39 260	38 813	39 047	38 956	38 691	39 084
Both Sexes, 16 to 19 Years											
Civilian noninstitutional population	14 527	14 223	14 520	14 073	13 840	13 935	14 196	14 511	14 934	15 365	15 644
Civilian labor force	8 031	7 954	7 792	7 265	7 096	7 170	7 481	7 765	7 806	7 932	8 256
Employed	6 805	6 759	6 581	5 906	5 669	5 805	6 161	6 419	6 500	6 661	7 051
Agriculture	273	250	264	247	237	224	249	275	261	244	261
Nonagricultural industries	6 532	6 510	6 317	5 659	5 432	5 580	5 912	6 144	6 239	6 417	6 790
Unemployed	1 226	1 194	1 212	1 359	1 427	1 365	1 320	1 346	1 306	1 271	1 205
Not in labor force	6 497	6 270	6 727	6 808	6 745	6 765	6 715	6 746	7 128	7 433	7 388
WHITE[1]											
Both Sexes											
Civilian noninstitutional population	158 194	159 338	160 625	161 759	162 972	164 289	165 555	166 914	168 317	169 993	171 478
Civilian labor force	104 756	106 355	107 447	107 743	108 837	109 700	111 082	111 950	113 108	114 693	115 415
Employed	99 812	101 584	102 261	101 182	101 669	103 045	105 190	106 490	107 808	109 856	110 931
Agriculture	2 965	2 996	2 998	3 026	3 018	2 895	3 162	3 194	3 276	3 208	3 160
Nonagricultural industries	96 846	98 588	99 263	98 157	98 650	100 150	102 027	103 296	104 532	106 648	107 770
Unemployed	4 944	4 770	5 186	6 560	7 169	6 655	5 892	5 459	5 300	4 836	4 484
Not in labor force	53 349	52 983	53 178	54 061	54 135	54 589	54 473	54 965	55 209	55 301	56 064
Men, 16 Years and Over											
Civilian noninstitutional population	75 855	76 468	77 369	77 977	78 651	79 371	80 059	80 733	81 489	82 577	83 352
Civilian labor force	58 317	58 988	59 638	59 656	60 168	60 484	60 727	61 146	61 783	62 639	63 034
Employed	55 550	56 352	56 703	55 797	55 959	56 656	57 452	58 146	58 888	59 998	60 604
Agriculture	2 318	2 345	2 353	2 384	2 378	2 286	2 347	2 347	2 436	2 389	2 376
Nonagricultural industries	53 232	54 007	54 350	53 413	53 580	54 370	55 104	55 800	56 452	57 608	58 228
Unemployed	2 766	2 636	2 935	3 859	4 209	3 828	3 275	2 999	2 896	2 641	2 431
Not in labor force	17 538	17 480	17 731	18 321	18 484	18 887	19 332	19 587	19 706	19 938	20 317
Men, 20 Years and Over											
Civilian noninstitutional population	69 887	70 654	71 457	72 274	73 040	73 721	74 311	74 879	75 454	76 320	76 966
Civilian labor force	54 734	55 441	56 116	56 387	56 976	57 284	57 411	57 719	58 340	59 126	59 421
Employed	52 466	53 292	53 685	53 103	53 357	54 021	54 676	55 254	55 977	56 986	57 500
Agriculture	2 104	2 149	2 148	2 192	2 197	2 114	2 151	2 132	2 224	2 201	2 182
Nonagricultural industries	50 362	51 143	51 537	50 912	51 160	51 907	52 525	53 122	53 753	54 785	55 319
Unemployed	2 268	2 149	2 431	3 284	3 620	3 263	2 735	2 465	2 363	2 140	1 920
Not in labor force	15 153	15 213	15 340	15 887	16 064	16 436	16 900	17 161	17 114	17 194	17 545

[1]Beginning in 2003, persons who selected this race group only; persons who selected more than one race group are not included. Prior to 2003, persons who reported more than one race group were included in the group they identified as the main race.

Table 1-3. Employment Status of the Civilian Noninstitutional Population, by Sex, Age, Race, and Hispanic Origin, 1988–2008—*Continued*

(Thousands of people.)

Characteristic	1999	2000	2001	2002	2003	2004	2005	2006	2007	2008
ALL RACES										
Both Sexes										
Civilian noninstitutional population	207 753	212 577	215 092	217 570	221 168	223 357	226 082	228 815	231 867	233 788
Civilian labor force	139 368	142 583	143 734	144 863	146 510	147 401	149 320	151 428	153 124	154 287
Employed	133 488	136 891	136 933	136 485	137 736	139 252	141 730	144 427	146 047	145 362
Agriculture	3 281	2 464	2 299	2 311	2 275	2 232	2 197	2 206	2 095	2 168
Nonagricultural industries	130 207	134 427	134 635	134 174	135 461	137 020	139 532	142 221	143 952	143 194
Unemployed	5 880	5 692	6 801	8 378	8 774	8 149	7 591	7 001	7 078	8 924
Not in labor force	68 385	69 994	71 359	72 707	74 658	75 956	76 762	77 387	78 743	79 501
Men, 16 Years and Over										
Civilian noninstitutional population	99 722	101 964	103 282	104 585	106 435	107 710	109 151	110 605	112 173	113 113
Civilian labor force	74 512	76 280	76 886	77 500	78 238	78 980	80 033	81 255	82 136	82 520
Employed	71 446	73 305	73 196	72 903	73 332	74 524	75 973	77 502	78 254	77 486
Agriculture	2 432	1 861	1 708	1 724	1 695	1 688	1 654	1 663	1 604	1 650
Nonagricultural industries	69 014	71 444	71 488	71 179	71 636	72 836	74 319	75 838	76 650	75 836
Unemployed	3 066	2 975	3 690	4 597	4 906	4 456	4 059	3 753	3 882	5 033
Not in labor force	25 210	25 684	26 396	27 085	28 197	28 730	29 119	29 350	30 036	30 593
Men, 20 Years and Over										
Civilian noninstitutional population	91 555	93 875	95 181	96 439	98 272	99 476	100 835	102 145	103 555	104 453
Civilian labor force	70 194	72 010	72 816	73 630	74 623	75 364	76 443	77 562	78 596	79 047
Employed	67 761	69 634	69 776	69 734	70 415	71 572	73 050	74 431	75 337	74 750
Agriculture	2 244	1 756	1 613	1 629	1 614	1 596	1 577	1 579	1 514	1 552
Nonagricultural industries	65 517	67 878	68 163	68 104	68 801	69 976	71 473	72 852	73 823	73 198
Unemployed	2 433	2 376	3 040	3 896	4 209	3 791	3 392	3 131	3 259	4 297
Not in labor force	21 362	21 864	22 365	22 809	23 649	24 113	24 392	24 584	24 959	25 406
Women, 16 Years and Over										
Civilian noninstitutional population	108 031	110 613	111 811	112 985	114 733	115 647	116 931	118 210	119 694	120 675
Civilian labor force	64 855	66 303	66 848	67 363	68 272	68 421	69 288	70 173	70 988	71 767
Employed	62 042	63 586	63 737	63 582	64 404	64 728	65 757	66 925	67 792	67 876
Agriculture	849	602	591	587	580	547	544	543	490	518
Nonagricultural industries	61 193	62 983	63 147	62 995	63 824	64 181	65 213	66 382	67 302	67 358
Unemployed	2 814	2 717	3 111	3 781	3 868	3 694	3 531	3 247	3 196	3 891
Not in labor force	43 175	44 310	44 962	45 621	46 461	47 225	47 643	48 037	48 707	48 908
Women, 20 Years and Over										
Civilian noninstitutional population	100 158	102 790	103 983	105 136	106 800	107 658	108 850	109 992	111 330	112 260
Civilian labor force	60 840	62 301	63 016	63 648	64 716	64 923	65 714	66 585	67 516	68 382
Employed	58 555	60 067	60 417	60 420	61 402	61 773	62 702	63 834	64 799	65 039
Agriculture	803	567	558	557	550	515	519	520	460	491
Nonagricultural industries	57 752	59 500	59 860	59 863	60 852	61 258	62 182	63 315	64 339	64 548
Unemployed	2 285	2 235	2 599	3 228	3 314	3 150	3 013	2 751	2 718	3 342
Not in labor force	39 318	40 488	40 967	41 488	42 083	42 735	43 136	43 407	43 814	43 878
Both Sexes, 16 to 19 Years										
Civilian noninstitutional population	16 040	15 912	15 929	15 994	16 096	16 222	16 398	16 678	16 982	17 075
Civilian labor force	8 333	8 271	7 902	7 585	7 170	7 114	7 164	7 281	7 012	6 858
Employed	7 172	7 189	6 740	6 332	5 919	5 907	5 978	6 162	5 911	5 573
Agriculture	234	141	128	124	111	121	100	108	121	125
Nonagricultural industries	6 938	7 049	6 611	6 207	5 808	5 786	5 877	6 054	5 790	5 448
Unemployed	1 162	1 081	1 162	1 253	1 251	1 208	1 186	1 119	1 101	1 285
Not in labor force	7 706	7 642	8 027	8 409	8 926	9 108	9 234	9 397	9 970	10 218
WHITE[1]										
Both Sexes										
Civilian noninstitutional population	173 085	176 220	178 111	179 783	181 292	182 643	184 446	186 264	188 253	189 540
Civilian labor force	116 509	118 545	119 399	120 150	120 546	121 086	122 299	123 834	124 935	125 635
Employed	112 235	114 424	114 430	114 013	114 235	115 239	116 949	118 833	119 792	119 126
Agriculture	3 083	2 320	2 174	2 171	2 148	2 103	2 077	2 063	1 953	2 021
Nonagricultural industries	109 152	112 104	112 256	111 841	112 087	113 136	114 872	116 769	117 839	117 104
Unemployed	4 273	4 121	4 969	6 137	6 311	5 847	5 350	5 002	5 143	6 509
Not in labor force	56 577	57 675	58 713	59 633	60 746	61 558	62 148	62 429	63 319	63 905
Men, 16 Years and Over										
Civilian noninstitutional population	83 930	85 370	86 452	87 361	88 249	89 044	90 027	91 021	92 073	92 725
Civilian labor force	63 413	64 466	64 966	65 308	65 509	65 994	66 694	67 613	68 158	68 351
Employed	61 139	62 289	62 212	61 849	61 866	62 712	63 763	64 883	65 289	64 624
Agriculture	2 273	1 743	1 606	1 611	1 597	1 583	1 562	1 554	1 501	1 539
Nonagricultural industries	58 866	60 546	60 606	60 238	60 269	61 129	62 201	63 330	63 788	63 085
Unemployed	2 274	2 177	2 754	3 459	3 643	3 282	2 931	2 730	2 869	3 727
Not in labor force	20 517	20 905	21 486	22 053	22 740	23 050	23 334	23 408	23 915	24 374
Men, 20 Years and Over										
Civilian noninstitutional population	77 432	78 966	80 029	80 922	81 860	82 615	83 556	84 466	85 420	86 056
Civilian labor force	59 747	60 850	61 519	62 067	62 473	62 944	63 705	64 540	65 214	65 483
Employed	57 934	59 119	59 245	59 124	59 348	60 159	61 255	62 259	62 806	62 304
Agriculture	2 094	1 640	1 512	1 519	1 517	1 495	1 488	1 473	1 417	1 447
Nonagricultural industries	55 839	57 479	57 733	57 605	57 831	58 664	59 767	60 785	61 389	60 857
Unemployed	1 813	1 731	2 275	2 943	3 125	2 785	2 450	2 281	2 408	3 179
Not in labor force	17 685	18 116	18 510	18 855	19 386	19 671	19 851	19 927	20 206	20 573

[1] Beginning in 2003, persons who selected this race group only; persons who selected more than one race group are not included. Prior to 2003, persons who reported more than one race group were included in the group they identified as the main race.

Table 1-3. Employment Status of the Civilian Noninstitutional Population, by Sex, Age, Race, and Hispanic Origin, 1988–2008—Continued

(Thousands of people.)

Characteristic	1988	1989	1990	1991	1992	1993	1994	1995	1996	1997	1998
WHITE[1]											
Women, 16 Years and Over											
Civilian noninstitutional population	82 340	82 871	83 256	83 781	84 321	84 918	85 496	86 181	86 828	87 417	88 126
Civilian labor force	46 439	47 367	47 809	48 087	48 669	49 216	50 356	50 804	51 325	52 054	52 380
Employed	44 262	45 232	45 558	45 385	45 710	46 390	47 738	48 344	48 920	49 859	50 327
Agriculture	648	651	645	641	640	609	815	847	840	819	784
Nonagricultural industries	43 614	44 581	44 913	44 744	45 070	45 780	46 923	47 497	48 080	49 040	49 543
Unemployed	2 177	2 135	2 251	2 701	2 959	2 827	2 617	2 460	2 404	2 195	2 053
Not in labor force	35 901	35 504	35 447	35 695	35 651	35 702	35 141	35 377	35 503	35 363	35 746
Women, 20 Years and Over											
Civilian noninstitutional population	76 470	77 154	77 539	78 285	78 928	79 490	79 980	80 567	81 041	81 492	82 073
Civilian labor force	43 081	44 105	44 648	45 111	45 839	46 311	47 314	47 686	48 162	48 847	49 029
Employed	41 316	42 346	42 796	42 862	43 327	43 910	45 116	45 643	46 164	47 063	47 342
Agriculture	599	608	598	601	594	572	772	799	798	771	729
Nonagricultural industries	40 717	41 738	42 198	42 261	42 733	43 339	44 344	44 844	45 366	46 292	46 612
Unemployed	1 766	1 758	1 852	2 248	2 512	2 400	2 197	2 042	1 998	1 784	1 688
Not in labor force	33 389	33 050	32 891	33 174	33 089	33 179	32 666	32 881	32 879	32 645	33 044
Both Sexes, 16 to 19 Years											
Civilian noninstitutional population	11 838	11 530	11 630	11 200	11 004	11 078	11 264	11 468	11 822	12 181	12 439
Civilian labor force	6 940	6 809	6 683	6 245	6 022	6 105	6 357	6 545	6 607	6 720	6 965
Employed	6 030	5 946	5 779	5 216	4 985	5 113	5 398	5 593	5 667	5 807	6 089
Agriculture	263	239	252	233	228	209	239	262	254	236	250
Nonagricultural industries	5 767	5 707	5 528	4 984	4 757	4 904	5 158	5 331	5 413	5 571	5 839
Unemployed	910	863	903	1 029	1 037	992	960	952	939	912	876
Not in labor force	4 897	4 721	4 947	4 955	4 982	4 973	4 907	4 923	5 215	5 462	5 475
BLACK[1]											
Both Sexes											
Civilian noninstitutional population	20 692	21 021	21 477	21 799	22 147	22 521	22 879	23 246	23 604	24 003	24 373
Civilian labor force	13 205	13 497	13 740	13 797	14 162	14 225	14 502	14 817	15 134	15 529	15 982
Employed	11 658	11 953	12 175	12 074	12 151	12 382	12 835	13 279	13 542	13 969	14 556
Agriculture	153	150	142	160	153	143	136	101	98	117	138
Nonagricultural industries	11 505	11 803	12 034	11 914	11 997	12 239	12 699	13 178	13 444	13 852	14 417
Unemployed	1 547	1 544	1 565	1 723	2 011	1 844	1 666	1 538	1 592	1 560	1 426
Not in labor force	7 487	7 524	7 737	8 002	7 985	8 296	8 377	8 429	8 470	8 474	8 391
Men, 16 Years and Over											
Civilian noninstitutional population	9 289	9 439	9 573	9 725	9 896	10 083	10 258	10 411	10 575	10 763	10 927
Civilian labor force	6 596	6 701	6 802	6 851	6 997	7 019	7 089	7 183	7 264	7 354	7 542
Employed	5 824	5 928	5 995	5 961	5 930	6 047	6 241	6 422	6 456	6 607	6 871
Agriculture	133	127	124	139	138	128	118	93	86	103	118
Nonagricultural industries	5 691	5 802	5 872	5 822	5 791	5 919	6 122	6 329	6 371	6 504	6 752
Unemployed	771	773	806	890	1 067	971	848	762	808	747	671
Not in labor force	2 694	2 738	2 772	2 874	2 899	3 064	3 169	3 228	3 311	3 409	3 386
Men, 20 Years and Over											
Civilian noninstitutional population	8 063	8 215	8 364	8 479	8 652	8 840	9 171	9 280	9 414	9 575	9 727
Civilian labor force	6 023	6 127	6 221	6 357	6 451	6 568	6 646	6 730	6 806	6 910	7 053
Employed	5 357	5 509	5 602	5 692	5 706	5 681	5 964	6 137	6 167	6 325	6 530
Agriculture	135	129	119	117	131	131	115	89	83	101	112
Nonagricultural industries	5 222	5 381	5 483	5 576	5 575	5 550	5 849	6 048	6 084	6 224	6 418
Unemployed	666	617	619	664	745	886	682	593	639	585	524
Not in labor force	2 040	2 089	2 143	2 122	2 202	801	2 525	2 550	2 608	2 665	2 673
Women, 16 Years and Over											
Civilian noninstitutional population	11 402	11 582	11 904	12 074	12 251	12 438	12 621	12 835	13 029	13 241	13 446
Civilian labor force	6 609	6 796	6 938	6 946	7 166	7 206	7 413	7 634	7 869	8 175	8 441
Employed	5 834	6 025	6 180	6 113	6 221	6 334	6 595	6 857	7 086	7 362	7 685
Agriculture	20	24	18	21	15	15	18	8	13	14	20
Nonagricultural industries	5 814	6 001	6 162	6 092	6 206	6 320	6 577	6 849	7 073	7 348	7 665
Unemployed	776	772	758	833	944	872	818	777	784	813	756
Not in labor force	4 793	4 786	4 965	5 129	5 086	5 231	5 208	5 201	5 159	5 066	5 005
Women, 20 Years and Over											
Civilian noninstitutional population	10 298	10 482	10 760	10 959	11 152	11 332	11 496	11 682	11 833	12 016	12 023
Civilian labor force	6 190	6 352	6 517	6 572	6 778	6 824	7 004	7 175	7 405	7 686	7 912
Employed	5 548	5 727	5 884	5 874	5 978	6 095	6 320	6 556	6 762	7 013	7 290
Agriculture	18	23	18	20	15	14	17	7	12	13	19
Nonagricultural industries	5 530	5 703	5 867	5 853	5 963	6 081	6 303	6 548	6 749	7 000	7 272
Unemployed	642	625	633	698	800	729	685	620	643	673	622
Not in labor force	4 108	4 130	4 243	4 388	4 374	4 508	4 492	4 507	4 428	4 330	4 291
Both Sexes, 16 to 19 Years											
Civilian noninstitutional population	2 179	2 176	2 238	2 187	2 155	2 181	2 211	2 284	2 356	2 412	2 443
Civilian labor force	889	925	866	774	816	807	852	911	923	933	1 017
Employed	601	625	598	494	492	494	552	586	613	631	736
Agriculture	7	8	7	8	7	9	1	5	3	3	8
Nonagricultural industries	594	617	591	486	485	485	547	581	611	611	728
Unemployed	288	300	268	280	324	313	300	325	310	310	281
Not in labor force	1 291	1 251	1 372	1 413	1 339	1 374	1 360	1 372	1 434	1 434	1 427

[1]Beginning in 2003, persons who selected this race group only; persons who selected more than one race group are not included. Prior to 2003, persons who reported more than one race group were included in the group they identified as the main race.

Table 1-3. Employment Status of the Civilian Noninstitutional Population, by Sex, Age, Race, and Hispanic Origin, 1988–2008—*Continued*

(Thousands of people.)

Characteristic	1999	2000	2001	2002	2003	2004	2005	2006	2007	2008
WHITE[1]										
Women, 16 Years and Over										
Civilian noninstitutional population	89 156	90 850	91 660	92 422	93 043	93 599	94 419	95 242	96 180	96 814
Civilian labor force	53 096	54 079	54 433	54 842	55 037	55 092	55 605	56 221	56 777	57 284
Employed	51 096	52 136	52 218	52 164	52 369	52 527	53 186	53 950	54 503	54 501
Agriculture	810	578	568	560	551	520	515	510	452	482
Nonagricultural industries	50 286	51 558	51 650	51 604	51 818	52 007	52 672	53 440	54 050	54 019
Unemployed	1 999	1 944	2 215	2 678	2 668	2 565	2 419	2 271	2 274	2 782
Not in labor force	36 060	36 770	37 227	37 581	38 006	38 508	38 814	39 021	39 403	39 531
Women, 20 Years and Over										
Civilian noninstitutional population	82 953	84 718	85 526	86 266	86 905	87 430	88 200	88 942	89 790	90 400
Civilian labor force	49 714	50 740	51 218	51 717	52 099	52 212	52 643	53 286	53 925	54 508
Employed	48 098	49 145	49 369	49 448	49 823	50 040	50 589	51 359	51 996	52 124
Agriculture	765	546	537	532	522	488	492	488	423	457
Nonagricultural industries	47 333	48 599	48 831	48 916	49 301	49 552	50 097	50 871	51 572	51 667
Unemployed	1 616	1 595	1 849	2 269	2 276	2 172	2 054	1 927	1 930	2 384
Not in labor force	33 239	33 978	34 308	34 548	34 806	35 218	35 557	35 656	35 864	35 892
Both Sexes, 16 to 19 Years										
Civilian noninstitutional population	12 700	12 535	12 556	12 596	12 527	12 599	12 690	12 856	13 043	13 084
Civilian labor force	7 048	6 955	6 661	6 366	5 973	5 929	5 950	6 009	5 795	5 644
Employed	6 204	6 160	5 817	5 441	5 064	5 039	5 105	5 215	4 990	4 697
Agriculture	224	135	125	121	109	116	97	102	113	118
Nonagricultural industries	5 980	6 025	5 692	5 320	4 955	4 923	5 008	5 113	4 877	4 580
Unemployed	844	795	845	925	909	890	845	794	805	947
Not in labor force	5 652	5 581	5 894	6 230	6 554	6 669	6 739	6 847	7 248	7 440
BLACK[1]										
Both Sexes										
Civilian noninstitutional population	24 855	24 902	25 138	25 578	25 686	26 065	26 517	27 007	27 485	27 843
Civilian labor force	16 365	16 397	16 421	16 565	16 526	16 638	17 013	17 314	17 496	17 740
Employed	15 056	15 156	15 006	14 872	14 739	14 909	15 313	15 765	16 051	15 953
Agriculture	117	77	62	69	63	50	51	60	53	55
Nonagricultural industries	14 939	15 079	14 944	14 804	14 676	14 859	15 261	15 705	15 998	15 898
Unemployed	1 309	1 241	1 416	1 693	1 787	1 729	1 700	1 549	1 445	1 788
Not in labor force	8 490	8 505	8 717	9 013	9 161	9 428	9 504	9 693	9 989	10 103
Men, 16 Years and Over										
Civilian noninstitutional population	11 143	11 129	11 172	11 391	11 454	11 656	11 882	12 130	12 361	12 516
Civilian labor force	7 652	7 702	7 647	7 794	7 711	7 773	7 998	8 128	8 252	8 347
Employed	7 027	7 082	6 938	6 959	6 820	6 912	7 155	7 354	7 500	7 398
Agriculture	99	67	56	63	52	43	43	51	46	49
Nonagricultural industries	6 952	7 015	6 882	6 896	6 768	6 869	7 111	7 303	7 454	7 350
Unemployed	671	620	709	835	891	860	844	774	752	949
Not in labor force	3 386	3 427	3 525	3 597	3 743	3 884	3 884	4 002	4 110	4 169
Men, 20 Years and Over										
Civilian noninstitutional population	9 926	9 952	9 993	10 196	10 278	11 656	10 659	10 864	11 057	11 194
Civilian labor force	7 182	7 240	7 200	7 347	7 346	7 773	7 600	7 720	7 867	7 962
Employed	6 702	6 741	6 627	6 652	6 586	6 912	6 901	7 079	7 245	7 151
Agriculture	96	67	55	62	51	274	43	49	45	47
Nonagricultural industries	6 606	6 675	55	6 591	6 535	6 638	6 858	7 030	7 201	7 104
Unemployed	480	499	573	695	760	860	699	640	622	811
Not in labor force	2 743	2 711	2 792	2 848	2 932	3 884	3 060	3 144	3 189	3 232
Women, 16 Years and Over										
Civilian noninstitutional population	13 711	13 772	13 966	14 187	14 232	14 409	14 635	14 877	15 124	15 328
Civilian labor force	8 713	8 695	8 774	8 772	8 815	8 865	9 014	9 186	9 244	9 393
Employed	8 029	8 073	8 068	7 914	7 919	7 997	8 158	8 410	8 551	8 554
Agriculture	18	10	6	6	11	7	8	9	7	6
Nonagricultural industries	8 011	8 064	8 062	7 907	7 908	7 990	8 150	8 402	8 544	8 548
Unemployed	684	621	706	858	895	868	856	775	693	839
Not in labor force	4 999	5 078	5 192	5 415	5 418	5 544	5 621	5 691	5 879	5 934
Women, 20 Years and Over										
Civilian noninstitutional population	12 451	12 561	12 758	12 966	13 026	14 409	13 377	13 578	13 788	13 974
Civilian labor force	8 224	8 215	8 323	8 348	8 409	8 865	8 610	8 723	8 828	8 991
Employed	7 663	7 703	7 741	7 610	7 636	7 997	7 876	8 068	8 240	8 260
Agriculture	17	9	6	5	10	7	7	7	7	6
Nonagricultural industries	7 646	7 694	7 735	7 604	7 626	7 701	7 868	8 060	8 233	8 254
Unemployed	561	512	582	738	772	868	734	656	588	732
Not in labor force	4 226	4 346	4 434	4 618	4 618	5 544	4 768	4 854	4 960	4 982
Both Sexes, 16 to 19 Years										
Civilian noninstitutional population	2 479	2 389	2 388	2 416	2 382	2 423	2 481	2 565	2 640	2 676
Civilian labor force	959	941	898	870	771	762	803	871	801	787
Employed	691	711	637	611	516	520	536	618	566	541
Agriculture	4	1	1	2	1	0	1	3	1	1
Nonagricultural industries	687	710	637	609	515	520	535	614	564	540
Unemployed	268	230	260	260	255	241	267	253	235	246
Not in labor force	1 520	1 448	1 490	1 546	1 611	1 661	1 677	1 694	1 839	1 889

[1]Beginning in 2003, persons who selected this race group only; persons who selected more than one race group are not included. Prior to 2003, persons who reported more than one race group were included in the group they identified as the main race.

Table 1-3. Employment Status of the Civilian Noninstitutional Population, by Sex, Age, Race, and Hispanic Origin, 1988–2008—*Continued*

(Thousands of people.)

Characteristic	1988	1989	1990	1991	1992	1993	1994	1995	1996	1997	1998
HISPANIC[2]											
Both Sexes											
Civilian noninstitutional population	13 325	13 791	15 904	16 425	16 961	17 532	18 117	18 629	19 213	20 321	21 070
Civilian labor force	8 982	9 323	10 720	10 920	11 338	11 610	11 975	12 267	12 774	13 796	14 317
Employed	8 250	8 573	9 845	9 828	10 027	10 361	10 788	11 127	11 642	12 726	13 291
Agriculture	407	440	517	512	524	523	560	604	609	660	742
Nonagricultural industries	7 843	8 133	9 328	9 315	9 503	9 838	10 227	10 524	11 033	12 067	12 549
Unemployed	732	750	876	1 092	1 311	1 248	1 187	1 140	1 132	1 069	1 026
Not in labor force	4 342	4 468	5 184	5 506	5 623	5 922	6 142	6 362	6 439	6 526	6 753
Men, 16 Years and Over											
Civilian noninstitutional population	6 604	6 825	8 041	8 296	8 553	8 824	9 104	9 329	9 604	10 368	10 734
Civilian labor force	5 409	5 595	6 546	6 664	6 900	7 076	7 210	7 376	7 646	8 309	8 571
Employed	4 972	5 172	6 021	5 979	6 093	6 328	6 530	6 725	7 039	7 728	8 018
Agriculture	356	393	449	453	468	469	494	527	537	571	651
Nonagricultural industries	4 616	4 779	5 572	5 526	5 625	5 860	6 036	6 198	6 502	7 157	7 367
Unemployed	437	423	524	685	807	747	680	651	607	582	552
Not in labor force	1 195	1 230	1 495	1 632	1 654	1 749	1 894	1 952	1 957	2 059	2 164
Men, 20 Years and Over											
Civilian noninstitutional population	5 921	6 114	7 126	7 392	7 655	7 930	8 178	8 375	8 611	9 250	9 573
Civilian labor force	5 031	5 195	6 034	6 198	6 432	6 621	6 747	6 898	7 150	7 779	8 005
Employed	4 680	4 853	5 609	5 623	5 757	5 992	6 189	6 367	6 655	7 307	7 570
Agriculture	327	366	415	419	437	441	466	501	510	544	621
Nonagricultural industries	4 353	4 487	5 195	5 204	5 320	5 551	5 722	5 866	6 145	6 763	6 949
Unemployed	351	342	425	575	675	629	558	530	495	471	436
Not in labor force	890	919	1 092	1 194	1 223	1 309	1 431	1 477	1 461	1 471	1 568
Women, 16 Years and Over											
Civilian noninstitutional population	6 721	6 965	7 863	8 130	8 408	8 708	9 014	9 300	9 610	9 953	10 335
Civilian labor force	3 573	3 728	4 174	4 256	4 439	4 534	4 765	4 891	5 128	5 486	5 746
Employed	3 278	3 401	3 823	3 848	3 934	4 033	4 258	4 403	4 602	4 999	5 273
Agriculture	51	48	68	59	57	55	66	76	72	89	91
Nonagricultural industries	3 227	3 353	3 755	3 789	3 877	3 978	4 191	4 326	4 531	4 910	5 182
Unemployed	296	327	351	407	504	501	508	488	525	488	473
Not in labor force	3 147	3 237	3 689	3 874	3 969	4 174	4 248	4 409	4 482	4 466	4 589
Women, 20 Years and Over											
Civilian noninstitutional population	6 050	6 278	7 041	7 301	7 569	7 846	8 122	8 382	8 654	8 950	9 292
Civilian labor force	3 448	3 857	3 941	4 110	4 218	4 421	4 520	5 106	5 106	5 304	5 666
Employed	3 047	3 172	3 567	3 603	3 693	3 800	3 989	4 116	4 341	4 705	4 928
Agriculture	49	44	62	53	51	49	61	72	69	83	85
Nonagricultural industries	2 998	3 128	3 505	3 549	3 642	3 751	3 928	4 044	4 272	4 622	4 843
Unemployed	234	276	289	339	418	418	431	404	438	401	376
Not in labor force	2 769	2 830	3 184	3 360	3 459	3 628	3 701	3 863	3 875	3 845	3 988
Both Sexes, 16 to 19 Years											
Civilian noninstitutional population	1 354	1 399	1 737	1 732	1 737	1 756	1 818	1 872	1 948	2 121	2 204
Civilian labor force	671	680	829	781	796	771	807	850	845	911	1 007
Employed	523	548	668	602	577	570	609	645	646	714	793
Agriculture	32	31	40	41	36	33	32	31	29	33	36
Nonagricultural industries	492	517	628	562	541	537	577	614	617	682	757
Unemployed	148	132	161	179	219	201	198	205	199	197	214
Not in labor force	683	719	907	951	941	985	1 010	1 022	1 103	1 210	1 197

[2]May be of any race.

Table 1-3. Employment Status of the Civilian Noninstitutional Population, by Sex, Age, Race, and Hispanic Origin, 1988–2008—*Continued*

(Thousands of people.)

Characteristic	1999	2000	2001	2002	2003	2004	2005	2006	2007	2008
HISPANIC[2]										
Both Sexes										
Civilian noninstitutional population	21 650	23 938	24 942	25 963	27 551	28 109	29 133	30 103	31 383	32 141
Civilian labor force	14 665	16 689	17 328	17 943	18 813	19 272	19 824	20 694	21 602	22 024
Employed	13 720	15 735	16 190	16 590	17 372	17 930	18 632	19 613	20 382	20 346
Agriculture	734	536	423	448	446	441	423	428	426	441
Nonagricultural industries	12 986	15 199	15 767	16 141	16 927	17 489	18 209	19 185	19 956	19 904
Unemployed	945	954	1 138	1 353	1 441	1 342	1 191	1 081	1 220	1 678
Not in labor force	6 985	7 249	7 614	8 020	8 738	8 837	9 310	9 409	9 781	10 116
Men, 16 Years and Over										
Civilian noninstitutional population	10 713	12 174	12 695	13 221	14 098	14 417	14 962	15 473	16 154	16 524
Civilian labor force	8 546	9 923	10 279	10 609	11 288	11 587	11 985	12 488	13 005	13 255
Employed	8 067	9 428	9 668	9 845	10 479	10 832	11 337	11 887	12 310	12 248
Agriculture	642	449	345	361	350	356	350	347	352	364
Nonagricultural industries	7 425	8 979	9 323	9 484	10 129	10 476	10 987	11 540	11 958	11 884
Unemployed	480	494	611	764	809	755	647	601	695	1 007
Not in labor force	2 167	2 252	2 416	2 613	2 810	2 831	2 977	2 985	3 149	3 270
Men, 20 Years and Over										
Civilian noninstitutional population	9 523	10 841	11 386	11 928	12 797	13 082	13 586	14 046	14 649	14 971
Civilian labor force	7 950	9 247	9 595	9 977	10 756	11 020	11 408	11 888	12 403	12 629
Employed	7 576	8 859	9 100	9 341	10 063	10 385	10 872	11 391	11 827	11 769
Agriculture	602	423	328	345	336	335	341	337	337	351
Nonagricultural industries	6 974	8 435	8 773	8 996	9 727	10 050	10 532	11 054	11 490	11 418
Unemployed	374	388	495	636	693	635	536	497	576	860
Not in labor force	1 573	1 595	1 791	1 951	2 041	2 061	2 177	2 157	2 246	2 342
Women, 16 Years and Over										
Civilian noninstitutional population	10 937	11 764	12 247	12 742	13 452	13 692	14 172	14 630	15 229	15 616
Civilian labor force	6 119	6 767	7 049	7 334	7 525	7 685	7 839	8 206	8 597	8 769
Employed	5 653	6 307	6 522	6 744	6 894	7 098	7 295	7 725	8 072	8 098
Agriculture	92	87	77	87	96	85	73	80	74	77
Nonagricultural industries	5 561	6 220	6 445	6 657	6 798	7 013	7 222	7 645	7 999	8 021
Unemployed	466	460	527	590	631	587	544	480	525	672
Not in labor force	4 819	4 997	5 198	5 408	5 928	6 007	6 333	6 424	6 632	6 847
Women, 20 Years and Over										
Civilian noninstitutional population	9 821	10 574	11 049	11 528	12 211	12 420	12 858	13 262	13 791	14 127
Civilian labor force	6 275	6 557	6 863	7 096	7 096	7 257	7 377	7 735	8 108	8 274
Employed	5 290	5 903	6 121	6 367	6 541	6 752	6 913	7 321	7 662	7 707
Agriculture	88	81	73	84	91	78	70	77	69	75
Nonagricultural industries	5 202	5 822	6 048	6 283	6 450	6 674	6 843	7 244	7 593	7 632
Unemployed	376	371	436	496	555	504	464	414	446	567
Not in labor force	4 155	4 299	4 492	4 666	5 114	5 163	5 481	5 527	5 682	5 853
Both Sexes, 16 to 19 Years										
Civilian noninstitutional population	2 307	2 523	2 508	2 507	2 543	2 608	2 689	2 796	2 944	3 042
Civilian labor force	1 049	1 168	1 176	1 103	960	995	1 038	1 071	1 091	1 121
Employed	854	973	969	882	768	792	847	900	894	870
Agriculture	45	31	22	19	19	25	13	14	20	15
Nonagricultural industries	809	942	947	863	749	767	834	887	874	855
Unemployed	196	194	208	221	192	203	191	170	197	251
Not in labor force	1 257	1 355	1 331	1 404	1 583	1 612	1 651	1 725	1 853	1 921

[2]May be of any race.

Table 1-4. Employment Status of the Civilian Noninstitutional Population, by Sex, Race, and Marital Status, 1988–2008

(Thousands of people.)

Race, marital status, and year	Men				Women			
	Civilian noninstitutional population	Civilian labor force			Civilian noninstitutional population	Civilian labor force		
		Total	Employed	Unemployed		Total	Employed	Unemployed
ALL RACES								
Single								
1988	24 572	18 345	16 521	1 824	20 961	14 194	12 979	1 215
1989	24 831	18 738	16 936	1 801	21 141	14 377	13 175	1 202
1990	25 870	19 357	17 405	1 952	21 901	14 612	13 336	1 276
1991	26 197	19 411	17 011	2 400	22 173	14 681	13 198	1 482
1992	26 436	19 709	17 098	2 611	22 475	14 872	13 263	1 609
1993	26 570	19 706	17 261	2 445	22 713	15 031	13 484	1 547
1994	26 786	19 786	17 604	2 181	23 000	15 333	13 847	1 486
1995	26 918	19 841	17 833	2 007	23 151	15 467	14 053	1 413
1996	27 387	20 071	18 055	2 016	23 623	15 842	14 403	1 439
1997	28 311	20 689	18 783	1 906	24 285	16 492	15 037	1 455
1998	28 693	21 037	19 240	1 798	24 941	17 087	15 755	1 332
1999	29 104	21 351	19 686	1 665	25 576	17 575	16 267	1 308
2000	29 887	22 002	20 339	1 663	25 920	17 849	16 628	1 221
2001	30 646	22 285	20 298	1 988	26 462	18 021	16 635	1 386
2002	31 072	22 289	19 983	2 306	26 999	18 203	16 583	1 621
2003	31 691	22 297	19 841	2 457	27 802	18 397	16 723	1 674
2004	32 422	22 776	20 395	2 381	28 228	18 616	16 995	1 621
2005	33 125	23 214	21 006	2 209	29 046	19 183	17 588	1 595
2006	33 931	23 974	21 907	2 067	29 624	19 474	17 978	1 496
2007	34 650	24 276	22 143	2 132	30 219	19 745	18 322	1 422
2008	35 274	24 643	21 938	2 705	30 980	20 231	18 513	1 717
Married, Spouse Present								
1988	53 246	41 832	40 472	1 360	52 775	29 921	28 756	1 166
1989	53 530	42 036	40 760	1 276	52 885	30 548	29 404	1 145
1990	53 793	42 275	40 829	1 446	52 917	30 901	29 714	1 188
1991	54 158	42 303	40 429	1 875	53 169	31 112	29 698	1 415
1992	54 509	42 491	40 341	2 150	53 501	31 700	30 100	1 600
1993	55 178	42 834	40 935	1 899	53 838	31 980	30 499	1 482
1994	55 560	43 005	41 414	1 592	54 155	32 888	31 536	1 352
1995	56 100	43 472	42 048	1 424	54 716	33 359	32 063	1 296
1996	56 363	43 739	42 417	1 322	54 970	33 618	32 406	1 211
1997	56 396	43 808	42 642	1 167	54 915	33 802	32 755	1 047
1998	56 670	43 957	42 923	1 034	55 331	33 857	32 872	985
1999	57 089	44 244	43 254	990	56 178	34 372	33 450	921
2000	58 167	44 987	44 078	908	57 557	35 146	34 209	937
2001	58 448	45 233	44 007	1 226	57 610	35 236	34 153	1 083
2002	59 102	45 766	44 116	1 650	58 165	35 477	34 153	1 323
2003	60 063	46 404	44 653	1 751	59 069	36 046	34 695	1 352
2004	60 412	46 550	45 084	1 466	59 278	35 845	34 600	1 244
2005	60 545	46 771	45 483	1 287	59 205	35 941	34 773	1 168
2006	60 751	46 842	45 700	1 142	59 576	36 314	35 272	1 042
2007	61 760	47 520	46 314	1 206	60 474	36 881	35 832	1 049
2008	61 794	47 450	45 860	1 590	60 554	37 194	35 869	1 325
Divorced, Widowed, or Separated								
1988	10 039	6 751	6 280	471	23 020	10 627	9 962	665
1989	10 401	7 066	6 618	448	23 604	11 104	10 448	656
1990	10 714	7 378	6 871	508	23 968	11 315	10 639	676
1991	10 924	7 454	6 783	671	24 304	11 385	10 600	786
1992	11 325	7 763	7 001	762	24 559	11 570	10 689	881
1993	11 584	7 864	7 153	711	24 955	11 784	10 927	856
1994	12 008	8 026	7 432	594	25 304	12 018	11 227	791
1995	12 160	8 048	7 496	551	25 539	12 118	11 407	712
1996	12 456	8 276	7 735	541	25 791	12 397	11 691	706
1997	13 009	8 764	8 260	504	26 218	12 742	12 082	660
1998	13 394	8 965	8 530	435	26 190	12 771	12 143	628
1999	13 528	8 918	8 507	411	26 276	12 909	12 324	585
2000	13 910	9 291	8 888	403	27 135	13 308	12 748	559
2001	14 188	9 367	8 892	476	27 738	13 592	12 949	642
2002	14 411	9 445	8 804	641	27 821	13 683	12 846	837
2003	14 680	9 537	8 838	699	27 862	13 828	12 986	842
2004	14 875	9 654	9 045	608	28 141	13 961	13 133	828
2005	15 481	10 048	9 484	563	28 680	14 163	13 396	768
2006	15 923	10 440	9 895	545	29 010	14 385	13 675	709
2007	15 763	10 341	9 797	544	29 001	14 362	13 638	724
2008	16 044	10 427	9 688	739	29 141	14 342	13 494	849

Note: See notes and definitions for information on historical comparability.

Table 1-4. Employment Status of the Civilian Noninstitutional Population, by Sex, Race, and Marital Status, 1988–2008—*Continued*

(Thousands of people.)

Race, marital status, and year	Men Civilian noninstitutional population	Men Civilian labor force Total	Employed	Unemployed	Women Civilian noninstitutional population	Women Civilian labor force Total	Employed	Unemployed
WHITE[1]								
Single								
1988	19 966	15 279	13 982	1 297	16 218	11 428	10 674	754
1989	20 076	15 511	14 249	1 263	16 289	11 474	10 741	734
1990	20 746	15 993	14 617	1 376	16 555	11 522	10 729	794
1991	20 899	15 989	14 233	1 756	16 569	11 497	10 557	939
1992	21 025	16 129	14 285	1 844	16 684	11 502	10 526	976
1993	20 974	16 033	14 303	1 730	16 768	11 613	10 633	980
1994	21 071	16 074	14 539	1 535	16 936	11 805	10 885	920
1995	21 132	16 080	14 674	1 406	17 046	11 830	10 967	864
1996	21 454	16 285	14 891	1 394	17 282	11 977	11 099	878
1997	22 236	16 810	15 507	1 303	17 728	12 322	11 443	879
1998	22 513	17 007	15 746	1 261	18 247	12 742	11 945	797
1999	22 788	17 272	16 116	1 157	18 635	13 029	12 206	823
2000	23 266	17 659	16 504	1 154	18 808	13 215	12 449	766
2001	23 979	17 970	16 561	1 409	19 253	13 368	12 491	877
2002	24 289	17 924	16 289	1 635	19 625	13 556	12 550	1 006
2003	24 419	17 755	16 031	1 723	19 924	13 462	12 461	1 001
2004	24 929	18 090	16 435	1 655	20 210	13 597	12 628	969
2005	25 436	18 338	16 833	1 505	20 702	13 906	12 957	949
2006	26 012	18 928	17 500	1 428	21 085	14 109	13 199	909
2007	26 431	19 063	17 580	1 483	21 408	14 255	13 357	897
2008	27 023	19 395	17 474	1 920	22 064	14 648	13 578	1 070
Married, Spouse Present								
1988	47 685	37 429	36 304	1 125	47 364	26 499	25 540	959
1989	47 883	37 589	36 545	1 044	47 382	27 030	26 083	947
1990	47 841	37 515	36 338	1 177	47 240	27 271	26 285	986
1991	48 137	37 507	35 923	1 585	47 456	27 479	26 290	1 189
1992	48 416	37 671	35 886	1 785	47 705	27 951	26 623	1 329
1993	48 937	37 953	36 396	1 557	47 944	28 221	26 993	1 228
1994	49 169	38 008	36 719	1 288	48 120	29 017	27 888	1 129
1995	49 597	38 376	37 211	1 165	48 497	29 360	28 290	1 070
1996	49 800	38 616	37 522	1 094	48 684	29 517	28 496	1 020
1997	49 719	38 593	37 636	957	48 542	29 664	28 809	855
1998	49 901	38 629	37 793	836	48 722	29 534	28 727	808
1999	50 091	38 765	37 968	797	49 296	29 806	29 056	749
2000	50 775	39 169	38 451	717	50 194	30 344	29 582	762
2001	50 850	39 246	38 265	981	50 077	30 336	29 472	864
2002	51 284	39 580	38 261	1 319	50 489	30 511	29 463	1 048
2003	51 859	39 908	38 529	1 379	50 957	30 805	29 740	1 065
2004	51 992	39 935	38 774	1 161	50 939	30 544	29 549	996
2005	52 034	40 141	39 130	1 011	50 865	30 599	29 676	922
2006	52 035	40 103	39 207	896	51 200	30 950	30 111	839
2007	52 775	40 559	39 594	965	51 868	31 363	30 533	830
2008	52 708	40 404	39 157	1 247	51 637	31 456	30 367	1 089
Divorced, Widowed, or Separated								
1988	8 204	5 608	5 265	344	18 758	8 512	8 047	464
1989	8 509	5 887	5 558	329	19 200	8 863	8 409	454
1990	8 782	6 131	5 748	382	19 461	9 016	8 544	471
1991	8 941	6 159	5 641	518	19 757	9 111	8 538	573
1992	9 210	6 368	5 788	580	19 931	9 216	8 561	654
1993	9 459	6 498	5 957	541	20 206	9 382	8 764	618
1994	9 819	6 644	6 193	451	20 439	9 533	8 965	569
1995	10 005	6 689	6 261	428	20 638	9 613	9 087	526
1996	10 234	6 883	6 474	408	20 862	9 831	9 325	506
1997	10 622	7 236	6 855	382	21 147	10 068	9 607	461
1998	10 937	7 398	7 064	334	21 157	10 104	9 656	449
1999	11 050	7 375	7 056	320	21 225	10 261	9 834	427
2000	11 329	7 638	7 333	305	21 847	10 521	10 105	416
2001	11 623	7 750	7 386	364	22 330	10 729	10 255	474
2002	11 789	7 804	7 299	505	22 308	10 775	10 151	624
2003	11 971	7 846	7 305	541	22 162	10 769	10 168	602
2004	12 124	7 969	7 503	466	22 450	10 950	10 350	600
2005	12 558	8 215	7 800	415	22 853	11 101	10 552	548
2006	12 974	8 583	8 176	407	22 957	11 162	10 640	523
2007	12 867	8 536	8 115	421	22 904	11 159	10 613	547
2008	12 995	8 552	7 992	560	23 112	11 180	10 556	624

Note: See notes and definitions for information on historical comparability.

[1]Beginning in 2003, persons who selected this race group only; persons who selected more than one race group are not included. Prior to 2003, persons who reported more than one race group were included in the group they identified as their main race.

Table 1-4. Employment Status of the Civilian Noninstitutional Population, by Sex, Race, and Marital Status, 1988–2008—*Continued*

(Thousands of people.)

Race, marital status, and year	Men				Women			
	Civilian noninstitutional population	Civilian labor force			Civilian noninstitutional population	Civilian labor force		
		Total	Employed	Unemployed		Total	Employed	Unemployed
BLACK AND OTHER RACES[1]								
Single								
1988	4 606	3 066	2 539	527	4 743	2 766	2 305	461
1989	4 755	3 227	2 687	538	4 852	2 903	2 434	468
1990	5 124	3 364	2 788	576	5 346	3 090	2 607	482
1991	5 298	3 422	2 778	644	5 604	3 184	2 641	543
1992	5 411	3 580	2 813	767	5 791	3 370	2 737	633
1993	5 596	3 673	2 958	715	5 945	3 418	2 851	567
1994	5 715	3 712	3 065	646	6 064	3 528	2 962	566
1995	5 786	3 761	3 159	601	6 105	3 637	3 086	549
1996	5 933	3 786	3 164	622	6 341	3 865	3 304	561
1997	6 075	3 879	3 276	603	6 557	4 170	3 594	576
1998	6 180	4 030	3 494	537	6 694	4 345	3 810	535
1999	6 316	4 079	3 570	508	6 941	4 546	4 061	485
2000	6 621	4 343	3 835	509	7 112	4 634	4 179	455
2001	6 667	4 315	3 737	579	7 209	4 653	4 144	509
2002	6 783	4 365	3 694	671	7 374	4 647	4 033	615
2003	7 272	4 542	3 810	734	7 878	4 935	4 262	673
2004	7 493	4 686	3 960	726	8 018	5 019	4 367	652
2005	7 689	4 876	4 173	704	8 344	5 277	4 631	646
2006	7 919	5 046	4 407	639	8 539	5 365	4 779	587
2007	8 219	5 213	4 563	649	8 811	5 490	4 965	525
2008	8 251	5 248	4 464	785	8 916	5 583	4 935	647
Married, Spouse Present								
1988	5 561	4 403	4 168	235	5 411	3 422	3 216	207
1989	5 647	4 447	4 215	232	5 503	3 518	3 321	198
1990	5 952	4 760	4 491	269	5 677	3 630	3 429	202
1991	6 021	4 796	4 506	290	5 713	3 633	3 408	226
1992	6 093	4 820	4 455	365	5 796	3 749	3 477	271
1993	6 241	4 881	4 539	342	5 894	3 759	3 506	254
1994	6 391	4 997	4 695	304	6 035	3 871	3 648	223
1995	6 503	5 096	4 837	259	6 219	3 999	3 773	226
1996	6 563	5 123	4 895	228	6 286	4 101	3 910	191
1997	6 677	5 215	5 006	210	6 373	4 138	3 946	192
1998	6 769	5 328	5 130	198	6 609	4 323	4 145	177
1999	6 998	5 479	5 286	193	6 882	4 566	4 394	172
2000	7 392	5 818	5 627	191	7 363	4 802	4 627	175
2001	7 598	5 987	5 742	245	7 533	4 900	4 681	219
2002	7 818	6 186	5 855	331	7 676	4 966	4 690	275
2003	8 204	6 496	6 124	372	8 112	5 241	4 955	287
2004	8 420	6 615	6 310	305	8 339	5 301	5 051	248
2005	8 511	6 630	6 353	276	8 340	5 342	5 097	246
2006	8 716	6 739	6 493	246	8 376	5 364	5 161	203
2007	8 985	6 961	6 720	241	8 606	5 518	5 299	219
2008	9 086	7 046	6 703	343	8 917	5 738	5 502	236
Divorced, Widowed, or Separated								
1988	1 835	1 143	1 015	127	4 262	2 115	1 915	201
1989	1 892	1 179	1 060	119	4 404	2 241	2 039	202
1990	1 932	1 247	1 123	126	4 507	2 299	2 095	205
1991	1 983	1 295	1 142	153	4 547	2 274	2 062	213
1992	2 115	1 395	1 213	182	4 628	2 354	2 128	227
1993	2 125	1 366	1 196	170	4 749	2 402	2 163	238
1994	2 189	1 382	1 239	143	4 865	2 485	2 262	222
1995	2 155	1 359	1 235	123	4 901	2 505	2 320	186
1996	2 222	1 393	1 261	133	4 929	2 566	2 366	200
1997	2 387	1 528	1 405	122	5 071	2 674	2 475	199
1998	2 457	1 567	1 466	101	5 033	2 667	2 487	179
1999	2 478	1 543	1 451	91	5 051	2 648	2 490	158
2000	2 581	1 653	1 555	98	5 288	2 787	2 643	143
2001	2 565	1 617	1 506	112	5 408	2 863	2 694	168
2002	2 622	1 641	1 505	136	5 513	2 908	2 695	213
2003	2 709	1 691	1 533	158	5 700	3 059	2 818	240
2004	2 751	1 685	1 542	142	5 691	3 011	2 783	228
2005	2 923	1 833	1 684	148	5 827	3 062	2 844	220
2006	2 949	1 857	1 719	138	6 053	3 223	3 035	186
2007	2 896	1 805	1 682	123	6 097	3 203	3 025	177
2008	3 049	1 875	1 696	179	6 029	3 162	2 938	225

Note: See notes and definitions for information on historical comparability.

[1]Beginning in 2003, persons who selected this race group only; persons who selected more than one race group are not included. Prior to 2003, persons who reported more than one race group were included in the group they identified as their main race.

Table 1-5. Employment Status of the Civilian Noninstitutional Population, by Region, Division, State, and Selected Territory, 2007–2008

(Thousands of people, percent.)

Region, division, and state	2007						2008					
	Civilian noninstitutional population	Civilian labor force					Civilian noninstitutional population	Civilian labor force				
		Total	Participation rate	Employed	Unemployed	Unemployment rate		Total	Participation rate	Employed	Unemployed	Unemployment rate
UNITED STATES[1]	231 867	153 124	66.0	146 047	7 078	4.6	233 788	154 287	66.0	145 362	8 924	5.8
Northeast	42 991	27 967	65.1	26 729	1 239	4.4	43 230	28 240	65.3	26 709	1 531	5.4
New England	11 255	7 633	67.8	7 293	340	4.5	11 319	7 669	67.8	7 254	415	5.4
Connecticut	2 713	1 850	68.2	1 766	85	4.6	2 728	1 876	68.8	1 769	107	5.7
Maine	1 057	703	66.5	670	33	4.6	1 061	707	66.6	669	38	5.4
Massachusetts	5 112	3 416	66.8	3 263	153	4.5	5 148	3 424	66.5	3 244	180	5.3
New Hampshire	1 038	738	71.1	712	26	3.5	1 045	739	70.7	711	28	3.8
Rhode Island	834	572	68.6	543	30	5.2	834	568	68.1	523	44	7.8
Vermont	502	354	70.5	340	14	4.0	504	355	70.4	339	17	4.8
Middle Atlantic	31 736	20 334	64.1	19 435	899	4.4	31 911	20 571	64.5	19 455	1 116	5.4
New Jersey	6 719	4 462	66.4	4 272	191	4.3	6 756	4 497	66.6	4 251	246	5.5
New York	15 259	9 575	62.7	9 141	434	4.5	15 351	9 680	63.1	9 153	527	5.4
Pennsylvania	9 758	6 297	64.5	6 023	274	4.4	9 804	6 395	65.2	6 051	344	5.4
Midwest	51 027	34 881	68.4	33 092	1 789	5.1	51 330	34 847	67.9	32 735	2 112	6.1
East North Central	35 657	24 005	67.3	22 678	1 327	5.5	35 833	23 919	66.8	22 343	1 576	6.6
Illinois	9 806	6 690	68.2	6 349	341	5.1	9 885	6 697	67.7	6 264	434	6.5
Indiana	4 834	3 221	66.6	3 074	147	4.6	4 873	3 230	66.3	3 040	191	5.9
Michigan	7 785	5 024	64.5	4 667	357	7.1	7 783	4 936	63.4	4 519	416	8.4
Ohio	8 875	5 977	67.3	5 641	336	5.6	8 904	5 972	67.1	5 582	390	6.5
Wisconsin	4 357	3 094	71.0	2 948	146	4.7	4 389	3 084	70.3	2 938	146	4.7
West North Central	15 370	10 876	70.8	10 414	463	4.3	15 497	10 928	70.5	10 393	536	4.9
Iowa	2 309	1 664	72.1	1 602	62	3.7	2 325	1 676	72.1	1 607	69	4.1
Kansas	2 100	1 485	70.7	1 425	60	4.1	2 117	1 497	70.7	1 431	66	4.4
Minnesota	4 007	2 911	72.6	2 776	135	4.6	4 043	2 933	72.5	2 773	160	5.4
Missouri	4 511	3 023	67.0	2 870	153	5.1	4 547	3 012	66.2	2 829	183	6.1
Nebraska	1 344	985	73.3	956	29	2.9	1 355	996	73.5	962	33	3.3
North Dakota	495	366	73.9	355	11	3.1	498	370	74.3	358	12	3.2
South Dakota	604	442	73.2	429	13	2.9	611	445	72.8	431	14	3.0
South	83 787	54 286	64.8	51 932	2 355	4.3	84 960	54 940	64.7	51 924	3 017	5.5
South Atlantic	44 423	29 154	65.6	27 935	1 219	4.2	44 992	29 480	65.5	27 797	1 683	5.7
Delaware	666	441	66.2	426	15	3.4	676	443	65.5	422	21	4.8
District of Columbia	478	327	68.4	309	18	5.5	482	333	69.1	310	23	7.0
Florida	14 318	9 088	63.5	8 717	372	4.1	14 454	9 231	63.9	8 660	572	6.2
Georgia	7 076	4 798	67.8	4 579	219	4.6	7 204	4 848	67.3	4 546	302	6.2
Maryland	4 331	2 988	69.0	2 882	105	3.5	4 357	2 998	68.8	2 867	131	4.4
North Carolina	6 880	4 506	65.5	4 293	213	4.7	7 011	4 544	64.8	4 257	287	6.3
South Carolina	3 367	2 125	63.1	2 006	119	5.6	3 431	2 153	62.8	2 004	149	6.9
Virginia	5 862	4 068	69.4	3 945	122	3.0	5 927	4 125	69.6	3 960	165	4.0
West Virginia	1 445	813	56.3	778	35	4.3	1 450	806	55.6	772	34	4.3
East South Central	13 745	8 532	62.1	8 115	417	4.9	13 891	8 561	61.6	8 035	526	6.1
Alabama	3 558	2 176	61.2	2 100	76	3.5	3 591	2 162	60.2	2 054	109	5.0
Kentucky	3 266	2 036	62.3	1 923	113	5.5	3 301	2 043	61.9	1 911	132	6.4
Mississippi	2 175	1 307	60.1	1 225	82	6.3	2 190	1 314	60.0	1 224	91	6.9
Tennessee	4 746	3 013	63.5	2 868	146	4.8	4 808	3 041	63.2	2 846	195	6.4
West South Central	25 619	16 600	64.8	15 881	719	4.3	26 077	16 899	64.8	16 092	807	4.8
Arkansas	2 160	1 361	63.0	1 292	69	5.1	2 180	1 370	62.8	1 301	70	5.1
Louisiana	3 294	2 026	61.5	1 949	76	3.8	3 337	2 079	62.3	1 983	96	4.6
Oklahoma	2 720	1 738	63.9	1 667	71	4.1	2 749	1 748	63.6	1 682	67	3.8
Texas	17 445	11 475	65.8	10 972	503	4.4	17 812	11 702	65.7	11 126	575	4.9
West	52 993	35 278	66.6	33 617	1 661	4.7	53 845	35 971	66.8	33 725	2 246	6.2
Mountain	16 040	10 887	67.9	10 486	401	3.7	16 378	11 133	68.0	10 579	554	5.0
Arizona	4 762	3 036	63.8	2 920	116	3.8	4 877	3 133	64.2	2 960	172	5.5
Colorado	3 702	2 686	72.6	2 582	104	3.9	3 778	2 730	72.3	2 596	134	4.9
Idaho	1 109	749	67.5	726	23	3.0	1 131	755	66.8	718	37	4.9
Montana	748	502	67.1	485	17	3.4	758	506	66.8	483	23	4.5
Nevada	1 932	1 323	68.5	1 260	62	4.7	1 971	1 373	69.7	1 282	91	6.7
New Mexico	1 487	946	63.6	912	34	3.5	1 507	959	63.6	919	40	4.2
Utah	1 897	1 357	71.5	1 320	37	2.7	1 945	1 384	71.2	1 336	48	3.4
Wyoming	403	288	71.5	280	8	2.9	410	293	71.5	284	9	3.1
Pacific	36 953	24 391	66.0	23 131	1 261	5.2	37 468	24 838	66.3	23 146	1 692	6.8
Alaska	497	352	70.8	330	22	6.2	502	357	71.1	333	24	6.7
California	27 541	18 078	65.6	17 109	969	5.4	27 910	18 392	65.9	17 060	1 332	7.2
Hawaii	981	646	65.9	629	17	2.6	991	654	66.0	628	26	3.9
Oregon	2 932	1 925	65.7	1 826	99	5.1	2 980	1 958	65.7	1 833	125	6.4
Washington	5 002	3 391	67.8	3 237	154	4.5	5 086	3 477	68.4	3 291	186	5.3

Note: Data refer to place of residence. Region and division data are derived from summing the component states. Sub-national data reflect revised population controls and model reestimation.

[1]Due to separate processing and weighing procedures, totals for the United States differ from the results obtained by aggregating data for regions, divisions, or states.

Table 1-6. Civilian Noninstitutional Population, by Age, Race, Sex, and Hispanic Origin, 1948–2008

(Thousands of people.)

Race, Hispanic origin, sex, and year	16 years and over	16 to 19 years			20 years and over						
		Total	16 to 17 years	18 to 19 years	Total	20 to 24 years	25 to 34 years	35 to 44 years	45 to 54 years	55 to 64 years	65 years and over
ALL RACES											
Both Sexes											
1948	103 068	8 449	4 265	4 185	94 618	11 530	22 610	20 097	16 771	12 885	10 720
1949	103 994	8 215	4 139	4 079	95 778	11 312	22 822	20 401	17 002	13 201	11 035
1950	104 995	8 143	4 076	4 068	96 851	11 080	23 013	20 681	17 240	13 469	11 363
1951	104 621	7 865	4 096	3 771	96 755	10 167	22 843	20 863	17 464	13 692	11 724
1952	105 231	7 922	4 234	3 689	97 305	9 389	23 044	21 137	17 716	13 889	12 126
1953	107 056	8 014	4 241	3 773	99 041	8 960	23 266	21 922	17 991	13 830	13 075
1954	108 321	8 224	4 336	3 889	100 095	8 885	23 304	22 135	18 305	14 085	13 375
1955	109 683	8 364	4 440	3 925	101 318	9 036	23 249	22 348	18 643	14 309	13 728
1956	110 954	8 434	4 482	3 953	102 518	9 271	23 072	22 567	19 012	14 516	14 075
1957	112 265	8 612	4 587	4 026	103 653	9 486	22 849	22 786	19 424	14 727	14 376
1958	113 727	8 986	4 872	4 114	104 737	9 733	22 563	23 025	19 832	14 923	14 657
1959	115 329	9 618	5 337	4 282	105 711	9 975	22 201	23 207	20 203	15 134	14 985
1960	117 245	10 187	5 573	4 615	107 056	10 273	21 998	23 437	20 601	15 409	15 336
1961	118 771	10 513	5 462	5 052	108 255	10 583	21 829	23 585	20 893	15 675	15 685
1962	120 153	10 652	5 503	5 150	109 500	10 852	21 503	23 797	20 916	15 874	16 554
1963	122 416	11 370	6 301	5 070	111 045	11 464	21 400	23 948	21 144	16 138	16 945
1964	124 485	12 111	6 974	5 139	112 372	12 017	21 367	23 940	21 452	16 442	17 150
1965	126 513	12 930	6 936	5 995	113 582	12 442	21 417	23 832	21 728	16 727	17 432
1966	128 058	13 592	6 914	6 679	114 463	12 638	21 543	23 579	21 977	17 007	17 715
1967	129 874	13 480	7 003	6 480	116 391	13 421	22 057	23 313	22 256	17 310	18 029
1968	132 028	13 698	7 200	6 499	118 328	13 891	22 912	23 036	22 534	17 614	18 338
1969	134 335	14 095	7 422	6 673	120 238	14 488	23 645	22 709	22 806	17 930	18 657
1970	137 085	14 519	7 643	6 876	122 566	15 323	24 435	22 489	23 059	18 250	19 007
1971	140 216	15 022	7 849	7 173	125 193	16 345	25 337	22 274	23 244	18 581	19 406
1972	144 126	15 510	8 076	7 435	128 614	17 143	26 740	22 358	23 338	19 007	20 023
1973	147 096	15 840	8 227	7 613	131 253	17 692	28 172	22 287	23 431	19 281	20 389
1974	150 120	16 180	8 373	7 809	133 938	17 994	29 439	22 461	23 578	19 517	20 945
1975	153 153	16 418	8 419	7 999	136 733	18 595	30 710	22 526	23 535	19 844	21 525
1976	156 150	16 614	8 442	8 171	139 536	19 109	31 953	23 409	23 409	20 185	22 083
1977	159 033	16 688	8 482	8 206	142 345	19 582	33 117	23 296	23 197	20 557	22 597
1978	161 910	16 695	8 484	8 211	145 216	20 007	34 091	24 099	22 977	20 875	23 166
1979	164 863	16 657	8 389	8 268	148 205	20 353	35 261	24 861	22 752	21 210	23 767
1980	167 745	16 543	8 279	8 264	151 202	20 635	36 558	25 578	22 563	21 520	24 350
1981	170 130	16 214	8 068	8 145	153 916	20 820	37 777	26 291	22 422	21 756	24 850
1982	172 271	15 763	7 714	8 049	156 508	20 845	38 492	27 611	22 264	21 909	25 387
1983	174 215	15 274	7 385	7 889	158 941	20 799	39 147	28 932	22 167	22 003	25 892
1984	176 383	14 735	7 196	7 538	161 648	20 688	39 999	30 251	22 226	22 052	26 433
1985	178 206	14 506	7 232	7 274	163 700	20 097	40 670	31 379	22 418	22 140	26 997
1986	180 587	14 496	7 386	7 110	166 091	19 569	41 731	32 550	22 732	22 011	27 497
1987	182 753	14 606	7 501	7 104	168 147	18 970	42 297	33 755	23 183	21 835	28 108
1988	184 613	14 527	7 284	7 243	170 085	18 434	42 611	34 784	24 004	21 641	28 612
1989	186 393	14 223	6 886	7 338	172 169	18 025	42 845	35 977	24 744	21 406	29 173
1990	189 164	14 520	6 893	7 626	174 644	18 902	42 976	37 719	25 081	20 719	29 247
1991	190 925	14 073	6 901	7 173	176 852	18 963	42 688	39 116	25 709	20 675	29 700
1992	192 805	13 840	6 907	6 933	178 965	18 846	42 278	39 852	27 206	20 604	30 179
1993	194 838	13 935	7 010	6 925	180 903	18 642	41 771	40 733	28 549	20 574	30 634
1994	196 814	14 196	7 245	6 951	182 619	18 353	41 306	41 534	29 778	20 635	31 012
1995	198 584	14 511	7 407	7 104	184 073	17 864	40 798	42 254	30 974	20 735	31 448
1996	200 591	14 934	7 678	7 256	185 656	17 409	40 252	43 086	32 167	20 990	31 751
1997	203 133	15 365	7 861	7 504	187 769	17 442	39 559	43 883	33 391	21 505	31 989
1998	205 220	15 644	7 895	7 749	189 576	17 593	38 778	44 299	34 373	22 296	32 237
1999	207 753	16 040	8 060	7 979	191 713	17 968	37 976	44 635	35 587	23 064	32 484
2000	212 577	15 912	7 978	7 934	196 664	18 311	38 703	44 312	37 642	24 230	33 466
2001	215 092	15 929	8 020	7 909	199 164	18 877	38 505	44 195	38 904	25 011	33 672
2002	217 570	15 994	8 099	7 895	201 576	19 348	38 472	43 894	39 711	26 343	33 808
2003	221 168	16 096	8 561	7 535	205 072	19 801	39 021	43 746	40 522	27 728	34 253
2004	223 357	16 222	8 574	7 648	207 134	20 197	38 939	43 226	41 245	28 919	34 609
2005	226 082	16 398	8 778	7 619	209 685	20 276	39 064	43 005	42 107	30 165	35 068
2006	228 815	16 678	9 089	7 589	212 137	20 265	39 230	42 753	42 901	31 375	35 613
2007	231 867	16 982	9 222	7 760	214 885	20 427	39 751	42 401	43 544	32 533	36 228
2008	233 788	17 075	9 133	7 942	216 713	20 409	39 993	41 699	43 960	33 491	37 161

Table 1-6. Civilian Noninstitutional Population, by Age, Race, Sex, and Hispanic Origin, 1948–2008
—Continued

(Thousands of people.)

Race, Hispanic origin, sex, and year	16 years and over	16 to 19 years			20 years and over						
		Total	16 to 17 years	18 to 19 years	Total	20 to 24 years	25 to 34 years	35 to 44 years	45 to 54 years	55 to 64 years	65 years and over
ALL RACES											
Men											
1948	49 996	4 078	2 128	1 951	45 918	5 527	10 767	9 798	8 290	6 441	5 093
1949	50 321	3 946	2 062	1 884	46 378	5 405	10 871	9 926	8 379	6 568	5 226
1950	50 725	3 962	2 043	1 920	46 763	5 270	10 963	10 034	8 472	6 664	5 357
1951	49 727	3 725	2 039	1 687	46 001	4 451	10 709	10 049	8 551	6 737	5 503
1952	49 700	3 767	2 121	1 647	45 932	3 788	10 855	10 164	8 655	6 798	5 670
1953	50 750	3 823	2 122	1 701	46 927	3 482	11 020	10 632	8 878	6 798	6 119
1954	51 395	3 953	2 174	1 780	47 441	3 509	11 067	10 718	9 018	6 885	6 241
1955	52 109	4 022	2 225	1 798	48 086	3 708	11 068	10 804	9 164	6 960	6 380
1956	52 723	4 020	2 238	1 783	48 704	3 970	10 983	10 889	9 322	7 032	6 505
1957	53 315	4 083	2 284	1 800	49 231	4 166	10 889	10 965	9 499	7 109	6 602
1958	54 033	4 293	2 435	1 858	49 740	4 339	10 787	11 076	9 675	7 179	6 683
1959	54 793	4 652	2 681	1 971	50 140	4 488	10 625	11 149	9 832	7 259	6 785
1960	55 662	4 963	2 805	2 159	50 698	4 679	10 514	11 230	10 000	7 373	6 901
1961	56 286	5 112	2 742	2 371	51 173	4 844	10 440	11 286	10 112	7 483	7 006
1962	56 831	5 150	2 764	2 386	51 681	4 925	10 207	11 389	10 162	7 610	7 386
1963	57 921	5 496	3 162	2 334	52 425	5 240	10 165	11 476	10 274	7 740	7 526
1964	58 847	5 866	3 503	2 364	52 981	5 520	10 144	11 466	10 402	7 873	7 574
1965	59 782	6 318	3 488	2 831	53 463	5 701	10 182	11 427	10 512	7 990	7 649
1966	60 262	6 658	3 478	3 180	53 603	5 663	10 224	11 294	10 598	8 099	7 723
1967	60 905	6 537	3 528	3 010	54 367	5 977	10 495	11 161	10 705	8 218	7 809
1968	61 847	6 683	3 634	3 049	55 165	6 127	10 944	11 040	10 819	8 336	7 897
1969	62 898	6 928	3 741	3 187	55 969	6 379	11 309	10 890	10 935	8 464	7 990
1970	64 304	7 145	3 848	3 299	57 157	6 861	11 750	10 810	11 052	8 590	8 093
1971	65 942	7 430	3 954	3 477	58 511	7 511	12 227	10 721	11 129	8 711	8 208
1972	67 835	7 705	4 081	3 624	60 130	8 061	12 911	10 762	11 167	8 895	8 330
1973	69 292	7 855	4 152	3 703	61 436	8 429	13 641	10 746	11 202	8 990	8 426
1974	70 808	8 012	4 231	3 781	62 796	8 600	14 262	10 834	11 315	9 140	8 641
1975	72 291	8 134	4 252	3 882	64 158	8 950	14 899	10 874	11 298	9 286	8 852
1976	73 759	8 244	4 266	3 978	65 515	9 237	15 528	11 010	11 243	9 444	9 053
1977	75 193	8 288	4 290	4 000	66 904	9 477	16 108	11 260	11 144	9 616	9 297
1978	76 576	8 309	4 295	4 014	68 268	9 693	16 598	11 665	11 045	9 758	9 509
1979	78 020	8 310	4 251	4 060	69 709	9 873	17 193	12 046	10 944	9 907	9 746
1980	79 398	8 260	4 195	4 064	71 138	10 023	17 833	12 400	10 861	10 042	9 979
1981	80 511	8 092	4 087	4 005	72 419	10 116	18 427	12 758	10 797	10 151	10 170
1982	81 523	7 879	3 911	3 968	73 644	10 136	18 787	13 410	10 726	10 215	10 371
1983	82 531	7 659	3 750	3 908	74 872	10 140	19 143	14 067	10 689	10 261	10 573
1984	83 605	7 386	3 655	3 731	76 219	10 108	19 596	14 719	10 724	10 285	10 788
1985	84 469	7 275	3 689	3 586	77 195	9 746	19 864	15 265	10 844	10 392	11 084
1986	85 798	7 275	3 768	3 507	78 523	9 498	20 498	15 858	10 986	10 336	11 347
1987	86 899	7 335	3 824	3 510	79 565	9 195	20 781	16 475	11 215	10 267	11 632
1988	87 857	7 304	3 715	3 588	80 553	8 931	20 937	17 008	11 625	10 193	11 859
1989	88 762	7 143	3 524	3 619	81 619	8 743	21 080	17 590	11 981	10 092	12 134
1990	90 377	7 347	3 534	3 813	83 030	9 320	21 117	18 529	12 238	9 778	12 049
1991	91 278	7 134	3 548	3 586	84 144	9 367	20 977	19 213	12 554	9 780	12 254
1992	92 270	7 023	3 542	3 481	85 247	9 326	20 792	19 585	13 271	9 776	12 496
1993	93 332	7 076	3 595	3 481	86 256	9 216	20 569	20 037	13 944	9 773	12 717
1994	94 355	7 203	3 718	3 486	87 151	9 074	20 361	20 443	14 545	9 810	12 918
1995	95 178	7 367	3 794	3 573	87 811	8 835	20 079	20 800	15 111	9 856	13 130
1996	96 206	7 600	3 955	3 645	88 606	8 611	19 775	21 222	15 674	9 997	13 327
1997	97 715	7 836	4 053	3 783	89 879	8 706	19 478	21 669	16 276	10 282	13 469
1998	98 758	7 968	4 059	3 909	90 790	8 804	19 094	21 857	16 773	10 649	13 613
1999	99 722	8 167	4 143	4 024	91 555	8 899	18 565	21 969	17 335	11 008	13 779
2000	101 964	8 089	4 096	3 993	93 875	9 101	19 106	21 683	18 365	11 583	14 037
2001	103 282	8 101	4 102	3 999	95 181	9 368	19 056	21 643	18 987	11 972	14 155
2002	104 585	8 146	4 140	4 006	96 439	9 627	19 037	21 523	19 379	12 641	14 233
2003	106 435	8 163	4 365	3 797	98 272	9 878	19 347	21 463	19 784	13 305	14 496
2004	107 710	8 234	4 318	3 916	99 476	10 125	19 358	21 255	20 160	13 894	14 684
2005	109 151	8 317	4 481	3 836	100 835	10 181	19 446	21 177	20 585	14 502	14 944
2006	110 605	8 459	4 613	3 846	102 145	10 191	19 568	21 082	20 991	15 095	15 219
2007	112 173	8 618	4 658	3 960	103 555	10 291	19 858	20 910	21 313	15 658	15 525
2008	113 113	8 660	4 625	4 035	104 453	10 249	19 999	20 567	21 512	16 123	16 002

Table 1-6. Civilian Noninstitutional Population, by Age, Race, Sex, and Hispanic Origin, 1948–2008
—Continued

(Thousands of people.)

Race, Hispanic origin, sex, and year	16 years and over	16 to 19 years			20 years and over						
		Total	16 to 17 years	18 to 19 years	Total	20 to 24 years	25 to 34 years	35 to 44 years	45 to 54 years	55 to 64 years	65 years and over
ALL RACES											
Women											
1948	53 071	4 371	2 137	2 234	48 700	6 003	11 843	10 299	8 481	6 444	5 627
1949	53 670	4 269	2 077	2 195	49 400	5 907	11 951	10 475	8 623	6 633	5 809
1950	54 270	4 181	2 033	2 148	50 088	5 810	12 050	10 647	8 768	6 805	6 006
1951	54 895	4 140	2 057	2 084	50 754	5 716	12 134	10 814	8 913	6 955	6 221
1952	55 529	4 155	2 113	2 042	51 373	5 601	12 189	10 973	9 061	7 091	6 456
1953	56 305	4 191	2 119	2 072	52 114	5 478	12 246	11 290	9 113	7 032	6 956
1954	56 925	4 271	2 162	2 109	52 654	5 376	12 237	11 417	9 287	7 200	7 134
1955	57 574	4 342	2 215	2 127	53 232	5 328	12 181	11 544	9 479	7 349	7 348
1956	58 228	4 414	2 244	2 170	53 814	5 301	12 089	11 678	9 690	7 484	7 570
1957	58 951	4 529	2 303	2 226	54 421	5 320	11 960	11 821	9 925	7 618	7 774
1958	59 690	4 693	2 437	2 256	54 997	5 394	11 776	11 949	10 157	7 744	7 974
1959	60 534	4 966	2 656	2 311	55 570	5 487	11 576	12 058	10 371	7 875	8 200
1960	61 582	5 224	2 768	2 456	56 358	5 594	11 484	12 207	10 601	8 036	8 435
1961	62 484	5 401	2 720	2 681	57 082	5 739	11 389	12 299	10 781	8 192	8 679
1962	63 321	5 502	2 739	2 764	57 819	5 927	11 296	12 408	10 754	8 264	9 168
1963	64 494	5 874	3 139	2 736	58 620	6 224	11 235	12 472	10 870	8 398	9 419
1964	65 637	6 245	3 471	2 775	59 391	6 497	11 223	12 474	11 050	8 569	9 576
1965	66 731	6 612	3 448	3 164	60 119	6 741	11 235	12 405	11 216	8 737	9 783
1966	67 795	6 934	3 436	3 499	60 860	6 975	11 319	12 285	11 379	8 908	9 992
1967	68 968	6 943	3 475	3 470	62 026	7 445	11 562	12 152	11 551	9 092	10 220
1968	70 179	7 015	3 566	3 450	63 164	7 764	11 968	11 996	11 715	9 278	10 441
1969	71 436	7 167	3 681	3 486	64 269	8 109	12 336	11 819	11 871	9 466	10 667
1970	72 782	7 373	3 796	3 578	65 408	8 462	12 684	11 679	12 008	9 659	10 914
1971	74 274	7 591	3 895	3 697	66 682	8 834	13 110	11 553	12 115	9 870	11 198
1972	76 290	7 805	3 994	3 811	68 484	9 082	13 829	11 597	12 171	10 113	11 693
1973	77 804	7 985	4 076	3 909	69 819	9 263	14 531	11 541	12 229	10 290	11 963
1974	79 312	8 168	4 142	4 028	71 144	9 393	15 177	11 627	12 263	10 377	12 304
1975	80 860	8 285	4 168	4 117	72 576	9 645	15 811	11 652	12 237	10 558	12 673
1976	82 390	8 370	4 176	4 194	74 020	9 872	16 425	11 786	12 166	10 742	13 030
1977	83 840	8 400	4 193	4 206	75 441	10 103	17 008	12 036	12 053	10 940	13 300
1978	85 334	8 386	4 189	4 197	76 948	10 315	17 493	12 435	11 932	11 118	13 658
1979	86 843	8 347	4 139	4 208	78 496	10 480	18 070	12 815	11 808	11 303	14 021
1980	88 348	8 283	4 083	4 200	80 065	10 612	18 725	13 177	11 701	11 478	14 372
1981	89 618	8 121	3 981	4 140	81 497	10 705	19 350	13 533	11 625	11 605	14 680
1982	90 748	7 884	3 804	4 081	82 864	10 709	19 705	14 201	11 538	11 694	15 017
1983	91 684	7 616	3 635	3 981	84 069	10 660	20 004	14 865	11 478	11 742	15 319
1984	92 778	7 349	3 542	3 807	85 429	10 580	20 403	15 532	11 501	11 768	15 645
1985	93 736	7 231	3 543	3 688	86 506	10 351	20 805	16 114	11 574	11 748	15 913
1986	94 789	7 221	3 618	3 603	87 567	10 072	21 233	16 692	11 746	11 675	16 150
1987	95 853	7 271	3 677	3 594	88 583	9 776	21 516	17 279	11 968	11 567	16 476
1988	96 756	7 224	3 569	3 655	89 532	9 503	21 674	17 776	12 378	11 448	16 753
1989	97 630	7 080	3 361	3 719	90 550	9 282	21 765	18 387	12 763	11 314	17 039
1990	98 787	7 173	3 359	3 813	91 614	9 582	21 859	19 190	12 843	10 941	17 198
1991	99 646	6 939	3 353	3 586	92 708	9 597	21 711	19 903	13 155	10 895	17 446
1992	100 535	6 818	3 366	3 452	93 718	9 520	21 486	20 267	13 935	10 828	17 682
1993	101 506	6 859	3 415	3 444	94 647	9 426	21 202	20 696	14 605	10 801	17 917
1994	102 460	6 993	3 528	3 465	95 467	9 279	20 945	21 091	15 233	10 825	18 094
1995	103 406	7 144	3 613	3 531	96 262	9 029	20 719	21 454	15 862	10 879	18 318
1996	104 385	7 335	3 723	3 612	97 050	8 798	20 477	21 865	16 493	10 993	18 424
1997	105 418	7 528	3 808	3 721	97 889	8 736	20 081	22 214	17 115	11 224	18 520
1998	106 462	7 676	3 835	3 840	98 786	8 790	19 683	22 442	17 600	11 646	18 625
1999	108 031	7 873	3 917	3 955	100 158	9 069	19 411	22 666	18 251	12 056	18 705
2000	110 613	7 823	3 882	3 941	102 790	9 211	19 597	22 628	19 276	12 647	19 430
2001	111 811	7 828	3 917	3 910	103 983	9 509	19 449	22 552	19 917	13 039	19 517
2002	112 985	7 848	3 959	3 889	105 136	9 721	19 435	22 371	20 332	13 703	19 575
2003	114 733	7 934	4 195	3 738	106 800	9 924	19 674	22 283	20 738	14 423	19 758
2004	115 647	7 989	4 257	3 732	107 658	10 072	19 581	21 970	21 085	15 025	19 925
2005	116 931	8 081	4 297	3 784	108 850	10 095	19 618	21 828	21 521	15 663	20 125
2006	118 210	8 218	4 476	3 742	109 992	10 074	19 662	21 671	21 910	16 280	20 394
2007	119 694	8 364	4 564	3 800	111 330	10 137	19 893	21 491	22 231	16 876	20 703
2008	120 675	8 415	4 508	3 907	112 260	10 160	19 994	21 132	22 448	17 367	21 160

Table 1-6. Civilian Noninstitutional Population, by Age, Race, Sex, and Hispanic Origin, 1948–2008
—Continued

(Thousands of people.)

Race, Hispanic origin, sex, and year	16 years and over	16 to 19 years			20 years and over						
		Total	16 to 17 years	18 to 19 years	Total	20 to 24 years	25 to 34 years	35 to 44 years	45 to 54 years	55 to 64 years	65 years and over
WHITE											
Both Sexes											
1954	97 705	7 180	3 786	3 394	90 524	7 794	20 818	19 915	16 569	12 993	12 438
1955	98 880	7 292	3 874	3 419	91 586	7 912	20 742	20 110	16 869	13 169	12 785
1956	99 976	7 346	3 908	3 438	92 629	8 106	20 564	20 314	17 198	13 341	13 105
1957	101 119	7 505	4 007	3 498	93 612	8 293	20 342	20 514	17 562	13 518	13 383
1958	102 392	7 843	4 271	3 573	94 547	8 498	20 063	20 734	17 924	13 681	13 645
1959	103 803	8 430	4 707	3 725	95 370	8 697	19 715	20 893	18 257	13 858	13 951
1960	105 282	8 924	4 909	4 016	96 355	8 927	19 470	21 049	18 578	14 070	14 260
1961	106 604	9 211	4 785	4 427	97 390	9 203	19 289	21 169	18 845	14 304	14 581
1962	107 715	9 343	4 818	4 526	98 371	9 484	18 974	21 293	18 872	14 450	15 297
1963	109 705	9 978	5 549	4 430	99 725	10 069	18 867	21 398	19 082	14 681	15 629
1964	111 534	10 616	6 137	4 481	100 916	10 568	18 838	21 375	19 360	14 957	15 816
1965	113 284	11 319	6 049	5 271	101 963	10 935	18 882	21 258	19 604	15 215	16 070
1966	114 566	11 862	5 993	5 870	102 702	11 094	18 989	21 005	19 822	15 469	16 322
1967	116 100	11 682	6 051	5 632	104 417	11 797	19 464	20 745	20 067	15 745	16 602
1968	117 948	11 840	6 225	5 616	106 107	12 184	20 245	20 474	20 310	16 018	16 875
1969	119 913	12 179	6 418	5 761	107 733	12 677	20 892	20 156	20 546	16 305	17 156
1970	122 174	12 521	6 591	5 931	109 652	13 359	21 546	19 929	20 760	16 591	17 469
1971	124 758	12 937	6 750	6 189	111 821	14 208	22 295	19 694	20 907	16 884	17 833
1972	127 906	13 301	6 910	6 392	114 603	14 897	23 555	19 673	20 950	17 250	18 278
1973	130 097	13 533	7 021	6 512	116 563	15 264	24 685	19 532	20 991	17 484	18 607
1974	132 417	13 784	7 114	6 671	118 632	15 502	25 711	19 628	21 061	17 645	19 085
1975	134 790	13 941	7 132	6 808	120 849	15 980	26 746	19 641	20 981	17 918	19 587
1976	137 106	14 055	7 125	6 930	123 050	16 368	27 757	19 827	20 816	18 220	20 064
1977	139 380	14 095	7 150	6 944	125 285	16 728	28 703	20 231	20 575	18 540	20 508
1978	141 612	14 060	7 132	6 928	127 552	17 038	29 453	20 932	20 322	18 799	21 007
1979	143 894	13 994	7 029	6 964	129 900	17 284	30 371	21 579	20 058	19 071	21 538
1980	146 122	13 854	6 912	6 943	132 268	17 484	31 407	22 174	19 837	19 316	22 050
1981	147 908	13 516	6 704	6 813	134 392	17 609	32 367	22 778	19 666	19 485	22 487
1982	149 441	13 076	6 383	6 693	136 366	17 579	32 863	23 910	19 478	19 591	22 945
1983	150 805	12 623	6 089	6 534	138 183	17 492	33 286	25 027	19 349	19 625	23 403
1984	152 347	12 147	5 918	6 228	140 200	17 304	33 889	26 124	19 348	19 629	23 906
1985	153 679	11 900	5 922	5 978	141 780	16 853	34 450	27 100	19 405	19 620	24 352
1986	155 432	11 879	6 036	5 843	143 553	16 353	35 293	28 062	19 587	19 477	24 780
1987	156 958	11 939	6 110	5 829	145 020	15 808	35 667	29 036	19 965	19 242	25 301
1988	158 194	11 838	5 893	5 945	146 357	15 276	35 876	29 818	20 652	18 996	25 739
1989	159 338	11 530	5 506	6 023	147 809	14 879	35 951	30 774	21 287	18 743	26 175
1990	160 625	11 630	5 464	6 166	148 996	15 538	35 661	31 739	21 535	18 204	26 319
1991	161 759	11 200	5 451	5 749	150 558	15 516	35 342	32 854	22 052	18 074	26 721
1992	162 972	11 004	5 478	5 526	151 968	15 354	34 885	33 305	23 364	17 951	27 108
1993	164 289	11 078	5 562	5 516	153 210	15 087	34 365	33 919	24 456	17 892	27 493
1994	165 555	11 264	5 710	5 554	154 291	14 708	33 865	34 582	25 435	17 924	27 776
1995	166 914	11 468	5 822	5 646	155 446	14 313	33 355	35 222	26 418	17 986	28 153
1996	168 317	11 822	6 026	5 796	156 495	13 907	32 852	35 810	27 403	18 136	28 387
1997	169 993	12 181	6 213	5 968	157 812	13 983	32 091	36 325	28 388	18 511	28 514
1998	171 478	12 439	6 264	6 176	159 039	14 138	31 286	36 610	29 132	19 231	28 642
1999	173 085	12 700	6 342	6 358	160 385	14 394	30 516	36 755	30 048	19 855	28 818
2000	176 220	12 535	6 264	6 271	163 685	14 552	30 948	36 261	31 550	20 757	29 617
2001	178 111	12 556	6 291	6 265	165 556	15 001	30 770	36 113	32 475	21 434	29 762
2002	179 783	12 596	6 346	6 250	167 187	15 360	30 676	35 750	33 012	22 540	29 849
2003	181 292	12 527	6 629	5 898	168 765	15 536	30 789	35 352	33 466	23 589	30 033
2004	182 643	12 599	6 561	6 038	170 045	15 817	30 585	34 845	34 005	24 549	30 245
2005	184 446	12 690	6 768	5 921	171 757	15 871	30 592	34 554	34 649	25 534	30 556
2006	186 264	12 856	6 981	5 875	173 408	15 848	30 661	34 217	35 228	26 486	30 968
2007	188 253	13 043	7 026	6 018	175 210	15 945	31 011	33 770	35 665	27 392	31 426
2008	189 540	13 084	6 962	6 122	176 456	15 914	31 234	33 093	35 941	28 109	32 165

Table 1-6. Civilian Noninstitutional Population, by Age, Race, Sex, and Hispanic Origin, 1948–2008
—Continued

(Thousands of people.)

Race, Hispanic origin, sex, and year	16 years and over	16 to 19 years			20 years and over						
		Total	16 to 17 years	18 to 19 years	Total	20 to 24 years	25 to 34 years	35 to 44 years	45 to 54 years	55 to 64 years	65 years and over
WHITE											
Men											
1954	46 462	3 455	1 902	1 553	43 007	3 074	9 948	9 688	8 172	6 341	5 787
1955	47 076	3 507	1 945	1 563	43 569	3 241	9 936	9 768	8 303	6 398	5 923
1956	47 602	3 500	1 955	1 546	44 102	3 464	9 851	9 848	8 446	6 455	6 038
1957	48 119	3 556	2 000	1 557	44 563	3 638	9 758	9 917	8 605	6 518	6 127
1958	48 745	3 747	2 140	1 607	44 998	3 783	9 656	10 018	8 765	6 574	6 203
1959	49 408	4 079	2 370	1 710	45 329	3 903	9 499	10 081	8 909	6 639	6 298
1960	50 065	4 349	2 476	1 874	45 716	4 054	9 373	10 131	9 042	6 721	6 395
1961	50 608	4 479	2 407	2 073	46 129	4 204	9 290	10 178	9 148	6 819	6 490
1962	51 054	4 520	2 426	2 094	46 534	4 306	9 080	10 239	9 191	6 917	6 801
1963	52 031	4 827	2 792	2 036	47 204	4 610	9 039	10 309	9 297	7 031	6 919
1964	52 869	5 148	3 090	2 059	47 721	4 862	9 024	10 301	9 417	7 153	6 963
1965	53 681	5 541	3 050	2 492	48 140	5 017	9 056	10 262	9 516	7 261	7 028
1966	54 061	5 820	3 023	2 798	48 241	4 974	9 085	10 136	9 592	7 362	7 092
1967	54 608	5 671	3 058	2 613	48 937	5 257	9 339	10 013	9 688	7 474	7 167
1968	55 434	5 787	3 153	2 635	49 647	5 376	9 752	9 902	9 790	7 585	7 242
1969	56 348	6 005	3 246	2 759	50 343	5 589	10 074	9 760	9 895	7 705	7 320
1970	57 516	6 179	3 329	2 851	51 336	5 988	10 441	9 678	9 999	7 822	7 409
1971	58 900	6 420	3 412	3 008	52 481	6 546	10 841	9 578	10 066	7 933	7 517
1972	60 473	6 627	3 503	3 125	53 845	7 042	11 495	9 568	10 078	8 089	7 573
1973	61 577	6 737	3 555	3 182	54 842	7 312	12 075	9 514	10 099	8 178	7 664
1974	62 791	6 851	3 604	3 247	55 942	7 476	12 599	9 564	10 165	8 288	7 849
1975	63 981	6 929	3 609	3 320	57 052	7 766	13 131	9 578	10 134	8 413	8 031
1976	65 132	6 993	3 609	3 384	58 138	7 987	13 655	9 674	10 063	8 556	8 203
1977	66 301	7 024	3 625	3 399	59 278	8 175	14 139	9 880	9 957	8 708	8 420
1978	67 401	7 022	3 619	3 404	60 378	8 335	14 528	10 236	9 845	8 826	8 608
1979	68 547	7 007	3 568	3 439	61 540	8 470	15 008	10 563	9 730	8 949	8 820
1980	69 634	6 941	3 508	3 433	62 694	8 581	15 529	10 863	9 636	9 059	9 027
1981	70 480	6 764	3 401	3 363	63 715	8 644	16 005	11 171	9 560	9 139	9 195
1982	71 211	6 556	3 249	3 307	64 655	8 621	16 260	11 756	9 463	9 188	9 367
1983	71 922	6 340	3 098	3 242	65 581	8 597	16 499	12 314	9 408	9 208	9 556
1984	72 723	6 113	3 019	3 094	66 610	8 522	16 816	12 853	9 434	9 217	9 768
1985	73 373	5 987	3 026	2 961	67 386	8 246	17 042	13 337	9 488	9 262	10 010
1986	74 390	5 977	3 084	2 894	68 413	8 002	17 564	13 840	9 578	9 201	10 229
1987	75 189	6 015	3 125	2 890	69 175	7 729	17 754	14 338	9 771	9 101	10 481
1988	75 855	5 968	3 015	2 953	69 887	7 473	17 867	14 743	10 114	9 001	10 688
1989	76 468	5 813	2 817	2 996	70 654	7 279	17 908	15 237	10 434	8 900	10 897
1990	77 369	5 913	2 809	3 103	71 457	7 764	17 766	15 770	10 598	8 680	10 879
1991	77 977	5 704	2 805	2 899	72 274	7 748	17 615	16 340	10 856	8 640	11 074
1992	78 651	5 611	2 819	2 792	73 040	7 676	17 403	16 579	11 513	8 602	11 268
1993	79 371	5 650	2 862	2 788	73 721	7 545	17 158	16 900	12 058	8 590	11 470
1994	80 059	5 748	2 938	2 810	74 311	7 357	16 915	17 247	12 545	8 618	11 629
1995	80 733	5 854	2 995	2 859	74 879	7 163	16 653	17 567	13 028	8 653	11 815
1996	81 489	6 035	3 099	2 936	75 454	6 971	16 395	17 868	13 518	8 734	11 968
1997	82 577	6 257	3 209	3 048	76 320	7 087	16 043	18 163	14 030	8 929	12 067
1998	83 352	6 386	3 233	3 153	76 966	7 170	15 644	18 310	14 400	9 286	12 155
1999	83 930	6 498	3 266	3 232	77 432	7 244	15 150	18 340	14 834	9 581	12 283
2000	85 370	6 404	3 224	3 181	78 966	7 329	15 528	18 003	15 578	10 028	12 501
2001	86 452	6 422	3 229	3 194	80 029	7 564	15 486	17 960	16 047	10 369	12 604
2002	87 361	6 439	3 251	3 189	80 922	7 750	15 470	17 792	16 317	10 918	12 676
2003	88 249	6 390	3 378	3 012	81 860	7 856	15 569	17 620	16 555	11 442	12 818
2004	89 044	6 429	3 301	3 129	82 615	8 024	15 486	17 404	16 834	11 922	12 946
2005	90 027	6 471	3 464	3 006	83 556	8 057	15 507	17 286	17 169	12 415	13 123
2006	91 021	6 555	3 551	3 004	84 466	8 052	15 567	17 143	17 467	12 891	13 346
2007	92 073	6 653	3 567	3 086	85 420	8 113	15 762	16 927	17 686	13 341	13 591
2008	92 725	6 669	3 550	3 120	86 056	8 072	15 884	16 599	17 830	13 698	13 972

Table 1-6. Civilian Noninstitutional Population, by Age, Race, Sex, and Hispanic Origin, 1948–2008
—Continued

(Thousands of people.)

Race, Hispanic origin, sex, and year	16 years and over	16 to 19 years			20 years and over						
		Total	16 to 17 years	18 to 19 years	Total	20 to 24 years	25 to 34 years	35 to 44 years	45 to 54 years	55 to 64 years	65 years and over
WHITE											
Women											
1954	51 242	3 725	1 884	1 841	47 517	4 720	10 870	10 227	8 397	6 652	6 651
1955	51 802	3 785	1 929	1 856	48 017	4 671	10 806	10 342	8 566	6 771	6 862
1956	52 373	3 846	1 953	1 892	48 527	4 642	10 713	10 466	8 752	6 886	7 067
1957	52 998	3 949	2 007	1 941	49 049	4 655	10 584	10 597	8 957	7 000	7 256
1958	53 645	4 096	2 131	1 966	49 549	4 715	10 407	10 716	9 159	7 107	7 442
1959	54 392	4 351	2 337	2 015	50 041	4 794	10 216	10 812	9 348	7 219	7 653
1960	55 214	4 575	2 433	2 142	50 639	4 873	10 097	10 918	9 536	7 349	7 865
1961	55 993	4 732	2 378	2 354	51 261	4 999	9 999	10 991	9 697	7 485	8 091
1962	56 660	4 823	2 392	2 432	51 837	5 178	9 894	11 054	9 681	7 533	8 496
1963	57 672	5 151	2 757	2 394	52 521	5 459	9 828	11 089	9 785	7 650	8 710
1964	58 663	5 468	3 047	2 422	53 195	5 706	9 814	11 074	9 943	7 804	8 853
1965	59 601	5 778	2 999	2 779	53 823	5 918	9 826	10 996	10 088	7 954	9 042
1966	60 503	6 042	2 970	3 072	54 461	6 120	9 904	10 869	10 230	8 107	9 230
1967	61 491	6 011	2 993	3 019	55 480	6 540	10 125	10 732	10 379	8 271	9 435
1968	62 512	6 053	3 072	2 981	56 460	6 809	10 493	10 572	10 520	8 433	9 633
1969	63 563	6 174	3 172	3 002	57 390	7 089	10 818	10 396	10 651	8 600	9 836
1970	64 656	6 342	3 262	3 080	58 315	7 370	11 105	10 251	10 761	8 769	10 060
1971	65 857	6 518	3 338	3 180	59 340	7 662	11 454	10 117	10 841	8 951	10 315
1972	67 431	6 673	3 407	3 267	60 758	7 855	12 060	10 105	10 872	9 161	10 705
1973	68 517	6 796	3 466	3 331	61 721	7 951	12 610	10 018	10 891	9 306	10 943
1974	69 623	6 933	3 510	3 424	62 690	8 026	13 112	10 064	10 896	9 356	11 236
1975	70 810	7 011	3 523	3 488	63 798	8 214	13 615	10 063	10 847	9 505	11 556
1976	71 974	7 062	3 516	3 546	64 912	8 381	14 102	10 153	10 752	9 664	11 860
1977	73 077	7 071	3 525	3 545	66 007	8 553	14 564	10 351	10 618	9 832	12 088
1978	74 213	7 038	3 513	3 524	67 174	8 704	14 926	10 696	10 476	9 974	12 399
1979	75 347	6 987	3 460	3 527	68 360	8 815	15 363	11 017	10 327	10 122	12 717
1980	76 489	6 914	3 403	3 511	69 575	8 904	15 878	11 313	10 201	10 256	13 022
1981	77 428	6 752	3 303	3 449	70 677	8 965	16 362	11 606	10 106	10 346	13 292
1982	78 230	6 519	3 134	3 385	71 711	8 959	16 603	12 154	10 015	10 402	13 579
1983	78 884	6 282	2 991	3 292	72 601	8 895	16 788	12 714	9 941	10 418	13 847
1984	79 624	6 034	2 899	3 135	73 590	8 782	17 073	13 271	9 914	10 412	14 138
1985	80 306	5 912	2 895	3 017	74 394	8 607	17 409	13 762	9 917	10 358	14 342
1986	81 042	5 902	2 953	2 949	75 140	8 351	17 728	14 223	10 009	10 277	14 551
1987	81 769	5 924	2 985	2 939	75 845	8 079	17 913	14 698	10 194	10 141	14 820
1988	82 340	5 869	2 878	2 991	76 470	7 804	18 009	15 074	10 537	9 994	15 052
1989	82 871	5 716	2 690	3 027	77 154	7 600	18 043	15 537	10 853	9 843	15 278
1990	83 256	5 717	2 654	3 063	77 539	7 774	17 895	15 969	10 937	9 524	15 440
1991	83 781	5 497	2 646	2 850	78 285	7 768	17 726	16 514	11 196	9 435	15 647
1992	84 321	5 393	2 659	2 734	78 928	7 678	17 482	16 727	11 851	9 350	15 841
1993	84 918	5 428	2 700	2 728	79 490	7 542	17 206	17 019	12 398	9 302	16 023
1994	85 496	5 516	2 772	2 744	79 980	7 351	16 950	17 335	12 890	9 306	16 148
1995	86 181	5 614	2 827	2 787	80 567	7 150	16 702	17 654	13 390	9 333	16 337
1996	86 828	5 787	2 927	2 860	81 041	6 936	16 457	17 943	13 884	9 402	16 419
1997	87 417	5 924	3 004	2 920	81 492	6 896	16 047	18 162	14 357	9 582	16 447
1998	88 126	6 053	3 031	3 023	82 073	6 969	15 642	18 300	14 732	9 944	16 486
1999	89 156	6 202	3 076	3 127	82 953	7 150	15 366	18 415	15 214	10 274	16 536
2000	90 850	6 131	3 041	3 090	84 718	7 223	15 420	18 258	15 972	10 729	17 116
2001	91 660	6 134	3 062	3 071	85 526	7 438	15 284	18 153	16 428	11 065	17 158
2002	92 422	6 157	3 096	3 061	86 266	7 611	15 207	17 958	16 695	11 622	17 173
2003	93 043	6 137	3 251	2 886	86 905	7 680	15 220	17 731	16 911	12 147	17 216
2004	93 599	6 169	3 260	2 909	87 430	7 794	15 099	17 441	17 170	12 627	17 299
2005	94 419	6 219	3 304	2 915	88 200	7 814	15 086	17 268	17 480	13 119	17 433
2006	95 242	6 301	3 429	2 871	88 942	7 796	15 094	17 074	17 760	13 596	17 623
2007	96 180	6 390	3 458	2 932	89 790	7 832	15 249	16 843	17 979	14 051	17 835
2008	96 814	6 414	3 412	3 003	90 400	7 842	15 349	16 493	18 111	14 411	18 193

Table 1-6. Civilian Noninstitutional Population, by Age, Race, Sex, and Hispanic Origin, 1948–2008
—*Continued*

(Thousands of people.)

Race, Hispanic origin, sex, and year	16 years and over	16 to 19 years			20 years and over						
		Total	16 to 17 years	18 to 19 years	Total	20 to 24 years	25 to 34 years	35 to 44 years	45 to 54 years	55 to 64 years	65 years and over
BLACK											
Both Sexes											
1972	14 526	2 018	1 061	956	12 508	2 027	2 809	2 329	2 139	1 601	1 605
1973	14 917	2 095	1 095	1 000	12 823	2 132	2 957	2 333	2 156	1 616	1 628
1974	15 329	2 137	1 122	1 014	13 192	2 137	3 103	2 382	2 202	1 679	1 689
1975	15 751	2 191	1 146	1 046	13 560	2 228	3 258	2 395	2 211	1 717	1 755
1976	16 196	2 264	1 165	1 098	13 932	2 303	3 412	2 435	2 220	1 736	1 826
1977	16 605	2 273	1 175	1 097	14 332	2 400	3 566	2 493	2 225	1 765	1 883
1978	16 970	2 270	1 169	1 101	14 701	2 483	3 717	2 547	2 226	1 794	1 932
1979	17 397	2 276	1 167	1 109	15 121	2 556	3 899	2 615	2 240	1 831	1 980
1980	17 824	2 289	1 171	1 119	15 535	2 606	4 095	2 687	2 249	1 870	2 030
1981	18 219	2 288	1 161	1 127	15 931	2 642	4 290	2 758	2 260	1 913	2 069
1982	18 584	2 252	1 119	1 134	16 332	2 697	4 438	2 887	2 263	1 935	2 113
1983	18 925	2 225	1 092	1 133	16 700	2 734	4 607	2 999	2 260	1 964	2 135
1984	19 348	2 161	1 056	1 105	17 187	2 783	4 789	3 167	2 288	1 977	2 183
1985	19 664	2 160	1 083	1 077	17 504	2 649	4 873	3 290	2 372	2 060	2 259
1986	19 989	2 137	1 090	1 048	17 852	2 625	5 026	3 410	2 413	2 079	2 298
1987	20 352	2 163	1 123	1 040	18 189	2 578	5 139	3 563	2 460	2 097	2 352
1988	20 692	2 179	1 130	1 049	18 513	2 527	5 234	3 716	2 524	2 110	2 402
1989	21 021	2 176	1 116	1 060	18 846	2 479	5 308	3 900	2 587	2 118	2 454
1990	21 477	2 238	1 101	1 138	19 239	2 554	5 407	4 328	2 618	1 970	2 362
1991	21 799	2 187	1 085	1 102	19 612	2 585	5 419	4 538	2 682	1 985	2 403
1992	22 147	2 155	1 086	1 069	19 992	2 615	5 404	4 722	2 809	1 996	2 446
1993	22 521	2 181	1 113	1 069	20 339	2 600	5 409	4 886	2 941	2 016	2 487
1994	22 879	2 211	1 168	1 044	20 668	2 616	5 362	5 038	3 084	2 045	2 524
1995	23 246	2 284	1 198	1 086	20 962	2 554	5 337	5 178	3 244	2 079	2 571
1996	23 604	2 356	1 238	1 118	21 248	2 519	5 311	5 290	3 408	2 110	2 609
1997	24 003	2 412	1 255	1 158	21 591	2 515	5 279	5 410	3 571	2 164	2 653
1998	24 373	2 443	1 241	1 202	21 930	2 546	5 221	5 510	3 735	2 224	2 695
1999	24 855	2 479	1 250	1 229	22 376	2 615	5 197	5 609	3 919	2 295	2 741
2000	24 902	2 389	1 205	1 183	22 513	2 611	5 089	5 488	4 168	2 407	2 750
2001	25 138	2 388	1 212	1 176	22 750	2 686	5 003	5 467	4 343	2 478	2 775
2002	25 578	2 416	1 235	1 181	23 162	2 779	5 015	5 460	4 513	2 571	2 823
2003	25 686	2 382	1 309	1 074	23 304	2 773	4 978	5 387	4 628	2 692	2 846
2004	26 065	2 423	1 350	1 072	23 643	2 821	5 020	5 335	4 739	2 827	2 899
2005	26 517	2 481	1 341	1 140	24 036	2 835	5 075	5 311	4 869	2 980	2 967
2006	27 007	2 565	1 408	1 157	24 442	2 851	5 133	5 302	4 992	3 137	3 027
2007	27 485	2 640	1 497	1 143	24 845	2 891	5 210	5 271	5 110	3 284	3 080
2008	27 843	2 676	1 459	1 217	25 168	2 914	5 262	5 198	5 183	3 429	3 182
BLACK											
Men											
1972	6 538	978	525	453	5 559	921	1 251	1 026	963	720	679
1973	6 704	1 007	539	468	5 697	979	1 327	1 027	962	718	684
1974	6 875	1 027	554	471	5 848	956	1 381	1 055	997	753	707
1975	7 060	1 051	565	486	6 009	1 002	1 452	1 060	997	769	730
1976	7 265	1 099	579	518	6 167	1 036	1 521	1 077	999	774	756
1977	7 431	1 102	586	516	6 329	1 080	1 589	1 102	998	786	774
1978	7 577	1 093	579	514	6 484	1 120	1 657	1 128	995	794	789
1979	7 761	1 100	581	519	6 661	1 151	1 738	1 159	998	809	804
1980	7 944	1 110	583	526	6 834	1 171	1 828	1 191	999	825	822
1981	8 117	1 110	577	534	7 007	1 189	1 914	1 224	1 003	844	835
1982	8 283	1 097	556	542	7 186	1 225	1 983	1 282	1 003	848	846
1983	8 447	1 087	542	545	7 360	1 254	2 068	1 333	1 000	857	847
1984	8 654	1 055	524	531	7 599	1 292	2 164	1 411	1 012	858	861
1985	8 790	1 059	543	517	7 731	1 202	2 180	1 462	1 060	924	902
1986	8 956	1 049	548	503	7 907	1 195	2 264	1 517	1 072	934	924
1987	9 128	1 065	566	499	8 063	1 173	2 320	1 587	1 092	944	947
1988	9 289	1 074	569	505	8 215	1 151	2 367	1 656	1 121	951	970
1989	9 439	1 075	575	501	8 364	1 128	2 403	1 741	1 145	956	989
1990	9 573	1 094	555	540	8 479	1 144	2 412	1 968	1 183	855	917
1991	9 725	1 072	546	526	8 652	1 168	2 417	2 060	1 211	864	933
1992	9 896	1 056	544	512	8 840	1 194	2 409	2 150	1 268	868	951
1993	10 083	1 075	559	516	9 008	1 181	2 425	2 228	1 330	874	969
1994	10 258	1 087	586	501	9 171	1 207	2 399	2 300	1 392	889	985
1995	10 411	1 131	601	530	9 280	1 161	2 388	2 362	1 462	901	1 006
1996	10 575	1 161	623	538	9 414	1 154	2 373	2 413	1 534	914	1 025
1997	10 763	1 188	634	553	9 575	1 153	2 363	2 471	1 607	936	1 045
1998	10 927	1 201	623	578	9 727	1 166	2 335	2 520	1 682	956	1 068
1999	11 143	1 218	628	589	9 926	1 197	2 321	2 566	1 765	986	1 091
2000	11 129	1 178	605	572	9 952	1 195	2 277	2 471	1 889	1 067	1 053
2001	11 172	1 179	606	573	9 993	1 224	2 212	2 440	1 960	1 096	1 060
2002	11 391	1 195	615	580	10 196	1 281	2 223	2 437	2 042	1 137	1 075
2003	11 454	1 176	661	515	10 278	1 291	2 210	2 401	2 094	1 189	1 093
2004	11 656	1 195	680	516	10 461	1 326	2 242	2 382	2 150	1 250	1 111
2005	11 882	1 223	682	541	10 659	1 341	2 277	2 372	2 202	1 319	1 148
2006	12 130	1 266	713	552	10 864	1 355	2 318	2 369	2 261	1 390	1 170
2007	12 361	1 305	742	563	11 057	1 380	2 366	2 352	2 318	1 454	1 186
2008	12 516	1 322	718	604	11 194	1 384	2 398	2 313	2 335	1 519	1 245

Table 1-6. Civilian Noninstitutional Population, by Age, Race, Sex, and Hispanic Origin, 1948–2008
—Continued

(Thousands of people.)

Race, Hispanic origin, sex, and year	16 years and over	16 to 19 years			20 years and over						
		Total	16 to 17 years	18 to 19 years	Total	20 to 24 years	25 to 34 years	35 to 44 years	45 to 54 years	55 to 64 years	65 years and over
BLACK											
Women											
1972	7 988	1 040	536	503	6 948	1 106	1 558	1 302	1 176	881	925
1973	8 214	1 088	556	532	7 126	1 153	1 631	1 306	1 194	898	944
1974	8 454	1 110	567	542	7 344	1 181	1 723	1 327	1 206	926	981
1975	8 691	1 141	581	560	7 550	1 226	1 806	1 334	1 213	948	1 025
1976	8 931	1 165	585	580	7 765	1 266	1 890	1 357	1 220	962	1 070
1977	9 174	1 171	590	581	8 003	1 320	1 978	1 390	1 228	979	1 108
1978	9 394	1 177	589	588	8 217	1 363	2 061	1 419	1 231	999	1 143
1979	9 636	1 176	586	589	8 460	1 405	2 160	1 455	1 242	1 022	1 176
1980	9 880	1 180	587	593	8 700	1 435	2 267	1 496	1 250	1 045	1 208
1981	10 102	1 178	584	593	8 924	1 453	2 376	1 534	1 257	1 069	1 234
1982	10 300	1 155	563	592	9 146	1 472	2 455	1 605	1 260	1 087	1 267
1983	10 477	1 138	550	588	9 340	1 480	2 539	1 666	1 260	1 107	1 288
1984	10 694	1 106	532	574	9 588	1 491	2 625	1 756	1 276	1 119	1 322
1985	10 873	1 101	540	560	9 773	1 447	2 693	1 828	1 312	1 136	1 357
1986	11 033	1 088	542	545	9 945	1 430	2 762	1 893	1 341	1 145	1 374
1987	11 224	1 098	557	541	10 126	1 405	2 819	1 976	1 368	1 153	1 405
1988	11 402	1 105	561	544	10 298	1 376	2 867	2 060	1 403	1 159	1 432
1989	11 582	1 100	541	559	10 482	1 351	2 905	2 159	1 441	1 162	1 464
1990	11 904	1 144	546	598	10 760	1 410	2 995	2 360	1 435	1 114	1 446
1991	12 074	1 115	539	576	10 959	1 417	3 003	2 478	1 471	1 121	1 470
1992	12 251	1 099	542	557	11 152	1 421	2 995	2 573	1 542	1 127	1 495
1993	12 438	1 106	554	552	11 332	1 419	2 983	2 659	1 611	1 142	1 518
1994	12 621	1 125	582	543	11 496	1 410	2 963	2 738	1 692	1 156	1 538
1995	12 835	1 153	597	556	11 682	1 392	2 948	2 816	1 782	1 178	1 565
1996	13 029	1 195	615	580	11 833	1 364	2 938	2 877	1 874	1 196	1 584
1997	13 241	1 225	620	604	12 016	1 362	2 916	2 939	1 964	1 228	1 608
1998	13 446	1 243	618	624	12 203	1 380	2 886	2 991	2 053	1 268	1 626
1999	13 711	1 261	621	640	12 451	1 418	2 876	3 043	2 153	1 310	1 650
2000	13 772	1 211	600	611	12 561	1 416	2 812	3 017	2 279	1 340	1 697
2001	13 966	1 209	606	603	12 758	1 462	2 790	3 026	2 383	1 382	1 714
2002	14 187	1 221	620	601	12 966	1 498	2 792	3 023	2 471	1 434	1 747
2003	14 232	1 206	648	558	13 026	1 482	2 768	2 986	2 534	1 504	1 753
2004	14 409	1 227	670	557	13 182	1 495	2 778	2 954	2 590	1 577	1 789
2005	14 635	1 258	659	598	13 377	1 494	2 797	2 939	2 666	1 661	1 819
2006	14 877	1 299	694	605	13 578	1 495	2 815	2 933	2 731	1 747	1 857
2007	15 124	1 336	755	581	13 788	1 511	2 844	2 918	2 792	1 830	1 893
2008	15 328	1 354	741	613	13 974	1 530	2 864	2 885	2 848	1 910	1 937
HISPANIC [1]											
Both Sexes											
1973	6 104	867	. . .	. . .	5 238	. . .	. . .	. . .	. . .	. . .	. . .
1974	6 564	926	. . .	. . .	5 645	. . .	. . .	. . .	. . .	. . .	. . .
1975	6 862	962	. . .	. . .	5 900	. . .	. . .	. . .	. . .	. . .	. . .
1976	6 910	953	494	480	6 075	1 053	1 775	1 261	936	570	479
1977	7 362	1 024	513	508	6 376	1 163	1 869	1 283	989	587	485
1978	7 912	1 076	561	515	6 836	1 265	2 004	1 378	1 033	627	529
1979	8 207	1 095	544	551	7 113	1 296	2 117	1 458	1 015	659	566
1980	9 598	1 281	638	643	8 317	1 564	2 508	1 575	1 190	782	698
1981	10 120	1 301	641	660	8 819	1 650	2 698	1 680	1 231	832	728
1982	10 580	1 307	639	668	9 273	1 724	2 871	1 779	1 264	880	755
1983	11 029	1 304	635	670	9 725	1 790	3 045	1 883	1 298	928	781
1984	11 478	1 300	633	667	10 178	1 839	3 224	1 996	1 336	973	810
1985	11 915	1 298	638	661	10 617	1 864	3 401	2 117	1 377	1 015	843
1986	12 344	1 302	658	644	11 042	1 899	3 510	2 239	1 496	1 023	875
1987	12 867	1 332	651	681	11 536	1 910	3 714	2 464	1 492	1 061	895
1988	13 325	1 354	662	692	11 970	1 948	3 807	2 565	1 571	1 159	920
1989	13 791	1 399	672	727	12 392	1 950	3 953	2 658	1 649	1 182	1 001
1990	15 904	1 737	821	915	14 167	2 428	4 589	3 001	1 817	1 247	1 084
1991	16 425	1 732	819	913	14 693	2 481	4 674	3 243	1 879	1 283	1 134
1992	16 961	1 737	836	901	15 224	2 444	4 806	3 458	1 980	1 321	1 216
1993	17 532	1 756	855	901	15 776	2 487	4 887	3 632	2 094	1 324	1 353
1994	18 117	1 818	902	916	16 300	2 518	5 000	3 756	2 223	1 401	1 401
1995	18 629	1 872	903	969	16 757	2 528	5 050	3 965	2 294	1 483	1 437
1996	19 213	1 948	962	986	17 265	2 524	5 181	4 227	2 275	1 546	1 512
1997	20 321	2 121	1 088	1 033	18 200	2 623	5 405	4 453	2 581	1 580	1 558
1998	21 070	2 204	1 070	1 135	18 865	2 731	5 447	4 636	2 775	1 615	1 662
1999	21 650	2 307	1 113	1 194	19 344	2 700	5 512	4 833	2 868	1 713	1 718
2000	23 938	2 523	1 214	1 309	21 415	3 255	6 466	5 189	3 061	1 736	1 708
2001	24 942	2 508	1 173	1 334	22 435	3 417	6 726	5 346	3 339	1 816	1 792
2002	25 963	2 507	1 216	1 291	23 456	3 508	7 010	5 606	3 494	1 953	1 885
2003	27 551	2 543	1 346	1 197	25 008	3 533	7 506	6 003	3 845	2 093	2 027
2004	28 109	2 608	1 337	1 270	25 502	3 666	7 470	6 055	3 987	2 208	2 115
2005	29 133	2 689	1 415	1 274	26 444	3 647	7 684	6 293	4 217	2 361	2 242
2006	30 103	2 796	1 518	1 277	27 307	3 603	7 856	6 519	4 466	2 516	2 347
2007	31 383	2 944	1 559	1 385	28 440	3 648	8 129	6 785	4 720	2 685	2 473
2008	32 141	3 042	1 620	1 422	29 098	3 620	8 147	6 946	4 937	2 840	2 609

[1] May be of any race.
. . . = Not available.

Table 1-6. Civilian Noninstitutional Population, by Age, Race, Sex, and Hispanic Origin, 1948–2008
—Continued

(Thousands of people.)

Race, Hispanic origin, sex, and year	16 years and over	16 to 19 years			20 years and over						
		Total	16 to 17 years	18 to 19 years	Total	20 to 24 years	25 to 34 years	35 to 44 years	45 to 54 years	55 to 64 years	65 years and over
HISPANIC[1]											
Men											
1973	2 891	...	...	...	2 472	...	...	...	...	...	...
1974	3 130	...	...	...	2 680	...	...	...	...	...	...
1975	3 219	...	...	...	2 741	...	...	...	...	...	...
1976	3 241	...	...	...	2 764	...	...	...	...	...	...
1977	3 483	...	...	...	2 982	...	...	...	...	...	...
1978	3 750	...	...	...	3 228	...	...	...	...	...	...
1979	3 917	...	...	...	3 362	...	...	...	...	...	...
1980	4 689	...	...	...	4 036	...	...	...	...	...	...
1981	4 968	...	...	...	4 306	...	...	...	...	...	...
1982	5 203	...	...	...	4 539	...	...	...	...	...	...
1983	5 432	...	...	...	4 771	...	...	...	...	...	...
1984	5 661	...	...	...	5 005	...	...	...	...	...	...
1985	5 885	...	...	...	5 232	...	...	...	...	...	...
1986	6 106	...	...	...	5 451	...	...	...	...	...	...
1987	6 371	...	...	...	5 700	...	...	...	...	...	...
1988	6 604	...	...	...	5 921	...	...	...	...	...	...
1989	6 825	...	...	...	6 114	...	...	...	...	...	...
1990	8 041	...	...	...	7 126	...	...	...	...	...	...
1991	8 296	...	...	...	7 392	...	...	...	...	...	...
1992	8 553	...	...	...	7 655	...	...	...	...	...	...
1993	8 824	...	...	...	7 930	...	...	...	...	...	...
1994	9 104	926	472	454	8 178	1 346	2 627	1 871	1 076	644	614
1995	9 329	954	481	473	8 375	1 337	2 657	1 966	1 127	668	619
1996	9 604	992	485	507	8 611	1 321	2 692	2 144	1 111	712	630
1997	10 368	1 119	585	534	9 250	1 439	2 872	2 275	1 266	747	651
1998	10 734	1 161	586	575	9 573	1 462	2 907	2 377	1 342	771	714
1999	10 713	1 190	571	619	9 523	1 398	2 805	2 407	1 397	767	749
2000	12 174	1 333	640	693	10 841	1 784	3 380	2 626	1 527	799	725
2001	12 695	1 310	619	690	11 386	1 846	3 529	2 765	1 650	848	749
2002	13 221	1 293	615	678	11 928	1 890	3 727	2 875	1 716	902	817
2003	14 098	1 301	674	627	12 797	1 905	4 033	3 098	1 910	989	862
2004	14 417	1 336	664	672	13 082	1 981	4 024	3 147	1 990	1 046	894
2005	14 962	1 376	730	646	13 586	1 956	4 155	3 284	2 114	1 123	953
2006	15 473	1 428	763	664	14 046	1 916	4 266	3 414	2 251	1 204	996
2007	16 154	1 505	790	714	14 649	1 928	4 430	3 563	2 384	1 287	1 058
2008	16 524	1 553	838	716	14 971	1 890	4 438	3 655	2 502	1 365	1 121
HISPANIC[1]											
Women											
1973	3 213	...	...	...	2 766	...	...	...	...	...	...
1974	3 434	...	...	...	2 959	...	...	...	...	...	...
1975	3 644	...	...	...	3 161	...	...	...	...	...	...
1976	3 669	...	...	...	3 263	...	...	...	...	...	...
1977	3 879	...	...	...	3 377	...	...	...	...	...	...
1978	4 159	...	...	...	3 608	...	...	...	...	...	...
1979	4 291	...	...	...	3 751	...	...	...	...	...	...
1980	4 909	...	...	...	4 281	...	...	...	...	...	...
1981	5 151	...	...	...	4 513	...	...	...	...	...	...
1982	5 377	...	...	...	4 734	...	...	...	...	...	...
1983	5 597	...	...	...	4 954	...	...	...	...	...	...
1984	5 816	...	...	...	5 173	...	...	...	...	...	...
1985	6 029	...	...	...	5 385	...	...	...	...	...	...
1986	6 238	...	...	...	5 591	...	...	...	...	...	...
1987	6 496	...	...	...	5 835	...	...	...	...	...	...
1988	6 721	...	...	...	6 050	...	...	...	...	...	...
1989	6 965	...	...	...	6 278	...	...	...	...	...	...
1990	7 863	...	...	...	7 041	...	...	...	...	...	...
1991	8 130	...	...	...	7 301	...	...	...	...	...	...
1992	8 408	...	...	...	7 569	...	...	...	...	...	...
1993	8 708	...	...	...	7 846	...	...	...	...	...	...
1994	9 014	892	430	462	8 122	1 173	2 373	1 885	1 147	757	787
1995	9 300	918	422	496	8 382	1 191	2 393	1 999	1 167	815	818
1996	9 610	956	477	479	8 654	1 203	2 489	2 082	1 164	834	882
1997	9 953	1 003	503	500	8 950	1 184	2 533	2 178	1 315	833	907
1998	10 335	1 044	483	560	9 292	1 269	2 539	2 259	1 433	844	948
1999	10 937	1 116	542	575	9 821	1 302	2 707	2 425	1 470	947	969
2000	11 764	1 190	574	616	10 574	1 471	3 086	2 564	1 534	937	982
2001	12 247	1 198	554	644	11 049	1 571	3 198	2 581	1 689	968	1 043
2002	12 742	1 214	601	613	11 528	1 617	3 283	2 732	1 777	1 051	1 068
2003	13 452	1 242	672	570	12 211	1 628	3 473	2 905	1 935	1 105	1 166
2004	13 692	1 272	674	598	12 420	1 685	3 447	2 908	1 997	1 162	1 221
2005	14 172	1 313	685	628	12 858	1 692	3 529	3 009	2 103	1 237	1 289
2006	14 630	1 368	755	613	13 262	1 688	3 590	3 105	2 215	1 313	1 351
2007	15 229	1 439	769	670	13 791	1 720	3 698	3 222	2 336	1 398	1 416
2008	15 616	1 489	782	706	14 127	1 730	3 710	3 291	2 435	1 475	1 488

[1]May be of any race.
. . . = Not available.

Table 1-7. Civilian Labor Force, by Age, Sex, Race, and Hispanic Origin, 1948–2008

(Thousands of people.)

Race, Hispanic origin, sex, and year	16 years and over	16 to 19 years			20 years and over						
		Total	16 to 17 years	18 to 19 years	Total	20 to 24 years	25 to 34 years	35 to 44 years	45 to 54 years	55 to 64 years	65 years and over
ALL RACES											
Both Sexes											
1948	60 621	4 435	1 780	2 654	56 187	7 392	14 258	13 397	10 914	7 329	2 897
1949	61 286	4 288	1 704	2 583	57 000	7 340	14 415	13 711	11 107	7 426	3 010
1950	62 208	4 216	1 659	2 557	57 994	7 307	14 619	13 954	11 444	7 633	3 036
1951	62 017	4 103	1 743	2 360	57 914	6 594	14 668	14 100	11 739	7 796	3 020
1952	62 138	4 064	1 806	2 257	58 075	5 840	14 904	14 383	11 961	7 980	3 005
1953	63 015	4 027	1 727	2 299	58 989	5 481	14 898	15 099	12 249	8 024	3 236
1954	63 643	3 976	1 643	2 300	59 666	5 475	14 983	15 221	12 524	8 269	3 192
1955	65 023	4 092	1 711	2 382	60 931	5 666	15 058	15 400	12 992	8 513	3 305
1956	66 552	4 296	1 878	2 418	62 257	5 940	14 961	15 694	13 407	8 830	3 423
1957	66 929	4 275	1 843	2 433	62 653	6 071	14 826	15 847	13 768	8 853	3 290
1958	67 639	4 260	1 818	2 442	63 377	6 272	14 668	16 028	14 179	9 031	3 199
1959	68 369	4 492	1 971	2 522	63 876	6 413	14 435	16 127	14 518	9 227	3 158
1960	69 628	4 841	2 095	2 747	64 788	6 702	14 382	16 269	14 852	9 385	3 195
1961	70 459	4 936	1 984	2 951	65 524	6 950	14 319	16 402	15 071	9 636	3 146
1962	70 614	4 916	1 919	2 997	65 699	7 082	14 023	16 589	15 096	9 757	3 154
1963	71 833	5 139	2 171	2 966	66 695	7 473	14 050	16 788	15 338	10 006	3 041
1964	73 091	5 388	2 449	2 940	67 702	7 963	14 056	16 771	15 637	10 182	3 090
1965	74 455	5 910	2 486	3 425	68 543	8 259	14 233	16 840	15 756	10 350	3 108
1966	75 770	6 558	2 664	3 893	69 219	8 410	14 458	16 738	15 984	10 575	3 053
1967	77 347	6 521	2 734	3 786	70 825	9 010	15 055	16 703	16 172	10 792	3 097
1968	78 737	6 619	2 817	3 803	72 118	9 305	15 708	16 591	16 397	10 964	3 153
1969	80 734	6 970	3 009	3 959	73 763	9 879	16 336	16 458	16 730	11 135	3 227
1970	82 771	7 249	3 135	4 115	75 521	10 597	17 036	16 437	16 949	11 283	3 222
1971	84 382	7 470	3 192	4 278	76 913	11 331	17 714	16 305	17 024	11 390	3 149
1972	87 034	8 054	3 420	4 636	78 980	12 130	18 960	16 398	16 967	11 412	3 114
1973	89 429	8 507	3 665	4 839	80 924	12 846	20 376	16 492	16 983	11 256	2 974
1974	91 949	8 871	3 810	5 059	83 080	13 314	21 654	16 763	17 131	11 284	2 934
1975	93 775	8 870	3 740	5 131	84 904	13 750	22 864	16 903	17 084	11 346	2 956
1976	96 158	9 056	3 767	5 288	87 103	14 284	24 203	17 317	16 982	11 422	2 895
1977	99 009	9 351	3 919	5 431	89 658	14 825	25 500	17 943	16 878	11 577	2 934
1978	102 251	9 652	4 127	5 526	92 598	15 370	26 703	18 821	16 891	11 744	3 070
1979	104 962	9 638	4 079	5 559	95 325	15 769	27 938	19 685	16 897	11 931	3 104
1980	106 940	9 378	3 883	5 496	97 561	15 922	29 227	20 463	16 910	11 985	3 054
1981	108 670	8 988	3 647	5 340	99 682	16 099	30 392	21 211	16 970	11 969	3 042
1982	110 204	8 526	3 336	5 189	101 679	16 082	31 186	22 431	16 889	12 062	3 030
1983	111 550	8 171	3 073	5 098	103 379	16 052	31 834	23 611	16 851	11 992	3 040
1984	113 544	7 943	3 050	4 894	105 601	16 046	32 723	24 933	17 006	11 961	2 933
1985	115 461	7 901	3 154	4 747	107 560	15 718	33 550	26 073	17 322	11 991	2 907
1986	117 834	7 926	3 287	4 639	109 908	15 441	34 591	27 232	17 739	11 894	3 010
1987	119 865	7 988	3 384	4 604	111 878	14 977	35 233	28 460	18 210	11 877	3 119
1988	121 669	8 031	3 286	4 745	113 638	14 505	35 503	29 435	19 104	11 808	3 284
1989	123 869	7 954	3 125	4 828	115 916	14 180	35 896	30 601	19 916	11 877	3 446
1990	125 840	7 792	2 937	4 856	118 047	14 700	35 929	32 145	20 248	11 575	3 451
1991	126 346	7 265	2 789	4 476	119 082	14 548	35 507	33 312	20 828	11 473	3 413
1992	128 105	7 096	2 769	4 327	121 009	14 521	35 369	33 899	22 160	11 587	3 473
1993	129 200	7 170	2 831	4 338	122 030	14 354	34 780	34 562	23 296	11 599	3 439
1994	131 056	7 481	3 134	4 347	123 576	14 131	34 353	35 226	24 318	11 713	3 834
1995	132 304	7 765	3 225	4 540	124 539	13 688	34 198	35 751	25 223	11 860	3 819
1996	133 943	7 806	3 263	4 543	126 137	13 377	33 833	36 556	26 397	12 146	3 828
1997	136 297	7 932	3 237	4 695	128 365	13 532	33 380	37 326	27 574	12 665	3 887
1998	137 673	8 256	3 335	4 921	129 417	13 638	32 813	37 536	28 368	13 215	3 847
1999	139 368	8 333	3 337	4 996	131 034	13 933	32 143	37 882	29 388	13 682	4 005
2000	142 583	8 271	3 261	5 010	134 312	14 250	32 755	37 567	31 071	14 356	4 312
2001	143 734	7 902	3 088	4 814	135 832	14 557	32 361	37 404	32 025	15 104	4 382
2002	144 863	7 585	2 870	4 715	137 278	14 781	32 196	36 926	32 597	16 309	4 469
2003	146 510	7 170	2 857	4 313	139 340	14 928	32 343	36 695	33 270	17 312	4 792
2004	147 401	7 114	2 747	4 367	140 287	15 154	32 207	36 158	33 758	18 013	4 998
2005	149 320	7 164	2 825	4 339	142 157	15 127	32 341	36 030	34 402	18 979	5 278
2006	151 428	7 281	2 952	4 329	144 147	15 113	32 573	35 848	35 146	19 984	5 484
2007	153 124	7 012	2 771	4 242	146 112	15 205	33 130	35 527	35 697	20 750	5 804
2008	154 287	6 858	2 552	4 306	147 429	15 174	33 332	35 061	36 003	21 615	6 243

Table 1-7. Civilian Labor Force, by Age, Sex, Race, and Hispanic Origin, 1948–2008—*Continued*

(Thousands of people.)

Race, Hispanic origin, sex, and year	16 years and over	16 to 19 years			20 years and over						
		Total	16 to 17 years	18 to 19 years	Total	20 to 24 years	25 to 34 years	35 to 44 years	45 to 54 years	55 to 64 years	65 years and over
ALL RACES											
Men											
1948	43 286	2 600	1 109	1 490	40 687	4 673	10 327	9 596	7 943	5 764	2 384
1949	43 498	2 477	1 056	1 420	41 022	4 682	10 418	9 722	8 008	5 748	2 454
1950	43 819	2 504	1 048	1 456	41 316	4 632	10 527	9 793	8 117	5 794	2 453
1951	43 001	2 347	1 081	1 266	40 655	3 935	10 375	9 799	8 205	5 873	2 469
1952	42 869	2 312	1 101	1 210	40 558	3 338	10 585	9 945	8 326	5 949	2 416
1953	43 633	2 320	1 070	1 249	41 315	3 053	10 736	10 437	8 570	5 975	2 543
1954	43 965	2 295	1 023	1 272	41 669	3 051	10 771	10 513	8 702	6 105	2 526
1955	44 475	2 369	1 070	1 299	42 106	3 221	10 806	10 595	8 838	6 122	2 526
1956	45 091	2 433	1 142	1 291	42 658	3 485	10 685	10 663	9 002	6 220	2 602
1957	45 197	2 415	1 127	1 289	42 780	3 629	10 571	10 731	9 153	6 222	2 477
1958	45 521	2 428	1 133	1 295	43 092	3 771	10 475	10 843	9 320	6 304	2 378
1959	45 886	2 596	1 206	1 390	43 289	3 940	10 346	10 899	9 438	6 345	2 322
1960	46 388	2 787	1 290	1 496	43 603	4 123	10 251	10 967	9 574	6 399	2 287
1961	46 653	2 794	1 210	1 583	43 860	4 253	10 176	11 012	9 668	6 530	2 220
1962	46 600	2 770	1 178	1 592	43 831	4 279	9 920	11 115	9 715	6 560	2 241
1963	47 129	2 907	1 321	1 586	44 222	4 514	9 876	11 187	9 836	6 675	2 135
1964	47 679	3 074	1 499	1 575	44 604	4 754	9 876	11 156	9 956	6 741	2 124
1965	48 255	3 397	1 532	1 866	44 857	4 894	9 903	11 120	10 045	6 763	2 132
1966	48 471	3 685	1 609	2 075	44 788	4 820	9 948	10 983	10 100	6 847	2 089
1967	48 987	3 634	1 658	1 976	45 354	5 043	10 207	10 859	10 189	6 937	2 118
1968	49 533	3 681	1 687	1 995	45 852	5 070	10 610	10 725	10 267	7 025	2 154
1969	50 221	3 870	1 770	2 100	46 351	5 282	10 941	10 556	10 344	7 058	2 170
1970	51 228	4 008	1 810	2 199	47 220	5 717	11 327	10 469	10 417	7 126	2 165
1971	52 180	4 172	1 856	2 315	48 009	6 233	11 731	10 347	10 451	7 155	2 090
1972	53 555	4 476	1 955	2 522	49 079	6 766	12 350	10 372	10 412	7 155	2 026
1973	54 624	4 693	2 073	2 618	49 932	7 183	13 056	10 338	10 416	7 028	1 913
1974	55 739	4 861	2 138	2 721	50 879	7 387	13 665	10 401	10 431	7 063	1 932
1975	56 299	4 805	2 065	2 740	51 494	7 565	14 192	10 398	10 401	7 023	1 914
1976	57 174	4 886	2 069	2 817	52 288	7 866	14 784	10 500	10 293	7 020	1 826
1977	58 396	5 048	2 155	2 893	53 348	8 109	15 353	10 771	10 158	7 100	1 857
1978	59 620	5 149	2 227	2 923	54 471	8 327	15 814	11 159	10 083	7 151	1 936
1979	60 726	5 111	2 192	2 919	55 615	8 535	16 387	11 531	10 008	7 212	1 943
1980	61 453	4 999	2 102	2 897	56 455	8 607	16 971	11 836	9 905	7 242	1 893
1981	61 974	4 777	1 957	2 820	57 197	8 648	17 479	12 166	9 868	7 170	1 866
1982	62 450	4 470	1 776	2 694	57 980	8 604	17 793	12 781	9 784	7 174	1 845
1983	63 047	4 303	1 621	2 682	58 744	8 601	18 038	13 398	9 746	7 119	1 842
1984	63 835	4 134	1 591	2 542	59 701	8 594	18 488	14 037	9 776	7 050	1 755
1985	64 411	4 134	1 663	2 471	60 277	8 283	18 808	14 506	9 870	7 060	1 750
1986	65 422	4 102	1 707	2 395	61 320	8 148	19 383	15 029	9 994	6 954	1 811
1987	66 207	4 112	1 745	2 367	62 095	7 837	19 656	15 587	10 176	6 940	1 899
1988	66 927	4 159	1 714	2 445	62 768	7 594	19 742	16 074	10 566	6 831	1 960
1989	67 840	4 136	1 630	2 505	63 704	7 458	19 905	16 622	10 919	6 783	2 017
1990	69 011	4 094	1 537	2 557	64 916	7 866	19 872	17 481	11 103	6 627	1 967
1991	69 168	3 795	1 452	2 343	65 374	7 820	19 641	18 077	11 362	6 550	1 924
1992	69 964	3 751	1 453	2 297	66 213	7 770	19 495	18 347	12 040	6 551	2 010
1993	70 404	3 762	1 497	2 265	66 642	7 671	19 214	18 713	12 562	6 502	1 980
1994	70 817	3 896	1 630	2 266	66 921	7 540	18 854	18 966	12 962	6 423	2 176
1995	71 360	4 036	1 668	2 368	67 324	7 338	18 670	19 189	13 421	6 504	2 201
1996	72 087	4 043	1 665	2 378	68 044	7 104	18 430	19 602	13 967	6 693	2 247
1997	73 261	4 095	1 676	2 419	69 166	7 184	18 110	20 058	14 564	6 952	2 298
1998	73 959	4 244	1 728	2 516	69 715	7 221	17 796	20 242	14 963	7 253	2 240
1999	74 512	4 318	1 732	2 587	70 194	7 291	17 318	20 382	15 394	7 477	2 333
2000	76 280	4 269	1 676	2 594	72 010	7 521	17 844	20 093	16 269	7 795	2 488
2001	76 886	4 070	1 568	2 501	72 816	7 640	17 671	20 018	16 804	8 171	2 511
2002	77 500	3 870	1 431	2 439	73 630	7 769	17 596	19 828	17 143	8 751	2 542
2003	78 238	3 614	1 405	2 209	74 623	7 906	17 767	19 762	17 352	9 144	2 692
2004	78 980	3 616	1 329	2 288	75 364	8 057	17 798	19 539	17 635	9 547	2 787
2005	80 033	3 590	1 368	2 222	76 443	8 054	17 837	19 495	18 053	10 045	2 959
2006	81 255	3 693	1 453	2 240	77 562	8 116	17 944	19 407	18 489	10 509	3 096
2007	82 136	3 541	1 354	2 187	78 596	8 095	18 308	19 299	18 801	10 904	3 188
2008	82 520	3 472	1 238	2 235	79 047	8 065	18 302	18 972	18 928	11 345	3 436

Table 1-7. Civilian Labor Force, by Age, Sex, Race, and Hispanic Origin, 1948–2008—*Continued*

(Thousands of people.)

Race, Hispanic origin, sex, and year	16 years and over	16 to 19 years			20 years and over						
		Total	16 to 17 years	18 to 19 years	Total	20 to 24 years	25 to 34 years	35 to 44 years	45 to 54 years	55 to 64 years	65 years and over
ALL RACES											
Women											
1948	17 335	1 835	671	1 164	15 500	2 719	3 931	3 801	2 971	1 565	513
1949	17 788	1 811	648	1 163	15 978	2 658	3 997	3 989	3 099	1 678	556
1950	18 389	1 712	611	1 101	16 678	2 675	4 092	4 161	3 327	1 839	583
1951	19 016	1 756	662	1 094	17 259	2 659	4 293	4 301	3 534	1 923	551
1952	19 269	1 752	705	1 047	17 517	2 502	4 319	4 438	3 635	2 031	589
1953	19 382	1 707	657	1 050	17 674	2 428	4 162	4 662	3 679	2 049	693
1954	19 678	1 681	620	1 028	17 997	2 424	4 212	4 708	3 822	2 164	666
1955	20 548	1 723	641	1 083	18 825	2 445	4 252	4 805	4 154	2 391	779
1956	21 461	1 863	736	1 127	19 599	2 455	4 276	5 031	4 405	2 610	821
1957	21 732	1 860	716	1 144	19 873	2 442	4 255	5 116	4 615	2 631	813
1958	22 118	1 832	685	1 147	20 285	2 501	4 193	5 185	4 859	2 727	821
1959	22 483	1 896	765	1 132	20 587	2 473	4 089	5 228	5 080	2 882	836
1960	23 240	2 054	805	1 251	21 185	2 579	4 131	5 302	5 278	2 986	908
1961	23 806	2 142	774	1 368	21 664	2 697	4 143	5 390	5 403	3 106	926
1962	24 014	2 146	741	1 405	21 868	2 803	4 103	5 474	5 381	3 197	913
1963	24 704	2 232	850	1 380	22 473	2 959	4 174	5 601	5 502	3 331	906
1964	25 412	2 314	950	1 365	23 098	3 209	4 180	5 615	5 681	3 441	966
1965	26 200	2 513	954	1 559	23 686	3 365	4 330	5 720	5 711	3 587	976
1966	27 299	2 873	1 055	1 818	24 431	3 590	4 510	5 755	5 884	3 728	964
1967	28 360	2 887	1 076	1 810	25 475	3 966	4 848	5 844	5 983	3 855	979
1968	29 204	2 938	1 130	1 808	26 266	4 235	5 098	5 866	6 130	3 939	999
1969	30 513	3 100	1 239	1 859	27 413	4 597	5 395	5 902	6 386	4 077	1 057
1970	31 543	3 241	1 325	1 916	28 301	4 880	5 708	5 968	6 532	4 157	1 056
1971	32 202	3 298	1 336	1 963	28 904	5 098	5 983	5 957	6 573	4 234	1 059
1972	33 479	3 578	1 464	2 114	29 901	5 364	6 610	6 027	6 555	4 257	1 089
1973	34 804	3 814	1 592	2 221	30 991	5 663	7 320	6 154	6 567	4 228	1 061
1974	36 211	4 010	1 672	2 338	32 201	5 926	7 989	6 362	6 699	4 221	1 002
1975	37 475	4 065	1 674	2 391	33 410	6 185	8 673	6 505	6 683	4 323	1 042
1976	38 983	4 170	1 698	2 470	34 814	6 418	9 419	6 817	6 689	4 402	1 069
1977	40 613	4 303	1 765	2 538	36 310	6 717	10 149	7 171	6 720	4 477	1 078
1978	42 631	4 503	1 900	2 603	38 128	7 043	10 888	7 662	6 807	4 593	1 134
1979	44 235	4 527	1 887	2 639	39 708	7 234	11 551	8 154	6 889	4 719	1 161
1980	45 487	4 381	1 781	2 599	41 106	7 315	12 257	8 627	7 004	4 742	1 161
1981	46 696	4 211	1 691	2 520	42 485	7 451	12 912	9 045	7 101	4 799	1 176
1982	47 755	4 056	1 561	2 495	43 699	7 477	13 393	9 651	7 105	4 888	1 185
1983	48 503	3 868	1 452	2 416	44 636	7 451	13 796	10 213	7 105	4 873	1 198
1984	49 709	3 810	1 458	2 351	45 900	7 451	14 234	10 896	7 230	4 911	1 177
1985	51 050	3 767	1 491	2 276	47 283	7 434	14 742	11 567	7 452	4 932	1 156
1986	52 413	3 824	1 580	2 244	48 589	7 293	15 208	12 204	7 746	4 940	1 199
1987	53 658	3 875	1 638	2 237	49 783	7 140	15 577	12 873	8 034	4 937	1 221
1988	54 742	3 872	1 572	2 300	50 870	6 910	15 761	13 361	8 537	4 977	1 324
1989	56 030	3 818	1 495	2 323	52 212	6 721	15 990	13 980	8 997	5 095	1 429
1990	56 829	3 698	1 400	2 298	53 131	6 834	16 058	14 663	9 145	4 948	1 483
1991	57 178	3 470	1 337	2 133	53 708	6 728	15 867	15 235	9 465	4 924	1 489
1992	58 141	3 345	1 316	2 030	54 796	6 750	15 875	15 552	10 120	5 035	1 464
1993	58 795	3 408	1 335	2 073	55 388	6 683	15 566	15 849	10 733	5 097	1 459
1994	60 239	3 585	1 504	2 081	56 655	6 592	15 499	16 259	11 357	5 289	1 658
1995	60 944	3 729	1 557	2 172	57 215	6 349	15 528	16 562	11 801	5 356	1 618
1996	61 857	3 763	1 599	2 164	58 094	6 273	15 403	16 954	12 430	5 452	1 581
1997	63 036	3 837	1 561	2 277	59 198	6 348	15 271	17 268	13 010	5 713	1 590
1998	63 714	4 012	1 607	2 405	59 702	6 418	15 017	17 294	13 405	5 962	1 607
1999	64 855	4 015	1 606	2 410	60 840	6 643	14 826	17 501	13 994	6 204	1 673
2000	66 303	4 002	1 585	2 416	62 301	6 730	14 912	17 473	14 802	6 561	1 823
2001	66 848	3 832	1 520	2 313	63 016	6 917	14 690	17 386	15 221	6 932	1 870
2002	67 363	3 715	1 439	2 277	63 648	7 012	14 600	17 098	15 454	7 559	1 926
2003	68 272	3 556	1 452	2 104	64 716	7 021	14 576	16 933	15 919	8 168	2 099
2004	68 421	3 498	1 418	2 080	64 923	7 097	14 409	16 619	16 123	8 466	2 211
2005	69 288	3 574	1 457	2 117	65 714	7 073	14 503	16 535	16 349	8 934	2 319
2006	70 173	3 588	1 499	2 089	66 585	6 997	14 628	16 441	16 656	9 475	2 388
2007	70 988	3 471	1 417	2 055	67 516	7 110	14 822	16 227	16 896	9 846	2 615
2008	71 767	3 385	1 314	2 071	68 382	7 109	15 030	16 089	17 075	10 270	2 808

Table 1-7. Civilian Labor Force, by Age, Sex, Race, and Hispanic Origin, 1948–2008—*Continued*

(Thousands of people.)

Race, Hispanic origin, sex, and year	16 years and over	16 to 19 years			20 years and over						
		Total	16 to 17 years	18 to 19 years	Total	20 to 24 years	25 to 34 years	35 to 44 years	45 to 54 years	55 to 64 years	65 years and over
WHITE											
Both Sexes											
1954	56 816	3 501	1 448	2 054	53 315	4 752	13 226	13 540	11 258	7 591	2 946
1955	58 085	3 598	1 511	2 087	54 487	4 941	13 267	13 729	11 680	7 810	3 062
1956	59 428	3 771	1 656	2 113	55 657	5 194	13 154	14 000	12 061	8 080	3 166
1957	59 754	3 775	1 637	2 135	55 979	5 283	13 044	14 117	12 382	8 091	3 049
1958	60 293	3 757	1 615	2 144	56 536	5 449	12 884	14 257	12 727	8 254	2 964
1959	60 952	4 000	1 775	2 225	56 952	5 544	12 670	14 355	13 048	8 411	2 925
1960	61 915	4 275	1 871	2 405	57 640	5 787	12 594	14 450	13 322	8 522	2 964
1961	62 656	4 362	1 767	2 594	58 294	6 026	12 503	14 557	13 517	8 773	2 917
1962	62 750	4 354	1 709	2 645	58 396	6 164	12 218	14 695	13 551	8 856	2 912
1963	63 830	4 559	1 950	2 608	59 271	6 537	12 229	14 859	13 789	9 067	2 790
1964	64 921	4 784	2 211	2 572	60 137	6 952	12 235	14 852	14 043	9 239	2 817
1965	66 137	5 267	2 221	3 044	60 870	7 189	12 391	14 900	14 162	9 392	2 839
1966	67 276	5 827	2 367	3 460	61 449	7 324	12 591	14 785	14 370	9 583	2 793
1967	68 699	5 749	2 432	3 318	62 950	7 886	13 123	14 765	14 545	9 817	2 821
1968	69 976	5 839	2 519	3 320	64 137	8 109	13 740	14 683	14 756	9 968	2 884
1969	71 778	6.168	2 698	3 470	65 611	8 614	14 289	14 564	15 057	10 132	2 954
1970	73 556	6 442	2 824	3 617	67 113	9 238	14 896	14 525	15 269	10 255	2 930
1971	74 963	6 681	2 894	3 787	68 282	9 889	15 445	14 374	15 343	10 351	2 880
1972	77 275	7 193	3 096	4 098	70 082	10 605	16 584	14 399	15 283	10 402	2 809
1973	79 151	7 579	3 320	4 260	71 572	11 182	17 764	14 440	15 256	10 240	2 687
1974	81 281	7 899	3 441	4 459	73 381	11 600	18 862	14 644	15 375	10 241	2 656
1975	82 831	7 899	3 375	4 525	74 932	12 019	19 897	14 753	15 308	10 287	2 668
1976	84 767	8 088	3 410	4 679	76 678	12 444	20 990	15 088	15 187	10 371	2 599
1977	87 141	8 352	3 562	4 790	78 789	12 892	22 099	15 604	15 053	10 495	2 647
1978	89 634	8 555	3 715	4 839	81 079	13 309	23 067	16 353	15 004	10 602	2 745
1979	91 923	8 548	3 668	4 881	83 375	13 632	24 101	17 123	14 965	10 767	2 787
1980	93 600	8 312	3 485	4 827	85 286	13 769	25 181	17 811	14 956	10 812	2 759
1981	95 052	7 962	3 274	4 688	87 089	13 926	26 208	18 445	14 993	10 764	2 753
1982	96 143	7 518	3 001	4 518	88 625	13 866	26 814	19 491	14 879	10 832	2 742
1983	97 021	7 186	2 765	4 421	89 835	13 816	27 237	20 488	14 798	10 732	2 766
1984	98 492	6 952	2 720	4 232	91 540	13 733	27 958	21 588	14 899	10 701	2 660
1985	99 926	6 841	2 777	4 065	93 085	13 469	28 640	22 591	15 101	10 679	2 605
1986	101 801	6 862	2 895	3 967	94 939	13 176	29 497	23 571	15 379	10 583	2 732
1987	103 290	6 893	2 963	3 931	96 396	12 764	29 956	24 581	15 792	10 497	2 806
1988	104 756	6 940	2 861	4 079	97 815	12 311	30 167	25 358	16 573	10 462	2 943
1989	106 355	6 809	2 685	4 124	99 546	11 940	30 388	26 312	17 278	10 533	3 094
1990	107 447	6 683	2 543	4 140	100 764	12 397	30 174	27 265	17 515	10 290	3 123
1991	107 743	6 245	2 432	3 813	101 498	12 248	29 794	28 213	18 028	10 129	3 086
1992	108 837	6 022	2 388	3 633	102 815	12 187	29 518	28 580	19 200	10 196	3 135
1993	109 700	6 105	2 458	3 647	103 595	11 987	29 027	29 056	20 181	10 215	3 129
1994	111 082	6,357	2 681	3 677	104 725	11 688	28 580	29 626	21 026	10 319	3 486
1995	111 950	6 545	2 749	3 796	105 404	11 266	28 325	30 112	21 804	10 432	3 466
1996	113 108	6 607	2 780	3 826	106 502	11 003	27 901	30 683	22 781	10 648	3 485
1997	114 693	6 720	2 779	3 941	107 973	11 127	27 362	31 171	23 709	11 086	3 517
1998	115 415	6 965	2 860	4 105	108 450	11 244	26 707	31 221	24 282	11 548	3 448
1999	116 509	7 048	2 849	4 199	109 461	11 436	25 978	31 391	25 102	11 960	3 595
2000	118 545	6 955	2 768	4 186	111 590	11 626	26 336	30 968	26 353	12 463	3 846
2001	119 399	6 661	2 626	4 035	112 737	11 883	26 010	30 778	27 062	13 121	3 883
2002	120 150	6 366	2 445	3 921	113 784	12 073	25 908	30 286	27 405	14 148	3 965
2003	120 546	5 973	2 414	3 560	114 572	12 064	25 752	29 788	27 786	14 944	4 238
2004	121 086	5 929	2 309	3 620	115 156	12 192	25 548	29 305	28 181	15 522	4 408
2005	122 299	5 950	2 390	3 560	116 349	12 109	25 548	29 107	28 685	16 275	4 624
2006	123 834	6 009	2 473	3 536	117 825	12 128	25 681	28 849	29 231	17 132	4 805
2007	124 935	5 795	2 326	3 470	119 139	12 176	26 076	28 394	29 627	17 782	5 085
2008	125 635	5 644	2 126	3 518	119 990	12 142	26 210	27 932	29 780	18 464	5 463

Table 1-7. Civilian Labor Force, by Age, Sex, Race, and Hispanic Origin, 1948–2008—*Continued*

(Thousands of people.)

Race, Hispanic origin, sex, and year	16 years and over	16 to 19 years			20 years and over						
		Total	16 to 17 years	18 to 19 years	Total	20 to 24 years	25 to 34 years	35 to 44 years	45 to 54 years	55 to 64 years	65 years and over
WHITE											
Men											
1954	39 759	1 989	896	1 095	37 770	2 654	9 695	9 516	7 913	5 653	2 339
1955	40 197	2 056	935	1 121	38 141	2 803	9 721	9 597	8 025	5 654	2 343
1956	40 734	2 114	1 002	1 110	38 620	3 036	9 595	9 661	8 175	5 736	2 417
1957	40 826	2 108	992	1 114	38 718	3 152	9 483	9 719	8 317	5 735	2 307
1958	41 080	2 116	1 001	1 116	38 964	3 278	9 386	9 822	8 465	5 800	2 213
1959	41 397	2 279	1 077	1 202	39 118	3 409	9 261	9 876	8 581	5 833	2 158
1960	41 743	2 433	1 140	1 293	39 310	3 559	9 153	9 919	8 689	5 861	2 129
1961	41 986	2 439	1 067	1 372	39 547	3 681	9 072	9 961	8 776	5 988	2 068
1962	41 931	2 432	1 041	1 391	39 499	3 726	8 846	10 029	8 820	5 995	2 082
1963	42 404	2 563	1 183	1 380	39 841	3 955	8 805	10 079	8 944	6 090	1 967
1964	42 894	2 716	1 345	1 371	40 178	4 166	8 800	10 055	9 053	6 161	1 942
1965	43 400	2 999	1 359	1 639	40 401	4 279	8 824	10 023	9 130	6 188	1 959
1966	43 572	3 253	1 423	1 830	40 319	4 200	8 859	9 892	9 189	6 250	1 928
1967	44 041	3 191	1 464	1 727	40 851	4 416	9 102	9 785	9 260	6 348	1 944
1968	44 553	3 236	1 504	1 732	41 318	4 432	9 477	9 662	9 340	6 427	1 981
1969	45 185	3 413	1 583	1 830	41 772	4 615	9 773	9 509	9 413	6 467	1 996
1970	46 035	3 551	1 629	1 922	42 483	4 988	10 099	9 414	9 487	6 517	1 978
1971	46 904	3 719	1 681	2 039	43 185	5 448	10 444	9 294	9 528	6 550	1 922
1972	48 118	3 980	1 758	2 223	44 138	5 937	11 039	9 278	9 473	6 562	1 846
1973	48 920	4 174	1 875	2 300	44 747	6 274	11 621	9 212	9 445	6 452	1 740
1974	49 843	4 312	1 922	2 391	45 532	6 470	12 135	9 246	9 455	6 464	1 759
1975	50 324	4 290	1 871	2 418	46 034	6 642	12 579	9 231	9 415	6 425	1 742
1976	51 033	4 357	1 869	2 489	46 675	6 890	13 092	9 289	9 310	6 437	1 657
1977	52 033	4 496	1 949	2 548	47 537	7 097	13 575	9 509	9 175	6 492	1 688
1978	52 955	4 565	2 002	2 563	48 390	7 274	13 939	9 858	9 068	6 508	1 744
1979	53 856	4 537	1 974	2 563	49 320	7 421	14 415	10 183	8 968	6 571	1 761
1980	54 473	4 424	1 881	2 543	50 049	7 479	14 893	10 455	8 877	6 618	1 727
1981	54 895	4 224	1 751	2 473	50 671	7 521	15 340	10 740	8 836	6 530	1 704
1982	55 133	3 933	1 602	2 331	51 200	7 438	15 549	11 289	8 727	6 520	1 677
1983	55 480	3 764	1 452	2 312	51 716	7 406	15 707	11 817	8 649	6 446	1 691
1984	56 062	3 609	1 420	2 189	52 453	7 370	16 037	12 348	8 683	6 410	1 606
1985	56 472	3 576	1 467	2 109	52 895	7 122	16 306	12 767	8 730	6 376	1 595
1986	57 217	3 542	1 502	2 040	53 675	6 986	16 769	13 207	8 791	6 260	1 663
1987	57 779	3 547	1 524	2 023	54 232	6 717	16 963	13 674	8 945	6 200	1 733
1988	58 317	3 583	1 487	2 095	54 734	6 468	17 018	14 068	9 285	6 108	1 787
1989	58 988	3 546	1 401	2 146	55 441	6 316	17 077	14 516	9 615	6 082	1 835
1990	59 638	3 522	1 333	2 189	56 116	6 688	16 920	15 026	9 713	5 957	1 811
1991	59 656	3 269	1 266	2 003	56 387	6 619	16 709	15 523	9 926	5 847	1 763
1992	60 168	3 192	1 260	1 932	56 976	6 542	16 512	15 701	10 570	5 821	1 830
1993	60 484	3 200	1 292	1 908	57 284	6 449	16 244	15 971	11 010	5 784	1 825
1994	60 727	3 315	1 403	1 912	57 411	6 294	15 879	16 188	11 327	5 726	1 998
1995	61 146	3 427	1 429	1 998	57 719	6 096	15 669	16 414	11 730	5 809	2 000
1996	61 783	3 444	1 421	2 023	58 340	5 922	15 475	16 728	12 217	5 943	2 054
1997	62 639	3 513	1 440	2 073	59 126	6 029	15 120	17 019	12 710	6 154	2 094
1998	63 034	3 614	1 487	2 127	59 421	6 063	14 770	17 157	13 003	6 415	2 013
1999	63 413	3 666	1 478	2 188	59 747	6 151	14 292	17 201	13 368	6 618	2 117
2000	64 466	3 615	1 422	2 193	60 850	6 244	14 666	16 880	13 977	6 840	2 243
2001	64 966	3 446	1 334	2 112	61 519	6 363	14 536	16 809	14 400	7 169	2 241
2002	65 308	3 241	1 215	2 026	62 067	6 444	14 499	16 583	14 615	7 665	2 261
2003	65 509	3 036	1 193	1 843	62 473	6 479	14 529	16 398	14 708	7 973	2 386
2004	65 994	3 050	1 127	1 923	62 944	6 586	14 429	16 192	14 934	8 326	2 478
2005	66 694	2 988	1 162	1 826	63 705	6 562	14 426	16 080	15 273	8 734	2 631
2006	67 613	3 074	1 222	1 852	64 540	6 597	14 469	15 962	15 606	9 152	2 753
2007	68 158	2 944	1 147	1 798	65 214	6 567	14 715	15 765	15 846	9 500	2 821
2008	68 351	2 868	1 040	1 829	65 483	6 526	14 715	15 436	15 905	9 855	3 046

Table 1-7. Civilian Labor Force, by Age, Sex, Race, and Hispanic Origin, 1948–2008—*Continued*

(Thousands of people.)

Race, Hispanic origin, sex, and year	16 years and over	16 to 19 years			20 years and over						
		Total	16 to 17 years	18 to 19 years	Total	20 to 24 years	25 to 34 years	35 to 44 years	45 to 54 years	55 to 64 years	65 years and over
WHITE											
Women											
1954	17 057	1 512	552	959	15 545	2 098	3 531	4 024	3 345	1 938	607
1955	17 888	1 542	576	966	16 346	2 138	3 546	4 132	3 655	2 156	719
1956	18 694	1 657	654	1 003	17 037	2 158	3 559	4 339	3 886	2 344	749
1957	18 928	1 667	645	1 021	17 261	2 131	3 561	4 398	4 065	2 356	742
1958	19 213	1 641	614	1 028	17 572	2 171	3 498	4 435	4 262	2 454	751
1959	19 555	1 721	698	1 023	17 834	2 135	3 409	4 479	4 467	2 578	767
1960	20 172	1 842	731	1 112	18 330	2 228	3 441	4 531	4 633	2 661	835
1961	20 670	1 923	700	1 222	18 747	2 345	3 431	4 596	4 741	2 785	849
1962	20 819	1 922	668	1 254	18 897	2 438	3 372	4 666	4 731	2 861	830
1963	21 426	1 996	767	1 228	19 430	2 582	3 424	4 780	4 845	2 977	823
1964	22 027	2 068	866	1 201	19 959	2 786	3 435	4 797	4 990	3 078	875
1965	22 737	2 268	862	1 405	20 469	2 910	3 567	4 877	5 032	3 204	880
1966	23 704	2 574	944	1 630	21 130	3 124	3 732	4 893	5 181	3 333	865
1967	24 658	2 558	968	1 591	22 100	3 471	4 021	4 980	5 285	3 469	877
1968	25 423	2 603	1 015	1 588	22 821	3 677	4 263	5 021	5 416	3 541	903
1969	26 593	2 755	1 115	1 640	23 839	3 999	4 516	5 055	5 644	3 665	958
1970	27 521	2 891	1 195	1 695	24 630	4 250	4 797	5 111	5 781	3 738	952
1971	28 060	2 962	1 213	1 748	25 097	4 441	5 001	5 080	5 816	3 801	958
1972	29 157	3 213	1 338	1 875	25 945	4 668	5 544	5 121	5 810	3 839	963
1973	30 231	3 405	1 445	1 960	26 825	4 908	6 143	5 228	5 811	3 788	947
1974	31 437	3 588	1 520	2 068	27 850	5 131	6 727	5 399	5 920	3 777	897
1975	32 508	3 610	1 504	2 107	28 898	5 378	7 318	5 522	5 892	3 862	926
1976	33 735	3 731	1 541	2 189	30 004	5 554	7 898	5 799	5 877	3 935	940
1977	35 108	3 856	1 614	2 243	31 253	5 795	8 523	6 095	5 877	4 003	959
1978	36 679	3 990	1 713	2 276	32 689	6 035	9 128	6 495	5 936	4 094	1 001
1979	38 067	4 011	1 694	2 318	34 056	6 211	9 687	6 940	5 997	4 196	1 024
1980	39 127	3 888	1 605	2 284	35 239	6 290	10 289	7 356	6 079	4 194	1 032
1981	40 157	3 739	1 523	2 216	36 418	6 406	10 868	7 704	6 157	4 235	1 049
1982	41 010	3 585	1 399	2 186	37 425	6 428	11 264	8 202	6 152	4 313	1 065
1983	41 541	3 422	1 314	2 109	38 119	6 410	11 530	8 670	6 149	4 285	1 074
1984	42 431	3 343	1 300	2 043	39 087	6 363	11 922	9 240	6 217	4 292	1 054
1985	43 455	3 265	1 310	1 955	40 190	6 348	12 334	9 824	6 371	4 303	1 010
1986	44 584	3 320	1 393	1 927	41 264	6 191	12 729	10 364	6 588	4 323	1 069
1987	45 510	3 347	1 439	1 908	42 164	6 047	12 993	10 907	6 847	4 297	1 073
1988	46 439	3 358	1 374	1 984	43 081	5 844	13 149	11 291	7 288	4 354	1 156
1989	47 367	3 262	1 284	1 978	44 105	5 625	13 311	11 796	7 663	4 451	1 259
1990	47 809	3 161	1 210	1 951	44 648	5 709	13 254	12 239	7 802	4 333	1 312
1991	48 087	2 976	1 166	1 810	45 111	5 629	13 085	12 689	8 101	4 282	1 324
1992	48 669	2 830	1 128	1 702	45 839	5 645	13 006	12 879	8 630	4 375	1 305
1993	49 216	2 905	1 167	1 739	46 311	5 539	12 783	13 085	9 171	4 430	1 304
1994	50 356	3 042	1 278	1 764	47 314	5 394	12 702	13 439	9 699	4 593	1 487
1995	50 804	3 118	1 320	1 798	47 686	5 170	12 656	13 697	10 074	4 622	1 466
1996	51 325	3 163	1 360	1 803	48 162	5 081	12 426	13 955	10 563	4 706	1 431
1997	52 054	3 207	1 339	1 867	48 847	5 099	12 242	14 153	10 999	4 932	1 422
1998	52 380	3 351	1 373	1 977	49 029	5 180	11 937	14 064	11 279	5 133	1 435
1999	53 096	3 382	1 371	2 010	49 714	5 285	11 685	14 190	11 734	5 342	1 478
2000	54 079	3 339	1 346	1 993	50 740	5 381	11 669	14 088	12 376	5 623	1 602
2001	54 433	3 215	1 292	1 923	51 218	5 519	11 474	13 969	12 662	5 952	1 642
2002	54 842	3 125	1 229	1 895	51 717	5 628	11 409	13 703	12 790	6 482	1 704
2003	55 037	2 937	1 221	1 716	52 099	5 584	11 223	13 390	13 078	6 970	1 852
2004	55 092	2 879	1 182	1 697	52 212	5 606	11 119	13 114	13 247	7 197	1 930
2005	55 605	2 962	1 228	1 733	52 643	5 546	11 123	13 027	13 413	7 542	1 993
2006	56 221	2 935	1 251	1 684	53 286	5 530	11 212	12 886	13 625	7 980	2 052
2007	56 777	2 851	1 179	1 672	53 925	5 609	11 360	12 629	13 781	8 282	2 264
2008	57 284	2 776	1 086	1 690	54 508	5 616	11 495	12 495	13 875	8 609	2 417

Table 1-7. Civilian Labor Force, by Age, Sex, Race, and Hispanic Origin, 1948–2008—*Continued*

(Thousands of people.)

Race, Hispanic origin, sex, and year	16 years and over	16 to 19 years			20 years and over						
		Total	16 to 17 years	18 to 19 years	Total	20 to 24 years	25 to 34 years	35 to 44 years	45 to 54 years	55 to 64 years	65 years and over
BLACK											
Both Sexes											
1972	8 707	788	293	496	7 919	1 393	2 107	1 735	1 496	909	281
1973	8 976	833	307	525	8 143	1 489	2 242	1 741	1 513	901	258
1974	9 167	851	317	534	8 317	1 492	2 358	1 777	1 517	917	253
1975	9 263	838	312	524	8 426	1 477	2 466	1 775	1 519	929	258
1976	9 561	837	304	532	8 724	1 544	2 646	1 824	1 518	925	268
1977	9 932	861	304	557	9 072	1 641	2 798	1 894	1 530	943	267
1978	10 432	930	341	589	9 501	1 739	2 961	1 975	1 560	978	289
1979	10 678	912	340	572	9 766	1 793	3 094	2 039	1 584	974	281
1980	10 865	891	326	565	9 975	1 802	3 259	2 081	1 596	978	257
1981	11 086	862	308	554	10 224	1 828	3 365	2 164	1 608	1 009	249
1982	11 331	824	268	556	10 507	1 849	3 492	2 303	1 610	1 012	243
1983	11 647	809	248	561	10 838	1 871	3 675	2 406	1 630	1 032	224
1984	12 033	827	268	558	11 206	1 926	3 800	2 565	1 671	1 020	224
1985	12 364	889	311	578	11 476	1 854	3 888	2 681	1 742	1 059	252
1986	12 654	883	322	562	11 770	1 881	4 028	2 793	1 793	1 051	224
1987	12 993	899	336	563	12 094	1 818	4 147	2 942	1 838	1 098	251
1988	13 205	889	344	545	12 316	1 782	4 226	3 069	1 894	1 069	276
1989	13 497	925	353	572	12 573	1 789	4 295	3 227	1 954	1 023	285
1990	13 740	866	306	560	12 874	1 758	4 307	3 566	2 003	977	262
1991	13 797	774	266	508	13 023	1 750	4 254	3 719	2 042	1 001	256
1992	14 162	816	285	532	13 346	1 763	4 309	3 843	2 142	1 029	259
1993	14 225	807	283	524	13 418	1 764	4 232	3 960	2 212	1 013	237
1994	14 502	852	351	501	13 650	1 800	4 199	4 068	2 308	1 007	267
1995	14 817	911	366	545	13 906	1 754	4 267	4 165	2 404	1 046	271
1996	15 134	923	366	556	14 211	1 738	4 305	4 287	2 553	1 073	255
1997	15 529	933	352	580	14 596	1 783	4 329	4 401	2 724	1 093	265
1998	15 982	1 017	370	646	14 966	1 797	4 332	4 531	2 863	1 163	278
1999	16 365	959	352	607	15 406	1 866	4 430	4 653	2 992	1 180	285
2000	16 397	941	356	585	15 456	1 873	4 281	4 515	3 203	1 264	320
2001	16 421	898	332	565	15 524	1 878	4 180	4 483	3 298	1 335	350
2002	16 565	870	297	574	15 695	1 908	4 134	4 458	3 435	1 407	353
2003	16 526	771	289	482	15 755	1 892	4 060	4 465	3 506	1 466	366
2004	16 638	762	272	489	15 876	1 926	4 076	4 380	3 578	1 538	380
2005	17 013	803	279	525	16 209	1 957	4 145	4 370	3 686	1 647	403
2006	17 314	871	318	553	16 443	1 960	4 197	4 348	3 785	1 739	414
2007	17 496	801	300	501	16 695	1 974	4 254	4 357	3 866	1 811	432
2008	17 740	787	270	517	16 953	1 981	4 328	4 316	3 945	1 908	476
BLACK											
Men											
1972	4 816	453	180	272	4 364	761	1 158	935	824	522	165
1973	4 924	460	175	286	4 464	819	1 217	935	842	499	153
1974	5 020	480	189	291	4 540	798	1 279	953	838	519	152
1975	5 016	447	168	279	4 569	790	1 328	948	833	520	150
1976	5 101	454	168	285	4 648	820	1 383	969	824	504	149
1977	5 263	476	178	299	4 787	856	1 441	1 003	818	515	154
1978	5 435	491	186	306	4 943	883	1 504	1 022	829	540	166
1979	5 559	480	179	301	5 079	928	1 577	1 049	844	524	156
1980	5 612	479	181	298	5 134	935	1 659	1 061	830	509	138
1981	5 685	462	169	293	5 223	940	1 702	1 093	829	524	134
1982	5 804	436	137	300	5 368	964	1 769	1 152	824	525	135
1983	5 966	433	134	300	5 533	997	1 840	1 196	845	536	119
1984	6 126	440	141	299	5 686	1 022	1 924	1 270	847	505	118
1985	6 220	471	162	310	5 749	950	1 937	1 313	879	544	125
1986	6 373	458	164	294	5 915	957	2 029	1 359	901	552	116
1987	6 486	463	179	284	6 023	914	2 074	1 406	915	586	130
1988	6 596	469	186	283	6 127	913	2 114	1 459	936	565	139
1989	6 701	480	190	291	6 221	904	2 157	1 544	945	530	141
1990	6 802	445	161	284	6 357	879	2 142	1 733	988	496	119
1991	6 851	400	140	260	6 451	896	2 111	1 806	1 010	507	122
1992	6 997	429	149	280	6 568	900	2 121	1 859	1 037	521	130
1993	7 019	425	154	270	6 594	875	2 118	1 918	1 065	506	112
1994	7 089	443	176	266	6 646	891	2 068	1 975	1 102	484	125
1995	7 183	453	184	269	6 730	866	2 089	1 987	1 148	490	150
1996	7 264	458	182	276	6 806	848	2 077	2 036	1 204	509	132
1997	7 354	444	178	266	6 910	832	2 052	2 096	1 287	508	134
1998	7 542	488	181	307	7 053	837	2 034	2 142	1 343	548	150
1999	7 652	470	180	291	7 182	835	2 069	2 206	1 387	547	138
2000	7 702	462	181	281	7 240	875	1 999	2 105	1 497	612	151
2001	7 647	447	166	281	7 200	853	1 915	2 073	1 537	645	177
2002	7 794	446	149	297	7 347	906	1 909	2 064	1 623	664	181
2003	7 711	365	138	228	7 346	918	1 872	2 058	1 627	685	186
2004	7 773	359	128	231	7 414	927	1 931	2 000	1 654	714	188
2005	7 998	399	139	260	7 600	940	1 948	2 028	1 732	756	196
2006	8 128	409	152	256	7 720	971	1 986	1 999	1 792	777	195
2007	8 252	384	137	247	7 867	981	2 037	2 030	1 822	791	206
2008	8 347	385	124	261	7 962	984	2 047	2 008	1 846	852	225

Table 1-7. Civilian Labor Force, by Age, Sex, Race, and Hispanic Origin, 1948–2008—*Continued*

(Thousands of people.)

Race, Hispanic origin, sex, and year	16 years and over	16 to 19 years			20 years and over						
		Total	16 to 17 years	18 to 19 years	Total	20 to 24 years	25 to 34 years	35 to 44 years	45 to 54 years	55 to 64 years	65 years and over
BLACK											
Women											
1972	3 890	335	113	224	3 555	632	949	800	672	387	116
1973	4 052	373	133	240	3 678	670	1 026	806	670	402	105
1974	4 148	371	128	243	3 777	694	1 079	824	679	398	100
1975	4 247	391	144	245	3 857	687	1 138	827	686	409	108
1976	4 460	384	136	247	4 076	723	1 264	855	694	421	119
1977	4 670	385	127	258	4 286	785	1 357	891	712	429	113
1978	4 997	439	155	283	4 558	856	1 456	953	731	439	124
1979	5 119	432	161	271	4 687	865	1 517	990	740	451	124
1980	5 253	412	144	267	4 841	867	1 600	1 020	767	469	119
1981	5 401	400	139	261	5 001	888	1 663	1 071	779	485	115
1982	5 527	387	131	256	5 140	885	1 723	1 151	786	487	108
1983	5 681	375	114	261	5 306	874	1 835	1 210	785	496	105
1984	5 907	387	127	260	5 520	904	1 876	1 294	823	515	106
1985	6 144	417	149	268	5 727	904	1 951	1 368	862	515	127
1986	6 281	425	157	268	5 855	924	1 999	1 434	892	499	107
1987	6 507	435	157	278	6 071	904	2 073	1 537	924	512	121
1988	6 609	419	158	262	6 190	869	2 112	1 610	958	504	137
1989	6 796	445	163	281	6 352	885	2 138	1 683	1 009	493	144
1990	6 938	421	145	276	6 517	879	2 165	1 833	1 015	481	143
1991	6 946	374	126	248	6 572	854	2 143	1 913	1 032	494	135
1992	7 166	387	135	252	6 778	863	2 188	1 985	1 105	508	129
1993	7 206	383	129	254	6 824	889	2 115	2 042	1 147	506	125
1994	7 413	409	174	235	7 004	909	2 131	2 093	1 206	523	142
1995	7 634	458	182	276	7 175	887	2 177	2 178	1 256	556	121
1996	7 869	464	184	280	7 405	890	2 228	2 251	1 349	565	122
1997	8 175	489	175	314	7 686	951	2 277	2 305	1 437	585	131
1998	8 441	528	189	339	7 912	960	2 298	2 390	1 520	615	128
1999	8 713	489	172	316	8 224	1 031	2 360	2 447	1 606	633	147
2000	8 695	479	175	305	8 215	998	2 282	2 409	1 706	652	168
2001	8 774	451	166	284	8 323	1 025	2 265	2 410	1 762	690	173
2002	8 772	424	148	276	8 348	1 002	2 225	2 394	1 812	743	171
2003	8 815	406	151	255	8 409	973	2 188	2 407	1 879	781	180
2004	8 865	403	144	259	8 462	999	2 144	2 380	1 924	824	192
2005	9 014	405	140	265	8 610	1 017	2 197	2 342	1 954	891	207
2006	9 186	462	166	297	8 723	989	2 211	2 349	1 993	963	218
2007	9 244	417	163	254	8 828	993	2 218	2 328	2 044	1 019	227
2008	9 393	402	146	256	8 991	997	2 281	2 308	2 099	1 056	251
HISPANIC[1]											
Both Sexes											
1973	3 673	407	. . .	. . .	. . .	. . .	. . .	. . .	. . .	. . .	. . .
1974	4 012	442	. . .	. . .	. . .	. . .	. . .	. . .	. . .	. . .	. . .
1975	4 171	444	. . .	. . .	. . .	. . .	. . .	. . .	. . .	. . .	. . .
1976	4 205	447	176	285	3 820	729	1 248	875	625	294	48
1977	4 536	493	184	305	4 059	813	1 325	916	656	293	55
1978	4 979	533	221	312	4 446	901	1 446	1 008	701	323	67
1979	5 219	551	207	343	4 668	960	1 532	1 062	704	339	72
1980	6 146	645	241	404	5 502	1 136	1 843	1 163	860	414	85
1981	6 492	603	215	388	5 888	1 231	2 015	1 239	886	430	87
1982	6 734	585	192	393	6 148	1 251	2 163	1 313	891	444	85
1983	7 033	590	189	401	6 442	1 282	2 267	1 380	931	495	86
1984	7 451	618	209	409	6 833	1 325	2 436	1 509	954	524	84
1985	7 698	579	199	379	7 119	1 358	2 571	1 595	985	527	82
1986	8 076	571	203	368	7 505	1 414	2 685	1 713	1 097	511	84
1987	8 541	610	206	404	7 931	1 425	2 890	1 904	1 086	545	81
1988	8 982	671	234	437	8 311	1 486	2 957	1 996	1 147	621	103
1989	9 323	680	224	456	8 643	1 483	3 118	2 092	1 205	625	120
1990	10 720	829	276	554	9 891	1 839	3 590	2 386	1 320	647	110
1991	10 920	781	249	532	10 139	1 835	3 596	2 539	1 376	681	111
1992	11 338	796	263	533	10 542	1 815	3 740	2 735	1 442	687	122
1993	11 610	771	246	525	10 839	1 811	3 800	2 865	1 534	684	145
1994	11 975	807	285	522	11 168	1 863	3 865	2 965	1 626	698	151
1995	12 267	850	291	559	11 417	1 818	3 943	3 113	1 671	720	152
1996	12 774	845	284	561	11 929	1 845	4 054	3 361	1 697	806	166
1997	13 796	911	315	596	12 884	2 004	4 298	3 601	1 945	850	186
1998	14 317	1 007	320	688	13 310	2 077	4 372	3 707	2 090	894	169
1999	14 665	1 049	333	717	13 616	2 052	4 330	3 929	2 178	927	199
2000	16 689	1 168	368	800	15 521	2 546	5 197	4 241	2 387	940	209
2001	17 328	1 176	352	824	16 152	2 616	5 380	4 377	2 583	1 000	195
2002	17 943	1 103	335	769	16 840	2 678	5 645	4 545	2 657	1 091	224
2003	18 813	960	322	638	17 853	2 672	5 960	4 867	2 894	1 201	259
2004	19 272	995	297	698	18 277	2 732	5 931	4 931	3 093	1 284	306
2005	19 824	1 038	331	708	18 785	2 651	6 080	5 110	3 256	1 378	311
2006	20 694	1 071	360	710	19 623	2 681	6 295	5 337	3 452	1 490	369
2007	21 602	1 091	347	744	20 511	2 728	6 559	5 552	3 707	1 569	395
2008	22 024	1 121	353	768	20 903	2 668	6 557	5 698	3 862	1 701	417

[1]May be any race.
. . . = Not available.

Table 1-7. Civilian Labor Force, by Age, Sex, Race, and Hispanic Origin, 1948–2008—*Continued*

(Thousands of people.)

Race, Hispanic origin, sex, and year	16 years and over	16 to 19 years			20 years and over						
		Total	16 to 17 years	18 to 19 years	Total	20 to 24 years	25 to 34 years	35 to 44 years	45 to 54 years	55 to 64 years	65 years and over
HISPANIC[1]											
Men											
1973	2 356	...	...	...	2 124	...	...	...	...	...	...
1974	2 556	...	...	...	2 306	...	...	...	...	...	...
1975	2 597	...	...	...	2 343	...	...	...	...	...	...
1976	2 580	260	104	155	2 326	433	771	541	398	189	34
1977	2 817	285	105	179	2 530	485	828	567	416	197	42
1978	3 041	299	129	171	2 742	546	882	620	425	217	52
1979	3 184	315	121	194	2 869	562	941	648	445	216	56
1980	3 818	392	147	245	3 426	697	1 161	713	522	270	62
1981	4 005	359	130	229	3 647	747	1 269	756	535	278	61
1982	4 148	333	111	221	3 815	759	1 361	808	539	290	58
1983	4 362	348	109	239	4 014	789	1 447	852	557	311	58
1984	4 563	345	113	232	4 218	822	1 540	910	570	325	51
1985	4 729	334	116	218	4 395	835	1 629	957	591	331	53
1986	4 948	336	114	222	4 612	888	1 669	1 015	661	323	56
1987	5 163	345	112	233	4 818	865	1 801	1 121	652	325	55
1988	5 409	378	123	255	5 031	897	1 834	1 189	686	355	69
1989	5 595	400	129	271	5 195	909	1 899	1 221	719	375	71
1990	6 546	512	165	346	6 034	1 182	2 230	1 403	775	380	65
1991	6 664	466	141	325	6 198	1 202	2 260	1 487	780	401	67
1992	6 900	468	154	314	6 432	1 141	2 366	1 593	844	414	74
1993	7 076	455	145	310	6 621	1 147	2 417	1 675	900	394	88
1994	7 210	463	163	300	6 747	1 184	2 430	1 713	922	410	89
1995	7 376	479	168	311	6 898	1 153	2 469	1 795	965	417	98
1996	7 646	496	156	340	7 150	1 132	2 510	1 966	967	469	105
1997	8 309	531	177	354	7 779	1 267	2 684	2 091	1 112	511	113
1998	8 571	565	188	377	8 005	1 288	2 733	2 173	1 164	541	106
1999	8 546	596	181	415	7 950	1 231	2 633	2 219	1 205	526	136
2000	9 923	676	204	471	9 247	1 590	3 181	2 451	1 337	555	134
2001	10 279	684	200	484	9 595	1 602	3 294	2 562	1 430	582	125
2002	10 609	632	183	449	9 977	1 627	3 484	2 647	1 478	607	134
2003	11 288	532	164	368	10 756	1 642	3 776	2 877	1 630	680	150
2004	11 587	567	156	410	11 020	1 671	3 765	2 934	1 736	728	186
2005	11 985	577	179	398	11 408	1 645	3 879	3 058	1 855	779	192
2006	12 488	600	189	411	11 888	1 646	4 014	3 203	1 960	838	228
2007	13 005	602	189	412	12 403	1 645	4 170	3 346	2 104	904	233
2008	13 255	626	202	424	12 629	1 594	4 172	3 425	2 216	979	243
HISPANIC[1]											
Women											
1973	1 317	...	...	...	1 142	...	...	...	...	...	...
1974	1 456	...	...	...	1 264	...	...	...	...	...	...
1975	1 574	...	...	...	1 384	...	...	...	...	...	...
1976	1 625	201	71	130	1 454	295	479	334	227	105	13
1977	1 720	204	80	125	1 523	327	497	349	240	96	13
1978	1 938	233	93	142	1 704	354	564	388	275	106	16
1979	2 035	235	86	149	1 800	397	590	413	258	124	15
1980	2 328	252	93	159	2 076	439	682	450	337	144	22
1981	2 486	244	85	159	2 242	484	745	483	351	152	27
1982	2 586	252	81	172	2 333	492	802	504	352	155	28
1983	2 671	242	80	162	2 429	493	820	529	374	184	29
1984	2 888	273	96	177	2 615	503	896	599	384	199	34
1985	2 970	245	84	161	2 725	524	943	639	394	196	29
1986	3 128	236	89	147	2 893	526	1 016	698	436	189	28
1987	3 377	265	94	171	3 112	559	1 090	783	434	220	27
1988	3 573	293	111	182	3 281	589	1 123	806	461	267	34
1989	3 728	280	95	185	3 448	574	1 219	871	486	251	49
1990	4 174	318	110	207	3 857	657	1 360	983	545	268	45
1991	4 256	315	107	207	3 941	633	1 336	1 052	596	279	44
1992	4 439	328	110	219	4 110	674	1 374	1 142	599	273	48
1993	4 534	316	101	215	4 218	664	1 383	1 190	633	290	57
1994	4 765	345	122	222	4 421	679	1 435	1 252	704	288	62
1995	4 891	371	123	249	4 520	666	1 473	1 318	706	303	54
1996	5 128	349	128	221	4 779	713	1 544	1 395	729	338	61
1997	5 486	381	138	242	5 106	737	1 614	1 510	833	338	73
1998	5 746	442	132	310	5 304	789	1 639	1 533	927	353	62
1999	6 119	453	151	302	5 666	821	1 698	1 710	973	401	63
2000	6 767	492	164	328	6 275	956	2 016	1 791	1 051	386	75
2001	7 049	492	152	340	6 557	1 014	2 086	1 815	1 153	418	70
2002	7 334	471	152	320	6 863	1 051	2 161	1 897	1 179	484	90
2003	7 525	428	158	271	7 096	1 030	2 183	1 990	1 264	520	109
2004	7 685	429	141	288	7 257	1 060	2 166	1 998	1 357	556	119
2005	7 839	462	152	310	7 377	1 005	2 201	2 052	1 401	599	119
2006	8 206	471	171	300	7 735	1 035	2 280	2 134	1 492	652	141
2007	8 597	489	158	332	8 108	1 083	2 389	2 205	1 604	665	162
2008	8 769	495	151	344	8 274	1 074	2 384	2 274	1 646	722	174

[1]May be any race.
. . . = Not available.

Table 1-8. Civilian Labor Force Participation Rates, by Age, Sex, Race, and Hispanic Origin, 1948–2008

(Percent.)

Race, Hispanic origin, sex, and year	16 years and over	16 to 19 years	20 years and over						
			Total	20 to 24 years	25 to 34 years	35 to 44 years	45 to 54 years	55 to 64 years	65 years and over
ALL RACES									
Both Sexes									
1948	58.8	52.5	59.4	64.1	63.1	66.7	65.1	56.9	27.0
1949	58.9	52.2	59.5	64.9	63.2	67.2	65.3	56.2	27.3
1950	59.2	51.8	59.9	65.9	63.5	67.5	66.4	56.7	26.7
1951	59.2	52.2	59.8	64.8	64.2	67.6	67.2	56.9	25.8
1952	59.0	51.3	59.7	62.2	64.7	68.0	67.5	57.5	24.8
1953	58.9	50.2	59.6	61.2	64.0	68.9	68.1	58.0	24.8
1954	58.8	48.3	59.6	61.6	64.3	68.8	68.4	58.7	23.9
1955	59.3	48.9	60.1	62.7	64.8	68.9	69.7	59.5	24.1
1956	60.0	50.9	60.7	64.1	64.8	69.5	70.5	60.8	24.3
1957	59.6	49.6	60.4	64.0	64.9	69.5	70.9	60.1	22.9
1958	59.5	47.4	60.5	64.4	65.0	69.6	71.5	60.5	21.8
1959	59.3	46.7	60.4	64.3	65.0	69.5	71.9	61.0	21.1
1960	59.4	47.5	60.5	65.2	65.4	69.4	72.2	60.9	20.8
1961	59.3	46.9	60.5	65.7	65.6	69.5	72.1	61.5	20.1
1962	58.8	46.1	60.0	65.3	65.2	69.7	72.2	61.5	19.1
1963	58.7	45.2	60.1	65.1	65.6	70.1	72.5	62.0	17.9
1964	58.7	44.5	60.2	66.3	65.8	70.0	72.9	61.9	18.0
1965	58.9	45.7	60.3	66.4	66.4	70.7	72.5	61.9	17.8
1966	59.2	48.2	60.5	66.5	67.1	71.0	72.7	62.2	17.2
1967	59.6	48.4	60.9	67.1	68.2	71.6	72.7	62.3	17.2
1968	59.6	48.3	60.9	67.0	68.6	72.0	72.8	62.2	17.2
1969	60.1	49.4	61.3	68.2	69.1	72.5	73.4	62.1	17.3
1970	60.4	49.9	61.6	69.2	69.7	73.1	73.5	61.8	17.0
1971	60.2	49.7	61.4	69.3	69.9	73.2	73.2	61.3	16.2
1972	60.4	51.9	61.4	70.8	70.9	73.3	72.7	60.0	15.6
1973	60.8	53.7	61.7	72.6	72.3	74.0	72.5	58.4	14.6
1974	61.3	54.8	62.0	74.0	73.6	74.6	72.7	57.8	14.0
1975	61.2	54.0	62.1	73.9	74.4	75.0	72.6	57.2	13.7
1976	61.6	54.5	62.4	74.7	75.7	76.0	72.5	56.6	13.1
1977	62.3	56.0	63.0	75.7	77.0	77.0	72.8	56.3	13.0
1978	63.2	57.8	63.8	76.8	78.3	78.1	73.5	56.3	13.3
1979	63.7	57.9	64.3	77.5	79.2	79.2	74.3	56.2	13.1
1980	63.8	56.7	64.5	77.2	79.9	80.0	74.9	55.7	12.5
1981	63.9	55.4	64.8	77.3	80.5	80.7	75.7	55.0	12.2
1982	64.0	54.1	65.0	77.1	81.0	81.2	75.9	55.1	11.9
1983	64.0	53.5	65.0	77.2	81.3	81.6	76.0	54.5	11.7
1984	64.4	53.9	65.3	77.6	81.8	82.4	76.5	54.2	11.1
1985	64.8	54.5	65.7	78.2	82.5	83.1	77.3	54.2	10.8
1986	65.3	54.7	66.2	78.9	82.9	83.7	78.0	54.0	10.9
1987	65.6	54.7	66.5	78.9	83.3	84.3	78.6	54.4	11.1
1988	65.9	55.3	66.8	78.7	83.3	84.6	79.6	54.6	11.5
1989	66.5	55.9	67.3	78.7	83.8	85.1	80.5	55.5	11.8
1990	66.5	53.7	67.6	77.8	83.6	85.2	80.7	55.9	11.8
1991	66.2	51.6	67.3	76.7	83.2	85.2	81.0	55.5	11.5
1992	66.4	51.3	67.6	77.0	83.7	85.1	81.5	56.2	11.5
1993	66.3	51.5	67.5	77.0	83.3	84.9	81.6	56.4	11.2
1994	66.6	52.7	67.7	77.0	83.2	84.8	81.7	56.8	12.4
1995	66.6	53.5	67.7	76.6	83.8	84.6	81.4	57.2	12.1
1996	66.8	52.3	67.9	76.8	84.1	84.8	82.1	57.9	12.1
1997	67.1	51.6	68.4	77.6	84.4	85.1	82.6	58.9	12.2
1998	67.1	52.8	68.3	77.5	84.6	84.7	82.5	59.3	11.9
1999	67.1	52.0	68.3	77.5	84.6	84.9	82.6	59.3	12.3
2000	67.1	52.0	68.3	77.8	84.6	84.8	82.5	59.2	12.9
2001	66.8	49.6	68.2	77.1	84.0	84.6	82.3	60.4	13.0
2002	66.6	47.4	68.1	76.4	83.7	84.1	82.1	61.9	13.2
2003	66.2	44.5	67.9	75.4	82.9	83.9	82.1	62.4	14.0
2004	66.0	43.9	67.7	75.0	82.7	83.6	81.8	62.3	14.4
2005	66.0	43.7	67.8	74.6	82.8	83.8	81.7	62.9	15.1
2006	66.2	43.7	67.9	74.6	83.0	83.8	81.9	63.7	15.4
2007	66.0	41.3	68.0	74.4	83.3	83.8	82.0	63.8	16.0
2008	66.0	40.2	68.0	74.4	83.3	84.1	81.9	64.5	16.8

Table 1-8. Civilian Labor Force Participation Rates, by Age, Sex, Race, and Hispanic Origin, 1948–2008
—Continued

(Percent.)

Race, Hispanic origin, sex, and year	16 years and over	16 to 19 years	20 years and over						
			Total	20 to 24 years	25 to 34 years	35 to 44 years	45 to 54 years	55 to 64 years	65 years and over
ALL RACES									
Men									
1948	86.6	63.7	88.6	84.6	95.9	97.9	95.8	89.5	46.8
1949	86.4	62.8	88.5	86.6	95.8	97.9	95.6	87.5	47.0
1950	86.4	63.2	88.4	87.9	96.0	97.6	95.8	86.9	45.8
1951	86.3	63.0	88.2	88.4	96.9	97.5	95.9	87.2	44.9
1952	86.3	61.3	88.3	88.1	97.5	97.8	96.2	87.5	42.6
1953	86.0	60.7	88.0	87.7	97.4	98.2	96.5	87.9	41.6
1954	85.5	58.0	87.8	86.9	97.3	98.1	96.5	88.7	40.5
1955	85.4	58.9	87.6	86.9	97.6	98.1	96.4	87.9	39.6
1956	85.5	60.5	87.6	87.8	97.3	97.9	96.6	88.5	40.0
1957	84.8	59.1	86.9	87.1	97.1	97.9	96.3	87.5	37.5
1958	84.2	56.6	86.6	86.9	97.1	97.9	96.3	87.8	35.6
1959	83.7	55.8	86.3	87.8	97.4	97.8	96.0	87.4	34.2
1960	83.3	56.1	86.0	88.1	97.5	97.7	95.7	86.8	33.1
1961	82.9	54.6	85.7	87.8	97.5	97.6	95.6	87.3	31.7
1962	82.0	53.8	84.8	86.9	97.2	97.6	95.6	86.2	30.3
1963	81.4	52.9	84.4	86.1	97.1	97.5	95.7	86.2	28.4
1964	81.0	52.4	84.2	86.1	97.3	97.3	95.7	85.6	28.0
1965	80.7	53.8	83.9	85.8	97.2	97.3	95.6	84.6	27.9
1966	80.4	55.3	83.6	85.1	97.3	97.2	95.3	84.5	27.1
1967	80.4	55.6	83.4	84.4	97.2	97.3	95.2	84.4	27.1
1968	80.1	55.1	83.1	82.8	96.9	97.1	94.9	84.3	27.3
1969	79.8	55.9	82.8	82.8	96.7	96.9	94.6	83.4	27.2
1970	79.7	56.1	82.6	83.3	96.4	96.9	94.3	83.0	26.8
1971	79.1	56.1	82.1	83.0	95.9	96.5	93.9	82.1	25.5
1972	78.9	58.1	81.6	83.9	95.7	96.4	93.2	80.4	24.3
1973	78.8	59.7	81.3	85.2	95.7	96.2	93.0	78.2	22.7
1974	78.7	60.7	81.0	85.9	95.8	96.0	92.2	77.3	22.4
1975	77.9	59.1	80.3	84.5	95.2	95.6	92.1	75.6	21.6
1976	77.5	59.3	79.8	85.2	95.2	95.4	91.6	74.3	20.2
1977	77.7	60.9	79.7	85.6	95.3	95.7	91.1	73.8	20.0
1978	77.9	62.0	79.8	85.9	95.3	95.7	91.3	73.3	20.4
1979	77.8	61.5	79.8	86.4	95.3	95.7	91.4	72.8	19.9
1980	77.4	60.5	79.4	85.9	95.2	95.5	91.2	72.1	19.0
1981	77.0	59.0	79.0	85.5	94.9	95.4	91.4	70.6	18.4
1982	76.6	56.7	78.7	84.9	94.7	95.3	91.2	70.2	17.8
1983	76.4	56.2	78.5	84.8	94.2	95.2	91.2	69.4	17.4
1984	76.4	56.0	78.3	85.0	94.4	95.4	91.2	68.5	16.3
1985	76.3	56.8	78.1	85.0	94.7	95.0	91.0	67.9	15.8
1986	76.3	56.4	78.1	85.8	94.6	94.8	91.0	67.3	16.0
1987	76.2	56.1	78.0	85.2	94.6	94.6	90.7	67.6	16.3
1988	76.2	56.9	77.9	85.0	94.3	94.5	90.9	67.0	16.5
1989	76.4	57.9	78.1	85.3	94.4	94.5	91.1	67.2	16.6
1990	76.4	55.7	78.2	84.4	94.1	94.3	90.7	67.8	16.3
1991	75.8	53.2	77.7	83.5	93.6	94.1	90.5	67.0	15.7
1992	75.8	53.4	77.7	83.3	93.8	93.7	90.7	67.0	16.1
1993	75.4	53.2	77.3	83.2	93.4	93.4	90.1	66.5	15.6
1994	75.1	54.1	76.8	83.1	92.6	92.8	89.1	65.5	16.8
1995	75.0	54.8	76.7	83.1	93.0	92.3	88.8	66.0	16.8
1996	74.9	53.2	76.8	82.5	93.2	92.4	89.1	67.0	16.9
1997	75.0	52.3	77.0	82.5	93.0	92.6	89.5	67.6	17.1
1998	74.9	53.3	76.8	82.0	93.2	92.6	89.2	68.1	16.5
1999	74.7	52.9	76.7	81.9	93.3	92.8	88.8	67.9	16.9
2000	74.8	52.8	76.7	82.6	93.4	92.7	88.6	67.3	17.7
2001	74.4	50.2	76.5	81.6	92.7	92.5	88.5	68.3	17.7
2002	74.1	47.5	76.3	80.7	92.4	92.1	88.5	69.2	17.9
2003	73.5	44.3	75.9	80.0	91.8	92.1	87.7	68.7	18.6
2004	73.3	43.9	75.8	79.6	91.9	91.9	87.5	68.7	19.0
2005	73.3	43.2	75.8	79.1	91.7	92.1	87.7	69.3	19.8
2006	73.5	43.7	75.9	79.6	91.7	92.1	88.1	69.6	20.3
2007	73.2	41.1	75.9	78.7	92.2	92.3	88.2	69.6	20.5
2008	73.0	40.1	75.7	78.7	91.5	92.2	88.0	70.4	21.5

Table 1-8. Civilian Labor Force Participation Rates, by Age, Sex, Race, and Hispanic Origin, 1948–2008
—*Continued*

(Percent.)

Race, Hispanic origin, sex, and year	16 years and over	16 to 19 years	20 years and over						
			Total	20 to 24 years	25 to 34 years	35 to 44 years	45 to 54 years	55 to 64 years	65 years and over
ALL RACES									
Women									
1948	32.7	42.0	31.8	45.3	33.2	36.9	35.0	24.3	9.1
1949	33.1	42.4	32.3	45.0	33.4	38.1	35.9	25.3	9.6
1950	33.9	41.0	33.3	46.0	34.0	39.1	37.9	27.0	9.7
1951	34.6	42.4	34.0	46.5	35.4	39.8	39.7	27.6	8.9
1952	34.7	42.2	34.1	44.7	35.4	40.4	40.1	28.7	9.1
1953	34.4	40.7	33.9	44.3	34.0	41.3	40.4	29.1	10.0
1954	34.6	39.4	34.2	45.1	34.4	41.2	41.2	30.0	9.3
1955	35.7	39.7	35.4	45.9	34.9	41.6	43.8	32.5	10.6
1956	36.9	42.2	36.4	46.3	35.4	43.1	45.5	34.9	10.8
1957	36.9	41.1	36.5	45.9	35.6	43.3	46.5	34.5	10.5
1958	37.1	39.0	36.9	46.3	35.6	43.4	47.8	35.2	10.3
1959	37.1	38.2	37.1	45.1	35.3	43.4	49.0	36.6	10.2
1960	37.7	39.3	37.6	46.1	36.0	43.4	49.9	37.2	10.8
1961	38.1	39.7	38.0	47.0	36.4	43.8	50.1	37.9	10.7
1962	37.9	39.0	37.8	47.3	36.3	44.1	50.0	38.7	10.0
1963	38.3	38.0	38.3	47.5	37.2	44.9	50.6	39.7	9.6
1964	38.7	37.0	38.9	49.4	37.2	45.0	51.4	40.2	10.1
1965	39.3	38.0	39.4	49.9	38.5	46.1	50.9	41.1	10.0
1966	40.3	41.4	40.1	51.5	39.8	46.8	51.7	41.8	9.6
1967	41.1	41.6	41.1	53.3	41.9	48.1	51.8	42.4	9.6
1968	41.6	41.9	41.6	54.5	42.6	48.9	52.3	42.4	9.6
1969	42.7	43.2	42.7	56.7	43.7	49.9	53.8	43.1	9.9
1970	43.3	44.0	43.3	57.7	45.0	51.1	54.4	43.0	9.7
1971	43.4	43.4	43.3	57.7	45.6	51.6	54.3	42.9	9.5
1972	43.9	45.8	43.7	59.1	47.8	52.0	53.9	42.1	9.3
1973	44.7	47.8	44.4	61.1	50.4	53.3	53.7	41.1	8.9
1974	45.7	49.1	45.3	63.1	52.6	54.7	54.6	40.7	8.1
1975	46.3	49.1	46.0	64.1	54.9	55.8	54.6	40.9	8.2
1976	47.3	49.8	47.0	65.0	57.3	57.8	55.0	41.0	8.2
1977	48.4	51.2	48.1	66.5	59.7	59.6	55.8	40.9	8.1
1978	50.0	53.7	49.6	68.3	62.2	61.6	57.1	41.3	8.3
1979	50.9	54.2	50.6	69.0	63.9	63.6	58.3	41.7	8.3
1980	51.5	52.9	51.3	68.9	65.5	65.5	59.9	41.3	8.1
1981	52.1	51.8	52.1	69.6	66.7	66.8	61.1	41.4	8.0
1982	52.6	51.4	52.7	69.8	68.0	68.0	61.6	41.8	7.9
1983	52.9	50.8	53.1	69.9	69.0	68.7	61.9	41.5	7.8
1984	53.6	51.8	53.7	70.4	69.8	70.1	62.9	41.7	7.5
1985	54.5	52.1	54.7	71.8	70.9	71.8	64.4	42.0	7.3
1986	55.3	53.0	55.5	72.4	71.6	73.1	65.9	42.3	7.4
1987	56.0	53.3	56.2	73.0	72.4	74.5	67.1	42.7	7.4
1988	56.6	53.6	56.8	72.7	72.7	75.2	69.0	43.5	7.9
1989	57.4	53.9	57.7	72.4	73.5	76.0	70.5	45.0	8.4
1990	57.5	51.6	58.0	71.3	73.5	76.4	71.2	45.2	8.6
1991	57.4	50.0	57.9	70.1	73.1	76.5	72.0	45.2	8.5
1992	57.8	49.1	58.5	70.9	73.9	76.7	72.6	46.5	8.3
1993	57.9	49.7	58.5	70.9	73.4	76.6	73.5	47.2	8.1
1994	58.8	51.3	59.3	71.0	74.0	77.1	74.6	48.9	9.2
1995	58.9	52.2	59.4	70.3	74.9	77.2	74.4	49.2	8.8
1996	59.3	51.3	59.9	71.3	75.2	77.5	75.4	49.6	8.6
1997	59.8	51.0	60.5	72.7	76.0	77.7	76.0	50.9	8.6
1998	59.8	52.3	60.4	73.0	76.3	77.1	76.2	51.2	8.6
1999	60.0	51.0	60.7	73.2	76.4	77.2	76.7	51.5	8.9
2000	59.9	51.2	60.6	73.1	76.1	77.2	76.8	51.9	9.4
2001	59.8	49.0	60.6	72.7	75.5	77.1	76.4	53.2	9.6
2002	59.6	47.3	60.5	72.1	75.1	76.4	76.0	55.2	9.8
2003	59.5	44.8	60.6	70.8	74.1	76.0	76.8	56.6	10.6
2004	59.2	43.8	60.3	70.5	73.6	75.6	76.5	56.3	11.1
2005	59.3	44.2	60.4	70.1	73.9	75.8	76.0	57.0	11.5
2006	59.4	43.7	60.5	69.5	74.4	75.9	76.0	58.2	11.7
2007	59.3	41.5	60.6	70.1	74.5	75.5	76.0	58.3	12.6
2008	59.5	40.2	60.9	70.0	75.2	76.1	76.1	59.1	13.3

Table 1-8. Civilian Labor Force Participation Rates, by Age, Sex, Race, and Hispanic Origin, 1948–2008
—Continued

(Percent.)

Race, Hispanic origin, sex, and year	16 years and over	16 to 19 years	20 years and over						
			Total	20 to 24 years	25 to 34 years	35 to 44 years	45 to 54 years	55 to 64 years	65 years and over
WHITE									
Both Sexes									
1954	58.2	48.8	58.9	61.0	63.5	68.0	67.9	58.4	23.7
1955	58.7	49.3	59.5	62.4	64.0	68.3	69.2	59.3	23.9
1956	59.4	51.3	60.1	64.1	64.0	68.9	70.1	60.6	24.2
1957	59.1	50.3	59.8	63.7	64.1	68.8	70.5	59.9	22.8
1958	58.9	47.9	59.8	64.1	64.2	68.8	71.0	60.3	21.7
1959	58.7	47.4	59.7	63.7	64.3	68.7	71.5	60.7	21.0
1960	58.8	47.9	59.8	64.8	64.7	68.6	71.7	60.6	20.8
1961	58.8	47.4	59.9	65.5	64.8	68.8	71.7	61.3	20.0
1962	58.3	46.6	59.4	65.0	64.4	69.0	71.8	61.3	19.0
1963	58.2	45.7	59.4	64.9	64.8	69.4	72.3	61.8	17.9
1964	58.2	45.1	59.6	65.8	64.9	69.5	72.5	61.8	17.8
1965	58.4	46.5	59.7	65.7	65.6	70.1	72.2	61.7	17.7
1966	58.7	49.1	59.8	66.0	66.3	70.4	72.5	61.9	17.1
1967	59.2	49.2	60.3	66.8	67.4	71.2	72.5	62.3	17.0
1968	59.3	49.3	60.4	66.6	67.9	71.7	72.7	62.2	17.1
1969	59.9	50.6	60.9	67.9	68.4	72.3	73.3	62.1	17.2
1970	60.2	51.4	61.2	69.2	69.1	72.9	73.5	61.8	16.8
1971	60.1	51.6	61.1	69.6	69.3	73.0	73.4	61.3	16.1
1972	60.4	54.1	61.2	71.2	70.4	73.2	72.9	60.3	15.4
1973	60.8	56.0	61.4	73.3	72.0	73.9	72.7	58.6	14.4
1974	61.4	57.3	61.9	74.8	73.4	74.6	73.0	58.0	13.9
1975	61.5	56.7	62.0	75.2	74.4	75.1	73.0	57.4	13.6
1976	61.8	57.5	62.3	76.0	75.6	76.1	73.0	56.9	13.0
1977	62.5	59.3	62.9	77.1	77.0	77.1	73.2	56.6	12.9
1978	63.3	60.8	63.6	78.1	78.3	78.1	73.8	56.4	13.1
1979	63.9	61.1	64.2	78.9	79.4	79.3	74.6	56.5	12.9
1980	64.1	60.0	64.5	78.7	80.2	80.3	75.4	56.0	12.5
1981	64.3	58.9	64.8	79.1	81.0	81.0	76.2	55.2	12.2
1982	64.3	57.5	65.0	78.9	81.6	81.5	76.4	55.3	12.0
1983	64.3	56.9	65.0	79.0	81.8	81.9	76.5	54.7	11.8
1984	64.6	57.2	65.3	79.4	82.5	82.6	77.0	54.5	11.1
1985	65.0	57.5	65.7	79.9	83.1	83.4	77.8	54.4	10.7
1986	65.5	57.8	66.1	80.6	83.6	84.0	78.5	54.3	11.0
1987	65.8	57.7	66.5	80.7	84.0	84.7	79.1	54.6	11.1
1988	66.2	58.6	66.8	80.6	84.1	85.0	80.3	55.1	11.4
1989	66.7	59.1	67.3	80.2	84.5	85.5	81.2	56.2	11.8
1990	66.9	57.5	67.6	79.8	84.6	85.9	81.3	56.5	11.9
1991	66.6	55.8	67.4	78.9	84.3	85.9	81.8	56.0	11.6
1992	66.8	54.7	67.7	79.4	84.6	85.8	82.2	56.8	11.6
1993	66.8	55.1	67.6	79.5	84.5	85.7	82.5	57.1	11.4
1994	67.1	56.4	67.9	79.5	84.4	85.7	82.7	57.6	12.5
1995	67.1	57.1	67.8	78.7	84.9	85.5	82.5	58.0	12.3
1996	67.2	55.9	68.1	79.1	84.9	85.7	83.1	58.7	12.3
1997	67.5	55.2	68.4	79.6	85.3	85.8	83.5	59.9	12.3
1998	67.3	56.0	68.2	79.5	85.4	85.3	83.4	60.1	12.0
1999	67.3	55.5	68.2	79.5	85.1	85.4	83.5	60.2	12.5
2000	67.3	55.5	68.2	79.9	85.1	85.4	83.5	60.0	13.0
2001	67.0	53.1	68.1	79.2	84.5	85.2	83.3	61.2	13.0
2002	66.8	50.5	68.1	78.6	84.5	84.7	83.0	62.8	13.3
2003	66.5	47.7	67.9	77.7	83.6	84.3	83.0	63.3	14.1
2004	66.3	47.1	67.7	77.1	83.5	84.1	82.9	63.2	14.6
2005	66.3	46.9	67.7	76.3	83.5	84.2	82.8	63.7	15.1
2006	66.5	46.7	67.9	76.5	83.8	84.3	83.0	64.7	15.5
2007	66.4	44.4	68.0	76.4	84.1	84.1	83.1	64.9	16.2
2008	66.3	43.1	68.0	76.3	83.9	84.4	82.9	65.7	17.0

Table 1-8. Civilian Labor Force Participation Rates, by Age, Sex, Race, and Hispanic Origin, 1948–2008
—Continued

(Percent.)

Race, Hispanic origin, sex, and year	16 years and over	16 to 19 years	20 years and over						
			Total	20 to 24 years	25 to 34 years	35 to 44 years	45 to 54 years	55 to 64 years	65 years and over
WHITE									
Men									
1954	85.6	57.6	87.8	86.3	97.5	98.2	96.8	89.1	40.4
1955	85.4	58.6	87.5	86.5	97.8	98.2	96.7	88.4	39.6
1956	85.6	60.4	87.6	87.6	97.4	98.1	96.8	88.9	40.0
1957	84.8	59.2	86.9	86.6	97.2	98.0	96.7	88.0	37.7
1958	84.3	56.5	86.6	86.7	97.2	98.0	96.6	88.2	35.7
1959	83.8	55.9	86.3	87.3	97.5	98.0	96.3	87.9	34.3
1960	83.4	55.9	86.0	87.8	97.7	97.9	96.1	87.2	33.3
1961	83.0	54.5	85.7	87.6	97.7	97.9	95.9	87.8	31.9
1962	82.1	53.8	84.9	86.5	97.4	97.9	96.0	86.7	30.6
1963	81.5	53.1	84.4	85.8	97.4	97.8	96.2	86.6	28.4
1964	81.1	52.7	84.2	85.7	97.5	97.6	96.1	86.1	27.9
1965	80.8	54.1	83.9	85.3	97.4	97.7	95.9	85.2	27.9
1966	80.6	55.9	83.6	84.4	97.5	97.6	95.8	84.9	27.2
1967	80.6	56.3	83.5	84.0	97.5	97.7	95.6	84.9	27.1
1968	80.4	55.9	83.2	82.4	97.2	97.6	95.4	84.7	27.4
1969	80.2	56.8	83.0	82.6	97.0	97.4	95.1	83.9	27.3
1970	80.0	57.5	82.8	83.3	96.7	97.3	94.9	83.3	26.7
1971	79.6	57.9	82.3	83.2	96.3	97.0	94.7	82.6	25.6
1972	79.6	60.1	82.0	84.3	96.0	97.0	94.0	81.1	24.4
1973	79.4	62.0	81.6	85.8	96.2	96.8	93.5	78.9	22.7
1974	79.4	62.9	81.4	86.6	96.3	96.7	93.0	78.0	22.4
1975	78.7	61.9	80.7	85.5	95.8	96.4	92.9	76.4	21.7
1976	78.4	62.3	80.3	86.3	95.9	96.0	92.5	75.2	20.2
1977	78.5	64.0	80.2	86.8	96.0	96.2	92.1	74.6	20.0
1978	78.6	65.0	80.1	87.3	95.9	96.3	92.1	73.7	20.3
1979	78.6	64.8	80.1	87.6	96.0	96.4	92.2	73.4	20.0
1980	78.2	63.7	79.8	87.2	95.9	96.2	92.1	73.1	19.1
1981	77.9	62.4	79.5	87.0	95.8	96.1	92.4	71.5	18.5
1982	77.4	60.0	79.2	86.3	95.6	96.0	92.2	71.0	17.9
1983	77.1	59.4	78.9	86.1	95.2	96.0	91.9	70.0	17.7
1984	77.1	59.0	78.7	86.5	95.4	96.1	92.0	69.5	16.4
1985	77.0	59.7	78.5	86.4	95.7	95.7	92.0	68.8	15.9
1986	76.9	59.3	78.5	87.3	95.5	95.4	91.8	68.0	16.3
1987	76.8	59.0	78.4	86.9	95.5	95.4	91.6	68.1	16.5
1988	76.9	60.0	78.3	86.6	95.2	95.4	91.8	67.9	16.7
1989	77.1	61.0	78.5	86.8	95.4	95.3	92.2	68.3	16.8
1990	77.1	59.6	78.5	86.2	95.2	95.3	91.7	68.6	16.6
1991	76.5	57.3	78.0	85.4	94.9	95.0	91.4	67.7	15.9
1992	76.5	56.9	78.0	85.2	94.9	94.7	91.8	67.7	16.2
1993	76.2	56.6	77.7	85.5	94.7	94.5	91.3	67.3	15.9
1994	75.9	57.7	77.3	85.5	93.9	93.9	90.3	66.4	17.2
1995	75.7	58.5	77.1	85.1	94.1	93.4	90.0	67.1	16.9
1996	75.8	57.1	77.3	85.0	94.4	93.6	90.4	68.0	17.2
1997	75.9	56.1	77.5	85.1	94.2	93.7	90.6	68.9	17.4
1998	75.6	56.6	77.2	84.6	94.4	93.7	90.3	69.1	16.6
1999	75.6	56.4	77.2	84.9	94.3	93.8	90.1	69.1	17.2
2000	75.5	56.5	77.1	85.2	94.5	93.8	89.7	68.2	17.9
2001	75.1	53.7	76.9	84.1	93.9	93.6	89.7	69.1	17.8
2002	74.8	50.3	76.7	83.2	93.7	93.2	89.6	70.2	17.8
2003	74.2	47.5	76.3	82.5	93.3	93.1	88.8	69.7	18.6
2004	74.1	47.4	76.2	82.1	93.2	93.0	88.7	69.8	19.1
2005	74.1	46.2	76.2	81.4	93.0	93.0	89.0	70.4	20.0
2006	74.3	46.9	76.4	81.9	92.9	93.1	89.3	71.0	20.6
2007	74.0	44.3	76.3	80.9	93.4	93.1	89.6	71.2	20.8
2008	73.7	43.0	76.1	80.8	92.6	93.0	89.2	71.9	21.8

Table 1-8. Civilian Labor Force Participation Rates, by Age, Sex, Race, and Hispanic Origin, 1948–2008
    —Continued

(Percent.)

Race, Hispanic origin, sex, and year	16 years and over	16 to 19 years	20 years and over						
			Total	20 to 24 years	25 to 34 years	35 to 44 years	45 to 54 years	55 to 64 years	65 years and over
WHITE									
Women									
1954	33.3	40.6	32.7	44.4	32.5	39.3	39.8	29.1	9.1
1955	34.5	40.7	34.0	45.8	32.8	40.0	42.7	31.8	10.5
1956	35.7	43.1	35.1	46.5	33.2	41.5	44.4	34.0	10.6
1957	35.7	42.2	35.2	45.8	33.6	41.5	45.4	33.7	10.2
1958	35.8	40.1	35.5	46.0	33.6	41.4	46.5	34.5	10.1
1959	36.0	39.6	35.6	44.5	33.4	41.4	47.8	35.7	10.0
1960	36.5	40.3	36.2	45.7	34.1	41.5	48.6	36.2	10.6
1961	36.9	40.6	36.6	46.9	34.3	41.8	48.9	37.2	10.5
1962	36.7	39.8	36.5	47.1	34.1	42.2	48.9	38.0	9.8
1963	37.2	38.7	37.0	47.3	34.8	43.1	49.5	38.9	9.4
1964	37.5	37.8	37.5	48.8	35.0	43.3	50.2	39.4	9.9
1965	38.1	39.2	38.0	49.2	36.3	44.4	49.9	40.3	9.7
1966	39.2	42.6	38.8	51.0	37.7	45.0	50.6	41.1	9.4
1967	40.1	42.5	39.8	53.1	39.7	46.4	50.9	41.9	9.3
1968	40.7	43.0	40.4	54.0	40.6	47.5	51.5	42.0	9.4
1969	41.8	44.6	41.5	56.4	41.7	48.6	53.0	42.6	9.7
1970	42.6	45.6	42.2	57.7	43.2	49.9	53.7	42.6	9.5
1971	42.6	45.4	42.3	58.0	43.7	50.2	53.6	42.5	9.3
1972	43.2	48.1	42.7	59.4	46.0	50.7	53.4	41.9	9.0
1973	44.1	50.1	43.5	61.7	48.7	52.2	53.4	40.7	8.7
1974	45.2	51.7	44.4	63.9	51.3	53.6	54.3	40.4	8.0
1975	45.9	51.5	45.3	65.5	53.8	54.9	54.3	40.6	8.0
1976	46.9	52.8	46.2	66.3	56.0	57.1	54.7	40.7	7.9
1977	48.0	54.5	47.3	67.8	58.5	58.9	55.3	40.7	7.9
1978	49.4	56.7	48.7	69.3	61.2	60.7	56.7	41.1	8.1
1979	50.5	57.4	49.8	70.5	63.1	63.0	58.1	41.5	8.1
1980	51.2	56.2	50.6	70.6	64.8	65.0	59.6	40.9	7.9
1981	51.9	55.4	51.5	71.5	66.4	66.4	60.9	40.9	7.9
1982	52.4	55.0	52.2	71.8	67.8	67.5	61.4	41.5	7.8
1983	52.7	54.5	52.5	72.1	68.7	68.2	61.9	41.1	7.8
1984	53.3	55.4	53.1	72.5	69.8	69.6	62.7	41.2	7.5
1985	54.1	55.2	54.0	73.8	70.9	71.4	64.2	41.5	7.0
1986	55.0	56.3	54.9	74.1	71.8	72.9	65.8	42.1	7.3
1987	55.7	56.5	55.6	74.8	72.5	74.2	67.2	42.4	7.2
1988	56.4	57.2	56.3	74.9	73.0	74.9	69.2	43.6	7.7
1989	57.2	57.1	57.2	74.0	73.8	75.9	70.6	45.2	8.2
1990	57.4	55.3	57.6	73.4	74.1	76.6	71.3	45.5	8.5
1991	57.4	54.1	57.6	72.5	73.8	76.8	72.4	45.4	8.5
1992	57.7	52.5	58.1	73.5	74.4	77.0	72.8	46.8	8.2
1993	58.0	53.5	58.3	73.4	74.3	76.9	74.0	47.6	8.1
1994	58.9	55.1	59.2	73.4	74.9	77.5	75.2	49.4	9.2
1995	59.0	55.5	59.2	72.3	75.8	77.6	75.2	49.5	9.0
1996	59.1	54.7	59.4	73.3	75.5	77.8	76.1	50.1	8.7
1997	59.5	54.1	59.9	73.9	76.3	77.9	76.6	51.5	8.6
1998	59.4	55.4	59.7	74.3	76.3	76.9	76.6	51.6	8.7
1999	59.6	54.5	59.9	73.9	76.0	77.1	77.1	52.0	8.9
2000	59.5	54.5	59.9	74.5	75.7	77.2	77.5	52.4	9.4
2001	59.4	52.4	59.9	74.2	75.1	77.0	77.1	53.8	9.6
2002	59.3	50.8	60.0	74.0	75.0	76.3	76.6	55.8	9.9
2003	59.2	47.9	59.9	72.7	73.7	75.5	77.3	57.4	10.8
2004	58.9	46.7	59.7	71.9	73.6	75.2	77.1	57.0	11.2
2005	58.9	47.6	59.7	71.0	73.7	75.4	76.7	57.5	11.4
2006	59.0	46.6	59.9	70.9	74.3	75.5	76.7	58.7	11.6
2007	59.0	44.6	60.1	71.6	74.5	75.0	76.6	58.9	12.7
2008	59.2	43.3	60.3	71.6	74.9	75.8	76.6	59.7	13.3

Table 1-8. Civilian Labor Force Participation Rates, by Age, Sex, Race, and Hispanic Origin, 1948–2008
—Continued

(Percent.)

Race, Hispanic origin, sex, and year	16 years and over	16 to 19 years	20 years and over						
			Total	20 to 24 years	25 to 34 years	35 to 44 years	45 to 54 years	55 to 64 years	65 years and over
BLACK									
Both Sexes									
1972	59.9	39.1	63.3	68.6	74.9	74.4	70.0	56.9	17.5
1973	60.2	39.8	63.4	69.7	75.7	74.5	70.3	55.9	16.0
1974	59.8	39.8	63.0	69.8	75.8	74.6	69.1	54.7	15.1
1975	58.8	38.2	62.0	66.1	75.6	74.1	69.0	54.3	14.9
1976	59.0	37.0	62.5	66.8	77.4	74.9	68.6	53.4	14.9
1977	59.8	37.9	63.2	68.2	78.3	75.9	69.0	53.7	14.5
1978	61.5	41.0	64.5	69.9	79.6	77.4	70.4	54.8	15.3
1979	61.4	40.1	64.5	70.0	79.2	77.9	71.1	53.5	14.5
1980	61.0	38.9	64.1	69.0	79.5	77.4	71.4	52.6	13.0
1981	60.8	37.7	64.2	69.2	78.5	78.4	71.2	52.8	12.0
1982	61.0	36.6	64.3	68.6	78.7	79.8	71.1	52.3	11.5
1983	61.5	36.4	64.9	68.4	79.8	80.2	72.1	52.5	10.5
1984	62.2	38.3	65.2	69.2	79.3	81.0	73.0	51.6	10.3
1985	62.9	41.2	65.6	70.0	79.8	81.5	73.4	51.4	11.2
1986	63.3	41.3	65.9	71.7	80.1	81.9	74.3	50.6	9.7
1987	63.8	41.6	66.5	70.5	80.7	82.6	74.7	52.4	10.7
1988	63.8	40.8	66.5	70.5	80.8	82.6	75.0	50.6	11.5
1989	64.2	42.5	66.7	72.2	80.9	82.7	75.5	48.3	11.6
1990	64.0	38.7	66.9	68.8	79.7	82.4	76.5	49.6	11.1
1991	63.3	35.4	66.4	67.7	78.5	82.0	76.2	50.4	10.7
1992	63.9	37.9	66.8	67.4	79.7	81.4	76.2	51.6	10.6
1993	63.2	37.0	66.0	67.8	78.3	81.0	75.2	50.2	9.5
1994	63.4	38.5	66.0	68.8	78.3	80.8	74.8	49.3	10.6
1995	63.7	39.9	66.3	68.7	80.0	80.4	74.1	50.3	10.5
1996	64.1	39.2	66.9	69.0	81.1	81.0	74.9	50.9	9.8
1997	64.7	38.7	67.6	70.9	82.0	81.4	76.3	50.5	10.0
1998	65.6	41.6	68.2	70.6	83.0	82.2	76.7	52.3	10.3
1999	65.8	38.7	68.9	71.4	85.2	83.0	76.4	51.4	10.4
2000	65.8	39.4	68.7	71.8	84.1	82.3	76.9	52.5	11.6
2001	65.3	37.6	68.2	69.9	83.6	82.0	75.9	53.9	12.6
2002	64.8	36.0	67.8	68.6	82.4	81.6	76.1	54.7	12.5
2003	64.3	32.4	67.6	68.2	81.6	82.9	75.8	54.4	12.9
2004	63.8	31.4	67.2	68.3	81.2	82.1	75.5	54.4	13.1
2005	64.2	32.4	67.4	69.0	81.7	82.3	75.7	55.3	13.6
2006	64.1	34.0	67.3	68.8	81.8	82.0	75.8	55.4	13.7
2007	63.7	30.3	67.2	68.3	81.7	82.7	75.7	55.1	14.0
2008	63.7	29.4	67.4	68.0	82.2	83.0	76.1	55.6	15.0
BLACK									
Men									
1972	73.6	46.3	78.5	82.7	92.7	91.1	85.4	72.5	24.2
1973	73.4	45.7	78.4	83.7	91.8	91.0	87.4	69.5	22.3
1974	72.9	46.7	77.6	83.6	92.8	90.4	84.0	68.9	21.6
1975	70.9	42.6	76.0	78.7	91.6	89.4	83.5	67.7	20.7
1976	70.0	41.3	75.4	79.0	90.9	89.9	82.4	65.1	19.8
1977	70.6	43.2	75.6	79.2	90.7	91.0	82.0	65.5	20.0
1978	71.5	44.9	76.2	78.8	90.9	90.5	83.2	67.9	21.1
1979	71.3	43.6	76.3	80.7	90.8	90.4	84.5	64.8	19.5
1980	70.3	43.2	75.1	79.9	90.9	89.1	83.0	61.9	16.9
1981	70.0	41.6	74.5	79.2	88.9	89.3	82.7	62.1	16.0
1982	70.1	39.8	74.7	78.7	89.2	89.8	82.2	61.9	15.9
1983	70.6	39.9	75.2	79.4	89.0	89.7	84.5	62.6	14.0
1984	70.8	41.7	74.8	79.1	88.9	90.0	83.7	58.9	13.7
1985	70.8	44.6	74.4	79.0	88.8	89.8	83.0	58.9	13.9
1986	71.2	43.7	74.8	80.1	89.6	89.6	84.1	59.1	12.6
1987	71.1	43.6	74.7	77.8	89.4	88.6	83.7	62.1	13.7
1988	71.0	43.8	74.6	79.3	89.3	88.2	83.5	59.4	14.3
1989	71.0	44.6	74.4	80.2	89.7	88.7	82.5	55.5	14.3
1990	71.0	40.7	75.0	76.8	88.8	88.1	83.5	58.0	13.0
1991	70.4	37.3	74.6	76.7	87.3	87.7	83.4	58.7	13.0
1992	70.7	40.6	74.3	75.4	88.0	86.5	81.8	60.0	13.7
1993	69.6	39.5	73.2	74.1	87.3	86.1	80.0	57.9	11.6
1994	69.1	40.8	72.5	73.9	86.2	85.9	79.1	54.5	12.7
1995	69.0	40.1	72.5	74.6	87.5	84.1	78.5	54.4	14.9
1996	68.7	39.5	72.3	73.4	87.5	84.4	78.5	55.6	12.9
1997	68.3	37.4	72.2	72.1	86.8	84.8	80.1	54.3	12.9
1998	69.0	40.7	72.5	71.8	87.1	85.0	79.9	57.3	14.0
1999	68.7	38.6	72.4	69.8	89.2	86.0	78.5	55.5	12.7
2000	69.2	39.2	72.8	73.3	87.8	85.2	79.2	57.4	14.4
2001	68.4	37.9	72.1	69.7	86.6	84.9	78.4	58.9	16.7
2002	68.4	37.3	72.1	70.7	85.9	84.7	79.5	58.4	16.9
2003	67.3	31.1	71.5	71.1	84.7	85.7	77.7	57.6	17.0
2004	66.7	30.0	70.9	69.9	86.1	84.0	76.9	57.1	17.0
2005	67.3	32.6	71.3	70.1	85.5	85.5	78.6	57.3	17.1
2006	67.0	32.3	71.1	71.6	85.7	84.4	79.2	55.9	16.7
2007	66.8	29.4	71.2	71.1	86.1	86.3	78.6	54.4	17.3
2008	66.7	29.1	71.1	71.1	85.3	86.8	79.1	56.1	18.1

Table 1-8. Civilian Labor Force Participation Rates, by Age, Sex, Race, and Hispanic Origin, 1948–2008
—*Continued*

(Percent.)

Race, Hispanic origin, sex, and year	16 years and over	16 to 19 years	20 years and over						
			Total	20 to 24 years	25 to 34 years	35 to 44 years	45 to 54 years	55 to 64 years	65 years and over
BLACK									
Women									
1972	48.7	32.2	51.2	57.0	60.8	61.4	57.2	44.0	12.6
1973	49.3	34.2	51.6	58.0	62.7	61.7	56.1	44.7	11.4
1974	49.0	33.4	51.4	58.8	62.4	62.2	56.4	42.8	10.4
1975	48.8	34.2	51.1	55.9	62.8	62.0	56.6	43.1	10.7
1976	49.8	32.9	52.5	56.9	66.7	63.0	56.8	43.7	11.3
1977	50.8	32.9	53.6	59.3	68.5	64.1	57.9	43.7	10.5
1978	53.1	37.3	55.5	62.7	70.6	67.2	59.4	43.8	11.1
1979	53.1	36.8	55.4	61.5	70.1	68.0	59.6	44.0	10.9
1980	53.1	34.9	55.6	60.2	70.5	68.1	61.4	44.8	10.2
1981	53.5	34.0	56.0	61.1	70.0	69.8	62.0	45.4	9.3
1982	53.7	33.5	56.2	60.1	70.2	71.7	62.4	44.8	8.5
1983	54.2	33.0	56.8	59.1	72.3	72.6	62.3	44.8	8.2
1984	55.2	35.0	57.6	60.7	71.5	73.7	64.5	46.1	8.0
1985	56.5	37.9	58.6	62.5	72.4	74.8	65.7	45.3	9.4
1986	56.9	39.1	58.9	64.6	72.4	75.8	66.5	43.6	7.8
1987	58.0	39.6	60.0	64.4	73.5	77.8	67.5	44.4	8.6
1988	58.0	37.9	60.1	63.2	73.7	78.1	68.3	43.4	9.6
1989	58.7	40.4	60.6	65.5	73.6	78.0	70.0	42.4	9.8
1990	58.3	36.8	60.6	62.4	72.3	77.7	70.7	43.2	9.9
1991	57.5	33.5	60.0	60.3	71.4	77.2	70.2	44.1	9.2
1992	58.5	35.2	60.8	60.8	73.1	77.1	71.7	45.1	8.6
1993	57.9	34.6	60.2	62.6	70.9	76.8	71.2	44.4	8.3
1994	58.7	36.3	60.9	64.5	71.9	76.4	71.3	45.3	9.2
1995	59.5	39.8	61.4	63.7	73.9	77.3	70.5	47.2	7.7
1996	60.4	38.9	62.6	65.2	75.9	78.2	72.0	47.2	7.7
1997	61.7	39.9	64.0	69.9	78.1	78.4	73.2	47.6	8.2
1998	62.8	42.5	64.8	69.6	79.6	79.9	74.0	48.5	7.9
1999	63.5	38.8	66.1	72.7	82.1	80.4	74.6	48.4	8.9
2000	63.1	39.6	65.4	70.5	81.1	79.9	74.9	48.6	9.9
2001	62.8	37.3	65.2	70.1	81.2	79.6	73.9	49.9	10.1
2002	61.8	34.7	64.4	66.9	79.7	79.2	73.3	51.8	9.8
2003	61.9	33.7	64.6	65.7	79.1	80.6	74.2	51.9	10.3
2004	61.5	32.8	64.2	66.8	77.2	80.6	74.3	52.3	10.7
2005	61.6	32.2	64.4	68.1	78.5	79.7	73.3	53.7	11.4
2006	61.7	35.6	64.2	66.2	78.6	80.1	73.0	55.1	11.8
2007	61.1	31.2	64.0	65.7	78.0	79.8	73.2	55.7	12.0
2008	61.3	29.7	64.3	65.2	79.6	80.0	73.7	55.3	13.0
HISPANIC[1]									
Both Sexes									
1973	60.2	46.9	. . .	. . .	. . .	. . .	. . .	. . .	. . .
1974	61.1	47.7	. . .	. . .	. . .	. . .	. . .	. . .	. . .
1975	60.8	46.2	. . .	. . .	. . .	. . .	. . .	. . .	. . .
1976	60.8	46.9	62.9	. . .	. . .	. . .	. . .	. . .	. . .
1977	61.6	48.2	63.7	. . .	. . .	. . .	. . .	. . .	. . .
1978	62.9	49.6	65.0	. . .	. . .	. . .	. . .	. . .	. . .
1979	63.6	50.3	65.6	. . .	. . .	. . .	. . .	. . .	. . .
1980	64.0	50.3	66.2	. . .	. . .	. . .	. . .	. . .	. . .
1981	64.1	46.4	66.8	. . .	. . .	. . .	. . .	. . .	. . .
1982	63.6	44.8	66.3	. . .	. . .	. . .	. . .	. . .	. . .
1983	63.8	45.3	66.2	. . .	. . .	. . .	. . .	. . .	. . .
1984	64.9	47.5	67.1	. . .	. . .	. . .	. . .	. . .	. . .
1985	64.6	44.6	67.1	. . .	. . .	. . .	. . .	. . .	. . .
1986	65.4	43.9	68.0	. . .	. . .	. . .	. . .	. . .	. . .
1987	66.4	45.8	68.8	. . .	. . .	. . .	. . .	. . .	. . .
1988	67.4	49.6	69.4	. . .	. . .	. . .	. . .	. . .	. . .
1989	67.6	48.6	69.7	. . .	. . .	. . .	. . .	. . .	. . .
1990	67.4	47.8	69.8	. . .	. . .	. . .	. . .	. . .	. . .
1991	66.5	45.1	69.0	. . .	. . .	. . .	. . .	. . .	. . .
1992	66.8	45.8	69.2	. . .	. . .	. . .	. . .	. . .	. . .
1993	66.2	43.9	68.7	. . .	. . .	. . .	. . .	. . .	. . .
1994	66.1	44.4	68.5	74.0	77.3	78.9	73.1	49.8	10.7
1995	65.8	45.4	68.1	71.9	78.1	78.5	72.8	48.6	10.5
1996	66.5	43.4	69.1	73.1	78.2	79.5	74.6	52.2	11.0
1997	67.9	43.0	70.8	76.4	79.5	80.9	75.4	53.8	11.9
1998	67.9	45.7	70.6	76.1	80.3	80.0	75.3	55.4	10.1
1999	67.7	45.5	70.4	76.0	78.6	81.3	75.9	54.1	11.6
2000	69.7	46.3	72.5	78.2	80.4	81.7	78.0	54.2	12.3
2001	69.5	46.9	72.0	76.6	80.0	81.9	77.4	55.1	10.9
2002	69.1	44.0	71.8	76.3	80.5	81.1	76.1	55.8	11.9
2003	68.3	37.7	71.4	75.6	79.4	81.1	75.3	57.4	12.8
2004	68.6	38.2	71.7	74.5	79.4	81.4	77.6	58.1	14.5
2005	68.0	38.6	71.0	72.7	79.1	81.2	77.2	58.4	13.9
2006	68.7	38.3	71.9	74.4	80.1	81.9	77.3	59.2	15.7
2007	68.8	37.1	72.1	74.8	80.7	81.8	78.6	58.5	16.0
2008	68.5	36.9	71.8	73.7	80.5	82.0	78.2	59.9	16.0

[1]May be of any race.
. . . = Not available.

Table 1-8. Civilian Labor Force Participation Rates, by Age, Sex, Race, and Hispanic Origin, 1948–2008
—Continued

(Percent.)

Race, Hispanic origin, sex, and year	16 years and over	16 to 19 years	20 years and over						
			Total	20 to 24 years	25 to 34 years	35 to 44 years	45 to 54 years	55 to 64 years	65 years and over
HISPANIC[1]									
Men									
1973	81.5	. . .	85.9	. . .	. . .	. . .	. . .	. . .	. . .
1974	81.7	. . .	86.0	. . .	. . .	. . .	. . .	. . .	. . .
1975	80.7	. . .	85.5	. . .	. . .	. . .	. . .	. . .	. . .
1976	79.6	. . .	84.2	. . .	. . .	. . .	. . .	. . .	. . .
1977	80.9	. . .	84.8	. . .	. . .	. . .	. . .	. . .	. . .
1978	81.1	. . .	84.9	. . .	. . .	. . .	. . .	. . .	. . .
1979	81.3	. . .	85.3	. . .	. . .	. . .	. . .	. . .	. . .
1980	81.4	. . .	84.9	. . .	. . .	. . .	. . .	. . .	. . .
1981	80.6	. . .	84.7	. . .	. . .	. . .	. . .	. . .	. . .
1982	79.7	. . .	84.0	. . .	. . .	. . .	. . .	. . .	. . .
1983	80.3	. . .	84.1	. . .	. . .	. . .	. . .	. . .	. . .
1984	80.6	. . .	84.3	. . .	. . .	. . .	. . .	. . .	. . .
1985	80.3	. . .	84.0	. . .	. . .	. . .	. . .	. . .	. . .
1986	81.0	. . .	84.6	. . .	. . .	. . .	. . .	. . .	. . .
1987	81.0	. . .	84.5	. . .	. . .	. . .	. . .	. . .	. . .
1988	81.9	. . .	85.0	. . .	. . .	. . .	. . .	. . .	. . .
1989	82.0	. . .	85.0	. . .	. . .	. . .	. . .	. . .	. . .
1990	81.4	. . .	84.7	. . .	. . .	. . .	. . .	. . .	. . .
1991	80.3	. . .	83.8	. . .	. . .	. . .	. . .	. . .	. . .
1992	80.7	. . .	84.0	. . .	. . .	. . .	. . .	. . .	. . .
1993	80.2	. . .	83.5	. . .	. . .	. . .	. . .	. . .	. . .
1994	79.2	50.0	82.5	88.0	92.5	91.5	85.7	63.6	14.4
1995	79.1	50.2	82.4	86.2	92.9	91.3	85.6	62.4	15.8
1996	79.6	50.0	83.0	85.7	93.2	91.7	87.0	65.9	16.7
1997	80.1	47.4	84.1	88.1	93.5	91.9	87.8	68.4	17.3
1998	79.8	48.7	83.6	88.1	94.0	91.4	86.7	70.2	14.9
1999	79.8	50.1	83.5	88.1	93.9	92.2	86.2	68.6	18.2
2000	81.5	50.7	85.3	89.1	94.1	93.3	87.6	69.4	18.5
2001	81.0	52.2	84.3	86.8	93.4	92.7	86.7	68.6	16.8
2002	80.2	48.8	83.6	86.1	93.5	92.1	86.1	67.3	16.3
2003	80.1	40.9	84.1	86.2	93.6	92.9	85.4	68.8	17.4
2004	80.4	42.4	84.2	84.4	93.6	93.2	87.2	69.6	20.8
2005	80.1	41.9	84.0	84.1	93.3	93.1	87.7	69.3	20.1
2006	80.7	42.0	84.6	85.9	94.1	93.8	87.1	69.6	22.9
2007	80.5	40.0	84.7	85.3	94.1	93.9	88.3	70.3	22.0
2008	80.2	40.3	84.4	84.3	94.0	93.7	88.6	71.7	21.7
HISPANIC[1]									
Women									
1973	41.0	. . .	41.3	. . .	. . .	. . .	. . .	. . .	. . .
1974	42.4	. . .	42.7	. . .	. . .	. . .	. . .	. . .	. . .
1975	43.2	. . .	43.8	. . .	. . .	. . .	. . .	. . .	. . .
1976	44.3	. . .	44.6	. . .	. . .	. . .	. . .	. . .	. . .
1977	44.3	. . .	45.1	. . .	. . .	. . .	. . .	. . .	. . .
1978	46.6	. . .	47.2	. . .	. . .	. . .	. . .	. . .	. . .
1979	47.4	. . .	48.0	. . .	. . .	. . .	. . .	. . .	. . .
1980	47.4	. . .	48.5	. . .	. . .	. . .	. . .	. . .	. . .
1981	48.3	. . .	49.7	. . .	. . .	. . .	. . .	. . .	. . .
1982	48.1	. . .	49.3	. . .	. . .	. . .	. . .	. . .	. . .
1983	47.7	. . .	49.0	. . .	. . .	. . .	. . .	. . .	. . .
1984	49.6	. . .	50.5	. . .	. . .	. . .	. . .	. . .	. . .
1985	49.3	. . .	50.6	. . .	. . .	. . .	. . .	. . .	. . .
1986	50.1	. . .	51.7	. . .	. . .	. . .	. . .	. . .	. . .
1987	52.0	. . .	53.3	. . .	. . .	. . .	. . .	. . .	. . .
1988	53.2	. . .	54.2	. . .	. . .	. . .	. . .	. . .	. . .
1989	53.5	. . .	54.9	. . .	. . .	. . .	. . .	. . .	. . .
1990	53.1	. . .	54.8	. . .	. . .	. . .	. . .	. . .	. . .
1991	52.4	. . .	54.0	. . .	. . .	. . .	. . .	. . .	. . .
1992	52.8	. . .	54.3	. . .	. . .	. . .	. . .	. . .	. . .
1993	52.1	. . .	53.8	. . .	. . .	. . .	. . .	. . .	. . .
1994	52.9	38.7	54.4	57.9	60.5	66.4	61.4	38.1	7.9
1995	52.6	40.4	53.9	55.9	61.6	65.9	60.5	37.2	6.6
1996	53.4	36.5	55.2	59.2	62.0	67.0	62.7	40.5	6.9
1997	55.1	38.0	57.0	62.3	63.7	69.3	63.3	40.6	8.1
1998	55.6	42.4	57.1	62.2	64.5	67.9	64.7	41.9	6.6
1999	55.9	40.6	57.7	63.0	62.7	70.5	66.2	42.4	6.5
2000	57.5	41.4	59.3	65.0	65.3	69.9	68.5	41.2	7.7
2001	57.6	41.1	59.3	64.6	65.2	70.3	68.3	43.2	6.7
2002	57.6	38.8	59.5	65.0	65.8	69.5	66.3	46.1	8.5
2003	55.9	34.5	58.1	63.3	62.9	68.5	65.3	47.1	9.4
2004	56.1	33.7	58.4	62.9	62.9	68.7	67.9	47.8	9.8
2005	55.3	35.2	57.4	59.4	62.4	68.2	66.6	48.4	9.3
2006	56.1	34.4	58.3	61.3	63.5	68.7	67.4	49.7	10.4
2007	56.5	34.0	58.8	62.9	64.6	68.4	68.7	47.6	11.4
2008	56.2	33.3	58.6	62.1	64.3	69.1	67.6	48.9	11.7

[1]May be of any race.
. . . = Not available.

Table 1-9. Employed and Unemployed Full- and Part-Time Workers, by Age, Sex, and Race, 1998–2008

(Thousands of people.)

Race, sex, age, and year	Employed[1]								Unemployed	
	Full-time workers				Part-time workers				Looking for full-time work	Looking for part-time work
	Total	At work		Not at work	Total	At work[2]		Not at work		
		35 hours or more	1 to 34 hours for economic or noneconomic reasons			For economic reasons	For noneconomic reasons			
ALL RACES										
Both Sexes, 16 Years and Over										
1998	108 202	91 880	12 260	4 062	23 261	2 497	19 239	1 524	4 916	1 293
1999	110 302	96 276	10 079	3 947	23 186	2 216	19 509	1 461	4 669	1 211
2000	113 846	100 533	9 125	4 188	23 044	2 003	19 548	1 493	4 538	1 154
2001	113 573	99 047	10 464	4 061	23 361	2 297	19 494	1 570	5 546	1 254
2002	112 700	99 042	9 746	3 912	23 785	2 755	19 549	1 481	7 063	1 314
2003	113 324	99 539	9 841	3 944	24 412	3 184	19 702	1 525	7 361	1 413
2004	114 518	100 496	10 053	3 969	24 734	3 113	20 109	1 513	6 762	1 388
2005	117 016	103 044	9 983	3 990	24 714	2 963	20 229	1 522	6 175	1 415
2006	119 688	105 328	10 223	4 137	24 739	2 774	20 356	1 609	5 675	1 326
2007	121 091	106 990	9 976	4 125	24 956	2 851	20 511	1 594	5 789	1 289
2008	120 030	105 575	10 426	4 030	25 332	3 814	20 009	1 509	7 446	1 478
Both Sexes, 20 Years and Over										
1998	105 882	89 966	11 915	4 001	18 530	2 197	15 007	1 326	4 332	672
1999	107 917	94 270	9 754	3 893	18 399	1 939	15 187	1 273	4 094	624
2000	111 353	98 439	8 787	4 127	18 348	1 747	15 297	1 304	3 978	632
2001	111 323	97 161	10 156	4 006	18 870	2 013	15 486	1 371	4 956	682
2002	110 679	97 342	9 474	3 862	19 475	2 448	15 704	1 322	6 395	730
2003	111 578	98 087	9 587	3 904	20 239	2 875	16 001	1 363	6 705	818
2004	112 747	99 034	9 789	3 924	20 598	2 817	16 436	1 345	6 178	764
2005	115 206	101 534	9 729	3 942	20 546	2 698	16 489	1 359	5 619	786
2006	117 844	103 779	9 974	4 090	20 421	2 510	16 478	1 433	5 117	765
2007	119 317	105 499	9 738	4 080	20 819	2 587	16 819	1 413	5 234	742
2008	118 404	104 212	10 204	3 989	21 385	3 492	16 543	1 350	6 790	849
Men, 16 Years and Over										
1998	63 189	55 080	6 136	1 973	7 504	1 063	6 026	416	2 707	559
1999	63 930	57 034	4 971	1 924	7 516	946	6 178	392	2 548	518
2000	65 930	59 345	4 555	2 030	7 375	856	6 105	414	2 486	488
2001	65 623	58 386	5 241	1 996	7 573	1 021	6 129	424	3 144	546
2002	65 205	58 318	4 971	1 916	7 697	1 246	6 050	401	4 029	568
2003	65 379	58 428	5 023	1 927	7 953	1 473	6 056	423	4 291	615
2004	66 444	59 363	5 148	1 933	8 080	1 405	6 258	417	3 843	613
2005	67 858	60 825	5 096	1 937	8 115	1 316	6 370	429	3 444	616
2006	69 307	62 087	5 237	1 984	8 194	1 232	6 510	452	3 192	561
2007	70 035	62 965	5 095	1 975	8 220	1 319	6 424	477	3 326	556
2008	68 853	61 436	5 443	1 974	8 634	1 842	6 349	442	4 396	637
Men, 20 Years and Over										
1998	61 837	53 947	5 950	1 940	5 297	925	4 050	322	2 366	214
1999	62 514	55 827	4 790	1 897	5 247	809	4 127	311	2 222	211
2000	64 464	58 095	4 370	2 000	5 170	733	4 109	328	2 162	214
2001	64 311	57 273	5 072	1 966	5 465	881	4 253	331	2 801	239
2002	64 006	57 302	4 815	1 889	5 728	1 093	4 299	336	3 642	254
2003	64 364	57 580	4 879	1 905	6 051	1 314	4 388	348	3 906	302
2004	65 377	58 471	5 000	1 906	6 196	1 251	4 600	345	3 511	281
2005	66 803	59 934	4 955	1 914	6 247	1 182	4 705	360	3 118	274
2006	68 193	61 140	5 095	1 958	6 238	1 100	4 762	376	2 861	270
2007	68 968	62 057	4 959	1 952	6 369	1 190	4 782	397	2 990	268
2008	67 895	60 625	5 315	1 955	6 855	1 675	4 802	378	3 994	303
Women, 16 Years and Over										
1998	45 014	36 800	6 124	2 090	15 757	1 435	13 214	1 108	2 210	734
1999	46 372	39 242	5 108	2 022	15 670	1 270	13 330	1 069	2 121	693
2000	47 916	41 188	4 570	2 158	15 670	1 147	13 443	1 080	2 052	666
2001	47 950	40 661	5 223	2 065	15 788	1 276	13 365	1 146	2 402	709
2002	47 494	40 723	4 775	1 996	16 088	1 509	13 498	1 080	3 034	747
2003	47 946	41 111	4 818	2 017	16 459	1 711	13 646	1 102	3 070	798
2004	48 073	41 133	4 905	2 036	16 654	1 708	13 851	1 096	2 919	775
2005	49 158	42 219	4 887	2 052	16 598	1 647	13 859	1 092	2 732	799
2006	50 380	43 241	4 986	2 153	16 545	1 542	13 846	1 157	2 483	764
2007	51 056	44 025	4 881	2 150	16 736	1 532	14 087	1 117	2 463	732
2008	51 178	44 139	4 983	2 056	16 698	1 972	13 660	1 067	3 050	841

Note: Beginning in January 2004, data reflect revised population controls used in the household survey. See notes and definitions for information on historical comparability.

[1] Employed persons are classified as full- or part-time workers based on their usual weekly hours at all jobs, regardless of the number of hours they were at work during the reference week. Persons absent from work are also classified according to their usual status.
[2] Includes some persons at work 35 hours or more classified by their reason for working part time.

Table 1-9. Employed and Unemployed Full- and Part-Time Workers, by Age, Sex, and Race, 1998–2008
—Continued

(Thousands of people.)

Race, sex, age, and year	Employed[1]								Unemployed	
	Full-time workers				Part-time workers					
		At work				At work[2]				
	Total	35 hours or more	1 to 34 hours for economic or noneconomic reasons	Not at work	Total	For economic reasons	For noneconomic reasons	Not at work	Looking for full-time work	Looking for part-time work
ALL RACES										
Women, 20 Years and Over										
1998	44 045	36 019	5 965	2 061	13 233	1 272	10 957	1 004	1 966	458
1999	45 403	38 443	4 964	1 996	13 152	1 131	11 059	962	1 872	413
2000	46 889	40 344	4 417	2 128	13 178	1 013	11 188	976	1 816	419
2001	47 012	39 889	5 083	2 040	13 405	1 132	11 233	1 040	2 155	444
2002	46 673	40 040	4 660	1 973	13 747	1 355	11 406	986	2 752	476
2003	47 215	40 507	4 708	2 000	14 188	1 560	11 613	1 015	2 799	515
2004	47 371	40 563	4 790	2 017	14 402	1 567	11 836	1 000	2 667	483
2005	48 403	41 600	4 774	2 028	14 299	1 516	11 784	999	2 501	512
2006	49 651	42 639	4 880	2 132	14 183	1 410	11 716	1 057	2 256	495
2007	50 349	43 442	4 779	2 128	14 450	1 397	12 037	1 016	2 244	474
2008	50 509	43 587	4 888	2 034	14 530	1 817	11 740	973	2 796	546
WHITE[3]										
Men, 16 Years and Over										
1998	54 206	47 239	5 257	1 709	6 398	829	5 209	360	1 999	432
1999	54 756	48 834	4 274	1 647	6 383	730	5 314	339	1 883	391
2000	56 068	50 434	3 896	1 738	6 221	656	5 213	351	1 798	379
2001	55 830	49 625	4 504	1 701	6 381	793	5 225	364	2 323	431
2002	55 369	49 459	4 267	1 644	6 480	980	5 150	350	3 017	443
2003	55 216	49 323	4 266	1 628	6 650	1 146	5 148	357	3 164	479
2004	55 926	49 891	4 396	1 638	6 786	1 092	5 331	363	2 805	477
2005	56 955	50 965	4 334	1 656	6 808	1 014	5 424	370	2 459	471
2006	58 063	51 894	4 484	1 685	6 820	947	5 481	393	2 299	432
2007	58 494	52 460	4 359	1 676	6 795	1 022	5 368	406	2 444	425
2008	57 432	51 104	4 653	1 675	7 192	1 433	5 379	379	3 235	492
Men, 20 Years and Over										
1998	53 017	46 240	5 095	1 682	4 483	716	3 487	280	1 756	164
1999	53 513	47 764	4 124	1 626	4 420	618	3 534	268	1 651	162
2000	54 778	49 335	3 733	1 710	4 341	558	3 505	278	1 566	165
2001	54 666	48 636	4 354	1 676	4 579	677	3 616	285	2 080	195
2002	54 333	48 581	4 133	1 619	4 790	857	3 640	293	2 743	200
2003	54 339	48 585	4 145	1 609	5 010	1 016	3 703	291	2 893	231
2004	55 005	49 124	4 267	1 614	5 154	961	3 895	299	2 567	217
2005	56 050	50 203	4 213	1 634	5 205	905	3 990	310	2 242	209
2006	57 108	51 081	4 365	1 662	5 150	840	3 987	324	2 074	208
2007	57 591	51 691	4 243	1 656	5 216	915	3 967	334	2 204	204
2008	56 623	50 421	4 542	1 660	5 681	1 302	4 055	324	2 944	235
Women, 16 Years and Over										
1998	36 553	29 792	5 039	1 722	13 774	1 089	11 695	990	1 481	572
1999	37 417	31 577	4 157	1 684	13 679	947	11 768	964	1 469	530
2000	38 438	32 942	3 729	1 767	13 698	867	11 870	961	1 422	521
2001	38 445	32 491	4 252	1 702	13 773	971	11 787	1 015	1 664	551
2002	38 152	32 623	3 896	1 633	14 011	1 152	11 903	956	2 084	595
2003	38 249	32 659	3 939	1 652	14 120	1 304	11 860	956	2 038	629
2004	38 240	32 555	4 018	1 667	14 287	1 280	12 038	969	1 968	597
2005	38 973	33 325	3 976	1 672	14 213	1 207	12 043	963	1 807	612
2006	39 813	33 980	4 082	1 751	14 137	1 157	11 967	1 013	1 670	601
2007	40 238	34 486	4 014	1 738	14 265	1 143	12 148	973	1 694	579
2008	40 292	34 569	4 076	1 647	14 209	1 518	11 761	931	2 119	664
Women, 20 Years and Over										
1998	35 738	29 130	4 910	1 698	11 604	953	9 749	902	1 318	370
1999	36 602	30 905	4 036	1 662	11 496	839	9 789	867	1 297	319
2000	37 585	32 242	3 600	1 743	11 560	754	9 935	872	1 256	339
2001	37 658	31 839	4 139	1 680	11 711	853	9 933	924	1 492	357
2002	37 467	32 049	3 803	1 615	11 981	1 029	10 079	873	1 888	381
2003	37 640	32 158	3 845	1 637	12 183	1 180	10 124	879	1 866	411
2004	37 663	32 085	3 927	1 652	12 377	1 166	10 326	885	1 795	377
2005	38 354	32 820	3 882	1 652	12 235	1 108	10 248	879	1 653	401
2006	39 232	33 500	3 998	1 733	12 128	1 050	10 151	927	1 524	402
2007	39 670	34 015	3 932	1 722	12 326	1 037	10 402	887	1 547	383
2008	39 765	34 128	4 005	1 632	12 359	1 392	10 116	851	1 949	435

Note: Beginning in January 2004, data reflect revised population controls used in the household survey. See notes and definitions for information on historical comparability.

[1]Employed persons are classified as full- or part-time workers based on their usual weekly hours at all jobs, regardless of the number of hours they were at work during the reference week. Persons absent from work are also classified according to their usual status.
[2]Includes some persons at work 35 hours or more classified by their reason for working part time.
[3]Beginning in 2003, persons who selected this race group only; persons who selected more than one race group are not included. Prior to 2003, persons who reported more than one race group were included in the group they identified as their main race.

Table 1-9. Employed and Unemployed Full- and Part-Time Workers, by Age, Sex, and Race, 1998–2008
—Continued

(Thousands of people.)

Race, sex, age, and year	Employed[1]								Unemployed	
	Full-time workers				Part-time workers					
		At work				At work[2]				
	Total	35 hours or more	1 to 34 hours for economic or noneconomic reasons	Not at work	Total	For economic reasons	For noneconomic reasons	Not at work	Looking for full-time work	Looking for part-time work
BLACK[3]										
Men, 16 Years and Over										
1998	6 148	5 322	637	189	723	168	520	34	572	99
1999	6 263	5 574	494	196	764	163	568	33	528	97
2000	6 350	5 704	445	202	732	144	548	41	542	78
2001	6 178	5 509	468	200	761	165	557	39	626	83
2002	6 194	5 541	480	173	765	188	546	30	749	86
2003	6 055	5 414	453	188	765	221	505	39	804	87
2004	6 177	5 538	460	179	736	205	499	32	763	98
2005	6 381	5 745	463	174	773	207	533	33	742	102
2006	6 529	5 907	446	176	825	201	590	34	681	93
2007	6 673	6 068	429	176	826	195	589	42	660	92
2008	6 548	5 935	440	173	850	276	542	32	849	100
Men, 20 Years and Over										
1998	6 023	5 218	620	185	507	147	334	25	487	37
1999	6 140	5 477	471	192	561	142	392	27	446	35
2000	6 222	5 594	429	199	520	125	363	32	468	31
2001	6 069	5 417	455	197	558	145	382	31	542	31
2002	6 073	5 437	465	171	579	166	387	26	660	35
2003	5 980	5 355	439	185	607	201	372	34	717	43
2004	6 089	5 463	449	177	592	189	376	27	689	44
2005	6 287	5 662	452	174	614	189	397	28	655	44
2006	6 424	5 816	433	175	655	185	441	30	596	44
2007	6 574	5 983	417	174	671	181	452	37	580	43
2008	6 461	5 860	430	171	690	252	409	29	764	46
Women, 16 Years and Over										
1998	6 281	5 166	828	288	1 404	278	1 045	81	624	131
1999	6 641	5 651	734	256	1 388	257	1 059	72	554	130
2000	6 780	5 862	632	287	1 293	211	1 005	77	515	106
2001	6 761	5 777	715	270	1 307	223	998	85	584	122
2002	6 588	5 685	640	263	1 326	259	991	76	744	114
2003	6 552	5 709	595	247	1 367	274	1 017	76	774	121
2004	6 597	5 740	611	246	1 399	306	1 022	71	744	124
2005	6 750	5 871	619	260	1 407	320	1 018	70	723	133
2006	7 001	6 131	605	265	1 410	274	1 054	82	655	120
2007	7 119	6 272	584	263	1 432	273	1 085	75	589	104
2008	7 105	6 238	596	272	1 449	302	1 070	77	717	122
Women, 20 Years and Over										
1998	6 159	5 073	803	283	1 131	256	807	68	555	66
1999	6 519	5 549	717	252	1 145	230	850	65	486	75
2000	6 651	5 753	615	283	1 052	197	788	67	456	56
2001	6 647	5 684	695	268	1 094	203	816	75	521	61
2002	6 492	5 605	626	261	1 117	234	816	68	671	67
2003	6 468	5 639	583	246	1 168	257	842	69	698	75
2004	6 512	5 674	595	243	1 195	287	844	64	679	76
2005	6 653	5 789	606	258	1 222	298	861	63	660	74
2006	6 893	6 042	588	263	1 175	255	848	72	588	67
2007	7 024	6 194	570	260	1 216	254	897	65	527	61
2008	7 006	6 160	580	267	1 254	283	902	68	654	78

Note: Beginning in January 2004, data reflect revised population controls used in the household survey. See notes and definitions for information on historical comparability.

[1]Employed persons are classified as full- or part-time workers based on their usual weekly hours at all jobs, regardless of the number of hours they were at work during the reference week. Persons absent from work are also classified according to their usual status.
[2]Includes some persons at work 35 hours or more classified by their reason for working part time.
[3]Beginning in 2003, persons who selected this race group only; persons who selected more than one race group are not included. Prior to 2003, persons who reported more than one race group were included in the group they identified as their main race.

Table 1-10. Persons Not in the Labor Force, by Age, Sex, and Desire and Availability for Work, 2003–2008

(Thousands of people.)

Category	Total		Age						Sex			
			16 to 24 years		25 to 54 years		55 years and over		Men		Women	
	2003	2004	2003	2004	2003	2004	2003	2004	2003	2004	2003	2004
TOTAL, NOT IN THE LABOR FORCE	74 658	75 956	13 800	14 151	20 980	21 288	39 878	40 517	28 197	28 730	46 461	47 225
Do Not Want a Job Now[1]	69 932	71 103	12 079	12 422	18 857	19 136	38 996	39 545	26 073	26 565	43 859	44 538
Want a Job[1]	4 726	4 852	1 721	1 729	2 124	2 152	882	971	2 124	2 165	2 603	2 687
Did not search for work in the previous year	2 631	2 715	882	886	1 129	1 145	620	684	1 127	1 126	1 503	1 590
Searched for work in the previous year[2]	2 096	2 137	838	843	995	1 006	262	288	996	1 040	1 099	1 097
Not available to work now	564	563	274	279	248	242	43	42	231	230	333	333
Available to work now	1 531	1 574	565	565	747	764	220	245	765	809	766	765
Reason not currently looking:												
Discouragement over job prospects[3]	457	466	134	142	248	240	75	84	266	288	190	178
Reasons other than discouragement	1 075	1 108	431	423	499	524	145	161	499	521	576	587
Family responsibilities	153	157	37	28	94	104	22	24	35	38	118	119
In school or training	239	244	194	199	42	43	3	2	125	131	114	112
Ill health or disability	113	123	15	18	72	71	26	35	51	56	62	67
Other[4]	570	584	184	178	292	306	94	100	288	296	282	2

Category	Total		Age						Sex			
			16 to 24 years		25 to 54 years		55 years and over		Men		Women	
	2005	2006	2005	2006	2005	2006	2005	2006	2005	2006	2005	2006
TOTAL, NOT IN THE LABOR FORCE	76 762	77 387	14 383	14 549	21 403	21 318	40 976	41 520	29 119	30 036	47 643	48 037
Do Not Want a Job Now[1]	71 777	72 602	12 585	12 867	19 238	19 221	39 954	40 514	26 926	27 914	44 851	45 354
Want a Job[1]	4 985	4 786	1 798	1 682	2 165	2 097	1 022	1 006	2 193	2 122	2 792	2 684
Did not search for work in the previous year	2 841	2 758	963	883	1 163	1 155	715	720	1 173	1 173	1 668	1 612
Searched for work in the previous year[2]	2 144	2 028	836	800	1 002	942	307	286	1 020	950	1 124	1 071
Not available to work now	599	580	285	282	260	252	54	46	231	223	368	354
Available to work now	1 545	1 448	551	518	742	690	252	240	789	726	756	717
Reason not currently looking:												
Discouragement over job prospects[3]	436	381	141	118	217	195	78	68	260	226	176	152
Reasons other than discouragement	1 109	1 067	410	399	525	495	175	172	529	500	580	565
Family responsibilities	159	152	32	31	105	97	22	24	36	37	123	117
In school or training	217	207	179	177	35	28	2	2	118	102	99	96
Ill health or disability	119	130	16	18	69	76	34	36	64	57	55	68
Other[4]	614	578	182	174	316	294	116	110	311	305	302	285

Category	Total		Age						Sex			
			16 to 24 years		25 to 54 years		55 years and over		Men		Women	
	2007	2008	2007	2008	2007	2008	2007	2008	2007	2008	2007	2008
TOTAL, NOT IN THE LABOR FORCE	78 743	79 501	15 192	15 452	21 343	21 255	42 207	42 794	30 036	30 593	48 707	48 908
Do Not Want a Job Now[1]	74 040	74 519	13 510	13 719	19 256	19 087	41 275	41 712	27 914	28 365	46 126	46 154
Want a Job[1]	4 703	4 983	1 683	1 733	2 088	2 168	933	1 082	2 122	2 228	2 581	2 755
Did not search for work in the previous year	2 748	2 826	931	913	1 148	1 145	668	768	1 173	1 187	1 575	1 639
Searched for work in the previous year[2]	1 955	2 157	751	819	939	1 023	264	314	950	1 041	1 005	1 115
Not available to work now	560	543	272	252	234	244	53	48	223	214	336	329
Available to work now	1 395	1 614	479	568	705	780	211	266	726	827	669	787
Reason not currently looking:												
Discouragement over job prospects[3]	369	462	110	145	199	226	61	90	226	282	143	180
Reasons other than discouragement	1 026	1 152	370	422	506	554	150	176	500	545	526	607
Family responsibilities	160	171	31	35	109	111	21	25	37	45	123	126
In school or training	180	218	149	173	27	42	3	3	102	108	78	109
Ill health or disability	114	124	11	16	66	68	37	40	57	55	58	69
Other[4]	572	640	178	199	304	332	90	108	305	337	267	303

[1]Includes some persons who were not asked if they wanted a job.
[2]Persons who had a job during the prior 12 months must have searched since the end of that job.
[3]Includes believes no work available, could not find work, lacks necessary schooling or training, employer thinks too young or old, and other types of discrimination.
[4]Includes those who did not actively look for work in the prior four weeks for reasons such as childcare and transportation problems, as well as a small number for whom reason for nonparticipation was not ascertained.

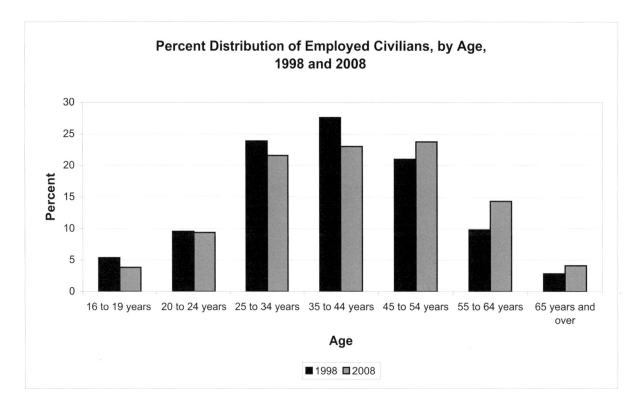

The change in the distribution of employed civilians by age reflects, in part, the aging of the baby-boom population. From 1998 to 2008, the proportion of employed persons age 45 years and over increased significantly, while the proportion of employed persons age 16 to 44 years declined. In 1998, workers 16 to 44 years of age made up 66.4 percent of employed civilians. In 2008, they made up 57.8 percent of employed civilians. (See Table 1-11.)

OTHER HIGHLIGHTS

- In 2008, employment decreased for only the third time since 1988 declining by 0.5 percent. (See Table 1-11.)

- Women made up 46.7 percent of total employed civilians in 2008 but made up the vast majority of those employed in the following occupations: health care support (88.8 percent), personal care and services (78.4 percent), office and administrative support (74.8 percent), and education, training, and library (74.0 percent). (See Table 1-13.)

- The number of employed persons age 25 years and over increased by 12.8 percent from 1998 to 2008. However, during this same period, the number of employed persons with a bachelor's degree or higher increased by 30.3 percent, while the number of employed persons with less than a high school diploma decreased by 5.1 percent. (See Table 1-16.)

- In 1970, only 15.7 percent of multiple jobholders were women. By 2008, the majority were women (51.3 percent). (See Table 1-17.)

Table 1-11. Employed Civilians, by Age, Sex, Race, and Hispanic Origin, 1948–2008

(Thousands of people.)

Race, Hispanic origin, sex, and year	16 years and over	16 to 19 years			20 years and over						
		Total	16 to 17 years	18 to 19 years	Total	20 to 24 years	25 to 34 years	35 to 44 years	45 to 54 years	55 to 64 years	65 years and over
ALL RACES											
Both Sexes											
1948	58 343	4 026	1 600	2 426	54 318	6 937	13 801	13 050	10 624	7 103	2 804
1949	57 651	3 712	1 466	2 246	53 940	6 660	13 639	13 108	10 636	7 042	2 864
1950	58 918	3 703	1 433	2 270	55 218	6 746	13 917	13 424	10 966	7 265	2 899
1951	59 961	3 767	1 575	2 192	56 196	6 321	14 233	13 746	11 421	7 558	2 917
1952	60 250	3 719	1 626	2 092	56 536	5 572	14 515	14 058	11 687	7 785	2 919
1953	61 179	3 720	1 577	2 142	57 460	5 225	14 519	14 774	11 969	7 806	3 166
1954	60 109	3 475	1 422	2 053	56 634	4 971	14 190	14 541	11 976	7 895	3 060
1955	62 170	3 642	1 500	2 143	58 528	5 270	14 481	14 879	12 556	8 158	3 185
1956	63 799	3 818	1 647	2 171	59 983	5 545	14 407	15 218	12 978	8 519	3 314
1957	64 071	3 778	1 613	2 167	60 291	5 641	14 253	15 348	13 320	8 553	3 179
1958	63 036	3 582	1 519	2 063	59 454	5 571	13 675	15 157	13 448	8 559	3 045
1959	64 630	3 838	1 670	2 168	60 791	5 870	13 709	15 454	13 915	8 822	3 023
1960	65 778	4 129	1 770	2 360	61 648	6 119	13 630	15 598	14 238	8 989	3 073
1961	65 746	4 108	1 621	2 486	61 638	6 227	13 429	15 552	14 320	9 120	2 987
1962	66 702	4 195	1 607	2 588	62 508	6 446	13 311	15 901	14 491	9 346	3 013
1963	67 762	4 255	1 751	2 504	63 508	6 815	13 318	16 114	14 749	9 596	2 915
1964	69 305	4 516	2 013	2 503	64 789	7 303	13 449	16 166	15 094	9 804	2 973
1965	71 088	5 036	2 075	2 962	66 052	7 702	13 704	16 294	15 320	10 028	3 005
1966	72 895	5 721	2 269	3 452	67 178	7 964	14 017	16 312	15 615	10 310	2 961
1967	74 372	5 682	2 334	3 348	68 690	8 499	14 575	16 281	15 789	10 536	3 011
1968	75 920	5 781	2 403	3 377	70 141	8 762	15 265	16 220	16 083	10 745	3 065
1969	77 902	6 117	2 573	3 543	71 785	9 319	15 883	16 100	16 410	10 919	3 155
1970	78 678	6 144	2 598	3 546	72 534	9 731	16 318	15 922	16 473	10 974	3 118
1971	79 367	6 208	2 596	3 613	73 158	10 201	16 781	15 675	16 451	11 009	3 040
1972	82 153	6 746	2 787	3 959	75 407	10 999	18 082	15 822	16 457	11 044	3 003
1973	85 064	7 271	3 032	4 239	77 793	11 839	19 509	16 041	16 553	10 966	2 886
1974	86 794	7 448	3 111	4 338	79 347	12 101	20 610	16 203	16 633	10 964	2 835
1975	85 846	7 104	2 941	4 162	78 744	11 885	21 087	15 953	16 190	10 827	2 801
1976	88 752	7 336	2 972	4 363	81 416	12 570	22 493	16 468	16 224	10 912	2 747
1977	92 017	7 688	3 138	4 550	84 329	13 196	23 850	17 157	16 212	11 126	2 787
1978	96 048	8 070	3 330	4 739	87 979	13 887	25 281	18 128	16 338	11 400	2 946
1979	98 824	8 083	3 340	4 743	90 741	14 327	26 492	18 981	16 357	11 585	2 999
1980	99 303	7 710	3 106	4 605	91 593	14 087	27 204	19 523	16 234	11 586	2 960
1981	100 397	7 225	2 866	4 359	93 172	14 122	28 180	20 145	16 255	11 525	2 945
1982	99 526	6 549	2 505	4 044	92 978	13 690	28 149	20 879	15 923	11 414	2 923
1983	100 834	6 342	2 320	4 022	94 491	13 722	28 756	21 960	15 812	11 315	2 927
1984	105 005	6 444	2 404	4 040	98 562	14 207	30 348	23 598	16 178	11 395	2 835
1985	107 150	6 434	2 492	3 941	100 716	13 980	31 208	24 732	16 509	11 474	2 813
1986	109 597	6 472	2 622	3 850	103 125	13 790	32 201	25 861	16 949	11 405	2 919
1987	112 440	6 640	2 736	3 905	105 800	13 524	33 105	27 119	17 487	11 465	3 041
1988	114 968	6 805	2 713	4 092	108 164	13 244	33 574	28 269	18 447	11 433	3 197
1989	117 342	6 759	2 588	4 172	110 582	12 962	34 045	29 443	19 279	11 499	3 355
1990	118 793	6 581	2 410	4 171	112 213	13 401	33 935	30 817	19 525	11 189	3 346
1991	117 718	5 906	2 202	3 704	111 812	12 975	33 061	31 593	19 882	11 001	3 300
1992	118 492	5 669	2 128	3 540	112 824	12 872	32 667	31 923	21 022	10 998	3 341
1993	120 259	5 805	2 226	3 579	114 455	12 840	32 385	32 666	22 175	11 058	3 331
1994	123 060	6 161	2 510	3 651	116 899	12 758	32 288	33 599	23 348	11 228	3 681
1995	124 900	6 419	2 573	3 846	118 481	12 443	32 356	34 202	24 378	11 435	3 666
1996	126 708	6 500	2 646	3 853	120 208	12 138	32 077	35 051	25 514	11 739	3 690
1997	129 558	6 661	2 648	4 012	122 897	12 380	31 809	35 908	26 744	12 296	3 761
1998	131 463	7 051	2 762	4 289	124 413	12 557	31 394	36 278	27 587	12 872	3 725
1999	133 488	7 172	2 793	4 379	126 316	12 891	30 865	36 728	28 635	13 315	3 882
2000	136 891	7 189	2 759	4 431	129 701	13 229	31 549	36 433	30 310	14 002	4 179
2001	136 933	6 740	2 558	4 182	130 194	13 348	30 863	36 049	31 036	14 645	4 253
2002	136 485	6 332	2 330	4 002	130 154	13 351	30 306	35 235	31 281	15 674	4 306
2003	137 736	5 919	2 312	3 607	131 817	13 433	30 383	34 881	31 914	16 598	4 608
2004	139 252	5 907	2 193	3 714	133 345	13 723	30 423	34 580	32 469	17 331	4 819
2005	141 730	5 978	2 284	3 694	135 752	13 792	30 680	34 630	33 207	18 349	5 094
2006	144 427	6 162	2 444	3 719	138 265	13 878	31 051	34 569	34 052	19 389	5 325
2007	146 047	5 911	2 286	3 625	140 136	13 964	31 586	34 302	34 563	20 108	5 614
2008	145 362	5 573	1 989	3 584	139 790	13 629	31 383	33 457	34 529	20 812	5 979

Table 1-11. Employed Civilians, by Age, Sex, Race, and Hispanic Origin, 1948–2008—*Continued*

(Thousands of people.)

Race, Hispanic origin, sex, and year	16 years and over	16 to 19 years			20 years and over						
		Total	16 to 17 years	18 to 19 years	Total	20 to 24 years	25 to 34 years	35 to 44 years	45 to 54 years	55 to 64 years	65 years and over
ALL RACES											
Men											
1948	41 725	2 344	996	1 348	39 382	4 349	10 038	9 363	7 742	5 587	2 303
1949	40 925	2 124	911	1 213	38 803	4 197	9 879	9 308	7 661	5 438	2 329
1950	41 578	2 186	909	1 277	39 394	4 255	10 060	9 445	7 790	5 508	2 336
1951	41 780	2 156	979	1 177	39 626	3 780	10 134	9 607	8 012	5 711	2 382
1952	41 682	2 107	985	1 121	39 578	3 183	10 352	9 753	8 144	5 804	2 343
1953	42 430	2 136	976	1 159	40 296	2 901	10 500	10 229	8 374	5 808	2 483
1954	41 619	1 985	881	1 104	39 634	2 724	10 254	10 082	8 330	5 830	2 414
1955	42 621	2 095	936	1 159	40 526	2 973	10 453	10 267	8 553	5 857	2 424
1956	43 379	2 164	1 008	1 156	41 216	3 245	10 337	10 385	8 732	6 004	2 512
1957	43 357	2 115	987	1 130	41 239	3 346	10 222	10 427	8 851	6 002	2 394
1958	42 423	2 012	948	1 064	40 411	3 293	9 790	10 291	8 828	5 955	2 254
1959	43 466	2 198	1 015	1 183	41 267	3 597	9 862	10 492	9 048	6 058	2 210
1960	43 904	2 361	1 090	1 271	41 543	3 754	9 759	10 552	9 182	6 105	2 191
1961	43 656	2 315	989	1 325	41 342	3 795	9 591	10 505	9 195	6 155	2 098
1962	44 177	2 362	990	1 372	41 815	3 898	9 475	10 711	9 333	6 260	2 138
1963	44 657	2 406	1 073	1 334	42 251	4 118	9 431	10 801	9 478	6 385	2 038
1964	45 474	2 587	1 242	1 345	42 886	4 370	9 531	10 832	9 637	6 478	2 039
1965	46 340	2 918	1 285	1 634	43 422	4 583	9 611	10 837	9 792	6 542	2 057
1966	46 919	3 253	1 389	1 863	43 668	4 599	9 709	10 764	9 904	6 668	2 024
1967	47 479	3 186	1 417	1 769	44 294	4 809	9 988	10 674	9 990	6 774	2 058
1968	48 114	3 255	1 453	1 802	44 859	4 812	10 405	10 554	10 102	6 893	2 093
1969	48 818	3 430	1 526	1 904	45 388	5 012	10 736	10 401	10 187	6 931	2 122
1970	48 990	3 409	1 504	1 905	45 581	5 237	10 936	10 216	10 170	6 928	2 094
1971	49 390	3 478	1 510	1 968	45 912	5 593	11 218	10 028	10 139	6 916	2 019
1972	50 896	3 765	1 598	2 167	47 130	6 138	11 884	10 088	10 139	6 929	1 953
1973	52 349	4 039	1 721	2 318	48 310	6 655	12 617	10 126	10 197	6 857	1 856
1974	53 024	4 103	1 744	2 359	48 922	6 739	13 119	10 135	10 181	6 880	1 869
1975	51 857	3 839	1 621	2 219	48 018	6 484	13 205	9 891	9 902	6 722	1 811
1976	53 138	3 947	1 626	2 321	49 190	6 915	13 869	10 069	9 881	6 724	1 732
1977	54 728	4 174	1 733	2 441	50 555	7 232	14 483	10 399	9 832	6 848	1 761
1978	56 479	4 336	1 800	2 535	52 143	7 559	15 124	10 845	9 806	6 954	1 855
1979	57 607	4 300	1 799	2 501	53 308	7 791	15 688	11 202	9 735	7 015	1 876
1980	57 186	4 085	1 672	2 412	53 101	7 532	15 832	11 355	9 548	6 999	1 835
1981	57 397	3 815	1 526	2 289	53 582	7 504	16 266	11 613	9 478	6 909	1 812
1982	56 271	3 379	1 307	2 072	52 891	7 197	16 002	11 902	9 234	6 781	1 776
1983	56 787	3 300	1 213	2 087	53 487	7 232	16 216	12 450	9 133	6 686	1 770
1984	59 091	3 322	1 244	2 078	55 769	7 571	17 166	13 309	9 326	6 694	1 703
1985	59 891	3 328	1 300	2 029	56 562	7 339	17 564	13 800	9 411	6 753	1 695
1986	60 892	3 323	1 352	1 971	57 569	7 250	18 092	14 266	9 554	6 654	1 753
1987	62 107	3 381	1 393	1 988	58 726	7 058	18 487	14 898	9 750	6 682	1 850
1988	63 273	3 492	1 403	2 089	59 781	6 918	18 702	15 457	10 201	6 591	1 911
1989	64 315	3 477	1 327	2 150	60 837	6 799	18 952	16 002	10 569	6 548	1 968
1990	65 104	3 427	1 254	2 173	61 678	7 151	18 779	16 771	10 690	6 378	1 909
1991	64 223	3 044	1 135	1 909	61 178	6 909	18 265	17 086	10 813	6 245	1 860
1992	64 440	2 944	1 096	1 848	61 496	6 819	17 966	17 230	11 365	6 173	1 943
1993	65 349	2 994	1 155	1 839	62 355	6 805	17 877	17 665	11 927	6 166	1 916
1994	66 450	3 156	1 288	1 868	63 294	6 771	17 741	18 111	12 439	6 142	2 089
1995	67 377	3 292	1 316	1 977	64 085	6 665	17 709	18 374	12 958	6 272	2 108
1996	68 207	3 310	1 318	1 992	64 897	6 429	17 527	18 816	13 483	6 470	2 172
1997	69 685	3 401	1 355	2 045	66 284	6 548	17 338	19 327	14 107	6 735	2 229
1998	70 693	3 558	1 398	2 161	67 135	6 638	17 097	19 634	14 544	7 052	2 171
1999	71 446	3 685	1 437	2 249	67 761	6 729	16 694	19 811	14 991	7 274	2 263
2000	73 305	3 671	1 394	2 276	69 634	6 974	17 241	19 537	15 871	7 606	2 406
2001	73 196	3 420	1 268	2 151	69 776	6 952	16 915	19 305	16 268	7 900	2 437
2002	72 903	3 169	1 130	2 040	69 734	6 978	16 573	18 932	16 419	8 378	2 455
2003	73 332	2 917	1 115	1 802	70 415	7 065	16 670	18 774	16 588	8 733	2 585
2004	74 524	2 952	1 037	1 915	71 572	7 246	16 818	18 700	16 951	9 174	2 683
2005	75 973	2 923	1 067	1 855	73 050	7 279	16 993	18 780	17 429	9 714	2 857
2006	77 502	3 071	1 182	1 888	74 431	7 412	17 134	18 765	17 920	10 192	3 008
2007	78 254	2 917	1 091	1 827	75 337	7 374	17 452	18 666	18 210	10 556	3 080
2008	77 486	2 736	926	1 810	74 750	7 145	17 183	18 097	18 124	10 919	3 282

Table 1-11. Employed Civilians, by Age, Sex, Race, and Hispanic Origin, 1948–2008—*Continued*

(Thousands of people.)

Race, Hispanic origin, sex, and year	16 years and over	16 to 19 years			20 years and over						
		Total	16 to 17 years	18 to 19 years	Total	20 to 24 years	25 to 34 years	35 to 44 years	45 to 54 years	55 to 64 years	65 years and over
ALL RACES											
Women											
1948	16 617	1 682	604	1 078	14 936	2 588	3 763	3 687	2 882	1 516	501
1949	16 723	1 588	555	1 033	15 137	2 463	3 760	3 800	2 975	1 604	535
1950	17 340	1 517	524	993	15 824	2 491	3 857	3 979	3 176	1 757	563
1951	18 181	1 611	596	1 015	16 570	2 541	4 099	4 139	3 409	1 847	535
1952	18 568	1 612	641	971	16 958	2 389	4 163	4 305	3 543	1 981	576
1953	18 749	1 584	601	983	17 164	2 324	4 019	4 545	3 595	1 998	683
1954	18 490	1 490	541	949	17 000	2 247	3 936	4 459	3 646	2 065	646
1955	19 551	1 547	564	984	18 002	2 297	4 028	4 612	4 003	2 301	761
1956	20 419	1 654	639	1 015	18 767	2 300	4 070	4 833	4 246	2 515	802
1957	20 714	1 663	626	1 037	19 052	2 295	4 031	4 921	4 469	2 551	785
1958	20 613	1 570	571	999	19 043	2 278	3 885	4 866	4 620	2 604	791
1959	21 164	1 640	655	985	19 524	2 273	3 847	4 962	4 867	2 764	813
1960	21 874	1 768	680	1 089	20 105	2 365	3 871	5 046	5 056	2 884	882
1961	22 090	1 793	632	1 161	20 296	2 432	3 838	5 047	5 125	2 965	889
1962	22 525	1 833	617	1 216	20 693	2 548	3 836	5 190	5 158	3 086	875
1963	23 105	1 849	678	1 170	21 257	2 697	3 887	5 313	5 271	3 211	877
1964	23 831	1 929	771	1 158	21 903	2 933	3 918	5 334	5 457	3 326	934
1965	24 748	2 118	790	1 328	22 630	3 119	4 093	5 457	5 528	3 486	948
1966	25 976	2 468	880	1 589	23 510	3 365	4 308	5 548	5 711	3 642	937
1967	26 893	2 496	917	1 579	24 397	3 690	4 587	5 607	5 799	3 762	953
1968	27 807	2 526	950	1 575	25 281	3 950	4 860	5 666	5 981	3 852	972
1969	29 084	2 687	1 047	1 639	26 397	4 307	5 147	5 699	6 223	3 988	1 033
1970	29 688	2 735	1 094	1 641	26 952	4 494	5 382	5 706	6 303	4 046	1 023
1971	29 976	2 730	1 086	1 645	27 246	4 609	5 563	5 647	6 313	4 093	1 021
1972	31 257	2 980	1 188	1 792	28 276	4 861	6 197	5 734	6 318	4 115	1 051
1973	32 715	3 231	1 310	1 920	29 484	5 184	6 893	5 915	6 356	4 109	1 029
1974	33 769	3 345	1 367	1 978	30 424	5 363	7 492	6 068	6 451	4 084	966
1975	33 989	3 263	1 320	1 943	30 726	5 401	7 882	6 061	6 288	4 105	989
1976	35 615	3 389	1 346	2 043	32 226	5 655	8 624	6 400	6 343	4 188	1 017
1977	37 289	3 514	1 403	2 110	33 775	5 965	9 367	6 758	6 380	4 279	1 027
1978	39 569	3 734	1 530	2 204	35 836	6 328	10 157	7 282	6 532	4 446	1 091
1979	41 217	3 783	1 541	2 242	37 434	6 538	10 802	7 779	6 622	4 569	1 124
1980	42 117	3 625	1 433	2 192	38 492	6 555	11 370	8 168	6 686	4 587	1 125
1981	43 000	3 411	1 340	2 070	39 590	6 618	11 914	8 532	6 777	4 616	1 133
1982	43 256	3 170	1 198	1 972	40 086	6 492	12 147	8 977	6 689	4 634	1 147
1983	44 047	3 043	1 107	1 935	41 004	6 490	12 540	9 510	6 678	4 629	1 157
1984	45 915	3 122	1 161	1 962	42 793	6 636	13 182	10 289	6 852	4 700	1 133
1985	47 259	3 105	1 193	1 913	44 154	6 640	13 644	10 933	7 097	4 721	1 118
1986	48 706	3 149	1 270	1 879	45 556	6 540	14 109	11 595	7 395	4 751	1 165
1987	50 334	3 260	1 343	1 917	47 074	6 466	14 617	12 281	7 737	4 783	1 191
1988	51 696	3 313	1 310	2 003	48 383	6 326	14 872	12 811	8 246	4 841	1 286
1989	53 027	3 282	1 261	2 021	49 745	6 163	15 093	13 440	8 711	4 950	1 388
1990	53 689	3 154	1 156	1 998	50 535	6 250	15 155	14 046	8 835	4 811	1 437
1991	53 496	2 862	1 067	1 794	50 634	6 066	14 796	14 507	9 069	4 756	1 440
1992	54 052	2 724	1 032	1 692	51 328	6 053	14 701	14 693	9 657	4 825	1 398
1993	54 910	2 811	1 071	1 740	52 099	6 035	14 508	15 002	10 248	4 892	1 414
1994	56 610	3 005	1 222	1 783	53 606	5 987	14 545	15 488	10 908	5 085	1 592
1995	57 523	3 127	1 258	1 869	54 396	5 779	14 647	15 828	11 421	5 163	1 558
1996	58 501	3 190	1 328	1 862	55 311	5 709	14 549	16 235	12 031	5 269	1 518
1997	59 873	3 260	1 293	1 967	56 613	5 831	14 471	16 581	12 637	5 561	1 532
1998	60 771	3 493	1 364	2 128	57 278	5 919	14 298	16 644	13 043	5 820	1 554
1999	62 042	3 487	1 357	2 130	58 555	6 163	14 171	16 917	13 644	6 041	1 619
2000	63 586	3 519	1 364	2 154	60 067	6 255	14 308	16 897	14 438	6 396	1 773
2001	63 737	3 320	1 289	2 031	60 417	6 396	13 948	16 744	14 768	6 745	1 815
2002	63 582	3 162	1 200	1 962	60 420	6 374	13 733	16 303	14 863	7 296	1 851
2003	64 404	3 002	1 197	1 805	61 402	6 367	13 714	16 106	15 326	7 866	2 023
2004	64 728	2 955	1 156	1 799	61 773	6 477	13 605	15 880	15 518	8 157	2 135
2005	65 757	3 055	1 217	1 838	62 702	6 513	13 687	15 850	15 779	8 635	2 238
2006	66 925	3 091	1 261	1 830	63 834	6 467	13 917	15 804	16 132	9 198	2 316
2007	67 792	2 994	1 195	1 798	64 799	6 590	14 133	15 636	16 353	9 553	2 534
2008	67 876	2 837	1 063	1 774	65 039	6 484	14 200	15 360	16 406	9 893	2 697

Table 1-11. Employed Civilians, by Age, Sex, Race, and Hispanic Origin, 1948–2008—*Continued*

(Thousands of people.)

| Race, Hispanic origin, sex, and year | 16 years and over | 16 to 19 years | | | 20 years and over | | | | | | |
		Total	16 to 17 years	18 to 19 years	Total	20 to 24 years	25 to 34 years	35 to 44 years	45 to 54 years	55 to 64 years	65 years and over
WHITE											
Both Sexes											
1954	53 957	3 078	1 257	1 822	50 879	4 358	12 616	13 000	10 811	7 262	2 831
1955	55 833	3 225	1 330	1 896	52 608	4 637	12 855	13 327	11 322	7 510	2 957
1956	57 269	3 389	1 465	1 922	53 880	4 897	12 748	13 637	11 706	7 822	3 068
1957	57 465	3 374	1 442	1 931	54 091	4 952	12 619	13 716	12 009	7 829	2 951
1958	56 613	3 216	1 370	1 847	53 397	4 908	12 128	13 571	12 113	7 849	2 828
1959	58 006	3 475	1 520	1 955	54 531	5 138	12 144	13 830	12 552	8 063	2 805
1960	58 850	3 700	1 598	2 103	55 150	5 331	12 021	13 930	12 820	8 192	2 855
1961	58 913	3 693	1 472	2 220	55 220	5 460	11 835	13 905	12 906	8 335	2 778
1962	59 698	3 774	1 447	2 327	55 924	5 676	11 703	14 173	13 066	8 511	2 795
1963	60 622	3 851	1 600	2 250	56 771	6 036	11 689	14 341	13 304	8 718	2 683
1964	61 922	4 076	1 846	2 230	57 846	6 444	11 794	14 380	13 596	8 916	2 717
1965	63 446	4 562	1 892	2 670	58 884	6 752	11 992	14 473	13 804	9 116	2 748
1966	65 021	5 176	2 052	3 124	59 845	6 986	12 268	14 449	14 072	9 356	2 713
1967	66 361	5 114	2 121	2 993	61 247	7 493	12 763	14 429	14 224	9 596	2 746
1968	67 750	5 195	2 193	3 002	62 555	7 687	13 410	14 386	14 487	9 781	2 804
1969	69 518	5 508	2 347	3 161	64 010	8 182	13 935	14 270	14 788	9 947	2 888
1970	70 217	5 571	2 386	3 185	64 645	8 559	14 326	14 092	14 854	9 979	2 835
1971	70 878	5 670	2 404	3 266	65 208	9 000	14 713	13 858	14 843	10 014	2 780
1972	73 370	6 173	2 581	3 592	67 197	9 718	15 904	13 940	14 845	10 077	2 714
1973	75 708	6 623	2 806	3 816	69 086	10 424	17 099	14 083	14 886	9 983	2 610
1974	77 184	6 796	2 881	3 916	70 388	10 676	18 040	14 196	14 948	9 958	2 568
1975	76 411	6 487	2 721	3 770	69 924	10 546	18 485	13 979	14 555	9 827	2 533
1976	78 853	6 724	2 762	3 962	72 129	11 119	19 662	14 407	14 549	9 923	2 470
1977	81 700	7 068	2 926	4 142	74 632	11 696	20 844	14 984	14 483	10 107	2 518
1978	84 936	7 367	3 085	4 282	77 569	12 251	22 008	15 809	14 550	10 311	2 642
1979	87 259	7 356	3 079	4 278	79 904	12 594	23 033	16 578	14 522	10 477	2 699
1980	87 715	7 021	2 861	4 161	80 694	12 405	23 653	17 071	14 405	10 475	2 684
1981	88 709	6 588	2 645	3 943	82 121	12 477	24 551	17 617	14 414	10 386	2 676
1982	87 903	5 984	2 317	3 667	81 918	12 097	24 531	18 268	14 083	10 283	2 656
1983	88 893	5 799	2 156	3 643	83 094	12 138	24 955	19 194	13 961	10 169	2 678
1984	92 120	5 836	2 209	3 627	86 284	12 451	26 235	20 552	14 239	10 227	2 580
1985	93 736	5 768	2 270	3 498	87 968	12 235	26 945	21 552	14 459	10 247	2 530
1986	95 660	5 792	2 386	3 406	89 869	12 027	27 746	22 515	14 750	10 176	2 654
1987	97 789	5 898	2 468	3 431	91 890	11 748	28 429	23 596	15 216	10 164	2 738
1988	99 812	6 030	2 424	3 606	93 782	11 438	28 796	24 468	16 054	10 153	2 874
1989	101 584	5 946	2 278	3 668	95 638	11 084	29 091	25 442	16 775	10 223	3 024
1990	102 261	5 779	2 141	3 638	96 481	11 498	28 773	26 282	16 933	9 960	3 035
1991	101 182	5 216	1 971	3 246	95 966	11 116	27 989	26 883	17 269	9 719	2 990
1992	101 669	4 985	1 904	3 081	96 684	11 031	27 552	27 097	18 285	9 701	3 019
1993	103 045	5 113	1 990	3 123	97 932	10 931	27 274	27 645	19 273	9 772	3 037
1994	105 190	5 398	2 210	3 188	99 792	10 736	27 101	28 442	20 247	9 912	3 354
1995	106 490	5 593	2 273	3 320	100 897	10 400	27 014	28 951	21 127	10 070	3 335
1996	107 808	5 667	2 325	3 343	102 141	10 149	26 678	29 566	22 071	10 313	3 364
1997	109 856	5 807	2 341	3 466	104 049	10 362	26 294	30 137	23 061	10 785	3 411
1998	110 931	6 089	2 436	3 653	104 842	10 512	25 729	30 320	23 662	11 272	3 347
1999	112 235	6 204	2 435	3 769	106 032	10 716	25 113	30 548	24 507	11 657	3 491
2000	114 424	6 160	2 383	3 777	108 264	10 944	25 500	30 151	25 762	12 169	3 738
2001	114 430	5 817	2 224	3 593	108 613	11 054	24 948	29 793	26 301	12 743	3 774
2002	114 013	5 441	2 037	3 404	108 572	11 096	24 568	29 049	26 401	13 630	3 828
2003	114 235	5 064	1 999	3 065	109 171	11 052	24 399	28 501	26 762	14 375	4 083
2004	115 239	5 039	1 895	3 145	110 199	11 233	24 337	28 176	27 228	14 965	4 260
2005	116 949	5 105	1 999	3 106	111 844	11 231	24 443	28 102	27 801	15 788	4 480
2006	118 833	5 215	2 099	3 117	113 618	11 296	24 652	27 929	28 419	16 652	4 670
2007	119 792	4 990	1 965	3 026	114 802	11 325	25 024	27 492	28 779	17 262	4 921
2008	119 126	4 697	1 703	2 994	114 428	11 055	24 875	26 736	28 686	17 829	5 247

Table 1-11. Employed Civilians, by Age, Sex, Race, and Hispanic Origin, 1948–2008—*Continued*

(Thousands of people.)

Race, Hispanic origin, sex, and year	16 years and over	16 to 19 years			20 years and over						
		Total	16 to 17 years	18 to 19 years	Total	20 to 24 years	25 to 34 years	35 to 44 years	45 to 54 years	55 to 64 years	65 years and over
WHITE											
Men											
1954	37 846	1 723	771	953	36 123	2 394	9 287	9 175	7 614	5 412	2 241
1955	38 719	1 824	821	1 004	36 895	2 607	9 461	9 351	7 792	5 431	2 254
1956	39 368	1 893	890	1 002	37 475	2 850	9 330	9 449	7 950	5 559	2 336
1957	39 349	1 865	874	990	37 484	2 930	9 226	9 480	8 067	5 542	2 234
1958	38 591	1 783	852	932	36 808	2 896	8 861	9 386	8 061	5 501	2 103
1959	39 494	1 961	915	1 046	37 533	3 153	8 911	9 560	8 261	5 588	2 060
1960	39 755	2 092	973	1 119	37 663	3 264	8 777	9 589	8 372	5 618	2 043
1961	39 588	2 055	891	1 164	37 533	3 311	8 630	9 566	8 394	5 670	1 961
1962	40 016	2 098	883	1 215	37 918	3 426	8 514	9 718	8 512	5 749	1 998
1963	40 428	2 156	972	1 184	38 272	3 646	8 463	9 782	8 650	5 844	1 887
1964	41 115	2 316	1 128	1 188	38 799	3 856	8 538	9 800	8 787	5 945	1 872
1965	41 844	2 612	1 159	1 453	39 232	4 025	8 598	9 795	8 924	5 998	1 892
1966	42 331	2 913	1 245	1 668	39 418	4 028	8 674	9 719	9 029	6 096	1 871
1967	42 833	2 849	1 278	1 571	39 985	4 231	8 931	9 632	9 093	6 208	1 892
1968	43 411	2 908	1 319	1 589	40 503	4 226	9 315	9 522	9 198	6 316	1 926
1969	44 048	3 070	1 385	1 685	40 978	4 401	9 608	9 379	9 279	6 359	1 953
1970	44 178	3 066	1 374	1 692	41 112	4 601	9 784	9 202	9 271	6 340	1 914
1971	44 595	3 157	1 393	1 764	41 438	4 935	10 026	9 026	9 256	6 339	1 856
1972	45 944	3 416	1 470	1 947	42 528	5 431	10 664	9 047	9 236	6 363	1 786
1973	47 085	3 660	1 590	2 071	43 424	5 863	11 268	9 046	9 257	6 299	1 689
1974	47 674	3 728	1 611	2 117	43 946	5 965	11 701	9 027	9 242	6 304	1 706
1975	46 697	3 505	1 502	2 002	43 192	5 770	11 783	8 818	9 005	6 160	1 656
1976	47 775	3 604	1 501	2 103	44 171	6 140	12 362	8 944	8 968	6 176	1 579
1977	49 150	3 824	1 607	2 217	45 326	6 437	12 893	9 212	8 898	6 279	1 605
1978	50 544	3 950	1 664	2 286	46 594	6 717	13 413	9 608	8 840	6 339	1 677
1979	51 452	3 904	1 654	2 250	47 546	6 868	13 888	9 930	8 748	6 406	1 707
1980	51 127	3 708	1 534	2 174	47 419	6 652	14 009	10 077	8 586	6 412	1 684
1981	51 315	3 469	1 402	2 066	47 846	6 652	14 398	10 307	8 518	6 309	1 662
1982	50 287	3 079	1 214	1 865	47 209	6 372	14 164	10 593	8 267	6 188	1 624
1983	50 621	3 003	1 124	1 879	47 618	6 386	14 297	11 062	8 152	6 084	1 637
1984	52 462	3 001	1 140	1 861	49 461	6 647	15 045	11 776	8 320	6 108	1 564
1985	53 046	2 985	1 185	1 800	50 061	6 428	15 374	12 214	8 374	6 118	1 552
1986	53 785	2 966	1 225	1 741	50 818	6 340	15 790	12 620	8 442	6 012	1 612
1987	54 647	2 999	1 252	1 747	51 649	6 150	16 084	13 138	8 596	5 991	1 690
1988	55 550	3 084	1 248	1 836	52 466	5 987	16 241	13 590	8 992	5 909	1 748
1989	56 352	3 060	1 171	1 889	53 292	5 839	16 383	14 046	9 335	5 891	1 797
1990	56 703	3 018	1 119	1 899	53 685	6 179	16 124	14 496	9 383	5 744	1 760
1991	55 797	2 694	1 017	1 677	53 103	5 942	15 644	14 743	9 488	5 578	1 707
1992	55 959	2 602	990	1 612	53 357	5 855	15 357	14 842	10 027	5 503	1 772
1993	56 656	2 634	1 031	1 603	54 021	5 830	15 230	15 178	10 497	5 514	1 772
1994	57 452	2 776	1 144	1 632	54 676	5 738	15 052	15 562	10 910	5 490	1 925
1995	58 146	2 892	1 169	1 723	55 254	5 613	14 958	15 793	11 359	5 609	1 921
1996	58 888	2 911	1 161	1 750	55 977	5 444	14 820	16 136	11 834	5 755	1 987
1997	59 998	3 011	1 206	1 806	56 986	5 590	14 567	16 470	12 352	5 972	2 037
1998	60 604	3 103	1 233	1 870	57 500	5 659	14 259	16 715	12 661	6 251	1 955
1999	61 139	3 205	1 254	1 951	57 934	5 753	13 851	16 781	13 046	6 447	2 056
2000	62 289	3 169	1 205	1 965	59 119	5 876	14 238	16 477	13 675	6 678	2 175
2001	62 212	2 967	1 102	1 865	59 245	5 870	13 989	16 280	13 987	6 941	2 178
2002	61 849	2 725	987	1 738	59 124	5 882	13 727	15 910	14 060	7 360	2 184
2003	61 866	2 518	972	1 546	59 348	5 890	13 731	15 675	14 117	7 640	2 295
2004	62 712	2 553	903	1 650	60 159	6 026	13 735	15 572	14 418	8 018	2 390
2005	63 763	2 508	942	1 566	61 255	6 041	13 840	15 544	14 810	8 471	2 550
2006	64 883	2 625	1 020	1 605	62 259	6 114	13 903	15 480	15 189	8 893	2 680
2007	65 289	2 483	951	1 531	62 806	6 066	14 112	15 287	15 399	9 215	2 727
2008	64 624	2 320	808	1 512	62 304	5 858	13 931	14 775	15 300	9 518	2 922

Table 1-11. Employed Civilians, by Age, Sex, Race, and Hispanic Origin, 1948–2008—*Continued*

(Thousands of people.)

Race, Hispanic origin, sex, and year	16 years and over	16 to 19 years			20 years and over						
		Total	16 to 17 years	18 to 19 years	Total	20 to 24 years	25 to 34 years	35 to 44 years	45 to 54 years	55 to 64 years	65 years and over
WHITE											
Women											
1954	16 111	1 355	486	869	14 756	1 964	3 329	3 825	3 197	1 850	590
1955	17 114	1 401	509	892	15 713	2 030	3 394	3 976	3 530	2 079	703
1956	17 901	1 496	575	920	16 405	2 047	3 418	4 188	3 756	2 263	732
1957	18 116	1 509	568	941	16 607	2 022	3 393	4 236	3 942	2 287	717
1958	18 022	1 433	518	915	16 589	2 012	3 267	4 185	4 052	2 348	725
1959	18 512	1 514	605	909	16 998	1 985	3 233	4 270	4 291	2 475	745
1960	19 095	1 608	625	984	17 487	2 067	3 244	4 341	4 448	2 574	812
1961	19 325	1 638	581	1 056	17 687	2 149	3 205	4 339	4 512	2 665	817
1962	19 682	1 676	564	1 112	18 006	2 250	3 189	4 455	4 554	2 762	797
1963	20 194	1 695	628	1 066	18 499	2 390	3 226	4 559	4 654	2 874	796
1964	20 807	1 760	718	1 042	19 047	2 588	3 256	4 580	4 809	2 971	845
1965	21 602	1 950	733	1 217	19 652	2 727	3 394	4 678	4 880	3 118	856
1966	22 690	2 263	807	1 456	20 427	2 958	3 594	4 730	5 043	3 260	842
1967	23 528	2 265	843	1 422	21 263	3 262	3 832	4 797	5 131	3 388	854
1968	24 339	2 287	874	1 413	22 052	3 461	4 095	4 864	5 289	3 465	878
1969	25 470	2 438	962	1 476	23 032	3 781	4 327	4 891	5 509	3 588	935
1970	26 039	2 505	1 012	1 493	23 534	3 959	4 542	4 890	5 582	3 640	921
1971	26 283	2 513	1 011	1 502	23 770	4 065	4 687	4 831	5 588	3 675	924
1972	27 426	2 755	1 111	1 645	24 669	4 286	5 240	4 893	5 608	3 714	928
1973	28 623	2 962	1 217	1 746	25 661	4 562	5 831	5 036	5 628	3 684	920
1974	29 511	3 069	1 269	1 799	26 442	4 711	6 340	5 169	5 706	3 654	862
1975	29 714	2 983	1 215	1 767	26 731	4 775	6 701	5 161	5 550	3 667	877
1976	31 078	3 120	1 260	1 860	27 958	4 978	7 300	5 462	5 580	3 746	891
1977	32 550	3 244	1 319	1 923	29 306	5 259	7 950	5 772	5 585	3 829	912
1978	34 392	3 416	1 420	1 996	30 975	5 535	8 595	6 201	5 710	3 972	964
1979	35 807	3 451	1 423	2 027	32 357	5 726	9 145	6 648	5 773	4 071	993
1980	36 587	3 314	1 327	1 986	33 275	5 753	9 644	6 994	5 818	4 064	1 001
1981	37 394	3 119	1 242	1 877	34 275	5 826	10 153	7 311	5 896	4 077	1 013
1982	37 615	2 905	1 103	1 802	34 710	5 724	10 367	7 675	5 816	4 095	1 032
1983	38 272	2 796	1 032	1 764	35 476	5 751	10 659	8 132	5 809	4 084	1 041
1984	39 659	2 835	1 069	1 766	36 823	5 804	11 190	8 776	5 920	4 118	1 015
1985	40 690	2 783	1 085	1 698	37 907	5 807	11 571	9 338	6 084	4 128	978
1986	41 876	2 825	1 160	1 665	39 050	5 687	11 956	9 895	6 307	4 164	1 042
1987	43 142	2 900	1 216	1 684	40 242	5 598	12 345	10 459	6 620	4 172	1 047
1988	44 262	2 946	1 176	1 770	41 316	5 450	12 555	10 878	7 062	4 244	1 126
1989	45 232	2 886	1 107	1 779	42 346	5 245	12 708	11 395	7 440	4 332	1 227
1990	45 558	2 762	1 023	1 739	42 796	5 319	12 649	11 785	7 551	4 217	1 275
1991	45 385	2 523	954	1 569	42 862	5 174	12 344	12 139	7 781	4 141	1 283
1992	45 710	2 383	915	1 468	43 327	5 176	12 195	12 254	8 258	4 198	1 246
1993	46 390	2 479	959	1 520	43 910	5 101	12 044	12 467	8 776	4 258	1 265
1994	47 738	2 622	1 066	1 556	45 116	4 997	12 049	12 880	9 338	4 423	1 429
1995	48 344	2 701	1 104	1 597	45 643	4 787	12 056	13 157	9 768	4 461	1 415
1996	48 920	2 756	1 164	1 592	46 164	4 705	11 858	13 430	10 237	4 558	1 376
1997	49 859	2 796	1 136	1 660	47 063	4 773	11 727	13 667	10 709	4 813	1 374
1998	50 327	2 986	1 203	1 783	47 342	4 853	11 470	13 604	11 001	5 021	1 392
1999	51 096	2 999	1 181	1 817	48 098	4 963	11 262	13 767	11 461	5 211	1 435
2000	52 136	2 991	1 178	1 813	49 145	5 068	11 262	13 674	12 087	5 490	1 564
2001	52 218	2 850	1 122	1 727	49 369	5 184	10 959	13 513	12 314	5 802	1 597
2002	52 164	2 716	1 050	1 665	49 448	5 214	10 842	13 138	12 341	6 269	1 644
2003	52 369	2 546	1 027	1 519	49 823	5 161	10 668	12 826	12 645	6 735	1 788
2004	52 527	2 486	991	1 495	50 040	5 207	10 602	12 604	12 810	6 947	1 870
2005	53 186	2 597	1 057	1 540	50 589	5 190	10 603	12 558	12 991	7 317	1 930
2006	53 950	2 590	1 079	1 512	51 359	5 182	10 750	12 449	13 230	7 758	1 991
2007	54 503	2 507	1 013	1 494	51 996	5 259	10 912	12 205	13 380	8 047	2 193
2008	54 501	2 377	895	1 482	52 124	5 197	10 943	11 961	13 386	8 312	2 325

Table 1-11. Employed Civilians, by Age, Sex, Race, and Hispanic Origin, 1948–2008—*Continued*

(Thousands of people.)

Race, Hispanic origin, sex, and year	16 years and over	16 to 19 years			20 years and over						
		Total	16 to 17 years	18 to 19 years	Total	20 to 24 years	25 to 34 years	35 to 44 years	45 to 54 years	55 to 64 years	65 years and over
BLACK											
Both Sexes											
1972	7 802	509	180	329	7 292	1 166	1 924	1 629	1 434	872	269
1973	8 128	570	194	378	7 559	1 258	2 062	1 659	1 460	872	249
1974	8 203	554	190	364	7 649	1 231	2 157	1 682	1 452	884	243
1975	7 894	507	183	325	7 386	1 115	2 145	1 617	1 393	874	241
1976	8 227	508	170	338	7 719	1 193	2 309	1 679	1 416	870	252
1977	8 540	508	169	339	8 031	1 244	2 443	1 754	1 448	892	251
1978	9 102	571	191	380	8 531	1 359	2 641	1 848	1 479	932	273
1979	9 359	579	204	376	8 780	1 424	2 759	1 902	1 502	927	266
1980	9 313	547	192	356	8 765	1 376	2 827	1 910	1 487	925	239
1981	9 355	505	170	335	8 849	1 346	2 872	1 957	1 489	954	231
1982	9 189	428	138	290	8 761	1 283	2 830	2 025	1 469	928	225
1983	9 375	416	123	294	8 959	1 280	2 976	2 107	1 456	937	204
1984	10 119	474	146	328	9 645	1 423	3 223	2 311	1 533	945	209
1985	10 501	532	175	356	9 969	1 399	3 325	2 427	1 598	985	235
1986	10 814	536	183	353	10 278	1 429	3 464	2 524	1 666	982	214
1987	11 309	587	203	385	10 722	1 421	3 614	2 695	1 714	1 036	241
1988	11 658	601	223	378	11 057	1 433	3 725	2 839	1 783	1 018	261
1989	11 953	625	237	388	11 328	1 467	3 801	2 981	1 844	970	265
1990	12 175	598	194	404	11 577	1 409	3 803	3 287	1 897	933	248
1991	12 074	494	161	334	11 580	1 373	3 714	3 401	1 892	957	243
1992	12 151	492	157	335	11 659	1 343	3 699	3 441	1 964	965	246
1993	12 382	494	171	323	11 888	1 377	3 700	3 584	2 059	941	226
1994	12 835	552	224	328	12 284	1 449	3 732	3 722	2 178	953	251
1995	13 279	586	223	363	12 693	1 443	3 844	3 861	2 288	1 004	253
1996	13 542	613	233	380	12 929	1 411	3 851	3 974	2 426	1 025	241
1997	13 969	631	229	401	13 339	1 456	3 903	4 094	2 588	1 048	249
1998	14 556	736	246	490	13 820	1 496	3 967	4 238	2 739	1 118	262
1999	15 056	691	243	448	14 365	1 594	4 091	4 404	2 872	1 134	271
2000	15 156	711	260	451	14 444	1 593	3 993	4 261	3 073	1 226	300
2001	15 006	637	230	408	14 368	1 571	3 840	4 200	3 139	1 283	335
2002	14 872	611	193	417	14 262	1 543	3 726	4 109	3 220	1 332	332
2003	14 739	516	196	320	14 222	1 516	3 618	4 080	3 289	1 373	346
2004	14 909	520	169	351	14 389	1 572	3 635	4 039	3 332	1 452	359
2005	15 313	536	164	372	14 776	1 599	3 722	4 060	3 464	1 555	375
2006	15 765	618	215	402	15 147	1 643	3 809	4 072	3 570	1 659	394
2007	16 051	566	202	364	15 485	1 674	3 888	4 120	3 658	1 732	413
2008	15 953	541	172	369	15 411	1 625	3 870	4 015	3 670	1 791	440
BLACK											
Men											
1972	4 368	309	114	195	4 058	648	1 074	890	793	499	156
1973	4 527	330	112	220	4 197	711	1 142	898	816	483	148
1974	4 527	322	114	209	4 204	668	1 176	912	803	500	145
1975	4 275	276	98	179	3 998	595	1 159	865	755	487	137
1976	4 404	283	100	184	4 120	635	1 217	897	763	472	137
1977	4 565	291	105	186	4 273	659	1 271	940	777	484	143
1978	4 796	312	106	206	4 483	697	1 357	969	788	516	155
1979	4 923	316	111	205	4 606	754	1 425	983	801	498	147
1980	4 798	299	109	191	4 498	713	1 438	975	770	478	126
1981	4 794	273	95	178	4 520	693	1 457	991	764	492	123
1982	4 637	223	65	158	4 414	660	1 414	997	750	471	122
1983	4 753	222	64	158	4 531	684	1 483	1 034	749	477	105
1984	5 124	252	79	173	4 871	750	1 635	1 138	780	460	108
1985	5 270	278	92	186	4 992	726	1 669	1 187	795	501	114
1986	5 428	278	96	182	5 150	732	1 756	1 211	831	507	112
1987	5 661	304	109	195	5 357	728	1 821	1 283	853	547	124
1988	5 824	316	122	193	5 509	736	1 881	1 348	878	536	131
1989	5 928	327	124	202	5 602	742	1 931	1 415	886	498	131
1990	5 995	303	99	204	5 692	702	1 895	1 586	926	469	114
1991	5 961	255	85	170	5 706	695	1 859	1 634	923	481	114
1992	5 930	249	78	170	5 681	679	1 819	1 650	930	478	124
1993	6 047	254	88	166	5 793	674	1 858	1 717	978	461	106
1994	6 241	276	107	169	5 964	718	1 850	1 795	1 030	455	115
1995	6 422	285	111	174	6 137	714	1 895	1 836	1 085	468	138
1996	6 456	289	109	180	6 167	685	1 867	1 878	1 129	482	126
1997	6 607	282	108	174	6 325	668	1 874	1 955	1 215	487	127
1998	6 871	341	120	221	6 530	686	1 886	2 008	1 284	524	142
1999	7 027	325	120	205	6 702	700	1 926	2 092	1 327	525	131
2000	7 082	341	129	211	6 741	730	1 865	1 984	1 425	596	142
2001	6 938	311	115	196	6 627	703	1 757	1 931	1 452	614	170
2002	6 959	306	95	212	6 652	725	1 729	1 899	1 503	624	172
2003	6 820	234	89	145	6 586	726	1 660	1 868	1 518	638	176
2004	6 912	231	76	155	6 681	739	1 720	1 840	1 534	668	180
2005	7 155	254	76	178	6 901	748	1 759	1 886	1 616	711	182
2006	7 354	275	99	175	7 079	804	1 797	1 882	1 680	734	184
2007	7 500	254	82	172	7 245	816	1 851	1 916	1 717	750	195
2008	7 398	247	70	177	7 151	794	1 805	1 854	1 703	792	204

Table 1-11. Employed Civilians, by Age, Sex, Race, and Hispanic Origin, 1948–2008—*Continued*

(Thousands of people.)

Race, Hispanic origin, sex, and year	16 years and over	16 to 19 years			20 years and over						
		Total	16 to 17 years	18 to 19 years	Total	20 to 24 years	25 to 34 years	35 to 44 years	45 to 54 years	55 to 64 years	65 years and over
BLACK											
Women											
1972	3 433	200	65	134	3 233	519	850	739	641	373	113
1973	3 601	239	81	158	3 362	546	920	761	644	389	101
1974	3 677	232	77	155	3 445	562	981	770	649	383	98
1975	3 618	231	85	146	3 388	520	985	752	638	387	104
1976	3 823	224	70	154	3 599	558	1 092	782	653	398	115
1977	3 975	217	64	153	3 758	585	1 172	814	671	408	109
1978	4 307	260	85	175	4 047	662	1 283	879	691	416	118
1979	4 436	263	92	171	4 174	670	1 333	919	702	428	119
1980	4 515	248	82	165	4 267	663	1 389	936	717	448	113
1981	4 561	232	75	157	4 329	653	1 415	966	725	462	108
1982	4 552	205	73	132	4 347	623	1 416	1 028	719	457	103
1983	4 622	194	59	136	4 428	596	1 493	1 073	707	460	99
1984	4 995	222	67	155	4 773	673	1 588	1 173	753	485	101
1985	5 231	254	83	171	4 977	673	1 656	1 240	804	484	121
1986	5 386	259	87	171	5 128	696	1 708	1 313	835	475	102
1987	5 648	283	93	190	5 365	693	1 793	1 412	860	489	117
1988	5 834	285	101	184	5 548	697	1 844	1 491	905	482	129
1989	6 025	298	113	185	5 727	725	1 870	1 566	959	472	134
1990	6 180	296	96	200	5 884	707	1 907	1 701	971	464	135
1991	6 113	239	76	164	5 874	677	1 855	1 768	969	476	129
1992	6 221	243	79	164	5 978	664	1 880	1 791	1 034	487	123
1993	6 334	239	82	157	6 095	703	1 842	1 867	1 081	480	121
1994	6 595	275	117	158	6 320	731	1 882	1 926	1 147	497	136
1995	6 857	301	112	189	6 556	729	1 949	2 025	1 202	536	114
1996	7 086	324	124	200	6 762	726	1 984	2 096	1 297	543	115
1997	7 362	349	122	227	7 013	789	2 029	2 139	1 373	561	122
1998	7 685	395	126	268	7 290	810	2 081	2 230	1 455	594	120
1999	8 029	366	123	243	7 663	893	2 165	2 312	1 545	609	139
2000	8 073	370	131	240	7 703	862	2 128	2 277	1 647	630	158
2001	8 068	327	115	212	7 741	868	2 084	2 269	1 686	668	165
2002	7 914	304	99	205	7 610	819	1 997	2 209	1 717	708	160
2003	7 919	283	107	175	7 636	790	1 959	2 211	1 770	735	171
2004	7 997	289	93	196	7 707	833	1 914	2 199	1 798	784	179
2005	8 158	282	88	194	7 876	852	1 964	2 175	1 848	844	193
2006	8 410	343	116	227	8 068	839	2 012	2 191	1 890	925	210
2007	8 551	311	120	191	8 240	858	2 037	2 205	1 941	982	218
2008	8 554	294	102	192	8 260	831	2 065	2 161	1 967	1 000	236
HISPANIC[1]											
Both Sexes											
1973	3 396	325	...	...	...	...	...	...	...	...	...
1974	3 687	355	...	...	...	...	...	...	...	...	...
1975	3 663	322	...	...	...	...	...	...	...	...	...
1976	3 720	341	124	230	3 436	614	1 135	803	573	269	42
1977	4 079	381	135	245	3 715	715	1 212	860	608	269	50
1978	4 527	423	159	264	4 104	803	1 330	942	661	307	62
1979	4 785	445	152	292	4 340	860	1 430	996	666	319	69
1980	5 527	500	174	325	5 028	998	1 675	1 074	811	389	80
1981	5 813	459	155	304	5 354	1 060	1 837	1 147	829	399	82
1982	5 805	410	119	291	5 394	1 030	1 896	1 173	816	399	80
1983	6 072	423	125	297	5 649	1 068	1 997	1 224	837	441	81
1984	6 651	468	148	320	6 182	1 160	2 201	1 385	883	474	79
1985	6 888	438	144	294	6 449	1 187	2 316	1 473	913	486	75
1986	7 219	430	146	284	6 789	1 231	2 427	1 570	1 011	474	76
1987	7 790	474	149	325	7 316	1 273	2 668	1 775	1 010	512	76
1988	8 250	523	171	353	7 727	1 341	2 749	1 876	1 078	585	97
1989	8 573	548	165	383	8 025	1 325	2 900	1 968	1 129	589	114
1990	9 845	668	208	460	9 177	1 672	3 327	2 229	1 235	611	103
1991	9 828	602	169	433	9 225	1 622	3 264	2 333	1 266	637	103
1992	10 027	577	169	408	9 450	1 575	3 350	2 468	1 316	628	112
1993	10 361	570	160	410	9 792	1 574	3 446	2 605	1 402	630	135
1994	10 788	609	195	415	10 178	1 643	3 517	2 737	1 495	647	139
1995	11 127	645	194	450	10 483	1 609	3 618	2 889	1 565	666	135
1996	11 642	646	199	447	10 996	1 628	3 758	3 115	1 595	748	152
1997	12 726	714	228	487	12 012	1 798	4 029	3 371	1 846	794	173
1998	13 291	793	230	563	12 498	1 883	4 113	3 504	1 994	846	158
1999	13 720	854	254	600	12 866	1 881	4 097	3 738	2 074	886	190
2000	15 735	973	285	688	14 762	2 356	4 950	4 052	2 308	898	197
2001	16 190	969	268	701	15 221	2 404	5 065	4 149	2 472	944	187
2002	16 590	882	254	628	15 708	2 413	5 272	4 273	2 511	1 029	209
2003	17 372	768	242	525	16 604	2 399	5 541	4 573	2 711	1 132	249
2004	17 930	792	211	581	17 138	2 477	5 560	4 671	2 932	1 210	288
2005	18 632	847	253	595	17 785	2 423	5 756	4 879	3 114	1 317	296
2006	19 613	900	287	614	18 712	2 487	6 001	5 106	3 324	1 441	354
2007	20 382	894	269	625	19 488	2 516	6 237	5 314	3 547	1 499	376
2008	20 346	870	248	622	19 476	2 361	6 119	5 371	3 620	1 619	385

[1]May be of any race.

. . . = Not available.

Table 1-11. Employed Civilians, by Age, Sex, Race, and Hispanic Origin, 1948–2008—*Continued*

(Thousands of people.)

Race, Hispanic origin, sex, and year	16 years and over	16 to 19 years			20 years and over						
		Total	16 to 17 years	18 to 19 years	Total	20 to 24 years	25 to 34 years	35 to 44 years	45 to 54 years	55 to 64 years	65 years and over
HISPANIC[1]											
Men											
1973	2 198	. . .	. . .	. . .	2 010	. . .	. . .	. . .	. . .	. . .	. . .
1974	2 369	. . .	. . .	. . .	2 165	. . .	. . .	. . .	. . .	. . .	. . .
1975	2 301	. . .	. . .	. . .	2 117	. . .	. . .	. . .	. . .	. . .	. . .
1976	2 303	199	74	125	2 109	364	708	504	369	173	. . .
1977	2 564	225	78	147	2 335	427	763	540	394	184	. . .
1978	2 808	241	93	147	2 568	494	824	590	405	207	. . .
1979	2 962	260	93	168	2 701	511	891	615	427	205	. . .
1980	3 448	306	109	198	3 142	611	1 065	662	491	254	. . .
1981	3 597	272	90	182	3 325	642	1 157	707	504	259	. . .
1982	3 583	229	66	162	3 354	621	1 192	729	498	261	. . .
1983	3 771	248	71	177	3 523	655	1 280	760	499	275	. . .
1984	4 083	258	78	180	3 825	718	1 398	841	530	292	. . .
1985	4 245	251	82	169	3 994	727	1 473	888	550	308	. . .
1986	4 428	254	82	172	4 174	773	1 510	929	614	297	. . .
1987	4 713	268	81	188	4 444	777	1 664	1 044	606	303	. . .
1988	4 972	292	87	205	4 680	815	1 706	1 120	645	331	. . .
1989	5 172	319	94	225	4 853	821	1 787	1 152	676	350	. . .
1990	6 021	412	126	286	5 609	1 083	2 076	1 312	722	355	. . .
1991	5 979	356	94	263	5 623	1 063	2 050	1 360	719	369	. . .
1992	6 093	336	97	238	5 757	985	2 127	1 437	768	372	. . .
1993	6 328	337	95	242	5 992	1 003	2 200	1 527	822	360	. . .
1994	6 530	341	109	233	6 189	1 056	2 227	1 600	847	379	79
1995	6 725	358	110	248	6 367	1 030	2 284	1 675	908	384	85
1996	7 039	384	107	277	6 655	1 015	2 345	1 842	918	438	96
1997	7 728	420	130	290	7 307	1 142	2 547	1 978	1 059	477	105
1998	8 018	449	133	315	7 570	1 173	2 592	2 077	1 115	512	101
1999	8 067	491	139	352	7 576	1 135	2 524	2 135	1 151	502	130
2000	9 428	570	159	411	8 859	1 486	3 063	2 358	1 295	532	126
2001	9 668	568	149	419	9 100	1 473	3 142	2 446	1 375	545	119
2002	9 845	504	141	363	9 341	1 476	3 271	2 503	1 396	569	125
2003	10 479	415	121	294	10 063	1 485	3 537	2 724	1 533	639	144
2004	10 832	446	108	338	10 385	1 514	3 557	2 801	1 654	687	174
2005	11 337	465	137	328	10 872	1 511	3 711	2 939	1 781	748	183
2006	11 887	496	146	350	11 391	1 535	3 845	3 088	1 894	809	220
2007	12 310	483	145	338	11 827	1 524	3 982	3 220	2 012	869	220
2008	12 248	479	140	340	11 769	1 406	3 897	3 233	2 080	929	224
HISPANIC[1]											
Women											
1973	1 198	. . .	. . .	. . .	1 060	. . .	. . .	. . .	. . .	. . .	. . .
1974	1 319	. . .	. . .	. . .	1 166	. . .	. . .	. . .	. . .	. . .	. . .
1975	1 362	. . .	. . .	. . .	1 224	. . .	. . .	. . .	. . .	. . .	. . .
1976	1 417	155	50	106	1 288	249	427	300	204	96	. . .
1977	1 516	155	57	98	1 370	288	449	320	214	86	. . .
1978	1 719	182	65	117	1 537	308	506	352	256	99	. . .
1979	1 824	185	60	125	1 638	349	539	381	241	115	. . .
1980	2 079	193	65	128	1 886	387	610	412	320	136	. . .
1981	2 216	187	65	122	2 029	418	680	440	326	139	. . .
1982	2 222	181	52	129	2 040	409	704	444	318	139	. . .
1983	2 301	175	54	120	2 127	413	717	464	338	166	. . .
1984	2 568	211	71	140	2 357	442	804	544	354	181	. . .
1985	2 642	187	62	125	2 456	460	843	585	362	178	. . .
1986	2 791	176	64	112	2 615	458	917	641	397	177	. . .
1987	3 077	206	69	137	2 872	496	1 004	732	405	209	. . .
1988	3 278	231	84	147	3 047	526	1 042	756	434	254	. . .
1989	3 401	229	71	158	3 172	504	1 114	816	453	239	. . .
1990	3 823	256	82	174	3 567	588	1 251	917	513	256	. . .
1991	3 848	246	76	170	3 603	559	1 214	972	548	268	. . .
1992	3 934	242	72	170	3 693	591	1 223	1 031	548	256	. . .
1993	4 033	233	65	168	3 800	571	1 246	1 077	581	269	. . .
1994	4 258	268	86	182	3 989	587	1 290	1 137	648	268	59
1995	4 403	287	85	202	4 116	579	1 334	1 213	657	282	50
1996	4 602	261	92	169	4 341	612	1 412	1 273	677	310	56
1997	4 999	294	98	196	4 705	656	1 482	1 393	787	318	69
1998	5 273	345	97	247	4 928	710	1 521	1 428	879	334	57
1999	5 653	363	115	248	5 290	746	1 574	1 603	923	384	60
2000	6 307	404	127	277	5 903	870	1 887	1 695	1 013	366	72
2001	6 522	401	119	282	6 121	931	1 923	1 703	1 097	398	67
2002	6 744	378	113	265	6 367	937	2 001	1 770	1 114	460	84
2003	6 894	353	121	231	6 541	914	2 004	1 849	1 178	493	105
2004	7 098	346	103	243	6 752	964	2 003	1 870	1 279	523	114
2005	7 295	382	116	266	6 913	912	2 045	1 940	1 333	569	113
2006	7 725	404	140	264	7 321	951	2 155	2 018	1 430	632	135
2007	8 072	410	124	287	7 662	991	2 255	2 094	1 535	631	155
2008	8 098	391	108	282	7 707	955	2 222	2 138	1 541	690	161

[1]May be of any race.
. . . = Not available.

Table 1-12. Civilian Employment-Population Ratios, by Sex, Age, Race, and Hispanic Origin, 1948–2008

(Percent.)

Race, Hispanic origin, and year	Both sexes			Men			Women		
	16 years and over	16 to 19 years	20 years and over	16 years and over	16 to 19 years	20 years and over	16 years and over	16 to 19 years	20 years and over
ALL RACES									
1948	56.6	47.7	57.4	83.5	57.5	85.8	31.3	38.5	30.7
1949	55.4	45.2	56.3	81.3	53.8	83.7	31.2	37.2	30.6
1950	56.1	45.5	57.0	82.0	55.2	84.2	32.0	36.3	31.6
1951	57.3	47.9	58.1	84.0	57.9	86.1	33.1	38.9	32.6
1952	57.3	46.9	58.1	83.9	55.9	86.2	33.4	38.8	33.0
1953	57.1	46.4	58.0	83.6	55.9	85.9	33.3	37.8	32.9
1954	55.5	42.3	56.6	81.0	50.2	83.5	32.5	34.9	32.3
1955	56.7	43.5	57.8	81.8	52.1	84.3	34.0	35.6	33.8
1956	57.5	45.3	58.5	82.3	53.8	84.6	35.1	37.5	34.9
1957	57.1	43.9	58.2	81.3	51.8	83.8	35.1	36.7	35.0
1958	55.4	39.9	56.8	78.5	46.9	81.2	34.5	33.5	34.6
1959	56.0	39.9	57.5	79.3	47.2	82.3	35.0	33.0	35.1
1960	56.1	40.5	57.6	78.9	47.6	81.9	35.5	33.8	35.7
1961	55.4	39.1	56.9	77.6	45.3	80.8	35.4	33.2	35.6
1962	55.5	39.4	57.1	77.7	45.9	80.9	35.6	33.3	35.8
1963	55.4	37.4	57.2	77.1	43.8	80.6	35.8	31.5	36.3
1964	55.7	37.3	57.7	77.3	44.1	80.9	36.3	30.9	36.9
1965	56.2	38.9	58.2	77.5	46.2	81.2	37.1	32.0	37.6
1966	56.9	42.1	58.7	77.9	48.9	81.5	38.3	35.6	38.6
1967	57.3	42.2	59.0	78.0	48.7	81.5	39.0	35.9	39.3
1968	57.5	42.2	59.3	77.8	48.7	81.3	39.6	36.0	40.0
1969	58.0	43.4	59.7	77.6	49.5	81.1	40.7	37.5	41.1
1970	57.4	42.3	59.2	76.2	47.7	79.7	40.8	37.1	41.2
1971	56.6	41.3	58.4	74.9	46.8	78.5	40.4	36.0	40.9
1972	57.0	43.5	58.6	75.0	48.9	78.4	41.0	38.2	41.3
1973	57.8	45.9	59.3	75.5	51.4	78.6	42.0	40.5	42.2
1974	57.8	46.0	59.2	74.9	51.2	77.9	42.6	41.0	42.8
1975	56.1	43.3	57.6	71.7	47.2	74.8	42.0	39.4	42.3
1976	56.8	44.2	58.3	72.0	47.9	75.1	43.2	40.5	43.5
1977	57.9	46.1	59.2	72.8	50.4	75.6	44.5	41.8	44.8
1978	59.3	48.3	60.6	73.8	52.2	76.4	46.4	44.5	46.6
1979	59.9	48.5	61.2	73.8	51.7	76.5	47.5	45.3	47.7
1980	59.2	46.6	60.6	72.0	49.5	74.6	47.7	43.8	48.1
1981	59.0	44.6	60.5	71.3	47.1	74.0	48.0	42.0	48.6
1982	57.8	41.5	59.4	69.0	42.9	71.8	47.7	40.2	48.4
1983	57.9	41.5	59.5	68.8	43.1	71.4	48.0	40.0	48.8
1984	59.5	43.7	61.0	70.7	45.0	73.2	49.5	42.5	50.1
1985	60.1	44.4	61.5	70.9	45.7	73.3	50.4	42.9	51.0
1986	60.7	44.6	62.1	71.0	45.7	73.3	51.4	43.6	52.0
1987	61.5	45.5	62.9	71.5	46.1	73.8	52.5	44.8	53.1
1988	62.3	46.8	63.6	72.0	47.8	74.2	53.4	45.9	54.0
1989	63.0	47.5	64.2	72.5	48.7	74.5	54.3	46.4	54.9
1990	62.8	45.3	64.3	72.0	46.6	74.3	54.3	44.0	55.2
1991	61.7	42.0	63.2	70.4	42.7	72.7	53.7	41.2	54.6
1992	61.5	41.0	63.0	69.8	41.9	72.1	53.8	40.0	54.8
1993	61.7	41.7	63.3	70.0	42.3	72.3	54.1	41.0	55.0
1994	62.5	43.4	64.0	70.4	43.8	72.6	55.3	43.0	56.2
1995	62.9	44.2	64.4	70.8	44.7	73.0	55.6	43.8	56.5
1996	63.2	43.5	64.7	70.9	43.6	73.2	56.0	43.5	57.0
1997	63.8	43.4	65.5	71.3	43.4	73.7	56.8	43.3	57.8
1998	64.1	45.1	65.6	71.6	44.7	73.9	57.1	45.5	58.0
1999	64.3	44.7	65.9	71.6	45.1	74.0	57.4	44.3	58.5
2000	64.4	45.2	66.0	71.9	45.4	74.2	57.5	45.0	58.4
2001	63.7	42.3	65.4	70.9	42.2	73.3	57.0	42.4	58.1
2002	62.7	39.6	64.6	69.7	38.9	72.3	56.3	40.3	57.5
2003	62.3	36.8	64.3	68.9	35.7	71.7	56.1	37.8	57.5
2004	62.3	36.4	64.4	69.2	35.9	71.9	56.0	37.0	57.4
2005	62.7	36.5	64.7	69.6	35.1	72.4	56.2	37.8	57.6
2006	63.1	36.9	65.2	70.1	36.3	72.9	56.6	37.6	58.0
2007	63.0	34.8	65.2	69.8	33.9	72.8	56.6	35.8	58.2
2008	62.2	32.6	64.5	68.5	31.6	71.6	56.2	33.7	57.9

Table 1-12. Civilian Employment-Population Ratios, by Sex, Age, Race, and Hispanic Origin, 1948–2008
—Continued

(Percent.)

Race, Hispanic origin, and year	Both sexes			Men			Women		
	16 years and over	16 to 19 years	20 years and over	16 years and over	16 to 19 years	20 years and over	16 years and over	16 to 19 years	20 years and over
WHITE[1]									
1954	55.2	42.9	56.2	81.5	49.9	84.0	31.4	36.4	31.1
1955	56.5	44.2	57.4	82.2	52.0	84.7	33.0	37.0	32.7
1956	57.3	46.1	58.2	82.7	54.1	85.0	34.2	38.9	33.8
1957	56.8	45.0	57.8	81.8	52.4	84.1	34.2	38.2	33.9
1958	55.3	41.0	56.5	79.2	47.6	81.8	33.6	35.0	33.5
1959	55.9	41.2	57.2	79.9	48.1	82.8	34.0	34.8	34.0
1960	55.9	41.5	57.2	79.4	48.1	82.4	34.6	35.1	34.5
1961	55.3	40.1	56.7	78.2	45.9	81.4	34.5	34.6	34.5
1962	55.4	40.4	56.9	78.4	46.4	81.5	34.7	34.8	34.7
1963	55.3	38.6	56.9	77.7	44.7	81.1	35.0	32.9	35.2
1964	55.5	38.4	57.3	77.8	45.0	81.3	35.5	32.2	35.8
1965	56.0	40.3	57.8	77.9	47.1	81.5	36.2	33.7	36.5
1966	56.8	43.6	58.3	78.3	50.1	81.7	37.5	37.5	37.5
1967	57.2	43.8	58.7	78.4	50.2	81.7	38.3	37.7	38.3
1968	57.4	43.9	59.0	78.3	50.3	81.6	38.9	37.8	39.1
1969	58.0	45.2	59.4	78.2	51.1	81.4	40.1	39.5	40.1
1970	57.5	44.5	59.0	76.8	49.6	80.1	40.3	39.5	40.4
1971	56.8	43.8	58.3	75.7	49.2	79.0	39.9	38.6	40.1
1972	57.4	46.4	58.6	76.0	51.5	79.0	40.7	41.3	40.6
1973	58.2	48.9	59.3	76.5	54.3	79.2	41.8	43.6	41.6
1974	58.3	49.3	59.3	75.9	54.4	78.6	42.4	44.3	42.2
1975	56.7	46.5	57.9	73.0	50.6	75.7	42.0	42.5	41.9
1976	57.5	47.8	58.6	73.4	51.5	76.0	43.2	44.2	43.1
1977	58.6	50.1	59.6	74.1	54.4	76.5	44.5	45.9	44.4
1978	60.0	52.4	60.8	75.0	56.3	77.2	46.3	48.5	46.1
1979	60.6	52.6	61.5	75.1	55.7	77.3	47.5	49.4	47.3
1980	60.0	50.7	61.0	73.4	53.4	75.6	47.8	47.9	47.8
1981	60.0	48.7	61.1	72.8	51.3	75.1	48.3	46.2	48.5
1982	58.8	45.8	60.1	70.6	47.0	73.0	48.1	44.6	48.4
1983	58.9	45.9	60.1	70.4	47.4	72.6	48.5	44.5	48.9
1984	60.5	48.0	61.5	72.1	49.1	74.3	49.8	47.0	50.0
1985	61.0	48.5	62.0	72.3	49.9	74.3	50.7	47.1	51.0
1986	61.5	48.8	62.6	72.3	49.6	74.3	51.7	47.9	52.0
1987	62.3	49.4	63.4	72.7	49.9	74.7	52.8	49.0	53.1
1988	63.1	50.9	64.1	73.2	51.7	75.1	53.8	50.2	54.0
1989	63.8	51.6	64.7	73.7	52.6	75.4	54.6	50.5	54.9
1990	63.7	49.7	64.8	73.3	51.0	75.1	54.7	48.3	55.2
1991	62.6	46.6	63.7	71.6	47.2	73.5	54.2	45.9	54.8
1992	62.4	45.3	63.6	71.1	46.4	73.1	54.2	44.2	54.9
1993	62.7	46.2	63.9	71.4	46.6	73.3	54.6	45.7	55.2
1994	63.5	47.9	64.7	71.8	48.3	73.6	55.8	47.5	56.4
1995	63.8	48.8	64.9	72.0	49.4	73.8	56.1	48.1	56.7
1996	64.1	47.9	65.3	72.3	48.2	74.2	56.3	47.6	57.0
1997	64.6	47.7	65.9	72.7	48.1	74.7	57.0	47.2	57.8
1998	64.7	48.9	65.9	72.7	48.6	74.7	57.1	49.3	57.7
1999	64.8	48.8	66.1	72.8	49.3	74.8	57.3	48.3	58.0
2000	64.9	49.1	66.1	73.0	49.5	74.9	57.4	48.8	58.0
2001	64.2	46.3	65.6	72.0	46.2	74.0	57.0	46.5	57.7
2002	63.4	43.2	64.9	70.8	42.3	73.1	56.4	44.1	57.3
2003	63.0	40.4	64.7	70.1	39.4	72.5	56.3	41.5	57.3
2004	63.1	40.0	64.8	70.4	39.7	72.8	56.1	40.3	57.2
2005	63.4	40.2	65.1	70.8	38.8	73.3	56.3	41.8	57.4
2006	63.8	40.6	65.5	71.3	40.0	73.7	56.6	41.1	57.7
2007	63.6	38.3	65.5	70.9	37.3	73.5	56.7	39.2	57.9
2008	62.8	35.9	64.8	69.7	34.8	72.4	56.3	37.1	57.7

[1]Beginning in 2003, persons who selected this race group only; persons who selected more than one race group are not included. Prior to 2003, persons who reported more than one race group were included in the group they identified as their main race.

Table 1-12. Civilian Employment-Population Ratios, by Sex, Age, Race, and Hispanic Origin, 1948–2008
—Continued

(Percent.)

Race, Hispanic origin, and year	Both sexes			Men			Women		
	16 years and over	16 to 19 years	20 years and over	16 years and over	16 to 19 years	20 years and over	16 years and over	16 to 19 years	20 years and over
BLACK[1]									
1972	53.7	25.2	58.3	66.8	31.6	73.0	43.0	19.2	46.5
1973	54.5	27.2	58.9	67.5	32.8	73.7	43.8	22.0	47.2
1974	53.5	25.9	58.0	65.8	31.4	71.9	43.5	20.9	46.9
1975	50.1	23.1	54.5	60.6	26.3	66.5	41.6	20.2	44.9
1976	50.8	22.4	55.4	60.6	25.8	66.8	42.8	19.2	46.4
1977	51.4	22.3	56.0	61.4	26.4	67.5	43.3	18.5	47.0
1978	53.6	25.2	58.0	63.3	28.5	69.1	45.8	22.1	49.3
1979	53.8	25.4	58.1	63.4	28.7	69.1	46.0	22.4	49.3
1980	52.3	23.9	56.4	60.4	27.0	65.8	45.7	21.0	49.1
1981	51.3	22.1	55.5	59.1	24.6	64.5	45.1	19.7	48.5
1982	49.4	19.0	53.6	56.0	20.3	61.4	44.2	17.7	47.5
1983	49.5	18.7	53.6	56.3	20.4	61.6	44.1	17.0	47.4
1984	52.3	21.9	56.1	59.2	23.9	64.1	46.7	20.1	49.8
1985	53.4	24.6	57.0	60.0	26.3	64.6	48.1	23.1	50.9
1986	54.1	25.1	57.6	60.6	26.5	65.1	48.8	23.8	51.6
1987	55.6	27.1	58.9	62.0	28.5	66.4	50.3	25.8	53.0
1988	56.3	27.6	59.7	62.7	29.4	67.1	51.2	25.8	53.9
1989	56.9	28.7	60.1	62.8	30.4	67.0	52.0	27.1	54.6
1990	56.7	26.7	60.2	62.6	27.7	67.1	51.9	25.8	54.7
1991	55.4	22.6	59.0	61.3	23.8	65.9	50.6	21.5	53.6
1992	54.9	22.8	58.3	59.9	23.6	64.3	50.8	22.1	53.6
1993	55.0	22.6	58.4	60.0	23.6	64.3	50.9	21.6	53.8
1994	56.1	24.9	59.4	60.8	25.4	65.0	52.3	24.5	55.0
1995	57.1	25.7	60.5	61.7	25.2	66.1	53.4	26.1	56.1
1996	57.4	26.0	60.8	61.1	24.9	65.5	54.4	27.1	57.1
1997	58.2	26.1	61.8	61.4	23.7	66.1	55.6	28.5	58.4
1998	59.7	30.1	63.0	62.9	28.4	67.1	57.2	31.8	59.7
1999	60.6	27.9	64.2	63.1	26.7	67.5	58.6	29.0	61.5
2000	60.9	29.8	64.2	63.6	28.9	67.7	58.6	30.6	61.3
2001	59.7	26.7	63.2	62.1	26.4	66.3	57.8	27.0	60.7
2002	58.1	25.3	61.6	61.1	25.6	65.2	55.8	24.9	58.7
2003	57.4	21.7	61.0	59.5	19.9	64.1	55.6	23.4	58.6
2004	57.2	21.5	60.9	59.3	19.3	63.9	55.5	23.6	58.5
2005	57.7	21.6	61.5	60.2	20.8	64.7	55.7	22.4	58.9
2006	58.4	24.1	62.0	60.6	21.7	65.2	56.5	26.4	59.4
2007	58.4	21.4	62.3	60.7	19.5	65.5	56.5	23.3	59.8
2008	57.3	20.2	61.2	59.1	18.7	63.9	55.8	21.7	59.1
HISPANIC[2]									
1973	55.6	. . .	. . .	. . .	. . .	. . .	. . .	. . .	. . .
1974	56.2	. . .	. . .	. . .	. . .	. . .	. . .	. . .	. . .
1975	53.4	. . .	. . .	. . .	. . .	. . .	. . .	. . .	. . .
1976	53.8	. . .	56.6	. . .	. . .	. . .	. . .	. . .	. . .
1977	55.4	. . .	58.3	. . .	. . .	. . .	. . .	. . .	. . .
1978	57.2	. . .	60.0	. . .	. . .	. . .	. . .	. . .	. . .
1979	58.3	. . .	61.0	. . .	. . .	. . .	. . .	. . .	. . .
1980	57.6	. . .	60.5	. . .	. . .	. . .	. . .	. . .	. . .
1981	57.4	. . .	60.7	. . .	. . .	. . .	. . .	. . .	. . .
1982	54.9	. . .	58.2	. . .	. . .	. . .	. . .	. . .	. . .
1983	55.1	. . .	58.1	. . .	. . .	. . .	. . .	. . .	. . .
1984	57.9	. . .	60.7	. . .	. . .	. . .	. . .	. . .	. . .
1985	57.8	. . .	60.7	. . .	. . .	. . .	. . .	. . .	. . .
1986	58.5	. . .	61.5	. . .	. . .	. . .	. . .	. . .	. . .
1987	60.5	. . .	63.4	. . .	. . .	. . .	. . .	. . .	. . .
1988	61.9	. . .	64.6	. . .	. . .	. . .	. . .	. . .	. . .
1989	62.2	. . .	64.8	. . .	. . .	. . .	. . .	. . .	. . .
1990	61.9	. . .	64.8	. . .	. . .	. . .	. . .	. . .	. . .
1991	59.8	. . .	62.8	. . .	. . .	. . .	. . .	. . .	. . .
1992	59.1	. . .	62.1	. . .	. . .	. . .	. . .	. . .	. . .
1993	59.1	. . .	62.1	. . .	. . .	. . .	. . .	. . .	. . .
1994	59.5	33.5	62.4	71.7	36.8	. . .	47.2	30.1	. . .
1995	59.7	34.4	62.6	72.1	37.5	. . .	47.3	31.3	. . .
1996	60.6	33.1	63.7	73.3	38.8	. . .	47.9	27.3	. . .
1997	62.6	33.7	66.0	74.5	37.6	. . .	50.2	29.3	. . .
1998	63.1	36.0	66.2	74.7	38.6	. . .	51.0	33.0	. . .
1999	63.4	37.0	66.5	75.3	41.2	. . .	51.7	32.5	. . .
2000	65.7	38.6	68.9	77.4	42.8	81.7	53.6	33.9	55.8
2001	64.9	38.6	67.8	76.2	43.3	79.9	53.3	33.5	55.4
2002	63.9	35.2	67.0	74.5	39.0	78.3	52.9	31.1	55.2
2003	63.1	30.2	66.4	74.3	31.9	78.6	51.2	28.4	53.6
2004	63.8	30.4	67.2	75.1	33.4	79.4	51.8	27.2	54.4
2005	64.0	31.5	67.3	75.8	33.8	80.0	51.5	29.1	53.8
2006	65.2	32.2	68.5	76.8	34.8	81.1	52.8	29.5	55.2
2007	64.9	30.4	68.5	76.2	32.1	80.7	53.0	28.5	55.6
2008	63.3	28.6	66.9	74.1	30.9	78.6	51.9	26.2	54.6

[1]Beginning in 2003, persons who selected this race group only; persons who selected more than one race group are not included. Prior to 2003, persons who reported more than one race group were included in the group they identified as their main race.
[2]May be of any race.
. . . = Not available.

Table 1-13. Employed Civilians, by Sex, Race, Hispanic Origin, and Occupation, 2006–2008

(Thousands of people.)

Year and occupation	Total	Men	Women	White[1]	Black[1]	Hispanic[2]
2006						
All Occupations	144 427	77 502	66 925	118 833	15 765	19 613
Management, professional, and related occupations	50 420	24 928	25 492	42 177	4 252	3 337
Management, business, and financial operations	21 233	12 347	8 886	18 298	1 547	1 477
Computer and mathematical occupations	3 209	2 354	855	2 392	233	3 209
Architecture and engineering occupations	2 830	2 418	412	2 368	158	167
Life, physical and social science occupations	1 434	813	620	1 146	81	1 434
Community and social service occupations	2 156	829	1 327	1 631	402	184
Legal occupations	1 637	791	846	1 455	107	93
Education, training, and library occupations	8 126	2 100	6 026	6 900	795	591
Arts, design, entertainment, sports, and media occupations	2 735	1 401	1 334	2 370	183	214
Healthcare practitioner and technical occupations	7 060	1 875	5 185	5 617	746	7 060
Healthcare support occupations	3 132	333	2 799	2 137	774	3 132
Protective service occupations	2 939	2 284	654	2 239	578	2 939
Food preparation and serving related occupations	7 606	3 297	4 309	6 071	892	7 606
Building and grounds cleaning and maintenance occupations	5 381	3 230	2 151	4 264	840	1 712
Personal care and service occupations	4 754	1 014	3 740	3 600	714	618
Sales and related occupations	16 641	8 478	8 163	14 026	1 503	1 839
Office and administrative support occupations	19 500	4 797	14 703	15 772	2 548	2 314
Farming, fishing, and forestry occupations	961	750	212	870	47	961
Construction and extraction occupations	9 507	9 216	8 481	8 235	624	2 790
Installation, maintenance, and repair occupations	5 362	5 114	248	4 674	408	5 362
Production occupations	9 378	6 529	2 850	7 548	1 148	1 936
Transportation and material moving occupations	8 846	7 533	1 313	6 974	1 438	1 645
2007						
All Occupations	146 047	78 254	67 792	119 792	16 051	20 382
Management, professional, and related occupations	51 788	25 593	26 195	43 235	4 343	3 621
Management, business, and financial operations	21 577	12 375	9 203	18 511	1 626	1 580
Computer and mathematical occupations	3 441	2 560	881	2 523	247	179
Architecture and engineering occupations	2 932	2 511	421	2 449	154	189
Life, physical and social science occupations	1 382	792	591	1 094	80	64
Community and social service occupations	2 265	890	1 375	1 720	416	216
Legal occupations	1 668	809	858	1 481	111	100
Education, training, and library occupations	8 485	2 267	6 218	7 215	814	646
Arts, design, entertainment, sports, and media occupations	2 789	1 476	1 313	2 453	159	241
Healthcare practitioner and technical occupations	7 248	1 913	5 335	5 788	736	407
Healthcare support occupations	3 138	338	2 800	2 182	753	441
Protective service occupations	3 071	2 380	691	2 347	581	307
Food preparation and serving related occupations	7 699	3 354	4 345	6 121	888	1 633
Building and grounds cleaning and maintenance occupations	5 469	3 280	2 189	4 325	833	1 875
Personal care and service occupations	4 760	986	3 774	3 612	678	648
Sales and related occupations	16 698	8 424	8 275	13 888	1 658	1 891
Office and administrative support occupations	19 513	4 840	14 673	15 772	2 543	2 415
Farming, fishing, and forestry occupations	960	759	201	859	47	388
Construction and extraction occupations	9 535	9 276	258	8 504	636	2 851
Installation, maintenance, and repair occupations	5 245	5 043	202	4 517	436	725
Production occupations	9 395	6 563	2 832	7 566	1 184	1 921
Transportation and material moving occupations	8 776	7 420	1 355	6 863	1 471	1 667
2008						
All Occupations	145 362	77 486	67 876	119 126	15 953	20 346
Management, professional, and related occupations	52 761	25 948	26 813	44 090	4 374	3 723
Management, business, and financial operations	22 059	12 647	9 412	18 938	1 599	1 652
Computer and mathematical occupations	3 676	2 765	911	2 730	267	188
Architecture and engineering occupations	2 931	2 536	395	2 446	148	196
Life, physical and social science occupations	1 307	704	603	1 030	93	62
Community and social service occupations	2 293	909	1 383	1 741	436	205
Legal occupations	1 671	803	867	1 481	116	110
Education, training, and library occupations	8 605	2 234	6 371	7 337	792	641
Arts, design, entertainment, sports, and media occupations	2 820	1 471	1 349	2 466	172	234
Healthcare practitioner and technical occupations	7 399	1 878	5 521	5 920	751	434
Healthcare support occupations	3 212	359	2 853	2 156	827	436
Protective service occupations	3 047	2 352	695	2 330	582	332
Food preparation and serving related occupations	7 824	3 443	4 381	6 199	946	1 645
Building and grounds cleaning and maintenance occupations	5 445	3 254	2 192	4 295	818	1 821
Personal care and service occupations	4 923	1 064	3 859	3 701	722	699
Sales and related occupations	35 544	13 067	22 477	29 160	4 075	4 361
Office and administrative support occupations	19 249	4 845	14 404	15 563	2 499	2 459
Farming, fishing, and forestry occupations	988	780	208	878	45	389
Construction and extraction occupations	8 667	8 448	219	7 747	545	2 564
Installation, maintenance, and repair occupations	5 152	4 953	199	4 451	437	749
Production occupations	8 973	6 313	2 661	7 210	1 093	1 892
Transportation and material moving occupations	8 827	7 507	1 319	6 909	1 487	1 736

[1]Beginning in 2003, persons who selected this race group only; persons who selected more than one race group are not included. Prior to 2003, persons who reported more than one race group were included in the group they identified as the main race.
[2]May be of any race.

Table 1-14. Employed Civilians, by Selected Occupation and Industry, 2006–2008

(Thousands of people.)

Year and industry	Total employed	Agriculture, forestry, fishing, and hunting	Mining	Construction	Manufacturing			Wholesale trade
					Total	Durable goods	Nondurable goods	
2006								
All Occupations	144 427	2 206	687	11 749	16 377	10 499	5 877	4 561
Management, professional, and related occupations	50 420	1 089	165	1 892	4 673	3 170	1 503	785
Management, business, and financial operations	21 233	1 042	87	1 693	2 587	1 638	949	585
Computer and mathematical occupations	3 209	2	9	14	474	379	95	80
Architecture and engineering occupations	2 830	4	41	135	1 055	902	153	47
Life, physical and social science occupations	1 434	35	22	13	238	54	184	19
Community and social service occupations	2 156	1	X	0	3	2	2	1
Legal occupations	1 637	1	3	5	23	14	9	2
Education, training, and library occupations	8 126	2	1	2	32	22	10	8
Arts, design, entertainment, sports, and media occupations	2 735	1	2	28	219	139	79	30
Healthcare practitioner and technical occupations	7 060	1	1	4	42	20	22	11
Healthcare support occupations	3 132	3	X	1	7	4	3	2
Protective service occupations	2 939	15	2	12	40	31	9	5
Food preparation and serving related occupations	7 606	3	1	4	29	10	18	6
Building and grounds cleaning and maintenance occupations	5 381	26	4	43	175	92	83	34
Personal care and service occupations	4 754	43	X	3	11	7	5	4
Sales and related occupations	16 641	8	8	105	626	343	283	1 630
Office and administrative support occupations	19 500	88	55	624	1 490	922	569	807
Farming, fishing, and forestry occupations	961	799	0	4	51	7	44	49
Construction and extraction occupations	9 507	15	248	8 026	337	284	53	40
Installation, maintenance, and repair occupations	5 362	16	72	565	807	520	287	232
Production occupations	9 378	33	34	182	6 786	4 345	2 441	153
Transportation and material moving occupations	8 846	69	99	286	1 344	765	579	815
2007								
All Occupations	146 047	2 095	736	11 856	16 302	10 363	5 938	4 367
Management, professional, and related occupations	51 788	1 013	171	1 931	4 654	3 169	1 485	704
Management, business, and financial operations	21 577	971	110	1 717	2 616	1 672	944	534
Computer and mathematical occupations	3 441	3	4	21	431	358	73	62
Architecture and engineering occupations	2 932	4	34	147	1 062	902	159	34
Life, physical and social science occupations	1 382	30	17	10	247	51	196	14
Community and social service occupations	2 265	1	X	0	3	3	1	X
Legal occupations	1 668	1	2	5	23	15	8	6
Education, training, and library occupations	8 485	1	X	5	25	16	9	6
Arts, design, entertainment, sports, and media occupations	2 789	1	1	24	210	132	78	35
Healthcare practitioner and technical occupations	7 248	2	2	2	36	19	17	13
Healthcare support occupations	3 138	0	X	0	11	5	5	2
Protective service occupations	3 071	26	1	15	38	24	14	6
Food preparation and serving related occupations	7 699	2	0	3	35	7	29	9
Building and grounds cleaning and maintenance occupations	5 469	22	4	48	129	74	55	22
Personal care and service occupations	4 760	29	X	3	8	3	5	3
Sales and related occupations	16 698	8	10	125	621	343	278	1 583
Office and administrative support occupations	19 513	77	59	621	1 521	931	590	19 513
Farming, fishing, and forestry occupations	960	785	1	6	65	11	54	47
Construction and extraction occupations	9 535	15	257	8 077	354	292	62	23
Installation, maintenance, and repair occupations	5 245	25	69	567	794	506	288	192
Production occupations	18 171	93	164	460	8 071	4 997	3 074	980
Transportation and material moving occupations	8 776	73	115	297	1 260	679	582	825
2008								
All Occupations	145 362	2 168	819	10 974	15 904	10 273	5 631	4 052
Management, professional, and related occupations	52 761	1 041	199	2 018	4 688	3 243	1 445	693
Management, business, and financial operations	22 059	996	117	1 804	2 523	1 639	884	553
Computer and mathematical occupations	3 676	4	8	18	513	425	88	56
Architecture and engineering occupations	2 931	4	45	159	1 107	955	152	24
Life, physical and social science occupations	1 307	24	20	7	242	47	194	12
Community and social service occupations	2 293	X	X	1	3	3	X	1
Legal occupations	1 671	1	4	2	24	13	11	7
Education, training, and library occupations	8 605	4	1	1	27	14	13	3
Arts, design, entertainment, sports, and media occupations	2 820	7	4	24	212	127	85	29
Healthcare practitioner and technical occupations	7 399	2	0	2	37	19	17	9
Healthcare support occupations	3 212	0	X	0	5	3	2	3
Protective service occupations	3 047	25	5	14	32	20	11	7
Food preparation and serving related occupations	7 824	2	1	2	38	11	27	14
Building and grounds cleaning and maintenance occupations	5 445	29	1	46	144	74	70	25
Personal care and service occupations	4 923	36	X	4	12	6	7	2
Sales and related occupations	16 295	11	11	81	625	334	291	1 468
Office and administrative support occupations	19 249	82	57	610	1 507	924	583	697
Farming, fishing, and forestry occupations	988	836	2	3	48	7	41	41
Construction and extraction occupations	8 667	6	285	7 241	322	254	68	38
Installation, maintenance, and repair occupations	5 152	19	74	527	798	538	260	151
Production occupations	8 973	14	63	169	6 434	4 158	2 275	123
Transportation and material moving occupations	8 827	66	120	260	1 250	700	551	788

X = Not applicable.

Table 1-14. Employed Civilians, by Selected Occupation and Industry, 2006–2008—*Continued*

(Thousands of people.)

Year and industry	Retail trade	Transportation and warehousing	Utilities	Information	Finance and insurance	Real estate and rental and leasing	Professional and technical services
2006							
All Occupations	16 767	6 269	1 186	3 573	7 254	3 237	8 776
Management, professional, and related occupations	1 797	668	351	1 804	3 506	997	6 734
Management, business, and financial operations	978	546	181	712	2 943	927	2 448
Computer and mathematical occupations	131	52	27	268	349	23	1 084
Architecture and engineering occupations	30	36	89	138	21	8	905
Life, physical and social science occupations	11	6	26	13	20	1	364
Community and social service occupations	2	0	1	1	18	5	14
Legal occupations	18	4	5	16	79	19	1 112
Education, training, and library occupations	20	10	6	126	26	4	45
Arts, design, entertainment, sports, and media occupations	211	11	12	528	21	10	602
Healthcare practitioner and technical occupations	396	3	3	1	28	2	161
Healthcare support occupations	36	0	X	1	6	3	49
Protective service occupations	67	40	11	8	36	21	15
Food preparation and serving related occupations	319	7	0	30	6	6	7
Building and grounds cleaning and maintenance occupations	144	60	9	25	15	215	28
Personal care and service occupations	43	181	2	37	4	25	X
Sales and related occupations	9 225	108	27	416	1 271	1 236	237
Office and administrative support occupations	2 538	1 593	218	679	2 331	399	1 379
Farming, fishing, and forestry occupations	14	3	1	X	X	X	2
Construction and extraction occupations	104	56	111	12	6	71	54
Installation, maintenance, and repair occupations	696	318	181	393	35	145	103
Production occupations	518	84	236	95	28	22	104
Transportation and material moving occupations	1 265	3 150	39	74	10	97	35
2007							
All Occupations	16 570	6 457	1 193	3 566	7 306	3 182	9 208
Management, professional, and related occupations	1 734	666	386	1 847	3 623	971	7 151
Management, business, and financial operations	916	550	195	714	3 017	893	2 597
Computer and mathematical occupations	142	45	42	315	379	29	4 554
Architecture and engineering occupations	17	31	100	133	14	6	1 004
Life, physical and social science occupations	18	5	22	12	23	3	341
Community and social service occupations	2	1	X	0	15	5	7
Legal occupations	21	3	6	12	90	17	1 089
Education, training, and library occupations	19	16	9	123	18	6	33
Arts, design, entertainment, sports, and media occupations	174	12	9	536	34	8	680
Healthcare practitioner and technical occupations	424	3	3	2	33	5	180
Healthcare support occupations	42	3	0	1	5	6	52
Protective service occupations	71	55	11	6	30	19	23
Food preparation and serving related occupations	327	18	1	33	4	22	5
Building and grounds cleaning and maintenance occupations	160	52	14	16	23	205	31
Personal care and service occupations	50	195	1	37	3	20	24
Sales and related occupations	9 269	112	18	413	1 259	1 229	262
Office and administrative support occupations	2 477	1 601	218	621	1 521	931	1 620
Farming, fishing, and forestry occupations	13	6	1	X	0	0	2
Construction and extraction occupations	114	61	123	15	11	58	52
Installation, maintenance, and repair occupations	646	336	165	415	31	154	97
Production occupations	1 688	3 312	268	147	29	130	152
Transportation and material moving occupations	1 177	3 214	56	65	12	105	36
2008							
All Occupations	16 533	6 501	1 225	3 481	7 279	2 949	9 362
Management, professional, and related occupations	1 746	726	380	1 815	3 679	878	7 367
Management, business, and financial operations	913	591	194	711	3 076	806	2 718
Computer and mathematical occupations	128	60	42	297	403	28	1 371
Architecture and engineering occupations	24	44	98	107	13	6	1
Life, physical and social science occupations	12	6	19	12	18	2	317
Community and social service occupations	4	1	X	X	18	5	7
Legal occupations	8	3	6	9	65	14	1 133
Education, training, and library occupations	24	12	5	109	24	3	39
Arts, design, entertainment, sports, and media occupations	209	8	10	565	29	8	641
Healthcare practitioner and technical occupations	425	2	6	4	33	5	156
Healthcare support occupations	46	3	X	2	3	5	51
Protective service occupations	60	40	11	4	30	15	30
Food preparation and serving related occupations	336	14	0	29	5	21	4
Building and grounds cleaning and maintenance occupations	153	53	20	21	22	215	30
Personal care and service occupations	51	183	1	36	6	19	22
Sales and related occupations	9 127	116	18	377	1 278	1 150	257
Office and administrative support occupations	2 481	1 610	217	657	2 198	329	1 321
Farming, fishing, and forestry occupations	13	4	X	0	1	0	0
Construction and extraction occupations	100	63	127	14	6	50	41
Installation, maintenance, and repair occupations	663	362	187	384	24	141	82
Production occupations	481	101	210	77	15	30	156
Transportation and material moving occupations	1 277	3 225	54	65	12	97	31

X = Not applicable.

Table 1-14. Employed Civilians, by Selected Occupation and Industry, 2006–2008—*Continued*

(Thousands of people.)

Year and industry	Management, administrative, and waste services	Educational services	Health care and social assistance	Arts, entertainment, and recreation	Accommodation and food services	Other services (except public administration)	Public administration
2006							
All Occupations	6 092	12 522	17 416	2 671	9 474	7 088	6 524
Management, professional, and related occupations	1 082	9 371	9 112	880	1 389	1 466	2 659
Management, business, and financial operations	726	1 113	1 410	235	1 309	563	1 148
Computer and mathematical occupations	96	180	123	16	14	33	235
Architecture and engineering occupations	46	42	23	7	7	20	175
Life, physical and social science occupations	23	217	215	9	2	15	186
Community and social service occupations	7	282	882	4	4	605	323
Legal occupations	24	9	25	1	1	16	274
Education, training, and library occupations	11	6 991	631	56	17	64	77
Arts, design, entertainment, sports, and media occupations	42	239	41	545	30	112	52
Healthcare practitioner and technical occupations	106	299	5 760	8	6	39	189
Healthcare support occupations	65	31	2 747	14	5	120	43
Protective service occupations	481	106	70	123	38	17	1 834
Food preparation and serving related occupations	22	446	376	251	6 003	67	25
Building and grounds cleaning and maintenance occupations	2 113	576	489	259	461	567	138
Personal care and service occupations	X	X	X	121	4	0	X
Sales and related occupations	320	69	62	166	660	437	28
Office and administrative support occupations	959	1 147	2 576	213	388	698	1 318
Farming, fishing, and forestry occupations	10	2	0	1	2	1	21
Construction and extraction occupations	122	76	57	18	14	36	105
Installation, maintenance, and repair occupations	178	140	106	72	55	1 099	149
Production occupations	233	51	148	24	101	477	70
Transportation and material moving occupations	480	258	117	48	241	341	79
2007							
All Occupations	6 412	12 828	17 834	2 833	9 582	6 972	6 746
Management, professional, and related occupations	1 200	9 727	9 411	947	1 425	1 488	2 738
Management, business, and financial operations	820	1 131	1 488	232	1 348	586	1 144
Computer and mathematical occupations	381	8 597	7 923	715	78	902	1 594
Architecture and engineering occupations	59	36	26	5	6	17	196
Life, physical and social science occupations	24	188	218	11	1	17	182
Community and social service occupations	9	297	914	6	2	647	354
Legal occupations	33	8	29	1	1	16	304
Education, training, and library occupations	14	7 396	615	71	16	36	77
Arts, design, entertainment, sports, and media occupations	36	209	48	591	28	104	49
Healthcare practitioner and technical occupations	113	273	5 922	11	8	27	189
Healthcare support occupations	72	26	2 735	16	8	117	42
Protective service occupations	515	108	69	127	39	15	1 899
Food preparation and serving related occupations	14	452	378	266	6 053	49	29
Building and grounds cleaning and maintenance occupations	2 250	554	486	269	476	569	135
Personal care and service occupations	33	206	1 613	658	92	1 711	74
Sales and related occupations	354	67	66	175	683	410	34
Office and administrative support occupations	1 404	1 219	2 683	389	1 100	1 099	1 383
Farming, fishing, and forestry occupations	9	2	2	2	0	4	14
Construction and extraction occupations	83	80	45	18	13	32	103
Installation, maintenance, and repair occupations	171	132	95	63	52	1 074	168
Production occupations	660	320	318	78	323	814	163
Transportation and material moving occupations	444	274	154	57	214	313	84
2008							
All Occupations	6 178	13 169	18 233	2 972	9 795	7 005	6 763
Management, professional, and related occupations	1 114	9 895	9 655	1 017	1 511	1 539	2 799
Management, business, and financial operations	795	1 164	1 540	305	1 439	641	1 174
Computer and mathematical occupations	67	195	163	15	14	33	260
Architecture and engineering occupations	X	X	0	X	X	X	0
Life, physical and social science occupations	24	184	202	12	2	12	181
Community and social service occupations	9	309	897	4	5	645	384
Legal occupations	34	14	25	2	1	18	300
Education, training, and library occupations	15	7 531	608	64	15	51	68
Arts, design, entertainment, sports, and media occupations	35	190	69	600	20	96	63
Healthcare practitioner and technical occupations	93	273	6 130	5	7	30	182
Healthcare support occupations	78	35	2 791	20	12	118	39
Protective service occupations	526	110	60	142	46	21	1 868
Food preparation and serving related occupations	19	452	382	252	6 168	48	37
Building and grounds cleaning and maintenance occupations	2 151	599	485	274	467	581	128
Personal care and service occupations	26	239	1 678	689	101	1 741	75
Sales and related occupations	307	75	64	184	711	401	36
Office and administrative support occupations	988	1 189	2 664	226	415	657	1 343
Farming, fishing, and forestry occupations	5	5	1	3	1	3	22
Construction and extraction occupations	103	63	38	14	18	38	99
Installation, maintenance, and repair occupations	185	137	101	59	52	1 053	154
Production occupations	678	369	314	92	292	805	164
Transportation and material moving occupations	463	314	137	72	189	310	96

X = Not applicable.

Table 1-15. Employed Civilians in Agriculture and Nonagricultural Industries, by Class of Worker and Sex, 1988–2008

(Thousands of people.)

Sex and year	Total employed	Agriculture				Nonagricultural industries						
		Total	Wage and salary workers	Self-employed workers	Unpaid family workers	Total	Wage and salary workers				Self-employed workers	Unpaid family workers
							Total	Government	Private household	Other industries except private households		
Both Sexes												
1988	114 969	3 169	1 621	1 398	150	111 800	103 021	17 114	1 153	84 754	8 519	260
1989	117 341	3 199	1 665	1 403	131	114 142	105 259	17 469	1 101	86 689	8 605	279
1990	118 793	3 223	1 740	1 378	105	115 570	106 598	17 769	1 027	87 802	8 719	253
1991	117 718	3 269	1 729	1 423	118	114 449	105 373	17 934	1 010	86 429	8 851	226
1992	118 492	3 247	1 750	1 385	112	115 245	106 437	18 136	1 135	87 166	8 575	233
1993	120 259	3 115	1 689	1 320	106	117 144	107 966	18 579	1 126	88 261	8 959	218
1994	123 060	3 409	1 715	1 645	49	119 651	110 517	18 293	966	91 258	9 003	131
1995	124 900	3 440	1 814	1 580	45	121 460	112 448	18 362	963	93 123	8 902	110
1996	126 707	3 443	1 869	1 518	56	123 264	114 171	18 217	928	95 026	8 971	122
1997	129 558	3 399	1 890	1 457	51	126 159	116 983	18 131	915	97 937	9 056	120
1998	131 463	3 378	2 000	1 341	38	128 085	119 019	18 383	962	99 674	8 962	103
1999	133 488	3 281	1 944	1 297	40	130 207	121 323	18 903	933	101 487	8 790	95
2000	136 891	2 464	1 421	1 010	33	134 427	125 114	19 248	718	105 148	9 205	108
2001	136 933	2 299	1 283	988	28	134 635	125 407	19 335	694	105 378	9 121	107
2002	136 485	2 311	1 282	1 003	26	134 174	125 156	19 636	757	104 764	8 923	95
2003	137 736	2 275	1 299	951	25	135 461	126 015	19 634	764	105 616	9 344	101
2004	139 252	2 232	1 242	964	27	137 020	127 463	19 983	779	106 701	9 467	90
2005	141 730	2 197	1 212	955	30	139 532	129 931	20 357	812	108 761	9 509	93
2006	144 427	2 206	1 287	901	18	142 221	132 449	20 337	803	111 309	9 685	87
2007	146 047	2 095	1 220	856	19	143 952	134 283	21 003	813	112 467	9 557	112
2008	145 362	2 168	1 279	860	28	143 194	133 882	21 258	805	111 819	9 219	93
Men												
1988	63 273	2 493	1 268	1 174	50	60 780	55 177	8 074	157	46 946	5 564	39
1989	64 315	2 513	1 302	1 167	44	61 802	56 202	8 116	156	47 930	5 562	38
1990	65 105	2 546	1 355	1 151	39	62 559	56 913	8 245	149	48 519	5 597	48
1991	64 223	2 589	1 359	1 185	45	61 634	55 899	8 300	143	47 456	5 700	35
1992	64 441	2 575	1 371	1 164	40	61 866	56 212	8 348	156	47 708	5 613	41
1993	65 349	2 478	1 323	1 117	39	62 871	56 926	8 435	146	48 345	5 894	50
1994	66 450	2 554	1 330	1 197	27	63 896	58 300	8 327	99	49 874	5 560	37
1995	67 377	2 559	1 395	1 138	26	64 818	59 332	8 267	96	50 969	5 461	25
1996	68 207	2 573	1 418	1 124	31	65 634	60 133	8 110	99	51 924	5 465	36
1997	69 685	2 552	1 439	1 084	29	67 133	61 595	8 015	81	53 499	5 506	31
1998	70 693	2 553	1 526	1 005	23	68 140	62 630	8 178	86	54 366	5 480	29
1999	71 446	2 432	1 450	962	20	69 014	63 624	8 278	74	55 272	5 366	25
2000	73 305	1 861	1 116	725	20	71 444	65 838	8 309	71	57 458	5 573	33
2001	73 196	1 708	990	703	15	71 488	65 930	8 342	63	57 524	5 527	31
2002	72 903	1 724	979	731	14	71 179	65 726	8 437	76	57 212	5 425	29
2003	73 332	1 695	991	694	11	71 636	65 871	8 368	59	57 444	5 736	30
2004	74 525	1 687	970	702	15	72 838	66 951	8 616	60	58 275	5 860	27
2005	75 973	1 654	949	688	17	74 319	68 345	8 760	67	59 518	5 944	30
2006	77 502	1 663	989	664	10	75 838	69 811	8 696	60	61 055	6 004	23
2007	78 254	1 604	973	623	8	76 650	70 697	9 022	76	61 599	5 920	32
2008	77 486	1 650	997	637	16	75 836	70 072	9 089	70	2 800	5 736	29
Women												
1988	51 696	676	353	224	99	51 020	47 844	9 039	996	37 809	2 955	220
1989	53 028	687	363	236	87	52 341	49 057	9 353	945	38 759	3 043	240
1990	53 689	678	385	227	66	53 011	49 685	9 524	879	39 282	3 122	205
1991	53 495	680	369	237	73	52 815	49 474	9 635	867	38 972	3 150	191
1992	54 052	672	379	221	73	53 380	50 225	9 788	979	39 458	2 963	192
1993	54 910	637	367	204	67	54 273	51 040	10 144	980	39 916	3 065	168
1994	56 610	855	384	448	23	55 755	52 217	9 965	867	41 385	3 443	95
1995	57 523	881	419	442	20	56 642	53 115	10 095	867	42 153	3 440	86
1996	58 501	871	452	394	25	57 630	54 037	10 107	830	43 100	3 506	87
1997	59 873	847	451	373	23	59 026	55 388	10 116	834	44 438	3 550	89
1998	60 770	825	474	336	15	59 945	56 389	10 205	876	45 308	3 482	74
1999	62 042	849	494	335	20	61 193	57 699	10 625	859	46 215	3 424	70
2000	63 586	602	305	285	12	62 983	59 277	10 939	647	47 690	3 631	76
2001	63 737	591	293	284	13	63 147	59 477	10 993	630	47 853	3 594	75
2002	63 582	587	303	272	12	62 995	59 431	11 199	680	47 552	3 499	66
2003	64 404	580	309	257	14	63 824	60 144	11 267	705	48 172	3 609	72
2004	64 728	546	271	262	12	64 182	60 512	11 367	719	48 426	3 607	63
2005	65 757	544	263	267	13	65 213	61 586	11 598	745	49 243	3 565	63
2006	66 925	543	298	237	8	66 382	62 638	11 641	742	50 254	3 681	64
2007	67 792	490	247	233	11	67 302	63 586	11 981	737	50 868	3 637	80
2008	67 876	518	282	224	12	67 358	63 810	12 169	735	50 907	3 483	65

Note: See notes and definitions for information on historical comparabilty.

Table 1-16. Number of Employed Persons Age 25 Years and Over, by Educational Attainment, Sex, Race, and Hispanic Origin, 1998–2008

(Thousands of people.)

Race, Hispanic origin, sex, and year	Total	Less than a high school diploma	High school graduate, no college	Some college, no degree	Associate's degree	College graduate or higher	
						Total	Bachelor's degree only
All Races							
1998	111 855	11 673	35 976	20 626	9 850	33 730	22 260
1999	113 425	11 294	36 017	21 129	10 079	34 905	22 973
2000	116 473	11 692	36 452	21 601	10 707	36 020	23 706
2001	116 846	11 669	36 078	21 459	11 127	36 514	23 907
2002	116 802	11 535	35 779	20 928	11 166	37 395	24 570
2003	118 385	11 537	35 857	21 107	11 313	38 570	25 188
2004	119 622	11 408	35 944	21 284	11 693	39 293	25 484
2005	121 960	11 712	36 398	21 380	12 245	40 225	26 027
2006	124 386	11 892	36 702	21 630	12 514	41 649	26 960
2007	126 172	11 521	36 857	22 076	12 535	43 182	28 055
2008	126 161	11 073	36 097	22 092	12 948	43 951	28 460
Men							
1998	60 497	7 238	19 188	10 684	4 731	18 656	12 028
1999	61 032	6 921	19 125	10 941	4 838	19 208	12 343
2000	62 661	7 199	19 388	11 260	5 013	19 800	12 742
2001	62 824	7 188	19 274	11 076	5 226	20 060	12 872
2002	62 756	7 220	19 154	10 811	5 221	20 350	13 076
2003	63 349	7 290	19 200	10 858	5 231	20 770	13 354
2004	64 326	7 276	19 535	10 896	5 426	21 192	13 575
2005	65 772	7 487	20 127	10 993	5 739	21 427	13 687
2006	67 019	7 614	20 345	11 110	5 835	22 114	14 138
2007	67 963	7 450	20 434	11 382	5 862	22 835	14 680
2008	67 605	7 108	20 093	11 356	6 021	23 027	14 845
Women							
1998	51 359	4 435	16 788	9 943	5 119	15 074	10 231
1999	52 392	4 372	16 893	10 189	5 242	15 697	10 630
2000	53 812	4 493	17 064	10 341	5 694	16 220	10 964
2001	54 021	4 480	16 804	10 383	5 901	16 453	11 035
2002	54 046	4 315	16 624	10 117	5 945	17 045	11 493
2003	55 035	4 248	16 657	10 249	6 081	17 800	11 834
2004	55 296	4 132	16 409	10 387	6 267	18 101	11 908
2005	56 188	4 226	16 271	10 388	6 506	18 798	12 340
2006	57 367	4 278	16 357	10 520	6 678	19 535	12 822
2007	58 209	4 071	16 423	10 695	6 674	20 346	13 375
2008	58 555	3 965	16 004	10 737	6 926	20 924	13 614
White[1]							
1998	94 330	9 510	30 249	17 101	8 426	29 044	19 107
1999	95 316	9 235	30 211	17 388	8 556	29 925	19 668
2000	97 320	9 544	30 438	17 770	9 075	30 493	20 078
2001	97 560	9 550	30 126	17 671	9 393	30 821	20 136
2002	97 476	9 394	29 836	17 209	9 440	31 597	20 670
2003	98 120	9 437	29 645	17 227	9 476	32 335	21 103
2004	98 967	9 335	29 571	17 445	9 817	32 799	21 299
2005	100 613	9 579	29 911	17 515	10 256	33 352	21 550
2006	102 322	9 720	30 188	17 632	10 424	34 357	22 272
2007	103 477	9 446	30 140	17 936	10 419	35 535	23 138
2008	103 373	9 036	29 495	17 873	10 742	36 228	23 511
Black[1]							
1998	12 324	1 579	4 504	2 776	1 020	2 446	1 741
1999	12 771	1 488	4 631	2 924	1 108	2 621	1 814
2000	12 852	1 499	4 571	2 910	1 160	2 713	1 866
2001	12 797	1 492	4 492	2 871	1 216	2 727	1 921
2002	12 719	1 498	4 453	2 843	1 210	2 715	1 955
2003	12 706	1 376	4 465	2 780	1 199	2 887	2 056
2004	12 817	1 326	4 606	2 717	1 195	2 973	2 097
2005	13 177	1 369	4 742	2 720	1 288	3 057	2 106
2006	13 504	1 389	4 697	2 816	1 338	3 263	2 243
2007	13 811	1 293	4 783	2 912	1 389	3 435	2 362
2008	13 786	1 234	4 719	2 972	1 439	3 423	2 354
Hispanic[2]							
1998	10 615	3 889	3 018	1 622	660	1 427	1 007
1999	10 985	3 926	3 213	1 696	660	1 491	1 034
2000	12 406	4 468	3 658	1 828	756	1 696	1 198
2001	12 817	4 601	3 796	1 916	781	1 723	1 223
2002	13 294	4 744	3 921	1 900	823	1 906	1 370
2003	14 205	5 073	4 169	2 037	889	2 039	1 468
2004	14 661	5 135	4 330	2 137	931	2 127	1 538
2005	15 362	5 367	4 535	2 230	997	2 232	1 595
2006	16 225	5 620	4 801	2 282	1 095	2 428	1 698
2007	16 973	5 677	5 110	2 382	1 160	2 644	1 898
2008	17 115	5 426	5 232	2 484	1 236	2 736	1 930

[1]Beginning in 2003, persons who selected this race group only; persons who selected more than one race group are not included. Prior to 2003, persons who reported more than one race group were included in the group they identified as their main race.
[2]May be of any race.

Table 1-16. Number of Employed Persons Age 25 Years and Over, by Educational Attainment, Sex, Race, and Hispanic Origin, 1998–2008—*Continued*

(Thousands of people.)

Race, Hispanic origin, sex, and year	Total	Less than a high school diploma	High school graduate, no college	Some college, no degree	Associate's degree	College graduate or higher	
						Total	Bachelor's degree only
White Men[1]							
1998	51 842	6 123	16 308	9 009	4 118	16 284	10 490
1999	52 180	5 883	16 193	9 182	4 160	16 763	10 806
2000	53 243	6 085	16 373	9 435	4 320	17 030	11 029
2001	53 375	6 080	16 292	9 344	4 501	17 158	11 060
2002	53 242	6 072	16 148	9 102	4 497	17 423	11 217
2003	53 458	6 192	16 068	9 042	4 431	17 725	11 461
2004	54 133	6 188	16 297	9 125	4 613	17 910	11 555
2005	55 214	6 368	16 750	9 225	4 851	18 021	11 551
2006	56 145	6 448	17 018	9 244	4 952	18 483	11 881
2007	56 740	6 364	17 039	9 409	4 964	18 964	12 260
2008	56 446	6 066	16 741	9 397	5 070	19 171	12 482
White Women[1]							
1998	42 488	3 387	13 941	8 092	4 308	12 760	8 618
1999	43 135	3 352	14 018	8 207	4 396	13 162	8 862
2000	44 077	3 459	14 065	8 335	4 755	13 463	9 049
2001	44 184	3 469	13 834	8 327	4 891	13 663	9 075
2002	44 234	3 322	13 688	8 107	4 944	14 173	9 453
2003	44 662	3 245	13 576	8 185	5 045	14 610	9 643
2004	44 834	3 146	13 275	8 320	5 203	14 888	9 744
2005	45 399	3 211	13 162	8 290	5 405	15 331	9 999
2006	46 177	3 272	13 171	8 388	5 473	15 874	10 391
2007	46 737	3 082	13 102	8 527	5 455	16 571	10 878
2008	46 928	2 970	12 753	8 477	5 672	17 056	11 029
Black Men[1]							
1998	5 844	811	2 248	1 267	413	1 104	802
1999	6 001	741	2 339	1 313	469	1 140	789
2000	6 011	755	2 253	1 326	466	1 210	828
2001	5 924	762	2 232	1 258	486	1 186	834
2002	5 928	785	2 212	1 264	482	1 185	855
2003	5 860	693	2 190	1 256	492	1 230	890
2004	5 942	676	2 287	1 172	503	1 305	931
2005	6 153	697	2 417	1 171	558	1 310	938
2006	6 276	720	2 338	1 249	535	1 433	1 002
2007	6 429	653	2 340	1 320	570	1 547	1 076
2008	6 357	616	2 358	1 296	579	1 508	1 036
Black Women[1]							
1998	6 480	768	2 256	1 509	607	1 341	939
1999	6 770	746	2 292	1 612	639	1 481	1 025
2000	6 841	743	2 318	1 583	694	1 503	1 038
2001	6 873	730	2 260	1 612	729	1 541	1 087
2002	6 791	713	2 241	1 579	729	1 530	1 101
2003	6 846	683	2 275	1 524	707	1 657	1 166
2004	6 874	650	2 319	1 545	691	1 668	1 166
2005	7 024	672	2 325	1 549	730	1 748	1 169
2006	7 228	669	2 359	1 567	803	1 830	1 241
2007	7 382	641	2 443	1 592	819	1 888	1 286
2008	7 429	617	2 361	1 676	859	1 915	1 318
Hispanic Men[2]							
1998	6 397	2 594	1 764	913	336	790	547
1999	6 441	2 554	1 839	917	334	797	540
2000	7 373	2 937	2 128	995	397	916	634
2001	7 628	3 041	2 174	1 082	386	945	669
2002	7 865	3 141	2 244	1 029	415	1 035	732
2003	8 578	3 424	2 461	1 105	451	1 137	806
2004	8 872	3 508	2 583	1 158	468	1 155	837
2005	9 361	3 639	2 775	1 251	503	1 193	847
2006	9 856	3 823	2 932	1 260	547	1 293	891
2007	10 303	3 947	3 100	1 285	567	1 403	1 000
2008	10 363	3 714	3 231	1 371	607	1 439	1 008
Hispanic Women[2]							
1998	4 219	1 295	1 254	708	325	637	459
1999	4 544	1 372	1 373	778	327	694	494
2000	5 033	1 531	1 529	833	359	780	564
2001	5 190	1 560	1 622	834	395	778	553
2002	5 429	1 604	1 676	871	408	871	638
2003	5 627	1 649	1 708	932	438	901	661
2004	5 789	1 628	1 746	980	463	972	701
2005	6 000	1 728	1 759	979	495	1 039	748
2006	6 370	1 797	1 868	1 021	548	1 135	807
2007	6 670	1 730	2 010	1 097	593	1 241	898
2008	6 752	1 712	2 001	1 113	629	1 297	922

[1]Beginning in 2003, persons who selected this race group only; persons who selected more than one race group are not included. Prior to 2003, persons who reported more than one race group were included in the group they identified as their main race.
[2]May be of any race.

Table 1-17. Multiple Jobholders and Multiple Jobholding Rates, by Selected Characteristics, May of Selected Years, 1970–2009

(Thousands of people, percent, not seasonally adjusted.)

Year	Total employed	Multiple jobholders				Multiple jobholding rate[1]						
		Total	Men	Women		Total	Men	Women	White	Black[2]	Asian	Hispanic[3]
				Number	Percent of all multiple jobholders							
1970	78 358	4 048	3 412	636	15.7	5.2	7.0	2.2	5.3	4.4	. . .	. . .
1971	78 708	4 035	3 270	765	19.0	5.1	6.7	2.6	5.3	3.8	. . .	. . .
1972	81 224	3 770	3 035	735	19.5	4.6	6.0	2.4	4.8	3.7	. . .	. . .
1973	83 758	4 262	3 393	869	20.4	5.1	6.6	2.7	5.1	4.7	. . .	. . .
1974	85 786	3 889	3 022	867	22.3	4.5	5.8	2.6	4.6	3.8	. . .	. . .
1975	84 146	3 918	2 962	956	24.4	4.7	5.8	2.9	4.8	3.7	. . .	. . .
1976	87 278	3 948	3 037	911	23.1	4.5	5.8	2.6	4.7	2.8	. . .	. . .
1977	90 482	4 558	3 317	1 241	27.2	5.0	6.2	3.4	5.3	2.6	. . .	. . .
1978	93 904	4 493	3 212	1 281	28.5	4.8	5.8	3.3	5.0	3.1	. . .	. . .
1979	96 327	4 724	3 317	1 407	29.8	4.9	5.9	3.5	5.1	3.0	. . .	. . .
1980	96 809	4 759	3 210	1 549	32.5	4.9	5.8	3.8	5.1	3.2	. . .	. . .
1985	106 878	5 730	3 537	2 192	38.3	5.4	5.9	4.7	5.7	3.2	. . .	. . .
1989	117 084	7 225	4 115	3 109	43.0	6.2	6.4	5.9	6.5	4.3	. . .	. . .
1991	116 626	7 183	4 054	3 129	43.6	6.2	6.4	5.9	6.4	4.9	. . .	. . .
1994	122 946	7 316	3 973	3 343	45.7	6.0	6.0	5.9	6.1	4.9	. . .	3.8
1995	124 554	7 952	4 225	3 727	46.9	6.4	6.3	6.5	6.6	5.2	. . .	3.6
1996	126 391	7 846	4 352	3 494	44.5	6.2	6.4	6.0	6.4	5.1	. . .	4.0
1997	129 565	8 197	4 398	3 800	46.4	6.3	6.3	6.4	6.5	5.7	. . .	4.1
1998	131 476	8 126	4 438	3 688	45.4	6.2	6.3	6.1	6.3	5.5	. . .	4.4
1999	133 411	7 895	4 117	3 778	47.9	5.9	5.8	6.1	6.0	5.5	. . .	3.6
2000	136 685	7 751	4 084	3 667	47.3	5.7	5.6	5.8	5.9	4.9	3.4	3.2
2001	137 121	7 540	3 914	3 626	48.1	5.5	5.3	5.7	5.6	5.3	3.7	3.4
2002	136 559	7 247	3 736	3 511	48.4	5.3	5.1	5.5	5.5	4.7	4.0	3.8
2003	137 567	7 338	3 841	3 498	47.7	5.3	5.3	5.4	5.5	4.3	4.2	3.4
2004	138 867	7 258	3 653	3 605	49.7	5.2	4.9	5.6	5.3	5.1	3.7	3.4
2005	141 591	7 348	3 741	3 607	49.1	5.2	4.9	5.5	5.4	4.4	3.5	2.8
2006	144 041	7 641	3 863	3 778	49.4	5.3	5.0	5.7	5.3	5.4	3.7	3.1
2007	145 004	7 093	3 835	3 858	50.1	5.3	4.9	5.7	5.5	4.4	3.7	3.0
2008	145 927	7 653	3 842	3 812	49.8	5.2	4.9	5.6	5.4	4.9	3.8	2.9
2009	140 363	7 265	3 540	3 725	51.3	5.2	4.8	5.6	5.3	4.8	3.9	3.0

Note: Data prior to 1985 reflect 1970 census–based population controls; years 1985–1991 reflect 1980 census–based controls; years 1994–1999 reflect 1990 census–based controls adjusted for the estimated undercount; and data for years 2000–2002 have been revised to incorporate population controls from the 2000 census. Prior to 1994, data on multiple jobholders were collected only through special periodic supplements to the Current Population Survey (CPS) in May of various years; these supplemental surveys were not conducted in 1981–1984, 1986–1988, 1990, or 1992–1993. Beginning in 1994, data reflect the introduction of a major redesign of the CPS, including the the collection of monthly data on multiple jobholders.

[1]Multiple jobholders as a percent of all employed persons in specified group.
[2]Data for years prior to 1977 refer to the Black-and-Other population group.
[3]May be of any race.
. . . = Not available.

Table 1-18. Multiple Jobholders, by Sex, Age, Marital Status, Race, Hispanic Origin, and Job Status, 2006–2008

(Thousands of people, percent.)

Characteristic	Both sexes Number 2005	2006	Rate[1] 2005	2006	Men Number 2005	2006	Rate[1] 2005	2006	Women Number 2005	2006	Rate[1] 2005	2006
Age												
Total, 16 years and over[2]	7 546	7 576	5.3	5.2	3 855	3 822	5.1	4.9	3 691	3 753	5.6	5.6
16 to 19 years	298	270	5.0	4.4	118	103	4.0	3.4	180	167	5.9	5.4
20 to 24 years	798	774	5.8	5.6	373	341	5.1	4.6	425	432	6.5	6.7
25 to 34 years	1 582	1 577	5.2	5.1	827	850	4.9	5.0	755	727	5.5	5.2
35 to 44 years	1 900	1 856	5.5	5.4	1 016	969	5.4	5.2	884	887	5.6	5.6
45 to 54 years	1 879	1 934	5.7	5.7	939	940	5.4	5.2	940	994	6.0	6.2
55 to 64 years	900	988	4.9	5.1	473	517	4.9	5.1	426	471	4.9	5.1
65 years and over	189	176	3.7	3.3	109	101	3.8	3.4	80	75	3.6	3.2
Marital Status												
Single	2 113	2 131	5.5	5.3	987	962	4.7	4.4	1 125	1 169	6.4	6.5
Married, spouse present	4 109	4 136	5.1	5.1	2 416	2 420	5.3	5.3	1 693	1 716	4.9	4.9
Widowed, divorced, or separated	1 324	1 308	5.8	5.6	452	440	4.8	4.4	872	868	6.5	6.3
Race and Hispanic Origin												
White[3]	6 342	6 321	5.4	5.3	3 268	3 199	5.1	4.9	3 074	3 122	5.8	5.8
Black[3]	763	818	5.0	5.2	363	404	5.1	5.5	400	415	4.9	4.9
Hispanic[4]	582	598	3.1	3.0	333	337	2.9	2.8	248	261	3.4	3.4
Full- or Part-Time Status												
Primary job full time, secondary job part time	3 942	3 981	...	...	2 219	3 822	...	...	1 724	3 753	...	...
Primary and secondary jobs, both part time	1 708	1 676	...	...	570	508	...	...	1 138	1 168	...	...
Primary and secondary jobs, both full time	294	310	...	...	188	208	...	...	105	102	...	...
Hours vary on primary or secondary job	1 558	1 564	...	...	859	849	...	...	698	715	...	...

Characteristic	Both sexes Number 2007	2008	Rate[1] 2007	2008	Men Number 2007	2008	Rate[1] 2007	2008	Women Number 2007	2008	Rate[1] 2007	2008
Age												
Total, 16 years and over[2]	7 655	7 620	5.2	5.2	3 833	3 837	4.9	5.0	3 822	3 783	5.6	5.6
16 to 19 years	249	225	4.2	4.0	96	94	3.3	3.4	153	131	5.1	4.6
20 to 24 years	738	752	5.3	5.5	309	329	4.2	4.6	429	423	6.5	6.5
25 to 34 years	1 662	1 555	5.3	5.0	876	846	5.0	4.9	786	710	5.6	5.0
35 to 44 years	1 844	1 841	5.4	5.5	948	941	5.1	5.2	896	900	5.7	5.9
45 to 54 years	1 926	1 958	5.6	5.7	959	959	5.3	5.3	967	999	5.9	6.1
55 to 64 years	1 022	1 067	5.1	5.1	522	539	4.9	4.9	501	528	5.2	5.3
65 years and over	214	223	3.8	3.7	123	129	4.0	3.9	91	94	3.6	3.5
Marital Status												
Single	2 101	2 089	5.2	5.2	952	989	4.3	4.5	1 149	1 100	6.3	5.9
Married, spouse present	4 215	4 166	5.1	5.1	2 435	2 386	5.3	5.2	1 780	1 780	5.0	5.0
Widowed, divorced, or separated	1 339	1 365	5.7	5.9	446	462	4.6	4.8	893	903	6.5	6.7
Race and Hispanic Origin												
White[3]	6 467	6 405	5.4	5.4	3 250	3 255	5.0	5.0	3 217	3 151	5.9	5.8
Black[3]	753	756	4.7	4.7	375	371	5.0	5.0	379	385	4.4	4.5
Hispanic[4]	638	671	3.1	3.3	353	377	2.9	3.1	284	294	3.5	3.6
Full- or Part-Time Status												
Primary job full time, secondary job part time	4 174	4 165	...	...	2 320	2 289	...	...	1 854	1 876	...	...
Primary and secondary jobs, both part time	1 764	1 791	...	...	531	588	...	...	1 233	1 203	...	...
Primary and secondary jobs, both full time	288	284	...	...	193	192	...	...	95	92	...	...
Hours vary on primary or secondary job	1 383	1 338	...	...	765	747	...	...	618	591	...	...

Note: Estimates for the above race groups (White or Black) do not sum to totals because data are not presented for all races. Beginning in January 2003, data reflect the revised population controls used in the household survey.

[1]Multiple jobholders as a percent of all employed persons in specified group.
[2]Includes a small number of persons who work part time at their primary job and full time at their secondary job(s), not shown separately.
[3]Beginning in 2003, persons who selected this race group only; persons who selected more than one race group are not included. Prior to 2003, persons who reported more than one race group were included in the group they identified as their main race.
[4]May be of any race.
. . . = Not available.

Table 1-19. Multiple Jobholders, by Sex and Industry of Principal Secondary Job, Annual Averages, 2006–2008

(Thousands of people.)

Year and industry of secondary job	Both sexes	Men	Women
2006			
All Nonagricultural Industries, Wage and Salary Workers	5 219	2 453	2 766
Mining	3	3	0
Construction	275	224	50
Manufacturing	175	111	64
Durable goods	106	76	30
Nondurable goods	68	34	34
Wholesale and retail trade	1 105	472	633
Wholesale trade	89	54	35
Retail trade	1 015	418	598
Transportation and utilities	178	138	41
Transportation and warehousing	171	131	40
Utilities	8	7	1
Information	195	115	80
Financial activities	416	245	171
Professional and business services	831	484	347
Education and health services	1 550	530	1 020
Leisure and hospitality	1 076	549	527
Other services	525	219	306
Other services, except private households	438	209	229
Other servces, private households	86	10	77
Public administration	214	138	77
2007			
All Nonagricultural Industries, Wage and Salary Workers	5 315	2 440	2 875
Mining	2	2	0
Construction	268	210	58
Manufacturing	177	106	71
Durable goods	93	65	28
Nondurable goods	84	41	43
Wholesale and retail trade	1 127	446	681
Wholesale trade	75	49	26
Retail trade	1 051	396	655
Transportation and utilities	210	157	53
Transportation and warehousing	194	146	48
Utilities	16	11	5
Information	175	118	57
Financial activities	400	227	173
Professional and business services	861	493	368
Education and health services	1 516	506	1 009
Leisure and hospitality	1 142	558	585
Other services	560	241	319
Other services, except private households	478	239	239
Other servces, private households	82	2	80
Public administration	199	134	65
2008			
All Nonagricultural Industries, Wage and Salary Workers	5 322	2 480	2 842
Mining	6	5	1
Construction	242	202	40
Manufacturing	173	108	65
Durable goods	101	72	29
Nondurable goods	72	36	36
Wholesale and retail trade	1 142	461	681
Wholesale trade	78	46	31
Retail trade	1 065	415	650
Transportation and utilities	188	145	43
Transportation and warehousing	171	133	39
Utilities	17	13	4
Information	135	89	46
Financial activities	354	215	139
Professional and business services	863	521	342
Education and health services	1 527	544	983
Leisure and hospitality	1 146	519	626
Other services	622	287	335
Other services, except private households	535	279	256
Other servces, private households	87	8	79
Public administration	190	123	67

Table 1-20. Employment and Unemployment in Families, by Race and Hispanic Origin, Annual Averages, 2000–2008

(Thousands of people, percent.)

Characteristic	2000	2001	2002	2003	2004	2005	2006	2007	2008
ALL RACES									
Total Families	71 680	73 306	74 169	75 301	75 872	76 443	77 017	77 894	77 943
With employed member(s)	59 626	60 707	61 121	61 761	62 424	62 933	63 492	64 330	64 058
As percent of total families	83.2	82.8	82.4	82.0	82.3	82.3	82.4	82.6	82.2
Some usually work full time[1]	55 683	56 519	56 742	57 229	57 813	58 276	58 918	59 616	59 116
With no employed member	12 054	12 600	13 048	13 540	13 447	13 509	13 525	13 564	13 884
As percent of total families	16.8	17.2	17.6	18.0	17.7	17.7	17.6	17.4	17.8
With unemployed member(s)	4 110	4 847	5 809	6 079	5 593	5 318	4 913	4 914	6 104
As percent of total families	5.7	6.6	7.8	8.1	7.4	7.0	6.4	6.3	7.8
Some member(s) employed	2 973	3 494	4 126	4 285	3 915	3 717	3 419	3 497	4 319
As percent of families with unemployed member(s)	72.3	72.1	71.0	70.5	70.0	69.9	69.6	71.2	70.8
Some usually work full time[1]	2 675	3 122	3 668	3 790	3 494	3 310	3 049	3 096	3 830
As percent of families with unemployed member(s)	65.1	64.4	63.1	62.3	62.5	62.2	62.1	63.0	62.7
WHITE[2]									
Total Families	59 918	60 921	61 494	61 995	62 250	62 567	62 977	63 667	63 490
With employed member(s)	49 877	50 505	50 785	51 002	51 350	51 645	52 054	52 669	52 273
As percent of total families	83.2	83.0	82.6	82.3	82.5	82.5	82.7	82.7	82.3
Some usually work full time[1]	46 639	47 060	47 193	47 356	47 620	47 883	48 395	48 879	48 271
With no employed member	10 042	10 416	10 709	10 993	10 900	10 922	10 923	10 997	11 217
As percent of total families	16.8	17.0	17.4	17.7	17.5	17.5	17.3	17.3	17.7
With unemployed member(s)	3 010	3 553	4 275	4 411	4 078	3 801	3 556	3 587	4 506
As percent of total families	5.0	5.8	7.0	7.1	6.6	6.1	5.6	5.6	7.1
Some member(s) employed	2 276	2 661	3 164	3 245	3 000	2 782	2 582	2 653	3 332
As percent of families with unemployed member(s)	75.6	74.9	74.0	73.6	73.6	73.2	72.6	73.9	74.0
Some usually work full time[1]	2 052	2 379	2 808	2 873	2 677	2 477	2 306	2 350	2 955
As percent of families with unemployed member(s)	68.2	67.0	65.7	65.1	65.7	65.2	64.8	65.5	65.6
BLACK[2]									
Total Families	8 600	8 674	8 845	8 869	8 860	8 952	9 058	9 184	9 297
With employed member(s)	6 964	6 933	6 987	6 906	6 920	6 986	7 078	7 249	7 290
As percent of total families	81.0	80.0	79.0	77.9	78.1	78.0	78.1	78.9	78.4
Some usually work full time[1]	6 401	6 373	6 390	6 270	6 292	6 353	6 437	6 608	6 622
With no employed member	1 636	1 742	1 858	1 963	1 940	1 966	1 980	1 935	2 006
As percent of total families	19.0	20.1	21.0	22.1	21.9	22.0	21.9	21.1	21.6
With unemployed member(s)	881	990	1 162	1 213	1 127	1 140	1 036	990	1 188
As percent of total families	10.2	11.4	13.1	13.7	12.7	12.7	11.4	10.8	12.8
Some member(s) employed	535	596	689	695	625	657	596	591	686
As percent of families with unemployed member(s)	60.8	60.2	59.3	57.3	55.5	57.7	57.6	59.7	57.8
Some usually work full time[1]	476	533	611	612	556	583	526	519	605
As percent of families with unemployed member(s)	54.1	53.8	52.6	50.5	49.3	51.1	50.8	52.4	50.9
HISPANIC[3]									
Total Families	7 581	8 140	8 650	9 185	9 305	9 603	9 905	10 332	10 500
With employed member(s)	6 633	7 100	7 485	7 907	8 071	8 312	8 641	9 048	9 135
As percent of total families	87.5	87.2	86.5	86.1	86.7	86.6	87.2	87.6	87.0
Some usually work full time[1]	6 255	6 692	6 989	7 383	7 566	7 786	8 129	8 492	8 466
With no employed member	947	1 040	1 165	1 277	1 235	1 291	1 264	1 285	1 365
As percent of total families	12.5	12.8	13.5	13.9	13.3	13.4	12.8	12.4	13.0
With unemployed member(s)	679	809	965	1 020	950	860	793	876	1 159
As percent of total families	9.0	9.9	11.2	11.1	10.2	9.0	8.0	8.5	11.0
Some member(s) employed	493	592	686	715	664	606	544	619	846
As percent of families with unemployed member(s)	72.7	73.2	71.1	70.1	69.9	70.5	68.6	70.6	73.0
Some usually work full time[1]	446	537	615	640	594	544	491	554	743
As percent of families with unemployed member(s)	65.8	66.4	63.7	62.7	62.5	63.2	61.9	63.2	64.1

Note: The race or ethnicity of the family is determined by the race of the householder. Estimates for the above race groups (White or Black) do not sum to totals because data are not presented for all races. Detail may not sum to total due to rounding. Data for 2003 reflect the revised population controls used in the Current Population Survey (CPS). Estimates for 2000 are not strictly comparable with data for later years due to population controls reflecting Census 2000 results.

[1] Usually work 35 hours or more a week at all jobs.
[2] Beginning in 2003, families where the householder selected this race group only; families where the householder selected more than one race group are excluded. Prior to 2003, families where the householder selected more than one race group were included in the group that the householder identified as the main race.
[3] May be of any race.

Table 1-21. Families, by Presence and Relationship of Employed Members and Family Type, Annual Averages, 2000–2008

(Thousands of people, percent.)

Characteristic	Number of families								
	2000	2001	2002	2003	2004	2005	2006	2007	2008
MARRIED-COUPLE FAMILIES									
Total	54 704	55 749	56 280	57 074	57 188	57 167	57 509	58 145	58 125
Member(s) employed, total	45 967	46 680	46 976	47 535	47 767	47 895	48 196	48 676	48 541
Husband only	10 500	10 833	11 174	11 403	11 712	11 562	11 399	11 509	11 351
Wife only	2 946	3 257	3 613	3 863	3 843	3 715	3 754	3 858	4 036
Husband and wife	29 128	29 241	28 873	29 077	28 991	29 330	29 799	30 055	29 854
Other employment combinations	3 394	3 350	3 317	3 193	3 222	3 288	3 244	3 254	3 300
No member(s) employed	8 737	9 068	9 303	9 539	9 420	9 272	9 313	9 469	9 585
FAMILIES MAINTAINED BY WOMEN[1]									
Total	12 775	13 037	13 215	13 450	13 614	14 035	14 208	14 423	14 383
Member(s) employed, total	10 026	10 131	10 169	10 187	10 358	10 609	10 796	11 087	10 929
Householder only	5 581	5 667	5 944	5 987	6 021	6 052	6 103	6 307	6 250
Householder and other member(s)	2 806	2 778	2 559	2 539	2 701	2 830	2 955	2 994	2 870
Other member(s), not householder	1 639	1 686	1 666	1 660	1 636	1 727	1 738	1 785	1 809
No member(s) employed	2 749	2 906	3 047	3 263	3 255	3 426	3 412	3 336	3 454
FAMILIES MAINTAINED BY MEN[1]									
Total	4 200	4 521	4 674	4 777	5 071	5 242	5 300	5 327	5 435
Member(s) employed, total	3 632	3 895	3 976	4 039	4 299	4 430	4 500	4 568	4 589
Householder only	1 761	1 875	1 939	1 954	2 060	2 093	2 089	2 170	2 178
Householder and other member(s)	1 358	1 450	1 440	1 427	1 557	1 639	1 715	1 696	1 659
Other member(s), not householder	514	570	598	658	682	698	696	701	752
No member(s) employed	567	625	698	739	772	812	800	759	845

Characteristic	Percent distribution								
	2000	2001	2002	2003	2004	2005	2006	2007	2008
MARRIED-COUPLE FAMILIES									
Total	100.0	100.0	100.0	100.0	100.0	100.0	100.0	100.0	100.0
Member(s) employed, total	84.0	83.7	83.5	83.3	83.5	83.8	83.8	83.7	83.5
Husband only	19.2	19.4	19.9	20.0	20.5	20.2	19.8	19.8	19.5
Wife only	5.4	5.8	6.4	6.8	6.7	6.5	6.5	6.6	6.9
Husband and wife	53.2	52.5	51.3	50.9	50.7	51.3	51.8	51.7	51.4
Other employment combinations	6.2	6.0	5.9	5.6	5.6	5.8	5.6	5.6	5.7
No member(s) employed	16.0	16.3	16.5	16.7	16.5	16.2	16.2	16.3	16.5
FAMILIES MAINTAINED BY WOMEN[1]									
Total	100.0	100.0	100.0	100.0	100.0	100.0	100.0	100.0	100.0
Member(s) employed, total	78.5	77.7	77.0	75.7	76.1	75.6	76.0	76.9	76.0
Householder only	43.7	43.5	45.0	44.5	44.2	43.1	43.0	43.7	43.5
Householder and other member(s)	22.0	21.3	19.4	18.9	19.8	20.2	20.8	20.8	20.0
Other member(s), not householder	12.8	12.9	12.6	12.3	12.0	12.3	12.2	12.4	12.6
No member(s) employed	21.5	22.3	23.1	24.3	23.9	24.4	24.0	23.1	24.0
FAMILIES MAINTAINED BY MEN[1]									
Total	100.0	100.0	100.0	100.0	100.0	100.0	100.0	100.0	100.0
Member(s) employed, total	86.5	86.2	85.1	84.6	84.8	84.5	84.9	85.7	84.4
Householder only	41.9	41.5	41.5	40.9	40.6	39.9	39.4	40.7	40.1
Householder and other member(s)	32.3	32.1	30.8	29.9	30.7	31.3	32.4	31.8	30.5
Other member(s), not householder	12.2	12.6	12.8	13.8	13.5	13.3	13.1	13.2	13.8
No member(s) employed	13.5	13.8	14.9	15.5	15.2	15.5	15.1	14.3	15.6

Note: Detail may not sum to total due to rounding. Estimates for 2000 are not strictly comparable with data for later years due to population controls reflecting Census 2000 results.

[1]No spouse present.

Table 1-22. Unemployment in Families, by Presence and Relationship of Employed Members and Family Type, Annual Averages, 2000–2008

(Thousands of people, percent.)

Characteristic	Number								
	2000	2001	2002	2003	2004	2005	2006	2007	2008
MARRIED-COUPLE FAMILIES									
With Unemployed Member(s), Total	2 584	3 081	3 772	3 857	3 521	3 243	2 968	2 978	3 796
No member employed	411	531	676	713	615	580	526	512	663
Some member(s) employed	2 174	2 550	3 096	3 144	2 906	2 664	2 442	2 467	3 133
Husband unemployed	836	1 160	1 523	1 600	1 333	1 190	1 061	1 110	1 439
Wife employed	531	736	993	1 023	850	753	679	725	927
Wife unemployed	789	918	1 117	1 129	1 041	1 004	898	902	1 114
Husband employed	694	809	969	991	913	873	772	783	975
Other family member unemployed	959	1 003	1 133	1 129	1 147	1 049	1 010	966	1 243
FAMILIES MAINTAINED BY WOMEN[1]									
With Unemployed Member(s), Total	1 194	1 324	1 504	1 612	1 521	1 539	1 429	1 416	1 666
No member employed	587	643	787	842	829	797	753	701	849
Some member(s) employed	607	681	717	770	692	743	675	714	817
Householder unemployed	522	593	737	791	758	746	688	650	796
Other member(s) employed	102	129	147	162	146	161	132	144	181
Other member(s) unemployed	672	731	767	821	764	793	740	766	870
FAMILIES MAINTAINED BY MEN[1]									
With Unemployed Member(s), Total	331	442	533	610	551	536	516	520	642
No member employed	139	178	220	239	234	225	215	205	274
Some member(s) employed	192	264	313	371	316	310	301	316	368
Householder unemployed	173	234	303	340	296	301	284	294	385
Other member(s) employed	67	96	129	158	117	122	118	137	164
Other member(s) unemployed	158	208	230	270	255	235	232	226	257

Characteristic	Percent distribution								
	2000	2001	2002	2003	2004	2005	2006	2007	2008
MARRIED-COUPLE FAMILIES									
With Unemployed Member(s), Total	100.0	100.0	100.0	100.0	100.0	100.0	100.0	100.0	100.0
No member employed	15.9	17.2	17.9	18.5	17.5	17.9	17.7	17.2	17.5
Some member(s) employed	84.1	82.8	82.1	81.5	82.5	82.1	82.3	82.8	82.5
Husband unemployed	32.3	37.7	40.4	41.5	37.9	36.7	35.7	37.3	37.9
Wife employed	20.5	23.9	26.3	26.5	24.2	23.2	22.9	24.3	24.4
Wife unemployed	30.5	29.8	29.6	29.3	29.6	31.0	30.3	30.3	29.3
Husband employed	26.8	26.3	25.7	25.7	25.9	26.9	26.0	26.3	25.7
Other family member unemployed	37.1	32.6	30.0	29.3	32.6	32.4	34.0	32.4	32.7
FAMILIES MAINTAINED BY WOMEN[1]									
With Unemployed Member(s), Total	100.0	100.0	100.0	100.0	100.0	100.0	100.0	100.0	100.0
No member employed	49.1	48.6	52.3	52.3	54.5	51.8	52.7	49.5	50.9
Some member(s) employed	50.9	51.4	47.7	47.8	45.5	48.2	47.3	50.5	49.1
Householder unemployed	43.7	44.8	49.0	49.1	49.8	48.5	48.2	45.9	47.8
Other member(s) employed	8.5	9.7	9.8	10.0	9.6	10.5	9.3	10.2	10.9
Other member(s) unemployed	56.3	55.2	51.0	50.9	50.2	51.5	51.8	54.1	52.2
FAMILIES MAINTAINED BY MEN[1]									
With Unemployed Member(s), Total	100.0	100.0	100.0	100.0	100.0	100.0	100.0	100.0	100.0
No member employed	42.0	40.3	41.3	39.2	42.5	42.1	41.7	39.3	42.7
Some member(s) employed	58.0	59.7	58.7	60.8	57.5	57.9	58.3	60.7	57.3
Householder unemployed	52.2	52.9	56.8	55.7	53.7	56.1	55.0	56.6	60.0
Other member(s) employed	20.4	21.7	24.2	25.9	21.3	22.8	22.8	26.3	25.6
Other member(s) unemployed	47.8	47.1	43.2	44.3	46.3	43.9	45.0	43.4	40.0

Note: Detail may not sum to total due to rounding. Estimates for 2000 are not strictly comparable with data for later years due to population controls reflecting Census 2000 results.

[1] No spouse present.

Table 1-23. Employment Status of the Population, by Sex, Marital Status, and Presence and Age of Own Children Under 18 Years, Annual Averages, 2000–2008

(Thousands of people, percent.)

Characteristic	2000 Both sexes	2000 Men	2000 Women	2001 Both sexes	2001 Men	2001 Women	2002 Both sexes	2002 Men	2002 Women	2003 Both sexes	2003 Men	2003 Women	2004 Both sexes	2004 Men	2004 Women
With Own Children Under 18 Years, Total															
Civilian noninstitutional population	63 267	27 673	35 595	64 100	28 076	36 024	64 399	28 137	36 263	64 932	28 402	36 530	64 758	28 272	36 486
Civilian labor force	51 944	26 202	25 742	52 489	26 551	25 938	52 566	26 529	26 036	52 727	26 739	25 988	52 288	26 607	25 681
Participation rate	82.1	94.7	72.3	81.9	94.6	72.0	81.6	94.3	71.8	81.2	94.1	71.1	80.7	94.1	70.4
Employed	50 259	25 622	24 637	50 455	25 750	24 704	50 022	25 474	24 549	50 103	25 638	24 466	49 957	25 696	24 261
Employment-population ratio	79.4	92.6	69.2	78.7	91.7	68.6	77.7	90.5	67.7	77.2	90.3	67.0	77.1	90.9	66.5
Full-time workers[1]	43 365	24 922	18 443	43 424	24 964	18 460	42 884	24 644	18 240	42 880	24 762	18 118	42 758	24 794	17 964
Part-time workers[2]	6 894	699	6 195	7 031	787	6 244	7 138	829	6 308	7 223	876	6 347	7 200	902	6 298
Unemployed	1 685	581	1 104	2 034	801	1 233	2 543	1 056	1 488	2 624	1 101	1 523	2 331	911	1 420
Unemployment rate	3.2	2.2	4.3	3.9	3.0	4.8	4.8	4.0	5.7	5.0	4.1	5.9	4.5	3.4	5.5
Married, Spouse Present															
Civilian noninstitutional population	51 415	25 540	25 874	51 981	25 796	26 185	51 947	25 781	26 166	52 476	26 049	26 427	52 109	25 852	26 258
Civilian labor force	42 361	24 290	18 072	42 712	24 512	18 201	42 492	24 425	18 067	42 776	24 638	18 138	42 247	24 449	17 798
Participation rate	82.4	95.1	69.8	82.2	95.0	69.5	81.8	94.7	69.0	81.5	94.6	68.6	81.1	94.6	67.8
Employed	41 357	23 816	17 541	41 431	23 849	17 581	40 867	23 533	17 334	41 128	23 712	17 416	40 847	23 703	17 144
Employment-population ratio	80.4	93.2	67.8	79.7	92.5	67.1	78.7	91.3	66.2	78.4	91.0	65.9	78.4	91.7	65.3
Full-time workers[1]	35 793	23 212	12 581	35 772	23 169	12 603	35 180	22 825	12 356	35 315	22 954	12 360	35 141	22 935	12 206
Part-time workers[2]	5 564	604	4 960	5 659	680	4 979	5 687	708	4 979	5 813	757	5 056	5 706	768	4 938
Unemployed	1 004	474	531	1 282	662	619	1 625	893	733	1 648	926	722	1 400	747	653
Unemployment rate	2.4	2.0	2.9	3.0	2.7	3.4	3.8	3.7	4.1	3.9	3.8	4.0	3.3	3.1	3.7
Other Marital Status[3]															
Civilian noninstitutional population	11 853	2 132	9 720	12 119	2 280	9 839	12 452	2 355	10 096	12 455	2 354	10 102	12 649	2 420	10 229
Civilian labor force	9 583	1 913	7 670	9 777	2 039	7 737	10 073	2 103	7 970	9 950	2 100	7 850	10 042	2 158	7 883
Participation rate	80.8	89.7	78.9	80.7	89.4	78.6	80.9	89.3	78.9	79.9	89.2	77.7	79.4	89.2	77.1
Employed	8 902	1 806	7 096	9 024	1 902	7 123	9 155	1 941	7 215	8 975	1 926	7 050	9 110	1 993	7 117
Employment-population ratio	75.1	84.7	73.0	74.5	83.4	72.4	73.5	82.4	71.5	72.1	81.8	69.8	72.0	82.4	69.6
Full-time workers[1]	7 572	1 710	5 862	7 652	1 795	5 857	7 704	1 820	5 885	7 566	1 807	5 759	7 617	1 859	5 757
Part-time workers[2]	1 330	96	1 234	1 372	107	1 265	1 451	122	1 329	1 411	118	1 291	1 494	134	1 360
Unemployed	681	107	574	752	138	614	918	163	755	976	175	800	931	165	766
Unemployment rate	7.1	5.6	7.5	7.7	6.8	7.9	9.1	7.8	9.5	9.8	8.3	10.2	9.3	7.6	9.7
With Own Children 6 to 17 Years, None Younger															
Civilian noninstitutional population	34 737	15 165	19 572	35 523	15 486	20 038	35 829	15 580	20 250	35 943	15 653	20 290	35 874	15 597	20 277
Civilian labor force	29 576	14 178	15 398	30 182	14 489	15 693	30 371	14 541	15 830	30 362	14 572	15 790	30 182	14 516	15 666
Participation rate	85.1	93.5	78.7	85.0	93.6	78.3	84.8	93.3	78.2	84.5	93.1	77.8	84.1	93.1	77.3
Employed	28 744	13 877	14 868	29 174	14 096	15 078	29 122	14 023	15 099	29 040	14 008	15 032	29 013	14 056	14 957
Employment-population ratio	82.7	91.5	76.0	82.1	91.0	75.2	81.3	90.0	74.6	80.8	89.5	74.1	80.9	90.1	73.8
Full-time workers[1]	25 042	13 513	11 529	25 382	13 689	11 693	25 225	13 586	11 638	25 116	13 558	11 557	25 069	13 597	11 473
Part-time workers[2]	3 703	364	3 339	3 792	407	3 385	3 898	437	3 461	3 925	450	3 475	3 944	459	3 485
Unemployed	832	302	530	1 008	393	615	1 249	518	731	1 322	564	758	1 170	460	709
Unemployment rate	2.8	2.1	3.4	3.3	2.7	3.9	4.1	3.6	4.6	4.4	3.9	4.8	3.9	3.2	4.5
With Own Children Under 6 Years															
Civilian noninstitutional population	28 530	12 508	16 022	28 577	12 590	15 986	28 570	12 557	16 013	28 988	12 749	16 240	28 884	12 675	16 210
Civilian labor force	22 368	12 024	10 344	22 307	12 062	10 245	22 194	11 988	10 206	22 365	12 167	10 198	22 106	12 091	10 014
Participation rate	78.4	96.1	64.6	78.1	95.8	64.1	77.7	95.5	63.7	77.2	95.4	62.8	76.5	95.4	61.8
Employed	21 515	11 745	9 770	21 280	11 654	9 626	20 900	11 450	9 450	21 063	11 630	9 433	20 944	11 640	9 304
Employment-population ratio	75.4	93.9	61.0	74.5	92.6	60.2	73.2	91.2	59.0	72.7	91.2	58.1	72.5	91.8	57.4
Full-time workers[1]	18 323	11 410	6 914	18 041	11 274	6 767	17 660	11 058	6 602	17 764	11 203	6 561	17 689	11 197	6 491
Part-time workers[2]	3 191	335	2 856	3 239	380	2 859	3 240	392	2 848	3 299	426	2 872	3 256	443	2 813
Unemployed	853	279	574	1 026	408	619	1 294	538	757	1 302	538	765	1 162	451	710
Unemployment rate	3.8	2.3	5.6	4.6	3.4	6.0	5.8	4.5	7.4	5.8	4.4	7.5	5.3	3.7	7.1
With No Own Children Under 18 Years															
Civilian noninstitutional population	145199	71 825	73 374	149643	73 857	75 786	151715	74 993	76 722	154714	76 510	78 204	156900	77 739	79 160
Civilian labor force	88 014	48 140	39 874	90 171	49 249	40 922	90 971	49 644	41 327	92 319	50 036	42 284	93 511	50 771	42 740
Participation rate	60.6	67.0	54.3	60.3	66.7	54.0	60.0	66.2	53.9	59.7	65.4	54.1	59.6	65.3	54.0
Employed	84 058	45 781	38 278	85 421	46 371	39 050	85 187	46 154	39 034	86 233	46 294	39 939	87 748	47 282	40 467
Employment-population ratio	57.9	63.7	52.2	57.1	62.8	51.5	56.1	61.5	50.9	55.7	60.5	51.1	55.9	60.8	51.1
Full-time workers[1]	68 046	39 136	28 910	69 074	39 596	29 478	68 574	39 319	29 254	69 073	39 245	29 827	70 244	40 134	30 110
Part-time workers[2]	16 012	6 645	9 367	16 347	6 776	9 572	16 614	6 834	9 779	17 160	7 049	10 111	17 505	7 148	10 357
Unemployed	3 956	2 359	1 596	4 750	2 878	1 872	5 784	3 491	2 293	6 087	3 741	2 345	5 763	3 489	2 274
Unemployment rate	4.5	4.9	4.0	5.3	5.8	4.6	6.4	7.0	5.5	6.6	7.5	5.5	6.2	6.9	5.3

Note: Own children include sons, daughters, stepchildren, and adopted children. Not included are nieces, nephews, grandchildren, and other related and unrelated children. Detail may not sum to total due to rounding. Estimates for 2000 are not strictly comparable with data for later years due to population controls reflecting Census 2000 results.

[1]Usually work 35 hours or more a week at all jobs.
[2]Usually work less than 35 hours a week at all jobs.
[3]Includes never-married, divorced, separated, and widowed persons.

Table 1-23. Employment Status of the Population, by Sex, Marital Status, and Presence and Age of Own Children Under 18 Years, Annual Averages, 2000–2008—*Continued*

(Thousands of people, percent.)

Characteristic	2005			2006			2007			2008		
	Both sexes	Men	Women	Both sexes	Men	Women	Both sexes	Men	Women	Both sexes	Men	Women
With Own Children Under 18 Years, Total												
Civilian noninstitutional population	64 482	28 065	36 417	65 941	29 449	36 492	66 801	29 684	37 117	65 655	29 142	36 513
Civilian labor force	52 056	26 399	25 657	53 590	27 730	25 861	54 370	28 002	26 368	53 506	27 422	26 085
Participation rate	80.7	94.1	70.5	81.3	94.2	70.9	81.4	94.3	71.0	81.5	94.1	71.4
Employed	49 882	25 587	24 294	51 561	26 948	24 614	52 373	27 216	25 157	51 017	26 380	24 637
Employment-population ratio	77.4	91.2	66.7	78.2	91.5	67.4	78.4	91.7	67.8	77.7	90.5	67.5
Full-time workers[1]	42 852	24 713	18 139	44 634	26 033	18 601	45 336	26 282	19 053	43 967	25 338	18 629
Part-time workers[2]	7 029	875	6 155	6 927	914	6 013	7 037	933	6 104	7 050	1 042	6 008
Unemployed	2 174	811	1 363	2 029	782	1 247	1 998	786	1 211	2 490	1 041	1 448
Unemployment rate	4.2	3.1	5.3	3.8	2.8	4.8	3.7	2.8	4.6	4.7	3.8	5.6
Married, Spouse Present												
Civilian noninstitutional population	51 519	25 578	25 942	52 930	26 908	26 022	53 432	27 205	26 227	52 433	26 647	25 786
Civilian labor force	41 905	24 215	17 690	43 336	25 494	17 842	43 824	25 784	18 041	43 137	25 205	17 933
Participation rate	81.3	94.7	68.2	81.9	94.7	68.6	82.0	94.8	68.8	82.3	94.6	69.5
Employed	40 614	23 556	17 058	42 134	24 854	17 280	42 625	25 134	17 492	41 611	24 353	17 258
Employment-population ratio	78.8	92.1	65.8	79.6	92.4	66.4	79.8	92.4	66.7	79.4	91.4	66.9
Full-time workers[1]	35 086	22 808	12 278	36 649	24 074	12 575	37 120	24 332	12 788	36 128	23 444	12 685
Part-time workers[2]	5 528	748	4 780	5 485	780	4 705	5 505	802	4 704	5 482	909	4 573
Unemployed	1 291	659	632	1 202	640	562	1 199	650	549	1 527	852	675
Unemployment rate	3.1	2.7	3.6	2.8	2.5	3.1	2.7	2.5	3.0	3.5	3.4	3.8
Other Marital Status[3]												
Civilian noninstitutional population	12 963	2 487	10 475	13 010	2 541	10 470	13 369	2 479	10 890	13 222	2 495	10 727
Civilian labor force	10 151	2 184	7 967	10 255	2 236	8 019	10 546	2 219	8 328	10 369	2 217	8 152
Participation rate	78.3	87.8	76.1	78.8	88.0	76.6	78.9	89.5	76.5	78.4	88.9	76.0
Employed	9 268	2 032	7 236	9 427	2 094	7 333	9 747	2 082	7 665	9 406	2 027	7 379
Employment-population ratio	71.5	81.7	69.1	72.5	82.4	70.0	72.9	84.0	70.4	71.1	81.3	68.8
Full-time workers[1]	7 766	1 905	5 861	7 985	1 960	6 026	8 216	1 950	6 266	7 838	1 894	5 944
Part-time workers[2]	1 502	127	1 375	1 442	134	1 308	1 531	132	1 400	1 568	133	1 435
Unemployed	883	152	731	827	142	686	799	137	662	963	190	773
Unemployment rate	8.7	7.0	9.2	8.1	6.3	8.5	7.6	6.2	8.0	9.3	8.6	9.5
With Own Children 6 to 17 Years, None Younger												
Civilian noninstitutional population	35 937	15 590	20 348	36 530	16 212	20 318	36 983	16 384	20 599	36 581	16 256	20 325
Civilian labor force	30 068	14 496	15 572	30 675	15 091	15 585	31 179	15 269	15 910	30 846	15 128	15 718
Participation rate	83.7	93.0	76.5	84.0	93.1	76.7	84.3	93.2	77.2	84.3	93.1	77.3
Employed	28 953	14 066	14 887	29 643	14 690	14 952	30 176	14 866	15 310	29 590	14 588	15 003
Employment-population ratio	80.6	90.2	73.2	81.1	90.6	73.6	81.6	90.7	74.3	80.9	89.7	73.8
Full-time workers[1]	25 074	13 606	11 468	25 835	14 206	11 629	26 288	14 378	11 910	25 733	14 054	11 679
Part-time workers[2]	3 880	460	3 419	3 808	485	3 323	3 888	488	3 400	3 858	534	3 324
Unemployed	1 115	430	684	1 032	400	632	1 003	403	600	1 255	541	715
Unemployment rate	3.7	3.0	4.4	3.4	2.7	4.1	3.2	2.6	3.8	4.1	3.6	4.5
With Own Children Under 6 Years												
Civilian noninstitutional population	28 545	12 475	16 070	29 411	13 237	16 174	29 818	13 299	16 518	29 074	12 886	16 188
Civilian labor force	21 988	11 903	10 085	22 915	12 639	10 276	23 192	12 733	10 458	22 661	12 293	10 367
Participation rate	77.0	95.4	62.8	77.9	95.5	63.5	77.8	95.7	63.3	77.9	95.4	64.0
Employed	20 928	11 521	9 407	21 919	12 257	9 661	22 197	12 350	9 847	21 426	11 792	9 634
Employment-population ratio	73.3	92.4	58.5	74.5	92.6	59.7	74.4	92.9	59.6	73.7	91.5	59.5
Full-time workers[1]	17 778	11 107	6 671	18 800	11 828	6 972	19 048	11 904	7 143	18 234	11 284	6 950
Part-time workers[2]	3 150	414	2 736	3 119	430	2 689	3 149	446	2 704	3 193	508	2 684
Unemployed	1 060	381	678	997	382	615	995	383	611	1 234	501	733
Unemployment rate	4.8	3.2	6.7	4.3	3.0	6.0	4.3	3.0	5.8	5.4	4.1	7.1
With No Own Children Under 18 Years												
Civilian noninstitutional population	159751	79 237	80 514	162874	81 156	81 718	165066	82 489	82 577	168133	83 971	84 162
Civilian labor force	95 545	51 914	43 631	97 837	53 525	44 312	98 754	54 134	44 620	100780	55 098	45 682
Participation rate	59.8	65.5	54.2	60.1	66.0	54.2	59.8	65.6	54.0	59.9	65.6	54.3
Employed	90 171	48 709	41 462	92 866	50 554	42 312	93 674	51 039	42 635	94 346	51 106	43 239
Employment-population ratio	56.4	61.5	51.5	57.0	62.3	51.8	56.7	61.9	51.6	56.1	60.9	51.4
Full-time workers[1]	72 515	41 496	31 019	75 054	43 274	31 780	75 755	43 752	32 003	76 064	43 515	32 549
Part-time workers[2]	17 657	7 213	10 444	17 812	7 280	10 532	17 919	7 286	10 632	18 282	7 592	10 690
Unemployed	5 374	3 205	2 169	4 971	2 971	2 000	5 080	3 095	1 984	6 435	3 992	2 443
Unemployment rate	5.6	6.2	5.0	5.1	5.6	4.5	5.1	5.7	4.4	6.4	7.2	5.3

Note: Own children include sons, daughters, stepchildren, and adopted children. Not included are nieces, nephews, grandchildren, and other related and unrelated children. Detail may not sum to total due to rounding. Estimates for 2000 are not strictly comparable with data for later years due to population controls reflecting Census 2000 results.

[1] Usually work 35 hours or more a week at all jobs.
[2] Usually work less than 35 hours a week at all jobs.
[3] Includes never-married, divorced, separated, and widowed persons.

Table 1-24. Employment Status of Mothers with Own Children Under 3 Years of Age, by Age of Youngest Child and Marital Status, Annual Averages, 2004–2008

(Thousands of people, percent.)

Year and characteristic	Civilian noninstitutional population	Civilian labor force		Employed				Unemployed	
		Total	Percent of population	Total	Percent of population	Full-time workers[1]	Part-time workers[2]	Number	Percent of labor force
2004									
Total Mothers with Own Children Under 3 Years	9 345	5 377	57.5	4 964	53.1	3 360	1 604	414	7.7
2 years	2 813	1 746	62.1	1 630	57.9	1 152	477	116	6.6
1 year	3 273	1 906	58.2	1 759	53.7	1 172	587	147	7.7
Under 1 year	3 259	1 725	52.9	1 575	48.3	1 035	540	151	8.7
Married, Spouse Present with Own Children Under 3 Years	7 071	3 910	55.3	3 740	52.9	2 513	1 227	170	4.4
2 years	2 111	1 246	59.0	1 200	56.8	839	361	46	3.7
1 year	2 519	1 401	55.6	1 337	53.1	877	459	65	4.6
Under 1 year	2 441	1 262	51.7	1 203	49.3	797	406	59	4.7
Other Marital Status with Own Children Under 3 Years[3]	2 274	1 467	64.5	1 224	53.8	847	377	243	16.6
2 years	702	499	71.1	430	61.2	314	116	70	13.9
1 year	754	505	66.9	422	56.0	295	127	82	16.3
Under 1 year	818	463	56.6	372	45.4	238	134	91	19.7
2005									
Total Mothers with Own Children Under 3 Years	9 365	5 470	58.4	5 077	54.2	3 501	1 576	393	7.2
2 years	2 845	1 773	62.3	1 654	58.1	1 162	492	119	6.7
1 year	3 287	1 958	59.6	1 823	55.5	1 247	576	135	6.9
Under 1 year	3 233	1 740	53.8	1 600	49.5	1 092	508	140	8.0
Married, Spouse Present with Own Children Under 3 Years	6 951	3 939	56.7	3 776	54.3	2 588	1 188	164	4.2
2 years	2 118	1 268	59.9	1 214	57.3	840	374	55	4.3
1 year	2 435	1 389	57.0	1 337	54.9	901	436	52	3.7
Under 1 year	2 398	1 282	53.5	1 225	51.1	847	378	58	4.5
Other Marital Status with Own Children Under 3 Years[3]	2 414	1 531	63.4	1 301	53.9	913	388	230	15.0
2 years	726	504	69.5	440	60.6	322	118	64	12.7
1 year	852	569	66.8	486	57.0	346	139	83	14.6
Under 1 year	836	457	54.7	375	44.9	245	130	82	18.0
2006									
Total Mothers with Own Children Under 3 Years	9 431	5 675	60.2	5 315	56.4	3 751	1 564	360	6.3
2 years	2 864	1 847	64.5	1 746	61.0	1 280	466	101	5.5
1 year	3 318	2 006	60.5	1 883	56.7	1 305	577	123	6.1
Under 1 year	3 248	1 822	56.1	1 686	51.9	1 166	520	136	7.4
Married, Spouse Present with Own Children Under 3 Years	6 998	4 076	58.2	3 933	56.2	2 756	1 177	143	3.5
2 years	2 114	1 305	61.7	1 265	59.8	910	354	40	3.1
1 year	2 494	1 456	58.4	1 404	56.3	962	442	52	3.6
Under 1 year	2 390	1 315	55.0	1 264	52.9	883	381	51	3.9
Other Marital Status with Own Children Under 3 Years[3]	2 433	1 600	65.7	1 382	56.8	996	386	217	13.6
2 years	750	543	72.3	481	64.2	369	112	61	11.3
1 year	824	550	66.7	479	58.1	344	135	71	13.0
Under 1 year	859	507	59.0	422	49.2	283	139	85	16.7
2007									
Total Mothers with Own Children Under 3 Years	9 659	5 721	59.2	5 354	55.4	3 783	1 571	367	6.4
2 years	2 812	1 808	64.3	1 694	60.2	1 225	469	114	6.3
1 year	3 501	2 068	59.1	1 938	55.4	1 350	589	130	6.3
Under 1 year	3 346	1 845	55.1	1 721	51.4	1 208	513	123	6.7
Married, Spouse Present with Own Children Under 3 Years	7 018	4 027	57.4	3 888	55.4	2 730	1 157	140	3.5
2 years	2 076	1 281	61.7	1 230	59.2	881	349	51	4.0
1 year	2 536	1 433	56.5	1 388	54.7	954	434	46	3.2
Under 1 year	2 406	1 313	54.6	1 270	52.8	896	374	43	3.3
Other Marital Status with Own Children Under 3 Years[3]	2 641	1 694	64.1	1 466	55.5	1 052	414	227	13.4
2 years	736	528	71.6	464	63.1	344	120	63	12.0
1 year	965	635	65.8	551	57.1	396	155	84	13.2
Under 1 year	940	531	56.5	451	48.0	312	139	80	15.1
2008									
Total Mothers with Own Children Under 3 Years	9 595	5 792	60.4	5 354	55.8	3 782	1 573	438	7.6
2 years	2 934	1 852	63.1	1 734	59.1	1 264	470	118	6.4
1 year	3 342	2 069	61.9	1 905	57.0	1 337	568	164	7.9
Under 1 year	3 319	1 871	56.4	1 715	51.7	1 180	535	156	8.4
Married, Spouse Present with Own Children Under 3 Years	6 868	4 035	58.7	3 848	56.0	2 717	1 132	186	4.6
2 years	2 088	1 255	60.1	1 206	57.8	871	335	49	3.9
1 year	2 414	1 450	60.1	1 380	57.2	970	410	70	4.8
Under 1 year	2 366	1 330	56.2	1 263	53.4	875	388	67	5.0
Other Marital Status with Own Children Under 3 Years[3]	2 727	1 758	64.4	1 506	55.2	1 065	441	252	14.3
2 years	847	597	70.5	528	62.4	393	135	69	11.5
1 year	928	619	66.7	525	56.6	367	159	94	15.1
Under 1 year	953	542	56.8	452	47.5	305	147	89	16.5

Note: Own children include sons, daughters, stepchildren, and adopted children. Not included are nieces, nephews, grandchildren, and other related and unrelated children. Detail may not sum to total due to rounding. Updated population controls are introduced annually with the release of January data.

[1] Usually work 35 hours or more a week at all jobs.
[2] Usually work less than 35 hours a week at all jobs.
[3] Includes never-married, divorced, separated, and widowed persons.

UNEMPLOYMENT

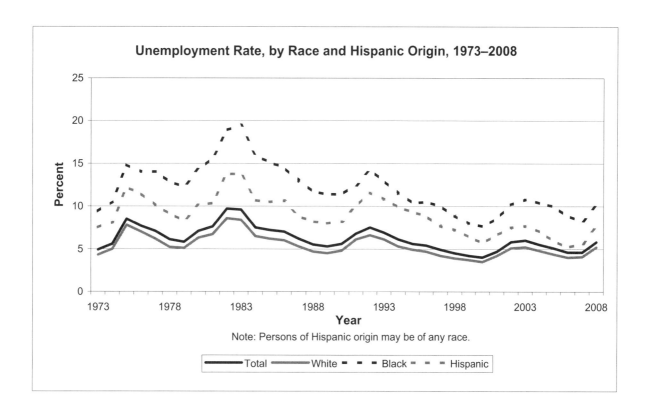

Unemployment Rate, by Race and Hispanic Origin, 1973–2008

Note: Persons of Hispanic origin may be of any race.

The unemployment rate increased for all racial and ethnic groups in 2008. Blacks continued to have the highest unemployment rate at 10.1 percent, followed by Hispanics (7.6 percent) and Whites (5.2 percent). From 2007 to 2008, the unemployment rate increased by 2.0 percentage points for Hispanics, 1.8 percentage points for Blacks, and 1.1 percentage points for Whites. (See Table 1-27.)

OTHER HIGHLIGHTS

- The unemployment rate increased dramatically in 2008, rising from 4.6 percent in 2007 to 5.8 percent in 2008. It was higher for men (6.1 percent) than for women (5.4 percent). (See Table 1-27.)

- The disparity in unemployment rates among age groups continued to be substantial, as younger workers experienced much higher levels of unemployment. In 2008, the unemployment rate for those age 16 to 19 years was 18.7 percent, while it was only 3.7 percent for those age 55 to 64 years. (See Table 1-27.)

- Among the major industries, construction had the highest unemployment rate at 10.6 percent, while government had the lowest at 2.4 percent. (See Table 1-29.)

- Michigan (8.4 percent), Rhode Island (7.8 percent), and California (7.2 percent) had the highest unemployment rates in 2008. From 2007 to 2008, the unemployment rate increased in 46 states and the District of Columbia and remained the same in three states: Arkansas, Wisconsin, and West Virginia. Oklahoma was the only state that experienced a decline in the unemployment rate from 2007 to 2008. (See Table 1-5.)

Table 1-25. Unemployment Rate, by Selected Characteristics, 1948–2008

(Unemployment as a percent of civilian labor force.)

Year	All civilian workers	Both sexes, 16 to 19 years	Men, 20 years and over	Women, 20 years and over	White[1]	Black[1]	Asian[1]	Hispanic[2]	Married men, spouse present	Married women, spouse present	Women who maintain families
1948	3.8	9.2	3.2	3.6	...	...	...	...	...	...	...
1949	5.9	13.4	5.4	5.3	...	...	...	...	...	...	...
1950	5.3	12.2	4.7	5.1	...	...	...	...	...	...	...
1951	3.3	8.2	2.5	4.0	...	...	...	...	...	...	...
1952	3.0	8.5	2.4	3.2	...	...	...	...	...	...	...
1953	2.9	7.6	2.5	2.9	...	...	...	...	...	...	...
1954	5.5	12.6	4.9	5.5	5.0	...	...	...	...	...	...
1955	4.4	11.0	3.8	4.4	3.9	...	...	...	2.6	3.7	...
1956	4.1	11.1	3.4	4.2	3.6	...	...	...	2.3	3.6	...
1957	4.3	11.6	3.6	4.1	3.8	...	...	...	2.8	4.3	...
1958	6.8	15.9	6.2	6.1	6.1	...	...	...	5.1	6.5	...
1959	5.5	14.6	4.7	5.2	4.8	...	...	...	3.6	5.2	...
1960	5.5	14.7	4.7	5.1	5.0	...	...	...	3.7	5.2	...
1961	6.7	16.8	5.7	6.3	6.0	...	...	...	4.6	6.4	...
1962	5.5	14.7	4.6	5.4	4.9	...	...	...	3.6	5.4	...
1963	5.7	17.2	4.5	5.4	5.0	...	...	...	3.4	5.4	...
1964	5.2	16.2	3.9	5.2	4.6	...	...	...	2.8	5.1	...
1965	4.5	14.8	3.2	4.5	4.1	...	...	...	2.4	4.5	...
1966	3.8	12.8	2.5	3.8	3.4	...	...	...	1.9	3.7	...
1967	3.8	12.9	2.3	4.2	3.4	...	...	...	1.8	4.5	4.9
1968	3.6	12.7	2.2	3.8	3.2	...	...	...	1.6	3.9	4.4
1969	3.5	12.2	2.1	3.7	3.1	...	...	...	1.5	3.9	4.4
1970	4.9	15.3	3.5	4.8	4.5	...	...	...	2.6	4.9	5.4
1971	5.9	16.9	4.4	5.7	5.4	...	...	...	3.2	5.7	7.3
1972	5.6	16.2	4.0	5.4	5.1	10.4	...	...	2.8	5.4	7.2
1973	4.9	14.5	3.3	4.9	4.3	9.4	...	7.5	2.3	4.7	7.1
1974	5.6	16.0	3.8	5.5	5.0	10.5	...	8.1	2.7	5.3	7.0
1975	8.5	19.9	6.8	8.0	7.8	14.8	...	12.2	5.1	7.9	10.0
1976	7.7	19.0	5.9	7.4	7.0	14.0	...	11.5	4.2	7.1	10.1
1977	7.1	17.8	5.2	7.0	6.2	14.0	...	10.1	3.6	6.5	9.4
1978	6.1	16.4	4.3	6.0	5.2	12.8	...	9.1	2.8	5.5	8.5
1979	5.8	16.1	4.2	5.7	5.1	12.3	...	8.3	2.8	5.1	8.3
1980	7.1	17.8	5.9	6.4	6.3	14.3	...	10.1	4.2	5.8	9.2
1981	7.6	19.6	6.3	6.8	6.7	15.6	...	10.4	4.3	6.0	10.4
1982	9.7	23.2	8.8	8.3	8.6	18.9	...	13.8	6.5	7.4	11.7
1983	9.6	22.4	8.9	8.1	8.4	19.5	...	13.7	6.5	7.0	12.2
1984	7.5	18.9	6.6	6.8	6.5	15.9	...	10.7	4.6	5.7	10.3
1985	7.2	18.6	6.2	6.6	6.2	15.1	...	10.5	4.3	5.6	10.4
1986	7.0	18.3	6.1	6.2	6.0	14.5	...	10.6	4.4	5.2	9.8
1987	6.2	16.9	5.4	5.4	5.3	13.0	...	8.8	3.9	4.3	9.2
1988	5.5	15.3	4.8	4.9	4.7	11.7	...	8.2	3.3	3.9	8.1
1989	5.3	15.0	4.5	4.7	4.5	11.4	...	8.0	3.0	3.7	8.1
1990	5.6	15.5	5.0	4.9	4.8	11.4	...	8.2	3.4	3.8	8.3
1991	6.8	18.7	6.4	5.7	6.1	12.5	...	10.0	4.4	4.5	9.3
1992	7.5	20.1	7.1	6.3	6.6	14.2	...	11.6	5.1	5.0	10.0
1993	6.9	19.0	6.4	5.9	6.1	13.0	...	10.8	4.4	4.6	9.7
1994	6.1	17.6	5.4	5.4	5.3	11.5	...	9.9	3.7	4.1	8.9
1995	5.6	17.3	4.8	4.9	4.9	10.4	...	9.3	3.3	3.9	8.0
1996	5.4	16.7	4.6	4.8	4.7	10.5	...	8.9	3.0	3.6	8.2
1997	4.9	16.0	4.2	4.4	4.2	10.0	...	7.7	2.7	3.1	8.1
1998	4.5	14.6	3.7	4.1	3.9	8.9	...	7.2	2.4	2.9	7.2
1999	4.2	13.9	3.5	3.8	3.7	8.0	...	6.4	2.2	2.7	6.4
2000	4.0	13.1	3.3	3.6	3.5	7.6	3.6	5.7	2.0	2.7	5.9
2001	4.7	14.7	4.2	4.1	4.2	8.6	4.5	6.6	2.7	3.1	6.6
2002	5.8	16.5	5.3	5.1	5.1	10.2	5.9	7.5	3.6	3.7	8.0
2003	6.0	17.5	5.6	5.1	5.2	10.8	6.0	7.7	3.8	3.7	8.5
2004	5.5	17.0	5.0	4.9	4.8	10.4	4.4	7.0	3.1	3.5	8.0
2005	5.1	16.6	4.4	4.6	4.4	10.0	4.0	6.0	2.8	3.3	7.8
2006	4.6	15.4	4.0	4.1	4.0	8.9	3.0	5.2	2.4	2.9	7.1
2007	4.6	15.7	4.1	4.0	4.1	8.3	3.2	5.6	2.5	2.8	6.5
2008	5.8	18.7	5.4	4.9	5.2	10.1	4.0	7.6	3.4	3.6	8.0

Note: See notes and definitions for information on historical comparability.

[1]Beginning in 2003, persons who selected this race group only; persons who selected more than one race group are not included. Prior to 2003, persons who reported more than one race group were included in the group they identified as their main race.
[2]May be of any race.
. . . = Not available.

Table 1-26. Unemployed Persons, by Age, Sex, Race, and Hispanic Origin, 1948–2008

(Thousands of people.)

Race, Hispanic origin, sex, and year	16 years and over	16 to 19 years			20 years and over						
		Total	16 to 17 years	18 to 19 years	Total	20 to 24 years	25 to 34 years	35 to 44 years	45 to 54 years	55 to 64 years	65 years and over
ALL RACES											
Both Sexes											
1948	2 276	409	180	228	1 869	455	457	347	290	226	93
1949	3 637	576	238	337	3 060	680	776	603	471	384	146
1950	3 288	513	226	287	2 776	561	702	530	478	368	137
1951	2 055	336	168	168	1 718	273	435	354	318	238	103
1952	1 883	345	180	165	1 539	268	389	325	274	195	86
1953	1 834	307	150	157	1 529	256	379	325	280	218	70
1954	3 532	501	221	247	3 032	504	793	680	548	374	132
1955	2 852	450	211	239	2 403	396	577	521	436	355	120
1956	2 750	478	231	247	2 274	395	554	476	429	311	109
1957	2 859	497	230	266	2 362	430	573	499	448	300	111
1958	4 602	678	299	379	3 923	701	993	871	731	472	154
1959	3 740	654	301	354	3 085	543	726	673	603	405	135
1960	3 852	712	325	387	3 140	583	752	671	614	396	122
1961	4 714	828	363	465	3 886	723	890	850	751	516	159
1962	3 911	721	312	409	3 191	636	712	688	605	411	141
1963	4 070	884	420	462	3 187	658	732	674	589	410	126
1964	3 786	872	436	437	2 913	660	607	605	543	378	117
1965	3 366	874	411	463	2 491	557	529	546	436	322	103
1966	2 875	837	395	441	2 041	446	441	426	369	265	92
1967	2 975	839	400	438	2 140	511	480	422	383	256	86
1968	2 817	838	414	426	1 978	543	443	371	314	219	88
1969	2 832	853	436	416	1 978	560	453	358	320	216	72
1970	4 093	1 106	537	569	2 987	866	718	515	476	309	104
1971	5 016	1 262	596	665	3 755	1 130	933	630	573	381	109
1972	4 882	1 308	633	676	3 573	1 132	878	576	510	368	111
1973	4 365	1 235	634	600	3 130	1 008	866	451	430	290	88
1974	5 156	1 422	699	722	3 733	1 212	1 044	559	498	321	99
1975	7 929	1 767	799	968	6 161	1 865	1 776	951	893	520	155
1976	7 406	1 719	796	924	5 687	1 714	1 710	849	758	510	147
1977	6 991	1 663	781	881	5 330	1 629	1 650	785	666	450	147
1978	6 202	1 583	796	787	4 620	1 483	1 422	694	552	345	123
1979	6 137	1 555	739	816	4 583	1 442	1 446	705	540	346	104
1980	7 637	1 669	778	890	5 969	1 835	2 024	940	676	399	94
1981	8 273	1 763	781	981	6 510	1 976	2 211	1 065	715	444	98
1982	10 678	1 977	831	1 145	8 701	2 392	3 037	1 552	966	647	107
1983	10 717	1 829	753	1 076	8 888	2 330	3 078	1 650	1 039	677	114
1984	8 539	1 499	646	854	7 039	1 838	2 374	1 335	828	566	97
1985	8 312	1 468	662	806	6 844	1 738	2 341	1 340	813	518	93
1986	8 237	1 454	665	789	6 783	1 651	2 390	1 371	790	489	91
1987	7 425	1 347	648	700	6 077	1 453	2 129	1 281	723	412	78
1988	6 701	1 226	573	653	5 475	1 261	1 929	1 166	657	375	87
1989	6 528	1 194	537	657	5 333	1 218	1 851	1 159	637	379	91
1990	7 047	1 212	527	685	5 835	1 299	1 995	1 328	723	386	105
1991	8 628	1 359	587	772	7 269	1 573	2 447	1 719	946	473	113
1992	9 613	1 427	641	787	8 186	1 649	2 702	1 976	1 138	589	132
1993	8 940	1 365	606	759	7 575	1 514	2 395	1 896	1 121	541	108
1994	7 996	1 320	624	696	6 676	1 373	2 067	1 627	971	485	153
1995	7 404	1 346	652	695	6 058	1 244	1 841	1 549	844	425	153
1996	7 236	1 306	617	689	5 929	1 239	1 757	1 505	883	406	139
1997	6 739	1 271	589	683	5 467	1 152	1 571	1 418	830	369	127
1998	6 210	1 205	573	632	5 005	1 081	1 419	1 258	782	343	122
1999	5 880	1 162	544	618	4 718	1 042	1 278	1 154	753	367	124
2000	5 692	1 081	502	579	4 611	1 022	1 207	1 133	762	355	132
2001	6 801	1 162	531	632	5 638	1 209	1 498	1 355	989	458	129
2002	8 378	1 253	540	714	7 124	1 430	1 890	1 691	1 315	635	163
2003	8 774	1 251	545	706	7 523	1 495	1 960	1 815	1 356	713	183
2004	8 149	1 208	554	653	6 942	1 431	1 784	1 578	1 288	682	179
2005	7 591	1 186	541	645	6 405	1 335	1 661	1 400	1 195	630	184
2006	7 001	1 119	509	610	5 882	1 234	1 521	1 279	1 094	595	159
2007	7 078	1 101	485	616	5 976	1 241	1 544	1 225	1 135	642	190
2008	8 924	1 285	563	722	7 639	1 545	1 949	1 604	1 473	803	264

Table 1-26. Unemployed Persons, by Age, Sex, Race, and Hispanic Origin, 1948–2008—Continued

(Thousands of people.)

Race, Hispanic origin, sex, and year	16 years and over	16 to 19 years			20 years and over						
		Total	16 to 17 years	18 to 19 years	Total	20 to 24 years	25 to 34 years	35 to 44 years	45 to 54 years	55 to 64 years	65 years and over
ALL RACES											
Men											
1948	1 559	256	113	142	1 305	324	289	233	201	177	81
1949	2 572	353	145	207	2 219	485	539	414	347	310	125
1950	2 239	318	139	179	1 922	377	467	348	327	286	117
1951	1 221	191	102	89	1 029	155	241	192	193	162	87
1952	1 185	205	116	89	980	155	233	192	182	145	73
1953	1 202	184	94	90	1 019	152	236	208	196	167	60
1954	2 344	310	142	168	2 035	327	517	431	372	275	112
1955	1 854	274	134	140	1 580	248	353	328	285	265	102
1956	1 711	269	134	135	1 442	240	348	278	270	216	90
1957	1 841	300	140	159	1 541	283	349	304	302	220	83
1958	3 098	416	185	231	2 681	478	685	552	492	349	124
1959	2 420	398	191	207	2 022	343	484	407	390	287	112
1960	2 486	426	200	225	2 060	369	492	415	392	294	96
1961	2 997	479	221	258	2 518	458	585	507	473	375	122
1962	2 423	408	188	220	2 016	381	445	404	382	300	103
1963	2 472	501	248	252	1 971	396	445	386	358	290	97
1964	2 205	487	257	230	1 718	384	345	324	319	263	85
1965	1 914	479	247	232	1 435	311	292	283	253	221	75
1966	1 551	432	220	212	1 120	221	239	219	196	179	65
1967	1 508	448	241	207	1 060	235	219	185	199	163	60
1968	1 419	426	234	193	993	258	205	171	165	132	61
1969	1 403	440	244	196	963	270	205	155	157	127	48
1970	2 238	599	306	294	1 638	479	391	253	247	198	71
1971	2 789	693	346	347	2 097	640	513	320	313	239	71
1972	2 659	711	357	355	1 948	628	466	284	272	227	73
1973	2 275	653	352	300	1 624	528	439	211	219	171	57
1974	2 714	757	394	362	1 957	649	546	266	250	183	63
1975	4 442	966	445	521	3 476	1 081	986	507	499	302	103
1976	4 036	939	443	496	3 098	951	914	431	411	296	94
1977	3 667	874	421	453	2 794	877	869	373	326	252	97
1978	3 142	813	426	388	2 328	768	691	314	277	198	81
1979	3 120	811	393	418	2 308	744	699	329	272	196	67
1980	4 267	913	429	485	3 353	1 076	1 137	482	357	243	58
1981	4 577	962	431	531	3 615	1 144	1 213	552	390	261	55
1982	6 179	1 090	469	621	5 089	1 407	1 791	879	550	393	69
1983	6 260	1 003	408	595	5 257	1 369	1 822	947	613	433	73
1984	4 744	812	348	464	3 932	1 023	1 322	728	450	356	53
1985	4 521	806	363	443	3 715	944	1 244	706	459	307	55
1986	4 530	779	355	424	3 751	899	1 291	763	440	301	58
1987	4 101	732	353	379	3 369	779	1 169	689	426	258	49
1988	3 655	667	311	356	2 987	676	1 040	617	366	240	49
1989	3 525	658	303	355	2 867	660	953	619	351	234	49
1990	3 906	667	283	384	3 239	715	1 092	711	413	249	59
1991	4 946	751	317	433	4 195	911	1 375	990	550	305	64
1992	5 523	806	357	449	4 717	951	1 529	1 118	675	378	67
1993	5 055	768	342	426	4 287	865	1 338	1 049	636	336	64
1994	4 367	740	342	398	3 627	768	1 113	855	522	281	88
1995	3 983	744	352	391	3 239	673	961	815	464	233	94
1996	3 880	733	347	387	3 146	675	903	786	484	223	76
1997	3 577	694	321	373	2 882	636	772	732	457	217	69
1998	3 266	686	330	355	2 580	583	699	609	420	201	69
1999	3 066	633	295	338	2 433	562	624	571	403	203	70
2000	2 975	599	281	317	2 376	547	602	557	398	189	83
2001	3 690	650	300	350	3 040	688	756	714	536	272	74
2002	4 597	700	301	399	3 896	792	1 023	897	725	373	87
2003	4 906	697	291	407	4 209	841	1 097	988	764	412	107
2004	4 456	664	292	372	3 791	811	980	839	684	373	104
2005	4 059	667	300	367	3 392	775	844	715	624	331	102
2006	3 753	622	271	352	3 131	705	810	642	569	318	88
2007	3 882	623	263	360	3 259	721	856	634	591	349	108
2008	5 033	736	312	425	4 297	920	1 119	875	804	425	153

Table 1-26. Unemployed Persons, by Age, Sex, Race, and Hispanic Origin, 1948–2008—*Continued*

(Thousands of people.)

Race, Hispanic origin, sex, and year	16 years and over	16 to 19 years			20 years and over						
		Total	16 to 17 years	18 to 19 years	Total	20 to 24 years	25 to 34 years	35 to 44 years	45 to 54 years	55 to 64 years	65 years and over
ALL RACES											
Women											
1948	717	153	67	86	564	131	168	114	89	49	12
1949	1 065	223	93	130	841	195	237	189	124	74	21
1950	1 049	195	87	108	854	184	235	182	151	82	20
1951	834	145	66	79	689	118	194	162	125	76	16
1952	698	140	64	76	559	113	156	133	92	50	13
1953	632	123	56	67	510	104	143	117	84	51	10
1954	1 188	191	79	79	997	177	276	249	176	99	20
1955	998	176	77	99	823	148	224	193	151	90	18
1956	1 039	209	97	112	832	155	206	198	159	95	19
1957	1 018	197	90	107	821	147	224	195	146	80	28
1958	1 504	262	114	148	1 242	223	308	319	239	123	30
1959	1 320	256	110	147	1 063	200	242	266	213	118	23
1960	1 366	286	125	162	1 080	214	260	256	222	102	26
1961	1 717	349	142	207	1 368	265	305	343	278	141	37
1962	1 488	313	124	189	1 175	255	267	284	223	111	38
1963	1 598	383	172	210	1 216	262	287	288	231	120	29
1964	1 581	385	179	207	1 195	276	262	281	224	115	32
1965	1 452	395	164	231	1 056	246	237	263	183	101	28
1966	1 324	405	175	229	921	225	202	207	173	86	27
1967	1 468	391	159	231	1 078	277	261	237	184	93	26
1968	1 397	412	180	233	985	285	238	200	149	87	27
1969	1 429	413	192	220	1 015	290	248	203	163	89	24
1970	1 855	506	231	275	1 349	387	327	262	229	111	33
1971	2 227	568	250	318	1 658	489	420	310	260	142	38
1972	2 222	598	276	322	1 625	503	413	293	237	141	38
1973	2 089	583	282	301	1 507	480	427	240	212	119	31
1974	2 441	665	305	360	1 777	564	497	294	248	137	36
1975	3 486	802	355	447	2 684	783	791	444	395	219	52
1976	3 369	780	352	429	2 588	763	795	417	346	214	53
1977	3 324	789	361	428	2 535	752	782	412	340	198	50
1978	3 061	769	370	399	2 292	714	731	381	275	148	43
1979	3 018	743	346	396	2 276	697	748	375	268	150	38
1980	3 370	755	349	407	2 615	760	886	459	318	155	36
1981	3 696	800	350	450	2 895	833	998	513	325	184	43
1982	4 499	886	362	524	3 613	985	1 246	673	416	254	38
1983	4 457	825	344	481	3 632	961	1 255	703	427	244	41
1984	3 794	687	298	390	3 107	815	1 052	607	378	211	45
1985	3 791	661	298	363	3 129	794	1 098	634	355	211	39
1986	3 707	675	310	365	3 032	752	1 099	609	350	189	33
1987	3 324	616	295	321	2 709	674	960	592	298	155	30
1988	3 046	558	262	297	2 487	585	889	550	291	136	38
1989	3 003	536	234	302	2 467	558	897	540	286	144	41
1990	3 140	544	243	301	2 596	584	902	617	310	137	46
1991	3 683	608	270	338	3 074	662	1 071	728	396	168	49
1992	4 090	621	283	338	3 469	698	1 173	858	463	210	66
1993	3 885	597	264	333	3 288	648	1 058	847	485	205	45
1994	3 629	580	282	298	3 049	605	954	772	449	204	66
1995	3 421	602	299	303	2 819	571	880	735	381	193	60
1996	3 356	573	270	303	2 783	564	854	720	399	183	63
1997	3 162	577	268	310	2 585	516	800	686	373	152	58
1998	2 944	519	242	277	2 424	498	720	650	362	141	53
1999	2 814	529	249	280	2 285	480	654	584	350	163	54
2000	2 717	483	221	262	2 235	475	604	577	364	165	50
2001	3 111	512	230	282	2 599	521	742	641	453	187	55
2002	3 781	553	238	315	3 228	638	866	795	591	263	76
2003	3 868	554	255	299	3 314	654	863	827	592	302	76
2004	3 694	543	262	281	3 150	619	804	739	605	309	75
2005	3 531	519	240	278	3 013	560	817	685	571	299	82
2006	3 247	496	238	258	2 751	530	711	637	524	277	71
2007	3 196	478	222	256	2 718	520	688	591	544	293	81
2008	3 891	549	251	297	3 342	625	830	730	669	377	111

Table 1-26. Unemployed Persons, by Age, Sex, Race, and Hispanic Origin, 1948–2008—*Continued*

(Thousands of people.)

Race, Hispanic origin, sex, and year	16 years and over	16 to 19 years			20 years and over						
		Total	16 to 17 years	18 to 19 years	Total	20 to 24 years	25 to 34 years	35 to 44 years	45 to 54 years	55 to 64 years	65 years and over
WHITE											
Both Sexes											
1954	2 859	423	191	232	2 436	394	610	540	447	329	115
1955	2 252	373	181	191	1 879	304	412	402	358	300	105
1956	2 159	382	191	191	1 777	297	406	363	355	258	98
1957	2 289	401	195	204	1 888	331	425	401	373	262	98
1958	3 680	541	245	297	3 139	541	756	686	614	405	136
1959	2 946	525	255	270	2 421	406	526	525	496	348	120
1960	3 065	575	273	302	2 490	456	573	520	502	330	109
1961	3 743	669	295	374	3 074	566	668	652	611	438	139
1962	3 052	580	262	318	2 472	488	515	522	485	345	117
1963	3 208	708	350	358	2 500	501	540	518	485	349	107
1964	2 999	708	365	342	2 291	508	441	472	447	323	100
1965	2 691	705	329	374	1 986	437	399	427	358	276	91
1966	2 255	651	315	336	1 604	338	323	336	298	227	80
1967	2 338	635	311	325	1 703	393	360	336	321	221	75
1968	2 226	644	326	318	1 582	422	330	297	269	187	80
1969	2 260	660	351	309	1 601	432	354	294	269	185	66
1970	3 339	871	438	432	2 468	679	570	433	415	275	95
1971	4 085	1 011	491	521	3 074	887	732	517	500	338	100
1972	3 906	1 021	515	506	2 885	887	679	459	439	324	95
1973	3 442	955	513	443	2 486	758	664	358	371	257	77
1974	4 097	1 104	561	544	2 993	925	821	448	427	283	88
1975	6 421	1 413	657	755	5 007	1 474	1 413	774	753	460	136
1976	5 914	1 364	649	715	4 550	1 326	1 329	682	637	448	128
1977	5 441	1 284	636	648	4 157	1 195	1 255	621	569	388	129
1978	4 698	1 189	631	558	3 509	1 059	1 059	543	453	290	104
1979	4 664	1 193	589	603	3 472	1 038	1 068	545	443	290	87
1980	5 884	1 291	625	666	4 593	1 364	1 528	740	550	335	74
1981	6 343	1 374	629	745	4 968	1 449	1 658	827	578	379	77
1982	8 241	1 534	683	851	6 707	1 770	2 283	1 223	796	549	86
1983	8 128	1 387	609	778	6 741	1 678	2 282	1 294	837	563	88
1984	6 372	1 116	510	605	5 256	1 282	1 723	1 036	660	475	81
1985	6 191	1 074	507	567	5 117	1 235	1 695	1 039	642	432	75
1986	6 140	1 070	509	561	5 070	1 149	1 751	1 056	629	407	78
1987	5 501	995	495	500	4 506	1 017	1 527	984	576	333	68
1988	4 944	910	437	473	4 033	874	1 371	890	520	309	69
1989	4 770	863	407	456	3 908	856	1 297	871	503	311	70
1990	5 186	903	401	502	4 283	899	1 401	983	582	330	88
1991	6 560	1 029	461	568	5 532	1 132	1 805	1 330	759	410	96
1992	7 169	1 037	484	553	6 132	1 156	1 967	1 483	915	495	116
1993	6 655	992	468	523	5 663	1 057	1 754	1 411	907	442	92
1994	5 892	960	471	489	4 933	952	1 479	1 184	779	407	132
1995	5 459	952	476	476	4 507	866	1 311	1 161	676	362	131
1996	5 300	939	456	484	4 361	854	1 223	1 117	709	336	122
1997	4 836	912	438	475	3 924	765	1 068	1 035	648	302	106
1998	4 484	876	424	451	3 608	731	978	901	620	276	101
1999	4 273	844	414	430	3 429	720	865	843	595	303	104
2000	4 121	795	386	409	3 326	682	835	817	591	294	107
2001	4 969	845	402	443	4 124	829	1 062	985	761	378	109
2002	6 137	925	407	518	5 212	977	1 340	1 237	1 004	518	137
2003	6 311	909	414	495	5 401	1 012	1 354	1 287	1 025	569	155
2004	5 847	890	414	476	4 957	959	1 211	1 130	953	557	148
2005	5 350	845	391	454	4 505	878	1 106	1 006	884	488	144
2006	5 002	794	375	419	4 208	832	1 029	920	813	480	135
2007	5 143	805	361	444	4 338	851	1 052	902	848	520	164
2008	6 509	947	422	524	5 562	1 087	1 336	1 196	1 094	634	216

Table 1-26. Unemployed Persons, by Age, Sex, Race, and Hispanic Origin, 1948–2008—*Continued*

(Thousands of people.)

Race, Hispanic origin, sex, and year	16 years and over	16 to 19 years			20 years and over						
		Total	16 to 17 years	18 to 19 years	Total	20 to 24 years	25 to 34 years	35 to 44 years	45 to 54 years	55 to 64 years	65 years and over
WHITE											
Men											
1954	1 913	266	125	142	1 647	260	408	341	299	241	98
1955	1 478	232	114	117	1 246	196	260	246	233	223	89
1956	1 366	221	112	108	1 145	186	265	212	225	177	81
1957	1 477	243	118	124	1 234	222	257	239	250	193	73
1958	2 489	333	149	184	2 156	382	525	436	404	299	110
1959	1 903	318	162	156	1 585	256	350	316	320	245	98
1960	1 988	341	167	174	1 647	295	376	330	317	243	86
1961	2 398	384	176	208	2 014	370	442	395	382	318	107
1962	1 915	334	158	176	1 581	300	332	311	308	246	84
1963	1 976	407	211	196	1 569	309	342	297	294	246	80
1964	1 779	400	217	183	1 379	310	262	255	266	216	70
1965	1 556	387	200	186	1 169	254	226	228	206	190	67
1966	1 241	340	178	162	901	172	185	173	160	154	57
1967	1 208	342	186	156	866	185	171	153	167	140	52
1968	1 142	328	185	143	814	206	162	140	142	111	55
1969	1 137	343	198	145	794	214	165	130	134	108	43
1970	1 857	485	255	230	1 372	388	316	212	216	177	64
1971	2 309	562	288	275	1 747	513	418	268	272	211	66
1972	2 173	564	288	276	1 610	506	375	231	237	199	60
1973	1 836	513	284	229	1 323	411	353	166	188	153	51
1974	2 169	584	311	274	1 585	505	434	218	213	161	53
1975	3 627	785	369	416	2 841	871	796	412	411	265	86
1976	3 258	754	368	385	2 504	750	730	346	341	259	78
1977	2 883	672	342	330	2 211	660	682	297	276	213	82
1978	2 411	615	338	277	1 797	558	525	250	227	169	68
1979	2 405	633	319	313	1 773	553	526	253	220	165	56
1980	3 345	716	347	369	2 629	827	884	378	291	206	44
1981	3 580	755	349	406	2 825	869	943	433	317	221	42
1982	4 846	854	387	467	3 991	1 066	1 385	696	460	331	53
1983	4 859	761	328	433	4 098	1 019	1 410	755	497	362	54
1984	3 600	608	280	328	2 992	722	991	572	363	302	42
1985	3 426	592	282	310	2 834	694	931	553	356	257	43
1986	3 433	576	276	299	2 857	645	978	586	349	248	51
1987	3 132	548	272	276	2 584	568	879	536	350	209	43
1988	2 766	499	239	260	2 268	480	777	477	293	200	40
1989	2 636	487	230	257	2 149	476	694	470	280	191	38
1990	2 935	504	214	290	2 431	510	796	530	330	214	51
1991	3 859	575	249	327	3 284	677	1 064	780	438	269	55
1992	4 209	590	270	319	3 620	686	1 155	858	543	318	58
1993	3 828	565	261	305	3 263	619	1 015	793	512	270	53
1994	3 275	540	259	280	2 735	555	827	626	417	236	74
1995	2 999	535	260	275	2 465	483	711	621	371	200	79
1996	2 896	532	260	273	2 363	478	655	592	383	188	67
1997	2 641	502	234	268	2 140	439	553	549	358	182	58
1998	2 431	510	254	257	1 920	405	512	441	342	164	58
1999	2 274	461	223	237	1 813	398	441	419	322	172	61
2000	2 177	446	217	229	1 731	368	428	403	302	162	68
2001	2 754	479	232	247	2 275	494	547	529	413	229	64
2002	3 459	516	228	288	2 943	562	772	672	554	305	77
2003	3 643	518	221	298	3 125	589	798	723	591	333	91
2004	3 282	497	224	274	2 785	560	694	620	516	307	88
2005	2 931	480	220	260	2 450	522	586	536	463	263	81
2006	2 730	449	202	247	2 281	483	567	482	417	259	73
2007	2 869	461	195	266	2 408	501	604	478	447	285	93
2008	3 727	548	231	317	3 179	668	784	662	604	337	124

Table 1-26. Unemployed Persons, by Age, Sex, Race, and Hispanic Origin, 1948–2008—*Continued*

(Thousands of people.)

Race, Hispanic origin, sex, and year	16 years and over	16 to 19 years			20 years and over						
		Total	16 to 17 years	18 to 19 years	Total	20 to 24 years	25 to 34 years	35 to 44 years	45 to 54 years	55 to 64 years	65 years and over
WHITE											
Women											
1954	946	157	66	90	789	134	202	199	148	88	17
1955	774	141	67	74	633	108	152	156	125	77	16
1956	793	161	79	83	632	111	141	151	130	81	17
1957	812	158	77	80	654	109	168	162	123	69	25
1958	1 191	208	96	113	983	159	231	250	210	106	26
1959	1 043	207	93	114	836	150	176	209	176	103	22
1960	1 077	234	106	128	843	161	197	190	185	87	23
1961	1 345	285	119	166	1 060	196	226	257	229	120	32
1962	1 137	246	104	142	891	188	183	211	177	99	33
1963	1 232	301	139	162	931	192	198	221	191	103	27
1964	1 220	308	148	159	912	198	179	217	181	107	30
1965	1 135	318	129	188	817	183	173	199	152	86	24
1966	1 014	311	137	174	703	166	138	163	138	73	23
1967	1 130	293	125	169	837	209	189	183	154	81	23
1968	1 084	316	141	175	768	216	168	157	127	76	25
1969	1 123	317	153	164	806	218	189	164	135	77	23
1970	1 482	386	183	202	1 096	291	254	221	199	98	31
1971	1 777	449	203	246	1 328	376	314	249	228	126	34
1972	1 733	457	227	230	1 275	381	304	227	202	125	35
1973	1 606	442	228	214	1 164	347	311	192	183	104	26
1974	1 927	519	250	270	1 408	420	387	230	214	122	35
1975	2 794	628	288	340	2 166	602	617	362	342	195	49
1976	2 656	611	280	330	2 045	577	598	336	296	188	49
1977	2 558	612	294	318	1 946	536	573	323	293	175	47
1978	2 287	574	292	281	1 713	500	533	294	226	122	37
1979	2 260	560	270	290	1 699	485	542	293	223	125	32
1980	2 540	576	278	298	1 964	537	645	362	259	129	31
1981	2 762	620	281	339	2 143	580	715	394	261	158	36
1982	3 395	680	296	384	2 715	704	898	527	337	217	33
1983	3 270	626	282	345	2 643	659	872	539	340	201	33
1984	2 772	508	231	277	2 264	559	731	464	297	173	39
1985	2 765	482	225	257	2 283	541	763	486	286	175	32
1986	2 708	495	233	262	2 213	504	773	470	281	159	27
1987	2 369	447	223	224	1 922	449	648	448	227	124	25
1988	2 177	412	198	214	1 766	393	594	413	227	110	30
1989	2 135	376	177	199	1 758	380	603	401	223	120	32
1990	2 251	399	187	212	1 852	389	605	453	251	116	37
1991	2 701	453	212	241	2 248	455	741	550	320	141	41
1992	2 959	447	214	233	2 512	469	811	625	372	177	58
1993	2 827	426	208	219	2 400	438	739	618	395	172	39
1994	2 617	420	211	208	2 197	397	652	558	361	170	58
1995	2 460	418	216	201	2 042	384	600	540	306	162	52
1996	2 404	407	196	211	1 998	376	568	525	326	148	55
1997	2 195	411	204	207	1 784	326	515	486	290	119	49
1998	2 053	365	171	195	1 688	327	467	460	279	112	43
1999	1 999	383	190	193	1 616	322	423	423	273	131	43
2000	1 944	349	168	180	1 595	314	407	414	289	133	39
2001	2 215	366	170	196	1 849	335	515	456	348	150	45
2002	2 678	409	179	230	2 269	415	567	565	449	213	60
2003	2 668	391	194	197	2 276	423	555	564	434	235	64
2004	2 565	393	191	202	2 172	399	516	510	437	250	60
2005	2 419	365	172	193	2 054	356	520	469	421	225	63
2006	2 271	345	173	172	1 927	349	462	437	395	222	62
2007	2 274	344	166	178	1 930	350	448	425	401	235	71
2008	2 782	399	191	207	2 384	419	552	534	489	298	92

Table 1-26. Unemployed Persons, by Age, Sex, Race, and Hispanic Origin, 1948–2008—*Continued*

(Thousands of people.)

Race, Hispanic origin, sex, and year	16 years and over	16 to 19 years			20 years and over						
		Total	16 to 17 years	18 to 19 years	Total	20 to 24 years	25 to 34 years	35 to 44 years	45 to 54 years	55 to 64 years	65 years and over
BLACK											
Both Sexes											
1972	906	279	113	167	627	226	183	106	62	37	12
1973	846	262	114	148	584	231	181	82	53	29	9
1974	965	297	127	170	666	261	201	95	65	33	10
1975	1 369	330	130	200	1 040	362	321	157	126	54	17
1976	1 334	330	134	195	1 005	350	338	145	101	54	16
1977	1 393	354	135	218	1 040	397	355	140	81	51	16
1978	1 330	360	150	210	972	379	320	127	82	47	17
1979	1 319	333	137	197	986	369	335	137	82	48	15
1980	1 553	343	134	210	1 209	426	433	171	109	53	18
1981	1 731	357	138	219	1 374	483	493	207	119	55	17
1982	2 142	396	130	266	1 747	565	662	278	141	84	17
1983	2 272	392	125	267	1 879	591	700	299	174	95	21
1984	1 914	353	122	230	1 561	504	577	253	138	75	15
1985	1 864	357	135	221	1 507	455	562	254	143	74	18
1986	1 840	347	138	209	1 493	453	564	269	127	69	10
1987	1 684	312	134	178	1 373	397	533	247	124	62	10
1988	1 547	288	121	167	1 259	349	502	230	111	51	15
1989	1 544	300	116	184	1 245	322	494	246	109	53	20
1990	1 565	268	112	156	1 297	349	505	278	106	44	14
1991	1 723	280	105	175	1 443	378	539	318	151	44	13
1992	2 011	324	127	197	1 687	421	610	402	178	64	13
1993	1 844	313	112	201	1 530	387	532	376	153	72	11
1994	1 666	300	127	173	1 366	351	468	346	130	55	16
1995	1 538	325	143	182	1 213	311	423	303	116	42	18
1996	1 592	310	133	177	1 282	327	454	313	127	48	13
1997	1 560	302	123	179	1 258	327	426	307	136	45	16
1998	1 426	281	124	156	1 146	301	366	294	125	45	16
1999	1 309	268	109	159	1 041	273	339	249	121	46	14
2000	1 241	230	96	134	1 011	281	289	254	131	38	20
2001	1 416	260	102	158	1 155	307	340	283	159	52	15
2002	1 693	260	103	156	1 433	365	407	349	215	76	21
2003	1 787	255	93	162	1 532	375	442	385	217	93	20
2004	1 729	241	103	138	1 487	353	441	341	245	86	21
2005	1 700	267	115	152	1 433	358	423	310	222	92	28
2006	1 549	253	102	151	1 296	318	388	276	214	81	19
2007	1 445	235	98	138	1 210	300	367	237	208	79	19
2008	1 788	246	98	148	1 542	355	458	301	275	117	36
BLACK											
Men											
1972	448	143	66	77	305	113	84	45	31	23	9
1973	395	128	62	66	267	108	75	37	27	16	5
1974	494	159	75	82	336	129	103	41	35	19	8
1975	741	170	71	100	571	195	169	83	78	33	13
1976	698	170	69	103	528	185	166	73	60	32	13
1977	698	187	73	114	512	197	170	63	40	31	12
1978	641	180	80	101	462	185	148	53	40	24	11
1979	636	164	68	97	473	174	152	66	44	27	10
1980	815	179	72	108	636	222	222	88	60	32	12
1981	891	188	73	115	703	248	245	102	65	32	10
1982	1 167	213	72	141	954	304	355	154	74	54	12
1983	1 213	211	70	142	1 002	313	358	162	96	59	14
1984	1 003	188	62	126	815	272	289	132	67	45	9
1985	951	193	69	124	757	224	268	127	85	43	11
1986	946	180	68	112	765	225	273	148	70	44	5
1987	826	160	70	90	666	186	253	122	61	39	6
1988	771	154	64	90	617	177	233	111	58	30	8
1989	773	153	65	88	619	162	226	129	59	33	10
1990	806	142	62	80	664	177	247	146	62	27	6
1991	890	145	54	91	745	201	252	172	87	25	7
1992	1 067	180	71	109	886	221	301	208	107	42	6
1993	971	170	66	104	801	201	260	201	87	46	7
1994	848	167	69	97	682	173	218	180	72	29	10
1995	762	168	73	95	593	153	195	150	63	21	11
1996	808	169	73	96	639	163	210	158	75	26	7
1997	747	162	70	92	585	165	178	141	72	22	7
1998	671	147	61	86	524	151	148	133	60	24	8
1999	626	145	60	85	480	135	143	114	60	22	7
2000	620	121	52	70	499	145	134	121	72	17	9
2001	709	136	51	85	573	150	159	142	84	31	7
2002	835	140	54	85	695	181	180	165	120	40	9
2003	891	132	49	83	760	192	212	189	109	47	10
2004	860	128	52	75	733	188	211	160	120	46	8
2005	844	145	63	82	699	192	189	143	116	45	14
2006	774	134	53	81	640	167	189	118	112	43	11
2007	752	130	55	75	622	166	186	114	106	41	10
2008	949	138	54	84	811	190	242	154	143	61	21

Table 1-26. Unemployed Persons, by Age, Sex, Race, and Hispanic Origin, 1948–2008—*Continued*

(Thousands of people.)

Race, Hispanic origin, sex, and year	16 years and over	16 to 19 years			20 years and over						
		Total	16 to 17 years	18 to 19 years	Total	20 to 24 years	25 to 34 years	35 to 44 years	45 to 54 years	55 to 64 years	65 years and over
BLACK											
Women											
1972	458	136	47	90	322	113	99	61	31	14	3
1973	451	134	51	82	317	123	105	45	26	13	4
1974	470	139	51	87	331	132	98	55	30	14	2
1975	629	160	60	100	469	167	153	75	48	22	4
1976	637	160	66	93	477	165	172	73	41	23	3
1977	695	167	63	104	528	200	185	77	41	21	4
1978	690	179	70	110	510	194	173	74	41	23	6
1979	683	169	69	100	513	195	183	71	38	21	5
1980	738	164	62	102	574	204	211	83	49	21	6
1981	840	169	65	104	671	235	248	105	54	23	7
1982	975	182	58	124	793	261	307	123	67	29	5
1983	1 059	181	56	125	878	278	342	137	77	36	7
1984	911	165	60	104	747	231	288	121	71	30	5
1985	913	164	66	98	750	231	295	127	58	31	7
1986	894	167	70	97	728	228	291	121	57	25	5
1987	858	152	64	88	706	211	280	125	63	23	4
1988	776	134	57	78	642	172	269	118	53	22	7
1989	772	147	51	96	625	160	267	118	50	21	9
1990	758	126	49	76	633	172	258	132	44	17	8
1991	833	135	51	84	698	177	288	145	64	19	6
1992	944	144	56	88	800	200	308	194	71	22	6
1993	872	143	46	97	729	186	272	175	66	26	5
1994	818	133	57	76	685	178	249	166	59	26	6
1995	777	157	. . .	87	620	158	228	153	53	20	7
1996	784	141	60	80	643	164	244	155	52	21	7
1997	813	140	53	87	673	163	248	166	64	24	9
1998	756	134	63	71	622	150	218	160	65	21	8
1999	684	123	49	74	561	138	196	135	61	25	7
2000	621	109	44	65	512	136	154	132	59	22	10
2001	706	124	52	72	582	157	181	141	75	21	8
2002	858	120	49	71	738	183	228	185	95	35	12
2003	895	123	44	79	772	183	230	195	109	46	10
2004	868	114	51	63	755	166	230	180	126	40	13
2005	856	123	52	70	734	166	233	168	106	47	14
2006	775	120	50	70	656	150	199	158	102	38	8
2007	693	106	43	63	588	135	181	123	103	38	9
2008	839	108	44	64	732	166	216	147	132	56	15
HISPANIC[1]											
Both Sexes											
1973	277	80	. . .	. . .	. . .	. . .	. . .	. . .	. . .	. . .	. . .
1974	325	88	. . .	. . .	. . .	. . .	. . .	. . .	. . .	. . .	. . .
1975	508	123	. . .	. . .	. . .	. . .	. . .	. . .	. . .	. . .	. . .
1976	485	106	51	55	385	116	113	72	53	26	6
1977	456	113	50	60	344	98	114	56	48	24	5
1978	452	110	63	47	342	98	116	65	41	16	5
1979	434	106	54	51	329	100	102	65	37	20	4
1980	620	145	66	79	474	138	168	90	49	24	5
1981	678	144	60	84	533	171	178	92	57	31	5
1982	929	175	73	102	754	221	267	140	75	45	6
1983	961	167	64	104	793	214	270	156	93	54	5
1984	800	149	60	88	651	164	235	124	71	51	5
1985	811	141	55	85	670	171	256	123	73	41	7
1986	857	141	57	84	716	183	258	143	85	38	9
1987	751	136	57	79	615	152	222	128	75	33	5
1988	732	148	63	84	585	145	209	120	69	36	6
1989	750	132	59	73	618	158	218	124	76	36	6
1990	876	161	68	94	714	167	263	156	85	36	7
1991	1 092	179	79	99	913	214	332	206	110	44	8
1992	1 311	219	94	124	1 093	240	390	267	126	59	10
1993	1 248	201	86	115	1 047	237	354	261	132	54	10
1994	1 187	198	90	108	989	220	348	227	132	51	12
1995	1 140	205	96	109	934	209	325	224	106	54	16
1996	1 132	199	85	114	933	217	296	246	101	59	14
1997	1 069	197	87	110	872	206	269	229	99	56	13
1998	1 026	214	89	125	812	194	260	203	96	48	11
1999	945	196	79	117	750	171	233	190	104	42	10
2000	954	194	83	112	759	190	247	189	79	42	12
2001	1 138	208	84	123	931	212	315	228	111	56	9
2002	1 353	221	81	140	1 132	265	373	271	146	62	15
2003	1 441	192	79	113	1 249	273	419	294	183	69	10
2004	1 342	203	86	117	1 139	255	371	261	161	74	18
2005	1 191	191	78	113	1 000	227	324	231	142	61	15
2006	1 081	170	74	97	911	194	294	231	128	49	14
2007	1 220	197	78	119	1 023	213	322	238	161	70	19
2008	1 678	251	105	146	1 427	307	437	328	242	81	32

[1]May be of any race.
. . . = Not available.

Table 1-26. Unemployed Persons, by Age, Sex, Race, and Hispanic Origin, 1948–2008—*Continued*

(Thousands of people.)

Race, Hispanic origin, sex, and year	16 years and over	16 to 19 years			20 years and over						
		Total	16 to 17 years	18 to 19 years	Total	20 to 24 years	25 to 34 years	35 to 44 years	45 to 54 years	55 to 64 years	65 years and over
HISPANIC[1]											
Men											
1973	158	. . .	. . .	. . .	114	. . .	. . .	. . .	. . .	. . .	. . .
1974	187	. . .	. . .	. . .	139	. . .	. . .	. . .	. . .	. . .	. . .
1975	296	. . .	. . .	. . .	225	. . .	. . .	. . .	. . .	. . .	. . .
1976	278	60	30	31	217	69	63	38	29	16	. . .
1977	253	60	27	33	195	57	65	28	22	15	. . .
1978	234	59	35	24	175	51	59	30	20	10	. . .
1979	223	55	29	27	168	52	50	33	19	11	. . .
1980	370	86	39	47	284	85	96	51	31	16	. . .
1981	408	87	40	47	321	105	113	49	31	19	. . .
1982	565	104	45	59	461	138	169	80	40	29	. . .
1983	591	100	38	62	491	134	168	92	57	36	. . .
1984	480	87	36	51	393	103	142	69	41	33	. . .
1985	483	82	34	49	401	108	156	69	40	23	. . .
1986	520	82	33	50	438	115	159	86	46	26	. . .
1987	451	77	32	45	374	88	137	77	46	22	. . .
1988	437	86	36	50	351	83	128	70	42	24	. . .
1989	423	81	36	45	342	88	113	69	43	25	. . .
1990	524	100	40	60	425	99	154	91	53	25	. . .
1991	685	110	47	62	575	139	210	126	62	33	. . .
1992	807	132	56	75	675	156	239	156	75	42	. . .
1993	747	118	50	68	629	144	217	148	79	33	. . .
1994	680	121	54	67	558	128	203	113	75	30	9
1995	651	121	59	63	530	123	185	120	57	33	13
1996	607	112	49	63	495	117	165	124	49	31	9
1997	582	110	47	63	471	125	137	113	54	35	8
1998	552	117	54	62	436	115	142	97	49	29	5
1999	480	106	42	63	374	96	109	83	54	24	7
2000	494	106	46	60	388	105	118	93	42	23	8
2001	611	117	52	65	495	129	152	116	55	36	6
2002	764	127	42	86	636	151	213	144	82	38	8
2003	809	116	42	74	693	157	239	153	98	41	5
2004	755	120	48	72	635	158	207	133	82	41	13
2005	647	112	42	70	536	134	168	119	74	31	9
2006	601	104	43	61	497	110	169	114	66	29	8
2007	695	119	44	74	576	121	189	126	92	35	13
2008	1 007	147	63	84	860	188	275	192	136	50	19
HISPANIC[1]											
Women											
1973	119	. . .	. . .	. . .	83	. . .	. . .	. . .	. . .	. . .	. . .
1974	137	. . .	. . .	. . .	98	. . .	. . .	. . .	. . .	. . .	. . .
1975	212	. . .	. . .	. . .	160	. . .	. . .	. . .	. . .	. . .	. . .
1976	207	45	22	24	166	47	52	33	22	10	. . .
1977	204	50	23	27	153	40	49	28	25	11	. . .
1978	219	51	28	23	168	46	58	36	20	8	. . .
1979	211	50	26	24	160	48	52	32	18	10	. . .
1980	249	59	28	31	190	53	72	39	18	8	. . .
1981	269	57	20	37	212	65	65	43	25	13	. . .
1982	364	71	28	43	293	83	98	60	35	16	. . .
1983	369	68	26	42	302	80	102	65	36	18	. . .
1984	320	62	25	37	258	61	93	55	30	17	. . .
1985	327	58	22	37	269	63	100	54	32	18	. . .
1986	337	59	25	35	278	68	99	57	39	12	. . .
1987	300	59	25	34	241	64	85	51	29	11	. . .
1988	296	62	27	34	234	63	81	50	27	12	. . .
1989	327	51	23	28	276	70	105	55	33	11	. . .
1990	351	62	28	34	289	68	109	65	32	11	. . .
1991	407	69	32	37	339	74	122	80	48	12	. . .
1992	504	87	38	49	418	84	151	111	51	17	. . .
1993	501	83	36	47	418	93	136	113	53	21	. . .
1994	508	77	36	40	431	92	145	115	57	21	2
1995	488	84	38	46	404	86	140	104	50	21	3
1996	525	88	36	52	438	100	131	122	52	27	5
1997	488	87	40	46	401	81	132	117	46	21	4
1998	473	98	35	63	376	80	118	106	48	19	5
1999	466	90	36	54	376	75	124	107	50	17	3
2000	460	88	37	51	371	86	129	96	38	19	4
2001	527	91	33	58	436	83	163	112	56	20	3
2002	590	94	39	54	496	113	160	127	65	24	7
2003	631	76	37	39	555	116	180	141	86	28	5
2004	587	83	38	45	504	97	164	128	78	32	5
2005	544	80	36	43	464	93	156	112	68	30	6
2006	480	67	31	36	414	84	125	116	62	20	6
2007	525	79	34	45	446	92	134	111	69	35	6
2008	672	104	42	62	567	119	162	136	105	32	13

[1]May be of any race.
. . . = Not available.

Table 1-27. Unemployment Rates of Civilian Workers, by Age, Sex, Race, and Hispanic Origin, 1948–2008

(Percent of labor force.)

Race, Hispanic origin, sex, and year	16 years and over	16 to 19 years			20 years and over						
		Total	16 to 17 years	18 to 19 years	Total	20 to 24 years	25 to 34 years	35 to 44 years	45 to 54 years	55 to 64 years	65 years and over
ALL RACES											
Both Sexes											
1948	3.8	9.2	10.1	8.6	3.3	6.2	3.2	2.6	2.7	3.1	3.2
1949	5.9	13.4	14.0	13.0	5.4	9.3	5.4	4.4	4.2	5.2	4.9
1950	5.3	12.2	13.6	11.2	4.8	7.7	4.8	3.8	4.2	4.8	4.5
1951	3.3	8.2	9.6	7.1	3.0	4.1	3.0	2.5	2.7	3.1	3.4
1952	3.0	8.5	10.0	7.3	2.7	4.6	2.6	2.3	2.3	2.4	2.9
1953	2.9	7.6	8.7	6.8	2.6	4.7	2.5	2.2	2.3	2.7	2.2
1954	5.5	12.6	13.5	10.7	5.1	9.2	5.3	4.5	4.4	4.5	4.1
1955	4.4	11.0	12.3	10.0	3.9	7.0	3.8	3.4	3.4	4.2	3.6
1956	4.1	11.1	12.3	10.2	3.7	6.6	3.7	3.0	3.2	3.5	3.2
1957	4.3	11.6	12.5	10.9	3.8	7.1	3.9	3.1	3.3	3.4	3.4
1958	6.8	15.9	16.4	15.5	6.2	11.2	6.8	5.4	5.2	5.2	4.8
1959	5.5	14.6	15.3	14.0	4.8	8.5	5.0	4.2	4.2	4.4	4.3
1960	5.5	14.7	15.5	14.1	4.8	8.7	5.2	4.1	4.1	4.2	3.8
1961	6.7	16.8	18.3	15.8	5.9	10.4	6.2	5.2	5.0	5.4	5.1
1962	5.5	14.7	16.3	13.6	4.9	9.0	5.1	4.1	4.0	4.2	4.5
1963	5.7	17.2	19.3	15.6	4.8	8.8	5.2	4.0	3.8	4.1	4.1
1964	5.2	16.2	17.8	14.9	4.3	8.3	4.3	3.6	3.5	3.7	3.8
1965	4.5	14.8	16.5	13.5	3.6	6.7	3.7	3.2	2.8	3.1	3.3
1966	3.8	12.8	14.8	11.3	2.9	5.3	3.1	2.5	2.3	2.5	3.0
1967	3.8	12.9	14.6	11.6	3.0	5.7	3.2	2.5	2.4	2.4	2.8
1968	3.6	12.7	14.7	11.2	2.7	5.8	2.8	2.2	1.9	2.0	2.8
1969	3.5	12.2	14.5	10.5	2.7	5.7	2.8	2.2	1.9	1.9	2.2
1970	4.9	15.3	17.1	13.8	4.0	8.2	4.2	3.1	2.8	2.7	3.2
1971	5.9	16.9	18.7	15.5	4.9	10.0	5.3	3.9	3.4	3.3	3.5
1972	5.6	16.2	18.5	14.6	4.5	9.3	4.6	3.5	3.0	3.2	3.6
1973	4.9	14.5	17.3	12.4	3.9	7.8	4.2	2.7	2.5	2.6	3.0
1974	5.6	16.0	18.3	14.3	4.5	9.1	4.8	3.3	2.9	2.8	3.4
1975	8.5	19.9	21.4	18.9	7.3	13.6	7.8	5.6	5.2	4.6	5.2
1976	7.7	19.0	21.1	17.5	6.5	12.0	7.1	4.9	4.5	4.5	5.1
1977	7.1	17.8	19.9	16.2	5.9	11.0	6.5	4.4	3.9	3.9	5.0
1978	6.1	16.4	19.3	14.2	5.0	9.6	5.3	3.7	3.3	2.9	4.0
1979	5.8	16.1	18.1	14.7	4.8	9.1	5.2	3.6	3.2	2.9	3.4
1980	7.1	17.8	20.0	16.2	6.1	11.5	6.9	4.6	4.0	3.3	3.1
1981	7.6	19.6	21.4	18.4	6.5	12.3	7.3	5.0	4.2	3.7	3.2
1982	9.7	23.2	24.9	22.1	8.6	14.9	9.7	6.9	5.7	5.4	3.5
1983	9.6	22.4	24.5	21.1	8.6	14.5	9.7	7.0	6.2	5.6	3.7
1984	7.5	18.9	21.2	17.4	6.7	11.5	7.3	5.4	4.9	4.7	3.3
1985	7.2	18.6	21.0	17.0	6.4	11.1	7.0	5.1	4.7	4.3	3.2
1986	7.0	18.3	20.2	17.0	6.2	10.7	6.9	5.0	4.5	4.1	3.0
1987	6.2	16.9	19.1	15.2	5.4	9.7	6.0	4.5	4.0	3.5	2.5
1988	5.5	15.3	17.4	13.8	4.8	8.7	5.4	4.0	3.4	3.2	2.7
1989	5.3	15.0	17.2	13.6	4.6	8.6	5.2	3.8	3.2	3.2	2.6
1990	5.6	15.5	17.9	14.1	4.9	8.8	5.6	4.1	3.6	3.3	3.0
1991	6.8	18.7	21.0	17.2	6.1	10.8	6.9	5.2	4.5	4.1	3.3
1992	7.5	20.1	23.1	18.2	6.8	11.4	7.6	5.8	5.1	5.1	3.8
1993	6.9	19.0	21.4	17.5	6.2	10.5	6.9	5.5	4.8	4.7	3.2
1994	6.1	17.6	19.9	16.0	5.4	9.7	6.0	4.6	4.0	4.1	4.0
1995	5.6	17.3	20.2	15.3	4.9	9.1	5.4	4.3	3.3	3.6	4.0
1996	5.4	16.7	18.9	15.2	4.7	9.3	5.2	4.1	3.3	3.3	3.6
1997	4.9	16.0	18.2	14.5	4.3	8.5	4.7	3.8	3.0	2.9	3.3
1998	4.5	14.6	17.2	12.8	3.9	7.9	4.3	3.4	2.8	2.6	3.2
1999	4.2	13.9	16.3	12.4	3.6	7.5	4.0	3.0	2.6	2.7	3.1
2000	4.0	13.1	15.4	11.6	3.4	7.2	3.7	3.0	2.5	2.5	3.1
2001	4.7	14.7	17.2	13.1	4.2	8.3	4.6	3.6	3.1	3.0	2.9
2002	5.8	16.5	18.8	15.1	5.2	9.7	5.9	4.6	4.0	3.9	3.6
2003	6.0	17.5	19.1	16.4	5.4	10.0	6.1	4.9	4.1	4.1	3.8
2004	5.5	17.0	20.2	15.0	4.9	9.4	5.5	4.4	3.8	3.8	3.6
2005	5.1	16.6	19.1	14.9	4.5	8.8	5.1	3.9	3.5	3.3	3.5
2006	4.6	15.4	17.2	14.1	4.1	8.2	4.7	3.6	3.1	3.0	2.9
2007	4.6	15.7	17.5	14.5	4.1	8.2	4.7	3.4	3.2	3.1	3.3
2008	5.8	18.7	22.1	16.8	5.2	10.2	5.8	4.6	4.1	3.7	4.2

Table 1-27. Unemployment Rates of Civilian Workers, by Age, Sex, Race, and Hispanic Origin, 1948–2008
—Continued

(Percent of labor force.)

Race, Hispanic origin, sex, and year	16 years and over	16 to 19 years			20 years and over						
		Total	16 to 17 years	18 to 19 years	Total	20 to 24 years	25 to 34 years	35 to 44 years	45 to 54 years	55 to 64 years	65 years and over
ALL RACES											
Men											
1948	3.6	9.8	10.2	9.5	3.2	6.9	2.8	2.4	2.5	3.1	3.4
1949	5.9	14.3	13.7	14.6	5.4	10.4	5.2	4.3	4.3	5.4	5.1
1950	5.1	12.7	13.3	12.3	4.7	8.1	4.4	3.6	4.0	4.9	4.8
1951	2.8	8.1	9.4	7.0	2.5	3.9	2.3	2.0	2.4	2.8	3.5
1952	2.8	8.9	10.5	7.4	2.4	4.6	2.2	1.9	2.2	2.4	3.0
1953	2.8	7.9	8.8	7.2	2.5	5.0	2.2	2.0	2.3	2.8	2.4
1954	5.3	13.5	13.9	13.2	4.9	10.7	4.8	4.1	4.3	4.5	4.4
1955	4.2	11.6	12.5	10.8	3.8	7.7	3.3	3.1	3.2	4.3	4.0
1956	3.8	11.1	11.7	10.5	3.4	6.9	3.3	2.6	3.0	3.5	3.5
1957	4.1	12.4	12.4	12.3	3.6	7.8	3.3	2.8	3.3	3.5	3.4
1958	6.8	17.1	16.3	17.8	6.2	12.7	6.5	5.1	5.3	5.5	5.2
1959	5.2	15.3	15.8	14.9	4.7	8.7	4.7	3.7	4.1	4.5	4.8
1960	5.4	15.3	15.5	15.0	4.7	8.9	4.8	3.8	4.1	4.6	4.2
1961	6.4	17.1	18.3	16.3	5.7	10.8	5.7	4.6	4.9	5.7	5.5
1962	5.2	14.7	16.0	13.8	4.6	8.9	4.5	3.6	3.9	4.6	4.6
1963	5.2	17.2	18.8	15.9	4.5	8.8	4.5	3.5	3.6	4.3	4.5
1964	4.6	15.8	17.1	14.6	3.9	8.1	3.5	2.9	3.2	3.9	4.0
1965	4.0	14.1	16.1	12.4	3.2	6.4	2.9	2.5	2.5	3.3	3.5
1966	3.2	11.7	13.7	10.2	2.5	4.6	2.4	2.0	1.9	2.6	3.1
1967	3.1	12.3	14.5	10.5	2.3	4.7	2.1	1.7	2.0	2.3	2.8
1968	2.9	11.6	13.9	9.7	2.2	5.1	1.9	1.6	1.6	1.9	2.8
1969	2.8	11.4	13.8	9.3	2.1	5.1	1.9	1.5	1.5	1.8	2.2
1970	4.4	15.0	16.9	13.4	3.5	8.4	3.5	2.4	2.4	2.8	3.3
1971	5.3	16.6	18.7	15.0	4.4	10.3	4.4	3.1	3.0	3.3	3.4
1972	5.0	15.9	18.3	14.1	4.0	9.3	3.8	2.7	2.6	3.2	3.6
1973	4.2	13.9	17.0	11.4	3.3	7.3	3.4	2.0	2.1	2.4	3.0
1974	4.9	15.6	18.4	13.3	3.8	8.8	4.0	2.6	2.4	2.6	3.3
1975	7.9	20.1	21.6	19.0	6.8	14.3	6.9	4.9	4.8	4.3	5.4
1976	7.1	19.2	21.4	17.6	5.9	12.1	6.2	4.1	4.0	4.2	5.1
1977	6.3	17.3	19.5	15.6	5.2	10.8	5.7	3.5	3.2	3.6	5.2
1978	5.3	15.8	19.1	13.3	4.3	9.2	4.4	2.8	2.7	2.8	4.2
1979	5.1	15.9	17.9	14.3	4.2	8.7	4.3	2.9	2.7	2.7	3.4
1980	6.9	18.3	20.4	16.7	5.9	12.5	6.7	4.1	3.6	3.4	3.1
1981	7.4	20.1	22.0	18.8	6.3	13.2	6.9	4.5	4.0	3.6	2.9
1982	9.9	24.4	26.4	23.1	8.8	16.4	10.1	6.9	5.6	5.5	3.7
1983	9.9	23.3	25.2	22.2	8.9	15.9	10.1	7.1	6.3	6.1	3.9
1984	7.4	19.6	21.9	18.3	6.6	11.9	7.2	5.2	4.6	5.0	3.0
1985	7.0	19.5	21.9	17.9	6.2	11.4	6.6	4.9	4.6	4.3	3.1
1986	6.9	19.0	20.8	17.7	6.1	11.0	6.7	5.1	4.4	4.3	3.2
1987	6.2	17.8	20.2	16.0	5.4	9.9	5.9	4.4	4.2	3.7	2.6
1988	5.5	16.0	18.2	14.6	4.8	8.9	5.3	3.8	3.5	3.5	2.5
1989	5.2	15.9	18.6	14.2	4.5	8.8	4.8	3.7	3.2	3.5	2.4
1990	5.7	16.3	18.4	15.0	5.0	9.1	5.5	4.1	3.7	3.8	3.0
1991	7.2	19.8	21.8	18.5	6.4	11.6	7.0	5.5	4.8	4.6	3.3
1992	7.9	21.5	24.6	19.5	7.1	12.2	7.8	6.1	5.6	5.8	3.3
1993	7.2	20.4	22.9	18.8	6.4	11.3	7.0	5.6	5.1	5.2	3.2
1994	6.2	19.0	21.0	17.6	5.4	10.2	5.9	4.5	4.0	4.4	4.0
1995	5.6	18.4	21.1	16.5	4.8	9.2	5.1	4.2	3.5	3.6	4.3
1996	5.4	18.1	20.8	16.3	4.6	9.5	4.9	4.0	3.5	3.3	3.4
1997	4.9	16.9	19.1	15.4	4.2	8.9	4.3	3.6	3.1	3.1	3.0
1998	4.4	16.2	19.1	14.1	3.7	8.1	3.9	3.0	2.8	2.8	3.1
1999	4.1	14.7	17.0	13.1	3.5	7.7	3.6	2.8	2.6	2.7	3.0
2000	3.9	14.0	16.8	12.2	3.3	7.3	3.4	2.8	2.4	2.4	3.3
2001	4.8	16.0	19.1	14.0	4.2	9.0	4.3	3.6	3.2	3.3	3.0
2002	5.9	18.1	21.1	16.4	5.3	10.2	5.8	4.5	4.2	4.3	3.4
2003	6.3	19.3	20.7	18.4	5.6	10.6	6.2	5.0	4.4	4.5	4.0
2004	5.6	18.4	22.0	16.3	5.0	10.1	5.5	4.3	3.9	3.9	3.7
2005	5.1	18.6	22.0	16.5	4.4	9.6	4.7	3.7	3.5	3.3	3.4
2006	4.6	16.9	18.6	15.7	4.0	8.7	4.5	3.3	3.1	3.0	2.8
2007	4.7	17.6	19.4	16.5	4.1	8.9	4.7	3.3	3.1	3.2	3.4
2008	6.1	21.2	25.2	19.0	5.4	11.4	6.1	4.6	4.2	3.8	4.5

Table 1-27. Unemployment Rates of Civilian Workers, by Age, Sex, Race, and Hispanic Origin, 1948–2008
—*Continued*

(Percent of labor force.)

Race, Hispanic origin, sex, and year	16 years and over	16 to 19 years			20 years and over						
		Total	16 to 17 years	18 to 19 years	Total	20 to 24 years	25 to 34 years	35 to 44 years	45 to 54 years	55 to 64 years	65 years and over
ALL RACES											
Women											
1948	4.1	8.3	10.0	7.4	3.6	4.8	4.3	3.0	3.0	3.1	2.3
1949	6.0	12.3	14.4	11.2	5.3	7.3	5.9	4.7	4.0	4.4	3.8
1950	5.7	11.4	14.2	9.8	5.1	6.9	5.7	4.4	4.5	4.5	3.4
1951	4.4	8.3	10.0	7.2	4.0	4.4	4.5	3.8	3.5	4.0	2.9
1952	3.6	8.0	9.1	7.3	3.2	4.5	3.6	3.0	2.5	2.5	2.2
1953	3.3	7.2	8.5	6.4	2.9	4.3	3.4	2.5	2.3	2.5	1.4
1954	6.0	11.4	12.7	7.7	5.5	7.3	6.6	5.3	4.6	4.6	3.0
1955	4.9	10.2	12.0	9.1	4.4	6.1	5.3	4.0	3.6	3.8	2.3
1956	4.8	11.2	13.2	9.9	4.2	6.3	4.8	3.9	3.6	3.6	2.3
1957	4.7	10.6	12.6	9.4	4.1	6.0	5.3	3.8	3.2	3.0	3.4
1958	6.8	14.3	16.6	12.9	6.1	8.9	7.3	6.2	4.9	4.5	3.7
1959	5.9	13.5	14.4	13.0	5.2	8.1	5.9	5.1	4.2	4.1	2.8
1960	5.9	13.9	15.5	12.9	5.1	8.3	6.3	4.8	4.2	3.4	2.9
1961	7.2	16.3	18.3	15.1	6.3	9.8	7.4	6.4	5.1	4.5	4.0
1962	6.2	14.6	16.7	13.5	5.4	9.1	6.5	5.2	4.1	3.5	4.2
1963	6.5	17.2	20.2	15.2	5.4	8.9	6.9	5.1	4.2	3.6	3.2
1964	6.2	16.6	18.8	15.2	5.2	8.6	6.3	5.0	3.9	3.3	3.3
1965	5.5	15.7	17.2	14.8	4.5	7.3	5.5	4.6	3.2	2.8	2.9
1966	4.8	14.1	16.6	12.6	3.8	6.3	4.5	3.6	2.9	2.3	2.8
1967	5.2	13.5	14.8	12.8	4.2	7.0	5.4	4.1	3.1	2.4	2.7
1968	4.8	14.0	15.9	12.9	3.8	6.7	4.7	3.4	2.4	2.2	2.7
1969	4.7	13.3	15.5	11.8	3.7	6.3	4.6	3.4	2.6	2.2	2.3
1970	5.9	15.6	17.4	14.4	4.8	7.9	5.7	4.4	3.5	2.7	3.1
1971	6.9	17.2	18.7	16.2	5.7	9.6	7.0	5.2	4.0	3.3	3.6
1972	6.6	16.7	18.8	15.2	5.4	9.4	6.2	4.9	3.6	3.3	3.5
1973	6.0	15.3	17.7	13.5	4.9	8.5	5.8	3.9	3.2	2.8	2.9
1974	6.7	16.6	18.2	15.4	5.5	9.5	6.2	4.6	3.7	3.2	3.6
1975	9.3	19.7	21.2	18.7	8.0	12.7	9.1	6.8	5.9	5.1	5.0
1976	8.6	18.7	20.8	17.4	7.4	11.9	8.4	6.1	5.2	4.9	5.0
1977	8.2	18.3	20.5	16.9	7.0	11.2	7.7	5.7	5.1	4.4	4.7
1978	7.2	17.1	19.5	15.3	6.0	10.1	6.7	5.0	4.0	3.2	3.8
1979	6.8	16.4	18.3	15.0	5.7	9.6	6.5	4.6	3.9	3.2	3.3
1980	7.4	17.2	19.6	15.6	6.4	10.4	7.2	5.3	4.5	3.3	3.1
1981	7.9	19.0	20.7	17.9	6.8	11.2	7.7	5.7	4.6	3.8	3.6
1982	9.4	21.9	23.2	21.0	8.3	13.2	9.3	7.0	5.9	5.2	3.2
1983	9.2	21.3	23.7	19.9	8.1	12.9	9.1	6.9	6.0	5.0	3.4
1984	7.6	18.0	20.4	16.6	6.8	10.9	7.4	5.6	5.2	4.3	3.8
1985	7.4	17.6	20.0	16.0	6.6	10.7	7.4	5.5	4.8	4.3	3.3
1986	7.1	17.6	19.6	16.3	6.2	10.3	7.2	5.0	4.5	3.8	2.8
1987	6.2	15.9	18.0	14.3	5.4	9.4	6.2	4.6	3.7	3.1	2.4
1988	5.6	14.4	16.6	12.9	4.9	8.5	5.6	4.1	3.4	2.7	2.9
1989	5.4	14.0	15.7	13.0	4.7	8.3	5.6	3.9	3.2	2.8	2.9
1990	5.5	14.7	17.4	13.1	4.9	8.5	5.6	4.2	3.4	2.8	3.1
1991	6.4	17.5	20.2	15.9	5.7	9.8	6.8	4.8	4.2	3.4	3.3
1992	7.0	18.6	21.5	16.6	6.3	10.3	7.4	5.5	4.6	4.2	4.5
1993	6.6	17.5	19.8	16.1	5.9	9.7	6.8	5.3	4.5	4.0	3.1
1994	6.0	16.2	18.7	14.3	5.4	9.2	6.2	4.7	4.0	3.9	4.0
1995	5.6	16.1	19.2	14.0	4.9	9.0	5.7	4.4	3.2	3.6	3.7
1996	5.4	15.2	16.9	14.0	4.8	9.0	5.5	4.2	3.2	3.4	4.0
1997	5.0	15.0	17.2	13.6	4.4	8.1	5.2	4.0	2.9	2.7	3.6
1998	4.6	12.9	15.1	11.5	4.1	7.8	4.8	3.8	2.7	2.4	3.3
1999	4.3	13.2	15.5	11.6	3.8	7.2	4.4	3.3	2.5	2.6	3.2
2000	4.1	12.1	13.9	10.8	3.6	7.1	4.1	3.3	2.5	2.5	2.7
2001	4.7	13.4	15.2	12.2	4.1	7.5	5.1	3.7	3.0	2.7	2.9
2002	5.6	14.9	16.6	13.8	5.1	9.1	5.9	4.6	3.8	3.5	3.9
2003	5.7	15.6	17.5	14.2	5.1	9.3	5.9	4.9	3.7	3.7	3.6
2004	5.4	15.5	18.5	13.5	4.9	8.7	5.6	4.4	3.7	3.6	3.4
2005	5.1	14.5	16.5	13.1	4.6	7.9	5.6	4.1	3.5	3.3	3.5
2006	4.6	13.8	15.9	12.4	4.1	7.6	4.9	3.9	3.1	2.9	3.0
2007	4.5	13.8	15.7	12.5	4.0	7.3	4.6	3.6	3.2	3.0	3.1
2008	5.4	16.2	19.1	14.3	4.9	8.8	5.5	4.5	3.9	3.7	3.9

Table 1-27. Unemployment Rates of Civilian Workers, by Age, Sex, Race, and Hispanic Origin, 1948–2008
—Continued

(Percent of labor force.)

Race, Hispanic origin, sex, and year	16 years and over	16 to 19 years			20 years and over						
		Total	16 to 17 years	18 to 19 years	Total	20 to 24 years	25 to 34 years	35 to 44 years	45 to 54 years	55 to 64 years	65 years and over
WHITE											
Both Sexes											
1954	5.0	12.1	13.2	11.3	4.6	8.3	4.6	4.0	4.0	4.3	3.9
1955	3.9	10.4	12.0	9.2	3.4	6.2	3.1	2.9	3.1	3.8	3.4
1956	3.6	10.1	11.5	9.0	3.2	5.7	3.1	2.6	2.9	3.2	3.1
1957	3.8	10.6	11.9	9.6	3.4	6.3	3.3	2.8	3.0	3.2	3.2
1958	6.1	14.4	15.2	13.9	5.6	9.9	5.9	4.8	4.8	4.9	4.6
1959	4.8	13.1	14.4	12.1	4.3	7.3	4.2	3.7	3.8	4.1	4.1
1960	5.0	13.5	14.6	12.6	4.3	7.9	4.5	3.6	3.8	3.9	3.7
1961	6.0	15.3	16.7	14.4	5.3	9.4	5.3	4.5	4.5	5.0	4.8
1962	4.9	13.3	15.3	12.0	4.2	7.9	4.2	3.6	3.6	3.9	4.0
1963	5.0	15.5	17.9	13.7	4.2	7.7	4.4	3.5	3.5	3.8	3.8
1964	4.6	14.8	16.5	13.3	3.8	7.3	3.6	3.2	3.2	3.5	3.5
1965	4.1	13.4	14.8	12.3	3.3	6.1	3.2	2.9	2.5	2.9	3.2
1966	3.4	11.2	13.3	9.7	2.6	4.6	2.6	2.3	2.1	2.4	2.9
1967	3.4	11.0	12.8	9.8	2.7	5.0	2.7	2.3	2.2	2.3	2.7
1968	3.2	11.0	12.9	9.6	2.5	5.2	2.4	2.0	1.8	1.9	2.8
1969	3.1	10.7	13.0	8.9	2.4	5.0	2.5	2.0	1.8	1.8	2.2
1970	4.5	13.5	15.5	11.9	3.7	7.3	3.8	3.0	2.7	2.7	3.2
1971	5.4	15.1	17.0	13.8	4.5	9.0	4.7	3.6	3.3	3.3	3.5
1972	5.1	14.2	16.6	12.3	4.1	8.4	4.1	3.2	2.9	3.1	3.4
1973	4.3	12.6	15.4	10.4	3.5	6.8	3.7	2.5	2.4	2.5	2.9
1974	5.0	14.0	16.3	12.2	4.1	8.0	4.4	3.1	2.8	2.8	3.3
1975	7.8	17.9	19.5	16.7	6.7	12.3	7.1	5.2	4.9	4.5	5.1
1976	7.0	16.9	19.0	15.3	5.9	10.7	6.3	4.5	4.2	4.3	4.9
1977	6.2	15.4	17.9	13.5	5.3	9.3	5.7	4.0	3.8	3.7	4.9
1978	5.2	13.9	17.0	11.5	4.3	8.0	4.6	3.3	3.0	2.7	3.8
1979	5.1	14.0	16.1	12.4	4.2	7.6	4.4	3.2	3.0	2.7	3.1
1980	6.3	15.5	17.9	13.8	5.4	9.9	6.1	4.2	3.7	3.1	2.7
1981	6.7	17.3	19.2	15.9	5.7	10.4	6.3	4.5	3.9	3.5	2.8
1982	8.6	20.4	22.8	18.8	7.6	12.8	8.5	6.3	5.4	5.1	3.1
1983	8.4	19.3	22.0	17.6	7.5	12.1	8.4	6.3	5.7	5.2	3.2
1984	6.5	16.0	18.8	14.3	5.7	9.3	6.2	4.8	4.4	4.4	3.0
1985	6.2	15.7	18.3	13.9	5.5	9.2	5.9	4.6	4.3	4.0	2.9
1986	6.0	15.6	17.6	14.1	5.3	8.7	5.9	4.5	4.1	3.8	2.9
1987	5.3	14.4	16.7	12.7	4.7	8.0	5.1	4.0	3.7	3.2	2.4
1988	4.7	13.1	15.3	11.6	4.1	7.1	4.5	3.5	3.1	3.0	2.4
1989	4.5	12.7	15.2	11.1	3.9	7.2	4.3	3.3	2.9	3.0	2.3
1990	4.8	13.5	15.8	12.1	4.3	7.3	4.6	3.6	3.3	3.2	2.8
1991	6.1	16.5	19.0	14.9	5.5	9.2	6.1	4.7	4.2	4.0	3.1
1992	6.6	17.2	20.3	15.2	6.0	9.5	6.7	5.2	4.8	4.9	3.7
1993	6.1	16.2	19.0	14.4	5.5	8.8	6.0	4.9	4.5	4.3	3.0
1994	5.3	15.1	17.6	13.3	4.7	8.1	5.2	4.0	3.7	3.9	3.8
1995	4.9	14.5	17.3	12.5	4.3	7.7	4.6	3.9	3.1	3.5	3.8
1996	4.7	14.2	16.4	12.6	4.1	7.8	4.4	3.6	3.1	3.2	3.5
1997	4.2	13.6	15.8	12.0	3.6	6.9	3.9	3.3	2.7	2.7	3.0
1998	3.9	12.6	14.8	11.0	3.3	6.5	3.7	2.9	2.6	2.4	2.9
1999	3.7	12.0	14.5	10.2	3.1	6.3	3.3	2.7	2.4	2.5	2.9
2000	3.5	11.4	13.9	9.8	3.0	5.9	3.2	2.6	2.2	2.4	2.8
2001	4.2	12.7	15.3	11.0	3.7	7.0	4.1	3.2	2.8	2.9	2.8
2002	5.1	14.5	16.7	13.2	4.6	8.1	5.2	4.1	3.7	3.7	3.5
2003	5.2	15.2	17.2	13.9	4.7	8.4	5.3	4.3	3.7	3.8	3.7
2004	4.8	15.0	17.9	13.1	4.3	7.9	4.7	3.9	3.4	3.6	3.3
2005	4.4	14.2	16.4	12.7	3.9	7.2	4.3	3.5	3.1	3.0	3.1
2006	4.0	13.2	15.1	11.9	3.6	6.9	4.0	3.2	2.8	2.8	2.8
2007	4.1	13.9	15.5	12.8	3.6	7.0	4.0	3.2	2.9	2.9	3.2
2008	5.2	16.8	19.9	14.9	4.6	9.0	5.1	4.3	3.7	3.4	4.0

Table 1-27. Unemployment Rates of Civilian Workers, by Age, Sex, Race, and Hispanic Origin, 1948–2008
—Continued

(Percent of labor force.)

Race, Hispanic origin, sex, and year	16 years and over	16 to 19 years			20 years and over						
		Total	16 to 17 years	18 to 19 years	Total	20 to 24 years	25 to 34 years	35 to 44 years	45 to 54 years	55 to 64 years	65 years and over
WHITE											
Men											
1954	4.8	13.4	14.0	13.0	4.4	9.8	4.2	3.6	3.8	4.3	4.2
1955	3.7	11.3	12.2	10.4	3.3	7.0	2.7	2.6	2.9	3.9	3.8
1956	3.4	10.5	11.2	9.7	3.0	6.1	2.8	2.2	2.8	3.1	3.4
1957	3.6	11.5	11.9	11.1	3.2	7.0	2.7	2.5	3.0	3.4	3.2
1958	6.1	15.7	14.9	16.5	5.5	11.7	5.6	4.4	4.8	5.2	5.0
1959	4.6	14.0	15.0	13.0	4.1	7.5	3.8	3.2	3.7	4.2	4.5
1960	4.8	14.0	14.6	13.5	4.2	8.3	4.1	3.3	3.6	4.1	4.0
1961	5.7	15.7	16.5	15.2	5.1	10.1	4.9	4.0	4.4	5.3	5.2
1962	4.6	13.7	15.2	12.7	4.0	8.1	3.8	3.1	3.5	4.1	4.0
1963	4.7	15.9	17.8	14.2	3.9	7.8	3.9	2.9	3.3	4.0	4.1
1964	4.1	14.7	16.1	13.3	3.4	7.4	3.0	2.5	2.9	3.5	3.6
1965	3.6	12.9	14.7	11.3	2.9	5.9	2.6	2.3	2.3	3.1	3.4
1966	2.8	10.5	12.5	8.9	2.2	4.1	2.1	1.7	1.7	2.5	3.0
1967	2.7	10.7	12.7	9.0	2.1	4.2	1.9	1.6	1.8	2.2	2.7
1968	2.6	10.1	12.3	8.3	2.0	4.6	1.7	1.4	1.5	1.7	2.8
1969	2.5	10.0	12.5	7.9	1.9	4.6	1.7	1.4	1.4	1.7	2.2
1970	4.0	13.7	15.7	12.0	3.2	7.8	3.1	2.3	2.3	2.7	3.2
1971	4.9	15.1	17.1	13.5	4.0	9.4	4.0	2.9	2.9	3.2	3.4
1972	4.5	14.2	16.4	12.4	3.6	8.5	3.4	2.5	2.5	3.0	3.3
1973	3.8	12.3	15.2	10.0	3.0	6.6	3.0	1.8	2.0	2.4	2.9
1974	4.4	13.5	16.2	11.5	3.5	7.8	3.6	2.4	2.2	2.5	3.0
1975	7.2	18.3	19.7	17.2	6.2	13.1	6.3	4.5	4.4	4.1	5.0
1976	6.4	17.3	19.7	15.5	5.4	10.9	5.6	3.7	3.7	4.0	4.7
1977	5.5	15.0	17.6	13.0	4.7	9.3	5.0	3.1	3.0	3.3	4.9
1978	4.6	13.5	16.9	10.8	3.7	7.7	3.8	2.5	2.5	2.6	3.9
1979	4.5	13.9	16.1	12.2	3.6	7.5	3.7	2.5	2.5	2.5	3.2
1980	6.1	16.2	18.5	14.5	5.3	11.1	5.9	3.6	3.3	3.1	2.5
1981	6.5	17.9	19.9	16.4	5.6	11.6	6.1	4.0	3.6	3.4	2.4
1982	8.8	21.7	24.2	20.0	7.8	14.3	8.9	6.2	5.3	5.1	3.2
1983	8.8	20.2	22.6	18.7	7.9	13.8	9.0	6.4	5.7	5.6	3.2
1984	6.4	16.8	19.7	15.0	5.7	9.8	6.2	4.6	4.2	4.7	2.6
1985	6.1	16.5	19.2	14.7	5.4	9.7	5.7	4.3	4.1	4.0	2.7
1986	6.0	16.3	18.4	14.7	5.3	9.2	5.8	4.4	4.0	4.0	3.0
1987	5.4	15.5	17.9	13.7	4.8	8.4	5.2	3.9	3.9	3.4	2.5
1988	4.7	13.9	16.1	12.4	4.1	7.4	4.6	3.4	3.2	3.3	2.2
1989	4.5	13.7	16.4	12.0	3.9	7.5	4.1	3.2	2.9	3.1	2.1
1990	4.9	14.3	16.1	13.2	4.3	7.6	4.7	3.5	3.4	3.6	2.8
1991	6.5	17.6	19.7	16.3	5.8	10.2	6.4	5.0	4.4	4.6	3.1
1992	7.0	18.5	21.5	16.5	6.4	10.5	7.0	5.5	5.1	5.5	3.2
1993	6.3	17.7	20.2	16.0	5.7	9.6	6.2	5.0	4.7	4.7	2.9
1994	5.4	16.3	18.5	14.7	4.8	8.8	5.2	3.9	3.7	4.1	3.7
1995	4.9	15.6	18.2	13.8	4.3	7.9	4.5	3.8	3.2	3.4	4.0
1996	4.7	15.5	18.3	13.5	4.1	8.1	4.2	3.5	3.1	3.2	3.2
1997	4.2	14.3	16.3	12.9	3.6	7.3	3.7	3.2	2.8	3.0	2.7
1998	3.9	14.1	17.1	12.1	3.2	6.7	3.5	2.6	2.6	2.6	2.9
1999	3.6	12.6	15.1	10.8	3.0	6.5	3.1	2.4	2.4	2.6	2.9
2000	3.4	12.3	15.3	10.4	2.8	5.9	2.9	2.4	2.2	2.4	3.0
2001	4.2	13.9	17.4	11.7	3.7	7.8	3.8	3.1	2.9	3.2	2.8
2002	5.3	15.9	18.8	14.2	4.7	8.7	5.3	4.1	3.8	4.0	3.4
2003	5.6	17.1	18.5	16.1	5.0	9.1	5.5	4.4	4.0	4.2	3.8
2004	5.0	16.3	19.8	14.2	4.4	8.5	4.8	3.8	3.5	3.7	3.5
2005	4.4	16.1	18.9	14.3	3.8	7.9	4.1	3.3	3.0	3.0	3.1
2006	4.0	14.6	16.5	13.4	3.5	7.3	3.9	3.0	2.7	2.8	2.7
2007	4.2	15.7	17.0	14.8	3.7	7.6	4.1	3.0	2.8	3.0	3.3
2008	5.5	19.1	22.2	17.3	4.9	10.2	5.3	4.3	3.8	3.4	4.1

Table 1-27. Unemployment Rates of Civilian Workers, by Age, Sex, Race, and Hispanic Origin, 1948–2008
—Continued

(Percent of labor force.)

Race, Hispanic origin, sex, and year	16 years and over	16 to 19 years			20 years and over						
		Total	16 to 17 years	18 to 19 years	Total	20 to 24 years	25 to 34 years	35 to 44 years	45 to 54 years	55 to 64 years	65 years and over
WHITE											
Women											
1954	5.5	10.4	12.0	9.4	5.1	6.4	5.7	4.9	4.4	4.5	2.8
1955	4.3	9.1	11.6	7.7	3.9	5.1	4.3	3.8	3.4	3.6	2.2
1956	4.2	9.7	12.1	8.3	3.7	5.1	4.0	3.5	3.3	3.5	2.3
1957	4.3	9.5	11.9	7.8	3.8	5.1	4.7	3.7	3.0	2.9	3.4
1958	6.2	12.7	15.6	11.0	5.6	7.3	6.6	5.6	4.9	4.3	3.5
1959	5.3	12.0	13.3	11.1	4.7	7.0	5.2	4.7	3.9	4.0	2.9
1960	5.3	12.7	14.5	11.5	4.6	7.2	5.7	4.2	4.0	3.3	2.8
1961	6.5	14.8	17.0	13.6	5.7	8.4	6.6	5.6	4.8	4.3	3.8
1962	5.5	12.8	15.6	11.3	4.7	7.7	5.4	4.5	3.7	3.5	4.0
1963	5.8	15.1	18.1	13.2	4.8	7.4	5.8	4.6	3.9	3.5	3.3
1964	5.5	14.9	17.1	13.2	4.6	7.1	5.2	4.5	3.6	3.5	3.4
1965	5.0	14.0	15.0	13.4	4.0	6.3	4.9	4.1	3.0	2.7	2.7
1966	4.3	12.1	14.5	10.7	3.3	5.3	3.7	3.3	2.7	2.2	2.7
1967	4.6	11.5	12.9	10.6	3.8	6.0	4.7	3.7	2.9	2.3	2.6
1968	4.3	12.1	13.9	11.0	3.4	5.9	3.9	3.1	2.3	2.1	2.8
1969	4.2	11.5	13.7	10.0	3.4	5.5	4.2	3.2	2.4	2.1	2.4
1970	5.4	13.4	15.3	11.9	4.4	6.9	5.3	4.3	3.4	2.6	3.3
1971	6.3	15.1	16.7	14.1	5.3	8.5	6.3	4.9	3.9	3.3	3.6
1972	5.9	14.2	17.0	12.3	4.9	8.2	5.5	4.4	3.5	3.3	3.7
1973	5.3	13.0	15.8	10.9	4.3	7.1	5.1	3.7	3.2	2.7	2.8
1974	6.1	14.5	16.4	13.0	5.1	8.2	5.8	4.3	3.6	3.2	3.9
1975	8.6	17.4	19.2	16.1	7.5	11.2	8.4	6.5	5.8	5.0	5.3
1976	7.9	16.4	18.2	15.1	6.8	10.4	7.6	5.8	5.0	4.8	5.3
1977	7.3	15.9	18.2	14.2	6.2	9.3	6.7	5.3	5.0	4.4	4.9
1978	6.2	14.4	17.1	12.4	5.2	8.3	5.8	4.5	3.8	3.0	3.7
1979	5.9	14.0	15.9	12.5	5.0	7.8	5.6	4.2	3.7	3.0	3.1
1980	6.5	14.8	17.3	13.1	5.6	8.5	6.3	4.9	4.3	3.1	3.0
1981	6.9	16.6	18.4	15.3	5.9	9.1	6.6	5.1	4.2	3.7	3.4
1982	8.3	19.0	21.2	17.6	7.3	10.9	8.0	6.4	5.5	5.0	3.1
1983	7.9	18.3	21.4	16.4	6.9	10.3	7.6	6.2	5.5	4.7	3.1
1984	6.5	15.2	17.8	13.6	5.8	8.8	6.1	5.0	4.8	4.0	3.7
1985	6.4	14.8	17.2	13.1	5.7	8.5	6.2	4.9	4.5	4.1	3.1
1986	6.1	14.9	16.7	13.6	5.4	8.1	6.1	4.5	4.3	3.7	2.6
1987	5.2	13.4	15.5	11.7	4.6	7.4	5.0	4.1	3.3	2.9	2.4
1988	4.7	12.3	14.4	10.8	4.1	6.7	4.5	3.7	3.1	2.5	2.6
1989	4.5	11.5	13.8	10.1	4.0	6.8	4.5	3.4	2.9	2.7	2.5
1990	4.7	12.6	15.5	10.9	4.1	6.8	4.6	3.7	3.2	2.7	2.8
1991	5.6	15.2	18.2	13.3	5.0	8.1	5.7	4.3	4.0	3.3	3.1
1992	6.1	15.8	18.9	13.7	5.5	8.3	6.2	4.9	4.3	4.0	4.5
1993	5.7	14.7	17.8	12.6	5.2	7.9	5.8	4.7	4.3	3.9	3.0
1994	5.2	13.8	16.6	11.8	4.6	7.4	5.1	4.2	3.7	3.7	3.9
1995	4.8	13.4	16.4	11.2	4.3	7.4	4.7	3.9	3.0	3.5	3.5
1996	4.7	12.9	14.4	11.7	4.1	7.4	4.6	3.8	3.1	3.1	3.8
1997	4.2	12.8	15.2	11.1	3.7	6.4	4.2	3.4	2.6	2.4	3.4
1998	3.9	10.9	12.4	9.8	3.4	6.3	3.9	3.3	2.5	2.2	3.0
1999	3.8	11.3	13.9	9.6	3.3	6.1	3.6	3.0	2.3	2.5	2.9
2000	3.6	10.4	12.5	9.0	3.1	5.8	3.5	2.9	2.3	2.4	2.4
2001	4.1	11.4	13.1	10.2	3.6	6.1	4.5	3.3	2.7	2.5	2.7
2002	4.9	13.1	14.6	12.1	4.4	7.4	5.0	4.1	3.5	3.3	3.5
2003	4.8	13.3	15.9	11.5	4.4	7.6	4.9	4.2	3.3	3.4	3.5
2004	4.7	13.6	16.1	11.9	4.2	7.1	4.6	3.9	3.3	3.5	3.1
2005	4.4	12.3	14.0	11.1	3.9	6.4	4.7	3.6	3.1	3.0	3.2
2006	4.0	11.7	13.8	10.2	3.6	6.3	4.1	3.4	2.9	2.8	3.0
2007	4.0	12.1	14.1	10.6	3.6	6.2	3.9	3.4	2.9	2.8	3.1
2008	4.9	14.4	17.6	12.3	4.4	7.5	4.8	4.3	3.5	3.5	3.8

Table 1-27. Unemployment Rates of Civilian Workers, by Age, Sex, Race, and Hispanic Origin, 1948–2008
—*Continued*

(Percent of labor force.)

Race, Hispanic origin, sex, and year	16 years and over	16 to 19 years			20 years and over						
		Total	16 to 17 years	18 to 19 years	Total	20 to 24 years	25 to 34 years	35 to 44 years	45 to 54 years	55 to 64 years	65 years and over
BLACK											
Both Sexes											
1972	10.4	35.4	38.7	33.6	7.9	16.3	8.7	6.1	4.2	4.1	4.3
1973	9.4	31.5	37.0	28.1	7.2	15.5	8.1	4.7	3.5	3.2	3.5
1974	10.5	35.0	40.0	31.8	8.0	17.5	8.5	5.4	4.3	3.6	3.9
1975	14.8	39.5	41.6	38.1	12.3	24.5	13.0	8.9	8.3	5.9	6.6
1976	14.0	39.3	44.2	36.7	11.5	22.7	12.8	8.0	6.7	5.9	5.9
1977	14.0	41.1	44.5	39.2	11.5	24.2	12.7	7.4	5.3	5.5	5.9
1978	12.8	38.7	43.9	35.7	10.2	21.8	10.8	6.4	5.2	4.8	5.8
1979	12.3	36.5	40.2	34.4	10.1	20.6	10.8	6.7	5.2	4.9	5.3
1980	14.3	38.5	41.1	37.1	12.1	23.6	13.3	8.2	6.8	5.4	6.9
1981	15.6	41.4	44.8	39.5	13.4	26.4	14.7	9.5	7.4	5.5	7.0
1982	18.9	48.0	48.6	47.8	16.6	30.6	19.0	12.1	8.7	8.3	7.1
1983	19.5	48.5	50.5	47.6	17.3	31.6	19.0	12.4	10.7	9.2	9.2
1984	15.9	42.7	45.7	41.2	13.9	26.1	15.2	9.9	8.2	7.4	6.5
1985	15.1	40.2	43.6	38.3	13.1	24.5	14.5	9.5	8.2	7.0	7.0
1986	14.5	39.3	43.0	37.2	12.7	24.1	14.0	9.6	7.1	6.6	4.5
1987	13.0	34.7	39.7	31.6	11.3	21.8	12.8	8.4	6.8	5.6	3.9
1988	11.7	32.4	35.1	30.7	10.2	19.6	11.9	7.5	5.9	4.8	5.5
1989	11.4	32.4	32.9	32.2	9.9	18.0	11.5	7.6	5.6	5.2	6.9
1990	11.4	30.9	36.5	27.8	10.1	19.9	11.7	7.8	5.3	4.6	5.3
1991	12.5	36.1	39.5	34.4	11.1	21.6	12.7	8.5	7.4	4.4	5.2
1992	14.2	39.7	44.7	37.1	12.6	23.8	14.2	10.5	8.3	6.2	4.9
1993	13.0	38.8	39.7	38.4	11.4	21.9	12.6	9.5	6.9	7.1	4.7
1994	11.5	35.2	36.1	34.6	10.0	19.5	11.1	8.5	5.6	5.4	6.2
1995	10.4	35.7	39.1	33.4	8.7	17.7	9.9	7.3	4.8	4.0	6.7
1996	10.5	33.6	36.3	31.7	9.0	18.8	10.5	7.3	5.0	4.4	5.3
1997	10.0	32.4	35.0	30.8	8.6	18.3	9.9	7.0	5.0	4.2	6.1
1998	8.9	27.6	33.6	24.2	7.7	16.8	8.4	6.5	4.4	3.9	5.6
1999	8.0	27.9	31.0	26.2	6.8	14.6	7.6	5.3	4.0	3.9	5.0
2000	7.6	24.5	26.9	22.9	6.5	15.0	6.7	5.6	4.1	3.0	6.1
2001	8.6	29.0	30.8	27.9	7.4	16.3	8.1	6.3	4.8	3.9	4.3
2002	10.2	29.8	34.9	27.2	9.1	19.1	9.9	7.8	6.3	5.4	5.9
2003	10.8	33.0	32.2	33.5	9.7	19.8	10.9	8.6	6.2	6.3	5.4
2004	10.4	31.7	37.8	28.3	9.4	18.4	10.8	7.8	6.9	5.6	5.5
2005	10.0	33.3	41.2	29.0	8.8	18.3	10.2	7.1	6.0	5.6	6.9
2006	8.9	29.1	32.2	27.3	7.9	16.2	9.3	6.3	5.7	4.6	4.7
2007	8.3	29.4	32.6	27.4	7.2	15.2	8.6	5.4	5.4	4.3	4.5
2008	10.1	31.2	36.3	28.5	9.1	17.9	10.6	7.0	7.0	6.1	7.5
BLACK											
Men											
1972	9.3	31.7	36.7	28.4	7.0	14.9	7.2	4.8	3.8	4.4	5.4
1973	8.0	27.8	35.7	23.0	6.0	13.2	6.2	3.9	3.2	3.2	3.3
1974	9.8	33.1	39.9	28.3	7.4	16.2	8.1	4.3	4.2	3.6	5.3
1975	14.8	38.1	41.9	35.9	12.5	24.7	12.7	8.7	9.3	6.3	8.7
1976	13.7	37.5	40.8	36.0	11.4	22.6	12.0	7.5	7.3	6.3	8.7
1977	13.3	39.2	41.0	38.2	10.7	23.0	11.8	6.2	4.9	6.0	7.8
1978	11.8	36.7	43.0	32.9	9.3	21.0	9.8	5.1	4.9	4.4	6.6
1979	11.4	34.2	37.9	32.2	9.3	18.7	9.6	6.3	5.2	5.1	6.4
1980	14.5	37.5	39.7	36.2	12.4	23.7	13.4	8.2	7.2	6.2	8.7
1981	15.7	40.7	43.2	39.2	13.5	26.4	14.4	9.3	7.8	6.1	7.5
1982	20.1	48.9	52.7	47.1	17.8	31.5	20.1	13.4	9.0	10.3	9.3
1983	20.3	48.8	52.2	47.3	18.1	31.4	19.4	13.5	11.4	11.0	11.8
1984	16.4	42.7	44.0	42.2	14.3	26.6	15.0	10.4	7.9	8.9	7.9
1985	15.3	41.0	42.9	40.0	13.2	23.5	13.8	9.6	9.7	7.9	8.9
1986	14.8	39.3	41.4	38.2	12.9	23.5	13.5	10.9	7.8	8.0	4.3
1987	12.7	34.4	39.0	31.6	11.1	20.3	12.2	8.7	6.7	6.6	4.3
1988	11.7	32.7	34.4	31.7	10.1	19.4	11.0	7.6	6.2	5.2	5.6
1989	11.5	31.9	34.4	30.3	10.0	17.9	10.5	8.4	6.2	6.2	7.4
1990	11.9	31.9	38.8	28.0	10.4	20.1	11.5	8.4	6.3	5.4	4.6
1991	13.0	36.3	39.0	34.8	11.5	22.4	11.9	9.5	8.6	5.0	6.1
1992	15.2	42.0	47.5	39.1	13.5	24.6	14.2	11.2	10.3	8.1	4.9
1993	13.8	40.1	42.7	38.6	12.1	23.0	12.3	10.5	8.1	9.0	5.8
1994	12.0	37.6	39.3	36.5	10.3	19.4	10.6	9.1	6.5	6.0	8.2
1995	10.6	37.1	39.7	35.4	8.8	17.6	9.3	7.6	5.5	4.4	7.6
1996	11.1	36.9	39.9	34.9	9.4	19.2	10.1	7.8	6.3	5.2	5.0
1997	10.2	36.5	39.5	34.4	8.5	19.8	8.7	6.7	5.6	4.2	5.5
1998	8.9	30.1	33.9	27.9	7.4	18.0	7.3	6.2	4.4	4.5	5.2
1999	8.2	30.9	33.3	29.4	6.7	16.2	6.9	5.2	4.3	3.9	5.0
2000	8.0	26.2	28.5	24.7	6.9	16.6	6.7	5.8	4.8	2.7	6.3
2001	9.3	30.4	30.5	30.4	8.0	17.6	8.3	6.9	5.5	4.8	4.0
2002	10.7	31.3	36.6	28.7	9.5	20.0	9.4	8.0	7.4	6.1	5.0
2003	11.6	36.0	35.6	36.3	10.3	20.9	11.3	9.2	6.7	6.8	5.6
2004	11.1	35.6	40.8	32.7	9.9	20.3	10.9	8.0	7.2	6.4	4.2
2005	10.5	36.3	45.1	31.5	9.2	20.5	9.7	7.0	6.7	5.9	7.1
2006	9.5	32.7	34.8	31.5	8.3	17.2	9.5	5.9	6.3	5.5	5.8
2007	9.1	33.8	40.1	30.2	7.9	16.9	9.1	5.6	5.8	5.2	5.0
2008	11.4	35.9	43.9	32.0	10.2	19.3	11.8	7.7	7.7	7.1	9.5

Table 1-27. Unemployment Rates of Civilian Workers, by Age, Sex, Race, and Hispanic Origin, 1948–2008
—Continued

(Percent of labor force.)

Race, Hispanic origin, sex, and year	16 years and over	16 to 19 years			20 years and over						
		Total	16 to 17 years	18 to 19 years	Total	20 to 24 years	25 to 34 years	35 to 44 years	45 to 54 years	55 to 64 years	65 years and over
BLACK											
Women											
1972	11.8	40.5	42.0	40.1	9.0	17.9	10.5	7.6	4.6	3.7	2.6
1973	11.1	36.1	38.6	34.2	8.6	18.4	10.3	5.6	3.9	3.3	3.7
1974	11.3	37.4	40.2	36.0	8.8	19.0	9.0	6.6	4.4	3.6	1.9
1975	14.8	41.0	41.2	40.6	12.2	24.3	13.4	9.0	7.0	5.3	3.6
1976	14.3	41.6	48.4	37.6	11.7	22.8	13.6	8.5	5.9	5.4	2.4
1977	14.9	43.4	49.5	40.4	12.3	25.5	13.6	8.7	5.8	4.8	3.4
1978	13.8	40.8	45.0	38.7	11.2	22.7	11.9	7.8	5.6	5.2	4.7
1979	13.3	39.1	42.7	36.9	10.9	22.6	12.1	7.2	5.2	4.7	3.9
1980	14.0	39.8	42.9	38.2	11.9	23.5	13.2	8.2	6.4	4.5	4.9
1981	15.6	42.2	46.5	39.8	13.4	26.4	14.9	9.8	6.9	4.7	6.0
1982	17.6	47.1	44.2	48.6	15.4	29.6	17.8	10.7	8.5	6.1	4.5
1983	18.6	48.2	48.6	48.0	16.5	31.8	18.6	11.4	9.9	7.3	6.3
1984	15.4	42.6	47.5	40.2	13.5	25.6	15.4	9.4	8.6	5.9	4.9
1985	14.9	39.2	44.3	36.4	13.1	25.6	15.1	9.3	6.8	6.0	5.2
1986	14.2	39.2	44.6	36.1	12.4	24.7	14.6	8.5	6.4	5.0	4.9
1987	13.2	34.9	40.5	31.7	11.6	23.3	13.5	8.1	6.9	4.5	3.4
1988	11.7	32.0	35.9	29.6	10.4	19.8	12.7	7.4	5.6	4.3	5.4
1989	11.4	33.0	31.1	34.0	9.8	18.1	12.5	7.0	5.0	4.2	6.4
1990	10.9	29.9	34.1	27.6	9.7	19.6	11.9	7.2	4.3	3.6	5.9
1991	12.0	36.0	40.1	33.9	10.6	20.7	13.4	7.6	6.2	3.8	4.4
1992	13.2	37.2	41.7	34.8	11.8	23.1	14.1	9.8	6.4	4.2	5.0
1993	12.1	37.4	36.1	38.1	10.7	20.9	12.9	8.6	5.8	5.1	3.6
1994	11.0	32.6	32.9	32.5	9.8	19.6	11.7	8.0	4.9	4.9	4.4
1995	10.2	34.3	38.5	31.5	8.6	17.8	10.5	7.0	4.2	3.6	. . .
1996	10.0	30.3	32.8	28.6	8.7	18.4	11.0	6.9	3.8	3.8	5.6
1997	9.9	28.7	30.3	27.8	8.8	17.1	10.9	7.2	4.4	4.1	6.6
1998	9.0	25.3	33.2	20.9	7.9	15.7	9.5	6.7	4.3	3.4	6.1
1999	7.8	25.1	28.5	23.3	6.8	13.4	8.3	5.5	3.8	3.9	5.0
2000	7.1	22.8	25.3	21.3	6.2	13.6	6.8	5.5	3.4	3.3	6.0
2001	8.1	27.5	31.2	25.4	7.0	15.3	8.0	5.8	4.3	3.1	4.6
2002	9.8	28.3	33.2	25.6	8.8	18.3	10.2	7.7	5.3	4.7	6.9
2003	10.2	30.3	29.1	31.1	9.2	18.8	10.5	8.1	5.8	5.9	5.3
2004	9.8	28.2	35.2	24.3	8.9	16.6	10.7	7.6	6.5	4.8	6.8
2005	9.5	30.3	37.3	26.6	8.5	16.3	10.6	7.2	5.4	5.3	6.6
2006	8.4	25.9	29.9	23.6	7.5	15.2	9.0	6.7	5.1	3.9	3.7
2007	7.5	25.3	26.4	24.7	6.7	13.6	8.1	5.3	5.0	3.7	4.0
2008	8.9	26.8	29.9	25.0	8.1	16.6	9.5	6.4	6.3	5.3	5.8
HISPANIC[1]											
Both Sexes											
1973	7.5	19.7	23.4	17.3	6.0	8.5	5.7	5.6	4.7	5.5	3.9
1974	8.1	19.8	23.5	17.2	6.6	9.8	6.3	5.9	4.6	6.1	6.3
1975	12.2	27.7	30.0	26.5	10.3	16.7	9.9	8.6	8.1	7.7	9.9
1976	11.5	23.8	29.2	19.2	10.1	15.9	9.1	8.2	8.4	8.8	12.6
1977	10.1	22.9	27.0	19.6	8.5	12.0	8.6	6.1	7.3	8.2	9.2
1978	9.1	20.7	28.3	15.1	7.7	10.9	8.0	6.5	5.8	5.0	7.5
1979	8.3	19.2	26.0	14.9	7.0	10.4	6.7	6.2	5.2	6.0	5.7
1980	10.1	22.5	27.6	19.5	8.6	12.1	9.1	7.7	5.7	5.9	6.0
1981	10.4	23.9	28.0	21.7	9.1	13.9	8.8	7.4	6.4	7.3	5.4
1982	13.8	29.9	38.1	25.9	12.3	17.7	12.3	10.7	8.4	10.1	6.5
1983	13.7	28.4	33.8	25.8	12.3	16.7	11.9	11.3	10.0	10.9	5.8
1984	10.7	24.1	28.9	21.6	9.5	12.4	9.7	8.2	7.5	9.7	6.1
1985	10.5	24.3	27.8	22.5	9.4	12.6	9.9	7.7	7.4	7.8	8.1
1986	10.6	24.7	28.1	22.9	9.5	12.9	9.6	8.4	7.8	7.3	10.1
1987	8.8	22.3	27.7	19.5	7.8	10.6	7.7	6.7	6.9	6.0	6.5
1988	8.2	22.0	27.1	19.3	7.0	9.8	7.1	6.0	6.0	5.8	5.6
1989	8.0	19.4	26.4	16.0	7.2	10.7	7.0	5.9	6.3	5.8	5.3
1990	8.2	19.5	24.5	16.9	7.2	9.1	7.3	6.6	6.4	5.6	6.0
1991	10.0	22.9	31.9	18.7	9.0	11.6	9.2	8.1	8.0	6.5	7.0
1992	11.6	27.5	35.7	23.4	10.4	13.2	10.4	9.8	8.8	8.6	8.1
1993	10.8	26.1	35.1	21.8	9.7	13.1	9.3	9.1	8.6	8.0	6.6
1994	9.9	24.5	31.7	20.6	8.9	11.8	9.0	7.7	8.1	7.3	7.9
1995	9.3	24.1	33.1	19.5	8.2	11.5	8.2	7.2	6.4	7.5	10.6
1996	8.9	23.6	30.0	20.3	7.8	11.8	7.3	7.3	6.0	7.3	8.2
1997	7.7	21.6	27.7	18.4	6.8	10.3	6.3	6.4	5.1	6.5	6.8
1998	7.2	21.3	28.0	18.1	6.1	9.4	5.9	5.5	4.6	5.3	6.4
1999	6.4	18.6	23.7	16.3	5.5	8.3	5.4	4.8	4.8	4.5	5.0
2000	5.7	16.6	22.5	13.9	4.9	7.5	4.8	4.5	3.3	4.5	5.7
2001	6.6	17.7	24.0	15.0	5.8	8.1	5.9	5.2	4.3	5.6	4.5
2002	7.5	20.1	24.2	18.2	6.7	9.9	6.6	6.0	5.5	5.7	6.8
2003	7.7	20.0	24.6	17.7	7.0	10.2	7.0	6.0	6.3	5.7	3.9
2004	7.0	20.4	29.0	16.8	6.2	9.3	6.3	5.3	5.2	5.8	6.0
2005	6.0	18.4	23.6	16.0	5.3	8.6	5.3	4.5	4.4	4.4	4.9
2006	5.2	15.9	20.4	13.6	4.6	7.2	4.7	4.3	3.7	3.3	3.9
2007	5.6	18.1	22.5	16.0	5.0	7.8	4.9	4.3	4.3	4.5	4.9
2008	7.6	22.4	29.8	19.0	6.8	11.5	6.7	5.8	6.3	4.8	7.8

[1]May be of any race.
. . . = Not available.

Table 1-27. Unemployment Rates of Civilian Workers, by Age, Sex, Race, and Hispanic Origin, 1948–2008
—Continued

(Percent of labor force.)

Race, Hispanic origin, sex, and year	16 years and over	16 to 19 years			20 years and over						
		Total	16 to 17 years	18 to 19 years	Total	20 to 24 years	25 to 34 years	35 to 44 years	45 to 54 years	55 to 64 years	65 years and over
HISPANIC[1]											
Men											
1973	6.7	19.0	20.9	17.7	5.4	8.2	5.0	4.2	4.5	5.4	. . .
1974	7.3	19.0	22.0	17.1	6.0	9.9	5.5	5.0	4.3	5.4	. . .
1975	11.4	27.6	29.3	26.5	9.6	16.3	9.6	7.9	7.0	6.8	. . .
1976	10.8	23.3	28.7	19.7	9.4	16.0	8.1	7.0	7.4	8.7	. . .
1977	9.0	20.9	25.9	18.2	7.7	11.7	7.9	4.9	5.4	7.4	. . .
1978	7.7	19.7	27.5	13.9	6.4	9.4	6.6	4.8	4.8	4.4	. . .
1979	7.0	17.5	23.5	13.8	5.8	9.2	5.3	5.1	4.4	5.0	. . .
1980	9.7	21.9	26.2	19.3	8.3	12.2	8.3	7.1	6.0	5.9	. . .
1981	10.2	24.3	30.9	20.3	8.8	14.1	8.9	6.5	5.9	6.7	. . .
1982	13.6	31.3	40.2	26.8	12.1	18.2	12.4	9.9	7.5	10.0	. . .
1983	13.6	28.7	34.7	25.9	12.2	17.0	11.6	10.8	10.3	11.7	. . .
1984	10.5	25.2	31.5	22.2	9.3	12.5	9.2	7.6	7.2	10.2	. . .
1985	10.2	24.7	29.1	22.4	9.1	12.9	9.6	7.2	6.8	7.0	. . .
1986	10.5	24.5	28.5	22.4	9.5	13.0	9.5	8.5	7.0	8.0	. . .
1987	8.7	22.2	28.2	19.3	7.8	10.2	7.6	6.9	7.1	6.7	. . .
1988	8.1	22.7	29.5	19.5	7.0	9.2	7.0	5.9	6.1	6.7	. . .
1989	7.6	20.2	27.6	16.8	6.6	9.7	5.9	5.7	6.0	6.6	. . .
1990	8.0	19.5	24.0	17.4	7.0	8.4	6.9	6.5	6.8	6.5	. . .
1991	10.3	23.5	33.6	19.2	9.3	11.6	9.3	8.5	7.9	8.1	. . .
1992	11.7	28.2	36.6	24.0	10.5	13.7	10.1	9.8	8.9	10.2	. . .
1993	10.6	25.9	34.5	21.9	9.5	12.6	9.0	8.8	8.8	8.5	. . .
1994	9.4	26.3	33.3	22.5	8.3	10.8	8.4	6.6	8.1	7.4	10.5
1995	8.8	25.3	34.8	20.2	7.7	10.6	7.5	6.7	5.9	7.9	12.9
1996	7.9	22.5	31.5	18.4	6.9	10.3	6.6	6.3	5.1	6.7	8.3
1997	7.0	20.8	26.5	17.9	6.1	9.8	5.1	5.4	4.8	6.8	7.2
1998	6.4	20.6	29.0	16.4	5.4	8.9	5.2	4.5	4.2	5.3	5.0
1999	5.6	17.8	23.4	15.3	4.7	7.8	4.1	3.8	4.5	4.6	5.0
2000	5.0	15.7	22.3	12.8	4.2	6.6	3.7	3.8	3.1	4.1	6.2
2001	5.9	17.1	25.8	13.4	5.2	8.1	4.6	4.5	3.8	6.3	4.8
2002	7.2	20.2	22.9	19.1	6.4	9.3	6.1	5.4	5.5	6.2	6.3
2003	7.2	21.9	25.9	20.1	6.4	9.6	6.3	5.3	6.0	6.0	3.6
2004	6.5	21.2	30.7	17.6	5.8	9.4	5.5	4.5	4.7	5.7	6.9
2005	5.4	19.3	23.4	17.5	4.7	8.2	4.3	3.9	4.0	4.0	4.8
2006	4.8	17.3	22.6	14.8	4.2	6.7	4.2	3.6	3.4	3.5	3.7
2007	5.3	19.7	23.4	18.0	4.6	7.4	4.5	3.8	4.4	3.9	5.5
2008	7.6	23.4	30.9	19.9	6.8	11.8	6.6	5.6	6.2	5.1	7.8
HISPANIC[1]											
Women											
1973	9.0	20.7	26.8	16.7	7.3	9.0	6.9	8.3	5.1	5.6	. . .
1974	9.4	20.8	25.3	17.4	7.7	9.7	7.7	7.5	5.3	7.5	. . .
1975	13.5	27.9	31.0	26.4	11.5	17.2	10.5	9.9	10.0	9.3	. . .
1976	12.7	22.2	30.3	18.7	11.4	15.8	10.8	10.0	9.8	9.0	. . .
1977	11.9	24.4	28.5	21.9	10.1	12.1	9.8	8.2	10.6	11.0	. . .
1978	11.3	21.8	29.9	16.6	9.8	13.0	10.3	9.2	7.4	7.2	. . .
1979	10.3	21.2	30.0	15.8	8.9	12.1	8.9	7.7	7.1	7.9	. . .
1980	10.7	23.4	29.7	19.8	9.2	12.0	10.6	8.6	5.3	5.8	. . .
1981	10.8	23.4	23.5	23.4	9.5	13.5	8.7	8.9	7.2	8.4	. . .
1982	14.1	28.2	35.1	25.0	12.5	16.8	12.2	11.9	9.9	10.4	. . .
1983	13.8	28.0	32.5	25.7	12.4	16.2	12.5	12.2	9.7	9.6	. . .
1984	11.1	22.8	26.1	21.0	9.9	12.2	10.3	9.1	7.9	8.8	. . .
1985	11.0	23.8	26.2	22.6	9.9	12.1	10.6	8.5	8.1	9.2	. . .
1986	10.8	25.1	27.6	23.6	9.6	12.9	9.8	8.2	8.9	6.2	. . .
1987	8.9	22.4	27.1	19.9	7.7	11.4	7.8	6.5	6.7	5.0	. . .
1988	8.3	21.0	24.5	18.9	7.1	10.7	7.2	6.2	5.9	4.6	. . .
1989	8.8	18.2	24.7	14.9	8.0	12.2	8.6	6.3	6.7	4.5	. . .
1990	8.4	19.4	25.4	16.2	7.5	10.4	8.0	6.7	6.0	4.3	. . .
1991	9.6	21.9	29.6	17.9	8.6	11.7	9.1	7.6	8.1	4.1	. . .
1992	11.4	26.4	34.5	22.4	10.2	12.4	11.0	9.7	8.5	6.2	. . .
1993	11.0	26.3	36.0	21.7	9.9	14.0	9.9	9.5	8.3	7.2	. . .
1994	10.7	22.2	29.7	18.1	9.8	13.5	10.1	9.2	8.0	7.1	3.6
1995	10.0	22.6	30.7	18.7	8.9	13.0	9.5	7.9	7.0	6.8	6.4
1996	10.2	25.1	28.2	23.3	9.2	14.1	8.5	8.7	7.2	8.1	8.0
1997	8.9	22.7	29.2	19.1	7.9	11.0	8.2	7.7	5.5	6.1	6.0
1998	8.2	22.1	26.4	20.2	7.1	10.1	7.2	6.9	5.1	5.4	8.8
1999	7.6	19.8	24.0	17.7	6.6	9.1	7.3	6.3	5.1	4.3	4.8
2000	6.8	18.0	22.7	15.6	5.9	9.0	6.4	5.4	3.6	5.0	4.8
2001	7.5	18.5	21.6	17.1	6.6	8.2	7.8	6.2	4.8	4.8	4.0
2002	8.0	19.9	25.8	17.0	7.2	10.8	7.4	6.7	5.5	5.0	7.5
2003	8.4	17.7	23.2	14.4	7.8	11.3	8.2	7.1	6.8	5.3	4.4
2004	7.6	19.3	27.0	15.5	7.0	9.1	7.6	6.4	5.8	5.8	4.6
2005	6.9	17.2	23.8	14.0	6.3	9.2	7.1	5.5	4.8	5.0	5.1
2006	5.9	14.1	18.1	11.9	5.3	8.1	5.5	5.5	4.2	3.1	4.2
2007	6.1	16.1	21.3	13.6	5.5	8.5	5.6	5.1	4.3	5.2	4.0
2008	7.7	21.1	28.1	18.0	6.9	11.1	6.8	6.0	6.4	4.4	7.7

[1]May be of any race.
. . . = Not available.

Table 1-28. Unemployed Persons and Unemployment Rates, by Selected Occupation, 2000–2008

(Thousands of people, percent of civilian labor force.)

Occupation	2000	2001	2002	2003	2004	2005	2006	2007	2008
Total Unemployed Persons, 16 Years and Over[1]	5 692	6 801	8 378	8 774	8 149	7 591	7 001	7 078	8 924
Management, professional, and related	827	1 102	1 482	1 556	1 346	1 172	1 065	1 090	1 463
Management, business, and financial operations	320	455	622	627	544	464	427	429	619
Professional and related	507	647	859	929	801	708	638	662	844
Services	1 132	1 311	1 544	1 681	1 617	1 587	1 485	1 521	1 769
Sales and office	1 446	1 652	2 110	2 070	1 937	1 820	1 667	1 638	2 006
Sales and related	673	779	998	995	912	874	812	835	980
Office and administrative support	773	873	1 112	1 076	1 025	946	856	804	1 026
Natural resources, construction, and maintenance	758	943	1 155	1 244	1 140	1 069	1 007	1 052	1 421
Farming, fishing, and forestry	133	163	142	136	132	103	101	89	112
Construction and extraction	507	626	788	814	786	751	699	781	1 067
Installation, maintenance, and repair	119	154	225	295	222	214	207	182	243
Production, transportation, and material moving	1 081	1 318	1 530	1 555	1 393	1 245	1 127	1 128	1 474
Production	575	759	848	807	714	677	544	564	746
Transportation and material moving	505	559	682	748	679	568	583	564	727
Total Unemployment Rate, 16 Years and Over[1]	4.0	4.7	5.8	6.0	5.5	5.1	4.6	4.6	5.8
Management, professional, and related	1.8	2.3	3.0	3.1	2.7	2.3	2.1	2.1	2.7
Management, business, and financial operations	1.6	2.2	3.0	3.1	2.6	2.2	2.0	1.9	2.7
Professional and related	1.9	2.3	3.0	3.2	2.8	2.4	2.1	2.1	2.7
Services	5.2	5.8	6.6	7.1	6.6	6.4	5.9	5.9	6.7
Sales and office	3.8	4.4	5.6	5.5	5.2	4.8	4.4	4.3	5.3
Sales and related	4.1	4.7	5.9	5.9	5.4	5.0	4.7	4.8	5.7
Office and administrative support	3.6	4.2	5.4	5.2	5.0	4.6	4.2	4.0	5.1
Natural resources, construction, and maintenance	5.3	6.4	7.8	8.1	7.3	6.5	6.0	6.3	8.8
Farming, fishing, and forestry	10.2	13.4	12.0	11.4	11.8	9.6	9.5	8.5	10.2
Construction and extraction	6.2	7.3	9.1	9.1	8.4	7.6	6.8	7.6	11.0
Installation, maintenance, and repair	2.4	3.2	4.6	5.5	4.2	3.9	3.7	3.4	4.5
Production, transportation, and material moving	5.1	6.4	7.6	7.9	7.2	6.5	5.8	5.8	7.6
Production	4.8	6.6	7.8	7.7	7.0	6.7	5.5	5.7	7.7
Transportation and material moving	5.6	6.2	7.4	8.2	7.4	6.2	6.2	6.0	7.6

[1]Includes persons with no work experience and persons whose last job was in the armed forces.

Table 1-29. Unemployed Persons and Unemployment Rates, by Class of Worker and Industry, 2000–2008

(Thousands of people, percent.)

Class of worker and industry	2000	2001	2002	2003	2004	2005	2006	2007	2008
Total Unemployed Persons, 16 Years and Over	5 692	6 801	8 378	8 774	8 149	7 591	7 001	7 078	8 924
Nonagricultural private wage and salary workers	4 483	5 540	6 926	7 131	6 484	5 989	5 523	5 559	7 118
Mining	21	23	33	37	21	20	22	25	25
Construction	513	609	800	810	769	712	671	757	1 030
Manufacturing	691	992	1 205	1 166	966	812	699	706	945
Durable goods	400	630	789	762	590	485	410	436	597
Nondurable goods	290	362	416	404	375	326	289	270	348
Wholesale trade and retail trade	837	945	1 202	1 237	1 197	1 137	1 039	975	1 205
Transportation and utilities	193	236	274	283	236	232	229	233	312
Information	124	190	253	246	189	163	126	120	167
Financial activities	208	252	320	319	332	272	264	289	380
Professional and business services	573	768	1 009	1 042	861	792	746	740	921
Education and health services	383	463	570	640	617	627	568	575	698
Leisure and hospitality	720	833	961	1 006	972	921	865	896	1 102
Other services	219	229	301	347	324	301	293	241	332
Agriculture and related private wage and salary workers	134	153	139	140	129	104	95	78	123
Government workers	422	430	512	568	548	534	473	505	534
Self-employed and unpaid family workers	219	218	265	294	303	298	293	309	383
Total Unemployment Rate, 16 Years and Over[1]	4.0	4.7	5.8	6.0	5.5	5.1	4.6	4.6	5.8
Nonagricultural private wage and salary workers	4.1	5.0	6.2	6.3	5.7	5.2	4.7	4.7	5.9
Mining	4.4	4.2	6.3	6.7	3.9	3.1	3.2	3.4	3.1
Construction	6.2	7.1	9.2	9.3	8.4	7.4	6.7	7.4	10.6
Manufacturing	3.5	5.2	6.7	6.6	5.7	4.9	4.2	4.3	5.8
Durable goods	3.2	5.2	6.9	6.9	5.5	4.6	3.9	4.2	5.6
Nondurable goods	4.0	5.2	6.2	6.1	5.9	5.3	4.8	4.5	6.0
Wholesale trade and retail trade	4.3	4.9	6.1	6.0	5.8	5.4	4.9	4.7	5.9
Transportation and utilities	3.4	4.3	4.9	5.3	4.4	4.1	4.0	3.9	5.1
Information	3.2	4.9	6.9	6.8	5.7	5.0	3.7	3.6	5.0
Financial activities	2.4	2.9	3.5	3.5	3.6	2.9	2.7	3.0	3.9
Professional and business services	4.8	6.1	7.9	8.2	6.8	6.2	5.6	5.3	6.5
Education and health services	2.5	2.8	3.4	3.6	3.4	3.4	3.0	3.0	3.5
Leisure and hospitality	6.6	7.5	8.4	8.7	8.3	7.8	7.3	7.4	8.6
Other services	3.9	4.0	5.1	5.7	5.3	4.8	4.7	3.9	5.3
Agriculture and related private wage and salary workers	9.0	11.2	10.1	10.2	9.9	8.3	7.2	6.3	9.2
Government workers	2.1	2.2	2.5	2.8	2.7	2.6	2.3	2.3	2.4
Self-employed and unpaid family workers	2.1	2.1	2.6	2.7	2.8	2.7	2.7	2.8	3.6

Note: See notes and definitions for information on historical comparability.

[1]Includes persons with no work experience and persons whose last job was in the armed forces.

Table 1-30. Unemployed Persons, by Duration of Unemployment, 1948–2008

(Thousands of people, number of weeks.)

Year	Total unemployed	Duration of unemployment					Average duration, in weeks	Median duration, in weeks
		Less than 5 weeks	5 to 14 weeks	15 weeks and over				
				Total	15 to 26 weeks	27 weeks and over		
1948	2 276	1 300	669	309	193	116	8.6	. . .
1949	3 637	1 756	1 194	684	428	256	10.0	. . .
1950	3 288	1 450	1 055	782	425	357	12.1	. . .
1951	2 055	1 177	574	303	166	137	9.7	. . .
1952	1 883	1 135	516	232	148	84	8.4	. . .
1953	1 834	1 142	482	210	132	78	8.0	. . .
1954	3 532	1 605	1 116	812	495	317	11.8	. . .
1955	2 852	1 335	815	702	366	336	13.0	. . .
1956	2 750	1 412	805	533	301	232	11.3	. . .
1957	2 859	1 408	891	560	321	239	10.5	. . .
1958	4 602	1 753	1 396	1 452	785	667	13.9	. . .
1959	3 740	1 585	1 114	1 040	469	571	14.4	. . .
1960	3 852	1 719	1 176	957	503	454	12.8	. . .
1961	4 714	1 806	1 376	1 532	728	804	15.6	. . .
1962	3 911	1 663	1 134	1 119	534	585	14.7	. . .
1963	4 070	1 751	1 231	1 088	535	553	14.0	. . .
1964	3 786	1 697	1 117	973	491	482	13.3	. . .
1965	3 366	1 628	983	755	404	351	11.8	. . .
1966	2 875	1 573	779	526	287	239	10.4	. . .
1967	2 975	1 634	893	448	271	177	8.7	2.3
1968	2 817	1 594	810	412	256	156	8.4	4.5
1969	2 832	1 629	827	375	242	133	7.8	4.4
1970	4 093	2 139	1 290	663	428	235	8.6	4.9
1971	5 016	2 245	1 585	1 187	668	519	11.3	6.3
1972	4 882	2 242	1 472	1 167	601	566	12.0	6.2
1973	4 365	2 224	1 314	826	483	343	10.0	5.2
1974	5 156	2 604	1 597	955	574	381	9.8	5.2
1975	7 929	2 940	2 484	2 505	1 303	1 203	14.2	8.4
1976	7 406	2 844	2 196	2 366	1 018	1 348	15.8	8.2
1977	6 991	2 919	2 132	1 942	913	1 028	14.3	7.0
1978	6 202	2 865	1 923	1 414	766	648	11.9	5.9
1979	6 137	2 950	1 946	1 241	706	535	10.8	5.4
1980	7 637	3 295	2 470	1 871	1 052	820	11.9	6.5
1981	8 273	3 449	2 539	2 285	1 122	1 162	13.7	6.9
1982	10 678	3 883	3 311	3 485	1 708	1 776	15.6	8.7
1983	10 717	3 570	2 937	4 210	1 652	2 559	20.0	10.1
1984	8 539	3 350	2 451	2 737	1 104	1 634	18.2	7.9
1985	8 312	3 498	2 509	2 305	1 025	1 280	15.6	6.8
1986	8 237	3 448	2 557	2 232	1 045	1 187	15.0	6.9
1987	7 425	3 246	2 196	1 983	943	1 040	14.5	6.5
1988	6 701	3 084	2 007	1 610	801	809	13.5	5.9
1989	6 528	3 174	1 978	1 375	730	646	11.9	4.8
1990	7 047	3 265	2 257	1 525	822	703	12.0	5.3
1991	8 628	3 480	2 791	2 357	1 246	1 111	13.7	6.8
1992	9 613	3 376	2 830	3 408	1 453	1 954	17.7	8.7
1993	8 940	3 262	2 584	3 094	1 297	1 798	18.0	8.3
1994	7 996	2 728	2 408	2 860	1 237	1 623	18.8	9.2
1995	7 404	2 700	2 342	2 363	1 085	1 278	16.6	8.3
1996	7 236	2 633	2 287	2 316	1 053	1 262	16.7	8.3
1997	6 739	2 538	2 138	2 062	995	1 067	15.8	8.0
1998	6 210	2 622	1 950	1 637	763	875	14.5	6.7
1999	5 880	2 568	1 832	1 480	755	725	13.4	6.4
2000	5 692	2 558	1 815	1 318	669	649	12.6	5.9
2001	6 801	2 853	2 196	1 752	951	801	13.1	6.8
2002	8 378	2 893	2 580	2 904	1 369	1 535	16.6	9.1
2003	8 774	2 785	2 612	3 378	1 442	1 936	19.2	10.1
2004	8 149	2 696	2 382	3 072	1 293	1 779	19.6	9.8
2005	7 591	2 667	2 304	2 619	1 130	1 490	18.4	8.9
2006	7 001	2 614	2 121	2 266	1 031	1 235	16.8	8.3
2007	7 078	2 542	2 232	2 303	1 061	1 243	16.8	8.5
2008	8 924	2 932	2 804	3 188	1 427	1 761	17.9	9.4

. . . = Not available.

Table 1-31. Long-Term Unemployment, by Industry and Selected Occupation, 2000–2008

(Thousands of people.)

Length of unemployment, industry, and occupation	2000	2001	2002	2003	2004	2005	2006	2007	2008
UNEMPLOYED 15 WEEKS AND OVER									
Total	1 318	1 752	2 904	3 378	3 072	2 619	2 266	2 303	3 188
Wage and Salary Workers, by Industry									
Agriculture and related	32	44	39	44	38	29	30	28	42
Mining	7	7	11	17	8	8	5	6	7
Construction	107	130	236	262	248	216	177	215	339
Manufacturing	184	303	528	575	467	326	257	259	385
Durable goods	99	183	348	389	293	199	140	162	246
Nondurable goods	86	120	180	186	174	127	116	97	139
Wholesale and retail trade	186	241	423	472	455	415	337	334	440
Transportation and utilities	57	71	124	132	114	91	87	95	142
Information	33	52	119	128	87	76	55	49	66
Financial activities	58	75	131	144	139	91	103	100	168
Professional and business services	143	217	377	440	345	299	266	247	346
Education and health services	124	149	232	300	304	271	263	253	320
Leisure and hospitality	146	196	279	328	321	277	259	274	356
Other services	54	58	95	132	126	117	97	80	132
Public administration	41	36	51	59	72	62	34	51	55
Experienced Workers, by Occupation									
Management, professional, and related	213	313	603	692	571	436	373	368	569
Services	246	323	447	564	565	511	464	482	595
Sales and office	331	419	759	810	750	641	561	560	741
Natural resources, construction, and maintenance	161	212	346	424	386	341	294	299	463
Production, transportation, and material moving	273	360	575	654	561	461	380	384	570
UNEMPLOYED 27 WEEKS AND OVER									
Total	649	801	1 535	1 936	1 779	1 490	1 235	1 243	1 761
Wage and Salary Workers, by Industry									
Agriculture and related	13	16	18	21	18	16	13	14	17
Mining	4	3	5	10	6	4	3	3	4
Construction	44	60	111	132	133	108	92	107	168
Manufacturing	100	132	291	366	302	195	140	152	230
Durable goods	50	75	191	255	196	124	75	93	150
Nondurable goods	50	57	100	111	106	71	64	58	80
Wholesale and retail trade	80	114	226	261	261	230	183	171	237
Transportation and utilities	27	33	67	74	63	50	42	58	77
Information	18	21	62	80	58	41	30	29	38
Financial activities	32	34	131	88	79	56	56	50	97
Professional and business services	67	90	377	262	193	172	144	130	184
Education and health services	63	71	232	167	168	156	144	132	182
Leisure and hospitality	69	90	279	166	169	148	135	142	196
Other services	26	31	95	71	76	74	51	43	73
Public administration	23	18	51	33	44	38	21	29	29
Experienced Workers, by Occupation									
Management, professional, and related	101	135	340	429	356	269	206	207	320
Services	128	156	225	295	307	284	249	251	329
Sales and office	151	185	397	459	419	354	299	285	411
Natural resources, construction, and maintenance	74	96	164	229	221	186	158	157	240
Production, transportation, and material moving	140	162	313	388	336	261	206	219	323

Note: Beginning in January 2004, data reflect revised population controls used in the household survey. See notes and definitions for information on historical comparability.

Table 1-32. Unemployed Persons and Unemployment Rates, by Reason for Unemployment, Sex, and Age, 1975–2008

(Thousands of people, percent.)

Sex, age, and year	Number of unemployed					Unemployed as a percent of the total civilian labor force			
	Total	Job losers and persons who completed temporary jobs	Job leavers	Entrants		Job losers and persons who completed temporary jobs	Job leavers	Entrants	
				Reentrants	New entrants			Reentrants	New entrants
Both Sexes, 16 Years and Over									
1975	7 929	4 386	827	1 892	823	4.7	0.9	2.0	0.9
1976	7 406	3 679	903	1 928	895	3.8	0.9	2.0	0.9
1977	6 991	3 166	909	1 963	953	3.2	0.9	2.0	1.0
1978	6 202	2 585	874	1 857	885	2.5	0.9	1.8	0.9
1979	6 137	2 635	880	1 806	817	2.5	0.8	1.7	0.8
1980	7 637	3 947	891	1 927	872	3.7	0.8	1.8	0.8
1981	8 273	4 267	923	2 102	981	3.9	0.8	1.9	0.9
1982	10 678	6 268	840	2 384	1 185	5.7	0.8	2.2	1.1
1983	10 717	6 258	830	2 412	1 216	5.6	0.7	2.2	1.1
1984	8 539	4 421	823	2 184	1 110	3.9	0.7	1.9	1.0
1985	8 312	4 139	877	2 256	1 039	3.6	0.8	2.0	0.9
1986	8 237	4 033	1 015	2 160	1 029	3.4	0.9	1.8	0.9
1987	7 425	3 566	965	1 974	920	3.0	0.8	1.6	0.8
1988	6 701	3 092	983	1 809	816	2.5	0.8	1.5	0.7
1989	6 528	2 983	1 024	1 843	677	2.4	0.8	1.5	0.5
1990	7 047	3 387	1 041	1 930	688	2.7	0.8	1.5	0.5
1991	8 628	4 694	1 004	2 139	792	3.7	0.8	1.7	0.6
1992	9 613	5 389	1 002	2 285	937	4.2	0.8	1.8	0.7
1993	8 940	4 848	976	2 198	919	3.8	0.8	1.7	0.7
1994	7 996	3 815	791	2 786	604	2.9	0.6	2.1	0.5
1995	7 404	3 476	824	2 525	579	2.6	0.6	1.9	0.4
1996	7 236	3 370	774	2 512	580	2.5	0.6	1.9	0.4
1997	6 739	3 037	795	2 338	569	2.2	0.6	1.7	0.4
1998	6 210	2 822	734	2 132	520	2.1	0.5	1.5	0.4
1999	5 880	2 622	783	2 005	469	1.9	0.6	1.4	0.3
2000	5 692	2 517	780	1 961	434	1.8	0.5	1.4	0.3
2001	6 801	3 476	835	2 031	459	2.4	0.6	1.4	0.3
2002	8 378	4 607	866	2 368	536	3.2	0.6	1.6	0.4
2003	8 774	4 838	818	2 477	641	3.3	0.6	1.7	0.4
2004	8 149	4 197	858	2 408	686	2.8	0.6	1.6	0.5
2005	7 591	3 667	872	2 386	666	2.5	0.6	1.6	0.4
2006	7 001	3 321	827	2 237	616	2.2	0.5	1.5	0.4
2007	7 078	3 515	793	2 142	627	2.3	0.5	1.4	0.4
2008	8 924	4 789	896	2 472	766	3.1	0.6	1.6	0.5
Both Sexes, 16 to 19 Years									
1975	1 767	450	155	529	634	5.1	1.7	6.0	7.1
1976	1 719	387	153	496	683	4.3	1.7	5.5	7.5
1977	1 663	318	156	477	711	3.4	1.7	5.1	7.6
1978	1 583	300	167	455	660	3.1	1.7	4.7	6.8
1979	1 555	319	184	452	599	3.3	1.9	4.7	6.2
1980	1 669	388	156	481	643	4.1	1.7	5.1	6.9
1981	1 763	385	162	487	728	4.3	1.8	5.4	8.1
1982	1 977	460	134	509	874	5.4	1.6	6.0	10.2
1983	1 829	370	110	482	867	4.6	1.3	5.9	10.6
1984	1 499	271	114	370	745	3.4	1.4	4.7	9.4
1985	1 468	275	113	390	689	3.5	1.4	4.9	8.7
1986	1 454	240	145	374	695	3.0	1.8	4.7	8.8
1987	1 347	210	146	375	617	2.7	1.8	4.7	7.7
1988	1 226	207	159	310	550	2.6	2.0	3.9	6.8
1989	1 194	198	200	345	452	2.5	2.5	4.3	5.7
1990	1 212	233	181	338	460	3.0	2.3	4.3	5.9
1991	1 359	289	180	365	524	4.0	2.5	5.0	7.2
1992	1 427	259	149	377	643	3.6	2.1	5.3	9.1
1993	1 365	233	151	353	628	3.3	2.1	4.9	8.8
1994	1 320	185	84	634	416	2.5	1.1	8.5	5.6
1995	1 346	214	102	615	415	2.8	1.3	7.9	5.3
1996	1 306	182	91	625	409	2.3	1.2	8.0	5.2
1997	1 271	174	104	606	388	2.2	1.3	7.6	4.9
1998	1 205	181	86	577	361	2.2	1.0	7.0	4.4
1999	1 162	173	114	547	328	2.1	1.4	6.6	3.9
2000	1 081	157	109	516	299	1.9	1.3	6.2	3.6
2001	1 162	185	98	568	311	2.3	1.2	7.2	3.9
2002	1 253	197	91	597	368	2.6	1.2	7.9	4.9
2003	1 251	188	85	554	424	2.6	1.2	7.7	5.9
2004	1 208	165	76	510	456	2.3	1.1	7.2	6.4
2005	1 186	155	76	489	466	2.2	1.1	6.8	6.5
2006	1 119	145	78	461	435	2.0	1.1	6.3	6.0
2007	1 101	176	71	435	419	2.5	1.0	6.2	6.0
2008	1 285	203	80	490	511	3.0	1.2	7.1	7.5

Note: See notes and definitions for information on historical comparability.

Table 1-32. Unemployed Persons and Unemployment Rates, by Reason for Unemployment, Sex, and Age, 1975–2008—*Continued*

(Thousands of people, percent.)

Sex, age, and year	Number of unemployed					Unemployed as a percent of the total civilian labor force			
	Total	Job losers and persons who completed temporary jobs	Job leavers	Entrants		Job losers and persons who completed temporary jobs	Job leavers	Entrants	
				Reentrants	New entrants			Reentrants	New entrants
Men, 20 Years and Over									
1975	3 476	2 598	298	506	76	5.0	0.6	1.0	0.1
1976	3 098	2 167	323	521	86	4.1	0.6	1.0	0.2
1977	2 794	1 816	335	540	103	3.4	0.6	1.0	0.2
1978	2 328	1 433	337	471	86	2.6	0.6	0.9	0.2
1979	2 308	1 464	325	446	73	2.6	0.6	0.8	0.1
1980	3 353	2 389	359	516	90	4.2	0.6	0.9	0.2
1981	3 615	2 565	356	592	102	4.5	0.6	1.0	0.2
1982	5 089	3 965	327	678	119	6.8	0.6	1.2	0.2
1983	5 257	4 088	336	695	138	6.9	0.6	1.2	0.2
1984	3 932	2 800	324	663	146	4.7	0.5	1.1	0.2
1985	3 715	2 568	352	671	124	4.3	0.6	1.1	0.2
1986	3 751	2 568	444	611	128	4.1	0.7	1.0	0.2
1987	3 369	2 289	413	558	108	3.7	0.7	0.9	0.2
1988	2 987	1 939	416	534	98	3.1	0.7	0.9	0.2
1989	2 867	1 843	394	541	88	2.9	0.6	0.8	0.1
1990	3 239	2 100	431	626	82	3.2	0.7	1.0	0.1
1991	4 195	2 982	411	698	105	4.6	0.6	1.1	0.2
1992	4 717	3 420	421	765	111	5.2	0.6	1.2	0.2
1993	4 287	2 996	429	747	114	4.5	0.6	1.1	0.2
1994	3 627	2 296	367	898	65	3.4	0.5	1.3	0.1
1995	3 239	2 051	356	775	57	3.0	0.5	1.2	0.1
1996	3 146	2 043	322	731	51	3.0	0.5	1.1	0.1
1997	2 882	1 795	358	675	55	2.6	0.5	1.0	0.1
1998	2 580	1 588	318	611	63	2.3	0.5	0.9	0.1
1999	2 433	1 459	336	592	46	2.1	0.5	0.8	0.1
2000	2 376	1 416	328	577	55	2.0	0.5	0.8	0.1
2001	3 040	1 999	372	612	56	2.7	0.5	0.8	0.1
2002	3 896	2 702	386	743	65	3.7	0.5	1.0	0.1
2003	4 209	2 899	376	846	88	3.9	0.5	1.1	0.1
2004	3 791	2 503	398	791	99	3.3	0.5	1.0	0.1
2005	4 059	2 188	445	1 067	359	2.7	0.5	1.0	0.1
2006	3 131	1 927	368	757	78	2.5	0.5	1.0	0.1
2007	3 259	2 064	371	723	101	2.6	0.5	0.9	0.1
2008	4 297	2 918	410	856	113	3.7	0.5	1.1	0.1
Women, 20 Years and Over									
1975	2 684	1 339	375	858	114	4.0	1.1	2.6	0.3
1976	2 588	1 124	427	912	126	3.2	1.2	2.6	0.4
1977	2 535	1 031	419	945	140	2.8	1.2	2.6	0.4
1978	2 292	852	371	930	138	2.2	1.0	2.4	0.4
1979	2 276	851	370	908	145	2.1	0.9	2.3	0.4
1980	2 615	1 170	376	930	139	2.8	0.9	2.3	0.3
1981	2 895	1 317	404	1 023	151	3.1	1.0	2.4	0.4
1982	3 613	1 844	379	1 197	192	4.2	0.9	2.7	0.4
1983	3 632	1 801	384	1 235	212	4.0	0.9	2.8	0.5
1984	3 107	1 350	386	1 151	220	2.9	0.8	2.5	0.5
1985	3 129	1 296	412	1 195	227	2.7	0.9	2.5	0.5
1986	3 032	1 225	426	1 175	206	2.5	0.9	2.4	0.4
1987	2 709	1 067	406	1 041	194	2.2	0.8	2.1	0.4
1988	2 487	946	408	965	168	1.9	0.8	1.9	0.3
1989	2 467	942	430	958	137	1.8	0.8	1.8	0.3
1990	2 596	1 054	429	966	146	2.0	0.8	1.8	0.3
1991	3 074	1 423	413	1 075	163	2.6	0.8	2.0	0.3
1992	3 469	1 710	433	1 142	183	3.1	0.8	2.1	0.3
1993	3 288	1 619	395	1 098	176	2.9	0.7	2.0	0.3
1994	3 049	1 334	339	1 253	122	2.4	0.6	2.2	0.2
1995	2 819	1 211	366	1 135	107	2.1	0.6	2.0	0.2
1996	2 783	1 145	361	1 156	120	2.0	0.6	2.0	0.2
1997	2 585	1 069	333	1 057	126	1.8	0.6	1.8	0.2
1998	2 424	1 053	330	944	97	1.8	0.6	1.6	0.2
1999	2 285	990	333	866	96	1.6	0.5	1.4	0.2
2000	2 235	943	343	868	80	1.5	0.6	1.4	0.1
2001	2 599	1 291	365	850	92	2.0	0.6	1.3	0.1
2002	3 228	1 708	389	1 028	102	2.7	0.6	1.6	0.2
2003	3 314	1 751	357	1 076	130	2.7	0.6	1.7	0.2
2004	3 150	1 529	384	1 107	131	2.4	0.6	1.7	0.2
2005	3 013	1 417	391	1 103	101	2.2	0.6	1.7	0.2
2006	2 751	1 249	380	1 019	103	1.9	0.6	1.5	0.2
2007	2 718	1 276	351	984	107	1.9	0.5	1.7	0.4
2007	3 342	1 668	406	1 126	143	2.4	0.6	1.6	0.2

Note: See notes and definitions for information on historical comparability.

Table 1-33. Percent of the Population with Work Experience During the Year, by Age and Sex, 1987–2008

(Percent.)

Sex and year	Total	16 to 17 years	18 to 19 years	20 to 24 years	25 to 34 years	35 to 44 years	45 to 54 years	55 to 59 years	60 to 64 years	65 to 69 years	70 years and over
Both Sexes											
1987	69.7	51.8	76.6	85.5	85.7	86.1	81.6	69.4	51.3	26.2	10.2
1988	70.2	50.6	75.5	85.7	86.0	86.8	82.2	70.5	52.2	27.9	10.3
1989	70.5	51.9	75.4	84.9	86.6	86.9	82.8	70.4	52.5	28.4	10.0
1990	70.2	48.6	74.2	84.1	86.2	87.0	82.8	70.9	53.4	28.3	10.2
1991	69.5	43.4	70.8	83.4	85.9	86.6	83.0	70.3	52.9	27.2	9.8
1992	69.1	43.8	69.9	82.7	85.2	85.9	82.8	70.8	53.5	25.5	9.8
1993	69.2	42.1	70.4	82.0	85.0	85.3	82.8	71.6	51.6	27.5	10.7
1994	69.6	44.1	71.5	82.5	85.5	85.6	83.8	72.2	52.8	27.5	10.0
1995	69.6	44.4	71.2	82.0	85.6	85.9	83.4	72.2	53.3	28.0	10.2
1996	69.9	43.3	70.5	83.1	86.1	85.7	84.3	73.3	54.3	27.8	10.4
1997	70.1	43.6	70.5	83.0	87.1	85.9	84.4	73.8	53.8	28.5	10.0
1998	70.1	42.1	69.9	82.9	86.7	86.3	84.2	73.7	54.5	29.2	10.6
1999	70.7	43.7	71.2	82.7	87.3	86.9	85.0	72.3	55.8	30.5	11.6
2000	70.5	42.2	69.6	82.6	87.1	87.0	84.6	72.9	55.1	30.8	11.4
2001	69.4	37.7	66.7	80.8	86.1	85.8	83.7	73.5	56.7	30.6	10.5
2002	68.5	34.5	62.8	78.5	84.4	85.0	83.7	74.7	56.8	33.1	10.4
2003	67.8	32.0	61.7	77.5	83.7	84.0	82.9	73.9	56.5	33.2	11.4
2004	67.7	32.6	59.8	76.9	83.3	84.2	82.6	73.9	57.0	32.7	12.2
2005	67.8	31.1	60.1	77.3	83.7	84.1	82.8	74.4	58.2	32.0	12.1
2006	67.9	30.9	58.3	76.9	84.4	84.3	82.8	74.5	58.2	33.6	12.6
2007	67.8	28.5	57.3	76.6	84.2	84.4	82.4	75.6	59.7	35.2	13.0
2008	67.1	24.6	55.3	76.0	84.1	83.9	81.8	74.6	60.3	34.9	13.5
Men											
1987	78.9	52.4	77.4	90.4	94.3	94.1	91.9	83.3	63.2	34.2	15.4
1988	79.1	51.8	78.9	90.7	94.3	94.6	91.6	82.1	63.1	35.6	15.6
1989	79.4	53.2	77.7	89.9	94.7	94.7	91.9	82.0	64.2	35.4	15.1
1990	78.9	50.3	76.7	88.7	94.4	94.7	91.3	82.0	65.8	35.8	14.0
1991	77.9	45.4	72.2	87.9	93.5	93.6	91.3	81.5	63.6	35.0	14.4
1992	77.4	46.6	73.7	87.1	93.3	92.8	89.9	80.9	63.2	32.4	14.3
1993	76.8	43.9	71.4	86.6	92.5	92.0	89.3	79.8	59.1	34.3	15.3
1994	77.2	44.4	74.7	87.2	92.9	92.0	90.0	81.3	61.4	33.9	14.8
1995	77.0	43.7	73.6	86.4	92.6	92.2	89.7	81.5	62.1	34.5	14.9
1996	77.2	44.1	71.8	86.7	93.4	92.1	90.4	81.8	62.5	33.6	15.2
1997	77.1	43.4	70.3	86.6	94.1	92.3	90.7	81.4	62.9	33.8	13.9
1998	76.9	40.4	71.6	86.4	93.5	92.7	90.1	81.7	63.5	35.5	14.7
1999	77.3	44.7	72.3	85.5	93.9	93.2	89.9	79.2	65.1	37.4	16.5
2000	77.1	42.1	70.2	85.1	93.4	93.6	89.8	80.6	64.4	38.4	16.0
2001	76.3	37.4	67.7	84.8	93.2	92.2	89.1	80.4	64.3	37.8	14.5
2002	75.2	34.7	62.8	82.1	91.6	91.8	88.9	80.7	64.3	39.3	14.6
2003	74.3	32.8	61.7	80.2	90.8	90.9	87.7	80.9	63.1	37.3	15.8
2004	74.2	32.1	58.9	80.2	91.0	91.1	87.9	80.1	64.5	37.1	16.7
2005	74.6	31.1	60.7	80.8	91.3	91.6	88.2	80.1	64.3	37.6	17.0
2006	74.5	30.9	57.9	80.1	91.9	91.8	88.0	80.6	64.1	38.3	17.3
2007	74.3	28.5	59.0	80.5	90.5	91.5	88.2	80.3	66.2	39.3	17.9
2008	73.2	24.4	55.1	78.7	90.7	91.1	86.4	79.3	66.0	40.3	17.9
Women											
1987	61.3	51.1	75.8	81.0	77.3	78.5	71.9	56.7	41.0	19.6	6.8
1988	62.1	49.3	72.2	81.0	78.1	79.4	73.5	60.0	42.5	21.4	6.8
1989	62.3	50.6	73.1	80.2	78.6	79.3	74.2	59.9	42.4	22.5	6.7
1990	62.2	46.8	71.7	79.6	78.0	79.6	74.9	60.4	42.5	22.1	7.7
1991	61.8	41.4	69.4	79.0	78.3	79.9	75.3	59.9	43.6	20.6	6.7
1992	61.5	40.9	66.1	78.4	77.2	79.1	76.1	61.5	44.4	20.0	6.7
1993	62.1	40.3	69.4	77.5	77.6	78.7	76.5	63.9	44.7	22.1	7.7
1994	62.5	43.7	68.4	77.8	78.1	79.4	78.0	63.9	45.0	22.2	6.8
1995	62.8	45.2	68.7	77.7	78.8	79.8	77.6	63.2	45.6	22.4	7.1
1996	63.2	42.5	69.2	79.5	78.9	79.5	78.4	65.4	46.9	23.0	7.1
1997	63.6	43.9	70.7	79.5	80.1	79.6	78.4	66.7	45.6	24.0	7.3
1998	63.7	44.1	68.2	79.4	80.1	80.0	78.6	66.3	46.2	23.8	7.8
1999	64.5	42.6	70.1	79.9	80.9	80.7	80.3	66.2	47.3	24.4	8.2
2000	64.3	42.3	69.0	80.2	80.9	80.5	79.5	65.7	47.0	23.9	8.2
2001	63.1	38.1	65.7	76.9	79.2	79.5	78.6	67.1	49.8	24.2	7.9
2002	62.3	34.3	62.8	74.9	77.2	78.4	78.7	69.1	50.0	27.8	7.4
2003	61.7	31.2	61.6	74.6	76.6	77.2	78.4	67.3	50.7	29.6	8.3
2004	61.5	33.1	60.7	73.7	75.6	77.4	77.5	68.2	50.3	28.7	9.0
2005	61.4	31.2	59.6	73.7	76.1	76.8	77.6	68.9	52.7	27.1	8.7
2006	61.6	30.9	58.7	73.7	76.9	76.9	77.9	68.8	53.0	29.5	9.3
2007	61.6	28.5	55.6	72.6	77.8	77.4	76.9	71.2	53.7	31.5	9.5
2008	61.3	24.8	55.4	73.2	77.3	76.7	77.3	70.1	55.0	30.1	10.3

Note: See notes and definitions for information on historical comparability.

Table 1-34. Persons with Work Experience During the Year, by Industry and Class of Worker of Job Held the Longest, 2002–2008

(Thousands of people.)

Industry and class of worker	2002	2003	2004	2005	2006	2007	2008
TOTAL	151 546	151 553	153 024	155 127	157 352	158 468	158 317
Agriculture	2 490	2 521	2 492	2 344	2 332	2 407	2 382
Wage and salary workers	1 583	1 605	1 549	1 501	1 495	1 525	1 522
Self-employed workers	875	894	918	829	812	846	824
Unpaid family workers	33	22	25	14	25	36	37
Nonagricultural Industries	149 055	149 032	150 532	152 783	155 021	156 061	155 934
Wage and salary workers	139 909	139 747	140 885	143 002	145 152	146 485	146 521
Mining	594	576	630	696	758	746	840
Construction	9 488	9 423	10 076	10 423	10 989	10 547	10 234
Manufacturing	17 660	17 349	17 196	17 243	17 112	16 641	16 332
Durable goods	11 013	10 622	10 814	10 930	10 995	10 687	10 477
Nondurable goods	6 647	6 727	6 382	6 313	6 116	5 954	5 855
Wholesale and retail trade	21 615	21 650	22 091	22 479	21 822	21 837	21 838
Wholesale trade	4 402	4 691	4 470	4 517	4 395	4 017	4 016
Retail trade	17 213	16 959	17 621	17 962	17 427	17 820	17 822
Transportation and utilities	7 039	6 934	7 040	7 248	7 413	8 023	7 675
Transportation and warehousing	5 745	5 736	5 827	6 095	6 197	6 750	6 365
Utilities	1 294	1 198	1 213	1 153	1 216	1 273	1 310
Information	3 989	3 755	3 359	3 495	3 710	3 687	3 455
Financial activities	9 591	9 822	9 956	9 748	10 101	10 013	9 671
Finance and insurance	6 986	7 135	7 192	7 011	7 190	7 347	6 994
Real estate and rental and leasing	2 605	2 687	2 764	2 737	2 912	2 666	2 677
Professional and business services	13 883	13 485	13 277	13 537	14 412	14 659	14 868
Professional, scientific, and technical services	7 989	7 855	7 793	7 768	8 294	8 676	8 742
Management, administration, and waste management services	5 894	5 629	5 484	5 769	6 118	5 982	6 127
Education and health services	29 343	29 571	29 814	30 552	31 314	31 921	32 828
Education services	12 765	13 026	13 169	13 282	13 659	13 989	14 396
Health care and social assistance services	16 578	16 544	16 645	17 270	17 655	17 932	18 432
Leisure and hospitality	13 260	13 110	13 345	13 405	13 455	13 959	14 242
Arts, entertainment, and recreation	2 852	2 789	2 888	2 877	2 797	3 124	3 047
Accommodation and food services	10 408	10 321	10 457	10 528	10 658	10 835	11 195
Other services and private household	6 416	6 529	6 473	6 490	6 341	6 603	6 590
Private households	873	897	907	866	912	888	912
Public administration	6 290	6 734	6 897	6 917	7 076	7 095	7 121
Self-employed workers	9 023	9 169	9 520	9 658	9 733	9 451	9 332
Unpaid family workers	124	116	128	123	135	126	82

Note: See notes and definitions for information on historical comparability.

Table 1-35. Number of Persons with Work Experience During the Year, by Extent of Employment and Sex, 1987–2008

(Thousands of people.)

Sex and year	Total	Full-time workers				Part-time workers			
		Total	50 to 52 weeks	27 to 49 weeks	1 to 26 weeks	Total	50 to 52 weeks	27 to 49 weeks	1 to 26 weeks
Both Sexes									
1987	128 315	100 288	77 015	13 361	9 912	28 027	10 973	6 594	10 460
1988	130 451	102 131	79 627	12 875	9 629	28 320	11 384	6 624	10 312
1989	132 817	104 876	81 117	14 271	9 488	27 941	11 275	6 987	9 679
1990	133 535	105 323	80 932	14 758	9 633	28 212	11 507	7 012	9 693
1991	133 410	104 472	80 385	14 491	9 596	28 938	11 946	7 003	9 989
1992	133 912	104 813	81 523	13 587	9 703	29 099	12 326	6 841	9 932
1993	136 354	106 299	83 384	13 054	9 861	30 055	12 818	6 777	10 460
1994	138 468	108 141	85 764	13 051	9 326	30 327	12 936	6 956	10 435
1995	139 724	110 063	88 173	12 970	8 920	29 661	12 725	6 831	10 105
1996	142 201	112 313	90 252	12 997	9 064	29 888	13 382	6 643	9 863
1997	143 968	113 879	92 631	12 508	8 740	30 089	13 810	6 565	9 714
1998	145 566	116 412	95 772	12 156	8 484	29 155	13 538	6 480	9 137
1999	148 295	119 096	97 941	12 294	8 861	29 199	13 680	6 317	9 202
2000	149 361	120 591	100 349	12 071	8 171	28 770	13 865	6 161	8 744
2001	151 042	121 921	100 357	13 172	8 392	29 121	14 038	6 139	8 944
2002	151 546	121 726	100 659	12 544	8 523	29 819	14 635	6 184	9 000
2003	151 553	121 158	100 700	11 972	8 486	30 395	15 333	6 027	9 035
2004	153 024	122 404	102 427	11 862	8 115	30 621	15 552	6 077	8 992
2005	155 127	124 683	104 876	11 816	7 991	30 444	15 374	6 161	8 909
2006	157 352	127 340	107 734	11 736	7 870	30 012	15 131	6 223	8 657
2007	158 468	128 332	108 617	11 901	7 814	30 136	15 477	6 194	8 466
2008	158 317	125 937	104 023	13 421	8 493	32 380	16 562	6 630	9 188
Men									
1987	69 144	59 736	47 040	7 503	5 193	9 408	3 260	2 191	3 957
1988	70 021	60 504	48 299	7 329	4 876	9 517	3 468	2 199	3 850
1989	71 640	62 108	49 693	7 642	4 773	9 532	3 619	2 254	3 659
1990	71 953	62 319	49 175	8 188	4 956	9 634	3 650	2 322	3 662
1991	71 700	61 636	47 895	8 324	5 417	10 064	3 820	2 342	3 902
1992	72 007	61 722	48 300	7 965	5 457	10 285	3 864	2 354	4 067
1993	72 872	62 513	49 832	7 317	5 364	10 359	4 005	2 144	4 210
1994	73 958	63 634	51 582	7 094	4 958	10 324	3 948	2 358	4 018
1995	74 381	64 145	52 671	6 973	4 501	10 236	4 034	2 257	3 945
1996	75 760	65 356	53 795	6 891	4 670	10 404	4 321	2 136	3 947
1997	76 408	66 089	54 918	6 638	4 533	10 319	4 246	2 274	3 799
1998	76 918	67 250	56 953	6 208	4 089	9 669	4 197	2 090	3 382
1999	78 145	68 347	57 520	6 401	4 426	9 797	4 297	2 062	3 438
2000	78 804	68 925	58 756	6 094	4 075	9 879	4 485	1 957	3 437
2001	79 971	70 074	58 715	7 087	4 272	9 897	4 306	1 989	3 602
2002	80 282	70 132	58 765	6 804	4 563	10 151	4 519	2 042	3 590
2003	80 317	69 766	58 778	6 479	4 509	10 551	5 042	1 872	3 637
2004	81 261	70 780	60 096	6 428	4 256	10 482	4 987	1 992	3 503
2005	82 735	72 056	61 510	6 299	4 247	10 679	5 153	2 074	3 452
2006	83 767	73 578	63 058	6 373	4 147	10 189	4 747	2 046	3 396
2007	84 292	73 734	62 994	6 583	4 157	10 558	4 933	2 165	3 460
2008	83 889	72 204	59 869	7 645	4 690	11 685	5 425	2 457	3 803
Women									
1987	59 171	40 552	29 975	5 858	4 719	18 619	7 713	4 403	6 503
1988	60 430	41 627	31 328	5 546	4 753	18 803	7 916	4 425	6 462
1989	61 178	42 768	31 424	6 629	4 715	18 410	7 656	4 733	6 021
1990	61 582	43 004	31 757	6 570	4 677	18 578	7 857	4 690	6 031
1991	61 712	42 837	32 491	6 167	4 179	18 875	8 126	4 662	6 087
1992	61 904	43 090	33 223	5 621	4 246	18 814	8 462	4 487	5 865
1993	63 481	43 785	33 552	5 736	4 497	19 696	8 813	4 633	6 250
1994	64 511	44 508	34 182	5 957	4 369	20 003	8 988	4 598	6 417
1995	65 342	45 917	35 502	5 997	4 418	19 425	8 691	4 574	6 160
1996	66 439	46 955	36 457	6 105	4 393	19 484	9 061	4 507	5 916
1997	67 559	47 790	37 713	5 870	4 207	19 769	9 564	4 291	5 914
1998	68 648	49 162	38 819	5 948	4 395	19 486	9 341	4 390	5 755
1999	70 150	50 748	40 421	5 892	4 435	19 402	9 383	4 255	5 764
2000	70 556	51 665	41 593	5 977	4 095	18 891	9 380	4 204	5 307
2001	71 071	51 848	41 642	6 085	4 120	19 223	9 731	4 150	5 342
2002	71 263	51 593	41 893	5 741	3 959	19 671	10 117	4 143	5 411
2003	71 236	51 391	41 921	5 493	3 977	19 844	10 291	4 155	5 398
2004	71 763	51 624	42 331	5 434	3 859	20 139	10 565	4 085	5 489
2005	72 392	52 627	43 366	5 517	3 744	19 765	10 222	4 087	5 456
2006	73 585	53 762	44 676	5 364	3 723	19 823	10 384	4 178	5 261
2007	74 176	54 598	45 622	5 318	3 657	19 579	10 543	4 029	5 006
2008	74 428	53 733	44 154	5 776	3 803	20 695	11 137	4 172	5 385

Note: See notes and definitions for information on historical comparability.

Table 1-36. Percent Distribution of the Population with Work Experience During the Year, by Extent of Employment and Sex, 1987–2008

(Percent of total people with work experience.)

Sex and year	Total	Full-time workers				Part-time workers			
		Total	50 to 52 weeks	27 to 49 weeks	1 to 26 weeks	Total	50 to 52 weeks	27 to 49 weeks	1 to 26 weeks
Both Sexes									
1987	100.0	78.1	60.0	10.4	7.7	21.9	8.6	5.1	8.2
1988	100.0	78.3	61.0	9.9	7.4	21.7	8.7	5.1	7.9
1989	100.0	78.9	61.1	10.7	7.1	21.1	8.5	5.3	7.3
1990	100.0	78.9	60.6	11.1	7.2	21.2	8.6	5.3	7.3
1991	100.0	78.4	60.3	10.9	7.2	21.7	9.0	5.2	7.5
1992	100.0	78.2	60.9	10.1	7.2	21.7	9.2	5.1	7.4
1993	100.0	78.0	61.2	9.6	7.2	22.1	9.4	5.0	7.7
1994	100.0	78.0	61.9	9.4	6.7	21.8	9.3	5.0	7.5
1995	100.0	78.8	63.1	9.3	6.4	21.2	9.1	4.9	7.2
1996	100.0	79.0	63.5	9.1	6.4	21.0	9.4	4.7	6.9
1997	100.0	79.1	64.3	8.7	6.1	20.9	9.6	4.6	6.7
1998	100.0	80.0	65.8	8.4	5.8	20.1	9.3	4.5	6.3
1999	100.0	80.3	66.0	8.3	6.0	19.7	9.2	4.3	6.2
2000	100.0	80.8	67.2	8.1	5.5	19.3	9.3	4.1	5.9
2001	100.0	80.7	66.4	8.7	5.6	19.3	9.3	4.1	5.9
2002	100.0	80.3	66.4	8.3	5.6	19.7	9.7	4.1	5.9
2003	100.0	79.9	66.4	7.9	5.6	20.1	10.1	4.0	6.0
2004	100.0	80.0	66.9	7.8	5.3	20.1	10.2	4.0	5.9
2005	100.0	80.4	67.6	7.6	5.2	19.6	9.9	4.0	5.7
2006	100.0	80.9	68.5	7.5	5.0	19.1	9.6	4.0	5.5
2007	100.0	81.0	68.5	7.5	4.9	19.0	9.8	3.9	5.3
2008	100.0	79.5	65.7	8.5	5.4	20.5	10.5	4.2	5.8
Men									
1987	100.0	86.4	68.0	10.9	7.5	13.6	4.7	3.2	5.7
1988	100.0	86.5	69.0	10.5	7.0	13.6	5.0	3.1	5.5
1989	100.0	86.8	69.4	10.7	6.7	13.3	5.1	3.1	5.1
1990	100.0	86.6	68.3	11.4	6.9	13.4	5.1	3.2	5.1
1991	100.0	86.0	66.8	11.6	7.6	14.0	5.3	3.3	5.4
1992	100.0	85.8	67.1	11.1	7.6	14.3	5.4	3.3	5.6
1993	100.0	85.8	68.4	10.0	7.4	14.2	5.5	2.9	5.8
1994	100.0	86.0	69.7	9.6	6.7	13.9	5.3	3.2	5.4
1995	100.0	86.3	70.8	9.4	6.1	13.7	5.4	3.0	5.3
1996	100.0	86.3	71.0	9.1	6.2	13.7	5.7	2.8	5.2
1997	100.0	86.5	71.9	8.7	5.9	13.6	5.6	3.0	5.0
1998	100.0	87.4	74.0	8.1	5.3	12.6	5.5	2.7	4.4
1999	100.0	87.5	73.6	8.2	5.7	12.5	5.5	2.6	4.4
2000	100.0	87.5	74.6	7.7	5.2	12.6	5.7	2.5	4.4
2001	100.0	87.6	73.4	8.9	5.3	12.4	5.4	2.5	4.5
2002	100.0	87.4	73.2	8.5	5.7	12.6	5.6	2.5	4.5
2003	100.0	86.9	73.2	8.1	5.6	13.1	6.3	2.3	4.5
2004	100.0	87.1	74.0	7.9	5.2	12.9	6.1	2.5	4.3
2005	100.0	87.0	74.3	7.6	5.1	12.9	6.2	2.5	4.2
2006	100.0	87.8	75.3	7.6	5.0	12.2	5.7	2.4	4.1
2007	100.0	87.5	74.7	7.8	4.9	12.5	5.9	2.6	4.1
2008	100.0	86.1	71.4	9.1	5.6	13.9	6.5	2.9	4.5
Women									
1987	100.0	68.6	50.7	9.9	8.0	31.4	13.0	7.4	11.0
1988	100.0	68.9	51.8	9.2	7.9	31.1	13.1	7.3	10.7
1989	100.0	69.9	51.4	10.8	7.7	30.0	12.5	7.7	9.8
1990	100.0	69.9	51.6	10.7	7.6	30.2	12.8	7.6	9.8
1991	100.0	69.4	52.6	10.0	6.8	30.7	13.2	7.6	9.9
1992	100.0	69.7	53.7	9.1	6.9	30.4	13.7	7.2	9.5
1993	100.0	69.0	52.9	9.0	7.1	31.0	13.9	7.3	9.8
1994	100.0	69.0	53.0	9.2	6.8	30.9	13.9	7.1	9.9
1995	100.0	70.3	54.3	9.2	6.8	29.7	13.3	7.0	9.4
1996	100.0	70.7	54.9	9.2	6.6	29.3	13.6	6.8	8.9
1997	100.0	70.7	55.8	8.7	6.2	29.4	14.2	6.4	8.8
1998	100.0	71.6	56.5	8.7	6.4	28.4	13.6	6.4	8.4
1999	100.0	72.3	57.6	8.4	6.3	27.7	13.4	6.1	8.2
2000	100.0	73.2	58.9	8.5	5.8	26.8	13.3	6.0	7.5
2001	100.0	73.0	58.6	8.6	5.8	27.0	13.7	5.8	7.5
2002	100.0	72.5	58.8	8.1	5.6	27.6	14.2	5.8	7.6
2003	100.0	72.1	58.8	7.7	5.6	27.8	14.4	5.8	7.6
2004	100.0	72.0	59.0	7.6	5.4	28.0	14.7	5.7	7.6
2005	100.0	72.7	59.9	7.6	5.2	27.2	14.1	5.6	7.5
2006	100.0	73.1	60.7	7.3	5.1	26.9	14.1	5.7	7.1
2007	100.0	73.6	61.5	7.2	4.9	26.4	14.2	5.4	6.7
2008	100.0	72.2	59.3	7.8	5.1	27.8	15.0	5.6	7.2

Note: See notes and definitions for information on historical comparability.

Table 1-37. Extent of Unemployment During the Year, by Sex, 1987–2008

(Thousands of people, percent.)

Sex and extent of unemployment	1987	1988	1989	1990	1991	1992	1993	1994	1995	1996	1997
BOTH SEXES											
Total Who Worked or Looked for Work	130 353	132 185	134 394	135 408	135 826	136 654	139 786	141 325	142 413	144 528	146 096
Percent with unemployment	14.1	12.9	12.9	14.6	15.7	15.7	14.7	13.4	12.7	11.6	10.7
Total with Unemployment	18 399	17 096	17 273	19 809	21 276	21 455	20 527	18 966	18 067	16 789	15 637
Did not work but looked for work	2 037	1 735	1 577	1 874	2 415	2 742	3 432	2 857	2 690	2 329	2 129
Worked during the year	16 362	15 362	15 697	17 936	18 861	18 714	17 094	16 109	15 377	14 460	13 508
Year-round workers with 1 or 2 weeks of unemployment	792	830	833	1 056	966	871	688	746	715	589	611
Part-year workers with unemployment	15 570	14 532	14 864	16 880	17 895	17 843	16 406	15 363	14 662	13 871	12 897
1 to 4 weeks	3 363	3 256	3 489	3 645	3 224	2 944	2 626	2 788	2 812	2 550	2 582
5 to 10 weeks	3 191	3 148	3 359	3 669	3 655	3 496	2 898	2 983	2 725	2 671	2 601
11 to 14 weeks	2 258	2 128	2 235	2 501	2 587	2 574	2 300	2 265	2 147	2 020	1 822
15 to 26 weeks	3 904	3 479	3 600	4 316	4 927	4 877	4 549	4 158	4 013	3 662	3 378
27 weeks or more	2 854	2 521	2 181	2 749	3 502	3 952	4 033	3 169	2 965	2 968	2 514
With 2 or more spells of unemployment	5 149	5 136	5 073	5 811	5 864	5 734	5 338	4 783	4 468	4 237	4 044
2 spells	2 442	2 460	2 460	2 855	2 738	2 698	2 572	2 207	1 963	1 982	1 853
3 or more spells	2 707	2 676	2 613	2 956	3 126	3 036	2 766	2 576	2 505	2 255	2 191
MEN											
Total Who Worked or Looked for Work	69 995	70 738	72 362	72 844	72 909	73 387	74 516	75 244	75 698	76 786	77 385
Percent with unemployment	15.0	13.7	13.5	15.5	17.3	17.5	15.7	14.1	13.2	11.9	11.1
Total with Unemployment	10 504	9 696	9 792	11 307	12 642	12 844	11 723	10 582	9 996	9 157	8 604
Did not work but looked for work	852	717	723	891	1 210	1 379	1 641	1 286	1 317	1 026	978
Worked during the year	9 653	8 978	9 071	10 415	11 432	11 466	10 082	9 296	8 679	8 130	7 626
Year-round workers with 1 or 2 weeks of unemployment	536	585	568	711	612	567	449	527	462	395	382
Part-year workers with unemployment	9 117	8 393	8 503	9 704	10 820	10 899	9 633	8 769	8 217	7 735	7 244
1 to 4 weeks	1 561	1 633	1 742	1 819	1 591	1 563	1 343	1 365	1 398	1 272	1 275
5 to 10 weeks	1 824	1 808	1 890	2 041	2 111	2 039	1 647	1 666	1 434	1 478	1 474
11 to 14 weeks	1 415	1 279	1 365	1 462	1 659	1 615	1 354	1 370	1 253	1 258	1 068
15 to 26 weeks	2 514	2 124	2 188	2 645	3 206	3 165	2 862	2 449	2 439	2 076	1 949
27 weeks or more	1 803	1 549	1 318	1 737	2 253	2 517	2 427	1 919	1 693	1 651	1 478
With 2 or more spells of unemployment	3 300	3 366	3 178	3 689	3 886	3 889	3 451	2 940	2 793	2 554	2 437
2 spells	1 488	1 560	1 517	1 676	1 742	1 781	1 580	1 266	1 110	1 109	1 078
3 or more spells	1 812	1 806	1 661	2 013	2 144	2 108	1 871	1 674	1 683	1 445	1 359
WOMEN											
Total Who Worked or Looked for Work	60 357	61 447	62 032	62 564	62 917	63 267	65 270	66 081	66 716	67 742	68 710
Percent with unemployment	13.1	12.0	12.1	13.6	13.7	13.6	13.5	12.7	12.1	11.3	10.2
Total with Unemployment	7 895	7 400	7 481	8 502	8 634	8 611	8 804	8 383	8 070	7 632	7 033
Did not work but looked for work	1 185	1 017	854	982	1 205	1 363	1 791	1 570	1 373	1 303	1 151
Worked during the year	6 710	6 382	6 628	7 520	7 427	7 247	7 014	6 813	6 696	6 330	5 882
Year-round workers with 1 or 2 weeks of unemployment	255	244	265	344	354	304	239	219	253	194	229
Part-year workers with unemployment	6 455	6 138	6 363	7 176	7 073	6 943	6 775	6 594	6 443	6 136	5 653
1 to 4 weeks	1 802	1 623	1 747	1 827	1 633	1 380	1 284	1 422	1 413	1 279	1 307
5 to 10 weeks	1 368	1 340	1 469	1 627	1 544	1 457	1 252	1 317	1 291	1 192	1 127
11 to 14 weeks	844	849	870	1 038	927	959	946	896	893	762	754
15 to 26 weeks	1 391	1 354	1 413	1 671	1 720	1 712	1 687	1 708	1 574	1 586	1 429
27 weeks or more	1 050	972	864	1 013	1 249	1 435	1 606	1 251	1 272	1 317	1 036
With 2 or more spells of unemployment	1 849	1 769	1 895	2 122	1 979	1 844	1 887	1 843	1 675	1 682	1 607
2 spells	954	899	943	1 179	997	916	992	941	853	872	775
3 or more spells	895	870	952	943	982	928	895	902	822	810	832

Table 1-37. Extent of Unemployment During the Year, by Sex, 1987–2008—*Continued*

(Thousands of people, percent.)

Sex and extent of unemployment	1998	1999	2000	2001	2002	2003	2004	2005	2006	2007	2008
BOTH SEXES											
Total Who Worked or Looked for Work	147 295	149 798	150 786	153 056	154 205	154 315	155 576	157 549	159 259	160 565	161 506
Percent with unemployment	9.5	8.7	8.1	10.4	10.9	10.7	9.7	9.2	9.1	9.4	13.1
Total with Unemployment	14 044	13 068	12 269	15 843	16 824	16 462	15 074	14 558	14 447	15 130	21 231
Did not work but looked for work	1 729	1 503	1 425	2 014	2 660	2 762	2 551	2 422	1 907	2 097	3 189
Worked during the year	12 316	11 566	10 845	13 829	14 164	13 699	12 522	12 136	12 540	13 033	18 042
Year-round workers with 1 or 2 weeks of unemployment	630	562	573	602	584	534	465	431	450	500	763
Part-year workers with unemployment	11 686	11 004	10 272	13 227	13 580	13 165	12 057	11 705	12 090	12 533	17 279
1 to 4 weeks	2 323	2 361	2 233	2 368	2 002	1 839	1 985	1 941	2 601	2 593	2 794
5 to 10 weeks	2 495	2 218	2 014	2 557	2 373	2 264	2 100	2 170	2 107	2 090	2 944
11 to 14 weeks	1 701	1 594	1 505	2 038	1 970	1 749	1 773	1 698	1 615	1 888	2 438
15 to 26 weeks	3 019	2 803	2 641	3 683	3 848	3 778	3 448	3 349	3 176	3 373	4 859
27 weeks or more	2 148	2 028	1 879	2 582	3 387	3 535	2 751	2 547	2 592	2 589	4 244
With 2 or more spells of unemployment	3 628	3 225	3 079	3 421	3 226	3 093	2 896	3 095	3 076	3 108	3 991
2 spells	1 650	1 449	1 397	1 643	1 556	1 585	1 344	1 477	1 564	1 427	1 987
3 or more spells	1 978	1 776	1 682	1 779	1 670	1 508	1 552	1 618	1 513	1 681	2 004
MEN											
Total Who Worked or Looked for Work	77 704	78 905	79 546	80 975	81 651	81 804	82 478	83 951	84 736	85 368	85 563
Percent with unemployment	9.4	9.0	8.6	11.0	11.8	11.4	10.0	9.7	9.6	10.2	14.4
Total with Unemployment	7 284	7 091	6 806	8 928	9 621	9 339	8 256	8 116	8 115	8 698	12 331
Did not work but looked for work	787	760	742	1 004	1 369	1 487	1 217	1 216	969	1 076	1 674
Worked during the year	6 497	6 332	6 064	7 924	8 252	7 854	7 039	6 899	7 146	7 622	10 656
Year-round workers with 1 or 2 weeks of unemployment	386	373	379	421	365	359	289	296	295	365	484
Part-year workers with unemployment	6 111	5 959	5 685	7 502	7 887	7 495	6 750	6 603	6 850	7 257	10 172
1 to 4 weeks	1 085	1 166	1 070	1 247	1 075	958	1 028	1 052	1 283	1 367	1 523
5 to 10 weeks	1 363	1 168	1 135	1 446	1 342	1 314	1 170	1 209	1 267	1 214	1 701
11 to 14 weeks	980	937	880	1 207	1 186	1 039	1 021	1 024	961	1 163	1 467
15 to 26 weeks	1 585	1 655	1 595	2 191	2 282	2 178	2 065	1 923	1 868	2 058	3 035
27 weeks or more	1 098	1 033	1 005	1 412	2 002	2 006	1 466	1 395	1 472	1 455	2 445
With 2 or more spells of unemployment	2 014	1 845	1 809	2 100	1 920	1 882	1 828	1 975	1 936	1 992	2 623
2 spells	880	787	804	1 002	914	946	808	940	945	847	1 234
3 or more spells	1 134	1 058	1 005	1 099	1 006	936	1 020	1 035	991	1 145	1 389
WOMEN											
Total Who Worked or Looked for Work	69 591	70 893	71 240	72 081	72 554	72 511	73 097	73 598	74 523	75 197	75 943
Percent with unemployment	9.7	8.4	7.7	9.6	9.9	9.8	9.3	8.8	8.5	8.6	11.7
Total with Unemployment	6 760	5 976	5 463	6 915	7 203	7 123	6 818	6 442	6 332	6 432	8 900
Did not work but looked for work	942	743	683	1 010	1 291	1 275	1 334	1 206	938	1 021	1 514
Worked during the year	5 816	5 234	4 779	5 905	5 913	5 848	5 484	5 236	5 394	5 411	7 385
Year-round workers with 1 or 2 weeks of unemployment	243	189	193	180	220	176	177	136	154	135	279
Part-year workers with unemployment	5 573	5 045	4 586	5 725	5 693	5 672	5 307	5 100	5 240	5 276	7 106
1 to 4 weeks	1 237	1 194	1 164	1 121	927	882	957	888	1 317	1 226	1 270
5 to 10 weeks	1 131	1 050	878	1 111	1 031	950	929	961	840	876	1 243
11 to 14 weeks	721	657	625	831	784	710	752	674	655	725	971
15 to 26 weeks	1 434	1 148	1 045	1 492	1 566	1 600	1 384	1 426	1 307	1 316	1 823
27 weeks or more	1 050	996	874	1 170	1 385	1 530	1 285	1 151	1 120	1 134	1 800
With 2 or more spells of unemployment	1 614	1 379	1 270	1 321	1 306	1 211	1 069	1 120	1 140	1 116	1 368
2 spells	770	662	593	641	642	639	537	537	619	580	753
3 or more spells	844	717	677	680	664	572	532	583	521	536	616

Table 1-38. Percent Distribution of Persons with Unemployment During the Year, by Sex and Extent of Unemployment, 1987–2008

(Percent.)

Sex and extent of unemployment	1987	1988	1989	1990	1991	1992	1993	1994	1995	1996	1997
BOTH SEXES											
Total with Unemployment Who Worked During the Year ...	100.0	100.0	100.0	100.0	100.0	100.0	100.0	100.0	100.0	100.0	100.0
Year-round workers with 1 or 2 weeks of unemployment	4.8	5.4	5.3	5.9	5.1	4.7	4.0	4.6	4.6	4.1	4.5
Part-year workers with unemployment	95.2	94.5	94.6	94.1	94.8	95.4	96.1	95.4	95.4	96.0	95.5
1 to 4 weeks	20.6	21.2	22.2	20.3	17.1	15.7	15.4	17.3	18.3	17.6	19.1
5 to 10 weeks	19.5	20.5	21.4	20.5	19.4	18.7	17.0	18.5	17.7	18.5	19.3
11 to 14 weeks	13.8	13.8	14.2	13.9	13.7	13.8	13.5	14.1	14.0	14.0	13.5
15 to 26 weeks	23.9	22.6	22.9	24.1	26.1	26.1	26.6	25.8	26.1	25.3	25.0
27 weeks or more	17.4	16.4	13.9	15.3	18.5	21.1	23.6	19.7	19.3	20.6	18.6
With 2 or more spells of unemployment	31.4	33.4	32.3	32.4	31.1	30.6	31.2	29.7	29.1	29.3	29.9
2 spells	14.9	16.0	15.7	15.9	14.5	14.4	15.0	13.7	12.8	13.7	13.7
3 or more spells	16.5	17.4	16.6	16.5	16.6	16.2	16.2	16.0	16.3	15.6	16.2
MEN											
Total with Unemployment Who Worked During the Year ...	100.0	100.0	100.0	100.0	100.0	100.0	100.0	100.0	100.0	100.0	100.1
Year-round workers with 1 or 2 weeks of unemployment	5.6	6.5	6.3	6.8	5.4	4.9	4.4	5.7	5.3	4.9	5.0
Part-year workers with unemployment	94.5	93.4	93.7	93.2	94.6	95.0	95.5	94.3	94.7	95.1	95.1
1 to 4 weeks	16.2	18.2	19.2	17.5	13.9	13.6	13.3	14.7	16.1	15.6	16.7
5 to 10 weeks	18.9	20.1	20.8	19.6	18.5	17.8	16.3	17.9	16.5	18.2	19.3
11 to 14 weeks	14.7	14.2	15.1	14.0	14.5	14.1	13.4	14.7	14.4	15.5	14.0
15 to 26 weeks	26.0	23.7	24.1	25.4	28.0	27.6	28.4	26.4	28.1	25.5	25.6
27 weeks or more	18.7	17.2	14.5	16.7	19.7	21.9	24.1	20.6	19.5	20.3	19.4
With 2 or more spells of unemployment	34.2	37.5	35.0	35.4	34.0	33.9	34.3	31.6	32.2	31.4	31.9
2 spells	15.4	17.4	16.7	16.1	15.2	15.5	15.7	13.6	12.8	13.6	14.1
3 or more spells	18.8	20.1	18.3	19.3	18.8	18.4	18.6	18.0	19.4	17.8	17.8
WOMEN											
Total With Unemployment Who Worked During the Year ...	100.0	100.0	100.0	100.0	100.0	100.0	100.0	100.0	100.0	100.0	100.0
Year-round workers with 1 or 2 weeks of unemployment	3.8	3.8	4.0	4.6	4.8	4.2	3.4	3.2	3.8	3.1	3.9
Part-year workers with unemployment	96.3	96.1	96.0	95.3	95.3	95.7	96.6	96.7	96.2	96.9	96.1
1 to 4 weeks	26.9	25.4	26.4	24.3	22.0	19.0	18.3	20.9	21.1	20.2	22.2
5 to 10 weeks	20.4	21.0	22.2	21.6	20.8	20.1	17.8	19.3	19.3	18.8	19.2
11 to 14 weeks	12.6	13.3	13.1	13.8	12.5	13.2	13.5	13.1	13.3	12.0	12.8
15 to 26 weeks	20.7	21.2	21.3	22.2	23.2	23.6	24.1	25.1	23.5	25.1	24.3
27 weeks or more	15.7	15.2	13.0	13.4	16.8	19.8	22.9	18.3	19.0	20.8	17.6
With 2 or more spells of unemployment	27.5	27.7	28.6	28.2	26.6	25.4	26.9	27.0	25.0	26.6	27.3
2 spells	14.2	14.1	14.2	15.7	13.4	12.6	14.1	13.8	12.7	13.8	13.2
3 or more spells	13.3	13.6	14.4	12.5	13.2	12.8	12.8	13.2	12.3	12.8	14.1

Table 1-38. Percent Distribution of Persons with Unemployment During the Year, by Sex and Extent of Unemployment, 1987–2008—*Continued*

(Percent.)

Sex and extent of unemployment	1998	1999	2000	2001	2002	2003	2004	2005	2006	2007	2008
BOTH SEXES											
Total with Unemployment Who Worked During the Year ...	100.0	100.0	100.0	100.0	100.0	100.0	100.0	100.0	100.0	100.0	100.0
Year-round workers with 1 or 2 weeks of unemployment	5.1	4.9	5.3	4.4	4.1	3.9	3.7	3.6	3.6	3.8	4.2
Part-year workers with unemployment	95.0	95.1	94.8	95.6	95.9	96.1	96.3	96.4	96.4	96.1	95.8
1 to 4 weeks	18.9	20.4	20.6	17.1	14.1	13.4	15.9	16.0	20.7	19.9	15.5
5 to 10 weeks	20.3	19.2	18.6	18.5	16.8	16.5	16.8	17.9	16.8	16.0	16.3
11 to 14 weeks	13.8	13.8	13.9	14.7	13.9	12.8	14.2	14.0	12.9	14.5	13.5
15 to 26 weeks	24.5	24.2	24.4	26.6	27.2	27.6	27.5	27.6	25.3	25.9	26.9
27 weeks or more	17.5	17.5	17.3	18.7	23.9	25.8	22.0	20.9	20.7	19.8	23.5
With 2 or more spells of unemployment	29.5	27.9	28.4	24.8	22.8	22.6	23.1	25.5	24.5	23.8	22.1
2 spells	13.4	12.5	12.9	11.9	11.0	11.6	10.7	12.2	12.5	10.9	11.0
3 or more spells	16.1	15.4	15.5	12.9	11.8	11.0	12.4	13.3	12.1	12.9	11.1
MEN											
Total with Unemployment Who Worked During the Year ...	100.0	100.0	100.0	100.0	100.0	100.0	100.0	100.0	100.0	100.0	100.0
Year-round workers with 1 or 2 weeks of unemployment	5.9	5.9	6.3	5.3	4.4	4.6	4.1	4.3	4.1	4.8	4.5
Part-year workers with unemployment	94.1	94.0	93.6	94.7	95.6	95.4	95.9	95.7	95.9	95.2	95.5
1 to 4 weeks	16.7	18.4	17.6	15.7	13.0	12.2	14.6	15.3	18.0	17.9	14.3
5 to 10 weeks	21.0	18.4	18.7	18.2	16.3	16.7	16.6	17.5	17.7	15.9	16.0
11 to 14 weeks	15.1	14.8	14.5	15.2	14.4	13.2	14.5	14.8	13.4	15.3	13.8
15 to 26 weeks	24.4	26.1	26.3	27.6	27.7	27.7	29.3	27.9	26.1	27.0	28.5
27 weeks or more	16.9	16.3	16.5	17.8	24.3	25.5	20.8	20.2	20.6	19.1	22.9
With 2 or more spells of unemployment	31.0	29.1	29.9	26.5	23.3	24.0	26.0	28.6	27.1	26.1	24.6
2 spells	13.5	12.4	13.3	12.6	11.1	12.1	11.5	13.6	13.2	11.1	11.6
3 or more spells	17.5	16.7	16.6	13.9	12.2	11.9	14.5	15.0	13.9	15.0	13.0
WOMEN											
Total With Unemployment Who Worked During the Year ...	100.0	100.0	100.0	100.0	100.0	100.0	100.0	100.0	100.0	100.0	100.0
Year-round workers with 1 or 2 weeks of unemployment	4.2	3.6	4.0	3.1	3.7	3.0	3.2	2.6	2.9	2.5	3.8
Part-year workers with unemployment	95.8	96.4	96.0	96.9	96.3	97.0	96.8	97.4	97.1	97.4	96.2
1 to 4 weeks	21.3	22.8	24.3	19.0	15.7	15.1	17.4	17.0	24.4	22.6	17.2
5 to 10 weeks	19.4	20.1	18.4	18.8	17.4	16.2	16.9	18.4	15.6	16.2	16.8
11 to 14 weeks	12.4	12.6	13.1	14.1	13.3	12.1	13.7	12.9	12.1	13.4	13.1
15 to 26 weeks	24.7	21.9	21.9	25.3	26.5	27.4	25.2	27.2	24.2	24.3	24.7
27 weeks or more	18.0	19.0	18.3	19.8	23.4	26.2	23.5	22.0	20.8	20.9	24.4
With 2 or more spells of unemployment	27.7	26.3	26.6	22.4	22.1	20.7	19.5	21.4	21.1	20.6	18.5
2 spells	13.2	12.6	12.4	10.9	10.9	10.9	9.8	10.3	11.5	10.7	10.2
3 or more spells	14.5	13.7	14.2	11.5	11.2	9.8	9.7	11.1	9.7	9.9	8.3

Table 1-39. Number and Median Annual Earnings of Year-Round, Full-Time Wage and Salary Workers, by Age, Sex, and Race, 1987–2008

(Thousands of people, dollars.)

Sex, age, and race	1987	1988	1989	1990	1991	1992	1993	1994	1995	1996	1997
NUMBER											
Both Sexes, 16 Years and Over	71 069	73 598	74 898	74 728	74 449	75 517	77 427	79 875	83 407	85 611	86 905
16 to 24 years	7 563	7 400	7 471	6 978	6 571	6 224	6 685	6 684	6 892	6 809	7 063
25 to 44 years	42 211	44 036	45 082	45 086	44 811	45 022	45 951	47 150	48 695	49 225	49 513
25 to 34 years	22 884	23 727	23 721	23 201	22 541	22 469	22 637	23 193	23 310	23 071	23 186
35 to 44 years	19 327	20 309	21 361	21 885	22 270	22 553	23 314	23 957	25 385	26 154	26 327
45 to 54 years	12 764	13 506	13 848	14 070	14 718	15 652	16 424	17 366	18 436	19 714	20 109
55 to 64 years	7 406	7 529	7 321	7 458	7 219	7 590	7 208	7 500	8 122	8 455	8 901
65 years and over	1 125	1 127	1 177	1 137	1 130	1 029	1 159	1 174	1 263	1 408	1 318
Men, 16 Years and Over	42 490	43 785	45 107	44 574	43 523	43 894	45 494	47 255	49 334	50 407	50 772
16 to 24 years	4 145	4 165	4 223	3 982	3 596	3 457	3 853	3 918	4 094	3 942	4 021
25 to 44 years	25 293	26 246	27 321	27 069	26 353	26 335	27 161	28 000	28 940	29 282	29 453
25 to 34 years	13 659	14 163	14 439	13 941	13 303	13 146	13 400	13 749	13 844	13 817	13 735
35 to 44 years	11 634	12 083	12 882	13 128	13 050	13 189	13 761	14 251	15 096	15 465	15 718
45 to 54 years	7 726	8 086	8 276	8 168	8 479	8 908	9 522	10 120	10 589	11 372	11 388
55 to 64 years	4 654	4 616	4 562	4 650	4 403	4 588	4 238	4 460	4 884	4 908	5 133
65 years and over	672	672	725	705	694	606	719	757	827	903	775
Women, 16 Years and Over	28 579	29 812	29 791	30 155	30 925	31 622	31 933	32 619	34 073	35 203	36 133
16 to 24 years	3 418	3 235	3 249	2 995	2 976	2 767	2 832	2 767	2 798	2 867	3 041
25 to 44 years	16 918	17 790	17 760	18 017	18 458	18 688	18 790	19 150	19 755	19 942	20 060
25 to 34 years	9 225	9 564	9 282	9 260	9 238	9 323	9 237	9 444	9 467	9 254	9 451
35 to 44 years	7 693	8 226	8 478	8 757	9 220	9 365	9 553	9 706	10 288	10 688	10 609
45 to 54 years	5 037	5 420	5 572	5 902	6 239	6 744	6 902	7 246	7 847	8 343	8 721
55 to 64 years	2 752	2 913	2 758	2 808	2 816	3 002	2 970	3 040	3 238	3 547	3 767
65 years and over	453	455	451	433	436	423	439	417	436	505	543
White, 16 Years and Over	61 546	63 357	64 246	64 128	63 926	64 706	65 656	67 370	70 430	72 068	72 650
Men	37 461	38 449	39 430	38 915	38 018	38 267	39 347	40 589	42 608	43 554	43 429
Women	24 085	24 908	24 815	25 213	25 908	26 439	26 309	26 782	27 822	28 514	29 221
Black, 16 Years and Over	7 440	7 907	8 140	8 027	7 941	7 995	8 478	9 074	9 446	9 706	10 248
Men	3 838	3 976	4 219	4 162	4 001	4 011	4 259	4 598	4 686	4 682	5 026
Women	3 602	3 931	3 920	3 865	3 940	3 984	4 219	4 476	4 759	5 024	5 222
MEDIAN ANNUAL EARNINGS											
Both Sexes, 16 Years and Over	21 000	22 000	23 000	24 000	25 000	25 871	26 000	26 620	27 000	28 000	30 000
16 to 24 years	13 000	13 500	14 000	14 400	14 100	15 000	15 000	15 000	15 500	15 600	16 000
25 to 34 years	20 000	21 000	22 000	22 000	23 000	24 000	24 000	24 480	25 000	25 300	27 000
35 to 44 years	25 000	26 000	27 000	27 970	28 000	29 483	30 000	30 000	30 000	31 000	32 000
45 to 54 years	25 000	26 000	27 000	28 000	29 000	30 000	30 500	32 343	32 000	33 000	35 000
55 to 64 years	23 000	24 000	26 000	26 000	27 000	27 430	28 000	30 000	30 000	30 000	32 000
65 years and over	18 000	19 500	23 000	23 841	22 000	24 000	24 000	24 377	29 600	26 496	28 200
Men, 16 Years and Over	25 900	26 570	27 300	28 000	29 120	30 000	30 000	30 000	31 000	32 000	34 000
16 to 24 years	14 000	14 200	15 000	15 000	15 000	15 000	15 000	15 000	16 000	17 000	17 000
25 to 34 years	23 000	24 000	24 000	25 000	25 000	26 000	25 000	26 000	27 000	28 000	29 852
35 to 44 years	30 000	31 000	32 000	32 000	33 000	34 000	35 000	35 000	35 000	36 000	37 000
45 to 54 years	31 200	32 000	34 000	35 000	36 000	37 000	38 000	40 000	40 000	40 000	41 000
55 to 64 years	29 181	30 000	32 000	31 875	33 000	33 000	34 000	36 000	36 000	36 000	39 000
65 years and over	24 000	25 000	30 000	29 000	28 000	30 000	28 000	30 000	36 000	33 000	36 400
Women, 16 Years and Over	17 000	18 000	18 574	20 000	20 000	21 500	22 000	22 150	23 000	24 000	25 000
16 to 24 years	12 000	13 000	13 167	13 392	13 800	14 000	14 872	14 560	15 000	15 000	15 000
25 to 34 years	17 000	18 000	19 000	19 500	20 000	21 000	21 000	22 000	22 000	23 000	24 000
35 to 44 years	19 000	20 000	20 200	22 000	22 510	23 397	24 000	25 000	25 000	25 000	26 000
45 to 54 years	18 148	19 000	20 000	21 000	22 000	24 000	24 000	25 000	25 000	26 000	27 040
55 to 64 years	17 000	17 000	18 000	19 000	20 000	22 000	21 500	22 000	22 500	24 000	24 800
65 years and over	16 000	15 600	17 566	18 586	17 000	18 500	20 000	19 000	23 290	20 800	24 000
White, 16 Years and Over	22 000	23 000	24 000	25 000	25 000	26 200	27 000	28 000	28 000	29 000	30 000
Men	26 500	27 489	28 500	29 000	30 000	31 000	30 700	32 000	32 000	33 000	35 000
Women	17 000	18 000	19 000	20 000	20 500	22 000	22 000	23 000	23 000	24 000	25 000
Black, 16 Years and Over	17 000	18 000	19 000	19 350	20 000	21 000	20 800	21 000	22 000	23 784	24 000
Men	18 850	20 000	20 000	20 800	22 000	22 312	23 000	23 500	24 500	26 000	26 000
Women	15 500	16 200	17 115	18 000	18 500	20 000	19 843	20 000	20 000	21 000	22 000

Table 1-39. Number and Median Annual Earnings of Year-Round, Full-Time Wage and Salary Workers, by Age, Sex, and Race, 1987–2008—Continued

(Thousands of people, dollars.)

Sex, age, and race	1998	1999	2000	2001	2002	2003	2004	2005	2006	2007	2008
NUMBER											
Both Sexes, 16 Years and Over	89 748	91 722	94 359	94 531	94 526	94 731	96 098	98 632	101 353	102 441	98 493
16 to 24 years	7 618	7 631	8 384	7 989	7 903	7 631	7 702	7 956	8 113	8 064	7 242
25 to 44 years	50 264	50 532	51 159	49 939	49 120	48 343	48 421	49 149	50 056	49 725	47 364
25 to 34 years	23 048	22 952	23 044	22 744	22 657	22 512	22 405	22 808	23 613	23 646	22 786
35 to 44 years	27 216	27 580	28 115	27 195	26 463	25 831	26 016	26 341	26 443	26 080	24 578
45 to 54 years	21 274	22 375	23 307	23 855	23 999	24 507	25 074	25 661	26 338	26 566	25 722
55 to 64 years	9 273	9 594	9 870	10 948	11 584	12 207	12 812	13 605	14 340	15 248	15 286
65 years and over	1 318	1 590	1 639	1 800	1 921	2 042	2 090	2 262	2 507	2 837	2 879
Men, 16 Years and Over	52 509	53 132	54 477	54 630	54 420	54 575	55 610	57 020	58 533	58 673	55 973
16 to 24 years	4 479	4 347	4 602	4 605	4 570	4 421	4 493	4 663	4 812	4 719	4 112
25 to 44 years	29 763	29 738	30 080	29 271	28 855	28 499	28 763	29 151	29 589	29 004	27 546
25 to 34 years	13 612	13 471	13 497	13 386	13 400	13 288	13 430	13 629	13 933	13 706	13 208
35 to 44 years	16 151	16 267	16 583	15 885	15 455	15 211	15 333	15 522	15 655	15 298	14 337
45 to 54 years	12 030	12 546	13 045	13 363	13 330	13 616	13 975	14 382	14 758	14 810	14 199
55 to 64 years	5 438	5 498	5 693	6 253	6 502	6 872	7 165	7 489	7 905	8 449	8 397
65 years and over	801	1 003	1 057	1 138	1 163	1 165	1 213	1 334	1 469	1 692	1 720
Women, 16 Years and Over	37 239	38 591	39 887	39 901	40 106	40 156	40 488	41 613	42 820	43 768	42 520
16 to 24 years	3 140	3 285	3 782	3 384	3 333	3 210	3 209	3 293	3 301	3 345	3 130
25 to 44 years	20 503	20 794	21 081	20 668	20 264	19 844	19 656	19 997	20 467	20 721	19 819
25 to 34 years	9 437	9 481	9 548	9 358	9 257	9 224	8 974	9 179	9 679	9 940	9 578
35 to 44 years	11 066	11 313	11 533	11 310	11 007	10 620	10 682	10 818	10 788	10 782	10 240
45 to 54 years	9 244	9 829	10 263	10 493	10 669	10 891	11 099	11 279	11 580	11 757	11 524
55 to 64 years	3 836	4 096	4 178	4 695	5 082	5 335	5 647	6 116	6 434	6 799	6 889
65 years and over	517	586	583	662	758	877	877	927	1 038	1 146	1 158
White, 16 Years and Over	75 046	76 203	77 790	78 306	77 632	77 545	78 236	80 546	82 411	83 139	79 980
Men	44 901	45 211	46 105	46 373	45 823	45 816	46 317	47 790	48 897	48 825	46 608
Women	30 145	30 992	31 685	31 933	31 809	31 729	31 919	32 756	33 513	34 314	33 372
Black, 16 Years and Over	10 532	11 145	11 899	11 001	10 966	10 979	11 301	11 417	11 988	11 987	11 424
Men	5 202	5 411	5 636	5 281	5 150	5 196	5 470	5 402	5 679	5 689	5 377
Women	5 329	5 734	6 264	5 720	5 816	5 783	5 832	6 015	6 309	6 299	6 046
MEDIAN ANNUAL EARNINGS											
Both Sexes, 16 Years and Over	30 000	31 000	32 000	34 000	35 000	35 000	35 672	36 400	38 000	40 000	40 000
16 to 24 years	18 000	18 000	19 000	20 000	20 000	20 000	20 000	20 000	21 000	22 421	24 000
25 to 34 years	28 500	30 000	30 000	31 000	31 800	32 000	33 000	33 000	35 000	35 000	36 500
35 to 44 years	33 000	34 992	35 000	36 000	37 000	39 000	40 000	40 000	41 000	43 000	45 000
45 to 54 years	35 000	36 000	38 000	39 500	40 000	40 000	40 000	42 000	44 000	45 000	45 000
55 to 64 years	34 000	35 000	35 000	36 400	39 145	40 000	40 000	40 000	41 000	43 000	46 000
65 years and over	26 000	30 000	32 000	32 000	33 000	32 000	35 000	35 000	35 001	40 000	42 000
Men, 16 Years and Over	35 000	36 000	37 600	38 500	40 000	40 000	40 000	40 051	42 000	45 000	46 000
16 to 24 years	18 720	19 000	20 000	20 000	20 000	20 800	20 800	20 800	22 000	23 000	25 000
25 to 34 years	30 000	32 000	33 500	34 000	34 740	35 000	35 000	35 000	36 000	38 000	40 000
35 to 44 years	38 000	40 000	40 000	42 000	43 000	43 900	45 000	45 000	48 000	50 000	50 000
45 to 54 years	42 000	44 616	45 000	45 000	47 000	48 000	48 000	50 000	50 000	50 000	52 000
55 to 64 years	40 000	40 853	44 000	45 000	47 000	50 000	50 000	50 000	50 000	52 000	54 000
65 years and over	35 000	36 000	35 999	35 000	37 861	42 000	40 000	41 000	44 000	44 000	50 000
Women, 16 Years and Over	25 000	26 000	27 500	29 000	30 000	30 000	30 001	32 000	33 000	35 000	35 000
16 to 24 years	17 000	17 000	18 000	19 000	19 000	20 000	20 000	20 000	20 000	22 000	22 000
25 to 34 years	25 000	26 000	27 000	28 080	29 500	30 000	30 000	30 000	31 000	33 000	34 000
35 to 44 years	27 200	28 000	29 000	30 000	30 400	32 000	32 800	35 000	35 000	36 000	38 000
45 to 54 years	28 132	30 000	30 000	32 000	32 000	33 466	34 771	35 000	36 000	37 163	38 000
55 to 64 years	25 775	27 000	28 000	30 000	31 410	32 000	33 000	33 000	35 000	37 100	39 000
65 years and over	22 000	20 800	24 000	25 000	28 000	28 000	26 000	27 000	28 768	27 878	31 000	34 193
White, 16 Years and Over	31 000	32 000	34 000	35 000	35 000	36 000	37 000	38 000	40 000	40 000	41 600
Men	36 000	37 200	39 000	40 000	40 000	40 000	42 000	42 000	44 707	45 000	48 000
Women	26 000	27 000	28 000	30 000	30 000	31 000	31 800	32 000	34 000	35 000	35 500
Black, 16 Years and Over	25 000	25 760	26 000	28 500	29 000	30 000	30 000	30 000	31 000	33 000	34 000
Men	27 000	30 000	30 000	30 000	30 000	32 000	30 000	33 000	34 000	35 000	37 500
Women	23 000	24 000	25 000	26 000	26 000	27 000	28 000	29 141	30 000	30 000	30 002

Table 1-40. Number and Median Annual Earnings of Year-Round, Full-Time Wage and Salary Workers, by Sex and Occupation of Job Held the Longest, 2002–2008

(Thousands of people, dollars.)

Sex and occupation	2002	2003	2004	2005	2006	2007	2008
Both Sexes, Number of Workers							
Management, business, and financial operations	15 707	15 552	15 575	16 299	16 806	17 115	17 259
Management	11 350	11 102	11 125	11 685	11 866	12 191	12 256
Business and financial operations	4 357	4 450	4 451	4 613	4 941	4 924	5 003
Professional and related	19 149	19 607	19 592	20 093	21 268	21 939	21 748
Computer and mathematical	2 644	2 598	2 680	2 779	2 888	3 180	3 089
Architecture and engineering	2 257	2 273	2 349	2 361	2 491	2 467	2 360
Life, physical, and social sciences	1 094	1 010	999	1 096	1 142	1 026	1 044
Community and social services	1 694	1 698	1 632	1 728	1 835	1 791	1 754
Legal	1 006	1 149	1 087	1 093	1 168	1 159	1 228
Education, training, and library	4 606	4 918	4 742	4 894	5 195	5 482	5 478
Arts, design, entertainment, sports, and media	1 453	1 374	1 416	1 362	1 633	1 554	1 415
Health care practitioner and technical	4 395	4 586	4 688	4 780	4 916	5 278	5 380
Services	12 011	11 990	12 457	13 117	13 236	13 553	13 034
Health care support	1 767	1 703	1 781	2 027	2 081	2 027	2 019
Protective services	2 042	2 385	2 406	2 429	2 506	2 511	2 472
Food preparation and serving related	3 592	3 223	3 383	3 586	3 646	3 769	3 504
Building and grounds cleaning and maintenance	2 843	2 942	3 116	3 285	3 120	3 198	3 027
Personal care and services	1 767	1 735	1 771	1 790	1 883	2 048	2 012
Sales and office	23 791	23 766	23 619	24 010	24 467	24 472	23 058
Sales and related	9 929	9 804	9 951	10 251	10 497	10 301	9 763
Office and administrative support	13 862	13 962	13 668	13 758	13 970	14 171	13 294
Natural resources, construction, and maintenance	9 823	9 709	10 574	10 864	11 295	10 745	10 002
Farming, fishing, and forestry	573	562	629	556	585	607	581
Construction and extraction	5 256	5 070	5 711	6 145	6 484	5 885	5 158
Installation, maintenance, and repair	3 994	4 077	4 234	4 163	4 226	4 252	4 264
Production, transportation, and material moving	13 386	13 391	13 648	13 586	13 704	13 907	12 649
Production	7 736	7 670	7 787	7 623	7 762	7 589	6 652
Transportation and material moving	5 650	5 721	5 861	5 963	5 942	6 318	5 997
Armed forces	658	717	632	664	576	709	744
Both Sexes, Median Annual Earnings							
Management, business, and financial operations	50 000	52 000	55 000	57 000	60 000	60 000	60 800
Management	55 000	58 000	60 000	60 000	62 500	65 000	65 000
Business and financial operations	44 000	45 000	45 000	49 000	50 000	50 000	52 000
Professional and related	46 000	46 000	48 000	50 000	50 000	51 000	54 000
Computer and mathematical	60 000	60 000	62 000	62 400	68 000	70 000	70 000
Architecture and engineering	59 400	62 000	60 000	65 000	69 000	70 000	70 000
Life, physical, and social sciences	50 000	50 000	50 000	53 500	57 000	60 000	57 532
Community and social services	34 000	34 349	36 000	36 000	36 780	39 000	40 000
Legal	61 860	75 000	70 000	72 000	70 000	70 000	75 000
Education, training, and library	38 000	39 000	40 000	40 000	40 282	44 984	45 000
Arts, design, entertainment, sports, and media	43 500	40 000	40 000	42 000	45 000	44 297	47 000
Health care practitioner and technical	46 000	48 000	50 000	50 000	52 000	52 800	55 000
Services	22 000	22 000	22 000	23 000	24 000	25 000	25 000
Health care support	22 100	22 000	22 000	22 000	23 000	24 500	26 000
Protective services	38 000	42 000	42 000	42 000	45 000	45 000	45 000
Food preparation and serving related	18 000	18 000	18 000	19 656	19 000	20 000	20 800
Building and grounds cleaning and maintenance	20 000	20 000	20 000	21 000	23 000	23 000	24 000
Personal care and services	21 840	20 678	22 537	23 000	23 000	25 000	25 000
Sales and office	30 000	30 000	30 000	31 200	32 002	34 000	35 000
Sales and related	35 000	35 000	35 000	35 000	37 000	38 000	38 500
Office and administrative support	28 000	29 000	30 000	30 000	30 000	32 000	32 500
Natural resources, construction, and maintenance	33 000	34 000	35 000	35 000	35 000	36 000	40 000
Farming, fishing, and forestry	20 000	20 000	20 000	21 000	20 000	24 000	24 000
Construction and extraction	31 200	32 000	33 000	32 000	35 000	35 000	39 000
Installation, maintenance, and repair	36 000	38 000	38 300	40 000	40 000	40 000	42 000
Production, transportation, and material moving	28 704	30 000	30 000	30 200	30 000	33 000	34 000
Production	28 000	30 000	30 000	30 000	30 000	33 000	34 000
Transportation and material moving	29 000	30 000	30 000	30 800	30 000	33 800	34 000
Armed forces	36 000	36 000	40 000	39 000	40 000	42 000	45 000

Table 1-40. Number and Median Annual Earnings of Year-Round, Full-Time Wage and Salary Workers, by Sex and Occupation of Job Held the Longest, 2002–2008—*Continued*

(Thousands of people, dollars.)

Sex and occupation	2002	2003	2004	2005	2006	2007	2008
Men, Number of Workers							
Management, business, and financial operations	9 178	8 961	8 849	9 496	9 519	9 784	9 836
Management	7 145	6 991	6 911	7 477	7 361	7 619	7 714
Business and financial operations	2 033	1 970	1 938	2 019	2 157	2 165	2 122
Professional and related	9 299	9 535	9 497	9 561	10 387	10 274	10 074
Computer and mathematical	1 953	1 913	1 972	2 060	2 159	2 378	2 348
Architecture and engineering	1 984	2 004	2 049	2 041	2 174	2 172	2 068
Life, physical, and social sciences	667	668	626	668	748	611	581
Community and social services	726	730	705	713	756	744	675
Legal	490	610	537	490	546	515	595
Education, training, and library	1 407	1 476	1 386	1 421	1 587	1 651	1 535
Arts, design, entertainment, sports, and media	847	811	848	789	953	790	782
Health care practitioner and technical	1 225	1 323	1 374	1 378	1 464	1 413	1 490
Services	5 988	6 204	6 314	6 658	6 715	6 871	6 389
Health care support	181	178	208	240	252	261	204
Protective services	1 689	1 967	1 906	1 919	1 998	2 000	1 930
Food preparation and serving related	1 836	1 638	1 716	1 873	1 991	1 985	1 816
Building and grounds cleaning and maintenance	1 788	1 914	2 002	2 153	1 939	2 048	1 911
Personal care and services	494	508	482	473	535	576	527
Sales and office	9 453	9 398	9 380	9 464	9 747	9 694	9 128
Sales and related	5 933	5 891	5 892	5 896	6 125	6 019	5 690
Office and administrative support	3 520	3 507	3 488	3 568	3 622	3 675	3 438
Natural resources, construction, and maintenance	9 434	9 348	10 178	10 503	10 904	10 343	9 627
Farming, fishing, and forestry	463	470	536	469	482	516	489
Construction and extraction	5 156	4 972	5 576	6 026	6 344	5 753	5 056
Installation, maintenance, and repair	3 815	3 905	4 065	4 008	4 078	4 074	4 081
Production, transportation, and material moving	10 472	10 492	10 812	10 747	10 733	11 047	10 226
Production	5 517	5 513	5 637	5 503	5 525	5 461	4 983
Transportation and material moving	4 955	4 979	5 176	5 244	5 208	5 585	5 242
Armed forces	600	636	580	591	528	660	696
Men, Median Annual Earnings							
Management, business, and financial operations	60 000	60 200	65 000	69 000	68 000	70 000	72 000
Management	65 000	65 000	70 000	70 000	70 000	75 000	75 000
Business and financial operations	52 000	51 000	55 000	60 000	60 000	60 000	65 000
Professional and related	55 000	58 000	58 000	60 000	61 000	62 000	67 000
Computer and mathematical	60 000	65 000	65 000	65 000	70 000	70 000	74 000
Architecture and engineering	60 000	64 558	61 785	66 921	70 000	72 000	74 000
Life, physical, and social sciences	52 000	50 801	55 000	62 000	61 000	65 000	65 000
Community and social services	35 000	35 000	38 000	40 000	39 000	40 000	44 085
Legal	100 000	100 000	101 000	108 000	100 000	104 146	130 000
Education, training, and library	45 600	48 000	47 000	50 000	50 000	50 000	54 000
Arts, design, entertainment, sports, and media	46 000	45 000	45 000	50 000	50 000	50 000	52 000
Health care practitioner and technical	72 000	65 500	70 000	70 000	72 000	75 000	75 000
Services	25 000	26 000	25 000	26 000	29 000	29 000	30 000
Health care support	24 000	22 537	20 400	22 880	25 000	25 000	28 000
Protective services	40 000	44 000	44 000	45 000	46 886	49 000	49 000
Food preparation and serving related	20 000	18 720	18 720	20 000	20 000	21 000	21 500
Building and grounds cleaning and maintenance	24 500	22 156	24 000	24 000	25 000	25 000	27 012
Personal care and services	30 000	28 559	26 000	30 000	30 000	30 000	30 500
Sales and office	38 000	39 000	40 000	40 000	40 000	42 000	40 000
Sales and related	41 600	41 000	44 000	42 000	45 000	45 000	48 000
Office and administrative support	32 000	32 000	34 000	34 000	35 000	36 000	35 000
Natural resources, construction, and maintenance	33 592	34 283	35 000	35 000	35 674	36 000	40 000
Farming, fishing, and forestry	22 000	22 000	22 000	22 500	20 000	24 000	24 000
Construction and extraction	31 304	32 000	33 000	32 000	35 000	35 000	40 000
Installation, maintenance, and repair	36 000	38 000	38 870	40 000	40 000	40 000	42 685
Production, transportation, and material moving	30 000	32 000	33 000	34 000	33 358	35 000	35 360
Production	30 360	32 000	34 000	35 000	35 000	36 000	36 000
Transportation and material moving	30 000	30 000	32 000	32 760	32 000	35 000	35 000
Armed forces	36 000	36 000	40 000	40 000	40 000	42 000	45 000

Table 1-40. Number and Median Annual Earnings of Year-Round, Full-Time Wage and Salary Workers, by Sex and Occupation of Job Held the Longest, 2002–2008—*Continued*

(Thousands of people, dollars.)

Sex and occupation	2002	2003	2004	2005	2006	2007	2008
Women, Number of Workers							
Management, business, and financial operations	6 529	6 591	6 726	6 803	7 287	7 332	7 423
Management	4 205	4 111	4 214	4 209	4 504	4 573	4 542
Business and financial operations	2 324	2 479	2 512	2 594	2 783	2 759	2 881
Professional and related	9 851	10 071	10 095	10 532	10 881	11 664	11 675
Computer and mathematical	691	685	708	718	729	802	741
Architecture and engineering	273	269	300	320	317	295	293
Life, physical, and social sciences	428	342	373	428	394	415	462
Community and social services	968	968	927	1 015	1 079	1 047	1 079
Legal	516	539	550	603	622	645	633
Education, training, and library	3 199	3 441	3 356	3 473	3 608	3 831	3 944
Arts, design, entertainment, sports, and media	606	563	568	573	681	764	633
Health care practitioner and technical	3 170	3 263	3 314	3 403	3 452	3 865	3 890
Services	6 026	5 786	6 144	6 459	6 522	6 682	6 645
Health care support	1 586	1 525	1 573	1 787	1 829	1 766	1 815
Protective services	354	419	500	510	509	511	541
Food preparation and serving related	1 757	1 585	1 668	1 713	1 655	1 784	1 688
Building and grounds cleaning and maintenance	1 055	1 029	1 115	1 132	1 181	1 150	1 116
Personal care and services	1 274	1 228	1 289	1 317	1 349	1 471	1 485
Sales and office	14 338	14 368	14 239	14 546	14 720	14 778	13 930
Sales and related	3 996	3 913	4 060	4 355	4 372	4 282	4 073
Office and administrative support	10 342	10 455	10 180	10 191	10 348	10 496	9 856
Natural resources, construction, and maintenance	391	361	396	360	391	402	376
Farming, fishing, and forestry	111	92	93	87	104	92	91
Construction and extraction	100	97	135	119	140	132	101
Installation, maintenance, and repair	180	172	169	155	148	178	183
Production, transportation, and material moving	2 914	2 899	2 835	2 839	2 971	2 861	2 423
Production	2 219	2 157	2 150	2 120	2 237	2 128	1 668
Transportation and material moving	695	742	685	719	734	733	755
Armed forces	58	81	52	73	48	49	49
Women, Median Annual Earnings							
Management, business, and financial operations	41 000	43 000	43 000	46 000	50 000	50 000	50 000
Management	44 000	47 000	46 000	50 000	52 000	52 000	55 000
Business and financial operations	38 500	40 000	40 000	41 000	46 000	45 000	48 000
Professional and related	40 000	40 000	40 000	42 000	43 000	45 000	46 000
Computer and mathematical	51 627	52 000	57 000	57 000	60 000	60 000	62 000
Architecture and engineering	50 000	48 000	47 500	55 000	52 000	55 000	50 000
Life, physical, and social sciences	44 000	45 000	45 995	50 000	48 000	48 000	49 000
Community and social services	33 000	33 000	35 000	35 000	36 000	37 000	37 700
Legal	45 000	45 000	46 000	47 500	50 000	47 500	52 001
Education, training, and library	35 000	35 000	37 000	38 000	38 632	41 000	42 000
Arts, design, entertainment, sports, and media	40 000	35 000	36 000	35 000	38 000	40 000	40 000
Health care practitioner and technical	41 000	43 000	45 000	46 000	48 000	50 000	50 000
Services	20 000	20 000	20 000	20 000	20 500	22 000	23 516
Health care support	22 000	22 000	22 000	21 000	23 000	24 500	26 000
Protective services	30 900	32 000	32 000	34 344	37 896	35 000	35 000
Food preparation and serving related	16 160	17 000	16 000	18 000	18 000	19 000	20 000
Building and grounds cleaning and maintenance	16 491	16 000	16 866	18 000	19 000	19 500	20 000
Personal care and services	20 000	20 000	21 000	20 800	20 000	24 000	24 000
Sales and office	26 989	28 000	28 000	29 000	30 000	30 000	30 600
Sales and related	25 000	26 000	26 000	26 000	26 000	28 000	29 000
Office and administrative support	27 000	28 000	28 000	29 800	30 000	30 002	32 000
Natural resources, construction, and maintenance	26 000	28 000	30 000	30 200	27 000	37 025	30 000
Farming, fishing, and forestry	17 000	16 000	15 700	18 000	18 808	24 117	24 685
Construction and extraction	26 000	29 500	40 000	31 200	24 980	40 000	34 500
Installation, maintenance, and repair	34 000	37 000	33 000	36 000	40 000	42 000	33 913
Production, transportation, and material moving	22 000	22 100	23 000	23 000	23 000	25 000	25 000
Production	21 632	22 000	23 000	23 400	23 000	25 000	25 000
Transportation and material moving	22 000	22 710	23 000	21 000	24 000	27 000	24 000
Armed forces	40 000	32 000	35 100	32 652	32 000	41 000	32 000

Table 1-41. Wage and Salary Workers Paid Hourly Rates with Earnings at or Below the Prevailing Federal Minimum Wage, by Selected Characteristics, 2007–2008

(Thousands of people, percent.)

Characteristic	Workers paid hourly rates				
	Total	Below prevailing federal minimum wage	At prevailing federal minimum wage	Total at or below prevailing federal minimum wage	
				Number	Percent of hourly-paid workers
2007					
Age and Sex					
Both sexes, 16 years and over	75 873	1 462	267	1 729	2.3
16 to 24 years	16 275	669	145	814	5.0
25 years and over	59 597	793	122	915	1.5
Men, 16 years and over	37 790	460	86	546	1.4
16 to 24 years	8 314	190	52	242	2.9
25 years and over	29 476	270	34	304	1.0
Women, 16 years and over	38 082	1 002	181	1 183	3.1
16 to 24 years	7 961	479	93	572	7.2
25 years and over	30 121	523	88	611	2.0
Race, Sex, and Hispanic Origin					
White, 16 years and over	61 061	1 216	204	1 420	2.3
Men	30 944	398	73	471	1.5
Women	30 117	818	131	949	3.2
Black, 16 years and over	9 965	150	55	205	2.1
Men	4 482	39	10	49	1.1
Women	5 483	111	45	156	2.8
Asian, 16 years and over	2 730	50	1	50	1.8
Men	1 260	14	. . .	14	1.1
Women	1 469	36	1	37	2.5
Hispanic,[1] 16 years and over	13 168	205	41	246	1.9
Men	7 796	95	19	114	1.5
Women	5 372	110	22	133	2.5
Full- and Part-Time Status[2] and Sex					
Full-time workers	57 745	658	94	751	1.3
Men	32 003	253	30	283	0.9
Women	25 743	405	64	468	1.8
Part-time workers	17 997	799	172	971	5.4
Men	5 721	204	56	260	4.5
Women	12 276	594	117	711	5.8
2008					
Age and Sex					
Both sexes, 16 years and over	75 305	1 940	286	2 226	3.0
16 to 24 years	15 680	961	161	1 122	7.2
25 years and over	59 626	979	125	1 104	1.9
Men, 16 years and over	37 334	638	90	728	2.0
16 to 24 years	7 978	326	58	384	4.8
25 years and over	29 356	313	32	345	1.2
Women, 16 years and over	37 972	1 302	196	1 497	3.9
16 to 24 years	7 701	635	103	738	9.6
25 years and over	30 270	666	93	759	2.5
Race, Sex, and Hispanic Origin					
White, 16 years and over	60 464	1 568	215	1 783	2.9
Men	30 533	495	65	560	1.8
Women	29 931	1 073	151	1 223	4.1
Black, 16 years and over	9 866	259	49	308	3.1
Men	4 408	105	17	123	2.8
Women	5 457	154	32	186	3.4
Asian, 16 years and over	2 844	58	11	69	2.4
Men	1 301	24	3	27	2.1
Women	1 543	34	8	41	2.7
Hispanic,[1] 16 years and over	13 070	285	39	324	2.5
Men	7 756	117	15	132	1.7
Women	5 313	168	23	191	3.6
Full- and Part-Time Status[2] and Sex					
Full-time workers	56 837	778	95	873	1.5
Men	31 363	313	27	341	1.1
Women	25 474	464	68	532	2.1
Part-time workers	18 334	1 162	191	1 353	7.4
Men	5 903	325	63	388	6.6
Women	12 431	837	128	965	7.8

Note: The prevailing federal minimum wage was $5.15 per hour from January 2007 to July 23, 2007. Beginning July 24, 2007, the prevailing federal minimum wage increased to $5.85 per hour. It remained $5.85 per hour until July 23, 2008. Beginning July 24, 2008, the prevailing federal minimum wage increased to $6.55 per hour. Data are for wage and salary workers, excluding the incorporated self-employed. The data refer to a person's earnings on the sole or principal job, and pertain only to workers who are paid hourly rates. Salaried workers and other nonhourly workers are not included. The presence of workers with hourly earnings below the minimum wage does not necessarily indicate violation of the Fair Labor Standards Act, as there are exceptions to the minimum wage provisions of the law. In addition, some survey respondents reported hourly earnings below the minimum wage even though they earned the minimum wage or higher. Updated population controls are introduced annually with the release of January data.

[1]May be of any race.
[2]The distinction between full- and part-time workers is based on the hours usually worked. These data will not sum to totals because full- or part-time status on the principal job is not identifiable for a small number of multiple jobholders.
. . . = Not available.

Table 1-42. Absences from Work of Employed Full-Time Wage and Salary Workers, by Age and Sex, 2006–2008

(Thousands of people, percent.)

Year, sex, and age	Total employed	Absence rate[1]			Lost worktime rate[2]		
		Total	Illness or injury	Other reasons	Total	Illness or injury	Other reasons
2006							
Both Sexes, 16 Years and Over	105 785	3.2	2.3	0.9	1.8	1.2	0.5
16 to 19 years	1 741	3.0	2.1	0.9	1.4	1.1	0.4
20 to 24 years	9 490	2.8	1.9	0.9	1.4	0.9	0.5
25 years and over	94 555	3.3	2.3	0.9	1.8	1.3	0.5
25 to 54 years	78 821	3.2	2.2	1.0	1.7	1.2	0.6
55 years and over	15 733	3.6	3.0	0.7	2.0	1.7	0.3
Men, 16 Years and Over	59 633	2.4	1.8	0.6	1.3	1.0	0.3
16 to 19 years	1 059	2.1	1.7	0.5	1.1	1.0	0.2
20 to 24 years	5 462	2.2	1.6	0.6	1.0	0.8	0.2
25 years and over	53 111	2.4	1.9	0.6	1.3	1.0	0.3
25 to 54 years	44 601	2.3	1.7	0.6	1.2	0.9	0.3
55 years and over	8 510	3.2	2.7	0.5	1.9	1.7	0.2
Women, 16 Years and Over	46 152	4.3	2.8	1.4	2.4	1.5	0.9
16 to 19 years	681	4.4	2.9	1.5	2.0	1.2	0.8
20 to 24 years	4 027	3.8	2.3	1.4	2.0	1.0	1.0
25 years and over	41 443	4.3	2.9	1.4	2.4	1.6	0.9
25 to 54 years	34 221	4.3	2.8	1.5	2.5	1.5	1.0
55 years and over	7 223	4.2	3.3	0.9	2.3	1.8	0.4
2007							
Both Sexes, 16 Years and Over	107 164	3.2	2.2	1.0	1.7	1.2	0.5
16 to 19 years	1 674	2.8	1.9	1.0	1.5	0.9	0.6
20 to 24 years	9 527	2.9	1.9	1.0	1.5	0.9	0.6
25 years and over	95 964	3.2	2.2	1.0	1.7	1.2	0.5
25 to 54 years	79 438	3.1	2.1	1.0	1.7	1.1	0.6
55 years and over	16 526	3.5	2.8	0.7	2.0	1.7	0.3
Men, 16 Years and Over	60 262	2.3	1.7	0.6	1.2	1.0	0.3
16 to 19 years	1 011	1.8	1.4	0.4	0.8	0.6	0.2
20 to 24 years	5 435	2.1	1.7	0.5	1.0	0.8	0.2
25 years and over	53 817	2.3	1.7	0.6	1.3	1.0	0.3
25 to 54 years	44 895	2.2	1.6	0.6	1.2	0.9	0.3
55 years and over	8 922	3.0	2.4	0.5	1.7	1.5	0.2
Women, 16 Years and Over	46 902	4.3	2.7	1.5	2.4	1.5	0.9
16 to 19 years	663	4.4	2.6	1.9	2.7	1.4	1.3
20 to 24 years	4 092	4.0	2.2	1.8	2.2	1.0	1.2
25 years and over	42 147	4.3	2.8	1.5	2.4	1.5	0.9
25 to 54 years	34 544	4.3	2.7	1.6	2.4	1.4	1.0
55 years and over	7 603	4.2	3.3	0.9	2.4	1.9	0.5
2008							
Both Sexes, 16 Years and Over	102 307	3.1	2.2	0.9	1.7	1.2	0.5
16 to 19 years	1 345	2.4	1.5	0.9	1.3	0.7	0.5
20 to 24 years	8 528	2.9	2.0	0.9	1.4	0.9	0.6
25 years and over	92 433	3.2	2.2	0.9	1.7	1.2	0.5
25 to 54 years	75 837	3.1	2.1	1.0	1.7	1.1	0.6
55 years and over	16 597	3.6	2.9	0.7	2.0	1.7	0.3
Men, 16 Years and Over	57 019	2.3	1.8	0.5	1.2	1.0	0.3
16 to 19 years	799	1.5	1.0	0.5	0.6	0.5	0.2
20 to 24 years	4 797	2.0	1.5	0.4	0.9	0.7	0.2
25 years and over	51 424	2.3	1.8	0.5	1.3	1.0	0.3
25 to 54 years	42 477	2.2	1.7	0.5	1.2	0.9	0.3
55 years and over	8 946	3.0	2.5	0.5	1.8	1.5	0.3
Women, 16 Years and Over	45 288	4.1	2.7	1.4	2.3	1.4	0.9
16 to 19 years	546	3.6	2.2	1.4	2.2	1.1	1.1
20 to 24 years	3 732	4.0	2.5	1.5	2.2	1.1	1.0
25 years and over	41 010	4.2	2.8	1.4	2.3	1.4	0.8
25 to 54 years	33 359	4.2	2.6	1.5	2.3	1.3	0.9
55 years and over	7 650	4.2	3.4	0.8	2.3	1.9	0.4

Note: Beginning in January 2003, data reflect the revised population controls used in the household survey.

[1] Absences are defined as instances when persons who usually work 35 or more hours a week worked less than 35 hours during the reference week for reasons including own illness, injury, or medical problems; childcare problems; other family or personal obligations; civic or military duty; and maternity or paternity leave. Excluded are situations in which work was missed due to vacation or personal days, holidays, labor disputes, and other reasons. For multiple jobholders, absence data refer only to work missed at their main jobs. The absence rate is the ratio of workers with absences to total full-time wage and salary employment. The estimates of full-time wage and salary employment shown in this table do not match those in other tables because the estimates in this table are based on the full Current Population Survey (CPS) sample. Those in the other tables are based on a quarter of the sample only.
[2] Hours absent as a percentage of hours usually worked.

Table 1-43. Median Years of Tenure with Current Employer for Employed Wage and Salary Workers, by Age and Sex, Selected Years, February 1996–January 2008

(Number of years.)

Sex and age	February 1996	February 1998	February 2000	January 2002	January 2004	January 2006	January 2008
Both Sexes							
16 years and over	3.8	3.6	3.5	3.7	4.0	4.0	4.1
16 to 17 years	0.7	0.6	0.6	0.7	0.7	0.6	0.7
18 to 19 years	0.7	0.7	0.7	0.8	0.8	0.7	0.8
20 to 24 years	1.2	1.1	1.1	1.2	1.3	1.3	1.3
25 years and over	5.0	4.7	4.7	4.7	4.9	4.9	5.1
25 to 34 years	2.8	2.7	2.6	2.7	2.9	2.9	2.7
35 to 44 years	5.3	5.0	4.8	4.6	4.9	4.9	4.9
45 to 54 years	8.3	8.1	8.2	7.6	7.7	7.3	7.6
55 to 64 years	10.2	10.1	10.0	9.9	9.6	9.3	9.9
65 years and over	8.4	7.8	9.4	8.6	9.0	8.8	10.2
Men							
16 years and over	4.0	3.8	3.8	3.9	4.1	4.1	4.2
16 to 17 years	0.6	0.6	0.6	0.8	0.7	0.7	0.7
18 to 19 years	0.7	0.7	0.7	0.8	0.8	0.7	0.8
20 to 24 years	1.2	1.2	1.2	1.4	1.3	1.4	1.4
25 years and over	5.3	4.9	4.9	4.9	5.1	5.0	5.2
25 to 34 years	3.0	2.8	2.7	2.8	3.0	2.9	2.8
35 to 44 years	6.1	5.5	5.3	5.0	5.2	5.1	5.2
45 to 54 years	10.1	9.4	9.5	9.1	9.6	8.1	8.2
55 to 64 years	10.5	11.2	10.2	10.2	9.8	9.5	10.1
65 years and over	8.3	7.1	9.0	8.1	8.2	8.3	10.4
Women							
16 years and over	3.5	3.4	3.3	3.4	3.8	3.9	3.9
16 to 17 years	0.7	0.6	0.6	0.7	0.6	0.6	0.6
18 to 19 years	0.7	0.7	0.7	0.8	0.8	0.7	0.8
20 to 24 years	1.2	1.1	1.0	1.1	1.3	1.2	1.3
25 years and over	4.7	4.4	4.4	4.4	4.7	4.8	4.9
25 to 34 years	2.7	2.5	2.5	2.5	2.8	2.8	2.6
35 to 44 years	4.8	4.5	4.3	4.2	4.5	4.6	4.7
45 to 54 years	7.0	7.2	7.3	6.5	6.4	6.7	7.0
55 to 64 years	10.0	9.6	9.9	9.6	9.2	9.2	9.8
65 years and over	8.4	8.7	9.7	9.4	9.6	9.5	9.9

Note: Data for 1996 and 1998 are based on population controls from the 1990 census. Data beginning in 2000 reflect the introduction of Census 2000 population controls and are not strictly comparable with data for prior years. In addition, data for 2004 reflect the introduction of revised population controls in January 2003 and January 2004, and data for January 2006 reflect the introduction of revisions to the population controls in January 2005 and 2006.

Table 1-44. Median Years of Tenure with Current Employer for Employed Wage and Salary Workers, by Industry, Selected Years, February 2000–January 2008

(Number of years.)

Industry	February 2000	January 2002	January 2004	January 2006	January 2008
TOTAL, 16 YEARS AND OVER	3.5	3.7	4.0	4.0	4.1
Private Sector	3.2	3.3	3.5	3.6	3.6
Agriculture and related industries	3.7	4.2	3.7	3.8	4.3
Nonagricultural industries	3.2	3.3	3.5	3.6	3.6
Mining	4.8	4.5	5.2	3.8	4.1
Construction	2.7	3.0	3.0	3.0	3.5
Manufacturing	4.9	5.4	5.8	5.5	5.9
Durable goods manufacturing	4.8	5.5	6.0	5.6	6.1
Nonmetallic mineral product	5.5	5.3	4.8	5.0	4.8
Primary metals and fabricated metal product	5.0	6.3	6.4	6.2	5.2
Machinery manufacturing	5.3	6.8	6.4	6.6	6.0
Computers and electronic product	3.9	4.7	5.2	5.9	6.7
Electrical equipment and appliances	5.0	5.5	9.8	6.2	6.2
Transportation equipment	6.4	7.0	7.7	7.2	7.8
Wood product	3.7	4.3	5.0	4.7	6.2
Furniture and fixtures	4.4	4.7	4.7	4.2	5.2
Miscellaneous manufacturing	3.7	4.5	4.6	3.9	4.7
Nondurable goods manufacturing	5.0	5.3	5.5	5.4	5.4
Food manufacturing	4.6	5.0	4.9	5.2	4.3
Beverage and tobacco product	5.5	4.6	8.0	5.4	6.9
Textiles, apparel, and leather	4.7	5.0	5.0	4.4	4.6
Paper and printing	5.1	6.2	6.9	6.3	5.5
Petroleum and coal product	9.5	9.8	11.4	5.0	4.3
Chemicals	6.0	5.7	5.3	6.1	7.6
Plastics and rubber product	4.6	5.3	5.7	5.0	5.3
Wholesale and retail trade	2.7	2.8	3.1	3.1	3.2
Wholesale trade	3.9	3.9	4.3	4.6	5.0
Retail trade	2.5	2.6	2.8	2.8	2.9
Transportation and utilities	4.7	4.9	5.3	4.9	5.1
Transportation and warehousing	4.0	4.3	4.7	4.3	4.6
Utilities	11.5	13.4	13.3	10.4	10.1
Information[1]	3.4	3.3	4.3	4.8	4.7
Publishing, except Internet	4.2	4.8	4.7	5.3	4.7
Motion picture and sound recording industries	1.6	2.3	2.2	1.9	1.9
Broadcasting, except Internet	3.6	3.1	4.0	4.6	3.4
Telecommunications	4.3	3.4	4.6	5.3	6.9
Financial activities	3.5	3.6	3.9	4.0	4.5
Finance and insurance	3.6	3.9	4.1	4.1	4.7
Finance	3.3	3.6	4.0	3.9	4.4
Insurance	4.4	4.5	4.4	4.7	5.2
Real estate and rental and leasing	3.1	3.0	3.3	3.4	3.7
Real estate	3.1	3.2	3.5	3.5	3.9
Rental and leasing services	3.0	2.2	2.9	3.1	3.0
Professional and business services	2.4	2.7	3.2	3.2	3.1
Professional and technical services	2.6	3.1	3.6	3.8	3.3
Management, administrative, and waste services[1]	2.0	2.1	2.6	2.5	2.5
Administrative and support services	1.8	1.9	2.4	2.4	2.4
Waste management and remediation services	3.6	4.3	3.4	4.1	4.1
Education and health services	3.4	3.5	3.6	4.0	4.1
Education services	3.2	3.6	3.8	4.0	4.3
Health care and social assistance	3.5	3.5	3.6	4.1	4.1
Hospitals	5.1	4.9	4.7	5.2	5.4
Health services, except hospitals	3.2	3.1	3.3	3.6	3.6
Social assistance	2.4	2.5	2.8	3.1	3.0
Leisure and hospitality	1.7	1.8	2.0	1.9	2.1
Arts, entertainment, and recreation	2.6	2.3	2.8	3.1	2.8
Accommodation and food services	1.5	1.6	1.9	1.6	1.9
Accommodation	2.8	2.7	3.1	2.5	3.1
Food services and drinking places	1.4	1.4	1.6	1.4	1.6
Other services	3.1	3.3	3.3	3.2	3.3
Other services, except private households	3.2	3.3	3.5	3.3	3.4
Repair and maintenance	3.0	3.0	3.2	2.9	3.0
Personal and laundry services	2.7	2.8	3.4	2.8	3.2
Membership associations and organizations	4.0	4.1	3.9	4.2	4.4
Other services, private households	3.0	2.7	2.3	2.8	2.8
Public Sector	7.1	6.7	6.9	6.9	7.2
Federal government	11.5	11.3	10.4	9.9	9.9
State government	5.5	5.4	6.4	6.3	6.5
Local government	6.7	6.2	6.4	6.6	7.1

Note: Data beginning in 2000 reflect the introduction of Census 2000 population controls. Data for 2004 forward reflect updated population controls introduced annually with the release of January data.

[1]Includes other industries not shown separately.

Table 1-45. Employment Status of the Population, by Sex and Marital Status, March 1990–March 2009

(Thousands of people, percent.)

Marital status and year	Men						Women					
	Population	Labor force					Population	Labor force				
		Total		Employed	Unemployed			Total		Employed	Unemployed	
		Number	Percent of population		Number	Percent of labor force			Number	Percent of population		Number	Percent of labor force
Single												
1990	25 757	18 829	73.1	16 893	1 936	10.3	21 088	14 003	66.4	12 856	1 147	8.2
1991	26 220	19 014	72.5	16 418	2 596	13.7	21 688	14 125	65.1	12 887	1 238	8.8
1992	26 529	19 229	72.5	16 401	2 828	14.7	21 738	14 072	64.7	12 793	1 279	9.1
1993	26 951	19 625	72.8	16 858	2 767	14.1	21 848	14 091	64.5	12 711	1 380	9.8
1994	28 350	20 365	71.8	17 826	2 539	12.5	22 885	14 903	65.1	13 419	1 484	10.0
1995	28 318	20 449	72.2	18 286	2 163	10.6	22 853	14 974	65.5	13 673	1 301	8.7
1996	28 695	20 561	71.7	18 097	2 464	12.0	23 632	15 417	65.2	14 084	1 333	8.6
1997	29 294	20 942	71.5	18 683	2 259	10.8	24 215	16 178	66.8	14 747	1 431	8.8
1998	29 558	21 255	71.9	19 124	2 131	10.0	24 808	16 885	68.1	15 626	1 259	7.5
1999	29 883	21 329	71.4	19 465	1 864	8.7	25 674	17 486	68.1	16 185	1 301	7.4
2000	30 232	21 641	71.6	19 823	1 818	8.4	25 863	17 749	68.6	16 446	1 303	7.3
2001	30 968	22 232	71.8	20 239	1 993	9.0	26 180	17 900	68.4	16 631	1 269	7.1
2002	32 220	22 761	70.6	20 066	2 695	11.8	26 942	18 079	67.1	16 499	1 580	8.7
2003	32 852	22 821	69.5	20 194	2 627	11.5	27 527	17 901	65.0	16 219	1 682	9.4
2004	33 786	23 212	68.7	20 434	2 778	12.0	28 033	18 089	64.5	16 506	1 583	8.8
2005	34 069	23 335	68.5	20 831	2 504	10.7	28 508	18 554	65.1	16 902	1 652	8.9
2006	34 906	24 369	69.8	21 961	2 408	9.9	29 357	18 989	64.7	17 444	1 545	8.1
2007	35 359	24 506	69.3	22 224	2 281	9.3	29 695	19 218	64.7	17 935	1 284	6.7
2008	36 522	25 229	69.1	22 695	2 534	10.0	30 772	19 889	64.6	18 369	1 520	7.6
2009	36 907	24 930	67.5	20 645	4 284	17.2	31 038	19 785	63.7	17 714	2 071	10.5
Married, Spouse Present												
1990	52 464	41 020	78.2	39 562	1 458	3.6	53 207	30 967	58.2	29 870	1 097	3.5
1991	52 460	40 883	77.9	38 843	2 040	5.0	53 176	31 103	58.5	29 668	1 435	4.6
1992	52 780	40 930	77.5	38 650	2 280	5.6	53 464	31 686	59.3	30 130	1 556	4.9
1993	53 488	41 255	77.1	39 069	2 186	5.3	54 146	32 158	59.4	30 757	1 401	4.4
1994	53 436	40 993	76.7	39 085	1 908	4.7	54 198	32 863	60.6	31 397	1 466	4.5
1995	54 166	41 806	77.2	40 262	1 544	3.7	54 902	33 563	61.1	32 267	1 296	3.9
1996	53 996	41 837	77.5	40 356	1 481	3.5	54 640	33 382	61.1	32 258	1 124	3.4
1997	53 981	41 967	77.7	40 628	1 339	3.2	54 611	33 907	62.1	32 836	1 071	3.2
1998	54 685	42 288	77.3	41 039	1 249	3.0	55 241	34 136	61.8	33 028	1 108	3.2
1999	55 256	42 557	77.0	41 476	1 081	2.5	55 801	34 349	61.6	33 403	946	2.8
2000	55 897	43 254	77.4	42 261	993	2.3	56 432	34 959	61.9	33 998	961	2.7
2001	56 152	43 463	77.4	42 245	1 218	2.8	56 740	35 234	62.1	34 273	961	2.7
2002	57 325	44 271	77.2	42 508	1 763	4.0	57 883	35 624	61.5	34 295	1 329	3.7
2003	57 940	44 700	77.1	42 797	1 903	4.3	58 545	36 185	61.8	34 806	1 379	3.8
2004	58 395	44 860	76.8	43 247	1 613	3.6	59 008	35 918	60.9	34 582	1 336	3.7
2005	58 854	45 263	76.9	43 763	1 500	3.3	59 449	35 809	60.2	34 738	1 071	3.0
2006	58 850	45 082	76.6	43 877	1 205	2.7	59 476	36 192	60.9	35 185	1 007	2.8
2007	60 126	46 129	76.7	44 813	1 317	2.9	60 656	37 335	61.6	36 370	965	2.6
2008	59 455	45 451	76.4	43 958	1 493	3.3	60 108	37 074	61.7	35 919	1 155	3.1
2009	60 132	45 741	76.1	42 667	3 074	6.7	60 818	37 536	61.7	35 540	1 996	5.3
Widowed, Divorced, or Separated												
1990	11 152	7 513	67.4	6 959	554	7.4	23 857	11 168	46.8	10 530	638	5.7
1991	11 588	7 804	67.3	6 985	819	10.5	24 105	11 145	46.2	10 386	759	6.8
1992	11 927	8 049	67.5	7 140	909	11.3	24 582	11 486	46.7	10 610	876	7.6
1993	11 861	7 956	67.1	7 055	901	11.3	24 661	11 308	45.9	10 528	780	6.9
1994	12 239	8 156	66.6	7 382	774	9.5	25 098	11 879	47.3	10 995	884	7.4
1995	12 410	8 315	67.0	7 632	683	8.2	25 373	12 001	47.3	11 308	693	5.8
1996	13 176	8 697	66.0	7 976	721	8.3	25 786	12 430	48.2	11 742	688	5.5
1997	14 113	9 420	66.7	8 715	705	7.5	26 301	12 814	48.7	12 071	743	5.8
1998	14 166	9 482	66.9	8 954	528	5.6	26 092	12 880	49.4	12 235	645	5.0
1999	14 225	9 449	66.4	8 971	478	5.1	26 199	12 951	49.4	12 307	644	5.0
2000	14 289	9 623	67.3	9 152	471	4.9	26 354	13 228	50.2	12 657	571	4.3
2001	14 392	9 421	65.5	8 927	494	5.2	26 747	13 454	50.3	12 887	567	4.2
2002	14 617	9 650	66.0	8 931	719	7.5	27 802	13 716	49.3	12 855	861	6.3
2003	15 180	9 855	64.9	9 020	835	8.5	28 240	14 154	50.1	13 240	914	6.5
2004	15 059	9 789	65.0	9 059	730	7.5	28 228	14 194	50.3	13 324	870	6.1
2005	15 779	10 256	65.0	9 569	687	6.7	28 576	14 233	49.8	13 472	761	5.3
2006	16 405	10 815	65.9	10 141	674	6.2	28 981	14 220	49.1	13 539	681	4.8
2007	16 247	10 799	66.5	10 150	650	6.0	28 950	14 320	49.5	13 620	700	4.9
2008	16 718	10 896	65.2	10 083	812	7.5	29 419	14 553	49.5	13 765	787	5.4
2009	16 719	10 687	63.9	9 224	1 463	13.7	29 471	14 449	49.0	13 169	1 281	8.9

Note: See notes and definitions for information on historical comparability.

Table 1-45. Employment Status of the Population, by Sex and Marital Status, March 1990–March 2009
—Continued

(Thousands of people, percent.)

Marital status and year	Men						Women					
	Population	Labor force					Population	Labor force				
		Total		Employed	Unemployed			Total		Employed	Unemployed	
		Number	Percent of population		Number	Percent of labor force		Number	Percent of population		Number	Percent of labor force
Widowed												
1990	2 331	519	22.3	490	29	5.6	11 477	2 243	19.5	2 149	94	4.2
1991	2 385	486	20.4	448	38	7.8	11 288	2 150	19.0	2 044	106	4.9
1992	2 529	566	22.4	501	65	11.5	11 325	2 131	18.8	2 029	102	4.8
1993	2 468	596	24.1	535	61	10.2	11 214	1 961	17.5	1 856	105	5.4
1994	2 220	474	21.4	440	34	7.2	11 073	1 945	17.6	1 825	120	6.2
1995	2 282	496	21.7	469	27	5.4	11 080	1 941	17.5	1 844	97	5.0
1996	2 476	487	19.7	466	21	4.3	11 070	1 916	17.3	1 820	96	5.0
1997	2 686	559	20.8	529	30	5.4	11 058	2 018	18.2	1 926	92	4.6
1998	2 567	563	21.9	551	12	2.1	11 027	2 157	19.6	2 071	86	4.0
1999	2 540	562	22.1	532	30	5.3	10 943	2 039	18.6	1 942	97	4.8
2000	2 601	583	22.4	547	36	6.2	11 061	2 011	18.2	1 911	100	5.0
2001	2 638	568	21.5	546	22	3.9	11 182	2 137	19.1	2 045	92	4.3
2002	2 635	629	23.9	581	48	7.6	11 411	2 001	17.5	1 887	114	5.7
2003	2 694	628	23.3	588	40	6.4	11 295	2 087	18.5	1 991	96	4.6
2004	2 651	581	21.9	558	23	4.0	11 159	2 157	19.3	2 048	109	5.1
2005	2 729	618	22.6	590	28	4.5	11 125	2 111	19.0	2 005	106	5.0
2006	2 626	610	23.2	563	47	7.7	11 305	2 164	19.1	2 094	70	3.2
2007	2 697	631	23.4	588	43	6.8	11 220	2 058	18.3	1 971	87	4.2
2008	2 911	656	22.5	611	44	6.8	11 399	2 218	19.5	2 101	117	5.3
2009	2 813	632	22.5	543	90	14.2	11 446	2 174	19.0	2 032	143	6.6
Divorced												
1990	6 256	5 004	80.0	4 639	365	7.3	8 845	6 678	75.5	6 333	345	5.2
1991	6 586	5 262	79.9	4 722	540	10.3	9 152	6 779	74.1	6 365	414	6.1
1992	6 743	5 418	80.3	4 823	595	11.0	9 569	7 076	73.9	6 578	498	7.0
1993	6 770	5 330	78.7	4 736	594	11.1	9 879	7 183	72.7	6 736	447	6.2
1994	7 222	5 548	76.8	5 028	520	9.4	10 113	7 473	73.9	6 962	511	6.8
1995	7 343	5 739	78.2	5 266	473	8.2	10 262	7 559	73.7	7 206	353	4.7
1996	7 734	5 954	77.0	5 468	486	8.2	10 508	7 829	74.5	7 468	361	4.6
1997	8 191	6 298	76.9	5 851	447	7.1	11 102	8 092	72.9	7 666	426	5.3
1998	8 307	6 378	76.8	6 045	333	5.2	11 065	8 038	72.6	7 687	351	4.4
1999	8 529	6 481	76.0	6 151	330	5.1	11 130	8 171	73.4	7 841	330	4.0
2000	8 532	6 583	77.2	6 279	304	4.6	11 061	8 505	76.9	8 217	288	3.4
2001	8 580	6 403	74.6	6 074	329	5.1	11 719	8 662	73.9	8 335	327	3.8
2002	8 643	6 519	75.4	6 053	466	7.1	12 227	8 902	72.8	8 416	486	5.5
2003	8 938	6 621	74.1	6 052	569	8.6	12 653	9 191	72.6	8 673	518	5.6
2004	8 942	6 622	74.1	6 104	518	7.8	12 817	9 246	72.1	8 706	540	5.8
2005	9 196	6 754	73.4	6 281	473	7.0	12 950	9 253	71.5	8 836	417	4.5
2006	9 646	7 065	73.2	6 631	434	6.1	13 107	9 188	70.1	8 799	389	4.2
2007	9 608	7 110	74.0	6 679	431	6.1	13 214	9 334	70.6	8 896	439	4.7
2008	9 767	7 106	72.8	6 607	499	7.0	13 551	9 387	69.3	8 938	449	4.8
2009	9 938	7 052	71.0	6 064	988	14.0	13 301	9 176	69.0	8 402	774	8.4
Separated												
1990	2 565	1 990	77.6	1 830	160	8.0	3 535	2 247	63.6	2 048	199	8.9
1991	2 616	2 057	78.6	1 816	241	11.7	3 665	2 216	60.5	1 977	239	10.8
1992	2 655	2 065	77.8	1 816	249	12.1	3 688	2 279	61.8	2 003	276	12.1
1993	2 623	2 030	77.4	1 784	246	12.1	3 568	2 165	60.7	1 937	228	10.5
1994	2 797	2 134	76.3	1 914	220	10.3	3 911	2 461	62.9	2 208	253	10.3
1995	2 784	2 081	74.7	1 898	183	8.8	4 031	2 501	62.0	2 258	243	9.7
1996	2 966	2 255	76.0	2 041	214	9.5	4 209	2 684	63.8	2 453	231	8.6
1997	3 236	2 563	79.2	2 335	228	8.9	4 141	2 705	65.3	2 480	225	8.3
1998	3 293	2 542	77.2	2 358	184	7.2	4 000	2 683	67.1	2 476	207	7.7
1999	3 156	2 405	76.2	2 287	118	4.9	4 126	2 740	66.4	2 523	217	7.9
2000	3 157	2 456	77.8	2 326	130	5.3	4 012	2 711	67.6	2 528	183	6.8
2001	3 174	2 450	77.2	2 307	143	5.8	3 846	2 654	69.0	2 507	147	5.5
2002	3 339	2 502	74.9	2 297	205	8.2	4 164	2 812	67.5	2 551	261	9.3
2003	3 548	2 606	73.4	2 380	226	8.7	4 293	2 877	67.0	2 576	301	10.5
2004	3 466	2 586	74.6	2 397	189	7.3	4 251	2 791	65.7	2 569	222	8.0
2005	3 855	2 884	74.8	2 698	186	6.4	4 501	2 870	63.8	2 632	238	8.3
2006	4 132	3 141	76.0	2 947	194	6.2	4 569	2 869	62.8	2 647	222	7.7
2007	3 943	3 058	77.6	2 883	176	5.7	4 516	2 927	64.8	2 753	174	6.0
2008	4 040	3 134	77.6	2 865	269	8.6	4 469	2 947	65.9	2 726	221	7.5
2009	3 968	3 002	75.7	2 617	386	12.8	4 725	3 099	65.6	2 734	364	11.8

Note: See notes and definitions for information on historical comparability.

Table 1-46. Employment Status of All Women and Single Women, by Presence and Age of Children, March 1990–March 2009

(Thousands of women, percent.)

Presence and age of children and year	All women							Single women						
	Civilian labor force	Civilian labor force as percent of population	Employed			Unemployed		Civilian labor force	Civilian labor force as percent of population	Employed			Unemployed	
			Number	Percent full time	Percent part time	Number	Percent of labor force			Number	Percent full time	Percent part time	Number	Percent of labor force
Women with No Children Under 18 Years														
1990	33 942	52.3	32 391	74.4	25.6	1 551	4.6	12 478	68.1	11 611	65.9	34.1	866	6.9
1991	34 047	52.0	32 167	74.0	26.0	1 880	5.5	12 472	67.0	11 529	66.2	33.8	943	7.6
1992	34 487	52.3	32 481	74.3	25.7	2 006	5.8	12 355	66.9	11 374	66.6	33.4	982	7.9
1993	34 495	52.1	32 476	74.6	25.4	2 020	5.9	12 223	66.4	11 201	66.1	33.9	1 022	8.4
1994	35 454	53.1	33 343	72.7	27.3	2 110	6.0	12 737	66.8	11 674	64.5	35.5	1 063	8.3
1995	35 843	52.9	34 054	72.9	27.1	1 789	5.0	12 870	67.1	11 919	64.5	35.5	951	7.4
1996	36 509	53.0	34 698	73.3	26.7	1 811	5.0	13 172	66.1	12 255	64.6	35.4	918	7.0
1997	37 295	53.6	35 572	73.7	26.3	1 723	4.6	13 405	66.5	12 442	64.0	36.0	964	7.2
1998	38 253	54.1	36 680	74.1	25.9	1 573	4.1	13 888	67.2	13 082	64.8	35.2	806	5.8
1999	39 316	54.3	37 589	74.6	25.4	1 727	4.4	14 435	67.1	13 491	65.6	34.4	944	6.5
2000	40 142	54.8	38 408	75.4	24.6	1 733	4.3	14 677	67.6	13 713	66.6	33.4	964	6.6
2001	40 836	54.9	39 219	75.7	24.3	1 617	4.0	14 877	67.4	13 993	67.3	32.7	884	5.9
2002	41 278	54.0	39 038	75.1	24.9	2 241	5.4	14 855	65.6	13 682	65.9	34.1	1 173	7.9
2003	42 039	54.1	39 667	74.8	25.2	2 372	5.6	14 678	63.5	13 430	65.1	34.9	1 249	8.5
2004	42 289	53.8	40 000	74.6	25.4	2 289	5.4	14 828	63.0	13 670	65.5	34.5	1 157	7.8
2005	42 039	54.1	39 667	74.8	25.2	2 372	5.6	14 678	63.5	13 430	65.1	34.9	1 249	8.5
2006	43 392	53.6	41 440	75.3	24.7	1 952	4.5	15 673	63.4	14 547	66.5	33.5	1 125	7.2
2007	44 039	53.9	42 279	75.3	24.7	1 760	4.0	15 704	63.4	14 801	66.4	33.6	903	5.7
2008	45 585	54.3	43 417	75.7	24.3	2 168	4.8	16 378	63.4	15 261	67.4	32.6	1 116	6.8
2009	45 649	53.8	42 343	73.3	26.7	3 306	7.2	16 112	62.1	14 607	64.9	35.1	1 506	9.3
Women with Children Under 18 Years														
1990	22 196	66.7	20 865	73.0	27.0	1 331	6.0	1 525	55.2	1 244	79.1	20.9	280	18.4
1991	22 327	66.6	20 774	73.0	27.0	1 552	7.0	1 654	53.6	1 358	76.4	23.6	296	17.9
1992	22 756	67.2	21 052	73.8	26.2	1 704	7.5	1 716	52.5	1 420	75.9	24.1	297	17.3
1993	23 063	66.9	21 521	73.9	26.1	1 541	6.7	1 869	54.4	1 510	74.8	25.2	359	19.2
1994	24 191	68.4	22 467	70.8	29.2	1 724	7.1	2 166	56.9	1 745	73.9	26.1	421	19.4
1995	24 695	69.7	23 195	71.7	28.3	1 500	6.1	2 104	57.5	1 754	73.6	26.4	350	16.6
1996	24 720	70.2	23 386	72.6	27.4	1 334	5.4	2 245	60.5	1 829	73.5	26.5	416	18.5
1997	25 604	72.1	24 082	74.1	25.9	1 522	5.9	2 772	68.1	2 305	76.6	23.4	467	16.8
1998	25 647	72.3	24 209	74.0	26.0	1 438	5.6	2 997	72.5	2 544	75.6	24.4	453	15.1
1999	25 469	72.1	24 305	74.1	25.9	1 165	4.6	3 051	73.4	2 694	75.8	24.2	357	11.7
2000	25 795	72.9	24 693	74.6	25.4	1 102	4.3	3 073	73.9	2 734	79.7	20.3	339	11.0
2001	25 751	73.1	24 572	75.6	24.4	1 179	4.6	3 022	73.8	2 638	81.8	18.2	385	12.7
2002	26 140	72.2	24 612	74.8	25.2	1 529	5.8	3 224	75.3	2 818	79.1	20.9	406	12.6
2003	26 202	71.7	24 598	74.3	25.7	1 603	6.1	3 222	73.1	2 789	79.5	20.5	433	13.4
2004	25 913	70.7	24 413	74.2	25.8	1 501	5.8	3 262	72.6	2 836	76.8	23.2	426	13.1
2005	26 202	71.7	24 598	74.3	25.7	1 603	6.1	3 222	73.1	2 789	79.5	20.5	433	13.4
2006	26 009	70.6	24 728	75.6	24.4	1 281	4.9	3 317	71.5	2 896	77.8	22.2	420	12.7
2007	26 834	71.3	25 646	75.2	24.8	1 188	4.4	3 514	71.4	3 133	76.4	23.6	381	10.8
2008	25 930	71.2	24 637	75.7	24.3	1 294	5.0	3 511	71.0	3 108	78.0	22.0	403	11.5
2009	26 122	71.6	24 079	74.6	25.4	2 043	7.8	3 673	72.0	3 108	75.8	24.2	566	18.2
Women with Children Under 6 Years														
1990	9 397	58.2	8 732	69.6	30.4	664	7.1	929	48.7	736	75.0	25.0	194	20.9
1991	9 636	58.4	8 758	69.5	30.5	878	9.1	1 050	48.8	819	72.2	27.8	231	22.0
1992	9 573	58.0	8 662	70.2	29.8	911	9.5	1 029	45.8	829	73.2	26.8	200	19.4
1993	9 621	57.9	8 764	70.1	29.9	857	8.9	1 125	47.4	869	70.0	30.0	257	22.8
1994	10 328	60.3	9 394	67.1	32.9	935	9.1	1 379	52.2	1 062	70.0	30.0	317	23.0
1995	10 395	62.3	9 587	67.5	32.5	809	7.8	1 328	53.0	1 069	68.6	31.4	259	19.5
1996	10 293	62.3	9 592	68.4	31.6	701	6.8	1 378	55.1	1 099	67.3	32.7	279	20.2
1997	10 610	65.0	9 800	70.5	29.5	810	7.6	1 755	65.1	1 424	71.6	28.4	330	18.8
1998	10 619	65.2	9 839	69.8	30.2	780	7.3	1 755	67.3	1 448	71.7	28.3	307	17.5
1999	10 322	64.4	9 674	69.0	31.0	648	6.3	1 811	68.1	1 565	71.0	29.0	246	13.6
2000	10 316	65.3	9 763	70.5	29.5	553	5.4	1 835	70.5	1 603	75.3	24.7	232	12.6
2001	10 200	64.9	9 618	71.2	28.8	582	5.7	1 783	69.7	1 542	79.1	20.9	242	13.6
2002	10 193	64.1	9 441	70.4	29.6	752	7.4	1 819	71.0	1 568	74.5	25.5	251	13.8
2003	10 209	62.9	9 433	70.0	30.0	776	7.6	1 893	70.2	1 614	75.2	24.8	279	14.7
2004	10 131	62.2	9 407	69.4	30.6	724	7.1	1 885	68.4	1 605	70.1	29.9	279	14.8
2005	10 209	62.9	9 433	70.0	30.0	776	7.6	1 893	70.2	1 614	75.2	24.8	279	14.7
2006	10 430	63.0	9 779	72.0	28.0	651	6.2	1 934	68.6	1 659	72.8	27.2	276	14.3
2007	10 894	63.5	10 305	71.9	28.1	589	5.4	2 066	67.4	1 827	72.7	27.3	239	11.6
2008	10 452	63.6	9 794	72.1	27.9	657	6.3	1 982	66.0	1 705	72.2	27.8	277	14.0
2009	10 497	63.6	9 517	71.8	28.2	980	9.3	2 137	67.8	1 754	70.3	29.7	383	17.9

Note: See notes and definitions for information on historical comparability.

Table 1-47. Employment Status of Ever-Married Women and Married Women, Spouse Present, by Presence and Age of Children, March 1990–March 2009

(Thousands of women, percent.)

Presence and age of children and year	Ever-married women[1]						Married women, spouse present						
	Civilian labor force	Civilian labor force as percent of population	Employed			Unemployed		Civilian labor force	Civilian labor force as percent of population	Employed			Unemployed	
			Number	Percent full time	Percent part time	Number	Percent of labor force			Number	Percent full time	Percent part time	Number	Percent of labor force

Women with No Children Under 18 Years

1990	21 464	46.1	20 779	79.1	20.9	685	3.2	14 467	51.1	14 068	77.3	22.7	399	2.8
1991	21 575	46.1	20 637	78.4	21.6	937	4.3	14 529	51.2	13 976	77.6	22.4	552	3.8
1992	22 132	46.6	21 108	78.5	21.5	1 024	4.6	14 851	51.9	14 247	77.8	22.2	604	4.1
1993	22 273	46.6	21 275	79.0	21.0	998	4.5	15 211	52.4	14 630	77.6	22.4	581	3.8
1994	22 716	47.6	21 669	77.1	22.9	1 047	4.6	15 234	53.2	14 641	75.6	24.4	593	3.9
1995	22 973	47.3	22 134	77.4	22.6	839	3.7	15 594	53.2	15 072	76.3	23.7	522	3.3
1996	23 337	47.7	22 444	78.1	21.9	893	3.8	15 628	53.4	15 123	76.8	23.2	506	3.2
1997	23 890	48.3	23 130	78.9	21.1	760	3.2	15 750	54.2	15 315	77.7	22.3	435	2.8
1998	24 366	48.7	23 598	79.3	20.7	767	3.1	16 007	54.1	15 581	78.3	21.7	426	2.7
1999	24 881	48.9	24 098	79.7	20.3	783	3.1	16 484	54.4	16 061	78.2	21.8	423	2.6
2000	25 465	49.4	24 695	80.3	19.7	769	3.0	16 786	54.7	16 357	79.1	20.9	429	2.6
2001	25 959	49.6	25 226	80.4	19.6	733	2.8	16 909	54.8	16 528	78.7	21.3	381	2.3
2002	26 423	49.1	25 356	80.0	20.0	1 068	4.0	17 353	54.8	16 780	78.4	21.6	573	3.3
2003	27 361	50.1	26 238	79.7	20.3	1 123	4.1	17 901	55.7	17 273	78.6	21.4	628	3.5
2004	27 461	49.8	26 329	79.3	20.7	1 131	4.1	17 965	55.0	17 367	78.6	21.4	598	3.3
2005	27 361	50.1	26 238	79.7	20.3	1 123	4.1	17 901	55.7	17 273	78.6	21.4	628	3.5
2006	27 719	49.3	26 893	80.1	19.9	827	3.0	18 124	54.8	17 691	79.3	20.7	434	2.4
2007	28 335	49.8	27 477	80.1	19.9	858	3.0	18 766	55.4	18 326	79.6	20.4	441	2.3
2008	29 207	50.3	28 156	80.2	19.8	1 052	3.6	19 188	55.9	18 650	79.8	20.2	539	2.8
2009	29 536	50.2	27 737	77.8	22.2	1 800	6.1	19 541	55.8	18 521	77.3	22.7	1 019	5.2

Women with Children Under 18 Years

1990	20 671	67.8	19 621	72.6	27.4	1 051	5.1	16 500	66.3	15 803	69.8	30.2	698	4.2
1991	20 673	67.9	19 416	72.8	27.2	1 257	6.1	16 575	66.8	15 692	70.1	29.9	883	5.3
1992	21 040	68.8	19 633	73.6	26.4	1 407	6.7	16 835	67.8	15 884	71.3	28.7	952	5.7
1993	21 194	68.3	20 011	73.9	26.1	1 183	5.6	16 947	67.5	16 127	71.4	28.6	820	4.8
1994	22 025	69.8	20 722	70.5	29.5	1 303	5.9	17 628	69.0	16 755	68.0	32.0	873	5.0
1995	22 591	71.1	21 441	71.5	28.5	1 150	5.1	17 969	70.2	17 195	68.8	31.2	774	4.3
1996	22 475	71.4	21 556	72.5	27.5	919	4.1	17 754	70.0	17 136	69.6	30.4	618	3.5
1997	22 831	72.6	21 777	73.9	26.1	1 054	4.6	18 157	71.1	17 521	71.6	28.4	636	3.5
1998	22 650	72.3	21 665	73.8	26.2	985	4.3	18 129	70.6	17 447	71.5	28.5	682	3.8
1999	22 419	71.9	21 611	73.9	26.1	808	3.6	17 865	70.1	17 342	71.5	28.5	523	2.9
2000	22 722	72.7	21 960	74.0	26.0	763	3.4	18 174	70.6	17 641	71.7	28.3	533	2.9
2001	22 729	73.0	21 934	74.9	25.1	795	3.5	18 325	70.8	17 745	72.6	27.4	580	3.2
2002	22 917	71.8	21 794	74.3	25.7	1 122	4.9	18 271	69.6	17 515	71.7	28.3	756	4.1
2003	22 979	71.5	21 809	73.7	26.3	1 170	5.1	18 284	69.2	17 533	71.0	29.0	751	4.1
2004	22 651	70.5	21 576	73.8	26.2	1 075	4.7	17 953	68.2	17 215	71.3	28.7	738	4.1
2005	22 979	71.5	21 809	73.7	26.3	1 170	5.1	18 284	69.2	17 533	71.0	29.0	751	4.1
2006	22 692	70.5	21 831	75.3	24.7	861	3.8	18 067	68.4	17 494	73.0	27.0	574	3.2
2007	23 320	71.3	22 513	75.0	25.0	807	3.5	18 569	69.3	18 045	72.6	27.4	524	2.8
2008	22 419	71.2	21 529	75.4	24.6	890	4.0	17 886	69.4	17 269	73.6	26.4	616	3.4
2009	22 449	71.5	20 972	74.5	25.5	1 477	6.6	17 995	69.8	17 018	73.1	26.9	977	5.4

Women with Children Under 6 Years

1990	8 467	59.5	7 996	69.1	30.9	471	5.6	7 247	58.9	6 901	67.4	32.6	346	4.8
1991	8 585	59.9	7 938	69.2	30.8	647	7.5	7 434	59.9	6 933	67.5	32.5	501	6.7
1992	8 544	60.0	7 832	69.9	30.1	711	8.3	7 333	59.9	6 819	68.5	31.5	514	7.0
1993	8 496	59.6	7 895	70.2	29.8	600	7.1	7 289	59.6	6 840	68.8	31.2	450	6.2
1994	8 949	61.8	8 332	66.7	33.3	617	6.9	7 723	61.7	7 291	65.4	34.6	432	5.6
1995	9 067	63.9	8 517	67.4	32.6	550	6.1	7 759	63.5	7 349	66.1	33.9	409	5.3
1996	8 915	63.6	8 493	68.6	31.4	422	4.7	7 590	62.7	7 297	66.5	33.5	293	3.9
1997	8 856	64.9	8 376	70.3	29.7	480	5.4	7 582	63.6	7 252	69.1	30.9	330	4.4
1998	8 864	64.8	8 391	69.5	30.5	473	5.3	7 655	63.7	7 309	68.1	31.9	346	4.5
1999	8 511	63.7	8 109	68.6	31.4	402	4.7	7 246	61.8	6 979	67.1	32.9	267	3.7
2000	8 481	64.3	8 159	69.5	30.5	321	3.8	7 341	62.8	7 087	68.1	31.9	254	3.5
2001	8 417	64.0	8 077	69.7	30.3	340	4.0	7 319	62.5	7 062	68.5	31.5	257	3.5
2002	8 373	62.8	7 873	69.6	30.4	501	6.0	7 166	60.8	6 804	67.7	32.3	363	5.1
2003	8 315	61.4	7 818	68.9	31.1	497	6.0	7 175	59.8	6 826	67.1	32.9	349	4.9
2004	8 246	61.0	7 801	69.3	30.7	445	5.4	7 107	59.3	6 774	68.1	31.9	332	4.7
2005	8 315	61.4	7 818	68.9	31.1	497	6.0	7 175	59.8	6 826	67.1	32.9	349	4.9
2006	8 496	61.9	8 121	71.8	28.2	375	4.4	7 366	60.3	7 092	70.6	29.4	274	3.7
2007	8 829	62.7	8 479	71.7	28.3	350	4.0	7 664	61.5	7 407	70.8	29.2	257	3.4
2008	8 470	63.0	8 089	72.1	27.9	381	4.5	7 285	61.6	6 999	70.9	29.1	285	3.9
2009	8 360	62.6	7 763	72.1	27.9	597	7.1	7 231	61.6	6 805	71.4	28.6	426	5.9

[1]Ever-married women are women who are, or have ever been, married.

Table 1-48. Employment Status of Women Who Maintain Families, by Marital Status and Presence and Age of Children, March 1990–March 2009

(Thousands of women, percent.)

Marital status, age of children, and year	Civilian noninstitutional population	Civilian labor force			Unemployed		Not in the labor force
		Number	Percent of the population	Employed	Number	Percent of the labor force	
Total, Women Who Maintain Families							
1990	11 309	7 088	62.7	6 471	617	8.7	4 221
1991	11 765	7 329	62.3	6 657	672	9.2	4 436
1992	12 214	7 517	61.5	6 798	719	9.6	4 697
1993	12 489	7 777	62.3	7 093	684	8.8	4 712
1994	12 963	8 214	63.4	7 413	801	9.8	4 750
1995	12 762	8 192	64.2	7 527	665	8.1	4 570
1996	12 993	8 460	65.1	7 832	628	7.4	4 532
1997	13 258	8 998	67.9	8 192	806	9.0	4 260
1998	13 102	8 976	68.5	8 309	667	7.4	4 127
1999	13 191	9 213	69.8	8 596	617	6.7	3 978
2000	13 145	9 226	70.2	8 592	634	6.9	3 918
2001	12 930	9 034	69.9	8 453	581	6.4	3 897
2002	13 489	9 523	70.6	8 755	768	8.1	3 966
2003	14 000	9 759	69.7	8 898	861	8.8	4 241
2004	14 165	9 869	69.7	9 054	815	8.3	4 297
2005	14 391	9 941	69.1	9 140	801	8.1	4 450
2006	14 485	9 966	68.8	9 227	739	7.4	4 520
2007	14 833	10 172	68.6	9 510	661	6.5	4 662
2008	14 820	10 166	68.6	9 447	719	7.1	4 654
2009	14 813	10 140	68.5	9 034	1 106	10.9	4 673
Women with No Children Under 18 Years							
1990	4 290	2 227	51.9	2 132	95	4.3	2 062
1991	4 447	2 364	53.2	2 231	133	5.6	2 083
1992	4 651	2 427	52.2	2 307	120	4.9	2 223
1993	4 708	2 466	52.4	2 339	127	5.2	2 242
1994	4 758	2 609	54.8	2 489	120	4.6	2 149
1995	4 610	2 471	53.6	2 394	77	3.1	2 139
1996	4 847	2 552	52.7	2 462	90	3.5	2 295
1997	4 909	2 663	54.2	2 571	92	3.5	2 246
1998	4 952	2 649	53.5	2 578	71	2.7	2 303
1999	4 942	2 667	54.0	2 556	111	4.2	2 275
2000	5 097	2 707	53.1	2 546	161	5.9	2 390
2001	5 185	2 772	53.5	2 668	104	3.8	2 413
2002	5 119	2 764	54.0	2 628	136	4.9	2 355
2003	5 457	2 934	53.8	2 728	206	7.0	2 522
2004	5 551	3 052	55.0	2 855	197	6.5	2 499
2005	5 692	3 095	54.4	2 961	134	4.3	2 597
2006	5 693	3 088	54.2	2 945	143	4.6	2 604
2007	5 823	3 124	53.7	2 990	134	4.3	2 699
2008	6 022	3 352	55.7	3 167	185	5.5	2 670
2009	6 068	3 332	54.9	3 075	258	7.7	2 735
Women with Children Under 18 Years							
1990	7 018	4 860	69.3	4 338	522	10.7	2 159
1991	7 318	4 965	67.8	4 426	539	10.9	2 353
1992	7 564	5 090	67.3	4 491	599	11.8	2 473
1993	7 781	5 311	68.3	4 755	556	10.5	2 470
1994	8 205	5 604	68.3	4 924	680	12.1	2 601
1995	8 152	5 720	70.2	5 132	588	10.3	2 431
1996	8 146	5 908	72.5	5 370	538	9.1	2 237
1997	8 348	6 335	75.9	5 621	714	11.3	2 014
1998	8 151	6 327	77.6	5 731	596	9.4	1 823
1999	8 248	6 546	79.4	6 040	506	7.7	1 702
2000	8 048	6 520	81.0	6 046	474	7.3	1 528
2001	7 746	6 261	80.8	5 785	476	7.6	1 484
2002	8 370	6 759	80.8	6 127	632	9.4	1 611
2003	8 543	6 825	79.9	6 170	655	9.6	1 718
2004	8 614	6 817	79.1	6 199	618	9.1	1 798
2005	8 699	6 846	78.7	6 179	667	9.7	1 853
2006	8 793	6 878	78.2	6 282	596	8.7	1 915
2007	9 010	7 047	78.2	6 520	527	7.5	1 963
2008	8 798	6 814	77.4	6 280	535	7.8	1 984
2009	8 745	6 807	77.8	5 959	848	12.5	1 938
Single Women with No Children Under 18 Years							
1990	642	450	70.1	425	25	5.6	192
1991	682	469	68.8	441	28	6.0	214
1992	745	505	67.8	475	30	5.9	241
1993	752	531	70.6	494	37	7.0	221
1994	704	490	69.6	451	39	8.0	213
1995	779	534	68.5	508	26	4.9	245
1996	895	588	65.7	572	16	2.7	308
1997	860	585	68.0	563	22	3.8	275
1998	893	637	71.3	613	24	3.8	256
1999	969	674	69.6	638	36	5.3	295
2000	1 004	720	71.7	642	78	10.8	284
2001	1 096	787	71.8	756	31	3.9	309
2002	1 154	796	69.0	747	49	6.2	358
2003	1 254	814	64.9	713	101	12.4	440
2004	1 381	977	70.7	887	90	9.2	404

Note: See notes and definitions for information on historical comparability.

Table 1-48. Employment Status of Women Who Maintain Families, by Marital Status and Presence and Age of Children, March 1990–March 2009—*Continued*

(Thousands of women, percent.)

Marital status, age of children, and year	Civilian noninstitutional population	Civilian labor force					Not in the labor force
		Number	Percent of the population	Employed	Unemployed		
					Number	Percent of the labor force	
Single Women with No Children Under 18 Years—*Continued*							
2005	1 388	926	66.7	855	71	7.7	463
2006	1 370	933	68.1	861	72	7.7	437
2007	1 413	986	69.8	930	57	5.7	427
2008	1 515	1 057	69.8	989	68	6.5	458
2009	1 531	1 069	69.8	967	102	9.6	462
Single Women with Children Under 18 Years							
1990	1 953	1 095	56.1	874	221	20.2	858
1991	2 208	1 187	53.8	985	202	17.0	1 021
1992	2 376	1 256	52.9	1 067	189	15.0	1 120
1993	2 445	1 414	57.8	1 161	253	17.9	1 031
1994	2 790	1 625	58.2	1 328	297	18.3	1 165
1995	2 613	1 510	57.8	1 261	249	16.5	1 102
1996	2 639	1 633	61.9	1 346	287	17.6	1 006
1997	3 012	2 087	69.3	1 749	338	16.2	925
1998	3 083	2 280	74.0	1 960	320	14.0	803
1999	3 163	2 415	76.4	2 146	269	11.1	748
2000	3 167	2 413	76.2	2 151	262	10.9	754
2001	3 097	2 351	75.9	2 055	296	12.6	745
2002	3 315	2 566	77.4	2 241	325	12.7	749
2003	3 421	2 584	75.5	2 272	312	12.1	837
2004	3 414	2 568	75.2	2 233	335	13.0	846
2005	3 591	2 708	75.4	2 325	383	14.1	882
2006	3 671	2 710	73.8	2 370	340	12.5	961
2007	3 748	2 782	74.2	2 491	291	10.4	966
2008	3 721	2 743	73.7	2 448	295	10.8	978
2009	3 872	2 877	74.3	2 448	429	14.9	995
Widowed, Divorced, or Separated Women with No Children Under 18 Years							
1990	3 648	1 778	48.7	1 708	70	3.9	1 870
1991	3 765	1 896	50.4	1 791	105	5.5	1 869
1992	3 905	1 923	49.2	1 832	91	4.7	1 982
1993	3 956	1 935	48.9	1 845	90	4.7	2 021
1994	4 054	2 118	52.2	2 037	81	3.8	1 936
1995	3 831	1 938	50.6	1 887	51	2.6	1 894
1996	3 952	1 964	49.7	1 890	74	3.8	1 988
1997	4 049	2 077	51.3	2 008	69	3.3	1 971
1998	4 058	2 011	49.6	1 965	46	2.3	2 047
1999	3 974	1 993	50.2	1 918	75	3.8	1 980
2000	4 093	1 987	48.5	1 904	83	4.2	2 106
2001	4 088	1 985	48.6	1 912	73	3.7	2 104
2002	3 964	1 968	49.6	1 882	86	4.4	1 997
2003	4 203	2 121	50.5	2 016	105	5.0	2 082
2004	4 170	2 075	49.8	1 968	107	5.2	2 095
2005	4 304	2 170	50.4	2 106	64	2.9	2 135
2006	4 323	2 156	49.9	2 084	72	3.3	2 168
2007	4 410	2 138	48.5	2 061	77	3.6	2 272
2008	4 507	2 295	50.9	2 178	117	5.1	2 213
2009	4 536	2 263	49.9	2 108	155	6.9	2 273
Widowed, Divorced, or Separated Women with Children Under 18 Years							
1990	5 065	3 765	74.3	3 464	301	8.0	1 301
1991	5 109	3 778	73.9	3 441	337	8.9	1 331
1992	5 187	3 834	73.9	3 424	410	10.7	1 353
1993	5 336	3 897	73.0	3 594	303	7.8	1 439
1994	5 415	3 979	73.5	3 596	383	9.6	1 436
1995	5 539	4 210	76.0	3 871	339	8.1	1 329
1996	5 507	4 275	77.6	4 024	251	5.9	1 231
1997	5 337	4 248	79.6	3 872	376	8.9	1 089
1998	5 068	4 047	79.9	3 771	276	6.8	1 020
1999	5 086	4 131	81.2	3 894	237	5.7	955
2000	4 881	4 107	84.1	3 895	212	5.2	774
2001	4 649	3 910	84.1	3 730	180	4.6	739
2002	5 056	4 193	82.9	3 886	307	7.3	862
2003	5 122	4 241	82.8	3 898	343	8.1	881
2004	5 201	4 249	81.7	3 966	283	6.7	952
2005	5 108	4 137	81.0	3 854	283	6.8	971
2006	5 121	4 167	81.4	3 912	255	6.1	955
2007	5 262	4 266	81.1	4 029	237	5.5	997
2008	5 077	4 071	80.2	3 832	239	5.9	1 006
2009	4 873	3 930	80.7	3 511	420	10.7	943

Note: See notes and definitions for information on historical comparability.

Table 1-49. Number and Age of Children in Families, by Type of Family and Labor Force Status of Mother, March 1990–March 2009

(Thousands of children.)

Age of children and year	Total children	Mother in labor force	Mother not in labor force	Married-couple families			Families maintained by women			Families maintained by men
				Total	Mother in labor force	Mother not in labor force	Total	Mother in labor force	Mother not in labor force	
Children Under 18 Years										
1990	59 596	36 712	21 110	45 898	29 077	16 820	11 925	7 635	4 290	1 774
1991	60 330	36 968	21 526	45 912	29 056	16 856	12 582	7 912	4 670	1 836
1992	61 262	38 081	21 176	45 966	29 882	16 084	13 291	8 199	5 093	2 005
1993	62 020	38 542	21 444	46 499	30 054	16 445	13 487	8 488	4 999	2 034
1994	63 407	40 186	21 188	47 247	31 279	15 968	14 127	8 907	5 220	2 033
1995	63 989	41 365	20 421	47 675	32 190	15 486	14 111	9 176	4 935	2 202
1996	64 506	41 573	20 449	47 484	31 764	15 720	14 538	9 809	4 729	2 484
1997	64 710	42 747	19 223	47 529	32 263	15 265	14 441	10 483	3 958	2 740
1998	65 043	43 156	19 069	47 909	32 533	15 376	14 317	10 623	3 694	2 818
1999	65 191	43 419	19 074	47 945	32 193	15 752	14 547	11 226	3 322	2 699
2000	65 601	44 188	18 674	48 902	33 149	15 753	13 960	11 039	2 921	2 739
2001	65 777	44 051	18 864	49 352	33 436	15 916	13 563	10 615	2 948	2 862
2002	65 978	43 821	19 243	48 836	32 673	16 163	14 228	11 149	3 079	2 914
2003	66 521	43 769	19 782	49 004	32 411	16 593	14 547	11 359	3 189	2 970
2004	66 386	43 144	20 229	48 656	31 892	16 764	14 717	11 252	3 465	3 014
2005	66 526	43 239	20 179	48 688	31 886	16 802	14 729	11 352	3 377	3 108
2006	66 883	43 278	20 440	48 853	31 946	16 908	14 865	11 332	3 532	3 165
2007	67 228	44 116	20 073	48 927	32 496	16 431	15 263	11 620	3 643	3 038
2008	67 153	43 798	19 966	48 303	32 110	16 193	15 461	11 688	3 773	3 388
2009	66 913	43 509	20 074	48 384	32 065	16 315	15 204	11 444	3 759	3 326
Children 6 to 17 Years										
1990	39 095	25 805	12 079	29 726	20 067	9 659	8 157	5 737	2 420	1 211
1991	39 470	25 806	12 392	29 598	19 907	9 691	8 599	5 899	2 701	1 272
1992	40 064	26 666	12 067	29 673	20 586	9 087	9 060	6 079	2 980	1 331
1993	40 622	27 046	12 291	30 233	20 796	9 437	9 104	6 249	2 854	1 285
1994	41 795	28 179	12 287	30 895	21 663	9 233	9 570	6 516	3 054	1 329
1995	42 423	28 931	12 000	31 298	22 239	9 059	9 633	6 692	2 941	1 492
1996	42 964	29 381	11 897	31 231	22 092	9 139	10 047	7 289	2 758	1 685
1997	43 488	30 308	11 400	31 509	22 602	8 906	10 199	7 705	2 493	1 781
1998	43 771	30 579	11 367	31 707	22 706	9 001	10 238	7 873	2 365	1 826
1999	44 110	30 885	11 370	31 975	22 706	9 269	10 281	8 179	2 101	1 855
2000	44 562	31 531	11 198	32 732	23 393	9 339	9 997	8 138	1 859	1 833
2001	44 458	31 411	11 153	32 957	23 599	9 358	9 608	7 813	1 795	1 894
2002	44 865	31 437	11 510	32 799	23 296	9 504	10 148	8 142	2 006	1 918
2003	45 273	31 559	11 635	32 782	23 160	9 622	10 412	8 399	2 013	2 080
2004	45 066	31 040	11 968	32 506	22 736	9 769	10 502	8 304	2 199	2 058
2005	45 027	30 930	11 995	32 412	22 565	9 847	10 514	8 366	2 148	2 102
2006	45 039	30 591	12 250	32 311	22 315	9 996	10 530	8 276	2 254	2 198
2007	45 155	31 252	11 855	32 417	22 788	9 629	10 690	8 464	2 226	2 048
2008	44 909	30 853	11 874	31 990	22 413	9 577	10 737	8 440	2 297	2 182
2009	44 595	30 600	11 811	31 966	22 425	9 537	10 449	8 175	2 274	2 180
Children Under 6 Years										
1990	20 502	10 907	9 031	16 171	9 010	7 161	3 767	1 897	1 870	563
1991	20 860	11 162	9 134	16 313	9 148	7 165	3 983	2 013	1 969	563
1992	21 198	11 415	9 109	16 293	9 296	6 997	4 232	2 119	2 112	674
1993	21 398	11 496	9 153	16 266	9 258	7 008	4 383	2 239	2 145	749
1994	21 612	12 007	8 901	16 352	9 617	6 735	4 556	2 391	2 166	704
1995	21 566	12 435	8 421	16 377	9 951	6 427	4 478	2 484	1 995	710
1996	21 542	12 192	8 552	16 253	9 672	6 581	4 491	2 520	1 971	799
1997	21 222	12 439	7 823	16 020	9 661	6 359	4 243	2 778	1 464	959
1998	21 272	12 577	7 703	16 201	9 827	6 375	4 079	2 751	1 328	992
1999	21 081	12 533	7 704	15 971	9 487	6 484	4 267	3 046	1 220	844
2000	21 039	12 657	7 476	16 170	9 757	6 413	3 963	2 901	1 062	906
2001	21 318	12 640	7 711	16 395	9 837	6 558	3 956	2 802	1 153	968
2002	21 113	12 384	7 733	16 037	9 377	6 660	4 080	3 007	1 073	996
2003	21 248	12 210	8 147	16 222	9 251	6 971	4 136	2 960	1 176	890
2004	21 321	12 104	8 261	16 151	9 156	6 995	4 214	2 948	1 266	956
2005	21 498	12 308	8 184	16 276	9 321	6 955	4 216	2 987	1 229	1 006
2006	21 844	12 687	8 190	16 542	9 631	6 911	4 335	3 057	1 278	968
2007	22 073	12 864	8 218	16 509	9 708	6 802	4 572	3 156	1 416	991
2008	22 244	12 946	8 092	16 313	9 697	6 616	4 724	3 248	1 476	1 207
2009	22 318	12 909	8 263	16 418	9 640	6 778	4 755	3 270	1 485	1 146

Note: See notes and definitions for information on historical comparability.

Table 1-50. Number of Families and Median Family Income, by Type of Family and Earner Status of Members, 1990–2008

(Thousands of families, dollars.)

Number and type of families and median family income	1990	1991	1992	1993	1994	1995	1996	1997	1998
NUMBER OF FAMILIES									
Married-Couple Families, Total	52 241	52 549	53 254	53 248	53 929	53 621	53 654	54 362	54 829
No earners	6 765	7 101	7 250	7 281	7 225	7 276	7 145	7 286	7 257
One earner	11 630	11 553	12 053	11 806	11 715	11 708	11 493	11 700	12 246
Husband	9 110	8 907	9 182	8 715	8 673	8 792	8 611	8 770	9 173
Wife	1 816	1 987	2 145	2 405	2 364	2 251	2 207	2 298	2 411
Other family member	703	659	726	686	678	666	674	632	662
Two earners	25 896	26 037	26 344	26 742	27 263	27 180	27 260	27 712	27 593
Husband and wife	23 697	23 880	24 255	24 543	25 123	25 274	25 274	25 731	25 696
Husband and other family member	1 711	1 633	1 447	1 582	1 565	1 393	1 483	1 406	1 306
Husband not an earner	487	524	642	617	574	513	502	575	590
Three earners or more	7 950	7 858	7 606	7 419	7 727	7 456	7 756	7 664	7 733
Husband and wife	7 029	7 052	6 882	6 723	6 987	6 770	7 126	7 023	7 102
Husband, not wife	756	595	550	535	543	531	479	478	456
Husband not an earner	165	211	175	162	196	155	150	163	176
Families Maintained by Women, Total	11 771	12 214	12 504	12 982	12 771	13 007	13 277	13 115	13 206
No earners	2 623	2 925	2 968	3 100	2 848	2 664	2 574	2 332	2 143
One earner	5 672	5 926	6 184	6 407	6 506	6 815	7 027	7 091	7 351
Householder	4 585	4 812	5 042	5 278	5 415	5 590	5 817	5 841	6 167
Other family member	1 087	1 114	1 142	1 129	1 091	1 225	1 211	1 251	1 183
Two earners or more	3 476	3 363	3 352	3 476	3 417	3 527	3 675	3 692	3 712
Householder and other family member(s)	3 146	3 058	2 998	3 139	3 126	3 225	3 431	3 398	3 399
Householder not an earner	330	305	354	337	291	302	245	294	313
Families Maintained by Men, Total	2 948	3 079	3 094	2 992	3 287	3 557	3 924	3 982	4 041
No earners	296	310	345	329	383	357	359	344	381
One earner	1 396	1 541	1 544	1 593	1 705	1 800	1 972	2 104	2 027
Householder	1 133	1 289	1 305	1 352	1 428	1 548	1 667	1 791	1 725
Other family member	263	253	239	241	277	253	305	313	302
Two earners or more	1 257	1 228	1 204	1 070	1 198	1 400	1 593	1 534	1 634
Householder and other family member(s)	1 180	1 157	1 117	1 002	1 128	1 302	1 469	1 427	1 532
Householder not an earner	76	71	88	67	71	98	124	107	102
MEDIAN FAMILY INCOME									
Married-Couple Families, Total	39 802	40 746	42 000	43 000	44 893	47 000	49 614	51 475	54 043
No earners	19 221	20 415	20 023	19 983	20 604	21 888	22 622	23 782	24 525
One earner	31 020	31 671	32 500	32 084	33 393	35 100	36 468	39 140	40 519
Husband	32 422	33 208	34 714	34 401	35 000	36 052	38 150	40 300	42 000
Wife	25 228	26 500	27 343	27 502	28 661	32 098	30 301	34 050	35 625
Other family member	33 262	33 042	33 622	30 254	32 578	37 784	39 644	40 317	42 414
Two earners	44 000	45 359	47 737	49 650	51 190	53 500	56 000	58 020	61 300
Husband and wife	44 031	45 516	48 050	49 980	51 500	53 626	56 392	58 564	61 900
Husband and other family member	42 602	45 000	45 694	48 862	48 517	52 530	49 610	53 854	57 680
Husband not an earner	39 494	40 495	40 124	38 800	42 800	47 121	46 990	47 979	50 955
Three earners or more	59 336	61 120	61 640	63 535	66 172	68 996	70 400	75 593	78 973
Husband and wife	55 846	61 448	62 674	64 099	66 674	69 371	71 148	76 105	79 907
Husband, not wife	59 675	60 592	57 015	60 712	63 633	60 360	61 824	68 890	71 001
Husband not an earner	49 107	44 874	47 551	54 805	54 655	61 196	55 495	62 684	63 205
Families Maintained by Women, Total	16 351	16 054	16 431	16 800	17 600	19 306	19 416	20 470	21 875
No earners	5 880	6 060	5 964	6 492	6 805	7 440	7 092	7 476	7 737
One earner	15 987	16 284	16 468	16 745	17 226	18 824	18 500	19 000	20 000
Householder	15 001	15 542	15 905	15 700	16 603	17 890	18 000	18 000	18 800
Other family member	20 173	20 220	19 709	20 800	21 300	23 166	21 000	22 870	25 981
Two earners or more	30 500	31 508	32 705	33 300	33 820	35 000	36 400	39 275	40 000
Householder and other family member(s)	30 367	31 550	33 280	33 165	33 357	34 674	36 400	39 000	39 713
Householder not an earner	32 800	29 477	30 460	35 394	37 531	39 444	38 249	47 471	43 725
Families Maintained by Men, Total	28 493	28 000	27 400	25 856	27 486	30 000	31 500	32 984	35 000
No earners	11 386	11 196	9 416	10 900	11 293	12 240	12 030	14 252	15 468
One earner	25 000	23 715	23 020	22 300	24 011	25 337	26 100	26 897	29 125
Householder	24 150	23 309	23 000	22 079	24 000	25 069	25 874	27 000	29 125
Other family member	27 620	25 720	24 359	26 916	26 253	27 291	28 584	25 486	28 241
Two earners or more	40 000	37 700	39 000	38 000	41 439	43 100	44 275	49 900	51 288
Householder and other family member(s)	40 256	37 550	39 300	38 363	41 534	43 000	43 065	50 000	50 954
Householder not an earner	34 064	40 000	36 445	33 700	37 386	55 133	47 001	44 786	68 257

Note: See notes and definitions for information on historical comparability.

Table 1-50. Number of Families and Median Family Income, by Type of Family and Earner Status of Members, 1990–2008—*Continued*

(Thousands of families, dollars.)

Number and type of families and median family income	1999	2000	2001	2002	2003	2004	2005	2006	2007	2008
NUMBER OF FAMILIES										
Married-Couple Families, Total	55 352	55 650	56 798	57 362	57 767	58 180	58 225	59 050	58 490	59 181
No earners	7 160	7 297	7 662	7 803	8 043	7 998	8 017	8 091	7 914	8 083
One earner	12 290	12 450	12 852	13 503	14 061	14 385	14 301	14 562	14 272	14 625
Husband	9 062	9 319	9 573	10 121	10 478	10 853	10 611	10 706	10 396	10 567
Wife	2 585	2 545	2 689	2 821	3 027	2 993	3 097	3 264	3 267	3 437
Other family member	643	586	590	560	557	539	593	591	608	620
Two earners	28 010	28 329	28 779	28 891	28 693	28 806	28 802	29 216	29 256	29 466
Husband and wife	26 134	26 447	26 829	26 966	26 860	26 758	26 833	27 241	27 264	27 531
Husband and other family member	1 325	1 277	1 424	1 391	1 322	1 462	1 376	1 358	1 393	1 308
Husband not an earner	552	605	526	534	511	586	594	616	599	627
Three earners or more	7 892	7 575	7 504	7 165	6 970	6 991	7 104	7 181	7 048	7 008
Husband and wife	7 220	6 917	6 859	6 565	6 349	6 459	6 535	6 620	6 452	6 393
Husband, not wife	528	537	530	455	467	381	445	397	452	432
Husband not an earner	144	120	115	145	154	152	124	165	144	182
Families Maintained by Women, Total	13 164	12 950	13 517	14 033	14 196	14 404	14 505	14 852	14 846	14 842
No earners	1 883	1 786	2 076	2 228	2 451	2 610	2 616	2 627	2 502	2 678
One earner	7 441	7 462	7 693	8 153	8 012	8 074	8 052	8 303	8 418	8 381
Householder	6 127	6 132	6 436	6 832	6 725	6 788	6 724	6 904	7 020	6 978
Other family member	1 314	1 331	1 257	1 321	1 286	1 285	1 329	1 398	1 398	1 404
Two earners or more	3 840	3 702	3 748	3 652	3 733	3 720	3 836	3 923	3 925	3 783
Householder and other family member(s)	3 508	3 376	3 442	3 290	3 364	3 399	3 468	3 547	3 572	3 467
Householder not an earner	332	325	306	362	369	321	368	376	353	316
Families Maintained by Men, Total	4 086	4 316	4 499	4 747	4 778	4 953	5 193	5 119	5 181	5 301
No earners	376	380	461	466	530	492	537	555	532	611
One earner	2 044	2 223	2 319	2 434	2 466	2 573	2 661	2 584	2 703	2 636
Householder	1 721	1 879	1 911	2 026	2 053	2 152	2 196	2 155	2 297	2 199
Other family member	323	344	408	408	413	421	464	429	406	437
Two earners or more	1 666	1 713	1 719	1 847	1 782	1 888	1 995	1 979	1 947	2 054
Householder and other family member(s)	1 522	1 585	1 629	1 709	1 625	1 736	1 848	1 828	1 812	1 889
Householder not an earner	143	128	90	138	157	152	147	152	134	165
MEDIAN FAMILY INCOME										
Married-Couple Families, Total	56 792	59 200	60 100	61 000	62 388	63 627	65 586	69 300	72 802	72 805
No earners	25 262	25 356	25 900	25 954	26 312	26 798	28 376	30 000	30 134	31 164
One earner	41 261	44 424	44 400	45 000	46 546	47 749	50 000	50 400	52 686	53 865
Husband	44 200	47 010	47 500	48 004	48 948	50 000	52 000	53 360	55 350	56 000
Wife	35 546	36 458	36 140	39 072	41 180	41 000	43 505	45 000	47 000	47 015
Other family member	41 120	45 492	44 270	40 927	45 936	46 324	50 263	49 352	48 922	55 114
Two earners	64 007	67 500	69 543	71 282	73 309	75 100	76 960	81 500	85 012	85 500
Husband and wife	64 950	68 132	70 000	72 150	74 500	76 000	77 539	82 762	86 000	86 842
Husband and other family member	53 541	56 503	65 240	62 848	60 100	66 120	67 350	68 828	71 573	68 755
Husband not an earner	52 466	53 430	58 725	54 840	58 000	63 050	65 622	63 657	68 032	66 445
Three earners or more	81 940	83 990	86 090	88 632	93 000	94 212	98 000	103 803	106 747	105 618
Husband and wife	83 000	84 634	87 000	89 962	94 353	95 524	99 800	104 045	107 630	106 493
Husband, not wife	69 561	79 050	76 230	82 180	77 316	87 000	79 417	91 965	101 771	99 731
Husband not an earner	69 275	68 050	80 661	68 400	91 771	73 137	84 638	97 510	92 428	93 961
Families Maintained by Women, Total	23 100	25 000	25 064	26 000	26 000	26 400	27 000	28 218	30 000	29 698
No earners	8 010	8 988	8 160	8 808	8 344	8 400	8 228	8 657	8 873	9 404
One earner	20 092	22 306	23 008	24 597	24 752	25 040	25 308	26 393	27 795	28 060
Householder	19 000	21 400	22 001	23 760	23 832	24 801	24 505	25 381	26 644	27 000
Other family member	26 800	27 524	28 476	29 524	28 857	29 700	31 700	31 462	31 950	34 814
Two earners or more	41 144	43 035	45 244	46 580	47 576	48 549	50 000	52 400	55 749	54 369
Householder and other family member(s)	40 855	43 000	44 842	46 000	46 701	47 974	48 989	51 479	55 010	54 306
Householder not an earner	48 004	45 600	51 000	51 248	57 267	56 799	64 805	61 699	64 094	54 978
Families Maintained by Men, Total	37 000	37 040	36 000	37 440	37 914	40 000	40 293	41 130	44 001	43 050
No earners	13 752	14 946	12 840	15 200	15 408	14 167	13 950	15 462	12 921	15 557
One earner	31 038	30 160	30 800	30 139	32 097	35 000	35 001	35 100	37 716	36 806
Householder	30 483	30 816	30 500	30 014	31 355	35 000	35 075	35 011	37 720	37 569
Other family member	34 756	29 118	31 052	32 000	35 525	35 438	35 000	37 840	37 522	34 404
Two earners or more	51 040	55 010	55 024	55 000	57 840	57 600	60 024	61 000	63 600	64 077
Householder and other family member(s)	50 960	55 400	54 850	55 220	57 400	57 058	60 000	61 000	64 000	63 416
Householder not an earner	57 407	51 945	61 824	49 852	64 658	65 400	70 879	62 000	60 498	69 794

Note: See notes and definitions for information on historical comparability.

Table 1-51. Employment Status of the Foreign-Born and Native-Born Populations, by Selected Characteristics, 2007–2008

(Thousands of people, percent.)

Year and characteristic	Civilian noninstitutional population	Civilian labor force				
		Total	Participation rate	Employed	Unemployed	
					Number	Rate
2007						
TOTAL						
Both sexes, 16 years and over	231 867	153 124	66.0	146 047	7 078	4.6
Men	112 173	82 136	73.2	78 254	3 882	4.7
Women	119 694	70 988	59.3	67 792	3 196	4.5
FOREIGN BORN						
Both sexes, 16 years and over	35 017	23 994	68.5	22 967	1 027	4.3
Men	17 670	14 470	81.9	13 883	588	4.1
Women	17 347	9 524	54.9	9 085	439	4.6
Age						
16 to 24 years	4 205	2 454	58.4	2 266	188	7.7
25 to 34 years	8 243	6 421	77.9	6 147	274	4.3
35 to 44 years	8 322	6 782	81.5	6 546	236	3.5
45 to 54 years	6 278	5 126	81.7	4 930	196	3.8
55 to 64 years	3 850	2 531	65.7	2 424	107	4.2
65 years and over	4 119	680	16.5	655	25	3.7
Race and Hispanic Origin						
White, non-Hispanic	7 492	4 599	61.4	4 428	171	3.7
Black, non-Hispanic	2 610	1 901	72.8	1 795	106	5.6
Asian, non-Hispanic	7 762	5 264	67.8	5 106	158	3.0
Hispanic[1]	16 817	11 987	71.3	11 405	582	4.9
Educational Attainment						
Total, 25 years and over	30 812	21 540	69.9	20 701	839	3.9
Less than a high school diploma	9 456	5 893	62.3	5 585	308	5.2
High school graduate, no college[2]	7 863	5 400	68.7	5 188	212	3.9
Some college or associate's degree	4 780	3 538	74.0	3 387	151	4.3
Bachelor's degree or higher[3]	8 713	6 709	77.0	6 541	168	2.5
NATIVE BORN						
Both sexes, 16 years and over	196 850	129 130	65.6	123 079	6 051	4.7
Men	94 503	67 666	71.6	64 372	3 294	4.9
Women	102 347	61 464	60.1	58 707	2 757	4.5
Age						
16 to 24 years	33 204	19 763	59.5	17 608	2 155	10.9
25 to 34 years	31 509	26 708	84.8	25 439	1 270	4.8
35 to 44 years	34 079	28 745	84.3	27 756	989	3.4
45 to 54 years	37 266	30 571	82.0	29 633	938	3.1
55 to 64 years	28 683	18 219	63.5	17 684	535	2.9
65 years and over	32 109	5 124	16.0	4 959	165	3.2
Race and Hispanic Origin						
White, non-Hispanic	151 596	100 279	66.1	96 411	3 868	3.9
Black, non-Hispanic	23 921	14 961	62.5	13 671	1 290	8.6
Asian, non-Hispanic	2 708	1 683	62.2	1 620	63	3.7
Hispanic[1]	14 566	9 615	66.0	8 977	638	6.6
Educational Attainment						
Total, 25 years and over	163 645	109 367	66.8	105 471	3 896	3.6
Less than a high school diploma	17 177	6 514	37.9	5 936	578	8.9
High school graduates, no college[2]	53 510	33 139	61.9	31 670	1 470	4.4
Some college or associate's degree	45 051	32 349	71.8	31 225	1 124	3.5
Bachelor's degree or higher[3]	47 908	37 365	78.0	36 640	725	1.9

Note: Due to the introduction of revised population controls in January 2008, estimated levels for 2008 are not strictly comparable with those for 2007.

[1]May be of any race.
[2]Includes persons with a high school diploma or equivalent.
[3]Includes persons with bachelor's, master's, professional, and doctoral degrees.

Table 1-51. Employment Status of the Foreign-Born and Native-Born Populations, by Selected Characteristics, 2007–2008—*Continued*

(Thousands of people, percent.)

Year and characteristic	Civilian noninstitutional population	Civilian labor force				
		Total	Participation rate	Employed	Unemployed	
					Number	Rate
2008						
TOTAL						
Both sexes, 16 years and over	233 788	154 287	66.0	145 362	8 924	5.8
Men	113 113	82 520	73.0	77 486	5 033	6.1
Women	120 675	71 767	59.5	67 876	3 891	5.4
FOREIGN BORN						
Both sexes, 16 years and over	35 317	24 063	68.1	22 660	1 403	5.8
Men	17 688	14 400	81.4	13 578	822	5.7
Women	17 629	9 663	54.8	9 082	581	6.0
Age						
16 to 24 years	3 845	2 211	57.5	1 979	232	10.5
25 to 34 years	7 992	6 236	78.0	5 866	371	5.9
35 to 44 years	8 327	6 814	81.8	6 473	341	5.0
45 to 54 years	6 602	5 380	81.5	5 083	297	5.5
55 to 64 years	4 126	2 700	65.4	2 580	120	4.5
65 years and over	4 424	721	16.3	679	42	5.9
Race and Hispanic Origin						
White, non-Hispanic	7 517	4 531	60.3	4 305	226	5.0
Black, non-Hispanic	2 743	2 007	73.2	1 863	144	7.2
Asian, non-Hispanic	7 894	5 382	68.2	5 185	197	3.7
Hispanic[1]	16 816	11 889	70.7	11 067	822	6.9
Educational Attainment						
Total, 25 years and over	31 472	21 852	69.4	20 681	1 171	5.4
Less than a high school diploma	9 420	5 759	61.1	5 316	443	7.7
High school graduates, no college[2]	8 098	5 514	68.1	5 201	312	5.7
Some college or associate degree	4 951	3 648	73.7	3 457	190	5.2
Bachelor's degree and higher[3]	9 003	6 931	77.0	6 705	226	3.3
NATIVE BORN						
Both sexes, 16 years and over	198 471	130 224	65.6	122 703	7 521	5.8
Men	95 424	68 119	71.4	63 908	4 211	6.2
Women	103 047	62 104	60.3	58 795	3 310	5.3
Age						
16 to 24 years	33 639	19 821	58.9	17 223	2 599	13.1
25 to 34 years	32 001	27 096	84.7	25 517	1 579	5.8
35 to 44 years	33 372	28 247	84.6	26 984	1 264	4.5
45 to 54 years	37 357	30 623	82.0	29 446	1 177	3.8
55 to 64 years	29 364	18 915	64.4	18 232	682	3.6
65 years and over	32 737	5 522	16.9	5 300	222	4.0
Race and Hispanic Origin						
White, non-Hispanic	152 157	100 679	66.2	95 909	4 770	4.7
Black, non-Hispanic	24 157	15 101	62.5	13 524	1 577	10.4
Asian, non-Hispanic	2 669	1 674	62.7	1 600	74	4.4
Hispanic[1]	15 325	10 135	66.1	9 279	856	8.4
Educational Attainment						
Total, 25 years and over	164 832	110 403	67.0	105 480	4 923	4.5
Less than a high school diploma	16 702	6 406	38.4	5 757	649	10.1
High school graduates, no college[2]	53 017	32 749	61.8	30 896	1 854	5.7
Some college or associate degree	46 153	33 070	71.7	31 582	1 488	4.5
Bachelor's degree or higher[3]	48 959	38 177	78.0	37 245	932	2.4

Note: Due to the introduction of revised population controls in January 2008, estimated levels for 2008 are not strictly comparable with those for 2007.

[1] May be of any race.
[2] Includes persons with a high school diploma or equivalent.
[3] Includes persons with bachelor's, master's, professional, and doctoral degrees.

Table 1-52. Employment Status of the Foreign-Born and Native-Born Populations Age 16 Years and Over, by Sex and Presence and Age of Youngest Child, Annual Averages, 2007–2008

(Thousands of people, percent.)

Characteristic	2007			2008		
	Both sexes	Men	Women	Both sexes	Men	Women
FOREIGN BORN						
With Own Children Under 18 Years						
Civilian noninstitutional population	13 970	6 640	7 329	13 864	6 618	7 245
Civilian labor force	10 667	6 260	4 407	10 626	6 228	4 399
Participation rate	76.4	94.3	60.1	76.6	94.1	60.7
Employed	10 245	6 055	4 190	10 047	5 929	4 118
Employment-population ratio	73.3	91.2	57.2	72.5	89.6	56.8
Unemployed	422	205	217	580	299	281
Unemployment rate	4.0	3.3	4.9	5.5	4.8	6.4
With Own Children 6 to 17 Years, None Younger						
Civilian noninstitutional population	6 974	3 252	3 722	7 173	3 359	3 814
Civilian labor force	5 640	3 029	2 611	5 791	3 123	2 668
Participation rate	80.9	93.1	70.2	80.7	93.0	69.9
Employed	5 431	2 935	2 497	5 505	2 985	2 520
Employment-population ratio	77.9	90.2	67.1	76.7	88.9	66.1
Unemployed	209	94	115	286	138	148
Unemployment rate	3.7	3.1	4.4	4.9	4.4	5.5
With Own Children Under 6 Years						
Civilian noninstitutional population	6 996	3 388	3 608	6 691	3 259	3 431
Civilian labor force	5 027	3 231	1 795	4 835	3 104	1 731
Participation rate	71.9	95.4	49.8	72.3	95.2	50.4
Employed	4 814	3 120	1 693	4 542	2 944	1 598
Employment-population ratio	68.8	92.1	46.9	67.9	90.3	46.6
Unemployed	213	111	102	294	161	133
Unemployment rate	4.2	3.4	5.7	6.1	5.2	7.7
With Own Children Under 3 Years						
Civilian noninstitutional population	4 087	1 982	2 105	3 923	1 927	1 996
Civilian labor force	2 821	1 888	933	2 727	1 837	890
Participation rate	69.0	95.3	44.3	69.5	95.3	44.6
Employed	2 700	1 825	876	2 558	1 745	813
Employment-population ratio	66.1	92.1	41.6	65.2	90.6	40.7
Unemployed	120	63	57	169	92	78
Unemployment rate	4.3	3.4	6.1	6.2	5.0	8.7
With No Own Children Under 18 Years						
Civilian noninstitutional population	21 047	11 030	10 018	21 453	11 070	10 383
Civilian labor force	13 327	8 210	5 117	13 436	8 173	5 264
Participation rate	63.3	74.4	51.1	62.6	73.8	50.7
Employed	12 722	7 828	4 895	12 613	7 650	4 964
Employment-population ratio	60.4	71.0	48.9	58.8	69.1	47.8
Unemployed	605	383	222	823	523	300
Unemployment rate	4.5	4.7	4.3	6.1	6.4	5.7

Note: Due to the introduction of revised population controls in January 2008, estimated levels for 2008 are not strictly comparable with those for 2007.

Table 1-52. Employment Status of the Foreign-Born and Native-Born Populations Age 16 Years and Over, by Sex and Presence and Age of Youngest Child, Annual Averages, 2007–2008—*Continued*

(Thousands of people, percent.)

Characteristic	2007			2008		
	Both sexes	Men	Women	Both sexes	Men	Women
NATIVE BORN						
With Own Children Under 18 Years						
Civilian noninstitutional population	52 683	22 996	29 686	51 642	22 467	29 175
Civilian labor force	43 578	21 699	21 879	42 762	21 144	21 617
Participation rate	82.7	94.4	73.7	82.8	94.1	74.1
Employed	42 005	21 119	20 887	40 859	20 403	20 455
Employment-population ratio	79.7	91.8	70.4	79.1	90.8	70.1
Unemployed	1 573	581	992	1 903	741	1 162
Unemployment rate	3.6	2.7	4.5	4.5	3.5	5.4
With Own Children 6 to 17 Years, None Younger						
Civilian noninstitutional population	29 861	13 085	16 775	29 259	12 841	16 418
Civilian labor force	25 413	12 197	13 216	24 936	11 955	12 981
Participation rate	85.1	93.2	78.8	85.2	93.1	79.1
Employed	24 622	11 889	12 733	23 974	11 555	12 419
Employment-population ratio	82.5	90.9	75.9	81.9	90.0	75.6
Unemployed	791	308	483	963	400	562
Unemployment rate	3.1	2.5	3.7	3.9	3.3	4.3
With Own Children Under 6 Years						
Civilian noninstitutional population	22 822	9 911	12 911	22 384	9 627	12 757
Civilian labor force	18 165	9 502	8 663	17 825	9 189	8 636
Participation rate	79.6	95.9	67.1	79.6	95.5	67.7
Employed	17 383	9 230	8 154	16 885	8 849	8 036
Employment-population ratio	76.2	93.1	63.2	75.4	91.9	63.0
Unemployed	782	272	509	940	340	600
Unemployment rate	4.3	2.9	5.9	5.3	3.7	6.9
With Own Children Under 3 Years						
Civilian noninstitutional population	13 406	5 851	7 554	13 358	5 758	7 600
Civilian labor force	10 412	5 624	4 788	10 419	5 517	4 902
Participation rate	77.7	96.1	63.4	78.0	95.8	64.5
Employed	9 935	5 457	4 478	9 841	5 299	4 542
Employment-population ratio	74.1	93.3	59.3	73.7	92.0	59.8
Unemployed	477	167	310	578	218	360
Unemployment rate	4.6	3.0	6.5	5.5	3.9	7.4
With No Own Children Under 18 Years						
Civilian noninstitutional population	144 167	71 506	72 661	146 829	72 957	73 872
Civilian labor force	85 552	45 967	39 585	87 462	46 975	40 487
Participation rate	59.3	64.3	54.5	59.6	64.4	54.8
Employed	81 074	43 253	37 821	81 844	43 505	38 339
Employment-population ratio	56.2	60.5	52.1	55.7	59.6	51.9
Unemployed	4 478	2 714	1 764	5 618	3 470	2 148
Unemployment rate	5.2	5.9	4.5	6.4	7.4	5.3

Note: Due to the introduction of revised population controls in January 2008, estimated levels for 2008 are not strictly comparable with those for 2007.

Table 1-53. Employment Status of the Foreign-Born and Native-Born Populations Age 25 Years and Over, by Educational Attainment, Race, and Hispanic Origin, Annual Averages, 2007–2008

(Thousands of people, percent.)

Characteristic	2007				2008			
	Less than a high school diploma	High school graduate, no college[1]	Some college or associate's degree	Bachelor's degree or higher[2]	Less than a high school diploma	High school graduate, no college[1]	Some college or associate's degree	Bachelor's degree or higher[2]
FOREIGN BORN								
White, Non-Hispanic								
Civilian noninstitutional population	895	1 850	1 338	2 701	891	1 884	1 360	2 744
Civilian labor force	306	1 035	882	1 991	276	990	885	2 024
Participation rate	34.1	55.9	65.9	73.7	30.9	52.5	65.1	73.7
Employed	292	993	850	1 937	253	939	838	1 952
Employment-population ratio	32.7	53.7	63.5	71.7	28.4	49.9	61.6	71.2
Unemployed	13	42	32	53	22	50	48	71
Unemployment rate	4.3	4.1	3.6	2.7	8.1	5.1	5.4	3.5
Black, Non-Hispanic								
Civilian noninstitutional population	318	712	570	654	334	758	629	677
Civilian labor force	193	515	474	566	192	561	501	582
Participation rate	60.7	72.2	83.2	86.6	57.4	74.0	79.7	86.0
Employed	177	491	445	549	176	516	466	559
Employment-population ratio	55.6	68.9	78.1	84.1	52.9	68.1	74.0	82.5
Unemployed	16	24	29	17	15	45	36	24
Unemployment rate	8.4	4.7	6.1	3.0	7.9	8.0	7.1	4.1
Asian, Non-Hispanic								
Civilian noninstitutional population	836	1 428	1 066	3 754	864	1 453	1 033	3 880
Civilian labor force	370	924	769	2 889	402	951	758	2 979
Participation rate	44.3	64.7	72.1	77.0	46.6	65.5	73.4	76.8
Employed	359	892	736	2 828	375	913	725	2 898
Employment-population ratio	43.0	62.5	69.0	75.3	43.4	62.8	70.2	74.7
Unemployed	11	32	33	61	27	39	33	81
Unemployment rate	3.0	3.5	4.3	2.1	6.8	4.1	4.4	2.7
Hispanic[3]								
Civilian noninstitutional population	7 368	3 801	1 726	1 508	7 292	3 940	1 852	1 579
Civilian labor force	5 001	2 877	1 352	1 189	4 871	2 967	1 439	1 245
Participation rate	67.9	75.7	78.3	78.9	66.8	75.3	77.7	78.9
Employed	4 736	2 764	1 297	1 155	4 495	2 790	1 368	1 198
Employment-population ratio	64.3	72.7	75.1	76.6	61.6	70.8	73.9	75.9
Unemployed	266	112	56	34	376	177	71	47
Unemployment rate	5.3	3.9	4.1	2.9	7.7	6.0	5.0	3.7
NATIVE BORN								
White, Non-Hispanic								
Civilian noninstitutional population	11 099	41 790	35 413	41 067	10 723	41 180	35 972	41 982
Civilian labor force	4 092	25 333	25 048	31 725	3 975	24 863	25 386	32 458
Participation rate	36.9	60.6	70.7	77.3	37.1	60.4	70.6	77.3
Employed	3 783	24 377	24 281	31 150	3 644	23 659	24 397	31 727
Employment-population ratio	34.1	58.3	68.6	75.9	34.0	57.5	67.8	75.6
Unemployed	309	955	767	575	331	1 204	990	731
Unemployment rate	7.5	3.8	3.1	1.8	8.3	4.8	3.9	2.3
Black, Non-Hispanic								
Civilian noninstitutional population	3 215	6 938	5 306	3 496	3 128	6 923	5 533	3 582
Civilian labor force	1 154	4 481	3 948	2 872	1 167	4 467	4 125	2 881
Participation rate	35.9	64.6	74.4	82.1	37.3	64.5	74.6	80.4
Employed	1 003	4 138	3 731	2 788	979	4 046	3 815	2 769
Employment-population ratio	31.2	59.6	70.3	79.7	31.3	58.4	69.0	77.3
Unemployed	151	343	216	84	187	420	310	113
Unemployment rate	13.1	7.7	5.5	2.9	16.0	9.4	7.5	3.9
Asian, Non-Hispanic								
Civilian noninstitutional population	143	397	399	953	147	360	442	929
Civilian labor force	58	223	287	757	57	210	308	737
Participation rate	40.6	56.0	72.0	79.4	38.9	58.2	69.6	79.3
Employed	56	218	281	734	55	200	301	715
Employment-population ratio	39.4	54.8	70.3	77.0	37.7	55.4	68.2	76.9
Unemployed	2	5	7	23	2	10	6	23
Unemployment rate	2.9	2.2	2.3	3.0	2.9	4.9	2.1	3.1
Hispanic[3]								
Civilian noninstitutional population	2 275	3 390	2 939	1 784	2 264	3 587	3 131	1 835
Civilian labor force	1 039	2 468	2 340	1 517	1 040	2 609	2 476	1 588
Participation rate	45.7	72.8	79.6	85.1	45.9	72.8	79.1	86.5
Employed	942	2 345	2 245	1 489	931	2 442	2 353	1 537
Employment-population ratio	41.4	69.2	76.4	83.5	41.1	68.1	75.2	83.8
Unemployed	97	122	94	29	109	167	123	50
Unemployment rate	9.4	5.0	4.0	1.9	10.4	6.4	5.0	3.2

Note: Due to the introduction of revised population controls in January 2008, estimated levels for 2008 are not strictly comparable with those for 2007. Data for race/ethnicity groups do not sum to total because data are not presented for all races.

[1]Includes persons with a high school diploma or equivalent.
[2]Includes persons with bachelor's, master's, professional, and doctoral degrees.
[3]May be of any race.

Table 1-54. Employed Foreign-Born and Native-Born Persons Age 16 Years and Over, by Occupation and Sex, 2007–2008 Annual Averages

(Thousands of people, percent.)

Occupation	2007					
	Foreign born			Native born		
	Both sexes	Male	Female	Both sexes	Male	Female
TOTAL EMPLOYED	22 967	13 883	9 085	123 079	64 372	58 707
Percent Employed	100.0	100.0	100.0	100.0	100.0	100.0
Management, professional, and related	27.2	25.1	30.4	37.0	34.4	39.9
Management, business, and financial operations	10.4	10.4	10.4	15.6	17.0	14.1
Management	7.4	8.1	6.3	11.2	13.3	8.9
Business and financial operations	3.0	2.3	4.1	4.4	3.7	5.2
Professional and related	16.8	14.7	20.0	21.4	17.4	25.9
Computer and mathematical	3.4	4.2	2.0	2.2	3.1	1.2
Architecture and engineering	2.0	2.8	0.9	2.0	3.3	0.6
Life, physical, and social sciences	1.1	1.1	1.2	0.9	1.0	0.8
Community and social services	0.9	0.6	1.3	1.7	1.3	2.1
Legal	0.4	0.2	0.7	1.3	1.2	1.4
Education, training, and library	3.2	2.0	5.1	6.3	3.1	9.8
Arts, design, entertainment, sports, and media	1.4	1.3	1.5	2.0	2.0	2.0
Health care practitioner and technical	4.4	2.6	7.2	5.1	2.4	8.0
Services	22.8	17.3	31.1	15.4	12.3	18.7
Health care support	2.5	0.6	5.4	2.1	0.4	3.9
Protective services	0.8	1.0	0.5	2.4	3.5	1.1
Food preparation and serving related	7.5	7.1	8.1	4.8	3.7	6.1
Building and grounds cleaning and maintenance	8.3	7.4	9.7	2.9	3.5	2.2
Personal care and services	3.6	1.2	7.4	3.2	1.3	5.3
Sales and office	17.5	12.4	25.1	26.2	17.9	35.2
Sales and related	9.1	7.8	11.0	11.9	11.4	12.4
Office and administrative support	8.4	4.7	14.1	14.3	6.5	22.8
Natural resources, construction, and maintenance	16.4	26.0	1.7	9.7	17.8	0.9
Farming, fishing, and forestry	1.6	2.1	0.9	0.5	0.7	0.2
Construction and extraction	11.8	19.1	0.5	5.6	10.3	0.4
Installation, maintenance, and repair	3.0	4.8	0.3	3.7	6.8	0.3
Production, transportation, and material moving	16.2	19.2	11.7	11.7	17.6	5.3
Production	9.3	9.6	8.8	5.9	8.1	3.5
Transportation and material moving	6.9	9.6	2.9	5.8	9.5	1.9

Occupation	2008					
	Foreign born			Native born		
	Both sexes	Male	Female	Both sexes	Male	Female
TOTAL EMPLOYED	22 660	13 578	9 082	122 703	63 908	58 795
Percent Employed	100.0	100.0	100.0	100.0	100.0	100.0
Management, professional, and related	28.2	25.9	31.5	37.8	35.1	40.7
Management, business, and financial operations	10.8	10.6	11.0	16.0	17.5	14.3
Management	7.7	8.3	6.8	11.5	13.8	9.0
Business and financial operations	3.1	2.3	4.2	4.5	3.8	5.3
Professional and related	17.4	15.3	20.5	21.8	17.6	26.4
Computer and mathematical	3.6	4.7	2.1	2.3	3.3	1.2
Architecture and engineering	2.0	2.9	0.8	2.0	3.4	0.6
Life, physical, and social sciences	1.2	1.2	1.2	0.9	0.9	0.8
Community and social services	0.9	0.7	1.1	1.7	1.3	2.2
Legal	0.4	0.3	0.7	1.3	1.2	1.4
Education, training, and library	3.3	1.8	5.4	6.4	3.1	10.0
Arts, design, entertainment, sports, and media	1.4	1.2	1.6	2.0	2.0	2.0
Health care practitioner and technical	4.6	2.6	7.8	5.2	2.4	8.2
Services	23.2	17.7	31.3	15.6	12.6	18.9
Health care support	2.5	0.5	5.4	2.2	0.5	4.0
Protective services	0.9	1.1	0.6	2.3	3.4	1.1
Food preparation and serving related	7.5	7.3	7.7	5.0	3.8	6.3
Building and grounds cleaning and maintenance	8.2	7.2	9.7	2.9	3.6	2.2
Personal care and services	4.1	1.5	7.9	3.3	1.3	5.3
Sales and office	17.2	12.4	24.3	25.8	17.8	34.5
Sales and related	8.9	7.8	10.6	11.6	11.2	12.1
Office and administrative support	8.3	4.6	13.8	14.2	6.6	22.4
Natural resources, construction, and maintenance	15.1	24.2	1.5	9.3	17.0	0.8
Farming, fishing, and forestry	1.7	2.2	0.9	0.5	0.7	0.2
Construction and extraction	10.4	17.2	0.4	5.1	9.6	0.3
Installation, maintenance, and repair	3.0	4.8	0.2	3.6	6.7	0.3
Production, transportation, and material moving	16.4	19.7	11.3	11.5	17.4	5.0
Production	9.3	9.9	8.4	5.6	7.8	3.2
Transportation and material moving	7.1	9.9	2.9	5.9	9.6	1.8

Note: Due to the introduction of revised population controls in January 2008, estimated levels for 2008 are not strictly comparable with those for 2007.

Table 1-55. Median Usual Weekly Earnings of Full-Time Wage and Salary Workers for the Foreign-Born and Native-Born Populations, by Selected Characteristics, 2007–2008 Annual Averages

(Thousands of people, dollars, percent.)

Year and characteristic	Foreign born		Native born		Earnings of foreign born as a percent of earnings of native born[1]
	Number	Median weekly earnings	Number	Median weekly earnings	
2007					
Both Sexes, 16 Years and Over	17 876	554	89 463	722	76.8
Men	11 329	585	48 969	809	72.3
Women	6 547	509	40 494	627	81.2
Age					
16 to 24 years	1 650	391	9 599	435	89.8
25 to 34 years	5 078	520	20 792	669	77.8
35 to 44 years	5 186	604	21 814	807	74.7
45 to 54 years	3 816	615	22 877	817	75.2
55 to 64 years	1 761	632	12 435	828	76.3
65 years and over	386	518	1 946	622	83.3
Race and Hispanic Origin					
White, non-Hispanic	3 084	805	68 484	762	105.6
Black, non-Hispanic	1 442	585	11 160	569	102.8
Asian, non-Hispanic	3 876	832	1 188	832	100.0
Hispanic[2]	9 297	448	6 904	605	74.0
Educational Attainment					
Total, 25 years and over	16 225	586	79 864	763	76.7
Less than a high school diploma	4 582	405	4 164	479	84.6
High school graduate, no college[3]	3 928	511	24 069	617	82.9
Some college	2 539	617	23 651	714	86.5
Bachelor's degree or higher[4]	5 177	1 057	27 980	1 075	98.3
2008					
Both Sexes, 16 Years and Over	17 328	595	89 320	744	79.9
Men	10 848	613	48 591	842	72.9
Women	6 480	557	40 729	651	85.5
Age					
16 to 24 years	1 337	402	9 284	451	89.1
25 to 34 years	4 786	572	20 857	689	83.0
35 to 44 years	5 118	635	21 290	842	75.4
45 to 54 years	3 846	663	22 794	848	78.2
55 to 64 years	1 849	661	12 914	849	77.9
65 years and over	392	568	2 181	659	86.2
Race and Hispanic Origin					
White, non-Hispanic	2 984	846	68 334	788	107.3
Black, non-Hispanic	1 472	601	10 905	588	102.2
Asian, non-Hispanic	3 988	864	1 184	865	99.8
Hispanic[2]	8 686	483	7 122	621	77.8
Educational Attainment					
Total, 25 years and over	15 992	614	80 036	788	78.0
Less than a high school diploma	4 213	417	3 908	493	84.6
High school graduates, no college[3]	3 920	523	23 472	633	82.7
Some college	2 582	651	23 944	729	89.3
Bachelor's degree and higher[4]	5 277	1 092	28 713	1 119	97.6

Note: Due to the introduction of revised population controls in January 2008, estimated levels for 2008 are not strictly comparable with those for 2007. Data for race/ethnicity groups do not sum to total because data are not presented for all races.

[1]These figures are computed using unrounded medians and may differ slightly from percentages computed using the rounded medians displayed in this table.
[2]May be of any race.
[3]Includes persons with a high school diploma or equivalent.
[4]Includes persons with bachelor's, master's, professional, and doctoral degrees.

Table 1-56. Percent Distribution of the Civilian Labor Force Age 25 to 64 Years, by Educational Attainment, Sex, and Race, March 1990–March 2009

(Thousands of people, percent.)

Sex, race, and year	Civilian labor force	Percent distribution				
		Total	Less than a high school diploma	4 years of high school only	1 to 3 years of college	4 or more years of college
Both Sexes						
1990	99 175	100.0	13.4	39.5	20.7	26.4
1991	100 480	100.0	13.0	39.4	21.1	26.5
1992	102 387	100.0	12.2	36.2	25.2	26.4
1993	103 504	100.0	11.5	35.2	26.3	27.0
1994	104 868	100.0	11.0	34.0	27.7	27.3
1995	106 519	100.0	10.8	33.1	27.8	28.3
1996	108 037	100.0	10.9	32.9	27.7	28.5
1997	110 514	100.0	10.9	33.0	27.4	28.6
1998	111 857	100.0	10.7	32.8	27.4	29.1
1999	112 542	100.0	10.3	32.3	27.4	30.0
2000	114 052	100.0	9.8	31.8	27.9	30.4
2001	115 073	100.0	9.8	31.4	28.1	30.7
2002	117 738	100.0	10.1	30.6	27.7	31.6
2003	119 261	100.0	10.1	30.1	27.8	31.9
2004	119 392	100.0	9.7	30.1	27.8	32.4
2005	120 461	100.0	9.8	30.1	27.8	32.3
2006	122 541	100.0	9.8	29.6	28.0	32.6
2007	124 581	100.0	9.8	29.3	27.3	33.6
2008	125 493	100.0	9.0	28.8	27.9	34.4
2009	125 655	100.0	9.0	28.7	27.9	34.3
Men						
1990	54 476	100.0	15.1	37.2	19.7	28.0
1991	55 165	100.0	14.7	37.5	20.2	27.6
1992	55 917	100.0	13.9	34.7	23.8	27.5
1993	56 544	100.0	13.2	33.9	24.7	28.1
1994	56 633	100.0	12.7	32.9	25.8	28.6
1995	57 454	100.0	12.2	32.3	25.7	29.7
1996	58 121	100.0	12.7	32.2	26.0	29.1
1997	59 268	100.0	12.8	32.2	25.8	29.2
1990	59 905	100.0	12.3	32.3	25.8	20.6
1999	60 030	100.0	11.7	32.0	25.8	30.5
2000	60 510	100.0	11.1	31.8	26.1	30.9
2001	61 091	100.0	11.0	31.6	26.3	31.1
2002	62 794	100.0	11.8	30.6	25.9	31.7
2003	63 466	100.0	12.0	30.1	25.8	32.1
2004	63 699	100.0	11.5	30.5	25.8	32.2
2005	64 562	100.0	11.6	31.4	25.4	31.6
2006	65 708	100.0	11.8	30.7	25.7	31.8
2007	66 742	100.0	11.7	30.6	25.1	32.7
2008	66 957	100.0	11.0	30.3	25.8	33.0
2009	66 843	100.0	10.8	30.4	26.0	32.8
Women						
1990	44 699	100.0	11.3	42.4	21.9	24.5
1991	45 315	100.0	10.9	41.6	22.2	25.2
1992	46 469	100.0	10.2	37.9	26.9	25.0
1993	46 961	100.0	9.3	36.7	28.2	25.8
1994	48 235	100.0	9.1	35.3	29.8	25.8
1995	49 065	100.0	9.1	34.1	30.2	26.6
1996	49 916	100.0	8.8	33.7	29.7	27.8
1997	51 246	100.0	8.7	34.0	29.3	28.0
1998	51 953	100.0	8.8	33.3	29.3	28.6
1999	52 512	100.0	8.7	32.7	29.2	29.5
2000	53 541	100.0	8.4	31.8	30.0	29.8
2001	53 982	100.0	8.5	31.1	30.1	30.2
2002	54 944	100.0	8.2	30.6	29.7	31.5
2003	55 795	100.0	8.0	30.1	30.1	31.8
2004	55 693	100.0	7.7	29.6	30.2	32.5
2005	55 899	100.0	7.8	28.6	30.5	33.1
2006	56 833	100.0	7.6	28.2	30.6	33.6
2007	57 839	100.0	7.5	27.9	29.9	34.6
2008	58 536	100.0	6.7	27.0	30.4	35.9
2009	58 811	100.0	7.0	26.9	30.2	35.9

Table 1-56. Percent Distribution of the Civilian Labor Force Age 25 to 64 Years, by Educational Attainment, Sex, and Race, March 1990–March 2009—*Continued*

(Thousands of people, percent.)

Sex, race, and year	Civilian labor force	Percent distribution				
		Total	Less than a high school diploma	4 years of high school only	1 to 3 years of college	4 or more years of college
White[1]						
1990	85 238	100.0	12.6	39.6	20.6	27.1
1991	86 344	100.0	12.2	39.3	21.1	27.4
1992	87 656	100.0	11.3	36.1	25.5	27.1
1993	88 457	100.0	10.7	35.0	26.4	27.9
1994	89 009	100.0	10.5	33.7	27.7	28.1
1995	90 192	100.0	10.0	32.8	27.8	29.3
1996	91 506	100.0	10.4	32.8	27.5	29.3
1997	93 179	100.0	10.4	32.8	27.3	29.5
1998	93 527	100.0	10.2	32.7	27.4	29.8
1999	94 216	100.0	9.8	32.2	27.2	30.8
2000	95 073	100.0	9.5	31.8	27.7	31.0
2001	95 562	100.0	9.5	31.0	28.0	31.4
2002	97 699	100.0	9.8	30.6	27.6	32.0
2003	98 241	100.0	9.9	30.0	27.7	32.4
2004	98 030	100.0	9.5	29.8	27.8	32.9
2005	98 581	100.0	9.7	29.8	27.8	32.7
2006	100 205	100.0	9.7	29.3	28.1	32.9
2007	101 548	100.0	9.7	29.1	27.3	33.9
2008	102 077	100.0	8.9	28.7	27.8	34.6
2009	102 261	100.0	9.1	28.6	27.7	34.6
Black[1]						
1990	10 537	100.0	19.9	42.5	22.1	15.5
1991	10 650	100.0	19.5	42.9	22.1	15.4
1992	10 936	100.0	19.2	40.3	24.9	15.6
1993	11 051	100.0	16.8	39.5	27.6	16.1
1994	11 368	100.0	14.5	39.3	29.2	17.0
1995	11 695	100.0	14.1	38.6	29.6	17.7
1996	11 891	100.0	14.2	37.2	31.2	17.4
1997	12 253	100.0	14.3	37.8	31.3	16.6
1998	12 893	100.0	14.3	37.3	30.1	18.2
1999	12 945	100.0	13.0	37.2	30.4	19.5
2000	13 383	100.0	11.8	36.1	31.5	20.7
2001	13 617	100.0	12.0	37.1	31.1	19.8
2002	13 319	100.0	12.4	34.5	32.0	21.0
2003	13 315	100.0	11.3	35.6	31.5	21.6
2004	13 372	100.0	11.0	36.6	30.5	21.9
2005	13 635	100.0	11.2	37.3	29.9	21.6
2006	13 855	100.0	10.9	35.6	30.4	23.0
2007	14 186	100.0	10.1	35.4	31.4	23.1
2008	14 356	100.0	9.5	34.3	32.1	24.1
2009	14 325	100.0	8.5	35.1	33.0	23.5

[1]Beginning in 2003, persons who selected this race group only; persons who selected more than one race group are not included. Prior to 2003, persons who reported more than one race group were included in the group they identified as their main race.

Table 1-57. Labor Force Participation Rates of Persons Age 25 to 64 Years, by Educational Attainment, Sex, and Race, March 1990–March 2009

(Civilian labor force as a percent of the civilian noninstitutional population.)

Sex, race, and year	Participation rates				
	Total	Less than a high school diploma	4 years of high school only	1 to 3 years of college	4 or more years of college
Both Sexes					
1990	78.6	60.7	78.2	83.3	88.4
1991	78.6	60.7	78.1	83.2	88.4
1992	79.0	60.3	78.3	83.5	88.4
1993	78.9	59.6	77.7	82.9	88.3
1994	78.9	58.3	77.8	83.2	88.2
1995	79.3	59.8	77.3	83.2	88.7
1996	79.4	60.2	77.9	83.7	87.8
1997	80.1	61.7	78.5	83.7	88.5
1998	80.2	63.0	78.4	83.5	88.0
1999	80.0	62.7	78.1	83.0	87.6
2000	80.3	62.7	78.4	83.2	87.8
2001	80.2	63.5	78.4	83.0	87.0
2002	79.7	63.5	77.7	82.1	86.7
2003	79.4	64.1	76.9	81.9	86.2
2004	78.8	63.2	76.1	81.2	85.9
2005	78.5	62.9	75.7	81.1	85.7
2006	78.7	63.2	75.9	81.0	85.9
2007	79.0	63.7	76.3	81.1	85.9
2008	79.0	62.5	76.0	80.9	86.1
2009	78.6	62.3	75.7	80.3	85.9
Men					
1990	88.8	75.1	89.9	91.5	94.5
1991	88.6	75.1	89.3	92.0	94.2
1992	88.6	75.1	89.0	91.8	93.7
1993	88.1	74.9	88.1	90.6	93.7
1994	87.0	71.5	86.8	90.3	93.2
1995	87.4	72.0	86.9	90.1	93.8
1996	87.5	74.3	86.9	90.0	92.9
1997	87.7	75.2	86.4	90.6	93.5
1998	87.8	75.3	86.7	90.0	93.4
1999	87.5	74.4	86.6	89.4	93.0
2000	87.5	74.9	86.2	88.9	93.3
2001	87.4	75.4	85.8	89.1	92.9
2002	87.0	75.5	85.3	88.8	92.4
2003	86.4	76.1	84.3	87.5	92.2
2004	85.9	75.2	83.8	87.0	91.9
2005	86.0	75.7	83.7	87.5	91.7
2006	86.0	76.3	83.4	87.8	91.7
2007	86.2	75.7	83.9	87.2	92.4
2008	85.8	74.8	83.6	86.5	91.9
2009	85.1	73.7	82.3	86.0	91.9
Women					
1990	68.9	46.2	68.7	75.9	81.1
1991	69.1	46.2	68.6	75.2	81.8
1992	70.0	45.6	69.1	76.2	82.2
1993	70.0	44.2	68.8	76.1	82.2
1994	71.1	44.7	70.0	77.0	82.5
1995	71.5	47.2	68.9	77.3	82.8
1996	71.8	45.7	69.8	78.1	82.3
1997	72.8	47.1	71.4	77.6	83.2
1998	73.0	49.8	70.9	77.8	82.3
1999	72.8	50.5	70.4	77.4	81.9
2000	73.5	50.4	71.2	78.3	82.0
2001	73.4	51.7	71.3	77.7	80.9
2002	72.7	50.4	70.4	76.4	81.0
2003	72.6	50.5	69.8	77.1	80.1
2004	72.0	49.7	68.6	76.2	80.0
2005	71.4	48.7	67.4	75.8	79.8
2006	71.7	48.3	68.2	75.3	80.4
2007	72.1	49.6	68.4	76.0	79.7
2008	72.5	47.9	68.2	76.1	80.9
2009	72.4	49.0	68.7	75.4	80.5

Table 1-57. Labor Force Participation Rates of Persons Age 25 to 64 Years, by Educational Attainment, Sex, and Race, March 1990–March 2009—*Continued*

(Civilian labor force as a percent of the civilian noninstitutional population.)

Sex, race, and year	Participation rates				
	Total	Less than a high school diploma	4 years of high school only	1 to 3 years of college	4 or more years of college
White[1]					
1990	79.2	62.5	78.4	83.3	88.3
1991	79.4	62.5	78.3	83.1	88.6
1992	79.8	61.5	78.7	83.8	88.7
1993	79.7	61.1	78.2	83.1	88.8
1994	79.8	60.3	78.3	83.5	88.5
1995	80.1	61.6	77.9	83.4	88.8
1996	80.4	62.5	78.6	83.9	88.2
1997	81.0	63.8	79.2	83.9	89.0
1998	80.6	63.8	78.6	83.5	88.3
1999	80.6	64.2	78.5	83.3	87.9
2000	80.8	64.2	78.7	83.1	87.9
2001	80.7	64.5	78.7	83.1	87.2
2002	80.3	65.0	78.2	82.4	87.0
2003	80.1	65.7	77.5	82.3	86.5
2004	79.5	64.6	76.7	81.6	86.2
2005	79.2	63.8	76.4	81.5	86.1
2006	79.5	65.1	76.5	81.4	86.2
2007	79.6	65.1	77.2	81.4	86.1
2008	79.6	63.8	76.8	81.2	86.3
2009	79.4	64.7	76.4	80.7	86.2
Black[1]					
1990	74.6	54.5	78.2	84.2	92.0
1991	73.9	53.9	77.1	84.1	90.2
1992	74.4	55.4	76.9	83.4	89.1
1993	73.8	53.4	74.7	83.0	89.6
1994	73.5	49.4	75.2	82.4	89.5
1995	74.2	51.0	74.5	82.8	90.9
1996	73.7	50.1	74.3	83.0	87.9
1997	74.9	52.9	75.0	83.8	89.0
1998	77.7	59.3	77.0	85.0	88.8
1999	76.5	55.1	76.5	82.9	88.6
2000	77.9	55.5	77.0	84.2	90.3
2001	78.1	58.7	76.8	83.0	90.5
2002	76.4	56.6	75.0	81.7	88.9
2003	75.8	55.4	73.9	81.2	88.2
2004	75.0	55.2	73.4	79.0	87.9
2005	75.2	58.2	72.6	79.5	87.2
2006	75.0	54.0	73.3	79.6	87.7
2007	75.6	55.3	72.5	80.7	88.0
2008	75.6	54.3	72.8	80.0	87.5
2009	74.4	50.0	72.6	78.7	86.2

[1]Beginning in 2003, persons who selected this race group only; persons who selected more than one race group are not included. Prior to 2003, persons who reported more than one race group were included in the group they identified as their main race.

Table 1-58. Unemployment Rates of Persons Age 25 to 64 Years, by Educational Attainment and Sex, March 1990–March 2009

(Unemployment as a percent of the civilian labor force.)

Sex, race, and year	Unemployment rates				
	Total	Less than a high school diploma	4 years of high school only	1 to 3 years of college	4 or more years of college
Both Sexes					
1990	4.5	9.6	4.9	3.7	1.9
1991	6.1	12.3	6.7	5.0	2.9
1992	6.7	13.5	7.7	5.9	2.9
1993	6.4	13.0	7.3	5.5	3.2
1994	5.8	12.6	6.7	5.0	2.9
1995	4.8	10.0	5.2	4.5	2.5
1996	4.8	10.9	5.5	4.1	2.2
1997	4.4	10.4	5.1	3.8	2.0
1998	4.0	8.5	4.8	3.6	1.8
1999	3.5	7.7	4.0	3.1	1.9
2000	3.3	7.9	3.8	3.0	1.5
2001	3.5	8.1	4.2	2.9	2.0
2002	5.0	10.2	6.1	4.5	2.8
2003	5.3	9.9	6.4	5.2	3.0
2004	5.1	10.5	5.9	4.9	2.9
2005	4.4	9.0	5.5	4.1	2.3
2006	4.1	8.3	4.7	3.9	2.3
2007	3.9	8.5	4.7	3.7	1.8
2008	4.4	10.1	5.8	4.2	2.1
2009	8.1	15.8	10.4	8.0	4.3
Men					
1990	4.8	9.6	5.3	3.9	2.1
1991	6.8	13.4	7.7	5.2	3.2
1992	7.5	14.8	8.8	6.4	3.2
1993	7.3	14.1	8.7	6.3	3.4
1994	6.2	12.8	7.2	5.3	2.9
1995	5.1	10.9	5.7	4.4	2.6
1996	5.3	11.0	6.4	4.5	2.3
1997	4.7	9.9	5.6	4.0	2.1
1998	4.1	8.0	5.1	3.7	1.7
1999	3.5	7.0	4.1	3.2	1.9
2000	3.3	7.1	3.9	3.1	1.6
2001	3.7	7.5	4.6	3.2	1.9
2002	5.5	9.9	6.7	4.9	3.0
2003	5.8	9.5	6.9	6.0	3.2
2004	5.4	9.4	6.6	5.4	3.0
2005	4.7	7.9	6.0	4.3	2.5
2006	4.3	7.6	5.0	4.2	2.4
2007	4.3	8.4	5.5	3.9	1.9
2008	4.9	10.9	6.3	4.2	2.0
2009	9.5	16.5	12.4	9.3	4.7
Women					
1990	4.2	9.5	4.6	3.5	1.7
1991	5.2	10.7	5.5	4.8	2.5
1992	5.7	11.4	6.5	5.3	2.5
1993	5.2	11.2	5.8	4.6	2.9
1994	5.4	12.4	6.2	4.7	2.9
1995	4.4	8.6	4.6	4.5	2.4
1996	4.1	10.7	4.4	3.8	2.1
1997	4.1	11.3	4.5	3.6	2.0
1998	3.9	9.3	4.4	3.5	1.9
1999	3.5	8.8	3.9	3.0	1.9
2000	3.2	9.1	3.6	2.9	1.4
2001	3.3	8.9	3.8	2.6	2.0
2002	4.6	10.6	5.4	4.1	2.6
2003	4.8	10.6	5.9	4.4	2.8
2004	4.7	12.2	5.2	4.3	2.9
2005	4.2	10.9	4.8	4.0	2.2
2006	3.8	9.4	4.4	3.7	2.1
2007	3.4	8.5	3.8	3.6	1.8
2008	4.0	8.5	5.1	4.2	2.1
2009	6.6	14.5	7.9	6.7	4.0

Table 1-58. Unemployment Rates of Persons Age 25 to 64 Years, by Educational Attainment and Sex, March 1990–March 2009—*Continued*

(Unemployment as a percent of the civilian labor force.)

Sex, race, and year	Unemployment rates				
	Total	Less than a high school diploma	4 years of high school only	1 to 3 years of college	4 or more years of college
White[1]					
1990	4.0	8.3	4.4	3.3	1.8
1991	5.6	11.6	6.2	4.6	2.7
1992	6.0	12.9	6.8	5.3	2.7
1993	5.8	12.4	6.5	5.0	3.1
1994	5.2	11.7	5.8	4.5	2.6
1995	4.3	9.2	4.6	4.2	2.3
1996	4.2	10.2	4.6	3.7	2.1
1997	3.9	9.4	4.6	3.4	1.8
1998	3.5	7.5	4.2	3.2	1.7
1999	3.1	7.0	3.4	2.8	1.7
2000	3.0	7.5	3.3	2.7	1.4
2001	3.1	7.2	3.6	2.7	1.8
2002	4.6	9.1	5.5	4.1	2.6
2003	4.7	9.0	5.7	4.5	2.7
2004	4.6	9.6	5.4	4.4	2.8
2005	3.9	7.7	4.9	3.6	2.2
2006	3.5	7.1	4.0	3.5	2.1
2007	3.5	7.8	4.2	3.3	1.7
2008	4.0	9.2	5.1	3.7	1.9
2009	7.6	15.2	9.9	7.4	4.0
Black[1]					
1990	8.6	15.9	8.6	6.5	1.9
1991	10.1	15.9	10.3	8.0	5.2
1992	12.4	17.2	14.1	10.7	4.8
1993	10.9	17.3	12.4	8.7	4.1
1994	10.6	17.4	12.2	8.3	4.9
1995	7.7	13.7	8.4	6.3	4.1
1996	8.9	15.3	10.8	6.9	3.3
1997	8.1	16.6	8.2	6.1	4.4
1998	7.3	13.4	8.4	6.4	2.1
1999	6.3	12.0	6.7	5.2	3.3
2000	5.4	10.4	6.3	4.3	2.5
2001	6.5	14.0	7.7	4.3	3.3
2002	8.1	15.4	9.7	6.0	4.1
2003	9.0	14.7	9.9	8.9	4.7
2004	8.4	15.8	9.3	7.9	3.7
2005	8.3	17.9	8.6	7.5	3.6
2006	7.8	16.4	9.0	6.5	3.6
2007	6.5	14.0	7.7	5.7	2.5
2008	7.6	16.7	9.3	6.5	3.3
2009	12.1	22.0	14.0	11.2	7.2

[1]Beginning in 2003, persons who selected this race group only; persons who selected more than one race group are not included. Prior to 2003, persons who reported more than one race group were included in the group they identified as their main race.

Table 1-59. Workers Age 25 to 64 Years, by Educational Attainment, Occupation of Longest Job Held, and Sex, 2007–2008

(Thousands of people with work experience during the year.)

Year, sex, and occupation	Total	Less than a high school diploma	4 years of high school only	1 to 3 years of college	4 or more years of college
2007					
Both Sexes	128 358	11 456	36 797	36 128	43 977
Management, business, and financial operations	20 278	434	3 324	5 157	11 363
Management	14 420	385	2 586	3 789	7 660
Business and financial operations	5 859	49	738	1 368	3 703
Professional and related	28 191	176	2 117	6 061	19 836
Computer and mathematical	3 493	12	280	747	2 454
Architecture and engineering	2 556	2	207	609	1 737
Life, physical, and social sciences	1 186	3	62	109	1 012
Community and social services	2 091	22	160	368	1 541
Legal	1 480	20	112	252	1 096
Education, training, and library	8 109	51	564	1 066	6 428
Arts, design, entertainment, sports, and media	2 462	33	271	620	1 538
Health care practitioner and technical	6 815	33	461	2 290	4 031
Services	18 888	3 361	7 197	5 755	2 574
Health care support	2 634	304	965	1 062	303
Protective services	2 636	70	732	1 145	689
Food preparation and serving related	4 900	1 097	2 023	1 237	543
Building and grounds cleaning and maintenance	4 820	1 456	2 080	933	351
Personal care and services	3 898	433	1 397	1 379	689
Sales and office	29 930	1 356	9 958	10 839	7 777
Sales and related	13 007	723	3 879	4 126	4 279
Office and administrative support	16 923	633	6 079	6 713	3 498
Natural resources, construction, and maintenance	13 972	2 994	6 058	3 917	1 002
Farming, fishing, and forestry	880	429	286	118	48
Construction and extraction	8 385	2 056	3 778	2 007	545
Installation, maintenance, and repair	4 706	510	1 994	1 792	410
Production, transportation, and material moving	16 522	3 127	8 010	4 139	1 246
Production	8 712	1 669	4 125	2 253	665
Transportation and material moving	7 810	1 457	3 885	1 887	581
Armed forces	577	7	132	259	179
Men	68 300	7 396	20 589	17 840	22 474
Management, business, and financial operations	11 322	327	1 895	2 584	6 516
Management	8 899	295	1 659	2 172	4 773
Business and financial operations	2 423	32	236	412	1 744
Professional and related	11 861	51	737	2 113	8 959
Computer and mathematical	2 569	7	188	562	1 812
Architecture and engineering	2 212	2	171	542	1 497
Life, physical, and social sciences	665	2	28	66	569
Community and social services	798	10	49	109	630
Legal	668	3	20	26	619
Education, training, and library	2 085	2	59	171	1 853
Arts, design, entertainment, sports, and media	1 239	20	157	336	727
Health care practitioner and technical	1 624	5	64	302	1 254
Services	7 977	1 391	2 831	2 517	1 238
Health care support	317	32	92	130	62
Protective services	2 008	53	511	906	538
Food preparation and serving related	2 128	523	801	560	244
Building and grounds cleaning and maintenance	2 783	743	1 185	611	243
Personal care and services	741	40	242	308	151
Sales and office	10 633	505	3 007	3 390	3 731
Sales and related	6 833	294	1 736	2 104	2 699
Office and administrative support	3 800	211	1 271	1 287	1 032
Natural resources, construction, and maintenance	13 347	2 853	5 841	3 741	911
Farming, fishing, and forestry	693	328	248	85	32
Construction and extraction	8 167	2 033	3 690	1 932	512
Installation, maintenance, and repair	4 487	492	1 903	1 724	367
Production, transportation, and material moving	12 630	2 262	6 152	3 255	961
Production	5 957	1 018	2 857	1 636	445
Transportation and material moving	6 674	1 244	3 295	1 618	516
Armed forces	529	7	125	240	156
Women	60 058	4 060	16 208	18 288	21 503
Management, business, and financial operations	8 956	107	1 430	2 573	4 846
Management	5 521	90	927	1 617	2 887
Business and financial operations	3 435	17	503	956	1 959
Professional and related	16 330	125	1 380	3 948	10 877
Computer and mathematical	924	5	92	184	643
Architecture and engineering	344	. . .	36	67	241
Life, physical, and social sciences	521	0	34	43	443
Community and social services	1 292	12	111	259	911
Legal	812	17	92	226	477
Education, training, and library	6 024	49	504	896	4 574
Arts, design, entertainment, sports, and media	1 222	14	114	284	811
Health care practitioner and technical	5 191	29	397	1 988	2 777
Services	10 911	1 971	4 366	3 238	1 336
Health care support	2 316	272	873	931	241
Protective services	628	18	221	238	151
Food preparation and serving related	2 772	575	1 222	677	299
Building and grounds cleaning and maintenance	2 037	713	894	322	108
Personal care and services	3 157	393	1 156	1 070	538
Sales and office	19 297	851	6 951	7 449	4 046
Sales and related	6 175	430	2 143	2 023	1 579
Office and administrative support	13 122	421	4 808	5 426	2 467
Natural resources, construction, and maintenance	625	141	217	176	91
Farming, fishing, and forestry	187	101	38	33	16
Construction and extraction	219	23	88	75	33
Installation, maintenance, and repair	219	18	91	68	42
Production, transportation, and material moving	3 892	865	1 858	885	285
Production	2 755	651	1 268	617	219
Transportation and material moving	1 137	214	590	268	66
Armed forces	48	. . .	7	18	22

. . . = Not available.

Table 1-59. Workers Age 25 to 64 Years, by Educational Attainment, Occupation of Longest Job Held, and Sex, 2007–2008—*Continued*

(Thousands of people with work experience during the year.)

Year, sex, and occupation	Total	Less than a high school diploma	4 years of high school only	1 to 3 years of college	4 or more years of college
2008					
Both Sexes	128 339	11 478	36 732	36 103	44 027
Management, business, and financial operations	20 566	406	3 516	5 037	11 608
Management	14 645	360	2 768	3 595	7 923
Business and financial operations	5 921	45	748	1 442	3 685
Professional and related	28 527	167	2 117	6 279	19 965
Computer and mathematical	3 494	14	240	828	2 412
Architecture and engineering	2 574	4	228	643	1 699
Life, physical, and social sciences	1 242	1	67	138	1 036
Community and social services	2 065	27	178	351	1 509
Legal	1 545	3	86	218	1 238
Education, training, and library	8 201	41	547	1 112	6 501
Arts, design, entertainment, sports, and media	2 404	49	293	552	1 510
Health care practitioner and technical	7 001	27	477	2 437	4 060
Services	19 346	3 536	7 368	5 877	2 565
Health care support	2 762	267	970	1 220	305
Protective services	2 594	90	707	1 089	708
Food preparation and serving related	5 056	1 143	2 129	1 227	557
Building and grounds cleaning and maintenance	4 886	1 496	2 118	958	313
Personal care and services	4 048	539	1 444	1 382	682
Sales and office	29 191	1 375	9 606	10 798	7 412
Sales and related	12 864	768	3 764	4 103	4 230
Office and administrative support	16 326	607	5 842	6 695	3 183
Natural resources, construction, and maintenance	13 756	2 878	6 121	3 773	984
Farming, fishing, and forestry	891	446	286	100	58
Construction and extraction	8 094	1 962	3 754	1 850	528
Installation, maintenance, and repair	4 771	470	2 081	1 822	398
Production, transportation, and material moving	16 323	3 112	7 869	4 066	1 276
Production	8 206	1 618	3 853	2 092	642
Transportation and material moving	8 117	1 494	4 016	1 974	633
Armed forces	631	4	136	274	217
Men	68 130	7 341	20 570	17 879	22 340
Management, business, and financial operations	11 549	286	1 937	2 646	6 680
Management	9 098	271	1 757	2 179	4 891
Business and financial operations	2 452	15	179	468	1 790
Professional and related	11 866	75	741	2 259	8 792
Computer and mathematical	2 593	13	172	607	1 801
Architecture and engineering	2 240	2	177	575	1 485
Life, physical, and social sciences	634	1	34	80	519
Community and social services	709	17	56	115	521
Legal	753	3	15	23	712
Education, training, and library	2 008	3	46	166	1 793
Arts, design, entertainment, sports, and media	1 240	30	178	306	727
Health care practitioner and technical	1 690	6	64	387	1 233
Services	7 910	1 455	2 902	2 365	1 188
Health care support	258	20	80	100	58
Protective services	1 961	59	517	863	522
Food preparation and serving related	2 139	511	864	522	242
Building and grounds cleaning and maintenance	2 784	802	1 171	620	191
Personal care and services	768	63	270	259	176
Sales and office	10 468	539	2 884	3 479	3 566
Sales and related	6 756	303	1 674	2 104	2 675
Office and administrative support	3 712	237	1 210	1 375	890
Natural resources, construction, and maintenance	13 166	2 735	5 910	3 612	909
Farming, fishing, and forestry	680	341	233	64	41
Construction and extraction	7 901	1 942	3 666	1 790	502
Installation, maintenance, and repair	4 585	452	2 011	1 757	365
Production, transportation, and material moving	12 591	2 248	6 071	3 265	1 008
Production	5 803	1 043	2 715	1 610	435
Transportation and material moving	6 788	1 204	3 356	1 655	573
Armed forces	579	3	126	253	197
Women	60 209	4 137	16 162	18 224	21 687
Management, business, and financial operations	9 017	120	1 579	2 391	4 927
Management	5 548	90	1 011	1 416	3 032
Business and financial operations	3 469	30	569	975	1 896
Professional and related	16 660	92	1 376	4 020	11 173
Computer and mathematical	902	1	68	221	611
Architecture and engineering	334	2	51	68	214
Life, physical, and social sciences	608	. . .	33	58	517
Community and social services	1 356	10	122	236	988
Legal	792	. . .	71	194	526
Education, training, and library	6 193	38	501	946	4 708
Arts, design, entertainment, sports, and media	1 164	19	115	247	783
Health care practitioner and technical	5 311	21	414	2 050	2 826
Services	11 435	2 081	4 465	3 512	1 377
Health care support	2 504	247	890	1 119	247
Protective services	632	31	189	226	186
Food preparation and serving related	2 918	633	1 264	706	315
Building and grounds cleaning and maintenance	2 102	694	947	338	123
Personal care and services	3 279	476	1 174	1 123	507
Sales and office	18 723	836	6 722	7 319	3 846
Sales and related	6 108	465	2 090	1 999	1 554
Office and administrative support	12 614	370	4 632	5 320	2 292
Natural resources, construction, and maintenance	591	142	212	161	75
Farming, fishing, and forestry	211	104	54	36	17
Construction and extraction	193	20	88	60	26
Installation, maintenance, and repair	186	18	70	65	32
Production, transportation, and material moving	3 731	865	1 798	801	267
Production	2 402	575	1 138	482	207
Transportation and material moving	1 329	290	660	319	61
Armed forces	52	1	10	21	20

. . . = Not available.

Table 1-60. Percent Distribution of Workers Age 25 to 64 Years, by Educational Attainment, Occupation of Longest Job Held, and Sex, 2007–2008

(Percent of total workers in occupation.)

Year, sex, and occupation	Total	Less than a high school diploma	4 years of high school only	1 to 3 years of college	4 or more years of college
2007					
Both Sexes	100.0	8.9	28.7	28.1	34.3
Management, business, and financial operations	100.0	2.1	16.4	25.4	56.0
Management	100.0	2.7	17.9	26.3	53.1
Business and financial operations	100.0	0.8	12.6	23.4	63.2
Professional and related	100.0	0.6	7.5	21.5	70.4
Computer and mathematical	100.0	0.3	8.0	21.4	70.3
Architecture and engineering	100.0	0.1	8.1	23.8	68.0
Life, physical, and social sciences	100.0	0.2	5.2	9.2	85.3
Community and social services	100.0	1.0	7.7	17.6	73.7
Legal	100.0	1.4	7.6	17.0	74.1
Education, training, and library	100.0	0.6	7.0	13.2	79.3
Arts, design, entertainment, sports, and media	100.0	1.4	11.0	25.2	62.5
Health care practitioner and technical	100.0	0.5	6.8	33.6	59.1
Services	100.0	17.8	38.1	30.5	13.6
Health care support	100.0	11.5	36.6	40.3	11.5
Protective services	100.0	2.7	27.8	43.4	26.1
Food preparation and serving related	100.0	22.4	41.3	25.2	11.1
Building and grounds cleaning and maintenance	100.0	30.2	43.1	19.4	7.3
Personal care and services	100.0	11.1	35.8	35.4	17.7
Sales and office	100.0	4.5	33.3	36.2	26.0
Sales and related	100.0	5.6	29.8	31.7	32.9
Office and administrative support	100.0	3.7	35.9	39.7	20.7
Natural resources, construction, and maintenance	100.0	21.4	43.4	28.0	7.2
Farming, fishing, and forestry	100.0	48.7	32.5	13.4	5.4
Construction and extraction	100.0	24.5	45.1	23.9	6.5
Installation, maintenance, and repair	100.0	10.8	42.4	38.1	8.7
Production, transportation, and material moving	100.0	18.9	48.5	25.1	7.5
Production	100.0	19.2	47.4	25.9	7.6
Transportation and material moving	100.0	18.7	49.7	24.2	7.4
Armed forces	100.0	1.2	23.0	44.8	31.0
Men	100.0	. . .	. . .	. . .	. . .
Management, business, and financial operations	100.0	2.9	16.7	22.8	57.6
Management	100.0	3.3	18.6	24.4	53.6
Business and financial operations	100.0	1.3	9.7	17.0	72.0
Professional and related	100.0	0.4	6.2	17.8	75.5
Computer and mathematical	100.0	0.3	7.3	21.9	70.5
Architecture and engineering	100.0	0.1	7.7	24.5	67.7
Life, physical, and social sciences	100.0	0.4	4.2	9.9	85.5
Community and social services	100.0	1.3	6.2	13.7	78.9
Legal	100.0	0.4	3.0	3.9	92.7
Education, training, and library	100.0	0.1	2.9	8.2	88.9
Arts, design, entertainment, sports, and media	100.0	1.6	12.7	27.1	58.6
Health care practitioner and technical	100.0	0.3	3.9	18.6	77.2
Services	100.0	17.4	35.5	31.5	15.5
Health care support	100.0	10.1	29.1	41.1	19.6
Protective services	100.0	2.6	25.4	45.1	26.8
Food preparation and serving related	100.0	24.6	37.6	26.3	11.5
Building and grounds cleaning and maintenance	100.0	26.7	42.6	22.0	8.7
Personal care and services	100.0	5.4	32.6	41.6	20.4
Sales and office	100.0	4.8	28.3	31.9	35.1
Sales and related	100.0	4.3	25.4	30.8	39.5
Office and administrative support	100.0	5.6	33.4	33.9	27.1
Natural resources, construction, and maintenance	100.0	21.4	43.8	28.0	6.8
Farming, fishing, and forestry	100.0	47.3	35.8	12.2	4.7
Construction and extraction	100.0	24.9	45.2	23.7	6.3
Installation, maintenance, and repair	100.0	11.0	42.4	38.4	8.2
Production, transportation, and material moving	100.0	17.9	48.7	25.8	7.6
Production	100.0	17.1	48.0	27.5	7.5
Transportation and material moving	100.0	18.6	49.4	24.3	7.7
Armed forces	100.0	1.3	23.7	45.4	29.6
Women	100.0	. . .	. . .	. . .	. . .
Management, business, and financial operations	100.0	1.2	16.0	28.7	54.1
Management	100.0	1.6	16.8	29.3	52.3
Business and financial operations	100.0	0.5	14.6	27.8	57.0
Professional and related	100.0	0.8	8.4	24.2	66.6
Computer and mathematical	100.0	0.6	9.9	19.9	69.6
Architecture and engineering	100.0	0.0	10.4	19.6	70.0
Life, physical, and social sciences	100.0	0.1	6.5	8.3	85.1
Community and social services	100.0	0.9	8.6	20.1	70.5
Legal	100.0	2.1	11.3	27.8	58.7
Education, training, and library	100.0	0.8	8.4	14.9	75.9
Arts, design, entertainment, sports, and media	100.0	1.1	9.3	23.3	66.3
Health care practitioner and technical	100.0	0.6	7.7	38.3	53.5
Services	100.0	18.1	40.0	29.7	12.2
Health care support	100.0	11.7	37.7	40.2	10.4
Protective services	100.0	2.8	35.2	37.9	24.0
Food preparation and serving related	100.0	20.7	44.1	24.4	10.8
Building and grounds cleaning and maintenance	100.0	35.0	43.9	15.8	5.3
Personal care and services	100.0	12.5	36.6	33.9	17.0
Sales and office	100.0	4.4	36.0	38.6	21.0
Sales and related	100.0	7.0	34.7	32.8	25.6
Office and administrative support	100.0	3.2	36.6	41.4	18.8
Natural resources, construction, and maintenance	100.0	22.6	34.7	28.1	14.6
Farming, fishing, and forestry	100.0	53.7	20.2	17.8	8.3
Construction and extraction	100.0	10.5	40.2	34.2	15.1
Installation, maintenance, and repair	100.0	8.1	41.6	30.9	19.4
Production, transportation, and material moving	100.0	22.2	47.7	22.7	7.3
Production	100.0	23.6	46.0	22.4	8.0
Transportation and material moving	100.0	18.8	51.9	23.6	5.8
Armed forces	100.0	. . .	15.0	38.2	46.7

. . . = Not available.

Table 1-60. Percent Distribution of Workers Age 25 to 64 Years, by Educational Attainment, Occupation of Longest Job Held, and Sex, 2007–2008—*Continued*

(Percent of total workers in occupation.)

Year, sex, and occupation	Total	Less than a high school diploma	4 years of high school only	1 to 3 years of college	4 or more years of college
2008					
Both Sexes	100.0	8.9	28.6	28.1	34.3
Management, business, and financial operations	100.0	2.0	17.1	24.5	56.4
Management	100.0	2.5	18.9	24.5	54.1
Business and financial operations	100.0	0.8	12.6	24.4	62.2
Professional and related	100.0	0.6	7.4	22.0	70.0
Computer and mathematical	100.0	0.4	6.9	23.7	69.0
Architecture and engineering	100.0	0.1	8.9	25.0	66.0
Life, physical, and social sciences	100.0	0.1	5.4	11.1	83.4
Community and social services	100.0	1.3	8.6	17.0	73.1
Legal	100.0	0.2	5.6	14.1	80.1
Education, training, and library	100.0	0.5	6.7	13.6	79.3
Arts, design, entertainment, sports, and media	100.0	2.0	12.2	23.0	62.8
Health care practitioner and technical	100.0	0.4	6.8	34.8	58.0
Services	100.0	18.3	38.1	30.4	13.3
Health care support	100.0	9.7	35.1	44.2	11.0
Protective services	100.0	3.5	27.2	42.0	27.3
Food preparation and serving related	100.0	22.6	42.1	24.3	11.0
Building and grounds cleaning and maintenance	100.0	30.6	43.3	19.6	6.4
Personal care and services	100.0	13.3	35.7	34.1	16.9
Sales and office	100.0	4.7	32.9	37.0	25.4
Sales and related	100.0	6.0	29.3	31.9	32.9
Office and administrative support	100.0	3.7	35.8	41.0	19.5
Natural resources, construction, and maintenance	100.0	20.9	44.5	27.4	7.2
Farming, fishing, and forestry	100.0	50.0	32.1	11.3	6.6
Construction and extraction	100.0	24.2	46.4	22.9	6.5
Installation, maintenance, and repair	100.0	9.9	43.6	38.2	8.3
Production, transportation, and material moving	100.0	19.1	48.2	24.9	7.8
Production	100.0	19.7	47.0	25.5	7.8
Transportation and material moving	100.0	18.4	49.5	24.3	7.8
Armed forces	100.0	0.7	21.5	43.5	34.4
Men	100.0	10.8	30.2	26.2	32.8
Management, business, and financial operations	100.0	2.5	16.8	22.9	57.8
Management	100.0	3.0	19.3	24.0	53.8
Business and financial operations	100.0	0.6	7.3	19.1	73.0
Professional and related	100.0	0.6	6.2	19.0	74.1
Computer and mathematical	100.0	0.5	6.6	23.4	69.4
Architecture and engineering	100.0	0.1	7.9	25.7	66.3
Life, physical, and social sciences	100.0	0.1	5.4	12.6	81.9
Community and social services	100.0	2.3	7.9	16.3	73.5
Legal	100.0	0.5	1.9	3.1	94.5
Education, training, and library	100.0	0.1	2.3	8.3	89.3
Arts, design, entertainment, sports, and media	100.0	2.4	14.3	24.7	58.6
Health care practitioner and technical	100.0	0.4	3.8	22.9	73.0
Services	100.0	18.4	36.7	29.9	15.0
Health care support	100.0	7.7	31.0	38.8	22.5
Protective services	100.0	3.0	26.4	44.0	26.6
Food preparation and serving related	100.0	23.9	40.4	24.4	11.3
Building and grounds cleaning and maintenance	100.0	28.8	42.0	22.3	6.8
Personal care and services	100.0	8.3	35.1	33.7	22.9
Sales and office	100.0	5.2	27.5	33.2	34.1
Sales and related	100.0	4.5	24.8	31.1	39.6
Office and administrative support	100.0	6.4	32.6	37.0	24.0
Natural resources, construction, and maintenance	100.0	20.8	44.9	27.4	6.9
Farming, fishing, and forestry	100.0	50.2	34.2	9.5	6.1
Construction and extraction	100.0	24.6	46.4	22.7	6.4
Installation, maintenance, and repair	100.0	9.9	43.9	38.3	8.0
Production, transportation, and material moving	100.0	17.9	48.2	25.9	8.0
Production	100.0	18.0	46.8	27.7	7.5
Transportation and material moving	100.0	17.7	49.4	24.4	8.4
Armed forces	100.0	0.5	21.8	43.8	34.0
Women	100.0	6.9	26.8	30.3	36.0
Management, business, and financial operations	100.0	1.3	17.5	26.5	54.6
Management	100.0	1.6	18.2	25.5	54.7
Business and financial operations	100.0	0.9	16.4	28.1	54.6
Professional and related	100.0	0.6	8.3	24.1	67.1
Computer and mathematical	100.0	0.1	7.5	24.6	67.8
Architecture and engineering	100.0	0.5	15.2	20.4	63.9
Life, physical, and social sciences	100.0	0.0	5.5	9.5	85.0
Community and social services	100.0	0.8	9.0	17.4	72.8
Legal	100.0	0.0	9.0	24.6	66.4
Education, training, and library	100.0	0.6	8.1	15.3	76.0
Arts, design, entertainment, sports, and media	100.0	1.7	9.9	21.2	67.3
Health care practitioner and technical	100.0	0.4	7.8	38.6	53.2
Services	100.0	18.2	39.0	30.7	12.0
Health care support	100.0	9.9	35.6	44.7	9.9
Protective services	100.0	4.9	29.9	35.8	29.4
Food preparation and serving related	100.0	21.7	43.3	24.2	10.8
Building and grounds cleaning and maintenance	100.0	33.0	45.1	16.1	5.8
Personal care and services	100.0	14.5	35.8	34.2	15.4
Sales and office	100.0	4.5	35.9	39.1	20.5
Sales and related	100.0	7.6	34.2	32.7	25.4
Office and administrative support	100.0	2.9	36.7	42.2	18.2
Natural resources, construction, and maintenance	100.0	24.1	35.8	27.3	12.8
Farming, fishing, and forestry	100.0	49.4	25.4	17.1	8.1
Construction and extraction	100.0	10.2	45.5	30.9	13.4
Installation, maintenance, and repair	100.0	9.9	37.6	35.1	17.3
Production, transportation, and material moving	100.0	23.2	48.2	21.5	7.2
Production	100.0	23.9	47.4	20.1	8.6
Transportation and material moving	100.0	21.8	49.7	24.0	4.6
Armed forces	100.0	2.6	18.6	40.2	38.6

Table 1-61. Median Annual Earnings of Year-Round, Full-Time Wage and Salary Workers Age 25 to 64 Years, by Educational Attainment and Sex, 1997–2008

(Thousands of workers, dollars.)

Year and sex	Total	Less than a high school diploma	4 years of high school only	1 to 3 years of college	4 or more years of college
1997					
Both Sexes					
Number of workers	78 524	7 218	25 432	21 742	24 131
Median annual earnings	30 000	19 000	25 740	30 000	44 000
Men					
Number of workers	45 976	4 873	14 686	12 126	14 291
Median annual earnings	35 000	21 840	30 000	35 000	50 000
Women					
Number of workers	32 548	2 345	10 746	9 617	9 840
Median annual earnings	25 000	15 000	21 000	25 000	36 000
1998					
Both Sexes					
Number of workers	80 812	7 353	25 595	22 526	25 338
Median annual earnings	32 000	19 000	26 300	31 619	45 000
Men					
Number of workers	47 230	4 872	14 744	12 473	15 142
Median annual earnings	36 400	22 000	30 000	36 000	52 000
Women					
Number of workers	33 582	2 482	10 851	10 053	10 197
Median annual earnings	27 000	15 000	22 000	26 500	38 000
1999					
Both Sexes					
Number of workers	82 501	7 208	25 792	23 380	26 120
Median annual earnings	33 000	20 000	27 000	33 000	48 000
Men					
Number of workers	47 781	4 693	14 806	12 824	15 459
Median annual earnings	38 500	22 000	32 000	39 000	55 600
Women					
Number of workers	34 720	2 516	10 986	10 556	10 662
Median annual earnings	27 040	15 000	22 000	27 280	40 000
2000					
Both Sexes					
Number of workers	84 337	7 354	26 144	24 064	26 775
Median annual earnings	35 000	20 000	28 600	34 000	50 000
Men					
Number of workers	48 816	4 738	15 057	13 242	15 780
Median annual earnings	40 000	22 500	33 000	40 000	60 000
Women					
Number of workers	35 521	2 616	11 087	10 822	10 995
Median annual earnings	29 000	16 000	24 000	28 000	40 000
2001					
Both Sexes					
Number of workers	84 743	7 623	25 522	23 719	27 879
Median annual earnings	35 000	20 800	29 000	35 000	50 000
Men					
Number of workers	48 887	5 049	14 655	12 968	16 215
Median annual earnings	40 000	24 000	33 800	40 000	60 000
Women					
Number of workers	35 856	2 574	10 867	10 751	11 664
Median annual earnings	30 000	17 000	24 000	30 000	42 000
2002					
Both Sexes					
Number of workers	84 702	7 578	25 078	23 604	28 443
Median annual earnings	36 000	21 000	30 000	35 100	52 000
Men					
Number of workers	48 687	5 102	14 306	12 677	16 602
Median annual earnings	41 000	23 400	34 000	41 500	61 000
Women					
Number of workers	36 015	2 476	10 772	10 927	11 841
Median annual earnings	30 000	18 000	25 000	30 000	43 500

Table 1-61. Median Annual Earnings of Year-Round, Full-Time Wage and Salary Workers Age 25 to 64 Years, by Educational Attainment and Sex, 1997–2008—*Continued*

(Thousands of workers, dollars.)

Year and sex	Total	Less than a high school diploma	4 years of high school only	1 to 3 years of college	4 or more years of college
2003					
Both Sexes					
Number of workers	85 058	7 245	25 352	23 702	28 759
Median annual earnings	37 752	21 000	30 000	36 000	53 000
Men					
Number of workers	48 988	4 879	14 657	12 766	16 686
Median annual earnings	42 000	24 000	35 000	42 000	62 000
Women					
Number of workers	36 070	2 366	10 695	10 936	12 073
Median annual earnings	32 000	18 000	25 111	31 000	45 000
2004					
Both Sexes					
Number of workers	86 306	7 648	25 786	23 897	28 976
Median annual earnings	38 000	21 840	30 000	37 000	55 000
Men					
Number of workers	49 904	5 178	15 263	12 822	16 642
Median annual earnings	42 900	24 000	35 000	43 000	65 000
Women					
Number of workers	36 402	2 470	10 523	11 074	12 334
Median annual earnings	32 000	18 000	25 280	31 200	45 000
2005					
Both Sexes					
Number of workers	88 415	7 758	26 023	24 623	30 012
Median annual earnings	39 768	22 880	31 000	38 000	55 000
Men					
Number of workers	51 022	5 376	15 451	13 199	16 996
Median annual earnings	44 000	25 000	35 360	45 000	65 000
Women					
Number of workers	37 393	2 381	10 571	11 424	13 016
Median annual earnings	33 644	18 200	26 000	32 000	46 700
2006					
Both Sexes					
Number of workers	90 733	7 951	26 233	24 737	31 812
Median annual earnings	40 000	23 000	32 000	39 482	57 588
Men					
Number of workers	52 252	5 485	15 525	13 204	18 038
Median annual earnings	45 000	25 000	36 665	45 000	68 000
Women					
Number of workers	38 481	2 466	10 708	11 533	13 774
Median annual earnings	35 000	19 000	26 800	33 000	49 000
2007					
Both Sexes					
Number of workers	91 540	7 123	25 925	25 574	32 918
Median annual earnings	41 000	24 000	33 000	40 000	60 000
Men					
Number of workers	52 262	4 902	15 390	13 655	18 316
Median annual earnings	47 000	25 000	38 000	45 188	70 000
Women					
Number of workers	39 277	2 221	10 535	11 919	14 603
Median annual earnings	35 000	19 200	27 120	35 000	50 000
2008					
Both Sexes					
Number of workers	88 373	6 600	24 531	24 887	32 355
Median annual earnings	42 000	24 000	34 000	40 000	60 000
Men					
Number of workers	50 141	4 503	14 480	13 283	17 876
Median annual earnings	49 564	27 000	39 040	47 000	72 000
Women					
Number of workers	38 231	2 097	10 051	11 604	14 479
Median annual earnings	36 000	19 567	28 000	35 000	50 000

Chapter Two

EMPLOYMENT, HOURS, AND EARNINGS

EMPLOYMENT AND HOURS

HIGHLIGHTS

The employment, hours, and earnings data in this section are presented by industry and state and are derived from the Current Employment Statistics (CES) survey, which covers approximately 390,000 individual worksites. The employment numbers differ from those presented in Chapter 1 from the household survey because of dissimilarities in methodology, concepts, definitions, and coverage. As the CES survey data are obtained from payroll records, they are consistent for industry classifications.

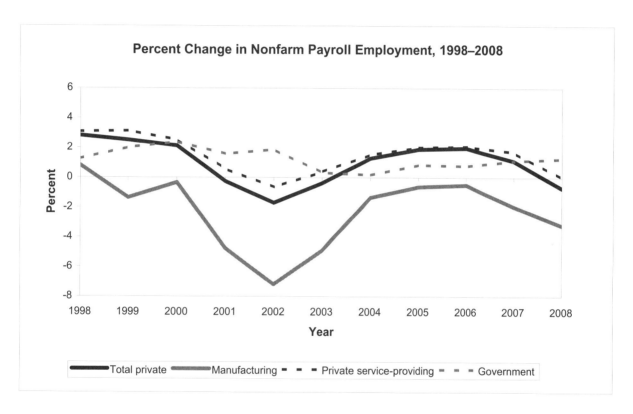

Percent Change in Nonfarm Payroll Employment, 1998–2008

In 2008, total employment declined for the first time since 2003, decreasing by 0.4 percent. While private-service providing employment was stable, employment in goods-producing industries declined by 3.7 percent overall and by 3.2 percent in manufacturing. Government employment increased slightly, growing by 1.3 percent. (See Table 2-1.)

OTHER HIGHLIGHTS:

- Construction employment continued to decline in 2008 after increasing every year from 1995 to 2006, except in 2002. In 2008, it declined by 5.4 percent compared to a 0.8 percent decline in 2007. (See Table 2-1.)

- While many sectors experienced a decline in employment from 2007 to 2008, employment increased by 2.9 percent in education and health services. Leisure and hospitality, government, mining, utilities, and other services all experienced modest gains. (See Table 2-1.)

- From 1998 to 2008, the number of women on nonfarm payrolls has increased has faster rate (11.4 percent) than the number of men (6.5 percent). (See Tables 2-1 and 2-2.)

- Average weekly hours of production workers on private nonfarm payrolls decreased in 2008. From 1998 to 2008, it has gradually decreased from 34.5 hours to 33.6 hours. (See Table 2-6.)

NOTES AND DEFINITIONS

EMPLOYMENT, HOURS, AND EARNINGS

Collection and Coverage

The Bureau of Labor Statistics (BLS) works with State Employment Security Agencies (SESAs) to conduct the Current Employment Statistics (CES), or establishment, survey. This survey collects monthly data on employment, hours, and earnings from a sample of nonfarm establishments (including government). The CES sample includes about 150,000 businesses and government agencies and covers approximately 390,000 individual worksites. The active CES sample includes approximately one-third of all nonfarm payroll workers. From these data, a large number of employment, hours, and earnings series with considerable industrial and geographic detail are prepared and published.

Data defined on the 790 form are submitted each month by the respondent and edited by the state agency. Data submitted on the schedule are used in developing statewide and major metropolitan area estimates. The state also transmits sample data and state-developed geographic estimates to Washington. All states' samples are combined to form a collective sample for developing national industry estimates. Statewide samples range from nearly 30,000 sample units in California to about 1,000 units in smaller states. It should be noted that state estimation procedures are designed to produce accurate data for each individual state. BLS independently develops the national employment series and does not force state estimates to sum to national totals nor vice versa.

Data are collected by telephone, touch-tone self response, computer-assisted interviews, fax technology, voice recognition, and mail. The use of electronic media has resulted in a more rapid response times and higher response rates.

Industry Classification

The CES survey completed a conversion from its original quota sample design to a probability-based sample survey design, and switched from the Standard Industrial Classification (SIC) system to the North American Industry Classification System (NAICS) in 2003. The industry-coding update included reconstruction of historical estimates in order to preserve time series for data users. The foundation of industrial classification with NAICS has changed how establishments are classified into industries and how businesses, as they exist today, are recognized. With the release of January 2008 data on February 1, 2008, the CES National Nonfarm Payroll series was updated to the 2007 North American Industry Classification System (NAICS) from the 2002 NAICS basis. This resulted in relatively minor changes.

Industry Employment

Employment data refer to persons on establishment payrolls who received pay for any part of the pay period containing the 12th day of the month. The data exclude proprietors, the self-employed, unpaid volunteer or family workers, farm workers, and domestic workers. Salaried officers of corporations are included. Government employment covers only civilian employees; military personnel are excluded. Employees of the Central Intelligence Agency, the National Security Agency, the National Imagery and Mapping Agency, and the Defense Intelligence Agency are also excluded.

Persons on establishment payrolls who were on paid sick leave (for cases in which pay is received directly from the firm), paid holiday, or vacation leave, or who work during part of the pay period despite being unemployed or on strike during the rest of the period were counted as employed. Not counted as employed were persons on layoff, on leave without pay, on strike for the entire period, or who had been hired but had not yet reported during to their new jobs.

Beginning with the June 2003 publication of May 2003 data, the CES national federal government employment series has been estimated from a sample of federal establishments and benchmarked annually to counts from unemployment insurance tax records. It reflects employee counts as of the pay period containing the 12th day of the month, which is consistent with other CES industry series. Previously, the national series was an end-of-month count produced by the Office of Personnel Management.

The exclusion of farm employment, self-employment, and domestic service employment accounts from the payroll survey accounts for the differences in employment figures between the household and payroll surveys. The payroll survey also excludes workers on leave without pay. (These workers are counted as employed in the household survey.) Persons who worked in more than one establishment during the reporting period are counted each time their names appear on payrolls; these persons are only counted once in the household survey.

Concepts and Definitions

Production and related workers. This category includes working supervisors and all nonsupervisory workers (including group leaders and trainees) engaged in fabricating, processing, assembling, inspecting, receiving, storing, handling, packing, warehousing, shipping, trucking, hauling, maintenance, repair, janitorial, guard services, product development, auxiliary production for plant's own use (such as a power plant), record- keeping, and other services closely associated with production operations.

Construction workers. This group includes the following employees in the construction division: working supervisors, qualified craft workers, mechanics, apprentices, helpers, and laborers engaged in new work, alterations, demolition, repair, maintenance, and the like, whether working at the site of construction or at jobs in shops or yards at jobs (such as precutting and pre-assembling) ordinarily performed by members of the construction trades.

Nonsupervisory workers. This category consists of employees such as office and clerical workers, repairers, salespersons, operators, drivers, physicians, lawyers, accountants, nurses, social workers, research aides, teachers, drafters, photographers, beauticians, musicians, restaurant workers, custodial workers, attendants, line installers and repairers, laborers, janitors, guards, and other employees at similar occupational levels whose services are closely associated with those of the employees listed. It excludes persons in executive, managerial, and supervisory positions.

Payroll. This refers to payments made to full- and part-time production, construction, or nonsupervisory workers who received pay for any part of the pay period containing the 12th day of the month. The payroll is reported before deductions of any kind, such as those for old age and unemployment insurance, group insurance, withholding tax, bonds, or union dues. Also included is pay for overtime, holidays, and vacation, as well as for sick leave paid directly by the firm. Bonuses (unless earned and paid regularly each pay period), other pay not earned in the pay period reported (such as retroactive pay), tips, and the value of free rent, fuel, meals, or other payment-in-kind are excluded. Employee benefits (such as health and other types of insurance and contributions to retirement, as paid by the employer) are also excluded.

Total hours. During the pay period, total hours include all hours worked (including overtime hours), hours paid for standby or reporting time, and equivalent hours for which employees received pay directly from the employer for sick leave, holidays, vacations, and other leave. Overtime and other premium pay hours are not converted to straight-time equivalent hours. The concept of total hours differs from those of scheduled hours and hours worked. The average weekly hours derived from paid total hours reflect the effects of such factors as unpaid absenteeism, labor turnover, part-time work, and work stoppages, as well as fluctuations in work schedules.

Average weekly hours. The workweek information relates to the average hours for which pay was received and is different from standard or scheduled hours. Such factors as unpaid absenteeism, labor turnover, part-time work, and work stoppages cause average weekly hours to be lower than scheduled hours of work for an establishment. Group averages further reflect changes in the workweeks of component industries.

Overtime hours. These are hours worked by production or related workers for which overtime premiums were paid because the hours were in excess of the number of hours of either the straight-time workday or the total workweek. Weekend and holiday hours are included only if overtime premiums were paid. Hours for which only shift differential, hazard, incentive, or other similar types of premiums were paid are excluded.

Average overtime hours. Overtime hours represent the portion of average weekly hours that exceeded regular hours and for which overtime premiums were paid. If an employee worked during a paid holiday at regular rates, receiving as total compensation his or her holiday pay plus straight-time pay for hours worked that day, no overtime hours would be reported.

Since overtime hours are premium hours by definition, weekly hours and overtime hours do not necessarily move in the same direction from month to month. Factors such as work stoppages, absenteeism, and labor turnover may not have the same influence on overtime hours as on average hours. Diverse trends at the industry group level may also be caused by a marked change in hours for a component industry in which little or no overtime was worked in both the previous and current months.

Industry hours and earnings. Average hours and earnings data are derived from reports of payrolls and hours for production and related workers in manufacturing and natural resources and mining, construction workers in construction, and nonsupervisory employees in private service-providing industries.

Indexes of aggregate weekly hours and payrolls. The indexes of aggregate weekly hours are calculated by dividing the current month's aggregate by the average of the 12 monthly figures for 2002. For basic industries, the hours aggregates are the product of average weekly hours and production worker or nonsupervisory worker employment. At all higher levels of industry aggregation, hours aggregates are the sum of the component aggregates.

The indexes of aggregate weekly payrolls are calculated by dividing the current month's aggregate by the average of the 12 monthly figures for 2002. For basic industries, the payroll aggregates are the product of average hourly earnings and aggregate weekly hours. At all higher levels of industry aggregation, payroll aggregates are the sum of the component aggregates.

Average hourly earnings. Average hourly earnings are on a "gross" basis. They reflect not only changes in basic hourly and incentive wage rates, but also such variable factors as premium pay for overtime and late-shift work and changes in output of workers paid on an incentive plan. They also reflect shifts in the number of employees between relatively high-paid and low-paid work and changes in workers' earnings in individual establishments. Averages for groups and divisions further reflect changes in average hourly earnings for individual industries.

Averages of hourly earnings differ from wage rates. Earnings are the actual return to the worker for a stated period; rates are the amount stipulated for a given unit of work or time. The earnings series do not measure the level of total labor costs on the part of the employer because the following items are excluded: irregular bonuses, retroactive items, payroll taxes paid by employers, and earnings for those employees not covered under the definitions of production workers, construction workers, or nonsupervisory employees.

Average hourly earnings, excluding overtime-premium pay, are computed by dividing the total production worker payroll for the industry group by the sum of total production worker hours and one-half of total overtime hours. No adjustments are made for other premium payment provisions, such as holiday pay, late-shift premiums, and overtime rates other than time and one-half.

Average weekly earnings. These estimates are derived by multiplying average weekly hours estimates by average hourly earnings estimates. Therefore, weekly earnings are affected not only by changes in average hourly earnings but also by changes in the length of the workweek. Monthly variations in factors, such as the proportion of part-time workers, work stoppages, labor turnover during the survey period, and absenteeism for which employees are not paid may cause the average workweek to fluctuate.

Long-term trends of average weekly earnings can be affected by structural changes in the makeup of the workforce. For example, persistent long-term increases in the proportion of part-time workers in retail trade and many of the services industries have reduced average workweeks in these industries and have affected the average weekly earnings series.

These earnings are in constant dollars and are calculated from the earnings averages for the current month using a deflator derived from the Consumer Price Index for Urban Wage Earnings and Clerical Workers (CPI-W). The reference year for these series is 1982.

Benchmarks

Employment estimates are adjusted annually to a complete count of jobs—called benchmarks—which are primarily derived from tax reports submitted by employers covered by state unemployment laws (which cover most establishments). A comprehensive account of employment is derived in March. In this re-anchoring of sample-based employment estimates to full population counts, the original sample-based estimates are replaced with the benchmark data from the previous year. The benchmark information is used to adjust monthly estimates between the new benchmark and the preceding benchmark, thereby preserving the continuity of the series and establishing the level of employment for the new benchmark month.

Experimental All Employee Hours and Earnings Series from the Current Employment Statistics Program

Background

The Current Employment Statistics (CES) program began work in 2005 to add new series on hours and earnings. New series have been developed to measure the average hourly earnings, average weekly hours, and gross monthly earnings of *all* nonfarm private sector employees. The new hours and earnings series are more comprehensive in coverage, thereby providing improved information for analyzing economic trends and improved input to productivity and personal income series.

Additionally, CES is adding average overtime hours in manufacturing. Historically, the CES program has published average hours and earnings series for production workers in the goods-producing industries and non-supervisory workers in the service-providing industries. These workers account for about 80 percent of total private nonfarm employment.

Experimental Designation and Future Publication Plans

BLS is designating the release of these new series as experimental because of the limited experience to date with the editing and review of the sample reports and the resultant estimates. BLS began the first collection of the all employee payroll, hours, and gross monthly earnings data from respondents late in 2005. There is not yet enough historical information to apply all of the edit and review techniques used in the published CES data to these new series, nor is there sufficient data to allow seasonal adjustment of the new series.

The first release of experimental series on April 6, 2007, included national level estimates at a total private sector level and limited industry detail from March 2006 through January 2007. Each month the experimental estimates are released on the same date as the Employment Situation news release (typically the first Friday of the month). In April 2008 BLS began releasing some first preliminary estimates. As BLS and data users gain more experience with these new experimental data series, additional industry detail may be released, and publication of second preliminary estimates may be added. BLS began publishing experimental estimates of hours and earnings for all employees in limited detail for all states on March 11, 2008.

By the end of 2009, BLS should have sufficient historical data to seasonally adjust the all employee payroll and hours series and is planning to publish them as official CES data in the Employment Situation news release and other BLS publications beginning in February 2010.

In order to publish all employee average weekly hours, average hourly earnings, and average weekly earnings, BLS is collecting all employees total payroll and all employees total hours from survey respondents. The definitions of these data items parallel the definitions used for the production worker payroll and hours data; the only difference is that they cover all employees, rather than just production or nonsupervisory workers.

Sources of Additional Information

For further information on sampling and estimation methods for national data visit the Employment, Hours, and Earnings homepage on the BLS Web site at <http://www.bls.gov/ces>. For more information on state and area data, please visit the BLS Web site at <http://www.bls.gov/sae>.

Table 2-1. Employees on Nonfarm Payrolls, by Super Sector and Selected Component Groups, NAICS Basis, 1995–2008

(Thousands of people.)

Industry	1995	1996	1997	1998	1999	2000	2001	2002	2003	2004	2005	2006	2007	2008
TOTAL	117 298	119 708	122 776	125 930	128 993	131 785	131 826	130 341	129 999	131 435	133 703	136 086	137 598	137 066
Total Private	97 865	100 169	103 113	106 021	108 686	110 995	110 708	108 828	108 416	109 814	111 899	114 113	115 380	114 566
Goods-Producing	23 156	23 409	23 886	24 354	24 465	24 649	23 873	22 557	21 816	21 882	22 190	22 531	22 233	21 419
Mining and Logging	641	637	654	645	598	599	606	583	572	591	628	684	724	774
Mining	558	556	571	565	517	520	533	512	503	523	562	620	664	717
Logging	83	81	82	80	81	79	74	70	69	68	65	64	60	57
Construction	5 274	5 536	5 813	6 149	6 545	6 787	6 826	6 716	6 735	6 976	7 336	7 691	7 630	7 215
Construction of buildings	1 325	1 380	1 435	1 509	1 586	1 633	1 589	1 575	1 576	1 630	1 712	1 805	1 774	1 659
Heavy and civil engineering	775	800	825	865	909	937	953	931	903	907	951	985	1 005	970
Specialty trade contractors	3 174	3 355	3 553	3 775	4 050	4 217	4 284	4 210	4 256	4 439	4 673	4 901	4 850	4 585
Manufacturing	17 241	17 237	17 419	17 560	17 322	17 263	16 441	15 259	14 510	14 315	14 226	14 155	13 879	13 431
Durable goods	10 373	10 486	10 705	10 911	10 831	10 877	10 336	9 485	8 964	8 925	8 956	8 981	8 808	8 476
Wood product	574	583	595	609	620	613	574	555	538	550	559	559	515	460
Nonmetallic mineral product	513	517	526	535	541	554	545	516	494	506	505	510	501	468
Primary metals	642	639	639	642	625	622	571	509	477	467	466	464	456	443
Fabricated metal product	1 623	1 648	1 696	1 740	1 728	1 753	1 676	1 549	1 479	1 497	1 522	1 553	1 563	1 528
Machinery	1 442	1 469	1 496	1 514	1 468	1 457	1 371	1 232	1 152	1 145	1 166	1 183	1 187	1 186
Computer and electronic product	1 688	1 747	1 803	1 831	1 781	1 820	1 749	1 507	1 355	1 323	1 316	1 308	1 273	1 248
Electrical equipment and appliances	593	591	586	592	588	591	557	497	460	445	434	433	429	425
Transportation equipment	1 979	1 975	2 028	2 078	2 089	2 057	1 939	1 830	1 775	1 767	1 772	1 769	1 712	1 607
Furniture and related product	609	607	618	644	668	683	645	607	576	576	568	560	531	481
Miscellaneous manufacturing	710	711	718	727	724	728	710	683	658	651	647	644	642	631
Nondurable goods	6 868	6 751	6 714	6 649	6 491	6 386	6 105	5 774	5 546	5 390	5 271	5 174	5 071	4 955
Food manufacturing	1 560	1 562	1 558	1 555	1 550	1 553	1 551	1 526	1 518	1 494	1 478	1 479	1 484	1 485
Beverage and tobacco product	203	204	206	209	208	207	209	207	200	195	192	194	198	199
Textile mills	469	443	436	425	397	378	333	291	261	237	218	195	170	151
Textile product mills	242	237	236	235	232	230	217	204	188	183	176	167	158	148
Apparel	791	722	681	621	541	484	415	350	304	278	251	232	215	198
Paper and paper product	640	631	631	625	616	605	578	547	516	496	484	471	458	446
Printing and related support activities	817	816	821	828	815	807	768	707	681	663	646	634	622	594
Petroleum and coal product	140	137	136	135	128	123	121	118	114	112	112	113	115	117
Chemicals	988	985	987	993	983	980	959	928	906	887	872	866	861	850
Plastics and rubber product	914	919	933	941	947	951	896	847	814	805	802	786	757	734
Private Service-Providing	74 710	76 760	79 227	81 667	84 221	86 346	86 834	86 271	86 600	87 932	89 709	91 582	93 147	93 146
Trade, Transportation, and Utilities	23 834	24 239	24 700	25 186	25 771	26 225	25 983	25 497	25 287	25 533	25 959	26 276	26 630	26 385
Wholesale Trade	5 433	5 522	5 664	5 795	5 893	5 933	5 773	5 652	5 608	5 663	5 764	5 905	6 015	5 964
Durable goods	2 909	2 978	3 072	3 162	3 220	3 251	3 130	3 008	2 941	2 951	2 999	3 075	3 122	3 061
Nondurable goods	1 969	1 978	2 008	2 033	2 061	2 065	2 031	2 015	2 005	2 010	2 022	2 041	2 062	2 053
Electronic markets, agents, and brokers	555	567	584	600	612	618	611	629	662	702	743	789	832	850
Retail Trade	13 897	14 143	14 389	14 609	14 970	15 280	15 239	15 025	14 917	15 058	15 280	15 353	15 520	15 356
Motor vehicle and parts dealers	1 627	1 686	1 723	1 741	1 797	1 847	1 855	1 879	1 883	1 902	1 919	1 910	1 908	1 845
Furniture and home furnishing stores	461	474	485	499	524	544	541	539	547	563	576	587	575	543
Electronic and appliance stores	449	470	494	510	542	564	555	525	512	516	536	541	549	550
Building material and garden supply stores	982	1 007	1 043	1 062	1 101	1 142	1 152	1 177	1 185	1 227	1 276	1 324	1 309	1 253
Food and beverage stores	2 880	2 928	2 957	2 966	2 985	2 993	2 951	2 882	2 838	2 822	2 818	2 821	2 844	2 858
Health and personal care stores	812	826	853	876	898	928	952	939	938	941	954	961	993	1 002
Gasoline stations	922	946	956	961	944	936	925	896	882	876	871	864	862	843
Clothing and clothing accessories stores	1 246	1 221	1 236	1 269	1 307	1 322	1 321	1 313	1 305	1 364	1 415	1 451	1 500	1 484
Sporting goods, hobby, and music stores	606	614	626	635	664	686	679	661	647	641	647	646	656	647
General merchandise stores	2 635	2 657	2 658	2 687	2 752	2 820	2 842	2 812	2 822	2 863	2 934	2 935	3 021	3 047
Miscellaneous store retailers	841	874	913	950	986	1 007	993	960	931	914	900	881	865	848
Nonstore retailers	435	439	445	453	472	492	474	444	427	429	435	433	438	436
Transportation and Warehousing	3 838	3 935	4 027	4 168	4 300	4 410	4 372	4 224	4 185	4 249	4 361	4 470	4 541	4 505
Air transportation	511	526	542	563	586	614	615	564	528	515	501	487	492	493
Rail transportation	233	225	221	225	229	232	227	218	218	226	228	228	234	230
Water transportation	51	51	51	51	52	56	54	53	55	56	61	63	66	65
Truck transportation	1 249	1 282	1 308	1 354	1 392	1 406	1 387	1 339	1 326	1 352	1 398	1 436	1 439	1 391
Transit and ground passenger transportation	328	339	350	363	371	372	375	381	382	385	389	399	412	418
Pipeline transportation	54	51	50	48	47	46	45	42	40	38	38	39	40	42
Scenic and sightseeing transportation	22	23	25	25	26	28	29	26	27	27	29	28	29	28
Support activities for transportation	430	446	473	497	518	537	539	525	520	535	552	571	584	590
Couriers and messengers	517	540	546	568	586	605	587	561	562	557	571	582	581	576
Warehousing and storage	444	452	462	474	494	514	514	517	528	558	595	638	665	673
Utilities	666	640	621	613	609	601	599	596	577	564	554	549	553	560
Information	2 843	2 940	3 084	3 218	3 419	3 630	3 629	3 395	3 188	3 118	3 061	3 038	3 032	2 997
Publishing industries, except Internet	911	927	956	982	1 005	1 035	1 021	964	925	909	904	902	901	883
Motion picture and sound recording industry	311	335	353	370	384	383	377	388	376	385	378	376	381	382
Broadcasting, except Internet	298	309	313	321	329	344	345	334	324	325	328	328	325	316
Internet publishing and broadcasting and web search portals	34	40	45	54	78	111	100	76	67	66	67	69	73	80
Telecommunications	1 009	1 038	1 108	1 167	1 271	1 397	1 424	1 281	1 167	1 115	1 071	1 048	1 031	1 021
Other information services	72	79	86	95	122	157	147	124	116	117	118	121	126	134

Table 2-1. Employees on Nonfarm Payrolls, by Super Sector and Selected Component Groups, NAICS Basis, 1995–2008—*Continued*

(Thousands of people.)

Industry	1995	1996	1997	1998	1999	2000	2001	2002	2003	2004	2005	2006	2007	2008
Financial Activities	6 827	6 969	7 178	7 462	7 648	7 687	7 808	7 847	7 977	8 031	8 153	8 328	8 301	8 146
Finance and insurance	5 069	5 151	5 302	5 529	5 665	5 677	5 769	5 814	5 919	5 945	6 019	6 156	6 132	6 015
Monetary authorities, central bank	23	23	22	22	23	23	23	23	23	22	22	21	22	22
Credit intermediation	2 314	2 368	2 434	2 532	2 591	2 548	2 598	2 686	2 792	2 817	2 869	2 925	2 866	2 736
Securities, commodity contracts, and investments	562	590	636	692	737	805	831	789	758	766	786	818	849	858
Insurance carriers and related activities	2 108	2 108	2 144	2 209	2 236	2 221	2 234	2 233	2 266	2 259	2 259	2 304	2 307	2 309
Funds, trusts, and other financial vehicles	61	63	67	73	78	81	84	82	80	82	84	88	89	90
Real estate and rental and leasing	1 758	1 817	1 876	1 934	1 983	2 011	2 038	2 033	2 058	2 086	2 134	2 173	2 169	2 130
Real estate	1 182	1 209	1 244	1 278	1 303	1 316	1 343	1 357	1 387	1 419	1 461	1 499	1 500	1 481
Rental and leasing services	557	588	610	631	653	667	666	649	643	641	646	646	640	621
Lessors of nonfinancial intangible assets	19	21	23	25	27	28	29	28	27	26	27	28	28	28
Professional and Business Services	12 844	13 462	14 335	15 147	15 957	16 666	16 476	15 976	15 987	16 394	16 954	17 566	17 942	17 778
Professional and technical services	5 078	5 313	5 629	5 992	6 345	6 702	6 871	6 649	6 603	6 747	7 025	7 357	7 660	7 830
Management of companies and enterprises	1 686	1 703	1 730	1 756	1 774	1 796	1 779	1 705	1 687	1 724	1 759	1 811	1 866	1 895
Administrative and waste services	6 080	6 447	6 977	7 398	7 838	8 168	7 826	7 622	7 697	7 923	8 170	8 398	8 416	8 054
Administrative and support services	5 806	6 165	6 686	7 099	7 527	7 855	7 509	7 304	7 375	7 594	7 833	8 050	8 061	7 694
Waste management and remediation services	273	282	291	299	311	313	317	318	322	329	338	348	355	360
Education and Health Services	13 289	13 683	14 087	14 446	14 798	15 109	15 645	16 199	16 588	16 953	17 372	17 826	18 322	18 855
Education services	2 010	2 078	2 155	2 233	2 320	2 390	2 511	2 643	2 695	2 763	2 836	2 901	2 941	3 037
Health care and social assistance	11 278	11 605	11 932	12 214	12 477	12 718	13 134	13 556	13 893	14 190	14 536	14 925	15 380	15 819
Ambulatory health care services	3 768	3 940	4 093	4 161	4 227	4 320	4 462	4 633	4 786	4 952	5 114	5 286	5 474	5 661
Hospitals	3 734	3 773	3 822	3 892	3 936	3 954	4 051	4 160	4 245	4 285	4 345	4 423	4 515	4 641
Nursing and residential health facilities	2 308	2 380	2 443	2 487	2 529	2 583	2 676	2 743	2 786	2 818	2 855	2 893	2 958	3 008
Social assistance	1 470	1 512	1 574	1 673	1 786	1 860	1 946	2 020	2 075	2 135	2 222	2 324	2 433	2 509
Leisure and Hospitality	10 501	10 777	11 018	11 232	11 543	11 862	12 036	11 986	12 173	12 493	12 816	13 110	13 427	13 459
Arts, entertainment, and recreation	1 459	1 522	1 600	1 645	1 709	1 788	1 824	1 783	1 813	1 850	1 892	1 929	1 969	1 969
Performing arts and spectator sports	308	329	350	350	361	382	382	364	372	368	376	399	405	406
Museums, historical sites	84	89	94	97	103	110	115	114	115	118	121	124	130	132
Amusements, gambling, and recreation	1 068	1 105	1 157	1 198	1 245	1 296	1 327	1 305	1 327	1 364	1 395	1 406	1 434	1 431
Accommodation and food services	9 042	9 254	9 418	9 586	9 834	10 074	10 211	10 203	10 360	10 643	10 923	11 181	11 457	11 489
Accommodation	1 653	1 699	1 730	1 774	1 832	1 884	1 852	1 779	1 775	1 790	1 819	1 832	1 867	1 857
Food services and drinking places	7 389	7 555	7 689	7 813	8 002	8 189	8 359	8 425	8 584	8 854	9 104	9 349	9 590	9 632
Other Services	4 572	4 690	4 825	4 976	5 087	5 168	5 258	5 372	5 401	5 409	5 395	5 438	5 494	5 528
Repair and maintenance	1 079	1 136	1 169	1 189	1 222	1 242	1 257	1 247	1 234	1 229	1 236	1 249	1 253	1 228
Personal and laundry services	1 144	1 166	1 180	1 206	1 220	1 243	1 255	1 257	1 264	1 273	1 277	1 288	1 310	1 327
Membership associations and organizations	2 349	2 389	2 475	2 581	2 644	2 683	2 746	2 868	2 904	2 908	2 882	2 901	2 931	2 973
Government	19 432	19 539	19 664	19 909	20 307	20 790	21 118	21 513	21 583	21 621	21 804	21 974	22 218	22 500
Federal	2 949	2 877	2 806	2 772	2 769	2 865	2 764	2 766	2 761	2 730	2 732	2 732	2 734	2 764
Federal, excluding U.S. Postal Service	2 099	2 010	1 940	1 891	1 880	1 985	1 891	1 924	1 952	1 948	1 957	1 963	1 965	2 017
State	4 635	4 606	4 582	4 612	4 709	4 786	4 905	5 029	5 002	4 982	5 032	5 075	5 122	5 178
State, excluding education	2 716	2 695	2 678	2 690	2 726	2 756	2 792	2 786	2 748	2 744	2 772	2 782	2 804	2 819
Local	11 849	12 056	12 276	12 525	12 829	13 139	13 449	13 718	13 820	13 909	14 041	14 167	14 362	14 557
Local, excluding education	5 396	5 464	5 517	5 604	5 709	5 845	5 970	6 063	6 110	6 144	6 185	6 254	6 376	6 482

Table 2-2. Women Employees on Nonfarm Payrolls, by Super Sector and Selected Component Groups, NAICS Basis, 1995–2008

(Thousands of people.)

Industry	1995	1996	1997	1998	1999	2000	2001	2002	2003	2004	2005	2006	2007	2008
TOTAL NONFARM	56 213	57 406	58 914	60 309	61 810	63 223	63 684	63 360	63 237	63 739	64 718	65 525	66 805	67 194
Total Private	45 514	46 574	47 923	49 144	50 358	51 452	51 669	51 033	50 901	51 404	52 329	53 307	54 227	54 291
Goods-Producing	6 225	6 214	6 294	6 353	6 299	6 297	5 961	5 486	5 192	5 117	5 104	5 082	5 041	4 880
Mining and logging	98	96	99	100	96	92	90	85	80	80	79	82	93	102
Construction	666	700	730	769	818	846	832	827	822	841	890	944	947	923
Manufacturing	5 462	5 418	5 466	5 484	5 386	5 359	5 039	4 574	4 290	4 197	4 135	4 057	4 001	3 855
Private Service-Providing	39 289	40 360	41 629	42 791	44 059	45 155	45 708	45 547	45 709	46 287	47 225	48 224	49 186	49 410
Trade, transportation, and utilities	9 870	10 043	10 230	10 413	10 658	10 859	10 768	10 466	10 321	10 364	10 535	10 627	10 849	10 826
Wholesale trade	1 668	1 701	1 746	1 778	1 809	1 827	1 770	1 718	1 700	1 714	1 738	1 796	1 831	1 827
Retail trade	7 020	7 142	7 272	7 380	7 543	7 680	7 635	7 449	7 339	7 387	7 524	7 587	7 758	7 750
Transportation and warehousing	1 018	1 042	1 060	1 103	1 154	1 202	1 212	1 149	1 134	1 117	1 130	1 098	1 110	1 097
Utilities	163	157	153	152	152	151	151	150	147	146	143	146	150	151
Information	1 380	1 433	1 481	1 514	1 600	1 697	1 684	1 554	1 428	1 366	1 333	1 306	1 285	1 265
Financial activities	4 164	4 241	4 359	4 515	4 605	4 638	4 726	4 755	4 830	4 831	4 896	5 031	4 959	4 816
Professional and business services	5 979	6 273	6 704	7 030	7 370	7 680	7 591	7 314	7 248	7 360	7 574	7 779	8 007	7 962
Education and health services	10 181	10 474	10 779	11 042	11 323	11 586	12 037	12 474	12 786	13 073	13 408	13 764	14 178	14 586
Leisure and hospitality	5 382	5 520	5 640	5 760	5 933	6 082	6 224	6 215	6 319	6 516	6 708	6 903	7 054	7 067
Other services	2 333	2 376	2 435	2 517	2 570	2 614	2 677	2 769	2 779	2 776	2 772	2 814	2 854	2 889
Government	10 698	10 832	10 991	11 164	11 452	11 771	12 015	12 327	12 337	12 335	12 389	12 218	12 578	12 904
Federal	1 285	1 261	1 240	1 184	1 174	1 231	1 148	1 155	1 173	1 168	1 177	1 194	1 202	1 226
State	2 326	2 316	2 324	2 354	2 412	2 464	2 534	2 621	2 599	2 562	2 575	2 630	2 651	2 686
Local	7 088	7 255	7 426	7 627	7 866	8 076	8 333	8 551	8 565	8 606	8 637	8 395	8 725	8 992

Table 2-3. Production Workers on Private Nonfarm Payrolls, by Super Sector, NAICS Basis, 1995–2008

(Thousands of people.)

Industry	1995	1996	1997	1998	1999	2000	2001	2002	2003	2004	2005	2006	2007	2008
TOTAL PRIVATE	79 845	81 773	84 158	86 316	88 430	90 336	89 983	88 393	87 658	88 937	91 135	93 451	94 903	94 509
Goods-Producing	17 137	17 318	17 698	18 008	18 067	18 169	17 466	16 400	15 732	15 821	16 145	16 559	16 405	15 791
Mining and logging	458	461	479	473	438	446	457	436	420	440	473	519	547	580
Construction	4 113	4 325	4 546	4 807	5 105	5 295	5 332	5 196	5 123	5 309	5 611	5 903	5 883	5 562
Manufacturing	12 567	12 532	12 673	12 729	12 524	12 428	11 677	10 768	10 189	10 072	10 060	10 137	9 975	9 649
Private Service-Providing	62 708	64 455	66 460	68 308	70 363	72 167	72 517	71 993	71 926	73 116	74 990	76 893	78 498	78 718
Trade, transportation, and utilities	19 984	20 325	20 698	21 059	21 576	21 965	21 709	21 337	21 078	21 319	21 830	22 166	22 546	22 415
Wholesale trade	4 361	4 423	4 523	4 605	4 673	4 686	4 555	4 474	4 396	4 444	4 584	4 724	4 851	4 839
Retail trade	11 841	12 057	12 274	12 440	12 772	13 040	12 952	12 774	12 655	12 788	13 030	13 110	13 317	13 197
Transportation and warehousing	3 260	3 339	3 407	3 522	3 642	3 753	3 718	3 611	3 563	3 637	3 774	3 889	3 935	3 928
Utilities	522	506	494	492	489	485	483	478	464	450	443	443	444	451
Information	2 007	2 096	2 181	2 217	2 351	2 502	2 531	2 398	2 347	2 371	2 386	2 399	2 403	2 398
Financial activities	5 165	5 279	5 415	5 605	5 728	5 737	5 810	5 872	5 967	5 989	6 090	6 281	6 326	6 271
Professional and business services	10 645	11 161	11 896	12 566	13 184	13 790	13 588	13 049	12 911	13 287	13 854	14 446	14 784	14 622
Education and health services	11 765	12 123	12 478	12 791	13 089	13 362	13 846	14 311	14 532	14 771	15 129	15 539	15 999	16 503
Leisure and hospitality	9 330	9 565	9 780	9 947	10 216	10 516	10 662	10 576	10 666	10 955	11 263	11 568	11 861	11 893
Other services	3 812	3 907	4 013	4 124	4 219	4 296	4 373	4 449	4 426	4 425	4 438	4 494	4 578	4 617

Table 2-4. Production Workers on Durable Goods Manufacturing Payrolls, by Industry, NAICS Basis, 1995–2008

(Thousands of people.)

Industry	1995	1996	1997	1998	1999	2000	2001	2002	2003	2004	2005	2006	2007	2008
Total Durable Goods	7 352	7 426	7 599	7 721	7 651	7 659	7 164	6 530	6 152	6 140	6 220	6 355	6 250	5 986
Wood product	478	485	497	508	514	506	468	449	433	444	453	450	406	359
Nonmetallic mineral product	400	405	413	421	426	440	427	399	375	388	387	391	384	366
Primary metals	500	500	502	505	492	490	447	396	370	364	363	363	358	349
Fabricated metal product	1 223	1 242	1 285	1 320	1 305	1 326	1 254	1 147	1 093	1 109	1 129	1 162	1 171	1 143
Machinery	970	985	1 007	1 016	978	961	891	787	732	730	749	770	774	771
Computer and electronic product	890	915	951	965	933	949	876	744	673	656	700	756	744	732
Electrical equipment and appliances	438	434	428	432	433	433	402	352	320	307	300	303	305	306
Transportation equipment	1 472	1 481	1 522	1 530	1 527	1 498	1 399	1 310	1 269	1 265	1 277	1 304	1 275	1 177
Furniture and related product	482	480	492	514	534	546	511	477	446	446	437	434	410	366
Miscellaneous manufacturing	499	500	503	511	509	510	490	469	442	432	424	423	425	417

Table 2-5. Production Workers on Nondurable Goods Manufacturing Payrolls, by Industry, NAICS Basis, 1995–2008

(Thousands of people.)

Industry	1995	1996	1997	1998	1999	2000	2001	2002	2003	2004	2005	2006	2007	2008
Total Nondurable Goods	5 214	5 106	5 075	5 008	4 872	4 769	4 513	4 238	4 037	3 932	3 841	3 782	3 725	3 663
Food manufacturing	1 221	1 228	1 228	1 228	1 229	1 228	1 221	1 202	1 193	1 178	1 170	1 172	1 184	1 187
Beverage and tobacco product	117	120	121	123	120	117	116	120	106	107	112	115	118	112
Textile mills	393	372	367	357	334	315	276	242	217	194	174	158	137	122
Textile product mills	198	193	193	190	187	183	174	162	148	147	143	135	123	116
Apparel	698	631	594	534	458	404	341	286	242	219	193	182	173	163
Leather and allied product	89	79	74	67	60	55	47	40	35	33	31	29	27	28
Paper and paper product	494	488	489	484	474	468	446	421	393	374	365	357	351	344
Printing and related support	599	594	597	598	585	576	544	493	471	460	447	447	443	425
Petroleum and coal product	89	87	88	87	85	83	81	78	74	77	75	72	73	77
Chemicals	988	985	987	993	983	980	959	928	906	887	872	866	861	850
Plastics and rubber product	914	919	933	941	947	951	896	847	814	805	802	786	757	734

Table 2-6. Average Weekly Hours of Production Workers on Private Nonfarm Payrolls, by Super Sector, NAICS Basis, 1995–2008

(Hours.)

Industry	1995	1996	1997	1998	1999	2000	2001	2002	2003	2004	2005	2006	2007	2008
TOTAL PRIVATE	34.3	34.3	34.5	34.5	34.3	34.3	34.0	33.9	33.7	33.7	33.8	33.9	33.9	33.6
Goods-Producing	40.8	40.8	41.1	40.8	40.8	40.7	39.9	39.9	39.8	40.0	40.1	40.5	40.6	40.2
Mining and logging	45.3	46.0	46.2	44.9	44.2	44.4	44.6	43.2	43.6	44.5	45.6	45.6	45.9	45.1
Construction	38.8	38.9	38.9	38.8	39.0	39.2	38.7	38.4	38.4	38.3	38.6	39.0	39.0	38.5
Manufacturing	41.3	41.3	41.7	41.4	41.4	41.3	40.3	40.5	40.4	40.8	40.7	41.1	41.2	40.8
Private Service-Providing	32.6	32.6	32.8	32.8	32.7	32.7	32.5	32.5	32.3	32.3	32.4	32.5	32.4	32.3
Trade, transportation, and utilities	34.1	34.1	34.3	34.2	33.9	33.8	33.5	33.6	33.6	33.5	33.4	33.4	33.3	33.2
Wholesale trade	38.6	38.6	38.8	38.6	38.6	38.8	38.4	38.0	37.9	37.8	37.7	38.0	38.2	38.2
Retail trade	30.8	30.7	30.9	30.9	30.8	30.7	30.7	30.9	30.9	30.7	30.6	30.5	30.2	30.0
Transportation and warehousing	38.9	39.1	39.4	38.7	37.6	37.4	36.7	36.6	36.8	37.2	37.0	36.9	37.0	36.4
Utilities	42.3	42.0	42.0	42.0	42.0	42.0	41.4	40.9	41.1	40.9	41.1	41.4	42.4	42.7
Information	36.0	36.4	36.3	36.6	36.7	36.8	36.9	36.5	36.2	36.3	36.5	36.6	36.5	36.7
Financial activities	35.5	35.5	35.7	36.0	35.8	35.9	35.8	35.6	35.5	35.5	35.9	35.7	35.9	35.8
Professional and business services	34.0	34.1	34.3	34.3	34.4	34.5	34.2	34.2	34.1	34.2	34.2	34.6	34.8	34.8
Education and health services	32.0	31.9	32.2	32.2	32.1	32.2	32.3	32.4	32.3	32.4	32.6	32.5	32.6	32.5
Leisure and hospitality	25.9	25.9	26.0	26.2	26.1	26.1	25.8	25.8	25.6	25.7	25.7	25.7	25.5	25.2
Other services	32.6	32.5	32.7	32.6	32.5	32.5	32.3	32.0	31.4	31.0	30.9	30.9	30.9	30.8

Table 2-7. Average Weekly Hours of Production Workers on Manufacturing Payrolls, by Industry, NAICS Basis, 1995–2008

(Hours.)

Industry	1995	1996	1997	1998	1999	2000	2001	2002	2003	2004	2005	2006	2007	2008
DURABLE GOODS														
Total	42.1	42.1	42.6	42.1	41.9	41.8	40.6	40.8	40.8	41.3	41.1	41.4	41.5	41.1
Wood product	41.0	41.2	41.4	41.4	41.3	41.0	40.2	39.9	40.4	40.7	40.0	39.8	39.4	38.6
Nonmetallic mineral product	41.8	42.0	41.9	42.2	42.1	41.6	41.6	42.0	42.2	42.4	42.2	43.0	42.3	42.1
Primary metals	43.4	43.6	44.3	43.5	43.8	44.2	42.4	42.4	42.3	43.1	43.1	43.6	42.9	42.2
Fabricated metal product	41.9	41.9	42.3	41.9	41.7	41.9	40.6	40.6	40.7	41.1	41.0	41.4	41.6	41.3
Machinery	43.5	43.3	44.0	43.1	42.3	42.3	40.9	40.5	40.8	42.0	42.1	42.4	42.6	42.3
Computer and electronic product	42.2	41.9	42.5	41.9	41.5	41.4	39.8	39.7	40.4	40.4	40.0	40.5	40.6	41.0
Electrical equipment and appliances	41.9	42.1	42.1	41.8	41.8	41.6	39.8	40.1	40.6	40.7	40.6	41.0	41.2	40.9
Transportation equipment	43.7	43.8	44.2	43.2	43.6	43.3	41.9	42.5	41.9	42.5	42.4	42.7	42.8	42.0
Furniture and related product	38.5	38.2	39.1	39.4	39.3	39.2	38.3	39.2	38.9	39.5	39.2	38.8	39.2	38.1
Miscellaneous manufacturing	39.2	39.1	39.7	39.2	39.3	39.0	38.8	38.6	38.4	38.5	38.7	38.7	38.9	38.9
NONDURABLE GOODS														
Total	40.1	40.1	40.5	40.5	40.4	40.3	39.9	40.0	39.8	40.0	39.9	40.6	40.8	40.4
Food manufacturing	39.6	39.5	39.8	40.1	40.2	40.1	39.6	39.6	39.3	39.3	39.0	40.1	40.7	40.5
Beverage and tobacco product	39.3	39.7	40.0	40.3	41.0	42.0	40.9	39.4	39.1	39.2	40.1	40.8	40.7	38.8
Textile mills	40.9	40.8	41.6	41.0	41.0	41.4	40.0	40.6	39.1	40.1	40.3	40.6	40.3	38.7
Textile product mills	38.6	38.7	39.2	39.2	39.1	38.7	38.4	39.0	39.3	38.7	38.9	39.8	39.7	38.6
Apparel	35.3	35.2	35.6	35.6	35.4	35.7	36.0	36.7	35.6	36.1	35.8	36.5	37.2	36.4
Leather and allied product	37.7	37.8	38.2	37.4	37.2	37.5	36.4	37.5	39.3	38.4	38.4	38.9	38.2	37.5
Paper and paper product	43.4	43.5	43.9	43.6	43.6	42.8	42.1	41.9	41.5	42.1	42.5	42.9	43.1	42.9
Printing and related support	39.1	39.1	39.5	39.3	39.1	39.2	38.7	38.4	38.2	38.4	38.4	39.2	39.1	38.3
Petroleum and coal product	43.7	43.7	43.1	43.6	42.6	42.7	43.8	43.0	44.5	44.9	45.5	45.0	44.1	44.6
Chemicals	43.3	43.3	43.4	43.2	42.7	42.2	41.9	42.3	42.4	42.8	42.3	42.5	41.9	41.5
Plastics and rubber product	41.1	41.0	41.4	41.3	41.3	40.8	40.0	40.6	40.4	40.4	40.0	40.6	41.3	41.0

Table 2-8. Average Weekly Overtime Hours of Production Workers on Manufacturing Payrolls, by Industry, NAICS Basis, 1995–2008

(Hours.)

Industry	1995	1996	1997	1998	1999	2000	2001	2002	2003	2004	2005	2006	2007	2008
TOTAL MANUFACTURING	4.7	4.8	5.1	4.9	4.9	4.7	4.0	4.2	4.2	4.6	4.6	4.4	4.2	3.7
Total Durable Goods	5.0	5.0	5.4	5.0	5.0	4.8	3.9	4.2	4.3	4.7	4.6	4.4	4.2	3.7
Wood product	3.9	4.0	4.0	4.0	4.2	4.1	3.7	3.9	4.1	4.4	4.1	3.8	3.6	3.1
Nonmetallic mineral product	5.7	6.1	6.0	6.4	6.1	6.1	5.5	5.9	5.8	6.1	6.3	5.7	5.3	4.8
Primary metals	5.7	5.8	6.3	5.9	6.3	6.5	5.5	5.6	5.5	6.5	6.3	6.3	5.4	5.3
Fabricated metal product	4.8	4.8	5.3	4.9	4.8	4.9	4.1	4.1	4.1	4.5	4.6	4.5	4.4	4.1
Machinery	5.3	5.2	5.8	5.1	5.0	5.1	3.9	4.0	4.2	4.8	5.0	4.6	4.6	3.8
Computer and electronic product	4.9	4.7	5.2	4.8	4.6	4.6	3.2	3.4	3.8	3.7	3.6	3.5	3.2	3.0
Electrical equipment and appliances	3.5	3.7	3.9	3.5	3.7	3.7	3.0	3.1	3.4	4.0	3.8	4.1	3.8	3.4
Transportation equipment	6.5	6.7	7.2	6.4	6.1	5.5	4.5	5.1	5.0	5.5	5.3	4.9	4.9	4.0
Furniture and related product	2.8	2.9	3.3	3.6	3.9	3.5	2.7	3.4	3.5	3.6	3.2	3.0	3.0	2.1
Miscellaneous manufacturing	3.4	3.4	3.7	3.4	3.7	3.1	2.8	2.9	2.7	3.2	3.3	2.9	2.8	2.8
Total Nondurable Goods	4.3	4.4	4.7	4.6	4.6	4.5	4.1	4.2	4.1	4.4	4.4	4.4	4.1	3.7
Food manufacturing	4.6	4.7	4.8	5.1	5.3	5.0	4.6	4.6	4.4	4.7	4.7	4.7	4.7	4.6
Beverage and tobacco product	4.8	5.0	4.8	5.0	5.3	5.8	4.9	4.8	4.0	4.3	5.7	5.5	4.9	3.5
Textile mills	5.0	5.0	5.5	5.2	5.0	4.8	3.8	4.2	4.0	4.4	3.9	3.8	3.5	3.1
Textile product mills	3.3	3.6	3.9	4.0	4.0	3.4	2.7	3.3	3.1	3.0	4.3	4.2	3.2	2.2
Apparel	2.2	2.3	2.4	2.2	2.5	2.1	1.8	2.3	2.1	2.1	2.1	2.3	2.3	1.5
Leather and allied product	4.0	4.0	4.7	4.7	4.1	4.6	2.2	2.9	2.7	2.2	2.2	3.6	2.0	1.8
Paper and paper product	5.5	5.7	6.0	5.8	5.9	5.7	4.9	5.1	5.1	5.4	5.6	5.6	5.4	4.9
Printing and related support	3.8	3.8	4.2	3.9	3.6	3.7	3.4	3.4	3.2	3.4	3.3	3.5	3.0	2.4
Petroleum and coal product	6.3	6.4	6.4	6.8	6.6	6.5	7.9	7.0	8.3	8.2	8.5	7.7	6.4	6.2
Chemicals	5.6	5.7	5.8	5.5	5.2	5.0	4.7	4.7	4.5	4.9	4.7	4.1	3.7	3.3
Plastics and rubber product	3.9	4.0	4.3	4.2	4.2	4.0	3.6	3.9	3.9	4.2	4.0	3.9	4.1	3.6

Table 2-9. Indexes of Aggregate Weekly Hours of Production Workers on Private Nonfarm Payrolls, by Super Sector, NAICS Basis, 1995–2008

(2002 = 100.)

Industry	1995	1996	1997	1998	1999	2000	2001	2002	2003	2004	2005	2006	2007	2008
TOTAL PRIVATE	91.6	93.8	97.1	99.4	101.5	103.6	102.1	100.0	98.7	100.2	102.8	105.8	107.3	106.2
Goods-Producing	106.8	108.1	111.2	112.3	112.6	113.1	106.6	100.0	95.7	96.8	98.9	102.5	101.7	96.9
Mining and logging	110.2	112.7	117.6	112.8	102.9	105.1	108.3	100.0	97.4	104.0	114.7	125.8	133.5	138.9
Construction	79.9	84.3	88.6	93.4	99.7	104.0	103.2	100.0	98.4	101.7	108.3	115.3	114.8	107.3
Manufacturing	119.0	118.8	121.4	121.0	118.9	117.7	108.1	100.0	94.5	94.3	93.9	95.6	94.4	90.4
Private Service-Providing	87.3	89.7	93.1	95.8	98.4	101.0	100.8	100.0	99.5	101.1	103.8	106.7	108.9	108.8
Trade, transportation, and utilities	95.1	96.6	98.8	100.3	101.9	103.5	101.5	100.0	98.6	99.6	101.6	103.3	104.8	103.6
Wholesale trade	99.2	100.7	103.4	104.8	106.2	107.1	102.9	100.0	98.0	98.9	101.8	105.7	109.2	109.0
Retail trade	92.3	93.7	95.9	97.2	99.5	101.3	100.5	100.0	98.9	99.4	100.8	101.1	101.8	100.3
Transportation and warehousing	95.6	98.2	101.0	102.6	103.2	105.6	102.7	100.0	98.8	101.9	105.2	107.9	109.4	107.6
Utilities	112.9	108.6	106.1	105.8	105.0	104.2	102.4	100.0	97.4	94.2	93.1	93.8	96.2	98.5
Information	82.5	87.0	90.4	92.6	98.5	105.0	106.6	100.0	97.0	98.3	99.4	100.2	100.2	100.4
Financial activities	87.8	89.8	92.6	96.5	98.0	98.5	99.5	100.0	101.5	101.9	104.7	107.4	108.7	107.6
Professional and business services	81.2	85.2	91.5	96.7	101.7	106.6	104.0	100.0	98.7	101.8	106.3	112.1	115.3	114.2
Education and health services	81.2	83.4	86.7	88.9	90.6	92.8	96.6	100.0	101.4	103.3	106.4	109.0	112.5	115.8
Leisure and hospitality	88.5	90.8	93.4	95.5	97.9	100.6	100.7	100.0	100.1	103.0	106.3	108.9	110.9	109.9
Other services	87.1	89.1	91.9	94.3	96.3	97.8	99.1	100.0	97.5	96.1	96.2	97.5	99.4	99.7

Table 2-10. Indexes of Aggregate Weekly Hours of Production Workers on Manufacturing Payrolls, by Industry, NAICS Basis, 1995–2008

(2002 = 100.)

Industry	1995	1996	1997	1998	1999	2000	2001	2002	2003	2004	2005	2006	2007	2008
DURABLE GOODS														
Total	116.3	117.5	121.6	122.0	120.5	120.3	109.3	100.0	94.3	95.2	96.1	98.9	97.4	92.3
Wood product	109.3	111.6	114.8	117.5	118.6	115.8	105.0	100.0	97.8	100.9	101.3	100.0	89.3	77.4
Nonmetallic mineral product	99.7	101.5	103.1	105.8	106.9	109.1	106.1	100.0	94.3	98.0	97.4	100.3	96.9	91.9
Primary metals	129.3	129.9	132.3	131.1	128.4	128.9	113.0	100.0	93.4	93.3	93.1	94.1	91.4	87.6
Fabricated metal product	109.9	111.6	116.6	118.6	116.7	119.1	109.3	100.0	95.3	97.7	99.3	103.1	104.5	101.3
Machinery	132.2	133.7	138.9	137.3	129.8	127.5	114.1	100.0	93.6	96.0	98.8	102.2	103.2	102.1
Computer and electronic product	127.1	129.9	136.8	136.7	131.1	133.0	117.9	100.0	92.1	89.7	94.8	103.6	102.1	101.5
Electrical equipment and appliances	130.3	129.4	127.7	127.8	128.3	127.7	113.4	100.0	92.0	88.7	86.4	88.0	89.1	88.7
Transportation equipment	115.4	116.4	120.7	118.7	119.5	116.3	105.3	100.0	95.4	96.4	97.3	99.9	98.0	88.6
Furniture and related product	99.2	98.3	102.9	108.4	112.6	114.7	104.7	100.0	93.0	94.3	91.8	90.3	86.1	74.8
Miscellaneous manufacturing	107.9	107.8	110.1	110.4	110.3	109.6	104.8	100.0	93.6	91.8	90.6	90.4	91.0	89.5
NONDURABLE GOODS														
Total	123.1	120.5	120.9	119.4	116.1	113.3	106.0	100.0	94.7	92.7	90.3	90.4	89.6	87.1
Food manufacturing	101.6	101.8	102.6	103.4	103.8	103.5	101.5	100.0	98.4	97.1	95.8	98.6	101.2	101.0
Beverage and tobacco product	97.9	101.4	103.1	104.9	104.7	104.2	100.3	100.0	88.4	88.8	94.8	99.3	102.2	92.3
Textile mills	163.5	154.1	155.2	148.9	139.1	132.4	112.2	100.0	86.3	79.0	71.3	65.1	56.3	47.9
Textile product mills	121.0	118.0	119.4	117.6	115.5	112.4	105.5	100.0	92.4	90.2	88.0	85.0	77.5	70.6
Apparel	235.0	211.5	201.3	181.0	154.6	137.6	117.1	100.0	82.0	75.1	65.7	63.4	61.5	56.6
Leather and allied product	221.8	197.5	187.1	166.6	148.3	138.4	113.3	100.0	91.3	83.6	79.0	74.1	69.3	69.8
Paper and paper product	121.4	120.1	121.5	119.5	117.1	113.4	106.6	100.0	92.4	89.2	87.9	86.9	85.7	83.6
Printing and related support	123.9	122.8	124.6	124.3	120.9	119.4	111.5	100.0	95.3	93.4	90.9	92.5	91.6	86.1
Petroleum and coal product	115.5	113.5	112.7	113.4	107.6	105.8	105.6	100.0	98.7	102.6	102.4	96.9	95.6	102.1
Chemicals	115.4	114.7	114.7	115.4	113.1	110.4	104.7	100.0	99.0	99.0	95.9	96.1	94.1	94.9
Plastics and rubber product	109.8	110.0	112.7	113.7	114.6	114.3	104.9	100.0	95.2	94.2	92.4	91.9	91.1	87.7

Table 2-11. Employees on Total Nonfarm Payrolls, by State and Selected Territory, 1968–2008

(Thousands of people.)

State	1968	1969	1970	1971	1972	1973	1974	1975	1976	1977	1978	1979	1980	1981	1982
UNITED STATES	68 023	70 512	71 006	71 335	73 798	76 912	78 389	77 069	79 502	82 593	86 826	89 932	90 528	91 289	89 677
Alabama	970	1 000	1 010	1 022	1 072	1 136	1 170	1 155	1 207	1 269	1 337	1 362	1 356	1 348	1 313
Alaska	80	87	93	98	104	110	128	162	172	163	164	167	169	186	200
Arizona	473	517	547	581	646	714	746	729	759	809	895	980	1 014	1 041	1 030
Arkansas	515	534	536	551	582	615	641	624	660	696	733	750	742	740	720
California	6 642	6 932	6 946	6 917	7 210	7 622	7 834	7 847	8 154	8 600	9 200	9 665	9 849	9 985	9 810
Colorado	687	721	750	787	869	936	960	964	1 003	1 058	1 150	1 218	1 251	1 295	1 317
Connecticut	1 158	1 194	1 198	1 164	1 190	1 239	1 264	1 223	1 240	1 282	1 346	1 398	1 427	1 438	1 429
Delaware	203	212	217	225	232	239	233	230	237	239	248	257	259	259	259
District of Columbia	583	575	567	567	572	574	580	577	576	579	596	613	616	611	598
Florida	1 932	2 070	2 152	2 276	2 513	2 779	2 864	2 746	2 784	2 933	3 181	3 381	3 576	3 736	3 762
Georgia	1 456	1 532	1 558	1 603	1 695	1 803	1 828	1 756	1 839	1 927	2 050	2 128	2 159	2 199	2 202
Hawaii	255	276	294	302	313	328	336	343	349	359	377	394	404	405	399
Idaho	193	201	208	217	237	252	267	273	291	307	331	338	330	328	312
Illinois	4 285	4 376	4 346	4 296	4 315	4 467	4 546	4 419	4 565	4 656	4 789	4 880	4 850	4 732	4 593
Indiana	1 817	1 880	1 849	1 841	1 922	2 028	2 031	1 942	2 024	2 114	2 206	2 236	2 130	2 115	2 028
Iowa	852	873	877	883	912	961	999	999	1 037	1 079	1 119	1 132	1 110	1 089	1 042
Kansas	672	687	679	678	718	763	790	801	835	871	913	947	945	950	921
Kentucky	869	896	910	932	988	1 039	1 066	1 058	1 103	1 148	1 210	1 245	1 210	1 196	1 161
Louisiana	1 021	1 033	1 034	1 056	1 129	1 176	1 221	1 250	1 314	1 365	1 464	1 517	1 579	1 631	1 607
Maine	323	330	332	332	344	355	362	357	375	388	406	416	418	419	416
Maryland	1 224	1 272	1 349	1 372	1 415	1 472	1 494	1 479	1 498	1 546	1 626	1 691	1 712	1 716	1 676
Massachusetts	2 188	2 249	2 244	2 211	2 252	2 333	2 354	2 273	2 324	2 416	2 526	2 604	2 654	2 672	2 642
Michigan	2 960	3 081	2 999	2 995	3 119	3 284	3 278	3 137	3 283	3 442	3 609	3 637	3 443	3 364	3 193
Minnesota	1 243	1 300	1 315	1 310	1 357	1 436	1 481	1 474	1 521	1 597	1 689	1 767	1 770	1 761	1 707
Mississippi	552	573	584	602	649	693	711	692	728	766	814	838	829	819	791
Missouri	1 631	1 672	1 668	1 661	1 700	1 771	1 789	1 741	1 798	1 862	1 953	2 011	1 970	1 957	1 923
Montana	193	196	199	205	215	224	234	238	251	265	280	284	280	282	274
Nebraska	459	474	484	491	517	541	562	558	572	594	610	631	628	623	610
Nevada	177	194	203	211	224	245	256	263	280	308	350	384	400	411	401
New Hampshire	252	259	259	260	279	298	300	293	313	337	360	379	385	395	394
New Jersey	2 485	2 570	2 606	2 608	2 673	2 760	2 783	2 700	2 754	2 837	2 962	3 027	3 060	3 099	3 093
New Mexico	277	288	293	306	328	346	360	370	390	415	444	461	465	476	474
New York	7 002	7 182	7 157	7 011	7 039	7 132	7 077	6 830	6 790	6 858	7 045	7 179	7 207	7 287	7 255
North Carolina	1 679	1 747	1 783	1 814	1 912	2 018	2 048	1 980	2 083	2 171	2 278	2 373	2 380	2 392	2 347
North Dakota	156	158	164	167	176	184	194	204	215	221	234	244	245	249	250
Ohio	3 751	3 887	3 881	3 840	3 938	4 113	4 169	4 016	4 095	4 230	4 395	4 485	4 367	4 318	4 124
Oklahoma	720	748	763	774	812	852	887	900	931	972	1 036	1 088	1 138	1 201	1 217
Oregon	679	709	711	729	775	816	838	837	879	937	1 009	1 056	1 045	1 019	961
Pennsylvania	4 264	4 375	4 352	4 291	4 400	4 507	4 515	4 436	4 513	4 565	4 716	4 806	4 753	4 729	4 580
Rhode Island	343	346	344	343	358	366	367	349	367	382	396	400	398	401	391
South Carolina	783	820	842	863	920	984	1 016	983	1 038	1 082	1 138	1 176	1 189	1 197	1 162
South Dakota	168	173	175	179	190	199	207	209	219	227	237	241	238	236	230
Tennessee	1 264	1 310	1 328	1 357	1 450	1 531	1 558	1 506	1 575	1 648	1 737	1 777	1 747	1 755	1 703
Texas	3 424	3 597	3 625	3 684	3 884	4 142	4 360	4 463	4 684	4 907	5 272	5 602	5 851	6 180	6 263
Utah	335	348	357	369	393	415	434	440	463	489	525	548	551	558	561
Vermont	140	146	148	148	154	161	163	162	168	178	191	198	200	204	203
Virginia	1 385	1 436	1 519	1 567	1 656	1 753	1 805	1 779	1 848	1 930	2 034	2 115	2 157	2 161	2 146
Washington	1 099	1 120	1 079	1 064	1 100	1 152	1 199	1 226	1 283	1 367	1 485	1 581	1 608	1 612	1 569
West Virginia	508	512	517	520	541	562	572	575	596	612	633	659	646	629	608
Wisconsin	1 472	1 525	1 530	1 525	1 581	1 661	1 703	1 677	1 726	1 799	1 887	1 960	1 938	1 923	1 867
Wyoming	103	107	108	111	117	126	137	146	157	171	187	201	210	224	218
Puerto Rico	. . .	. . .	. . .	. . .	. . .	. . .	. . .	. . .	. . .	. . .	. . .	. . .	693	680	642
Virgin Islands	. . .	. . .	. . .	. . .	. . .	. . .	. . .	33	31	32	34	36	37	38	37

. . . = Not available.

Table 2-11. Employees on Total Nonfarm Payrolls, by State and Selected Territory, 1968–2008—*Continued*

(Thousands of people.)

State	1983	1984	1985	1986	1987	1988	1989	1990	1991	1992	1993	1994	1995
UNITED STATES	90 280	94 530	97 511	99 474	102 088	105 345	108 014	109 487	108 375	108 726	110 844	114 291	117 298
Alabama	1 329	1 388	1 427	1 463	1 508	1 559	1 601	1 636	1 642	1 674	1 717	1 759	1 804
Alaska	214	226	231	221	210	214	227	238	243	247	253	259	262
Arizona	1 078	1 182	1 279	1 338	1 386	1 419	1 455	1 483	1 491	1 517	1 584	1 692	1 793
Arkansas	741	780	797	814	837	865	893	924	937	963	994	1 034	1 070
California	9 918	10 390	10 770	11 086	11 473	11 912	12 239	12 500	12 359	12 154	12 045	12 160	12 422
Colorado	1 327	1 402	1 419	1 408	1 413	1 436	1 482	1 521	1 545	1 597	1 671	1 756	1 835
Connecticut	1 444	1 517	1 558	1 598	I 638	1 667	I 666	1 620	1 557	1 526	1 531	1 544	1 562
Delaware	266	280	293	303	321	334	345	347	342	341	349	356	366
District of Columbia	597	614	629	640	656	674	681	686	677	674	670	659	643
Florida	3 905	4 204	4 410	4 599	4 848	5 067	5 261	5 376	5 283	5 348	5 560	5 788	5 985
Georgia	2 280	2 449	2 570	2 672	2 782	2 876	2 941	2 992	2 938	2 987	3 109	3 266	3 402
Hawaii	406	413	426	439	460	478	506	528	539	543	539	536	533
Idaho	318	331	336	328	333	349	366	385	398	415	433	459	475
Illinois	4 531	4 672	4 755	4 791	4 928	5 098	5 214	5 288	5 233	5 235	5 330	5 463	5 593
Indiana	2 030	2 122	2 169	2 222	2 305	2 396	2 479	2 522	2 507	2 554	2 627	2 713	2 787
Iowa	1 040	1 075	1 074	1 074	1 109	1 156	1 200	1 226	1 238	1 253	1 279	1 320	1 358
Kansas	922	961	968	985	1 005	1 035	1 064	1 092	1 097	1 116	1 135	1 167	1 200
Kentucky	1 152	1 214	1 250	1 274	1 328	1 382	1 433	1 471	1 475	1 509	1 548	1 597	1 643
Louisiana	1 565	1 602	1 591	1 519	1 484	1 512	1 539	1 588	1 611	1 625	1 657	1 720	1 770
Maine	425	446	458	477	501	527	542	535	514	512	519	532	538
Maryland	1 724	1 814	1 888	1 952	2 028	2 102	2 155	2 173	2 103	2 084	2 104	2 148	2 184
Massachusetts	2 697	2 856	2 931	2 992	3 071	3 138	3 118	2 988	2 824	2 798	2 843	2 907	2 980
Michigan	3 223	3 381	3 562	3 657	3 736	3 819	3 922	3 947	3 884	3 919	3 999	4 142	4 269
Minnesota	1 718	1 820	1 866	1 893	1 963	2 028	2 087	2 136	2 146	2 194	2 252	2 320	2 388
Mississippi	793	821	839	· 848	864	896	919	937	938	960	1 002	1 056	1 075
Missouri	1 937	2 033	2 095	2 143	2 198	2 259	2 315	2 345	2 309	2 334	2 395	2 470	2 521
Montana	276	281	279	275	274	283	291	297	304	317	326	340	352
Nebraska	611	635	651	653	667	688	708	731	740	752	769	798	819
Nevada	403	426	446	468	500	538	581	621	629	639	672	738	786
New Hampshire	410	442	466	490	513	529	529	508	482	487	502	523	540
New Jersey	3 165	3 329	3 414	3 488	3 576	3 651	3 690	3 635	3 499	3 458	3 493	3 553	3 601
New Mexico	480	503	520	526	529	548	562	580	585	602	626	657	682
New York	7 313	7 570	7 751	7 908	8 059	8 187	8 247	8 214	7 888	7 732	7 762	7 833	7 894
North Carolina	2 419	2 565	2 651	2 744	2 863	2 987	3 074	3 122	3 076	3 140	3 243	3 351	3 451
North Dakota	251	253	252	250	252	257	260	266	271	277	285	295	302
Ohio	4 093	4 260	4 373	4 472	4 583	4 701	4 818	4 882	4 819	4 848	4 918	5 076	5 221
Oklahoma	1 171	1 180	1 165	1 124	1 109	1 132	1 164	1 189	1 204	1 215	1 240	1 273	1 309
Oregon	967	1 007	1 030	1 059	1 100	1 153	1 206	1 256	1 254	1 277	1 318	1 372	1 428
Pennsylvania	4 524	4 655	4 730	4 791	4 915	5 042	5 139	5 170	5 084	5 076	5 123	5 192	5 253
Rhode Island	396	416	429	443	452	459	462	454	424	424	430	434	439
South Carolina	1 189	1 263	1 296	1 338	1 392	1 449	1 500	1 540	1 510	1 525	1 568	1 605	1 644
South Dakota	235	247	249	252	257	266	276	289	296	308	318	331	342
Tennessee	1 719	1 812	1 868	1 930	2 012	2 092	2 167	2 193	2 184	2 245	2 328	2 423	2 499
Texas	6 194	6 492	6 663	6 564	6 517	6 678	6 840	7 101	7 181	7 276	7 488	7 758	8 029
Utah	567	601	624	634	640	660	691	724	745	769	810	860	908
Vermont	206	215	225	234	246	256	262	258	249	251	257	264	270
Virginia	2 207	2 333	2 455	2 558	2 680	2 773	2 862	2 894	2 829	2 848	2 919	3 004	3 070
Washington	1 586	1 660	1 710	1 770	1 852	1 941	2 047	2 143	2 177	2 222	2 253	2 304	2 347
West Virginia	582	597	597	598	599	610	615	630	629	640	652	674	688
Wisconsin	1 867	1 949	1 983	2 024	2 090	2 169	2 236	2 292	2 302	2 358	2 413	2 491	2 559
Wyoming	203	204	207	196	183	189	193	199	203	206	210	217	219
Puerto Rico	646	684	693	728	764	818	837	846	838	858	872	898	930
Virgin Islands	36	37	37	38	40	42	42	43	44	45	49	44	42

Table 2-11. Employees on Total Nonfarm Payrolls, by State and Selected Territory, 1968–2008—*Continued*

(Thousands of people.)

State	1996	1997	1998	1999	2000	2001	2002	2003	2004	2005	2006	2007	2008
UNITED STATES	119 708	122 776	125 930	128 993	131 785	131 826	130 341	129 999	131 435	133 703	136 086	137 598	137 066
Alabama	1 829	1 866	1 898	1 920	1 931	1 909	1 883	1 876	1 902	1 945	1 980	2 006	1 994
Alaska	264	269	275	278	284	289	295	299	304	310	315	318	322
Arizona	1 892	1 985	2 075	2 163	2 243	2 265	2 265	2 296	2 381	2 509	2 635	2 674	2 616
Arkansas	1 087	1 105	1 122	1 142	1 159	1 154	1 146	1 145	1 158	1 178	1 199	1 205	1 204
California	12 743	13 130	13 596	13 992	14 488	14 602	14 458	14 393	14 533	14 801	15 060	15 174	14 994
Colorado	1 901	1 980	2 058	2 133	2 214	2 227	2 184	2 153	2 180	2 226	2 279	2 331	2 349
Connecticut	1 582	1 608	1 643	1 669	1 693	1 681	1 665	1 645	1 650	1 662	1 681	1 698	1 700
Delaware	376	388	400	413	420	419	415	415	424	431	436	436	433
District of Columbia	623	618	614	627	650	654	664	666	674	682	688	694	705
Florida	6 172	6 403	6 625	6 816	7 070	7 160	7 169	7 250	7 499	7 800	8 002	8 018	7 764
Georgia	3 527	3 614	3 741	3 855	3 949	3 943	3 870	3 845	3 899	4 001	4 089	4 146	4 103
Hawaii	531	532	531	535	551	555	557	568	583	602	617	625	619
Idaho	489	506	521	539	560	568	568	572	588	611	638	655	648
Illinois	5 685	5 771	5 899	5 959	6 045	5 995	5 884	5 811	5 816	5 862	5 933	5 980	5 948
Indiana	2 814	2 858	2 917	2 970	3 000	2 933	2 901	2 895	2 929	2 955	2 974	2 986	2 958
Iowa	1 383	1 407	1 443	1 469	1 478	1 466	1 447	1 440	1 457	1 481	1 504	1 519	1 523
Kansas	1 228	1 270	1 314	1 328	1 346	1 349	1 336	1 313	1 325	1 333	1 354	1 380	1 391
Kentucky	1 672	1 711	1 753	1 795	1 827	1 805	1 789	1 783	1 799	1 825	1 847	1 867	1 854
Louisiana	1 808	1 848	1 887	1 894	1 918	1 915	1 896	1 906	1 918	1 892	1 853	1 916	1 940
Maine	542	554	569	586	604	608	607	607	612	612	615	618	616
Maryland	2 213	2 269	2 326	2 392	2 455	2 472	2 480	2 487	2 518	2 556	2 589	2 608	2 598
Massachusetts	3 039	3 114	3 184	3 243	3 329	3 339	3 259	3 198	3 195	3 212	3 246	3 281	3 285
Michigan	4 353	4 439	4 514	4 585	4 677	4 564	4 488	4 417	4 400	4 390	4 327	4 268	4 159
Minnesota	2 443	2 500	2 564	2 622	2 685	2 690	2 665	2 660	2 681	2 723	2 758	2 771	2 759
Mississippi	1 089	1 107	1 134	1 153	1 154	1 130	1 124	1 115	1 125	1 130	1 141	1 153	1 147
Missouri	2 567	2 639	2 684	2 727	2 749	2 730	2 699	2 681	2 695	2 735	2 774	2 795	2 792
Montana	362	367	376	384	391	392	396	401	411	421	433	445	447
Nebraska	837	856	878	894	911	917	908	911	918	930	942	957	965
Nevada	843	891	926	983	1 027	1 051	1 052	1 088	1 153	1 223	1 280	1 293	1 266
New Hampshire	554	570	589	606	622	627	618	618	627	636	642	646	646
New Jersey	3 639	3 725	3 801	3 901	3 995	3 997	3 984	3 979	3 999	4 039	4 071	4 079	4 058
New Mexico	695	708	720	730	745	757	766	776	794	809	832	844	847
New York	7 941	8 069	8 239	8 459	8 638	8 595	8 462	8 410	8 465	8 537	8 618	8 734	8 795
North Carolina	3 536	3 653	3 759	3 849	3 915	3 894	3 836	3 789	3 836	3 915	4 041	4 145	4 130
North Dakota	309	314	319	324	328	330	330	333	338	345	352	358	367
Ohio	5 296	5 392	5 482	5 564	5 625	5 543	5 445	5 398	5 408	5 427	5 436	5 428	5 368
Oklahoma	1 347	1 387	1 432	1 453	1 480	1 494	1 474	1 445	1 461	1 500	1 540	1 568	1 595
Oregon	1 485	1 537	1 563	1 586	1 618	1 606	1 585	1 574	1 607	1 655	1 704	1 731	1 721
Pennsylvania	5 306	5 406	5 495	5 586	5 691	5 683	5 641	5 611	5 644	5 702	5 756	5 798	5 801
Rhode Island	441	450	458	466	477	478	479	484	489	491	493	493	482
South Carolina	1 673	1 718	1 783	1 830	1 859	1 823	1 804	1 807	1 833	1 867	1 907	1 944	1 928
South Dakota	347	353	360	370	378	379	378	378	384	390	399	407	411
Tennessee	2 533	2 584	2 638	2 685	2 729	2 688	2 664	2 663	2 706	2 743	2 783	2 797	2 776
Texas	8 263	8 614	8 944	9 160	9 432	9 514	9 416	9 370	9 497	9 741	10 066	10 395	10 617
Utah	954	994	1 023	1 049	1 075	1 081	1 073	1 074	1 104	1 148	1 204	1 253	1 255
Vermont	275	279	285	292	299	302	299	299	303	306	308	308	306
Virginia	3 136	3 232	3 320	3 412	3 517	3 517	3 494	3 498	3 584	3 664	3 727	3 761	3 758
Washington	2 416	2 515	2 595	2 649	2 711	2 697	2 654	2 658	2 701	2 777	2 859	2 934	2 959
West Virginia	699	708	719	726	736	735	733	728	737	747	756	758	761
Wisconsin	2 601	2 656	2 718	2 784	2 834	2 814	2 782	2 775	2 807	2 842	2 866	2 884	2 870
Wyoming	221	225	228	233	239	245	248	250	255	264	277	289	299
Puerto Rico	973	989	997	1 011	1 025	1 009	1 005	1 022	1 046	1 048	1 041	1 026	1 010
Virgin Islands	41	42	42	41	42	44	43	42	43	44	46	46	46

Table 2-12. Employees on Manufacturing Payrolls, by State and Selected Territory, NAICS Basis, 1995–2008

(Thousands of people.)

State	1995	1996	1997	1998	1999	2000	2001	2002	2003	2004	2005	2006	2007	2008
UNITED STATES	17 241	17 237	17 419	17 560	17 322	17 263	16 441	15 259	14 510	14 315	14 226	14 155	13 879	13 431
Alabama	370	362	364	365	358	351	326	307	294	292	299	303	296	285
Alaska	15	14	14	13	12	12	12	11	12	12	13	13	13	13
Arizona	191	199	205	211	207	210	202	184	175	177	182	186	182	175
Arkansas	246	241	241	242	241	240	227	214	206	203	201	199	189	183
California	1 719	1 777	1 826	1 856	1 829	1 856	1 781	1 634	1 545	1 523	1 505	1 490	1 464	1 425
Colorado	179	181	187	191	187	189	180	164	154	152	150	149	147	144
Connecticut	249	245	245	248	240	236	227	211	200	197	195	194	191	188
Delaware	43	41	43	44	44	42	39	37	36	35	33	34	33	32
District of Columbia	5	5	4	4	4	4	3	3	3	2	2	2	2	2
Florida	479	485	486	482	478	477	455	428	410	411	416	416	399	373
Georgia	547	552	555	553	550	538	505	471	452	448	450	448	431	408
Hawaii	16	16	16	16	16	16	16	15	15	15	15	15	15	15
Idaho	63	66	68	69	69	70	69	66	62	62	64	66	66	63
Illinois	894	899	902	906	882	871	815	754	714	697	688	683	675	660
Indiana	653	647	652	658	666	665	615	588	573	572	571	565	550	522
Iowa	237	235	239	251	253	251	240	227	220	223	229	231	230	228
Kansas	180	186	198	206	204	201	195	184	175	177	180	183	186	188
Kentucky	299	298	302	307	309	310	292	275	265	264	262	261	256	245
Louisiana	182	183	185	185	181	177	172	161	156	153	152	153	157	152
Maine	83	81	81	81	81	80	75	68	64	63	61	60	59	59
Maryland	175	172	173	173	172	172	166	155	145	141	139	135	132	128
Massachusetts	412	411	412	413	400	403	389	349	324	313	305	300	295	286
Michigan	875	868	875	892	900	898	823	764	720	701	680	651	620	575
Minnesota	375	381	391	397	395	397	379	356	343	343	347	346	342	335
Mississippi	241	231	228	234	233	223	201	188	179	180	178	176	170	160
Missouri	377	376	377	378	373	365	345	325	315	311	309	307	300	289
Montana	21	22	22	22	23	23	21	20	19	19	20	20	21	20
Nebraska	110	111	112	114	113	114	111	106	102	101	101	102	101	102
Nevada	36	38	40	41	41	43	44	43	44	46	48	50	50	48
New Hampshire	97	99	102	104	101	103	97	85	80	80	80	78	78	76
New Jersey	449	437	435	429	422	422	401	368	350	338	330	324	311	299
New Mexico	43	43	43	43	41	42	41	38	37	36	36	38	37	35
New York	810	797	797	792	773	751	708	652	613	597	581	568	553	534
North Carolina	828	809	800	796	777	758	704	644	599	577	565	553	539	514
North Dakota	20	21	22	23	23	24	24	24	24	25	26	26	26	26
Ohio	1 037	1 030	1 027	1 030	1 028	1 021	953	885	843	822	812	796	771	740
Oklahoma	161	162	168	175	177	177	170	152	143	142	145	149	151	151
Oregon	211	218	227	229	224	225	216	202	195	200	204	207	204	195
Pennsylvania	881	867	871	874	864	864	822	760	712	691	679	670	659	644
Rhode Island	80	77	76	75	72	71	68	62	59	57	55	53	51	48
South Carolina	347	339	339	341	336	336	314	290	276	268	261	253	250	242
South Dakota	44	44	44	44	44	44	41	38	38	39	40	42	42	43
Tennessee	524	507	503	504	500	493	454	429	413	412	409	399	380	362
Texas	994	1 016	1 044	1 077	1 063	1 067	1 026	948	899	890	897	924	934	924
Utah	117	122	126	127	126	126	122	114	112	115	118	123	128	126
Vermont	41	43	44	45	45	46	46	41	38	37	37	36	36	35
Virginia	373	371	374	376	367	364	341	320	305	299	296	288	278	265
Washington	311	325	350	361	343	332	316	285	267	264	273	286	293	291
West Virginia	78	78	77	78	77	76	72	69	65	63	62	61	59	56
Wisconsin	567	568	579	593	595	594	560	528	504	503	505	506	501	493
Wyoming	10	10	10	10	10	10	10	10	9	9	10	10	10	10
Puerto Rico	. . .	. . .	. . .	. . .	. . .	. . .	132	121	118	118	115	110	107	102
Virgin Islands	2	2	2	2	2	2	2	2	2	2	2	2	2	2

. . . = Not available.

Table 2-13. Employees on Government Payrolls, by State and Selected Territory, NAICS Basis, 1995–2008

(Thousands of people.)

State	1995	1996	1997	1998	1999	2000	2001	2002	2003	2004	2005	2006	2007	2008
UNITED STATES	19 432	19 539	19 664	19 909	20 307	20 790	21 118	21 513	21 583	21 621	21 804	21 974	22 218	22 500
Alabama	343	343	346	347	351	352	352	355	358	359	363	370	377	383
Alaska	73	73	73	74	74	74	79	81	82	81	81	81	82	83
Arizona	310	318	328	341	354	367	378	390	394	399	403	409	421	434
Arkansas	177	180	183	185	187	191	194	195	199	200	204	208	211	214
California	2 107	2 113	2 141	2 166	2 239	2 318	2 382	2 447	2 426	2 398	2 420	2 452	2 495	2 519
Colorado	304	309	316	322	328	337	344	355	356	359	363	367	375	384
Connecticut	221	223	226	228	235	242	244	249	246	243	244	246	249	252
Delaware	51	52	53	54	55	57	57	57	57	58	59	61	61	62
District of Columbia	255	240	233	226	222	224	226	232	231	231	234	233	231	235
Florida	918	928	942	955	966	1 002	1 023	1 039	1 053	1 066	1 081	1 099	1 123	1 128
Georgia	570	570	577	586	590	597	610	625	632	637	650	663	677	694
Hawaii	111	111	112	112	113	115	115	118	119	120	120	121	122	125
Idaho	96	97	100	103	105	109	110	112	113	114	115	116	117	119
Illinois	799	809	808	816	826	840	850	861	853	845	846	846	849	855
Indiana	387	386	387	394	398	405	410	417	423	426	426	426	431	440
Iowa	230	233	235	236	239	243	245	244	245	245	245	247	250	253
Kansas	237	234	236	240	240	245	248	251	250	251	251	255	258	260
Kentucky	287	289	291	295	301	308	312	315	313	310	314	318	323	323
Louisiana	358	362	364	367	370	373	374	375	379	382	374	348	356	363
Maine	93	93	93	95	97	100	102	103	104	105	105	104	104	104
Maryland	423	423	423	433	444	450	457	465	462	463	466	471	478	487
Massachusetts	404	409	414	422	428	435	440	436	426	422	425	429	433	437
Michigan	641	644	647	656	667	681	685	687	685	680	674	665	656	648
Minnesota	387	389	389	391	397	408	409	414	413	412	415	416	415	418
Mississippi	215	217	219	223	227	234	238	240	241	242	241	239	244	248
Missouri	390	401	413	414	421	426	429	431	432	429	429	434	440	446
Montana	78	79	80	81	82	84	84	85	86	87	86	86	87	88
Nebraska	151	151	152	151	151	154	157	159	160	160	161	162	162	164
Nevada	97	101	107	112	117	122	127	131	135	139	144	150	157	162
New Hampshire	76	78	79	80	82	84	86	88	90	90	91	92	93	95
New Jersey	573	571	570	572	578	589	603	614	622	633	642	647	648	651
New Mexico	166	171	177	178	180	183	186	191	195	198	201	198	195	198
New York	1 416	1 400	1 406	1 424	1 445	1 467	1 467	1 492	1 487	1 484	1 489	1 485	1 501	1 512
North Carolina	544	554	569	587	597	615	629	634	634	645	656	672	688	708
North Dakota	71	70	70	70	71	73	73	74	75	75	75	76	76	76
Ohio	749	752	758	763	772	785	794	800	803	802	800	800	797	796
Oklahoma	270	271	276	278	283	288	296	301	296	302	312	320	323	325
Oregon	250	257	260	266	272	279	282	286	280	282	285	286	290	299
Pennsylvania	712	713	715	712	716	725	728	739	746	744	745	746	745	749
Rhode Island	61	61	63	63	63	64	65	66	66	66	65	65	64	64
South Carolina	294	295	299	309	315	323	323	326	326	325	328	331	337	345
South Dakota	70	69	69	69	70	71	73	74	75	75	75	75	76	76
Tennessee	373	382	380	386	390	399	403	410	411	415	413	417	421	426
Texas	1 446	1 458	1 483	1 504	1 535	1 562	1 586	1 626	1 646	1 656	1 684	1 707	1 735	1 777
Utah	164	167	172	177	180	185	190	195	197	199	202	205	207	212
Vermont	45	45	46	46	48	49	50	51	52	52	53	54	54	54
Virginia	598	596	597	602	611	625	629	635	638	651	662	675	683	695
Washington	444	451	458	466	474	483	505	516	521	524	527	530	534	545
West Virginia	136	139	139	141	141	143	141	143	143	143	144	145	145	147
Wisconsin	379	384	387	393	399	406	414	415	413	412	415	415	416	421
Wyoming	58	58	58	58	59	61	62	63	64	65	65	65	67	69
Puerto Rico	. . .	. . .	. . .	. . .	. . .	. . .	282	295	301	307	305	300	297	299
Virgin Islands	14	14	14	14	13	13	12	13	13	12	12	13	13	13

. . . = Not available.

Table 2-14. Average Weekly Hours of Production Workers on Manufacturing Payrolls, by State and Selected Territory, NAICS Basis, 2001–2008

(Hours.)

State	2001	2002	2003	2004	2005	2006	2007	2008
UNITED STATES	40.3	40.5	40.4	40.8	40.7	41.1	41.2	40.8
Alabama	41.0	41.4	41.0	40.8	40.8	40.9	40.2	40.2
Alaska	43.1	37.4	43.0	40.6	32.9	40.6	44.7	47.0
Arizona	40.3	40.0	40.4	40.5	40.7	40.6	41.0	40.6
Arkansas	39.9	39.7	39.6	39.9	39.9	41.0	39.7	40.4
California	39.6	39.6	39.7	40.0	39.9	40.3	40.6	40.7
Colorado	40.7	40.6	40.4	40.4	38.5	39.2	39.9	40.2
Connecticut	41.7	41.6	41.4	41.8	42.2	42.2	42.3	42.4
Delaware	39.7	40.0	40.3	40.1	39.7	39.9	39.4	39.0
District of Columbia	. . .	. . .	. . .	. . .	. . .	. . .	. . .	. . .
Florida	40.6	42.1	41.0	41.1	41.7	41.5	41.2	39.8
Georgia	40.4	40.9	39.8	39.2	39.0	39.5	39.3	39.4
Hawaii	36.0	35.6	37.2	37.9	38.4	38.6	37.3	37.1
Idaho	39.1	39.6	41.3	40.5	40.3	41.7	41.4	39.4
Illinois	41.0	41.4	40.6	41.0	40.8	41.1	41.0	41.0
Indiana	41.0	42.4	42.1	42.1	41.9	41.7	41.7	41.2
Iowa	40.9	41.3	41.7	42.2	41.6	40.8	41.3	39.8
Kansas	40.7	40.8	40.5	41.0	41.1	43.0	44.5	42.3
Kentucky	41.5	42.2	41.7	40.8	40.6	41.1	41.3	41.1
Louisiana	43.1	43.9	44.1	43.9	42.0	43.0	42.1	42.2
Maine	39.8	39.9	40.0	39.6	39.6	41.4	41.9	41.4
Maryland	. . .	. . .	39.5	40.1	40.1	40.6	40.4	40.0
Massachusetts	40.3	40.8	40.6	41.1	41.5	40.7	40.7	40.6
Michigan	. . .	. . .	42.1	42.4	41.7	42.2	42.5	42.2
Minnesota	39.6	39.7	40.2	40.9	40.9	41.0	41.0	40.4
Mississippi	39.7	40.6	39.9	40.1	40.1	39.4	40.6	40.6
Missouri	40.3	39.3	40.5	40.2	39.6	39.3	40.3	40.2
Montana	38.8	38.2	38.4	38.3	40.1	39.9	39.9	39.4
Nebraska	41.2	41.9	41.6	41.6	40.0	40.9	42.6	42.3
Nevada	38.7	38.8	39.0	40.1	39.8	39.4	39.3	38.7
New Hampshire	40.6	39.8	40.0	40.0	41.2	41.2	40.3	38.8
New Jersey	40.6	40.9	41.0	42.1	42.0	42.1	41.2	41.7
New Mexico	39.0	39.9	39.4	39.6	39.1	39.2	39.0	39.0
New York	39.8	40.3	40.0	39.7	39.6	41.1	40.8	39.6
North Carolina	39.4	40.2	39.8	40.3	40.0	40.0	41.6	40.4
North Dakota	40.9	40.2	40.0	39.3	39.2	39.0	39.9	38.6
Ohio	41.2	41.4	41.0	41.7	41.4	41.4	41.7	40.8
Oklahoma	39.4	39.2	39.3	40.5	39.4	39.9	39.8	41.3
Oregon	39.1	39.1	39.3	39.1	40.2	40.5	40.1	39.1
Pennsylvania	40.4	40.3	40.0	40.3	40.5	40.8	41.1	41.1
Rhode Island	39.4	38.7	39.3	39.2	38.4	38.9	39.2	38.4
South Carolina	. . .	. . .	41.3	39.5	39.7	41.0	42.1	42.3
South Dakota	41.7	42.3	42.5	42.0	42.3	42.1	41.8	43.0
Tennessee	38.9	40.1	39.8	40.0	39.2	39.4	40.0	40.6
Texas	41.6	41.1	41.4	39.8	40.0	40.9	41.5	41.8
Utah	38.4	37.8	39.7	38.1	39.2	41.1	41.1	39.5
Vermont	39.6	40.0	40.0	40.2	39.2	39.6	39.4	39.4
Virginia	40.1	40.8	40.8	41.5	41.4	41.3	42.0	42.8
Washington	40.0	40.1	39.5	40.0	39.7	40.6	42.0	42.4
West Virginia	. . .	. . .	41.3	41.4	41.4	41.3	41.3	41.3
Wisconsin	40.2	40.5	40.3	40.3	40.4	40.7	40.2	40.0
Wyoming	38.6	39.3	40.2	39.7	40.5	41.2	41.8	42.4
Puerto Rico	39.9	40.6	40.9	41.0	40.8	40.5	40.9	40.6
Virgin Islands	43.9	43.7	42.8	46.4	43.7	43.9	42.2	43.3

. . . = Not available.

Table 2-15. Average Weekly Hours of All Employees on Private Nonfarm Payrolls, by Major Industry Sector and Selected Industry Detail, Not Seasonally Adjusted, Experimental Series, 2007–2008

(Hours.)

Industry	2007											
	January	February	March	April	May	June	July	August	September	October	November	December
TOTAL PRIVATE	34.1	34.2	34.3	34.7	34.4	34.7	34.9	34.7	35.0	34.5	34.5	34.9
Goods-Producing	38.8	38.6	39.2	39.3	39.5	39.8	39.6	39.7	40.0	39.7	39.6	39.8
Natural resources and mining	41.8	42.3	42.7	45.0	44.0	44.4	44.3	44.4	45.4	44.5	44.2	44.1
Construction	37.0	36.5	37.6	37.5	38.3	38.5	38.4	38.6	38.6	38.6	38.2	37.8
Manufacturing	39.6	39.4	39.9	40.0	40.0	40.2	40.0	40.2	40.5	40.0	40.2	40.6
Overtime hours	3.0	3.0	3.2	3.1	3.2	3.5	3.2	3.4	3.5	3.4	3.4	3.5
Durable goods	39.9	39.7	40.2	40.3	40.3	40.6	40.2	40.5	40.7	40.3	40.4	40.8
Overtime hours	3.0	3.0	3.2	3.1	3.2	3.5	3.2	3.5	3.4	3.4	3.4	3.5
Nondurable goods	39.0	39.0	39.3	39.4	39.3	39.5	39.5	39.6	40.0	39.5	39.8	40.2
Overtime hours	2.9	3.0	3.2	3.1	3.2	3.4	3.3	3.4	3.6	3.4	3.5	3.5
Private Service-Providing	33.0	33.1	33.2	33.6	33.2	33.5	33.8	33.5	33.8	33.3	33.3	33.8
Trade, transportation, and utilities	33.9	34.0	34.2	34.5	34.4	34.8	35.0	34.8	35.1	34.4	34.4	35.1
Wholesale trade	37.3	37.6	37.7	38.4	38.0	38.1	38.5	38.0	38.6	38.0	38.1	38.9
Retail trade	31.2	31.0	31.3	31.6	31.6	32.0	32.3	32.1	32.2	31.6	31.5	32.2
Transportation and warehousing	37.8	38.0	38.1	38.2	38.3	38.7	38.8	38.7	39.0	38.3	38.6	39.2
Utilities	41.1	41.7	41.4	42.0	42.0	42.0	41.8	41.9	42.4	41.4	41.6	42.1
Information	35.8	35.9	35.8	36.5	35.4	35.8	36.9	36.1	36.7	35.8	35.9	36.6
Financial activities	36.4	36.4	36.3	37.1	36.0	36.4	37.2	36.3	37.1	36.2	36.1	37.3
Professional and business services	34.7	35.2	35.2	35.9	35.3	35.5	35.7	35.4	35.9	35.3	35.3	35.8
Education and health services	33.3	33.3	33.3	33.7	33.4	33.4	33.7	33.5	33.8	33.5	33.6	33.9
Leisure and hospitality	25.5	25.7	25.9	26.3	26.0	26.4	26.9	26.6	26.2	25.9	25.7	25.9
Other services	32.7	32.7	32.7	32.8	32.7	32.8	33.0	32.9	33.2	32.8	32.8	33.1

Industry	2008											
	January	February	March	April	May	June	July	August	September	October	November	December
TOTAL PRIVATE	34.1	34.2	34.8	34.4	34.4	34.9	34.5	34.6	34.4	34.4	34.6	34.1
Goods-Producing	39.0	38.9	39.5	39.3	39.3	39.8	39.3	39.7	39.4	39.4	39.1	38.7
Natural resources and mining	43.0	43.0	44.2	43.5	43.4	44.0	43.4	44.0	43.6	44.2	44.7	43.1
Construction	37.3	37.1	37.8	37.7	37.8	38.5	38.3	38.6	38.0	38.1	37.4	36.9
Manufacturing	39.6	39.6	40.2	39.9	39.8	40.3	39.6	40.0	39.9	39.8	39.7	39.4
Overtime hours	3.1	3.0	3.1	3.1	3.0	3.1	2.9	3.2	3.1	2.9	2.7	2.5
Durable goods	40.0	39.9	40.5	40.2	40.1	40.6	39.8	40.4	40.1	40.1	39.9	39.7
Overtime hours	3.1	3.1	3.1	3.1	3.0	3.1	2.9	3.1	3.0	2.8	2.5	2.5
Nondurable goods	39.1	39.1	39.7	39.3	39.3	39.7	39.3	39.4	39.6	39.4	39.4	38.9
Overtime hours	3.1	3.0	3.1	3.1	3.1	3.2	3.0	3.2	3.3	3.1	3.0	2.7
Private Service-Providing	33.0	33.2	33.7	33.3	33.2	33.8	33.4	33.5	33.2	33.3	33.6	33.1
Trade, transportation, and utilities	34.1	34.1	34.7	34.3	34.4	35.0	34.6	34.7	34.5	34.3	34.4	34.2
Wholesale trade	38.0	38.1	38.8	38.3	38.3	39.0	38.4	38.5	38.2	38.3	38.9	38.1
Retail trade	31.1	31.1	31.6	31.3	31.4	32.0	31.7	31.8	31.5	31.2	31.2	31.1
Transportation and warehousing	38.0	38.1	38.6	38.2	38.3	39.2	38.5	38.7	38.7	38.4	38.7	38.6
Utilities	42.4	42.2	42.5	42.4	42.0	42.5	41.7	41.2	41.9	41.5	41.8	41.5
Information	36.3	36.3	37.0	36.3	36.0	36.9	36.5	36.6	36.5	36.5	37.1	36.4
Financial activities	36.3	36.4	37.1	36.3	36.3	37.2	36.2	36.4	36.1	36.2	37.2	36.2
Professional and business services	34.7	34.9	35.6	35.2	35.1	35.9	35.1	35.3	35.0	35.3	35.7	34.8
Education and health services	33.5	33.6	33.9	33.6	33.6	33.8	33.7	33.7	33.7	33.6	34.0	33.6
Leisure and hospitality	25.3	25.6	26.0	25.8	25.9	26.5	26.3	26.4	25.6	25.8	25.8	25.2
Other services	32.6	32.7	33.0	32.7	32.7	33.1	32.8	33.1	32.8	32.8	33.1	32.6

EARNINGS

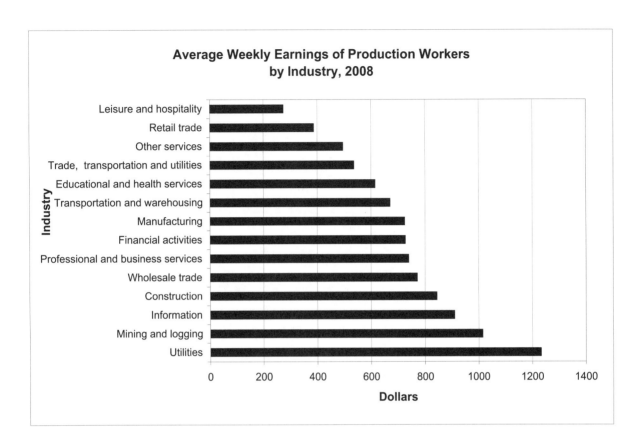

Average weekly earnings of production workers rose to $607.99 in 2008 from $590.04 in 2007. However, when adjusted for inflation, real wages actually fell. Average weekly earnings ranged from $273.27 in leisure and hospitality to $1,231.19 in utilities—more than double the average for all private workers. (See Table 2-18.)

OTHER HIGHLIGHTS

- Average weekly earnings for production workers on manufacturing payrolls increased by 1.8 percent to $724.23 in 2008. Wages ranged from a low of $535.30 in Rhode Island to a high of $933.04 in Michigan. (See Table 2-21.)

- While average weekly earnings was $724.23 in the manufacturing sector, the highest amount within that sector was in the petroleum and coal product industry ($1,224.26), and the lowest was in the apparel industry ($415.17). (See Table 2-19.)

- In 2008, covered workers in utilities had the highest average annual pay at $84,153, followed by workers in financial activities at $74,133 and those in information at $70,787. Covered workers in leisure and hospitality had the lowest average annual pay, earning only $18,946 per year. (See Table 2-23.)

Table 2-16. Average Hourly Earnings of Production Workers on Private Nonfarm Payrolls, by Super Sector, NAICS Basis, 1995–2008

(Dollars.)

Industry	1995	1996	1997	1998	1999	2000	2001	2002	2003	2004	2005	2006	2007	2008
TOTAL PRIVATE	11.65	12.04	12.51	13.01	13.49	14.02	14.54	14.97	15.37	15.69	16.13	16.76	17.43	18.08
Goods-Producing	12.96	13.38	13.82	14.23	14.71	15.27	15.78	16.33	16.80	17.19	17.60	18.02	18.67	19.33
Natural resources and mining	14.78	15.10	15.57	16.20	16.33	16.55	17.00	17.19	17.56	18.07	18.72	19.90	20.97	22.50
Construction	14.73	15.11	15.67	16.23	16.80	17.48	18.00	18.52	18.95	19.23	19.46	20.02	20.95	21.87
Manufacturing	12.34	12.75	13.14	13.45	13.85	14.32	14.76	15.29	15.74	16.14	16.56	16.81	17.26	17.74
Private Service-Providing	11.21	11.59	12.07	12.61	13.09	13.62	14.18	14.59	14.99	15.29	15.74	16.42	17.11	17.77
Trade, transportation, and utilities	11.10	11.46	11.90	12.39	12.82	13.31	13.70	14.02	14.34	14.58	14.92	15.39	15.78	16.16
Wholesale trade	13.34	13.80	14.41	15.07	15.62	16.28	16.77	16.98	17.36	17.65	18.16	18.91	19.59	20.14
Retail trade	8.85	9.21	9.59	10.05	10.45	10.86	11.29	11.67	11.90	12.08	12.36	12.57	12.75	12.87
Transportation and warehousing	13.18	13.45	13.78	14.12	14.55	15.05	15.33	15.76	16.25	16.52	16.70	17.28	17.72	18.41
Utilities	19.19	19.78	20.59	21.48	22.03	22.75	23.58	23.96	24.77	25.61	26.68	27.40	27.88	28.84
Information	15.68	16.30	17.14	17.67	18.40	19.07	19.80	20.20	21.01	21.40	22.06	23.23	23.96	24.77
Financial activities	12.28	12.71	13.22	13.93	14.47	14.98	15.59	16.17	17.14	17.52	17.95	18.80	19.64	20.27
Professional and business services	12.53	13.00	13.57	14.27	14.85	15.52	16.33	16.81	17.21	17.48	18.08	19.13	20.15	21.19
Education and health services	11.80	12.17	12.56	13.00	13.44	13.95	14.64	15.21	15.64	16.15	16.71	17.38	18.11	18.88
Leisure and hospitality	6.79	6.99	7.32	7.67	7.96	8.32	8.57	8.81	9.00	9.15	9.38	9.75	10.41	10.84
Other services	10.51	10.85	11.29	11.79	12.26	12.73	13.27	13.72	13.84	13.98	14.34	14.77	15.42	16.08

Table 2-17. Average Hourly Earnings of Production Workers on Manufacturing Payrolls, by Industry, NAICS Basis, 1995–2008

(Dollars.)

Industry	1995	1996	1997	1998	1999	2000	2001	2002	2003	2004	2005	2006	2007	2008
DURABLE GOODS														
Total	13.05	13.45	13.83	14.07	14.46	14.92	15.38	16.02	16.45	16.82	17.33	17.68	18.20	18.70
Wood product	9.92	10.24	10.52	10.85	11.18	11.63	11.99	12.33	12.71	13.03	13.16	13.39	13.68	14.20
Nonmetallic mineral product	12.38	12.80	13.17	13.59	13.97	14.53	14.86	15.40	15.76	16.25	16.61	16.59	16.93	16.90
Primary metals	14.75	15.12	15.39	15.66	16.00	16.64	17.06	17.68	18.13	18.57	18.94	19.36	19.66	20.18
Fabricated metal product	11.91	12.26	12.64	12.97	13.34	13.77	14.19	14.68	15.01	15.31	15.80	16.17	16.53	16.99
Machinery	13.13	13.49	13.94	14.23	14.77	15.21	15.48	15.92	16.29	16.67	17.02	17.20	17.72	17.97
Computer and electronic product	12.29	12.75	13.24	13.85	14.37	14.73	15.42	16.20	16.69	17.27	18.39	18.94	19.94	21.03
Electrical equipment and appliances	11.25	11.80	12.24	12.51	12.90	13.23	13.78	13.98	14.36	14.90	15.24	15.53	15.93	15.78
Transportation equipment	17.21	17.66	17.99	17.91	18.24	18.89	19.48	20.63	21.22	21.48	22.09	22.41	23.04	23.83
Furniture and related product	9.75	10.09	10.50	10.88	11.28	11.73	12.14	12.62	12.99	13.16	13.45	13.80	14.32	14.54
Miscellaneous manufacturing	10.23	10.59	10.88	11.17	11.55	11.93	12.45	12.91	13.30	13.84	14.07	14.36	14.66	15.19
NONDURABLE GOODS														
Total	11.30	11.68	12.04	12.45	12.85	13.31	13.75	14.15	14.63	15.05	15.27	15.33	15.67	16.15
Food manufacturing	10.27	10.50	10.77	11.09	11.40	11.77	12.18	12.55	12.80	12.98	13.04	13.13	13.55	14.00
Beverage and tobacco product	15.40	15.73	16.00	16.03	16.54	17.40	17.67	17.73	17.96	19.14	18.76	18.18	18.54	19.35
Textile mills	9.63	9.88	10.22	10.58	10.90	11.23	11.40	11.73	11.99	12.13	12.38	12.55	13.00	13.57
Textile product mills	8.60	8.95	9.30	9.61	10.04	10.31	10.49	10.85	11.15	11.31	11.61	11.86	11.78	11.73
Apparel	7.22	7.45	7.76	8.05	8.35	8.61	8.83	9.11	9.58	9.77	10.26	10.65	11.05	11.40
Leather and allied product	8.50	8.94	9.31	9.68	9.93	10.35	10.69	11.00	11.66	11.63	11.50	11.44	12.04	12.96
Paper and paper product	13.94	14.38	14.76	15.20	15.58	15.91	16.38	16.85	17.33	17.91	17.99	18.01	18.44	18.88
Printing and related support	12.08	12.41	12.78	13.20	13.67	14.09	14.48	14.93	15.37	15.71	15.74	15.80	16.15	16.75
Petroleum and coal product	20.24	20.18	21.10	21.75	22.22	22.80	22.90	23.04	23.63	24.39	24.47	24.11	25.21	27.46
Chemicals	14.86	15.37	15.78	16.23	16.40	17.09	17.57	17.97	18.50	19.17	19.67	19.60	19.55	19.49
Plastics and rubber product	10.86	11.17	11.48	11.79	12.25	12.70	13.21	13.55	14.18	14.59	14.80	14.97	15.39	15.85

Table 2-18. Average Weekly Earnings of Production Workers on Nonfarm Payrolls, by Industry, in Current and 1982 Dollars, NAICS Basis, 1995–2008

(Dollars.)

Industry	1995	1996	1997	1998	1999	2000	2001	2002	2003	2004	2005	2006	2007	2008
TOTAL PRIVATE														
Current dollars	400.07	413.28	431.86	448.56	463.15	481.01	493.79	506.75	518.06	529.09	544.33	567.87	590.04	607.99
1982 dollars	258.78	259.92	265.60	272.18	275.03	275.97	275.71	279.20	279.13	277.88	276.17	279.19	281.97	279.14
Goods-Producing														
Current dollars	528.62	546.48	568.43	580.99	599.99	621.86	630.01	651.61	669.13	688.13	705.31	730.16	757.34	776.60
1982 dollars	341.93	343.70	349.59	352.54	356.29	356.78	351.76	359.01	360.52	361.41	357.84	358.98	361.92	356.56
Mining and logging														
Current dollars	670.32	695.07	720.11	727.28	721.74	734.92	757.92	741.97	765.94	803.82	853.71	907.95	962.64	1 013.78
1982 dollars	433.58	437.15	442.87	441.31	428.59	421.64	423.18	408.80	412.68	422.17	433.14	446.39	460.03	465.45
Construction														
Current dollars	571.57	588.48	609.48	629.75	655.11	685.78	695.89	711.82	726.83	735.55	750.22	781.21	816.66	842.36
1982 dollars	369.71	370.11	374.83	382.13	389.02	393.45	388.55	392.19	391.61	386.32	380.63	384.08	390.27	386.75
Manufacturing														
Current dollars	509.26	526.55	548.22	557.12	573.14	590.77	595.19	618.75	635.99	658.49	673.30	691.02	711.56	724.23
1982 dollars	329.40	331.16	337.16	338.06	340.34	338.94	332.32	340.91	342.67	345.85	341.60	339.73	340.05	332.51
Private Service-Providing														
Current dollars	364.80	377.37	395.51	413.50	427.98	445.74	461.08	473.80	484.68	494.22	509.58	532.78	554.89	574.31
1982 dollars	235.96	237.34	243.24	250.91	254.14	255.73	257.44	261.05	261.14	259.57	258.54	261.94	265.18	263.68
Trade, transportation, and utilities														
Current dollars	378.79	390.64	407.54	423.30	434.31	449.88	459.53	471.27	481.14	488.42	498.43	514.34	526.07	535.79
1982 dollars	245.01	245.69	250.64	256.86	257.90	258.11	256.58	259.65	259.23	256.52	252.88	252.87	251.40	246.00
Wholesale trade														
Current dollars	515.14	533.29	559.39	582.21	602.77	631.40	643.45	644.38	657.29	667.09	685.00	718.63	748.94	769.91
1982 dollars	333.21	335.40	344.03	353.28	357.94	362.25	359.27	355.03	354.14	350.36	347.54	353.31	357.91	353.49
Retail trade														
Current dollars	272.56	282.76	295.97	310.34	321.63	333.38	346.16	360.81	367.15	371.13	377.58	383.02	385.11	386.39
1982 dollars	176.30	177.84	182.02	188.31	190.99	191.27	193.28	198.79	197.82	194.92	191.57	188.31	184.04	177.40
Transportation and warehousing														
Current dollars	513.37	525.64	542.55	546.86	547.97	562.31	562.70	579.88	598.41	614.96	618.58	636.97	654.95	670.33
1982 dollars	332.06	330.59	333.67	331.83	325.40	322.61	314.18	319.49	322.42	322.98	313.84	313.16	312.99	307.77
Utilities														
Current dollars	811.52	830.74	865.26	902.94	924.59	955.66	977.18	979.09	1 017.27	1 048.44	1 095.90	1 135.34	1 182.65	1 231.19
1982 dollars	524.92	522.48	532.14	547.90	549.04	548.28	545.61	539.44	548.10	550.65	556.01	558.18	565.17	565.27
Information														
Current dollars	564.92	592.72	622.37	646.34	675.47	700.86	730.88	737.77	760.45	777.25	805.08	850.42	874.65	908.44
1982 dollars	365.41	372.78	382.76	392.20	401.11	402.10	408.08	406.48	409.73	408.22	408.46	418.10	417.98	417.09
Financial activities														
Current dollars	436.12	451.49	472.37	500.98	517.57	537.37	557.92	575.54	609.08	622.87	644.99	672.21	705.13	726.37
1982 dollars	282.10	283.96	290.51	303.99	307.35	308.30	311.51	317.10	328.17	327.14	327.24	330.49	336.97	333.50
Professional and business services														
Current dollars	426.44	442.81	465.51	490.00	510.99	535.07	557.84	574.66	587.02	597.56	618.87	662.27	700.82	738.25
1982 dollars	275.83	278.50	286.29	297.33	303.44	306.98	311.47	316.62	316.28	313.84	313.99	325.60	334.91	338.95
Education and health services														
Current dollars	377.73	388.27	404.65	418.82	431.35	449.29	473.39	492.74	505.69	523.78	544.59	564.94	590.09	614.30
1982 dollars	244.33	244.19	248.86	254.14	256.15	257.77	264.32	271.48	272.46	275.09	276.30	277.75	282.00	282.04
Leisure and hospitality														
Current dollars	175.74	180.98	190.52	200.82	208.05	217.20	220.73	227.17	230.42	234.86	241.36	250.34	265.52	273.27
1982 dollars	113.67	113.82	117.17	121.86	123.55	124.61	123.24	125.16	124.15	123.35	122.46	123.08	126.89	125.47
Other services														
Current dollars	342.36	352.62	368.63	384.25	398.77	413.41	428.64	439.76	434.41	433.04	443.37	456.50	477.06	494.99
1982 dollars	221.45	221.77	226.71	233.16	236.80	237.18	239.33	242.29	234.06	227.44	224.95	224.43	227.98	227.26

Table 2-19. Average Weekly Earnings of Production Workers on Manufacturing Payrolls, by Industry, NAICS Basis, 1995–2008

(Dollars.)

Industry	1995	1996	1997	1998	1999	2000	2001	2002	2003	2004	2005	2006	2007	2008
TOTAL MANUFACTURING	509.26	526.55	548.22	557.10	573.10	590.77	595.19	618.75	635.99	658.49	673.30	691.02	711.60	724.23
Total Durable Goods	549.49	566.53	589.06	591.77	606.55	624.22	624.47	652.94	671.21	694.06	712.95	732.00	754.77	767.56
Wood product	406.51	422.32	435.74	449.78	461.61	477.13	481.36	492.00	514.10	530.16	526.62	533.11	539.34	547.81
Nonmetallic mineral product	517.69	538.03	551.70	573.00	587.42	604.87	618.91	646.87	664.92	688.30	700.64	712.67	716.78	711.30
Primary metals	639.70	658.81	681.52	681.68	700.93	734.79	723.82	749.32	767.45	799.77	815.90	843.63	843.26	850.84
Fabricated metal product	498.48	513.57	534.48	543.20	555.86	576.68	576.60	596.38	610.37	628.80	647.34	668.98	687.20	701.47
Machinery	571.04	584.59	613.31	613.69	625.19	643.81	632.56	645.38	664.48	699.42	716.42	728.84	754.19	759.92
Computer and electronic product	518.26	534.39	562.80	579.90	596.49	609.73	613.22	642.90	674.72	697.86	735.75	766.96	808.80	861.43
Electrical equipment and appliances	471.72	496.69	515.77	522.54	538.98	550.48	548.03	560.33	583.27	607.00	618.88	637.04	656.46	645.60
Transportation equipment	751.78	773.51	795.60	774.42	795.73	817.52	816.90	877.66	889.03	912.56	937.78	957.65	986.79	999.94
Furniture and related product	375.13	385.75	410.45	428.66	443.61	459.95	464.69	494.17	505.47	519.72	527.43	535.90	560.84	554.20
Miscellaneous manufacturing	400.96	414.03	431.77	437.83	454.20	464.86	483.04	498.84	510.62	533.30	545.04	555.90	569.99	591.73
Total Nondurable Goods	452.77	467.88	487.04	504.02	519.95	536.82	548.41	566.72	582.61	602.53	609.24	621.97	639.99	652.20
Food manufacturing	406.75	414.70	428.58	444.81	458.63	472.06	481.67	496.94	502.92	509.52	508.55	525.99	551.32	566.91
Beverage and tobacco product	605.00	624.82	639.69	646.26	679.06	730.35	721.68	698.39	702.45	751.20	751.54	741.34	755.22	750.18
Textile mills	394.17	403.08	425.53	434.15	447.38	464.51	456.64	476.52	469.33	486.68	498.47	509.39	524.40	524.93
Textile product mills	332.30	346.80	364.16	376.16	392.41	399.13	402.47	423.08	438.58	438.08	451.14	467.77	453.12	415.17
Apparel	255.12	261.95	276.01	286.26	295.68	307.69	317.74	334.24	340.95	352.21	366.71	389.17	411.39	415.17
Leather and allied product	319.98	337.86	355.63	361.87	369.80	388.46	388.83	412.99	457.83	446.66	441.96	445.47	459.50	486.49
Paper and paper product	604.74	625.38	647.55	662.20	679.24	681.34	690.06	705.62	719.73	754.14	764.04	772.39	795.58	809.21
Printing and related support	472.37	484.99	504.46	518.32	534.15	552.15	560.89	573.05	587.58	603.97	604.73	618.92	632.02	642.50
Petroleum and coal product	883.68	881.24	908.50	949.28	947.60	973.53	1 003.34	990.88	1 052.32	1 095.00	1 114.51	1 085.50	1 112.73	1 224.26
Chemicals	644.37	666.10	685.39	700.70	700.55	721.87	735.42	759.53	784.07	819.66	831.76	833.51	819.54	808.80
Plastics and rubber product	445.88	458.29	474.94	487.04	505.42	517.84	528.73	550.03	572.32	590.06	591.71	608.41	635.63	649.04

Table 2-20. Average Hourly Earnings of Production Workers on Manufacturing Payrolls, by State and Selected Territory, NAICS Basis, 2001–2008

(Dollars.)

State	2001	2002	2003	2004	2005	2006	2007	2008
UNITED STATES	14.76	15.29	15.74	16.14	16.56	16.81	17.26	17.74
Alabama	12.76	13.10	13.56	14.33	14.93	15.56	15.75	15.68
Alaska	11.70	13.24	12.18	12.01	14.22	14.31	16.37	17.31
Arizona	13.80	14.16	14.38	14.20	14.55	14.88	15.61	16.45
Arkansas	12.90	13.30	13.55	13.49	13.71	13.35	14.06	14.17
California	14.69	14.89	15.04	15.36	15.70	15.77	16.28	16.79
Colorado	14.72	15.44	16.89	16.46	15.91	16.59	17.77	19.78
Connecticut	16.42	17.24	17.74	18.35	18.96	19.78	20.63	21.42
Delaware	16.56	16.60	16.91	17.66	17.74	18.11	17.83	17.24
District of Columbia	. . .	. . .	. . .	. . .	. . .	. . .	. . .	. . .
Florida	12.68	13.30	14.09	13.84	13.89	14.75	16.12	18.31
Georgia	12.50	13.38	14.08	14.54	14.56	14.74	14.88	14.83
Hawaii	13.18	13.07	12.90	13.50	14.34	15.89	17.06	18.93
Idaho	13.85	13.80	13.72	14.15	14.96	16.89	19.01	19.94
Illinois	14.66	14.99	15.20	15.61	15.84	16.03	16.47	16.44
Indiana	16.42	17.15	17.84	17.92	18.14	18.57	18.70	18.47
Iowa	14.67	15.32	15.70	16.17	16.25	16.40	16.84	16.63
Kansas	15.48	15.98	15.83	16.57	17.14	17.69	18.07	18.73
Kentucky	15.44	15.73	16.01	16.50	16.65	16.92	16.92	17.38
Louisiana	16.18	17.03	16.86	16.40	17.30	17.94	19.34	19.99
Maine	14.71	15.55	16.28	16.97	17.28	18.58	19.19	19.72
Maryland	. . .	. . .	15.74	16.47	16.98	17.88	17.65	17.97
Massachusetts	15.75	16.25	16.53	16.89	17.66	18.26	19.26	20.33
Michigan	. . .	. . .	21.20	21.51	21.50	21.84	22.06	22.11
Minnesota	14.76	15.06	15.43	16.04	16.63	17.24	17.39	17.74
Mississippi	11.93	12.32	12.89	13.12	13.53	13.78	13.79	14.43
Missouri	16.11	16.80	18.22	17.92	17.42	17.16	16.99	17.70
Montana	14.03	14.43	14.02	14.87	15.62	15.90	15.88	16.66
Nebraska	13.64	14.05	14.86	15.19	15.44	15.04	15.19	15.26
Nevada	13.79	14.62	14.63	14.60	14.98	15.46	15.54	15.56
New Hampshire	13.98	14.21	14.85	15.48	15.87	16.57	17.09	17.31
New Jersey	14.74	15.19	15.45	15.89	16.33	16.56	17.22	17.88
New Mexico	13.27	13.41	13.19	13.13	13.66	14.06	14.40	14.72
New York	16.24	16.75	16.78	17.29	17.77	18.29	18.49	18.58
North Carolina	12.81	13.18	13.66	14.25	14.38	14.57	15.08	15.49
North Dakota	12.77	13.17	14.04	14.35	15.29	14.98	14.70	15.14
Ohio	16.79	17.49	17.99	18.47	19.07	19.17	19.35	19.37
Oklahoma	13.66	14.11	14.13	14.24	14.56	14.77	14.56	14.74
Oregon	14.74	15.06	15.20	15.34	15.49	15.57	16.45	16.91
Pennsylvania	14.37	14.75	14.99	15.16	15.26	15.38	15.48	15.77
Rhode Island	12.68	12.75	12.88	13.03	13.12	13.42	13.78	13.94
South Carolina	. . .	. . .	14.19	14.73	15.23	15.03	15.72	15.92
South Dakota	12.11	12.60	13.13	13.37	13.47	13.75	14.27	14.64
Tennessee	12.88	13.15	13.56	13.84	14.02	14.04	14.39	14.69
Texas	14.04	13.93	13.94	13.98	14.03	14.00	14.07	14.37
Utah	13.76	14.12	14.90	15.38	14.73	15.25	16.71	17.87
Vermont	14.18	14.33	14.54	14.60	15.06	15.79	16.49	16.51
Virginia	14.50	15.20	15.90	16.11	16.40	16.75	17.60	18.33
Washington	17.96	18.15	18.02	18.28	18.83	19.91	20.51	21.06
West Virginia	. . .	. . .	16.05	16.57	17.14	17.89	18.71	19.02
Wisconsin	15.44	15.86	16.12	16.19	16.29	16.54	17.37	17.94
Wyoming	17.26	17.72	16.75	16.58	17.08	17.44	18.02	20.36
Puerto Rico	9.84	10.30	10.46	10.84	11.10	11.48	11.94	12.09
Virgin Islands	22.57	22.98	23.37	23.35	23.49	26.53	26.35	28.05

. . . = Not available.

Table 2-21. Average Weekly Earnings of Production Workers on Manufacturing Payrolls, by State, NAICS Basis, 2001–2008

(Dollars.)

State	2001	2002	2003	2004	2005	2006	2007	2008
UNITED STATES	595.19	618.75	635.99	658.49	673.30	691.02	711.56	724.23
Alabama	523.16	542.34	555.96	584.66	609.14	636.40	633.15	630.34
Alaska	504.27	495.18	523.74	487.61	467.84	580.99	731.74	813.57
Arizona	556.14	566.40	580.95	575.10	592.19	604.13	640.01	667.87
Arkansas	514.71	528.01	536.58	538.25	547.03	547.35	558.18	572.47
California	581.72	589.64	597.09	614.40	626.43	635.53	660.97	683.35
Colorado	599.10	626.86	682.36	664.98	612.54	650.33	709.02	795.16
Connecticut	684.71	717.18	734.44	767.03	800.11	834.72	872.65	908.21
Delaware	657.43	664.00	681.47	708.17	704.28	722.59	702.50	672.36
District of Columbia	. . .	. . .	. . .	. . .	. . .	. . .	. . .	. . .
Florida	514.81	559.93	577.69	568.82	579.21	612.13	664.14	728.74
Georgia	505.00	547.24	560.38	569.97	567.84	582.23	584.78	584.30
Hawaii	474.48	465.29	479.88	511.65	550.66	613.35	636.34	702.30
Idaho	541.54	546.48	566.64	573.08	602.89	704.31	787.01	785.64
Illinois	601.06	620.59	617.12	640.01	646.27	658.83	675.27	674.04
Indiana	673.22	727.16	751.06	754.43	760.07	774.37	779.79	760.96
Iowa	600.00	632.72	654.69	682.37	676.00	669.12	695.49	661.87
Kansas	630.04	651.98	641.12	679.37	704.45	760.67	804.12	792.28
Kentucky	640.76	663.81	667.62	673.20	675.99	695.41	698.80	714.32
Louisiana	697.36	747.62	743.53	719.96	726.60	771.42	814.21	843.58
Maine	585.46	620.45	651.20	672.01	684.29	769.21	804.06	816.41
Maryland	. . .	. . .	621.73	660.45	680.90	725.93	713.06	718.80
Massachusetts	634.73	663.00	671.12	694.18	732.89	743.18	783.88	825.40
Michigan	. . .	. . .	892.52	912.02	896.55	921.65	937.55	933.04
Minnesota	584.50	597.88	620.29	656.04	680.17	706.84	712.99	716.70
Mississippi	473.62	500.19	514.31	526.11	542.55	542.93	559.87	585.86
Missouri	649.23	660.24	737.91	720.38	689.83	674.39	684.70	711.54
Montana	544.36	551.23	538.37	569.52	626.36	634.41	633.61	656.40
Nebraska	561.97	588.70	618.18	631.90	617.60	615.14	647.09	645.50
Nevada	533.67	567.26	570.57	585.46	596.20	609.12	610.72	602.17
New Hampshire	567.59	565.56	594.00	619.20	653.84	682.68	688.73	671.63
New Jersey	598.44	621.27	633.45	668.97	685.86	697.18	709.46	745.60
New Mexico	517.53	535.06	519.69	519.95	534.11	551.15	561.60	574.08
New York	646.35	675.03	671.20	686.41	703.69	751.72	754.39	735.77
North Carolina	504.71	529.84	543.67	574.28	575.20	582.80	627.33	625.80
North Dakota	522.29	529.43	561.60	563.96	599.37	584.22	586.53	584.40
Ohio	691.75	724.09	737.59	770.20	789.50	793.64	806.90	790.30
Oklahoma	538.20	553.11	555.31	576.72	573.66	589.32	579.49	608.76
Oregon	576.33	588.85	597.36	599.79	622.70	630.59	659.65	661.18
Pennsylvania	580.55	594.43	599.60	610.95	618.03	627.50	636.23	648.15
Rhode Island	499.59	493.43	506.18	510.78	503.81	522.04	540.18	535.30
South Carolina	. . .	. . .	586.05	581.84	604.63	616.23	661.81	673.42
South Dakota	504.99	532.98	558.03	561.54	569.78	578.88	596.49	629.52
Tennessee	501.03	527.32	539.69	553.60	549.58	553.18	575.60	596.41
Texas	584.06	572.52	577.12	556.40	561.20	572.60	583.91	600.67
Utah	528.38	533.74	591.53	585.98	577.42	626.78	686.78	705.87
Vermont	561.53	573.20	581.60	586.92	590.35	625.28	649.71	650.49
Virginia	581.30	621.30	647.70	668.57	678.96	691.78	739.20	784.52
Washington	718.40	727.82	711.79	731.20	747.55	808.35	861.42	892.94
West Virginia	. . .	. . .	662.87	686.00	709.60	738.86	772.72	785.53
Wisconsin	620.69	642.33	649.64	652.46	658.12	673.18	698.27	717.60
Wyoming	666.24	696.40	673.35	658.23	691.74	718.53	753.24	863.26
Puerto Rico	392.62	418.18	427.81	444.44	452.88	464.94	488.35	490.85
Virgin Islands	990.82	1 004.23	1 000.24	1 083.44	1 026.51	1 164.67	1 111.97	1 214.57

. . . = Not available.

Table 2-22. Average Hourly Earnings of All Employees on Private Nonfarm Payrolls, by Industry Sector and Selected Industry Detail, Not Seasonally Adjusted, Experimental Series, 2007–2008

(Dollars.)

Industry	2007											
	January	February	March	April	May	June	July	August	September	October	November	December
TOTAL PRIVATE	20.64	20.73	20.82	21.05	20.83	20.82	20.98	20.84	21.17	21.06	21.12	21.36
Goods-Producing	21.86	21.90	21.90	22.09	22.01	22.03	22.16	22.10	22.27	22.18	22.32	22.60
Mining and logging	24.93	25.18	25.00	25.17	24.71	24.87	24.86	24.58	24.63	24.76	24.79	25.31
Construction	22.65	22.71	22.72	22.80	22.88	22.85	23.00	23.04	23.26	23.21	23.33	23.68
Manufacturing	21.32	21.34	21.33	21.56	21.40	21.42	21.54	21.44	21.61	21.48	21.65	21.91
Private Service-Providing	20.30	20.40	20.51	20.76	20.49	20.47	20.65	20.48	20.86	20.74	20.78	21.02
Trade, transportation, and utilities	18.44	18.54	18.46	18.75	18.47	18.53	18.65	18.48	18.81	18.68	18.59	18.65
Wholesale trade	23.74	23.76	23.63	24.13	23.73	23.84	24.08	23.87	24.25	24.03	24.13	24.32
Retail trade	15.11	15.16	15.12	15.30	15.11	15.13	15.15	15.02	15.30	15.17	15.03	14.98
Transportation and warehousing	19.47	19.58	19.50	19.68	19.42	19.64	19.83	19.66	19.90	19.83	19.87	20.08
Utilities	29.36	29.45	29.87	30.47	30.16	29.86	30.34	30.06	30.59	30.73	30.67	31.36
Information	27.91	27.93	27.88	28.33	28.06	27.79	28.06	27.92	28.32	28.26	28.09	28.29
Financial activities	25.03	25.30	25.28	25.77	25.51	25.47	25.78	25.60	26.02	25.71	25.84	26.15
Professional and business services	24.42	24.56	24.45	24.83	24.44	24.43	24.81	24.40	24.86	24.59	24.74	25.26
Education and health services	20.35	20.36	21.28	21.32	21.24	21.30	21.44	21.41	21.63	21.61	21.71	21.82
Leisure and hospitality	12.21	12.30	12.24	12.30	12.35	12.26	12.28	12.27	12.45	12.52	12.60	12.88
Other services	17.51	17.50	17.48	17.66	17.50	17.51	17.59	17.59	17.78	17.70	17.72	17.90

Industry	2008											
	January	February	March	April	May	June	July	August	September	October	November	December
TOTAL PRIVATE	21.35	21.43	21.58	21.49	21.46	21.53	21.49	21.54	21.74	21.78	22.03	22.02
Goods-Producing	22.50	22.53	22.70	22.64	22.70	22.76	22.85	22.92	23.04	23.16	23.40	23.58
Mining and logging	25.73	25.16	26.57	25.28	25.12	25.59	26.40	26.65	26.37	26.35	27.38	27.50
Construction	23.48	23.57	23.60	23.60	23.72	23.69	23.87	24.11	24.26	24.32	24.45	24.78
Manufacturing	21.83	21.88	22.02	21.99	22.02	22.10	22.07	22.05	22.19	22.33	22.60	22.73
Private Service-Providing	21.04	21.13	21.28	21.18	21.12	21.19	21.12	21.16	21.38	21.40	21.67	21.62
Trade, transportation, and utilities	18.76	18.87	18.90	18.92	18.88	18.99	18.92	18.92	19.05	18.95	19.07	18.91
Wholesale trade	24.21	24.23	24.37	24.22	24.11	24.29	24.32	24.43	24.40	24.36	24.79	24.80
Retail trade	15.10	15.20	15.20	15.28	15.27	15.27	15.20	15.21	15.37	15.21	15.23	15.05
Transportation and warehousing	20.08	20.10	20.15	20.20	20.21	20.43	20.50	20.31	20.37	20.33	20.35	20.25
Utilities	31.48	32.19	31.86	31.57	31.81	32.62	31.95	32.28	32.58	32.52	32.91	32.96
Information	28.33	28.31	28.85	28.57	28.48	28.65	28.67	28.70	28.85	28.81	28.88	28.70
Financial activities	25.85	26.04	26.24	26.11	26.12	26.21	26.04	26.08	26.19	26.19	26.41	26.19
Professional and business services	25.33	25.48	25.72	25.46	25.47	25.73	25.60	25.67	25.91	26.07	26.75	26.76
Education and health services	21.80	21.81	22.02	22.01	21.97	21.99	22.14	22.15	22.35	22.33	22.46	22.59
Leisure and hospitality	12.77	12.85	12.80	12.78	12.77	12.65	12.56	12.61	12.79	12.80	12.88	13.00
Other services	17.83	17.89	18.18	18.14	18.11	18.18	18.12	18.14	18.28	18.28	18.44	18.48

NOTES AND DEFINITIONS

QUARTERLY CENSUS OF EMPLOYMENT AND WAGES

The Quarterly Census of Employment and Wages (QCEW), often referred to as the ES-202 program, is a cooperative endeavor of the Bureau of Labor Statistics (BLS) and the State Employment Security Agencies (SESAs). Using quarterly data submitted by the agencies, BLS summarizes the employment and wage data for workers covered by state unemployment insurance laws and civilian workers covered by the Unemployment Compensation for Federal Employees (UCFE) program.

Since the introduction of 2001 data, the QCEW data have been coded according to the North American Classification System, either NAICS 2002, which was used for the data up through 2006, or NAICS 2007 which will be used for data for the period from 2007 forward. NAICS is the statistical classification standard underlying all establishment-based federal economic statistics classified by industry. Before 2001, QCEW data were coded according to the Standard Industrial Classification (SIC) system. Due to the differences in the classification systems, data coded according to NAICS are often not directly comparable to SIC coded data.

Most industry definitions remained the same under NAICS 2007 as they were under NAICS 2002. However, there were a few industries with substantial changes. As QCEW data coded to the NAICS 2007 system become available, users will need to exercise caution in making comparisons that span the transition.

The QCEW data series is the most complete universe of employment and wage information by industry, county, and state. It includes 99.7% of all wage and salary civilian employment. These data serve as the basic source of benchmark information for employment by industry in the Current Employment Statistics (CES) survey, which is described in the first section of notes in this chapter. Therefore, the entire employment series is not presented here. The wage series is presented because the CES only provides earnings only for production and nonsupervisory employees. The QCEW is more comprehensive. BLS aggregates the data by industry and ownership; these aggregations are available at the national, state, county, and metropolitan statistical area (MSA) levels.

Collection and Coverage

Employment data under the QCEW program represent the number of covered workers who worked during, or received pay for, the pay period including the 12th of the month. Excluded are members of the armed forces, the self-employed, proprietors, domestic workers, unpaid family workers, and railroad workers covered by the railroad unemployment insurance system. Wages represent total compensation paid during the calendar quarter, regardless of when services were performed. Included in wages are pay for vacation and other paid leave, bonuses, stock options, tips, the cash value of meals and lodging, and in some states, contributions to deferred compensation plans (such as 401(k) plans). The QCEW program does provide partial information on agricultural industries and employees in private households.

Data from the QCEW program serve as an important input to many BLS programs. The QCEW data are used as the benchmark source for employment by the Current Employment Statistics program and the Occupational employment statistics program. The UI administrative records collected under the QCEW program serve as a sampling frame for BLS establishment surveys.

In addition, data from the QCEW program serve as an input to other federal and state programs. The Bureau of Economic Analysis (BEA) of the Department of Commerce uses QCEW data as the base for developing the wage and salary component of personal income. The Employment and Training Administration (ETA) of the Department of Labor and the SESAs use QCEW data to administer the employment security program. The QCEW data accurately reflect the extent of coverage of the state UI laws and are used to measure UI revenues; national, state and local area employment; and total and UI taxable wage trends.

Sources of Additional Information

Additional information is available on the BLS Web site at <http://www.bls.gov/cew>.

Table 2-23. Employment and Average Annual Pay for Covered Workers,[1] by Industry, NAICS Basis, 2003–2008

(Number, dollars.)

Industry	2003		2004		2005	
	Employment	Average annual pay	Employment	Average annual pay	Employment	Average annual pay
Total Private	107 065 553	37 508	108 490 066	39 134	110 611 016	40 505
Agriculture, forestry, fishing, and hunting	1 156 242	21 366	1 155 106	22 337	1 163 629	23 117
Mining and logging	1 656 345	33 729	1 675 038	36 086	1 724 044	39 080
Construction	6 672 360	39 509	6 916 398	40 521	7 269 317	42 100
Manufacturing	14 459 712	45 916	14 257 380	47 861	14 190 394	49 287
Wholesale trade	5 589 032	50 835	5 642 537	53 310	5 752 802	55 262
Retail trade	14 930 765	23 804	15 060 686	24 415	15 256 340	24 930
Transportation and warehousing	3 946 170	37 436	4 009 165	38 834	4 098 553	39 515
Utilities	575 877	68 651	563 931	72 403	550 593	75 208
Information	3 180 752	58 002	3 099 633	60 722	3 056 431	62 853
Financial activities	7 826 930	57 143	7 890 786	61 487	8 037 850	64 398
Professional and business services	15 858 457	45 052	16 294 776	47 401	16 869 852	49 574
Education and health services	15 738 013	35 071	16 084 963	36 548	16 479 482	37 654
Leisure and hospitality	12 162 238	16 138	12 467 597	16 624	12 739 466	17 068
Other services	4 261 165	24 348	4 287 999	25 152	4 324 015	25 883
Total Government	20 730 273	39 094	20 788 110	40 500	20 960 607	41 585
Federal	2 764 275	54 239	2 739 596	57 782	2 733 675	59 864
State	4 481 845	40 057	4 484 997	41 118	4 527 514	42 249
Local	13 484 153	35 669	13 563 517	36 805	13 699 418	37 718

Industry	2006		2007		2008	
	Employment	Average annual pay	Employment	Average annual pay	Employment	Average annual pay
Total Private	112 718 858	42 414	114 012 221	44 362	113 188 643	45 371
Agriculture, forestry, fishing, and hunting	1 160 179	24 132	1 166 333	25 191	1 169 029	25 986
Mining and logging	1 776 777	42 904	1 826 609	45 733	1 882 426	49 170
Construction	7 602 148	44 496	7 562 732	46 784	7 124 886	49 013
Manufacturing	14 110 663	51 427	13 833 022	53 489	13 382 697	54 400
Wholesale trade	5 885 194	58 046	5 987 206	60 719	5 954 915	61 843
Retail trade	15 370 040	25 567	15 509 017	26 124	15 307 933	26 179
Transportation and warehousing	4 204 514	40 848	4 292 445	42 615	4 271 969	42 962
Utilities	546 521	78 341	549 539	82 275	557 983	84 153
Information	3 040 577	65 962	3 029 789	69 140	2 989 161	70 787
Financial activities	8 162 063	68 901	8 145 981	73 980	7 968 376	74 133
Professional and business services	17 469 679	51 974	17 859 796	55 139	17 705 280	57 476
Education and health services	16 916 228	39 115	17 433 162	40 528	17 954 103	41 984
Leisure and hospitality	13 024 615	17 781	13 327 559	18 495	13 395 477	18 946
Other services	4 364 889	26 923	4 438 439	27 970	4 484 907	28 773
Total Government	21 114 976	43 180	21 353 885	44 968	21 617 017	46 568
Federal	2 728 974	62 274	2 726 300	64 871	2 762 055	66 293
State	4 565 908	43 875	4 611 395	45 903	4 642 650	47 980
Local	13 820 093	39 179	14 016 190	40 790	14 212 311	42 274

[1]Includes workers covered by unemployment insurance (UI) and Unemployment Compensation for Federal Employees (UCFE) programs.

Table 2-24. Employment and Average Annual Pay for Covered Workers,[1] by State and Selected Territory, 2003–2008

(Number, dollars.)

State	2003 Employment	2003 Average annual pay	2004 Employment	2004 Average annual pay	2005 Employment	2005 Average annual pay
UNITED STATES	127 795 827	37 765	129 278 176	39 354	131 571 623	40 677
Alabama	1 823 573	32 236	1 851 769	33 414	1 894 616	34 598
Alaska	291 797	37 804	296 292	39 062	302 330	40 216
Arizona	2 272 393	35 056	2 354 660	36 646	2 489 462	38 154
Arkansas	1 115 891	28 893	1 129 018	30 245	1 147 615	31 266
California	14 807 656	42 592	14 953 022	44 641	15 234 188	46 211
Colorado	2 117 773	38 942	2 142 352	40 276	2 189 516	41 601
Connecticut	1 625 801	48 328	1 631 240	51 007	1 644 274	52 954
Delaware	402 166	40 954	411 298	42 487	417 692	44 622
District of Columbia	651 088	60 417	659 542	63 887	667 512	66 696
Florida	7 248 097	33 544	7 463 255	35 186	7 747 729	36 800
Georgia	3 783 232	36 626	3 840 663	37 866	3 932 315	39 096
Hawaii	569 532	33 742	585 131	35 198	603 668	36 353
Idaho	575 889	28 677	591 355	29 871	614 548	30 777
Illinois	5 698 184	40 540	5 700 643	42 277	5 748 355	43 744
Indiana	2 821 879	33 379	2 848 873	34 694	2 873 795	35 431
Iowa	1 404 377	30 708	1 422 454	32 097	1 446 568	33 070
Kansas	1 284 726	31 489	1 296 618	32 738	1 305 440	33 864
Kentucky	1 714 060	31 855	1 729 015	33 165	1 757 997	33 965
Louisiana	1 855 554	30 782	1 865 164	31 880	1 841 046	33 566
Maine	591 372	30 750	597 238	31 906	594 481	32 701
Maryland	2 434 245	40 686	2 459 362	42 579	2 497 487	44 368
Massachusetts	3 141 089	46 323	3 138 738	48 916	3 159 934	50 095
Michigan	4 321 094	39 433	4 301 743	40 373	4 297 017	41 214
Minnesota	2 576 452	38 610	2 600 360	40 398	2 640 326	40 800
Mississippi	1 096 802	27 591	1 105 915	28 535	1 111 269	29 763
Missouri	2 615 848	33 788	2 627 401	34 845	2 664 447	35 951
Montana	393 541	26 907	403 432	27 830	413 460	29 150
Nebraska	875 251	30 382	882 263	31 507	892 397	32 422
Nevada	1 080 624	35 329	1 145 762	37 106	1 215 783	38 763
New Hampshire	604 340	37 321	613 310	39 176	620 893	40 551
New Jersey	3 850 590	46 351	3 873 787	48 064	3 917 397	49 471
New Mexico	745 935	30 202	760 449	31 411	778 233	32 605
New York	8 224 387	47 247	8 271 927	49 941	8 348 739	51 937
North Carolina	3 719 444	33 532	3 777 872	34 791	3 856 748	35 912
North Dakota	314 283	27 628	321 108	28 987	328 097	29 956
Ohio	5 281 390	35 153	5 292 088	36 441	5 308 808	37 333
Oklahoma	1 411 640	29 699	1 427 618	30 743	1 465 969	31 721
Oregon	1 563 725	34 450	1 595 003	35 630	1 652 773	36 588
Pennsylvania	5 471 255	36 995	5 496 599	38 555	5 552 301	39 661
Rhode Island	472 586	36 415	475 628	37 651	477 420	38 751
South Carolina	1 766 861	30 750	1 789 447	31 839	1 819 217	32 927
South Dakota	364 263	27 210	369 632	28 281	375 707	29 149
Tennessee	2 598 748	33 581	2 644 749	34 925	2 685 491	35 879
Texas	9 208 473	36 968	9 323 537	38 511	9 583 457	40 150
Utah	1 041 938	31 106	1 071 855	32 171	1 115 375	33 328
Vermont	294 395	32 086	298 454	33 274	300 919	34 197
Virginia	3 410 834	38 585	3 495 767	40 534	3 578 558	42 287
Washington	2 653 237	39 021	2 694 933	39 361	2 766 451	40 721
West Virginia	677 901	29 284	686 936	30 382	695 382	31 347
Wisconsin	2 687 919	33 425	2 714 847	34 743	2 744 006	35 471
Wyoming	241 699	29 924	248 051	31 210	254 418	33 251
Puerto Rico	1 023 102	21 548	1 043 949	22 259	1 048 004	22 859
Virgin Islands	41 961	30 994	43 156	31 846	44 464	33 404

[1]Includes workers covered by the unemployment insurance (UI) and Unemployment Compensation for Federal Employees (UCFE) programs.

Table 2-24. Employment and Average Annual Pay for Covered Workers,¹ by State and Selected Territory, 2003–2008—*Continued*

(Number, dollars.)

State	2006 Employment	2006 Average annual pay	2007 Employment	2007 Average annual pay	2008 Employment	2008 Average annual pay
UNITED STATES	133 833 834	42 535	135 366 106	44 458	134 805 659	45 563
Alabama	1 928 281	36 204	1 952 091	37 492	1 936 489	38 734
Alaska	307 637	41 750	310 810	43 972	315 285	45 805
Arizona	2 614 344	40 019	2 647 691	41 551	2 583 215	42 518
Arkansas	1 167 925	32 389	1 173 852	34 118	1 172 208	34 919
California	15 503 144	48 345	15 640 575	50 538	15 494 915	51 487
Colorado	2 242 012	43 506	2 292 630	45 396	2 310 865	46 614
Connecticut	1 672 109	54 814	1 686 043	58 029	1 687 902	58 395
Delaware	422 187	46 285	423 412	47 308	423 083	47 569
District of Columbia	671 143	70 151	678 119	73 450	685 069	76 518
Florida	7 952 023	38 485	7 945 162	39 746	7 666 374	40 568
Georgia	4 024 699	40 370	4 077 184	42 178	4 031 467	42 585
Hawaii	618 178	37 799	625 862	39 466	619 703	40 675
Idaho	643 671	32 580	660 683	33 544	653 108	33 897
Illinois	5 821 022	45 650	5 869 157	47 685	5 841 692	48 719
Indiana	2 892 419	36 553	2 905 725	37 528	2 872 442	38 403
Iowa	1 470 742	34 320	1 485 627	35 738	1 490 575	36 964
Kansas	1 327 677	35 696	1 356 966	37 044	1 366 878	38 178
Kentucky	1 779 202	35 201	1 801 907	36 480	1 791 017	37 434
Louisiana	1 807 563	36 604	1 868 986	38 229	1 890 007	40 381
Maine	598 525	33 794	602 321	35 129	602 074	36 317
Maryland	2 530 011	46 162	2 547 351	48 241	2 537 752	49 535
Massachusetts	3 194 914	52 435	3 234 357	55 244	3 245 983	56 746
Michigan	4 235 650	42 157	4 179 122	43 357	4 070 914	44 245
Minnesota	2 670 222	42 185	2 687 482	44 375	2 679 527	45 826
Mississippi	1 122 474	31 194	1 135 336	32 291	1 131 096	33 508
Missouri	2 699 860	37 143	2 719 380	38 603	2 715 183	40 361
Montana	426 182	30 596	436 656	32 224	437 591	33 305
Nebraska	902 383	33 814	916 580	35 238	922 929	36 243
Nevada	1 271 634	40 070	1 284 502	42 149	1 252 987	42 984
New Hampshire	627 371	42 447	630 204	43 863	628 763	44 912
New Jersey	3 951 210	51 645	3 961 341	53 853	3 934 789	55 280
New Mexico	807 063	34 567	821 484	36 379	825 736	37 910
New York	8 429 519	55 479	8 554 012	59 439	8 608 351	60 288
North Carolina	3 965 479	37 439	4 062 955	38 909	4 043 486	39 740
North Dakota	335 718	31 316	341 705	33 086	350 440	35 075
Ohio	5 314 572	38 568	5 306 812	39 917	5 235 972	40 784
Oklahoma	1 507 196	34 022	1 534 802	35 491	1 550 489	37 284
Oregon	1 699 932	38 077	1 727 886	39 569	1 713 764	40 500
Pennsylvania	5 607 139	41 349	5 652 547	43 239	5 658 771	44 381
Rhode Island	480 570	40 454	480 132	41 646	469 701	43 029
South Carolina	1 855 842	34 281	1 891 255	35 393	1 876 081	36 252
South Dakota	383 876	30 291	392 060	31 655	397 108	32 822
Tennessee	2 728 694	37 564	2 745 099	39 082	2 721 990	39 996
Texas	9 922 313	42 458	10 231 906	44 695	10 452 907	45 939
Utah	1 170 587	35 130	1 219 207	37 054	1 221 052	37 980
Vermont	303 205	35 542	303 448	36 956	302 627	38 328
Virginia	3 636 417	44 051	3 672 958	45 995	3 665 654	47 241
Washington	2 850 073	42 897	2 925 908	45 021	2 950 773	46 569
West Virginia	705 189	32 728	706 172	34 106	709 657	35 987
Wisconsin	2 767 141	36 821	2 780 924	38 050	2 772 889	39 119
Wyoming	266 894	36 662	277 721	39 254	286 333	41 487
Puerto Rico	1 036 802	23 707	1 016 362	24 741	1 001 120	25 554
Virgin Islands	45 114	35 357	45 922	36 521	45 796	37 005

¹Includes workers covered by the unemployment insurance (UI) and Unemployment Compensation for Federal Employees (UCFE) programs.

BUSINESS EMPLOYMENT DYNAMICS

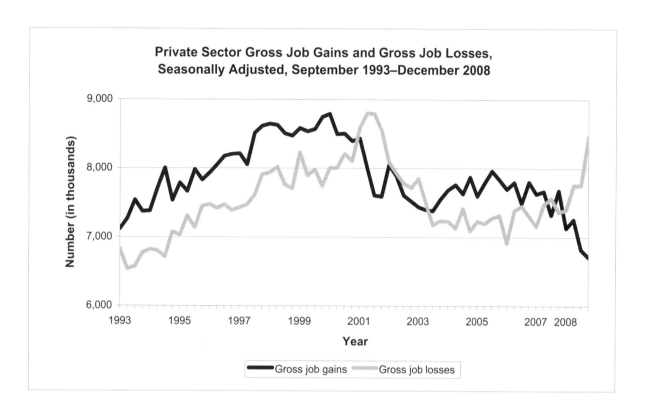

The change in the number of jobs is the net result of the gross increase in the number of jobs from expanding and opening establishments and the gross decrease in jobs from contracting and closing establishments. The net loss of 1.755 million in the fourth quarter of 2008 resulted from 6.712 million gross job gains and 8.467 million gross job losses. There was a net loss in all four quarters of 2008, the first time that there has been a net loss in all four quarters since 2002. By the end of the fourth quarter in 2008, job losses had exceeded job gains in five of the last six quarters. (See Table 2-25.)

OTHER HIGHLIGHTS

- The only major sectors that experienced more job gains than job losses in the fourth quarter of 2008 were utilities and educational and health services. In utilities, gross job gains only exceeded gross job losses by 1,000. However, in education and health services the change was more significant; gross job gains exceeded gross job losses by 176,000. (See Table 2-27.)

- In the goods-producing industries, gross job loss exceeded gross job gains by 761,000 in the fourth quarter of 2008. The net employment change in construction was -337,000 and in manufacturing it was -423,000. (See Table 2-27.)

- In the fourth quarter of 2008, gross job losses exceeded gross job gains in every state and the District of Columbia, except for Louisiana and North Dakota, which had a net employment change of 14,026 and 242, respectively. (See Table 2-28.)

NOTES AND DEFINITIONS

BUSINESS EMPLOYMENT DYNAMICS (BED)

The Business Employment Dynamics (BED) data are a set of statistics generated from the federal-state cooperative program known as the Quarterly Census of Employment and Wages (QCEW), or the ES-202 program. These quarterly data series consist of gross job gains and gross job losses statistics from 1992 forward.

The Bureau of Labor Statistics (BLS) compiles the BED data from existing quarterly state unemployment insurance (UI) records. Most employers in the United States are required to file quarterly reports on the employment and wages of workers covered by UI laws and to pay quarterly UI taxes. The quarterly UI reports are sent by the State Workforce Agencies (SWAs) to BLS. These reports form the basis of the BLS establishment universe-sampling frame.

In the BED program, the quarterly UI records are linked across quarters to provide a longitudinal history for each establishment. The linkage process allows the tracking of net employment changes at the establishment level, which in turn allows estimations of jobs gained at opening and expanding establishments and of jobs lost at closing and contracting establishments. BLS publishes three different establishment-based employment measures for every given quarter. Each of these measures—the Current Employment Statistics (CES) survey, the QCEW program, and the BED data each make use of the quarterly UI employment reports. However, each measure has somewhat different types of universal coverage, estimation procedures, and publication products. (See the notes and corresponding tables for CES and QCEW in earlier sections of this chapter.)

Concepts and Definitions

The BED data measure the net change in employment at the establishment level. These changes can come about in four different ways. A net increase in employment can come from either opening establishments or expanding establishments. A net decrease in employment can come from either closing establishments or contracting establishments.

Gross job gains include the sum of all jobs added at either opening or expanding establishments.

Gross job losses include the sum of all jobs lost in either closing or contracting establishments. The net change in employment is the difference between gross job gains and gross job losses.

Openings consist of establishments with positive third-month employment for the first time in the current quarter, with no links to the prior quarter, or with positive third-month employment in the current quarter, following zero employment in the previous quarter.

Expansions include establishments with positive employment in the third month in both the previous and current quarters, with a net increase in employment over this period.

Closings consist of establishments with positive third-month employment in the previous quarter, with no employment or zero employment reported in the current quarter.

Contractions include establishments with positive employment in the third month in both the previous and current quarters, with a net decrease in employment over this period.

Sources of Additional Information

For additional information, see BLS news release 09-0978, "Business Employment Dynamics: Fourth Quarter 2008." An extensive article on the BED data appeared in the April 2004 edition of the *Monthly Labor Review*. These resources can be found on the BLS Web site at <http://www.bls.gov>.

Table 2-25. Private Sector Gross Job Gains and Job Losses, Seasonally Adjusted, March 1993– December 2008

(Thousands of jobs.)

Year and month	Net change[1]	Gross job gains			Gross job losses		
		Total	Expanding establishments	Opening establishments	Total	Contracting establishments	Closing establishments
1993							
March	288	7 117	5 404	1 713	6 829	5 364	1 465
June	734	7 275	5 782	1 493	6 541	5 155	1 386
September	965	7 539	5 926	1 613	6 574	5 265	1 309
December	603	7 375	5 822	1 553	6 772	5 411	1 361
1994							
March	559	7 381	5 800	1 581	6 822	5 401	1 421
June	905	7 709	6 041	1 668	6 804	5 315	1 489
September	1 288	8 002	6 277	1 725	6 714	5 426	1 288
December	460	7 535	5 978	1 557	7 075	5 642	1 433
1995							
March	758	7 787	6 124	1 663	7 029	5 652	1 377
June	358	7 666	6 006	1 660	7 308	5 840	1 468
September	845	7 983	6 341	1 642	7 138	5 645	1 493
December	378	7 830	6 140	1 690	7 452	5 929	1 523
1996							
March	457	7 933	6 179	1 754	7 476	5 967	1 509
June	631	8 051	6 282	1 769	7 420	5 903	1 517
September	704	8 177	6 373	1 804	7 473	5 942	1 531
December	816	8 206	6 396	1 810	7 390	5 875	1 515
1997							
March	784	8 214	6 407	1 807	7 430	5 886	1 544
June	584	8 055	6 330	1 725	7 471	5 931	1 540
September	901	8 515	6 718	1 797	7 614	5 927	1 687
December	708	8 617	6 697	1 920	7 909	6 024	1 885
1998							
March	711	8 648	6 599	2 049	7 937	6 077	1 860
June	610	8 629	6 552	2 077	8 019	6 224	1 795
September	742	8 508	6 607	1 901	7 766	6 093	1 673
December	768	8 475	6 737	1 738	7 707	6 025	1 682
1999							
March	353	8 585	6 626	1 959	8 232	6 395	1 837
June	644	8 539	6 661	1 878	7 895	6 210	1 685
September	588	8 571	6 734	1 837	7 983	6 250	1 733
December	1 005	8 749	6 956	1 793	7 744	6 076	1 668
2000							
March	789	8 792	6 924	1 868	8 003	6 341	1 662
June	492	8 499	6 814	1 685	8 007	6 387	1 620
September	296	8 506	6 728	1 778	8 210	6 483	1 727
December	295	8 400	6 702	1 698	8 105	6 433	1 672
2001							
March	-156	8 436	6 694	1 742	8 592	6 717	1 875
June	-792	8 009	6 319	1 690	8 801	7 050	1 751
September	-1 184	7 608	5 917	1 691	8 792	6 991	1 801
December	-960	7 591	5 932	1 659	8 551	6 858	1 693
2002							
March	-39	8 049	6 259	1 790	8 088	6 424	1 664
June	-38	7 890	6 164	1 726	7 928	6 290	1 638
September	-171	7 608	6 015	1 593	7 779	6 248	1 531
December	-198	7 522	5 960	1 562	7 720	6 171	1 549
2003							
March	-412	7 439	5 917	1 522	7 851	6 311	1 540
June	-104	7 401	5 928	1 473	7 505	6 040	1 465
September	204	7 383	5 918	1 465	7 179	5 818	1 361
December	309	7 549	6 016	1 533	7 240	5 802	1 438
2004							
March	450	7 683	6 189	1 494	7 233	5 799	1 434
June	631	7 760	6 234	1 526	7 129	5 648	1 481
September	215	7 630	6 057	1 573	7 415	5 877	1 538
December	781	7 872	6 256	1 616	7 091	5 660	1 431
2005							
March	363	7 595	6 123	1 472	7 232	5 806	1 426
June	585	7 783	6 231	1 552	7 198	5 785	1 413
September	680	7 962	6 387	1 575	7 282	5 834	1 448
December	516	7 833	6 263	1 570	7 317	5 945	1 372
2006							
March	787	7 697	6 278	1 419	6 910	5 635	1 275
June	410	7 795	6 274	1 521	7 385	6 009	1 376
September	36	7 488	6 052	1 436	7 452	6 099	1 353
December	492	7 801	6 262	1 539	7 309	5 953	1 356
2007							
March	470	7 627	6 228	1 399	7 157	5 872	1 285
June	192	7 665	6 250	1 415	7 473	6 066	1 407
September	-241	7 323	5 849	1 474	7 564	6 209	1 355
December	310	7 676	6 220	1 456	7 366	6 010	1 356
2008							
March	-270	7 130	5 731	1 399	7 400	6 047	1 353
June	-493	7 258	5 858	1 400	7 751	6 277	1 474
September	-932	6 822	5 504	1 318	7 754	6 383	1 371
December	-1 755	6 712	5 367	1 345	8 467	6 977	1 490

[1]Net change is the difference between total gross job gains and total gross job losses.

Table 2-26. Private Sector Gross Job Gains and Job Losses, as a Percent of Employment,[1] Seasonally Adjusted, March 1993–December 2008

(Percent.)

Year and month	Net change[2]	Gross job gains			Gross job losses		
		Total	Expanding establishments	Opening establishments	Total	Contracting establishments	Closing establishments
1993							
March	0.3	7.9	6.0	1.9	7.6	6.0	1.6
June	0.8	8.0	6.4	1.6	7.2	5.7	1.5
September	1.1	8.3	6.5	1.8	7.2	5.8	1.4
December	0.6	8.0	6.3	1.7	7.4	5.9	1.5
1994							
March	0.7	8.0	6.3	1.7	7.3	5.8	1.5
June	1.0	8.3	6.5	1.8	7.3	5.7	1.6
September	1.3	8.4	6.6	1.8	7.1	5.7	1.4
December	0.5	7.9	6.3	1.6	7.4	5.9	1.5
1995							
March	0.8	8.1	6.4	1.7	7.3	5.9	1.4
June	0.3	7.9	6.2	1.7	7.6	6.1	1.5
September	0.9	8.2	6.5	1.7	7.3	5.8	1.5
December	0.3	8.0	6.3	1.7	7.7	6.1	1.6
1996							
March	0.5	8.1	6.3	1.8	7.6	6.1	1.5
June	0.7	8.2	6.4	1.8	7.5	6.0	1.5
September	0.7	8.2	6.4	1.8	7.5	6.0	1.5
December	0.8	8.2	6.4	1.8	7.4	5.9	1.5
1997							
March	0.9	8.2	6.4	1.8	7.3	5.8	1.5
June	0.6	7.9	6.2	1.7	7.3	5.8	1.5
September	1.0	8.4	6.6	1.8	7.4	5.8	1.6
December	0.8	8.4	6.5	1.9	7.6	5.8	1.8
1998							
March	0.7	8.4	6.4	2.0	7.7	5.9	1.8
June	0.6	8.3	6.3	2.0	7.7	6.0	1.7
September	0.7	8.1	6.3	1.8	7.4	5.8	1.6
December	0.7	8.0	6.4	1.6	7.3	5.7	1.6
1999							
March	0.3	8.0	6.2	1.8	7.7	6.0	1.7
June	0.6	8.0	6.2	1.8	7.4	5.8	1.6
September	0.6	8.0	6.3	1.7	7.4	5.8	1.6
December	1.0	8.1	6.4	1.7	7.1	5.6	1.5
2000							
March	0.7	8.0	6.3	1.7	7.3	5.8	1.5
June	0.4	7.7	6.2	1.5	7.3	5.8	1.5
September	0.2	7.7	6.1	1.6	7.5	5.9	1.6
December	0.3	7.6	6.1	1.5	7.3	5.8	1.5
2001							
March	-0.1	7.7	6.1	1.6	7.8	6.1	1.7
June	-0.8	7.2	5.7	1.5	8.0	6.4	1.6
September	-1.2	6.9	5.4	1.5	8.1	6.4	1.7
December	-0.9	7.0	5.5	1.5	7.9	6.3	1.6
2002							
March	0.0	7.5	5.8	1.7	7.5	6.0	1.5
June	0.0	7.3	5.7	1.6	7.3	5.8	1.5
September	-0.1	7.1	5.6	1.5	7.2	5.8	1.4
December	0.0	7.1	5.6	1.5	7.1	5.7	1.4
2003							
March	-0.4	6.9	5.5	1.4	7.3	5.9	1.4
June	-0.1	7.0	5.6	1.4	7.1	5.7	1.4
September	0.2	6.9	5.5	1.4	6.7	5.4	1.3
December	0.3	7.0	5.6	1.4	6.7	5.4	1.3
2004							
March	0.5	7.2	5.8	1.4	6.7	5.4	1.3
June	0.6	7.2	5.8	1.4	6.6	5.2	1.4
September	0.3	7.1	5.6	1.5	6.8	5.4	1.4
December	0.7	7.2	5.7	1.5	6.5	5.2	1.3
2005							
March	0.3	6.9	5.6	1.3	6.6	5.3	1.3
June	0.5	7.1	5.7	1.4	6.6	5.3	1.3
September	0.6	7.2	5.8	1.4	6.6	5.3	1.3
December	0.4	7.0	5.6	1.4	6.6	5.4	1.2
2006							
March	0.8	6.9	5.6	1.3	6.1	5.0	1.1
June	0.5	7.0	5.6	1.4	6.5	5.3	1.2
September	0.1	6.7	5.4	1.3	6.6	5.4	1.2
December	0.4	6.9	5.5	1.4	6.5	5.3	1.2
2007							
March	0.4	6.7	5.5	1.2	6.3	5.2	1.1
June	0.2	6.7	5.5	1.2	6.5	5.3	1.2
September	-0.3	6.4	5.1	1.3	6.7	5.5	1.2
December	0.3	6.8	5.5	1.3	6.5	5.3	1.2
2008							
March	-0.3	6.2	5.0	1.2	6.5	5.3	1.2
June	-0.4	6.4	5.2	1.2	6.8	5.5	1.3
September	-0.8	6.1	4.9	1.2	6.9	5.7	1.2
December	-1.6	6.0	4.8	1.2	7.6	6.3	1.3

[1] The rates measure gross job gains and job losses as a percentage of the average of the previous and current employment.
[2] Net change is the difference between total gross job gains and total gross job losses.

Table 2-27. Three-Month Private Sector Job Gains and Losses, by Industry, Seasonally Adjusted, December 2007–December 2008

(Thousands of jobs.)

Industry	Gross job gains and job losses (3 months ended)					Gross job gains and losses as a percent of employment (3 months ended)				
	December 2007	March 2008	June 2008	September 2008	December 2008	December 2007	March 2008	June 2008	September 2008	December 2008
TOTAL PRIVATE[1]										
Gross job gains	7 676	7 130	7 258	6 822	6 712	6.8	6.2	6.4	6.1	6.0
Gross job losses	7 366	7 400	7 751	7 754	8 467	6.5	6.5	6.8	6.9	7.6
Net employment change	310	-270	-493	-932	-1 755	0.3	-0.3	-0.4	-0.8	-1.6
Goods-Producing										
Gross job gains	1 573	1 493	1 494	1 397	1 302	6.8	6.5	6.6	6.2	6.0
Gross job losses	1 701	1 758	1 778	1 767	2 063	7.4	7.6	7.8	7.9	9.4
Net employment change	-128	-265	-284	-370	-761	-0.6	-1.1	-1.2	-1.7	-3.4
Natural Resources and Mining										
Gross job gains	292	274	280	274	285	15.8	14.5	14.9	14.6	15.0
Gross job losses	261	293	268	255	286	14.1	15.5	14.3	13.6	15.0
Net employment change	31	-19	12	19	-1	1.7	-1.0	0.6	1.0	0.0
Construction										
Gross job gains	784	763	737	698	639	10.5	10.2	10.1	9.8	9.4
Gross job losses	875	869	922	876	976	11.7	11.7	12.6	12.4	14.2
Net employment change	-91	-106	-185	-178	-337	-1.2	-1.5	-2.5	-2.6	-4.8
Manufacturing										
Gross job gains	497	456	477	425	378	3.6	3.3	3.5	3.2	2.9
Gross job losses	565	596	588	636	801	4.1	4.4	4.3	4.8	6.1
Net employment change	-68	-140	-111	-211	-423	-0.5	-1.1	-0.8	-1.6	-3.2
Service-Providing[1]										
Gross job gains	6 103	5 637	5 764	5 425	5 410	6.7	6.2	6.3	6.0	6.1
Gross job losses	5 665	5 642	5 973	5 987	6 404	6.3	6.2	6.6	6.6	7.1
Net employment change	438	-5	-209	-562	-994	0.4	0.0	-0.3	-0.6	-1.0
Wholesale Trade										
Gross job gains	321	294	295	272	259	5.4	4.9	4.9	4.5	4.4
Gross job losses	301	306	314	313	364	5.0	5.1	5.3	5.2	6.2
Net employment change	20	-12	-19	-41	-105	0.4	-0.2	-0.4	-0.7	-1.8
Retail Trade										
Gross job gains	1 022	954	939	892	835	6.6	6.2	6.0	5.8	5.6
Gross job losses	1 011	979	1 080	1 062	1 181	6.5	6.3	6.9	6.9	7.8
Net employment change	11	-25	-141	-170	-346	0.1	-0.1	-0.9	-1.1	-2.2
Transportation and Warehousing										
Gross job gains	254	208	225	208	238	5.8	4.8	5.2	4.8	5.6
Gross job losses	229	250	253	250	283	5.3	5.8	5.9	5.9	6.6
Net employment change	25	-42	-28	-42	-45	0.5	-1.0	-0.7	-1.1	-1.0
Utilities										
Gross job gains	15	13	16	14	13	2.8	2.4	2.9	2.5	2.3
Gross job losses	11	10	12	13	12	2.0	1.8	2.2	2.3	2.2
Net employment change	4	3	4	1	1	0.8	0.6	0.7	0.2	0.1
Information										
Gross job gains	145	154	162	135	137	4.7	5.1	5.4	4.5	4.6
Gross job losses	155	153	161	168	191	5.1	5.1	5.4	5.6	6.4
Net employment change	-10	1	1	-33	-54	-0.4	0.0	0.0	-1.1	-1.8
Financial Activities										
Gross job gains	432	412	394	376	388	5.3	5.1	4.9	4.7	4.9
Gross job losses	486	436	455	460	497	6.0	5.4	5.7	5.7	6.3
Net employment change	-54	-24	-61	-84	-109	-0.7	-0.3	-0.8	-1.0	-1.4
Professional and Business Services										
Gross job gains	1 440	1 239	1 345	1 231	1 234	8.0	6.8	7.5	6.9	7.1
Gross job losses	1 337	1 358	1 433	1 411	1 619	7.5	7.6	8.1	7.9	9.2
Net employment change	103	-119	-88	-180	-385	0.5	-0.8	-0.6	-1.0	-2.1
Education and Health Services										
Gross job gains	814	785	788	799	841	4.6	4.4	4.4	4.5	4.6
Gross job losses	666	667	715	706	665	3.7	3.8	4.0	4.0	3.7
Net employment change	148	118	73	93	176	0.9	0.6	0.4	0.5	0.9
Leisure and Hospitality										
Gross job gains	1 247	1 158	1 183	1 114	1 111	9.3	8.6	8.7	8.3	8.4
Gross job losses	1 148	1 154	1 218	1 259	1 235	8.5	8.6	9.1	9.4	9.3
Net employment change	99	4	-35	-145	-124	0.8	0.0	-0.4	-1.1	-0.9
Other Services										
Gross job gains	296	290	300	280	265	7.6	7.5	7.7	7.1	6.8
Gross job losses	287	289	293	307	322	7.3	7.4	7.5	7.8	8.3
Net employment change	9	1	7	-27	-57	0.3	0.1	0.2	-0.7	-1.5

[1]Includes unclassified sector, not shown separately.

Table 2-28. Private Sector Gross Job Gains and Losses, by State and Selected Territory, Seasonally Adjusted, December 2007–December 2008

(Number.)

State	Gross job gains (3 months ended)					Gross job losses (3 months ended)				
	December 2007	March 2008	June 2008	September 2008	December 2008	December 2007	March 2008	June 2008	September 2008	December 2008
UNITED STATES	7 676 000	7 130 000	7 258 000	6 822 000	6 712 000	7 366 000	7 400 000	7 751 000	7 754 000	8 467 000
Alabama	107 871	96 431	92 858	94 018	83 012	104 544	102 216	103 750	106 097	119 055
Alaska	24 875	24 026	27 326	23 290	25 991	26 209	21 293	23 152	25 878	26 540
Arizona	157 454	131 093	135 186	136 644	127 435	173 557	157 425	169 011	160 041	194 334
Arkansas	60 518	57 573	55 808	59 307	54 192	57 447	55 687	61 899	60 203	65 356
California	991 318	883 486	924 534	823 743	820 811	917 701	970 184	992 365	968 431	1 021 575
Colorado	147 704	144 403	142 518	136 670	128 334	142 396	139 549	143 312	148 638	161 291
Connecticut	84 896	75 774	81 956	74 507	71 865	82 717	75 913	79 403	86 469	91 586
Delaware	26 057	22 843	22 931	23 365	23 185	23 286	23 490	26 415	29 015	27 529
District of Columbia	26 858	27 668	29 566	27 587	24 920	26 855	24 968	26 545	26 265	30 282
Florida	503 784	462 893	456 432	437 465	439 888	557 019	508 941	559 962	548 854	582 767
Georgia	246 217	241 910	235 469	223 052	214 679	257 581	248 694	265 860	259 344	299 093
Hawaii	27 626	27 444	26 659	24 608	23 763	26 283	28 861	35 007	34 248	33 212
Idaho	46 957	43 825	40 999	41 167	38 841	42 462	47 387	48 725	46 527	49 607
Illinois	289 963	257 263	279 798	251 615	244 677	284 241	277 394	274 501	293 498	330 096
Indiana	147 408	128 823	148 823	142 552	129 136	152 272	151 313	156 699	160 977	191 303
Iowa	76 423	75 913	75 492	72 202	71 402	72 570	75 739	77 074	75 503	85 180
Kansas	72 455	85 756	73 245	66 962	74 781	72 803	76 089	76 424	75 491	78 274
Kentucky	98 760	89 802	92 385	82 716	85 906	91 580	94 167	94 347	98 439	106 165
Louisiana	114 566	105 843	106 666	101 375	119 844	102 061	101 310	110 348	117 794	105 818
Maine	39 812	35 386	39 310	35 228	38 175	36 533	38 311	38 951	42 054	41 665
Maryland	133 972	129 204	130 724	127 690	125 257	137 186	132 403	144 023	142 439	156 325
Massachusetts	163 903	156 011	170 476	151 905	146 760	169 769	152 572	161 310	172 780	188 813
Michigan	226 325	207 642	227 833	205 970	201 544	249 067	242 937	245 121	263 868	295 072
Minnesota	140 089	139 026	141 178	131 850	118 610	143 481	142 695	144 422	145 373	155 252
Mississippi	65 791	57 582	55 524	54 090	57 009	57 571	58 523	68 125	66 097	68 718
Missouri	138 451	137 642	142 593	133 936	133 000	141 379	139 452	147 646	144 905	167 561
Montana	32 517	30 702	27 908	27 599	28 115	28 468	30 160	31 601	28 770	31 199
Nebraska	47 931	46 332	44 468	45 474	44 255	47 536	42 107	47 868	45 394	50 122
Nevada	85 876	76 077	71 885	66 270	62 916	77 350	85 232	84 034	86 950	99 850
New Hampshire	39 237	35 433	38 576	34 837	33 804	38 422	37 137	38 970	38 872	41 707
New Jersey	227 637	202 756	230 667	196 277	189 705	218 322	213 561	225 045	234 424	247 770
New Mexico	47 752	44 333	43 833	44 736	39 679	44 620	41 459	47 977	45 529	51 967
New York	492 874	435 576	471 669	440 884	441 693	439 494	450 588	466 336	470 365	511 515
North Carolina	233 942	222 100	207 441	206 032	199 409	217 800	221 137	237 807	240 101	266 928
North Dakota	20 281	21 771	19 325	20 897	19 509	17 305	17 438	18 918	18 489	19 267
Ohio	270 727	243 918	271 662	245 865	228 707	274 342	283 287	273 471	281 477	320 542
Oklahoma	80 007	86 731	81 885	80 037	77 009	77 962	72 919	80 295	77 491	83 065
Oregon	107 206	97 406	89 219	97 615	86 078	103 814	100 289	110 881	98 568	126 138
Pennsylvania	289 282	267 831	287 681	267 451	255 471	275 587	274 187	282 520	290 479	310 328
Rhode Island	25 807	23 562	26 773	24 724	21 871	28 218	26 635	27 873	28 605	30 457
South Carolina	103 048	99 070	92 276	87 937	84 926	105 799	100 963	107 813	108 041	123 569
South Dakota	21 382	21 942	21 298	21 110	20 975	20 270	19 382	21 663	20 789	22 676
Tennessee	141 888	133 791	131 679	126 191	117 983	133 361	138 012	150 958	158 301	162 740
Texas	568 802	535 846	529 866	499 414	534 436	487 640	484 274	520 811	533 886	563 061
Utah	81 880	71 826	70 125	67 227	65 565	75 317	71 419	77 237	73 222	82 140
Vermont	20 368	17 728	18 395	17 109	17 491	18 694	19 372	18 709	19 096	20 345
Virginia	184 806	186 117	185 464	176 537	169 652	186 717	181 561	190 261	198 251	209 325
Washington	185 367	185 681	160 249	172 149	156 619	164 540	167 911	188 699	163 055	203 989
West Virginia	40 109	36 735	35 116	38 356	37 530	36 420	37 112	37 914	36 140	38 723
Wisconsin	136 739	133 678	138 886	129 435	127 923	135 453	136 642	144 751	150 913	162 478
Wyoming	23 500	23 351	19 438	21 024	19 620	18 010	19 803	23 122	18 684	19 854
Puerto Rico	49 548	43 097	43 855	42 205	44 854	49 977	56 195	52 124	47 635	50 209
Virgin Islands	2 261	2 193	2 119	1 927	1 881	2 234	2 157	2 482	2 302	2 197

Table 2-29. Private Sector Gross Job Gains and Losses as a Percent of Total Employment, by State and Selected Territory, Seasonally Adjusted, December 2007–December 2008

(Percent.)

State	Gross job gains (3 months ended)					Gross job losses (3 months ended)				
	December 2007	March 2008	June 2008	September 2008	December 2008	December 2007	March 2008	June 2008	September 2008	December 2008
UNITED STATES	6.8	6.2	6.4	6.1	6.0	6.5	6.5	6.8	6.9	7.6
Alabama	6.8	6.0	5.9	5.9	5.4	6.5	6.5	6.6	6.7	7.7
Alaska	10.6	10.2	11.5	9.7	10.9	11.2	9.0	9.7	10.8	11.2
Arizona	7.0	5.9	6.2	6.3	6.0	7.7	7.1	7.7	7.3	9.1
Arkansas	6.2	5.8	5.7	6.1	5.6	5.8	5.7	6.3	6.2	6.8
California	7.7	6.8	7.2	6.5	6.5	7.0	7.5	7.7	7.6	8.1
Colorado	7.6	7.4	7.3	7.0	6.7	7.3	7.1	7.3	7.7	8.3
Connecticut	5.9	5.3	5.7	5.2	5.1	5.7	5.3	5.5	6.0	6.5
Delaware	7.1	6.2	6.3	6.5	6.6	6.4	6.4	7.3	8.0	7.8
District of Columbia	6.0	6.2	6.6	6.1	5.6	6.1	5.6	5.9	5.8	6.8
Florida	7.4	6.8	6.8	6.6	6.9	8.1	7.5	8.4	8.3	9.0
Georgia	7.3	7.1	7.0	6.7	6.6	7.5	7.3	7.9	7.7	9.1
Hawaii	5.4	5.4	5.3	4.9	4.9	5.2	5.7	6.9	6.9	6.8
Idaho	8.5	8.0	7.5	7.6	7.3	7.7	8.6	8.9	8.6	9.4
Illinois	5.7	5.0	5.5	5.0	4.9	5.6	5.4	5.4	5.8	6.7
Indiana	5.9	5.2	6.0	5.7	5.4	6.0	6.1	6.3	6.6	7.9
Iowa	6.1	6.0	6.0	5.7	5.7	5.8	6.0	6.1	6.1	6.8
Kansas	6.5	7.7	6.5	6.0	6.7	6.6	6.7	6.8	6.7	7.0
Kentucky	6.6	5.9	6.1	5.6	5.8	6.1	6.3	6.3	6.6	7.2
Louisiana	7.4	6.9	6.9	6.6	7.8	6.7	6.5	7.1	7.7	6.8
Maine	8.0	7.0	7.8	7.0	7.7	7.3	7.6	7.8	8.4	8.4
Maryland	6.4	6.2	6.3	6.2	6.1	6.6	6.4	7.0	6.9	7.6
Massachusetts	5.9	5.6	6.0	5.4	5.2	6.1	5.5	5.8	6.2	6.8
Michigan	6.4	5.9	6.5	5.9	5.9	7.0	6.9	6.9	7.6	8.7
Minnesota	6.0	6.0	6.1	5.7	5.2	6.2	6.1	6.2	6.3	6.8
Mississippi	7.3	6.3	6.2	6.1	6.6	6.4	6.5	7.6	7.4	7.8
Missouri	6.0	6.0	6.2	5.9	5.9	6.2	6.1	6.4	6.4	7.4
Montana	9.0	8.5	7.8	7.7	7.9	8.0	8.4	8.8	8.1	8.8
Nebraska	6.3	6.0	5.8	6.0	5.7	6.2	5.5	6.2	6.0	6.6
Nevada	7.6	6.7	6.5	6.0	5.8	6.8	7.6	7.6	8.0	9.3
New Hampshire	7.2	6.5	7.1	6.4	6.3	7.1	6.8	7.2	7.2	7.8
New Jersey	6.8	6.1	6.9	5.9	5.8	6.5	6.3	6.7	7.0	7.5
New Mexico	7.5	6.9	6.8	7.0	6.2	7.0	6.5	7.5	7.2	8.2
New York	6.9	6.1	6.6	6.1	6.2	6.2	6.3	6.5	6.5	7.1
North Carolina	6.8	6.5	6.1	6.1	6.0	6.4	6.5	7.0	7.2	8.1
North Dakota	7.2	7.7	6.8	7.3	6.8	6.2	6.1	6.7	6.4	6.7
Ohio	6.0	5.4	6.1	5.5	5.1	6.1	6.3	6.0	6.2	7.2
Oklahoma	6.5	7.0	6.6	6.4	6.2	6.4	5.9	6.5	6.2	6.8
Oregon	7.3	6.7	6.2	6.8	6.1	7.1	6.9	7.7	6.9	8.9
Pennsylvania	5.8	5.4	5.8	5.4	5.2	5.6	5.6	5.7	5.9	6.4
Rhode Island	6.2	5.7	6.5	6.1	5.5	6.8	6.4	6.8	7.0	7.5
South Carolina	6.6	6.3	5.9	5.7	5.6	6.7	6.5	6.9	7.1	8.2
South Dakota	6.6	6.7	6.5	6.5	6.4	6.2	5.9	6.7	6.4	7.0
Tennessee	6.1	5.7	5.7	5.5	5.2	5.7	5.8	6.5	6.9	7.2
Texas	6.7	6.1	6.1	5.8	6.2	5.6	5.6	6.0	6.2	6.5
Utah	7.9	7.0	6.8	6.6	6.5	7.3	6.9	7.5	7.1	8.1
Vermont	8.2	7.0	7.4	6.9	7.1	7.5	7.7	7.4	7.7	8.2
Virginia	6.1	6.2	6.2	5.9	5.8	6.2	6.0	6.3	6.6	7.1
Washington	7.7	7.6	6.7	7.2	6.6	6.8	7.0	7.8	6.8	8.5
West Virginia	7.0	6.4	6.2	6.8	6.6	6.3	6.5	6.6	6.3	6.8
Wisconsin	5.7	5.6	5.8	5.4	5.4	5.7	5.7	6.1	6.4	6.8
Wyoming	10.8	10.5	8.7	9.5	8.8	8.2	8.9	10.4	8.4	8.9
Puerto Rico	6.7	5.9	6.1	5.9	6.3	6.8	7.6	7.2	6.6	7.0
Virgin Islands	6.8	6.6	6.5	5.9	5.8	6.8	6.5	7.5	7.1	6.7

Chapter Three

OCCUPATIONAL EMPLOYMENT AND WAGES

OCCUPATIONAL EMPLOYMENT AND WAGES

HIGHLIGHTS

This chapter presents employment and wage statistics from the Bureau of Labor Statistics Occupational Employment Statistics (OES) program.

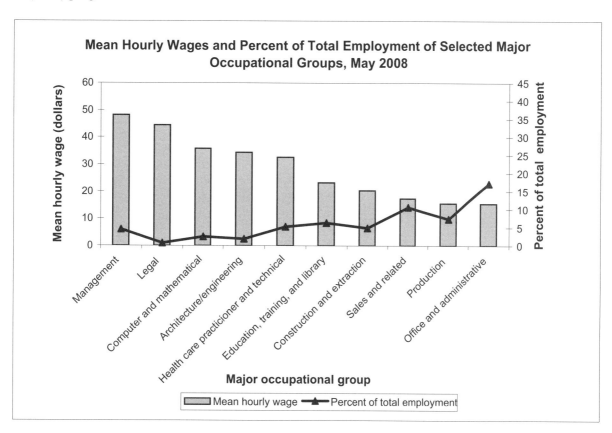

The mean hourly wage for all occupations was $20.32, while the mean annual wage was $42,270 in May 2008. Office and administration support occupations continued to employ the largest percentage of workers in any major group (17.2 percent). The mean hourly wage for office and administration support occupations ($15.49) ranked 16th (from highest to lowest) among the 22 major occupational groups compared. Management workers continued to have the highest mean hourly wage at $48.23. (Table 3-1.)

OTHER HIGHLIGHTS

- Food preparation workers, the third largest occupational group with 8.5 percent of workers, continued to be the lowest paying occupational group in May 2008, with a mean hourly wage of only $9.72. (See Table 3-1.)

- In addition to food preparation and serving-related occupations, the following occupational groups all had a mean hourly wage under $12.00: farming, forestry, and fishing; building and grounds cleaning and maintenance; and personal care and services. (See Table 3-1.)

- Medical doctors typically had the highest mean annual wage of all workers. Mean annual wages ranged from $153,370 for pediatricians to $206,770 for surgeons. Physician assistants had a mean annual salary of $81,610. (See Table 3-3.)

- There was a wide variation in the mean annual wages of sales and related occupations. Securities, commodities, and financial service agents had a mean annual wage of $92,050, while cashiers had a mean annual wage of only $18,800. (See Table 3-5.)

NOTES AND DEFINITIONS

Collection and Coverage

The Occupational Employment Statistics (OES) survey is a federal-state cooperative program conducted by the Bureau of Labor Statistics (BLS) and the State Workforce Agencies (SWAs). The OES program collects data on wage and salary workers in nonfarm establishments in order to produce employment and wage estimates for about 800 occupations. Data from self-employed persons are not collected and are not included in the estimates. BLS funds the survey and provides procedural and technical support, while the SWAs collect the necessary data.

With the exception of the May 2008 panel, each OES panel includes approximately 200,000 establishments. Due to budget constraints, the May 2008 sample was reduced to approximately 174,000 establishments. To reduce respondent burden, the collection is on a three-year survey cycle that ensures that establishments are surveyed at most once every three years. The estimates for occupations in nonfarm establishments are based on OES data collected for the reference months of May and November.

Scope of the Survey

Prior to 1996, the OES program collected only occupational employment data for selected industries in each year of the three-year survey cycle, and produced only industry-specific estimates of occupational employment. The 1996 survey round was the first year that the OES program began collecting occupational employment and wage data in every state. In addition, the program's three-year survey cycle was modified to collect data from all covered industries each year. In 1997, the OES program began producing estimates of cross-industry as well as industry-specific occupational employment and wages.

In 1999, the OES survey began using the Standard Occupational Classification (SOC) system. The SOC system is the first occupational classification system for federal agencies required by the Office of Management and Budget (OMB). The SOC system consists of 821 detailed occupations grouped into 449 broad occupations, 96 minor occupational groups, and 23 major occupational groups. The OES survey uses 22 of the 23 major occupational groups from the SOC to categorize workers into 801 detailed occupations. Military-specific occupations, which are not covered by the OES survey, are not included.

In 2002, the OES survey switched from the Standard Industrial Classification System (SIC) to the North American Industry Classification System (NAICS). In 2008, the OES survey switched to the 2007 NAICS from the 2002 NAICS. The most significant revisions were in the infor-

mation sector, particularly within the telecommunications area. More information about NAICS can be found on the BLS Web site at <http://www.bls.gov/bls/naics.htm>.

Concepts and Definitions

Employment is the estimate of total wage and salary employment in an occupation across the industries in which it was reported. The OES survey defines employment as the number of workers who can be classified as full-time or part-time employees, including workers on paid vacations or other types of leave; workers on unpaid short-term absences; employees who are salaried officers, executives, or staff members of incorporated firms; employees temporarily assigned to other units; and employees for whom the reporting unit is their permanent duty station regardless of whether that unit prepares their paycheck. Self-employed owners, partners in unincorporated firms, household workers, and unpaid family workers are excluded.

Occupations are classified based on work performed and required skills. Employees are assigned to an occupation based on the work they perform and not on their education or training. For example, an employee trained as an engineer but working as a drafter is reported as a drafter. Employees who perform the duties of two or more occupations are reported as being in either the occupation that requires the highest level of skill or the occupation in which the most time is spent (if there is no measurable difference in skill requirements).

Wages are money that is paid or received for work or services performed in a specified period. Base rate, cost-of-living allowances, guaranteed pay, hazardous-duty pay, incentive pay (including commissions and production bonuses), tips, and on-call pay are included. Excluded are back pay, jury duty pay, overtime pay, severance pay, shift differentials, nonproduction bonuses, employer cost of supplementary benefits, and tuition reimbursements.

Mean wage refers to an average wage; an occupational mean wage estimate is calculated by summing the wages of all the employees in a given occupation and then dividing the total wages by the number of employees.

An *establishment* is defined as an economic unit that processes goods or provides services, such as a factory, store, or mine. The establishment is generally at a single physical location and is primarily engaged in one type of economic activity.

An *industry* is a group of establishments that produce similar products or provide similar services. For example, all establishments that manufacture automobiles are in the same industry. A given industry, or even a particular establishment in that industry, might have employees in dozens of occupations. The North American Industry Classification System (NAICS) groups similar establishments into industries.

Additional Information

For additional data including area data, see BLS news release USDL 09-0457, "Occupational Employment and Wages, 2008," and special reports on the BLS Web site at <http://www.bls.gov/OES/>.

Table 3-1. Employment and Wages, by Major Occupational Group, May 2005–May 2008

(Number, percent, dollars.)

Occupation	May 2005				May 2006			
	Employment		Mean hourly wage	Mean annual wage[1]	Employment		Mean hourly wage	Mean annual wage[1]
	Number	Percent			Number	Percent		
All Occupations	130 307 850	100.0	18.21	37 870	132 604 980	100.0	18.84	39 190
Management	5 960 560	4.6	42.52	88 450	5 892 900	4.4	44.20	91 930
Business and financial operations	5 410 410	4.2	27.85	57 930	5 826 140	4.4	28.85	60 000
Computer and mathematical sciences	2 952 740	2.3	32.26	67 100	3 076 200	2.3	33.29	69 240
Architecture and engineering	2 382 480	1.8	30.73	63 910	2 430 250	1.8	31.82	66 190
Life, physical, and social sciences	1 185 730	0.9	27.90	58 030	1 231 070	0.9	28.68	59 660
Community and social services	1 692 950	1.3	18.04	37 530	1 749 210	1.3	18.75	39 000
Legal	986 740	0.8	38.98	81 070	976 740	0.7	41.04	85 360
Education, training, and library	8 078 500	6.2	20.89	43 450	8 206 440	6.2	21.79	45 320
Arts, design, entertainment, sports, and media	1 683 310	1.3	21.30	44 310	1 727 380	1.3	22.17	46 110
Health care practitioner and technical	6 547 350	5.0	28.45	59 170	6 713 780	5.1	29.82	62 030
Health care support	3 363 800	2.6	11.47	23 850	3 483 270	2.6	11.83	24 610
Protective services	3 056 660	2.3	17.19	35 750	3 024 840	2.3	17.81	37 040
Food preparation and serving related	10 797 700	8.3	8.58	17 840	11 029 280	8.3	8.86	18 430
Building and grounds cleaning and maintenance	4 342 550	3.3	10.55	21 930	4 396 250	3.3	10.86	22 580
Personal care and services	3 188 850	2.4	10.67	22 180	3 249 760	2.5	11.02	22 920
Sales and related	13 930 320	10.7	15.77	32 800	14 114 860	10.6	16.52	34 350
Office and administrative support	22 784 330	17.5	14.28	29 710	23 077 190	17.4	14.60	30 370
Farming, fishing, and forestry	443 070	0.3	10.10	21 010	450 040	0.3	10.49	21 810
Construction and extraction	6 370 400	4.9	18.39	38 260	6 680 710	5.0	18.89	39 290
Installation, maintenance, and repair	5 305 260	4.1	18.30	38 050	5 352 420	4.0	18.78	39 060
Production	10 249 220	7.9	14.37	29 890	10 268 510	7.7	14.65	30 480
Transportation and material moving	9 594 920	7.4	13.85	28 820	9 647 730	7.3	14.16	29 460

Occupation	May 2007				May 2008			
	Employment		Mean hourly wage	Mean annual wage[1]	Employment		Mean hourly wage	Mean annual wage[1]
	Number	Percent			Number	Percent		
All Occupations	134 354 250	100.0	19.56	40 690	135 185 230	100.0	20.32	42 270
Management	6 003 930	4.5	46.22	96 150	6 152 650	4.6	48.23	100 310
Business and financial operations	6 015 500	4.5	30.01	62 410	6 135 520	4.5	31.12	64 720
Computer and mathematical sciences	3 191 360	2.4	34.71	72 190	3 308 260	2.4	35.82	74 500
Architecture and engineering	2 486 020	1.9	33.11	68 880	2 521 630	1.9	34.34	71 430
Life, physical, and social sciences	1 255 670	0.9	29.82	62 020	1 296 840	1.0	30.90	64 280
Community and social services	1 793 040	1.3	19.49	40 540	1 861 750	1.4	20.09	41 790
Legal	998 590	0.7	42.53	88 450	1 003 270	0.7	44.36	92 270
Education, training, and library	8 316 360	6.2	22.41	46 610	8 451 250	6.3	23.30	48 460
Arts, design, entertainment, sports, and media	1 761 270	1.3	23.27	48 410	1 804 940	1.3	24.36	50 670
Health care practitioner and technical	6 877 680	5.1	31.26	65 020	7 076 800	5.2	32.64	67 890
Health care support	3 625 240	2.7	12.31	25 600	3 779 280	2.8	12.66	26 340
Protective services	3 087 650	2.3	18.63	38 750	3 128 960	2.3	19.33	40 200
Food preparation and serving related	11 273 850	8.4	9.35	19 440	11 438 550	8.5	9.72	20 220
Building and grounds cleaning and maintenance	4 403 900	3.3	11.33	23 560	4 429 870	3.3	11.72	24 370
Personal care and services	3 339 510	2.5	11.53	23 980	3 437 520	2.5	11.59	24 120
Sales and related	14 332 020	10.7	11.41	35 240	14 336 430	10.6	17.35	36 080
Office and administrative support	23 270 810	17.3	15.00	31 200	23 231 750	17.2	15.49	32 220
Farming, fishing, and forestry	448 000	0.3	10.89	22 640	438 490	0.3	11.32	23 560
Construction and extraction	6 708 200	5.0	19.53	40 620	6 548 760	4.8	20.36	42 350
Installation, maintenance, and repair	5 390 090	4.0	19.20	39 930	5 374 850	4.0	19.82	41 230
Production	10 146 560	7.6	15.05	31 310	9 919 120	7.3	15.54	32 320
Transportation and material moving	9 629 030	7.2	14.75	30 680	9 508 750	7.0	15.12	31 450

[1]The annual wage has been calculated by multiplying the hourly mean wage by a "year-round, full-time" hours figure of 2,080 hours; for occupations with no published hourly mean wage, the annual wage has been directly calculated from the reported survey data.

Table 3-2. Distribution of Employment, by Wage Range and Occupational Group, May 2007–May 2008

(Percent distribution.)

Occupation	Total	Wage range, May 2007								
		Under $9.50	$9.50 to $11.99	$12.00 to $15.24	$15.25 to $19.24	$19.25 to $24.49	$24.50 to $30.99	$31.00 to $39.24	$39.25 to $49.74	$49.75 and over
Management	100.0	1.1	0.9	2.5	5.0	8.7	13.0	16.4	17.5	34.9
Business and financial operations	100.0	1.5	2.1	6.2	12.9	19.2	21.1	17.4	11.0	8.6
Computer and mathematical sciences	100.0	0.6	1.4	3.8	7.5	12.9	17.8	21.7	19.5	14.8
Architecture and engineering	100.0	0.7	1.6	4.4	8.4	14.3	20.1	20.8	17.3	12.3
Life, physical, and social sciences	100.0	1.7	3.0	7.7	13.6	17.8	18.7	15.9	11.6	10.3
Community and social services	100.0	6.5	10.9	18.7	20.9	19.3	13.6	7.0	2.4	0.7
Legal	100.0	1.2	2.3	5.9	10.2	13.2	13.3	11.7	10.9	31.2
Education, training, and library	100.0	10.7	8.7	10.6	15.2	19.8	16.2	10.6	4.9	3.4
Arts, design, entertainment, sports, and media	100.0	12.4	9.1	12.8	15.6	15.9	13.2	9.4	5.8	5.8
Health care practitioner and technical	100.0	2.1	4.4	8.1	12.0	17.8	20.4	15.2	8.2	11.6
Health care support	100.0	25.9	30.2	24.6	12.6	4.8	1.5	0.4	0.1	-
Protective services	100.0	16.4	15.0	15.2	14.1	14.1	12.7	8.1	3.3	0.9
Food preparation and serving related	100.0	67.6	16.4	9.3	4.1	1.8	0.6	0.2	-	-
Building and grounds cleaning and maintenance	100.0	42.4	24.7	17.0	9.3	4.6	1.5	0.4	0.1	-
Personal care and services	100.0	50.0	21.2	12.5	7.0	4.1	2.8	1.3	0.7	0.3
Sales and related	100.0	37.9	15.1	11.6	9.6	8.1	6.2	4.5	3.1	4.0
Office and administrative support	100.0	16.7	19.0	23.8	19.4	13.8	5.1	1.6	0.4	0.1
Farming, fishing, and forestry	100.0	58.3	15.5	11.1	7.6	4.7	1.9	0.7	0.2	-
Construction and extraction	100.0	6.7	12.1	19.5	19.4	17.6	13.0	8.1	2.9	0.8
Installation, maintenance, and repair	100.0	7.6	10.7	17.3	20.3	20.4	15.2	6.5	1.6	0.3
Production	100.0	19.6	19.7	21.6	17.6	11.4	6.8	2.4	0.6	0.2
Transportation and material moving	100.0	27.0	18.8	19.3	15.2	10.7	5.5	1.9	0.7	0.9

Occupation	Total	Wage range, May 2008								
		Under $9.50	$9.50 to $11.99	$12.00 to $15.24	$15.25 to $19.24	$19.25 to $24.49	$24.50 to $30.99	$31.00 to $39.24	$39.25 to $49.74	$49.75 and over
Management	100.0	1.1	0.7	2.1	4.5	8.1	12.2	16.1	17.5	37.7
Business and financial operations	100.0	1.3	1.8	5.5	11.9	18.3	20.9	18.4	12.0	9.9
Computer and mathematical sciences	100.0	0.5	1.3	3.5	7.0	12.0	17.2	21.4	20.1	17.1
Architecture and engineering	100.0	0.5	1.5	4.2	7.9	13.4	19.4	20.5	17.8	14.8
Life, physical, and social sciences	100.0	1.5	2.9	7.3	12.4	17.1	18.3	16.5	12.2	11.8
Community and social services	100.0	6.0	9.8	17.7	20.9	19.4	14.4	7.7	3.0	0.9
Legal	100.0	0.9	1.8	5.5	9.9	12.9	13.4	12.1	10.7	32.7
Education, training, and library	100.0	9.7	8.1	10.2	14.4	19.7	16.9	11.5	5.6	3.9
Arts, design, entertainment, sports, and media	100.0	10.5	8.9	12.7	15.3	16.1	13.6	10.0	6.2	6.7
Health care practitioner and technical	100.0	1.8	4.0	7.7	11.3	16.7	20.0	16.2	9.3	13.1
Health care support	100.0	23.2	29.2	25.7	14.1	5.5	1.8	0.5	0.1	-
Protective services	100.0	14.5	14.6	15.5	14.0	14.2	12.9	8.8	4.1	1.3
Food preparation and serving related	100.0	63.8	18.1	10.3	4.8	2.0	0.7	0.2	0.1	-
Building and grounds cleaning and maintenance	100.0	38.5	25.2	18.4	10.3	5.2	1.7	0.5	0.1	-
Personal care and services	100.0	46.1	22.7	14.3	7.9	4.8	2.6	1.2	0.3	0.1
Sales and related	100.0	35.9	15.9	11.9	9.8	8.2	6.2	4.6	3.2	4.2
Office and administrative support	100.0	15.0	17.9	23.9	20.1	13.5	7.0	1.9	0.5	0.1
Farming, fishing, and forestry	100.0	53.3	18.4	12.1	7.9	5.0	2.2	0.8	0.2	-
Construction and extraction	100.0	5.6	10.6	18.9	19.6	17.7	13.7	9.1	3.8	1.1
Installation, maintenance, and repair	100.0	6.5	9.8	16.6	20.3	20.5	16.3	7.4	2.1	0.5
Production	100.0	17.2	19.2	22.0	18.5	12.1	7.2	2.8	0.8	0.2
Transportation and material moving	100.0	24.3	18.3	19.7	16.1	11.3	6.3	2.3	0.8	0.9

- = Quantity represents or rounds to zero.

Table 3-3. Employment and Wages, by Occupation, May 2007 and May 2008

(Number of people, dollars.)

Occupation	May 2007				May 2008			
	Employ-ment	Median hourly wage	Mean hourly wage	Mean annual wage[1]	Employ-ment	Median hourly wage	Mean hourly wage	Mean annual wage[1]
ALL OCCUPATIONS	134 354 250	15.10	19.56	40 690	135 185 230	15.57	20.32	42 270
Management								
Chief executives	299 160	([2])	72.77	151 370	301 930	76.23	77.13	160 440
General and operations managers	1 655 410	42.64	49.89	103 780	1 697 690	44.02	51.91	107 970
Legislators	61 110	([3])	([3])	33 880	64 650	([3])	([3])	37 980
Advertising and promotions managers	36 300	37.62	43.80	91 100	36 100	38.57	45.54	94 720
Marketing managers	165 240	50.19	54.52	113 400	166 790	52.20	56.81	118 160
Sales managers	322 170	45.63	51.34	106 790	333 910	46.76	53.07	110 390
Public relations managers	47 210	41.57	46.71	97 170	51 730	43.00	48.66	101 220
Administrative services managers	239 360	34.13	36.72	76 370	246 930	35.35	38.22	79 500
Computer and information systems managers	264 990	51.96	54.75	113 880	276 820	53.95	57.07	118 710
Financial managers	484 390	45.82	51.06	106 200	500 590	47.76	53.19	110 640
Compensation and benefits managers	41 780	39.14	42.50	88 400	38 810	41.59	44.91	93 410
Training and development managers	28 170	40.55	43.41	90 300	29 350	42.16	45.11	93 830
Human resources managers, all other	58 100	44.57	47.98	99 810	60 980	46.22	49.96	103 920
Industrial production managers	152 870	38.73	42.09	87 550	154 030	40.04	43.85	91 200
Purchasing managers	65 600	41.08	43.47	90 430	67 150	42.86	45.34	94 300
Transportation, storage, and distribution managers	92 790	36.69	39.41	81 980	96 300	37.98	40.64	84 520
Farm, ranch, and other agricultural managers	3 480	25.83	29.34	61 030	3 410	27.03	30.00	62 400
Farmers and ranchers	340	16.04	20.43	42 480	490	16.13	23.62	49 140
Construction managers	216 120	36.65	41.26	85 830	220 550	38.39	43.16	89 770
Education administrators, preschool and childcare center/programs	47 980	18.55	21.36	44 430	49 630	19.20	22.29	46 370
Education administrators, elementary and secondary schools	218 820	([3])	([3])	82 120	219 100	([3])	([3])	86 060
Education administrators, postsecondary	101 160	36.43	41.29	85 870	97 410	38.79	44.67	92 920
Education administrators, all other	28 640	33.32	35.69	74 230	28 090	34.44	37.13	77 220
Engineering managers	184 410	53.37	55.58	115 610	182 300	55.42	57.97	120 580
Food service managers	191 460	21.43	23.39	48 660	196 080	22.27	24.19	50 320
Funeral directors	24 020	24.21	27.72	57 660	25 680	25.10	28.27	58 810
Gaming managers	3 740	30.97	33.46	69 600	3 790	32.83	35.33	73 480
Lodging managers	31 890	21.27	24.59	51 140	32 460	22.02	25.26	52 550
Medical and health services managers	242 640	37.01	40.86	84 980	258 130	38.58	42.67	88 750
Natural sciences managers	39 370	50.02	54.41	113 170	43 060	54.23	59.20	123 140
Postmasters and mail superintendents	26 500	27.84	27.81	57 850	26 410	28.52	28.44	59 150
Property, real estate, and community association managers	159 660	21.00	25.74	53 530	159 700	22.18	27.05	56 250
Social and community service managers	112 330	26.22	28.40	59 070	117 150	26.92	29.12	60 570
Managers, all other	356 690	41.67	44.23	91 990	365 460	43.38	46.10	95 890
Business and Financial Operations								
Agents and business managers of artists, performers, and athletes	11 680	31.94	39.77	82 730	12 110	30.26	39.21	81 550
Purchasing agents and buyers, farm products	12 930	23.27	25.95	53 980	13 010	23.88	28.25	58 760
Wholesale and retail buyers, except farm products	132 550	22.58	25.76	53 580	132 420	23.42	26.70	55 540
Purchasing agents, except wholesale, retail, and farm products	281 950	25.22	26.95	56 060	286 990	25.93	27.70	57 630
Claims adjusters, examiners, and investigators	279 400	25.75	26.67	55 470	277 230	26.81	27.67	57 550
Insurance appraisers, auto damage	12 150	24.76	25.01	52 020	11 280	25.69	25.95	53 980
Compliance officers, except agriculture, construction, health and safety, and transportation	231 910	23.27	25.35	52 740	242 270	23.50	25.85	53 760
Cost estimators	219 070	26.41	28.19	58 640	218 400	27.17	29.00	60 320
Emergency management specialists	11 610	23.26	24.75	51 470	12 260	24.26	25.70	53 460
Employment, recruitment, and placement specialists	193 620	21.34	25.34	52 710	205 800	21.86	25.90	53 870
Compensation, benefits, and job analysis specialists	109 870	25.08	26.80	55 740	116 250	25.89	27.43	57 060
Training and development specialists	202 820	23.86	25.50	53 040	206 890	24.73	26.36	54 830
Human resources, training, and labor relations specialists, all other	211 770	26.10	27.28	56 740	217 440	26.79	28.00	58 230
Logisticians	90 340	30.89	31.85	66 240	98 590	31.96	32.98	68 600
Management analysts	499 640	34.21	38.68	80 460	535 850	35.37	39.87	82 920
Meeting and convention planners	45 490	20.93	22.68	47 180	47 960	21.28	22.84	47 500
Business operations specialists, all other	1 017 640	27.45	29.88	62 140	1 030 320	28.81	31.25	64 990
Accountants and auditors	1 115 010	27.43	30.37	63 180	1 133 580	28.57	31.65	65 840
Appraisers and assessors of real estate	66 210	22.18	25.14	52 290	66 260	22.77	25.68	53 410
Budget analysts	62 400	30.50	31.88	66 310	62 630	31.41	32.76	68 140
Credit analysts	70 890	26.24	30.20	62 820	74 400	26.56	31.05	64 580
Financial analysts	228 300	33.85	39.28	81 700	236 720	35.17	40.76	84 780
Personal financial advisers	132 460	32.53	42.89	89 220	146 690	33.20	44.69	92 970
Insurance underwriters	98 920	26.22	28.91	60 120	98 690	27.31	30.09	62 600
Financial examiners	25 510	32.05	35.36	73 550	26 020	34.10	37.59	78 180
Loan counselors	30 150	17.57	20.19	41 990	29 430	18.02	20.18	41 970
Loan officers	356 990	25.48	30.10	62 610	321 850	26.30	30.55	63 540
Tax examiners, collectors, and revenue agents	65 750	22.56	24.76	51 510	66 030	23.12	25.53	53 090
Tax preparers	61 890	13.71	16.78	34 890	63 030	14.14	17.08	35 520
Financial specialists, all other	136 570	26.63	29.69	61 760	145 110	27.48	30.71	63 880

[1]Annual wages have been calculated by multiplying the hourly mean wage by a "year-round, full-time" hours figure of 2,080 hours; for occupations with no published hourly mean wage, the annual wage has been directly calculated from the reported survey data.
[2]Median hourly wage is equal to or greater than $70.00 per hour.
[3]Wages for some occupations that do not generally entail year-round, full-time employment are reported as either hourly wages or annual salaries (depending on how employees are typically paid).

Table 3-3. Employment and Wages, by Occupation, May 2007 and May 2008—*Continued*

(Number of people, dollars.)

Occupation	May 2007				May 2008			
	Employ-ment	Median hourly wage	Mean hourly wage	Mean annual wage[1]	Employ-ment	Median hourly wage	Mean hourly wage	Mean annual wage[1]
Computer and Mathematical Sciences								
Computer and information scientists, research	28 720	47.10	48.39	100 640	26 610	47.10	48.51	100 900
Computer programmers	394 710	32.73	34.62	72 010	394 230	33.47	35.32	73 470
Computer software engineers, applications	495 810	39.97	41.18	85 660	494 160	41.07	42.26	87 900
Computer software engineers, systems software	349 140	42.82	43.65	90 780	381 830	44.44	45.44	94 520
Computer support specialists	525 570	20.39	21.78	45 300	545 520	20.89	22.29	46 370
Computer systems analysts	464 440	35.14	36.48	75 890	489 890	36.30	37.90	78 830
Database administrators	116 340	32.33	33.78	70 260	115 770	33.53	35.05	72 900
Network and computer systems administrators	309 660	31.10	32.62	67 850	327 850	31.88	33.45	69 570
Network systems and data communications analysts	216 050	32.80	34.02	70 760	230 410	34.18	35.50	73 830
Computer specialists, all other	182 690	34.38	34.77	72 310	191 780	36.13	36.54	76 000
Actuaries	18 030	41.20	45.87	95 420	18 220	40.77	46.14	95 980
Mathematicians	3 160	43.69	43.72	90 930	2 770	45.75	45.65	94 960
Operations research analysts	58 750	32.19	34.44	71 640	60 860	33.17	35.68	74 220
Statisticians	20 270	33.61	34.69	72 150	20 680	34.91	35.96	74 790
Mathematical technicians	1 080	18.54	23.31	48 490	1 100	18.46	20.24	42 100
Mathematical scientists, all other	6 930	25.90	29.38	61 100	6 600	26.44	31.55	65 630
Architecture and Engineering								
Architects, except landscape and naval	106 830	32.51	35.41	73 650	110 990	33.81	36.90	76 750
Landscape architects	21 890	27.68	29.93	62 250	21 130	28.35	30.77	64 000
Cartographers and photogrammetrists	11 460	24.02	26.19	54 480	11 690	24.60	27.87	57 980
Surveyors	56 670	24.82	26.18	54 450	55 780	25.47	26.91	55 980
Aerospace engineers	85 510	43.71	44.57	92 700	67 800	44.48	45.18	93 980
Agricultural engineers	2 480	32.55	33.88	70 460	2 640	33.04	35.02	72 850
Biomedical engineers	15 400	36.27	38.28	79 610	15 220	37.21	39.00	81 120
Chemical engineers	28 780	39.18	40.50	84 240	30 970	40.71	42.67	88 760
Civil engineers	247 370	34.48	36.17	75 230	261 360	35.87	37.77	78 560
Computer hardware engineers	79 330	44.16	45.32	94 270	73 370	46.83	48.16	100 180
Electrical engineers	148 800	38.10	39.47	82 090	154 670	39.50	41.04	85 350
Electronics engineers, except computer	133 870	40.07	41.13	85 550	139 930	41.52	42.63	88 670
Environmental engineers	51 210	34.78	35.97	74 820	52 590	35.59	37.49	77 970
Health and safety engineers, except mining safety engineers and inspectors	24 770	33.45	34.12	70 970	25 190	34.85	35.50	73 830
Industrial engineers	204 210	34.34	35.33	73 490	214 580	35.49	36.41	75 740
Marine engineers and naval architects	6 620	36.64	37.60	78 200	6 480	35.64	37.46	77 920
Materials engineers	21 910	37.10	37.90	78 840	24 160	39.34	40.48	84 200
Mechanical engineers	222 330	34.76	36.12	75 130	233 610	36.02	37.59	78 200
Mining and geological engineers, including mining safety engineers	7 150	35.74	38.23	79 520	6 900	36.52	38.42	79 910
Nuclear engineers	14 300	45.40	46.70	97 130	16 640	46.68	47.96	99 750
Petroleum engineers	16 060	49.98	54.75	113 890	20 880	51.93	57.28	119 140
Engineers, all other	169 950	40.99	41.07	85 430	169 240	42.58	42.83	89 080
Architectural and civil drafters	111 460	20.82	21.77	45 280	114 910	21.39	22.30	46 390
Electrical and electronics drafters	32 350	23.68	24.86	51 710	32 710	24.67	25.85	53 770
Mechanical drafters	74 260	21.51	22.45	46 690	77 070	22.42	23.36	48 600
Drafters, all other	23 280	21.49	22.76	47 340	20 720	21.60	22.73	47 290
Aerospace engineering and operations technicians	7 870	26.41	27.30	56 780	8 540	26.46	27.06	56 280
Civil engineering technicians	88 030	20.47	21.10	43 890	88 140	21.29	21.98	45 730
Electrical and electronic engineering technicians	162 460	25.07	25.23	52 470	162 330	25.60	25.96	53 990
Electromechanical technicians	15 730	22.41	23.14	48 120	16 290	22.27	23.13	48 110
Environmental engineering technicians	21 970	19.56	20.95	43 570	20 740	19.76	21.36	44 440
Industrial engineering technicians	74 930	22.83	24.72	51 410	72 880	22.69	24.07	50 070
Mechanical engineering technicians	46 230	22.73	23.70	49 290	45 770	23.14	24.06	50 040
Engineering technicians, except drafters, all other	78 140	26.95	26.80	55 730	73 870	27.33	27.19	56 560
Surveying and mapping technicians	72 410	16.17	17.26	35 900	71 920	16.88	18.03	37 500
Life, Physical, and Social Sciences								
Animal scientists	4 210	23.25	26.10	54 290	2 760	26.94	29.64	61 640
Food scientists and technologists	9 910	27.82	30.09	62 580	10 510	28.61	31.06	64 610
Soil and plant scientists	10 270	27.89	30.28	62 970	10 790	28.07	30.82	64 110
Biochemists and biophysicists	19 490	38.11	41.01	85 290	22 230	39.83	42.53	88 450
Microbiologists	14 610	29.17	31.94	66 430	15 750	30.94	33.73	70 150
Zoologists and wildlife biologists	17 830	26.49	28.11	58 480	17 780	26.58	28.28	58 820
Biological scientists, all other	27 070	30.45	31.85	66 240	28 290	31.29	32.71	68 030
Conservation scientists	16 570	27.00	27.51	57 220	15 830	28.23	28.93	60 170
Foresters	10 510	25.21	25.98	54 030	10 160	25.84	26.46	55 040
Epidemiologists	3 960	28.85	30.58	63 600	4 370	29.50	31.01	64 500
Medical scientists, except epidemiologists	87 440	30.87	35.65	74 160	99 750	34.90	39.36	81 870
Life scientists, all other	12 470	28.37	32.18	66 930	12 030	29.55	33.18	69 020
Astronomers	1 520	47.61	47.21	98 200	1 280	48.70	47.95	99 730
Physicists	13 980	46.56	48.03	99 900	14 810	49.47	51.17	106 440
Atmospheric and space scientists	8 750	37.69	37.96	78 960	8 860	39.08	39.46	82 080
Chemists	79 860	30.52	32.94	68 520	83 080	31.84	34.17	71 070
Materials scientists	9 740	36.62	37.47	77 930	9 650	38.57	39.23	81 600
Environmental scientists and specialists, including health	80 070	28.07	30.71	63 870	80 120	28.72	31.39	65 280
Geoscientists, except hydrologists and geographers	31 390	36.44	40.43	84 100	31 260	38.06	42.93	89 300
Hydrologists	7 670	32.76	33.77	70 250	7 590	34.35	35.36	73 540

[1]Annual wages have been calculated by multiplying the hourly mean wage by a "year-round, full-time" hours figure of 2,080 hours; for occupations with no published hourly mean wage, the annual wage has been directly calculated from the reported survey data.

Table 3-3. Employment and Wages, by Occupation, May 2007 and May 2008—*Continued*

(Number of people, dollars.)

Occupation	May 2007 Employment	May 2007 Median hourly wage	May 2007 Mean hourly wage	May 2007 Mean annual wage[1]	May 2008 Employment	May 2008 Median hourly wage	May 2008 Mean hourly wage	May 2008 Mean annual wage[1]
Life, Physical, and Social Sciences—*Continued*								
Physical scientists, all other	23 300	42.15	42.41	88 210	22 900	43.99	44.16	91 850
Economists	12 740	38.57	41.68	86 700	12 600	40.19	43.67	90 830
Market research analysts	220 740	28.99	32.20	66 980	230 070	29.36	32.37	67 340
Survey researchers	22 140	17.70	20.62	42 880	21 100	17.42	20.22	42 060
Clinical, counseling, and school psychologists	95 120	29.91	32.76	68 150	97 880	30.84	33.74	70 190
Industrial-organizational psychologists	1 240	38.85	41.64	86 610	1 460	37.03	41.57	86 460
Psychologists, all other	9 470	38.26	40.20	83 610	9 870	41.41	43.49	90 460
Sociologists	3 680	29.39	32.37	67 330	4 390	32.96	36.28	75 460
Urban and regional planners	35 040	27.87	29.08	60 480	37 120	28.75	30.00	62 400
Anthropologists and archeologists	5 250	25.52	26.68	55 490	5 230	25.92	27.55	57 300
Geographers	1 010	31.58	31.94	66 440	1 120	32.02	32.13	66 830
Historians	3 600	24.42	26.26	54 630	3 700	26.22	27.49	57 180
Political scientists	3 940	44.03	43.29	90 050	3 530	50.06	47.75	99 320
Social scientists and related workers, all other	30 410	32.31	33.52	69 720	28 680	33.04	34.49	71 730
Agricultural and food science technicians	19 280	16.17	17.08	35 520	18 930	16.34	17.53	36 470
Biological technicians	69 110	18.18	19.35	40 240	72 200	18.46	19.67	40 900
Chemical technicians	64 450	19.58	20.39	42 420	65 830	20.25	21.02	43 710
Geological and petroleum technicians	13 060	24.50	26.60	55 330	14 570	25.65	27.44	57 080
Nuclear technicians	5 920	31.80	31.66	65 850	6 360	32.64	32.17	66 910
Social science research assistants	16 070	17.24	18.33	38 120	18 120	17.14	18.23	37 920
Environmental science and protection technicians, including health	33 950	18.93	20.28	42 190	33 370	19.34	20.76	43 180
Forensic science technicians	12 030	22.92	24.19	50 310	11 990	23.97	25.46	52 960
Forest and conservation technicians	26 900	16.12	17.20	35 770	30 850	15.39	16.98	35 320
Life, physical, and social science technicians, all other	59 910	18.33	19.82	41 230	58 070	19.25	20.63	42 910
Community and Social Services								
Substance abuse and behavioral disorder counselors	76 830	17.10	18.19	37 830	79 180	17.80	19.07	39 670
Educational, vocational, and school counselors	232 260	23.77	24.85	51 690	243 100	24.54	25.74	53 540
Marriage and family therapists	23 340	20.96	21.78	45 310	24 520	21.44	22.56	46 930
Mental health counselors	95 970	17.31	18.97	39 450	104 650	17.70	19.36	40 270
Rehabilitation counselors	123 890	14.25	16.03	33 350	112 700	14.87	16.64	34 600
Counselors, all other	28 900	18.60	19.57	40 710	29 980	19.20	20.31	42 240
Child, family, and school social workers	265 090	18.57	20.15	41 920	274 140	19.01	20.73	43 120
Medical and public health social workers	120 060	21.48	22.27	46 320	131 730	21.95	22.87	47 560
Mental health and substance abuse social workers	118 690	17.62	18.93	39 380	131 010	17.89	19.05	39 630
Social workers, all other	64 990	22.02	22.68	47 170	68 230	22.22	23.16	48 180
Health educators	61 290	20.63	22.76	47 340	62 120	21.16	23.36	48 590
Probation officers and correctional treatment specialists	94 120	21.40	23.07	47 980	97 130	22.07	23.81	49 520
Social and human service assistants	316 380	12.80	13.68	28 450	332 880	13.12	14.03	29 170
Community and social service specialists, all other	109 970	17.51	18.56	38 590	107 910	18.11	19.21	39 950
Clergy	40 960	19.45	21.02	43 720	42 040	20.06	21.85	45 440
Directors, religious activities and education	14 780	17.00	18.98	39 470	14 790	17.35	19.36	40 260
Religious workers, all other	5 520	12.82	15.22	31 660	5 640	13.30	15.56	32 360
Legal								
Lawyers	555 770	51.02	56.87	118 280	553 690	53.17	59.98	124 750
Administrative law judges, adjudicators, and hearing officers	14 100	35.66	37.81	78 650	13 370	36.99	38.88	80 870
Arbitrators, mediators, and conciliators	8 810	23.48	27.10	56 380	9 570	24.36	28.68	59 650
Judges, magistrate judges, and magistrates	25 500	51.55	47.73	99 270	25 470	52.99	48.29	100 450
Paralegals and legal assistants	241 270	21.63	22.88	47 600	253 040	22.18	23.46	48 790
Court reporters	20 120	21.79	23.26	48 380	17 930	23.90	24.98	51 960
Law clerks	31 160	18.06	19.65	40 880	31 500	17.85	19.51	40 580
Title examiners, abstractors, and searchers	62 200	17.88	19.78	41 140	59 390	18.41	20.24	42 090
Legal support workers, all other	39 670	23.30	26.23	54 560	39 310	24.16	27.24	56 660
Education, Training, and Library								
Business teachers, postsecondary	67 700	(3)	(3)	73 240	69 690	(3)	(3)	77 340
Computer science teachers, postsecondary	33 840	(3)	(3)	69 660	32 520	(3)	(3)	74 050
Mathematical science teachers, postsecondary	44 560	(3)	(3)	65 450	45 710	(3)	(3)	68 130
Architecture teachers, postsecondary	6 070	(3)	(3)	71 480	6 430	(3)	(3)	75 450
Engineering teachers, postsecondary	32 360	(3)	(3)	85 260	32 070	(3)	(3)	90 070
Agricultural sciences teachers, postsecondary	10 700	(3)	(3)	80 280	10 000	(3)	(3)	77 770
Biological science teachers, postsecondary	52 560	(3)	(3)	84 130	51 930	(3)	(3)	83 270
Forestry and conservation science teachers, postsecondary	2 640	(3)	(3)	67 530	2 450	(3)	(3)	67 400
Atmospheric, earth, marine, and space sciences teachers, postsecondary	9 030	(3)	(3)	78 890	9 650	(3)	(3)	81 470
Chemistry teachers, postsecondary	19 800	(3)	(3)	72 900	19 950	(3)	(3)	76 310
Environmental science teachers, postsecondary	4 470	(3)	(3)	75 220	4 870	(3)	(3)	74 610
Physics teachers, postsecondary	12 530	(3)	(3)	77 440	12 350	(3)	(3)	81 880
Anthropology and archeology teachers, postsecondary	5 290	(3)	(3)	69 420	5 500	(3)	(3)	73 410
Area, ethnic, and cultural studies teachers, postsecondary	7 280	(3)	(3)	67 770	7 570	(3)	(3)	70 560
Economics teachers, postsecondary	12 840	(3)	(3)	83 030	12 540	(3)	(3)	88 330

[1]Annual wages have been calculated by multiplying the hourly mean wage by a "year-round, full-time" hours figure of 2,080 hours; for occupations with no published hourly mean wage, the annual wage has been directly calculated from the reported survey data.
[3]Wages for some occupations that do not generally entail year-round, full-time employment are reported as either hourly wages or annual salaries (depending on how employees are typically paid).

Table 3-3. Employment and Wages, by Occupation, May 2007 and May 2008—*Continued*

(Number of people, dollars.)

Occupation	May 2007				May 2008			
	Employ-ment	Median hourly wage	Mean hourly wage	Mean annual wage[1]	Employ-ment	Median hourly wage	Mean hourly wage	Mean annual wage[1]
Education, Training, and Library—*Continued*								
Geography teachers, postsecondary	4 050	([3])	([3])	65 810	4 030	([3])	([3])	67 480
Political science teachers, postsecondary	14 160	([3])	([3])	70 350	14 340	([3])	([3])	75 960
Psychology teachers, postsecondary	30 590	([3])	([3])	66 460	31 420	([3])	([3])	69 560
Sociology teachers, postsecondary	16 130	([3])	([3])	65 230	16 440	([3])	([3])	68 900
Social sciences teachers, postsecondary, all other	5 460	([3])	([3])	70 000	5 720	([3])	([3])	74 720
Health specialties teachers, postsecondary	114 070	([3])	([3])	95 440	125 100	([3])	([3])	102 000
Nursing instructors and teachers, postsecondary	42 660	([3])	([3])	60 850	46 890	([3])	([3])	62 660
Education teachers, postsecondary	54 420	([3])	([3])	59 250	55 880	([3])	([3])	60 080
Library science teachers, postsecondary	4 080	([3])	([3])	59 690	3 960	([3])	([3])	61 630
Criminal justice and law enforcement teachers, postsecondary	11 110	([3])	([3])	57 510	11 630	([3])	([3])	59 830
Law teachers, postsecondary	12 610	([3])	([3])	95 510	12 490	([3])	([3])	101 170
Social work teachers, postsecondary	7 510	([3])	([3])	61 140	7 930	([3])	([3])	64 680
Art, drama, and music teachers, postsecondary	73 890	([3])	([3])	61 050	76 810	([3])	([3])	65 030
Communications teachers, postsecondary	23 690	([3])	([3])	58 610	24 360	([3])	([3])	63 330
English language and literature teachers, postsecondary	60 910	([3])	([3])	60 580	62 230	([3])	([3])	63 610
Foreign language and literature teachers, postsecondary	25 100	([3])	([3])	62 540	26 400	([3])	([3])	65 280
History teachers, postsecondary	20 760	([3])	([3])	65 410	21 020	([3])	([3])	68 360
Philosophy and religion teachers, postsecondary	18 140	([3])	([3])	61 700	18 370	([3])	([3])	65 140
Graduate teaching assistants	119 790	([3])	([3])	30 080	124 380	([3])	([3])	31 710
Home economics teachers, postsecondary	4 770	([3])	([3])	63 790	4 820	([3])	([3])	70 420
Recreation and fitness studies teachers, postsecondary	17 500	([3])	([3])	57 540	17 410	([3])	([3])	60 700
Vocational education teachers, postsecondary	112 300	22.05	([3])	49 150	112 940	22.76	24.46	50 870
Postsecondary teachers, all other	265 500	([3])	([3])	71 950	242 780	([3])	([3])	71 320
Preschool teachers, except special education	380 930	11.12	12.40	25 800	392 170	11.48	12.80	26 610
Kindergarten teachers, except special education	170 880	([3])	([3])	47 750	174 530	([3])	([3])	49 770
Elementary school teachers, except special education	1 538 030	([3])	([3])	50 040	1 544 270	([3])	([3])	52 240
Middle school teachers, except special and vocational education	652 560	([3])	([3])	50 630	661 820	([3])	([3])	52 570
Vocational education teachers, middle school	15 260	([3])	([3])	48 460	15 720	([3])	([3])	50 150
Secondary school teachers, except special and vocational education	1 058 870	([3])	([3])	52 450	1 090 490	([3])	([3])	54 390
Vocational education teachers, secondary school	97 550	([3])	([3])	52 250	99 800	([3])	([3])	53 700
Special education teachers, preschool, kindergarten, and elementary school	219 930	([3])	([3])	51 230	226 250	([3])	([3])	52 970
Special education teachers, middle school	100 160	([3])	([3])	51 610	100 650	([3])	([3])	53 540
Special education teachers, secondary school	141 330	([3])	([3])	53 020	147 210	([3])	([3])	55 050
Adult literacy, remedial education, and GED teachers and instructors	72 240	21.50	23.00	47 830	73 050	22.26	23.95	49 830
Self-enrichment education teachers	156 960	16.62	19.04	39 600	163 190	17.17	19.68	40 920
Teachers and instructors, all other	555 460	([3])	([3])	37 840	574 540	([3])	([3])	40 770
Archivists	5 420	20.73	22.32	46 420	5 330	21.64	23.18	48 220
Curators	10 120	22.11	24.06	50 040	10 820	22.70	24.78	51 540
Museum technicians and conservators	9 950	17.00	18.84	39 180	10 200	17.63	19.59	40 750
Librarians	148 800	24.51	25.41	52 850	151 170	25.26	26.30	54 700
Library technicians	114 150	13.31	13.96	29 040	113 510	13.86	14.49	30 130
Audio-visual collections specialists	6 530	20.42	21.04	43 770	6 160	20.86	21.90	45 540
Farm and home management advisers	12 050	20.11	21.30	44 300	10 760	19.97	21.46	44 630
Instructional coordinators	117 940	26.57	27.92	58 070	122 180	27.35	28.74	59 780
Teacher assistants	1 251 610	([3])	([3])	22 820	1 266 900	([3])	([3])	23 560
Education, training, and library workers, all other	98 790	15.88	17.77	36 950	99 900	17.07	19.50	40 560
Arts, Design, Entertainment, Sports, and Media								
Art directors	32 290	34.77	40.01	83 230	33 670	37.01	42.55	88 510
Craft artists	5 390	12.59	14.48	30 110	5 440	13.98	15.66	32 570
Fine artists, including painters, sculptors, and illustrators	10 500	20.23	23.13	48 110	9 380	20.51	23.22	48 300
Multimedia artists and animators	29 440	26.23	29.33	61 010	31 500	27.08	29.99	62 380
Artists and related workers, all other	7 910	21.53	24.29	50 520	8 470	24.81	26.51	55 140
Commercial and industrial designers	34 800	27.19	29.11	60 540	32 940	27.57	29.60	61 580
Fashion designers	16 460	30.20	34.22	71 170	16 920	29.41	34.33	71 400
Floral designers	59 530	10.84	11.51	23 950	57 500	11.17	11.78	24 510
Graphic designers	201 080	19.85	21.80	45 340	209 290	20.39	22.48	46 750
Interior designers	52 620	21.14	24.13	50 190	53 290	21.61	24.53	51 020
Merchandise displayers and window trimmers	68 660	11.94	13.16	27 370	63 320	12.47	13.73	28 560
Set and exhibit designers	8 620	20.78	22.89	47 620	7 940	21.47	23.40	48 660
Designers, all other	11 890	21.01	24.24	50 420	11 160	21.07	24.10	50 130
Actors	44 860	14.28	23.91	([3])	44 360	16.59	29.05	([3])
Producers and directors	72 390	29.37	37.05	77 070	78 060	30.98	39.92	83 030
Athletes and sports competitors	12 670	([3])	([3])	71 920	13 960	([3])	([3])	79 460
Coaches and scouts	165 410	([3])	([3])	34 720	175 720	([3])	([3])	35 580
Umpires, referees, and other sports officials	13 630	([3])	([3])	29 850	12 970	([3])	([3])	28 330
Dancers	12 530	10.72	14.74	([3])	11 370	12.22	15.06	([3])
Choreographers	15 250	17.11	19.04	39 600	13 860	18.52	20.13	41 870

[1]Annual wages have been calculated by multiplying the hourly mean wage by a "year-round, full-time" hours figure of 2,080 hours; for occupations with no published hourly mean wage, the annual wage has been directly calculated from the reported survey data.
[3]Wages for some occupations that do not generally entail year-round, full-time employment are reported as either hourly wages or annual salaries (depending on how employees are typically paid).

Table 3-3. Employment and Wages, by Occupation, May 2007 and May 2008—*Continued*

(Number of people, dollars.)

Occupation	May 2007				May 2008			
	Employ-ment	Median hourly wage	Mean hourly wage	Mean annual wage[1]	Employ-ment	Median hourly wage	Mean hourly wage	Mean annual wage[1]
Arts, Design, Entertainment, Sports, and Media—*Continued*								
Music directors and composers	9 110	19.30	25.95	53 970	9 120	19.84	26.36	54 840
Musicians and singers	47 520	19.92	27.27	([3])	47 030	21.24	28.28	([3])
Entertainers and performers, sports and related workers, all other	32 040	13.99	15.67	([3])	36 190	14.62	17.91	([3])
Radio and television announcers	39 500	12.53	18.92	39 360	37 290	12.95	19.43	40 410
Public address system and other announcers	8 490	12.43	17.26	35 890	8 280	13.18	18.04	37 530
Broadcast news analysts	6 550	23.59	33.83	70 370	6 310	24.65	34.00	70 730
Reporters and correspondents	51 620	16.68	20.76	43 170	50 690	16.75	21.17	44 030
Public relations specialists	225 880	23.94	27.45	57 100	240 610	24.65	28.34	58 960
Editors	105 920	23.23	26.45	55 020	110 010	24.04	27.49	57 180
Technical writers	46 740	29.04	30.18	62 780	47 460	29.62	30.87	64 210
Writers and authors	44 310	24.36	28.90	60 120	44 170	25.51	31.04	64 560
Interpreters and translators	33 680	18.02	20.05	41 690	36 610	18.68	20.74	43 130
Media and communication workers, all other	24 420	20.07	21.98	45 720	24 470	19.99	22.97	47 770
Audio and video equipment technicians	40 360	17.33	18.88	39 260	45 200	18.30	19.86	41 310
Broadcast technicians	34 250	15.50	18.00	37 440	33 550	15.82	18.30	38 070
Radio operators	1 110	19.33	19.54	40 650	820	17.85	18.52	38 520
Sound engineering technicians	15 490	22.38	26.07	54 220	16 600	22.83	25.53	53 110
Photographers	62 370	13.32	16.35	34 010	61 670	14.15	17.14	35 640
Camera operators, television, video, and motion picture	19 990	20.12	22.39	46 570	19 270	20.03	22.94	47 710
Film and video editors	17 410	23.02	29.42	61 180	18 720	24.31	30.05	62 500
Media and communication equipment workers, all other	18 580	24.93	26.00	54 090	19 770	25.45	26.98	56 120
Health Care Practitioner and Technical								
Chiropractors	27 190	31.68	39.13	81 390	27 050	31.97	39.11	81 340
Dentists, general	85 260	66.17	70.68	147 010	85 910	68.69	74.17	154 270
Oral and maxillofacial surgeons	5 040	([2])	85.79	178 440	4 760	([2])	91.55	190 420
Orthodontists	5 350	([2])	89.11	185 340	5 500	([2])	93.72	194 930
Prosthodontists	380	([2])	81.42	169 360	370	([2])	81.64	169 810
Dentists, all other specialists	4 490	50.69	57.87	120 360	4 770	66.33	68.30	142 070
Dietitians and nutritionists	52 800	23.56	24.05	50 030	53 630	24.32	24.75	51 470
Optometrists	24 900	45.09	48.96	101 840	25 970	46.31	50.58	105 200
Pharmacists	253 110	48.31	47.58	98 960	266 410	51.16	50.13	104 260
Anesthesiologists	31 030	([2])	92.68	192 780	34 230	([2])	94.99	197 570
Family and general practitioners	113 250	([2])	73.86	153 640	106 210	75.60	77.64	161 490
Internists, general	46 260	([2])	80.42	167 270	46 980	([2])	84.97	176 740
Obstetricians and gynecologists	21 340	([2])	88.27	183 600	19 750	([2])	92.68	192 780
Pediatricians, general	28 890	67.64	69.81	145 210	29 170	70.21	73.74	153 370
Psychiatrists	21 790	([2])	70.97	147 620	22 140	74.13	74.06	154 050
Surgeons	50 260	([2])	92.03	191 410	47 070	([2])	99.41	206 770
Physicians and surgeons, all other	237 400	([2])	74.59	155 150	262 850	([2])	79.33	165 000
Physician assistants	67 160	37.72	37.41	77 800	71 950	39.05	39.24	81 610
Podiatrists	9 320	([2])	57.59	119 790	9 670	54.60	60.46	125 760
Registered nurses	2 468 340	28.85	30.04	62 480	2 542 760	30.03	31.31	65 130
Audiologists	11 360	28.58	30.61	63 660	12 480	29.82	31.49	65 500
Occupational therapists	91 920	30.67	31.51	65 540	94 800	32.10	32.65	67 920
Physical therapists	161 850	33.54	34.39	71 520	167 300	35.00	35.77	74 410
Radiation therapists	14 620	33.66	34.61	71 990	14 850	35.05	36.28	75 450
Recreational therapists	23 240	17.76	18.43	38 330	22 510	18.45	19.20	39 930
Respiratory therapists	101 180	24.07	24.49	50 930	103 870	25.10	25.55	53 150
Speech-language pathologists	103 810	29.18	30.64	63 740	107 340	30.25	31.80	66 130
Therapists, all other	11 580	24.10	25.45	52 930	12 960	24.37	26.32	54 750
Veterinarians	50 790	36.17	40.43	84 090	53 110	38.01	43.00	89 450
Health diagnosing and treating practitioners, all other	44 350	30.64	38.93	80 980	34 890	31.67	37.76	78 540
Medical and clinical laboratory technologists	163 270	24.87	25.20	52 410	166 510	25.72	25.99	54 050
Medical and clinical laboratory technicians	145 890	16.48	17.36	36 110	149 670	17.01	17.86	37 150
Dental hygienists	168 600	31.12	31.21	64 910	173 090	32.00	32.19	66 950
Cardiovascular technologists and technicians	46 980	21.61	22.37	46 530	48 040	22.60	23.38	48 640
Diagnostic medical sonographers	46 770	28.78	29.13	60 590	48 920	29.80	30.12	62 660
Nuclear medicine technologists	20 410	31.09	31.43	65 380	21 200	32.05	32.44	67 480
Radiologic technologists and technicians	200 370	24.16	24.59	51 150	208 570	25.10	25.59	53 230
Emergency medical technicians and paramedics	201 200	13.66	14.84	30 870	207 610	14.10	15.38	31 980
Dietetic technicians	24 540	11.90	12.83	26 680	24 620	12.54	13.26	27 580
Pharmacy technicians	301 950	12.85	13.25	27 560	324 110	13.32	13.70	28 500
Psychiatric technicians	60 690	14.27	15.21	31 640	54 800	14.06	15.48	32 190
Respiratory therapy technicians	17 610	19.52	20.00	41 590	16 210	20.40	21.00	43 670
Surgical technologists	86 000	18.05	18.66	38 800	89 600	18.62	19.27	40 070
Veterinary technologists and technicians	73 240	13.45	13.90	28 920	78 920	13.89	14.35	29 850
Licensed practical and licensed vocational nurses	719 240	18.24	18.72	38 940	730 500	18.77	19.28	40 110

[1]Annual wages have been calculated by multiplying the hourly mean wage by a "year-round, full-time" hours figure of 2,080 hours; for occupations with no published hourly mean wage, the annual wage has been directly calculated from the reported survey data.
[2]Median hourly wage is equal to or greater than $70.00 per hour.
[3]Wages for some occupations that do not generally entail year-round, full-time employment are reported as either hourly wages or annual salaries (depending on how employees are typically paid).

Table 3-3. Employment and Wages, by Occupation, May 2007 and May 2008—*Continued*

(Number of people, dollars.)

Occupation	May 2007				May 2008			
	Employ-ment	Median hourly wage	Mean hourly wage	Mean annual wage¹	Employ-ment	Median hourly wage	Mean hourly wage	Mean annual wage¹
Health Care Practitioner and Technical—*Continued*								
Medical records and health information technicians	165 590	14.08	15.12	31 450	168 650	14.71	15.85	32 960
Opticians, dispensing	62 420	15.11	16.10	33 480	59 470	15.77	16.85	35 060
Orthotists and prosthetists	5 600	29.10	30.90	64 280	5 490	30.09	31.76	66 060
Health technologists and technicians, all other	73 730	17.61	19.17	39 870	74 990	18.25	19.89	41 380
Occupational health and safety specialists	46 460	28.91	29.48	61 310	53 250	29.93	30.31	63 030
Occupational health and safety technicians	10 260	21.16	22.21	46 200	10 540	21.81	22.79	47 410
Athletic trainers	14 970	(³)	(³)	40 720	15 070	(³)	(³)	41 620
Health care practitioners and technical workers, all other	53 640	19.49	22.94	47 710	55 750	20.98	24.28	50 510
Health Care Support								
Home health aides	834 580	9.62	10.03	20 850	892 410	9.84	10.31	21 440
Nursing aides, orderlies, and attendants	1 390 260	11.14	11.50	23 920	1 422 720	11.46	11.84	24 620
Psychiatric aides	58 310	12.25	12.54	26 080	59 050	12.77	13.10	27 260
Occupational therapist assistants	25 130	21.66	21.72	45 180	25 610	23.19	23.29	48 440
Occupational therapist aides	7 640	12.54	13.91	28 930	7 410	12.96	14.22	29 580
Physical therapist assistants	59 120	21.22	21.32	44 340	61 820	22.18	22.26	46 300
Physical therapist aides	43 350	11.05	11.58	24 080	44 410	11.42	11.91	24 770
Massage therapists	45 920	16.76	19.39	40 330	51 250	16.78	19.16	39 850
Dental assistants	283 680	15.17	15.52	32 280	293 090	15.57	15.95	33 170
Medical assistants	434 540	13.19	13.59	28 270	475 950	13.60	13.97	29 060
Medical equipment preparers	43 790	13.00	13.43	27 940	44 340	13.66	14.08	29 290
Medical transcriptionists	86 990	15.02	15.44	32 120	86 200	15.41	15.84	32 960
Pharmacy aides	49 630	9.39	10.15	21 120	53 190	9.66	10.34	21 500
Veterinary assistants and laboratory animal caretakers	71 190	9.98	10.66	22 180	71 950	10.20	10.96	22 790
Health care support workers, all other	191 110	13.62	14.24	29 620	189 890	14.11	14.74	30 650
Protective Services								
First-line supervisors/managers of correctional officers	41 000	26.79	27.17	56 510	40 840	27.58	28.07	58 380
First-line supervisors/managers of police and detectives	91 510	34.91	35.39	73 620	92 840	36.29	36.93	76 820
First-line supervisors/managers of fire fighting and prevention workers	52 160	31.27	32.38	67 350	53 300	32.42	34.07	70 860
First-line supervisors/managers of protective service workers, all other	45 750	20.68	22.55	46 910	49 310	20.95	22.93	47 700
Firefighters	289 710	20.75	21.22	44 130	298 900	21.28	21.97	45 700
Fire inspectors and investigators	12 980	24.44	25.31	52 640	12 920	25.50	26.37	54 840
Forest fire inspectors and prevention specialists	1 600	15.11	17.20	35 770	1 580	15.09	17.50	36 400
Bailiffs	18 830	17.74	18.52	38 510	19 290	18.18	18.79	39 090
Correctional officers and jailers	431 980	17.78	19.22	39 970	428 040	18.45	19.88	41 340
Detectives and criminal investigators	103 320	28.81	30.05	62 500	104 480	29.29	30.69	63 840
Fish and game wardens	7 500	23.00	26.79	55 720	7 720	23.53	26.94	56 030
Parking enforcement workers	9 910	15.13	15.78	32 830	9 530	15.57	16.36	34 020
Police and sheriff's patrol officers	625 880	23.86	24.36	50 670	633 710	24.72	25.39	52 810
Transit and railroad police	5 530	22.29	23.80	49 500	3 830	22.44	23.34	48 540
Animal control workers	14 890	14.10	14.84	30 860	15 480	14.57	15.38	31 990
Private detectives and investigators	37 410	18.09	20.51	42 660	35 820	20.08	22.35	46 480
Gaming surveillance officers and gaming investigators	9 030	13.19	14.59	30 350	9 100	13.87	15.17	31 550
Security guards	1 032 260	10.85	11.94	24 840	1 046 760	11.28	12.42	25 840
Crossing guards	67 570	10.65	11.28	23 460	68 530	10.96	11.68	24 290
Lifeguards, ski patrol, and other recreational protective service workers	107 420	8.64	9.34	19 430	111 560	8.87	9.58	19 930
Protective service workers, all other	81 410	13.58	15.27	31 760	85 440	14.00	15.66	32 580
Food Preparation and Serving Related								
Chefs and head cooks	100 130	17.87	19.57	40 700	98 040	18.64	20.39	42 410
First-line supervisors/managers of food preparation and serving workers	788 750	13.48	14.39	29 930	805 360	13.93	14.81	30 810
Cooks, fast food	575 510	7.75	8.11	16 860	559 160	8.12	8.47	17 620
Cooks, institution and cafeteria	372 450	10.26	10.74	22 340	370 920	10.68	11.19	23 260
Cooks, private household	950	11.67	13.59	28 260	960	11.57	14.91	31 020
Cooks, restaurant	878 990	10.20	10.56	21 960	899 620	10.57	10.94	22 750
Cooks, short order	177 450	8.96	9.41	19 580	168 770	9.26	9.73	20 230
Cooks, all other	15 440	10.64	11.62	24 170	17 340	11.09	11.91	24 770
Food preparation workers	873 470	8.73	9.30	19 350	880 480	8.96	9.54	19 850
Bartenders	498 090	8.22	9.49	19 740	503 420	8.54	9.84	20 460
Combined food preparation and serving workers, including fast food	2 602 950	7.57	8.03	16 700	2 708 840	7.90	8.36	17 400
Counter attendants, cafeteria, food concession, and coffee shop	541 370	8.12	8.57	17 820	527 530	8.42	8.90	18 520
Waiters and waitresses	2 357 040	7.62	8.93	18 570	2 371 750	8.01	9.41	19 580
Food servers, nonrestaurant	185 530	9.06	9.93	20 660	188 390	9.32	10.19	21 190
Dining room and cafeteria attendants and bartender helpers	401 070	7.71	8.36	17 380	416 410	8.05	8.72	18 140
Dishwashers	509 550	7.89	8.20	17 060	521 150	8.19	8.54	17 750
Hosts and hostesses, restaurant, lounge, and coffee shop	342 960	8.07	8.54	17 770	349 990	8.42	8.93	18 570
Food preparation and serving related workers, all other	52 160	8.93	9.83	20 450	50 420	9.39	10.32	21 460

¹Annual wages have been calculated by multiplying the hourly mean wage by a "year-round, full-time" hours figure of 2,080 hours; for occupations with no published hourly mean wage, the annual wage has been directly calculated from the reported survey data.
³Wages for some occupations that do not generally entail year-round, full-time employment are reported as either hourly wages or annual salaries (depending on how employees are typically paid).

Table 3-3. Employment and Wages, by Occupation, May 2007 and May 2008—*Continued*

(Number of people, dollars.)

Occupation	May 2007				May 2008			
	Employ-ment	Median hourly wage	Mean hourly wage	Mean annual wage[1]	Employ-ment	Median hourly wage	Mean hourly wage	Mean annual wage[1]
Building and Grounds Cleaning and Maintenance								
First-line supervisors/managers of housekeeping and janitorial workers	179 850	15.79	16.93	35 220	183 560	16.34	17.46	36 310
First-line supervisors/managers of landscaping, lawn service, and groundskeeping workers	110 340	18.62	20.06	41 730	108 940	19.19	20.67	42 990
Janitors and cleaners, except maids and housekeeping cleaners	2 112 870	10.00	10.92	22 710	2 145 320	10.31	11.30	23 500
Maids and housekeeping cleaners	915 890	8.82	9.40	19 550	917 120	9.13	9.76	20 290
Building cleaning workers, all other	14 320	13.02	14.45	30 060	13 580	13.09	13.78	28 660
Pest control workers	63 440	13.96	14.56	30 280	63 180	14.37	14.92	31 040
Landscaping and groundskeeping workers	932 730	10.69	11.53	23 980	921 900	11.13	11.95	24 860
Pesticide handlers, sprayers, and applicators, vegetation	25 560	13.73	14.60	30 370	25 060	14.31	15.01	31 210
Tree trimmers and pruners	30 670	14.33	14.96	31 110	35 420	14.41	15.12	31 450
Grounds maintenance workers, all other	18 230	10.27	12.33	25 640	15 790	10.76	13.07	27 180
Personal Care and Services								
First-line supervisors/managers of personal service workers	126 870	16.30	17.88	37 190	129 070	16.78	18.38	38 230
Gaming supervisors	25 800	20.66	21.29	44 290	26 110	21.87	22.40	46 600
Slot key persons	13 680	11.42	12.45	25 900	15 390	12.24	13.68	28 460
Animal trainers	9 110	12.59	14.61	30 390	10 030	13.11	14.99	31 190
Nonfarm animal caretakers	118 760	9.08	10.18	21 180	126 740	9.31	10.36	21 550
Gaming dealers	86 210	7.51	8.71	18 120	91 130	7.84	9.56	19 890
Gaming and sports book writers and runners	17 370	9.27	10.64	22 120	16 140	9.46	10.96	22 800
Gaming service workers, all other	14 270	11.09	12.17	25 310	13 910	11.58	12.16	25 290
Motion picture projectionists	10 840	8.84	10.33	21 500	10 200	9.46	10.91	22 700
Ushers, lobby attendants, and ticket takers	106 700	7.85	8.60	17 880	106 570	8.35	9.18	19 100
Amusement and recreation attendants	245 380	8.10	8.76	18 220	258 820	8.40	9.10	18 930
Costume attendants	4 570	12.64	14.85	30 890	5 120	12.62	15.46	32 150
Locker room, coatroom, and dressing room attendants	17 830	9.18	9.99	20 780	18 170	9.48	10.33	21 490
Embalmers	8 930	17.69	18.66	38 810	8 090	18.32	18.90	39 320
Funeral attendants	33 100	10.07	10.80	22 470	33 060	10.63	11.19	23 270
Barbers	12 110	11.31	12.43	25 860	10 330	11.56	12.79	26 610
Hairdressers, hairstylists, and cosmetologists	343 320	10.68	12.38	25 760	355 990	11.13	12.82	26 660
Makeup artists, theatrical and performance	1 400	16.95	19.57	40 710	1 930	12.63	18.76	39 020
Manicurists and pedicurists	52 730	9.60	10.59	22 020	51 590	9.46	10.60	22 040
Shampooers	15 310	7.93	8.41	17 490	15 570	8.32	8.80	18 300
Skin care specialists	24 960	13.07	14.71	30 600	26 300	13.81	15.40	32 040
Baggage porters and bellhops	49 700	9.25	10.88	22 620	49 770	9.49	11.14	23 170
Concierges	19 770	12.28	12.93	26 900	20 380	13.07	13.52	28 120
Tour guides and escorts	31 620	10.63	11.57	24 060	31 760	11.19	12.09	25 150
Travel guides	3 520	14.74	16.09	33 470	4 510	14.60	16.18	33 660
Flight attendants	97 010	(3)	(3)	62 880	99 480	(3)	(3)	39 840
Transportation attendants, except flight attendants and baggage porters	20 690	9.76	10.60	22 040	21 870	9.98	10.76	22 370
Childcare workers	576 680	8.82	9.46	19 670	581 670	9.12	9.79	20 350
Personal and home care aides	595 350	8.89	9.11	18 940	614 190	9.22	9.47	19 690
Fitness trainers and aerobics instructors	219 990	13.31	15.86	32 990	229 030	14.04	16.50	34 310
Recreation workers	278 070	10.20	11.44	23 790	282 680	10.56	11.81	24 570
Residential advisers	51 630	11.08	12.00	24 960	52 240	11.26	12.17	25 320
Personal care and service workers, all other	64 210	9.22	10.72	22 300	75 780	9.59	10.88	22 630
Sales and Related								
First-line supervisors/managers of retail sales workers	1 156 540	16.57	18.85	39 210	1 186 270	16.97	19.19	39 910
First-line supervisors/managers of non-retail sales workers	280 770	32.22	37.58	78 170	275 390	32.74	38.40	79 870
Cashiers	3 545 330	8.25	8.84	18 380	3 545 610	8.49	9.08	18 880
Gaming change persons and booth cashiers	24 640	10.04	10.55	21 940	22 280	10.57	11.00	22 890
Counter and rental clerks	462 040	9.65	11.47	23 850	448 480	10.05	11.74	24 430
Parts salespersons	230 480	13.52	14.68	30 540	226 530	13.71	14.83	30 850
Retail salespersons	4 429 060	9.69	11.79	24 530	4 426 280	9.86	12.04	25 050
Advertising sales agents	161 440	20.59	25.14	52 290	161 550	20.90	25.56	53 170
Insurance sales agents	321 920	21.21	28.16	58 580	327 780	21.84	29.06	60 440
Securities, commodities, and financial services sales agents	268 480	32.90	43.49	90 470	271 900	33.02	44.26	92 050
Travel agents	85 580	14.49	15.48	32 190	86 420	14.70	15.61	32 470
Sales representatives, services, all other	556 430	23.34	27.64	57 480	569 130	23.77	28.38	59 030
Sales representatives, wholesale and manufacturing, technical and scientific products	403 320	32.82	36.76	76 460	415 120	33.75	38.11	79 260
Sales representatives, wholesale and manufacturing, except technical and scientific products	1 505 930	24.40	28.94	60 190	1 493 760	24.68	29.55	61 470
Demonstrators and product promoters	83 270	10.85	12.77	26 570	83 540	11.18	13.05	27 150
Models	2 060	10.83	12.04	25 040	1 660	13.18	14.50	30 160
Real estate brokers	49 270	28.30	38.36	79 800	51 390	27.64	37.13	77 240
Real estate sales agents	172 030	19.52	26.49	55 090	164 080	19.30	26.16	54 410
Sales engineers	75 940	38.59	41.51	86 350	78 030	39.95	43.16	89 770
Telemarketers	354 000	10.28	11.75	24 430	345 220	10.56	11.91	24 770
Door-to-door sales workers, news and street vendors, and related workers	11 600	9.33	12.59	26 190	9 520	10.09	13.27	27 600
Sales and related workers, all other	151 890	16.80	20.13	41 870	146 480	16.99	20.10	41 810

[1]Annual wages have been calculated by multiplying the hourly mean wage by a "year-round, full-time" hours figure of 2,080 hours; for occupations with no published hourly mean wage, the annual wage has been directly calculated from the reported survey data.
[3]Wages for some occupations that do not generally entail year-round, full-time employment are reported as either hourly wages or annual salaries (depending on how employees are typically paid).

Table 3-3. Employment and Wages, by Occupation, May 2007 and May 2008—*Continued*

(Number of people, dollars.)

Occupation	May 2007				May 2008			
	Employ-ment	Median hourly wage	Mean hourly wage	Mean annual wage[1]	Employ-ment	Median hourly wage	Mean hourly wage	Mean annual wage[1]
Office and Adminstrative Support								
First-line supervisors/managers of office and administrative support workers	1 378 240	21.47	22.89	47 620	1 404 330	22.02	23.42	48 700
Switchboard operators, including answering service	160 200	11.28	11.76	24 460	153 860	11.65	12.14	25 250
Telephone operators	23 840	15.18	15.72	32 690	22 820	15.23	16.25	33 800
Communications equipment operators, all other	3 830	16.23	17.06	35 470	3 500	16.85	17.79	37 000
Bill and account collectors	409 570	14.42	15.21	31 630	408 760	14.73	15.47	32 180
Billing and posting clerks and machine operators	515 060	14.41	14.94	31 080	512 120	14.88	15.44	32 120
Bookkeeping, accounting, and auditing clerks	1 858 500	15.17	15.76	32 780	1 855 010	15.63	16.25	33 800
Gaming cage workers	17 120	11.30	11.83	24 610	17 060	11.97	12.48	25 970
Payroll and timekeeping clerks	201 940	16.26	16.59	34 500	203 210	16.74	17.07	35 500
Procurement clerks	77 180	16.40	16.62	34 570	79 610	16.72	16.96	35 280
Tellers	607 960	11.02	11.36	23 620	600 380	11.35	11.66	24 250
Brokerage clerks	71 170	17.96	19.23	39 990	68 430	18.61	19.89	41 370
Correspondence clerks	15 550	14.18	14.71	30 600	13 450	14.73	15.04	31 280
Court, municipal, and license clerks	109 080	15.54	16.44	34 190	115 070	15.96	16.88	35 120
Credit authorizers, checkers, and clerks	67 480	14.25	15.00	31 200	65 020	14.61	15.37	31 980
Customer service representatives	2 193 430	13.96	14.93	31 040	2 233 270	14.36	15.28	31 790
Eligibility interviewers, government programs	107 220	18.80	18.86	39 240	112 510	18.90	19.16	39 850
File clerks	214 590	11.06	11.76	24 450	204 760	11.44	12.16	25 290
Hotel, motel, and resort desk clerks	223 210	9.11	9.66	20 100	230 230	9.37	9.92	20 630
Interviewers, except eligibility and loan	227 220	13.14	13.55	28 190	224 690	13.53	13.96	29 040
Library assistants, clerical	112 300	10.71	11.42	23 750	114 740	10.88	11.68	24 290
Loan interviewers and clerks	239 810	15.23	15.97	33 220	212 340	15.61	16.29	33 890
New accounts clerks	88 880	14.24	14.64	30 450	87 300	14.53	14.90	30 990
Order clerks	255 670	12.94	13.71	28 510	248 030	13.46	14.08	29 300
Human resources assistants, except payroll and timekeeping	161 970	16.81	17.31	36 000	164 340	17.19	17.70	36 810
Receptionists and information clerks	1 100 790	11.40	11.82	24 580	1 097 610	11.80	12.21	25 400
Reservation and transportation ticket agents and travel clerks	167 390	14.34	14.94	31 080	163 880	14.94	15.41	32 060
All other information and record clerks	233 180	15.44	16.15	33 580	215 780	16.15	16.78	34 910
Cargo and freight agents	81 380	17.82	18.64	38 760	85 950	17.92	18.67	38 830
Couriers and messengers	100 820	10.75	11.54	24 000	96 110	11.22	12.07	25 100
Police, fire, and ambulance dispatchers	93 670	15.70	16.38	34 060	96 360	16.19	16.99	35 340
Dispatchers, except police, fire, and ambulance	190 190	15.93	17.07	35 500	193 210	16.28	17.58	36 560
Meter readers, utilities	46 220	15.29	16.12	33 520	44 730	15.84	16.77	34 890
Postal service clerks	79 500	21.66	21.29	44 290	78 250	24.54	24.11	50 150
Postal service mail carriers	348 070	21.39	21.17	44 030	354 570	23.94	22.58	46 970
Postal service mail sorters, processors, and processing machine operators	201 430	21.01	19.66	40 890	185 770	24.05	21.87	45 490
Production, planning, and expediting clerks	283 930	19.08	19.74	41 050	281 660	19.46	20.26	42 150
Shipping, receiving, and traffic clerks	755 790	12.98	13.66	28 410	760 950	13.30	14.03	29 180
Stock clerks and order fillers	1 817 650	9.85	10.93	22 720	1 873 390	10.00	11.13	23 140
Weighers, measurers, checkers, and samplers, record-keeping	76 000	12.56	13.37	27 810	72 720	12.95	13.70	28 500
Executive secretaries and administrative assistants	1 517 410	18.58	19.57	40 700	1 491 520	19.24	20.35	42 340
Legal secretaries	266 180	18.66	19.50	40 550	257 810	19.16	20.02	41 640
Medical secretaries	424 670	13.92	14.45	30 050	454 500	14.27	14.81	30 800
Secretaries, except legal, medical, and executive	1 832 490	13.57	14.04	29 190	1 872 070	13.96	14.42	29 990
Computer operators	117 380	16.64	17.34	36 080	107 450	17.11	17.82	37 070
Data entry keyers	286 540	12.20	12.67	26 350	272 810	12.56	13.04	27 110
Word processors and typists	139 420	14.61	15.18	31 580	128 010	15.09	15.73	32 710
Desktop publishers	29 320	17.07	18.02	37 470	26 210	17.59	18.62	38 740
Insurance claims and policy processing clerks	232 700	15.41	16.24	33 780	237 800	15.91	16.75	34 830
Mail clerks and mail machine operators, except postal service	138 990	11.73	12.32	25 630	137 350	12.07	12.70	26 420
Office clerks, general	2 980 350	11.76	12.48	25 960	2 906 600	12.17	12.90	26 830
Office machine operators, except computer	87 240	12.13	12.85	26 730	79 470	12.40	13.13	27 310
Proofreaders and copy markers	15 650	13.90	14.87	30 930	15 300	14.66	15.50	32 240
Statistical assistants	19 210	15.64	16.45	34 220	16 900	16.76	17.32	36 020
Office and administrative support workers, all other	266 220	13.70	14.75	30 680	272 190	14.10	15.15	31 510
Farming, Fishing, and Forestry								
First-line supervisors/managers of farming, fishing, and forestry workers	20 860	18.52	19.75	41 080	20 800	19.11	20.55	42 740
Farm labor contractors	1 450	14.39	15.95	33 180	1 110	16.10	17.62	36 640
Agricultural inspectors	14 510	19.13	19.15	39 830	14 340	19.80	19.87	41 330
Animal breeders	2 320	12.78	15.56	32 370	2 080	13.02	15.90	33 070
Graders and sorters, agricultural products	40 770	8.64	9.42	19 590	37 500	9.06	9.85	20 490
Agricultural equipment operators	22 490	10.18	11.13	23 140	22 110	10.92	11.77	24 490
Farmworkers and laborers, crop, nursery, and greenhouse	239 380	8.19	8.82	18 350	242 390	8.64	9.27	19 280
Farmworkers, farm and ranch animals	43 120	9.78	10.51	21 860	38 110	10.13	11.02	22 920
Agricultural workers, all other	7 960	12.45	13.16	27 370	7 680	12.00	13.13	27 310
Fishers and related fishing workers	960	13.43	13.59	28 280	1 110	13.44	13.68	28 460
Forest and conservation workers	8 770	9.86	11.62	24 160	8 280	10.98	12.55	26 110
Fallers	7 500	14.41	16.37	34 060	7 120	14.66	16.43	34 180
Logging equipment operators	27 700	14.83	15.35	31 920	27 010	15.18	15.76	32 780
Log graders and scalers	4 430	15.45	16.16	33 620	3 610	15.64	16.51	34 330
Logging workers, all other	5 740	15.52	15.48	32 210	5 180	15.96	15.82	32 900

[1]Annual wages have been calculated by multiplying the hourly mean wage by a "year-round, full-time" hours figure of 2,080 hours; for occupations with no published hourly mean wage, the annual wage has been directly calculated from the reported survey data.

Table 3-3. Employment and Wages, by Occupation, May 2007 and May 2008—*Continued*

(Number of people, dollars.)

Occupation	May 2007				May 2008			
	Employ-ment	Median hourly wage	Mean hourly wage	Mean annual wage[1]	Employ-ment	Median hourly wage	Mean hourly wage	Mean annual wage[1]
Construction and Extraction								
First-line supervisors/managers of construction trades and extraction workers	577 130	26.90	28.54	59 360	577 390	27.95	29.46	61 280
Boilermakers	18 650	24.38	24.72	51 420	20 400	25.13	25.53	53 100
Brickmasons and blockmasons	116 290	21.19	22.02	45 800	106 270	21.94	22.95	47 740
Stonemasons	18 760	17.76	18.98	39 470	18 910	18.17	19.68	40 930
Carpenters	969 670	18.11	19.84	41 260	899 920	18.72	20.64	42 940
Carpet installers	34 630	17.33	19.21	39 960	34 390	17.80	19.87	41 330
Floor layers, except carpet, wood, and hard tiles	14 070	16.88	18.74	38 980	14 250	17.50	19.03	39 580
Floor sanders and finishers	8 220	15.04	16.08	33 460	8 220	15.41	16.93	35 220
Tile and marble setters	52 790	18.61	19.62	40 810	51 210	18.85	20.13	41 870
Cement masons and concrete finishers	213 850	16.27	17.93	37 300	201 730	16.87	18.75	39 000
Terrazzo workers and finishers	5 920	16.54	18.17	37 790	5 550	17.25	18.90	39 300
Construction laborers	1 053 060	13.13	14.88	30 950	1 020 290	13.71	15.51	32 250
Paving, surfacing, and tamping equipment operators	63 850	15.56	17.04	35 450	61 230	16.00	17.54	36 490
Pile-driver operators	5 050	22.86	24.80	51 580	4 790	23.01	24.83	51 640
Operating engineers and other construction equipment operators	403 620	18.33	20.22	42 060	398 910	18.88	20.97	43 630
Drywall and ceiling tile installers	137 570	17.56	18.94	39 400	128 740	18.12	19.68	40 940
Tapers	37 280	20.22	21.09	43 870	31 850	21.03	22.07	45 900
Electricians	624 560	21.53	23.12	48 100	633 010	22.32	23.98	49 890
Glaziers	50 800	16.94	18.60	38 680	51 730	17.11	18.74	38 990
Insulation workers, floor, ceiling, and wall	29 660	15.04	16.45	34 220	28 390	15.34	16.79	34 920
Insulation workers, mechanical	29 110	17.58	19.94	41 480	30 150	17.95	19.99	41 570
Painters, construction and maintenance	260 260	15.42	16.94	35 230	250 310	15.85	17.56	36 510
Paperhangers	5 970	16.62	18.67	38 820	4 610	16.76	19.00	39 520
Pipelayers	56 890	15.04	16.70	34 750	54 440	15.72	17.45	36 300
Plumbers, pipefitters, and steamfitters	435 010	21.20	22.76	47 350	437 540	21.94	23.65	49 200
Plasterers and stucco masons	49 310	17.52	18.84	39 190	43 290	18.01	19.27	40 070
Reinforcing iron and rebar workers	28 270	18.21	20.50	42 640	28 620	19.18	21.34	44 380
Roofers	123 180	15.98	17.47	36 340	120 200	16.17	18.00	37 430
Sheet metal workers	167 730	18.85	20.50	42 640	163 480	19.37	21.30	44 310
Structural iron and steel workers	65 100	20.26	21.99	45 730	68 670	20.68	22.68	47 170
Helpers—brickmasons, blockmasons, stonemasons, and tile and marble setters	57 870	12.63	13.69	28 480	53 300	13.19	14.24	29 610
Helpers—carpenters	96 180	11.70	12.18	25 330	81 260	12.21	12.69	26 390
Helpers—electricians	101 370	11.96	12.51	26 010	104 050	12.69	13.20	27 450
Helpers—painters, paperhangers, plasterers, and stucco masons	22 770	10.72	11.21	23 320	19 900	11.23	11.70	24 330
Helpers—pipelayers, plumbers, pipefitters, and steamfitters	83 380	12.19	12.74	26 500	79 870	12.73	13.10	27 260
Helpers—roofers	21 250	10.97	11.37	23 650	18 730	11.47	11.85	24 660
Helpers—construction trades, all other	33 870	11.49	12.43	25 850	27 210	12.01	13.04	27 130
Construction and building inspectors	95 890	23.24	24.25	50 440	96 000	24.12	25.08	52 160
Elevator installers and repairers	22 950	32.69	31.89	66 330	25 070	33.35	32.57	67 750
Fence erectors	26 650	12.85	13.79	28 690	25 710	13.49	14.49	30 130
Hazardous materials removal workers	39 530	17.47	18.85	39 210	42 500	17.94	19.37	40 290
Highway maintenance workers	137 140	15.67	16.21	33 710	136 420	16.35	16.84	35 040
Rail-track laying and maintenance equipment operators	14 050	20.25	20.00	41 600	15 020	21.26	21.57	44 870
Septic tank servicers and sewer pipe cleaners	23 440	15.74	16.39	34 100	24 730	16.19	17.09	35 550
Segmental pavers	1 090	12.65	12.95	26 940	1 170	13.17	13.68	28 450
Construction and related workers, all other	58 040	15.01	16.16	33 620	55 820	15.65	16.91	35 170
Derrick operators, oil and gas	19 410	18.17	18.98	39 480	23 590	20.15	20.18	41 980
Rotary drill operators, oil and gas	22 600	20.91	21.90	45 560	27 020	23.94	26.14	54 370
Service unit operators, oil, gas, and mining	30 440	16.73	18.55	38 580	36 850	18.07	19.86	41 320
Earth drillers, except oil and gas	19 760	17.46	18.85	39 200	20 220	18.39	19.88	41 360
Explosives workers, ordnance handling experts, and blasters	5 750	19.96	20.68	43 020	6 060	20.18	21.39	44 490
Continuous mining machine operators	9 830	21.09	21.06	43 800	10 920	22.09	21.91	45 570
Mine cutting and channeling machine operators	8 460	19.20	18.92	39 360	9 190	19.94	19.96	41 510
Mining machine operators, all other	4 170	19.40	20.03	41 660	4 650	20.62	20.79	43 240
Rock splitters, quarry	4 100	13.49	14.69	30 550	4 210	13.41	14.50	30 160
Roof bolters, mining	4 130	20.80	21.15	43 990	4 950	21.74	21.97	45 690
Roustabouts, oil and gas	54 200	13.71	14.66	30 480	62 540	14.72	15.70	32 660
Helpers—extraction workers	24 670	14.37	15.23	31 670	25 550	15.74	16.36	34 030
Extraction workers, all other	8 890	18.73	20.19	41 990	7 800	18.49	19.89	41 370
Installation, Maintenance, and Repair								
First-line supervisors/managers of mechanics, installers, and repairers	443 790	26.63	27.60	57 400	443 840	27.55	28.44	59 160
Computer, automated teller, and office machine repairers	132 750	17.84	18.61	38 710	122 400	18.18	18.95	39 420
Radio mechanics	5 570	18.89	20.20	42 020	5 440	19.36	20.45	42 530
Telecommunications equipment installers and repairers, except line installers	189 290	25.99	24.88	51 760	195 170	26.73	25.31	52 650
Avionics technicians	16 300	23.13	23.19	48 240	18 360	23.71	23.73	49 360
Electric motor, power tool, and related repairers	22 150	16.41	17.40	36 180	23 400	16.96	17.84	37 110
Electrical and electronics installers and repairers, transportation equipment	18 160	21.12	21.25	44 210	15 860	21.37	21.60	44 940
Electrical and electronics repairers, commercial and industrial equipment	79 150	22.65	22.90	47 630	77 270	23.29	23.68	49 260
Electrical and electronics repairers, powerhouse, substation, and relay	23 320	28.35	27.98	58 200	23 180	29.34	29.18	60 700
Electronic equipment installers and repairers, motor vehicles	19 310	13.53	14.60	30 360	19 980	13.29	14.31	29 770

[1]Annual wages have been calculated by multiplying the hourly mean wage by a "year-round, full-time" hours figure of 2,080 hours; for occupations with no published hourly mean wage, the annual wage has been directly calculated from the reported survey data.

Table 3-3. Employment and Wages, by Occupation, May 2007 and May 2008—*Continued*

(Number of people, dollars.)

Occupation	May 2007				May 2008			
	Employ-ment	Median hourly wage	Mean hourly wage	Mean annual wage[1]	Employ-ment	Median hourly wage	Mean hourly wage	Mean annual wage[1]
Installation, Maintenance, and Repair—*Continued*								
Electronic home entertainment equipment installers and repairers	38 170	15.03	15.94	33 160	38 680	15.42	16.26	33 830
Security and fire alarm systems installers	60 700	17.02	17.93	37 290	62 720	17.63	18.57	38 630
Aircraft mechanics and service technicians	118 780	23.56	23.88	49 670	116 310	24.71	24.83	51 650
Automotive body and related repairers	152 790	17.16	18.53	38 530	147 200	17.81	19.21	39 950
Automotive glass installers and repairers	18 340	15.13	15.80	32 870	18 330	15.44	15.95	33 180
Automotive service technicians and mechanics	650 780	16.43	17.54	36 480	649 460	16.88	18.05	37 540
Bus and truck mechanics and diesel engine specialists	250 370	18.58	19.04	39 610	248 620	18.94	19.57	40 710
Farm equipment mechanics	29 660	14.75	15.23	31 670	30 240	15.32	15.79	32 850
Mobile heavy equipment mechanics, except engines	124 180	19.93	20.57	42 790	125 930	20.59	21.30	44 300
Rail car repairers	23 190	21.62	21.69	45 120	20 780	21.48	21.59	44 920
Motorboat mechanics	19 610	16.45	17.06	35 490	19 640	16.60	17.35	36 080
Motorcycle mechanics	16 800	14.57	15.49	32 210	16 850	15.08	16.10	33 490
Outdoor power equipment and other small engine mechanics	27 560	13.49	13.94	29 000	26 440	13.91	14.41	29 970
Bicycle repairers	9 130	10.49	11.08	23 040	9 690	11.15	11.61	24 140
Recreational vehicle service technicians	14 030	15.27	16.19	33 670	13 400	15.14	16.05	33 380
Tire repairers and changers	100 510	10.52	11.24	23 380	98 520	10.80	11.46	23 830
Mechanical door repairers	18 280	15.33	16.42	34 140	17 530	16.11	17.00	35 360
Control and valve installers and repairers, except mechanical door	43 160	22.18	22.23	46 240	43 900	22.62	22.72	47 260
Heating, air-conditioning, and refrigeration mechanics and installers	262 570	18.44	19.54	40 630	261 610	19.08	20.31	42 240
Home appliance repairers	39 130	16.14	16.92	35 200	37 300	16.30	17.16	35 690
Industrial machinery mechanics	266 550	20.36	21.16	44 020	280 620	20.99	21.77	45 280
Maintenance and repair workers, general	1 308 350	15.66	16.51	34 350	1 305 170	16.21	17.13	35 630
Maintenance workers, machinery	78 760	17.11	18.00	37 450	73 650	17.69	18.56	38 610
Millwrights	49 360	22.16	23.40	48 660	46 250	22.87	24.05	50 030
Refractory materials repairers, except brickmasons	2 700	19.74	20.15	41 910	2 450	19.78	20.07	41 750
Electrical power line installers and repairers	109 990	25.27	24.85	51 690	111 580	26.49	26.11	54 300
Telecommunications line installers and repairers	160 250	22.70	22.39	46 570	168 050	23.12	22.75	47 330
Camera and photographic equipment repairers	3 870	17.23	18.06	37 570	3 820	16.49	18.27	37 990
Medical equipment repairers	34 080	19.38	20.95	43 580	34 260	19.96	21.17	44 030
Musical instrument repairers and tuners	5 410	15.40	16.50	34 330	5 310	15.90	17.28	35 950
Watch repairers	2 840	15.92	17.40	36 200	2 770	16.66	18.08	37 600
Precision instrument and equipment repairers, all other	13 640	22.80	23.23	48 320	12 990	23.54	24.23	50 400
Coin, vending, and amusement machine servicers and repairers	42 150	13.97	14.45	30 050	41 280	14.39	14.89	30 970
Commercial divers	1 980	20.01	24.76	51 510	2 370	22.28	26.42	54 940
Fabric menders, except garment	990	13.49	13.74	28 580	960	13.69	13.42	27 920
Locksmiths and safe repairers	18 750	15.98	16.55	34 430	18 500	16.57	17.26	35 900
Manufactured building and mobile home installers	9 150	12.83	13.60	28 280	8 290	13.58	14.17	29 460
Riggers	12 390	18.95	19.58	40 720	13 490	19.77	20.49	42 620
Signal and track switch repairers	6 090	24.58	24.66	51 290	6 570	23.89	23.59	49 060
Helpers—installation, maintenance, and repair workers	153 320	11.02	11.94	24 840	149 350	11.46	12.34	25 670
Installation, maintenance, and repair workers, all other	141 980	15.87	17.26	35 910	139 100	16.46	17.89	37 220
Production								
First-line supervisors/managers of production and operating workers	666 850	23.40	24.88	51 740	658 500	24.25	25.72	53 500
Aircraft structure, surfaces, rigging, and systems assemblers	34 410	21.84	21.24	44 180	43 330	21.22	20.96	43 600
Coil winders, tapers, and finishers	22 300	13.03	13.44	27 960	22 160	13.33	13.81	28 720
Electrical and electronic equipment assemblers	216 470	12.76	13.75	28 590	215 230	13.22	14.14	29 410
Electromechanical equipment assemblers	64 570	13.73	14.41	29 970	62 310	14.11	14.67	30 520
Engine and other machine assemblers	41 100	15.14	15.99	33 260	39 270	15.70	16.78	34 900
Structural metal fabricators and fitters	107 830	14.92	15.52	32 290	111 620	15.58	16.28	33 860
Fiberglass laminators and fabricators	31 810	12.80	13.21	27 490	30 890	13.48	13.79	28 680
Team assemblers	1 167 150	11.84	12.72	26 470	1 131 060	12.32	13.28	27 630
Timing device assemblers, adjusters, and calibrators	2 710	13.67	14.40	29 940	2 700	13.73	14.76	30 710
Assemblers and fabricators, all other	330 940	13.42	15.72	32 700	318 060	13.37	15.79	32 840
Bakers	141 560	10.86	11.71	24 360	141 130	11.20	12.03	25 020
Butchers and meat cutters	128 510	13.21	13.87	28 840	128 210	13.60	14.28	29 700
Meat, poultry, and fish cutters and trimmers	150 190	10.12	10.45	21 730	166 150	10.49	10.77	22 400
Slaughterers and meat packers	110 020	10.82	10.83	22 520	97 000	11.07	11.19	23 270
Food and tobacco roasting, baking, and drying machine operators and tenders	18 130	12.18	13.04	27 130	17 870	12.81	13.76	28 610
Food batchmakers	99 650	11.41	12.39	25 770	99 170	11.62	12.64	26 290
Food cooking machine operators and tenders	41 790	10.78	11.42	23 750	39 300	11.00	11.59	24 110
Computer-controlled machine tool operators, metal and plastic	140 380	15.65	16.20	33 690	143 030	16.03	16.60	34 520
Numerical tool and process control programmers	17 280	20.44	21.54	44 800	16 990	21.30	22.29	46 360
Extruding and drawing machine setters, operators, and tenders, metal and plastic	95 330	13.82	14.44	30 030	92 160	14.31	14.92	31 030
Forging machine setters, operators, and tenders, metal and plastic	30 130	14.54	15.08	31 360	28 800	14.90	15.56	32 370
Rolling machine setters, operators, and tenders, metal and plastic	37 950	15.67	16.33	33 960	34 970	16.40	17.02	35 410
Cutting, punching, and press machine setters, operators, and tenders, metal and plastic	254 160	13.10	13.72	28 540	242 970	13.54	14.15	29 420
Drilling and boring machine tool setters, operators, and tenders, metal and plastic	37 680	14.54	15.41	32 050	33 550	14.83	15.64	32 520
Grinding, lapping, polishing, and buffing machine tool setters, operators, and tenders, metal and plastic	96 730	13.77	14.60	30 360	91 990	14.16	15.01	31 230
Lathe and turning machine tool setters, operators, and tenders, metal and plastic	61 140	15.61	16.12	33 520	56 500	15.84	16.38	34 070
Milling and planing machine setters, operators, and tenders, metal and plastic	26 430	15.36	15.92	33 100	26 220	16.00	16.56	34 450
Machinists	410 900	16.94	17.49	36 370	419 070	17.41	18.03	37 490
Metal refining furnace operators and tenders	19 180	16.63	16.98	35 330	19 280	17.47	17.94	37 310

[1]Annual wages have been calculated by multiplying the hourly mean wage by a "year-round, full-time" hours figure of 2,080 hours; for occupations with no published hourly mean wage, the annual wage has been directly calculated from the reported survey data.

Table 3-3. Employment and Wages, by Occupation, May 2007 and May 2008—*Continued*

(Number of people, dollars.)

Occupation	May 2007				May 2008			
	Employ-ment	Median hourly wage	Mean hourly wage	Mean annual wage[1]	Employ-ment	Median hourly wage	Mean hourly wage	Mean annual wage[1]
Production—*Continued*								
Pourers and casters, metal	15 470	15.20	15.69	32 640	15 320	15.66	16.11	33 510
Model makers, metal and plastic	9 270	19.51	21.15	43 990	8 990	19.55	21.49	44 700
Patternmakers, metal and plastic	7 250	17.44	18.83	39 160	6 220	17.75	18.98	39 490
Foundry mold and coremakers	15 000	14.04	14.60	30 370	15 240	14.13	14.61	30 390
Molding, coremaking, and casting machine setters, operators, and tenders, metal and plastic	147 850	12.70	13.62	28 330	145 760	13.17	14.07	29 270
Multiple machine tool setters, operators, and tenders, metal and plastic	91 090	14.61	15.52	32 280	87 800	14.87	15.76	32 780
Tool and die makers	92 560	21.68	22.36	46 520	85 610	22.32	23.17	48 180
Welders, cutters, solderers, and brazers	385 740	15.51	16.33	33 960	392 520	16.13	17.01	35 370
Welding, soldering, and brazing machine setters, operators, and tenders	50 820	14.90	15.96	33 200	51 840	15.20	16.20	33 700
Heat treating equipment setters, operators, and tenders, metal and plastic	25 500	15.03	15.47	32 180	23 630	15.40	15.93	33 140
Lay out workers, metal and plastic	9 190	16.93	17.67	36 760	8 340	16.79	17.87	37 170
Plating and coating machine setters, operators, and tenders, metal and plastic	41 370	13.40	14.20	29 540	40 300	13.65	14.46	30 090
Tool grinders, filers, and sharpeners	17 240	14.90	15.75	32 760	16 410	15.37	16.29	33 880
Metal workers and plastic workers, all other	47 100	15.75	17.56	36 530	43 690	15.61	17.10	35 570
Bindery workers	62 990	12.73	13.56	28 200	60 560	13.17	13.99	29 100
Bookbinders	6 230	13.82	15.38	31 980	6 150	14.92	16.33	33 970
Job printers	43 320	15.69	16.45	34 220	42 640	16.21	16.98	35 330
Prepress technicians and workers	65 540	16.34	17.08	35 520	61 170	16.84	17.52	36 440
Printing machine operators	199 790	15.14	16.08	33 450	193 510	15.46	16.42	34 150
Laundry and dry-cleaning workers	218 060	8.86	9.41	19 570	221 230	9.14	9.72	20 230
Pressers, textile, garment, and related materials	69 260	8.87	9.27	19 280	67 500	9.15	9.55	19 860
Sewing machine operators	200 340	9.31	10.13	21 080	190 440	9.55	10.43	21 690
Shoe and leather workers and repairers	7 880	10.37	11.10	23 080	8 170	11.00	11.60	24 130
Shoe machine operators and tenders	4 130	11.73	11.78	24 510	4 910	12.06	12.22	25 420
Sewers, hand	8 530	10.10	10.70	22 250	7 050	10.58	11.14	23 170
Tailors, dressmakers, and custom sewers	31 550	11.58	12.49	25 980	31 700	12.01	12.94	26 920
Textile bleaching and dyeing machine operators and tenders	18 050	11.36	11.63	24 180	16 180	11.38	11.77	24 480
Textile cutting machine setters, operators, and tenders	21 080	10.79	11.31	23 510	20 170	10.88	11.45	23 810
Textile knitting and weaving machine setters, operators, and tenders	33 400	11.78	12.00	24 960	30 250	12.21	12.33	25 650
Textile winding, twisting, and drawing-out machine setters, operators, and tenders	40 450	11.23	11.44	23 790	36 540	11.53	11.83	24 600
Extruding and forming machine setters, operators, and tenders, synthetic and glass fibers	15 240	14.34	14.79	30 760	14 440	14.98	15.29	31 800
Fabric and apparel patternmakers	8 370	17.18	19.67	40 900	7 500	18.15	20.28	42 190
Upholsterers	40 290	13.50	14.24	29 620	39 090	13.94	14.69	30 560
Textile, apparel, and furnishings workers, all other	21 760	11.48	12.53	26 060	17 430	11.85	13.20	27 450
Cabinetmakers and bench carpenters	128 730	13.45	14.25	29 640	120 960	13.93	14.72	30 620
Furniture finishers	23 470	12.42	13.19	27 440	21 630	12.93	13.66	28 410
Model makers, wood	1 610	14.45	17.05	35 470	1 740	15.06	17.16	35 690
Patternmakers, wood	2 040	15.63	16.98	35 320	1 930	16.35	18.61	38 720
Sawing machine setters, operators, and tenders, wood	58 160	11.94	12.58	26 160	51 830	12.41	13.01	27 070
Woodworking machine setters, operators, and tenders, except sawing	95 220	11.63	12.23	25 430	88 510	11.89	12.44	25 880
Woodworkers, all other	11 470	11.25	12.40	25 790	11 260	11.57	12.78	26 570
Nuclear power reactor operators	4 220	33.85	34.24	71 220	4 970	35.25	35.34	73 510
Power distributors and dispatchers	9 410	30.44	30.33	63 100	9 820	31.68	31.76	66 070
Power plant operators	34 400	27.23	27.41	57 020	34 700	28.11	28.05	58 340
Stationary engineers and boiler operators	40 370	22.90	23.42	48 700	39 000	23.94	24.36	50 660
Water and liquid waste treatment plant and system operators	108 290	17.83	18.44	38 360	110 300	18.48	19.21	39 950
Chemical plant and system operators	48 030	24.45	24.49	50 950	44 600	25.23	25.07	52 150
Gas plant operators	13 190	26.27	26.21	54 510	14 500	26.81	26.61	55 350
Petroleum pump system operators, refinery operators, and gaugers	43 270	25.49	25.68	53 420	45 710	26.45	26.42	54 950
Plant and system operators, all other	13 290	22.47	22.49	46 780	12 370	23.37	23.36	48 590
Chemical equipment operators and tenders	52 620	21.18	21.28	44 250	52 890	21.76	21.92	45 580
Separating, filtering, clarifying, precipitating, and still machine setters, operators, and tenders	44 310	17.28	17.91	37 260	41 200	17.64	18.27	38 010
Crushing, grinding, and polishing machine setters, operators, and tenders	42 360	13.79	14.52	30 210	41 270	14.38	15.08	31 360
Grinding and polishing workers, hand	42 750	11.95	12.58	26 160	40 290	12.36	13.03	27 100
Mixing and blending machine setters, operators, and tenders	139 370	14.59	15.24	31 710	140 120	15.04	15.70	32 650
Cutters and trimmers, hand	26 180	11.19	12.25	25 480	24 700	11.38	12.28	25 540
Cutting and slicing machine setters, operators, and tenders	80 260	13.70	14.51	30 180	76 500	13.85	14.44	30 020
Extruding, forming, pressing, and compacting machine setters, operators, and tenders	88 600	13.46	14.20	29 540	85 130	13.92	14.63	30 430
Furnace, kiln, oven, dryer, and kettle operators and tenders	24 590	14.78	15.40	32 030	22 950	15.31	15.84	32 950
Inspectors, testers, sorters, samplers, and weighers	472 900	14.57	15.86	32 980	467 010	15.02	16.29	33 890
Jewelers and precious stone and metal workers	27 160	15.00	16.35	34 010	24 780	15.84	17.00	35 360
Dental laboratory technicians	44 530	16.10	17.23	35 850	42 640	16.43	17.78	36 990
Medical appliance technicians	11 900	15.69	17.31	36 010	12 930	16.57	18.58	38 640
Ophthalmic laboratory technicians	30 900	12.76	13.71	28 530	32 930	13.08	14.01	29 130
Packaging and filling machine operators and tenders	368 320	11.42	12.43	25 860	357 480	11.73	12.76	26 550
Coating, painting, and spraying machine setters, operators, and tenders	102 600	13.24	13.89	28 900	103 310	13.66	14.27	29 680
Painters, transportation equipment	51 260	17.31	18.69	38 870	50 310	17.86	19.37	40 300
Painting, coating, and decorating workers	31 740	11.15	12.05	25 060	31 200	11.57	12.54	26 090
Photographic process workers	21 090	11.99	13.58	28 250	21 040	12.51	14.14	29 410
Photographic processing machine operators	50 690	9.48	10.51	21 860	49 550	9.79	10.93	22 740

[1]Annual wages have been calculated by multiplying the hourly mean wage by a "year-round, full-time" hours figure of 2,080 hours; for occupations with no published hourly mean wage, the annual wage has been directly calculated from the reported survey data.

Table 3-3. Employment and Wages, by Occupation, May 2007 and May 2008—*Continued*

(Number of people, dollars.)

Occupation	May 2007				May 2008			
	Employ-ment	Median hourly wage	Mean hourly wage	Mean annual wage[1]	Employ-ment	Median hourly wage	Mean hourly wage	Mean annual wage[1]
Production—*Continued*								
Semiconductor processors	36 690	15.32	16.74	34 820	32 230	15.49	16.43	34 170
Cementing and gluing machine operators and tenders	21 670	12.64	13.35	27 770	19 640	13.23	13.96	29 030
Cleaning, washing, and metal pickling equipment operators and tenders	16 850	11.07	12.12	25 210	18 870	11.53	12.57	26 140
Cooling and freezing equipment operators and tenders	9 610	11.38	12.34	25 660	9 940	12.05	13.11	27 260
Etchers and engravers	11 130	12.76	13.81	28 720	10 760	13.22	14.14	29 400
Molders, shapers, and casters, except metal and plastic	41 650	12.81	13.51	28 100	41 900	13.40	13.98	29 090
Paper goods machine setters, operators, and tenders	111 250	15.41	15.89	33 050	104 170	15.91	16.35	34 010
Tire builders	20 530	20.06	19.01	39 540	21 740	19.35	18.31	38 080
Helpers—production	524 440	10.14	10.86	22 600	499 870	10.48	11.21	23 320
Production workers, all other	288 480	12.33	14.18	29 500	280 160	12.86	14.57	30 310
Transportation and Material Moving								
Aircraft cargo handling supervisors	4 690	18.16	21.46	44 630	4 950	19.23	22.43	46 660
First-line supervisors/managers of helpers, laborers, and material movers, hand	184 400	19.54	20.69	43 020	186 230	20.18	21.33	44 380
First-line supervisors/managers of transportation and material moving machine and vehicle operators	223 710	23.97	25.25	52 510	218 480	24.67	25.94	53 960
Airline pilots, copilots, and flight engineers	78 250	(3)	(3)	148 810	77 090	(3)	(3)	119 750
Commercial pilots	29 180	(3)	(3)	71 270	31 250	(3)	(3)	75 500
Air traffic controllers	24 180	(3)	(3)	107 780	24 260	53.78	51.97	108 090
Airfield operations specialists	6 210	18.42	19.68	40 930	8 050	19.88	20.46	42 550
Ambulance drivers and attendants, except emergency medical technicians	21 520	10.16	10.73	22 310	21 790	10.77	11.25	23 400
Bus drivers, transit and intercity	189 050	15.94	16.42	34 150	184 160	16.32	17.16	35 700
Bus drivers, school	461 590	12.43	12.59	26 190	460 100	12.79	13.01	27 060
Driver/sales workers	382 360	10.28	12.11	25 190	372 720	10.70	12.52	26 050
Truck drivers, heavy and tractor-trailer	1 693 590	17.41	18.06	37 560	1 672 580	17.92	18.62	38 720
Truck drivers, light or delivery services	922 900	12.68	13.86	28 820	908 960	13.27	14.55	30 260
Taxi drivers and chauffeurs	165 590	10.01	10.93	22 740	170 520	10.36	11.32	23 540
Motor vehicle operators, all other	77 660	11.63	13.40	27 870	78 610	11.97	14.26	29 650
Locomotive engineers	41 760	27.65	30.38	63 180	42 760	23.29	25.71	53 470
Locomotive firers	580	21.78	23.88	49 660	970	23.17	25.46	52 950
Rail yard engineers, dinkey operators, and hostlers	4 950	18.76	19.48	40 510	5 480	15.68	16.76	34 850
Railroad brake, signal, and switch operators	23 120	24.59	26.22	54 530	24 610	22.94	23.75	49 400
Railroad conductors and yardmasters	37 540	28.20	29.56	61 480	39 580	25.40	26.02	54 120
Subway and streetcar operators	6 600	24.29	22.95	47 740	7 430	25.59	23.72	49 330
Rail transportation workers, all other	5 210	18.87	18.62	38 730	4 660	21.12	21.25	44 200
Sailors and marine oilers	32 550	15.66	16.37	34 050	32 420	16.53	17.25	35 880
Captains, mates, and pilots of water vessels	30 540	27.50	30.15	62 720	30 600	29.79	32.56	67 730
Motorboat operators	3 250	15.66	17.58	36 570	3 380	15.34	17.54	36 480
Ship engineers	13 710	26.97	29.65	61 680	11 190	29.18	31.80	66 140
Bridge and lock tenders	4 750	18.86	18.33	38 120	4 490	19.54	19.20	39 930
Parking lot attendants	131 860	8.66	9.29	19 320	136 470	9.04	9.67	20 120
Service station attendants	93 140	8.79	9.48	19 720	84 480	9.11	9.78	20 340
Traffic technicians	6 550	18.69	19.30	40 150	7 030	19.00	20.10	41 810
Transportation inspectors	24 130	24.73	27.43	57 050	24 940	26.56	28.46	59 200
Transportation workers, all other	46 720	15.51	16.51	34 330	43 330	15.87	17.11	35 590
Conveyor operators and tenders	45 580	13.49	13.95	29 020	41 920	13.95	14.46	30 090
Crane and tower operators	45 720	19.36	20.65	42 940	44 490	20.13	21.84	45 430
Dredge operators	1 910	16.46	18.42	38 320	1 910	16.70	18.77	39 040
Excavating and loading machine and dragline operators	68 040	16.37	17.79	36 990	65 160	16.93	18.36	38 180
Loading machine operators, underground mining	2 770	18.79	20.18	41 980	3 670	20.54	21.26	44 230
Hoist and winch operators	3 220	16.72	18.84	39 190	2 810	17.50	19.87	41 340
Industrial truck and tractor operators	630 700	13.47	14.31	29 760	620 450	13.98	14.78	30 750
Cleaners of vehicles and equipment	336 210	8.98	10.03	20 870	330 850	9.35	10.43	21 700
Laborers and freight, stock, and material movers, hand	2 363 440	10.53	11.46	23 840	2 335 510	10.89	11.87	24 690
Machine feeders and offbearers	143 140	11.48	12.15	25 260	144 820	12.29	12.92	26 880
Packers and packagers, hand	798 450	8.80	9.77	20 320	777 630	9.16	10.15	21 100
Gas compressor and gas pumping station operators	4 230	21.82	21.44	44 590	4 050	21.45	21.35	44 410
Pump operators, except wellhead pumpers	10 400	18.75	19.55	40 660	9 280	18.81	19.72	41 020
Wellhead pumpers	15 780	17.65	18.12	37 680	17 050	18.20	18.96	39 430
Refuse and recyclable material collectors	126 270	14.15	15.10	31 410	129 080	14.93	15.76	32 790
Shuttle car operators	2 660	19.67	19.86	41 300	3 050	20.29	20.53	42 700
Tank car, truck, and ship loaders	14 870	15.93	17.22	35 820	12 330	18.14	19.00	39 510
Material moving workers, all other	43 840	14.74	15.95	33 170	41 140	15.68	16.68	34 700

[1]Annual wages have been calculated by multiplying the hourly mean wage by a "year-round, full-time" hours figure of 2,080 hours; for occupations with no published hourly mean wage, the annual wage has been directly calculated from the reported survey data.
[3]Wages for some occupations that do not generally entail year-round, full-time employment are reported as either hourly wages or annual salaries (depending on how employees are typically paid).

Chapter Four

LABOR FORCE AND EMPLOYMENT PROJECTIONS BY INDUSTRY AND OCCUPATION

LABOR FORCE AND EMPLOYMENT PROJECTIONS BY INDUSTRY AND OCCUPATION

HIGHLIGHTS

Every two years, the Bureau of Labor Statistics (BLS) develops decade-long projections for industry output, employment, and occupations. This chapter presents the employment outlook for the 2008–2018 period. The projections are based on a set of explicit assumptions and an application of a model of economic relationships.

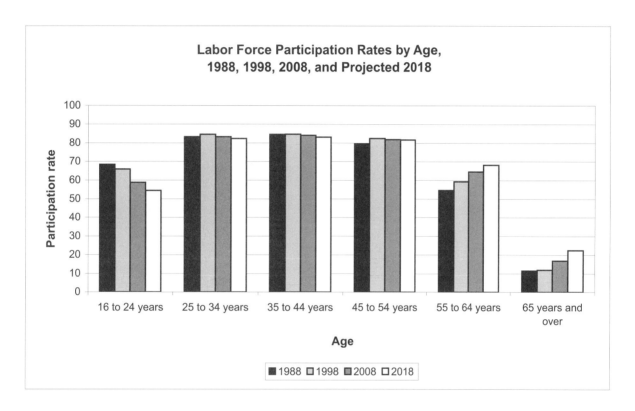

Labor Force Participation Rates by Age, 1988, 1998, 2008, and Projected 2018

The civilan labor force is projected to grow by 8.2 percent from 2008 to 2018, a much slower rate than the 12.1 percent increase from 1998 to 2008 or the 13.2 percent increase from 1988 to 1998. The aging of baby boomers has lead to a significant projected increase in the labor force of older workers. The labor force of those age 55 years and over is expected to grow by 43.0 percent and 81.4 percent for those in the 65- to 74-year age group. (See Table 4-1.)

OTHER HIGHLIGHTS

- The labor force in 2018 is expected to more diverse. From 2008 to 2018, the number of Hispanics in the labor force is projected to increase by 33.1 percent, followed by the number of Asians at 29.8 percent and the number of Blacks at 14.1 percent. Meanwhile, the number of non-Hispanic Whites in the labor force is only projected to increase by 1.5 percent. (Hispanics may be of any race.) (See Table 4-1.)

- While the number of women in the labor force is projected to increase from 2008 to 2018, the number is increasing at declining rate. From 1988 to 1998, the number of women in the labor force increased 16.4 percent and from 1998 to 2008, the number increased 12.6 percent. It is projected that the number of women will increase by only 9.0 percent from 2008 to 2018. (See Table 4-1.)

- The number of 16- to 24-year-olds as well as the number of 35- to 54-year-olds in the labor force is expected to decline from 2008 to 2018. (See Table 4-1.)

NOTES AND DEFINITIONS

The Bureau of Labor Statistics (BLS) develops long-term projections of likely employment patterns in the U.S. economy. Since the early 1970s, projections have been prepared on a 2-year cycle. The projections cover the future size and composition of the labor force, aggregate economic growth, detailed estimates of industry production, and industry and occupational employment. The resulting data serve a variety of users who need information about expected patterns of economic growth and the effects these patterns are expected to have on employment. For example, information about future employment opportunities by occupation is used by counselors, educators, and others helping people choose a career and by officials who plan education and training programs.

The labor force projections are a function of two components—projections of the population and projections of labor force participation rates. Population projections are provided by the Census Bureau for detailed age, sex, race, and ethnicity groupings. BLS extrapolates participation rates for these same categories by applying well-specified smoothing and time series techniques to historical time series for the detailed participation rates.

Concepts and Definitions

Employment. In the employment projections survey, employment is defined as a count of jobs, not a count of individual workers.

Employment change. The numerical change in employment measures the projected number of job gains or losses.

Employment change, percent. The percent change in employment measures the projected rate of change of employment in an occupation. A rapidly growing occupation usually indicates favorable prospects for employment. However, even modest employment growth in a large occupation can result in many more job openings due to growth than can rapid employment growth in a small occupation.

Job openings due to growth and replacement needs. Estimates of the projected number of net entrants into an occupation. For occupations that require training, the data may be used to assess the minimum number of workers who will need to be trained. The number of openings due to growth is the positive employment change from 2008 to 2018. If employment declines, then there are no job openings due to growth. The number of openings due to replacement needs is the net number of workers leaving an occupation who will need to be replaced. Replacement needs are calculated from monthly CPS data for 1999 to 2008.

Median annual wages quartile. This measure indicates where the median annual wages of an occupation rank in compar-

ison to the wages for all workers across the Nation. Occupations in which the median wage is higher than that earned by 75 percent of all workers are classified as having "very high" (VH) earnings. Occupations in which the median wage is above the national median for all workers are classified as having "high" (H) earnings. Occupations with a median wage below the national median are classified as having "low" (L) earnings, and occupations in which the median wage falls into the lowest 25 percent of national wages are classified as occupations with "very low" (VL) earnings.

Short-term on-the-job training. Skills needed for a worker to become fully qualified can be acquired during a short demonstration of job duties or during 1 month or less of on-the-job experience or instruction. Examples include retail salespersons and waiters and waitresses.

Moderate-term on-the-job training. Skills needed for a worker to become fully qualified can be acquired during 1 to 12 months of combined on-the-job experience and informal training. Examples include heavy and tractor-trailer truck-drivers and medical secretaries.

Long-term on-the-job training. More than 12 months of on-the-job training or, alternatively, combined work experience and formal classroom instruction are needed for workers to develop the skills to become fully qualified. This category includes formal or informal apprenticeships that may last up to 5 years. Long-term on-the-job training also includes intensive occupation-specific, employer-sponsored programs that workers must complete. Such programs include those offered by fire and police academies and schools for air traffic controllers and flight attendants. In other occupations—nuclear power reactor operators, for example—trainees take formal courses, often provided at the jobsite, to prepare for the required licensing exams. Individuals undergoing training usually are considered to be employed in the occupation. Also included in this category is the development of some natural ability—such as that possessed by musicians, athletes, actors, and other entertainers—that must be cultivated over several years, frequently in a nonwork setting.

Sources of Additional Information

A complete presentation of the projections, including analysis of results and additional tables and a comprehensive description of the methodology, can be found in the November 2009 edition of the *Monthly Labor Review*, which is available on the BLS Web site at <http://www.bls.gov/opub/mlr/2009/11/home.htm>. In addition, more information on employment projections can be found on the BLS Web site at <http://www.bls.gov/emp/>.

Table 4-1. Civilian Labor Force, by Age, Sex, Race, and Hispanic Origin, 1988, 1998, 2008, and Projected 2018

(Numbers in thousands, percent.)

Age, sex, race, and Hispanic origin	Labor force				Change			Percent change		
	1988	1998	2008	2018	1988–1998	1998–2008	2008–2018	1988–1998	1998–2008	2008–2018
Both Sexes, 16 Years and Over	121 669	137 673	154 287	166 911	16 004	16 614	12 624	13.2	12.1	8.2
16 to 24 years	22 536	21 894	22 032	21 131	-642	138	-901	-2.8	0.6	-4.1
16 to 19 years	8 031	8 256	6 858	5 868	225	-1 398	-990	2.8	-16.9	-14.4
20 to 24 years	14 505	13 638	15 174	15 263	-867	1 536	89	-6.0	11.3	0.6
25 to 54 years	84 041	98 718	104 396	105 944	14 677	5 678	1 548	17.5	5.8	1.5
25 to 34 years	35 503	32 813	33 332	36 814	-2 690	519	3 482	-7.6	1.6	10.4
35 to 44 years	29 435	37 536	35 061	34 787	8 101	-2 475	-274	27.5	-6.6	-0.8
45 to 54 years	19 104	28 368	36 003	34 343	9 264	7 635	-1 660	48.5	26.9	-4.6
55 years and over	15 092	17 062	27 858	39 836	1 970	10 796	11 978	13.1	63.3	43.0
55 to 64 years	11 808	13 215	21 615	28 754	1 407	8 400	7 139	11.9	63.6	33.0
65 to 74 years	2 814	3 179	4 985	9 045	365	1 806	4 060	13.0	56.8	81.4
75 years and over	471	668	1 258	2 037	197	590	779	41.8	88.3	61.9
Men, 16 Years and Over	66 927	73 959	82 520	88 682	7 032	8 561	6 162	10.5	11.6	7.5
16 to 24 years	11 752	11 464	11 538	10 987	-288	74	-551	-2.5	0.6	-4.8
16 to 19 years	4 159	4 244	3 472	2 923	85	-772	-549	2.0	-18.2	-15.8
20 to 24 years	7 594	7 221	8 065	8 064	-373	844	-1	-4.9	11.7	0.0
25 to 54 years	46 382	53 002	56 202	57 309	6 620	3 200	1 107	14.3	6.0	2.0
25 to 34 years	19 742	17 796	18 302	20 173	-1 946	506	1 871	-9.9	2.8	10.2
35 to 44 years	16 074	20 242	18 972	19 109	4 168	-1 270	137	25.9	-6.3	0.7
45 to 54 years	10 566	14 963	18 928	18 027	4 397	3 965	-901	41.6	26.5	-4.8
55 years and over	8 793	9 493	14 780	20 386	700	5 287	5 606	8.0	55.7	37.9
55 to 64 years	6 831	7 253	11 345	14 479	422	4 092	3 134	6.2	56.4	27.6
65 to 74 years	1 657	1 826	2 724	4 753	169	898	2 029	10.2	49.2	74.5
75 years and over	304	413	711	1 154	109	298	443	35.9	72.2	62.3
Women, 16 Years and Over	54 742	63 714	71 767	78 229	8 972	8 053	6 462	16.4	12.6	9.0
16 to 24 years	10 783	10 430	10 494	10 144	-353	64	-350	-3.3	0.6	-3.3
16 to 19 years	3 872	4 012	3 385	2 946	140	-627	-439	3.6	-15.6	-13.0
20 to 24 years	6 910	6 418	7 109	7 198	-492	691	89	-7.1	10.8	1.3
25 to 54 years	37 659	45 716	48 195	48 635	8 057	2 479	440	21.4	5.4	0.9
25 to 34 years	15 761	15 017	15 030	16 641	-744	13	1 611	-4.7	0.1	10.7
35 to 44 years	13 361	17 294	16 089	15 678	3 933	-1 205	-411	29.4	-7.0	-2.6
45 to 54 years	8 537	13 405	17 075	16 316	4 868	3 670	-759	57.0	27.4	-4.4
55 years and over	6 301	7 569	13 078	19 449	1 268	5 509	6 371	20.1	72.8	48.7
55 to 64 years	4 977	5 962	10 270	14 275	985	4 308	4 005	19.8	72.3	39.0
65 to 74 years	1 157	1 352	2 261	4 291	195	909	2 030	16.9	67.2	89.8
75 years and over	167	255	547	883	88	292	336	52.7	114.5	61.4
White, 16 Years and Over	104 756	115 415	125 635	132 490	10 659	10 220	6 855	10.2	8.9	5.5
Men	58 317	63 034	68 351	71 731	4 717	5 317	3 380	8.1	8.4	4.9
Women	46 439	52 380	57 284	60 759	5 941	4 904	3 475	12.8	9.4	6.1
Black, 16 Years and Over	13 205	15 982	17 740	20 244	2 777	1 758	2 504	21.0	11.0	14.1
Men	6 596	7 542	8 347	9 579	946	805	1 232	14.3	10.7	14.8
Women	6 609	8 441	9 393	10 665	1 832	952	1 272	27.7	11.3	13.5
Asian, 16 Years and Over	3 718	6 278	7 202	9 345	2 560	924	2 143	68.9	14.7	29.8
Men	2 017	3 383	3 852	4 895	1 366	469	1 043	67.7	13.9	27.1
Women	1 701	2 895	3 350	4 450	1 194	455	1 100	70.2	15.7	32.8
All Other Groups,[1] 16 Years and Over	. . .	. . .	3 710	4 832	. . .	. . .	1 122	. . .	. . .	30.2
Men	. . .	. . .	1 970	2 477	. . .	. . .	507	. . .	. . .	25.7
Women	. . .	. . .	1 740	2 355	. . .	. . .	615	. . .	. . .	35.3
Hispanic,[2] 16 Years and Over	8 982	14 317	22 024	29 304	5 335	7 707	7 280	59.4	53.8	33.1
Men	5 409	8 571	13 255	17 051	3 162	4 684	3 796	58.5	54.6	28.6
Women	3 573	5 746	8 769	12 253	2 173	3 023	3 484	60.8	52.6	39.7
Non-Hispanic, 16 Years and Over	112 687	123 356	132 263	137 607	10 669	8 907	5 344	9.5	7.2	4.0
Men	61 518	65 388	69 265	71 631	3 870	3 877	2 366	6.3	5.9	3.4
Women	51 169	57 968	62 998	65 976	6 799	5 030	2 978	13.3	8.7	4.7
White Non-Hispanic, 16 Years and Over	96 141	101 767	105 210	106 834	5 626	3 443	1 624	5.9	3.4	1.5
Men	53 122	54 833	55 971	57 075	1 711	1 138	1 104	3.2	2.1	2.0
Women	43 018	46 935	49 238	49 759	3 917	2 303	521	9.1	4.9	1.1

[1] The "All other groups" category includes respondents who reported the racial categories of "American Indian and Alaska Native" or "Native Hawaiian and Other Pacific Islander," as well as those who reported two or more races. This category was not defined prior to 2003.
[2] May be of any race.
. . . = Not available.

Table 4-1. Civilian Labor Force, by Age, Sex, Race, and Hispanic Origin, 1988, 1998, 2008, and Projected 2018—*Continued*

(Numbers in thousands, percent.)

Age, sex, race, and Hispanic origin	Percent distribution				Annual growth rate (percent)		
	1988	1998	2008	2018	1988–1998	1998–2008	2008–2018
Both Sexes, 16 Years and Over	100.0	100.0	100.0	100.0	1.2	1.1	0.8
16 to 24 years	18.5	15.9	14.3	12.7	-0.3	0.1	-0.4
16 to 19 years	6.6	6.0	4.4	3.5	0.3	-1.8	-1.5
20 to 24 years	11.9	9.9	9.8	9.1	-0.6	1.1	0.1
25 to 54 years	69.1	71.7	67.7	63.5	1.6	0.6	0.1
25 to 34 years	29.2	23.8	21.6	22.1	-0.8	0.2	1.0
35 to 44 years	24.2	27.3	22.7	20.8	2.5	-0.7	-0.1
45 to 54 years	15.7	20.6	23.3	20.6	4.0	2.4	-0.5
55 years and over	12.4	12.4	18.1	23.9	1.2	5.0	3.6
55 to 64 years	9.7	9.6	14.0	17.2	1.1	5.0	2.9
65 to 74 years	2.3	2.3	3.2	5.4	1.2	4.6	6.1
75 years and over	0.4	0.5	0.8	1.2	3.6	6.5	4.9
Men, 16 Years and Over	55.0	53.7	53.5	53.1	1.0	1.1	0.7
16 to 24 years	9.7	8.3	7.5	6.6	-0.2	0.1	-0.5
16 to 19 years	3.4	3.1	2.3	1.8	0.2	0.0	-1.7
20 to 24 years	6.2	5.2	5.2	4.8	-0.5	1.1	0.0
25 to 54 years	38.1	38.5	36.4	34.3	1.3	0.6	0.2
25 to 34 years	16.2	12.9	11.9	12.1	-1.0	0.3	1.0
35 to 44 years	13.2	14.7	12.3	11.4	2.3	-0.6	0.1
45 to 54 years	8.7	10.9	12.3	10.8	3.5	2.4	-0.5
55 years and over	7.2	6.9	9.6	12.2	0.8	4.5	3.3
55 to 64 years	5.6	5.3	7.4	8.7	0.6	4.6	2.5
65 to 74 years	1.4	1.3	1.8	2.8	1.0	4.1	5.7
75 years and over	0.2	0.3	0.5	0.7	3.1	5.6	5.0
Women, 16 Years and Over	45.0	46.3	46.5	46.9	1.5	1.2	0.9
16 to 24 years	8.9	7.6	6.8	6.1	-0.3	0.1	-0.3
16 to 19 years	3.2	2.9	2.2	1.8	0.4	-1.7	-1.4
20 to 24 years	5.7	4.7	4.6	4.3	-0.7	1.0	0.1
25 to 54 years	31.0	33.2	31.2	29.1	2.0	0.5	0.1
25 to 34 years	13.0	10.9	9.7	10.0	-0.5	0.0	1.0
35 to 44 years	11.0	12.6	10.4	9.4	2.6	-0.7	-0.3
45 to 54 years	7.0	9.7	11.1	9.8	4.6	2.4	-0.5
55 years and over	5.2	5.5	8.5	11.7	1.9	5.6	4.0
55 to 64 years	4.1	4.3	6.7	8.6	1.8	5.6	3.3
65 to 74 years	1.0	1.0	1.5	2.6	1.6	5.3	6.6
75 years and over	0.1	0.2	0.4	0.5	4.3	7.9	4.9
White, 16 Years and Over	86.1	83.8	81.4	79.4	1.0	0.9	0.5
Men	47.9	45.8	44.3	43.0	0.8	0.8	0.5
Women	38.2	38.0	37.1	36.4	1.2	0.9	0.6
Black, 16 Years and Over	10.9	11.6	11.5	12.1	1.9	1.0	1.3
Men	5.4	5.5	5.4	5.7	1.3	1.0	1.4
Women	5.4	6.1	6.1	6.4	2.5	1.1	1.3
Asian, 16 Years and Over	3.1	4.6	4.7	5.6	5.4	1.4	2.6
Men	1.7	2.5	2.5	2.9	5.3	1.3	2.4
Women	1.4	2.1	2.2	2.7	5.5	1.5	2.9
All Other Groups,[1] 16 Years and Over	. . .	. . .	2.4	2.9	. . .	. . .	2.7
Men	. . .	. . .	1.3	1.5	. . .	. . .	2.3
Women	. . .	. . .	1.1	1.4	. . .	. . .	3.1
Hispanic,[2] 16 Years and Over	7.4	10.4	14.3	17.6	4.8	4.4	2.9
Men	4.4	6.2	8.6	10.2	4.7	4.5	2.6
Women	2.9	4.2	5.7	7.3	4.9	4.3	3.4
Non-Hispanic, 16 Years and Over	92.6	89.6	85.7	82.4	0.9	0.7	0.4
Men	50.6	47.5	44.9	42.9	0.6	0.6	0.3
Women	42.1	42.1	40.8	39.5	1.3	0.8	0.5
White Non-Hispanic, 16 Years and Over	79.0	73.9	68.2	64.0	0.6	0.3	0.2
Men	43.7	39.8	36.3	34.2	0.3	0.2	0.2
Women	35.4	34.1	31.9	29.8	0.9	0.5	0.1

[1]The "All other groups" category includes respondents who reported the racial categories of "American Indian and Alaska Native" or "Native Hawaiian and Other Pacific Islander," as well as those who reported two or more races. This category was not defined prior to 2003.
[2]May be of any race.
. . . = Not available.

PROJECTED EMPLOYMENT

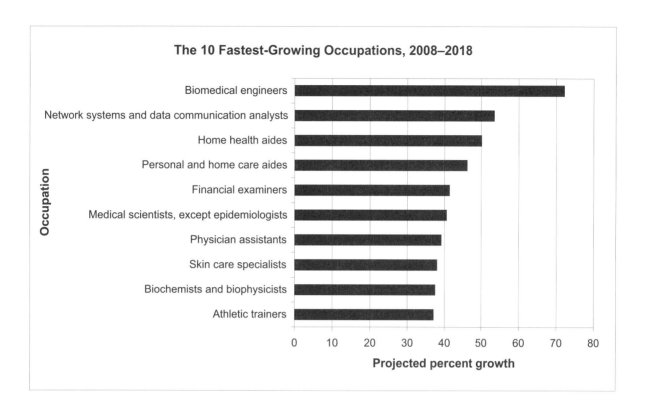

Although biomedical engineering is the fastest-growing occupation, employment is only projected to be at 28,000 in 2018. In contrast, network systems and data communications analysts—the second fastest-growing occupation—is projected to provide 448,000 jobs in 2018. (See Table 4-2.)

OTHER HIGHLIGHTS:

- Of the ten occupations with the fastest job growth, seven require a bachelor's degree or more, two require short-term on-the-job training, and one requires a postsecondary vocational award. (See Table 4-2.)

- Many of the largest declines in employment can be found in the manufacturing sector. Employment in semiconductor and other electronic component manufacturing is projected to decline by 146,000, while employment in motor vehicle parts manufacturing is projected to decline by 101,000 between 2008 and 2018. (See Table 4-4.)

- The occupations projected to add the most jobs from 2008 to 2018 are registered nurses (582,000), home health aides (461,000), and customer service representatives (400,000). Seventeen of the thirty fastest-growing occupations are related to health care or medical research. (See Table 4-7.)

Table 4-2. Fastest-Growing Occupations, 2008–2018

(Numbers in thousands, percent.)

Occupation	Occupational group	Employment		Change		Most significant source of postsecondary education or training[1]
		2008	2018	Number	Percent	
Biomedical engineers	Professional and related	16	28	12	72.0	Bachelor's degree
Network systems and data communications analysts	Professional and related	292	448	156	53.4	Bachelor's degree
Home health aides	Service	922	1 383	461	50.0	Short-term on-the-job training
Personal and home care aides	Service	817	1 193	376	46.0	Short-term on-the-job training
Financial examiners	Management, business, and financial	27	38	11	41.2	Bachelor's degree
Medical scientists, except epidemiologists	Professional and related	109	154	44	40.4	Doctoral degree
Physician assistants	Professional and related	75	104	29	39.0	Master's degree
Skin care specialists	Service	39	54	15	37.9	Postsecondary vocational award
Biochemists and biophysicists	Professional and related	23	32	9	37.4	Doctoral degree
Athletic trainers	Professional and related	16	22	6	37.0	Bachelor's degree
Physical therapist aides	Service	46	63	17	36.3	Short-term on-the-job training
Dental hygienists	Professional and related	174	237	63	36.1	Associate's degree
Veterinary technologists and technicians	Professional and related	80	108	29	35.8	Associate's degree
Dental assistants	Service	295	401	106	35.8	Moderate-term on-the-job training
Computer software engineers, applications	Professional and related	515	690	175	34.0	Bachelor's degree
Medical assistants	Service	484	648	164	33.9	Moderate-term on-the-job-training
Physical therapist assistants	Service	64	85	21	33.3	Associate's degree
Veterinarians	Professional and related	60	79	20	33.0	First professional degree
Self-enrichment education teachers	Professional and related	254	335	81	32.1	Work experience
Compliance officers, except agriculture, construction, health and safety, and transportation	Management, business, and financial	260	341	81	31.1	Long-term on-the-job training
Occupational therapist aides	Service	8	10	2	30.7	Short-term on-the-job training
Environmental engineers	Professional and related	54	71	17	30.6	Bachelor's degree
Pharmacy technicians	Professional and related	326	426	100	30.6	Moderate-term on-the-job training
Computer software engineers, systems software	Professional and related	395	515	120	30.4	Bachelor's degree
Survey researchers	Professional and related	23	31	7	30.4	Bachelor's degree
Physical therapists	Professional and related	186	242	56	30.3	Master's degree
Personal financial advisors	Management, business, and financial	208	271	63	30.1	Bachelor's degree
Environmental engineering technicians	Professional and related	21	28	6	30.1	Associate's degree
Occupational therapist assistants	Service	27	35	8	29.8	Associate's degree
Fitness trainers and aerobics instructors	Service	261	338	77	29.4	Post-secondary vocational award

[1]An occupation is placed into 1 of 11 categories that best describes the education or training needed by most workers to become fully qualified in that occupation.

Table 4-3. Occupations with the Largest Job Growth, 2008–2018

(Numbers in thousands, percent.)

Occupation	Occupational group	Employment		Change		Most significant source of postsecondary education or training[1]
		2008	2018	Number	Percent	
Registered nurses	Professional and related	2 619	3 200	582	22.2	Associate's degree
Home health aides	Service	922	1 383	461	50.0	Short-term on-the-job training
Customer service representatives	Office and administrative support	2 252	2 652	400	17.7	Moderate-term on-the-job training
Combined food preparation and serving workers, including fast food	Service	2 702	3 096	394	14.6	Short-term on-the-job training
Personal and home care aides	Service	817	1 193	376	46.0	Short-term on-the-job training
Retail salespersons	Sales and related	4 489	4 864	375	8.4	Short-term on-the-job training
Office clerks, general	Office and adminstrative support	3 024	3 383	359	11.9	Short-term on-the-job training
Accountants and auditors	Management, business, and financial	1 291	1 570	279	21.7	Bachelor's degree
Nursing aides, orderlies, and attendants	Service	1 470	1 746	276	18.8	Postsecondary vocational award
Postsecondary teachers	Professional and related	1 699	1 956	257	15.1	Doctoral degree
Construction laborers	Construction and extraction	1 249	1 505	256	20.5	Moderate-term on-the-job training
Elementary school teachers, except special education ..	Professional and related	1 550	1 794	244	15.8	Bachelor's degree
Truck drivers, heavy and tractor-trailer	Transportation and material moving	1 798	2 031	233	13.0	Short-term on-the-job training
Landscaping and groundskeeping workers	Service	1 206	1 423	217	18.0	Short-term on-the-job training
Bookkeeping, accounting, and auditing clerks	Office and administrative support	2 064	2 276	212	10.3	Moderate-term on-the-job training
Executive secretaries and administrative assistants	Office and administrative support	1 594	1 799	204	12.8	Work experience
Management analysts	Management, business, and financial	747	925	178	23.9	Bachelor's or higher degree
Computer software engineers, applications	Professional and related	515	690	175	34.0	Bachelor's degree
Receptionists and information clerks	Office and administrative support	1 139	1 312	173	15.2	Short term on-the-job training
Carpenters	Construction and extraction	1 285	1 450	165	12.9	Long-term on-the-job training
Medical assistants	Service	484	648	164	33.9	Moderate-term on-the-job training
First-line supervisors/managers of office and, administrative support workers	Office and administrative support	1 457	1 618	160	11.0	Work experience
Network systems and data communications analysts	Professional and related	292	448	156	53.4	Bachelor's degree
Licensed practical and licensed vocational nurses	Professional and related	754	909	156	20.7	Post secondary vocational award
Security guards	Service	1 077	1 229	153	14.2	Short-term on-the-job-training
Waiters and waitresses	Service	2 382	2 533	152	6.4	Short-term on-the-job training
Maintenance and repair workers, general	Installation, maintenance, and repair occupations	1 361	1 509	148	10.9	Moderate-term on-the-job training
Physicians and surgeons	Professional and related	661	806	144	21.8	First professional degree
Child care workers	Service	1 302	1 444	142	10.9	Short-term on-the-job training
Teacher assistants	Professional and related	1 313	1 448	135	10.3	Short-term on-the-job training

[1]An occupation is placed into 1 of 11 categories that best describes the education or training needed by most workers to become fully qualified in that occupation.

Table 4-4. Industries with the Largest Wage and Salary Employment Growth and Declines, 2008–2018

(Number in thousands, percent.)

Industry	Sector	Employment		Change	
		2008	2018	Number	Percent
Largest Growth					
Management, scientific, and technical consulting services	Professional and business services	1 009	1 844	835	82.8
Offices of physicians	Health care and social assistance	2 266	3 038	772	34.1
Computer systems design and related services	Professional and business services	1 450	2 107	656	45.3
Other general merchandise stores	Retail trade	1 490	2 097	607	40.7
Employment services	Professional and business services	3 144	3 744	600	19.1
Local government, excluding education and hospitals	Government	5 819	6 306	487	8.4
Home health care services	Health care and social assistance	958	1 399	441	46.1
Services for the elderly and persons with disabilities	Health care and social assistance	585	1 016	431	73.8
Nursing care facilities	Health care and social assistance	1 614	2 007	394	24.4
Full-service restaurants	Accommodation and food services	4 598	4 942	343	7.5
Largest Declines					
Department stores	Retail trade	1 557	1 398	-159	-10.2
Semiconductor and other electronic component manufacturing	Manufacturting	432	287	-146	-33.7
Motor vehicle parts manufacturing	Manufacturting	544	443	-101	-18.6
Postal service	Government	748	650	-98	-13.0
Printing and related support activities	Manufacturing	594	499	-95	-16.0
Cut and sew apparel manufacturing	Manufacturing	155	67	-89	-57.0
Newspaper publishers	Information	326	245	-81	-24.8
Support activities for mining	Mining	328	252	-76	-23.2
Gasoline stations	Retail trade	843	769	-75	-8.9
Wired telecommunications carriers	Information	666	593	-73	-11.0

Table 4-5. Employment and Total Job Openings, by Education Cluster, 2008–2018

(Numbers in thousands, percent, dollars.)

Education cluster	Employment				Change in employment, 2008–2018		Total job openings due to growth and net replacements[1]		May 2008 median annual wages[2]
	Number		Percent distribution		Number	Percent	Number	Percent distribution	
	2008	2018	2008	2018					
TOTAL, ALL OCCUPATIONS	150 932	166 206	100.0	100.0	15 274	10.1	50 929	100.0	32 390
First professional degree	2 001	2 354	1.3	1.4	353	17.6	746	1.5	122 550
Doctoral degree	2 085	2 430	1.4	1.5	345	16.6	743	1.5	61 200
Master's degree	2 531	2 995	1.7	1.8	464	18.3	1 008	2.0	55 170
Bachelor's or higher degree, plus work experience	6 519	7 068	4.3	4.3	550	8.4	2 106	4.1	89 720
Bachelor's degree	18 584	21 669	12.3	13.0	3 085	16.6	7 072	13.9	57 770
Associate's degree	6 129	7 297	4.1	4.4	1 168	19.1	2 372	4.7	54 320
Postsecondary vocational award	8 787	9 952	5.8	6.0	1 164	13.2	2 927	5.7	32 380
Work experience in a related occupation	14 517	15 697	9.6	9.4	1 180	8.1	4 196	8.2	45 650
Long-term on-the-job training	10 815	11 621	7.2	7.0	806	7.5	3 081	6.1	39 630
Moderate-term on-the-job training	24 569	26 531	16.3	16.0	1 963	8.0	7 059	13.9	30 640
Short-term on-the-job training	54 396	58 593	36.0	35.3	4 197	7.7	19 619	38.5	21 320

[1]Total job openings are given by the sum of net employment increases and net replacements. If employment change is negative, job openings due to growth are zero and total job openings equal net replacements.
[2] Data for wage and salary workers are derived from the Occupational Employment Statistics Survey.

Table 4-6. Employment and Output, by Industry, 1998, 2008, and Projected 2018

(Number, percent, dollars.)

| Industry | Employment | | | | | | | Output | | | | |
| | Number of jobs (thousands) | | | Change | | Average annual rate of change (percent) | | Billions of chained (2000) dollars | | | Average annual rate of change (percent) | |
	1998	2008	2018	1998–2018	2008–2018	1998–2008	2008–2018	1998	2008	2018	1998–2008	2008–2018
TOTAL[1,2]	140 564	150 932	166 206	10 368	15 274	0.7	1.0	17 050	21 028	27 703	2.0	2.8
Nonagriculture Wage and Salary Workers	126 625	137 815	152 444	11 190	14 629	0.9	1.0	16 785	20 735	27 371	2.1	2.8
Mining	565	717	613	152	-104	2.4	-1.6	205	232	227	1.2	-0.2
Oil and gas extraction	141	162	136	21	-26	1.4	-1.7	131	126	122	-0.5	-0.3
Mining (except oil and gas)	243	228	226	-15	-2	-0.7	-0.1	49	46	56	-0.7	2.0
Coal mining	85	81	84	-5	3.0	-0.6	0.4	20	20	24	0.5	1.5
Metal ore mining	46	40	36	-6	-4	-1.5	-1.1	11	8	8	-3.5	0.6
Nonmetallic mineral mining and quarrying	12	107	106	-4	-1	-0.4	-0.1	19	18	23	-0.7	2.8
Mining support activities	181	328	252	147	-76	6.1	-2.6	25	56	54	8.4	-0.3
Utilities	613	560	501	-54	-59	-0.9	-1.1	299	319	349	0.7	0.9
Electric power generation, transmission, and distribution	444	405	346	-39	-59	-0.9	-1.6	206	247	282	1.8	1.3
Natural gas distribution	129	107	101	-22	-6	-1.8	-0.6	85	68	67	-2.3	-0.1
Water, sewage, and other systems	41	48	54	7	6	1.6	1.2	7	8	10	1.2	1.6
Construction	6 149	7 215	8 552	1 066	1 337	1.6	1.7	852	861	1 141	0.1	2.9
Manufacturing	17 560	13 431	12 225	-4 128	-1 206	-2.6	-0.9	4 061	3 985	4 923	-0.2	2.1
Food	1 555	1 485	1 483	-70	-2	-0.5	0.0	417	434	533	0.4	2.1
Animal food	55	51	49	-4	-2	-0.8	-0.4	24	21	32	-1.4	4.2
Grain and oilseed milling	68	63	61	-5	-1	-0.8	-0.2	44	34	52	-2.4	4.2
Sugar and confectionery product	98	71	64	-28	-7	-3.2	-1.1	25	25	29	0.0	1.7
Fruit and vegetable preserving and specialty food	203	174	155	-29	-19	-1.5	-1.1	50	56	66	1.1	1.7
Dairy product	131	129	126	-2	-3	-0.2	-0.2	59	59	64	0.1	0.8
Animal slaughtering and processing	499	512	539	13	27	0.3	0.5	110	126	145	1.3	1.4
Seafood product preparation and packaging	47	41	45	-7	4	-1.5	1.0	8	10	12	2.4	2.0
Bakery and tortilla	306	281	275	-25	-6	-0.8	-0.2	46	45	57	-0.2	2.4
Other food	148	164	169	16	5	1.1	0.3	52	62	79	1.9	2.4
Beverage and tobacco product	209	199	181	-10	-18	-0.5	-0.9	168	144	140	-1.5	-0.3
Beverage	171	177	164	6	-13	0.4	-0.8	72	81	98	1.1	2.0
Tobacco	38	22	17	-16	-5	-5.3	-2.7	96	65	50	-3.9	-2.6
Textile mills	425	151	79	-273	-72	-9.8	-6.3	56	31	29	-5.8	-0.4
Fiber, yarn, and thread mills	87	37	21	-50	-17	-8.1	-5.7	12	8	8	-4.2	0.5
Fabric mills	221	65	35	-156	-30	-11.5	-6.1	29	15	14	-6.5	-0.2
Textile fabric finishing/fabric coating mills	116	48	24	-68	-25	-8.4	-7.0	15	8	7	-5.8	-1.5
Textile product mills	235	148	91	-87	-56	-4.5	-4.7	31	23	24	-3.0	0.6
Textile furnishings mills	127	75	42	-51	-34	-5.1	-5.7	21	16	18	-2.4	1.1
Other textile product mills	108	72	49	-36	-23	-4.0	-3.7	10	6	6	-4.4	-0.8
Apparel	622	198	88	-423	-110	-10.8	-7.8	67	31	22	-7.3	-3.6
Apparel knitting mills	87	26	13	-60	-14	-11.3	-7.1	9	5	3	-6.0	-3.0
Cut and sew apparel	498	155	67	-343	-89	-11.0	-8.1	54	25	16	-7.5	-4.1
Apparel accessories and other apparel	37	17	9	-20	-8	-7.5	-6.0	5	2	2	-8.0	0.2
Leather and allied product	83	34	23	-49	-11	-8.6	-3.7	23	12	11	-6.7	-0.4
Leather and hide tanning and finishing	43	18	13	-25	-5	-8.5	-3.1	8	4	4	-6.9	-0.4
Footwear	40	16	10	-24	-6	-8.8	-4.5	16	8	8	-6.6	-0.4
Wood product	609	460	424	-150	-35	-2.8	-0.8	92	91	95	-0.2	0.4
Sawmills and wood preservation	135	104	85	-31	-19	-2.6	-2.0	28	30	31	0.6	0.5
Veneer, plywood, and engineered wood product	113	91	100	-22	9	-2.1	0.9	20	21	22	0.4	0.3
Other wood product	362	265	240	-97	-26	-3.1	-1.0	44	40	42	-1.0	0.5
Paper	625	446	338	-179	-108	-3.3	-2.7	165	142	128	-1.5	-1.0
Pulp, paper, and paperboard mills	208	126	82	-82	-44	-4.9	-4.2	78	67	62	-1.5	-0.7
Converted paper product	417	320	256	-97	-64	-2.6	-2.2	88	75	66	-1.6	-1.2
Printing and related support activities	828	594	499	-234	-95	-3.3	-1.7	107	92	80	-1.5	-1.4
Petroleum and coal product	135	117	91	-17	-26	-1.4	-2.5	226	224	279	-0.1	2.2
Chemical	993	850	793	-143	-57	-1.5	-0.7	430	464	613	0.8	2.8
Basic chemical	213	152	100	-61	-52	-3.3	-4.1	112	104	136	-0.7	2.7
Resin, synthetic rubber, and artificial and synthetic fiber and filament	140	105	95	-35	-10	-2.8	-1.0	70	66	85	-0.5	2.5
Pesticide, fertilizer, and other agricultural chemical	50	36	35	-14	-1	-3.2	-0.3	24	17	19	-3.5	1.6
Pharmaceutical and medicine	247	290	307	43	18	1.6	0.6	108	141	195	2.6	3.3
Paint, coating, and adhesive	78	63	65	-15	3	-2.1	0.4	27	26	30	-0.2	1.4
Soap, cleaning compound, and toilet preparation	131	108	101	-22	-7	-1.9	-0.7	55	75	98	3.1	2.8
Other chemical product and preparation	135	95	89	-39	-6	-3.4	-0.7	35	40	49	1.3	1.9
Plastics and rubber product	941	734	678	-207	-56	-2.5	-0.8	165	160	227	-0.3	3.5
Plastics product	728	589	555	-139	-34	-2.1	-0.6	130	138	193	0.6	3.4
Rubber product	214	145	123	-68	-23	-3.8	-1.7	34	22	33	-4.3	4.2
Nonmetallic mineral product	535	468	480	-67	12	-1.3	0.3	95	85	104	-1.1	2.0
Clay product and refractory	82	52	54	-30	2	-4.4	0.3	9	8	9	-1.9	1.9
Glass and glass product	142	97	84	-45	-13	-3.8	-1.4	23	22	30	-0.4	3.0
Cement and concrete product	217	223	248	6	24	0.3	1.0	40	36	45	-1.3	2.3
Lime and gypsum product	94	96	95	2	-1	0.2	-0.1	22	21	22	-0.7	0.7
Primary metal	642	443	400	-198	-44	-3.6	-1.0	162	152	144	-0.6	-0.6
Iron and steel mills ferroalloy	144	99	80	-45	-19	-3.7	-2.1	52	45	47	-1.5	0.4
Steel product from purchased steel	73	60	59	-12	-1	-1.9	-0.2	19	15	16	-2.6	0.6
Alumina and aluminum production and processing	100	68	65	-32	-3	-3.8	-0.5	33	42	40	2.5	-0.5
Nonferrous (except aluminum) production and processing	102	67	63	-35	-5	-4.1	-0.7	29	24	16	-1.9	-4.1
Foundries	223	149	133	-74	-16	-4.0	-1.1	30	30	28	0.3	-0.9

[1] Employment data for wage and salary workers are from the BLS Current Employment Statistics (CES) Survey, which counts jobs, whereas data for self-employed, unpaid family workers, and agriculture, forestry, fishing, and hunting workers are from the Current Population Survey (CPS, or household, survey), which counts workers.
[2] Output subcategories do not necessarily add to higher categories as a by-product of chain weighting.

Table 4-6. Employment and Output, by Industry, 1998, 2008, and Projected 2018—*Continued*

(Number, percent, dollars.)

Industry	Employment							Output				
	Number of jobs (thousands)			Change		Average annual rate of change (percent)		Billions of chained (2000) dollars			Average annual rate of change (percent)	
	1998	2008	2018	1998–2018	2008–2018	1998–2008	2008–2018	1998	2008	2018	1998–2008	2008–2018
Manufacturing—*Continued*												
Fabricated metal product	1 740	1 528	1 399	-211	-129	-1.3	-0.9	255	251	286	-0.2	1.3
Forging and stamping	146	108	85	-38	-23	-3.0	-2.4	26	24	25	-0.6	0.3
Cutlery and handtool	80	49	36	-31	-13	-4.7	-3.1	11	11	11	-0.4	0.3
Architectural and structural metals	396	409	429	14	20	0.3	0.5	57	59	75	0.3	2.4
Boiler, tank, and shipping container	109	96	89	-13	-7	-1.2	-0.7	24	21	24	-1.3	1.3
Hardware	54	29	24	-24	-5	-5.8	-2.0	11	10	10	-0.8	0.0
Spring and wire product	83	52	42	-31	-10	-4.6	-2.0	9	7	9	-2.0	2.2
Machine shops; turned product; and screw, nut, and bolt	371	360	320	-11	-41	-0.3	-1.2	45	47	56	0.4	1.7
Coating, engraving, heat treating, and allied activities	173	144	125	-29	-19	-1.8	-1.4	20	23	25	1.4	1.0
Other fabricated metal product	330	282	250	-48	-32	-1.6	-1.2	52	49	53	-0.6	0.7
Machinery	1 514	1 186	1 095	-329	-90	-2.4	-0.8	276	280	334	0.2	1.8
Agriculture, construction, and mining machinery	241	242	250	1	8	0.0	0.3	57	57	77	0.0	3.0
Industrial machinery	171	121	93	-50	-28	-3.4	-2.6	32	34	32	0.7	-0.5
Ventilation, heating, air-conditioning, and commercial refrigeration	186	150	113	-36	-37	-2.1	-2.8	32	35	38	0.8	0.9
Metalworking machinery	289	192	190	-97	-2	-4.0	-0.1	32	28	33	-1.1	1.4
Engine, turbine, and power transmission equipment	114	104	97	-10	-7	-0.9	-0.7	32	38	54	1.7	3.4
Other general purpose machinery	365	273	249	-92	-24	-2.9	-0.9	64	64	74	0.0	1.4
Computer and electronic product	1 831	1 248	1 007	-583	-241	-3.8	-2.1	407	515	946	2.4	6.3
Computer and peripheral equipment	322	183	125	-139	-58	-5.5	-3.8	88	201	967	8.6	17.0
Communications equipment	237	129	120	-108	-9	-5.9	-0.7	81	75	109	-0.8	3.8
Audio and video equipment	53	27	15	-26	-12	-6.6	-6.0	8	5	11	-4.7	8.4
Semiconductor and other electronic component	650	432	287	-217	-146	-4.0	-4.0	127	173	309	3.2	5.9
Navigational, measuring, electromedical, and control instruments	509	442	434	-68	-7	-1.4	-0.2	94	92	128	-0.1	3.3
Manufacturing and reproducing magnetic and optical media	59	35	26	-24	-9	-5.1	-2.9	11	10	13	-0.1	1.8
Electrical equipment, appliance, and component	592	425	368	-167	-57	-3.3	-1.4	114	100	113	-1.4	1.3
Electric lighting equipment	85	57	46	-28	-11	-3.9	-2.2	13	13	15	-0.3	1.9
Household appliance	108	72	55	-36	-17	-4.0	-2.7	21	24	30	1.0	2.5
Electrical equipment	215	159	129	-56	-29	-3.0	-2.0	36	28	30	-2.4	0.6
Other electrical equipment and component	184	137	138	-47	1	-2.9	0.0	44	36	39	-2.1	0.8
Transportation equipment	2 078	1 607	1 437	-472	-169	-2.5	-1.1	638	583	744	-0.9	2.5
Motor vehicle	284	191	160	-93	-31	-3.9	-1.8	239	237	322	-0.1	3.1
Motor vehicle body and trailer	170	142	131	-28	-11	-1.8	-0.8	32	28	36	-1.2	2.7
Motor vehicle parts	818	544	443	-274	-101	-4.0	-2.0	179	169	190	-0.6	1.2
Aerospace product and parts	579	504	502	-75	-2	-1.4	0.0	154	115	148	-2.8	2.5
Railroad rolling stock	35	28	18	-7	-11	-2.0	-4.7	9	5	7	-6.2	3.9
Ship and boat building	154	157	140	3	-17	0.2	-1.1	18	16	24	-0.8	3.9
Other transportation equipment	40	41	44	1	3	0.2	0.8	10	13	22	2.8	5.7
Furniture and related product	644	481	512	-163	31	-2.9	0.6	70	63	95	-1.1	4.2
Household and institutional furniture and kitchen cabinet	418	306	339	-112	33	-3.1	1.0	40	36	57	-1.2	4.8
Office furniture (including fixtures)	173	131	130	-42	-1	-2.7	-0.1	23	21	30	-0.9	3.4
Other furniture related product	53	44	42	-9	-2	-1.8	-0.3	7	6	8	-1.4	2.7
Miscellaneous	727	631	759	-96	128	-1.4	1.9	105	134	222	2.4	5.2
Medical equipment and supplies	301	310	360	8	50	0.3	1.5	49	72	133	3.9	6.3
Other miscellaneous	426	321	399	-105	78	-2.8	2.2	56	61	89	0.9	3.8
Wholesale Trade	5 795	5 964	6 220	169	256	0.3	0.4	780	1 064	1 777	3.2	5.3
Retail Trade	14 610	15 356	16 010	747	654	0.5	0.4	872	1 232	1 864	3.5	4.2
Transportation and Warehousing	4 168	4 505	4 950	337	446	0.8	0.9	595	678	906	1.3	2.9
Air transportation	563	493	529	-70	37	-1.3	0.7	121	102	152	-1.7	4.1
Rail transportation	225	230	240	5	11	0.2	0.5	44	50	59	1.5	1.6
Water transportation	51	65	67	15.0	2	2.6	0.3	28	21	32	-2.9	4.2
Truck transportation	1 354	1 391	1 534	37	143	0.3	1.0	199	275	375	3.3	3.1
Transit and ground passenger transportation	363	418	471	55	53	1.4	1.2	32	38	47	1.9	2.1
Pipeline transportation	48	42	38	-6	-4	-1.3	-0.9	20	17	17	-1.8	-0.1
Scenic and sightseeing transportation	522	618	726	96	108	1.7	1.6	116	137	173	1.7	2.3
Support activities for transportation	881	748	650	-133	-98	-1.6	-1.4	62	57	62	-0.8	0.9
Couriers and messengers	568	576	588	8	12	0.1	0.2	59	72	95	2.1	2.7
Warehousing and storage	474	673	756	199	83	3.6	1.2	36	43	55	1.9	2.5
Information	3 218	2 997	3 115	-222	118	-0.7	0.4	769	1 106	1 865	3.7	5.4
Publishing industries, except Internet	982	883	842	-100	-41	-1.1	-0.5	224	308	468	3.2	4.3
Newspaper, periodical, book, and directory publishers	767	619	499	-149	-120	-2.1	-2.1	136	127	120	-0.7	-0.6
Software publishers	215	264	343	49	79	2.1	2.7	88	195	530	8.2	10.5
Motion picture, video, and sound recording industries	369	382	428	12	46	0.3	1.1	74	87	116	1.7	2.9
Broadcasting, except Internet	321	316	340	-5	24	-0.2	0.7	63	85	104	2.9	2.1
Telecommunications	1 167	1 022	932	-146	-90	-1.3	-0.9	351	480	822	3.2	5.5
Data processing, hosting, related services, and other information services	378	395	574	17	179	0.4	3.8	58	142	345	9.3	9.3
Finance and Insurance	5 529	6 015	6 337	487	322	0.8	0.5	58	142	345	9.3	9.3
Monetary authorities, credit intermediation, and related activities	2 554	2 758	2 896	205	137	0.8	0.5	560	847	1 217	4.2	3.7
Securities, commodity contracts, and other financial investments and related activities	692	858	959	166	101	2.2	1.1	199	436	883	8.1	7.3
Insurance carriers	1 443	1 402	1 338	-41	-64	-0.3	-0.5	309	362	421	1.6	1.5
Agencies, brokerages, and other insurance-related activities	766	907	1 038	141	131	1.7	1.4	112	124	161	1.0	2.7
Funds, trusts, and other financial vehicles	73	90	106	17	16	2.1	1.6	71	88	99	2.1	1.2
Real estate	1 278	1 481	1 677	203	196	1.5	1.3	690	859	1 065	2.2	2.2
Automotive equipment rental and leasing	189	195	215	6	20	0.3	1.0	37	40	53	0.8	3.0
Consumer goods rental and general rental centers	344	298	308	-46	10	-1.4	0.3	22	24	30	0.8	2.3
Commercial and industrial machinery and equipment rental and leasing	98	128	128	30	0	2.7	0.0	36	45	52	2.3	1.3
Lessors of nonfinancial intangible assets (except copyrighted works)	25	28	38	3	10	1.1	3.0	92	146	235	4.8	4.9

Table 4-6. Employment and Output, by Industry, 1998, 2008, and Projected 2018—*Continued*

(Number, percent, dollars.)

Industry	Employment							Output				
	Number of jobs (thousands)			Change		Average annual rate of change (percent)		Billions of chained (2000) dollars			Average annual rate of change (percent)	
	1998	2008	2018	1998–2018	2008–2018	1998–2008	2008–2018	1998	2008	2018	1998–2008	2008–2018
Professional, Scientific, and Technical Services	5 992	7 830	10 486	1 838	2 657	2.7	3.0	877	1 279	1 752	3.8	3.2
Legal services	1 021	1 164	1 417	143	253	1.3	2.0	183	202	249	1.0	2.1
Accounting, tax preparation, bookkeeping, and payroll services	802	950	1 149	148	199	1.7	1.9	90	108	118	1.9	0.9
Architectural, engineering, and related services	1 115	1 445	1 770	330	325	2.6	2.0	148	229	269	4.5	1.6
Specialized design services	120	143	209	23	66	1.8	3.8	21	26	35	2.2	3.0
Computer systems design and related services	975	1 450	2 107	475	656	4.1	3.8	143	207	302	3.8	3.8
Management, scientific, and technical consulting services	590	1 009	1 844	419	835	5.5	6.2	96	172	287	6.0	5.3
Scientific research and development services	486	622	779	136	157	2.5	2.3	66	159	289	9.2	6.1
Advertising and related services	453	462	499	9	37	0.2	0.8	68	96	131	3.4	3.2
Other professional, scientific, and technical services	430	585	713	155	128	3.1	2.0	64	87	107	3.2	2.1
Management of companies and enterprises	1 756	1 895	1 997	139	102	0.8	0.5	379	634	964	5.3	4.3
Administrative and support and waste management and remediation services	7 398	8 054	9 485	656	1 431	0.9	1.6	422	593	837	3.5	3.5
Administrative and support services	7 099	7 694	9 034	595	1 340	0.8	1.6	370	526	731	3.6	3.3
Office administrative services	265	403	483	139	80	4.3	1.8	23	50	68	8.2	3.1
Facilities support services	89	133	174	44	41	4.1	2.7	12	17	18	3.4	0.6
Employment services	3 246	3 144	3 744	-101	600	-0.3	1.8	130	174	238	2.9	3.2
Business support services	772	823	948	51	125	0.6	1.4	43	57	68	2.9	1.8
Travel arrangement and reservation services	304	228	225	-77	-3	-2.9	-0.1	26	28	37	0.7	2.7
Investigation and security services	659	807	960	148	153	2.0	1.8	28	40	54	3.6	3.0
Services to buildings and dwellings	1 460	1 847	2 183	387	336	2.4	1.7	77	121	198	4.6	5.0
Other support services	304	308	317	5	9	0.2	0.3	31	39	51	2.3	2.7
Waste management and remediation services	299	360	451	61	91	1.9	2.3	52	67	105	2.6	4.6
Education services	2 233	3 037	3 842	804	806	3.1	2.4	123	156	184	2.4	1.7
Elementary and secondary schools	651	855	1 090	204	235	2.8	2.5	26	30	37	1.5	2.2
Junior colleges, colleges, universities, and professional schools	1 234	1 603	1 857	369	255	2.6	1.5	68	92	102	3.0	1.0
Other education services	348	579	895	231	316	5.2	4.5	29	34	44	1.7	2.7
Health care and social assistance	12 214	15 819	19 816	3 605	3 997	2.6	2.3	924	1 302	1 861	3.5	3.6
Ambulatory health care services	4 161	5 661	7 676	1 500	2 015	3.1	3.1	426	636	973	4.1	4.3
Offices of health practitioners	2 815	3 713	4 979	898	1 265	2.8	3.0	312	468	714	4.2	4.3
Home health care services	660	958	1 399	299	441	3.8	3.9	33	53	79	4.8	4.1
Outpatient, laboratory, and other ambulatory services	687	990	1 298	303	308	3.7	2.8	82	116	180	3.5	4.5
Hospitals, private	3 892	4 641	5 192	749	551	1.8	1.1	306	426	580	3.4	3.2
Nursing and residential care facilities	2 487	3 008	3 645	521	637	1.9	1.9	111	131	160	1.6	2.0
Nursing care facilities	. . .	. . .	. . .	. . .	. . .	. . .	. . .	. . .	. . .	. . .	. . .	. . .
Residential care facilities	. . .	. . .	. . .	. . .	. . .	. . .	. . .	. . .	. . .	. . .	. . .	. . .
Social assistance	1 673	2 509	3 303	836	794	4.1	2.8	81	111	157	3.2	3.5
Individual and family services	597	1 109	1 639	511	530	6.4	4.0	32	46	69	3.7	4.1
Community, and vocational rehabilitation services	460	541	672	81	131	1.6	2.2	18	24	40	3.2	5.2
Child day care services	615	859	992	244	133	3.4	1.4	31	41	49	2.7	1.9
Arts, entertainment, and recreation	1 645	1 970	2 274	324	304	1.8	1.4	134	173	209	2.6	1.9
Performing arts, spectator sports, and related industries	350	406	468	56	62	1.5	1.4	70	78	89	1.2	1.3
Performing arts companies	128	118	127	-10	9	-0.8	0.7	13	10	11	-3.2	1.2
Spectator sports	110	129	146	19	17	1.6	1.3	22	27	33	2.0	2.1
Promoters of events, and agents and managers	77	109	131	32	21	3.5	1.8	15	21	21	3.4	0.0
Independent artists, writers, and performers	35	50	65	15	14	3.7	2.5	20	21	25	0.8	1.6
Museums, historical sites, and similar institutions	97	132	161	34	29	3.1	2.0	5	7	8	2.5	1.2
Amusement, gambling, and recreation industries	1 198	1 431	1 645	233	214	1.8	1.4	59	88	113	4.1	2.5
Accommodation and food services	9 586	11 489	12 327	1 903	838	1.8	0.7	473	575	675	2.0	1.6
Accommodation	1 774	1 857	1 957	84	99	0.5	0.5	129	145	176	1.1	2.0
Food services and drinking places	7 813	9 632	10 371	1 819	739	2.1	0.7	344	430	499	2.3	1.5
Other services	5 750	6 333	7 142	583	809	1.0	1.2	401	463	539	1.4	1.5
Repair and maintenance	1 189	1 228	1 291	39	63	0.3	0.5	141	157	180	1.1	1.4
Automotive repair and maintenance	828	858	912	30	54	0.4	0.6	88	99	105	1.2	0.6
Electronic and precision equipment repair and maintenance	113	104	111	-9	6	-0.8	0.6	20	21	23	0.6	1.0
Commercial and industrial machinery and equipment (except automotive and electronic) repair and maintenance	163	192	200	28	8	1.6	0.4	17	23	41	3.2	6.0
Personal and household goods repair and maintenance	85	74	68	-11	-6	-1.3	-0.8	17	14	14	-1.5	-0.4
Personal and laundry services	1 206	1 327	1 589	121	262	1.0	1.8	105	124	153	1.6	2.2
Personal care services	469	622	819	153	198	2.9	2.8	33	40	54	1.8	3.0
Death care services	134	136	145	3	9	0.2	0.6	13	11	9	-2.0	-1.1
Dry-cleaning and laundry services	383	335	348	-48	13	-1.3	0.4	22	22	22	-0.2	0.3
Other personal services	220	234	276	14	42	0.6	1.7	37	52	70	3.3	3.0
Religious, grantmaking, civic, professional, and similar organizations	2 581	2 973	3 353	392	379	1.4	1.2	140	168	189	1.9	1.2
Religious organizations	1 460	1 684	1 882	224	198	1.4	1.1	47	51	57	0.9	1.1
Grantmaking and giving services and social advocacy organizations	265	351	387	87	36	2.9	1.0	29	44	47	4.4	0.5
Civic, social, professional, and similar organizations	857	938	1 083	81	145	0.9	1.5	64	73	86	1.3	1.6
Private households	774	805	910	31	105	0.4	1.2	15	14	17	-0.4	2.0
Federal Government	2 772	2 764	2 859	-8	95	0.0	0.3	573	760	868	2.9	1.3
Postal Service	881	748	650	-133	-98	-1.6	-1.4	62	57	62	-0.8	0.9
Federal electric utilities	30	24	19	-6	-5	-2.1	-2.3	10	11	12	1.3	0.7
Federal enterprises except Postal Service and electric utilities	86	64	45	-22	-19	-3.0	-3.4	8	11	13	3.5	1.4
Federal government except enterprises	1 776	1 929	2 145	153	216	0.8	1.1	495	681	785	3.2	1.4
Federal defense government	550	496	547	-54	51.0	-1.0	1.0	323	463	548	3.7	1.7
Federal non-defense government except enterprises	1 226	1 433	1 598	207	165	1.6	1.1	172	225	246	2.7	0.9

. . . = Not available.

Table 4-6. Employment and Output, by Industry, 1998, 2008, and Projected 2018—*Continued*

(Number, percent, dollars.)

Industry	Employment							Output				
	Number of jobs (thousands)			Change		Average annual rate of change (percent)		Billions of chained (2000) dollars			Average annual rate of change (percent)	
	1998	2008	2018	1998–2018	2008–2018	1998–2008	2008–2018	1998	2008	2018	1998–2008	2008–2018
State and Local Government	17 137	19 735	21 327	2 598	1 592	1.4	0.8	1 254	1 504	1 728	1.8	1.4
Local government passenger transit	214	269	343	55	74	2.3	2.5	8	9	11	1.1	2.1
Local government enterprises except passenger transit	1 078	1 326	1 499	249	173	2.1	1.2	140	176	211	2.3	1.8
Local government hospitals	630	663	669	32	6	0.5	0.1	23	27	29	1.9	0.6
Local government educational services	6 921	8 076	8 728	1 155	653	1.6	0.8	271	305	323	1.2	0.6
Local government excluding enterprises, educational services, and hospitals	3 682	4 224	4 464	542	240	1.4	0.6	164	185	189	1.2	0.2
State government enterprises	504	534	578	30	45	0.6	0.8	21	25	30	2.1	1.8
State government hospitals-compensation	346	363	377	17	14	0.5	0.4	19	20	21	0.1	0.9
State government	1 922	2 359	2 584	437	225	2.1	0.9	75	87	89	1.4	0.2
State government, other compensation	1 840	1 922	2 084	81	162	0.4	0.8	97	101	103	0.4	0.2
State and local government capital services	. . .	. . .	. . .	. . .	. . .	. . .	. . .	77	109	139	3.5	2.4
General state and local government except compensation and capital services	. . .	. . .	. . .	. . .	. . .	. . .	. . .	360	462	590	2.5	2.5
Owner-Occupied Dwellings	. . .	. . .	. . .	. . .	. . .	. . .	. . .	699	899	1 093	2.6	2.0
Agriculture, Forestry, Fishing, and Hunting	2 528	2 098	2 020	-430	-78.0	-1.8	-0.4	265	293	319	1.0	0.9
Crop production	1 085	951	881	-135	-70	-1.3	-0.8	110	131	141	1.8	0.7
Animal production	1 120	861	824	-259	-37	-2.6	-0.4	104	115	128	1.0	1.1
Forestry	17	17	18	0	1	-0.2	0.7	7	6	8	-1.7	3.2
Logging	123	82	100	-41	18	-4.0	2.0	24	23	23	-0.7	0.1
Fishing, hunting and trapping	58	47	47	-11	0	-2.0	0.0	6	7	6	1.1	-1.1
Support activities for agriculture and forestry	126	141	150	16	9	1.2	0.6	13	8	11	-4.0	2.9
Nonagriculture Self-Employed and Unpaid Family Worker[3]	9 342	9 313	9 943	-30	631	0.0	0.7	. . .	. . .	. . .	. . .	. . .
Secondary Wage and Salary Jobs in Agriculture and Private Household Industries[4]	173	182	192	9	10	0.5	0.5	. . .	. . .	. . .	. . .	. . .
Secondary Jobs as a Self-Employed or Unpaid Family Worker[5]	1 897	1 524	1 607	-372	83	-2.2	0.5	. . .	. . .	. . .	. . .	. . .

[3]Comparable estimate of output growth is not available.
[4]Workers who hold a secondary wage and salary job in agricultural production, forestry, fishing, and private household industries.
[5]Wage and salary workers who hold a secondary job as a self-employed or unpaid family worker.
. . . = Not available.

Table 4-7. Employment, by Occupation, 2008 and Projected 2018

(Numbers in thousands, percent.)

Occupation	Employment				Change, 2008–2018		Total job openings due to growth and net replacements, 2008–2018[1]
	Number		Percent distribution		Number	Percent	
	2008	2018	2008	2018			
ALL OCCUPATIONS	150 932	166 206	100.0	100.0	15 274	10.1	50 929
Management, Business, and Financial	15 747	17 411	10.4	10.5	1 664	10.6	5 035
Management	8 912	9 367	5.9	5.6	454	5.1	2 460
Top executives	2 201	2 194	1.5	1.3	-7	-0.3	634
Chief executives	400	395	0.3	0.2	-6	-1.4	113
General and operations managers	1 733	1 731	1.1	1.0	-2	-0.1	502
Legislators	68	68	0.0	0.0	1	0.7	20
Advertising, marketing, promotions, public relations, and sales managers	624	704	0.4	0.4	80	12.9	217
Advertising and promotions managers	45	44	0.0	0.0	-1	-1.7	11
Marketing and sales managers	522	596	0.3	0.4	74	14.1	186
Marketing managers	176	198	0.1	0.1	22	12.5	60
Sales managers	347	399	0.2	0.2	52	14.9	127
Public relations managers	57	64	0.0	0.0	7	12.9	21
Operations specialties managers	1 552	1 672	1.0	1.0	120	7.7	467
Administrative services managers	259	292	0.2	0.2	32	12.5	87
Computer and information systems managers	293	343	0.2	0.2	50	16.9	97
Financial managers	539	581	0.4	0.3	41	7.6	138
Human resources managers	134	147	0.1	0.1	13	9.6	41
Compensation and benefits managers	41	44	0.0	0.0	3	8.5	12
Training and development managers	30	34	0.0	0.0	4	11.9	10
Human resources managers, all other	63	69	0.0	0.0	6	9.2	19
Industrial production managers	156	144	0.1	0.1	-12	-7.6	55
Purchasing managers	70	71	0.0	0.0	1	1.5	21
Transportation, storage, and distribution managers	100	94	0.1	0.1	-5	-5.3	27
Other management occupations	4 536	4 797	3.0	2.9	261	5.8	1 141
Agricultural managers	1 234	1 169	0.8	0.7	-65	-5.2	125
Farm, ranch, and other agricultural managers	248	263	0.2	0.2	15	5.9	65
Farmers and ranchers	986	907	0.7	0.5	-79	-8.0	60
Construction managers	551	646	0.4	0.4	95	17.2	138
Education administrators	445	483	0.3	0.3	37	8.3	170
Education administrators, preschool and childcare center/program	59	66	0.0	0.0	7	11.8	25
Education administrators, elementary and secondary school	231	250	0.2	0.2	20	8.6	89
Education administrators, postsecondary	125	127	0.1	0.1	3	2.3	40
Education administrators, all other	31	39	0.0	0.0	8	23.9	17
Engineering managers	184	195	0.1	0.1	11	6.2	49
Food service managers	339	357	0.2	0.2	18	5.3	84
Funeral directors	30	34	0.0	0.0	4	11.9	10
Gaming managers	6	7	0.0	0.0	1	11.8	20
Lodging managers	60	63	0.0	0.0	3	4.7	16
Medical and health services managers	284	329	0.2	0.2	45	16.0	99
Natural sciences managers	45	52	0.0	0.0	7	15.5	2
Postmasters and mail superintendents	26	22	0.0	0.0	-4	-15.1	5
Property, real estate, and community association managers	304	330	0.2	0.2	26	8.4	78
Social and community service managers	131	149	0.1	0.1	18	13.8	48
Managers, all other	898	964	0.6	0.6	66	7.3	298
Business and Financial Operations	6 834	8 044	4.5	4.8	1 210	17.7	2 575
Business operations specialists	4 043	4 762	2.7	2.9	720	17.8	1 609
Agents and business managers of artists, performers, and athletes	23	28	0.0	0.0	5	22.4	10
Buyers and purchasing agents	457	495	0.3	0.3	37	8.2	159
Purchasing agents and buyers, farm products	14	14	0.0	0.0	0	-1.1	3
Wholesale and retail buyers, except farm products	148	144	0.1	0.1	-3	-2.2	37
Purchasing agents, except wholesale, retail, and farm products	295	336	0.2	0.2	41	13.9	119
Claims adjusters, appraisers, examiners, and investigators	306	327	0.2	0.2	21	6.8	99
Claims adjusters, examiners, and investigators	295	316	0.2	0.2	21	7.1	96
Insurance appraisers, auto damage	12	12	0.0	0.0	0	0.5	3
Compliance officers, except agriculture, construction, health and safety, and transportation	260	341	0.2	0.2	81	31.0	109
Cost estimators	218	273	0.1	0.2	55	25.3	104
Emergency management specialists	13	16	0.0	0.0	3	21.7	6
Human resources, training, and labor relations specialists	771	956	0.5	0.6	185	23.9	386
Employment, recruitment, and placement specialists	208	266	0.1	0.2	58	27.9	112
Compensation, benefits, and job analysis specialists	122	151	0.1	0.1	29	23.6	61
Training and development specialists	217	267	0.1	0.2	51	23.3	107
Human resources, training, and labor relations specialists, all other	225	272	0.1	0.2	47	21.0	106
Logisticians	100	120	0.1	0.1	20	19.5	42
Management analysts	747	925	0.5	0.6	178	23.9	307
Meeting and convention planners	57	65	0.0	0.0	9	15.6	21
Business operation specialists, all other	1 091	1 217	0.7	0.7	126	11.5	368
Financial specialists	2 792	3 282	1.8	2.0	491	17.6	966
Accountants and auditors	1 291	1 570	0.9	0.9	279	21.6	498
Appraisers and assessors of real estate	92	97	0.1	0.1	4	4.6	21
Budget analysts	67	77	0.0	0.0	10	15.1	22
Credit analysts	73	84	0.0	0.1	11	15.0	24
Financial analysts and advisers	562	670	0.4	0.4	108	19.2	210
Financial analysts	251	300	0.2	0.2	50	19.8	95
Personal financial advisers	208	271	0.1	0.2	63	30.1	85
Insurance underwriters	103	99	0.1	0.1	-4	-4.1	30
Financial examiners	27	38	0.0	0.0	11	41.2	16
Loan counselors and officers	360	399	0.2	0.2	38	10.6	78
Loan counselors	32	38	0.0	0.0	5	16.3	9
Loan officers	328	361	0.2	0.2	33	10.1	69
Tax examiners, collectors, preparers, and revenue agents	169	181	0.1	0.1	12	7.3	54
Tax examiners, collectors, and revenue agents	73	82	0.0	0.0	10	13.0	35
Tax preparers	96	99	0.1	0.1	3	2.9	19
Financial specialists, all other	151	166	0.1	0.1	16	10.5	43

Note: Data may not sum to totals or 100 percent due to rounding.

[1]Total job openings represent the sum of employment increases and net replacements. If employment change is negative, job openings due to growth are zero and total job openings equal net replacements.

Table 4-7. Employment, by Occupation, 2008 and Projected 2018—*Continued*

(Numbers in thousands, percent.)

Occupation	Employment				Change, 2008–2018		Total job openings due to growth and net replacements, 2008–2018[1]
	Number		Percent distribution		Number	Percent	
	2008	2018	2008	2018			
Computer and Mathematical Sciences	3 540	4 326	2.3	2.6	786	22.2	1 441
Computer specialists	3 424	4 187	2.3	2.5	763	22.3	1 384
Computer and information scientists, research	29	36	0.0	0.0	7	24.2	13
Computer programmers	427	414	0.3	0.2	-12	-2.9	80
Computer software engineers	910	1 205	0.6	0.7	295	32.5	372
Computer software engineers, applications	515	690	0.3	0.4	175	34.0	218
Computer software engineers, systems software	395	515	0.3	0.3	120	30.4	153
Computer support specialists	566	644	0.4	0.4	78	13.8	235
Computer systems analysts	532	640	0.4	0.4	108	20.3	223
Database administrators	120	145	0.1	0.1	24	20.3	44
Network and computer systems administrators	340	418	0.2	0.3	79	23.2	136
Network systems and data communications analysts	292	448	0.2	0.3	156	53.4	208
Computer specialists, all other	209	237	0.1	0.1	28	13.1	73
Mathematical science occupations	116	139	0.1	0.1	23	19.8	57
Actuaries	20	24	0.0	0.0	4	21.4	10
Mathematicians	3	4	0.0	0.0	1	22.5	2
Operations research analysts	63	77	0.0	0.0	14	22.0	32
Statisticians	23	26	0.0	0.0	3	13.1	10
Miscellaneous mathematical science occupations	8	9	0.0	0.0	1	16.2	4
Mathematical technicians	1	1	0.0	0.0	0	8.5	1
Mathematical scientists, all other	7	8	0.0	0.0	1	17.6	3
Architecture and engineering	2 636	2 907	1.7	1.7	271	10.3	838
Architects, surveyors, and cartographers	238	278	0.2	0.2	40	16.8	86
Architects, except naval	168	196	0.1	0.1	28	16.8	57
Architects, except landscape and naval	141	164	0.1	0.1	23	16.2	47
Landscape architects	27	32	0.0	0.0	5	19.7	10
Surveyors, cartographers, and photogrammetrists	70	82	0.0	0.0	12	17.0	30
Cartographers and photogrammetrists	12	16	0.0	0.0	3	26.8	6
Surveyors	58	66	0.0	0.0	9	14.9	23
Engineers	1 572	1 750	1.0	1.1	178	11.3	531
Aerospace engineers	72	79	0.0	0.0	7	10.4	22
Agricultural engineers	3	3	0.0	0.0	0	12.1	1
Biomedical engineers	16	28	0.0	0.0	12	72.0	15
Chemical engineers	32	31	0.0	0.0	-1	-2.0	8
Civil engineers	278	346	0.2	0.2	68	24.3	115
Computer hardware engineers	75	78	0.0	0.0	3	3.8	24
Electrical and electronics engineers	302	305	0.2	0.2	3	1.0	72
Electrical engineers	158	161	0.1	0.1	3	1.7	39
Electronics engineers, except computer	144	144	0.1	0.1	0	0.3	33
Environmental engineers	54	71	0.0	0.0	17	30.6	28
Industrial engineers, including health and safety	240	274	0.2	0.2	33	13.8	95
Health and safety engineers, except mining safety engineers and inspectors	26	28	0.0	0.0	3	10.3	9
Industrial engineers	215	245	0.1	0.1	31	14.2	85
Marine engineers and naval architects	9	9	0.0	0.0	1	5.8	2
Materials engineers	24	27	0.0	0.0	2	9.3	8
Mechanical engineers	239	253	0.2	0.2	14	6.0	76
Mining and geological engineers, including mining safety engineers	7	8	0.0	0.0	1	15.3	3
Nuclear engineers	17	19	0.0	0.0	2	10.9	5
Petroleum engineers	22	26	0.0	0.0	4	18.4	9
Engineers, all other	183	195	0.1	0.1	12	6.7	50
Drafters, engineering, and mapping technicians	826	878	0.5	0.5	52	6.3	220
Drafters	252	263	0.2	0.2	11	4.2	66
Architectural and civil drafters	118	129	0.1	0.1	11	9.1	36
Electrical and electronics drafters	34	34	0.0	0.0	0	0.8	8
Mechanical drafters	79	78	0.1	0.0	-1	-1.1	17
Drafters, all other	21	22	0.0	0.0	1	2.3	5
Engineering technicians, except drafters	497	523	0.3	0.3	26	5.2	125
Aerospace engineering and operations technicians	9	9	0.0	0.0	0	2.3	2
Civil engineering technicians	92	107	0.1	0.1	16	16.9	33
Electrical and electronic engineering technicians	164	160	0.1	0.1	-4	-2.2	31
Electromechanical technicians	16	16	0.0	0.0	-1	-4.9	3
Environmental engineering technicians	21	28	0.0	0.0	6	30.1	10
Industrial engineering technicians	73	77	0.0	0.0	5	6.6	19
Mechanical engineering technicians	46	46	0.0	0.0	-1	-1.5	9
Engineering technicians, except drafters, all other	77	81	0.1	0.0	4	5.2	19
Surveying and mapping technicians	77	93	0.1	0.1	16	20.4	29
Life, Physical, and Social Sciences	1 461	1 738	1.0	1.0	277	19.0	715
Life scientists	279	354	0.2	0.2	75	26.7	144
Agricultural and food scientists	31	36	0.0	0.0	5	15.6	16
Animal scientists	4	4	0.0	0.0	1	13.1	2
Food scientists and technologists	13	16	0.0	0.0	2	16.3	7
Soil and plant scientists	14	16	0.0	0.0	2	15.5	7
Biological scientists	91	111	0.1	0.1	19	21.0	49
Biochemists and biophysicists	23	32	0.0	0.0	9	37.4	16
Microbiologists	17	19	0.0	0.0	2	12.2	8
Zoologists and wildlife biologists	20	22	0.0	0.0	3	12.8	9
Biological scientists, all other	32	38	0.0	0.0	6	18.8	16
Conservation scientists and foresters	30	33	0.0	0.0	4	12.0	7
Conservation scientists	18	21	0.0	0.0	2	11.9	4
Foresters	12	13	0.0	0.0	1	12.1	3
Medical scientists	114	159	0.1	0.1	45	39.3	68
Epidemiologists	5	6	0.0	0.0	1	15.1	2
Medical scientists, except epidemiologists	109	154	0.1	0.1	44	40.4	66
Life scientists, all other	13	15	0.0	0.0	2	16.3	5

Note: Data may not sum to totals or 100 percent due to rounding.

[1]Total job openings represent the sum of employment increases and net replacements. If employment change is negative, job openings due to growth are zero and total job openings equal net replacements.

Table 4-7. Employment, by Occupation, 2008 and Projected 2018—*Continued*

(Numbers in thousands, percent.)

Occupation	Employment				Change, 2008–2018		Total job openings due to growth and net replacements, 2008–2018¹
	Number		Percent distribution		Number	Percent	
	2008	2018	2008	2018			
Life, Physical, and Social Sciences—*Continued*							
Physical scientists	276	317	0.2	0.2	42	15.1	123
Astronomers and physicists	17	20	0.0	0.0	3	15.9	8
Astronomers	2	2	0.0	0.0	0	16.0	1
Physicists	16	18	0.0	0.0	3	15.9	7
Atmospheric and space scientists	9	11	0.0	0.0	1	14.7	3
Chemists and materials scientists	94	97	0.1	0.1	3	3.5	34
Chemists	84	86	0.1	0.1	2	2.5	30
Materials scientists	10	11	0.0	0.0	1	11.9	4
Environmental scientists and geoscientists	128	159	0.1	0.1	31	24.5	68
Environmental scientists and specialists, including health	86	110	0.1	0.1	24	27.9	48
Geoscientists, except hydrologists and geologists	34	39	0.0	0.0	6	17.5	15
Hydrologists	8	10	0.0	0.0	2	18.3	4
Physical scientists, all other	27	30	0.0	0.0	3	11.1	10
Social scientists and related	549	666	0.4	0.4	117	21.3	275
Economists	15	16	0.0	0.0	1	5.8	5
Market and survey researchers	273	351	0.2	0.2	77	28.3	151
Market research analysts	250	320	0.2	0.2	70	28.1	137
Survey researchers	23	31	0.0	0.0	7	30.4	13
Psychologists	170	190	0.1	0.1	20	11.6	68
Clinical, counseling, and school psychologists	152	169	0.1	0.1	17	11.1	60
Industrial-organizational psychologists	2	3	0.0	0.0	1	26.3	1
Psychologists, all other	16	18	0.0	0.0	2	14.4	7
Sociologists	5	6	0.0	0.0	1	21.9	2
Urban and regional planners	38	46	0.0	0.0	7	19.0	15
Miscellaneous social scientists and related workers	48	59	0.0	0.0	11	22.0	35
Anthropologists and archeologists	6	7	0.0	0.0	2	28.1	5
Geographers	1	2	0.0	0.0	0	26.2	1
Historians	4	5	0.0	0.0	1	11.5	3
Political scientists	40	5	0.0	0.0	1	19.5	3
Social scientists and related workers, all other	33	40	0.0	0.0	7	22.4	24
Life, physical, and social science technicians	357	401	0.2	0.2	44	12.4	173
Agricultural and food science technicians	22	24	0.0	0.0	2	8.8	10
Biological technicians	80	94	0.1	0.1	14	17.6	42
Chemical technicians	66	66	0.0	0.0	-1	-0.8	13
Geological and petroleum technicians	15	15	0.0	0.0	0	1.5	6
Nuclear technicians	6	7	0.0	0.0	1	9.2	3
Social science research assistants	21	25	0.0	0.0	4	17.8	13
Other life, physical, and social science technicians	147	171	0.1	0.1	24	16.5	87
Environmental science and protection technicians, including health	35	45	0.0	0.0	10	28.9	25
Forensic science technicians	13	15	0.0	0.0	3	19.6	8
Forest and conservation technicians	34	37	0.0	0.0	3	8.6	18
Life, physical, and social science technicians, all other	65	73	0.0	0.0	9	13.3	36
Community and Social Services	2 724	3 172	1.8	1.9	448	16.5	1 033
Counselors, social workers, and other community and social service specialists	1 945	2 295	1.3	1.4	350	18.0	780
Counselors	666	782	0.4	0.5	117	17.5	251
Substance abuse and behavioral disorder counselors	86	104	0.1	0.1	18	21.0	36
Educational, vocational, and school counselors	276	314	0.2	0.2	39	14.0	94
Marriage and family therapists	27	31	0.0	0.0	4	14.5	10
Mental health counselors	113	140	0.1	0.1	27	24.0	50
Rehabilitation counselors	130	154	0.1	0.1	25	18.9	51
Counselors, all other	33	38	0.0	0.0	4	13.1	11
Social workers	642	745	0.4	0.4	103	16.1	265
Child, family, and school social workers	293	329	0.2	0.2	36	12.3	110
Medical and public health social workers	139	170	0.1	0.1	31	22.4	66
Mental health and substance abuse social workers	137	164	0.1	0.1	27	19.5	61
Social workers, all other	73	83	0.0	0.0	9	12.8	28
Miscellaneous community and social service specialists	637	767	0.4	0.5	130	20.3	265
Health educators	66	78	0.0	0.0	12	18.1	26
Probation officers and correctional treatment specialists	103	123	0.1	0.1	20	19.3	42
Social and human service assistants	352	432	0.2	0.3	79	22.6	154
Community and social service specialists, all other	116	134	0.1	0.1	18	15.7	43
Religious workers	779	878	0.5	0.5	99	12.7	252
Clergy	670	755	0.4	0.5	85	12.7	218
Directors, religious activities and education	80	91	0.1	0.1	10	12.6	26
Religious workers, all other	28	32	0.0	0.0	4	12.5	8
Legal	1 251	1 439	0.8	0.9	188	15.1	397
Lawyers, judges, and related workers	810	911	0.5	0.5	100	12.4	253
Lawyers	759	858	0.5	0.5	99	13.0	240
Judges, magistrates, and other judicial workers	51	53	0.0	0.0	2	3.6	12
Administrative law judges, adjudicators, and hearing officers	14	16	0.0	0.0	1	8.0	4
Arbitrators, mediators, and conciliators	10	11	0.0	0.0	1	13.9	3
Judges, magistrate judges, and magistrates	27	26	0.0	0.0	-1	-2.6	5
Legal support workers	441	529	0.3	0.3	88	20.0	145
Paralegals and legal assistants	264	338	0.2	0.2	74	28.1	104
Miscellaneous legal support workers	177	191	0.1	0.1	14	7.9	41
Court reporters	22	25	0.0	0.0	4	18.3	7
Law clerks	38	43	0.0	0.0	5	13.9	11
Title examiners, abstractors, and searchers	70	69	0.0	0.0	-1	-0.7	10
Legal support workers, all other	48	53	0.0	0.0	5	11.0	12

Note: Data may not sum to totals or 100 percent due to rounding.

¹Total job openings represent the sum of employment increases and net replacements. If employment change is negative, job openings due to growth are zero and total job openings equal net replacements.

Table 4-7. Employment, by Occupation, 2008 and Projected 2018—*Continued*

(Numbers in thousands, percent.)

Occupation	Employment				Change, 2008–2018		Total job openings due to growth and net replacements, 2008–2018[1]
	Number		Percent distribution		Number	Percent	
	2008	2018	2008	2018			
Education, Training, and Library	9 210	10 534	6.1	6.3	1 324	14.4	3 332
Postsecondary teachers	1 699	1 956	1.1	1.2	257	15.1	553
Primary, secondary, and special education teachers	4 522	5 169	3.0	3.1	647	14.3	1 748
Preschool and kindergarten teachers	637	750	0.4	0.5	114	17.8	241
Preschool teachers, except special education	457	544	0.3	0.3	87	19.0	178
Kindergarten teachers, except special education	180	207	0.1	0.1	27	15.0	63
Elementary and middle school teachers	2 225	2 571	1.5	1.5	346	15.5	852
Elementary school teachers, except special education	1 550	1 794	1.0	1.1	244	15.8	597
Middle school teachers, except special and vocational education	660	761	0.4	0.5	101	15.3	251
Vocational education teachers, middle school	16	16	0.0	0.0	1	3.2	4
Secondary school teachers	1 187	1 293	0.8	0.8	106	8.9	451
Secondary school teachers, except special and vocational education	1 088	1 184	0.7	0.7	96	8.9	412
Vocational education teachers, secondary school	99	109	0.1	0.1	10	9.6	39
Special education teachers	473	555	0.3	0.3	82	17.3	205
Special education teachers, preschool, kindergarten, and elementary school	226	270	0.1	0.2	44	19.6	103
Special education teachers, middle school	100	118	0.1	0.1	18	18.1	44
Special education teachers, secondary school	147	166	0.1	0.1	20	13.3	58
Other teachers and instructors	1 099	1 306	0.7	0.8	206	18.8	375
Adult literacy, remedial education, and GED teachers and instructors	96	110	0.1	0.1	15	15.1	29
Self-enrichment education teachers	254	335	0.2	0.2	81	32.0	120
Teachers and instructors, all other	750	860	0.5	0.5	110	14.7	226
Archivists, curators, and librarians	310	339	0.2	0.2	29	9.4	134
Archivists, curators, and museum technicians	29	35	0.0	0.0	6	20.4	15
Archivists	6	7	0.0	0.0	0	6.5	2
Curators	12	14	0.0	0.0	3	23.0	6
Museum technicians and conservators	11	14	0.0	0.0	3	25.6	6
Librarians	160	172	0.1	0.1	13	7.8	55
Library technicians	121	131	0.1	0.1	11	8.8	65
Other education, training, and library	1 580	1 765	1.0	1.1	185	11.7	521
Audio-visual collections specialists	7	8	0.0	0.0	1	10.3	2
Farm and home management advisers	13	13	0.0	0.0	0	1.2	3
Instructional coordinators	134	165	0.1	0.1	31	23.2	61
Teacher assistants	1 313	1 448	0.9	0.9	135	10.3	413
Education, training, and library workers, all other	113	131	0.1	0.1	18	15.8	43
Arts, Design, Entertainment, Sports, and Media	2 741	3 073	1.8	1.8	333	12.1	1 030
Art and design	834	922	0.6	0.6	88	10.6	328
Artists and related workers	222	248	0.1	0.1	26	11.6	76
Art directors	84	94	0.1	0.1	10	11.7	29
Craft artists	14	15	0.0	0.0	1	7.2	4
Fine artists, including painters, sculptors, and illustrators	24	26	0.0	0.0	2	9.0	7
Multimedia artists and animators	79	90	0.1	0.1	11	14.2	29
Artists and related workers, all other	22	23	0.0	0.0	2	7.9	7
Designers	612	674	0.4	0.4	62	10.2	252
Commercial and industrial designers	44	48	0.0	0.0	4	9.0	18
Fashion designers	23	23	0.0	0.0	0	0.8	7
Floral designers	76	74	0.1	0.0	-2	-2.5	23
Graphic designers	286	323	0.2	0.2	37	12.9	125
Interior designers	72	86	0.0	0.1	14	19.4	36
Merchandise displayers and window trimmers	85	91	0.1	0.1	6	7.1	32
Set and exhibit designers	11	13	0.0	0.0	2	16.6	5
Designers, all other	15	17	0.0	0.0	2	9.6	6
Entertainers and performers, sports and related	741	845	0.5	0.5	105	14.1	274
Actors, producers, and directors	155	172	0.1	0.1	17	10.9	61
Actors	57	64	0.0	0.0	7	12.8	21
Producers and directors	99	108	0.1	0.1	10	9.8	40
Athletes, coaches, umpires, and related workers	258	318	0.2	0.2	60	23.1	109
Athletes and sports competitors	17	18	0.0	0.0	2	11.8	5
Coaches and scouts	226	282	0.1	0.2	56	24.8	99
Umpires, referees, and other sports officials	16	18	0.0	0.0	2	10.4	5
Dancers and choreographers	29	31	0.0	0.0	2	6.0	15
Dancers	13	14	0.0	0.0	1	6.8	7
Choreographers	16	17	0.0	0.0	1	5.3	8
Musicians, singers, and related workers	240	260	0.2	0.2	20	8.2	68
Music directors and composers	54	59	0.0	0.0	5	10.0	16
Musicians and singers	186	201	0.1	0.1	14	7.6	52
Entertainers and performers, sports and related, all other	58	65	0.0	0.0	7	11.8	21
Media and communication	827	933	0.5	0.6	105	12.7	311
Announcers	67	65	0.0	0.0	-2	-3.5	20
Radio and television announcers	55	52	0.0	0.0	-3	-6.1	16
Public address system and other announcers	12	13	0.0	0.0	1	8.2	5
News analysts, reporters, and correspondents	69	65	0.0	0.0	-4	-6.3	19
Broadcast news analysts	8	8	0.0	0.0	0	4.1	2
Reporters and correspondents	62	57	0.0	0.0	-5	-7.6	17
Public relations specialists	275	341	0.2	0.2	66	24.0	131
Writers and editors	330	361	0.2	0.2	31	9.4	105
Editors	130	129	0.1	0.1	0	-0.3	34
Technical writers	49	58	0.0	0.0	9	18.2	17
Writers and authors	152	174	0.1	0.1	23	14.8	54
Miscellaneous media and communication workers	85	100	0.1	0.1	15	17.4	35
Interpreters and translators	51	62	0.0	0.0	11	22.2	23
Media and communication workers, all other	34	38	0.0	0.0	4	10.4	12

Note: Data may not sum to totals or 100 percent due to rounding.

[1]Total job openings represent the sum of employment increases and net replacements. If employment change is negative, job openings due to growth are zero and total job openings equal net replacements.

Table 4-7. Employment, by Occupation, 2008 and Projected 2018—*Continued*

(Numbers in thousands, percent.)

Occupation	Employment				Change, 2008–2018		Total job openings due to growth and net replacements, 2008–2018[1]
	Number		Percent distribution		Number	Percent	
	2008	2018	2008	2018			
Arts, Design, Entertainment, Sports, and Media—*Continued*							
Media and communication equipment occupations	339	374	0.2	0.2	35	10.2	117
Broadcast and sound engineering technicians and radio operators	115	124	0.1	0.1	9	7.8	44
Audio and video equipment technicians	55	62	0.0	0.0	7	12.6	24
Broadcast technicians	39	39	0.0	0.0	1	1.8	12
Radio operators	1	1	0.0	0.0	0	9.0	0
Sound engineering technicians	20	21	0.0	0.0	1	6.3	7
Photographers	152	170	0.1	0.1	18	11.5	48
Television, video, and motion picture camera operators and editors	52	57	0.0	0.0	5	10.5	18
Camera operators, television, video, and motion picture	26	29	0.0	0.0	2	9.2	9
Film and video editors	26	29	0.0	0.0	3	11.9	9
Media and communication equipment workers, all other	21	23	0.0	0.0	3	12.5	8
Health Care Practitioner and Technical	7 491	9 091	5.0	5.5	1 600	21.4	3 139
Health diagnosing and treating practitioners	4 630	5 646	3.1	3.4	1 015	21.9	1 866
Chiropractors	49	59	0.0	0.0	10	19.5	18
Dentists	142	164	0.1	0.1	22	15.6	62
Dentists, general	120	139	0.1	0.1	18	15.3	52
Oral and maxillofacial surgeons	7	8	0.0	0.0	1	15.3	3
Orthodontists	8	9	0.0	0.0	2	19.8	4
Prosthodontists	1	1	0.0	0.0	0	27.7	0
Dentists, all other specialists	7	8	0.0	0.0	1	14.7	3
Dietitians and nutritionists	60	66	0.0	0.0	6	9.2	26
Optometrists	35	43	0.0	0.0	9	24.4	20
Pharmacists	270	316	0.2	0.2	46	17.0	106
Physicians and surgeons	661	806	0.4	0.5	144	21.8	261
Physician assistants	75	104	0.0	0.1	29	39.0	43
Podiatrists	12	13	0.0	0.0	1	9.0	3
Registered nurses	2 619	3 200	1.7	1.9	582	22.2	1 039
Therapists	599	740	0.4	0.4	142	23.7	244
Audiologists	13	16	0.0	0.0	3	25.0	6
Occupational therapists	105	131	0.1	0.1	27	25.6	46
Physical therapists	186	242	0.1	0.1	56	30.3	79
Radiation therapists	15	19	0.0	0.0	4	27.1	7
Recreational therapists	23	27	0.0	0.0	3	14.6	12
Respiratory therapists	106	128	0.1	0.1	22	20.9	41
Speech-language pathologists	119	141	0.1	0.1	22	18.5	44
Therapists, all other	32	36	0.0	0.0	4	11.5	10
Veterinarians	60	79	0.0	0.0	20	33.0	30
Health diagnosing and treating practitioners, all other	49	55	0.0	0.0	6	13.0	15
Health technologists and technicians	2 719	3 280	1.8	2.0	561	20.6	1 202
Clinical laboratory technologists and technicians	328	374	0.2	0.2	46	13.9	108
Medical and clinical laboratory technologists	172	193	0.1	0.1	21	11.9	53
Medical and clinical laboratory technicians	156	181	0.1	0.1	25	16.1	55
Dental hygienists	174	237	0.1	0.1	63	36.1	98
Diagnostic related technologists and technicians	336	398	0.2	0.2	62	18.3	110
Cardiovascular technologists and technicians	50	61	0.0	0.0	12	24.1	19
Diagnostic medical sonographers	50	60	0.0	0.0	9	18.3	17
Nuclear medicine technologists	22	25	0.0	0.0	4	16.3	7
Radiologic technologists and technicians	215	252	0.1	0.2	37	17.2	68
Emergency medical technicians and paramedics	211	230	0.1	0.1	19	9.0	62
Health diagnosing and treating practitioner support technicians	596	753	0.4	0.5	157	26.4	308
Dietetic technicians	25	29	0.0	0.0	4	13.9	10
Pharmacy technicians	326	426	0.2	0.3	100	30.6	182
Psychiatric technicians	57	60	0.0	0.0	2	4.2	17
Respiratory therapy technicians	17	16	0.0	0.0	0	-1.1	4
Surgical technologists	92	115	0.1	0.1	23	25.3	46
Veterinary technologists and technicians	80	108	0.1	0.1	29	35.8	49
Licensed practical and licensed vocational nurses	754	909	0.5	0.5	156	20.6	391
Medical records and health information technicians	173	208	0.1	0.1	35	20.3	70
Opticians, dispensing	60	68	0.0	0.0	8	13.4	20
Miscellaneous health technologists and technicians	88	104	0.1	0.1	16	18.5	34
Orthotists and prosthetists	6	7	0.0	0.0	1	15.5	2
Health care technologists and technicians, all other	82	97	0.1	0.1	15	18.7	32
Other health care practitioner and technical	142	165	0.1	0.1	23	16.4	71
Occupational health and safety specialists and technicians	67	75	0.0	0.0	8	11.7	30
Occupational health and safety specialists	56	62	0.0	0.0	6	11.2	25
Occupational health and safety technicians	11	13	0.0	0.0	2	14.4	5
Miscellaneous health care practitioner and technical	75	91	0.0	0.1	15	20.5	41
Athletic trainers	16	22	0.0	0.0	6	36.9	12
Health care practitioner and technical workers, all other	59	68	0.0	0.0	9	15.9	29
Health Care Support	3 982	5 130	2.6	3.1	1 147	28.8	1 595
Nursing, psychiatric, and home health aides	2 454	3 194	1.6	1.9	741	30.2	985
Home health aides	922	1 383	0.6	0.8	461	50.0	553
Nursing aides, orderlies, and attendants	1 470	1 746	1.0	1.1	276	18.8	422
Psychiatric aides	63	66	0.0	0.0	4	5.8	10
Occupational and physical therapist assistants and aides	144	193	0.1	0.1	48	33.5	69
Occupational therapist assistants and aides	34	45	0.0	0.0	10	30.0	15
Occupational therapist assistants	27	35	0.0	0.0	8	29.8	12
Occupational therapist aides	8	10	0.0	0.0	2	30.7	4
Physical therapist assistants and aides	110	148	0.1	0.1	38	34.5	54
Physical therapist assistants	64	85	0.0	0.1	21	33.3	31
Physical therapist aides	46	63	0.0	0.0	17	36.3	23

Note: Data may not sum to totals or 100 percent due to rounding.

[1]Total job openings represent the sum of employment increases and net replacements. If employment change is negative, job openings due to growth are zero and total job openings equal net replacements.

Table 4-7. Employment, by Occupation, 2008 and Projected 2018—*Continued*

(Numbers in thousands, percent.)

Occupation	Employment				Change, 2008–2018		Total job openings due to growth and net replacements, 2008–2018[1]
	Number		Percent distribution		Number	Percent	
	2008	2018	2008	2018			
Health Care Support—*Continued*							
Other health care support	1 384	1 743	0.9	1.0	358	25.9	541
Massage therapists	122	146	0.1	0.1	23	18.9	40
Miscellaneous health care support	1 262	1 597	0.8	1.0	335	26.6	502
Dental assistants	295	401	0.2	0.2	106	35.8	161
Medical assistants	484	648	0.3	0.4	164	33.9	218
Medical equipment preparers	47	53	0.0	0.0	6	12.8	11
Medical transcriptionists	105	117	0.1	0.1	12	11.1	24
Pharmacy aides	55	52	0.0	0.0	-4	-6.3	6
Veterinary assistants and laboratory animal caretakers	75	92	0.0	0.1	17	22.8	26
Health care support workers, all other	201	235	0.1	0.1	34	17.1	57
Protective Services	3 270	3 670	2.2	2.2	400	12.2	1 304
First-line supervisors/managers of protective service workers	252	274	0.2	0.2	23	9.0	129
First-line supervisors/managers of law enforcement workers	141	152	0.1	0.1	12	8.2	70
First-line supervisors/managers of correctional officers	44	47	0.0	0.0	4	8.5	19
First-line supervisors/managers of police and detectives	97	105	0.1	0.1	8	8.1	51
First-line supervisors/managers of fire fighting and prevention workers	55	60	0.0	0.0	5	8.2	33
First-line supervisors/managers of protective service workers, all other	56	62	0.0	0.0	7	12.0	27
Fire fighting and prevention workers	327	386	0.2	0.2	59	18.1	159
Firefighters	310	368	0.2	0.2	58	18.5	153
Fire inspectors	17	18	0.0	0.0	2	9.2	6
Fire inspectors and investigators	15	16	0.0	0.0	1	9.3	5
Forest fire inspectors and prevention specialists	2	2	0.0	0.0	0	8.4	1
Law enforcement workers	1 271	1 393	0.8	0.8	122	9.6	426
Bailiffs, correctional officers, and jailers	475	519	0.3	0.3	45	9.4	150
Bailiffs	20	22	0.0	0.0	2	8.4	6
Correctional officers and jailers	455	498	0.3	0.3	43	9.4	144
Detectives and criminal investigators	112	131	0.1	0.1	19	16.6	42
Fish and game wardens	8	9	0.0	0.0	1	8.3	3
Parking enforcement workers	10	10	0.0	0.0	0	-0.1	2
Police officers	666	723	0.4	0.4	58	8.6	229
Police and sheriff's patrol officers	662	719	0.4	0.4	57	8.7	228
Transit and railroad police	4	5	0.0	0.0	0	5.3	1
Other protective services	1 420	1 617	0.9	1.0	197	13.9	590
Animal control workers	16	18	0.0	0.0	2	9.0	6
Private detectives and investigators	46	56	0.0	0.0	10	22.0	19
Security guards and gaming surveillance officers	1 086	1 240	0.7	0.7	154	14.1	377
Gaming surveillance officers and gaming investigators	9	10	0.0	0.0	1	11.7	3
Security guards	1 077	1 229	0.7	0.7	153	14.2	374
Miscellaneous protective services	273	305	0.2	0.2	32	11.7	188
Crossing guards	70	77	0.0	0.0	7	9.4	26
Lifeguards, ski patrol, and other recreational protective service workers	115	128	0.1	0.1	13	11.2	91
Protective service workers, all other	88	100	0.1	0.1	12	14.0	72
Food Preparation and Serving Related	11 552	12 560	7.7	7.6	1 008	8.7	5 101
Supervisors of food preparation and serving workers	942	997	0.6	0.6	55	5.9	145
Chefs and head cooks	108	109	0.1	0.1	0	0.2	11
First-line supervisors/managers of food preparation and serving workers	833	889	0.6	0.5	55	6.6	134
Cooks and food preparation workers	2 958	3 150	2.0	1.9	192	6.5	1 040
Cooks	2 066	2 220	1.4	1.3	154	7.4	682
Cooks, fast food	566	608	0.4	0.4	42	7.5	187
Cooks, institution and cafeteria	392	430	0.3	0.3	38	9.7	138
Cooks, private household	5	5	0.0	0.0	0	4.3	2
Cooks, restaurant	914	984	0.6	0.6	70	7.7	304
Cooks, short order	171	172	0.1	0.1	0	0.0	44
Cooks, all other	18	21	0.0	0.0	3	16.3	8
Food preparation workers	892	930	0.6	0.6	38	4.2	357
Food and beverage serving workers	6 307	6 962	4.2	4.2	655	10.4	3 142
Bartenders	509	550	0.3	0.3	41	8.0	222
Fast food and counter workers	3 227	3 670	2.1	2.2	443	13.7	1 402
Combined food preparation and serving workers, including fast food	2 702	3 096	1.8	1.9	394	14.6	967
Counter attendants, cafeteria, food concession, and coffee shop	525	574	0.3	0.3	49	9.3	435
Waiters and waitresses	2 382	2 533	1.6	1.5	152	6.4	1 466
Food servers, nonrestaurant	190	209	0.1	0.1	19	10.2	52
Other food preparation and serving related workers	1 345	1 451	0.9	0.9	106	7.9	774
Dining room and cafeteria attendants and bartender helpers	421	444	0.3	0.3	23	5.5	206
Dishwashers	523	583	0.3	0.4	60	11.6	276
Hosts and hostesses, restaurant, lounge, and coffee shop	351	373	0.2	0.2	23	6.5	267
Food preparation and serving related workers, all other	51	50	0.0	0.0	-1	-1.7	26
Building and Grounds Cleaning and Maintenance	5 727	6 211	3.8	3.7	484	8.4	1 434
Supervisors of building and grounds cleaning and maintenance workers	469	514	0.3	0.3	45	9.6	95
First-line supervisors/managers of housekeeping and janitorial workers	251	264	0.2	0.2	13	5.1	39
First-line supervisors/managers of landscaping, lawn service, and groundskeeping workers	218	250	0.1	0.2	32	14.9	56
Building cleaning and pest control workers	3 956	4 157	2.6	2.5	202	5.1	946
Building cleaning workers	3 888	4 079	2.6	2.5	192	4.9	912
Janitors and cleaners, except maids and housekeeping workers	2 375	2 479	1.6	1.5	104	4.4	553
Maids and housekeeping cleaners	1 498	1 584	1.0	1.0	86	5.7	354
Building cleaning workers, all other	15	16	0.0	0.0	2	12.1	5
Pest control workers	68	78	0.0	0.0	10	15.3	34
Grounds maintenance	1 303	1 540	0.9	0.9	237	18.2	394
Landscaping and groundskeeping	1 206	1 423	0.8	0.9	217	18.0	362
Pesticide handlers, sprayers, and applicators, vegetation	31	36	0.0	0.0	5	17.7	9
Tree trimmers and pruners	45	57	0.0	0.0	12	26.3	17
Grounds maintenance workers, all other	21	24	0.0	0.0	3	11.8	5

Note: Data may not sum to totals or 100 percent due to rounding.

[1]Total job openings represent the sum of employment increases and net replacements. If employment change is negative, job openings due to growth are zero and total job openings equal net replacements.

Table 4-7. Employment, by Occupation, 2008 and Projected 2018—*Continued*

(Numbers in thousands, percent.)

Occupation	Employment				Change, 2008–2018		Total job openings due to growth and net replacements, 2008–2018[1]
	Number		Percent distribution		Number	Percent	
	2008	2018	2008	2018			
Personal Care and Services	5 044	6 075	3.3	3.7	1 031	20.4	2 284
Supervisors of personal care and service workers	278	317	0.2	0.2	38	13.7	111
First-line supervisors/managers of gaming workers	65	71	0.0	0.0	6	8.4	20
Gaming supervisors	41	46	0.0	0.0	5	11.8	14
Slot key persons	24	25	0.0	0.0	1	2.8	6
First-line supervisors/managers of personal service workers	213	246	0.1	0.1	33	15.4	91
Animal care and service workers	220	266	0.1	0.2	46	20.6	93
Animal trainers	47	57	0.0	0.0	10	20.4	19
Nonfarm animal caretakers	173	209	0.1	0.1	36	20.7	74
Entertainment attendants and related workers	569	652	0.4	0.4	83	14.6	378
Gaming services workers	121	142	0.1	0.1	21	17.4	73
Gaming dealers	91	108	0.1	0.1	17	19.0	56
Gaming and sports book writers and runners	16	18	0.0	0.0	2	13.2	9
Gaming service workers, all other	14	16	0.0	0.0	2	11.7	8
Motion picture projectionists	11	11	0.0	0.0	0	0.6	5
Ushers, lobby attendants, and ticket takers	106	121	0.1	0.1	15	13.7	82
Miscellaneous entertainment attendants and related workers	331	378	0.2	0.2	47	14.3	219
Amusement and recreation attendants	263	298	0.2	0.2	35	13.3	171
Costume attendants	5	6	0.0	0.0	1	13.8	3
Locker room, coatroom, and dressing room attendants	19	21	0.0	0.0	2	13.2	12
Funeral service	43	53	0.0	0.0	10	22.1	30
Embalmers	9	9	0.0	0.0	0	5.2	5
Funeral attendants	35	44	0.0	0.0	9	26.2	26
Personal appearance	825	991	0.5	0.6	166	20.1	287
Barbers and cosmetologists	684	817	0.5	0.5	133	19.5	234
Barbers	54	60	0.0	0.0	6	11.6	14
Hairdressers, hairstylists, and cosmetologists	631	758	0.4	0.5	127	20.1	220
Miscellaneous personal appearance	141	173	0.1	0.1	33	23.3	53
Makeup artists, theatrical and performance	3	3	0.0	0.0	1	16.9	1
Manicurists and pedicurists	76	90	0.1	0.1	14	18.8	25
Shampooers	23	26	0.0	0.0	3	14.6	7
Skin care specialists	39	54	0.0	0.0	15	37.9	20
Transportation, tourism, and lodging attendants	236	261	0.2	0.2	25	10.5	89
Baggage porters, bellhops, and concierges	71	81	0.0	0.0	9	13.0	28
Baggage porters and bellhops	51	57	0.0	0.0	6	12.7	20
Concierges	21	24	0.0	0.0	3	13.7	8
Tour and travel guides	44	49	0.0	0.0	5	10.4	23
Tour guides and escorts	38	43	0.0	0.0	5	11.7	21
Travel guides	6	6	0.0	0.0	0	1.7	2
Transportation attendants	120	131	0.1	0.1	11	9.1	38
Flight attendants	99	107	0.1	0.1	8	8.1	30
Transportation attendants, except flight attendants and baggage porters	22	25	0.0	0.0	3	13.3	8
Other personal care and services	2 873	3 537	1.9	2.1	664	23.1	1 297
Childcare workers	1 302	1 444	0.9	0.9	142	10.9	523
Personal and home care aides	817	1 193	0.5	0.7	376	46.0	478
Recreation and fitness workers	589	714	0.4	0.4	125	21.2	231
Fitness trainers and aerobics instructors	261	338	0.2	0.2	77	29.4	124
Recreation workers	328	376	0.2	0.2	48	14.7	107
Residential advisers	57	62	0.0	0.0	5	9.1	25
Personal care and service workers, all other	109	124	0.1	0.1	16	14.3	40
Sales and Related	15 903	16 883	10.5	10.2	980	6.2	5 713
Supervisors of sales workers	2 192	2 305	1.5	1.4	113	5.1	580
First-line supervisors/managers of retail sales workers	1 686	1 774	1.1	1.1	88	5.2	450
First-line supervisors/managers of non-retail sales workers	507	531	0.3	0.3	24	4.8	130
Retail sales	8 737	9 251	5.8	5.6	514	5.9	3 573
Cashiers	3 572	3 696	2.4	2.2	123	3.4	1 730
Cashiers, except gaming	3 550	3 676	2.4	2.2	126	3.5	1 720
Gaming change persons and booth cashiers	22	20	0.0	0.0	-2	-10.4	10
Counter and rental clerks and parts salespersons	676	692	0.4	0.4	16	2.4	216
Counter and rental clerks	448	462	0.3	0.3	14	3.1	134
Parts salespersons	228	230	0.2	0.1	2	1.0	83
Retail salespersons	4 489	4 864	3.0	2.9	375	8.3	1 627
Sales representatives, services	1 614	1 788	1.1	1.1	174	10.8	561
Advertising sales agents	167	179	0.1	0.1	12	7.2	45
Insurance sales agents	435	486	0.3	0.3	52	11.9	153
Securities, commodities, and financial services sales agents	317	347	0.2	0.2	30	9.3	127
Travel agents	105	104	0.1	0.1	-1	-1.1	8
Sales representatives, services, all other	590	672	0.4	0.4	82	13.9	228
Sales representatives, wholesale and manufacturing	1 973	2 116	1.3	1.3	143	7.3	600
Sales representatives, wholesale and manufacturing, technical and scientific products	433	475	0.3	0.3	42	9.7	142
Sales representatives, wholesale and manufacturing, except technical and scientific products	1 540	1 641	1.0	1.0	101	6.6	458
Other sales and related workers	1 386	1 423	0.9	0.9	37	2.6	400
Models, demonstrators, and product promoters	105	113	0.1	0.1	8	7.3	38
Demonstrators and product promoters	103	110	0.1	0.1	7	7.1	37
Models	2	3	0.0	0.0	0	16.0	1
Real estate brokers and sales agents	518	592	0.3	0.4	74	14.4	159
Real estate brokers	123	134	0.1	0.1	11	8.6	31
Real estate sales agents	394	458	0.3	0.3	64	16.2	128
Sales engineers	78	85	0.1	0.1	7	8.8	35
Telemarketers	342	304	0.2	0.2	-38	-11.1	86

Note: Data may not sum to totals or 100 percent due to rounding.

[1]Total job openings represent the sum of employment increases and net replacements. If employment change is negative, job openings due to growth are zero and total job openings equal net replacements.

Table 4-7. Employment, by Occupation, 2008 and Projected 2018—*Continued*

(Numbers in thousands, percent.)

Occupation	Employment				Change, 2008–2018		Total job openings due to growth and net replacements, 2008–2018[1]
	Number		Percent distribution		Number	Percent	
	2008	2018	2008	2018			
Sales and Related—*Continued*							
Miscellaneous sales and related	344	329	0.2	0.2	-15	-4.2	82
Door-to-door sales workers, news and street vendors, and related workers	182	155	0.1	0.1	-27	-14.8	33
Sales and related workers, all other	162	175	0.1	0.1	12	7.6	49
Office and Administrative Support	24 101	25 943	16.0	15.6	1 842	7.6	7 255
Supervisors of office and administrative support workers	1 457	1 618	1.0	1.0	160	11.0	489
First-line supervisors/managers of office and administrative support workers	1 457	1 618	1.0	1.0	160	11.0	489
Communications equipment operators	182	163	0.1	0.1	-18	-10.0	37
Switchboard operators, including answering service	155	138	0.1	0.1	-17	-10.9	32
Telephone operators	23	22	0.0	0.0	-1	-3.6	4
Communications equipment operators, all other	4	3	0.0	0.0	0	-12.2	1
Financial clerks	3 911	4 313	2.6	2.6	402	10.3	1 152
Bill and account collectors	411	491	0.3	0.3	80	19.3	157
Billing and posting clerks and machine operators	529	610	0.4	0.4	81	15.3	168
Bookkeeping, accounting, and auditing clerks	2 064	2 276	1.4	1.4	212	10.3	460
Gaming cage workers	17	15	0.0	0.0	-2	-10.4	3
Payroll and timekeeping clerks	209	198	0.1	0.1	-11	-5.2	50
Procurement clerks	82	86	0.1	0.1	5	5.8	30
Tellers	601	638	0.4	0.4	38	6.2	284
Information and record clerks	5 685	6 230	3.8	3.7	546	9.6	2 352
Brokerage clerks	68	66	0.0	0.0	-2	-2.6	19
Correspondence clerks	14	12	0.0	0.0	-2	-13.8	4
Court, municipal, and license clerks	122	132	0.1	0.1	10	8.2	45
Credit authorizers, checkers, and clerks	64	66	0.0	0.0	2	2.8	20
Customer service representatives	2 252	2 652	1.5	1.6	400	17.7	1 108
Eligibility interviewers, government programs	120	131	0.1	0.1	11	9.2	39
File clerks	212	163	0.1	0.1	-50	-23.4	52
Hotel, motel, and resort desk clerks	230	262	0.2	0.2	32	13.7	110
Interviewers, except eligibility and loan	233	270	0.2	0.2	36	15.6	92
Library assistants, clerical	122	136	0.1	0.1	14	11.1	64
Loan interviewers and clerks	210	219	0.1	0.1	9	4.3	61
New accounts clerks	87	87	0.1	0.1	0	0.1	25
Order clerks	246	182	0.2	0.1	-64	-26.1	70
Human resources assistants, except payroll and timekeeping	170	160	0.1	0.1	-10	-5.7	48
Receptionists and information clerks	1 139	1 312	0.8	0.8	173	15.2	480
Reservation and transportation ticket agents and travel clerks	168	182	0.1	0.1	14	8.1	52
Information and record clerks, all other	227	200	0.2	0.1	-27	-11.8	64
Material recording, scheduling, dispatching, and distributing occupations	4 113	4 145	2.7	2.5	32	0.8	1 147
Cargo and freight agents	86	107	0.1	0.1	21	23.9	40
Couriers and messengers	122	122	0.1	0.1	0	-0.3	28
Dispatchers	296	308	0.2	0.2	13	4.3	79
Police, fire, and ambulance dispatchers	100	118	0.1	0.1	18	17.8	38
Dispatchers, except police, fire, and ambulance	196	191	0.1	0.1	-5	-2.6	40
Meter readers, utilities	45	36	0.0	0.0	-9	-20.0	13
Postal service workers	599	527	0.4	0.3	-72	-12.0	140
Postal service clerks	751	62	0.1	0.0	-14	-18.0	16
Postal service mail carriers	343	339	0.2	0.2	-4	-1.1	107
Postal service mail sorters, processors, and processing machine operators	180	125	0.1	0.1	-55	-30.3	17
Production, planning, and expediting clerks	284	288	0.2	0.2	4	1.5	74
Shipping, receiving, and traffic clerks	751	701	0.5	0.4	-49	-6.6	186
Stock clerks and order fillers	1 859	1 993	1.2	1.2	134	7.2	563
Weighers, measurers, checkers, and samplers, recordkeeping	72	62	0.0	0.0	-9	-13.1	25
Secretaries and administrative assistants	4 348	4 820	2.9	2.9	472	10.8	1 057
Executive secretaries and administrative assistants	1 594	1 799	1.1	1.1	204	12.8	419
Legal secretaries	263	311	0.2	0.2	48	18.4	84
Medical secretaries	471	597	0.3	0.4	126	26.6	189
Secretaries, except legal, medical, and executive	2 020	2 113	1.3	1.3	93	4.6	366
Other office and administrative support	4 405	4 654	2.9	2.8	249	5.7	1 021
Computer operators	110	90	0.1	0.1	-21	-18.6	12
Data entry and information processing	426	401	0.3	0.2	-26	-6.0	70
Data entry keyers	284	267	0.2	0.2	-17	-6.1	59
Word processors and typists	142	134	0.1	0.1	-8	-5.7	11
Desktop publishers	26	20	0.0	0.0	-6	-22.5	4
Insurance claims and policy processing clerks	254	254	0.2	0.2	1	0.3	34
Mail clerks and mail machine operators, except postal service	141	125	0.1	0.1	-17	-11.8	26
Office clerks, general	3 024	3 383	2.0	2.0	359	11.9	771
Office machine operators, except computer	80	74	0.1	0.0	-6	-7.6	27
Proofreaders and copy markers	18	17	0.0	0.0	-1	-6.1	3
Statistical assistants	18	19	0.0	0.0	1	5.1	4
Office and administrative support workers, all other	307	271	0.2	0.2	-36	-11.6	70
Farming, Fishing, and Forestry	1 035	1 026	0.7	0.6	-9	-0.9	291
Supervisors of farming, fishing, and forestry workers	49	52	0.0	0.0	4	7.8	16
Agricultural workers	872	857	0.6	0.5	-15	-1.7	239
Agricultural inspectors	17	19	0.0	0.0	2	12.8	6
Animal breeders	15	16	0.0	0.0	1	5.8	5
Graders and sorters, agricultural products	33	34	0.0	0.0	0	0.2	7
Miscellaneous agricultural	807	789	0.5	0.5	-18	-2.3	222
Fishing and hunting	36	33	0.0	0.0	-3	-7.6	9
Fishers and related fishing	36	33	0.0	0.0	-3	-7.7	9
Forest, conservation, and logging	79	84	0.1	0.1	5	6.3	27
Forest and conservation	13	14	0.0	0.0	1	8.5	5
Logging	66	70	0.0	0.0	4	5.9	22
Fallers	11	11	0.0	0.0	0	-2.9	3
Logging equipment operators	42	45	0.0	0.0	3	7.7	14
Log graders and scalers	6	5	0.0	0.0	0	-1.8	2
Logging workers, all other	8	9	0.0	0.0	1	13.5	3

Note: Data may not sum to totals or 100 percent due to rounding.

[1]Total job openings represent the sum of employment increases and net replacements. If employment change is negative, job openings due to growth are zero and total job openings equal net replacements.

Table 4-7. Employment, by Occupation, 2008 and Projected 2018—*Continued*

(Numbers in thousands, percent.)

Occupation	Employment				Change, 2008–2018		Total job openings due to growth and net replacements, 2008–2018[1]
	Number		Percent distribution		Number	Percent	
	2008	2018	2008	2018			
Construction and Extraction	7 810	8 829	5.2	5.3	1 019	13.0	2 396
Supervisors of construction and extraction workers	698	805	0.5	0.5	107	15.4	242
First-line supervisors/managers of construction and extraction workers	698	805	0.5	0.5	107	15.4	242
Construction trades and related	6 018	6 826	4.0	4.1	808	13.4	1 777
Boilermakers	20	24	0.0	0.0	4	18.8	8
Brickmasons, blockmasons, and stonemasons	160	179	0.1	0.1	19	11.5	59
Brickmasons and blockmasons	136	152	0.1	0.1	16	11.5	50
Stonemasons	24	27	0.0	0.0	3	11.6	9
Carpenters	1 285	1 450	0.9	0.9	165	12.9	325
Carpet, floor, and tile installers and finishers	161	172	0.1	0.1	11	7.1	54
Carpet installers	51	51	0.0	0.0	-1	-1.1	13
Floor layers, except carpet, wood, and hard tiles	21	21	0.0	0.0	0	-1.0	6
Floor sanders and finishers	12	14	0.0	0.0	1	11.3	5
Tile and marble setters	76	87	0.1	0.1	11	14.3	31
Cement masons, concrete finishers, and terrazzo workers	207	233	0.1	0.1	27	12.9	79
Cement masons and concrete finishers	201	227	0.1	0.1	26	12.9	76
Terrazzo workers and finishers	6	6	0.0	0.0	1	12.7	2
Construction laborers	1 249	1 505	0.8	0.9	256	20.5	339
Construction equipment operators	469	526	0.3	0.3	56	12.0	136
Paving, surfacing, and tamping equipment operators	60	67	0.0	0.0	7	11.5	17
Pile-driver operators	5	5	0.0	0.0	1	13.1	1
Operating engineers and other construction equipment operators	405	453	0.3	0.3	49	12.0	118
Drywall installers, ceiling tile installers, and tapers	189	214	0.1	0.1	25	13.4	46
Drywall and ceiling tile installers	151	172	0.1	0.1	21	13.5	37
Tapers	37	42	0.0	0.0	5	13.0	9
Electricians	695	778	0.5	0.5	83	11.9	251
Glaziers	54	58	0.0	0.0	4	7.7	24
Insulation workers	57	67	0.0	0.0	10	17.4	29
Insulation workers, floor, ceiling, and wall	28	32	0.0	0.0	4	15.2	13
Insulation workers, mechanical	30	36	0.0	0.0	6	19.4	16
Painters and paperhangers	450	480	0.3	0.3	30	6.6	107
Painters, construction and maintenance	443	474	0.3	0.3	31	7.0	107
Paperhangers	7	6	0.0	0.0	-1	-14.5	0
Pipelayers, plumbers, pipefitters, and steamfitters	556	642	0.4	0.4	86	15.5	198
Pipelayers	61	72	0.0	0.0	11	17.2	23
Plumbers, pipefitters, and steamfitters	495	571	0.3	0.3	76	15.3	176
Plasterers and stucco masons	49	52	0.0	0.0	3	6.6	11
Reinforcing iron and rebar workers	28	31	0.0	0.0	4	12.6	8
Roofers	149	155	0.1	0.1	6	3.8	30
Sheet metal workers	171	182	0.1	0.1	11	6.5	52
Structural iron and steel workers	70	79	0.0	0.0	9	12.4	20
Helpers—construction trades	382	456	0.3	0.3	75	19.5	156
Helpers—brickmasons, blockmasons, stonemasons, and tile and marble setters	51	59	0.0	0.0	8	16.4	19
Helpers—carpenters	80	99	0.1	0.1	19	23.3	35
Helpers—electricians	106	132	0.1	0.1	26	24.7	48
Helpers—painters, paperhangers, plasterers, and stucco masons	19	19	0.0	0.0	-1	-3.4	4
Helpers—pipelayers, plumbers, pipefitters, and steamfitters	80	101	0.1	0.1	21	25.7	37
Helpers—roofers	19	17	0.0	0.0	-2	-9.4	4
Helpers—construction trades, all other	27	30	0.0	0.0	3	12.3	9
Other construction and related	456	514	0.3	0.3	59	12.9	174
Construction and building inspectors	106	124	0.1	0.1	18	16.8	40
Elevator installers and repairers	25	27	0.0	0.0	2	9.2	9
Fence erectors	34	38	0.0	0.0	5	13.6	8
Hazardous materials removal	43	49	0.0	0.0	6	14.8	18
Highway maintenance	146	158	0.1	0.1	12	8.5	52
Rail-track laying and maintenance equipment operators	16	18	0.0	0.0	2	14.8	7
Septic tank servicers and sewer pipe cleaners	26	32	0.0	0.0	6	23.8	13
Miscellaneous construction and related	61	68	0.0	0.0	7	11.0	27
Segmental pavers	1	1	0.0	0.0	0	7.1	1
Construction and related workers, all other	60	66	0.0	0.0	7	11.1	27
Extraction workers	257	227	0.2	0.1	-30	-11.7	47
Derrick, rotary drill, and service unit operators, oil, gas, and mining	93	75	0.1	0.0	-18	-19.0	16
Derrick operators, oil and gas	25	19	0.0	0.0	-6	-23.0	4
Rotary drill operators, oil and gas	29	23	0.0	0.0	-6	-21.5	5
Service unit operators, oil, gas, and mining	39	33	0.0	0.0	-6	-14.7	7
Earth drillers, except oil and gas	23	25	0.0	0.0	2	7.1	6
Explosives workers, ordnance handling experts, and blasters	6	7	0.0	0.0	0	4.0	1
Mining machine operators	25	25	0.0	0.0	0	-0.8	5
Continuous mining machine operators	11	11	0.0	0.0	-1	-5.5	2
Mine cutting and channeling machine operators	9	10	0.0	0.0	0	4.4	2
Mining machine operators, all other	5	5	0.0	0.0	0	-0.4	1
Rock splitters, quarry	4	4	0.0	0.0	0	-1.7	1
Roof bolters, mining	5	5	0.0	0.0	0	-5.7	1
Roustabouts, oil and gas	66	57	0.0	0.0	-8	-12.5	11
Helpers—extraction workers	26	21	0.0	0.0	-5	-19.2	5
Extraction workers, all other	8	8	0.0	0.0	-1	-7.3	1
Installation, Maintenance, and Repair	5 798	6 238	3.8	3.8	440	7.6	1 586
Supervisors of installation, maintenance, and repair workers	449	468	0.3	0.3	19	4.3	137
First-line supervisors/managers of mechanics, installers, and repairers	449	468	0.3	0.3	19	4.3	137
Electrical and electronic equipment mechanics, installers, and repairers	659	683	0.4	0.4	24	3.7	150
Computer, automated teller, and office machine repairers	153	146	0.1	0.1	-7	-4.4	26
Radio and telecommunications equipment installers and reporters	209	208	0.1	0.1	-1	-0.3	37
Radio mechanics	6	6	0.0	0.0	0	-4.0	1
Telecommunications equipment installers and repairers, except line installers	203	203	0.1	0.1	-1	-0.2	36
Miscellaneous electrical and electronic equipment mechanics, installers, and repairers	297	329	0.2	0.2	32	10.6	87
Avionics technicians	19	21	0.0	0.0	2	10.6	5

Note: Data may not sum to totals or 100 percent due to rounding.

[1]Total job openings represent the sum of employment increases and net replacements. If employment change is negative, job openings due to growth are zero and total job openings equal net replacements.

Table 4-7. Employment, by Occupation, 2008 and Projected 2018—*Continued*

(Numbers in thousands, percent.)

Occupation	Employment				Change, 2008–2018		Total job openings due to growth and net replacements, 2008–2018[1]
	Number		Percent distribution		Number	Percent	
	2008	2018	2008	2018			
Installation, Maintenance, and Repair—*Continued*							
Electric motor, power tool, and related repairers	24	25	0.0	0.0	1	5.1	9
Electrical and electronics installers and repairers, transportation equipment	16	17	0.0	0.0	1	4.1	3
Electrical and electronics repairers, commercial and industrial equipment	78	81	0.1	0.0	3	3.8	16
Electrical and electronics repairers, powerhouse, substation, and relay	23	26	0.0	0.0	3	11.5	7
Electronic equipment installers and repairers, motor vehicles	20	20	0.0	0.0	0	0.1	3
Electronic home entertainment equipment installers and repairers	51	57	0.0	0.0	6	10.8	14
Security and fire alarm systems installers	66	83	0.0	0.0	16	24.8	28
Vehicle and mobile equipment mechanics, installers, and repairers	1 722	1 806	1.1	1.1	84	4.9	438
Aircraft mechanics and service technicians	122	129	0.1	0.1	8	6.4	31
Automotive technicians and repairers	950	987	0.6	0.6	37	3.9	230
Automotive body and related repairers	166	167	0.1	0.1	1	0.5	44
Automotive glass installers and repairers	20	20	0.0	0.0	0	1.8	4
Automotive service technicians and mechanics	764	800	0.5	0.5	36	4.7	182
Bus and truck mechanics and diesel engine specialists	263	278	0.2	0.2	15	5.7	75
Heavy vehicle and mobile equipment service technicians and mechanics	191	206	0.1	0.1	16	8.1	52
Farm equipment mechanics	31	33	0.0	0.0	2	6.9	8
Mobile heavy equipment mechanics, except engines	136	148	0.1	0.1	12	8.7	38
Rail car repairers	23	25	0.0	0.0	2	6.5	6
Small engine mechanics	70	75	0.0	0.0	5	6.8	19
Motorboat mechanics	22	23	0.0	0.0	1	5.6	6
Motorcycle mechanics	19	21	0.0	0.0	2	8.8	6
Outdoor power equipment and other small engine mechanics	29	31	0.0	0.0	2	6.4	8
Miscellaneous vehicle and mobile equipment mechanics, installers, and repairers	127	131	0.1	0.1	4	2.9	30
Bicycle repairers	10	12	0.0	0.0	2	19.3	4
Recreational vehicle service technicians	14	15	0.0	0.0	1	6.6	4
Tire repairers and changers	103	104	0.1	0.1	1	0.9	22
Other installation, maintenance, and repair occupations	2 969	3 282	2.0	2.0	313	10.6	863
Control and valve installers and repairers	62	63	0.0	0.0	1	2.1	11
Mechanical door repairers	17	19	0.0	0.0	2	10.9	5
Control and valve installers and repairers, except mechanical door	45	44	0.0	0.0	-1	-1.3	7
Heating, air-conditioning, and refrigeration mechanics and installers	308	395	0.2	0.2	87	28.1	136
Home appliance repairers	50	51	0.0	0.0	1	2.2	9
Industrial machinery installation, repair, and maintenance	1 772	1 945	1.2	1.2	173	9.7	445
Industrial machinery mechanics	288	309	0.2	0.2	21	7.3	62
Maintenance and repair workers, general	1 361	1 509	0.9	0.9	148	10.9	358
Maintenance workers, machinery	75	79	0.0	0.0	3	4.6	15
Millwrights	45	46	0.0	0.0	1	1.4	10
Refractory materials repairers, except brickmasons	3	2	0.0	0.0	0	-6.4	0
Line installers and repairers	285	292	0.2	0.2	7	2.3	73
Electrical power line installers and repairers	114	119	0.1	0.1	5	4.5	46
Telecommunications line installers and repairers	171	173	0.1	0.1	2	0.9	28
Precision instrument and equipment repairers	71	82	0.0	0.0	11	14.7	32
Camera and photographic equipment repairers	5	4	0.0	0.0	-1	-15.4	1
Medical equipment repairers	41	53	0.0	0.0	11	27.2	23
Musical instrument repairers and tuners	6	6	0.0	0.0	0	0.1	2
Watch repairers	3	3	0.0	0.0	0	-13.8	1
Precision instrument and equipment repairers, all other	16	16	0.0	0.0	0	2.5	5
Miscellaneous installation, maintenance, and repair	421	455	0.3	0.3	34	8.2	156
Coin, vending, and amusement machine servicers and repairers	44	47	0.0	0.0	3	7.0	18
Commercial divers	2	3	0.0	0.0	0	5.8	1
Fabric menders, except garment	1	1	0.0	0.0	0	-29.8	0
Locksmiths and safe repairers	22	25	0.0	0.0	3	12.0	6
Manufactured building and mobile home installers	10	11	0.0	0.0	1	5.2	1
Riggers	14	14	0.0	0.0	0	0.3	2
Signal and track switch repairers	7	7	0.0	0.0	0	1.2	1
Helpers—installation, maintenance, and repair	151	164	0.1	0.1	13	8.3	85
Installation, maintenance, and repair workers, all other	170	186	0.1	0.1	16	9.2	42
Production	10 083	9 734	6.7	5.9	-349	-3.5	2 156
Supervisors of production workers	681	646	0.5	0.4	-36	-5.2	92
First-line supervisors/managers of production and operating workers	681	646	0.5	0.4	-36	-5.2	92
Assemblers and fabricators	1 951	1 913	1.3	1.2	-38	-1.9	426
Aircraft structure, surfaces, rigging, and systems assemblers	44	48	0.0	0.0	4	9.4	13
Electrical, electronics, and electromechanical assemblers	298	254	0.2	0.2	-43	-14.5	46
Coil winders, tapers, and finishers	22	17	0.0	0.0	-6	-25.2	3
Electrical and electronic equipment assemblers	213	182	0.1	0.1	-31	-14.7	33
Electromechanical equipment assemblers	62	56	0.0	0.0	-6	-10.3	10
Engine and other machine assemblers	40	37	0.0	0.0	-3	-8.0	8
Structural metal fabricators and fitters	114	114	0.1	0.1	0	-0.4	24
Miscellaneous assemblers and fabricators	1 455	1 460	1.0	0.9	5	0.3	334
Fiberglass laminators and fabricators	30	29	0.0	0.0	-1	-4.6	7
Team assemblers	1 112	1 113	0.7	0.7	0	0.0	251
Timing device assemblers, adjusters, and calibrators	3	3	0.0	0.0	0	-4.4	1
Assemblers and fabricators, all other	310	316	0.2	0.2	6	1.9	76
Food processing	707	734	0.5	0.4	27	3.9	234
Bakers	152	152	0.1	0.1	0	0.2	39
Butchers and other meat, poultry, and fish processing	397	414	0.3	0.2	17	4.2	144
Butchers and meat cutters	129	131	0.1	0.1	2	1.5	43
Meat, poultry, and fish cutters and trimmers	170	180	0.1	0.1	11	6.4	65
Slaughterers and meat packers	98	103	0.1	0.1	4	4.2	36
Miscellaneous food processing	158	168	0.1	0.1	10	6.5	51
Food and tobacco roasting, baking, and drying machine operators and tenders	18	18	0.0	0.0	0	0.3	5
Food batchmakers	101	109	0.1	0.1	9	8.7	33
Food cooking machine operators and tenders	39	41	0.0	0.0	2	3.8	13
Metal workers and plastic	2 159	1 999	1.4	1.2	-159	-7.4	443
Computer control programmers and operators	158	165	0.1	0.1	7	4.2	40
Computer-controlled machine tool operators, metal and plastic	141	150	0.1	0.1	9	6.6	37

Note: Data may not sum to totals or 100 percent due to rounding.

[1]Total job openings represent the sum of employment increases and net replacements. If employment change is negative, job openings due to growth are zero and total job openings equal net replacements.

Table 4-7. Employment, by Occupation, 2008 and Projected 2018—*Continued*

(Numbers in thousands, percent.)

Occupation	Employment				Change, 2008–2018		Total job openings due to growth and net replacements, 2008–2018[1]
	Number		Percent distribution		Number	Percent	
	2008	2018	2008	2018			
Production—*Continued*							
Numerical tool and process control programmers	17	14	0.0	0.0	-3	-15.4	3
Forming machine setters, operators, and tenders, metal and plastic	153	138	0.1	0.1	-16	-10.1	30
Extruding and drawing machine setters, operators, and tenders, metal and plastic	91	86	0.1	0.1	-5	-5.2	18
Forging machine setters, operators, and tenders, metal and plastic	28	23	0.0	0.0	-6	-19.5	6
Rolling machine setters, operators, and tenders, metal and plastic	34	29	0.0	0.0	-5	-15.5	7
Machine tool cutting setters, operators, and tenders, metal and plastic	444	368	0.3	0.2	-76	-17.1	77
Cutting, punching, and press machine setters, operators, and tenders, metal and plastic	237	204	0.2	0.1	-33	-14.1	47
Drilling and boring machine tool setters, operators, and tenders, metal and plastic	33	24	0.0	0.0	-9	-26.9	3
Grinding, lapping, polishing, and buffing machine, tool setters, operators, and tenders, metal and plastic	93	78	0.1	0.0	-15	-15.9	14
Lathe and turning machine tool setters, operators, and tenders, metal and plastic	56	41	0.0	0.0	-15	-26.7	9
Milling and planing machine setters, operators, and tenders, metal and plastic	26	22	0.0	0.0	-4	-15.8	5
Machinists	422	402	0.3	0.2	-19	-4.6	56
Metal furnace and kiln operators and tenders	34	31	0.0	0.0	-3	-9.1	7
Metal-refining furnace operators and tenders	19	17	0.0	0.0	-2	-8.6	4
Pourers and casters, metal	15	14	0.0	0.0	-2	-9.6	3
Model makers and patternmakers, metal and plastic	17	16	0.0	0.0	-1	-5.8	1
Model makers, metal and plastic	10	10	0.0	0.0	-1	-5.9	1
Patternmakers, metal and plastic	7	7	0.0	0.0	0	-5.7	0
Molders and molding machine setters, operators, and tenders, metal and plastic	159	151	0.1	0.1	-8	-5.1	33
Foundry mold and coremakers	15	13	0.0	0.0	-2	-12.0	3
Molding, coremaking, and casting machine setters, operators and tenders, metal and plastic	144	137	0.1	0.1	-6	-4.4	30
Multiple machine tool setters, operators, and tenders, metal and plastic	86	73	0.1	0.0	-13	-14.7	17
Tool and die makers	84	78	0.1	0.0	-7	-8.0	5
Welding, soldering, and brazing	466	456	0.3	0.3	-11	-2.3	143
Welders, cutters, solderers, and brazers	412	406	0.3	0.2	-7	-1.6	126
Welding, soldering, and brazing machine setters, operators, and tenders	54	50	0.0	0.0	-4	-7.0	17
Miscellaneous metalworkers and plastic	135	122	0.1	0.1	-13	-9.7	35
Heat treating equipment setters, operators, and tenders, matal and plastic	23	21	0.0	0.0	-3	-10.6	11
Lay out workers, metal and plastic	8	7	0.0	0.0	-1	-11.6	2
Plating and coating machine setters, operators, and tenders, metal and plastic	40	35	0.0	0.0	-5	-12.4	11
Tool grinders, filers, and sharpeners	19	17	0.0	0.0	-1	-7.5	6
Metal workers and plastic workers, all other	45	42	0.0	0.0	-3	-7.4	6
Printing occupations	369	331	0.2	0.2	-38	-10.3	60
Bookbinders and bindery workers	67	54	0.0	0.0	-13	-19.3	10
Bindery workers	60	48	0.0	0.0	-12	-20.1	9
Bookbinders	6	5	0.0	0.0	-1	-12.1	1
Printers	303	278	0.2	0.2	-25	-8.3	50
Job printers	46	42	0.0	0.0	-4	-7.6	2
Prepress technicians and workers	61	50	0.0	0.0	-11	-17.7	8
Printing machine operators	196	185	0.1	0.1	-11	-5.5	41
Textile, apparel, and furnishings occupations	788	668	0.5	0.4	-120	-15.2	96
Laundry and dry-cleaning	235	242	0.2	0.1	7	2.8	48
Pressers, textile, garment, and related materials	67	61	0.0	0.0	-6	-8.2	3
Sewing machine operators	212	141	0.1	0.1	-72	-33.7	12
Shoe and leather	14	11	0.0	0.0	-3	-21.3	2
Shoe and leather workers and repairers	9	8	0.0	0.0	-1	-14.3	1
Shoe machine operators and tenders	5	3	0.0	0.0	-2	-34.8	1
Tailors, dressmakers, and sewers	67	65	0.0	0.0	-2	-3.1	7
Sewers, hand	12	11	0.0	0.0	-1	-8.2	1
Tailors, dressmakers, and custom sewers	55	54	0.0	0.0	-1	-2.0	6
Textile machine setters, operators, and tenders	100	61	0.1	0.0	-39	-39.0	13
Textile bleaching and dyeing machine operators and tenders	16	9	0.0	0.0	-7	-44.8	2
Textile cutting machine setters, operators, and tenders	19	13	0.0	0.0	-6	-31.0	3
Textile knitting and weaving machine setters, operators, and tenders	29	18	0.0	0.0	-12	-39.3	2
Textile winding, twisting, and drawing out machine setters, operators, and tenders	35	21	0.0	0.0	-14	-40.7	6
Miscellaneous textile, apparel, and furnishings workers	93	87	0.1	0.1	-6	-6.1	12
Extruding and forming machine setters, operators, and tenders, synthetic or glass fibers	14	9	0.0	0.0	-5	-33.9	2
Fabric and apparel patternmakers	8	6	0.0	0.0	-2	-27.2	1
Upholsterers	53	56	0.0	0.0	4	6.8	7
Textile, apparel, and furnishings workers, all other	18	16	0.0	0.0	-2	-12.7	3
Woodworkers	323	344	0.2	0.2	21	6.4	89
Cabinetmakers and bench carpenters	132	144	0.1	0.1	12	9.1	42
Furniture finishers	27	28	0.0	0.0	1	4.5	7
Model makers and patternmakers, wood	4	4	0.0	0.0	0	-0.6	1
Model makers, wood	2	2	0.0	0.0	0	2.4	0
Patternmakers, wood	2	2	0.0	0.0	0	-3.2	0
Woodworking machine setters, operators, and tenders	138	145	0.1	0.1	7	4.9	34
Sawing machine setters, operators, and tenders, wood	53	53	0.0	0.0	1	1.4	10
Woodworking machine setters, operators, and tenders, except sawing	86	92	0.1	0.1	6	7.0	24
Woodworkers, all other	23	24	0.0	0.0	1	3.3	6
Plant and system operators	325	332	0.2	0.2	7	2.2	102
Power plant operators, distributors, and dispatchers	50	51	0.0	0.0	0	0.4	18
Nuclear power reactor operators	5	6	0.0	0.0	1	18.9	3
Power distributors and dispatchers	10	10	0.0	0.0	0	-2.2	4
Power plant operators	35	35	0.0	0.0	-1	-1.6	12
Stationary engineers and boiler operators	42	44	0.0	0.0	2	5.2	9
Water and liquid waste treatment plant and system operators	113	136	0.1	0.1	23	19.8	47
Miscellaneous plant and system operators	120	102	0.1	0.1	-18	-14.7	28
Chemical plant and system operators	45	36	0.0	0.0	-9	-20.6	10
Gas plant operators	15	14	0.0	0.0	-1	-4.2	3
Petroleum pump system operators, refinery operators, and gaugers	47	40	0.0	0.0	-7	-15.2	11
Plant and system operators, all other	13	12	0.0	0.0	-1	-4.7	3

Note: Data may not sum to totals or 100 percent due to rounding.

[1]Total job openings represent the sum of employment increases and net replacements. If employment change is negative, job openings due to growth are zero and total job openings equal net replacements.

Table 4-7. Employment, by Occupation, 2008 and Projected 2018—*Continued*

(Numbers in thousands, percent.)

Occupation	Employment				Change, 2008–2018		Total job openings due to growth and net replacements, 2008–2018[1]
	Number		Percent distribution		Number	Percent	
	2008	2018	2008	2018			
Production—*Continued*							
Other production	2 781	2 767	1.8	1.7	-14	-0.5	614
Chemical processing machine setters, operators, and tenders	94	92	0.1	0.1	-2	-2.2	12
Chemical equipment operators and tenders	53	47	0.0	0.0	-6	-12.1	4
Separating, filtering, clarifying, precipitating, and still machine setters, operators, and tenders	41	45	0.0	0.0	4	10.6	8
Crushing, grinding, polishing, mixing, and blending	223	247	0.1	0.1	24	11.0	63
Crushing, grinding, and polishing machine setters, operators, and tenders	41	41	0.0	0.0	-1	-1.4	7
Grinding and polishing workers, hand	40	43	0.0	0.0	3	7.6	10
Mixing and blending machine setters, operators, and tenders	142	164	0.1	0.1	22	15.5	46
Cutting	99	93	0.1	0.1	-7	-6.8	21
Cutters and trimmers, hand	24	21	0.0	0.0	-3	-13.1	5
Cutting and slicing machine setters, operators, and tenders	75	72	0.0	0.0	-4	-4.8	16
Extruding, forming, pressing, and compacting machine setters, operators, and tenders	83	96	0.1	0.1	13	15.0	30
Furnace, kiln, oven, drier, and kettle operators and tenders	25	23	0.0	0.0	-2	-7.0	3
Inspectors, testers, sorters, samplers, and weighers	465	448	0.3	0.3	-17	-3.6	78
Jewelers and precious stone and metal	52	55	0.0	0.0	3	5.3	14
Medical, dental, and ophthalmic laboratory technicians	95	108	0.1	0.1	13	13.8	32
Dental laboratory technicians	46	52	0.0	0.0	6	13.9	15
Medical appliance technicians	14	15	0.0	0.0	2	10.9	4
Ophthalmic laboratory technicians	35	40	0.0	0.0	5	14.7	12
Packaging and filling machine operators and tenders	349	347	0.2	0.2	-2	-0.7	59
Painting workers	193	200	0.1	0.1	7	3.8	58
Coating, painting, and spraying machine setters, operators, and tenders	108	111	0.1	0.1	4	3.3	32
Painters, transportation equipment	52	53	0.0	0.0	0	0.8	14
Painting, coating, and decorating workers	33	36	0.0	0.0	3	10.2	12
Photographic process workers and processing machine operators	73	61	0.0	0.0	-12	-16.1	19
Photographic process workers	22	22	0.0	0.0	1	3.1	6
Photographic processing machine operators	51	39	0.0	0.0	-13	-24.3	13
Semiconductor processors	32	22	0.0	0.0	-10	-31.5	7
Miscellaneous production	999	976	0.7	0.6	-22	-2.2	221
Cementing and gluing machine operators and tenders	20	18	0.0	0.0	-2	-11.4	5
Cleaning, washing, and metal pickling equipment operators, and tenders	18	17	0.0	0.0	-1	-3.5	4
Cooling and freezing equipment operators and tenders	10	10	0.0	0.0	0	-0.4	2
Etchers and engravers	12	12	0.0	0.0	0	0.0	1
Molders, shapers, and casters, except metal and plastic	48	50	0.0	0.0	1	2.8	25
Paper goods machine setters, operators, and tenders	103	81	0.1	0.0	-22	-21.5	22
Tire builders	21	18	0.0	0.0	-4	-17.6	7
Helpers—production	484	484	0.3	0.3	0	-0.1	85
Production workers, all other	282	288	0.2	0.2	6	2.0	71
Transportation and Material Moving	9 826	10 217	6.5	6.1	391	4.0	2 857
Supervisors of transportation and material moving workers	406	405	0.3	0.2	-1	-0.3	77
Aircraft cargo handling supervisors	5	5	0.0	0.0	0	7.2	1
First-line supervisors/managers of helpers, laborers, and material movers, hand	184	190	0.1	0.1	7	3.6	39
First-line supervisors/managers of transportation and material moving machine and vehicle operators	218	210	0.1	0.1	-8	-3.7	38
Air transportation	150	169	0.1	0.1	18	12.1	69
Aircraft pilots and flight engineers	116	130	0.1	0.1	14	11.8	53
Airline pilots, copilots, and flight engineers	77	83	0.1	0.1	6	8.4	33
Commercial pilots	39	47	0.0	0.0	7	18.5	21
Air traffic controllers and airfield operations specialists	34	39	0.0	0.0	5	13.0	16
Air traffic controllers	26	30	0.0	0.0	3	13.0	12
Airfield operations specialists	8	9	0.0	0.0	1	13.0	4
Motor vehicle operators	4 171	4 552	2.8	2.7	381	9.1	1 124
Ambulance drivers and attendants, except emergency medical technicians	22	25	0.0	0.0	2	10.3	6
Bus drivers	648	691	0.4	0.4	44	6.8	157
Bus drivers, transit and intercity	194	210	0.1	0.1	16	8.2	50
Bus drivers, school	454	482	0.3	0.3	28	6.2	107
Driver/sales workers and truck drivers	3 189	3 481	2.1	2.1	292	9.2	863
Driver/sales workers	406	424	0.3	0.3	18	4.4	90
Truck drivers, heavy and tractor trailer	1 798	2 031	1.2	1.2	233	12.9	555
Truck drivers, light or delivery services	985	1 026	0.7	0.6	41	4.2	218
Taxi drivers and chauffeurs	232	268	0.2	0.2	36	15.5	77
Motor vehicle operators, all other	80	86	0.1	0.1	7	8.4	21
Rail transportation	131	142	0.1	0.1	12	9.2	55
Locomotive engineers and operators	51	56	0.0	0.0	5	9.9	22
Railroad brake, signal, and switch operators	26	28	0.0	0.0	2	9.4	11
Railroad conductors and yardmasters	41	44	0.0	0.0	3	6.9	17
Subway and streetcar operators	8	9	0.0	0.0	1	18.8	4
Rail transportation workers, all other	5	5	0.0	0.0	0	4.2	2
Water transportation	81	93	0.1	0.1	12	14.8	46
Sailors and marine oilers	33	37	0.0	0.0	4	11.7	18
Ship and boat captains and operators	37	43	0.0	0.0	6	16.3	21
Captains, mates, and pilots of water vessels	33	39	0.0	0.0	6	17.3	20
Motorboat operators	4	4	0.0	0.0	0	8.1	2
Ship engineers	12	14	0.0	0.0	2	18.6	7
Other transportation	303	319	0.2	0.2	16	5.2	128
Bridge and lock tenders	5	5	0.0	0.0	0	8.4	2
Parking lot attendants	136	142	0.1	0.1	6	4.2	55
Service station attendants	83	82	0.1	0.0	-2	-2.2	35
Traffic technicians	7	8	0.0	0.0	1	10.3	3
Transportation inspectors	27	32	0.0	0.0	5	18.3	11
Transportation workers, all other	44	50	0.0	0.0	6	12.7	22

Note: Data may not sum to totals or 100 percent due to rounding.

[1]Total job openings represent the sum of employment increases and net replacements. If employment change is negative, job openings due to growth are zero and total job openings equal net replacements.

Table 4-7. Employment, by Occupation, 2008 and Projected 2018—*Continued*

(Numbers in thousands, percent.)

Occupation	Employment				Change, 2008–2018		Total job openings due to growth and net replacements, 2008–2018[1]
	Number		Percent distribution		Number	Percent	
	2008	2018	2008	2018			
Transportation and Material Moving—*Continued*							
Material moving	4 584	4 537	3.0	2.7	-47	-1.0	1 357
Conveyor operators and tenders	41	37	0.0	0.0	-4	-9.3	12
Crane and tower operators	44	41	0.0	0.0	-3	-6.7	10
Dredge, excavating, and loading machine operators	82	89	0.1	0.1	6	7.7	31
Dredge operators	2	2	0.0	0.0	0	7.0	1
Excavating and loading machine and dragline operators	76	82	0.1	0.0	7	8.6	29
Loading machine operators, underground mining	4	4	0.0	0.0	0	-7.4	1
Hoist and winch operators	3	3	0.0	0.0	0	-8.0	1
Industrial truck and tractor operators	610	627	0.4	0.4	17	2.7	199
Laborers and material movers, hand	3 566	3 485	2.4	2.1	-80	-2.3	1 016
Cleaners of vehicles and equipment	349	353	0.2	0.2	4	1.0	128
Laborers and freight, stock, and material movers hand	2 317	2 299	1.5	1.4	-19	-0.8	746
Machine feeders and offbearers	141	110	0.1	0.1	-31	-22.2	16
Packers and packagers, hand	759	725	0.5	0.4	-34	-4.5	126
Pumping station operators	33	25	0.0	0.0	-8	-24.7	10
Gas compressor and gas pumping station operators	4	3	0.0	0.0	-1	-20.6	1
Laborers and freight, stock, and material movers, hand	10	8	0.0	0.0	-2	-19.6	3
Wellhead pumpers	19	13	0.0	0.0	-5	-28.4	5
Refuse and recyclable material collectors	149	177	0.1	0.1	28	18.6	71
Shuttle car operators	3	3	0.0	0.0	0	-4.0	1
Tank car, truck, and ship loaders	12	11	0.0	0.0	-1	-7.4	4
Material moving workers, all other	41	40	0.0	0.0	-1	-2.4	5

Note: Data may not sum to totals or 100 percent due to rounding.

[1]Total job openings represent the sum of employment increases and net replacements. If employment change is negative, job openings due to growth are zero and total job openings equal net replacements.

Chapter Five

PRODUCTIVITY AND COSTS

PRODUCTIVITY AND COSTS

HIGHLIGHTS

This chapter covers two kinds of productivity measures produced by the Bureau of Labor Statistics (BLS): output per hour (or labor productivity) and multifactor productivity. Multifactor productivity is designed to combine the joint influence of technological change, efficiency improvements, returns to scale, and other factors on economic growth. Industry data are based on the North American Industry Classification System (NAICS).

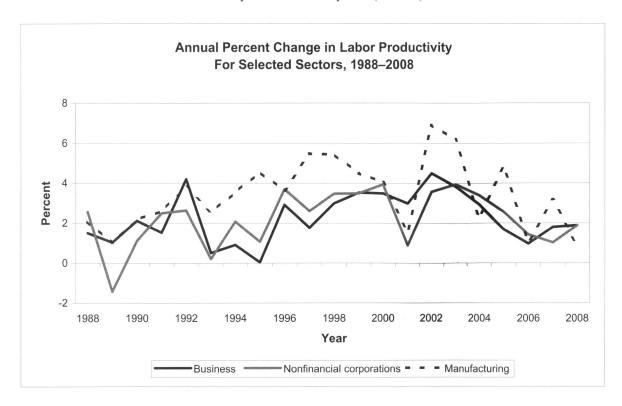

The levels of the output indexes for business, nonfinancial corporations, and manufacturing are not directly comparable because of different sources of the data. However trends can be examined in output per hour or labor productivity. In 2008, labor productivity grew slowly in all sectors. Nonfinancial corporations had the fastest growth at 1.9, percent followed by business at 1.8 percent. Manufacturing productivity grew the slowest at 0.8 percent. In 2007, labor productivity grew much faster in manufacturing (3.2 percent) than in business (1.8 percent). (See Table 5-1.)

OTHER HIGHLIGHTS:

- Labor productivity declined in wholesale trade (-0.3 percent), retail trade (-1.8 percent) and food services and drinking places (-0.7 percent) from 2007 to 2008. However from 1987 to 2008, the average annual percentage change was positive for all three industries. (See Table 5-3.)

- In 2007, output per hour increased in 31 of the 45 detailed service-providing industries and in 2 of the 5 detailed mining industries studied. Output rose in 66 percent of the industries in 2007, while labor hours declined in 48 percent. (See Table 5-2.)

- Multifactor productivity grew 1.2 percent in the private business sector and by more than 1.1 percent in the private nonfarm business sector in 2008, the largest annual rates of growth since 2005. (See Table 5-4.)

NOTES AND DEFINITIONS

PRODUCTIVITY AND COSTS

The Bureau of Labor Statistics (BLS) publishes three sets of productivity measures for the major sectors and subsectors of the U.S. economy, each using a distinct methodology. One measure includes labor productivity for the major sectors of business, nonfarm business, and nonfinancial corporations and for the subsectors of total, durable, and nondurable manufacturing. The second set includes multifactor productivity for major sectors; and the third measures multifactor productivity for total industries. Each set of measures involves a comparison of output and input measures.

Indexes of labor productivity show changes in the ratio of output to hours of labor input. These measures are used in economic analysis, public and private policymaking, and forecasting and analysis of prices, wages, and technological change.

Concepts and Definitions

Business sector output is constructed by excluding the following outputs from gross domestic product (GDP): general government, nonprofit institutions, paid employees of private households, and the rental value of owner-occupied dwellings. Corresponding exclusions are also made in labor inputs. These activities are excluded because theoretical or practical difficulties make it impossible to use them as a basis for the computation of meaningful productivity measures.

Hourly compensation costs are defined as the sum of wage and salary accruals and supplements to wages and salaries. Wage and salary accruals consist of the monetary remuneration of employees, including the compensation of corporate officers; commissions, tips, and bonuses; voluntary employee contributions to certain deferred compensation plans, such as 401(k) plans; employee gains from exercising nonqualified stock options; and receipts in kind that represent income. Supplements to wages and salaries consist of employer contributions for social insurance and employer payments (including payments in kind) to private pension and profit-sharing plans, group health and life insurance plans, privately administered workers' compensation plans. For employees (wage and salary workers), hourly compensation is measured relative to hours at work and includes payments made by employers for time not at work, such as vacation, holiday, and sick pay. Because compensation costs for the business and nonfarm business sectors would otherwise be severely understated, an estimate of the hourly compensation of proprietors of unincorporated businesses is made by assuming that their hourly compensation is equal to that of employees in the same sector.

Hours at work include paid time working, traveling between job sites, coffee breaks, and machine downtime.

Hours at work, however, exclude hours for which employees are paid but not at work.

The *nonfarm business sector* is a subset of the domestic economy and excludes the economic activities of the following: general government, private households, nonprofit organizations serving individuals, and farms.

Nonfinancial corporations are a subset of the domestic economy and excludes the economic activities of the following: general government, private households, nonprofit organizations serving individuals, and those corporations classified as offices of bank holding companies, offices of other holding companies, or offices in the finance and insurance sector.

Nonlabor payments include profits, consumption of fixed capital, taxes on production and imports less subsidies, net interest and miscellaneous payments, business current transfer payments, rental income of persons, and the current surplus of government enterprises.

Output is measured as an annual-weighted index of the changes in the various products or services (in real terms) provided for sale outside the industry. Real industry output is usually derived by deflating nominal sales or values of production using BLS price indexes, but for some industries it is measured by physical quantities of output. Industry output measures are constructed primarily using data from the economic censuses and annual surveys of the U.S. Census Bureau, U.S. Department of Commerce, together with information on price changes primarily from BLS. Output measures for some mining and utilities industries are based on physical quantity data from the Energy Information Administration, U.S. Department of Energy, while output measures for some transportation industries are based on physical quantity data from the Bureau of Transportation Statistics, U.S. Department of Transportation. Other data sources for some industries include the U.S. Geological Survey, U.S. Department of the Interior; the U.S. Postal Service; the Federal Deposit Insurance Corporation; and the Postal Rate Commission.

Productivity measures describe the relationship between industry output and the labor time involved in its production. They show the changes from period to period in the amount of goods and services produced per hour. Although the labor productivity measures relate output to hours of employees or all persons in an industry, they do not measure the specific contribution of labor or any other factor of production. Rather, they reflect the joint effects of many influences, including changes in technology; capital investment; utilization of capacity, energy, and materials; the use of purchased services inputs, including contract employment services; the organization of production; managerial skill; and the characteristics and effort of the workforce.

Unit labor costs show the growth in compensation relative to that of real output. These costs are calculated by dividing total labor compensation by real output. Changes in unit labor costs can be approximated by subtracting the change in productivity from the change in hourly compensation.

Multifactor Productivity Concepts and Definitions

Multifactor productivity (MFP) indexes for private business and private nonfarm business are derived by dividing an output index by an index of labor input and capital services. The output indexes are computed as chained superlative indexes of components of real output. BLS adjusts output measures from the Bureau of Economic Analysis (BEA) to remove the output of government enterprises.

Capital services measures the services derived from the stock of physical assets and software. The assets included are computers, software, communications and other information processing equipment, other fixed business equipment, structures, inventories, rental residences, and land. Investments, depreciation, capital income, and rental prices are estimated for each of these eight aggregates. Rental prices reflect the nominal rates of return and rates of economic depreciation and revaluation for the specific asset. Rental prices are adjusted for the effects of taxes. Data on investments in physical assets are obtained from BEA. Capital input measures constructed for the preliminary MFP measures are based on less detail than those for full MFP measure.

Combined inputs involve combining labor and capital inputs using a Tornqvist index. Growth rates of labor and capital input are combined with weights that represent each component's share of total costs. Total costs are defined as the value of output (Gross Product Originating) less a portion of taxes on production and imports. Most taxes on pro-

duction and imports, such as excise taxes, are excluded from costs; however, property and motor vehicle taxes remain in total costs. The index uses changing weights: The share in each year is averaged with the preceding year's share.

Labor input is total hours worked multiplied by a labor composition index. Hours paid of employees are largely obtained from BLS's Current Employment Survey (CES). These hours of employees are then converted to an at-work basis by using information from the Employment Cost Index (ECI) of the National Compensation Survey (NCS) and the Hours at Work Survey. Hours at work for non-production and supervisory workers are derived using data from the CPS, the CES, and the NCS. The hours at work of proprietors, unpaid family workers, and farm employees are derived from the Current Population Survey.

Multifactor productivity measures describe the relationship between output in real terms and the inputs involved in its production. They do not measure the specific contributions of labor, capital, or any other factor of production. Rather, multifactor productivity is designed to measure the joint influences of output, capital, and labor on economic growth of technological change, efficiency improvements, returns to scale, reallocation of resources due to shifts in factor inputs across industries, and other factors. The multifactor productivity indexes for private business and private nonfarm business are derived by dividing an output index by an index of labor input and capital services. The output indexes are computed as chained superlative indexes (Fisher Ideal indexes) of components of real output. BLS adjusts BEA output measures to remove the output of government enterprises.

Sources of Additional Information

Productivity concepts and methodology are described in Chapters 10 and 11 of the *BLS Handbook of Methods*. More information on productivity can be found in BLS news releases on the BLS Web site at <http://www.bls.gov/lpc/>.

Table 5-1. Indexes of Productivity and Related Data, 1947–2008

(1992 = 100.)

Year	Business											
	Output per hour	Output	Hours	Hourly compen-sation	Real hourly compen-sation	Unit labor costs	Unit nonlabor payments	Implicit price deflator	Employment	Output per person	Compen-sation in current dollars	Nonlabor payments in current dollars
1947	32.2	20.4	63.4	7.0	41.2	21.8	18.5	20.6	55.6	36.8	4.5	3.8
1948	33.7	21.5	63.8	7.6	41.3	22.6	20.6	21.9	56.2	38.3	4.9	4.4
1949	34.5	21.3	61.8	7.7	42.4	22.4	20.4	21.6	54.9	38.8	4.8	4.4
1950	37.4	23.4	62.6	8.3	44.8	22.1	21.5	21.9	55.5	42.2	5.2	5.0
1951	38.5	24.9	64.6	9.1	45.5	23.5	23.7	23.6	56.9	43.8	5.9	5.9
1952	39.6	25.7	64.8	9.6	47.4	24.3	23.1	23.8	57.2	44.9	6.2	5.9
1953	41.1	26.9	65.6	10.2	50.0	24.9	22.5	24.0	58.0	46.4	6.7	6.1
1954	41.9	26.6	63.4	10.6	51.3	25.2	22.4	24.1	56.6	47.0	6.7	6.0
1955	43.7	28.7	65.8	10.8	52.8	24.8	23.9	24.5	58.2	49.4	7.1	6.9
1956	43.8	29.2	66.8	11.5	55.4	26.4	23.4	25.3	59.4	49.2	7.7	6.8
1957	45.1	29.7	65.8	12.3	57.1	27.2	24.1	26.1	59.3	50.1	8.1	7.2
1958	46.4	29.2	62.9	12.8	58.0	27.6	24.6	26.5	57.1	51.1	8.1	7.2
1959	48.2	31.6	65.5	13.4	60.0	27.7	25.1	26.7	58.8	53.7	8.7	7.9
1960	49.1	32.2	65.6	13.9	61.4	28.4	24.7	27.0	59.1	54.4	9.1	8.0
1961	50.8	32.8	64.6	14.5	63.2	28.5	25.1	27.2	58.5	56.1	9.3	8.2
1962	53.1	34.9	65.8	15.1	65.3	28.4	25.9	27.5	59.3	58.9	9.9	9.1
1963	55.2	36.5	66.2	15.6	66.8	28.3	26.5	27.7	59.6	61.3	10.4	9.7
1964	57.0	38.9	68.1	16.2	68.4	28.5	27.2	28.0	60.7	64.0	11.1	10.6
1965	59.1	41.6	70.4	16.8	69.8	28.5	28.3	28.4	62.4	66.6	11.9	11.8
1966	61.5	44.4	72.3	18.0	72.4	29.2	28.9	29.1	64.3	69.1	13.0	12.8
1967	62.8	45.3	72.1	19.0	74.3	30.2	29.4	29.9	65.2	69.5	13.7	13.3
1968	65.0	47.5	73.2	20.5	77.0	31.6	30.3	31.1	66.5	71.5	15.0	14.4
1969	65.3	49.0	75.0	22.0	78.1	33.6	30.7	32.5	68.5	71.4	16.5	15.0
1970	66.6	49.0	73.5	23.6	79.6	35.5	31.3	33.9	68.3	71.6	17.4	15.3
1971	69.3	50.8	73.3	25.1	81.0	36.2	33.9	35.4	68.5	74.2	18.4	17.2
1972	71.6	54.1	75.6	26.7	83.5	37.3	35.4	36.6	70.5	76.8	20.2	19.2
1973	73.7	57.9	78.5	29.0	85.2	39.3	37.3	38.5	73.5	78.8	22.7	21.6
1974	72.5	57.0	78.7	31.8	84.1	43.8	39.7	42.3	74.6	76.4	25.0	22.7
1975	75.1	56.5	75.3	35.0	85.0	46.6	46.0	46.4	72.4	78.0	26.3	26.0
1976	77.5	60.2	77.8	38.0	87.3	49.1	48.4	48.8	74.6	80.7	29.6	29.2
1977	78.8	63.6	80.7	41.1	88.5	52.1	51.2	51.8	77.9	81.7	33.1	32.6
1978	79.6	67.6	84.9	44.6	89.9	56.0	54.5	55.4	82.2	82.3	37.9	36.8
1979	79.6	69.8	87.7	48.9	89.9	61.4	58.0	60.1	85.4	81.8	42.9	40.5
1980	79.4	69.1	87.0	54.1	89.5	68.1	61.2	65.6	85.6	80.7	47.0	42.3
1981	81.1	71.0	87.6	59.2	89.5	73.1	69.1	71.6	86.4	82.1	51.9	49.1
1982	80.4	68.8	85.6	63.5	90.5	79.0	70.1	75.7	85.0	81.0	54.3	48.2
1983	83.3	72.5	87.1	66.1	90.3	79.4	76.4	78.3	85.8	84.6	57.6	55.4
1984	85.5	78.8	92.2	68.9	90.5	80.6	80.4	80.5	90.1	87.5	63.5	63.4
1985	87.5	82.5	94.3	72.1	91.6	82.5	82.4	82.4	92.3	89.3	68.0	67.9
1986	90.0	85.6	95.1	75.8	94.5	84.3	82.9	83.8	93.9	91.2	72.1	71.0
1987	90.3	88.4	97.9	78.6	94.8	87.1	83.7	85.8	96.4	91.7	76.9	73.9
1988	91.6	92.2	100.6	82.7	96.2	90.3	85.6	88.5	99.3	92.8	83.2	78.9
1989	92.6	95.6	103.3	84.9	94.7	91.7	91.9	91.8	101.5	94.2	87.7	87.8
1990	94.5	97.1	102.7	90.3	96.0	95.6	94.1	95.0	102.2	95.0	92.7	91.4
1991	96.0	96.2	100.2	95.0	97.4	98.9	96.7	98.1	100.6	95.7	95.2	93.1
1992	100.0	100.0	100.0	100.0	100.0	100.0	100.0	100.0	100.0	100.0	100.0	100.0
1993	100.5	103.2	102.7	102.2	99.8	101.7	102.4	102.0	102.1	101.1	105.0	105.7
1994	101.4	108.3	106.8	103.8	99.2	102.3	106.1	103.7	105.6	102.6	110.8	114.9
1995	101.5	111.3	109.7	105.9	98.8	104.4	107.6	105.6	108.5	102.6	116.2	119.8
1996	104.4	116.4	111.5	109.5	99.5	104.9	111.3	107.3	110.9	105.0	122.1	129.6
1997	106.3	122.4	115.2	113.1	100.6	106.4	113.3	109.0	113.9	107.5	130.3	138.7
1998	109.4	128.6	117.5	120.0	105.3	109.6	109.8	109.7	116.2	110.6	140.9	141.2
1999	113.3	135.7	119.8	125.4	107.8	110.7	110.5	110.6	118.1	114.9	150.2	149.9
2000	117.2	141.9	121.0	134.6	111.9	114.8	108.9	112.6	120.1	118.1	162.9	154.5
2001	120.7	143.0	118.4	140.9	114.0	116.7	111.0	114.6	119.2	120.0	166.9	158.7
2002	126.2	145.8	115.6	145.3	115.6	115.1	116.1	115.5	116.5	125.1	167.9	169.3
2003	131.0	150.3	114.7	152.3	118.6	116.2	118.7	117.1	116.2	129.4	174.7	178.4
2004	134.9	156.5	116.1	157.6	119.5	116.9	125.8	120.2	117.7	133.1	182.9	196.9
2005	137.1	161.8	118.0	163.8	120.2	119.5	131.9	124.1	119.7	135.2	193.3	213.4
2006	138.5	166.8	120.4	170.1	120.8	122.8	135.9	127.7	121.9	136.8	204.8	226.6
2007	141.0	170.5	120.9	177.3	122.4	125.7	140.0	131.0	122.7	138.9	214.4	238.6
2008	143.6	170.5	118.7	182.1	121.1	126.8	143.6	133.0	121.1	140.7	216.1	244.8

Table 5-1. Indexes of Productivity and Related Data, 1947–2008—*Continued*

(1992 = 100.)

Year	Nonfarm business											
	Output per hour	Output	Hours	Hourly compen-sation	Real hourly compen-sation	Unit labor costs	Unit nonlabor payments	Implicit price deflator	Employment	Output per person	Compen-sation in current dollars	Nonlabor payments in current dollars
1947	37.0	20.1	54.2	7.5	43.8	20.2	17.8	19.3	47.1	42.6	4.1	3.6
1948	38.1	21.0	55.1	8.1	44.0	21.3	19.4	20.6	48.1	43.5	4.5	4.1
1949	39.3	20.8	53.0	8.4	45.9	21.3	19.9	20.8	46.8	44.5	4.4	4.2
1950	42.0	22.9	54.7	8.9	48.0	21.1	20.8	21.0	47.9	47.9	4.8	4.8
1951	43.1	24.7	57.2	9.6	48.3	22.3	22.4	22.4	50.0	49.3	5.5	5.5
1952	43.9	25.4	57.9	10.2	50.0	23.2	22.3	22.8	50.7	50.1	5.9	5.6
1953	44.9	26.6	59.3	10.7	52.4	23.9	22.2	23.3	52.2	51.0	6.4	5.9
1954	45.7	26.2	57.3	11.1	53.7	24.2	22.2	23.5	50.8	51.6	6.3	5.8
1955	47.7	28.4	59.6	11.5	55.9	24.1	23.6	23.9	52.3	54.3	6.8	6.7
1956	47.3	28.9	61.1	12.2	58.4	25.7	23.0	24.7	53.8	53.7	7.4	6.7
1957	48.5	29.5	60.7	12.9	59.8	26.5	23.8	25.5	54.1	54.5	7.8	7.0
1958	49.6	28.9	58.2	13.4	60.5	27.0	24.0	25.9	52.2	55.3	7.8	6.9
1959	51.5	31.4	60.9	13.9	62.4	27.0	24.9	26.2	54.1	58.0	8.5	7.8
1960	52.1	31.9	61.2	14.5	64.0	27.8	24.2	26.5	54.6	58.4	8.9	7.7
1961	53.7	32.5	60.6	15.0	65.5	27.9	24.7	26.7	54.2	60.0	9.1	8.0
1962	56.2	34.8	61.9	15.6	67.4	27.7	25.7	27.0	55.2	63.0	9.6	8.9
1963	58.1	36.4	62.6	16.1	68.8	27.7	26.2	27.2	55.9	65.2	10.1	9.5
1964	59.8	38.8	64.9	16.6	70.0	27.8	27.1	27.5	57.2	67.9	10.8	10.5
1965	61.7	41.6	67.4	17.2	71.2	27.8	28.0	27.9	59.2	70.2	11.6	11.6
1966	63.9	44.6	69.8	18.2	73.3	28.5	28.6	28.5	61.6	72.4	12.7	12.7
1967	65.0	45.3	69.7	19.3	75.3	29.6	29.1	29.4	62.6	72.4	13.4	13.2
1968	67.2	47.7	71.0	20.8	77.9	30.9	30.1	30.6	64.1	74.5	14.7	14.4
1969	67.3	49.2	73.0	22.2	78.9	32.9	30.3	32.0	66.4	74.1	16.2	14.9
1970	68.3	49.1	71.9	23.8	80.0	34.8	31.0	33.4	66.4	73.9	17.1	15.2
1971	71.1	51.0	71.7	25.3	81.5	35.6	33.5	34.8	66.6	76.5	18.1	17.1
1972	73.4	54.4	74.0	26.9	84.1	36.7	34.7	35.9	68.6	79.2	19.9	18.8
1973	75.7	58.3	77.0	29.1	85.6	38.4	35.1	37.2	71.7	81.4	22.4	20.5
1974	74.5	57.5	77.2	31.9	84.6	42.9	37.9	41.0	72.8	78.9	24.6	21.8
1975	76.6	56.6	73.9	35.2	85.4	45.9	44.6	45.4	70.7	80.0	26.0	25.2
1976	79.1	60.5	76.5	38.1	87.5	48.2	47.5	47.9	73.2	82.7	29.2	28.7
1977	80.4	63.9	79.5	41.2	88.9	51.3	50.4	51.0	76.5	83.5	32.8	32.2
1978	81.4	68.1	83.7	44.9	90.4	55.1	53.1	54.4	80.7	84.3	37.5	36.2
1979	81.1	70.2	86.6	49.1	90.2	60.5	56.3	59.0	84.2	83.5	42.5	39.6
1980	80.9	69.5	85.9	54.3	89.9	67.2	60.4	64.7	84.4	82.3	46.7	42.0
1981	82.0	71.0	86.6	59.6	90.0	72.7	67.8	70.9	85.4	83.1	51.6	48.1
1982	81.1	68.7	84.7	63.8	90.9	78.7	69.4	75.3	84.0	81.8	54.0	47.6
1983	84.7	73.1	86.3	66.5	90.9	78.5	76.2	77.7	84.9	86.1	57.4	55.7
1984	86.4	79.1	91.6	69.2	90.9	80.1	79.5	79.9	89.4	88.5	63.4	62.9
1985	87.8	82.5	94.0	72.3	91.8	82.3	81.9	82.2	92.0	89.7	67.9	67.6
1986	90.5	85.7	94.7	76.1	94.9	84.1	82.7	83.6	93.6	91.6	72.1	70.9
1987	90.8	88.6	97.6	78.8	95.1	86.8	83.4	85.6	96.2	92.1	76.9	73.9
1988	92.3	92.6	100.4	82.8	96.3	89.7	85.5	88.2	99.3	93.3	83.1	79.2
1989	93.0	95.9	103.1	84.9	94.7	91.3	91.5	91.4	101.5	94.5	87.6	87.7
1990	94.7	97.3	102.7	90.2	95.8	95.2	93.9	94.7	102.2	95.1	92.6	91.4
1991	96.2	96.4	100.2	94.9	97.3	98.7	96.9	98.1	100.5	95.9	95.1	93.4
1992	100.0	100.0	100.0	100.0	100.0	100.0	100.0	100.0	100.0	100.0	100.0	100.0
1993	100.6	103.5	102.9	102.0	99.6	101.4	102.9	102.0	102.4	101.1	105.0	106.5
1994	101.6	108.3	106.6	103.8	99.2	102.2	106.6	103.8	105.7	102.5	110.7	115.5
1995	102.0	111.8	109.6	106.0	98.9	103.9	108.7	105.7	108.7	102.8	116.2	121.5
1996	104.6	116.7	111.5	109.5	99.5	104.6	111.4	107.1	111.2	104.9	122.1	130.0
1997	106.2	122.6	115.4	112.9	100.4	106.3	114.0	109.1	114.4	107.2	130.3	139.8
1998	109.4	128.9	117.9	119.7	105.0	109.4	110.9	110.0	116.9	110.3	141.1	143.0
1999	113.0	136.1	120.5	124.8	107.3	110.5	112.0	111.0	119.0	114.4	150.4	152.5
2000	116.8	142.2	121.7	134.1	111.5	114.8	110.5	113.2	121.1	117.4	163.2	157.0
2001	120.2	143.4	119.3	140.1	113.3	116.5	112.6	115.1	120.3	119.2	167.1	161.5
2002	125.7	146.2	116.3	144.5	115.0	115.0	118.1	116.1	117.6	124.3	168.0	172.6
2003	130.3	150.6	115.5	151.4	117.9	116.2	120.1	117.6	117.4	128.3	174.9	180.8
2004	134.0	156.8	117.0	156.6	118.7	116.8	126.7	120.4	118.9	131.9	183.1	198.6
2005	136.2	162.0	118.9	162.8	119.4	119.5	133.6	124.7	121.0	133.9	193.6	216.5
2006	137.5	167.1	121.5	169.0	120.0	122.9	138.0	128.5	123.2	135.6	205.3	230.6
2007	140.1	171.0	122.1	176.0	121.6	125.7	141.4	131.5	124.2	137.7	214.9	241.7
2008	142.6	170.7	119.7	181.0	120.4	126.9	144.8	133.5	122.5	139.4	216.6	247.2

Table 5-1. Indexes of Productivity and Related Data, 1947–2008—*Continued*

(1992 = 100.)

Year	Nonfinancial corporations												
	Output per hour	Output	Hours	Hourly compensation	Real hourly compensation	Unit labor costs	Unit nonlabor costs	Unit profits	Implicit price deflator	Employment	Output per person	Compensation in current dollars	Nonlabor payments in current dollars
1947	. . .	. . .	. . .	. . .	. . .	. . .	. . .	. . .	. . .	. . .	. . .	. . .	. . .
1948	. . .	. . .	. . .	. . .	. . .	. . .	. . .	. . .	. . .	. . .	. . .	. . .	. . .
1949	. . .	. . .	. . .	. . .	. . .	. . .	. . .	. . .	. . .	. . .	. . .	. . .	. . .
1950	. . .	. . .	. . .	. . .	. . .	. . .	. . .	. . .	. . .	. . .	. . .	. . .	. . .
1951	. . .	. . .	. . .	. . .	. . .	. . .	. . .	. . .	. . .	. . .	. . .	. . .	. . .
1952	. . .	. . .	. . .	. . .	. . .	. . .	. . .	. . .	. . .	. . .	. . .	. . .	. . .
1953	. . .	. . .	. . .	. . .	. . .	. . .	. . .	. . .	. . .	. . .	. . .	. . .	. . .
1954	. . .	. . .	. . .	. . .	. . .	. . .	. . .	. . .	. . .	. . .	. . .	. . .	. . .
1955	. . .	. . .	. . .	. . .	. . .	. . .	. . .	. . .	. . .	. . .	. . .	. . .	. . .
1956	. . .	. . .	. . .	. . .	. . .	. . .	. . .	. . .	. . .	. . .	. . .	. . .	. . .
1957	. . .	. . .	. . .	. . .	. . .	. . .	. . .	. . .	. . .	. . .	. . .	. . .	. . .
1958	51.6	24.8	48.0	15.0	67.8	29.1	24.5	46.0	29.5	43.6	56.9	7.2	7.5
1959	54.2	27.6	50.9	15.6	69.9	28.7	23.5	53.6	29.7	45.6	60.5	7.9	8.7
1960	55.1	28.5	51.7	16.2	71.5	29.4	24.0	49.4	29.9	46.6	61.2	8.4	8.8
1961	56.9	29.2	51.3	16.7	73.0	29.4	24.4	49.5	30.0	46.3	63.0	8.6	9.1
1962	59.4	31.7	53.3	17.4	75.1	29.2	24.1	53.4	30.2	47.9	66.1	9.3	10.2
1963	61.6	33.6	54.5	17.9	76.4	29.1	23.9	56.5	30.3	48.9	68.7	9.8	11.0
1964	62.6	35.9	57.5	18.2	76.9	29.2	23.9	58.6	30.6	50.7	70.9	10.5	12.0
1965	64.1	38.9	60.7	18.8	77.8	29.3	23.7	63.0	31.0	53.3	73.0	11.4	13.4
1966	65.3	41.7	63.9	19.8	79.9	30.4	23.8	62.7	31.7	56.3	74.0	12.7	14.3
1967	66.3	42.8	64.6	20.9	81.9	31.6	25.3	58.6	32.5	57.9	73.9	13.5	14.7
1968	68.7	45.6	66.4	22.5	84.5	32.8	26.8	58.4	33.7	60.0	76.1	15.0	16.2
1969	68.8	47.5	69.0	24.1	85.6	34.9	29.0	52.9	35.1	62.7	75.7	16.6	16.9
1970	69.3	47.1	67.9	25.7	86.7	37.1	32.6	43.2	36.6	62.8	74.9	17.5	16.7
1971	72.3	49.0	67.8	27.3	88.2	37.8	34.2	48.8	38.0	63.0	77.8	18.6	18.7
1972	73.8	52.8	71.6	28.8	90.0	39.1	34.1	53.0	39.1	66.1	79.8	20.6	20.7
1973	74.5	56.0	75.2	31.0	91.3	41.6	36.0	53.6	41.3	69.8	80.3	23.3	22.8
1974	73.0	55.1	75.5	34.0	90.0	46.5	41.3	47.5	45.3	71.2	77.5	25.6	23.7
1975	75.8	54.3	71.7	37.3	90.6	49.2	47.0	61.5	49.8	68.5	79.4	26.7	27.7
1976	78.4	58.8	75.0	40.3	92.6	51.5	46.7	69.5	52.0	71.5	82.2	30.3	31.1
1977	80.5	63.1	78.4	43.5	93.9	54.1	48.4	75.9	54.7	75.1	84.0	34.2	35.3
1978	81.5	67.3	82.5	47.6	95.9	58.4	50.8	78.7	58.4	79.4	84.7	39.3	39.3
1979	80.8	69.3	85.8	51.9	95.4	64.2	55.4	73.9	62.9	83.3	83.2	44.5	41.9
1980	80.5	68.6	85.2	57.1	94.5	70.9	64.9	66.3	69.0	83.6	82.0	48.6	44.8
1981	82.6	71.3	86.4	62.2	94.0	75.4	73.9	79.0	75.4	85.0	83.9	53.8	53.7
1982	82.8	69.6	84.1	66.3	94.5	80.1	82.0	72.9	79.9	83.1	83.7	55.8	55.3
1983	85.4	72.9	85.3	68.8	94.0	80.5	82.2	88.6	81.7	83.5	87.3	58.7	61.2
1984	87.4	79.3	90.8	71.6	94.0	82.0	81.4	106.4	84.1	88.4	89.7	65.0	70.0
1985	89.2	82.8	92.9	74.8	95.0	83.9	83.6	101.8	85.5	90.9	91.1	69.5	73.3
1986	91.1	84.9	93.2	78.6	97.9	86.2	87.5	87.3	86.6	92.2	92.0	73.2	74.2
1987	93.0	89.3	96.1	81.2	97.9	87.3	86.6	98.3	88.1	94.8	94.2	78.0	80.2
1988	95.4	94.5	99.1	84.6	98.4	88.7	87.7	108.8	90.3	97.9	96.5	83.8	88.3
1989	94.0	96.0	102.2	86.7	96.6	92.2	93.3	99.7	93.2	100.4	95.7	88.5	91.3
1990	95.1	97.5	102.5	90.8	96.5	95.6	97.5	95.9	96.1	102.2	95.4	93.2	94.6
1991	97.4	97.0	99.6	95.4	97.8	97.9	102.6	94.4	98.7	100.0	97.0	95.0	97.4
1992	100.0	100.0	100.0	100.0	100.0	100.0	100.0	100.0	100.0	100.0	100.0	100.0	100.0
1993	100.2	102.6	102.4	101.8	99.3	101.6	99.3	114.4	102.2	102.0	100.6	104.2	106.1
1994	102.3	109.2	106.8	103.6	99.0	101.3	99.6	134.0	103.9	105.7	103.3	110.6	119.0
1995	103.4	114.4	110.6	105.4	98.4	102.0	100.0	139.0	104.9	109.5	104.5	116.7	126.5
1996	107.2	120.7	112.6	108.5	98.6	101.3	99.4	150.4	105.3	112.3	107.5	122.2	136.8
1997	110.0	128.6	116.9	111.9	99.5	101.7	99.4	154.0	105.9	115.8	111.0	130.7	146.8
1998	113.8	136.0	119.5	118.6	104.0	104.2	99.8	135.1	105.9	118.7	114.6	141.7	148.7
1999	117.8	143.9	122.2	123.8	106.4	105.1	102.2	125.2	106.2	121.2	118.8	151.3	156.1
2000	122.4	151.5	123.8	132.9	110.5	108.6	105.8	104.2	107.5	123.6	122.5	164.5	159.7
2001	123.5	148.7	120.4	137.3	111.0	111.2	112.3	84.0	109.0	122.1	121.9	165.3	155.6
2002	127.9	149.4	116.8	140.9	112.2	110.2	112.9	96.6	109.6	118.6	126.0	164.6	162.1
2003	133.0	153.1	115.1	147.3	114.7	110.8	112.7	107.3	110.9	117.4	130.3	169.6	170.2
2004	137.5	160.3	116.6	150.9	114.4	109.7	111.3	142.7	113.1	118.9	134.9	175.9	192.1
2005	141.0	167.3	118.6	155.7	114.2	110.4	115.4	161.1	116.3	121.2	138.0	184.7	213.8
2006	143.0	173.5	121.3	160.2	113.8	112.0	118.9	179.9	119.9	123.5	140.5	194.3	235.1
2007	144.5	176.5	122.1	166.0	114.6	114.9	125.8	162.1	121.9	124.7	141.5	202.7	239.5
2008	147.2	177.2	120.3	170.9	113.7	116.1	130.5	135.7	121.4	123.3	143.7	205.7	233.7

. . . = Not available.

Table 5-1. Indexes of Productivity and Related Data, 1947–2008—*Continued*

(1992 = 100.)

Year	Manufacturing											
	Output per hour	Output	Hours	Hourly compensation	Real hourly compensation	Unit labor costs	Unit nonlabor payments	Implicit price deflator	Employment	Output per person	Compensation in current dollars	Nonlabor payments in current dollars
1947	. . .	. . .	. . .	. . .	. . .	. . .	. . .	. . .	. . .	. . .	. . .	. . .
1948	. . .	. . .	. . .	. . .	. . .	. . .	. . .	. . .	. . .	. . .	. . .	. . .
1949	. . .	. . .	. . .	. . .	. . .	. . .	. . .	. . .	. . .	. . .	. . .	. . .
1950	. . .	. . .	. . .	. . .	. . .	. . .	. . .	. . .	. . .	. . .	. . .	. . .
1951	. . .	. . .	. . .	. . .	. . .	. . .	. . .	. . .	. . .	. . .	. . .	. . .
1952	. . .	. . .	. . .	. . .	. . .	. . .	. . .	. . .	. . .	. . .	. . .	. . .
1953	. . .	. . .	. . .	. . .	. . .	. . .	. . .	. . .	. . .	. . .	. . .	. . .
1954	. . .	. . .	. . .	. . .	. . .	. . .	. . .	. . .	. . .	. . .	. . .	. . .
1955	. . .	. . .	. . .	. . .	. . .	. . .	. . .	. . .	. . .	. . .	. . .	. . .
1956	. . .	. . .	. . .	. . .	. . .	. . .	. . .	. . .	. . .	. . .	. . .	. . .
1957	. . .	. . .	. . .	. . .	. . .	. . .	. . .	. . .	. . .	. . .	. . .	. . .
1958	. . .	. . .	. . .	. . .	. . .	. . .	. . .	. . .	. . .	. . .	. . .	. . .
1959	. . .	. . .	. . .	. . .	. . .	. . .	. . .	. . .	. . .	. . .	. . .	. . .
1960	. . .	. . .	. . .	. . .	. . .	. . .	. . .	. . .	. . .	. . .	. . .	. . .
1961	. . .	. . .	. . .	. . .	. . .	. . .	. . .	. . .	. . .	. . .	. . .	. . .
1962	. . .	. . .	. . .	. . .	. . .	. . .	. . .	. . .	. . .	. . .	. . .	. . .
1963	. . .	. . .	. . .	. . .	. . .	. . .	. . .	. . .	. . .	. . .	. . .	. . .
1964	. . .	. . .	. . .	. . .	. . .	. . .	. . .	. . .	. . .	. . .	. . .	. . .
1965	. . .	. . .	. . .	. . .	. . .	. . .	. . .	. . .	. . .	. . .	. . .	. . .
1966	. . .	. . .	. . .	. . .	. . .	. . .	. . .	. . .	. . .	. . .	. . .	. . .
1967	. . .	. . .	. . .	. . .	. . .	. . .	. . .	. . .	. . .	. . .	. . .	. . .
1968	. . .	. . .	. . .	. . .	. . .	. . .	. . .	. . .	. . .	. . .	. . .	. . .
1969	. . .	. . .	. . .	. . .	. . .	. . .	. . .	. . .	. . .	. . .	. . .	. . .
1970	. . .	. . .	. . .	. . .	. . .	. . .	. . .	. . .	. . .	. . .	. . .	. . .
1971	. . .	. . .	. . .	. . .	. . .	. . .	. . .	. . .	. . .	. . .	. . .	. . .
1972	. . .	. . .	. . .	. . .	. . .	. . .	. . .	. . .	. . .	. . .	. . .	. . .
1973	. . .	. . .	. . .	. . .	. . .	. . .	. . .	. . .	. . .	. . .	. . .	. . .
1974	. . .	. . .	. . .	. . .	. . .	. . .	. . .	. . .	. . .	. . .	. . .	. . .
1975	. . .	. . .	. . .	. . .	. . .	. . .	. . .	. . .	. . .	. . .	. . .	. . .
1976	. . .	. . .	. . .	. . .	. . .	. . .	. . .	. . .	. . .	. . .	. . .	. . .
1977	. . .	. . .	. . .	. . .	. . .	. . .	. . .	. . .	. . .	. . .	. . .	. . .
1978	. . .	. . .	. . .	. . .	. . .	. . .	. . .	. . .	. . .	. . .	. . .	. . .
1979	. . .	. . .	. . .	. . .	. . .	. . .	. . .	. . .	. . .	. . .	. . .	. . .
1980	. . .	. . .	. . .	. . .	. . .	. . .	. . .	. . .	. . .	. . .	. . .	. . .
1981	. . .	. . .	. . .	. . .	. . .	. . .	. . .	. . .	. . .	. . .	. . .	. . .
1982	. . .	. . .	. . .	. . .	. . .	. . .	. . .	. . .	. . .	. . .	. . .	. . .
1983	. . .	. . .	. . .	. . .	. . .	. . .	. . .	. . .	. . .	. . .	. . .	. . .
1984	. . .	. . .	. . .	. . .	. . .	. . .	. . .	. . .	. . .	. . .	. . .	. . .
1985	. . .	. . .	. . .	. . .	. . .	. . .	. . .	. . .	. . .	. . .	. . .	. . .
1986	. . .	. . .	. . .	. . .	. . .	. . .	. . .	. . .	. . .	. . .	. . .	. . .
1987	89.1	92.4	103.8	80.6	97.2	90.5	87.2	88.3	104.5	88.4	83.6	80.6
1988	90.9	97.2	106.9	83.5	97.1	91.8	90.5	90.9	106.4	91.4	89.2	87.9
1989	91.9	98.8	107.6	86.0	95.9	93.6	95.6	94.9	107.0	92.4	92.5	94.4
1990	93.9	98.5	104.9	90.1	95.7	96.0	99.2	98.2	105.4	93.4	94.6	97.7
1991	96.3	96.8	100.5	95.5	97.9	99.1	98.6	98.8	101.7	95.2	96.0	95.4
1992	100.0	100.0	100.0	100.0	100.0	100.0	100.0	100.0	100.0	100.0	100.0	100.0
1993	102.6	103.9	101.3	102.3	99.8	99.7	101.0	100.6	100.1	103.8	103.6	105.0
1994	106.2	110.1	103.7	104.8	100.1	98.7	102.8	101.4	101.4	108.6	108.7	113.1
1995	111.0	115.9	104.4	106.5	99.3	95.9	106.6	103.1	102.8	112.7	111.2	123.5
1996	115.0	119.8	104.2	108.3	98.4	94.1	108.5	103.8	102.7	116.7	112.8	130.0
1997	121.3	128.7	106.0	110.9	98.7	91.4	108.1	102.7	103.6	124.2	117.6	139.1
1998	127.9	135.3	105.8	117.8	103.4	92.1	103.0	99.4	104.5	129.5	124.6	139.4
1999	133.7	140.4	105.1	123.0	105.7	92.0	103.1	99.5	102.9	136.5	129.2	144.8
2000	139.1	144.2	103.7	132.5	110.2	95.3	104.3	101.4	102.6	140.6	137.4	150.4
2001	141.2	136.9	96.9	137.5	111.2	97.4	102.1	100.6	97.8	140.0	133.3	139.8
2002	151.0	136.0	90.1	145.1	115.5	96.1	101.2	99.5	90.8	149.9	130.7	137.6
2003	160.4	137.3	85.6	156.7	122.0	97.7	103.3	101.5	86.5	158.8	134.2	141.9
2004	164.0	139.7	85.2	157.9	119.7	96.3	111.3	106.4	85.3	163.8	134.6	155.5
2005	171.9	144.8	84.3	163.2	119.7	94.9	122.5	113.5	84.9	170.7	137.5	177.5
2006	173.7	147.5	84.9	166.4	118.2	95.8	128.0	117.4	84.4	174.8	141.3	188.8
2007	179.2	149.5	83.4	173.6	119.9	96.9	. . .	. . .	82.9	180.3	144.8	. . .
2008	180.7	144.9	80.2	178.7	118.9	98.9	. . .	. . .	80.1	180.9	143.3	. . .

. . . = Not available.

Table 5-2. Average Annual Percent Change in Output Per Hour and Related Series, Selected Industries, 1987–2007 and 2006–2007

(Number, percent.)

Industry	NAICS code	2007 employment (thousands)	Average annual percent change, 1987–2007			Annual percent change, 2006–2007		
			Output per hour	Output	Hours	Output per hour	Output	Hours
Mining								
Mining	21	664	-0.2	-0.3	-0.1	-6.4	0.0	6.9
Oil and gas extraction	211	146	1.0	-0.9	-1.8	-3.3	1.3	4.8
Mining, except oil and gas	212	223	2.1	0.9	-1.2	-5.3	-3.8	1.6
Coal mining	2121	77	2.8	0.0	-2.8	1.2	-2.6	-3.7
Metal ore mining	2122	36	1.9	1.9	0.0	-15.4	0.6	18.8
Nonmetallic mineral mining and quarrying	2123	110	1.1	1.1	0.0	-8.5	-7.7	0.8
Support activities for mining	213	294	3.5	5.9	2.3	6.7	19.7	12.2
Utilities								
Power generation and supply	2211	398	2.8	1.2	-1.5	-1.8	1.0	2.9
Natural gas distribution	2212	107	2.9	1.3	-1.5	0.5	6.5	6.0
Transportation and Warehousing								
Air transportation	481	433	3.2	3.4	0.3	1.8	3.1	1.3
Line-haul railroads	482111	186	4.3	2.3	-2.0	-4.5	-4.4	0.1
General freight trucking, long-distance	48412	920	1.5	3.2	1.7	1.8	0.5	-1.3
Used household and office goods moving	48421	102	-0.7	0.3	1.0	4.9	-4.1	-8.5
Postal service	491	762	1.1	1.0	0.0	0.7	-1.3	-1.9
Couriers and messengers	492	614	-0.6	2.5	3.1	-5.6	-3.6	2.1
Warehousing and storage	493	670	2.8	6.2	3.3	-3.3	1.4	4.9
General warehousing and storage	49311	566	4.8	8.2	3.2	-4.5	1.0	5.8
Refrigerated warehousing and storage	49312	49	-0.6	3.0	3.6	5.9	3.8	-2.0
Information								
Publishing	511	936	4.3	4.9	0.5	4.0	4.0	0.0
Newspaper, book, and directory publishers	5111	679	0.4	-0.4	-0.8	1.7	-0.7	-2.3
Software publishers	5112	257	15.6	23.5	6.9	3.3	9.4	5.9
Motion picture and video exhibition	51213	137	1.0	1.7	0.7	3.1	-2.5	-5.5
Broadcasting, except internet	515	337	1.5	2.7	1.3	7.9	5.7	-2.1
Radio and television broadcasting	5151	246	0.6	0.8	0.2	3.7	2.1	-1.5
Cable and other subscription programming	5152	91	3.0	8.2	5.0	14.5	10.8	-3.2
Wired telecommunications carriers	5171	489	4.7	2.9	-1.7	-0.1	-1.5	-1.4
Wireless telecommunications carriers	5172	207	9.4	23.3	12.7	5.8	10.9	4.9
Cable and other program distribution	5175	142	0.8	6.0	5.1	11.9	9.5	-2.1
Finance and Insurance								
Commercial banking	52211	1 351	2.6	2.6	0.0	0.9	3.9	3.0
Real Estate and Rental and Leasing								
Passenger car rental	532111	130	1.7	3.3	1.6	16.8	1.1	-13.4
Truck, trailer and RV rental and leasing	53212	58	5.4	4.6	-0.7	2.9	-1.7	-4.4
Video tape and disc rental	53223	123	5.5	5.9	0.4	26.5	1.3	-19.9
Professional and Technical Services								
Tax preparation services	541213	150	1.8	4.3	2.5	13.7	6.6	-6.2
Architectural services	54131	241	1.6	4.3	2.6	4.7	11.1	6.1
Engineering services	54133	961	1.0	3.3	2.3	-2.7	2.4	5.2
Advertising agencies	54181	199	1.9	2.4	0.5	3.7	8.5	4.6
Photography studios, portrait	541921	79	0.3	2.7	2.4	5.8	3.8	-1.9
Administrative and Waste Services								
Employment placement agencies	56131	294	3.2	5.5	2.3	7.2	4.7	-2.4
Travel agencies	56151	119	3.9	2.9	-1.0	3.9	1.3	-2.5
Janitorial services	56172	1 228	2.5	4.6	2.1	5.4	8.1	2.6
Healthcare and Social Assistance								
Medical and diagnostic laboratories	6215	223	3.1	6.6	3.4	-2.6	1.1	3.8
Medical laboratories	621511	148	2.7	5.6	2.8	2.1	2.4	0.3
Diagnostic imaging centers	621512	75	3.4	8.4	4.8	-11.4	-0.7	12.0
Arts, Entertainment, and Recreation								
Amusement and theme parks	71311	135	-0.4	2.7	3.1	5.6	4.5	-1.0
Bowling centers	71395	78	0.7	-0.9	-1.7	19.7	9.2	-8.7
Accommodation and Food Services								
Accommodation and food services	72	11 766	0.7	2.4	1.6	-0.7	0.9	1.6
Accommodation	721	1 907	1.2	2.5	1.3	-1.6	-0.1	1.5
Traveler accommodation	7211	1 829	1.3	2.6	1.3	-1.8	-0.2	1.6
Food services and drinking places	722	9 859	0.6	2.4	1.7	-0.4	1.3	1.7
Full-service restaurants	7221	4 618	0.6	2.4	1.8	-1.4	0.8	2.2
Limited-service eating places	7222	4 167	0.6	2.5	1.9	0.0	1.5	1.5
Special food services	7223	703	1.5	2.6	1.1	2.1	3.1	1.0
Drinking places (alcoholic beverages)	7224	372	0.0	-0.1	-0.1	2.5	0.8	-1.7
Other Services								
Automotive repair and maintenance	8111	1 170	1.3	2.2	0.9	-0.9	-0.8	0.1
Reupholstery and furniture repair	81142	26	0.0	-1.8	-1.8	5.7	-6.2	-11.3
Hair, nail and skin care services	81211	923	2.4	3.4	0.9	3.7	1.9	-1.7
Funeral homes and funeral services	81221	105	-0.3	-0.2	0.2	-2.4	-6.3	-4.0
Drycleaning and laundry services	8123	376	0.8	0.5	-0.3	-4.3	-1.4	3.1
Photofinishing	81292	26	0.7	-4.6	-5.3	-1.0	-0.1	0.9

Table 5-2. Average Annual Percent Change in Output Per Hour and Related Series, Selected Industries, 1987–2007 and 2006–2007—*Continued*

(Number, percent.)

Industry	NAICS code	2007 employment (thousands)	Average annual percent change, 1987–2007			Annual percent change, 2006–2007		
			Output per hour	Output	Hours	Output per hour	Output	Hours
Manufacturing								
Food	311	1 515	1.1	1.5	0.3	-2.6	-0.6	2.1
Animal food	3111	50	3.2	2.1	-1.0	1.0	-2.8	-3.8
Grain and oilseed milling	3112	61	2.3	1.2	-1.1	1.7	3.3	1.6
Sugar and confectionery products	3113	75	1.3	0.3	-0.9	-8.9	-6.6	2.5
Fruit and vegetable preserving and specialty	3114	174	1.8	1.5	-0.3	6.6	3.7	-2.7
Dairy products	3115	136	1.3	0.9	-0.3	-1.2	1.1	2.4
Animal slaughtering and processing	3116	514	0.8	2.3	1.5	-3.3	-0.9	2.5
Seafood product preparation and packaging	3117	43	2.1	1.3	-0.8	-10.5	-1.0	10.7
Bakeries and tortilla manufacturing	3118	293	0.9	0.5	-0.3	-2.4	-1.8	0.6
Other food products	3119	168	0.4	2.1	1.7	-7.8	-0.1	8.3
Beverages and tobacco products	312	201	0.7	0.0	-0.7	-3.1	-1.5	1.6
Beverages	3121	178	1.9	1.8	-0.1	0.1	3.3	3.2
Tobacco and tobacco products	3122	22	1.2	-2.7	-3.9	-0.6	-11.1	-10.6
Textile mills	313	179	3.7	-1.9	-5.5	1.5	-10.1	-11.4
Fiber, yarn, and thread mills	3131	42	4.3	-0.8	-4.9	9.7	-5.1	-13.5
Fabric mills	3132	82	4.7	-2.1	-6.5	0.6	-12.6	-13.1
Textile and fabric finishing mills	3133	55	1.3	-2.7	-3.9	-3.8	-10.7	-7.1
Textile product mills	314	176	0.9	-0.8	-1.7	-11.2	-17.8	-7.5
Textile furnishings mills	3141	91	0.7	-1.0	-1.7	-7.3	-18.8	-12.5
Other textile product mills	3149	85	1.4	-0.2	-1.6	-14.6	-15.8	-1.4
Apparel	315	245	-0.9	-7.5	-6.6	-29.7	-31.4	-2.4
Apparel knitting mills	3151	35	-0.4	-6.3	-5.9	-32.8	-35.2	-3.5
Cut and sew apparel	3152	191	-0.9	-7.8	-6.9	-29.4	-30.8	-2.0
Accessories and other apparel	3159	19	-2.9	-6.7	-3.9	-25.7	-28.7	-4.0
Leather and allied products	316	39	2.1	-4.3	-6.3	-5.5	-11.5	-6.3
Leather and hide tanning and finishing	3161	5	0.9	-4.3	-5.2	30.3	12.8	-13.4
Footwear	3162	17	1.3	-6.5	-7.7	-19.8	-18.0	2.2
Other leather products	3169	17	2.1	-2.4	-4.4	-2.5	-14.4	-12.2
Wood products	321	548	1.5	0.8	-0.7	0.3	-7.1	-7.3
Sawmills and wood preservation	3211	118	2.4	0.6	-1.7	-5.0	-10.3	-5.6
Plywood and engineered wood products	3212	109	1.0	0.9	0.0	3.7	-9.3	-12.5
Other wood products	3219	321	1.3	0.9	-0.4	1.9	-4.4	-6.1
Paper and paper products	322	459	2.1	0.4	-1.6	3.6	1.0	-2.6
Pulp, paper, and paperboard mills	3221	132	3.1	0.0	-3.0	2.9	-2.0	-4.8
Converted paper products	3222	326	1.6	0.7	-0.9	4.6	2.9	-1.6
Printing and related support activities	323	658	1.4	0.4	-1.0	3.1	1.0	-2.1
Petroleum and coal products	3241	115	2.8	1.2	-1.6	1.4	0.0	-1.4
Chemicals	325	869	2.2	1.6	-0.6	6.9	5.1	-1.7
Basic chemicals	3251	149	3.6	1.2	-2.4	15.5	13.7	-1.5
Resin, rubber, and artificial fibers	3252	109	2.8	1.3	-1.5	3.0	5.8	2.7
Agricultural chemicals	3253	36	2.9	1.0	-1.8	6.0	-3.9	-9.3
Pharmaceuticals and medicines	3254	296	0.8	3.4	2.6	-2.3	-0.9	1.5
Paints, coatings, and adhesives	3255	66	1.2	0.1	-1.2	-2.1	-4.0	-1.9
Soaps, cleaning compounds, and toiletries	3256	112	3.5	2.9	-0.6	20.7	13.5	-6.0
Other chemical products and preparations	3259	101	2.7	0.5	-2.1	15.5	6.8	-7.5
Plastics and rubber products	326	762	2.4	2.3	-0.1	-0.5	-2.0	-1.5
Plastics products	3261	612	2.3	2.6	0.3	-1.6	-2.7	-1.2
Rubber products	3262	150	2.6	1.1	-1.5	4.6	1.7	-2.8
Nonmetallic mineral products	327	515	1.4	1.3	-0.1	0.7	-1.7	-2.4
Clay products and refractories	3271	63	1.2	-0.9	-2.1	-5.7	-10.6	-5.2
Glass and glass products	3272	102	2.3	0.7	-1.6	-0.6	-4.4	-3.8
Cement and concrete products	3273	246	0.8	2.0	1.3	3.7	-0.4	-4.0
Lime and gypsum products	3274	19	1.2	0.5	-0.8	-4.6	-4.4	0.1
Other nonmetallic mineral products	3279	85	1.6	1.8	0.2	-2.7	3.2	6.1
Primary metals	331	458	3.1	1.1	-1.9	8.0	3.8	-3.9
Iron and steel mills and ferroalloy production	3311	101	5.2	2.4	-2.7	3.0	4.8	1.7
Steel products from purchased steel	3312	61	-0.9	-1.4	-0.6	-2.1	-4.1	-2.0
Alumina and aluminum production	3313	71	3.0	0.8	-2.2	7.2	0.3	-6.4
Other nonferrous metal production	3314	69	1.2	-1.1	-2.3	21.5	13.0	-7.0
Foundries	3315	156	2.6	0.9	-1.6	1.1	-4.4	-5.5
Fabricated metal products	332	1 598	1.8	1.8	0.1	1.7	3.0	1.3
Forging and stamping	3321	111	3.2	2.2	-0.9	5.7	3.0	-2.6
Cutlery and hand tools	3322	53	1.8	-0.2	-2.0	12.2	2.3	-8.8
Architectural and structural metals	3323	424	1.3	2.2	0.9	-0.4	2.7	3.0
Boilers, tanks, and shipping containers	3324	97	0.9	0.4	-0.5	3.2	6.7	3.4
Hardware	3325	34	0.9	-2.0	-2.9	-14.6	-14.2	0.4
Spring and wire products	3326	57	2.6	1.0	-1.5	-1.9	-3.8	-2.0
Machine shops and threaded products	3327	376	2.4	3.5	1.1	2.4	3.6	1.2
Coating, engraving, and heat treating metals	3328	149	3.1	3.6	0.4	2.6	4.7	2.1
Other fabricated metal products	3329	297	1.4	0.8	-0.5	0.6	2.5	1.9
Machinery	333	1 204	2.7	2.0	-0.7	0.2	1.2	1.0
Agriculture, construction, and mining machinery	3331	232	2.8	3.4	0.6	-3.3	5.2	8.8
Industrial machinery	3332	128	3.2	2.5	-0.7	2.3	3.3	1.0

Table 5-2. Average Annual Percent Change in Output Per Hour and Related Series, Selected Industries, 1987–2007 and 2006–2007—*Continued*

(Number, percent.)

Industry	NAICS code	2007 employment (thousands)	Average annual percent change, 1987–2007			Annual percent change, 2006–2007		
			Output per hour	Output	Hours	Output per hour	Output	Hours
Manufacturing—*Continued*								
Commercial and service industry machinery	3333	110	1.3	-0.2	-1.5	-10.0	-6.5	3.9
HVAC and commercial refrigeration equipment	3334	155	2.2	1.9	-0.3	-3.7	-5.7	-2.0
Metalworking machinery	3335	200	2.2	0.6	-1.6	5.0	-0.7	-5.5
Turbine and power transmission equipment	3336	102	2.3	1.9	-0.3	-0.3	-1.6	-1.3
Other general purpose machinery	3339	278	2.9	2.1	-0.8	2.2	3.0	0.7
Computer and electronic products	334	1 280	12.5	9.9	-2.3	8.0	4.7	-3.0
Computer and peripheral equipment	3341	187	24.3	19.2	-4.1	22.3	18.4	-3.1
Communications equipment	3342	129	7.8	4.6	-3.0	-4.6	-14.3	-10.1
Audio and video equipment	3343	30	4.8	1.2	-3.4	-27.3	-30.2	-3.9
Semiconductors and electronic components	3344	450	17.4	15.8	-1.4	15.6	11.0	-4.0
Electronic instruments	3345	445	4.3	2.2	-2.0	7.3	8.5	1.1
Magnetic media manufacturing and reproduction	3346	39	2.6	1.7	-0.9	2.7	-7.8	-10.2
Electrical equipment and appliances	335	432	2.9	0.7	-2.2	2.6	2.3	-0.3
Electric lighting equipment	3351	59	2.1	0.5	-1.6	0.9	3.3	2.4
Household appliances	3352	77	4.4	1.5	-2.7	-2.9	-2.1	0.8
Electrical equipment	3353	158	3.2	0.7	-2.4	5.5	6.2	0.7
Other electrical equipment and components	3359	139	2.2	0.3	-1.8	4.3	1.1	-3.1
Transportation equipment	336	1 726	3.2	2.1	-1.0	6.4	3.3	-2.9
Motor vehicles	3361	221	4.2	2.5	-1.6	4.8	-0.7	-5.2
Motor vehicle bodies and trailers	3362	168	1.6	2.5	0.9	6.9	-5.0	-11.2
Motor vehicle parts	3363	613	3.1	2.9	-0.2	3.2	-3.1	-6.1
Aerospace products and parts	3364	492	2.0	-0.4	-2.4	12.0	16.8	4.3
Railroad rolling stock	3365	28	4.7	5.3	0.7	-0.8	-0.3	0.5
Ship and boat building	3366	163	1.5	1.1	-0.4	1.8	1.9	0.2
Other transportation equipment	3369	42	5.7	6.1	0.3	21.0	17.0	-3.3
Furniture and related products	337	568	1.7	1.0	-0.7	-2.7	-6.9	-4.3
Household and institutional furniture	3371	380	1.6	0.8	-0.8	-3.6	-9.3	-5.9
Office furniture and fixtures	3372	139	1.7	1.1	-0.6	-2.7	-3.6	-0.9
Other furniture-related products	3379	49	2.2	2.5	0.3	-0.9	-2.0	-1.1
Miscellaneous manufacturing	339	710	2.9	2.9	0.0	-3.3	-4.4	-1.1
Medical equipment and supplies	3391	320	3.5	4.7	1.2	-3.5	-2.1	1.5
Other miscellaneous manufacturing	3399	390	2.3	1.5	-0.8	-3.7	-6.8	-3.3

Table 5-3.   Average Annual Percent Change in Output Per Hour and Related Series, Wholesale Trade, Retail Trade, Food Service, and Drinking Places, 1987–2008 and 2007–2008

(Number, percent.)

Industry	NAICS code	2008 employment (thousands)	Average annual percent change, 1987–2008			Annual percent change, 2007–2008		
			Output per hour	Output	Hours	Output per hour	Output	Hours
Wholesale Trade								
Wholesale trade	42	6 166	3.0	3.7	0.7	-0.3	-0.8	-0.5
Durable goods	423	3 171	4.9	5.4	0.5	0.4	-1.1	-1.5
Motor vehicles and parts	4231	351	3.1	2.9	-0.2	-7.7	-10.9	-3.5
Furniture and furnishings	4232	122	1.2	1.7	0.6	-15.9	-10.3	6.8
Lumber and construction supplies	4233	240	0.7	1.9	1.2	-1.1	-10.3	-9.3
Commercial equipment	4234	665	14.9	15.5	0.5	9.2	8.8	-0.3
Metals and minerals	4235	136	-0.9	-0.3	0.6	-8.5	-7.4	1.2
Electric goods	4236	362	8.5	8.5	0.0	2.7	3.4	0.7
Hardware and plumbing	4237	258	0.5	1.6	1.1	-7.3	-9.6	-2.5
Machinery and supplies	4238	697	2.5	2.6	0.2	6.5	4.7	-1.7
Miscellaneous durable goods	4239	340	1.4	2.7	1.3	2.9	2.6	-0.2
Nondurable goods	424	2 141	0.9	1.3	0.4	-0.4	-0.5	-0.1
Paper and paper products	4241	143	2.1	1.5	-0.6	-8.5	-3.1	6.0
Druggists' goods	4242	215	2.1	4.3	2.2	7.0	3.2	-3.6
Apparel and piece goods	4243	157	2.5	2.4	-0.1	4.6	2.2	-2.3
Grocery and related products	4244	766	0.7	1.7	1.0	-3.5	-1.9	1.6
Farm product raw materials	4245	79	1.8	-0.7	-2.5	1.7	3.3	1.5
Chemicals	4246	134	-0.4	0.3	0.7	0.8	-3.3	-4.1
Petroleum	4247	104	2.6	0.3	-2.3	1.7	4.4	2.6
Alcoholic beverages	4248	164	0.2	2.0	1.8	-4.2	0.6	5.0
Miscellaneous nondurable goods	4249	379	-0.2	-0.1	0.1	-6.9	-10.4	-3.8
Electronic markets and agents and brokers	425	854	2.0	4.7	2.6	-2.6	-0.2	2.5
Retail Trade								
Retail trade	44-45	16 328	3.0	3.7	0.6	-1.8	-3.6	-1.8
Motor vehicle and parts dealers	441	1 931	2.0	2.8	0.8	-8.9	-12.5	-3.9
Automobile dealers	4411	1 240	1.8	2.7	0.8	-9.3	-14.2	-5.4
Other motor vehicle dealers	4412	175	3.3	5.3	2.0	1.6	-4.2	-5.7
Auto parts, accessories, and tire stores	4413	516	2.0	2.6	0.5	-3.9	-3.6	0.4
Furniture and home furnishings stores	442	579	3.8	4.3	0.4	0.3	-7.4	-7.6
Furniture stores	4421	281	3.3	3.7	0.4	-1.3	-6.6	-5.4
Home furnishings stores	4422	298	4.6	5.1	0.5	1.9	-8.3	-10.0
Electronics and appliance stores	443	577	13.5	15.0	1.3	15.9	7.8	-7.0
Electronics and appliance stores	4431	577	13.5	15.0	1.3	15.9	7.8	-7.0
Building material and garden supply stores	444	1 305	3.0	4.4	1.3	0.8	-4.2	-4.9
Building material and supplies dealers	4441	1 147	2.7	4.4	1.6	-2.1	-7.1	-5.1
Lawn and garden equipment and supplies store	4442	158	5.2	4.7	-0.5	20.8	16.6	-3.5
Food and beverage stores	445	2 978	0.4	0.3	-0.1	-1.8	-0.6	1.2
Grocery stores	4451	2 558	0.3	0.3	0.0	-1.4	-0.6	0.8
Specialty food stores	4452	257	-0.1	-0.4	-0.3	-8.1	-7.0	1.2
Beer, wine and liquor stores	4453	163	2.2	1.0	-1.2	-4.9	2.9	8.2
Health and personal care stores	446	1 048	2.4	3.8	1.4	0.4	1.9	1.5
Health and personal care stores	4461	1 048	2.4	3.8	1.4	0.4	1.9	1.5
Gasoline stations	447	860	2.0	1.2	-0.7	-0.6	-4.4	-3.8
Clothing and clothing accessories stores	448	1 577	4.9	4.5	-0.3	3.2	-2.4	-5.4
Clothing stores	4481	1 179	5.2	5.2	-0.1	6.9	-0.8	-7.2
Shoe stores	4482	197	3.7	2.6	-1.1	-1.2	-0.6	0.6
Jewelry, luggage, and leather goods stores	4483	201	3.9	3.5	-0.4	-9.1	-11.8	-2.9
Sporting goods, hobby, book, and music stores	451	727	4.1	4.7	0.6	3.2	0.7	-2.4
Sporting goods and musical instrument stores	4511	532	4.7	5.5	0.7	3.4	2.6	-0.8
Book, periodical, and music stores	4512	194	2.6	2.9	0.3	2.6	-4.1	-6.5
General merchandise stores	452	3 070	3.4	5.3	1.8	-0.8	1.8	2.6
Department stores	4521	1 557	0.6	2.1	1.4	-6.7	-4.5	2.4
Other general merchandise stores	4529	1 513	6.9	9.2	2.2	2.4	5.3	2.8
Miscellaneous store retailers	453	1 013	4.5	4.6	0.1	2.2	-1.2	-3.3
Florists	4531	111	3.5	1.0	-2.5	19.0	0.5	-15.5
Office supplies, stationery and gift stores	4532	389	6.0	5.8	-0.2	-2.9	-6.0	-3.1
Used merchandise stores	4533	172	5.8	6.6	0.7	12.7	5.9	-6.1
Other miscellaneous store retailers	4539	342	2.5	3.9	1.3	-1.5	0.7	2.2
Nonstore retailers	454	665	8.5	8.7	0.2	1.5	-0.4	-1.9
Electronic shopping and mail-order houses	4541	305	11.2	15.2	3.6	-3.4	3.7	7.5
Vending machine operators	4542	58	2.1	-0.7	-2.7	13.1	-2.2	-13.5
Direct selling establishments	4543	303	3.1	1.5	-1.6	-0.5	-9.8	-9.4
Food Services and Drinking Places								
Food services and drinking places	722	9 877	0.6	2.2	1.6	-0.7	-1.0	-0.2
Full-service restaurants	7221	4 640	0.6	2.3	1.7	0.5	-0.5	-0.9
Limited-service eating places	7222	4 191	0.4	2.3	1.8	-3.1	-2.6	0.5
Special food services	7223	683	1.5	2.6	1.1	1.8	1.8	0.0
Drinking places, alcoholic beverages	7224	364	0.2	0.1	-0.1	4.1	4.1	-0.1

Table 5-4. Indexes of Multifactor Productivity and Related Measures, 1987–2008

(2000 = 100.)

Sector	1987	1988	1989	1990	1991	1992	1993	1994	1995	1996	1997
PRIVATE BUSINESS											
Productivity											
Output per hour of all persons	77.3	78.5	79.3	81.0	82.4	86.0	86.4	87.2	87.4	90.0	91.7
Output per unit of capital services	108.1	108.7	108.5	106.8	103.2	105.0	105.2	106.6	105.3	105.3	105.3
Multifactor productivity	89.9	90.6	90.8	91.4	90.7	93.1	93.2	93.9	93.7	95.3	96.2
Real value-added output	62.4	65.2	67.6	68.6	68.1	70.9	73.2	76.8	79.2	82.8	87.2
Inputs											
Labor input	75.5	78.1	80.6	80.5	79.7	80.5	83.0	86.7	89.0	90.8	94.4
Capital services	57.8	60.0	62.3	64.3	66.0	67.5	69.6	72.1	75.2	78.7	82.9
Combined input quantity	69.5	71.9	74.4	75.1	75.1	76.2	78.6	81.9	84.5	86.9	90.7
Capital hours ratio	71.5	72.2	73.1	75.9	79.9	81.8	82.1	81.8	83.1	85.5	87.1
PRIVATE NONFARM BUSINESS											
Productivity											
Output per hour of all persons	78.0	79.3	79.9	81.4	82.9	86.3	86.7	87.7	88.2	90.5	92.0
Output per unit of capital services	110.1	111.0	110.6	108.6	104.7	106.2	106.5	107.7	106.5	106.1	105.8
Multifactor productivity	90.7	91.7	91.7	92.0	91.3	93.5	93.7	94.4	94.5	95.8	96.5
Real value-added output	62.4	65.3	67.6	68.6	68.1	70.8	73.2	76.7	79.3	82.8	87.2
Inputs											
Labor input	74.9	77.5	80.1	80.2	79.2	80.1	82.7	86.1	88.4	90.4	94.0
Capital services	56.7	58.8	61.2	63.2	65.0	66.6	68.7	71.3	74.5	78.1	82.4
Combined input quantity	68.8	71.3	73.8	74.6	74.6	75.7	78.2	81.3	83.9	86.5	90.4
Capital hours ratio	70.8	71.4	72.3	75.0	79.1	81.2	81.4	81.5	82.8	85.3	86.9
MANUFACTURING											
Productivity											
Output per unit of labor	64.1	65.4	66.1	67.5	69.3	71.9	73.8	76.4	79.8	82.7	87.3
Output per unit of capital	96.4	99.7	99.1	96.1	92.2	93.0	94.3	97.2	98.7	98.0	100.6
Multifactor productivity	85.0	86.4	86.0	85.4	85.1	84.6	86.8	89.2	90.8	91.2	93.8
Sector output	64.1	67.4	68.5	68.3	67.1	69.3	72.0	76.3	80.3	83.1	89.2
Inputs											
Labor hours	100.0	103.1	103.7	101.1	96.9	96.4	97.7	100.0	100.6	100.4	102.2
Combined input quantity	75.4	78.0	79.7	80.0	78.9	82.0	83.0	85.6	88.5	91.1	95.1
Energy	99.1	103.1	102.9	105.1	104.7	103.7	107.1	110.4	113.7	110.4	108.2
Materials	63.2	64.1	65.3	66.2	65.8	71.5	72.1	74.9	78.9	86.0	92.9
Capital services	66.5	67.6	69.2	71.1	72.8	74.5	76.4	78.5	81.4	84.8	88.7
Purchased services	65.2	71.0	75.2	76.6	76.0	81.5	81.6	84.7	88.8	88.5	92.1

Table 5-4. Indexes of Multifactor Productivity and Related Measures, 1987–2008—*Continued*

(2000 = 100.)

Sector	1998	1999	2000	2001	2002	2003	2004	2005	2006	2007	2008
PRIVATE BUSINESS											
Productivity											
Output per hour of all persons	94.3	97.2	100.0	102.8	107.1	111.2	114.5	116.6	117.6	119.5	122.7
Output per unit of capital services	103.8	102.3	100.0	96.0	94.7	95.5	97.2	98.1	98.4	97.7	95.6
Multifactor productivity	97.4	98.8	100.0	100.4	102.5	105.4	108.2	109.7	110.3	110.7	112.0
Real value-added output	91.5	96.2	100.0	100.5	102.0	105.2	109.7	113.6	117.1	119.5	120.4
Inputs											
Labor input	96.5	98.8	100.0	98.2	96.2	95.8	96.9	98.8	101.2	102.3	100.3
Capital services	88.2	94.1	100.0	104.6	107.7	110.2	112.9	115.8	119.1	122.3	125.9
Combined input quantity	93.9	97.4	100.0	100.0	99.5	99.9	101.4	103.6	106.2	108.0	107.6
Capital hours ratio	90.9	95.0	100.0	107.0	113.1	116.5	117.8	118.9	119.6	122.3	128.3
PRIVATE NONFARM BUSINESS											
Productivity											
Output per hour of all persons	94.5	97.3	100.0	102.7	107.1	111.1	114.2	116.1	117.2	118.9	122.3
Output per unit of capital services	104.2	102.6	100.0	96.0	94.5	95.2	96.9	97.7	97.9	97.0	95.1
Multifactor productivity	97.7	99.0	100.0	100.4	102.5	105.2	108.0	109.3	109.9	110.1	111.4
Real value-added output	91.5	96.3	100.0	100.5	102.1	105.2	109.6	113.5	117.1	119.4	120.4
Inputs											
Labor input	96.3	98.8	100.0	98.4	96.4	96.0	97.1	99.1	101.6	102.8	100.9
Capital services	87.8	93.9	100.0	104.7	107.9	110.5	113.1	116.1	119.6	123.1	126.7
Combined input quantity	93.7	97.3	100.0	100.2	99.6	100.0	101.5	103.8	106.6	108.4	108.1
Capital hours ratio	90.7	94.8	100.0	107.0	113.2	116.7	117.8	118.9	119.7	122.6	128.8
MANUFACTURING											
Productivity											
Output per unit of labor	92.0	96.1	100.0	101.6	108.6	115.3	117.9	123.5	125.0	. . .	. . .
Output per unit of capital	100.7	100.4	100.0	93.5	92.3	93.2	95.4	98.9	100.2	. . .	. . .
Multifactor productivity	95.9	96.7	100.0	98.7	102.4	105.2	108.0	108.4	110.1	. . .	. . .
Sector output	93.8	97.4	100.0	94.9	94.3	95.2	96.9	100.4	102.3	. . .	. . .
Inputs											
Labor hours	101.9	101.3	100.0	93.5	86.8	82.6	82.2	81.3	81.8	. . .	. . .
Combined input quantity	97.8	100.7	100.0	96.2	92.1	90.5	89.7	92.7	92.9	. . .	. . .
Energy	105.4	105.5	100.0	90.6	89.3	84.4	84.0	91.6	86.6	. . .	. . .
Materials	97.7	102.6	100.0	93.3	88.4	87.7	87.3	92.4	91.5	. . .	. . .
Capital services	93.2	97.0	100.0	101.5	102.1	102.1	101.6	101.5	102.0	. . .	. . .
Purchased services	95.0	100.0	100.0	100.7	98.2	99.1	97.0	104.5	106.6	. . .	. . .

. . . = Not available.

Chapter Six

COMPENSATION OF EMPLOYEES

COMPENSATION OF EMPLOYEES

HIGHLIGHTS

This chapter discusses the Employment Cost Index (ECI), which covers changes in wages and salaries and benefits; the Employer Costs for Employee Compensation (ECEC); employee participation in various benefit plans; and occupational and hourly wage percentiles wages from the National Compensation Survey.

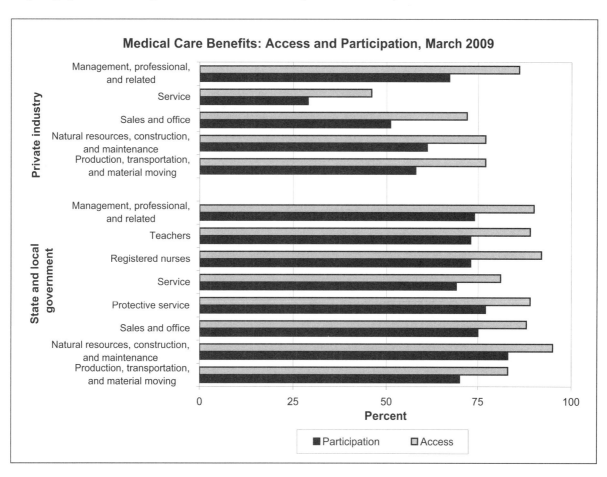

Seventy-one percent of private industry employees had access to paid medical care benefits, compared with 88 percent of state and local government employees. Among those that had access to the plan, 74 percent of private industry workers participated compared to 84 percent of state and government workers. (See Table 6-12.)

OTHER HIGHLIGHTS

- From September 2001 to September 2009, the ECI for total compensation rose 32.0 percent for union workers and 26.0 percent for nonunion workers. The change in the ECI for benefits accounted for much of the difference. While the ECI for wages and salaries grew at similar rates for union (24.8 percent) and nonunion workers (23.9 percent), the ECI for benefits grew 44.8 percent for union workers and 32.6 percent for nonunion workers. (See Tables 6-2 and 6-5.)

- Total employer compensation costs per hour varied among the different Census divisions, ranging from $33.29 in the New England states (Connecticut, Maine, Massachusetts, New Hampshire, Rhode Island, and Vermont) to $20.76 in the East South Central states (Alabama, Kentucky, Mississippi, and Tennessee). (See Table 6-7.)

- While only 67 percent of workers in the private industry had access to retirement benefits, 90 percent of state government workers did. (See Table 6-11.)

NOTES AND DEFINITIONS

NATIONAL COMPENSATION SURVEY

The National Compensation Survey (NCS) is an establishment-based survey that provides data for the Employment Cost Index (ECI), the Employer Costs for Employee Compensation (ECEC), an experimental series, the occupational earnings series, and the employee benefits survey.

The NCS surveys workers in private industry establishments, and in state and local government, in each state and the District of Columbia. For the NCS, the term *civilian workers* denotes workers in private industry and workers in state and local government. Establishments with one or more workers are included in the survey. Major exclusions from the survey are workers in the federal government, military personnel, agricultural workers, workers in private households, the self-employed, volunteers, unpaid workers, individuals receiving long-term disability compensation, and U.S. citizens working overseas. Currently, the NCS also excludes individuals who set their own pay (for example, proprietors, owners, major stockholders, and partners in unincorporated firms) and family members being paid token wages; however, these exclusions are being reevaluated.

The NCS, which originally used the Standard Industrial Classification (SIC) system, began a transition from SIC to the 2002 version of North American Industry Classification System (NAICS) in 2004; the transition was completed in July 2007. NAICS revises its industry classifications every 5 years to stay current with industrial taxonomy in North America. In August 2007, the NCS began collecting and coding data under the 2007 NAICS. The 2007 NAICS includes revisions across several sectors. The most significant revisions are in the information sector, particularly within the telecommunications area; overall, the change from 2002 NAICS to 2007 NAICS had little effect on the resulting NCS estimates.

EMPLOYMENT COST INDEX

The Employment Cost Index (ECI) is a measure of the change in the cost of labor, free from the influence of employment shifts among occupations and industries. The compensation series includes changes in wages and salaries and employer costs for employee benefits. The wage and salary series and the benefit cost series are the two components of compensation.

The ECI provides data for the civilian economy, which includes the total private nonfarm economy excluding private households, and the public sector excluding the federal government. The private industry series and the state and local government series provide data for the two sectors separately.

To be included in the ECI, employees in occupations must receive cash payments from the establishment for services performed and the establishment must pay the employer's portion of Medicare taxes on that individual's wages. Major exclusions from the survey are the self-employed, individuals who set their own pay (for example, proprietors, owners, major stockholders, and partners in unincorporated firms), volunteers, unpaid workers, family members being paid token wages, individuals receiving long-term disability compensation, and U.S. citizens working overseas.

Data for the September 2009 reference period were collected from a probability sample of approximately 62,700 occupational observations selected from a sample of about 13,200 establishments in private industry and approximately 11,700 occupations from a sample of about 1,900 establishments in state and local governments. The state and local government sample, which is replaced less frequently than the private industry sample, was replaced in its entirety in September 2007. The private industry sample is rotated over approximately 5 years, which makes the sample more representative of the economy and reduces respondent burden. Data are collected for the pay period including the 12th day of the survey months of March, June, September, and December. The sample is replaced on a cross-area, cross-industry basis.

Beginning with the release of the March 2006 data, indexes were rebased to December 2005 = 100 from June 1989 = 100. The percentage changes shown in the current and constant-dollar historical tables were calculated from the rebased indexes. Thus, changes may differ from those published in previous edition of the handbook because of rounding.

The ECI state and local government sample consists of 152 areas that represent the Nation's 361 metropolitan statistical areas and 573 micropolitan statistical areas as defined by OMB in December 2003 and the remaining portions of the 50 states. The private industry estimates started the conversion to December 2003 OMB areas definitions in the December 2008 reference period with replacement of one-fifth of the sample under the new area definitions.

Concepts and Definitions

Wages and salaries are defined as the hourly straight-time wage rate or, for workers not paid on an hourly basis, straight-time earnings divided by the corresponding hours. Straight-time wage and salary rates are total earnings before payroll deductions, excluding premium pay for overtime and for work on weekends and holidays, shift differentials, and nonproduction bonuses such as lump-sum payments provided in lieu of wage increases. Production bonuses, incentive earnings, commission payments, and cost-of-living adjustments are included in straight-time wage and salary rates.

Benefits covered by the ECI are: paid leave—vacations, holidays, sick leave, and personal leave; supplemental pay—premium pay for work in addition to the regular work schedule (such as overtime, weekends, and holidays), shift differentials, and nonproduction bonuses (such as referral bonuses and attendance bonuses); insurance benefits—life, health, short-term disability, and long-term disability; retirement and savings benefits—defined benefit and defined contribution plans; and legally required benefits—Social Security, Medicare, federal and state unemployment insurance, and workers' compensation.

Sources of Additional Information

Additional information on ECI methodology and more tables are available in Chapter 8 of the *BLS Handbook of Methods* and BLS new releases. The BLS publication *Compensation and Working Conditions* contains articles on all aspects of the NCS. All of these resources are on the BLS Web site at <http://www.bls.gov/ncs/ect/>.

Table 6-1. Employment Cost Index, Private Industry Workers, Total Compensation[1] and Wages and Salaries, by Industry and Occupation, 2001–2009

(December 2005 = 100.)

Characteristic and year	Total compensation					Wages and salaries				
	Indexes				Percent change for 12 months (ended December)	Indexes				Percent change for 12 months (ended December)
	March	June	September	December		March	June	September	December	
WORKERS BY INDUSTRY										
Total Private										
2001	85.0	85.8	86.7	87.3	4.1	87.6	88.4	89.2	89.9	3.8
2002	88.2	89.2	89.7	90.0	3.1	90.7	91.6	92.0	92.2	2.6
2003	91.4	92.3	93.2	93.6	4.0	93.3	94.0	94.8	95.1	3.1
2004	94.9	95.9	96.7	97.2	3.8	95.7	96.5	97.3	97.6	2.6
2005	98.2	98.9	99.5	100.0	2.9	98.3	98.9	99.5	100.0	2.5
2006	100.8	101.7	102.5	103.2	3.2	100.7	101.7	102.5	103.2	3.2
2007	104.0	104.9	105.7	106.3	3.0	104.3	105.1	106.0	106.6	3.3
2008	107.3	108.0	108.7	108.9	2.4	107.6	108.4	109.1	109.4	2.6
2009	109.3	109.6	110.0	. . .	. . .	109.8	110.1	110.6	. . .	. . .
Goods-Producing[2]										
2001	83.9	84.7	85.3	86.0	3.6	87.9	88.8	89.3	90.0	3.6
2002	87.0	87.7	88.2	89.0	3.5	90.7	91.4	91.9	92.6	2.9
2003	90.5	91.5	92.1	92.6	4.0	93.3	94.1	94.6	94.9	2.5
2004	94.5	95.4	96.5	96.9	4.6	95.6	96.2	97.2	97.2	2.4
2005	98.0	99.0	99.8	100.0	3.2	97.9	98.7	99.5	100.0	2.9
2006	100.3	101.3	102.0	102.5	2.5	100.7	101.8	102.3	102.9	2.9
2007	102.9	103.9	104.4	105.0	2.4	103.9	104.7	105.4	106.0	3.0
2008	106.1	106.8	107.2	107.5	2.4	107.1	108.0	108.6	109.0	2.8
2009	107.9	108.2	108.4	. . .	. . .	109.2	109.5	109.8	. . .	. . .
Service-Providing[3]										
2001	85.4	86.2	87.1	87.8	4.4	87.4	88.3	89.2	89.8	3.8
2002	88.7	89.7	90.2	90.4	3.0	90.7	91.7	92.0	92.1	2.6
2003	91.7	92.5	93.6	94.0	4.0	93.3	93.9	94.9	95.2	3.4
2004	95.1	96.1	96.8	97.3	3.5	95.8	96.6	97.3	97.7	2.6
2005	98.3	98.9	99.5	100.0	2.8	98.4	99.0	99.5	100.0	2.4
2006	101.0	101.8	102.7	103.4	3.4	100.8	101.7	102.6	103.3	3.3
2007	104.3	105.2	106.1	106.7	3.2	104.4	105.3	106.1	106.8	3.4
2008	107.7	108.5	109.1	109.4	2.5	107.7	108.6	109.3	109.6	2.6
2009	109.8	110.1	110.5	. . .	. . .	110.0	110.3	110.8	. . .	. . .
WORKERS BY OCCUPATION										
Management, Professional, and Related[4]										
2001	85.0	86.0	86.8	87.4	4.5	87.0	88.0	88.9	89.5	4.1
2002	88.3	89.2	89.5	89.7	2.6	90.4	91.3	91.6	91.7	2.5
2003	91.6	92.3	93.3	93.8	4.6	93.3	94.0	94.8	95.3	3.9
2004	94.9	95.7	96.5	97.1	3.5	96.0	96.5	97.3	97.8	2.6
2005	98.5	99.1	99.6	100.0	3.0	98.6	99.2	99.6	100.0	2.2
2006	101.1	101.9	102.9	103.5	3.5	101.1	102.0	103.0	103.6	3.6
2007	104.6	105.5	106.4	106.8	3.2	104.9	105.8	106.7	107.2	3.5
2008	108.1	108.9	109.6	109.9	2.9	108.5	109.3	110.1	110.5	3.1
2009	111.1	111.2	111.4	. . .	. . .	111.1	111.1	111.3	. . .	. . .
Management, Business, and Financial										
2001	86.1	87.1	87.8	88.5	4.4	87.3	88.3	89.1	89.8	4.1
2002	89.5	90.7	90.7	90.6	2.4	90.8	92.2	92.4	92.1	2.6
2003	93.3	93.9	94.9	95.4	5.3	94.8	95.5	96.4	96.7	5.0
2004	95.9	96.8	97.3	97.9	2.6	96.8	97.5	98.1	98.5	1.9
2005	99.1	99.6	99.7	100.0	2.1	99.2	99.7	99.5	100.0	1.5
2006	101.3	102.0	102.7	103.1	3.1	101.3	102.2	102.8	103.1	3.1
2007	104.3	105.1	106.0	106.3	3.1	104.7	105.5	106.3	106.6	3.4
2008	108.0	108.7	109.3	109.5	3.0	108.2	109.0	109.7	110.0	3.2
2009	109.6	109.7	109.7	. . .	. . .	110.3	110.3	110.4	. . .	. . .
Professional and Related										
2001	84.1	85.0	86.0	86.5	4.7	86.9	87.8	88.7	89.3	4.1
2002	87.3	87.9	88.5	89.1	3.0	90.1	90.5	91.0	91.4	2.4
2003	90.3	91.0	92.0	92.6	3.9	92.1	92.7	93.6	94.2	3.1
2004	94.1	94.8	95.8	96.5	4.2	95.3	95.7	96.7	97.2	3.2
2005	98.0	98.8	99.5	100.0	3.6	98.2	98.8	99.6	100.0	2.9
2006	101.0	101.8	103.1	103.9	3.9	100.9	101.8	103.1	104.0	4.0
2007	104.9	105.9	106.7	107.3	3.3	105.1	106.0	107.0	107.6	3.5
2008	108.3	109.0	109.9	110.3	2.8	108.7	109.5	110.4	110.9	3.1
2009	111.0	111.1	111.4	. . .	. . .	111.6	111.8	112.1	. . .	. . .

[1]Includes wages, salaries, and employer costs for employee benefits.
[2]Includes mining, construction, and manufacturing.
[3]Includes the following industries: wholesale trade; retail trade; transportation and warehousing; utilities; information; finance and insurance; real estate and rental and leasing; professional, scientific, and technical services; management of companies and enterprises; administrative and support and waste management and remediation services; education services; health care and social assistance; arts, entertainment, and recreation; accommodation and food services; and other services, except public administration.
[4]Includes the following occupational groups: management, business, and financial; professional and related; sales and related; and office and administrative support.
. . . = Not available.

Table 6-1. Employment Cost Index, Private Industry Workers, Total Compensation¹ and Wages and Salaries, by Industry and Occupation, 2001–2009—*Continued*

(December 2005 = 100.)

Characteristic and year	Total compensation					Wages and salaries				
	Indexes				Percent change for 12 months (ended December)	Indexes				Percent change for 12 months (ended December)
	March	June	September	December		March	June	September	December	
Sales and Office										
2001	84.5	85.4	86.1	86.9	4.1	86.9	87.8	88.4	89.1	3.5
2002	87.8	89.0	89.5	89.8	3.3	90.0	91.2	91.5	91.7	2.9
2003	90.8	91.9	93.0	93.1	3.7	92.4	93.3	94.4	94.3	2.8
2004	94.4	95.7	96.6	96.8	4.0	95.1	96.1	97.2	97.2	3.1
2005	97.8	98.5	99.3	100.0	3.3	97.8	98.5	99.3	100.0	2.9
2006	100.5	101.6	102.3	102.9	2.9	100.4	101.6	102.4	103.0	3.0
2007	103.7	104.7	105.3	106.1	3.1	103.8	104.8	105.3	106.2	3.1
2008	106.6	107.5	107.9	107.9	1.7	106.7	107.7	108.0	108.0	1.7
2009	107.9	108.3	108.8	. . .	. . .	107.9	108.3	109.0	. . .	. . .
Sales and Related										
2001	84.9	86.0	86.3	87.2	3.3	86.8	88.0	87.9	88.6	2.4
2002	87.7	89.7	89.7	89.7	2.9	89.2	91.0	91.0	90.9	2.6
2003	90.6	91.7	93.2	92.9	3.6	91.5	92.5	94.3	93.8	3.2
2004	94.0	95.4	96.8	96.2	3.6	94.4	95.7	97.4	96.6	3.0
2005	97.2	97.9	99.2	100.0	4.0	97.3	97.8	99.2	100.0	3.5
2006	99.9	101.1	101.7	102.3	2.3	99.8	101.3	102.0	102.6	2.6
2007	102.4	103.6	104.2	105.2	2.8	102.8	104.0	104.4	105.5	2.8
2008	105.0	106.2	106.0	105.5	0.3	105.3	106.6	106.4	105.7	0.2
2009	104.3	104.5	105.3	. . .	. . .	104.3	104.7	105.7	. . .	. . .
Office and Administrative Support										
2001	84.2	84.9	85.9	86.6	4.6	87.0	87.7	88.8	89.4	4.2
2002	87.9	88.6	89.3	89.9	3.8	90.7	91.3	91.8	92.4	3.4
2003	91.0	92.0	92.8	93.3	3.8	93.1	93.9	94.4	94.7	2.5
2004	94.7	95.8	96.5	97.2	4.2	95.6	96.4	97.1	97.6	3.1
2005	98.1	98.9	99.5	100.0	2.9	98.2	99.0	99.4	100.0	2.5
2006	100.9	101.9	102.7	103.4	3.4	100.9	101.9	102.6	103.3	3.3
2007	104.5	105.4	106.0	106.7	3.2	104.5	105.4	106.0	106.7	3.3
2008	107.8	108.5	109.2	109.6	2.7	107.7	108.5	109.2	109.7	2.8
2009	110.5	110.9	111.3	. . .	. . .	110.6	111.1	111.4	. . .	. . .
Natural Resources, Construction, and Maintenance										
2001	84.3	85.0	86.4	86.6	4.0	87.6	88.4	89.9	90.0	3.8
2002	87.4	88.5	89.3	89.7	3.6	90.5	91.7	92.3	92.6	2.9
2003	90.8	92.0	92.8	93.3	4.0	93.2	94.1	94.8	95.2	2.8
2004	94.8	96.1	96.5	97.1	4.1	95.8	96.7	97.1	97.5	2.4
2005	97.9	98.9	99.5	100.0	3.0	97.8	98.7	99.4	100.0	2.6
2006	100.8	102.1	103.0	103.6	3.6	100.7	101.8	102.8	103.4	3.4
2007	104.0	105.0	105.9	106.7	3.0	104.2	105.1	106.2	107.1	3.6
2008	107.6	108.3	109.0	109.6	2.7	108.1	109.0	109.8	110.5	3.2
2009	109.9	110.3	110.9	. . .	. . .	110.6	111.0	111.6	. . .	. . .
Construction, Extraction, Farming, Fishing, and Forestry										
2001	84.2	85.1	86.2	86.4	3.8	87.8	88.9	89.8	90.0	3.6
2002	87.3	88.1	88.8	89.5	3.6	90.6	91.3	91.9	92.4	2.7
2003	90.3	91.6	92.5	93.1	4.0	92.7	93.7	94.6	94.9	2.7
2004	94.7	95.8	96.4	97.2	4.4	95.8	96.6	96.9	97.5	2.7
2005	97.7	98.7	99.5	100.0	2.9	97.8	98.5	99.3	100.0	2.6
2006	100.7	102.2	103.1	103.7	3.7	100.7	102.0	103.0	103.7	3.7
2007	104.4	105.7	106.5	107.4	3.6	104.7	105.8	106.7	107.8	4.0
2008	108.6	109.7	110.3	110.8	3.2	109.2	110.1	110.8	111.5	3.4
2009	110.9	111.5	112.0	. . .	. . .	111.4	111.7	112.3	. . .	. . .
Installation, Maintenance, and Repair										
2001	84.4	84.9	86.8	86.8	4.1	87.4	87.9	90.1	90.1	4.3
2002	87.4	89.1	90.0	90.1	3.8	90.4	92.2	92.9	92.9	3.1
2003	91.4	92.5	93.1	93.6	3.9	93.8	94.6	95.1	95.5	2.8
2004	95.0	96.3	96.7	97.0	3.6	95.9	96.8	97.3	97.4	2.0
2005	98.1	99.3	99.6	100.0	3.1	97.8	99.1	99.5	100.0	2.7
2006	100.9	102.1	103.0	103.4	3.4	100.7	101.6	102.6	103.0	3.0
2007	103.5	104.1	105.2	105.8	2.3	103.7	104.2	105.6	106.1	3.0
2008	106.3	106.6	107.4	108.1	2.2	106.8	107.6	108.5	109.3	3.0
2009	108.6	108.9	109.4	. . .	. . .	109.7	110.2	110.7	. . .	. . .

¹Includes wages, salaries, and employer costs for employee benefits.
. . . = Not available.

Table 6-1. Employment Cost Index, Private Industry Workers, Total Compensation[1] and Wages and Salaries, by Industry and Occupation, 2001–2009—*Continued*

(December 2005 = 100.)

Characteristic and year	Total compensation					Wages and salaries				
	Indexes				Percent change for 12 months (ended December)	Indexes				Percent change for 12 months (ended December)
	March	June	September	December		March	June	September	December	
Production, Transportation, and Material Moving										
2001	85.3	85.8	86.7	87.4	3.6	88.7	89.4	90.2	91.0	3.9
2002	88.4	89.1	89.7	90.3	3.3	91.9	92.4	92.8	93.3	2.5
2003	91.5	92.4	93.2	93.6	3.7	94.0	94.6	95.1	95.4	2.3
2004	95.5	96.5	97.4	97.8	4.5	96.0	96.7	97.6	97.8	2.5
2005	98.5	99.0	99.7	100.0	2.2	98.3	98.9	99.6	100.0	2.2
2006	100.4	101.1	101.7	102.3	2.3	100.6	101.2	101.8	102.4	2.4
2007	102.5	103.3	103.9	104.5	2.2	103.1	103.8	104.5	105.0	2.5
2008	105.5	106.0	106.6	106.9	2.3	106.0	106.8	107.5	107.8	2.7
2009	107.7	108.1	108.6	. . .	. . .	108.3	108.8	109.4	. . .	. . .
Production										
2001	84.9	85.2	86.0	86.7	3.2	88.4	89.1	89.7	90.5	3.7
2002	87.7	88.3	88.8	89.4	3.1	91.3	91.8	92.3	92.8	2.5
2003	91.0	91.7	92.5	93.0	4.0	93.6	94.1	94.8	95.1	2.5
2004	95.3	96.4	97.4	97.7	5.1	95.6	96.5	97.4	97.5	2.5
2005	98.6	99.1	99.6	100.0	2.4	98.3	98.9	99.5	100.0	2.6
2006	100.4	101.0	101.6	102.0	2.0	100.7	101.2	101.7	102.2	2.2
2007	102.1	102.8	103.2	104.0	2.0	103.1	103.6	104.2	104.6	2.3
2008	104.8	105.2	105.8	106.1	2.0	105.6	106.4	107.2	107.4	2.7
2009	107.1	107.6	108.0	. . .	. . .	108.1	108.5	109.0	. . .	. . .
Transportation and Material Moving										
2001	85.8	86.7	87.7	88.5	4.2	89.0	89.9	90.8	91.6	4.1
2002	89.5	90.2	90.9	91.4	3.3	92.6	93.1	93.6	94.0	2.6
2003	92.4	93.4	94.0	94.4	3.3	94.7	95.3	95.6	95.8	1.9
2004	95.7	96.7	97.5	97.9	3.7	96.4	97.1	97.9	98.2	2.5
2005	98.3	99.0	99.8	100.0	2.1	98.5	98.9	99.7	100.0	1.8
2006	100.4	101.2	102.0	102.6	2.6	100.4	101.2	102.0	102.6	2.6
2007	103.1	104.1	104.9	105.3	2.6	103.2	104.1	105.0	105.4	2.7
2008	106.4	107.2	107.7	107.9	2.5	106.5	107.4	108.0	108.3	2.8
2009	108.4	108.9	109.6	. . .	. . .	108.5	109.2	109.9	. . .	. . .
Service										
2001	87.1	87.7	88.2	89.4	3.8	89.7	90.2	90.6	91.7	3.4
2002	90.2	90.6	91.5	92.0	2.9	92.5	92.8	93.4	93.9	2.4
2003	93.0	93.4	94.4	95.0	3.3	94.5	94.8	95.6	96.1	2.3
2004	95.9	96.7	97.2	97.7	2.8	96.4	96.9	97.4	97.9	1.9
2005	98.5	99.0	99.5	100.0	2.4	98.6	99.0	99.6	100.0	2.1
2006	100.8	101.5	102.3	103.1	3.1	100.6	101.3	102.0	102.9	2.9
2007	104.5	105.2	106.4	107.0	3.8	104.6	105.3	106.5	107.1	4.1
2008	107.8	108.7	109.4	109.8	2.6	107.9	108.8	109.7	110.1	2.8
2009	110.7	110.9	111.7	. . .	. . .	111.0	111.2	112.1	. . .	. . .

[1]Includes wages, salaries, and employer costs for employee benefits.
. . . = Not available.

Table 6-2. Employment Cost Index, Private Industry Workers, Total Compensation[1] and Wages and Salaries, by Bargaining Status and Industry, 2001–2009

(December 2005 = 100.)

Characteristic and year	Total compensation					Wages and salaries				
	Indexes				Percent change for 12 months (ended December)	Indexes				Percent change for 12 months (ended December)
	March	June	September	December		March	June	September	December	
WORKERS BY BARGAINING STATUS AND INDUSTRY										
Union Workers										
2001	82.0	82.9	83.7	84.8	4.2	86.5	87.4	88.3	89.6	4.3
2002	85.7	86.5	87.5	88.2	4.0	90.2	91.1	91.9	92.6	3.3
2003	89.5	90.7	91.6	92.3	4.6	93.0	93.8	94.4	94.9	2.5
2004	94.5	95.9	96.7	97.3	5.4	95.6	96.4	97.1	97.6	2.8
2005	97.9	98.8	99.6	100.0	2.8	97.9	98.7	99.5	100.0	2.5
2006	100.5	101.8	102.4	103.0	3.0	100.3	101.2	101.7	102.3	2.3
2007	102.7	103.9	104.4	105.1	2.0	102.8	103.7	104.4	104.7	2.3
2008	105.9	106.7	107.4	108.0	2.8	105.5	106.7	107.4	108.1	3.2
2009	109.1	109.8	110.5	. . .	. . .	108.8	109.6	110.2	. . .	. . .
Union Workers, Goods-Producing[2]										
2001	81.9	82.7	83.4	84.0	2.9	87.2	88.2	88.9	89.5	3.5
2002	84.8	85.5	86.4	87.1	3.7	90.0	90.9	91.7	92.4	3.2
2003	88.9	90.2	90.9	91.7	5.3	92.9	94.0	94.5	95.0	2.8
2004	94.6	95.9	96.7	97.2	6.0	95.4	96.3	96.9	97.1	2.2
2005	97.7	98.8	99.6	100.0	2.9	97.5	98.5	99.2	100.0	3.0
2006	99.9	101.2	101.8	102.2	2.2	100.5	101.6	101.9	102.3	2.3
2007	101.5	102.8	103.1	104.0	1.8	102.7	103.6	104.3	104.3	2.0
2008	104.6	105.6	106.2	106.9	2.8	105.2	106.4	107.1	107.7	3.3
2009	108.0	108.9	109.5	. . .	. . .	108.2	108.8	109.5	. . .	. . .
Union Workers, Manufacturing										
2001	81.1	81.4	82.0	83.0	2.7	87.3	88.1	88.8	89.7	3.7
2002	84.1	84.7	85.4	86.5	4.2	90.3	90.8	91.6	92.5	3.1
2003	88.6	89.5	90.1	91.0	5.2	93.3	94.2	94.5	95.0	2.7
2004	95.6	96.7	97.5	97.8	7.5	95.5	96.2	97.0	97.1	2.2
2005	98.3	99.1	99.7	100.0	2.2	97.6	98.3	99.0	100.0	3.0
2006	99.3	100.1	100.5	100.8	0.8	100.6	101.2	101.4	101.7	1.7
2007	99.2	100.0	100.0	101.0	0.2	102.0	102.5	102.9	102.6	0.9
2008	101.4	101.7	102.1	102.8	1.8	103.4	104.4	104.9	105.5	2.8
2009	104.4	104.8	105.4	. . .	. . .	106.0	106.4	107.0	. . .	. . .
Union Workers, Service-Providing[3]										
2001	82.0	83.0	84.0	85.5	5.2	85.9	86.8	87.8	89.6	4.9
2002	86.4	87.3	88.4	89.1	4.2	90.3	91.2	92.0	92.7	3.5
2003	90.1	91.1	92.3	92.8	4.2	93.1	93.6	94.4	94.8	2.3
2004	94.4	95.8	96.6	97.3	4.8	95.7	96.5	97.3	98.0	3.4
2005	98.1	98.8	99.6	100.0	2.8	98.2	99.0	99.7	100.0	2.0
2006	101.0	102.2	102.9	103.6	3.6	100.1	100.9	101.6	102.2	2.2
2007	103.7	104.7	105.4	106.0	2.3	102.9	103.8	104.6	104.9	2.6
2008	107.0	107.5	108.3	108.8	2.6	105.8	106.9	107.7	108.3	3.2
2009	109.9	110.6	111.3	. . .	. . .	109.2	110.1	110.8	. . .	. . .
Nonunion Workers										
2001	85.5	86.3	87.2	87.8	4.2	87.7	88.6	89.3	89.9	3.7
2002	88.7	89.6	90.0	90.3	2.8	90.8	91.7	92.0	92.2	2.6
2003	91.8	92.5	93.5	93.9	4.0	93.3	94.0	94.9	95.1	3.1
2004	95.0	95.9	96.7	97.2	3.5	95.8	96.5	97.3	97.6	2.6
2005	98.3	98.9	99.5	100.0	2.9	98.3	98.9	99.5	100.0	2.5
2006	100.9	101.7	102.6	103.2	3.2	100.8	101.8	102.7	103.3	3.3
2007	104.2	105.1	105.9	106.5	3.2	104.5	105.3	106.2	106.9	3.5
2008	107.5	108.3	108.9	109.1	2.4	107.9	108.7	109.4	109.6	2.5
2009	109.4	109.6	109.9	. . .	. . .	110.0	110.2	110.6	. . .	. . .
Nonunion, Goods-Producing[2]										
2001	84.7	85.5	86.0	86.7	3.8	88.1	89.0	89.5	90.1	3.6
2002	87.8	88.5	88.8	89.7	3.5	91.0	91.6	91.9	92.7	2.9
2003	91.1	91.9	92.6	92.9	3.6	93.4	94.1	94.6	94.9	2.4
2004	94.5	95.2	96.4	96.8	4.2	95.6	96.2	97.3	97.3	2.5
2005	98.1	99.0	99.9	100.0	3.3	98.0	98.7	99.6	100.0	2.8
2006	100.5	101.4	102.0	102.5	2.5	100.7	101.9	102.4	103.0	3.0
2007	103.3	104.2	104.8	105.4	2.8	104.2	105.0	105.8	106.4	3.3
2008	106.5	107.1	107.6	107.7	2.2	107.7	108.4	109.0	109.3	2.7
2009	107.9	108.0	108.0	. . .	. . .	109.5	109.7	109.9	. . .	. . .

[1]Includes wages, salaries, and employer costs for employee benefits.
[2]Includes mining, construction, and manufacturing.
[3]Includes the following industries: wholesale trade; retail trade; transportation and warehousing; utilities; information; finance and insurance; real estate and rental and leasing; professional, scientific, and technical services; management of companies and enterprises; administrative and support and waste management and remediation services; education services; health care and social assistance; arts, entertainment, and recreation; accommodation and food services; and other services, except public administration.
. . . = Not available.

Table 6-2. Employment Cost Index, Private Industry Workers, Total Compensation[1] and Wages and Salaries, by Bargaining Status and Industry, 2001–2009—*Continued*

(December 2005 = 100.)

Characteristic and year	Total compensation					Wages and salaries				
	Indexes				Percent change for 12 months (ended December)	Indexes				Percent change for 12 months (ended December)
	March	June	September	December		March	June	September	December	
Nonunion Workers, Manufacturing										
2001	84.5	85.3	85.8	86.3	3.6	88.5	89.4	89.8	90.3	3.4
2002	87.6	88.4	88.7	89.4	3.6	91.4	92.0	92.4	92.9	2.9
2003	91.2	91.9	92.6	92.8	3.8	93.9	94.5	94.9	95.2	2.5
2004	94.4	95.3	96.4	96.6	4.1	95.8	96.5	97.5	97.5	2.4
2005	98.2	99.1	99.8	100.0	3.5	98.4	99.0	99.8	100.0	2.6
2006	100.3	101.3	101.7	102.1	2.1	100.7	101.8	102.0	102.5	2.5
2007	102.8	103.7	104.1	104.6	2.4	103.6	104.2	104.9	105.5	2.9
2008	105.6	106.2	106.6	106.8	2.1	106.6	107.3	108.0	108.2	2.6
2009	107.1	107.3	107.3	. . .	. . .	108.6	108.9	109.1	. . .	. . .
Nonunion, Service-Providing[3]										
2001	85.7	86.5	87.5	88.0	4.1	87.6	88.5	89.3	89.9	3.8
2002	88.9	89.9	90.4	90.5	2.8	90.8	91.7	92.0	92.1	2.4
2003	91.9	92.7	93.7	94.1	4.0	93.3	94.0	94.9	95.2	3.4
2004	95.2	96.1	96.9	97.3	3.4	95.8	96.6	97.3	97.7	2.6
2005	98.3	98.9	99.4	100.0	2.8	98.4	99.0	99.5	100.0	2.4
2006	101.0	101.8	102.7	103.4	3.4	100.8	101.7	102.7	103.4	3.4
2007	104.4	105.3	106.2	106.8	3.3	104.6	105.4	106.3	107.0	3.5
2008	107.7	108.6	109.2	109.4	2.4	107.9	108.8	109.4	109.7	2.5
2009	109.8	110.0	110.4	. . .	. . .	110.1	110.3	110.8	. . .	. . .

[1]Includes wages, salaries, and employer costs for employee benefits.
[3]Includes the following industries: wholesale trade; retail trade; transportation and warehousing; utilities; information; finance and insurance; real estate and rental and leasing; professional, scientific, and technical services; management of companies and enterprises; administrative and support and waste management and remediation services; education services; health care and social assistance; arts, entertainment, and recreation; accommodation and food services; and other services, except public administration.
. . . = Not available.

Table 6-3. Employment Cost Index, Private Industry Workers, Total Compensation[1] and Wages and Salaries, by Region, and Metropolitan Area Status, 2001–2009

(December 2005 = 100.)

Geography type and year	Total compensation					Wages and salaries				
	Indexes				Percent change for 12 months (ended December)	Indexes				Percent change for 12 months (ended December)
	March	June	September	December		March	June	September	December	
CENSUS REGIONS AND DIVISIONS[1]										
Northeast										
2001	84.3	85.3	86.2	86.7	3.8	86.8	87.8	88.6	89.2	3.8
2002	87.7	88.6	88.9	89.3	3.0	90.2	91.0	91.1	91.5	2.6
2003	90.6	91.4	92.4	92.9	4.0	92.4	93.2	94.1	94.5	3.3
2004	94.2	95.5	96.3	96.6	4.0	95.3	96.3	97.1	97.2	2.9
2005	97.6	98.5	99.2	100.0	3.5	97.8	98.6	99.2	100.0	2.9
2006	100.9	101.8	102.5	103.3	3.3	100.8	101.7	102.5	103.1	3.1
2007	104.0	105.1	106.2	106.8	3.4	104.0	105.0	106.1	106.6	3.4
2008	107.4	108.1	108.7	109.5	2.5	107.5	108.2	108.7	109.6	2.8
2009	109.8	110.2	110.7	. . .	. . .	109.9	110.3	110.8	. . .	. . .
New England										
2006	100.7	101.4	102.1	103.1	3.1	100.7	101.5	102.3	103.1	3.1
2007	103.6	104.8	105.4	106.1	2.9	103.6	104.8	105.7	106.3	3.1
2008	106.7	107.1	107.8	109.5	3.2	107.1	107.6	108.3	110.3	3.8
2009	109.9	110.2	111.2	. . .	. . .	110.5	110.6	111.7	. . .	. . .
Middle Atlantic										
2006	100.9	101.9	102.6	103.3	3.3	100.8	101.7	102.5	103.1	3.1
2007	104.2	105.3	106.5	107.1	3.7	104.2	105.1	106.4	106.7	3.5
2008	107.8	108.6	109.1	109.5	2.2	107.6	108.4	109.0	109.4	2.5
2009	109.8	110.2	110.6	. . .	. . .	109.7	110.1	110.4	. . .	. . .
South										
2001	86.4	87.2	88.1	88.7	4.2	88.9	89.7	90.5	91.0	3.6
2002	89.5	90.5	91.2	91.2	2.8	91.8	92.7	93.3	93.2	2.4
2003	92.0	92.7	93.6	93.9	3.0	93.5	94.1	94.9	95.0	1.9
2004	95.2	96.2	97.1	97.7	4.0	95.8	96.7	97.5	98.0	3.2
2005	98.9	99.3	99.7	100.0	2.4	98.9	99.3	99.7	100.0	2.0
2006	101.0	101.6	102.8	103.5	3.5	101.0	101.6	102.9	103.6	3.6
2007	104.3	105.3	106.1	106.7	3.1	104.6	105.6	106.5	107.0	3.3
2008	107.8	108.5	109.1	109.3	2.4	108.1	109.1	109.8	110.0	2.8
2009	109.8	110.1	110.6	. . .	. . .	110.4	110.7	111.3	. . .	. . .
South Atlantic										
2006	101.2	101.9	103.1	103.8	3.8	101.3	101.9	103.2	103.9	3.9
2007	104.9	106.0	106.8	107.3	3.4	105.0	106.1	106.9	107.5	3.5
2008	108.5	109.1	109.7	109.8	2.3	108.6	109.5	110.2	110.3	2.6
2009	110.3	110.7	111.3	. . .	. . .	110.8	111.3	111.9	. . .	. . .
East South Central										
2006	100.7	100.9	101.5	102.3	2.3	100.7	101.5	102.1	103.1	3.1
2007	103.3	103.8	104.8	105.4	3.0	104.2	104.5	105.6	106.3	3.1
2008	106.5	107.2	108.0	108.0	2.5	107.2	107.9	109.0	109.0	2.5
2009	108.5	108.7	109.2	. . .	. . .	109.2	109.5	110.1	. . .	. . .
West South Central										
2006	100.7	101.4	102.7	103.4	3.4	100.6	101.2	102.7	103.4	3.4
2007	103.7	104.8	105.6	106.1	2.6	104.1	105.3	106.1	106.6	3.1
2008	107.3	108.2	108.7	109.0	2.7	107.8	108.8	109.4	109.8	3.0
2009	109.4	109.5	109.9	. . .	. . .	110.1	110.2	110.8	. . .	. . .
Midwest										
2001	84.8	85.4	86.1	86.7	3.5	86.8	87.6	88.3	88.9	3.3
2002	88.0	88.7	89.0	89.5	3.2	90.3	91.0	91.3	91.7	3.1
2003	92.1	92.8	93.6	94.0	5.0	94.2	94.7	95.2	95.5	4.1
2004	95.0	95.9	96.6	96.9	3.1	95.6	96.1	96.9	97.1	1.7
2005	97.8	98.4	99.5	100.0	3.2	97.8	98.2	99.4	100.0	3.0
2006	100.7	101.7	102.3	102.8	2.8	100.4	101.4	102.0	102.6	2.6
2007	103.3	104.2	104.6	105.3	2.4	103.6	104.4	105.0	105.6	2.9
2008	106.0	107.0	107.4	107.6	2.2	106.3	107.5	107.9	108.0	2.3
2009	107.9	108.1	108.4	. . .	. . .	108.4	108.6	108.9	. . .	. . .
East North Central										
2006	100.7	101.7	102.3	102.8	2.8	100.3	101.4	101.9	102.5	2.5
2007	103.2	104.1	104.4	105.0	2.1	103.6	104.4	104.7	105.3	2.7
2008	105.5	106.5	106.9	107.0	1.9	105.8	107.0	107.3	107.4	2.0
2009	107.0	107.3	107.5	. . .	. . .	107.5	107.7	108.0	. . .	. . .
West North Central										
2006	100.6	101.5	102.4	102.7	2.7	100.6	101.5	102.4	102.7	2.7
2007	103.5	104.3	105.3	105.9	3.1	103.8	104.5	105.6	106.3	3.5
2008	107.3	108.4	108.8	109.0	2.9	107.9	108.9	109.5	109.7	3.2
2009	109.9	110.2	110.6	. . .	. . .	110.7	110.8	111.2	. . .	. . .

[1] Includes wages, salaries, and employer costs for employee benefits.
. . . = Not available.

Table 6-3. Employment Cost Index, Private Industry Workers, Total Compensation[1] and Wages and Salaries, by Region, and Metropolitan Area Status, 2001–2009—*Continued*

(December 2005 = 100.)

Geography type and year	Total compensation					Wages and salaries				
	Indexes				Percent change for 12 months (ended December)	Indexes				Percent change for 12 months (ended December)
	March	June	September	December		March	June	September	December	
West										
2001	84.1	85.0	85.9	86.9	5.2	87.4	88.3	89.2	90.2	4.8
2002	87.4	88.5	89.1	89.8	3.3	90.4	91.5	92.0	92.4	2.4
2003	90.9	92.0	93.2	93.8	4.5	93.0	93.9	95.1	95.5	3.4
2004	95.3	96.2	96.9	97.4	3.8	96.4	97.0	97.7	98.0	2.6
2005	98.4	99.3	99.7	100.0	2.7	98.4	99.3	99.6	100.0	2.0
2006	100.6	101.8	102.5	103.0	3.0	100.7	102.1	102.7	103.2	3.2
2007	104.2	104.9	105.7	106.5	3.4	104.8	105.4	106.2	107.0	3.7
2008	107.8	108.4	109.3	109.4	2.7	108.3	108.9	109.9	110.1	2.9
2009	109.9	110.1	110.3	. . .	. . .	110.5	110.8	111.2	. . .	. . .
Mountain										
2006	101.0	101.8	102.7	103.1	3.1	100.6	101.7	102.8	103.2	3.2
2007	105.2	105.2	106.6	107.5	4.3	105.3	105.5	106.7	107.8	4.5
2008	108.4	109.4	110.3	110.4	2.7	108.9	109.9	110.8	111.0	3.0
2009	110.5	110.6	110.9	. . .	. . .	111.1	111.4	111.9	. . .	. . .
Pacific										
2006	100.5	101.8	102.5	103.0	3.0	100.8	102.2	102.7	103.3	3.3
2007	103.9	104.8	105.4	106.1	3.0	104.6	105.3	106.0	106.8	3.4
2008	107.6	108.1	108.9	109.1	2.8	108.1	108.6	109.6	109.8	2.8
2009	109.7	109.9	110.1	. . .	. . .	110.3	110.6	111.0	. . .	. . .
Metropolitan Areas										
2006	100.8	101.7	102.5	103.1	3.1	100.7	101.7	102.5	103.1	3.1
2007	103.9	104.9	105.7	106.3	3.1	104.3	105.1	105.9	106.5	3.3
2008	107.2	108.0	108.6	108.9	2.4	107.5	108.4	109.0	109.3	2.6
2009	109.2	109.5	109.9	. . .	. . .	109.7	110.0	110.4	. . .	. . .
Nonmetropolitan Areas										
2006	100.8	101.7	102.5	103.1	3.3	100.9	101.6	102.6	103.5	3.5
2007	103.9	104.9	105.7	106.3	3.1	104.4	105.2	106.2	107.0	3.4
2008	107.2	108.0	108.6	108.9	2.7	108.1	108.9	109.9	110.3	3.1
2009	109.2	109.5	109.9	. . .	. . .	110.8	111.1	112.0	. . .	. . .

[1]Includes wages, salaries, and employer costs for employee benefits.
. . . = Not available.

Table 6-4. Employment Cost Index, State and Local Government Workers, Total Compensation[1] and Wages and Salaries, by Industry and Occupation, 2001–2009

(December 2005 = 100.)

Characteristic and year	Total compensation					Wages and salaries				
	Indexes				Percent change for 12 months (ended December)	Indexes				Percent change for 12 months (ended December)
	March	June	September	December		March	June	September	December	
WORKERS BY INDUSTRY[1]										
Total State and Local Government										
2001	83.6	84.1	85.8	86.2	4.1	87.6	88.0	89.7	90.2	3.8
2002	86.7	87.0	89.0	89.7	4.1	90.5	90.8	92.4	93.0	3.1
2003	90.4	90.7	92.3	92.8	3.5	93.4	93.6	94.6	95.0	2.2
2004	93.5	93.9	95.4	96.1	3.6	95.4	95.6	96.6	97.0	2.1
2005	96.9	97.2	99.1	100.0	4.1	97.6	97.8	99.1	100.0	3.1
2006	100.5	100.9	103.2	104.1	4.1	100.3	100.8	102.8	103.5	3.5
2007	105.1	105.7	107.6	108.4	4.1	104.1	104.6	106.4	107.1	3.5
2008	108.9	109.4	111.3	111.6	3.0	107.7	108.2	110.1	110.4	3.1
2009	112.3	112.9	114.0	. . .	. . .	110.9	111.5	112.4	. . .	. . .
Education and Health Services										
2001	84.3	84.7	86.9	87.1	3.9	87.8	88.1	90.2	90.4	3.6
2002	87.4	87.6	89.7	90.4	3.8	90.6	90.8	92.8	93.3	3.2
2003	90.8	91.1	92.7	93.2	3.1	93.5	93.6	94.7	95.0	1.8
2004	93.7	93.8	95.5	96.1	3.1	95.3	95.4	96.6	97.0	2.1
2005	96.7	97.0	99.0	100.0	4.1	97.4	97.6	99.0	100.0	3.1
2006	100.3	100.8	103.7	104.3	4.3	100.2	100.7	103.1	103.6	3.6
2007	104.8	105.3	107.5	108.2	3.7	104.0	104.2	106.3	107.1	3.4
2008	108.6	109.1	111.2	111.5	3.0	107.5	108.1	110.2	110.5	3.2
2009	111.9	112.4	113.7	. . .	. . .	110.7	111.1	112.1	. . .	. . .
Education Services										
2001	84.4	84.7	86.9	87.2	3.9	87.9	88.2	90.3	90.5	3.4
2002	87.3	87.5	89.7	90.4	3.7	90.6	90.8	92.9	93.3	3.1
2003	90.8	91.1	92.7	93.1	3.0	93.4	93.6	94.7	95.0	1.8
2004	93.6	93.8	95.4	96.1	3.2	95.3	95.4	96.6	96.9	2.0
2005	96.6	96.9	98.9	100.0	4.1	97.3	97.5	98.9	100.0	3.2
2006	100.2	100.5	103.5	104.1	4.1	100.1	100.4	103.0	103.4	3.4
2007	104.6	105.0	107.4	108.0	3.7	103.7	103.9	106.1	106.8	3.3
2008	108.4	108.8	111.0	111.2	3.0	107.2	107.7	109.9	110.1	3.1
2009	111.8	112.1	113.5	. . .	. . .	110.4	110.7	111.7	. . .	. . .
Schools[2]										
2001	84.4	84.7	87.0	87.2	3.9	87.9	88.2	90.3	90.5	3.4
2002	87.3	87.5	89.7	90.4	3.7	90.6	90.8	92.9	93.3	3.1
2003	90.8	91.1	92.7	93.1	3.0	93.4	93.6	94.7	95.0	1.8
2004	93.6	93.8	95.5	96.1	3.2	95.3	95.4	96.6	96.9	2.0
2005	96.6	96.9	98.9	100.0	4.1	97.3	97.5	98.9	100.0	3.2
2006	100.2	100.5	103.5	104.1	4.1	100.1	100.4	103.0	103.4	3.4
2007	104.6	104.9	107.4	108.0	3.7	103.6	103.9	106.1	106.8	3.3
2008	108.4	108.8	111.0	111.2	3.0	107.2	107.7	109.9	110.1	3.1
2009	111.8	112.1	113.5	. . .	. . .	110.4	110.7	111.7	. . .	. . .
Elementary and Secondary Schools										
2001	84.1	84.3	86.5	86.7	3.5	87.8	88.2	90.0	90.3	3.1
2002	86.8	87.0	89.3	89.9	3.7	90.5	90.6	92.8	93.2	3.2
2003	90.3	90.6	92.4	92.7	3.1	93.2	93.4	94.6	94.8	1.7
2004	93.2	93.4	95.3	96.0	3.6	95.1	95.2	96.5	96.9	2.2
2005	96.4	96.6	98.8	100.0	4.2	97.1	97.2	98.9	100.0	3.2
2006	100.2	100.5	103.6	104.2	4.2	100.0	100.3	103.0	103.4	3.4
2007	104.7	105.0	107.4	108.0	3.6	103.6	103.8	106.0	106.6	3.1
2008	108.3	108.8	111.1	111.4	3.1	106.9	107.5	109.8	110.1	3.3
2009	112.0	112.2	114.0	. . .	. . .	110.3	110.5	112.0	. . .	. . .
Health Care and Social Assistance[3]										
2001	83.4	84.5	86.0	86.8	5.0	86.1	87.1	88.6	89.5	4.8
2002	87.8	88.2	89.5	90.6	4.4	90.7	91.1	92.2	93.0	3.9
2003	91.2	91.4	92.9	93.5	3.2	93.5	93.9	94.7	95.3	2.5
2004	94.2	94.7	96.3	96.5	3.2	95.7	96.0	97.1	97.3	2.1
2005	97.6	98.0	99.5	100.0	3.6	98.1	98.5	99.4	100.0	2.8
2006	101.3	102.9	105.1	105.7	5.7	101.0	103.0	104.8	105.5	5.5
2007	107.1	107.6	108.6	109.3	3.4	106.6	107.2	108.2	109.2	3.5
2008	110.1	111.1	112.7	113.2	3.6	110.1	111.0	112.8	113.4	3.8
2009	113.3	114.8	115.3	. . .	. . .	113.1	114.8	115.2	. . .	. . .

[1]Includes wages, salaries, and employer costs for employee benefits.
[2]Includes elementary and secondary schools, junior colleges, colleges, universities, and professional schools.
[3]Includes ambulatory health care services and social assistance, not shown separately.
. . . = Not available.

Table 6-4. Employment Cost Index, State and Local Government Workers, Total Compensation[1] and Wages and Salaries, by Industry and Occupation, 2001–2009—*Continued*

(December 2005 = 100.)

Characteristic and year	Total compensation					Wages and salaries				
	Indexes				Percent change for 12 months (ended December)	Indexes				Percent change for 12 months (ended December)
	March	June	September	December		March	June	September	December	
Hospitals										
2001	83.0	84.4	85.9	86.6	4.5	85.3	86.6	88.0	88.8	4.3
2002	87.6	88.1	89.3	90.6	4.6	90.0	90.6	91.7	92.8	4.5
2003	91.0	91.1	92.8	93.4	3.1	93.1	93.5	94.5	95.2	2.6
2004	93.9	94.4	96.1	96.7	3.5	95.6	95.9	97.1	97.7	2.6
2005	97.6	98.0	99.5	100.0	3.4	98.3	98.6	99.4	100.0	2.4
2006	100.9	101.3	103.3	104.3	4.3	100.9	101.4	103.1	104.4	4.4
2007	105.6	106.3	107.5	108.2	3.7	105.7	106.5	107.6	108.6	4.0
2008	109.2	109.7	110.8	111.3	2.9	109.8	110.3	111.4	112.1	3.2
2009	112.4	113.5	114.0	. . .	. . .	112.8	114.0	114.4	. . .	. . .
WORKERS BY OCCUPATION										
Management, Professional, and Related[4]										
2001	84.1	84.6	86.5	86.8	4.1	87.5	88.0	89.8	90.2	3.8
2002	87.2	87.4	89.5	90.3	4.0	90.4	90.6	92.5	93.1	3.2
2003	90.8	91.1	92.6	93.1	3.1	93.4	93.6	94.6	95.0	2.0
2004	93.8	94.0	95.5	96.2	3.3	95.3	95.5	96.6	97.0	2.1
2005	97.0	97.3	99.0	100.0	4.0	97.5	97.8	99.0	100.0	3.1
2006	100.3	100.8	103.3	104.0	4.0	100.2	100.7	102.9	103.5	3.5
2007	104.9	105.4	107.5	108.3	4.1	104.0	104.3	106.3	107.0	3.4
2008	108.8	109.3	111.3	111.6	3.0	107.6	108.2	110.1	110.4	3.2
2009	112.0	112.6	113.7	. . .	. . .	110.7	111.2	112.1	. . .	. . .
Professional and Related										
2001	84.0	84.4	86.4	86.7	4.0	87.5	87.9	89.8	90.1	3.7
2002	87.0	87.2	89.4	90.2	4.0	90.2	90.5	92.4	93.0	3.2
2003	90.7	91.0	92.5	93.0	3.1	93.3	93.4	94.5	94.9	2.0
2004	93.6	93.9	95.5	96.1	3.3	95.3	95.4	96.6	96.9	2.1
2005	96.8	97.1	98.9	100.0	4.1	97.4	97.7	98.9	100.0	3.2
2006	100.2	100.8	103.4	104.0	4.0	100.2	100.7	103.0	103.6	3.6
2007	104.8	105.3	107.5	108.2	4.0	103.9	104.2	106.3	107.0	3.3
2008	108.6	109.1	111.1	111.4	3.0	107.5	108.1	110.1	110.3	3.1
2009	111.9	112.4	113.7	. . .	. . .	110.6	111.1	112.1	. . .	. . .
Sales and Office										
2001	82.8	83.1	84.5	85.2	3.9	87.4	87.8	89.1	89.6	3.1
2002	86.1	86.5	88.3	89.1	4.6	90.4	90.8	92.3	92.9	3.7
2003	89.8	90.3	92.4	92.8	4.2	93.5	93.8	95.1	95.4	2.7
2004	93.7	94.4	95.7	96.5	4.0	96.0	96.2	97.3	97.6	2.3
2005	97.5	97.6	99.3	100.0	3.6	98.1	98.0	99.4	100.0	2.5
2006	100.9	101.5	103.3	104.1	4.1	100.6	101.2	102.6	103.2	3.2
2007	105.6	106.2	107.9	108.6	4.3	104.5	104.8	106.3	107.0	3.7
2008	108.8	109.3	111.0	111.3	2.5	107.4	107.9	109.3	109.7	2.5
2009	112.4	113.0	114.3	. . .	. . .	110.5	111.2	112.1	. . .	. . .
Office and Administration Support										
2001	82.6	82.9	84.4	85.1	3.9	87.4	87.8	89.1	89.7	3.1
2002	86.0	86.5	88.2	88.9	4.5	90.5	91.0	92.4	92.8	3.5
2003	89.6	90.0	92.1	92.6	4.2	93.4	93.7	95.0	95.3	2.7
2004	93.5	94.2	95.6	96.4	4.1	95.9	96.1	97.1	97.5	2.3
2005	97.4	97.5	99.2	100.0	3.7	98.0	97.9	99.3	100.0	2.6
2006	101.0	101.6	103.5	104.2	4.2	100.7	101.4	102.7	103.4	3.4
2007	105.7	106.4	108.2	108.9	4.5	104.7	105.0	106.5	107.3	3.8
2008	109.3	109.8	111.4	111.8	2.7	107.8	108.3	109.7	110.1	2.6
2009	112.8	113.3	114.7	. . .	. . .	111.0	111.6	112.6	. . .	. . .
Service										
2001	82.1	82.6	84.1	84.7	4.7	87.8	88.3	89.7	90.3	3.8
2002	85.2	85.8	87.4	88.0	3.9	90.8	91.2	92.1	92.4	2.3
2003	88.8	89.3	91.0	91.6	4.1	93.1	93.6	94.3	94.9	2.7
2004	92.3	92.7	94.9	95.5	4.3	95.3	95.4	96.4	96.8	2.0
2005	96.2	96.7	99.1	100.0	4.7	97.3	97.7	99.3	100.0	3.3
2006	100.6	101.2	103.1	104.5	4.5	100.3	100.8	102.4	103.9	3.9
2007	105.4	106.3	108.0	109.1	4.4	104.5	105.2	106.5	107.7	3.7
2008	109.7	110.0	111.9	112.4	3.0	108.3	108.6	110.4	110.9	3.0
2009	113.4	114.0	114.9	. . .	. . .	112.0	112.7	113.3	. . .	. . .

[1]Includes wages, salaries, and employer costs for employee benefits.
[4]Includes the following occupational groups: management, business, and financial; professional and related; sales and related; and office and administrative support.
. . . = Not available.

Table 6-5. Employment Cost Index, Benefits, by Industry and Occupation, 2001–2009

(December 2005 = 100.)

Characteristic and year	Indexes				Percent change for 12 months (ended December)
	March	June	September	December	
Civilian Workers[1]					
2001	78.1	78.8	80.0	80.6	5.1
2002	81.6	82.5	83.6	84.3	4.6
2003	86.4	87.4	88.9	89.7	6.4
2004	92.2	93.6	94.8	95.7	6.7
2005	97.6	98.3	99.5	100.0	4.5
2006	100.9	101.6	102.8	103.6	3.6
2007	104.0	105.1	106.1	106.8	3.1
2008	107.6	108.1	108.9	109.1	2.2
2009	109.7	110.0	110.6	. . .	. . .
Total Private					
2001	78.9	79.6	80.6	81.3	5.2
2002	82.4	83.4	84.1	84.7	4.2
2003	87.1	88.2	89.4	90.2	6.5
2004	93.0	94.6	95.4	96.2	6.7
2005	98.1	99.0	99.7	100.0	4.0
2006	101.0	101.7	102.5	103.1	3.1
2007	103.2	104.3	105.0	105.6	2.4
2008	106.5	107.0	107.5	107.7	2.0
2009	108.2	108.4	108.7	. . .	. . .
State and Local Government Workers					
2001	75.3	75.8	77.7	78.1	5.1
2002	78.9	79.3	81.8	83.0	6.3
2003	84.1	84.7	87.3	88.2	6.3
2004	89.5	90.3	93.0	94.1	6.7
2005	95.5	96.0	99.0	100.0	6.3
2006	100.7	101.3	104.1	105.2	5.2
2007	107.0	108.0	110.3	111.0	5.5
2008	111.4	111.8	113.9	114.2	2.9
2009	115.2	115.8	117.5	. . .	. . .
WORKERS BY OCCUPATION					
Management, Professional, and Related					
2001	79.8	80.7	81.5	82.0	5.8
2002	82.9	83.8	84.1	84.7	3.3
2003	87.4	88.1	89.4	90.1	6.4
2004	92.2	93.5	94.4	95.4	5.9
2005	98.2	99.0	99.8	100.0	4.8
2006	101.3	101.8	102.8	103.4	3.4
2007	103.8	104.9	105.6	106.0	2.5
2008	107.3	107.9	108.5	108.5	2.4
2009	108.8	108.8	108.9	. . .	. . .
Sales and Office					
2001	78.1	78.9	80.1	81.1	6.0
2002	82.0	83.4	84.2	84.7	4.4
2003	86.8	88.2	89.3	90.0	6.3
2004	92.6	94.4	95.2	95.8	6.4
2005	97.6	98.5	99.3	100.0	4.4
2006	100.8	101.6	102.0	102.9	2.9
2007	103.4	104.3	105.2	106.0	3.0
2008	106.5	107.0	107.6	107.8	1.7
2009	108.0	108.1	108.5	. . .	. . .
Natural Resources, Construction, and Maintainance					
2001	77.7	78.3	79.7	79.8	4.0
2002	81.2	82.3	83.5	84.1	5.4
2003	86.0	87.9	88.8	89.8	6.8
2004	92.9	94.9	95.4	96.4	7.3
2005	98.0	99.3	99.8	100.0	3.7
2006	101.1	102.7	103.5	104.0	4.0
2007	103.4	104.8	105.3	105.9	1.8
2008	106.5	107.0	107.5	107.7	1.7
2009	108.2	108.8	109.3	. . .	. . .
Production, Transportation, and Material Moving					
2001	78.8	79.0	80.1	80.7	3.1
2002	82.0	82.9	83.7	84.5	4.7
2003	86.8	88.3	89.4	90.2	6.7
2004	94.5	96.1	97.1	97.7	8.3
2005	98.7	99.3	100.0	100.0	2.4
2006	100.1	101.0	101.6	102.0	2.0
2007	101.2	102.4	102.7	103.7	1.7
2008	104.4	104.5	104.8	105.1	1.4
2009	106.4	106.8	107.1	. . .	. . .

[1]Includes workers in the private nonfarm economy, except those in private households, and workers in the public sector, except those in the federal government.
. . . = Not available.

Table 6-5. Employment Cost Index, Benefits, by Industry and Occupation, 2001–2009—*Continued*

(December 2005 = 100.)

Characteristic and year	Indexes				Percent change for 12 months (ended December)
	March	June	September	December	
Service					
2001	79.7	80.5	81.3	82.5	5.4
2002	83.7	84.4	85.9	86.5	4.8
2003	88.8	89.4	90.7	91.7	6.0
2004	94.6	95.9	96.7	97.0	5.8
2005	98.3	98.9	99.5	100.0	3.1
2006	101.5	102.2	103.0	103.6	3.6
2007	104.2	105.1	106.0	106.7	3.0
2008	107.6	108.5	108.7	108.8	2.0
2009	109.7	110.0	110.4	. . .	. . .
WORKERS BY INDUSTRY					
Goods-producing industries[2]					
2001	76.5	77.1	77.9	78.5	3.7
2002	80.0	80.6	81.3	82.3	4.8
2003	85.3	86.5	87.5	88.2	7.2
2004	92.5	93.9	95.0	96.3	9.2
2005	98.3	99.6	100.4	100.0	3.8
2006	99.6	100.4	101.3	101.7	1.7
2007	100.9	102.2	102.4	103.2	1.5
2008	104.0	104.4	104.6	104.7	1.5
2009	105.4	105.7	105.7	. . .	. . .
Manufacturing					
2001	75.5	75.8	76.4	77.2	3.5
2002	78.8	79.7	80.2	81.3	5.3
2003	84.7	85.8	86.7	87.3	7.4
2004	92.8	94.1	95.3	96.0	10.0
2005	98.3	99.4	100.0	100.0	4.2
2006	99.0	99.7	100.5	100.8	0.8
2007	99.6	101.0	100.7	101.7	0.9
2008	102.3	102.2	102.3	102.5	0.8
2009	103.5	103.6	103.4	. . .	. . .
Aircraft Manufacturing					
2001	45.9	46.0	45.0	46.7	6.6
2002	48.4	48.9	48.9	51.8	10.9
2003	59.4	59.3	59.6	57.2	10.4
2004	70.0	70.7	71.1	71.1	24.3
2005	97.1	97.2	97.4	100.0	40.6
2006	79.1	79.2	84.3	83.2	-16.8
2007	72.6	73.4	68.5	68.6	-17.5
2008	71.1	71.3	73.1	73.3	6.9
2009	73.4	73.5	72.0	. . .	. . .
Service-Providing[3]					
2001	79.9	80.7	81.8	82.4	5.6
2002	83.4	84.5	85.3	85.8	4.1
2003	87.8	88.9	90.2	91.0	6.1
2004	93.2	94.9	95.5	96.1	5.6
2005	98.1	98.7	99.4	100.0	4.1
2006	101.5	102.3	103.0	103.7	3.7
2007	104.1	105.2	106.0	106.6	2.8
2008	107.6	108.1	108.7	108.9	2.2
2009	109.3	109.5	109.9	. . .	. . .
WORKERS BY BARGAINING STATUS					
Union					
2001	74.8	75.7	76.6	77.3	3.9
2002	78.6	79.3	80.5	81.2	5.0
2003	83.9	85.7	87.2	88.1	8.5
2004	92.8	95.0	96.0	96.8	9.9
2005	98.0	98.9	99.8	100.0	3.3
2006	100.8	102.7	103.4	104.2	4.2
2007	102.4	104.1	104.3	105.8	1.5
2008	106.6	106.6	107.2	107.8	1.9
2009	109.5	110.3	110.9	. . .	. . .
Nonunion					
2001	79.9	80.5	81.6	82.2	5.4
2002	83.2	84.3	84.9	85.5	4.0
2003	87.8	88.8	89.9	90.6	6.0
2004	93.0	94.5	95.2	96.0	6.0
2005	98.2	99.0	99.6	100.0	4.2
2006	101.0	101.5	102.3	102.9	2.9
2007	103.4	104.3	105.1	105.6	2.6
2008	106.5	107.1	107.6	107.6	1.9
2009	107.9	108.0	108.2	. . .	. . .

[2]Includes mining, construction, and manufacturing.
[3]Includes the following industries: wholesale trade; retail trade; transportation and warehousing; utilities; information; finance and insurance; real estate and rental and leasing; professional, scientific, and technical services; management of companies and enterprises; administrative and support and waste management and remediation services; education services; health care and social assistance; arts, entertainment, and recreation; accommodation and food services; and other services, except public administration.
. . . = Not available.

NOTES AND DEFINITIONS

EMPLOYER COSTS FOR EMPLOYEE COMPENSATION

The Employer Costs for Employee Compensation (ECEC) measures the average cost per employee hour worked that employers pay for wages and salaries and benefits.

Survey Scope

The ECEC consists of data for the civilian economy, obtained from both private industry and state and local government. Excluded from private industry are the self-employed and farm and private household workers. Federal government workers are excluded from the public sector. The private industry series and the state and local government series provide separate data for the two sectors.

The cost levels for June 2009 were collected from a probability sample of 63,200 occupations selected from a sample of about 13,300 establishments in private industry and approximately 11,700 occupations from a sample of about 1,900 establishments in state and local governments. The state and local government sample, which is replaced less frequently than the private industry sample, was replaced in its entirety in September 2007. The private industry sample is rotated over approximately 5 years, which makes the sample more representative of the economy and reduces respondent burden. Data are collected for the pay period including the 12th day of the survey months of March, June, September, and December. The sample is replaced on a cross-area, cross-industry basis.

To be included in the ECEC, employees in occupations must receive cash payments from the establishment for services performed and the establishment must pay the employer's portion of Medicare taxes on that individual's wages. Major exclusions from the survey are the self-employed, individuals who set their own pay (for example, proprietors, owners, major stockholders, and partners in unincorporated firms), volunteers, unpaid workers, family members being paid token wages, individuals receiving long-term disability compensation, and U.S. citizens working overseas.

Current employment weights are used to calculate cost levels. These weights are derived from two BLS programs: the Quarterly Census of Employment and Wages (QCEW) and the Current Employment Statistics (CES). Combined, these programs provide the appropriate industry coverage and currency of data needed to match the ECEC.

Sources of Additional Information

Additional information may be obtained from BLS news release 09-1098 "Employer Costs for Employee Compensation—June 2009," and in various articles in the BLS e-publication, Compensation and Working Conditions. These resources are available on the BLS Web site at <http://www.bls.gov/ncs/ect/>.

Table 6-6. Employer Compensation Costs Per Hour Worked for Employee Compensation and Costs as a Percent of Total Compensation: Private Industry Workers, by Major Industry Group, June 2009

(Dollars, percent of total cost.)

Compensation component	All workers		Goods-producing[1]						Service-providing[2]			
			All goods-producing[1]		Construction		Manufacturing		All service-providing[2]		Trade, transportation, and utilities	
	Cost	Percent	Cost	Percent	Cost	Percent	Cost	Percent	Cost	Percent	Cost	Percent
TOTAL COMPENSATION	27.42	100.0	32.29	100.0	31.35	100.0	32.05	100.0	26.33	100.0	23.09	100.0
Wages and Salaries	19.39	70.7	21.63	67.0	21.68	69.1	21.22	66.2	18.90	71.8	16.39	71.0
Total Benefits	8.02	29.3	10.66	33.0	9.67	30.9	10.83	33.8	7.44	28.2	6.70	29.0
Paid leave	1.85	6.8	2.07	6.4	1.13	3.6	2.46	7.7	1.80	6.9	1.40	6.1
Vacation	0.96	3.5	1.10	3.4	0.63	2.0	1.29	4.0	0.93	3.5	0.73	3.2
Holiday	0.60	2.2	0.74	2.3	0.39	1.2	0.89	2.8	0.56	2.1	0.44	1.9
Sick	0.23	0.8	0.18	0.6	0.08	0.3	0.22	0.7	0.24	0.9	0.19	0.8
Personal	0.07	0.3	0.05	0.2	0.03	0.1	0.06	0.2	0.07	0.3	0.04	0.2
Supplemental pay	0.83	3.0	1.20	3.7	1.07	3.4	1.20	3.8	0.75	2.8	0.56	2.4
Overtime and premium pay[3]	0.27	1.0	0.57	1.8	0.61	1.9	0.53	1.7	0.20	0.8	0.28	1.2
Shift differentials	0.07	0.2	0.09	0.3	([4])	([5])	0.13	0.4	0.06	0.2	0.02	0.1
Nonproduction bonuses	0.49	1.8	0.54	1.7	0.45	1.4	0.54	1.7	0.48	1.8	0.26	1.1
Insurance	2.13	7.8	3.01	9.3	2.34	7.5	3.26	10.2	1.94	7.4	1.91	8.3
Life insurance	0.04	0.2	0.07	0.2	0.05	0.2	0.07	0.2	0.04	0.2	0.03	0.1
Health insurance	1.99	7.3	2.81	8.7	2.22	7.1	3.04	9.5	1.81	6.9	1.81	7.8
Short-term disability	0.05	0.2	0.09	0.3	0.06	0.2	0.10	0.3	0.05	0.2	0.03	0.1
Long-term disability	0.04	0.2	0.04	0.1	([4])	([5])	0.05	0.2	0.04	0.2	0.03	0.2
Retirement and savings	0.95	3.4	1.46	4.5	1.65	5.3	1.28	4.0	0.83	3.2	0.80	3.5
Defined benefit plans	0.41	1.5	0.85	2.6	1.12	3.6	0.67	2.1	0.31	1.2	0.36	1.6
Defined contribution plans	0.53	1.9	0.61	1.9	0.53	1.7	0.61	1.9	0.52	2.0	0.44	1.9
Legally required benefits	2.26	8.3	2.92	9.0	3.49	11.1	2.62	8.2	2.12	8.0	2.03	8.8
Social Security and Medicare	1.63	6.0	1.85	5.7	1.80	5.7	1.84	5.8	1.58	6.0	1.37	5.9
Social Security[6]	1.31	4.8	1.49	4.6	1.45	4.6	1.48	4.6	1.27	4.8	1.10	4.8
Medicare	0.32	1.2	0.36	1.1	0.34	1.1	0.36	1.1	0.31	1.2	0.27	1.1
Federal unemployment insurance	0.03	0.1	0.03	0.1	0.03	0.1	0.03	0.1	0.03	0.1	0.04	0.2
State unemployment insurance	0.15	0.5	0.20	0.6	0.25	0.8	0.18	0.6	0.14	0.5	0.14	0.6
Workers' compensation	0.45	1.6	0.84	2.6	1.41	4.5	0.57	1.8	0.36	1.4	0.49	2.1

Compensation component	Service-providing[2]											
	Information		Financial activities		Professional and business services		Education and health services		Leisure and hospitality		Other services	
	Cost	Percent	Cost	Percent	Cost	Percent	Cost	Percent	Cost	Percent	Cost	Percent
TOTAL COMPENSATION	40.75	100.0	36.32	100.0	33.64	100.0	29.46	100.0	12.09	100.0	24.55	100.0
Wages and Salaries	28.03	68.8	24.63	67.8	24.38	72.5	21.16	71.8	9.53	78.8	18.21	74.2
Total Benefits	12.71	31.2	11.69	32.2	9.26	27.5	8.30	28.2	2.57	21.2	6.33	25.8
Paid leave	3.78	9.3	3.00	8.3	2.34	6.9	2.23	7.6	0.40	3.3	1.54	6.3
Vacation	1.93	4.7	1.54	4.3	1.21	3.6	1.12	3.8	0.23	1.9	0.74	3.0
Holiday	1.01	2.5	0.92	2.5	0.78	2.3	0.67	2.3	0.12	1.0	0.57	2.3
Sick	0.49	1.2	0.41	1.1	0.28	0.8	0.33	1.1	0.04	0.3	0.20	0.8
Personal	0.35	0.9	0.13	0.4	0.06	0.2	0.11	0.4	([4])	([5])	0.04	0.2
Supplemental pay	1.08	2.7	1.85	5.1	1.27	3.8	0.59	2.0	0.14	1.2	0.50	2.0
Overtime and premium pay[3]	0.36	0.9	0.15	0.4	0.21	0.6	0.22	0.7	0.07	0.6	0.14	0.6
Shift differentials	0.06	0.1	([4])	([5])	0.04	0.1	0.20	0.7	([4])	([5])	([4])	([5])
Nonproduction bonuses	0.66	1.6	1.69	4.7	1.02	3.0	0.17	0.6	0.06	0.5	0.34	1.4
Insurance	3.55	8.7	2.90	8.0	2.05	6.1	2.30	7.8	0.65	5.3	1.54	6.3
Life insurance	0.05	0.1	0.06	0.2	0.06	0.2	0.03	0.1	([4])	([5])	0.07	0.3
Health insurance	3.25	8.0	2.69	7.4	1.87	5.6	2.17	7.4	0.62	5.1	1.40	5.7
Short-term disability	0.19	0.5	0.08	0.2	0.07	0.2	0.04	0.1	([4])	([5])	0.03	0.1
Long-term disability	0.06	0.2	0.06	0.2	0.05	0.2	0.05	0.2	([4])	([5])	0.04	0.1
Retirement and savings	1.43	3.5	1.52	4.2	1.04	3.1	0.91	3.1	0.11	0.9	0.66	2.7
Defined benefit plans	0.55	1.4	0.58	1.6	0.40	1.2	0.27	0.9	0.02	0.2	0.23	0.9
Defined contribution plans	0.88	2.2	0.94	2.6	0.64	1.9	0.64	2.2	0.09	0.7	0.43	1.7
Legally required benefits	2.86	7.0	2.41	6.6	2.56	7.6	2.27	7.7	1.27	10.5	2.10	8.6
Social Security and Medicare	2.39	5.9	2.04	5.6	2.00	6.0	1.77	6.0	0.86	7.1	1.52	6.2
Social Security[6]	1.91	4.7	1.62	4.5	1.60	4.8	1.42	4.8	0.70	5.8	1.22	5.0
Medicare	0.47	1.2	0.42	1.2	0.40	1.2	0.35	1.2	0.17	1.4	0.30	1.2
Federal unemployment insurance	0.03	0.1	0.03	0.1	0.03	0.1	0.03	0.1	0.04	0.3	0.03	0.1
State unemployment insurance	0.16	0.4	0.14	0.4	0.16	0.5	0.13	0.4	0.12	1.0	0.12	0.5
Workers' compensation	0.28	0.7	0.19	0.5	0.36	1.1	0.35	1.2	0.25	2.1	0.43	1.8

Note: Individual items may not sum to totals due to rounding.

[1]Includes mining, construction, and manufacturing. The agriculture, forestry, farming, and hunting sector is excluded.
[2]Includes utilities; wholesale trade; retail trade; transportation and warehousing; information; finance and insurance; real estate and rental and leasing; professional and technical services; management of companies and enterprises; administrative and waste services; education services; health care and social assistance; arts, entertainment, and recreation; accommodation and food services; and other services, except public administration.
[3]Includes premium pay for work in addition to the regular work schedule (such as overtime, weekends, and holidays).
[4]Cost per hour worked is $0.01 or less.
[5]Less than 0.05 percent.
[6]Comprises the Old Age, Survivors, and Disability Insurance (OASDI) program.

Table 6-7. Employer Compensation Costs Per Hour Worked for Employee Compensation and Costs as a Percent of Total Compensation: Private Industry Workers, by Census Region and Area, June 2009

(Dollars, percent of total costs.)

Compensation component	Census region and division[1]					
	Northeast		Northeast divisions			
			New England		Middle Atlantic	
	Cost	Percent	Cost	Percent	Cost	Percent
TOTAL COMPENSATION	32.14	100.0	33.29	100.0	31.69	100.0
Wages and Salaries	22.20	69.1	22.80	68.5	21.96	69.3
Total Benefits	9.94	30.9	10.48	31.5	9.73	30.7
Paid leave	2.41	7.5	2.47	7.4	2.39	7.5
Vacation	1.21	3.8	1.25	3.8	1.19	3.8
Holiday	0.77	2.4	0.82	2.4	0.75	2.4
Sick	0.32	1.0	0.28	0.9	0.33	1.1
Personal	0.12	0.4	0.12	0.4	0.12	0.4
Supplemental pay	1.29	4.0	1.81	5.4	1.08	3.4
Overtime and premium pay[2]	0.29	0.9	0.28	0.8	0.29	0.9
Shift differentials	0.07	0.2	0.06	0.2	0.07	0.2
Nonproduction bonuses	0.93	2.9	1.47	4.4	0.72	2.3
Insurance	2.47	7.7	2.46	7.4	2.48	7.8
Life insurance	0.05	0.1	0.05	0.2	0.05	0.1
Health insurance	2.30	7.2	2.28	6.8	2.31	7.3
Short-term disability	0.08	0.2	0.07	0.2	0.08	0.3
Long-term disability	0.04	0.1	0.05	0.2	0.04	0.1
Retirement and savings	1.18	3.7	1.14	3.4	1.19	3.8
Defined benefit plans	0.51	1.6	0.48	1.4	0.52	1.6
Defined contribution plans	0.67	2.1	0.66	2.0	0.67	2.1
Legally required benefits	2.59	8.1	2.60	7.8	2.59	8.2
Social Security and Medicare	1.87	5.8	1.94	5.8	1.84	5.8
Social Security	1.49	4.6	1.54	4.6	1.48	4.7
Medicare	0.38	1.2	0.40	1.2	0.37	1.2
Federal unemployment insurance	0.03	0.1	0.03	0.1	0.03	0.1
State unemployment insurance	0.23	0.7	0.23	0.7	0.22	0.7
Workers' compensation	0.46	1.4	0.40	1.2	0.49	1.5

Compensation component	Census region and division[1]							
	South		South divisions					
			South Atlantic		East South Central		West South Central	
	Cost	Percent	Cost	Percent	Cost	Percent	Cost	Percent
TOTAL COMPENSATION	24.26	100.0	25.33	100.0	20.76	100.0	24.35	100.0
Wages and Salaries	17.48	72.0	18.26	72.1	14.84	71.5	17.60	72.3
Total Benefits	6.78	28.0	7.08	27.9	5.92	28.5	6.75	27.7
Paid leave	1.56	6.4	1.67	6.6	1.27	6.1	1.55	6.4
Vacation	0.80	3.3	0.85	3.3	0.68	3.3	0.79	3.3
Holiday	0.51	2.1	0.54	2.1	0.40	1.9	0.52	2.1
Sick	0.19	0.8	0.21	0.8	0.13	0.6	0.19	0.8
Personal	0.06	0.2	0.06	0.3	0.05	0.2	0.05	0.2
Supplemental pay	0.65	2.7	0.65	2.6	0.50	2.4	0.74	3.0
Overtime and premium pay[2]	0.25	1.1	0.26	1.0	0.22	1.0	0.27	1.1
Shift differentials	0.06	0.3	0.07	0.3	0.07	0.4	0.05	0.2
Nonproduction bonuses	0.34	1.4	0.33	1.3	0.21	1.0	0.42	1.7
Insurance	1.83	7.6	1.88	7.4	1.84	8.9	1.74	7.2
Life insurance	0.05	0.2	0.04	0.2	0.05	0.2	0.05	0.2
Health insurance	1.70	7.0	1.75	6.9	1.71	8.2	1.61	6.6
Short-term disability	0.05	0.2	0.05	0.2	0.05	0.2	0.04	0.2
Long-term disability	0.04	0.2	0.04	0.2	0.03	0.2	0.04	0.2
Retirement and savings	0.77	3.2	0.83	3.3	0.54	2.6	0.82	3.3
Defined benefit plans	0.30	1.2	0.31	1.2	0.19	0.9	0.34	1.4
Defined contribution plans	0.48	2.0	0.52	2.0	0.35	1.7	0.48	2.0
Legally required benefits	1.95	8.1	2.05	8.1	1.77	8.5	1.90	7.8
Social Security and Medicare	1.47	6.1	1.53	6.0	1.31	6.3	1.45	6.0
Social Security	1.18	4.9	1.23	4.9	1.06	5.1	1.16	4.8
Medicare	0.29	1.2	0.30	1.2	0.25	1.2	0.29	1.2
Federal unemployment insurance	0.03	0.1	0.03	0.1	0.03	0.2	0.03	0.1
State unemployment insurance	0.09	0.4	0.09	0.4	0.08	0.4	0.08	0.3
Workers' compensation	0.37	1.5	0.39	1.5	0.34	1.7	0.33	1.4

Note: Individual items may not sum to totals due to rounding.

[1]The states that comprise the Census divisions are: New England—Connecticut, Maine, Massachusetts, New Hampshire, Rhode Island, and Vermont; Middle Atlantic—New Jersey, New York, and Pennsylvania; South Atlantic—Delaware, District of Columbia, Florida, Georgia, Maryland, North Carolina, South Carolina, Virginia, and West Virginia; East South Central—Alabama, Kentucky, Mississippi, and Tennessee; West South Central—Arkansas, Louisiana, Oklahoma, and Texas; East North Central—Illinois, Indiana, Michigan, Ohio, and Wisconsin; West North Central—Iowa, Kansas, Minnesota, Missouri, Nebraska, North Dakota, and South Dakota; Mountain—Arizona, Colorado, Idaho, Montana, Nevada, New Mexico, Utah, and Wyoming; and Pacific—Alaska, California, Hawaii, Oregon, and Washington.
[2]Comprises the Old-Age, Survivors, and Disability Insurance (OASDI) program.

Table 6-7. Employer Compensation Costs Per Hour Worked for Employee Compensation and Costs as a Percent of Total Compensation: Private Industry Workers, by Census Region and Area, June 2009—*Continued*

(Dollars, percent of total costs.)

Compensation component	Census region and division[1]					
	Midwest		Midwest divisions			
			East North Central		West North Central	
	Cost	Percent	Cost	Percent	Cost	Percent
TOTAL COMPENSATION	26.29	100.0	26.72	100.0	25.35	100.0
Wages and Salaries	18.46	70.2	18.68	69.9	17.99	71.0
Total Benefits	7.83	29.8	8.05	30.1	7.36	29.0
Paid leave	1.73	6.6	1.78	6.7	1.63	6.4
Vacation	0.92	3.5	0.92	3.4	0.91	3.6
Holiday	0.56	2.1	0.59	2.2	0.50	2.0
Sick	0.19	0.7	0.19	0.7	0.18	0.7
Personal	0.07	0.3	0.08	0.3	0.04	0.2
Supplemental pay	0.72	2.7	0.75	2.8	0.65	2.6
Overtime and premium pay[2]	0.28	1.1	0.29	1.1	0.26	1.0
Shift differentials	0.08	0.3	0.08	0.3	0.07	0.3
Nonproduction bonuses	0.36	1.4	0.37	1.4	0.33	1.3
Insurance	2.27	8.6	2.34	8.8	2.12	8.4
Life insurance	0.05	0.2	0.05	0.2	0.04	0.2
Health insurance	2.12	8.1	2.19	8.2	1.99	7.8
Short-term disability	0.06	0.2	0.07	0.2	0.04	0.2
Long-term disability	0.04	0.2	0.04	0.2	0.05	0.2
Retirement and savings	0.94	3.6	0.96	3.6	0.89	3.5
Defined benefit plans	0.43	1.6	0.47	1.8	0.35	1.4
Defined contribution plans	0.51	1.9	0.49	1.8	0.54	2.1
Legally required benefits	2.17	8.3	2.22	8.3	2.07	8.2
Social Security and Medicare	1.56	5.9	1.59	6.0	1.48	5.9
Social Security	1.26	4.8	1.29	4.8	1.19	4.7
Medicare	0.30	1.2	0.31	1.2	0.29	1.2
Federal unemployment insurance	0.03	0.1	0.03	0.1	0.03	0.1
State unemployment insurance	0.16	0.6	0.17	0.6	0.14	0.6
Workers' compensation	0.42	1.6	0.43	1.6	0.41	1.6

Compensation component	Census region and division[1]					
	West		West divisions			
			Mountain		Pacific	
	Cost	Percent	Cost	Percent	Cost	Percent
TOTAL COMPENSATION	29.40	100.0	26.18	100.0	30.78	100.0
Wages and Salaries	20.93	71.2	19.01	72.6	21.76	70.7
Total Benefits	8.47	28.8	7.17	27.4	9.02	29.3
Paid leave	1.93	6.6	1.59	6.1	2.08	6.7
Vacation	1.02	3.5	0.84	3.2	1.09	3.5
Holiday	0.61	2.1	0.52	2.0	0.65	2.1
Sick	0.25	0.9	0.19	0.7	0.28	0.9
Personal	0.05	0.2	0.04	0.2	0.05	0.2
Supplemental pay	0.82	2.8	0.78	3.0	0.84	2.7
Overtime and premium pay[2]	0.27	0.9	0.22	0.8	0.30	1.0
Shift differentials	0.06	0.2	0.05	0.2	0.06	0.2
Nonproduction bonuses	0.49	1.7	0.51	1.9	0.48	1.6
Insurance	2.14	7.3	1.79	6.8	2.29	7.4
Life insurance	0.04	0.1	0.04	0.2	0.04	0.1
Health insurance	2.02	6.9	1.68	6.4	2.17	7.0
Short-term disability	0.04	0.1	0.03	0.1	0.05	0.1
Long-term disability	0.04	0.1	0.04	0.2	0.04	0.1
Retirement and savings	1.02	3.5	0.82	3.1	1.10	3.6
Defined benefit plans	0.48	1.6	0.32	1.2	0.55	1.8
Defined contribution plans	0.54	1.8	0.51	1.9	0.55	1.8
Legally required benefits	2.56	8.7	2.18	8.3	2.72	8.8
Social Security and Medicare	1.75	6.0	1.58	6.0	1.82	5.9
Social Security	1.41	4.8	1.27	4.9	1.46	4.8
Medicare	0.34	1.2	0.31	1.2	0.36	1.2
Federal unemployment insurance	0.03	0.1	0.03	0.1	0.03	0.1
State unemployment insurance	0.17	0.6	0.12	0.5	0.19	0.6
Workers' compensation	0.61	2.1	0.45	1.7	0.68	2.2

Note: Individual items may not sum to totals due to rounding.

[1]The states that comprise the Census divisions are: New England—Connecticut, Maine, Massachusetts, New Hampshire, Rhode Island, and Vermont; Middle Atlantic—New Jersey, New York, and Pennsylvania; South Atlantic—Delaware, District of Columbia, Florida, Georgia, Maryland, North Carolina, South Carolina, Virginia, and West Virginia; East South Central—Alabama, Kentucky, Mississippi, and Tennessee; West South Central—Arkansas, Louisiana, Oklahoma, and Texas; East North Central—Illinois, Indiana, Michigan, Ohio, and Wisconsin; West North Central—Iowa, Kansas, Minnesota, Missouri, Nebraska, North Dakota, and South Dakota; Mountain—Arizona, Colorado, Idaho, Montana, Nevada, New Mexico, Utah, and Wyoming; and Pacific—Alaska, California, Hawaii, Oregon, and Washington.
[2]Comprises the Old-Age, Survivors, and Disability Insurance (OASDI) program.

Table 6-8. Employer Compensation Costs Per Hour Worked for Employee Compensation and Costs as a Percent of Total Compensation: State and Local Government, by Major Occupational and Industry Group, June 2009

(Dollars, percent of total cost.)

Compensation component	All workers		Occupational group[1]						Industry group	
	Cost	Percent	Management, professional, and related		Sales and office		Service		Service-providing[2]	
			Cost	Percent	Cost	Percent	Cost	Percent	Cost	Percent
TOTAL COMPENSATION	39.66	100.0	48.67	100.0	27.11	100.0	29.31	100.0	39.71	100.0
Wages and Salaries	26.01	65.6	33.02	67.9	16.73	61.7	17.73	60.5	26.06	65.6
Total Benefits	13.65	34.4	15.65	32.1	10.39	38.3	11.58	39.5	13.65	34.4
Paid leave	3.27	8.2	3.86	7.9	2.45	9.0	2.62	9.0	3.27	8.2
Vacation	1.15	2.9	1.18	2.4	1.09	4.0	1.13	3.9	1.15	2.9
Holiday	1.07	2.7	1.27	2.6	0.78	2.9	0.85	2.9	1.07	2.7
Sick	0.82	2.1	1.08	2.2	0.48	1.8	0.52	1.8	0.82	2.1
Personal	0.23	0.6	0.33	0.7	0.10	0.4	0.13	0.4	0.23	0.6
Supplemental pay	0.34	0.9	0.26	0.5	0.20	0.7	0.57	1.9	0.34	0.9
Overtime and premium pay[3]	0.18	0.5	0.08	0.2	0.11	0.4	0.37	1.2	0.18	0.4
Shift differentials	0.05	0.1	0.03	0.1	0.02	0.1	0.09	0.3	0.05	0.1
Nonproduction bonuses	0.12	0.3	0.14	0.3	0.07	0.3	0.11	0.4	0.12	0.3
Insurance	4.51	11.4	5.00	10.3	4.10	15.1	3.66	12.5	4.51	11.4
Life insurance	0.09	0.2	0.12	0.3	0.05	0.2	0.04	0.2	0.09	0.2
Health insurance	4.34	10.9	4.78	9.8	3.99	14.7	3.56	12.2	4.34	10.9
Short-term disability	0.02	0.1	0.03	0.1	0.02	0.1	0.02	0.1	0.02	0.1
Long-term disability	0.05	0.1	0.07	0.1	0.04	0.1	0.03	0.1	0.05	0.1
Retirement and savings	3.17	8.0	3.81	7.8	1.93	7.1	2.78	9.5	3.17	8.0
Defined benefit plans	2.85	7.2	3.42	7.0	1.69	6.2	2.55	8.7	2.86	7.2
Defined contribution plans	0.31	0.8	0.39	0.8	0.23	0.9	0.23	0.8	0.32	0.8
Legally required benefits	2.36	6.0	2.72	5.6	1.71	6.3	1.95	6.7	2.36	5.9
Social Security and Medicare	1.83	4.6	2.25	4.6	1.32	4.9	1.29	4.4	1.83	4.6
Social Security[4]	1.41	3.6	1.73	3.5	1.04	3.8	1.00	3.4	1.41	3.6
Medicare	0.42	1.1	0.53	1.1	0.28	1.0	0.29	1.0	0.42	1.1
Federal unemployment insurance	([5])	([6])	([5])	([6])	([5])	([6])	([5])	([6])	([5])	([6])
State unemployment insurance	0.06	0.2	0.06	0.1	0.06	0.2	0.07	0.2	0.06	0.2
Workers' compensation	0.46	1.2	0.41	0.8	0.33	1.2	0.59	2.0	0.46	1.2

Note: Individual items may not sum to totals due to rounding.

[1]This table presents data for the three major occupational groups in state and local government: management, professional, and related occupations, including teachers; sales and office occupations, including clerical workers; and service occupations, including police and firefighters.
[2]Service-providing industries, which include health and education services, employ a large proportion of the state and local government workforce.
[3]Includes premium pay for work in addition to the regular work schedule (such as overtime, weekends, and holidays).
[4]Comprises the Old Age, Survivors, and Disability Insurance (OASDI) program.
[5]Cost per hour worked is $0.01 or less.
[6]Less than 0.05 percent.

Table 6-9. Employer Compensation Costs Per Hour Worked for Employee Compensation and Costs as a Percent of Total Compensation: State and Local Government, by Major Occupational and Industry Group, June 2009

(Dollars, percent of total compensation.)

Characteristic	Total compensation	Wages and salaries	Cost per hour worked					
			Total	Paid leave	Supplemental pay	Insurance	Retirement and savings	Legally required benefits
COSTS PER HOUR WORKED								
State and Local Government Workers	39.66	26.01	13.65	3.27	0.34	4.51	3.17	2.36
Occupational Group								
Management, professional, and related	48.67	33.02	15.65	3.86	0.26	5.00	3.81	2.72
Professional and related	47.97	32.64	15.32	3.64	0.24	5.00	3.80	2.64
Teachers[1]	54.72	38.08	16.64	3.73	0.14	5.53	4.37	2.88
Primary, secondary, and special education school teachers	52.64	37.23	15.41	2.48	0.15	5.81	4.26	2.70
Sales and office	27.11	16.73	10.39	2.45	0.20	4.10	1.93	1.71
Office and administrative support	27.30	16.80	10.50	2.48	0.20	4.16	1.96	1.70
Service	29.31	17.73	11.58	2.62	0.57	3.66	2.78	1.95
Industry Group								
Education and health services	42.21	28.52	13.69	3.18	0.21	4.72	3.24	2.34
Education services	42.58	28.95	13.63	3.06	0.15	4.82	3.29	2.32
Elementary and secondary schools	41.72	28.71	13.01	2.27	0.15	4.97	3.37	2.25
Junior colleges, colleges, and universities	46.06	30.03	16.03	6.02	0.13	4.27	3.04	2.57
Health care and social assistance	39.96	25.88	14.08	3.91	0.60	4.14	2.92	2.50
Hospitals	36.28	23.33	12.96	3.49	0.74	4.31	2.09	2.33
Public administration	36.94	22.87	14.08	3.55	0.55	4.28	3.29	2.40
PERCENT OF TOTAL COMPENSATION								
State and Local Government Workers	100.0	65.6	34.4	8.2	0.9	11.4	8.0	6.0
Occupational Group								
Management, professional, and related	100.0	67.9	32.1	7.9	0.5	10.3	7.8	5.6
Professional and related	100.0	68.1	31.9	7.6	0.5	10.4	7.9	5.5
Teachers[1]	100.0	69.6	30.4	6.8	0.3	10.1	8.0	5.3
Primary, secondary, and special education school teachers	100.0	70.7	29.3	4.7	0.3	11.0	8.1	5.1
Sales and office	100.0	61.7	38.3	9.0	0.7	15.1	7.1	6.3
Office and administrative support	100.0	61.5	38.5	9.1	0.7	15.3	7.2	6.2
Service	100.0	60.5	39.5	9.0	1.9	12.5	9.5	6.7
Industry Group								
Education and health services	100.0	67.6	32.4	7.5	0.5	11.2	7.7	5.5
Education services	100.0	68.0	32.0	7.2	0.3	11.3	7.7	5.4
Elementary and secondary schools	100.0	68.8	31.2	5.4	0.4	11.9	8.1	5.4
Junior colleges, colleges, and universities	100.0	65.2	34.8	13.1	0.3	9.3	6.6	5.6
Health care and social assistance	100.0	64.8	35.2	9.8	1.5	10.4	7.3	6.3
Hospitals	100.0	64.3	35.7	9.6	2.0	11.9	5.8	6.4
Public administration	100.0	61.9	38.1	9.6	1.5	11.6	8.9	6.5

Note: Individual items may not sum to totals due to rounding.

[1]Includes postsecondary teachers; primary, secondary, and special education teachers; and other teachers and instructors.

Table 6-10. Employer Costs Per Hour Worked for Employee Compensation and Costs as a Percent of Total Compensation: Private Industry Workers, by Establishment Employment Size, June 2009

(Dollars, percent.)

Compensation component	1–99 workers					
	1–99 workers		1–49 workers		50–99 workers	
	Cost	Percent	Cost	Percent	Cost	Percent
TOTAL COMPENSATION	22.67	100.0	22.02	100.0	24.57	100.0
Wages and Salaries	16.71	73.7	16.37	74.4	17.68	72.0
Total Benefits	5.96	26.3	5.65	25.6	6.88	28.0
Paid leave	1.23	5.4	1.16	5.3	1.43	5.8
Vacation	0.61	2.7	0.58	2.6	0.71	2.9
Holiday	0.43	1.9	0.40	1.8	0.49	2.0
Sick	0.14	0.6	0.13	0.6	0.18	0.7
Personal	0.04	0.2	0.04	0.2	0.06	0.2
Supplemental pay	0.65	2.9	0.63	2.9	0.68	2.8
Overtime and premium pay	0.20	0.9	0.18	0.8	0.26	1.0
Shift differentials	0.02	0.1	-2.00	-3.0	0.03	0.1
Nonproduction bonuses	0.43	1.9	0.44	2.0	0.39	1.6
Insurance	1.50	6.6	1.38	6.3	1.85	7.5
Life insurance	0.03	0.1	0.03	0.1	0.04	0.2
Health insurance	1.41	6.2	1.30	5.9	1.73	7.1
Short-term disability	0.03	0.1	0.03	0.1	0.05	0.2
Long-term disability	0.02	0.1	0.02	0.1	0.03	0.1
Retirement and savings	0.56	2.5	0.49	2.2	0.75	3.1
Defined benefit plans	0.21	0.9	0.17	0.8	0.32	1.3
Defined contribution plans	0.35	1.5	0.32	1.5	0.43	1.8
Legally required benefits	2.03	9.0	1.98	9.0	2.17	8.8
Social Security and Medicare	1.39	6.1	1.36	6.2	1.49	6.1
Social Security	1.12	4.9	1.09	5.0	1.20	4.9
Medicare	0.27	1.2	0.26	1.2	0.29	1.2
Federal unemployment insurance	0.04	0.2	0.04	0.2	0.03	0.1
State unemployment insurance	0.15	0.7	0.15	0.7	0.15	0.6
Workers' compensation	0.45	2.0	0.44	2.0	0.49	2.0

Table 6-10. Employer Costs Per Hour Worked for Employee Compensation and Costs as a Percent of Total Compensation: Private Industry Workers, by Establishment Employment Size, June 2009—*Continued*

(Dollars, percent.)

Compensation component	100 workers or more					
	100 workers or more		100–499 workers		500 workers or more	
	Cost	Percent	Cost	Percent	Cost	Percent
TOTAL COMPENSATION	32.76	100.0	28.13	100.0	38.73	100.0
Wages and Salaries	22.42	68.4	19.69	70.0	25.93	66.9
Total Benefits	10.35	31.6	8.44	30.0	12.81	33.1
Paid leave	2.56	7.8	1.93	6.9	3.36	8.7
Vacation	1.34	4.1	1.00	3.5	1.79	4.6
Holiday	0.79	2.4	0.63	2.2	0.99	2.6
Sick	0.33	1.0	0.24	0.8	0.44	1.1
Personal	0.10	0.3	0.07	0.2	0.14	0.4
Supplemental pay	1.04	3.2	0.83	2.9	1.31	3.4
Overtime and premium pay	0.35	1.1	0.33	1.2	0.38	1.0
Shift differentials	0.12	0.4	0.07	0.3	0.18	0.5
Nonproduction bonuses	0.56	1.7	0.43	1.5	0.74	1.9
Insurance	2.84	8.7	2.39	8.5	3.43	8.9
Life insurance	0.06	0.2	0.05	0.2	0.07	0.2
Health insurance	2.65	8.1	2.24	7.9	3.18	8.2
Short-term disability	0.08	0.2	0.06	0.2	0.10	0.3
Long-term disability	0.06	0.2	0.04	0.2	0.08	0.2
Retirement and savings	1.38	4.2	0.97	3.4	1.92	4.9
Defined benefit plans	0.64	1.9	0.41	1.5	0.93	2.4
Defined contribution plans	0.74	2.3	0.56	2.0	0.98	2.5
Legally required benefits	2.53	7.7	2.33	8.3	2.79	7.2
Social Security and Medicare	1.90	5.8	1.64	5.8	2.23	5.8
Social Security	1.52	4.6	1.32	4.7	1.79	4.6
Medicare	0.38	1.2	0.32	1.2	0.45	1.2
Federal unemployment insurance ...	0.03	0.1	0.03	0.1	0.03	0.1
State unemployment insurance	0.15	0.5	0.16	0.6	0.14	0.4
Workers' compensation	0.45	1.4	0.49	1.8	0.39	1.0

NOTES AND DEFINITIONS

EMPLOYEE BENEFITS SURVEY

The Employee Benefits Survey provides data on the incidence and provisions of selected employee benefit plans.

Collection and Coverage

The March 2009 the National Compensation Survey (NCS) benefits survey represented about 122 million civilian workers; of this number, about 102 million were private industry workers and 19 million, state and local government workers. The survey included a sample of 18,287 establishments.

Definitions

Access to a benefit is determined on an occupational basis within an establishment. An employee is considered to have access to a benefit if it is available for his or her use.

Participation refers to the proportion of employees covered by a benefit. There will be cases where employees with access to a plan will not participate. For example, some employees may decline to participate in a health insurance plan if there is an employee cost involved.

A *private establishment* is an economic unit that produces goods or services, a central administrative office, or an auxiliary unit providing support services to a company. For private industries, the establishment is usually at a single physical location. For state and local governments, an establishment is defined as an agency or entity such as a school district, college, university, hospital, nursing home, administrative body, court, police department, fire department, health or social service operation, highway maintenance operation, urban transit operation, or other governmental unit. It provides services under the authority of a specific state or local government organization within a defined geographic area or jurisdiction.

Take-up rates are the percentage of workers with access to a plan who participate in the plan. They are computed by using the number of workers participating in a plan divided by the number of workers with access to the plan, times 100 and rounded to the nearest one percent. Since the computation of take-up rates is based on the number of workers collected, rather the rounded percentage estimates, the take-up rates in the tables may not equal the ratio of participation to access estimates.

An employee is considered to be a *union worker* when all the following conditions are met: 1.) a labor organization is recognized as the bargaining agent for all workers in the occupation. 2.) wage and salary rates are determined through collective bargaining or negotiations. 3.) settlement terms, which must include earnings provisions and may include benefit provisions, are embodied in a signed, mutually binding collective bargaining agreement

Sources of Additional Information

For more information, see Bureau of Labor Statistics (BLS) news release USDL 09-0872, "Employee Benefits in the United States, March 2009." For a listing of selected benefit definitions, see the *Glossary of Compensation Terms*. These resources are available on the BLS Web site at <http://www.bls.gov/ncs/ebs/>.

Table 6-11. Retirement Benefits:[1] Access, Participation, and Take-Up Rates,[2] March 2009

(Percent.)

Characteristic	Civilian[3]			Private industry			State and local government		
	Access	Participation	Take-up rate	Access	Participation	Take-up rate	Access	Participation	Take-up rate
ALL WORKERS	71	57	80	67	51	77	90	86	95
Worker Characteristics									
Management, professional, and related	83	75	89	80	69	87	92	87	95
Management, business, and financial	87	79	91	86	77	90	. . .	. . .	. . .
Professional and related	82	73	89	77	65	85	91	87	95
Teachers	85	81	94	. . .	. . .	. . .	91	88	96
Primary, secondary, and special education school teachers	92	88	96	. . .	. . .	. . .	97	94	97
Registered nurses	81	69	85	. . .	. . .	. . .	94	86	92
Service	51	34	67	45	26	57	84	79	95
Protective service	71	59	84	44	23	51	91	86	95
Sales and office	73	57	78	71	54	75	90	87	96
Sales and related	67	44	66	67	44	66	. . .	. . .	. . .
Office and administrative support	77	64	84	74	60	81	91	88	96
Natural resources, construction, and maintenance	70	57	81	68	53	79	94	91	97
Construction, extraction, farming, fishing, and forestry	67	53	79	64	49	76	. . .	. . .	. . .
Installation, maintenance, and repair	74	61	83	72	59	81	. . .	. . .	. . .
Production, transportation, and material moving	70	54	78	69	53	77	88	85	97
Production	70	57	80	70	56	80	. . .	. . .	. . .
Transportation and material moving	69	52	76	68	50	74	. . .	. . .	. . .
Full-time workers	80	67	84	76	61	80	99	95	96
Part-time workers	40	23	59	39	22	55	41	37	89
Union workers	92	87	95	87	82	94	97	94	96
Nonunion workers	67	51	77	65	48	74	84	79	95
Average Wage Within the Following Percentiles[4]									
Less than 10	34	15	44	35	15	43	58	54	92
10 to under 25	46	26	57	43	23	52	74	69	94
25 to under 50	72	56	78	69	50	73	94	89	95
50 to under 75	80	68	86	76	63	83	95	91	96
75 to under 90	88	81	91	84	75	89	97	94	96
90 or greater	90	82	92	86	78	90	97	94	96
Establishment Characteristics									
Goods-producing industries	75	63	83	75	62	83	. . .	. . .	. . .
Service-providing industries	70	56	80	65	49	75	90	85	95
Education and health services	79	68	86	71	56	79	91	87	95
Educational services	88	83	94	75	63	84	91	87	96
Elementary and secondary schools	91	87	96	. . .	. . .	. . .	93	90	97
Junior colleges, colleges, and universities	87	79	91	88	78	88	86	79	92
Health care and social assistance	72	57	80	70	55	78	92	83	90
Hospitals	89	77	87	. . .	. . .	. . .	93	83	90
Public administration	89	85	96	. . .	. . .	. . .	89	85	96
1 to 99 workers	54	38	71	53	36	69	78	75	96
1 to 49 workers	49	35	70	48	33	69	72	68	95
50 to 99 workers	68	48	71	66	46	69	88	85	97
100 workers or more	85	73	86	83	68	82	91	87	95
100 to 499 workers	80	64	80	79	61	77	87	83	95
500 workers or more	90	81	91	88	77	88	93	89	95
Geographic Areas[5]									
New England	66	55	83	63	50	80	86	83	97
Middle Atlantic	72	62	86	69	58	84	92	86	94
East North Central	72	59	81	70	55	78	85	82	97
West North Central	73	60	81	70	55	79	89	81	91
South Atlantic	72	56	77	68	49	72	91	85	94
East South Central	73	56	77	69	49	71	90	86	96
West South Central	67	51	77	62	44	71	90	88	98
Mountain	69	55	80	66	50	76	89	86	97
Pacific	68	55	82	63	49	77	92	89	97

[1]Includes defined benefit pension plans and defined contribution retirement plans. Workers are considered as having access or as participating if they have access to or participate in at least one of these plan types.
[2]The take-up rate is an estimate of the percentage of workers with access to a plan who participate in the plan, rounded for presentation.
[3]Includes workers in the private nonfarm economy except those in private households, and workers in the public sector, except the federal government.
[4]The percentile groupings are based on the average wage for each occupation surveyed, which may include workers both above and below the threshold.
[5]The states that comprise the Census divisions are: New England—Connecticut, Maine, Massachusetts, New Hampshire, Rhode Island, and Vermont; Middle Atlantic—New Jersey, New York, and Pennsylvania; South Atlantic—Delaware, District of Columbia, Florida, Georgia, Maryland, North Carolina, South Carolina, Virginia, and West Virginia; East South Central—Alabama, Kentucky, Mississippi, and Tennessee; West South Central—Arkansas, Louisiana, Oklahoma, and Texas; East North Central—Illinois, Indiana, Michigan, Ohio, and Wisconsin; West North Central—Iowa, Kansas, Minnesota, Missouri, Nebraska, North Dakota, and South Dakota; Mountain—Arizona, Colorado, Idaho, Montana, Nevada, New Mexico, Utah, and Wyoming; and Pacific—Alaska, California, Hawaii, Oregon, and Washington.
. . . = Not available or not applicable.

Table 6-12. Medical Care Benefits: Access, Participation, and Take-Up Rates,[1] March 2009

(Percent.)

Characteristic	Civilian[2]			Private industry			State and local government		
	Access	Participation	Take-up rate	Access	Participation	Take-up rate	Access	Participation	Take-up rate
ALL WORKERS	74	56	76	71	52	74	88	73	84
Worker Characteristics									
Management, professional, and related	87	69	80	86	67	78	90	74	82
Management, business, and financial	94	76	81	94	76	81	...	...	...
Professional and related	84	67	79	82	63	77	89	73	82
Teachers	84	67	80	...	...	...	89	73	82
Primary, secondary, and special education school teachers	92	73	80	...	...	...	95	77	82
Registered nurses	78	60	77	...	...	...	92	73	79
Service	51	35	69	46	29	63	81	69	85
Protective service	75	60	80	56	36	65	89	77	87
Sales and office	73	53	72	72	51	70	88	75	84
Sales and related	63	41	65	63	41	65	...	...	...
Office and administrative support	79	59	75	78	57	73	89	75	84
Natural resources, construction, and maintenance	78	63	81	77	61	80	95	83	88
Construction, extraction, farming, fishing, and forestry	73	59	82	70	57	81	...	...	...
Installation, maintenance, and repair	85	68	80	84	66	79	...	...	...
Production, transportation, and material moving	77	59	76	77	58	76	83	70	84
Production	82	66	81	82	66	81	...	...	...
Transportation and material moving	72	52	71	72	51	71	...	...	...
Full-time workers	88	68	77	86	65	75	99	83	84
Part-time workers	24	14	58	24	13	56	27	19	71
Union workers	92	78	84	90	76	85	95	80	84
Nonunion workers	70	51	73	69	49	72	81	68	83
Average Wage Within the Following Percentiles[3]									
Less than 10	26	13	51	25	13	50	51	40	78
10 to under 25	42	25	59	38	22	57	68	56	81
25 to under 50	79	58	74	77	54	71	91	79	86
50 to under 75	87	69	80	86	67	78	95	79	84
75 to under 90	92	74	81	89	72	81	97	80	83
90 or greater	92	75	81	90	73	80	97	80	83
Establishment Characteristics									
Goods-producing industries	85	70	82	85	70	82	...	...	...
Service-providing industries	71	53	74	68	48	71	88	73	83
Education and health services	80	61	76	75	53	71	89	73	82
Educational services	86	70	81	78	58	75	88	72	82
Elementary and secondary schools	88	70	80	...	...	...	89	72	81
Junior colleges, colleges, and universities	87	73	83	90	71	79	86	74	86
Health care and social assistance	76	55	72	74	53	71	91	76	83
Hospitals	88	69	79	...	...	...	94	76	81
Public administration	88	76	86	...	...	...	88	76	86
1 to 99 workers	60	43	72	59	42	72	75	64	86
1 to 49 workers	56	40	72	55	39	71	69	59	86
50 to 99 workers	72	53	73	71	51	72	85	73	85
100 workers or more	86	66	77	84	63	75	89	74	83
100 to 499 workers	81	61	75	81	59	73	84	72	86
500 workers or more	89	71	80	88	69	78	91	75	82
Geographic Areas[4]									
New England	72	53	73	70	50	71	85	69	81
Middle Atlantic	75	59	79	72	55	76	87	78	90
East North Central	73	54	74	72	53	73	81	63	78
West North Central	71	54	77	68	52	75	83	68	82
South Atlantic	75	55	74	72	51	71	91	75	83
East South Central	78	60	78	74	56	75	93	79	84
West South Central	70	52	74	66	47	71	90	76	84
Mountain	72	51	71	69	48	70	87	69	79
Pacific	75	59	79	72	56	78	90	77	86

[1]The take-up rate is an estimate of the percentage of workers with access to a plan who participate in the plan, rounded for presentation.
[2]Includes workers in the private nonfarm economy except those in private households, and workers in the public sector, except the federal government.
[3]The percentile groupings are based on the average wage for each occupation surveyed, which may include workers both above and below the threshold.
[4]The states that comprise the Census divisions are: New England—Connecticut, Maine, Massachusetts, New Hampshire, Rhode Island, and Vermont; Middle Atlantic—New Jersey, New York, and Pennsylvania; South Atlantic—Delaware, District of Columbia, Florida, Georgia, Maryland, North Carolina, South Carolina, Virginia, and West Virginia; East South Central—Alabama, Kentucky, Mississippi, and Tennessee; West South Central—Arkansas, Louisiana, Oklahoma, and Texas; East North Central—Illinois, Indiana, Michigan, Ohio, and Wisconsin; West North Central—Iowa, Kansas, Minnesota, Missouri, Nebraska, North Dakota, and South Dakota; Mountain—Arizona, Colorado, Idaho, Montana, Nevada, New Mexico, Utah, and Wyoming; and Pacific—Alaska, California, Hawaii, Oregon, and Washington.
. . . = Not available or not applicable.

Table 6-13. Medical Plans: Share of Premiums Paid by Employer and Employee for Single Coverage, March 2009

(Percent.)

Characteristic	Civilian[1]		Private industry		State and local government	
	Employer share of premium	Employee share of premium	Employer share of premium	Employee share of premium	Employer share of premium	Employee share of premium
ALL WORKERS	82	18	80	20	90	10
Worker Characteristics						
Management, professional, and related	84	16	81	19	90	10
Management, business, and financial	83	17	81	19	. . .	. . .
Professional and related	84	16	81	19	89	11
Teachers	89	11	. . .	. . .	90	10
Primary, secondary, and special education school teachers	89	11	. . .	. . .	90	10
Registered nurses	82	18	. . .	. . .	87	13
Service	82	18	78	22	90	10
Protective service	85	15	71	29	90	10
Sales and office	80	20	79	21	90	10
Sales and related	76	24	76	24	. . .	. . .
Office and administrative support	82	18	81	19	90	10
Natural resources, construction, and maintenance	83	17	82	18	90	10
Construction, extraction, farming, fishing, and forestry	85	15	85	15	. . .	. . .
Installation, maintenance, and repair	81	19	80	20	. . .	. . .
Production, transportation, and material moving	82	18	82	18	91	9
Production	82	18	82	18	. . .	. . .
Transportation and material moving	83	17	82	18	. . .	. . .
Full-time workers	83	17	81	19	90	10
Part-time workers	79	21	78	22	88	12
Union workers	91	9	90	10	91	9
Nonunion workers	80	20	79	21	89	11
Average Wage Within the Following Percentiles[2]						
Less than 10	75	25	75	25	89	11
10 to under 25	77	23	76	24	90	10
25 to under 50	81	19	79	21	90	10
50 to under 75	83	17	81	19	90	10
75 to under 90	85	15	83	17	90	10
90 or greater	85	15	82	18	91	9
Establishment Characteristics						
Goods-producing industries	82	18	82	18	. . .	. . .
Service-providing industries	82	18	80	20	90	10
Education and health services	85	15	82	18	90	10
Educational services	88	12	82	18	90	10
Elementary and secondary schools	89	11	. . .	. . .	90	10
Junior colleges, colleges, and universities	87	13	80	20	90	10
Health care and social assistance	83	17	82	18	87	13
Hospitals	82	18	. . .	. . .	88	12
Public administration	90	10	. . .	. . .	90	10
1 to 99 workers	81	19	80	20	91	9
1 to 49 workers	81	19	81	19	92	8
50 to 99 workers	81	19	79	21	91	9
100 workers or more	83	17	81	19	90	10
100 to 499 workers	82	18	80	20	90	10
500 workers or more	85	15	81	19	89	11
Geographic Areas[3]						
New England	79	21	78	22	87	13
Middle Atlantic	84	16	82	18	93	7
East North Central	81	19	79	21	90	10
West North Central	82	18	80	20	91	9
South Atlantic	81	19	79	21	88	12
East South Central	81	19	78	22	91	9
West South Central	83	17	82	18	87	13
Mountain	82	18	79	21	92	8
Pacific	85	15	84	16	89	11

[1]Includes workers in the private nonfarm economy except those in private households, and workers in the public sector, except the federal government.
[2]The percentile groupings are based on the average wage for each occupation surveyed, which may include workers both above and below the threshold.
[3]The states that comprise the Census divisions are: New England—Connecticut, Maine, Massachusetts, New Hampshire, Rhode Island, and Vermont; Middle Atlantic—New Jersey, New York, and Pennsylvania; South Atlantic—Delaware, District of Columbia, Florida, Georgia, Maryland, North Carolina, South Carolina, Virginia, and West Virginia; East South Central—Alabama, Kentucky, Mississippi, and Tennessee; West South Central—Arkansas, Louisiana, Oklahoma, and Texas; East North Central—Illinois, Indiana, Michigan, Ohio, and Wisconsin; West North Central—Iowa, Kansas, Minnesota, Missouri, Nebraska, North Dakota, and South Dakota; Mountain—Arizona, Colorado, Idaho, Montana, Nevada, New Mexico, Utah, and Wyoming; and Pacific—Alaska, California, Hawaii, Oregon, and Washington.
. . . = Not available or not applicable.

Table 6-14. Access to Paid Sick Leave, Vacation, and Holidays, March 2009

(Percent.)

Characteristic	Civilian[1]			Private industry			State and local government		
	Paid sick leave	Paid vacation	Paid holidays	Paid sick leave	Paid vacation	Paid holidays	Paid sick leave	Paid vacation	Paid holidays
ALL WORKERS	66	75	76	61	78	77	89	60	68
Worker Characteristics									
Management, professional, and related	86	74	79	84	87	89	90	44	56
Management, business, and financial	90	94	95	89	96	96	...	...	...
Professional and related	85	67	73	82	83	85	90	37	51
Teachers	84	17	35	...	...	...	88	12	32
Primary, secondary, and special education school teachers	91	13	32	...	...	...	93	9	28
Registered nurses	78	80	82	...	...	...	92	79	81
Service	49	63	57	42	61	53	85	75	77
Protective service	66	78	74	35	65	59	89	87	86
Sales and office	69	81	82	66	80	81	90	85	87
Sales and related	56	72	71	56	72	71	...	...	...
Office and administrative support	76	86	88	74	86	88	91	86	87
Natural resources, construction, and maintenance	53	78	79	49	76	77	94	95	95
Construction, extraction, farming, fishing, and forestry	39	66	67	33	63	64	...	...	...
Installation, maintenance, and repair	69	91	92	67	91	91	...	...	...
Production, transportation, and material moving	53	82	84	52	83	84	88	64	76
Production	53	90	91	52	90	91	...	...	...
Transportation and material moving	54	75	77	52	76	78	...	...	...
Full-time workers	77	86	87	73	91	89	98	67	75
Part-time workers	28	36	38	26	38	39	42	20	31
Union workers	82	73	79	69	85	86	97	57	70
Nonunion workers	63	76	75	61	77	76	83	62	66
Average Wage Within the Following Percentiles[2]									
Less than 10	22	43	37	21	42	36	60	39	46
10 to under 25	37	56	54	33	55	52	75	55	63
25 to under 50	68	83	84	64	85	84	92	84	87
50 to under 75	77	88	89	73	89	89	94	72	77
75 to under 90	86	77	80	81	88	88	96	37	51
90 or greater	88	74	77	84	88	88	98	35	47
Establishment Characteristics									
Goods-producing industries	53	86	87	52	86	87	...	...	...
Service-providing industries	68	73	74	63	76	75	89	60	68
Education and health services	82	66	72	77	80	82	90	43	56
Educational services	87	40	54	76	54	64	90	36	51
Elementary and secondary schools	90	27	44	...	...	...	90	27	43
Junior colleges, colleges, and universities	86	69	79	82	73	81	88	66	78
Health care and social assistance	78	85	85	77	84	84	91	91	91
Hospitals	88	91	89	...	...	...	92	94	93
Public administration	89	88	87	...	...	...	89	88	87
1 to 99 workers	53	70	69	52	71	69	79	66	70
1 to 49 workers	52	69	68	51	69	68	73	69	69
50 to 99 workers	56	75	74	54	76	74	88	63	71
100 workers or more	77	79	81	72	86	86	91	59	67
100 to 499 workers	70	80	81	67	84	84	87	59	63
500 workers or more	84	78	82	80	90	89	92	59	69
Geographic Areas[3]									
New England	73	73	75	70	77	78	87	49	55
Middle Atlantic	71	76	78	67	79	81	90	58	63
East North Central	60	74	76	56	78	77	85	53	65
West North Central	66	73	74	62	77	75	88	55	68
South Atlantic	64	78	78	59	80	78	93	67	78
East South Central	63	77	77	55	79	77	92	69	75
West South Central	65	75	75	61	79	80	86	52	53
Mountain	62	72	71	59	75	74	84	55	59
Pacific	70	75	74	65	77	74	93	67	76

[1]Includes workers in the private nonfarm economy except those in private households, and workers in the public sector, except the federal government.
[2]The percentile groupings are based on the average wage for each occupation surveyed, which may include workers both above and below the threshold.
[3]The states that comprise the Census divisions are: New England—Connecticut, Maine, Massachusetts, New Hampshire, Rhode Island, and Vermont; Middle Atlantic—New Jersey, New York, and Pennsylvania; South Atlantic—Delaware, District of Columbia, Florida, Georgia, Maryland, North Carolina, South Carolina, Virginia, and West Virginia; East South Central—Alabama, Kentucky, Mississippi, and Tennessee; West South Central—Arkansas, Louisiana, Oklahoma, and Texas; East North Central—Illinois, Indiana, Michigan, Ohio, and Wisconsin; West North Central—Iowa, Kansas, Minnesota, Missouri, Nebraska, North Dakota, and South Dakota; Mountain—Arizona, Colorado, Idaho, Montana, Nevada, New Mexico, Utah, and Wyoming; and Pacific—Alaska, California, Hawaii, Oregon, and Washington.
. . . = Not available or not applicable.

NOTES AND DEFINITIONS

OCCUPATIONAL EARNINGS

Collection and Coverage

Tables 6-15, 6-16, and 6-17 present occupational pay estimates for the nation. The data were compiled from locality data collected between December 2007 and January 2009. The average reference period is July 2008.

Concepts and Definitions

Earnings are regular payments from the employer to the employee as compensation for straight-time hourly work, or for any salaried work performed. The following components were included as part of earnings:

- Incentive pay, including commissions, production bonuses, and piece rates
- Cost-of-living allowances
- Hazard pay
- Payments of income deferred due to participation in a salary reduction plan
- Deadhead pay, defined as pay given to transportation workers returning in a vehicle without freight or passengers

Work levels are standardized measures of duties and responsibilities that apply to all occupations.

Percentiles designate position in the earnings distribution and are calculated from individual worker earnings and the hours those workers are scheduled to work. Tables 6-16 and 6-17 provide estimates on the mean hourly wage for the 10th percentile, the 25th percentile, the 50th percentile (the median), the 75th percentile, and the 90th percentile of occupational wages, by ownership sector and for full- and part-time workers within the sectors.

An *incentive worker* is any employee whose earnings are at least partly tied to commissions, piece rates, production bonuses, or other incentives based on production or sales.

A *time-based worker* is any employee whose earnings are tied to an hourly rate or salary, and not to a specific level of production.

Sources of Additional Information

An extensive description of the sampling, weighting and estimation steps and many additional detailed tables are available in BLS Bulletin 2720, "National Compensation Survey: Occupational Earnings in the United States, 2008," which is available on the BLS Web site at <http://www.bls.gov>.

Table 6-15. Mean Hourly Earnings[1] and Weekly Hours, by Selected Worker and Establishment Characteristics, National Compensation Survey, 2008

(Dollars, number of hours.)

Characteristic	Civilian workers		Private workers		State and local government workers	
	Mean hourly earnings	Mean weekly hours[2]	Mean hourly earnings	Mean weekly hours[2]	Mean hourly earnings	Mean weekly hours[2]
TOTAL	20.62	35.5	19.92	35.4	25.08	36.2
Worker Characteristics[3]						
Management, professional, and related occupations	33.56	37.0	34.13	37.4	31.83	35.9
Management, business, and financial occupations	37.57	39.6	38.17	39.9	34.08	37.5
Professional and related occupations	31.67	35.9	31.82	36.0	31.30	35.6
Service occupations	11.68	31.2	10.29	30.3	18.46	36.5
Sales and office occupations	16.31	34.9	16.27	34.7	16.76	36.4
Sales and related occupations	17.34	32.6	17.35	32.6	16.26	34.2
Office and administrative support occupations	15.74	36.2	15.60	36.2	16.78	36.5
Natural resources, construction, and maintenance occupations	20.81	39.2	20.88	39.3	20.11	38.8
Construction and extraction occupations	20.91	39.2	21.05	39.3	19.38	38.6
Installation, maintenance, and repair occupations	20.84	39.3	20.82	39.4	21.04	39.2
Production, transportation, and material moving occupations	15.53	37.4	15.43	37.5	18.59	34.4
Production occupations	15.92	38.8	15.85	38.8	20.62	39.0
Transportation and material moving occupations	15.11	35.9	14.97	36.0	17.95	33.2
Full-time workers	21.90	39.6	21.25	39.7	25.72	38.9
Part-time workers	11.76	20.6	11.43	20.8	15.99	18.5
Union workers	24.74	36.7	22.44	36.6	28.18	37.0
Nonunion workers	19.89	35.3	19.62	35.2	22.59	35.6
Time workers	20.32	35.3	19.53	35.2	25.06	36.2
Incentive workers	25.93	38.1	25.89	38.1	111.64	26.7
Establishment Characteristics						
Goods-producing	(4)	(4)	21.58	39.5	(4)	(4)
Service-providing	(4)	(4)	19.44	34.3	(4)	(4)
1–49 workers	17.42	34.0	17.38	34.1	18.90	32.9
50–99 workers	18.77	34.9	18.68	34.8	20.26	35.9
100–499 workers	20.18	36.2	19.79	36.2	23.23	36.0
500 workers or more	25.79	37.0	25.35	37.2	26.69	36.7

[1]Earnings are the straight-time hourly wages or salaries paid to employees. They include incentive pay, cost-of-living adjustments, and hazard pay. Excluded are premium pay for overtime, vacations, and holidays; nonproduction bonuses; and tips. The mean is computed by totaling the pay of all workers and dividing by the number of workers, weighted by hours.
[2]Mean weekly hours are the hours an employee is scheduled to work in a week, not including overtime.
[3]Employees are classified as working either a full-time or part-time schedule based on the definition used by each establishment. Union workers are those whose wages are determined through collective bargaining. Wages of time workers are based solely on hourly rate or salary; incentive workers are those whose wages are at least partly based on productivity payments such as piece rates, commissions, and production bonuses.
[4]Classification of establishments into goods-producing and service-producing industries applies to private industry only.

Table 6-16. Private Industry Workers: Hourly Wage Percentiles,[1] 2008

(Dollars.)

Occupation	Wages fall at or below the following percentiles:				
	10	25	50	75	90
ALL OCCUPATIONS	8.00	10.50	15.50	24.22	36.43
Management	20.80	27.78	38.82	54.23	69.74
Chief executives	32.81	52.56	81.21	125.48	158.65
General and operations managers	22.95	29.86	41.67	61.38	87.05
Advertising and promotions managers	19.01	24.04	33.65	48.07	62.05
Marketing and sales managers	24.86	33.12	43.43	58.89	74.17
Marketing managers	28.85	36.06	46.81	61.51	74.17
Sales managers	23.50	30.38	41.25	57.07	74.35
Public relations managers	18.13	22.19	35.70	51.52	76.73
Administrative services managers	20.19	25.48	30.87	38.89	51.01
Computer and information systems managers	32.19	42.83	53.41	64.17	74.54
Financial managers	22.16	28.38	38.95	55.66	72.92
Human resources managers	22.36	28.10	39.08	48.60	64.69
Compensation and benefits managers	19.00	25.53	31.73	42.55	57.69
Training and development managers	24.94	33.00	35.73	46.49	71.48
Industrial production managers	27.34	33.44	41.67	48.34	60.03
Purchasing managers	23.08	29.70	39.09	50.80	62.60
Transportation, storage, and distribution managers	20.63	25.38	34.61	49.62	61.50
Agricultural managers	16.25	16.25	23.39	43.75	56.73
Farm, ranch, and other agricultural managers	16.25	16.25	23.39	43.75	56.73
Construction managers	22.30	27.93	36.10	45.43	53.85
Education administrators	16.82	21.18	28.61	34.62	53.22
Education administrators, preschool and child care center/program	14.19	17.00	22.78	30.52	30.52
Education administrators, elementary and secondary school	27.04	28.15	33.65	44.47	54.47
Education administrators, postsecondary	22.14	25.01	31.71	48.34	62.08
Engineering managers	36.00	44.35	57.47	64.98	71.64
Food service managers	14.43	17.63	23.22	29.37	40.59
Funeral directors	17.31	19.12	20.37	34.31	35.42
Lodging managers	12.19	17.09	18.88	32.69	39.76
Medical and health services managers	20.00	27.27	35.51	47.44	55.71
Natural sciences managers	30.95	38.00	41.48	54.97	70.09
Property, real estate, and community association managers	15.80	19.21	23.08	32.24	38.46
Social and community service managers	16.49	18.12	24.04	29.95	37.61
Business and Financial Operations	18.09	22.04	28.09	35.77	47.19
Buyers and purchasing agents	18.89	21.59	25.99	32.60	41.39
Purchasing agents and buyers, farm products	20.74	23.81	27.91	41.39	41.39
Wholesale and retail buyers, except farm products	17.79	20.19	24.71	31.91	43.54
Purchasing agents, except wholesale, retail, and farm products	19.19	22.10	26.44	32.45	40.83
Claims adjusters, appraisers, examiners, and investigators	17.31	19.85	25.00	30.93	38.46
Claims adjusters, examiners, and investigators	17.24	19.85	24.81	30.88	38.46
Insurance appraisers, auto damage	18.00	20.00	27.77	30.96	34.54
Compliance officers, except agriculture, construction, health and safety, and transportation	19.84	22.57	24.42	34.08	38.46
Cost estimators	18.85	21.88	29.37	38.46	45.70
Human resources, training, and labor relations specialists	17.75	21.70	27.86	33.06	41.88
Employment, recruitment, and placement specialists	16.00	19.16	24.63	33.65	40.78
Compensation, benefits, and job analysis specialists	18.43	20.02	25.00	32.98	37.09
Training and development specialists	17.45	23.17	28.74	32.28	41.35
Logisticians	19.30	21.69	31.06	38.57	47.12
Management analysts	21.84	26.44	34.55	46.45	56.32
Meeting and convention planners	16.90	18.03	23.30	28.00	29.04
Accountants and auditors	18.15	22.11	27.55	34.53	44.71
Appraisers and assessors of real estate	17.36	18.24	24.04	33.18	40.87
Budget analysts	20.51	27.83	27.83	35.49	45.48
Credit analysts	18.67	20.90	24.85	30.58	38.94
Financial analysts and advisors	19.43	23.96	30.77	41.44	56.98
Financial analysts	22.56	25.64	32.64	43.87	59.39
Personal financial advisors	16.12	19.00	23.10	37.02	56.98
Insurance underwriters	19.67	22.37	29.51	39.65	49.65
Financial examiners	19.15	22.13	25.72	30.26	34.72
Loan counselors and officers	15.42	18.27	25.21	37.94	60.16
Loan counselors	12.50	17.50	21.62	34.75	42.42
Loan officers	15.42	18.27	25.48	38.46	60.16
Tax examiners, collectors, preparers, and revenue agents	9.00	9.00	13.06	17.64	29.50
Tax preparers	9.00	9.00	13.06	17.64	29.50
Computer and Mathematical Science	20.29	26.44	35.85	44.67	53.73
Computer and information scientists, research	26.83	36.55	48.08	58.70	72.12
Computer programmers	21.31	25.77	34.34	40.98	50.48
Computer software engineers	28.59	34.78	42.22	50.10	58.94
Computer software engineers, applications	27.89	33.61	41.12	50.00	58.56
Computer software engineers, systems software	31.29	35.90	43.22	50.35	59.05
Computer support specialists	14.42	18.50	23.37	31.62	42.41
Computer systems analysts	25.48	30.72	38.46	45.48	54.48
Database administrators	22.16	25.41	36.30	44.32	50.21
Network and computer systems administrators	20.30	24.04	30.70	38.86	45.94
Network systems and data communications analysts	22.41	26.40	33.33	42.31	48.51
Actuaries	25.64	32.83	40.53	51.07	61.31
Operations research analysts	19.79	25.21	34.29	45.19	50.12
Statisticians	18.44	29.53	35.10	50.18	55.64

[1]Percentiles designate position in the earnings distribution and are calculated from individual worker earnings and the hours they are scheduled to work.

Table 6-16. Private Industry Workers: Hourly Wage Percentiles,[1] 2008—*Continued*

(Dollars.)

Occupation	Wages fall at or below the following percentiles:				
	10	25	50	75	90
Architecture and Engineering	18.73	25.00	32.89	42.87	53.29
Architects, except naval	20.00	23.37	28.93	38.85	50.92
Architects, except landscape and naval	20.19	23.65	30.77	40.10	51.15
Landscape architects	20.00	20.30	25.65	29.92	32.80
Surveyors, cartographers, and photogrammetrists	17.10	19.67	26.05	37.35	52.68
Surveyors	19.67	24.00	27.97	37.35	52.68
Engineers	25.96	31.54	39.17	47.60	58.12
Aerospace engineers	34.44	41.46	50.50	59.68	70.00
Chemical engineers	31.25	32.32	41.16	52.97	60.52
Civil engineers	23.32	25.96	34.85	42.66	50.26
Computer hardware engineers	28.80	35.89	45.86	54.04	64.92
Electrical and electronics engineers	26.79	32.69	38.59	46.12	56.20
Electrical engineers	24.72	32.23	38.46	45.91	55.08
Electronics engineers, except computer	28.45	33.03	39.20	46.32	57.50
Environmental engineers	24.04	30.24	41.96	47.63	53.30
Industrial engineers, including health and safety	24.54	29.97	35.89	43.00	50.91
Health and safety engineers, except mining safety engineers and inspectors	30.03	31.75	36.54	50.91	58.78
Industrial engineers	24.22	29.02	35.41	42.04	48.56
Materials engineers	26.44	28.60	35.21	48.12	58.26
Mechanical engineers	25.41	29.49	34.97	42.09	50.00
Nuclear engineers	34.71	38.10	42.01	45.85	52.99
Petroleum engineers	29.75	39.37	50.71	76.97	83.56
Drafters	14.78	18.00	22.42	29.13	38.24
Architectural and civil drafters	14.78	17.50	21.39	29.65	35.90
Electrical and electronics drafters	13.89	15.43	22.81	25.92	30.66
Mechanical drafters	17.57	20.00	22.68	29.13	32.60
Engineering technicians, except drafters	13.61	19.01	25.24	29.56	35.28
Aerospace engineering and operations technicians	22.00	25.00	27.72	32.36	36.70
Civil engineering technicians	12.00	13.25	15.45	24.52	27.50
Electrical and electronic engineering technicians	13.61	18.54	24.62	29.03	33.08
Electro-mechanical technicians	19.71	23.63	26.45	29.56	31.80
Environmental engineering technicians	14.00	14.00	18.00	20.90	28.45
Industrial engineering technicians	17.19	20.03	25.00	29.27	34.38
Mechanical engineering technicians	18.50	20.08	24.74	33.18	41.84
Surveying and mapping technicians	12.50	14.00	21.00	25.48	40.50
Life, Physical, and Social Science	16.66	21.00	27.61	38.47	52.00
Life scientists	18.53	23.01	32.41	44.62	64.04
Agricultural and food scientists	15.87	32.41	40.94	44.62	44.62
Biological scientists	18.27	21.22	34.24	41.83	58.61
Biochemists and biophysicists	17.65	21.64	38.91	54.12	88.38
Conservation scientists and foresters	16.83	21.64	26.25	28.52	53.18
Medical scientists	19.54	23.63	31.20	46.15	66.34
Physical scientists	20.67	25.25	32.26	45.29	55.67
Astronomers and physicists	25.23	46.12	50.30	73.45	75.94
Physicists	25.23	46.12	49.90	73.45	75.94
Chemists and materials scientists	21.64	25.63	31.58	43.13	57.65
Chemists	21.64	25.23	30.35	39.50	55.59
Materials scientists	30.93	34.07	49.47	55.63	64.66
Environmental scientists and geoscientists	19.23	23.83	31.67	41.54	50.43
Environmental scientists and specialists, including health	18.51	21.64	28.05	36.20	47.89
Geoscientists, except hydrologists and geographers	22.82	28.85	34.68	48.08	50.77
Economists	21.64	21.64	35.48	43.27	100.96
Market and survey researchers	19.88	23.61	29.86	43.42	53.62
Market research analysts	21.64	24.04	29.90	45.40	53.62
Psychologists	16.41	17.39	23.03	33.47	56.81
Clinical, counseling, and school psychologists	17.39	17.39	24.50	40.63	56.81
Miscellaneous social scientists and related workers	21.63	22.60	30.07	45.48	64.11
Agricultural and food science technicians	14.00	15.00	16.96	21.46	34.66
Biological technicians	12.00	15.16	19.51	24.04	27.48
Chemical technicians	14.00	17.05	21.97	26.89	31.39
Geological and petroleum technicians	13.87	23.33	26.22	37.07	43.27
Nuclear technicians	27.50	31.17	36.37	43.87	44.93
Social science research assistants	15.41	20.00	23.00	25.00	30.00
Miscellaneous life, physical, and social science technicians	15.00	16.45	20.59	26.71	32.87
Environmental science and protection technicians, including health	16.50	21.20	26.71	32.87	32.87
Community and Social Services	11.00	13.57	16.69	21.00	27.81
Counselors	11.00	13.37	16.82	20.33	26.50
Substance abuse and behavioral disorder counselors	13.22	15.00	16.93	20.24	22.26
Educational, vocational, and school counselors	13.10	14.98	18.50	24.04	35.93
Mental health counselors	11.89	15.01	18.42	22.18	30.00
Rehabilitation counselors	10.35	11.25	14.31	17.35	18.59
Social workers	13.48	15.85	18.40	24.00	29.28
Child, family, and school social workers	12.50	14.29	16.83	19.87	24.73
Medical and public health social workers	15.40	18.83	23.23	28.92	31.86
Mental health and substance abuse social workers	13.85	15.87	17.31	22.00	30.29
Miscellaneous community and social service specialists	9.50	11.40	14.01	16.83	20.95
Health educators	9.93	22.66	35.00	41.00	48.06
Social and human service assistants	9.22	10.44	12.98	15.03	18.00
Clergy	9.65	13.00	14.87	20.67	24.76
Directors, religious activities and education	16.00	20.93	24.57	25.00	41.46

[1]Percentiles designate position in the earnings distribution and are calculated from individual worker earnings and the hours they are scheduled to work.

Table 6-16. Private Industry Workers: Hourly Wage Percentiles,[1] 2008—*Continued*

(Dollars.)

Occupation	Wages fall at or below the following percentiles:				
	10	25	50	75	90
Legal	16.15	19.70	30.29	52.55	81.73
Lawyers	26.44	35.58	53.83	77.88	97.84
Paralegals and legal assistants	15.38	17.44	21.64	29.33	34.62
Miscellaneous legal support workers	14.73	16.74	20.87	26.16	33.91
Law clerks	13.00	14.00	16.75	39.26	39.26
Title examiners, abstractors, and searchers	14.90	17.20	20.87	26.32	30.91
Education, Training, and Library	9.37	11.89	20.47	33.98	49.68
Postsecondary teachers	22.77	29.85	40.29	55.29	83.73
Business teachers, postsecondary	20.94	26.16	33.68	59.60	90.55
Math and computer teachers, postsecondary	24.70	33.76	35.99	53.29	72.07
Computer science teachers, postsecondary	20.83	27.73	37.84	59.69	82.84
Mathematical science teachers, postsecondary	33.66	33.76	33.76	49.74	68.42
Engineering and architecture teachers, postsecondary	38.11	47.47	81.41	90.58	103.86
Engineering teachers, postsecondary	38.11	49.71	81.41	92.63	103.86
Life sciences teachers, postsecondary	30.58	42.58	48.04	55.70	130.13
Biological science teachers, postsecondary	30.58	42.41	47.64	55.70	132.13
Physical sciences teachers, postsecondary	39.09	45.90	54.95	68.27	87.83
Chemistry teachers, postsecondary	39.09	43.56	50.50	58.43	75.93
Physics teachers, postsecondary	48.41	52.40	55.43	87.83	87.83
Social sciences teachers, postsecondary	31.04	34.19	44.51	54.61	72.92
Economics teachers, postsecondary	34.80	38.87	59.52	69.33	72.31
Political science teachers, postsecondary	26.29	45.55	47.39	49.04	50.94
Psychology teachers, postsecondary	27.33	31.04	41.84	55.27	74.42
Sociology teachers, postsecondary	35.14	40.49	41.15	55.96	96.61
Health teachers, postsecondary	28.48	37.49	63.75	86.55	115.25
Health specialties teachers, postsecondary	28.48	56.86	70.46	89.43	132.21
Nursing instructors and teachers, postsecondary	28.36	31.88	36.08	38.65	40.77
Education and library science teachers, postsecondary	24.52	31.73	41.53	41.53	44.36
Education teachers, postsecondary	24.52	31.73	41.53	41.53	44.36
Law, criminal justice, and social work teachers, postsecondary	32.88	33.22	68.17	88.72	107.53
Law teachers, postsecondary	52.61	68.17	80.84	101.68	107.53
Arts, communications, and humanities teachers, postsecondary	26.66	31.77	39.91	47.69	58.94
Art, drama, and music teachers, postsecondary	26.97	32.04	38.20	42.45	43.27
Communications teachers, postsecondary	21.16	21.84	31.72	59.47	75.28
English language and literature teachers, postsecondary	28.63	34.09	42.07	52.46	66.07
Foreign language and literature teachers, postsecondary	29.51	36.44	48.77	55.07	78.38
History teachers, postsecondary	28.40	30.20	44.21	50.70	63.06
Philosophy and religion teachers, postsecondary	26.61	30.59	36.18	44.75	58.54
Miscellaneous postsecondary teachers	19.00	23.09	30.48	38.43	57.28
Recreation and fitness studies teachers, postsecondary	10.00	18.00	26.97	31.01	31.01
Vocational education teachers, postsecondary	17.05	21.00	24.11	31.88	33.38
Primary, secondary, and special education school teachers	9.84	13.04	19.50	31.23	38.29
Preschool and kindergarten teachers	9.00	10.50	13.37	15.63	23.00
Preschool teachers, except special education	9.00	10.50	13.37	15.63	23.00
Kindergarten teachers, except special education	7.70	7.70	13.08	18.77	23.93
Elementary and middle school teachers	16.37	20.90	26.39	33.60	38.86
Elementary school teachers, except special education	16.77	21.04	26.16	33.27	37.19
Middle school teachers, except special and vocational education	10.85	20.07	28.21	36.01	42.48
Secondary school teachers	18.05	24.67	32.99	41.04	52.30
Secondary school teachers, except special and vocational education	20.44	25.21	33.24	41.57	52.38
Special education teachers	17.02	20.14	25.78	32.27	60.00
Special education teachers, preschool, kindergarten, and elementary school	18.03	20.14	25.44	31.67	36.11
Special education teachers, secondary school	10.50	25.15	32.15	53.85	66.98
Other teachers and instructors	9.61	14.00	19.78	26.89	36.06
Self-enrichment education teachers	10.25	18.67	19.23	21.00	27.00
Archivists, curators, and museum technicians	14.28	22.94	25.28	30.13	32.69
Archivists	12.85	14.36	23.87	23.87	32.69
Curators	22.94	23.85	26.96	30.24	38.32
Librarians	19.51	21.59	29.21	39.69	54.83
Library technicians	13.47	14.35	16.99	23.70	27.06
Instructional coordinators	20.43	20.47	25.48	34.96	38.27
Teacher assistants	8.16	9.17	10.09	11.89	13.04
Arts, Design, Entertainment, Sports, and Media	11.50	15.63	22.21	31.39	44.09
Artists and related workers	14.85	16.83	25.05	37.96	48.76
Art directors	16.83	21.64	29.42	42.86	48.76
Multi-media artists and animators	15.08	17.00	27.38	34.62	47.03
Designers	11.50	15.51	21.00	30.37	38.73
Commercial and industrial designers	23.52	28.30	33.26	41.40	45.33
Fashion designers	20.83	24.04	33.65	48.08	49.23
Floral designers	7.85	8.50	10.35	12.00	15.00
Graphic designers	14.00	16.83	19.50	26.99	34.40
Interior designers	16.00	18.38	27.92	31.39	38.73
Merchandise displayers and window trimmers	10.00	11.60	15.00	20.37	25.12
Set and exhibit designers	18.03	18.03	20.33	49.91	65.00
Actors, producers, and directors	11.00	17.43	22.96	46.09	86.09
Producers and directors	11.77	17.43	22.96	46.09	86.09
Athletes, coaches, umpires, and related workers	9.00	12.00	19.33	26.87	34.38
Coaches and scouts	9.25	12.00	19.71	28.05	35.54
Umpires, referees, and other sports officials	5.34	8.31	26.67	26.67	26.67
Dancers and choreographers	7.00	10.35	17.84	25.00	30.35
Dancers	7.00	7.00	10.35	30.35	30.35
Choreographers	11.16	15.60	17.84	25.00	27.00
Musicians, singers, and related workers	15.58	21.96	30.44	40.45	53.04
Music directors and composers	15.58	21.96	21.96	26.44	31.39
Musicians and singers	13.26	30.44	32.92	41.35	58.03

[1]Percentiles designate position in the earnings distribution and are calculated from individual worker earnings and the hours they are scheduled to work.

Table 6-16. Private Industry Workers: Hourly Wage Percentiles,[1] 2008—*Continued*

(Dollars.)

Occupation	Wages fall at or below the following percentiles:				
	10	25	50	75	90
Arts, Design, Entertainment, Sports, and Media—*Continued*					
Announcers	8.50	12.00	18.00	26.14	50.48
Radio and television announcers	8.50	12.00	18.00	27.12	60.64
News analysts, reporters and correspondents	11.71	14.22	23.08	38.48	68.17
Reporters and correspondents	11.67	14.00	22.34	34.71	63.07
Public relations specialists	18.69	21.30	25.99	33.18	50.48
Writers and editors	14.72	18.75	27.05	33.65	48.01
Editors	14.69	18.13	24.52	33.49	46.15
Technical writers	16.59	20.80	28.79	37.76	49.14
Writers and authors	17.30	18.43	23.98	29.57	51.28
Miscellaneous media and communication workers	18.06	21.29	23.25	25.00	28.36
Interpreters and translators	18.06	21.35	21.35	31.00	32.50
Broadcast and sound engineering technicians and radio operators	9.27	15.39	21.14	33.92	39.01
Audio and video equipment technicians	10.00	13.19	20.90	30.00	39.01
Broadcast technicians	8.63	13.52	20.83	31.15	37.08
Photographers	8.61	9.38	12.00	15.36	17.20
Television, video, and motion picture camera operators and editors	14.26	17.00	24.02	28.60	31.20
Camera operators, television, video, and motion picture	12.27	15.50	18.00	27.04	31.20
Healthcare Practitioner and Technical	15.00	19.58	26.51	35.04	49.01
Dentists	42.81	50.48	50.48	69.71	91.10
Dentists, general	42.81	50.48	50.48	67.64	91.21
Dietitians and nutritionists	18.83	21.64	23.01	27.16	34.11
Optometrists	44.01	44.47	54.76	67.31	67.31
Pharmacists	43.86	48.79	51.88	54.11	56.52
Physicians and surgeons	24.51	37.74	79.40	109.81	154.22
Anesthesiologists	25.01	108.03	142.35	182.69	225.82
Family and general practitioners	30.50	63.33	76.92	100.96	145.19
Internists, general	22.96	23.23	66.10	82.83	132.21
Pediatricians, general	25.22	25.22	64.69	79.81	93.75
Psychiatrists	64.54	74.52	83.15	83.15	83.15
Surgeons	63.71	63.71	154.22	165.35	165.35
Physician assistants	29.81	34.29	40.87	48.00	60.10
Registered nurses	22.06	25.77	30.28	36.43	43.60
Therapists	20.15	23.65	29.33	35.92	43.14
Audiologists	19.68	24.51	25.45	27.69	30.00
Occupational therapists	25.00	28.50	31.85	37.99	46.50
Physical therapists	22.07	28.97	33.77	37.95	45.00
Radiation therapists	26.39	29.61	41.67	48.99	49.99
Recreational therapists	14.94	15.04	16.93	23.07	23.32
Respiratory therapists	19.65	22.08	23.96	27.16	30.43
Speech-language pathologists	23.73	26.00	30.45	37.91	50.00
Veterinarians	38.46	40.88	43.27	47.12	50.04
Clinical laboratory technologists and technicians	12.80	15.30	19.10	24.81	29.39
Medical and clinical laboratory technologists	16.60	20.70	24.65	28.83	32.72
Medical and clinical laboratory technicians	11.76	14.31	16.58	19.94	24.77
Dental hygienists	22.50	28.00	33.00	39.00	45.00
Diagnostic related technologists and technicians	15.63	21.39	26.55	32.60	39.00
Cardiovascular technologists and technicians	11.85	13.72	24.17	34.00	43.04
Diagnostic medical sonographers	24.00	27.39	31.29	36.78	41.60
Nuclear medicine technologists	30.77	31.00	35.99	40.39	43.72
Radiologic technologists and technicians	16.66	21.06	25.67	30.37	35.45
Emergency medical technicians and paramedics	9.95	10.83	13.00	15.52	23.23
Health diagnosing and treating practitioner support technicians	10.50	13.00	16.00	19.14	22.39
Dietetic technicians	7.50	8.23	11.52	12.56	12.56
Pharmacy technicians	10.39	12.22	14.25	16.26	18.01
Psychiatric technicians	9.20	11.28	13.11	16.84	19.67
Respiratory therapy technicians	17.20	19.20	21.17	25.22	27.54
Surgical technologists	14.38	16.71	19.14	21.62	23.36
Veterinary technologists and technicians	8.18	11.50	14.76	16.00	18.00
Licensed practical and licensed vocational nurses	14.67	16.83	18.75	21.67	25.18
Medical records and health information technicians	10.12	12.52	15.00	18.53	22.08
Opticians, dispensing	10.91	12.23	19.00	24.08	26.50
Miscellaneous health technologists and technicians	12.17	13.92	17.00	21.00	25.13
Occupational health and safety specialists and technicians	16.00	24.48	29.03	29.03	37.24
Occupational health and safety specialists	14.98	22.48	28.35	34.91	45.47
Miscellaneous healthcare practitioner and technical workers	18.99	19.22	27.47	37.63	37.63
Athletic trainers	17.03	18.99	18.99	23.95	27.47
Healthcare Support	8.50	9.85	11.54	14.50	17.69
Nursing, psychiatric, and home health aides	8.00	9.28	10.50	12.38	14.71
Home health aides	6.55	8.00	9.60	10.60	12.00
Nursing aides, orderlies, and attendants	8.75	9.80	11.08	12.98	15.41
Psychiatric aides	8.00	9.00	10.00	11.19	13.67
Occupational therapist assistants and aides	9.67	10.49	16.94	28.00	28.94
Occupational therapist assistants	12.28	16.82	22.94	28.94	28.94
Occupational therapist aides	9.67	9.67	10.49	16.94	16.94
Physical therapist assistants and aides	9.50	10.47	16.18	24.00	35.00
Physical therapist assistants	10.76	17.25	21.61	31.00	36.00
Physical therapist aides	8.00	9.50	10.51	12.77	15.99
Massage therapists	8.49	12.92	20.00	21.28	38.44
Miscellaneous healthcare support occupations	9.50	11.33	13.81	16.60	19.50
Dental assistants	11.95	14.92	16.87	19.50	21.50
Medical assistants	9.90	11.00	13.00	15.81	18.27
Medical equipment preparers	10.82	12.29	14.14	16.89	18.95
Medical transcriptionists	11.02	13.26	14.98	17.51	20.00
Pharmacy aides	8.32	9.27	11.00	13.00	15.00

[1]Percentiles designate position in the earnings distribution and are calculated from individual worker earnings and the hours they are scheduled to work.

Table 6-16. Private Industry Workers: Hourly Wage Percentiles,[1] 2008—*Continued*

(Dollars.)

Occupation	Wages fall at or below the following percentiles:				
	10	25	50	75	90
Healthcare Support—*Continued*					
Veterinary assistants and laboratory animal caretakers	8.00	9.50	12.00	12.75	15.81
Protective service occupations	8.00	9.00	10.50	13.00	16.50
First-line supervisors/managers, law enforcement workers	9.74	10.00	11.00	12.91	15.11
Bailiffs, correctional officers, and jailers	8.72	8.96	9.58	10.69	11.98
Correctional officers and jailers	8.72	8.96	9.58	10.69	11.98
Police officers	15.37	17.71	20.76	22.60	24.02
Police and sheriff's patrol officers	15.37	17.71	20.76	22.60	24.02
Private detectives and investigators	10.66	12.00	14.28	14.28	15.66
Security guards and gaming surveillance officers	8.00	9.11	10.35	12.50	15.50
Security guards	8.00	9.05	10.27	12.41	15.43
Miscellaneous protective service workers	7.00	7.50	8.50	10.00	13.07
Lifeguards, ski patrol, and other recreational protective service workers	7.00	7.35	8.00	9.00	11.00
Food preparation and serving related occupations	3.74	6.55	8.00	9.79	12.92
First-line supervisors/managers, food preparation and serving workers	9.50	11.68	14.42	18.53	22.65
Chefs and head cooks	10.75	12.00	16.30	22.12	27.30
First-line supervisors/managers of food preparation and serving workers	9.36	11.61	14.31	18.22	21.78
Cooks	7.15	8.00	9.75	12.00	13.93
Cooks, fast food	6.55	7.15	7.84	8.70	10.00
Cooks, institution and cafeteria	8.00	9.15	10.93	13.16	16.14
Cooks, restaurant	7.75	9.00	10.50	12.45	14.00
Cooks, short order	7.14	7.30	9.00	11.00	13.25
Food preparation workers	7.00	7.54	8.50	10.10	12.18
Food service, tipped	2.15	3.23	5.25	7.95	8.83
Bartenders	4.00	5.00	7.14	8.75	10.15
Waiters and waitresses	2.13	2.68	4.02	6.55	8.00
Dining room and cafeteria attendants and bartender helpers	4.09	6.15	7.65	8.50	10.00
Fast food and counter workers	6.33	7.00	7.70	8.60	10.00
Combined food preparation and serving workers, including fast food	6.28	7.00	7.52	8.50	9.96
Counter attendants, cafeteria, food concession, and coffee shop	6.57	7.15	8.00	9.00	11.14
Food servers, nonrestaurant	3.90	7.25	8.49	10.15	14.31
Dishwashers	7.00	7.50	8.05	9.00	10.50
Hosts and hostesses, restaurant, lounge, and coffee shop	4.25	6.77	7.95	9.00	11.00
Building and grounds cleaning and maintenance occupations	7.50	8.40	10.10	13.10	16.97
First-line supervisors/managers, building and grounds cleaning and maintenance workers	10.71	12.97	15.50	21.01	26.33
First-line supervisors/managers of housekeeping and janitorial workers	10.44	12.50	14.50	20.50	24.22
First-line supervisors/managers of landscaping, lawn service, and groundskeeping workers	12.75	15.39	17.83	21.88	30.28
Building cleaning workers	7.30	8.18	9.91	12.45	16.15
Janitors and cleaners, except maids and housekeeping cleaners	7.36	8.50	10.45	12.94	16.75
Maids and housekeeping cleaners	7.25	7.90	8.75	10.36	12.98
Pest control workers	12.00	13.27	16.52	17.56	20.15
Grounds maintenance workers	8.00	8.95	10.00	13.00	16.80
Landscaping and groundskeeping workers	8.00	8.95	10.00	12.50	16.33
Tree trimmers and pruners	12.34	14.00	15.00	16.00	24.50
Personal care and service occupations	6.15	7.29	9.00	12.00	17.40
First-line supervisors/managers of gaming workers	10.00	11.50	13.35	17.98	21.44
Gaming supervisors	10.93	14.42	16.49	20.67	21.44
Slot key persons	9.50	10.36	11.85	12.36	13.19
First-line supervisors/managers of personal service workers	10.00	12.81	14.50	17.00	21.66
Nonfarm animal caretakers	7.00	8.00	9.35	10.25	13.87
Gaming services workers	5.26	5.70	6.47	7.47	8.07
Gaming dealers	5.25	5.66	6.33	7.33	7.91
Gaming and sports book writers and runners	7.87	7.87	8.00	11.25	16.67
Motion picture projectionists	7.00	7.35	8.25	11.25	35.60
Ushers, lobby attendants, and ticket takers	6.55	7.96	9.46	13.66	14.90
Miscellaneous entertainment attendants and related workers	6.55	7.14	8.00	10.08	12.74
Amusement and recreation attendants	6.50	7.00	7.75	9.15	12.74
Locker room, coatroom, and dressing room attendants	7.43	7.87	9.34	12.18	17.64
Funeral attendants	8.50	8.75	12.50	13.00	13.75
Barbers and cosmetologists	7.34	8.97	12.24	17.55	24.50
Hairdressers, hairstylists, and cosmetologists	7.34	8.82	12.43	17.68	25.24
Miscellaneous personal appearance workers	7.14	8.00	12.22	18.25	29.75
Manicurists and pedicurists	7.14	8.78	10.83	13.54	16.89
Shampooers	7.15	8.00	8.00	8.00	10.00
Skin care specialists	6.55	12.50	20.06	21.11	29.75
Baggage porters, bellhops, and concierges	6.33	7.47	9.00	12.50	18.94
Baggage porters and bellhops	6.33	6.60	7.90	9.17	11.75
Concierges	9.00	10.50	14.05	18.94	18.94
Tour and travel guides	7.15	9.00	12.77	15.00	19.25
Tour guides and escorts	7.15	9.00	11.00	14.25	17.02
Transportation attendants	16.18	29.37	37.97	42.72	48.72
Flight attendants	20.00	30.73	37.97	43.22	49.28
Transportation attendants, except flight attendants and baggage porters	5.85	8.50	10.93	11.82	20.03
Child care workers	7.00	7.75	8.75	10.25	12.00
Personal and home care aides	6.75	7.50	9.50	11.00	11.86
Recreation and fitness workers	7.15	8.40	10.89	15.24	20.00
Fitness trainers and aerobics instructors	8.00	9.70	13.92	18.66	25.00
Recreation workers	6.67	8.00	9.77	13.00	17.16
Residential advisors	5.25	5.25	10.10	13.40	18.46

[1]Percentiles designate position in the earnings distribution and are calculated from individual worker earnings and the hours they are scheduled to work.

Table 6-16. Private Industry Workers: Hourly Wage Percentiles,[1] 2008—*Continued*

(Dollars.)

Occupation	Wages fall at or below the following percentiles:				
	10	25	50	75	90
Sales and Related	7.50	8.73	12.00	19.04	32.00
First-line supervisors/managers, sales workers	10.60	13.25	17.01	22.65	33.66
First-line supervisors/managers of retail sales workers	10.60	12.76	16.37	20.07	27.23
First-line supervisors/managers of non-retail sales workers	11.29	16.73	24.04	35.32	54.11
Retail sales workers	7.15	8.00	9.54	12.50	17.40
Cashiers, all workers	7.00	7.65	8.60	10.35	12.85
Cashiers	7.00	7.60	8.50	10.12	12.50
Gaming change persons and booth cashiers	9.96	11.50	13.55	14.18	15.28
Counter and rental clerks and parts salespersons	7.50	8.75	11.25	15.52	20.66
Counter and rental clerks	6.81	7.88	9.28	11.85	15.15
Parts salespersons	9.00	10.89	14.50	18.78	23.75
Retail salespersons	7.50	8.50	10.46	14.07	20.00
Advertising sales agents	11.13	14.42	21.64	27.96	43.03
Insurance sales agents	12.50	16.62	21.01	31.78	49.73
Securities, commodities, and financial services sales agents	15.83	21.33	38.38	67.98	118.69
Travel agents	7.15	10.73	13.75	19.15	25.00
Sales representatives, wholesale and manufacturing	14.42	18.86	26.04	38.86	53.74
Sales representatives, wholesale and manufacturing, technical and scientific products	17.63	23.77	35.05	50.00	61.72
Sales representatives, wholesale and manufacturing except technical and scientific products	13.76	18.00	23.60	34.60	48.93
Models, demonstrators, and product promoters	9.23	11.35	14.61	18.00	24.64
Demonstrators and product promoters	9.23	11.33	14.61	18.00	24.64
Real estate brokers and sales agents	10.00	11.50	15.80	21.80	37.76
Real estate brokers	6.94	13.05	13.08	26.26	37.76
Real estate sales agents	10.35	11.50	15.80	21.63	37.20
Sales engineers	20.84	26.39	32.22	41.92	49.72
Telemarketers	7.61	8.48	10.04	14.00	17.23
Miscellaneous sales and related workers	8.00	9.14	13.63	20.78	30.53
Door-to-door sales workers, news and street vendors, and related workers	8.45	10.00	10.86	13.55	15.96
Office and Administrative Support	9.50	11.50	14.50	18.49	23.00
First line supervisors/managers of support workers	14.78	17.74	21.21	26.82	31.02
Switchboard operators, including answering service	8.00	9.61	11.00	13.64	17.00
Telephone operators	9.00	9.35	12.00	18.14	21.46
Financial clerks	10.00	11.60	14.42	17.68	21.00
Bill and account collectors	8.16	11.75	14.64	18.40	22.56
Billing and posting clerks and machine operators	10.83	12.67	14.82	17.00	19.95
Bookkeeping, accounting, and auditing clerks	10.96	12.75	15.39	18.89	22.15
Gaming cage workers	9.00	9.18	9.75	10.50	12.62
Payroll and timekeeping clerks	12.50	15.43	17.45	20.60	22.62
Procurement clerks	11.00	13.54	16.69	18.53	20.53
Tellers	9.34	10.03	11.31	13.06	15.15
Brokerage clerks	12.36	15.30	17.78	20.75	23.91
Correspondence clerks	12.98	13.95	16.00	19.33	23.95
Credit authorizers, checkers, and clerks	11.01	12.34	14.65	18.15	22.35
Customer service representatives	9.78	11.76	14.56	18.41	23.61
Eligibility interviewers, government programs	10.50	14.19	17.02	19.77	21.28
File clerks	9.00	10.10	11.37	14.92	15.99
Hotel, motel, and resort desk clerks	7.50	8.25	9.50	10.61	12.50
Interviewers, except eligibility and loan	8.53	10.00	12.24	14.70	17.58
Library assistants, clerical	8.97	9.40	13.24	16.04	18.54
Loan interviewers and clerks	11.04	13.00	15.86	18.39	21.55
New accounts clerks	10.64	12.00	14.00	16.01	20.26
Order clerks	10.00	11.50	14.44	18.41	21.29
Human resources assistants, except payroll and timekeeping	12.11	14.87	18.04	19.56	23.99
Receptionists and information clerks	9.00	10.25	12.03	14.49	17.07
Reservation and transportation ticket agents and travel clerks	9.00	10.29	14.63	19.30	21.54
Cargo and freight agents	13.13	14.21	17.78	23.59	39.00
Couriers and messengers	8.00	8.40	10.41	12.63	14.50
Dispatchers	9.50	12.50	16.45	21.00	24.81
Police, fire, and ambulance dispatchers	10.00	11.49	12.50	17.80	18.13
Dispatchers, except police, fire, and ambulance	9.50	12.75	16.47	21.44	25.00
Meter readers, utilities	10.00	13.08	16.25	19.38	26.54
Production, planning, and expediting clerks	12.49	14.75	18.61	23.71	26.90
Shipping, receiving, and traffic clerks	8.70	10.15	12.55	15.75	19.10
Stock clerks and order fillers	7.50	8.73	11.14	14.03	16.97
Weighers, measurers, checkers, and samplers, recordkeeping	9.00	11.36	13.00	16.52	21.39
Secretaries and administrative assistants	11.51	14.25	18.00	22.55	27.89
Executive secretaries and administrative assistants	15.00	17.50	21.30	25.72	30.14
Legal secretaries	14.00	17.28	21.80	28.49	33.69
Medical secretaries	10.00	12.00	14.50	18.00	21.42
Secretaries, except legal, medical, and executive	10.60	13.00	15.67	19.14	22.45
Computer operators	12.50	14.00	16.86	19.80	21.98
Data entry and information processing workers	10.00	11.35	12.93	15.14	18.41
Data entry keyers	9.90	11.00	12.57	14.50	17.19
Word processors and typists	11.64	12.10	15.24	19.63	26.43
Desktop publishers	11.40	14.31	18.55	22.76	27.14
Insurance claims and policy processing clerks	11.26	13.00	15.61	18.68	22.51
Mail clerks and mail machine operators, except postal service	8.48	10.04	11.58	14.48	17.18
Office clerks, general	9.50	11.00	13.50	16.83	20.50
Office machine operators, except computer	9.14	10.80	13.01	15.44	18.50
Proofreaders and copy markers	9.00	9.00	12.64	14.38	17.59
Statistical assistants	11.47	15.67	19.34	22.75	26.49

[1]Percentiles designate position in the earnings distribution and are calculated from individual worker earnings and the hours they are scheduled to work.

Table 6-16. Private Industry Workers: Hourly Wage Percentiles,[1] 2008—*Continued*

(Dollars.)

Occupation	Wages fall at or below the following percentiles:				
	10	25	50	75	90
Farming, Fishing, and Forestry	7.25	8.00	10.10	15.00	19.89
First-line supervisors/managers of farming, fishing, and forestry workers	12.00	18.35	21.15	25.06	29.93
Graders and sorters, agricultural products	6.92	7.30	9.00	10.29	15.44
Miscellaneous agricultural workers	7.29	7.85	9.50	12.50	15.00
Farmworkers and laborers, crop, nursery, and greenhouse	7.00	7.85	9.54	12.00	15.00
Farmworkers, farm and ranch animals	7.29	7.29	7.29	10.00	11.07
Logging workers	10.00	13.34	17.08	18.55	24.29
Construction and Extraction	10.98	14.00	18.96	26.33	34.70
First-line supervisors/managers of construction trades and extraction workers	18.03	22.00	27.66	35.00	41.49
Boilermakers	14.84	15.20	18.31	21.04	28.46
Brickmasons, blockmasons, and stonemasons	18.00	22.00	25.36	28.65	34.05
Brickmasons and blockmasons	18.00	22.02	25.36	28.65	34.05
Carpenters	13.69	16.00	20.00	26.51	35.49
Carpet, floor, and tile installers and finishers	13.00	16.78	19.00	24.00	38.63
Carpet installers	17.86	20.00	20.00	24.85	38.67
Tile and marble setters	13.00	16.00	16.97	22.00	25.73
Cement masons, concrete finishers, and terrazzo workers	13.50	15.50	19.00	24.57	29.00
Cement masons and concrete finishers	13.50	15.50	19.00	24.00	29.00
Construction laborers	9.00	10.67	14.00	21.00	27.25
Construction equipment operators	11.76	14.50	17.90	24.00	29.79
Paving, surfacing, and tamping equipment operators	10.72	12.50	15.25	20.00	25.00
Operating engineers and other construction equipment operators	12.75	14.86	18.51	26.29	30.86
Drywall installers, ceiling tile installers, and tapers	14.00	16.82	19.75	26.58	35.48
Drywall and ceiling tile installers	13.52	16.82	19.94	26.58	35.48
Tapers	16.50	17.22	17.22	25.00	31.43
Electricians	13.00	16.00	21.75	32.79	38.60
Glaziers	6.25	12.66	18.00	26.49	30.11
Insulation workers	10.50	14.56	16.70	20.50	24.50
Insulation workers, floor, ceiling, and wall	9.39	9.50	13.40	18.50	26.50
Insulation workers, mechanical	14.57	15.00	18.00	20.68	23.63
Painters and paperhangers	10.16	12.50	15.00	19.00	23.00
Painters, construction and maintenance	10.16	12.50	15.00	19.00	23.00
Pipelayers, plumbers, pipefitters, and steamfitters	13.31	16.86	22.57	32.25	37.32
Pipelayers	10.68	13.00	14.50	26.87	28.00
Plumbers, pipefitters, and steamfitters	13.75	17.95	23.00	32.25	38.41
Plasterers and stucco masons	12.28	15.50	16.44	18.64	18.99
Reinforcing iron and rebar workers	11.50	13.00	16.50	20.25	30.51
Roofers	10.00	11.59	16.00	21.06	28.50
Sheet metal workers	12.00	15.00	18.72	26.05	35.11
Structural iron and steel workers	14.79	19.05	26.00	31.23	55.71
Helpers, construction trades	9.13	10.73	12.50	16.00	20.00
Helpers, brickmasons, blockmasons, stonemasons, and tile and marble setters	9.00	10.00	14.00	22.99	24.63
Helpers–carpenters	9.80	12.00	13.18	16.00	16.48
Helpers–electricians	9.25	10.00	11.00	13.00	14.06
Helpers–painters, paperhangers, plasterers, and stucco masons	8.40	10.00	11.00	12.00	13.00
Helpers–pipelayers, plumbers, pipefitters, and steamfitters	9.13	11.00	12.90	14.80	18.00
Helpers–roofers	9.00	9.40	12.00	12.00	13.64
Construction and building inspectors	17.00	20.19	27.59	33.17	39.66
Elevator installers and repairers	26.51	35.22	38.46	52.66	52.66
Hazardous materials removal workers	10.50	11.50	17.00	21.00	33.63
Highway maintenance workers	8.50	18.50	20.72	22.66	23.20
Miscellaneous construction and related workers	10.34	12.25	15.84	20.00	25.98
mining	12.10	12.10	24.88	34.41	34.41
Service unit operators, oil, gas, and mining	15.13	19.00	25.00	31.70	31.70
Earth drillers, except oil and gas	15.30	15.30	16.46	20.50	22.00
Mining machine operators	18.88	20.50	21.85	25.51	33.01
Continuous mining machine operators	20.50	20.50	25.51	25.51	33.44
Roustabouts, oil and gas	10.78	10.78	18.00	29.30	31.16
Helpers–extraction workers	13.10	15.00	15.75	20.50	20.50
Installation, Maintenance, and Repair	11.50	15.00	19.41	26.00	31.26
First-line supervisors/managers of mechanics	17.96	20.19	25.15	32.89	40.84
Computer, automated teller, and office machine repairers	10.00	13.76	16.72	21.15	24.77
Radio and telecommunications equipment installers and repairers	18.06	25.00	29.43	31.92	33.77
Telecommunications equipment installers and repairers	18.06	25.00	29.43	31.92	33.77
Miscellaneous electrical and electronic equipment mechanics, installers, and repairers	11.55	14.04	19.50	26.51	31.71
Avionics technicians	7.45	7.90	14.70	20.84	28.14
Electric motor, power tool, and related repairers	10.00	11.50	13.64	15.09	20.75
Electrical and electronics installers and repairers, transportation equipment	20.00	23.00	25.66	29.02	32.00
Electrical and electronics installers and repairers, commercial and industrial equipment	14.04	17.45	23.27	29.49	31.71
Electrical and electronics installers and repairers, powehouse, substation, and relay	21.93	28.95	35.85	36.92	37.72
Electronic equipment installers and repairers, motor vehicles	12.39	13.05	17.00	17.00	24.19
Electronic home entertainment equipment installers and repairers	10.00	11.98	13.25	17.00	23.00
Security and fire alarm systems installers	13.00	17.00	20.60	24.50	28.75
Aircraft mechanics and service technicians	17.50	21.25	27.29	31.37	40.27
Automotive technicians and repairers	10.75	13.00	17.50	22.00	27.50
Automotive body and related repairers	12.00	12.75	16.26	20.50	27.91
Automotive glass installers and repairers	13.00	18.00	20.00	20.86	24.62
Automotive service technicians and mechanics	10.42	13.00	18.00	22.50	27.88

[1] Percentiles designate position in the earnings distribution and are calculated from individual worker earnings and the hours they are scheduled to work.

Table 6-16. Private Industry Workers: Hourly Wage Percentiles,[1] 2008—Continued

(Dollars.)

Occupation	Wages fall at or below the following percentiles:				
	10	25	50	75	90
Installation, Maintenance, and Repair—Continued					
Bus and truck mechanics and diesel engine specialists	14.00	16.50	19.23	23.12	27.87
Heavy vehicle and mobile equipment service technicians and mechanics	13.00	16.70	19.22	23.10	27.07
Farm equipment mechanics	10.50	11.75	15.43	18.85	21.50
Mobile heavy equipment mechanics, except engines	15.50	17.64	20.53	23.50	28.16
Rail car repairers	14.50	17.00	18.41	22.35	28.08
Small engine mechanics	10.00	12.15	16.37	19.50	25.00
Motorboat mechanics	10.45	11.50	17.00	19.50	20.25
Motorcycle mechanics	10.00	11.00	15.25	27.50	36.76
Outdoor power equipment and other small engine mechanics	9.00	14.00	17.10	18.30	20.65
Miscellaneous vehicle and mobile equipment mechanic, installers, and repairers	7.36	8.50	10.00	12.75	16.45
Tire repairers and changers	7.50	8.50	10.00	12.50	14.90
Control and valve installers and repairers	12.07	17.25	20.97	25.55	33.79
Control and valve installers and repairers, except mechanical door	17.13	19.37	22.65	28.76	35.69
Heating, air conditioning, and refrigeration mechanics and installers	12.07	15.00	19.34	26.21	32.07
Home appliance repairers	14.10	17.00	19.31	21.30	21.30
Industrial machinery installation, repair, and maintenance workers	12.40	15.50	19.12	24.00	29.71
Industrial machinery mechanics	16.12	18.78	21.91	27.26	31.59
Maintenance and repair workers, general	11.00	13.16	17.00	20.96	26.68
Maintenance workers, machinery	12.75	14.62	16.80	21.00	25.33
Millwrights	18.00	19.27	25.06	29.18	38.71
Line installers and repairers	16.86	22.91	28.38	30.58	33.24
Electrical power-line installers and repairers	18.04	25.31	29.35	33.93	38.38
Telecommunications line installers and repairers	15.75	22.38	27.69	30.33	31.30
Precision instrument and equipment repairers	13.50	15.50	19.80	28.98	35.74
Medical equipment repairers	11.11	14.99	16.43	24.86	28.43
Musical instrument repairers and tuners	12.60	15.00	18.50	19.50	25.20
Miscellaneous installation, maintenance, and repair workers	9.00	11.25	14.71	19.07	24.99
Coin, vending, and amusement machine servicers and repairers	11.00	11.00	14.78	18.21	19.76
Locksmiths and safe repairers	12.00	13.00	15.00	19.95	26.07
Manufactured building and mobile home installers	8.68	10.00	11.00	12.50	17.00
Riggers	10.93	11.50	15.00	24.00	26.57
Helpers–installation, maintenance, and repair workers	8.00	9.68	12.00	14.78	18.00
Production	8.80	10.81	14.21	19.14	25.95
First-line supervisors/managers of production and operating workers	14.71	18.45	22.90	29.14	35.12
Aircraft structure, surfaces, rigging, and systems assemblers	14.23	18.71	23.01	29.85	31.85
Electrical, electronics, and electromechanical assemblers	8.99	10.46	12.32	15.69	19.92
Coil winders, tapers, and finishers	9.00	10.00	11.53	14.15	19.92
Electrical and electronic equipment assemblers	8.66	10.18	12.32	14.85	20.28
Electromechanical equipment assemblers	9.85	11.06	13.83	17.62	19.20
Engine and other machine assemblers	11.75	14.28	17.00	25.22	29.48
Structural metal fabricators and fitters	11.00	13.86	15.64	20.00	26.79
Miscellaneous assemblers and fabricators	8.50	10.24	13.35	18.16	28.75
Fiberglass laminators and fabricators	10.87	11.00	12.76	16.00	17.00
Team assemblers	9.22	11.48	13.90	21.95	29.10
Bakers	8.00	9.25	11.55	14.08	18.78
Butchers and other meat, poultry, and fish processing workers	8.00	9.68	11.97	14.25	17.92
Butchers and meat cutters	9.00	12.00	15.30	17.92	21.25
Meat, poultry, and fish cutters and trimmers	7.09	8.25	9.68	10.85	12.00
Slaughterers and meat packers	9.65	10.85	12.15	12.80	14.65
Miscellaneous food processing workers	8.50	9.35	12.75	16.59	20.19
Food and tobacco roasting, baking, and drying machiner operators	8.56	8.81	12.67	16.09	20.70
Food batchmakers	8.61	10.85	14.25	17.80	20.28
Food cooking machine operators and tenders	7.50	9.00	9.75	13.02	17.79
Computer control programmers and operators	11.00	13.50	17.75	21.22	26.29
Computer-controlled machine tool operators, metal and plastic	10.98	13.00	17.05	20.00	24.47
Numerical tool and process control programmers	18.87	20.00	23.56	31.35	32.55
Forming machine setters, operators, and tenders, metal and plastic	11.00	12.80	15.77	18.85	21.38
Extruding and drawing machine setters, operators, and tenders, metal and plastic	11.05	13.16	15.31	18.85	20.59
Forging machine setters, operators, and tenders, metal and plastic	10.75	11.81	15.04	19.60	22.25
Rolling machine setters, operators, and tenders, metal and plastic	11.00	12.50	16.50	19.94	22.40
Machine tool cutting setters, operators, and tenders, metal and plastic	9.12	11.70	14.29	18.00	20.78
Cutting, punching, and press machine setters, operators, and tenders, metal and plastic	8.93	11.51	13.40	16.81	20.25
Drilling and boring machine tool setters, operators, and tenders, metal and plastic	9.12	10.42	14.50	18.98	22.83
Grinding, lapping, polishing, and buffing machine tool setters, operators, and tenders, metal and plastic	10.25	11.59	14.12	17.00	19.00
Lathe and turning machine tool setters, operators, and tenders, metal and plastic	9.50	13.00	17.44	20.04	23.00
Milling and planing machine setters, operators, and tenders, metal and plastic	8.15	16.00	19.00	21.29	22.50
Machinists	14.02	17.00	20.33	25.00	29.38
Metal furnace and kiln operators and tenders	10.75	13.27	17.53	19.98	23.54
Metal-refining furnace operators and tenders	11.00	12.93	18.98	21.20	25.47
Pourers and casters, metal	8.50	16.92	17.45	18.98	19.98
Model makers and patternmakers, metal and plastic	13.80	15.05	22.25	30.51	34.39
Model makers, metal and plastic	15.05	16.10	24.62	31.72	34.39
Patternmakers, metal and plastic	13.80	13.80	14.00	21.00	32.58
Molders and molding machine setters, operators, and tenders, metal and plastic	8.11	10.25	12.50	15.83	19.95
Foundry mold and coremakers	13.70	14.90	17.05	17.73	19.54
Molding, coremaking, and casting machine setters, operators, and tenders, metal and plastic	8.00	9.86	12.35	15.50	20.00
Multiple machine tool setters, operators, and tenders, metal and plastic	9.83	11.50	14.10	18.64	24.50
Tool and die makers	17.51	20.56	24.31	27.00	33.29
Welding, soldering, and brazing workers	11.00	13.50	16.49	19.10	23.74

[1]Percentiles designate position in the earnings distribution and are calculated from individual worker earnings and the hours they are scheduled to work.

Table 6-16. Private Industry Workers: Hourly Wage Percentiles,[1] 2008—*Continued*

(Dollars.)

Occupation	Wages fall at or below the following percentiles:				
	10	25	50	75	90
Welders, cutters, solderers, and brazers	11.21	13.60	16.50	19.36	23.33
Welding, soldering, and brazing machine setters, operators, and tenders	10.76	12.75	15.70	18.00	25.90
Miscellaneous metalworkers and plastic workers	8.30	11.00	14.56	17.80	21.75
Heat treating equipment setters, operators, and tenders, metal and plastic	9.00	10.50	16.15	18.89	23.75
Lay-out workers, metal and plastic	14.10	15.00	16.00	19.84	36.89
Plating and coating machine setters, operators, and tenders, metal and plastic	9.00	10.13	13.36	18.50	25.37
Tool grinders, filers, and sharpeners	9.60	14.80	17.22	19.04	25.00
Bookbinders and bindery workers	7.75	9.70	12.57	17.14	21.00
Bindery workers	7.75	9.70	12.57	17.14	21.00
Printers	9.99	12.65	16.25	20.60	24.53
Job printers	10.51	16.00	18.40	20.84	22.50
Prepress technicians and workers	10.00	13.13	18.27	22.89	26.13
Printing machine operators	9.62	12.41	15.50	20.00	23.95
Laundry and dry-cleaning workers	7.45	8.00	9.25	10.70	12.50
Pressers, textile, garment, and related materials	7.00	7.50	8.50	10.67	12.36
Sewing machine operators	7.50	8.95	10.51	14.07	16.61
Tailors, dressmakers, and sewers	9.00	10.95	13.00	18.85	23.35
Tailors, dressmakers, and custom sewers	9.00	10.95	13.00	18.15	23.35
Textile machine setters, operators, and tenders	9.42	10.35	12.05	13.90	15.59
Textile bleaching and dyeing machine operators and tenders	8.75	9.58	11.07	12.50	13.50
Textile cutting machine setters, operators, and tenders	8.61	9.42	10.39	12.35	15.24
Textile knitting and weaving machine setters, operators, and tenders, synthetic, and glass fibers	9.68	11.11	13.90	14.98	15.71
Textile winding, twisting, and drawing out machine setters, operators, and tenders	9.66	10.38	11.90	12.97	16.25
Miscellaneous textile, apparel, and furnishings workers	8.50	10.11	11.80	17.00	20.17
Extruding and forming machine setters, operators, and tenders, synthetic and glass fibers	9.34	12.18	16.97	19.55	19.55
Fabric and apparel patternmakers	16.01	17.06	20.65	23.75	32.50
Upholsterers	9.02	11.00	15.76	19.57	21.74
Cabinetmakers and bench carpenters	10.44	11.67	14.93	16.65	18.20
Furniture finishers	10.50	11.56	12.45	15.50	18.27
Woodworking machine setters, operators, and tenders	8.50	10.50	12.50	14.98	17.15
Sawing machine setters, operators, and tenders, wood	8.25	9.56	11.85	14.00	17.00
Woodworking machine setters, operators, and tenders, except sawing	8.75	11.30	13.50	15.06	18.00
Power plant operators, distributors, and dispatchers	24.90	27.87	33.47	33.85	38.93
Power distributors and dispatchers	30.13	32.68	36.49	43.14	45.10
Power plant operators	19.00	27.19	27.87	32.73	35.84
Stationary engineers and boiler operators	15.41	21.67	28.66	30.77	34.16
Water and liquid waste treatment plant and system operators	16.73	18.38	20.81	26.13	33.00
Miscellaneous plant and system operators	17.64	21.89	27.97	31.07	33.40
Chemical plant and system operators	16.98	17.90	25.83	30.10	31.58
Gas plant operators	25.42	27.74	32.50	33.40	33.40
Petroleum pump system operators, refinery operators, and gaugers	9.50	27.11	29.25	31.15	33.58
Chemical processing machine setters, operators, and tenders	11.00	16.00	20.26	26.83	30.31
Chemical equipment operators and tenders	10.50	14.26	19.38	24.67	26.43
Separating, filtering, clarifying, precipitating, and still machine setters, operators, and tenders	12.73	17.24	21.25	29.40	31.27
Crushing, grinding, polishing, mixing, and blending workers	10.00	12.25	15.53	19.60	22.85
Crushing, grinding, and polishing machine setters, operators, and tenders	10.00	12.75	16.60	19.50	27.69
Grinding and polishing workers, hand	9.01	10.75	13.00	14.50	19.71
Mixing and blending machine setters, operators, and tenders	11.00	13.48	16.32	21.18	22.91
Cutting workers	9.49	11.00	14.50	17.10	20.15
Cutters and trimmers, hand	8.40	10.50	13.00	15.78	18.00
Cutting and slicing machine setters, operators, and tenders	9.58	11.80	14.50	17.75	20.34
Extruding, forming, pressing, and compacting machine setters, operators, and tenders	8.80	10.00	13.72	16.68	23.10
Furnace, kiln, oven, drier, and kettle operators and tenders	8.94	11.62	14.52	19.37	26.37
Inspectors, testers, sorters, samplers, and weighers	9.45	11.68	14.85	19.46	25.71
Jewelers and precious stone and metal workers	10.22	11.97	18.35	24.50	31.00
Medical, dental, and ophthalmic laboratory technicians	10.21	11.50	15.00	16.57	20.26
Dental laboratory technicians	10.50	12.00	15.43	17.50	20.26
Ophthalmic laboratory technicians	10.05	10.21	11.51	15.00	15.24
Packaging and filling machine operators and tenders	8.75	11.00	14.43	17.80	21.33
Painting workers	9.25	10.90	14.00	17.47	21.50
Coating, painting, and spraying machine setters, operators, and tenders	9.25	11.00	13.35	16.75	18.70
Painters, transportation equipment	11.69	14.50	18.26	24.99	28.57
Painting, coating, and decorating workers	7.50	8.00	10.57	14.64	17.78
Photographic process workers and processing machine operators	7.94	8.90	11.24	14.20	17.50
Photographic process workers	10.00	11.24	11.50	17.00	27.29
Photographic processing machine operators	7.94	8.19	9.88	14.20	15.00
Semiconductor processors	11.95	14.31	17.45	19.68	22.77
Miscellaneous production workers	8.05	9.50	11.85	16.40	21.60
Cementing and gluing machine operators and tenders	9.20	10.53	14.28	18.04	21.53
Cleaning, washing, and metal pickling equipment operators and tenders	11.24	11.95	15.00	24.09	29.28
Cooling and freezing equipment operators and tenders	8.75	8.75	12.20	19.08	24.65
Etchers and engravers	10.25	13.92	14.00	14.47	21.25
Molders, shapers, and casters, except metal and plastic	8.00	10.00	14.00	16.03	25.00
Paper goods machine setters, operators, and tenders	8.71	10.76	16.65	20.46	25.58
Tire builders	10.00	11.54	17.32	20.00	22.09
Helpers–production workers	7.75	9.11	10.75	13.22	17.07

[1]Percentiles designate position in the earnings distribution and are calculated from individual worker earnings and the hours they are scheduled to work.

Table 6-16. Private Industry Workers: Hourly Wage Percentiles,[1] 2008—*Continued*

(Dollars.)

Occupation	Wages fall at or below the following percentiles:				
	10	25	50	75	90
Transportation and Material Moving	8.00	9.78	13.00	17.52	22.82
First-line supervisors/managers of helpers, laborers, and material movers, hand	13.50	15.13	19.47	23.75	29.89
First-line supervisors/managers of transportation and material-moving machine and vehicle operators	15.48	18.50	23.50	28.26	34.56
Aircraft pilots and flight engineers	22.00	32.00	89.27	146.61	161.47
Airline pilots, copilots, and flight engineers	22.00	75.96	111.62	151.43	163.12
Commercial pilots	19.35	24.96	32.00	34.91	43.46
technicians	9.09	10.00	10.35	12.86	16.41
Bus drivers	10.40	12.00	14.47	16.56	19.00
Bus drivers, transit and intercity	10.40	12.00	14.47	16.65	23.35
Bus drivers, school	10.40	11.44	14.08	16.56	18.46
Driver/sales workers and truck drivers	9.25	12.00	16.00	20.53	25.24
Driver/sales workers	6.55	7.50	11.00	16.58	21.65
Truck drivers, heavy and tractor-trailer	12.00	14.50	17.25	21.50	25.23
Truck drivers, light or delivery services	8.50	10.14	13.25	18.90	28.17
Taxi drivers and chauffeurs	7.21	8.24	9.50	12.00	16.00
Locomotive engineers and operators	15.54	15.54	22.99	36.64	50.35
Locomotive engineers	15.54	15.54	23.75	38.47	51.69
Railroad brake, signal, and switch operators	15.18	17.38	22.42	30.69	34.81
Railroad conductors and yardmasters	14.43	14.43	21.95	35.51	40.03
Sailors and marine oilers	9.00	10.42	11.67	14.97	15.63
Ship and boat captains and operators	15.00	19.58	26.67	28.75	35.13
Captains, mates, and pilots of water vessels	15.00	19.58	26.92	28.75	35.13
Parking lot attendants	6.46	7.43	8.35	9.61	11.07
Service station attendants	7.50	8.00	8.82	12.50	16.02
Transportation inspectors	10.44	19.75	23.04	30.96	31.74
Conveyor operators and tenders	8.75	10.25	12.50	15.62	17.60
Crane and tower operators	13.75	16.00	20.00	25.20	31.10
Dredge, excavating, and loading machine operators	11.00	13.92	16.11	18.50	23.00
Excavating and loading machine and dragline operators	11.00	13.92	16.00	18.50	22.69
Hoist and winch operators	10.75	12.86	20.28	30.03	39.85
Industrial truck and tractor operators	9.50	11.34	13.71	16.87	21.03
Laborers and material movers, hand	7.50	8.45	10.24	13.06	16.60
Cleaners of vehicles and equipment	7.45	8.40	10.00	12.65	15.45
Laborers and freight, stock, and material movers, hand	7.75	8.89	10.65	13.65	17.51
Machine feeders and offbearers	7.80	8.61	10.54	13.28	15.81
Packers and packagers, hand	7.00	7.78	9.06	11.54	14.11
Pumping station operators	16.54	21.68	22.91	22.91	27.61
Refuse and recyclable material collectors	8.17	9.34	10.50	14.21	17.14
Tank car, truck, and ship loaders	14.00	16.00	20.22	20.22	31.30

[1]Percentiles designate position in the earnings distribution and are calculated from individual worker earnings and the hours they are scheduled to work.

Table 6-17. State and Local Government Workers: Hourly Wage Percentiles,[1] 2008

(Dollars.)

Occupation	Wages fall at or below the following percentiles:				
	10	25	50	75	90
ALL WORKERS	11.35	14.98	21.43	31.55	43.23
Management	21.41	29.00	38.31	49.72	59.54
Chief executives	27.95	40.72	52.95	68.50	87.06
General and operations managers	21.99	26.19	34.59	49.21	61.60
Legislators	11.56	17.33	25.72	32.50	42.31
Public relations managers	19.03	23.18	32.96	41.77	50.01
Administrative services managers	22.28	26.56	33.28	42.37	47.45
Computer and information systems managers	28.40	33.68	42.33	50.63	66.81
Financial managers	23.00	31.32	41.09	50.77	59.54
Human resources managers	22.72	30.51	37.64	42.64	55.66
Compensation and benefits managers	27.27	29.71	34.39	45.19	48.34
Training and development managers	21.80	22.30	32.23	32.28	61.89
Purchasing managers	23.01	23.38	28.53	34.33	44.10
Transportation, storage, and distribution managers	23.81	32.12	38.24	44.19	52.69
Construction managers	21.36	28.60	35.28	42.86	47.63
Education administrators	25.75	34.06	43.45	52.35	60.84
Education administrators, preschool and child care center/program	15.77	16.31	25.85	27.80	39.11
Education administrators, elementary and secondary school	32.89	38.62	46.59	54.24	60.97
Education administrators, postsecondary	21.54	26.34	37.29	49.50	66.83
Engineering managers	38.47	41.60	53.28	57.41	63.33
Food service managers	18.27	19.95	23.47	29.27	31.37
Medical and health services managers	25.01	30.21	41.76	52.48	85.82
Natural sciences managers	24.33	27.67	33.96	53.85	54.88
Property, real estate, and community association managers	15.39	22.89	26.42	29.62	33.51
Social and community service managers	21.85	29.15	33.64	38.07	45.58
Business and Financial Operations	16.35	19.53	24.00	30.45	37.53
Buyers and purchasing agents	18.94	20.49	24.40	30.66	37.01
Purchasing agents, except wholesale, retail, and farm products	18.94	20.49	24.40	30.66	36.56
Claims adjusters, appraisers, examiners, and investigators	18.01	22.58	26.15	30.02	36.59
Claims adjusters, examiners, and investigators	18.01	22.58	26.15	30.02	36.59
Compliance officers, except agriculture, construction, health and safety, and transportation	14.55	18.10	20.76	26.37	31.04
Emergency management specialists	16.86	20.19	32.08	48.89	48.89
Human resources, training, and labor relations specialists	15.45	18.99	23.58	32.70	41.81
Employment, recruitment, and placement specialists	12.97	15.17	16.61	21.39	24.42
Compensation, benefits, and job analysis specialists	18.34	21.18	23.74	34.14	40.40
Training and development specialists	16.99	19.68	24.20	34.59	43.64
Management analysts	18.17	20.44	24.15	32.12	38.38
Meeting and convention planners	21.31	21.45	23.19	32.69	37.86
Accountants and auditors	17.53	19.99	24.44	29.00	37.24
Appraisers and assessors of real estate	10.82	16.60	20.81	28.56	34.94
Budget analysts	21.12	23.58	27.45	31.93	37.07
Financial analysts and advisors	15.72	20.63	24.59	27.02	34.97
Financial analysts	20.32	20.91	24.57	33.63	34.97
Insurance underwriters	13.90	19.10	25.34	25.38	26.73
Financial examiners	18.08	19.72	25.74	36.05	42.68
Loan counselors and officers	19.47	21.38	23.44	24.62	29.43
Loan counselors	19.47	21.38	23.44	24.62	29.43
Tax examiners, collectors, preparers, and revenue agents	12.90	15.54	20.65	26.97	33.84
Tax examiners, collectors, and revenue agents	13.09	15.67	20.65	26.97	33.84
Computer and Mathematical Science	18.41	22.15	27.54	33.98	39.79
Computer programmers	20.67	24.44	30.75	36.03	42.13
Computer software engineers	19.23	24.02	34.06	37.22	40.15
Computer software engineers, applications	18.97	21.84	33.54	35.42	38.89
Computer software engineers, systems software	25.74	34.06	34.06	37.27	44.26
Computer support specialists	15.86	19.44	22.62	26.66	29.76
Computer systems analysts	20.84	26.06	32.20	38.37	43.72
Database administrators	19.01	25.23	30.26	33.65	37.60
Network and computer systems administrators	19.20	22.93	28.53	32.69	40.06
Network systems and data communications analysts	20.60	22.40	28.32	34.80	37.02
Operations research analysts	25.93	27.04	27.04	27.04	31.78
Architecture and Engineering	18.46	23.08	28.94	36.04	43.86
Architects, except naval	29.20	31.89	34.47	42.64	46.21
Architects, except landscape and naval	31.89	31.89	39.27	42.64	46.21
Surveyors, cartographers, and photogrammetrists	19.78	24.19	25.71	32.88	43.95
Surveyors	22.31	25.71	32.88	39.27	45.31
Engineers	24.79	28.93	33.12	39.91	45.16
Civil engineers	24.79	28.99	33.29	41.30	45.09
Electrical and electronics engineers	27.45	30.64	36.30	42.78	47.70
Electrical engineers	26.78	27.99	31.92	36.30	45.61
Environmental engineers	24.03	26.76	30.55	38.42	45.05
Industrial engineers, including health and safety	20.84	32.40	39.44	41.94	53.62
Drafters	17.85	20.03	24.81	29.31	30.55
Architectural and civil drafters	16.33	20.54	26.22	30.55	30.55
Engineering technicians, except drafters	14.75	18.39	22.56	26.82	31.98
Civil engineering technicians	13.95	17.01	21.51	25.12	28.39
Electrical and electronic engineering technicians	20.06	22.59	28.48	34.34	38.82
Surveying and mapping technicians	14.81	17.05	21.91	25.61	28.19

[1]Percentiles designate position in the earnings distribution and are calculated from individual worker earnings and the hours they are scheduled to work.

Table 6-17. State and Local Government Workers: Hourly Wage Percentiles,[1] 2008—*Continued*

(Dollars.)

Occupation	Wages fall at or below the following percentiles:				
	10	25	50	75	90
Life, Physical, and Social Science	16.46	19.93	25.56	33.46	43.23
Life scientists	17.47	19.53	23.16	28.66	34.22
Agricultural and food scientists	16.75	16.80	17.47	17.96	21.77
Biological scientists	19.29	21.92	24.31	28.66	34.22
Biochemists and biophysicists	17.72	19.71	23.60	28.66	28.66
Zoologists and wildlife biologists	19.39	22.55	24.18	25.05	33.60
Conservation scientists and foresters	19.53	21.82	24.97	29.00	33.39
Conservation scientists	19.53	21.08	24.29	27.68	32.06
Foresters	22.70	27.65	28.34	51.66	56.16
Medical scientists	18.74	20.48	21.33	28.76	36.38
Physical scientists	20.08	23.30	26.94	34.49	42.56
Chemists and materials scientists	21.92	26.07	26.07	29.68	32.89
Chemists	21.92	26.07	26.07	29.68	32.89
Environmental scientists and geoscientists	19.38	22.87	28.14	36.06	42.56
Environmental scientists and specialists, including health	18.62	22.55	28.48	37.93	42.56
Psychologists	25.01	29.29	36.59	46.60	56.08
Clinical, counseling, and school psychologists	24.98	29.28	36.59	46.93	56.97
Urban and regional planners	22.21	24.50	31.26	38.45	54.21
Miscellaneous social scientists and related workers	11.63	12.62	16.51	25.57	39.61
Agricultural and food science technicians	9.02	9.84	14.88	20.03	23.60
Biological technicians	14.41	17.60	20.83	24.14	26.52
Chemical technicians	16.32	18.61	23.67	24.07	25.39
Social science research assistants	7.41	7.41	12.75	15.14	18.64
Miscellaneous life, physical, and social science technicians	13.16	16.46	19.41	25.16	30.98
Environmental science and protection technicians, including health	15.02	17.55	22.36	27.02	32.56
Forensic science technicians	19.08	22.51	25.91	30.98	34.83
Forest and conservation technicians	8.67	15.29	17.50	19.50	21.80
Community and Social Services	14.80	17.46	21.88	29.74	39.21
Counselors	16.68	20.72	27.97	38.74	48.27
Substance abuse and behavioral disorder counselors	15.63	17.80	23.25	38.43	46.23
Educational, vocational, and school counselors	18.91	24.88	34.28	43.24	54.39
Mental health counselors	14.42	15.63	18.96	23.12	29.96
Rehabilitation counselors	15.57	18.73	22.79	26.66	30.94
Social workers	15.04	17.25	20.46	27.30	33.82
Child, family, and school social workers	15.34	17.53	20.81	28.78	37.61
Medical and public health social workers	14.53	16.22	18.91	23.49	29.14
Mental health and substance abuse social workers	14.08	16.35	19.42	26.85	33.34
Miscellaneous community and social service specialists	13.71	15.67	19.81	24.87	31.95
Health educators	17.82	18.23	23.26	26.60	31.86
Probation officers and correctional treatment specialists	14.98	17.74	22.81	28.38	36.18
Social and human service assistants	11.49	13.85	16.40	20.15	23.35
Clergy	20.64	23.38	26.38	28.36	29.92
Legal	17.17	21.28	30.35	43.55	60.13
Lawyers	22.53	29.15	37.17	47.86	59.40
Judges, magistrates, and other judicial workers	22.29	30.64	43.12	62.75	81.87
Administrative law judges, adjudicators, and hearing officers	24.28	29.39	32.66	41.32	62.75
Judges, magistrate judges, and magistrates	22.29	40.97	59.78	71.25	86.24
Paralegals and legal assistants	13.60	18.15	21.28	24.34	29.75
Miscellaneous legal support workers	15.37	17.48	20.19	26.76	32.74
Court reporters	13.65	16.52	24.02	28.49	41.44
Law clerks	17.67	19.20	21.53	25.35	30.58
Education, Training, and Library	12.88	23.31	32.05	42.10	54.36
Postsecondary teachers	23.81	31.90	43.06	57.86	77.03
Business teachers, postsecondary	25.19	49.19	67.74	72.63	74.73
Math and computer teachers, postsecondary	32.05	35.35	41.43	55.50	64.51
Computer science teachers, postsecondary	31.62	37.80	60.31	73.16	104.13
Mathematical science teachers, postsecondary	32.77	35.35	39.79	47.44	57.84
Engineering and architecture teachers, postsecondary	29.58	34.17	51.22	67.59	78.60
Engineering teachers, postsecondary	29.58	34.17	49.94	67.84	81.14
Life sciences teachers, postsecondary	22.80	29.38	39.52	57.64	78.30
Biological science teachers, postsecondary	20.89	28.43	37.44	55.98	84.14
Physical sciences teachers, postsecondary	30.75	37.25	45.89	58.81	68.29
Atmospheric, earth, marine, and space sciences teachers, postsecondary	19.20	19.20	19.20	68.29	75.29
Chemistry teachers, postsecondary	30.95	40.47	45.89	58.81	71.10
Physics teachers, postsecondary	36.57	37.70	38.67	49.17	65.68
Social sciences teachers, postsecondary	32.06	33.69	42.23	56.01	76.73
Economics teachers, postsecondary	33.69	49.96	56.01	81.90	84.07
Political science teachers, postsecondary	32.06	33.15	35.14	42.26	51.93
Psychology teachers, postsecondary	28.84	38.82	40.19	40.19	43.56
Sociology teachers, postsecondary	35.94	42.41	52.44	64.94	79.25
Health teachers, postsecondary	26.36	31.30	44.14	74.44	104.74
Health specialties teachers, postsecondary	27.61	40.10	53.22	81.73	125.93
Nursing instructors and teachers, postsecondary	25.67	27.74	31.41	40.23	52.63
Education and library science teachers, postsecondary	21.11	28.27	32.42	42.35	57.64
Education teachers, postsecondary	21.11	28.27	32.42	42.35	57.64
Law, criminal justice, and social work teachers, postsecondary	35.92	56.80	88.18	115.19	130.29
Criminal justice and law enforcement teachers, postsecondary	31.54	31.54	44.26	56.80	56.80
Law teachers, postsecondary	65.89	84.09	98.50	130.29	130.29

[1]Percentiles designate position in the earnings distribution and are calculated from individual worker earnings and the hours they are scheduled to work.

Table 6-17. State and Local Government Workers: Hourly Wage Percentiles,[1] 2008—*Continued*

(Dollars.)

Occupation	Wages fall at or below the following percentiles:				
	10	25	50	75	90
Education, Training, and Library—*Continued*					
Arts, communications, and humanities teachers, postsecondary	28.66	34.52	39.98	45.25	45.25
Arts, communications, and humanities teachers, postsecondary	26.55	34.62	43.53	51.74	67.13
Art, drama, and music teachers, postsecondary	28.52	33.43	41.34	51.73	68.40
Communications teachers, postsecondary	32.48	32.48	38.91	41.48	47.33
English language and literature teachers, postsecondary	13.50	30.26	42.82	46.47	60.03
Foreign language and literature teachers, postsecondary	27.20	38.84	47.62	51.74	66.22
History teachers, postsecondary	36.71	37.30	45.78	59.42	71.09
Miscellaneous postsecondary teachers	19.46	26.80	37.96	49.58	64.55
Graduate teaching assistants	14.42	14.42	14.42	14.42	15.87
Recreation and fitness studies teachers, postsecondary	17.00	26.15	31.18	39.24	47.35
Vocational education teachers, postsecondary	20.83	20.83	28.49	44.29	58.13
Primary, secondary, and special education school teachers	24.54	28.77	34.33	42.86	52.69
Preschool and kindergarten teachers	20.47	25.78	31.57	38.76	49.18
Preschool teachers, except special education	13.23	18.88	27.49	34.89	42.40
Kindergarten teachers, except special education	24.35	27.60	32.74	39.96	50.10
Elementary and middle school teachers	24.13	28.52	34.48	42.94	52.55
Elementary school teachers, except special education	23.83	28.48	34.40	43.11	52.38
Middle school teachers, except special and vocational education	24.86	28.70	34.66	42.24	53.10
Secondary school teachers	25.21	29.09	34.46	43.02	52.44
Secondary school teachers, except special and vocational education	25.20	29.13	34.38	43.02	52.72
Vocational education teachers, secondary school	25.35	28.62	34.59	42.87	48.30
Special education teachers	24.66	28.84	34.48	43.75	54.14
Special education teachers, preschool, kindergarten, and elementary school	24.26	28.57	34.17	43.63	53.95
Special education teachers, middle school	26.85	30.58	34.89	43.87	54.39
Special education teachers, secondary school	24.66	28.84	35.47	43.83	54.87
Other teachers and instructors	10.48	17.27	32.35	48.88	62.25
Adult literacy, remedial education, and GED teachers and instructors	16.60	22.22	27.02	35.47	48.23
Self-enrichment education teachers	18.51	28.42	32.35	37.30	53.82
Archivists, curators, and museum technicians	12.96	15.62	19.16	31.90	37.32
Curators	14.75	19.16	24.19	30.89	31.90
Librarians	15.25	21.27	25.51	34.57	43.51
Library technicians	10.28	12.50	14.70	18.75	23.20
Farm and home management advisors	16.17	16.83	17.31	20.32	23.41
Instructional coordinators	22.88	25.91	33.07	40.64	48.47
Teacher assistants	9.43	10.81	12.67	15.32	18.83
Arts, Design, Entertainment, Sports, and Media	14.00	17.25	21.12	24.72	34.28
Designers	19.99	24.14	27.33	31.53	46.02
Graphic designers	19.99	24.14	27.33	31.53	46.02
Actors, producers, and directors	15.67	15.67	18.90	24.04	28.37
Producers and directors	15.67	15.67	18.90	24.04	28.37
Athletes, coaches, umpires, and related workers	9.30	14.42	17.98	24.72	47.32
Coaches and scouts	14.42	16.19	19.84	29.46	47.32
Umpires, referees, and other sports officials	7.00	8.00	10.00	15.00	21.00
Public relations specialists	16.92	17.77	23.62	28.52	34.28
Writers and editors	20.95	22.30	24.26	26.62	35.03
Miscellaneous media and communication workers	9.62	12.79	19.48	24.60	35.31
Interpreters and translators	9.62	11.50	20.60	24.60	35.31
Broadcast and sound engineering technicians and radio operators	15.08	17.18	20.10	21.70	23.61
Audio and video equipment technicians	15.70	17.18	20.59	22.70	24.01
Healthcare Practitioner and Technical	14.08	18.22	24.50	31.81	43.28
Dietitians and nutritionists	15.09	16.82	23.46	26.15	26.15
Pharmacists	44.78	46.37	50.48	53.88	54.00
Physicians and surgeons	11.43	18.17	25.53	75.34	93.94
Family and general practitioners	10.98	11.43	75.00	91.35	117.80
Psychiatrists	32.02	70.79	74.59	79.67	97.06
Registered nurses	20.64	24.02	28.70	34.52	43.28
Therapists	23.21	27.34	32.76	40.40	49.18
Occupational therapists	28.09	29.95	33.28	42.67	54.39
Physical therapists	28.49	31.27	35.24	39.01	43.98
Recreational therapists	12.72	14.13	18.20	28.20	30.26
Respiratory therapists	23.62	26.32	27.27	30.07	32.16
Speech-language pathologists	26.24	30.86	36.70	45.08	51.92
Clinical laboratory technologists and technicians	13.50	16.50	20.17	22.47	25.60
Medical and clinical laboratory technologists	14.42	16.96	21.60	25.41	26.88
Medical and clinical laboratory technicians	12.74	15.12	19.01	21.65	22.57
Diagnostic related technologists and technicians	18.03	21.50	25.45	29.15	36.75
Cardiovascular technologists and technicians	10.47	11.83	17.09	22.19	22.46
Radiologic technologists and technicians	19.16	22.08	25.82	28.80	32.40
Emergency medical technicians and paramedics	9.38	12.72	16.68	21.24	25.41
Health diagnosing and treating practitioner support technicians	11.42	12.73	15.16	20.67	24.63
Pharmacy technicians	11.68	12.51	13.85	17.11	20.73
Psychiatric technicians	10.57	12.23	17.93	23.92	26.45
Surgical technologists	14.30	15.16	16.18	18.26	18.98
Veterinary technologists and technicians	12.83	13.77	14.52	16.00	16.74
Licensed practical and licensed vocational nurses	13.34	14.45	16.89	19.67	22.44
Medical records and health information technicians	11.50	13.67	15.98	18.53	20.38
Miscellaneous health technologists and technicians	11.30	14.68	17.92	20.81	21.45
Occupational health and safety specialists and technicians	15.37	18.67	25.23	30.03	32.95
Occupational health and safety specialists	15.37	18.31	24.30	30.32	32.95
Miscellaneous healthcare practitioner and technical workers	14.08	14.90	18.27	19.23	21.19
Athletic trainers	14.08	14.90	18.27	19.23	21.19
Healthcare support	8.93	10.13	12.55	15.75	19.00
Nursing, psychiatric, and home health aides	8.75	9.84	11.94	15.22	17.66

[1]Percentiles designate position in the earnings distribution and are calculated from individual worker earnings and the hours they are scheduled to work.

Table 6-17. State and Local Government Workers: Hourly Wage Percentiles,[1] 2008—*Continued*

(Dollars.)

Occupation	Wages fall at or below the following percentiles:				
	10	25	50	75	90
Healthcare Practitioner and Technical—*Continued*					
Home health aides	8.87	9.32	10.06	13.35	15.87
Nursing aides, orderlies, and attendants	8.37	9.56	11.14	13.95	16.51
Psychiatric aides	9.81	11.42	14.35	17.05	19.27
Occupational therapist assistants and aides	10.85	14.76	16.46	24.40	24.40
Physical therapist assistants and aides	12.83	13.71	22.27	25.58	29.99
Physical therapist assistants	19.49	19.49	24.65	29.69	29.99
Miscellaneous healthcare support	9.64	11.35	13.39	15.79	21.37
Dental assistants	11.04	13.52	15.00	17.16	22.07
Medical assistants	10.70	11.90	13.39	15.79	17.17
Medical equipment preparers	10.00	13.46	15.60	20.27	24.22
Medical transcriptionists	10.00	10.24	12.45	19.22	20.31
Protective Service	12.98	16.03	21.48	28.88	35.78
First-line supervisors/managers, law enforcement workers	19.51	25.64	33.09	40.87	49.19
First-line supervisors/managers of correctional officers	15.81	19.42	25.94	31.26	40.56
First-line supervisors/managers of police and detectives	21.39	28.18	35.15	42.48	50.77
First-line supervisors/managers of fire fighting and prevention workers	15.85	20.94	26.56	32.57	40.83
Fire fighters	11.85	15.00	20.15	24.57	30.79
Fire inspectors	20.67	21.04	21.04	27.16	35.56
Fire inspectors and investigators	21.04	21.04	21.07	27.16	31.73
Bailiffs, correctional officers, and jailers	12.95	14.59	17.30	23.33	30.10
Bailiffs	14.23	22.01	25.43	32.12	32.12
Correctional officers and jailers	12.95	14.56	17.16	23.13	29.54
Detectives and criminal investigators	16.33	18.60	27.02	34.45	40.96
Fish and game wardens	10.00	18.69	23.59	23.59	27.36
Parking enforcement workers	10.34	12.09	14.10	17.24	21.23
Police officers	15.35	19.70	25.68	31.48	37.02
Police and sheriff's patrol officers	15.35	19.70	25.68	31.48	37.02
Animal control workers	9.84	11.88	13.48	14.76	20.96
Security guards and gaming surveillance officers	10.53	11.90	14.94	18.72	20.88
Security guards	10.50	11.90	14.94	18.67	20.88
Miscellaneous protective service workers	7.65	9.06	13.13	18.46	24.41
Crossing guards	7.15	8.98	10.53	14.65	17.34
Lifeguards, ski patrol, and other recreational protective service workers	6.90	7.75	9.53	16.54	25.00
Food Preparation and Serving Related	8.00	9.50	11.40	14.41	18.01
First-line supervisors/managers, food preparation and serving workers	9.83	12.82	16.38	19.72	24.56
First-line supervisors/managers of food preparation and serving workers	9.83	12.98	16.63	19.72	25.03
Cooks	7.75	9.40	11.14	13.44	17.25
Cooks, institution and cafeteria	7.69	9.36	11.15	13.60	17.35
Food preparation workers	8.62	10.15	12.01	14.16	15.66
Food service, tipped	6.00	8.00	9.98	12.73	13.08
Waiters and waitresses	5.15	5.15	6.55	7.33	8.11
Dining room and cafeteria attendants and bartender helpers	8.59	9.90	12.05	13.08	13.54
Fast food and counter workers	8.10	9.50	10.90	12.93	15.41
Combined food preparation and serving workers, including fast food	8.53	9.60	11.00	12.92	15.23
Counter attendants, cafeteria, food concession, and coffee shop	7.24	7.83	9.59	12.93	16.40
Food servers, nonrestaurant	7.75	8.56	9.73	13.37	15.95
Dishwashers	7.00	8.27	8.95	10.02	11.60
Building and Grounds Cleaning and Maintenance	8.96	10.27	13.17	16.73	20.81
First-line supervisors/managers, building and grounds cleaning and maintenance workers	13.64	16.81	19.44	22.54	30.55
First-line supervisors/managers of housekeeping and janitorial workers	14.29	16.67	19.43	21.64	34.53
First-line supervisors/managers of landscaping, lawn service, and groundskeeping workers	13.52	17.51	19.54	23.67	28.87
Building cleaning workers	8.84	10.02	12.72	15.95	19.27
Janitors and cleaners, except maids and housekeeping cleaners	8.98	10.13	12.91	16.10	19.44
Maids and housekeeping cleaners	7.69	8.61	10.03	12.20	14.14
Pest control workers	10.00	11.50	12.95	15.98	20.55
Grounds maintenance workers	8.88	10.50	13.11	18.39	23.32
Landscaping and groundskeeping workers	8.96	10.50	13.11	17.38	23.41
Tree trimmers and pruners	15.14	19.22	19.22	23.32	25.36
Personal Care and Service	7.15	8.66	11.50	15.58	19.24
First-line supervisors/managers of gaming workers	10.01	11.81	15.58	20.38	26.00
First-line supervisors/managers of personal service workers	13.94	15.44	17.89	17.89	22.37
Nonfarm animal caretakers	7.00	7.15	8.00	8.66	9.96
Gaming services workers	5.15	6.00	8.00	12.00	13.09
Gaming dealers	5.15	5.15	6.57	8.00	8.24
Ushers, lobby attendants, and ticket takers	6.98	7.28	8.00	9.46	9.46
Miscellaneous entertainment attendants and related workers	6.25	7.00	8.23	11.29	15.87
Amusement and recreation attendants	6.25	6.81	8.15	11.29	15.87
Transportation attendants	8.30	9.00	10.41	12.69	16.16
Transportation attendants, except flight attendants and baggage porters	8.30	9.00	10.41	12.69	16.16
Child care workers	7.79	9.45	12.00	13.68	17.47
Personal and home care aides	8.82	10.22	11.25	14.94	14.94
Recreation and fitness workers	8.00	9.06	12.80	16.64	20.00
Fitness trainers and aerobics instructors	8.64	9.99	13.00	15.87	17.27
Recreation workers	8.00	9.03	12.80	16.69	20.00
Residential advisors	15.27	16.31	16.94	19.06	21.87

[1]Percentiles designate position in the earnings distribution and are calculated from individual worker earnings and the hours they are scheduled to work.

Table 6-17. State and Local Government Workers: Hourly Wage Percentiles,[1] **2008**—*Continued*

(Dollars.)

Occupation	Wages fall at or below the following percentiles:				
	10	25	50	75	90
Sales and Related	9.21	11.00	15.00	19.48	25.96
First-line supervisors/managers, sales workers	17.16	17.16	21.08	26.60	29.10
First-line supervisors/managers of retail sales workers	17.16	17.16	21.08	26.60	29.10
Retail sales workers	8.54	10.42	12.61	17.93	20.84
Cashiers, all workers	9.11	10.42	12.47	17.93	21.00
Cashiers	9.25	10.69	12.82	17.93	21.00
Retail salespersons	8.50	12.35	14.23	18.52	19.48
Office and Administrative Support	10.89	12.87	16.01	19.69	23.54
First-line supervisors/managers of office and administrative support workers	14.28	16.59	19.49	23.54	27.66
Switchboard operators, including answering service	9.04	9.04	13.88	17.25	20.32
Financial clerks	11.74	14.04	17.46	20.15	22.97
Bill and account collectors	10.42	11.25	13.98	18.02	22.28
Billing and posting clerks and machine operators	10.99	12.45	15.13	18.21	20.62
Bookkeeping, accounting, and auditing clerks	12.02	14.46	18.00	20.33	23.05
Payroll and timekeeping clerks	14.00	16.20	18.40	20.14	23.66
Procurement clerks	11.58	11.77	16.56	21.38	24.36
Court, municipal, and license clerks	11.14	12.88	16.04	19.40	24.29
Customer service representatives	11.25	13.23	15.81	18.35	20.00
Eligibility interviewers, government programs	12.72	14.73	17.13	20.25	22.32
File clerks	9.62	11.71	13.62	17.39	20.08
Interviewers, except eligibility and loan	9.65	10.68	11.65	14.46	16.97
Library assistants, clerical	8.00	9.85	11.90	14.09	18.11
Human resources assistants, except payroll and timekeeping	12.00	14.64	17.77	21.75	24.70
Receptionists and information clerks	9.85	11.18	13.69	16.79	20.52
Couriers and messengers	5.85	8.20	11.40	17.19	20.51
Dispatchers	10.76	13.32	16.47	21.51	26.90
Police, fire, and ambulance dispatchers	10.76	13.04	16.19	20.38	26.10
Dispatchers, except police, fire, and ambulance	13.00	14.52	20.60	26.90	33.07
Meter readers, utilities	8.65	10.40	15.78	20.02	22.12
Production, planning, and expediting clerks	11.09	14.89	14.90	18.56	24.61
Shipping, receiving, and traffic clerks	10.45	11.76	13.71	18.27	25.34
Stock clerks and order fillers	10.27	12.97	16.92	18.25	22.03
Weighers, measurers, checkers, and samplers, recordkeeping	14.10	14.88	15.74	16.65	18.10
Secretaries and administrative assistants	11.60	13.96	16.92	20.67	24.93
Executive secretaries and administrative assistants	12.94	15.15	18.59	22.40	26.74
Legal secretaries	11.54	14.85	19.24	22.87	29.97
Medical secretaries	10.98	12.57	14.07	16.10	21.05
Secretaries, except legal, medical, and executive	11.30	13.37	15.93	19.49	22.77
Computer operators	11.08	11.08	11.94	14.78	20.66
Data entry and information processing workers	11.32	13.18	15.88	18.18	20.29
Data entry keyers	10.58	12.60	15.35	18.78	19.84
Word processors and typists	11.68	13.33	16.06	18.03	21.03
Insurance claims and policy processing clerks	11.50	15.32	19.88	20.36	23.43
Mail clerks and mail machine operators, except postal service	8.55	9.35	12.14	14.75	15.39
Office clerks, general	10.44	12.41	14.68	17.90	20.65
Office machine operators, except computer	8.17	8.18	12.00	14.62	14.62
Statistical assistants	15.92	19.60	20.60	22.81	24.53
Farming, Fishing, and Forestry	8.00	12.77	18.75	21.37	24.74
Forest and conservation workers	7.96	8.00	11.48	22.69	23.41
Construction and Extraction	12.00	13.95	17.74	23.14	30.35
First-line supervisors/managers of construction trades and extraction workers	15.75	18.51	23.10	28.98	31.07
Carpenters	12.07	16.80	17.73	21.74	30.00
Construction laborers	8.67	10.38	12.91	19.59	29.67
Construction equipment operators	11.71	13.16	15.51	19.72	23.85
Paving, surfacing, and tamping equipment operators	11.49	11.97	12.09	17.31	24.09
Operating engineers and other construction equipment operators	11.74	13.30	15.81	19.79	23.85
Electricians	16.64	20.34	23.94	30.42	36.44
Painters and paperhangers	13.26	16.09	20.61	35.00	35.00
Painters, construction and maintenance	13.26	16.09	20.61	35.00	35.00
Pipelayers, plumbers, pipefitters, and steamfitters	12.77	14.33	18.13	26.74	30.40
Pipelayers	10.53	11.83	13.91	14.51	16.93
Plumbers, pipefitters, and steamfitters	12.91	15.44	21.95	27.79	34.95
Helpers, construction trades	10.23	12.92	15.96	19.35	23.08
Construction and building inspectors	15.97	17.72	21.87	27.20	32.27
Highway maintenance workers	11.97	12.82	16.07	20.00	23.35
Septic tank servicers and sewer pipe cleaners	12.13	13.36	16.54	25.01	28.34
Miscellaneous construction and related workers	9.65	15.49	22.67	26.29	26.89
Installation, Maintenance, and Repair	12.82	15.70	19.64	25.46	30.44
First-line supervisors/managers of mechanics, installers, and repairers	18.24	20.96	25.78	30.04	38.24
Computer, automated teller, and office machine repairers	11.59	19.21	19.21	19.21	19.21
Radio and telecommunications equipment installers and repairers	19.35	21.71	26.69	28.66	34.19
Miscellaneous electrical and electronic equipment mechanics, installers, and repairers	16.09	18.41	25.48	32.17	37.98
Electrical and electronics repairers, commercial and industrial equipment	15.00	18.61	24.34	27.09	35.80
Electrical and electronics repairers, powerhouse, substation, and relay	18.38	18.41	26.30	35.73	46.03
Automotive technicians and repairers	13.65	16.19	19.70	22.49	27.52
Automotive service technicians and mechanics	13.65	15.44	19.70	22.15	27.37
Bus and truck mechanics and diesel engine specialists	13.91	16.75	21.04	26.47	29.34
Heavy vehicle and mobile equipment service technicians and mechanics	15.01	17.04	23.41	26.47	35.93
Mobile heavy equipment mechanics, except engines	15.01	15.01	21.90	24.73	35.93
Control and valve installers and repairers	12.22	12.71	16.36	21.51	24.04

[1]Percentiles designate position in the earnings distribution and are calculated from individual worker earnings and the hours they are scheduled to work.

Table 6-17. State and Local Government Workers: Hourly Wage Percentiles,[1] 2008—*Continued*

(Dollars.)

Occupation	Wages fall at or below the following percentiles:				
	10	25	50	75	90
Installation, Maintenance, and Repair—*Continued*					
Heating, air conditioning, and refrigeration mechanics and installers	12.22	12.71	16.36	21.51	24.04
Heating, air conditioning, and refrigeration mechanics and installers	15.67	18.50	21.93	26.67	41.37
Industrial machinery installation, repair, and maintenance workers	11.90	14.66	18.17	22.75	28.34
Industrial machinery mechanics	17.26	19.58	26.99	32.84	35.51
Maintenance and repair workers, general	11.86	14.19	17.71	21.52	26.11
Line installers and repairers	13.96	22.47	26.55	31.27	33.73
Electrical power-line installers and repairers	13.96	22.47	26.55	31.55	33.73
Miscellaneous installation, maintenance, and repair workers	12.07	13.73	18.10	23.31	28.26
Helpers–installation, maintenance, and repair workers	10.69	12.28	13.35	18.67	19.84
Production	12.51	15.10	19.25	24.62	31.24
First-line supervisors/managers of production and operating workers	15.10	16.23	19.91	24.64	32.85
Welding, soldering, and brazing workers	14.67	18.98	26.00	27.41	46.67
Welders, cutters, solderers, and brazers	14.67	18.98	25.67	27.00	46.67
Printers	13.96	13.96	17.81	21.68	22.08
Laundry and dry-cleaning workers	8.42	9.33	12.44	14.06	17.24
Power plant operators, distributors, and dispatchers	14.49	19.55	27.10	29.24	35.00
Power plant operators	14.49	18.62	27.38	31.00	35.43
Stationary engineers and boiler operators	17.95	21.00	23.90	31.24	38.44
Water and liquid waste treatment plant and system operators	12.63	15.05	18.28	21.93	25.92
Inspectors, testers, sorters, samplers, and weighers	13.60	17.35	17.40	21.60	27.53
Miscellaneous production workers	7.71	10.40	14.69	15.94	16.63
Helpers–production workers	7.47	7.71	9.89	10.12	10.97
Transportation and Material Moving	10.89	13.04	16.70	22.22	26.92
First-line supervisors/managers of helpers, laborers, and material movers, hand	19.89	21.21	22.09	26.19	29.25
First-line supervisors/managers of transportation and material-moving machine and vehicle operators	8.79	13.00	22.74	28.55	32.36
Bus drivers	11.56	13.44	16.36	20.44	25.62
Bus drivers, transit and intercity	13.46	16.90	22.88	26.16	26.92
Bus drivers, school	11.41	12.85	15.25	18.16	21.13
Driver/sales workers and truck drivers	12.48	13.84	16.20	20.80	24.46
Truck drivers, heavy and tractor-trailer	12.88	14.23	16.53	20.86	25.94
Truck drivers, light or delivery services	11.71	12.95	15.49	19.20	21.15
Taxi drivers and chauffeurs	9.91	10.58	11.77	12.94	16.37
Subway and streetcar operators	19.45	24.24	26.55	28.65	28.65
Parking lot attendants	5.15	7.81	9.75	12.83	13.01
Transportation inspectors	21.05	22.23	27.10	29.91	31.84
Dredge, excavating, and loading machine operators	10.71	12.42	16.57	19.96	21.77
Excavating and loading machine and dragline operators	10.71	12.42	16.57	19.96	21.77
Industrial truck and tractor operators	11.69	12.77	15.27	19.69	23.86
Laborers and material movers, hand	8.00	9.40	12.13	16.08	21.25
Laborers and freight, stock, and material movers, hand	8.00	9.39	11.81	15.50	21.25
Refuse and recyclable material collectors	9.44	11.67	15.73	24.09	29.84

[1]Percentiles designate position in the earnings distribution and are calculated from individual worker earnings and the hours they are scheduled to work.

Chapter Seven

RECENT TRENDS IN THE LABOR MARKET

RECENT TRENDS IN THE LABOR MARKET

HIGHLIGHTS

This chapter contains information on mass layoff events, initial claimants for unemployment insurance, movement of work, job openings, hires, and separations.

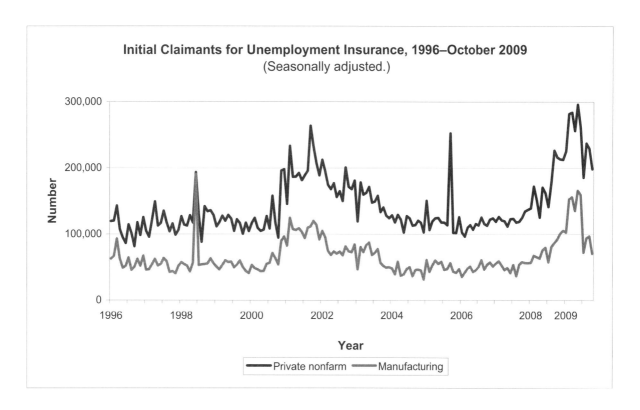

From December 2007 through October 2009, the total number of mass layoff events (seasonally adjusted) was 49,357, and the number of initial claims filed (seasonally adjusted) in those events was 5,021,824. December 2007 was the start of a recession as designated by the National Bureau of Economic Research. (See Table 7-1.)

OTHER HIGHLIGHTS

- In 2009, from January through October, the number of mass layoff events (seasonally adjusted), reached 25,872 while the number of initial claims rose to 2,627,390. Both were the highest totals on record from January through October since the Mass Layoff Statistics (MLS) program began recording data in April 1995. (See Table 7-1.)

- The manufacturing sector accounted for 29 percent of all mass layoff events and 36 percent of initial claims filed in October 2009; a year earlier, manufacturing made up 32 percent of events and 45 percent of initial claims. (See Table 7-3.)

- Of the four census regions, the West had the highest number of initial claims in October 2009 (64,631), followed by the Midwest (60,792), the South (45,772), and the Northeast (22,709). (See Table 7-4.)

- From January 2008 to September 2009, the number of job openings fell significantly. In January 2008, there were 4.3 million job openings and by September 2009, there were less than 2.5 million. (See Table 7-7.)

NOTES AND DEFINITIONS

MASS LAYOFFS

Collection and Coverage

The Mass Layoff Statistics (MLS) program is a federal-state program that identifies, describes, and tracks the effects of major job cutbacks, using data from each state's unemployment insurance database. Employers that have at least 50 initial claims filed against them during a consecutive 5-week period are contacted by the state agency to determine whether these separations are of at least 31 days duration, and, if so, information is obtained on the total number of persons separated, the reasons for these separations, and recall expectations. Employers are identified according to industry classification and location, and unemployment insurance claimants are identified by such demographic factors as age, race, gender, ethnic group, and place of residence. The program yields information on an individual's entire spell of unemployment, to the point when regular unemployment insurance benefits are exhausted.

A given month contains an aggregation of the weekly unemployment insurance claims filings for the Sunday through Saturday weeks in that month. All weeks are included for the particular month, except if the first day of the month falls on Saturday. In this case, the week is included in the prior month's tabulations. This means that some months will contain 4 weeks and others, 5 weeks, the number of weeks in a given month may be different from year to year, and the number of weeks in a year may vary. Therefore, analysis of over-the-month and over-the-year change in not seasonally adjusted series should take this calendar effect into consideration.

The latest quarterly data in these tables are considered preliminary. After the initial publication of quarterly information, more data are collected as remaining employer interviews for the quarter are completed and additional initial claimant information associated with extended layoff events is received.

The MLS program discontinued the collection of "domestic relocation" and "overseas relocation" as standard reasons for layoff beginning with data for the first quarter 2004. It was felt these reasons do not reflect an economic reason, and instead relate to the effect of the actual reason.

Concepts and Definitions

Employers in the MLS program include those covered by state unemployment insurance laws. Information on employers is obtained from the Quarterly Census of Employment and Wages (QCEW) program.

Extended layoff event is when there are fifty or more initial claims for unemployment insurance benefits from an employer during a 5-week period, with at least 50 workers separated for more than 30 days.

Initial claimant is a person who files any notice of unemployment to initiate a request either for a determination of entitlement to and eligibility for compensation, or for a subsequent period of unemployment within a benefit year or period of eligibility.

Layoff is the separation of persons from an employer as part of a mass layoff event. Such layoffs involve both persons subject to recall and those who are terminated by the establishment.

Mass layoff event is when there are fifty or more initial claims for unemployment insurance benefits from an employer during a five-week period, regardless of duration.

Movement-of-work action is relocation of work within the same company or to other companies, domestically or outside the United States. Because employers may cite more than one location to which work is moving, a layoff event may have more than one action associated with it.

Movement-of-work separations is the number of separations specifically associated with movement-of-work actions.

Outsourcing is the movement of work that was formerly conducted in-house by employees paid directly by a company to a different company under a contractual arrangement.

Seasonal adjustment is the process of estimating and removing the effect on time series data of regularly recurring seasonal events such as changes in the weather, holidays, and the beginning and ending of the school year. The use of seasonal adjustment makes it easier to observe fundamental changes in time series, particularly those associated with general economic expansions and contractions.

Separations is the total number of people laid-off in an extended mass layoff event for more than 30 days, according to the employer.

Worksite closure is the complete closure of either multi-unit or single-unit employers or the partial closure of a multi-unit employer where entire worksites affected by layoffs are closed or planned to be closed.

Sources of Additional Information

For more extensive information see BLS news release USDL 09-1404 "Mass Layoffs (Monthly)" and USDL 09-1358 "Extended Mass Layoffs (Quarterly)" on the BLS Web site at <http://www.bls.gov/mls/>.

Table 7-1. Mass Layoff Events and Initial Claimants for Unemployment Insurance, 1996–October 2009, Seasonally Adjusted

(Number.)

Year and month	Total		Private nonfarm		Manufacturing	
	Events	Initial claimants	Events	Initial claimants	Events	Initial claimants
1996						
January	1 333	130 495	1 231	119 544	563	62 626
February	1 250	131 011	1 116	120 274	544	66 635
March	1 226	151 775	1 110	142 847	581	93 175
April	1 078	115 314	977	107 408	507	62 617
May	1 005	98 129	956	94 957	460	48 972
June	1 071	95 156	956	86 476	435	51 901
July	1 143	121 576	1 047	114 533	475	64 477
August	1 138	111 018	1 015	101 550	470	45 750
September	1 098	89 262	992	81 578	437	50 320
October	1 269	128 505	1 105	117 632	479	62 133
November	1 124	107 614	1 006	98 567	479	52 019
December	1 364	136 382	1 204	125 521	524	67 104
1997						
January	1 154	117 136	985	105 049	355	45 970
February	985	104 805	868	95 846	383	46 614
March	1 233	134 334	1 051	121 521	399	54 344
April	1 353	162 965	1 165	149 073	504	62 166
May	1 229	123 446	1 102	112 769	452	52 241
June	1 383	137 275	1 106	117 005	467	54 828
July	1 436	153 734	1 220	135 080	484	63 442
August	1 197	129 375	1 040	117 754	485	58 941
September	1 132	118 918	933	104 136	337	42 572
October	1 235	130 351	1 050	116 063	377	43 911
November	1 157	109 533	1 018	99 067	378	40 752
December	1 238	118 146	1 072	106 346	430	51 879
1998						
January	1 316	143 061	1 089	126 988	406	57 309
February	1 234	129 602	1 046	114 166	438	54 440
March	1 181	124 912	1 030	112 851	436	52 061
April	1 362	145 440	1 142	128 241	428	43 403
May	1 248	129 030	1 089	117 332	466	56 728
June	1 332	205 228	1 162	193 631	684	190 810
July	1 422	147 574	1 187	128 085	444	53 057
August	1 076	100 917	887	88 347	433	54 085
September	1 268	150 904	1 139	141 911	450	54 589
October	1 389	153 632	1 174	134 417	468	55 517
November	1 331	151 957	1 138	135 741	467	63 022
December	1 400	150 760	1 115	128 451	415	55 676
1999						
January	1 399	129 104	1 122	111 713	429	50 593
February	1 321	136 296	1 074	117 827	404	46 526
March	1 354	148 022	1 112	127 562	460	53 087
April	1 251	134 118	1 058	120 142	457	60 125
May	1 278	146 682	1 063	128 874	438	57 589
June	1 217	138 397	1 053	123 191	446	58 202
July	1 136	117 941	951	104 930	358	49 567
August	1 188	140 981	1 000	122 361	408	53 579
September	1 355	134 430	1 152	116 756	374	59 783
October	995	115 894	797	100 478	344	50 194
November	1 258	138 992	1 025	117 116	337	44 140
December	1 174	119 033	973	104 519	298	40 825
2000						
January	1 100	126 440	968	116 846	371	53 270
February	1 280	151 107	1 018	124 497	379	48 372
March	1 159	126 309	965	109 445	393	46 564
April	1 030	115 068	913	104 865	407	43 829
May	1 196	126 525	976	106 893	376	44 019
June	1 220	145 766	1 020	127 239	406	54 672
July	1 065	118 649	922	108 499	417	56 465
August	1 282	178 789	1 060	157 762	423	71 141
September	1 260	134 153	1 045	117 266	407	63 394
October	938	107 676	798	94 783	385	54 006
November	1 643	215 381	1 447	196 166	599	89 869
December	1 691	214 601	1 514	197 944	575	96 295
2001						
January	1 288	158 580	1 144	145 584	529	82 504
February	1 912	253 943	1 684	233 524	828	124 430
March	1 761	202 344	1 569	186 565	800	107 481
April	1 622	200 683	1 484	186 898	776	106 255
May	1 676	206 062	1 523	192 500	750	108 773
June	1 608	195 802	1 432	181 264	740	103 468
July	1 710	201 363	1 574	189 030	721	93 949
August	1 732	207 416	1 568	195 777	791	109 611
September	2 407	277 955	2 236	263 773	841	111 520
October	2 177	242 507	2 051	232 371	923	119 873
November	2 104	218 378	1 940	206 999	948	113 776
December	1 824	200 677	1 673	188 836	746	92 019
2002						
January	1 841	224 765	1 711	212 461	764	104 909
February	1 823	207 788	1 663	194 840	701	95 406
March	1 697	187 212	1 525	174 281	604	74 492
April	1 666	183 005	1 494	167 848	584	68 282
May	1 730	190 129	1 561	176 744	613	73 612
June	1 632	171 213	1 436	155 960	547	70 137
July	1 632	179 407	1 461	164 741	557	73 479
August	1 468	161 431	1 324	149 847	563	67 831
September	1 918	217 299	1 737	200 635	615	81 292
October	1 749	187 851	1 573	171 346	611	73 940
November	1 651	178 739	1 507	167 723	590	72 329
December	1 834	194 852	1 646	180 976	676	84 247

Table 7-1. Mass Layoff Events and Initial Claimants for Unemployment Insurance, 1996–October 2009, Seasonally Adjusted—*Continued*

(Number.)

Year and month	Total		Private nonfarm		Manufacturing	
	Events	Initial claimants	Events	Initial claimants	Events	Initial claimants
2003						
January	1 336	132 819	1 160	119 199	382	46 839
February	1 831	191 434	1 650	178 003	650	80 285
March	1 784	175 384	1 589	159 467	609	72 679
April	1 702	172 252	1 555	162 323	637	83 268
May	1 744	185 159	1 556	171 221	646	87 077
June	1 726	164 597	1 518	147 553	640	68 197
July	1 661	165 130	1 450	149 233	567	71 319
August	1 546	171 996	1 383	157 968	563	77 405
September	1 571	149 250	1 370	133 276	479	56 454
October	1 525	157 759	1 319	140 086	422	51 872
November	1 370	139 572	1 225	127 963	379	49 219
December	1 395	136 166	1 226	124 009	428	49 789
2004						
January	1 414	145 593	1 221	128 305	396	47 882
February	1 257	130 205	1 111	117 788	365	39 214
March	1 362	138 397	1 222	129 094	396	58 213
April	1 349	136 837	1 175	121 841	347	37 115
May	1 240	116 392	1 077	102 443	340	39 208
June	1 397	139 975	1 231	127 229	370	46 998
July	1 315	135 186	1 165	123 768	371	49 945
August	1 417	127 814	1 226	112 867	344	36 298
September	1 275	124 279	1 149	113 689	337	45 732
October	1 265	129 312	1 153	120 337	366	46 319
November	1 306	129 014	1 161	117 300	374	44 939
December	1 163	114 258	1 009	102 732	285	31 445
2005						
January	1 474	159 945	1 341	150 403	387	60 842
February	1 087	117 129	964	106 399	350	42 747
March	1 204	129 993	1 056	119 466	368	52 667
April	1 244	134 425	1 111	123 958	396	60 052
May	1 264	137 475	1 121	124 468	397	54 998
June	1 196	126 416	1 082	117 568	367	58 003
July	1 241	130 331	1 094	117 510	354	46 056
August	1 143	125 536	1 000	113 465	342	47 255
September	2 250	296 913	2 035	252 291	420	55 974
October	1 109	111 202	991	102 111	320	43 387
November	1 162	113 502	1 027	102 058	325	41 493
December	1 263	136 751	1 135	125 700	358	46 940
2006						
January	1 112	111 601	986	102 359	293	35 390
February	960	104 045	872	96 317	317	41 810
March	1 078	118 270	976	109 842	320	48 026
April	1 198	123 674	1 062	113 849	366	50 747
May	1 132	116 808	1 013	106 743	312	42 958
June	1 156	124 955	1 044	115 491	356	45 280
July	1 204	123 172	1 077	113 324	381	50 109
August	1 278	136 289	1 117	125 064	376	60 524
September	1 167	124 083	1 054	115 451	390	46 470
October	1 195	121 439	1 081	112 777	401	53 597
November	1 209	131 459	1 096	122 136	402	57 084
December	1 201	133 311	1 100	124 019	369	51 113
2007						
January	1 261	129 190	1 116	118 890	406	55 341
February	1 240	134 524	1 130	126 105	404	58 861
March	1 261	129 480	1 151	120 923	407	52 356
April	1 281	130 263	1 145	119 683	381	45 654
May	1 200	119 259	1 097	111 585	368	48 682
June	1 256	132 078	1 138	122 726	356	41 135
July	1 288	131 556	1 182	123 322	405	53 318
August	1 262	125 334	1 162	117 557	331	36 577
September	1 279	125 527	1 183	118 917	440	54 006
October	1 346	133 514	1 224	124 666	436	57 527
November	1 352	143 419	1 233	134 445	408	56 330
December	1 469	145 916	1 354	136 914	447	56 152
2008						
January	1 476	149 068	1 350	139 076	435	56 579
February	1 669	183 038	1 532	172 013	526	67 235
March	1 585	161 497	1 471	151 550	483	65 252
April	1 344	135 352	1 215	125 074	487	63 247
May	1 701	180 558	1 563	170 538	538	75 520
June	1 717	174 748	1 561	162 071	555	79 744
July	1 535	152 499	1 390	141 239	455	57 648
August	1 887	188 951	1 735	178 479	626	80 913
September	2 290	240 721	2 114	226 492	643	86 617
October	2 204	230 330	2 042	216 095	687	92 256
November	2 333	225 639	2 185	213 288	868	100 643
December	2 275	226 117	2 100	212 559	871	105 402
2009						
January	2 227	237 902	2 070	225 490	738	102 577
February	2 769	295 477	2 628	281 500	1 235	152 618
March	2 933	299 388	2 751	283 989	1 259	155 909
April	2 712	271 226	2 519	256 111	1 111	135 252
May	2 933	312 880	2 736	296 108	1 331	165 802
June	2 763	279 231	2 536	260 747	1 235	159 310
July	2 157	206 791	1 928	185 718	621	72 266
August	2 690	259 307	2 428	237 302	900	93 892
September	2 561	248 006	2 324	229 371	856	97 066
October	2 127	217 182	1 918	198 453	619	70 572

Table 7-2. Mass Layoff Events and Initial Claimants for Unemployment Insurance, 1996–October 2009, Not Seasonally Adjusted

(Number.)

Year and month	Total		Private nonfarm		Manufacturing	
	Events	Initial claimants	Events	Initial claimants	Events	Initial claimants
1996						
January	1 763	176 285	1 660	163 469	689	80 410
February	947	77 661	805	68 713	395	37 403
March	994	129 068	902	121 900	499	82 182
April	1 030	109 572	943	101 740	405	57 084
May	942	80 366	897	77 488	358	33 421
June	924	80 232	812	71 421	257	26 491
July	1 534	192 155	1 410	182 196	783	128 214
August	918	83 166	844	77 872	347	32 573
September	513	42 376	463	39 170	231	21 860
October	1 289	131 850	1 006	110 287	402	54 937
November	1 433	130 774	1 181	111 923	563	62 962
December	1 824	204 123	1 691	194 665	776	101 952
1997						
January	2 139	212 860	1 950	197 137	727	82 978
February	755	63 352	632	55 848	277	26 507
March	783	84 069	678	76 804	265	33 141
April	1 269	152 168	1 111	139 164	402	55 181
May	1 152	101 476	1 037	91 900	352	35 472
June	1 238	121 256	952	99 210	277	28 786
July	1 899	237 410	1 623	211 580	794	124 062
August	973	99 513	878	92 768	363	42 472
September	548	59 062	447	52 310	181	18 881
October	1 414	139 297	1 108	116 157	408	47 579
November	1 156	100 051	953	86 994	386	39 757
December	1 634	172 029	1 500	161 797	639	78 387
1998						
January	2 360	255 203	2 117	235 263	823	104 790
February	970	81 455	773	68 345	315	31 692
March	762	78 210	673	71 258	289	31 369
April	1 253	132 476	1 076	117 601	342	37 312
May	1 180	107 952	1 038	97 493	365	38 553
June	1 208	183 590	1 012	169 411	409	103 501
July	2 220	286 055	1 903	255 245	1 014	152 044
August	617	53 665	558	50 149	259	26 593
September	637	79 629	564	74 941	248	25 134
October	1 553	160 830	1 220	132 258	507	60 529
November	1 368	144 343	1 076	123 066	478	62 829
December	1 776	207 661	1 552	188 787	618	82 871
1999						
January	2 421	226 995	2 142	206 615	861	94 887
February	1 067	89 800	810	73 846	289	28 322
March	880	91 890	737	80 063	302	31 317
April	1 270	136 885	1 100	123 987	450	56 668
May	1 032	102 738	895	93 006	303	32 958
June	1 140	130 951	925	109 848	268	32 610
July	1 741	221 334	1 496	201 412	808	137 688
August	698	75 691	638	70 285	246	26 606
September	717	75 288	592	64 942	212	28 968
October	1 098	118 938	814	97 984	373	55 222
November	1 336	139 508	977	110 200	347	45 431
December	1 509	162 381	1 353	150 171	446	60 349
2000						
January	1 934	223 322	1 807	212 805	741	100 397
February	1 045	103 898	780	81 103	268	30 358
March	986	106 748	827	92 565	329	38 434
April	924	101 359	838	93 631	323	34 061
May	984	92 193	841	81 125	262	25 838
June	1 597	192 025	1 269	160 685	404	60 258
July	1 333	164 978	1 159	152 243	664	100 874
August	751	97 215	679	90 877	256	35 687
September	936	106 842	767	93 327	319	46 865
October	874	103 755	684	84 922	321	48 877
November	1 697	216 514	1 397	190 626	617	93 966
December	2 677	326 743	2 477	311 623	1 074	166 928
2001						
January	1 522	200 343	1 405	188 504	632	107 028
February	1 501	172 908	1 285	156 183	576	79 784
March	1 527	171 466	1 371	158 108	659	86 874
April	1 450	176 265	1 353	166 167	608	78 845
May	1 434	159 365	1 331	151 186	528	64 887
June	2 107	253 826	1 784	226 022	737	116 005
July	2 117	273 807	1 952	259 128	1 144	168 877
August	1 490	166 148	1 386	158 307	603	79 515
September	1 327	160 402	1 214	151 161	485	58 544
October	1 831	215 483	1 676	202 053	742	107 030
November	2 721	295 956	2 373	270 268	1 122	151 969
December	2 440	268 893	2 319	259 497	1 103	136 820
2002						
January	2 146	263 777	2 028	252 245	892	128 825
February	1 382	138 808	1 253	129 849	481	58 784
March	1 460	161 316	1 335	151 305	500	59 613
April	1 506	165 814	1 378	153 216	461	50 897
May	1 723	179 799	1 571	166 801	488	52 720
June	1 584	162 189	1 266	136 424	336	42 130
July	2 042	245 294	1 819	226 892	907	135 271
August	1 248	128 103	1 151	119 874	427	48 668
September	1 062	124 522	957	114 736	352	43 755
October	1 497	171 100	1 270	149 327	493	64 655
November	2 153	240 171	1 860	216 237	719	92 712
December	2 474	264 158	2 324	252 807	984	126 826

Table 7-2. Mass Layoff Events and Initial Claimants for Unemployment Insurance, 1996–October 2009, Not Seasonally Adjusted—*Continued*

(Number.)

Year and month	Total		Private nonfarm		Manufacturing	
	Events	Initial claimants	Events	Initial claimants	Events	Initial claimants
2003						
January	2 315	225 430	2 130	210 918	822	90 244
February	1 363	124 965	1 222	116 264	435	48 161
March	1 207	113 026	1 099	104 468	390	41 063
April	1 581	161 412	1 470	152 937	499	62 349
May	1 703	174 204	1 538	160 729	499	61 278
June	1 691	157 552	1 336	127 743	389	40 845
July	2 087	226 435	1 815	206 901	946	136 410
August	1 258	133 839	1 163	124 131	405	52 620
September	868	82 647	756	73 914	271	31 428
October	1 523	158 240	1 265	137 706	438	53 741
November	1 438	138 543	1 234	123 524	408	48 419
December	1 929	192 633	1 793	182 750	648	77 915
2004						
January	2 428	239 454	2 226	220 687	848	89 551
February	941	84 201	832	76 577	240	23 043
March	920	92 554	847	87 782	258	34 686
April	1 458	157 314	1 316	142 657	343	36 172
May	988	87 501	878	78 786	219	22 141
June	1 379	134 588	1 077	110 804	222	27 307
July	2 094	253 929	1 860	234 877	885	145 895
August	809	69 033	745	63 876	194	17 698
September	708	68 972	637	63 102	189	25 808
October	1 242	127 918	1 101	117 375	372	48 265
November	1 399	130 423	1 201	115 549	412	44 243
December	1 614	161 271	1 487	152 092	436	50 726
2005						
January	2 564	263 952	2 421	253 409	823	108 985
February	810	74 644	722	68 372	230	24 931
March	806	88 937	733	83 793	246	33 030
April	1 373	158 582	1 263	148 133	395	59 129
May	986	101 358	891	93 332	249	30 424
June	1 157	120 463	941	103 307	216	32 783
July	1 981	244 216	1 745	222 377	856	136 210
August	645	67 582	598	63 484	188	22 531
September	1 662	213 281	1 505	179 042	318	47 497
October	905	91 941	757	80 694	249	37 276
November	1 254	116 127	1 079	102 182	363	41 442
December	2 323	254 258	2 168	242 753	706	96 382
2006						
January	1 245	117 946	1 123	108 701	331	35 097
February	719	66 555	658	62 208	210	24 892
March	921	111 838	856	106 177	285	44 688
April	1 140	121 589	1 038	112 964	296	39 538
May	872	84 809	794	78 663	192	23 570
June	1 489	164 761	1 224	140 687	319	41 095
July	1 511	166 857	1 335	154 342	648	96 152
August	708	72 844	656	69 054	203	28 494
September	865	87 699	785	81 274	296	39 076
October	964	98 804	820	88 133	311	46 737
November	1 315	136 186	1 172	125 009	455	58 473
December	2 249	254 503	2 126	244 783	735	105 462
2007						
January	1 407	134 984	1 263	124 475	456	53 615
February	935	86 696	861	82 097	273	36 170
March	1 082	123 974	1 015	118 431	367	49 886
April	1 219	127 444	1 115	118 040	309	35 229
May	923	85 816	856	81 153	224	26 527
June	1 599	172 810	1 318	148 669	313	36 571
July	1 599	175 419	1 450	164 939	684	101 390
August	963	93 458	908	88 345	220	23 361
September	717	67 385	667	64 026	246	29 381
October	1 083	108 455	929	97 716	338	50 918
November	1 799	198 220	1 593	181 184	514	75 413
December	2 167	224 214	2 071	216 898	699	91 754
2008						
January	1 647	154 503	1 520	144 191	488	54 418
February	1 269	119 508	1 178	113 587	361	42 527
March	1 089	114 541	1 039	110 147	333	43 740
April	1 272	130 810	1 172	121 625	394	48 188
May	1 552	159 471	1 438	150 462	388	51 698
June	1 622	166 742	1 315	140 916	309	42 097
July	1 891	200 382	1 687	186 018	760	108 733
August	1 427	139 999	1 343	133 146	414	51 912
September	1 292	129 586	1 202	122 505	361	46 391
October	2 125	221 784	1 917	205 553	689	100 457
November	2 574	241 589	2 389	226 657	997	107 620
December	3 377	351 305	3 232	340 220	1 378	172 529
2009						
January	3 806	388 813	3 633	375 293	1 461	172 757
February	2 262	218 438	2 173	210 755	945	103 588
March	2 191	228 387	2 107	221 397	940	114 747
April	2 547	256 930	2 385	243 321	887	100 872
May	2 738	289 628	2 572	274 047	1 005	123 683
June	2 519	256 357	2 051	216 063	674	85 726
July	3 054	336 654	2 659	296 589	1 133	154 208
August	1 428	125 024	1 334	117 193	436	41 151
September	1 371	123 177	1 258	115 141	448	51 126
October	1 934	193 904	1 678	172 883	566	69 655

Table 7-3. Industry Distribution: Mass Layoff Events and Initial Claimants for Unemployment Insurance, 1996–October 2009

(Number, not seasonally adjusted.)

Industry	1996	1997	1998	1999	2000	2001	2002	2003	2004	2005	2006	2007
						Mass layoff events						
ALL INDUSTRIES	14 111	14 960	15 904	14 909	15 738	21 467	20 277	18 963	15 980	16 466	13 998	15 493
Total, Private	13 641	14 164	15 098	14 197	15 028	20 763	19 376	17 846	15 018	15 534	13 238	14 714
Agriculture, forestry, fishing and hunting	1 027	1 295	1 536	1 718	1 503	1 314	1 164	1 025	811	711	651	668
Total, private nonfarm	12 614	12 869	13 562	12 479	13 525	19 449	18 212	16 821	14 207	14 823	12 587	14 046
Mining, quarrying, and oil and gas extraction	78	81	152	176	102	115	176	101	69	75	58	66
Utilities	44	31	40	31	37	33	44	40	25	25	20	20
Construction	1 248	1 512	1 477	1 509	1 638	1 688	1 939	2 013	1 821	1 975	1 546	1 952
Manufacturing	5 705	5 071	5 667	4 905	5 578	8 939	7 040	6 150	4 618	4 839	4 281	4 643
Food	841	924	909	830	826	879	826	850	797	751	648	595
Beverage and tobacco products	75	74	79	68	61	74	79	82	75	66	56	58
Textile mills	228	153	245	218	209	352	272	245	169	160	143	146
Textile product mills	83	82	84	70	83	91	113	111	93	86	66	63
Apparel	706	625	605	463	424	433	346	295	220	179	128	131
Leather and allied products	106	104	94	83	76	79	48	48	42	41	26	27
Wood products	243	296	271	240	377	355	377	345	225	273	339	418
Paper	144	121	142	91	148	212	167	156	82	98	86	78
Printing and related support activities	134	104	103	93	95	156	156	125	118	98	74	90
Petroleum and coal products	36	44	30	32	39	25	39	30	27	24	34	28
Chemicals	99	74	82	92	84	156	122	105	101	77	69	75
Plastics and rubber products	263	229	268	200	278	482	331	328	282	300	250	265
Nonmetallic mineral products	177	175	159	150	186	239	219	233	167	204	172	215
Primary metals	238	187	256	214	274	568	399	366	194	222	184	225
Fabricated metal products	264	233	284	268	327	675	482	397	322	311	288	293
Machinery	295	238	321	349	324	781	555	425	235	272	255	287
Computer and electronic products	367	253	489	344	231	1 050	817	481	230	217	173	190
Electrical equipment and appliance manufacturing	207	193	202	152	195	391	313	231	137	167	136	135
Transportation equipment	844	672	756	678	1 004	1 410	961	927	821	1 034	925	1 068
Furniture and related products	180	148	125	130	187	329	255	223	169	164	150	184
Miscellaneous manufacturing	175	142	163	140	150	202	163	147	112	95	79	72
Wholesale trade	264	245	234	228	236	334	336	318	222	251	184	220
Retail trade	960	1 023	935	830	906	1 249	1 351	1 327	1 165	1 196	991	1 048
Transportation and warehousing	546	712	661	595	717	908	947	965	853	1 011	934	982
Information	297	397	412	336	358	736	719	598	454	383	350	383
Finance and insurance	195	199	187	229	218	325	432	384	322	272	310	510
Real estate and rental and leasing	38	49	49	42	64	99	91	91	79	92	54	71
Professional and technical services	260	300	332	324	348	591	634	522	420	427	352	420
Management of companies and enterprises	32	31	26	43	40	47	40	35	38	27	28	42
Administrative and waste services	1 174	1 468	1 649	1 536	1 644	2 333	2 428	2 266	2 035	1 989	1 741	1 862
Educational services	209	32	36	35	34	51	69	82	60	70	63	67
Health care and social assistance	432	422	472	434	405	374	480	499	522	585	415	450
Arts, entertainment, and recreation	166	230	213	205	162	229	277	285	287	293	245	240
Accommodation and food services	649	811	790	738	729	1 032	916	886	980	1 083	844	905
Other services, except public administration	124	161	146	148	148	171	221	217	198	201	148	155
Unclassified	193	94	84	135	161	195	72	42	39	29	23	10
Government	470	796	806	712	710	704	901	1 117	962	932	760	779
Local	200	450	466	393	386	396	605	778	643	582	511	509

Table 7-3. Industry Distribution: Mass Layoff Events and Initial Claimants for Unemployment Insurance, 1996–October 2009—*Continued*

(Number, not seasonally adjusted.)

Industry	2008	January 2009	February 2009	March 2009	April 2009	May 2009	June 2009	July 2009	August 2009	September 2009	October 2009
						Mass layoff events					
ALL INDUSTRIES	21 137	3 806	2 262	2 191	2 547	2 738	2 519	3 054	1 428	1 371	1 934
Total, Private	20 130	3 709	2 215	2 140	2 464	2 599	2 101	2 752	1 356	1 285	1 806
Agriculture, forestry, fishing and hunting	698	76	42	33	79	27	50	93	22	27	128
Total, private nonfarm	19 432	3 633	2 173	2 107	2 385	2 572	2 051	2 659	1 334	1 258	1 678
Mining, quarrying, and oil and gas extraction	103	50	35	31	39	32	15	22	9	10	15
Utilities	28	(1)	(1)	3	(1)	4	4	(1)	(1)	6	6
Construction	2 393	388	199	166	194	255	136	170	160	167	205
Manufacturing	6 872	1 461	945	940	887	1 005	674	1 133	436	448	566
Food	678	84	57	63	81	65	48	67	41	50	91
Beverage and tobacco products	78	6	8	9	(1)	7	(1)	8	5	5	12
Textile mills	179	35	19	29	16	13	11	21	4	12	9
Textile product mills	69	19	8	6	9	8	4	8	5	3	3
Apparel	149	33	16	9	19	17	16	26	15	7	7
Leather and allied products	22	6	3	(1)	(1)	(1)	(1)	4	(1)	(1)	. . .
Wood products	557	104	57	62	39	43	29	42	19	36	41
Paper	146	38	34	27	26	30	13	17	8	15	14
Printing and related support activities	132	38	21	23	25	34	18	16	9	10	17
Petroleum and coal products	37	8	(1)	(1)	(1)	5	(1)	6	. . .	. . .	3
Chemicals	122	26	20	21	21	23	13	19	10	9	8
Plastics and rubber products	501	110	48	60	51	52	35	74	17	13	35
Nonmetallic mineral products	316	56	40	46	34	35	25	29	18	12	16
Primary metals	352	98	59	71	70	77	45	89	31	30	44
Fabricated metal products	574	151	99	88	97	100	74	114	43	44	49
Machinery	402	121	106	110	100	118	74	132	74	63	51
Computer and electronic products	285	76	78	68	69	60	60	63	77	30	28	29
Electrical equipment and appliance manufacturing	220	53	35	47	43	37	30	45	18	23	29
Transportation equipment	1 647	316	171	155	148	238	139	275	68	53	72
Furniture and related products	288	48	44	24	21	24	24	35	13	22	22
Miscellaneous manufacturing	118	35	20	19	14	17	9	29	6	11	14
Wholesale trade	363	86	62	59	55	64	50	78	34	32	50
Retail trade	1 457	329	193	178	153	202	155	161	111	139	124
Transportation and warehousing	1 267	236	80	91	231	89	184	131	101	47	61
Information	545	69	72	75	75	67	53	90	46	45	57
Finance and insurance	552	88	74	57	67	71	34	84	47	43	49
Real estate and rental and leasing	118	26	17	16	13	14	20	12	7	-2	13
Professional and technical services	564	87	82	81	97	83	53	95	32	31	57
Management of companies and enterprises	6l	l2	14	10	10	12	8	14	5	5	6
Administrative and waste services	2 699	473	235	227	300	310	239	351	195	142	260
Educational services	100	14	8	8	9	10	28	31	13	7	3
Health care and social assistance	580	41	33	24	49	87	173	101	31	23	37
Arts, entertainment, and recreation	311	49	10	17	47	37	45	38	19	29	34
Accommodation and food services	1 238	197	95	115	134	189	136	124	74	73	126
Other services, except public administration	174	25	18	9	23	41	42	19	13	7	9
Unclassified	7	1	. . .	. . .	1	. . .	2	2	. . .	2	. . .
Government	1 007	97	47	51	83	139	418	302	72	86	128
Local	705	59	23	35	57	77	365	253	39	50	68

[1]Data do not meet BLS or state agency disclosure standards.
. . . = Not available.

Table 7-3. Industry Distribution: Mass Layoff Events and Initial Claimants for Unemployment Insurance, 1996–October 2009—*Continued*

(Number, not seasonally adjusted.)

Industry	1996	1997	1998	1999	2000	2001	2002	2003	2004	2005	2006	2007
	Initial claimants											
ALL INDUSTRIES	1437628	1 542 543	1 771 069	1 572 399	1 835 592	2 514 862	2 245 051	1 888 926	1 607 158	1 795 341	1484391	1598875
Total, Private	1393548	1 470 612	1 695 163	1 509 503	1 768 743	2 447 154	2 158 413	1 790 713	1 520 157	1 691 217	1418452	1533920
Agriculture, forestry, fishing and hunting	72 704	88 943	111 346	127 144	123 211	100 570	88 700	68 728	55 993	50 339	46 457	47 947
Total, private nonfarm	1320844	1 381 669	1 583 817	1 382 359	1 645 532	2 346 584	2 069 713	1 721 985	1 464 164	1 640 878	1371995	1485973
Mining, quarrying, and oil and gas extraction	6 132	6 680	12 206	19 537	9 271	14 887	16 672	9 852	5 985	6 483	5 582	5 327
Utilities	4 271	2 211	3 257	2 224	3 361	3 898	4 275	2 963	2 827	3 173	1 336	1 462
Construction	89 208	109 238	110 128	119 706	136 328	139 958	158 366	146 602	134 486	149 893	116 283	142 618
Manufacturing	719 489	613 203	757 217	631 026	782 543	1 236 178	904 856	744 473	565 535	670 620	583 274	610 215
Food	79 762	91 643	93 292	87 309	90 972	98 013	98 251	87 353	82 114	76 926	62 852	62 141
Beverage and tobacco products	6 762	5 995	6 421	7 229	5 955	6 242	6 564	6 775	6 594	4 714	4 404	4 679
Textile mills	31 004	18 001	32 403	33 744	33 064	57 009	43 511	37 734	19 669	22 213	19 070	19 527
Textile product mills	6 229	7 827	8 264	6 977	8 542	10 233	16 234	11 611	11 101	9 801	6 044	6 681
Apparel	67 511	61 019	65 714	47 715	40 474	50 423	41 320	29 887	24 729	21 889	14 170	11 508
Leather and allied products	9 939	11 507	12 343	8 492	8 204	7 867	3 903	5 170	4 733	4 960	2 757	3 077
Wood products	22 132	32 024	28 639	22 964	42 774	37 390	42 177	34 820	26 220	32 590	34 728	41 604
Paper	15 180	10 272	13 789	9 191	14 592	25 345	17 165	14 031	6 686	8 430	7 468	6 439
Printing and related support activities	10 763	8 002	8 624	8 981	9 030	13 799	15 019	9 976	10 534	8 005	6 131	7 414
Petroleum and coal products	3 253	3 713	2 500	2 761	3 609	2 518	3 611	2 292	2 343	2 262	2 874	2 333
Chemicals	9 015	6 557	8 980	9 338	8 960	15 659	11 161	10 811	8 707	7 713	6 164	6 665
Plastics and rubber products	30 792	25 645	27 693	26 551	35 828	59 024	38 596	35 054	28 409	30 714	26 098	24 611
Nonmetallic mineral products	17 514	16 103	16 125	16 035	19 272	25 246	21 712	22 031	15 389	18 956	15 980	19 204
Primary metals	26 620	19 810	29 975	26 928	38 835	81 601	48 671	40 641	23 193	27 469	21 866	27 016
Fabricated metal products	24 812	21 956	27 657	28 437	34 543	66 862	49 228	35 884	30 672	28 137	26 090	26 674
Machinery	41 002	38 032	43 662	72 480	57 793	121 724	87 710	60 370	28 407	33 713	40 069	45 831
Computer and electronic products	35 079	23 102	51 875	33 422	24 638	133 552	85 958	46 888	21 230	20 249	15 326	16 439
Electrical equipment and appliance manufacturing	30 460	30 270	30 547	31 223	39 205	60 387	48 413	36 496	24 443	30 804	24 503	23 274
Transportation equipment	215 740	151 398	214 826	123 741	228 380	303 139	176 505	178 282	163 026	253 681	221 257	228 213
Furniture and related products	20 122	17 393	15 887	14 799	23 821	40 267	34 743	25 225	16 379	18 168	17 499	19 510
Miscellaneous manufacturing	15 798	12 934	18 001	12 709	14 052	19 878	14 404	13 142	10 957	9 226	7 924	7 375
Wholesale trade	19 849	20 105	22 232	19 091	20 576	27 973	31 224	25 422	19 861	20 780	13 856	17 922
Retail trade	90 290	98 984	98 261	83 419	95 451	131 316	149 363	138 457	114 588	113 748	96 999	96 787
Transportation and warehousing	57 323	92 783	97 816	70 147	79 430	106 358	124 699	103 499	94 588	113 279	106 708	109 104
Information	33 766	91 162	99 124	55 890	80 618	103 122	100 982	80 715	72 820	72 100	64 365	64 404
Finance and insurance	15 514	15 787	14 619	17 804	17 532	27 881	36 099	27 870	24 954	20 884	22 213	40 917
Real estate and rental and leasing	2 675	3 710	2 816	2 991	4 564	7 611	7 324	6 412	6 329	7 615	4 082	5 139
Professional and technical services	21 803	29 105	33 922	47 941	57 135	77 862	82 223	52 700	49 547	49 719	40 739	49 223
Management of companies and enterprises	3 176	2 765	2 653	3 845	4 601	5 540	5 668	3 777	4 729	2 864	2 310	3 258
Administrative and waste services	99 598	142 440	175 144	154 902	191 073	258 542	257 530	206 765	184 369	187 156	153 655	168 460
Educational services	17 183	1 847	2 251	2 611	2 486	3 571	4 855	5 862	4 315	5 641	5 081	5 667
Health care and social assistance	33 842	33 920	36 658	36 229	36 759	32 255	40 364	38 108	40 118	51 371	33 972	38 848
Arts, entertainment, and recreation	12 419	16 501	17 040	16 629	14 399	20 542	23 517	21 387	21 191	27 564	16 531	16 874
Accommodation and food services	55 489	76 876	76 129	68 550	71 713	110 234	92 575	83 856	96 509	117 107	89 947	94 928
Other services, except public administration	9 420	12 093	11 802	12 806	13 287	15 742	20 049	18 617	18 226	18 753	13 478	13 936
Unclassified	29 397	12 259	10 542	17 011	24 405	23 114	9 072	4 648	3 187	2 128	1 584	884
Government	44 080	71 931	75 906	62 896	66 849	67 708	86 638	98 213	87 001	104 124	65 939	64 955
Local	15 763	37 458	38 545	30 264	32 271	35 003	53 323	66 279	57 331	69 351	41 689	40 690

Table 7-3. Industry Distribution: Mass Layoff Events and Initial Claimants for Unemployment Insurance, 1996–October 2009—*Continued*

(Number, not seasonally adjusted.)

Industry	2008	January 2009	February 2009	March 2009	April 2009	May 2009	June 2009	July 2009	August 2009	September 2009	October 2009
						Initial claimants					
ALL INDUSTRIES	2 130 220	388 813	218 438	228 387	256 930	289 628	256 357	336 654	125 024	123 177	193 904
Total, Private	2 046 011	380 158	213 548	223 981	250 548	276 113	219 548	304 108	118 920	116 813	181 476
Agriculture, forestry, fishing and hunting	50 984	4 865	2 793	2 584	7 227	2 066	3 485	7 519	1 727	1 672	8 593
Total, private nonfarm	1 995 027	375 293	210 755	221 397	243 321	274 047	216 063	296 589	117 193	115 141	172 883
Mining, quarrying, and oil and gas extraction	9 273	4 538	3 379	3 751	3 267	3 057	1 147	1 816	603	918	1 038
Utilities	2 299	(¹)	(¹)	234	(¹)	466	246	446	(¹)	448	550
Construction	173 627	27 762	14 040	11 612	13 490	19 684	9 343	12 415	11 904	10 637	15 258
Manufacturing	870 310	172 757	103 588	114 747	100 872	123 683	85 726	154 208	41 151	51 126	69 655
Food	72 081	8 083	5 379	6 077	8 371	7 211	4 395	8 076	3 632	5 044	8 999
Beverage and tobacco products	6 466	511	606	1 305	(¹)	607	(¹)	624	937	306	1 001
Textile mills	21 620	4 322	1 833	3 108	2 409	1 059	1 563	2 424	538	1 197	1 407
Textile product mills	6 810	2 811	769	554	765	775	214	875	557	267	419
Apparel	13 970	3 189	1 545	883	1 610	1 360	1 683	2 926	1 317	572	438
Leather and allied products	2 862	504	234	(¹)	(¹)	(¹)	(¹)	(¹)	(¹)	(¹)	...
Wood products	56 278	9 870	5 348	5 799	3 437	4 219	2 435	3 453	1 423	2 653	4 326
Paper	14 707	3 977	3 129	2 749	2 584	3 854	968	1 439	576	1 287	1 216
Printing and related support activities	12 000	4 187	1 758	2 124	2 275	3 521	1 552	1 950	714	828	1 337
Petroleum and coal products	3 114	515	(¹)	(¹)	(¹)	415	(¹)	373	...	...	312
Chemicals	10 227	1 883	1 806	1 746	1 453	2 146	1 013	1 722	843	540	533
Plastics and rubber products	49 196	11 156	4 878	6 151	6 393	5 187	3 697	9 776	1 532	1 195	2 672
Nonmetallic mineral products	27 834	4 441	2 788	4 095	3 192	2 388	1 645	3 044	1 147	763	1 172
Primary metals	37 765	9 660	6 523	8 681	8 636	8 785	6 496	9 850	2 742	3 330	4 703
Fabricated metal products	49 757	13 746	8 735	8 186	7 698	9 483	6 846	10 798	3 501	3 856	4 702
Machinery	53 673	14 120	14 921	18 081	18 614	12 472	14 644	29 528	6 608	12 389	10 892
Computer and electronic products	26 270	6 747	7 439	8 130	5 770	5 732	6 145	7 823	2 535	1 986	2 169
Electrical equipment and appliance manufacturing	37 732	5 807	5 399	6 476	5 169	3 506	4 344	5 992	1 853	2 740	3 394
Transportation equipment	323 622	57 173	22 440	26 012	19 246	46 816	24 865	47 322	9 076	7 331	17 069
Furniture and related products	33 617	6 928	6 333	3 020	1 783	2 568	2 337	3 311	941	3 481	1 865
Miscellaneous manufacturing	10 709	3 127	1 607	1 354	1 118	1 402	644	2 596	577	1 117	1 029
Wholesale trade	28 849	7 612	4 243	4 696	4 343	6 022	4 858	6 201	2 714	2 422	4 645
Retail trade	136 209	33 622	17 538	19 491	16 211	18 360	15 318	17 388	10 173	13 094	12 914
Transportation and warehousing	136 178	25 081	7 864	8 809	28 962	7 835	23 792	11 279	9 131	4 807	5 541
Information	70 066	9 405	8 476	8 559	7 934	9 132	6 018	13 941	6 067	4 572	9 567
Finance and insurance	42 152	7 683	5 685	4 469	6 220	6 374	2 239	6 700	4 434	3 308	3 716
Real estate and rental and leasing	8 754	1 870	1 083	980	1 078	985	1 590	819	404	-2	870
Professional and technical services	57 144	7 032	7 895	7 191	10 085	7 030	4 503	10 555	2 302	1 998	5 974
Management of companies and enterprises	5 818	972	990	923	854	1 329	1 164	2 289	401	495	812
Administrative and waste services	246 670	46 646	23 566	18 762	25 498	32 973	19 150	35 419	15 604	11 525	25 694
Educational services	9 025	1 952	489	467	1 568	758	2 295	2 540	1 796	371	226
Health care and social assistance	44 139	4 279	2 032	1 820	3 343	8 402	13 948	7 010	1 947	1 573	2 165
Arts, entertainment, and recreation	21 550	4 421	655	1 259	4 074	2 676	2 671	2 611	1 403	2 209	2 435
Accommodation and food services	118 247	17 360	8 080	13 090	13 168	21 484	18 499	9 651	6 034	4 981	11 346
Other services, except public administration	14 310	2 155	1 083	537	2 168	3 797	3 424	1 212	1 076	409	477
Unclassified	407	49	...	...	86	...	132	89	...	86	...
Government	84 209	8 655	4 890	4 406	6 382	13 515	36 809	32 546	6 104	6 364	12 428
Local	58 272	5 198	2 553	2 870	4 290	6 745	32 864	28 404	3 006	3 679	6 445

¹Data do not meet BLS or state agency disclosure standards.
. . . = Not available.

Table 7-4. Mass Layoff Events and Initial Claimants for Unemployment Insurance, by Region and State, 1996–October 2009

(Number.)

Region and state	1996	1997	1998	1999	2000	2001	2002	2003	2004	2005	2006	2007
						Mass layoff events						
UNITED STATES[1]	14 111	14 960	15 904	14 909	15 738	21 467	20 277	18 963	15 980	16 466	13 998	15 493
Northeast	2 877	2 719	2 550	2 058	2 226	3 157	3 073	3 139	2 630	2 806	2 514	2 775
New England	413	376	395	383	427	691	615	493	359	426	352	358
Middle Atlantic	2 464	2 343	2 155	1 675	1 799	2 466	2 458	2 646	2 271	2 380	2 162	2 417
South	2 908	2 811	3 107	2 930	3 166	4 601	4 829	4 198	3 587	4 035	2 789	3 260
South Atlantic	1 603	1 536	1 608	1 423	1 538	2 249	2 275	2 068	1 802	1 585	1 475	1 727
East South Central	332	299	436	413	626	902	1 060	858	798	893	699	857
West South Central	973	976	1 063	1 094	1 002	1 450	1 494	1 272	987	1 557	615	676
Midwest	3 560	3 425	3 336	3 520	4 223	5 945	4 828	4 644	4 135	4 512	4 026	4 258
East North Central	2 825	2 594	2 591	2 710	3 309	4 682	3 679	3 622	3 292	3 585	3 183	3 381
West North Central	735	831	745	810	914	1 263	1 149	1 022	843	927	843	877
West	4 766	6 005	6 911	6 401	6 123	7 764	7 547	6 982	5 628	5 113	4 669	5 200
Mountain	454	478	481	508	596	836	726	638	512	537	443	558
Pacific	4 312	5 527	6 430	5 893	5 527	6 928	6 821	6 344	5 116	4 576	4 226	4 642
Alabama	67	45	90	105	119	169	428	332	274	244	138	276
Alaska	33	35	41	37	30	31	36	36	35	24	30	19
Arizona	139	120	105	103	107	161	170	146	110	109	72	99
Arkansas	127	115	105	103	85	95	76	60	54	52	40	69
California	3 841	5 049	5 881	5 342	5 008	6 145	6 045	5 651	4 547	4 104	3 702	4 130
Colorado	76	78	72	69	62	143	126	104	74	72	65	80
Connecticut	56	51	35	41	45	73	73	80	49	55	60	51
Delaware	20	17	13	13	13	33	19	23	13	9	9	17
District of Columbia	15	12	16	20	14	24	14	14	8	7	5	6
Florida	464	580	579	503	525	870	936	866	876	700	593	795
Georgia	141	143	155	165	164	215	310	403	323	323	317	350
Hawaii	50	57	53	62	38	77	74	55	37	33	48	46
Idaho	99	86	106	101	117	144	126	122	90	82	65	92
Illinois	649	571	532	549	647	870	824	775	663	647	600	641
Indiana	280	280	235	236	333	497	460	506	434	443	403	375
Iowa	105	142	153	196	230	319	251	249	169	212	188	192
Kansas	101	74	56	71	92	110	129	119	102	103	88	92
Kentucky	62	77	130	124	261	409	363	277	289	328	330	346
Louisiana	167	145	155	129	185	225	241	204	206	956	134	107
Maine	61	63	91	58	48	50	45	44	48	43	33	40
Maryland	151	162	67	57	68	73	85	94	80	55	120	128
Massachusetts	172	171	186	188	188	356	325	262	152	178	123	128
Michigan	593	467	489	791	969	1 359	612	604	866	1 032	922	949
Minnesota	196	194	172	162	198	304	279	260	213	237	205	199
Mississippi	66	42	95	53	102	121	82	81	61	155	71	80
Missouri	315	392	336	344	352	432	374	292	256	276	289	329
Montana	29	31	30	16	25	35	32	46	36	48	40	49
Nebraska	8	8	15	14	24	50	80	65	71	72	48	32
Nevada	75	97	92	148	214	246	178	148	121	138	117	135
New Hampshire	26	29	32	27	37	79	61	31	29	40	29	31
New Jersey	398	414	402	317	405	427	509	481	449	485	452	503
New Mexico	11	39	47	39	31	37	40	44	42	44	49	55
New York	560	621	446	311	244	441	765	932	836	806	717	733
North Carolina	146	114	124	123	172	288	245	246	167	166	129	93
North Dakota	7	16	6	12	10	30	24	22	22	14	18	22
Ohio	573	583	635	527	653	963	901	913	699	761	608	716
Oklahoma	26	61	74	74	61	122	122	121	86	58	55	69
Oregon	158	224	255	244	277	410	368	342	282	202	246	258
Pennsylvania	1 506	1 308	1 307	1 047	1 150	1 598	1 184	1 233	986	1 089	993	1 181
Rhode Island	69	59	47	58	71	82	72	41	51	65	52	54
South Carolina	349	225	369	334	288	452	364	170	159	142	140	177
South Dakota	3	5	7	11	8	18	12	15	10	13	7	11
Tennessee	137	135	121	131	144	203	187	168	174	166	160	155
Texas	653	655	729	788	671	1 008	1 055	887	641	491	386	431
Utah	24	26	29	30	39	66	50	24	33	37	30	43
Vermont	29	3	4	11	38	51	39	35	30	45	55	54
Virginia	279	266	258	200	271	275	263	229	156	170	143	142
Washington	230	162	200	208	174	265	298	260	215	213	200	189
West Virginia	38	17	27	8	23	19	39	23	20	13	19	19
Wisconsin	730	693	700	607	707	993	882	824	630	702	650	700
Wyoming	(²)	(²)	. . .	(²)	(²)	4	4	4	6	7	5	5

[1]Data for all states and the District of Columbia.
[2]Data do not meet BLS or state agency disclosure standards.
. . . = Not available.

Table 7-4. Mass Layoff Events and Initial Claimants for Unemployment Insurance, by Region and State, 1996–October 2009—*Continued*

(Number.)

Region and state	2008	January 2009	February 2009	March 2009	April 2009	May 2009	June 2009	July 2009	August 2009	September 2009	October 2009
						Mass layoff events					
UNITED STATES[1]	21 137	3 806	2 262	2 191	2 547	2 738	2 519	3 054	1 428	1 371	1 934
Northeast	3 257	787	348	317	504	451	428	511	279	233	260
New England	427	97	78	68	88	67	63	82	32	29	30
Middle Atlantic	2 830	690	270	249	416	384	365	429	247	204	230
South	5 153	1 052	624	589	655	742	620	725	342	334	499
South Atlantic	2 561	574	295	276	368	370	354	389	204	182	279
East South Central	1 392	279	172	158	160	171	128	213	57	71	87
West South Central	1 200	199	157	155	127	201	138	123	81	81	133
Midwest	5 751	1 024	561	607	608	826	592	805	350	309	483
East North Central	4 551	821	434	466	482	649	469	635	273	240	375
West North Central	1 200	203	127	141	126	177	123	170	77	69	108
West	6 976	943	729	678	780	719	879	1 013	457	495	692
Mountain	831	149	128	109	125	135	90	112	63	53	103
Pacific	6 145	794	601	569	655	584	789	901	394	442	589
Alabama	444	100	33	45	27	40	49	75	23	22	27
Alaska	27	10	7	([2])	5	12	6	([2])	4	7	8
Arizona	146	24	23	22	41	28	27	35	10	7	20
Arkansas	116	13	6	10	12	18	8	11	4	([2])	17
California	5 403	651	515	498	567	487	714	812	340	395	514
Colorado	93	24	15	13	19	15	11	15	5	14	19
Connecticut	65	14	12	11	11	17	15	15	4	4	9
Delaware	38	5	4	4	11	3	8	5	([2])	([2])	3
District of Columbia	11	([2])	([2])	([2])	([2])	([2])	3	...	([2])	...	([2])
Florida	1 333	235	155	107	152	181	182	192	104	91	167
Georgia	476	137	45	46	50	56	43	62	23	35	39
Hawaii	88	14	15	5	10	8	10	9	8	6	7
Idaho	145	21	10	16	10	9	5	8	9	4	10
Illinois	871	130	115	109	105	135	116	110	82	71	93
Indiana	680	117	59	68	80	86	45	87	30	21	37
Iowa	303	64	33	38	30	31	33	48	17	18	35
Kansas	136	21	18	19	7	31	15	22	14	15	13
Kentucky	540	80	78	72	83	85	49	97	22	32	36
Louisiana	311	29	19	16	27	35	26	21	18	10	24
Maine	33	18	4	9	6	7	3	4	([2])	3	3
Maryland	85	31	11	8	12	10	13	11	10	7	6
Massachusetts	162	33	32	25	38	23	20	31	13	12	9
Michigan	1 156	229	79	87	74	180	121	185	43	40	70
Minnesota	245	41	24	30	35	38	26	31	13	15	24
Mississippi	167	25	8	12	15	9	11	14	5	5	10
Missouri	433	62	38	42	46	54	39	61	28	16	31
Montana	54	14	11	7	4	7	6	5	3	3	11
Nebraska	47	5	7	3	4	13	3	4	([2])	3	4
Nevada	251	33	43	27	26	52	18	37	30	15	19
New Hampshire	42	7	9	9	10	7	5	17	6	([2])	3
New Jersey	518	90	47	39	66	45	88	101	27	31	37
New Mexico	73	13	13	9	14	13	15	5	4	7	11
New York	897	279	82	70	182	112	83	126	106	58	68
North Carolina	196	41	34	44	28	33	28	23	19	8	19
North Dakota	26	4	3	4	([2])	8	6	4	([2])	([2])	([2])
Ohio	1 027	199	91	93	115	145	94	138	58	47	75
Oklahoma	79	21	19	17	14	13	11	16	8	4	7
Oregon	367	76	43	42	43	41	43	49	21	15	35
Pennsylvania	1 415	321	141	140	168	227	194	202	114	115	125
Rhode Island	64	17	9	9	8	7	10	10	5	3	3
South Carolina	284	102	33	48	60	31	38	59	20	18	19
South Dakota	10	6	4	5	([2])	([2])	([2])	...	([2])	...	...
Tennessee	241	74	53	29	35	37	19	27	7	12	14
Texas	694	136	113	112	74	135	93	75	51	65	85
Utah	61	19	11	14	10	10	8	7	([2])	3	9
Vermont	61	8	([2])	5	15	6	([2])	5	([2])	([2])	3
Virginia	116	15	8	14	42	49	31	35	21	22	22
Washington	260	43	21	23	30	36	16	29	21	19	25
West Virginia	22	7	3	4	12	5	8	([2])	4	...	3
Wisconsin	817	146	90	109	108	103	93	115	60	61	100
Wyoming	8	([2])	([2])	([2])	([2])	([2])	...	...	...	...	4

[1]Data for all states and the District of Columbia.
[2]Data do not meet BLS or state agency disclosure standards.
. . . = Not available.

Table 7-4. Mass Layoff Events and Initial Claimants for Unemployment Insurance, by Region and State, 1996–October 2009—*Continued*

(Number.)

Region and state	1996	1997	1998	1999	2000	2001	2002	2003	2004	2005	2006	2007
	Initial claimants											
UNITED STATES[1]	1437628	1542543	1771069	1572399	1835592	2514862	2245051	1888926	1607158	1795341	1484391	1598875
Northeast	276 781	268 831	264 063	207 057	235 083	340 246	338 965	306 462	270 788	280 628	254 684	273 079
New England	42 426	36 796	40 074	40 473	56 909	75 283	67 846	50 708	35 020	45 064	37 359	34 860
Middle Atlantic	234 355	232 035	223 989	166 584	178 174	264 963	271 119	255 754	235 768	235 564	217 325	238 219
South	314 049	296 850	347 332	314 556	360 330	546 222	545 907	435 387	355 561	485 505	312 892	356 812
South Atlantic	181 035	154 809	173 436	155 192	185 615	257 113	247 353	206 290	165 280	159 131	152 443	163 761
East South Central	33 443	29 120	48 496	41 403	69 619	107 661	127 477	98 450	91 565	131 138	95 861	115 114
West South Central	99 571	112 921	125 400	117 961	105 096	181 448	171 077	130 647	98 716	195 236	64 588	77 937
Midwest	466 075	425 657	504 413	474 132	583 290	841 597	614 121	552 140	485 255	571 950	508 798	509 431
East North Central	381 479	326 665	390 667	359 364	465 917	663 997	457 002	414 489	387 065	457 592	406 432	414 919
West North Central	84 596	98 992	113 746	114 768	117 373	177 600	157 119	137 651	98 190	114 358	102 366	94 512
West	380 723	551 205	655 261	576 654	656 889	786 797	746 058	594 937	495 554	457 258	408 017	459 553
Mountain	43 676	47 055	45 541	51 863	61 090	94 490	76 484	58 247	47 929	50 830	41 696	49 308
Pacific	337 047	504 150	609 720	524 791	595 799	692 307	669 574	536 690	447 625	406 428	366 321	410 245
Alabama	7 576	4 480	10 721	10 175	13 491	18 228	59 821	44 523	34 012	29 603	14 530	30 543
Alaska	2 543	2 961	3 246	3 565	2 706	2 814	2 846	2 973	2 930	2 326	2 770	1 798
Arizona	12 621	11 915	11 350	11 710	10 782	16 148	17 775	12 566	11 020	11 831	7 950	10 839
Arkansas	13 755	13 557	11 819	13 896	9 050	11 328	6 868	6 131	5 926	7 611	5 056	8 647
California	290 546	460 613	556 078	469 814	536 673	600 501	576 110	467 573	394 114	360 138	317 907	357 994
Colorado	10 037	7 136	7 181	7 024	5 967	14 127	12 601	9 422	6 856	6 759	5 905	6 567
Connecticut	6 493	4 098	3 084	3 847	4 393	6 122	7 360	7 054	4 203	4 972	6 595	4 975
Delaware	4 600	1 307	5 764	3 477	8 271	8 200	4 927	8 084	3 764	5 034	4 185	4 522
District of Columbia	1 986	1 279	1 514	2 052	1 572	2 301	1 688	1 160	807	565	346	418
Florida	30 584	38 237	43 184	36 724	39 407	70 889	71 635	61 863	63 087	51 535	42 593	55 696
Georgia	12 934	13 319	16 992	15 903	16 967	22 141	41 888	49 009	33 406	40 854	35 947	39 624
Hawaii	4 056	4 714	5 148	5 107	3 042	7 803	7 467	5 151	2 938	2 692	3 706	3 988
Idaho	9 282	9 959	9 845	11 264	13 121	17 144	15 579	13 690	8 148	7 233	5 665	8 245
Illinois	80 557	72 749	74 206	86 768	108 726	135 126	116 592	90 181	75 763	71 399	75 118	80 477
Indiana	42 401	35 260	35 329	38 252	50 892	71 521	67 134	70 393	58 853	62 574	56 395	47 923
Iowa	10 341	16 912	19 467	30 779	32 479	44 997	35 460	32 744	18 126	30 291	27 804	23 637
Kansas	12 691	6 834	8 198	8 189	13 145	21 657	18 186	16 102	10 782	9 740	9 785	10 654
Kentucky	8 504	9 615	14 988	14 485	33 975	60 327	42 094	34 709	37 809	55 078	61 246	59 399
Louisiana	14 207	13 803	15 544	9 869	14 799	28 373	22 113	17 329	16 519	120 600	12 915	13 042
Maine	5 888	4 738	7 471	5 875	7 407	4 713	4 377	3 828	4 293	3 445	2 622	3 035
Maryland	18 588	24 521	10 295	4 527	5 868	6 259	9 386	7 911	7 951	4 998	11 771	12 172
Massachusetts	17 503	18 942	20 599	19 879	27 907	36 693	33 705	25 352	13 960	18 114	11 188	10 785
Michigan	89 651	60 558	101 297	99 284	129 640	196 459	63 350	66 866	99 124	131 411	127 964	125 942
Minnesota	20 145	21 462	29 806	19 936	24 169	38 739	33 348	27 725	24 607	26 689	25 729	19 231
Mississippi	5 683	3 541	9 651	4 576	8 684	10 501	7 162	5 239	4 384	29 971	5 242	9 647
Missouri	40 041	50 781	52 631	51 518	43 765	60 026	57 373	50 379	35 034	37 005	29 324	33 557
Montana	2 102	2 782	2 744	1 501	3 489	4 048	3 570	4 379	3 600	4 567	3 726	3 873
Nebraska	614	522	2 045	1 325	2 102	6 363	8 371	6 761	6 764	8 332	5 907	3 440
Nevada	7 059	9 121	7 652	14 611	21 976	32 414	19 115	12 897	11 795	13 224	11 130	11 344
New Hampshire	3 447	2 344	2 790	3 279	4 615	10 903	8 080	3 030	2 726	4 666	2 996	3 053
New Jersey	45 270	48 294	48 119	34 439	45 173	52 530	63 369	49 815	51 252	48 732	51 128	52 738
New Mexico	645	3 364	3 536	3 036	2 243	3 045	2 894	3 129	3 071	3 469	4 226	4 619
New York	62 325	63 296	50 700	70 925	22 318	46 404	85 578	93 583	95 228	87 649	76 638	77 353
North Carolina	16 701	11 947	11 723	18 592	23 902	33 021	27 324	28 977	14 435	16 670	13 316	10 694
North Dakota	531	1 684	961	2 022	912	4 303	3 140	2 577	1 980	1 184	3 065	2 992
Ohio	86 321	86 040	92 045	65 449	94 419	139 218	103 577	102 864	86 850	113 165	80 291	83 429
Oklahoma	2 867	7 287	9 646	9 889	7 531	21 086	16 203	17 502	14 124	10 090	7 234	9 627
Oregon	13 642	21 410	25 005	24 260	32 159	55 449	44 944	35 508	28 401	22 231	24 386	29 391
Pennsylvania	126 760	120 445	125 170	101 392	110 683	166 029	122 172	112 356	89 288	99 183	89 559	108 128
Rhode Island	6 870	6 341	5 675	6 788	8 441	10 851	9 567	5 251	6 907	9 151	8 211	7 362
South Carolina	50 285	26 108	49 051	46 724	45 084	74 891	51 006	21 001	22 241	17 450	16 909	21 787
South Dakota	233	797	638	999	801	1 515	1 241	1 363	897	1 117	752	1 001
Tennessee	11 680	11 484	13 136	12 167	13 469	18 605	18 400	13 979	15 360	16 486	14 561	15 525
Texas	68 742	78 274	88 391	84 307	73 716	120 661	125 893	89 685	62 147	56 935	39 383	46 621
Utah	1 867	2 703	3 233	2 590	3 457	7 260	4 642	1 892	2 959	3 266	2 765	3 464
Vermont	2 225	333	455	805	4 146	6 001	4 757	6 193	2 931	4 716	5 747	5 650
Virginia	42 169	36 645	32 636	26 515	42 651	37 911	36 059	26 377	17 802	20 927	25 642	17 496
Washington	26 260	14 452	20 243	22 045	21 219	25 740	38 207	25 485	19 242	19 041	17 552	17 074
West Virginia	3 188	1 446	2 277	678	1 893	1 500	3 440	1 908	1 787	1 098	1 734	1 352
Wisconsin	82 549	72 058	87 790	69 611	82 240	121 673	106 349	84 185	66 475	79 043	66 664	77 148
Wyoming	(²)	(²)	. . .	(²)	(²)	304	308	272	480	481	329	357

[1]Data for all states and the District of Columbia.
[2]Data do not meet BLS or state agency disclosure standards.
. . . = Not available.

Table 7-4. Mass Layoff Events and Initial Claimants for Unemployment Insurance, by Region and State, 1996–October 2009—*Continued*

(Number.)

Region and state	2008	January 2009	February 2009	March 2009	April 2009	May 2009	June 2009	July 2009	August 2009	September 2009	October 2009
						Initial claimants					
UNITED STATES[1]	2130220	388 813	218 438	228 387	256 930	289 628	256 357	336 654	125 024	123 177	193 904
Northeast	316 191	77 142	32 131	29 493	56 253	41 413	46 593	45 526	26 444	18 617	22 709
New England	40 915	8 414	7 744	7 021	9 192	5 865	6 516	7 194	2 953	2 762	2 134
Middle Atlantic	275 276	68 728	24 387	22 472	47 061	35 548	40 077	38 332	23 491	15 855	20 575
South	533 687	115 630	55 542	61 432	62 714	72 375	61 962	71 648	29 486	28 943	45 772
South Atlantic	225 596	58 892	23 842	27 819	33 338	34 117	31 988	34 220	17 732	14 927	23 144
East South Central	180 702	32 215	17 840	15 629	16 166	18 081	16 589	25 153	4 820	6 844	9 545
West South Central	127 389	24 523	13 860	17 984	13 210	20 177	13 385	12 275	6 934	7 172	13 083
Midwest	676 591	114 195	64 973	81 957	72 383	105 264	76 301	117 188	32 197	38 137	60 792
East North Central	538 429	93 852	52 690	64 595	60 241	84 281	59 347	94 516	25 962	30 304	49 277
West North Central	138 162	20 343	12 283	17 362	12 142	20 983	16 954	22 672	6 235	7 833	11 515
West	603 751	81 846	65 792	55 505	65 580	70 576	71 501	102 292	36 897	37 480	64 631
Mountain	75 567	12 657	11 381	10 991	11 993	13 290	7 184	11 241	6 116	3 924	9 020
Pacific	528 184	69 189	54 411	44 514	53 587	57 286	64 317	91 051	30 781	33 556	55 611
Alabama	57 324	10 588	4 690	4 985	2 745	4 037	7 837	8 324	1 997	2 044	3 179
Alaska	2 888	788	557	(2)	828	1 230	431	(2)	295	849	755
Arizona	14 274	1 941	2 185	2 483	4 985	2 484	2 137	3 469	977	463	1 666
Arkansas	11 914	1 462	1 156	806	1 057	2 319	583	1 033	260	(2)	1 954
California	446 480	54 153	45 557	38 130	43 675	47 091	56 138	82 085	26 082	28 797	48 169
Colorado	8 200	1 814	1 237	1 578	1 696	1 762	832	1 536	374	1 036	1 554
Connecticut	5 505	1 349	824	928	884	1 389	1 487	1 056	334	323	671
Delaware	6 335	1 052	484	509	988	172	882	347	(2)	(2)	251
District of Columbia	1 195	(2)	(2)	(2)	(2)	(2)	195	...	(2)	...	(2)
Florida	94 656	19 301	9 779	8 594	11 010	12 446	15 785	14 929	7 795	5 975	11 851
Georgia	48 603	16 654	3 830	4 152	6 006	5 187	3 809	7 636	2 202	2 817	3 880
Hawaii	9 590	998	1 211	376	934	900	992	670	872	465	630
Idaho	13 591	1 746	591	1 664	754	680	342	759	1 305	306	1 088
Illinois	103 685	13 443	19 469	18 096	17 550	19 717	20 576	25 119	7 432	10 743	12 917
Indiana	80 027	10 734	6 776	10 781	9 659	10 416	4 643	10 131	3 182	2 895	4 759
Iowa	43 574	7 353	4 374	6 140	2 636	4 379	3 765	8 730	1 359	2 384	4 732
Kansas	17 243	2 447	1 582	2 259	737	3 551	4 071	2 088	945	2 880	1 562
Kentucky	89 953	12 492	8 794	7 861	9 194	9 894	6 240	14 128	2 006	3 394	4 656
Louisiana	31 664	3 396	1 498	1 411	2 670	3 160	3 005	1 768	1 698	887	2 169
Maine	2 536	1 618	348	835	493	644	280	256	(2)	268	177
Maryland	7 116	2 535	800	531	1 115	1 201	1 325	987	759	463	479
Massachusetts	14 911	2 782	2 873	2 422	3 770	2 281	1 777	2 972	1 357	985	596
Michigan	132 468	26 453	7 392	11 121	7 139	26 344	12 218	23 929	3 593	6 167	9 543
Minnesota	23 370	3 289	1 777	3 665	3 103	4 224	2 318	3 229	948	1 122	1 985
Mississippi	13 818	2 353	458	745	1 350	726	895	803	349	323	602
Missouri	43 451	5 239	3 538	3 430	4 719	6 336	5 446	7 647	2 549	1 018	2 556
Montana	4 731	1 491	753	667	335	856	476	481	258	227	1 062
Nebraska	5 204	1 070	500	286	390	1 306	658	418	(2)	210	559
Nevada	22 389	2 805	3 881	2 351	2 123	5 297	1 686	3 212	2 879	1 201	1 361
New Hampshire	3 873	465	1 020	1 213	848	526	630	1 564	454	(2)	263
New Jersey	51 623	7 179	3 777	3 217	7 334	4 394	14 033	8 366	2 162	2 844	2 850
New Mexico	6 253	822	1 868	858	909	1 089	1 013	252	191	487	761
New York	95 612	31 893	8 927	6 974	24 349	10 762	7 681	11 886	11 405	4 424	6 961
North Carolina	21 037	4 149	3 833	6 277	2 582	5 351	2 505	1 950	2 523	918	1 672
North Dakota	4 354	415	207	1 259	(2)	869	640	560	(2)	(2)	(2)
Ohio	131 813	27 971	9 065	13 067	14 791	16 920	10 818	19 704	5 941	4 745	10 569
Oklahoma	10 187	2 772	1 437	1 483	2 464	1 772	1 052	2 013	679	401	582
Oregon	42 780	9 005	5 321	4 118	5 554	4 775	5 525	5 492	1 691	1 402	3 936
Pennsylvania	128 041	29 656	11 683	12 281	15 378	20 392	18 363	18 080	9 924	8 587	10 764
Rhode Island	7 040	1 526	1 291	889	1 649	563	(2)	965	(2)	260	173
South Carolina	32 063	10 703	3 471	6 157	6 482	3 021	4 087	5 359	2 133	2 831	2 692
South Dakota	966	530	305	323	(2)	(2)	(2)	...	(2)	...	...
Tennessee	19 607	6 782	3 898	2 038	2 877	3 424	1 617	1 898	468	1 083	1 108
Texas	73 624	16 893	9 769	14 284	7 019	12 926	8 745	7 461	4 297	5 715	8 378
Utah	5 604	1 978	753	1 313	1 055	1 020	698	1 532	(2)	204	1 058
Vermont	7 050	674	1 388	734	1 548	462	965	381	(2)	507	254
Virginia	12 738	3 313	786	1 229	4 052	6 168	2 817	2 873	1 652	1 868	1 955
Washington	26 446	4 245	1 765	1 833	2 596	3 290	1 231	2 549	1 841	2 043	2 121
West Virginia	1 853	1 127	681	301	1 028	429	583	(2)	272	...	250
Wisconsin	90 436	15 251	9 988	11 530	11 102	10 884	11 092	15 633	5 814	5 754	11 489
Wyoming	525	(2)	(2)	(2)	(2)	(2)	...	...	...	...	470

[1] Data for all states and the District of Columbia.
[2] Data do not meet BLS or state agency disclosure standards.
. . . = Not available.

Table 7-5. Extended Mass Layoff Events and Separations, Selected Measures, 2004–2009

(Number.)

| Year and quarter | Layoff events | | | | | |
| | Total, private nonfarm | Total, excluding seasonal and vacation events[1] | Total, movement of work[2] | Movement of work actions | | |
				Total	With separations reported	With separations unknown
2004						
Quarter 1	1 339	980	113	127	117	10
Quarter 2	1 358	787	86	112	82	30
Quarter 3	886	695	84	103	88	15
Quarter 4	1 427	760	83	138	95	43
2005						
Quarter 1	1 142	769	71	90	66	24
Quarter 2	1 203	635	73	98	74	24
Quarter 3	1 136	953	68	83	62	21
Quarter 4	1 400	619	65	92	57	35
2006						
Quarter 1	963	715	53	80	51	29
Quarter 2	1 353	750	72	103	66	37
Quarter 3	929	752	58	72	49	23
Quarter 4	1 640	943	69	94	66	28
2007						
Quarter 1	1 110	849	70	86	61	25
Quarter 2	1 421	772	65	89	66	23
Quarter 3	1 018	800	63	87	60	27
Quarter 4	1 814	1 062	69	90	66	24
2008						
Quarter 1	1 340	1 094	59	76	41	35
Quarter 2	1 756	1 105	71	100	78	22
Quarter 3[3]	1 581	1 365	84	106	78	28
Quarter 4	3 582	2 713	118	161	122	39
2009						
Quarter 1	3 979	3 639	92	124	87	37
Quarter 2[3]	3 396	2 639	117	160	104	56
Quarter 3[4]	1 776	1 518	75	107	72	35

| Year and quarter | Separations | | | | | |
| | Total, private nonfarm | Total, excluding seasonal and vacation events[1] | Total, movement of work[2] | Movement of work actions | | |
				Total	With separations reported	With separations unknown
2004						
Quarter 1	276 503	213 031	19 978	. . .	16 674	. . .
Quarter 2	278 831	151 447	16 240	. . .	11 098	. . .
Quarter 3	164 608	133 322	17 400	. . .	13 999	. . .
Quarter 4	273 967	144 108	19 599	. . .	13 351	. . .
2005						
Quarter 1	186 506	129 261	13 980	. . .	9 422	. . .
Quarter 2	246 099	108 372	12 040	. . .	9 527	. . .
Quarter 3	201 878	164 224	15 578	. . .	8 035	. . .
Quarter 4	250 178	111 818	12 051	. . .	7 210	. . .
2006						
Quarter 1	183 089	141 448	10 519	. . .	7 080	. . .
Quarter 2	295 964	139 737	16 610	. . .	9 674	. . .
Quarter 3	160 254	132 563	12 840	. . .	6 820	. . .
Quarter 4	296 662	167 130	15 782	. . .	10 462	. . .
2007						
Quarter 1	225 600	186 345	11 438	. . .	8 467	. . .
Quarter 2	278 719	123 843	11 352	. . .	7 401	. . .
Quarter 3	160 024	119 663	12 367	. . .	7 159	. . .
Quarter 4	301 592	171 808	11 302	. . .	7 152	. . .
2008						
Quarter 1	230 098	186 991	13 314	. . .	6 180	. . .
Quarter 2	354 713	198 389	12 317	. . .	7 346	. . .
Quarter 3[3]	290 453	246 532	14 943	. . .	9 631	. . .
Quarter 4	641 714	491 941	20 382	. . .	11 919	. . .
2009						
Quarter 1	705 133	648 908	15 501	. . .	9 089	. . .
Quarter 2[3]	650 679	490 658	21 720	. . .	11 533	. . .
Quarter 3[4]	277 924	231 223	12 107	. . .	6 755	. . .

[1]The questions on movement of work were not asked of employers when the reason for layoff was either seasonal work or vacation period.
[2]Movement of work can involve more than one action.
[3]Revised.
[4]Preliminary.
. . . = Not available.

Table 7-6. Movement of Work Actions by Type of Separation Where Number of Separations Is Known by Employers, 2004–2009

(Number.)

Actions[1]

Year and quarter	With separations reported	Location — Out-of-country relocations			Location — Domestic relocations			Unable to assign place of relocation	Company — Within company				Company — Different company			
		Total	Within company	Different company	Total	Within company	Different company		Total	Domestic	Out of country	Unable to assign	Total	Domestic	Out of country	Unable to assign
2004																
Quarter 1	117	34	21	13	80	64	16	3	87	64	21	2	30	16	13	1
Quarter 2	82	19	13	6	59	46	13	4	63	46	13	4	19	13	6	. . .
Quarter 3	88	18	13	5	68	63	5	2	78	63	13	2	10	5	5	. . .
Quarter 4	95	32	29	3	63	55	8	. . .	84	55	29	. . .	11	8	3	. . .
2005																
Quarter 1	66	21	17	4	45	37	8	. . .	54	37	17	. . .	12	8	4	. . .
Quarter 2	74	28	19	9	42	35	7	4	58	35	19	4	16	7	9	. . .
Quarter 3	62	20	15	5	42	32	10	. . .	47	32	15	. . .	15	10	5	. . .
Quarter 4	57	22	17	5	35	28	7	. . .	45	28	17	. . .	12	7	5	. . .
2006																
Quarter 1	51	22	17	5	29	24	5	. . .	41	24	17	. . .	10	5	5	. . .
Quarter 2	66	23	21	2	43	35	8	. . .	56	35	21	. . .	10	8	2	. . .
Quarter 3	49	12	9	3	37	31	6	. . .	40	31	9	. . .	9	6	3	. . .
Quarter 4	66	27	24	3	39	35	4	. . .	59	35	24	. . .	7	4	3	. . .
2007																
Quarter 1	61	14	13	1	46	41	5	1	55	41	13	1	6	5	1	. . .
Quarter 2	66	23	22	1	43	34	9	. . .	56	34	22	. . .	10	9	1	. . .
Quarter 3	60	21	11	10	38	34	4	1	46	34	11	1	14	4	10	. . .
Quarter 4	66	27	26	1	39	38	1	. . .	64	38	26	. . .	2	1	1	. . .
2008																
Quarter 1	41	15	12	3	26	24	2	. . .	36	24	12	. . .	5	2	3	. . .
Quarter 2	78	25	23	2	52	47	5	1	70	47	23	. . .	8	5	2	1
Quarter 3	78	19	17	2	59	50	9	. . .	67	50	17	. . .	11	9	2	. . .
Quarter 4	122	36	31	5	86	79	7	. . .	110	79	31	. . .	12	7	5	. . .
2009																
Quarter 1	87	25	23	2	62	57	5	. . .	80	57	23	. . .	7	5	2	. . .
Quarter 2[2]	104	22	21	1	82	75	7	. . .	96	75	21	. . .	8	7	1	. . .
Quarter 3[3]	72	18	15	3	54	43	11	. . .	58	43	15	. . .	14	11	3	. . .

Separations

Year and quarter	With separations reported	Location — Out-of-country relocations			Location — Domestic relocations			Unable to assign place of relocation	Company — Within company				Company — Different company			
		Total	Within company	Different company	Total	Within company	Different company		Total	Domestic	Out of country	Unable to assign	Total	Domestic	Out of country	Unable to assign
2004																
Quarter 1	16 674	4 906	2 976	1 930	10815	8 671	2 144	953	11 947	8 671	2 976	300	4 727	2 144	1 930	653
Quarter 2	11 098	2 415	1 882	533	8 257	5 982	2 275	426	8 290	5 982	1 882	426	2 808	2 275	533	. . .
Quarter 3	13 999	3 618	3 222	396	9 081	8 831	250	1 300	13 353	8 831	3 222	1 300	646	250	396	. . .
Quarter 4	13 351	5 258	4 825	433	8 093	7 285	808	. . .	12 110	7 285	4 825	. . .	1 241	808	433	. . .
2005																
Quarter 1	9 422	3 811	3 353	458	5 611	4 626	985	. . .	7 979	4 626	3 353	. . .	1 443	985	458	. . .
Quarter 2	9 527	2 815	1 938	877	6 018	5 330	688	694	7 962	5 330	1 938	694	1 565	688	877	. . .
Quarter 3	8 035	2 702	2 137	565	5 333	3 075	2 258	. . .	5 212	3 075	2 137	. . .	2 823	2 258	565	. . .
Quarter 4	7 210	2 702	2 010	692	4 508	4 104	404	. . .	6 114	4 104	2 010	. . .	1 096	404	692	. . .
2006																
Quarter 1	7 080	2 682	2 408	274	4 398	3 873	525	. . .	6 281	3 873	2 408	. . .	799	525	274	. . .
Quarter 2	9 674	3 033	2 912	121	6 641	5 823	818	. . .	8 735	5 823	2 912	. . .	939	818	121	. . .
Quarter 3	6 820	2 071	1 030	1 041	4 749	4 020	729	. . .	5 050	4 020	1 030	. . .	1 770	729	1 041	. . .
Quarter 4	10 462	5 581	5 426	155	4 881	4 494	387	. . .	9 920	4 494	5 426	. . .	542	387	155	. . .
2007																
Quarter 1	8 467	2 135	2 086	49	6 261	5 221	1 040	71	7 378	5 221	2 086	71	1 089	1 040	49	. . .
Quarter 2	7 401	3 537	3 387	150	3 864	3 254	610	. . .	6 641	3 254	3 387	. . .	760	610	150	. . .
Quarter 3	7 159	3 187	1 504	1 683	3 793	3 396	397	179	5 079	3 396	1 504	179	2 080	397	1 683	. . .
Quarter 4	7 152	2 997	2 910	87	4 155	3 975	180	. . .	6 885	3 975	2 910	. . .	267	180	87	. . .
2008																
Quarter 1	6 180	1 901	1 602	299	4 279	3 364	915	. . .	4 966	3 364	1 602	. . .	1 214	915	299	. . .
Quarter 2	7 346	3 159	2 935	224	3 912	3 694	218	275	6 629	3 694	2 935	. . .	717	218	224	275
Quarter 3	9 631	2 312	2 135	177	7 319	6 522	797	. . .	8 657	6 522	2 135	. . .	974	797	177	. . .
Quarter 4	11 919	4 059	3 720	339	7 860	7 363	497	. . .	11 083	7 363	3 720	. . .	836	497	339	. . .
2009																
Quarter 1	9 089	3 967	3 794	173	5 122	4 776	346	. . .	8 570	4 776	3 794	. . .	519	346	173	. . .
Quarter 2[2]	11 533	2 849	2 759	90	8 684	7 461	1 223	. . .	10 220	7 461	2 759	. . .	1 313	1 223	90	. . .
Quarter 3[3]	6 755	1 691	1 471	220	5 064	3 694	1 370	. . .	5 165	3 694	1 471	. . .	1 590	1 370	220	. . .

[1]Only actions for which separations associated with the movement of work were reported are shown.
[2]Revised.
[3]Preliminary.
. . . = Not available.

NOTES AND DEFINITIONS

JOB OPENINGS AND LABOR TURNOVER SURVEY

The data for the Job Openings and Labor Turnover Survey (JOLTS) are collected and compiled monthly from a sample of business establishments by the Bureau of Labor Statistics (BLS). Each month, data are collected in a survey of business establishments for total employment, job openings, hires, quits, layoffs and discharges, and other separations. Data collection methods include computer-assisted telephone interviewing, touchtone data entry, fax, and mail.

Concepts and Definitions

The JOLTS program covers all private nonfarm establishments such as factories, offices, and stores, as well as federal, state, and local government entities in the 50 states and the District of Columbia.

Industry classification is in accordance with the 2007 version of the North American Industry Classification System (NAICS). In order to ensure the highest possible quality of data, state workforce agencies verify with employers and update, if necessary, the industry code, location, and ownership classification of all establishments on a 3-year cycle. Changes in establishment characteristics resulting from the verification process are always introduced into the JOLTS sampling frame with the data reported for the first month of the year.

Employment includes persons on the payroll who worked or received pay for the pay period that includes the 12th day of the reference month. Full-time, part-time, permanent, short-term, seasonal, salaried, and hourly employees are included, as are employees on paid vacations or other paid leave. Proprietors or partners of unincorporated businesses, unpaid family workers, or persons on leave without pay or on strike for the entire pay period, are not counted as employed. Employees of temporary help agencies, employee leasing companies, outside contractors, and consultants are counted by their employer of record, not by the establishment where they are working.

Job openings information is submitted by establishments for the last business day of the reference month. A job opening requires that: 1) a specific position exists and there is work available for that position, 2) work could start within 30 days regardless of whether a suitable candidate is found, and 3) the employer is actively recruiting from outside the establishment to fill the position. Included are full-time, part-time, permanent, short-term, and seasonal openings. Active recruiting means that the establishment is taking steps to fill a position by advertising in newspapers or on the Internet, posting help-wanted signs, accepting applications, or using other similar methods.

Jobs to be filled only by internal transfers, promotions, demotions, or recall from layoffs are excluded. Also excluded are jobs with start dates more than 30 days in the future, jobs for which employees have been hired but have not yet reported for work, and jobs to be filled by employees of temporary help agencies, employee leasing companies, outside contractors, or consultants. The job openings rate is computed by dividing the number of job openings by the sum of employment and job openings and multiplying that quotient by 100.

Hires are the total number of additions to the payroll occurring at any time during the reference month, including both new and rehired employees, full-time and part-time, permanent, short-term and seasonal employees, employees recalled to the location after a layoff lasting more than 7 days, on-call or intermittent employees who returned to work after having been formally separated, and transfers from other locations. The hires count does not include transfers or promotions within the reporting site, employees returning from strike, employees of temporary help agencies or employee leasing companies, outside contractors, or consultants. The hires rate is computed by dividing the number of hires by employment and multiplying that quotient by 100.

Separations are the total number of terminations of employment occurring at any time during the reference month, and are reported by type of separation—quits, layoffs and discharges, and other separations. Quits are voluntary separations by employees (except for retirements, which are reported as other separations). Layoffs and discharges are involuntary separations initiated by the employer and include layoffs with no intent to rehire, formal layoffs lasting or expected to last more than 7 days, discharges resulting from mergers, downsizing, or closings, firings or other discharges for cause, terminations of permanent or short-term employees, and terminations of seasonal employees. Other separations include retirements, transfers to other locations, deaths, and separations due to disability. Separations do not include transfers within the same location or employees on strike.

The separations rate is computed by dividing the number of separations by employment and multiplying that quotient by 100. The quits, layoffs and discharges, and other separations rates are computed similarly, dividing the number by employment and multiplying by 100.

The JOLTS annual level estimates for hires, quits, layoffs and discharges, other separations, and total separations are the sum of the 12 published monthly levels. The annual rate estimates are computed by dividing the annual level by the

Current Employment Statistics (CES) annual average employment level, and multiplying that quotient by 100. This figure will be approximately equal to the sum of the 12 monthly rates.

Annual estimates are not calculated for job openings because job openings are a stock, or point-in-time, measurement for the last business day of each month. Only jobs still open on the last day of the month are counted. For the same reason job openings cannot be cumulated throughout each month, annual figures for job openings cannot be created by summing the monthly estimates. Hires and separations are flow measures and are cumulated over the month with a total reported for the month. Therefore, the annual figures can be created by summing the monthly estimates.

Sources of Additional Information

For more extensive information see BLS news release USDL 09-1359 "Job Openings and Labor Turnover (Monthly)" on the BLS Web site at <http://www.bls.gov/jlt/>.

Table 7-7. Job Openings Levels and Rates, by Industry, December 2000–September 2009

(Seasonally adjusted, levels in thousands, rates per 100.)

Year and month	Level											
	Total[1]	Total private[1]	Construction	Manufacturing	Trade, transportation, and utilities[2]	Retail trade	Professional and business services	Education and health services	Leisure and hospitality[3]	Accommodation and food services	Government[4]	State and local government
2000												
December	4 949	4 558	230	435	874	544	831	845	584	555	398	341
2001												
January	5 138	4 648	196	439	940	496	689	788	661	597	477	400
February	4 862	4 390	228	415	907	520	798	808	634	568	470	400
March	4 923	4 431	199	392	678	430	1 045	790	669	569	476	417
April	4 940	4 446	232	324	911	552	835	727	594	547	499	435
May	4 602	4 090	221	320	702	465	813	774	585	521	500	446
June	4 509	3 943	185	338	693	437	747	761	534	468	549	474
July	4 457	3 944	190	312	669	409	622	796	604	511	503	467
August	4 308	3 802	112	273	626	404	596	928	588	533	502	455
September	4 166	3 741	145	320	590	359	646	762	640	560	443	373
October	3 626	3 171	127	262	600	363	512	756	439	381	458	411
November	3 655	3 204	139	237	570	350	560	708	479	419	457	405
December	3 693	3 244	122	237	564	370	520	733	461	411	468	412
2002												
January	3 596	3 205	114	255	559	374	564	763	430	370	393	361
February	3 566	3 114	108	260	556	352	496	753	440	359	449	402
March	3 678	3 222	128	239	582	354	596	740	425	355	439	391
April	3 477	3 058	98	239	574	353	535	725	409	354	427	384
May	3 641	3 173	111	252	557	341	654	657	431	364	459	413
June	3 489	3 075	129	251	545	340	526	733	398	342	409	363
July	3 431	3 025	102	260	514	346	598	701	408	362	409	366
August	3 502	3 041	111	245	533	323	599	707	400	350	458	410
September	3 410	2 986	131	245	505	315	588	724	382	345	441	373
October	3 620	3 217	133	228	593	396	726	667	407	353	406	358
November	3 636	3 178	120	245	506	294	674	734	418	380	464	394
December	3 272	2 897	86	233	434	247	556	660	378	321	379	347
2003												
January	3 551	3 130	114	209	518	313	855	644	394	361	418	353
February	3 503	3 103	100	204	568	360	776	613	355	286	393	344
March	3 202	2 793	87	199	469	302	658	592	360	332	393	329
April	3 250	2 880	137	198	457	295	521	636	436	354	375	340
May	3 198	2 858	92	200	497	309	622	658	376	344	338	288
June	3 394	2 969	113	192	507	334	620	606	490	411	421	336
July	3 178	2 848	154	182	522	322	704	579	345	288	345	271
August	3 220	2 900	108	222	538	337	731	562	360	315	320	260
September	3 179	2 850	66	210	565	356	651	553	396	341	333	281
October	3 214	2 871	85	221	557	362	599	610	417	371	343	301
November	3 345	3 017	91	271	583	374	612	585	398	362	325	278
December	3 375	3 047	100	230	596	346	620	525	455	404	326	295
2004												
January	3 453	3 032	147	234	561	350	594	641	422	363	415	339
February	3 556	3 184	121	224	569	392	659	611	459	386	362	310
March	3 522	3 145	126	249	607	390	586	612	438	393	362	319
April	3 584	3 212	136	263	606	388	667	623	410	378	372	302
May	3 737	3 338	138	288	632	425	657	608	443	375	394	356
June	3 520	3 167	102	267	637	407	730	528	466	420	354	279
July	3 892	3 519	116	279	681	425	756	612	479	429	389	345
August	3 741	3 380	128	281	650	434	673	609	503	426	364	317
September	3 830	3 462	123	276	725	472	708	611	468	395	375	317
October	3 916	3 498	155	287	660	452	749	655	450	401	417	363
November	3 448	3 061	147	262	552	313	594	625	407	363	386	336
December	3 915	3 506	154	275	645	414	712	636	460	392	419	352
2005												
January	3 902	3 507	162	302	663	450	697	638	520	464	386	354
February	3 915	3 532	154	282	734	447	698	630	513	443	374	335
March	3 939	3 557	147	282	690	466	729	671	501	436	371	323
April	4 241	3 840	133	294	720	472	798	649	590	527	397	339
May	3 923	3 542	139	277	683	405	769	693	502	437	377	331
June	4 175	3 778	143	294	693	426	882	658	533	449	395	336
July	4 148	3 774	155	320	688	414	796	693	517	421	404	353
August	4 102	3 709	151	306	675	424	818	674	480	415	398	347
September	4 263	3 833	172	332	691	392	825	693	504	448	437	369
October	4 254	3 873	180	282	748	456	820	642	497	427	380	336
November	4 366	3 962	207	383	838	531	859	668	509	462	404	353
December	4 390	3 953	177	353	702	471	882	672	544	485	444	387

[1]Includes natural resources and mining, information, financial activities, and other services, not shown separately.
[2]Includes wholesale trade and transportation, warehousing, and utilities, not shown separately.
[3]Includes arts, entertainment, and recreation, not shown separately.
[4]Includes federal government, not shown separately.

Table 7-7. Job Openings Levels and Rates, by Industry, December 2000–September 2009—*Continued*

(Seasonally adjusted, levels in thousands, rates per 100.)

Year and month	Rate											
	Total[1]	Total private[1]	Construc-tion	Manufac-turing	Trade, transpor-tation, and utilities[2]	Retail trade	Profes-sional and business services	Education and health services	Leisure and hospitality[3]	Accommo-dation and food services	Govern-ment[4]	State and local govern-ment
2000												
December	3.6	3.9	3.3	2.5	3.2	3.4	4.7	5.2	4.7	5.2	1.9	1.9
2001												
January	3.7	4.0	2.8	2.5	3.5	3.1	3.9	4.9	5.2	5.5	2.2	2.2
February	3.5	3.8	3.2	2.4	3.3	3.3	4.5	5.0	5.0	5.3	2.2	2.2
March	3.6	3.8	2.8	2.3	2.5	2.7	5.9	4.9	5.3	5.3	2.2	2.2
April	3.6	3.8	3.3	1.9	3.4	3.5	4.8	4.5	4.7	5.1	2.3	2.3
May	3.4	3.5	3.1	1.9	2.6	3.0	4.7	4.7	4.6	4.8	2.3	2.4
June	3.3	3.4	2.6	2.0	2.6	2.8	4.3	4.6	4.2	4.4	2.5	2.5
July	3.3	3.4	2.7	1.9	2.5	2.6	3.6	4.8	4.8	4.7	2.3	2.5
August	3.2	3.3	1.6	1.7	2.4	2.6	3.5	5.6	4.6	4.9	2.3	2.4
September	3.1	3.3	2.1	1.9	2.2	2.3	3.8	4.6	5.0	5.2	2.0	2.0
October	2.7	2.8	1.8	1.6	2.3	2.3	3.1	4.6	3.5	3.6	2.1	2.2
November	2.7	2.8	2.0	1.5	2.2	2.3	3.4	4.3	3.8	4.0	2.1	2.1
December	2.7	2.9	1.8	1.5	2.2	2.4	3.1	4.4	3.7	3.9	2.1	2.2
2002												
January	2.7	2.9	1.7	1.6	2.1	2.4	3.4	4.6	3.5	3.5	1.8	1.9
February	2.7	2.8	1.6	1.6	2.1	2.3	3.0	4.5	3.6	3.4	2.1	2.1
March	2.7	2.9	1.9	1.5	2.2	2.3	3.6	4.4	3.4	3.4	2.0	2.1
April	2.6	2.7	1.4	1.5	2.2	2.3	3.2	4.3	3.3	3.4	2.0	2.0
May	2.7	2.8	1.6	1.6	2.1	2.2	3.9	3.9	3.5	3.5	2.1	2.2
June	2.6	2.7	1.9	1.6	2.1	2.2	3.2	4.3	3.2	3.3	1.9	1.9
July	2.6	2.7	1.5	1.7	2.0	2.3	3.6	4.1	3.3	3.4	1.9	1.9
August	2.6	2.7	1.6	1.6	2.0	2.1	3.6	4.2	3.2	3.3	2.1	2.1
September	2.6	2.7	1.9	1.6	1.9	2.1	3.6	4.3	3.1	3.3	2.0	1.9
October	2.7	2.9	2.0	1.5	2.3	2.6	4.3	3.9	3.3	3.3	1.8	1.9
November	2.7	2.8	1.8	1.6	2.0	1.9	4.1	4.3	3.3	3.6	2.1	2.1
December	2.5	2.6	1.3	1.5	1.7	1.6	3.4	3.9	3.0	3.0	1.7	1.8
2003												
January	2.7	2.8	1.7	1.4	2.0	2.1	5.1	3.8	3.1	3.4	1.9	1.8
February	2.6	2.8	1.5	1.4	2.2	2.4	4.6	3.6	2.8	2.7	1.8	1.8
March	2.4	2.5	1.3	1.3	1.8	2.0	4.0	3.5	2.9	3.1	1.8	1.7
April	2.4	2.6	2.0	1.3	1.8	1.9	3.2	3.7	3.5	3.3	1.7	1.8
May	2.4	2.6	1.4	1.4	1.9	2.0	3.8	3.8	3.0	3.2	1.5	1.5
June	2.5	2.7	1.7	1.3	2.0	2.2	3.7	3.5	3.9	3.8	1.9	1.8
July	2.4	2.6	2.2	1.2	2.0	2.1	4.2	3.4	2.8	2.7	1.6	1.4
August	2.4	2.6	1.6	1.5	2.1	2.2	4.4	3.3	2.9	3.0	1.5	1.4
September	2.4	2.6	1.0	1.4	2.2	2.3	3.9	3.2	3.1	3.2	1.5	1.5
October	2.4	2.6	1.2	1.5	2.2	2.4	3.6	3.5	3.3	3.4	1.6	1.6
November	2.5	2.7	1.3	1.9	2.3	2.4	3.7	3.4	3.1	3.3	1.5	1.5
December	2.5	2.7	1.4	1.6	2.3	2.3	3.7	3.0	3.6	3.7	1.5	1.5
2004												
January	2.6	2.7	2.1	1.6	2.2	2.3	3.6	3.7	3.3	3.3	1.9	1.8
February	2.7	2.8	1.7	1.5	2.2	2.5	3.9	3.5	3.6	3.5	1.7	1.6
March	2.6	2.8	1.8	1.7	2.3	2.5	3.5	3.5	3.4	3.6	1.7	1.7
April	2.7	2.9	1.9	1.8	2.3	2.5	3.9	3.6	3.2	3.4	1.7	1.6
May	2.8	3.0	1.9	2.0	2.4	2.7	3.9	3.5	3.4	3.4	1.8	1.9
June	2.6	2.8	1.4	1.8	2.4	2.6	4.3	3.0	3.6	3.8	1.6	1.5
July	2.9	3.1	1.6	1.9	2.6	2.7	4.4	3.5	3.7	3.9	1.8	1.8
August	2.8	3.0	1.8	1.9	2.5	2.8	3.9	3.5	3.9	3.8	1.7	1.7
September	2.8	3.0	1.7	1.9	2.8	3.0	4.1	3.5	3.6	3.6	1.7	1.7
October	2.9	3.1	2.1	2.0	2.5	2.9	4.3	3.7	3.5	3.6	1.9	1.9
November	2.5	2.7	2.0	1.8	2.1	2.0	3.5	3.5	3.1	3.3	1.7	1.7
December	2.9	3.1	2.1	1.9	2.4	2.7	4.1	3.6	3.5	3.5	1.9	1.8
2005												
January	2.9	3.1	2.2	2.1	2.5	2.9	4.0	3.6	3.9	4.1	1.7	1.8
February	2.9	3.1	2.1	1.9	2.8	2.9	4.0	3.5	3.9	3.9	1.7	1.7
March	2.9	3.1	2.0	1.9	2.6	3.0	4.2	3.8	3.8	3.9	1.7	1.7
April	3.1	3.3	1.8	2.0	2.7	3.0	4.5	3.6	4.4	4.6	1.8	1.7
May	2.9	3.1	1.9	1.9	2.6	2.6	4.4	3.9	3.8	3.9	1.7	1.7
June	3.0	3.3	1.9	2.0	2.6	2.7	5.0	3.7	4.0	3.9	1.8	1.7
July	3.0	3.3	2.1	2.2	2.6	2.6	4.5	3.8	3.9	3.7	1.8	1.8
August	3.0	3.2	2.0	2.1	2.5	2.7	4.6	3.7	3.6	3.6	1.8	1.8
September	3.1	3.3	2.3	2.3	2.6	2.5	4.6	3.8	3.8	3.9	2.0	1.9
October	3.1	3.3	2.4	2.0	2.8	2.9	4.6	3.5	3.7	3.8	1.7	1.7
November	3.1	3.4	2.7	2.6	3.1	3.3	4.8	3.7	3.8	4.0	1.8	1.8
December	3.2	3.4	2.3	2.4	2.6	3.0	4.9	3.7	4.0	4.2	2.0	2.0

[1]Includes natural resources and mining, information, financial activities, and other services, not shown separately.
[2]Includes wholesale trade and transportation, warehousing, and utilities, not shown separately.
[3]Includes arts, entertainment, and recreation, not shown separately.
[4]Includes federal government, not shown separately.

Table 7-7. Job Openings Levels and Rates, by Industry, December 2000–September 2009—*Continued*

(Seasonally adjusted, levels in thousands, rates per 100.)

Year and month	Level											
	Total[1]	Total private[1]	Construc-tion	Manufac-turing	Trade, transpor-tation, and utilities[2]	Retail trade	Profes-sional and business services	Education and health services	Leisure and hospitality[3]	Accommo-dation and food services	Govern-ment[4]	State and local govern-ment
2006												
January	4 351	3 963	155	332	717	450	842	692	557	497	366	321
February	4 455	4 028	148	377	712	427	846	755	569	521	427	368
March	4 631	4 176	186	380	749	435	787	747	575	503	449	399
April	4 680	4 225	185	372	796	462	740	736	573	517	447	403
May	4 600	4 149	172	314	785	460	900	690	569	505	445	397
June	4 463	3 985	195	358	740	447	695	727	530	468	469	415
July	4 118	3 665	187	317	700	387	611	648	557	489	483	432
August	4 551	4 088	203	353	747	431	724	776	581	528	468	421
September	4 621	4 151	193	358	885	456	734	786	563	435	476	427
October	4 647	4 197	179	371	778	434	769	816	599	514	451	401
November	4 556	4 099	140	344	754	405	807	790	672	620	459	407
December	4 606	4 149	120	372	872	540	732	774	606	534	459	413
2007												
January	4 648	4 175	288	367	877	466	776	737	551	480	433	395
February	4 592	4 133	288	374	768	443	665	710	553	476	467	408
March	4 771	4 301	197	369	865	421	838	723	586	518	471	423
April	4 628	4 164	188	353	833	402	818	747	569	493	456	400
May	4 573	4 109	190	371	720	369	785	761	590	518	461	410
June	4 815	4 343	169	364	848	488	800	798	618	542	465	423
July	4 414	4 032	160	374	798	438	705	739	606	549	428	386
August	4 596	4 118	149	346	796	408	781	784	637	567	485	432
September	4 568	4 127	137	337	782	419	776	860	665	575	441	390
October	4 371	3 920	144	292	706	365	760	736	631	567	453	402
November	4 429	3 959	134	342	751	398	805	750	644	575	473	402
December	4 382	3 918	135	316	785	415	784	794	586	529	462	399
2008												
January	4 332	3 873	131	302	734	367	759	740	596	539	406	372
February	4 248	3 813	136	278	722	378	766	806	558	487	446	397
March	4 073	3 644	90	233	659	391	763	760	551	488	431	376
April	3 967	3 547	109	274	630	388	749	719	520	470	413	383
May	4 009	3 577	162	280	649	402	681	728	575	491	435	379
June	3 850	3 429	117	268	608	361	713	714	516	468	420	359
July	3 912	3 552	126	257	686	400	696	818	457	403	410	341
August	3 722	3 314	84	300	638	393	692	707	438	378	421	357
September	3 346	2 913	152	236	525	297	608	624	427	374	431	352
October	3 390	2 964	79	230	564	363	603	646	417	370	427	344
November	3 311	2 928	76	203	624	410	505	697	302	284	378	337
December	3 224	2 861	66	188	495	337	562	685	315	274	345	312
2009												
January	2 920	2 461	55	115	488	362	501	636	272	242	417	328
February	2 973	2 606	58	141	488	334	482	589	332	302	367	317
March	2 633	2 269	51	115	414	265	428	537	289	263	353	291
April	2 513	2 042	29	95	332	205	461	515	322	312	461	307
May	2 523	2 191	39	105	466	319	451	530	265	239	310	267
June	2 513	2 163	56	113	469	308	445	531	276	254	322	273
July	2 408	2 090	47	110	393	260	431	553	256	237	314	266
August	2 423	2 128	65	122	422	273	438	520	238	216	300	269
September[5]	2 480	2 232	62	136	414	268	455	547	299	274	267	221

[1]Includes natural resources and mining, information, financial activities, and other services, not shown separately.
[2]Includes wholesale trade and transportation, warehousing, and utilities, not shown separately.
[3]Includes arts, entertainment, and recreation, not shown separately.
[4]Includes federal government, not shown separately.
[5]Preliminary.

Table 7-7. Job Openings Levels and Rates, by Industry, December 2000–September 2009—*Continued*

(Seasonally adjusted, levels in thousands, rates per 100.)

Year and month	Rate											
	Total[1]	Total private[1]	Construc-tion	Manufac-turing	Trade, transpor-tation, and utilities[2]	Retail trade	Profes-sional and business services	Education and health services	Leisure and hospitality[3]	Accommo-dation and food services	Govern-ment[4]	State and local govern-ment
2006												
January	3.1	3.4	2.0	2.3	2.7	2.9	4.6	3.8	4.1	4.3	1.6	1.6
February	3.2	3.4	1.9	2.6	2.6	2.7	4.6	4.1	4.2	4.5	1.9	1.9
March	3.3	3.5	2.4	2.6	2.8	2.7	4.3	4.0	4.2	4.3	2.0	2.0
April	3.3	3.6	2.3	2.5	2.9	2.9	4.1	4.0	4.2	4.4	2.0	2.1
May	3.3	3.5	2.2	2.2	2.9	2.9	4.9	3.7	4.2	4.3	2.0	2.0
June	3.2	3.4	2.5	2.5	2.7	2.8	3.8	3.9	3.9	4.0	2.1	2.1
July	2.9	3.1	2.4	2.2	2.6	2.5	3.3	3.5	4.1	4.2	2.1	2.2
August	3.2	3.5	2.6	2.4	2.8	2.7	3.9	4.2	4.2	4.5	2.1	2.1
September	3.3	3.5	2.4	2.5	3.3	2.9	4.0	4.2	4.1	3.7	2.1	2.2
October	3.3	3.5	2.3	2.6	2.9	2.7	4.2	4.3	4.3	4.4	2.0	2.0
November	3.2	3.5	1.8	2.4	2.8	2.6	4.3	4.2	4.8	5.2	2.0	2.1
December	3.3	3.5	1.5	2.6	3.2	3.4	3.9	4.1	4.4	4.5	2.0	2.1
2007												
January	3.3	3.5	3.6	2.6	3.2	2.9	4.2	3.9	4.0	4.1	1.9	2.0
February	3.2	3.5	3.6	2.6	2.8	2.8	3.6	3.8	4.0	4.0	2.1	2.1
March	3.4	3.6	2.5	2.6	3.1	2.6	4.5	3.8	4.2	4.4	2.1	2.1
April	3.3	3.5	2.4	2.5	3.0	2.5	4.4	3.9	4.1	4.1	2.0	2.0
May	3.2	3.4	2.4	2.6	2.6	2.3	4.2	4.0	4.2	4.3	2.0	2.1
June	3.4	3.6	2.2	2.6	3.1	3.0	4.3	4.2	4.4	4.5	2.0	2.1
July	3.1	3.4	2.1	2.6	2.9	2.7	3.8	3.9	4.3	4.6	1.9	1.9
August	3.2	3.4	1.9	2.4	2.9	2.6	4.2	4.1	4.5	4.7	2.1	2.2
September	3.2	3.5	1.8	2.4	2.8	2.6	4.1	4.5	4.7	4.8	1.9	2.0
October	3.1	3.3	1.9	2.1	2.6	2.3	4.1	3.8	4.5	4.7	2.0	2.0
November	3.1	3.3	1.7	2.4	2.7	2.5	4.3	3.9	4.5	4.7	2.1	2.0
December	3.1	3.3	1.8	2.2	2.9	2.6	4.1	4.1	4.1	4.4	2.0	2.0
2008												
January	3.0	3.2	1.7	2.1	2.7	2.3	4.0	3.8	4.2	4.5	1.8	1.9
February	3.0	3.2	1.8	2.0	2.6	2.4	4.1	4.1	4.0	4.1	2.0	2.0
March	2.9	3.1	1.2	1.7	2.4	2.5	4.1	3.9	3.9	4.1	1.9	1.9
April	2.8	3.0	1.5	2.0	2.3	2.4	4.0	3.7	3.7	3.9	1.8	1.9
May	2.8	3.0	2.2	2.0	2.4	2.5	3.7	3.7	4.1	4.1	1.9	1.9
June	2.7	2.9	1.6	1.9	2.2	2.3	3.8	3.7	3.7	3.9	1.8	1.8
July	2.8	3.0	1.7	1.9	2.5	2.5	3.8	4.1	3.3	3.4	1.8	1.7
August	2.6	2.8	1.2	2.2	2.4	2.5	3.8	3.6	3.2	3.2	1.8	1.8
September	2.4	2.5	2.1	1.7	2.0	1.9	3.3	3.2	3.1	3.2	1.9	1.7
October	2.4	2.5	1.1	1.7	2.1	2.3	3.3	3.3	3.0	3.1	1.9	1.7
November	2.4	2.5	1.1	1.5	2.3	2.6	2.8	3.5	2.2	2.4	1.6	1.7
December	2.3	2.5	0.9	1.4	1.9	2.2	3.1	3.5	2.3	2.4	1.5	1.6
2009												
January	2.1	2.2	0.8	0.9	1.9	2.4	2.8	3.2	2.0	2.1	1.8	1.6
February	2.2	2.3	0.9	1.1	1.9	2.2	2.8	3.0	2.4	2.6	1.6	1.6
March	1.9	2.0	0.8	0.9	1.6	1.8	2.5	2.7	2.1	2.3	1.5	1.5
April	1.9	1.8	0.5	0.8	1.3	1.4	2.7	2.6	2.4	2.7	2.0	1.5
May	1.9	2.0	0.6	0.9	1.8	2.1	2.6	2.7	2.0	2.1	1.4	1.3
June	1.9	1.9	0.9	0.9	1.8	2.0	2.6	2.7	2.1	2.2	1.4	1.4
July	1.8	1.9	0.8	0.9	1.5	1.7	2.5	2.8	1.9	2.1	1.4	1.3
August	1.8	1.9	1.1	1.0	1.6	1.8	2.6	2.6	1.8	1.9	1.3	1.4
September[5]	1.9	2.0	1.0	1.1	1.6	1.8	2.7	2.8	2.2	2.4	1.2	1.1

[1]Includes natural resources and mining, information, financial activities, and other services, not shown separately.
[2]Includes wholesale trade and transportation, warehousing, and utilities, not shown separately.
[3]Includes arts, entertainment, and recreation, not shown separately.
[4]Includes federal government, not shown separately.
[5]Preliminary.

Table 7-8. Hires Levels[1] and Rates,[2] by Industry, December 2000–September 2009

(Seasonally adjusted, levels in thousands, rates per 100.)

Year and month	Level[3]											
	Total[4]	Total private[4]	Construction	Manufacturing	Trade, transportation, and utilities[5]	Retail trade	Professional and business services	Education and health services	Leisure and hospitality[6]	Accommodation and food services	Government[7]	State and local government
2000												
December	5 379	4 978	427	538	1 159	860	950	518	936	807	406	382
2001												
January	5 578	5 243	473	504	1 160	840	1 082	472	953	807	351	284
February	5 497	5 120	468	458	1 097	770	970	531	950	803	399	371
March	5 805	5 449	543	461	1 125	832	1 164	576	977	836	362	333
April	5 459	5 095	449	438	1 132	800	804	509	1 084	922	372	339
May	5 479	5 092	440	408	1 252	887	1 014	500	950	795	390	347
June	5 269	4 884	443	399	1 107	810	940	510	926	768	378	334
July	5 339	4 991	455	366	1 116	792	905	531	939	774	361	313
August	5 167	4 756	401	361	1 059	764	939	526	882	740	370	323
September	5 124	4 765	412	357	1 086	794	915	525	932	802	356	331
October	5 107	4 723	426	376	1 093	776	918	508	848	706	360	315
November	5 018	4 690	493	361	1 007	717	880	502	856	729	347	311
December	4 913	4 555	445	375	945	665	894	479	835	717	346	301
2002												
January	4 927	4 605	405	374	1 020	726	903	507	868	739	338	293
February	5 034	4 692	426	402	1 036	707	903	485	848	725	348	304
March	4 781	4 440	406	359	941	654	942	480	813	672	336	298
April	5 026	4 674	421	408	1 050	729	920	503	837	712	359	312
May	5 020	4 656	402	418	1 039	726	986	487	821	697	368	313
June	4 948	4 618	433	402	1 039	719	864	498	811	680	334	293
July	5 297	4 986	475	417	1 055	739	1 006	494	887	719	328	287
August	4 945	4 562	397	379	999	700	961	453	838	707	354	299
September	4 929	4 617	446	402	1 023	720	954	455	815	702	322	270
October	4 866	4 495	432	355	999	701	957	461	808	692	344	275
November	4 977	4 609	421	380	1 005	713	996	456	814	676	399	333
December	5 019	4 687	442	371	1 033	733	970	496	823	688	319	279
2003												
January	5 029	4 687	447	414	953	673	959	516	897	731	351	293
February	4 894	4 575	360	365	978	743	937	463	807	683	312	271
March	4 538	4 204	411	338	921	643	738	463	783	643	320	266
April	4 720	4 409	447	330	916	653	926	449	831	685	308	282
May	4 678	4 380	441	326	941	656	811	484	869	698	301	260
June	4 774	4 459	433	346	969	682	883	477	831	709	323	277
July	4 708	4 409	426	342	950	639	893	461	747	637	321	281
August	4 665	4 462	492	356	1 007	687	871	460	838	706	240	201
September	4 830	4 566	467	344	1 025	687	892	501	800	700	293	261
October	5 052	4 673	412	350	1 133	784	921	491	858	720	348	295
November	4 781	4 485	441	370	970	671	879	481	830	695	304	249
December	5 078	4 742	451	372	1 061	738	899	472	896	783	332	286
2004												
January	4 970	4 603	441	375	1 123	759	888	487	849	700	367	310
February	4 904	4 567	435	379	1 034	733	736	488	872	725	332	286
March	5 324	4 969	523	405	1 135	762	935	492	907	772	346	314
April	5 197	4 879	431	416	1 139	798	980	482	871	745	320	266
May	5 059	4 754	448	397	1 080	742	914	468	896	752	307	278
June	5 064	4 758	470	378	1 058	695	916	453	862	732	316	278
July	5 040	4 712	418	388	1 086	759	889	473	862	724	347	305
August	5 170	4 851	450	405	1 104	743	970	492	881	746	318	278
September	5 092	4 723	434	394	1 086	738	920	459	889	740	372	346
October	5 226	4 830	484	375	1 117	773	919	495	911	764	360	303
November	5 246	4 903	449	377	1 170	812	949	503	881	763	362	316
December	5 274	4 933	464	371	1 157	813	1 007	513	860	751	345	291
2005												
January	5 565	5 188	482	383	1 175	788	1 038	515	979	813	373	343
February	5 358	5 022	515	371	1 141	799	1 031	506	846	732	328	289
March	5 347	5 009	462	378	1 167	833	1 017	532	887	761	318	279
April	5 368	5 026	507	367	1 147	797	998	532	877	737	353	302
May	5 352	5 022	501	375	1 169	806	1 007	516	874	741	331	292
June	5 460	5 144	470	354	1 155	809	1 048	526	975	799	322	281
July	5 396	5 079	425	381	1 156	827	1 036	502	910	776	338	297
August	5 532	5 206	531	379	1 158	826	1 116	519	914	779	327	283
September	5 459	5 146	524	392	1 128	781	1 071	535	936	796	334	295
October	5 124	4 767	515	401	1 091	752	882	487	881	761	323	272
November	5 287	4 942	489	390	1 089	704	940	523	959	826	359	309
December	5 213	4 866	466	362	1 131	751	931	512	906	793	353	300

[1]Hires are the number of hires during the entire month.
[2]The hires rate is the number of hires during the entire month as a percent of total employment.
[3]Detail will not necessarily add to totals because of the independent seasonal adjustment of the various series.
[4]Includes natural resources and mining, information, financial activities, and other services, not shown separately.
[5]Includes wholesale trade and transportation, warehousing, and utilities, not shown separately.
[6]Includes arts, entertainment, and recreation, not shown separately.
[7]Includes federal government, not shown separately.

Table 7-8. Hires Levels[1] and Rates,[2] by Industry, December 2000–September 2009—*Continued*

(Seasonally adjusted, levels in thousands, rates per 100.)

Year and month	Rate											
	Total[4]	Total private[4]	Construc-tion	Manufac-turing	Trade, transpor-tation, and utilities[5]	Retail trade	Profes-sional and business services	Education and health services	Leisure and hospitality[6]	Accommo-dation and food services	Govern-ment[7]	State and local govern-ment
2000												
December	4.1	4.5	6.3	3.1	4.4	5.6	5.6	3.4	7.8	7.9	2.0	2.1
2001												
January	4.2	4.7	6.9	2.9	4.4	5.5	6.4	3.1	8.0	7.9	1.7	1.6
February	4.1	4.6	6.8	2.7	4.2	5.0	5.8	3.4	7.9	7.9	1.9	2.0
March	4.4	4.9	7.9	2.7	4.3	5.4	6.9	3.7	8.1	8.2	1.7	1.8
April	4.1	4.6	6.6	2.6	4.3	5.2	4.8	3.3	9.0	9.0	1.8	1.9
May	4.1	4.6	6.4	2.4	4.8	5.8	6.1	3.2	7.9	7.8	1.9	1.9
June	4.0	4.4	6.5	2.4	4.3	5.3	5.7	3.3	7.7	7.5	1.8	1.8
July	4.0	4.5	6.7	2.2	4.3	5.2	5.5	3.4	7.8	7.5	1.7	1.7
August	3.9	4.3	5.9	2.2	4.1	5.0	5.7	3.3	7.3	7.2	1.7	1.7
September	3.9	4.3	6.0	2.2	4.2	5.2	5.6	3.3	7.7	7.8	1.7	1.8
October	3.9	4.3	6.3	2.4	4.2	5.1	5.7	3.2	7.1	6.9	1.7	1.7
November	3.8	4.3	7.3	2.3	3.9	4.7	5.5	3.2	7.1	7.2	1.6	1.7
December	3.8	4.2	6.6	2.4	3.7	4.4	5.6	3.0	7.0	7.1	1.6	1.6
2002												
January	3.8	4.2	6.0	2.4	4.0	4.8	5.6	3.2	7.2	7.3	1.6	1.6
February	3.9	4.3	6.3	2.6	4.1	4.7	5.7	3.0	7.1	7.1	1.6	1.6
March	3.7	4.1	6.0	2.3	3.7	4.3	5.9	3.0	6.8	6.6	1.6	1.6
April	3.9	4.3	6.3	2.7	4.1	4.8	5.7	3.1	7.0	7.0	1.7	1.7
May	3.9	4.3	6.0	2.7	4.1	4.8	6.2	3.0	6.9	6.9	1.7	1.7
June	3.8	4.2	6.5	2.6	4.1	4.8	5.4	3.1	6.8	6.7	1.6	1.6
July	4.1	4.6	7.1	2.7	4.1	4.9	6.3	3.0	7.4	7.1	1.5	1.5
August	3.8	4.2	5.9	2.5	3.9	4.7	6.0	2.8	7.0	6.9	1.6	1.6
September	3.8	4.2	6.7	2.7	4.0	4.8	6.0	2.8	6.8	6.9	1.5	1.4
October	3.7	4.1	6.5	2.4	3.9	4.7	6.0	2.8	6.7	6.7	1.6	1.5
November	3.8	4.2	6.3	2.5	4.0	4.8	6.2	2.8	6.7	6.6	1.8	1.8
December	3.9	4.3	6.6	2.5	4.1	4.9	6.1	3.0	6.8	6.7	1.5	1.5
2003												
January	3.9	4.3	6.7	2.8	3.8	4.5	6.0	3.1	7.4	7.1	1.6	1.6
February	3.8	4.2	5.4	2.5	3.9	5.0	5.9	2.8	6.7	6.6	1.4	1.4
March	3.5	3.9	6.2	2.3	3.6	4.3	4.6	2.8	6.5	6.2	1.5	1.4
April	3.6	4.1	6.7	2.3	3.6	4.4	5.8	2.7	6.9	6.7	1.4	1.5
May	3.6	4.0	6.6	2.2	3.7	4.4	5.1	2.9	7.2	6.8	1.4	1.4
June	3.7	4.1	6.4	2.4	3.8	4.6	5.5	2.9	6.9	6.9	1.5	1.5
July	3.6	4.1	6.3	2.4	3.8	4.3	5.6	2.8	6.2	6.2	1.5	1.5
August	3.6	4.1	7.3	2.5	4.0	4.6	5.4	2.8	6.0	6.8	1.1	1.1
September	3.7	4.2	6.9	2.4	4.1	4.6	5.6	3.0	6.6	6.7	1.4	1.4
October	3.9	4.3	6.1	2.4	4.5	5.2	5.7	2.9	7.0	6.9	1.6	1.6
November	3.7	4.1	6.5	2.6	3.8	4.5	5.5	2.9	6.8	6.6	1.4	1.3
December	3.9	4.4	6.6	2.6	4.2	4.9	5.6	2.8	7.3	7.5	1.5	1.5
2004												
January	3.8	4.2	6.4	2.6	4.4	5.1	5.5	2.9	6.9	6.7	1.7	1.6
February	3.8	4.2	6.4	2.7	4.1	4.9	4.6	2.9	7.1	6.9	1.5	1.5
March	4.1	4.5	7.6	2.8	4.5	5.1	5.8	2.9	7.3	7.3	1.6	1.7
April	4.0	4.5	6.2	2.9	4.5	5.3	6.0	2.9	7.0	7.0	1.5	1.4
May	3.9	4.3	6.4	2.8	4.2	4.9	5.6	2.8	7.2	7.1	1.4	1.5
June	3.9	4.3	6.8	2.6	4.1	4.6	5.6	2.7	6.9	6.9	1.5	1.5
July	3.8	4.3	6.0	2.7	4.3	5.0	5.4	2.8	6.9	6.8	1.6	1.6
August	3.9	4.4	6.4	2.8	4.3	4.9	5.9	2.9	7.1	7.0	1.5	1.5
September	3.9	4.3	6.2	2.8	4.2	4.9	5.6	2.7	7.1	6.9	1.7	1.8
October	4.0	4.4	6.8	2.6	4.4	5.1	5.5	2.9	7.2	7.1	1.7	1.6
November	4.0	4.4	6.3	2.6	4.6	5.4	5.7	2.9	7.0	7.1	1.7	1.7
December	4.0	4.5	6.5	2.6	4.5	5.4	6.1	3.0	6.8	7.0	1.6	1.5
2005												
January	4.2	4.7	6.8	2.7	4.6	5.2	6.2	3.0	7.7	7.5	1.7	1.8
February	4.0	4.5	7.2	2.6	4.4	5.3	6.2	2.9	6.7	6.8	1.5	1.5
March	4.0	4.5	6.4	2.6	4.5	5.5	6.1	3.1	7.0	7.0	1.5	1.5
April	4.0	4.5	7.0	2.6	4.4	5.2	5.9	3.1	6.9	6.8	1.6	1.6
May	4.0	4.5	6.9	2.6	4.5	5.3	6.0	3.0	6.8	6.8	1.5	1.5
June	4.1	4.6	6.4	2.5	4.4	5.3	6.2	3.0	7.6	7.3	1.5	1.5
July	4.0	4.5	5.8	2.7	4.4	5.4	6.1	2.9	7.1	7.1	1.5	1.6
August	4.1	4.6	7.2	2.7	4.4	5.4	6.6	3.0	7.1	7.1	1.5	1.5
September	4.1	4.6	7.1	2.8	4.3	5.1	6.3	3.1	7.3	7.3	1.5	1.5
October	3.8	4.2	6.9	2.8	4.2	4.9	5.1	2.8	6.9	7.0	1.5	1.4
November	3.9	4.4	6.5	2.7	4.2	4.6	5.5	3.0	7.4	7.5	1.6	1.6
December	3.9	4.3	6.2	2.6	4.3	4.9	5.4	2.9	7.0	7.2	1.6	1.6

[1]Hires are the number of hires during the entire month.
[2]The hires rate is the number of hires during the entire month as a percent of total employment.
[4]Includes natural resources and mining, information, financial activities, and other services, not shown separately.
[5]Includes wholesale trade and transportation, warehousing, and utilities, not shown separately.
[6]Includes arts, entertainment, and recreation, not shown separately.
[7]Includes federal government, not shown separately.

Table 7-8. Hires Levels[1] and Rates,[2] by Industry, December 2000–September 2009—*Continued*

(Seasonally adjusted, levels in thousands, rates per 100.)

| Year and month | Level[3] | | | | | | | | | | | |
	Total[4]	Total private[4]	Construc-tion	Manufac-turing	Trade, transpor-tation, and utilities[5]	Retail trade	Profes-sional and business services	Education and health services	Leisure and hospitality[6]	Accommo-dation and food services	Govern-ment[7]	State and local govern-ment
2006												
January	5 137	4 845	483	385	1 099	769	929	484	941	817	287	246
February	5 489	5 130	479	382	1 198	838	966	510	987	874	360	303
March	5 389	5 007	474	422	1 141	799	928	493	972	838	385	329
April	5 213	4 860	457	372	1 150	818	886	518	878	758	367	308
May	5 559	5 184	482	393	1 174	823	1 159	577	891	751	373	307
June	5 436	5 040	398	408	1 190	856	973	515	926	783	383	319
July	5 634	5 277	460	394	1 172	789	1 003	572	955	805	370	300
August	5 358	4 968	430	385	1 168	777	984	534	912	783	373	309
September	5 433	4 982	408	357	1 135	785	1 032	543	871	773	427	362
October	5 366	4 984	409	340	1 139	788	983	551	940	802	357	302
November	5 523	5 172	469	369	1 158	801	1 123	536	1 041	895	362	307
December	5 342	5 000	466	388	1 067	752	1 007	546	992	852	345	299
2007												
January	5 327	4 968	415	392	1 122	794	1 001	526	941	796	349	296
February	5 289	4 914	333	408	1 133	789	981	533	934	802	384	315
March	5 408	5 030	458	378	1 176	791	979	533	921	786	384	304
April	5 262	4 898	390	363	1 091	734	955	528	970	827	380	305
May	5 380	4 975	402	386	1 128	806	995	542	936	808	400	316
June	5 320	4 922	416	386	1 090	719	820	567	954	805	383	312
July	5 240	4 898	411	382	1 048	702	943	523	914	790	356	257
August	5 268	4 816	397	377	1 061	746	951	549	916	790	411	338
September	5 252	4 861	396	386	1 085	757	963	527	912	782	383	311
October	5 327	4 951	393	384	1 110	763	976	539	946	803	363	309
November	5 219	4 875	393	410	1 146	791	994	551	920	773	348	300
December	5 074	4 711	379	357	1 025	729	914	513	912	779	381	332
2008												
January	4 995	4 657	368	349	1 030	714	897	562	880	747	324	290
February	5 035	4 694	375	325	1 031	708	851	581	927	787	335	292
March	4 870	4 540	397	316	1 013	686	886	558	860	731	321	289
April	4 955	4 635	401	337	1 035	699	903	554	868	750	319	292
May	4 726	4 406	381	318	910	640	868	540	900	759	317	293
June	4 811	4 498	394	318	996	679	869	547	820	707	321	295
July	4 715	4 426	394	271	1 002	686	850	557	826	702	303	275
August	4 654	4 378	424	285	973	662	810	554	838	692	305	279
September	4 505	4 263	365	305	959	649	787	506	814	708	278	259
October	4 486	4 160	380	290	933	624	788	544	769	651	318	275
November	4 226	3 928	340	257	852	576	783	528	706	620	281	251
December	4 508	4 214	366	252	891	595	786	528	711	605	271	253
2009												
January	4 460	4 141	381	237	949	587	762	539	743	627	306	261
February	4 339	4 042	370	257	814	563	730	527	704	614	275	252
March	4 099	3 799	343	244	883	595	668	483	693	607	271	247
April	4 117	3 822	341	236	888	655	733	475	691	603	340	246
May	3 942	3 739	365	206	842	575	721	473	695	606	273	257
June	3 919	3 654	277	225	744	519	644	530	695	590	262	237
July	4 228	3 930	355	272	819	547	686	522	716	582	282	253
August	4 040	3 779	297	243	818	557	715	538	695	591	261	233
September[8]	4 010	3 758	353	262	832	525	699	524	653	556	258	235

[1]Hires are the number of hires during the entire month.
[2]The hires rate is the number of hires during the entire month as a percent of total employment.
[3]Detail will not necessarily add to totals because of the independent seasonal adjustment of the various series.
[4]Includes natural resources and mining, information, financial activities, and other services, not shown separately.
[5]Includes wholesale trade and transportation, warehousing, and utilities, not shown separately.
[6]Includes arts, entertainment, and recreation, not shown separately.
[7]Includes federal government, not shown separately.
[8]Preliminary.

Table 7-8. Hires Levels[1] and Rates,[2] by Industry, December 2000–September 2009—*Continued*

(Seasonally adjusted, levels in thousands, rates per 100.)

Year and month	Rate											
	Total[4]	Total private[4]	Construction	Manufacturing	Trade, transportation, and utilities[5]	Retail trade	Professional and business services	Education and health services	Leisure and hospitality[6]	Accommodation and food services	Government[7]	State and local government
2006												
January	3.8	4.3	6.3	2.7	4.2	5.0	5.4	2.7	7.3	7.4	1.3	1.3
February	4.1	4.5	6.2	2.7	4.6	5.5	5.6	2.9	7.6	7.9	1.6	1.6
March	4.0	4.4	6.2	3.0	4.4	5.2	5.3	2.8	7.5	7.5	1.8	1.7
April	3.8	4.3	5.9	2.6	4.4	5.3	5.1	2.9	6.7	6.8	1.7	1.6
May	4.1	4.5	6.3	2.8	4.5	5.4	6.6	3.2	6.8	6.7	1.7	1.6
June	4.0	4.4	5.2	2.9	4.5	5.6	5.5	2.9	7.1	7.0	1.7	1.7
July	4.1	4.6	6.0	2.8	4.5	5.2	5.7	3.2	7.3	7.2	1.7	1.6
August	3.9	4.3	5.6	2.7	4.4	5.1	5.6	3.0	6.9	7.0	1.7	1.6
September	4.0	4.4	5.3	2.5	4.3	5.1	5.8	3.0	6.6	6.9	1.9	1.9
October	3.9	4.4	5.3	2.4	4.3	5.1	5.6	3.1	7.1	7.1	1.6	1.6
November	4.0	4.5	6.1	2.6	4.4	5.2	6.3	3.0	7.9	7.9	1.6	1.6
December	3.9	4.4	6.0	2.8	4.0	4.9	5.7	3.0	7.5	7.5	1.6	1.5
2007												
January	3.9	4.3	5.4	2.8	4.2	5.1	5.6	2.9	7.1	7.0	1.6	1.5
February	3.9	4.3	4.4	2.9	4.3	5.1	5.5	2.9	7.0	7.0	1.7	1.6
March	3.9	4.4	5.9	2.7	4.4	5.1	5.5	2.9	6.9	6.9	1.7	1.6
April	3.8	4.2	5.1	2.6	4.1	4.7	5.3	2.9	7.3	7.2	1.7	1.6
May	3.9	4.3	5.2	2.8	4.2	5.2	5.5	3.0	7.0	7.1	1.8	1.6
June	3.9	4.3	5.4	2.8	4.1	4.6	4.6	3.1	7.1	7.0	1.7	1.6
July	3.8	4.2	5.4	2.8	3.9	4.5	5.3	2.9	6.8	6.9	1.6	1.3
August	3.8	4.2	5.2	2.7	4.0	4.8	5.3	3.0	6.8	6.9	1.9	1.7
September	3.8	4.2	5.2	2.8	4.1	4.9	5.4	2.9	6.8	6.8	1.7	1.6
October	3.9	4.3	5.2	2.8	4.2	4.9	5.4	2.9	7.0	7.0	1.6	1.6
November	3.8	4.2	5.2	3.0	4.3	5.1	5.5	3.0	6.8	6.7	1.6	1.5
December	3.7	4.1	5.0	2.6	3.8	4.7	5.0	2.8	6.7	6.7	1.7	1.7
2008												
January	3.6	4.0	4.9	2.5	3.9	4.6	5.0	3.0	6.5	6.5	1.4	1.5
February	3.7	4.1	5.0	2.4	3.9	4.6	4.7	3.1	6.9	6.8	1.5	1.5
March	3.5	3.9	5.4	2.3	3.8	4.4	4.9	3.0	6.4	6.3	1.4	1.5
April	3.6	4.0	5.5	2.5	3.9	4.5	5.0	3.0	6.4	6.5	1.4	1.5
May	3.4	3.8	5.2	2.3	3.4	4.1	4.9	2.9	6.7	6.6	1.4	1.5
June	3.5	3.9	5.5	2.4	3.8	4.4	4.9	2.9	6.1	6.1	1.4	1.5
July	3.4	3.9	5.5	2.0	3.8	4.5	4.8	2.9	6.1	6.1	1.3	1.4
August	3.4	3.8	5.9	2.1	3.7	4.3	4.6	2.9	6.2	6.0	1.4	1.4
September	3.3	3.7	5.1	2.3	3.7	4.2	4.5	2.7	6.1	6.2	1.2	1.3
October	3.3	3.7	5.4	2.2	3.6	4.1	4.5	2.9	5.7	5.7	1.4	1.4
November	3.1	3.5	4.9	2.0	3.3	3.8	4.5	2.8	5.3	5.4	1.2	1.3
December	3.3	3.7	5.3	2.0	3.4	4.0	4.5	2.8	5.3	5.3	1.2	1.3
2009												
January	3.3	3.7	5.7	1.9	3.7	3.9	4.4	2.8	5.6	5.5	1.4	1.3
February	3.2	3.6	5.6	2.1	3.2	3.8	4.3	2.8	5.3	5.4	1.2	1.3
March	3.1	3.4	5.3	2.0	3.5	4.0	4.0	2.5	5.3	5.4	1.2	1.2
April	3.1	3.5	5.4	1.9	3.5	4.4	4.4	2.5	5.3	5.4	1.5	1.2
May	3.0	3.4	5.8	1.7	3.3	3.9	4.3	2.5	5.3	5.4	1.2	1.3
June	3.0	3.3	4.5	1.9	2.9	3.5	3.9	2.8	5.3	5.2	1.2	1.2
July	3.2	3.6	5.8	2.3	3.3	3.7	4.1	2.7	5.4	5.2	1.3	1.3
August	3.1	3.5	4.9	2.1	3.3	3.8	4.3	2.8	5.3	5.2	1.2	1.2
September[8]	3.1	3.5	5.9	2.2	3.3	3.6	4.2	2.7	5.0	4.9	1.2	1.2

[1]Hires are the number of hires during the entire month.
[2]The hires rate is the number of hires during the entire month as a percent of total employment.
[4]Includes natural resources and mining, information, financial activities, and other services, not shown separately.
[5]Includes wholesale trade and transportation, warehousing, and utilities, not shown separately.
[6]Includes arts, entertainment, and recreation, not shown separately.
[7]Includes federal government, not shown separately.
[8]Preliminary.

Table 7-9. Separations Levels[1] and Rates,[2] by Industry, December 2000–September 2009

(Seasonally adjusted, levels in thousands, rates per 100.)

Year and month	Level[3]											
	Total[4]	Total private[4]	Construction	Manufacturing	Trade, transportation, and utilities[5]	Retail trade	Professional and business services	Education and health services	Leisure and hospitality[6]	Accommodation and food services	Government[7]	State and local government
2000												
December	5 391	5 084	432	543	1 135	838	951	506	920	794	406	377
2001												
January	5 653	5 327	440	551	1 249	868	1 079	427	962	822	348	279
February	5 492	5 159	466	534	1 125	772	993	496	877	733	337	299
March	5 855	5 366	489	561	1 225	904	1 218	508	984	853	328	292
April	5 636	5 309	457	558	1 219	869	914	461	1 004	896	320	288
May	5 565	5 232	445	546	1 230	867	1 133	435	908	774	350	303
June	5 412	5 119	460	558	1 165	818	1 016	480	893	732	310	275
July	5 439	5 154	452	509	1 177	834	973	474	949	789	309	266
August	5 269	4 907	408	503	1 044	756	979	461	893	744	361	319
September	5 351	5 073	427	461	1 146	806	997	464	1 026	836	276	238
October	5 604	5 230	428	562	1 218	814	1 005	485	898	766	360	318
November	5 294	4 994	527	493	1 083	724	948	468	905	753	277	253
December	4 987	4 742	444	488	1 024	707	928	412	837	713	315	267
2002												
January	5 124	4 818	419	476	1 077	754	954	462	836	709	328	290
February	5 130	4 796	444	474	1 064	724	930	450	850	720	339	286
March	4 747	4 333	395	436	997	687	932	431	810	679	307	256
April	5 091	4 755	460	449	1 029	710	904	460	840	710	338	294
May	5 109	4 815	434	471	1 035	734	1 059	447	804	680	311	265
June	4 941	4 600	423	450	1 046	727	878	396	824	684	333	286
July	5 359	5 051	488	467	1 044	729	1 093	460	905	727	334	283
August	4 924	4 615	375	460	1 037	750	911	439	807	673	311	266
September	4 977	4 642	445	444	1 043	737	964	431	793	688	322	272
October	4 867	4 521	438	446	1 018	699	924	442	725	641	339	292
November	4 905	4 559	407	436	1 033	716	969	421	796	666	340	295
December	5 113	4 858	450	452	1 012	708	1 035	467	812	684	308	270
2003												
January	4 951	4 635	452	449	1 007	708	904	469	844	700	339	280
February	4 968	4 652	401	442	1 045	790	915	434	820	685	315	267
March	4 643	4 232	406	400	990	696	814	441	797	656	338	279
April	4 792	4 468	408	437	896	620	932	390	813	678	322	273
May	4 733	4 419	430	377	968	664	812	461	837	694	323	267
June	4 831	4 541	421	411	1 004	685	875	481	791	668	296	254
July	4 724	4 432	413	439	973	640	855	458	749	642	318	273
August	4 756	4 420	452	380	969	661	856	457	801	665	321	276
September	4 776	4 454	444	373	972	662	825	458	809	674	313	273
October	4 950	4 635	406	388	1 126	768	870	450	811	686	302	252
November	4 728	4 402	439	382	999	691	817	451	818	676	320	260
December	4 904	4 628	414	385	1 069	731	848	433	859	743	317	285
2004												
January	4 815	4 433	432	380	1 037	729	880	452	832	700	409	328
February	4 778	4 457	449	382	1 034	730	733	471	829	690	321	269
March	4 962	4 581	455	399	1 071	738	918	447	855	729	316	279
April	4 976	4 672	410	384	1 091	768	895	443	829	704	285	262
May	4 794	4 501	407	370	1 038	708	851	444	842	718	304	252
June	4 988	4 646	460	386	1 017	667	915	434	837	708	334	290
July	4 988	4 636	402	392	1 090	775	871	440	874	736	382	333
August	5 015	4 713	409	397	1 068	734	920	456	883	745	288	256
September	5 014	4 680	412	411	1 017	710	873	472	882	694	327	294
October	4 966	4 630	434	388	1 091	750	808	408	887	747	330	282
November	5 178	4 843	444	398	1 166	803	923	487	851	732	326	291
December	5 189	4 872	434	389	1 140	820	976	463	841	715	340	290
2005												
January	5 269	4 974	519	397	1 128	758	985	478	951	804	320	291
February	5 121	4 792	455	353	1 072	755	979	493	820	703	323	286
March	5 226	4 860	423	382	1 145	853	1 004	519	865	742	325	291
April	5 088	4 741	431	382	1 070	741	969	499	773	669	328	280
May	5 204	4 905	467	377	1 129	774	981	471	866	736	313	271
June	5 139	4 820	435	381	1 110	767	985	461	913	764	321	275
July	4 997	4 745	406	395	1 084	787	977	453	889	763	302	255
August	5 298	4 946	479	396	1 123	806	1 029	483	877	763	323	288
September	5 460	5 140	491	420	1 136	808	970	486	997	811	324	277
October	5 085	4 742	467	390	1 085	757	869	470	900	779	338	303
November	5 003	4 677	428	388	1 061	685	817	482	912	789	320	279
December	5 102	4 772	455	351	1 129	744	883	489	894	764	339	281

[1]Total separations are the number of separations during the entire month.
[2]The total separations rate is the number of total separations during the entire month as a percent of total employment.
[3]Detail will not necessarily add to totals because of the independent seasonal adjustment of the various series.
[4]Includes natural resources and mining, information, financial activities, and other services, not shown separately.
[5]Includes wholesale trade and transportation, warehousing, and utilities, not shown separately.
[6]Includes arts, entertainment, and recreation, not shown separately.
[7]Includes federal government, not shown separately.

Table 7-9. Separations Levels[1] and Rates,[2] by Industry, December 2000–September 2009—*Continued*

(Seasonally adjusted, levels in thousands, rates per 100.)

Year and month	Rate											
	Total[4]	Total private[4]	Construction	Manufacturing	Trade, transportation, and utilities[5]	Retail trade	Professional and business services	Education and health services	Leisure and hospitality[6]	Accommodation and food services	Government[7]	State and local government
2000												
December	4.1	4.6	6.4	3.2	4.3	5.4	5.6	3.3	7.7	7.8	2.0	2.1
2001												
January	4.3	4.8	6.5	3.2	4.8	5.7	6.4	2.8	8.0	8.1	1.7	1.5
February	4.1	4.6	6.8	3.1	4.3	5.0	5.9	3.2	7.3	7.2	1.6	1.6
March	4.4	4.8	7.1	3.3	4.7	5.9	7.3	3.3	8.2	8.4	1.6	1.6
April	4.3	4.8	6.7	3.3	4.7	5.7	5.5	3.0	8.3	8.8	1.5	1.6
May	4.2	4.7	6.5	3.3	4.7	5.7	6.8	2.8	7.5	7.6	1.7	1.7
June	4.1	4.6	6.7	3.4	4.5	5.4	6.1	3.1	7.4	7.1	1.5	1.5
July	4.1	4.7	6.6	3.1	4.5	5.5	5.9	3.0	7.8	7.7	1.5	1.4
August	4.0	4.4	6.0	3.1	4.0	5.0	6.0	2.9	7.4	7.3	1.7	1.7
September	4.1	4.6	6.3	2.9	4.4	5.3	6.1	2.9	8.5	8.2	1.3	1.3
October	4.3	4.8	6.3	3.5	4.7	5.4	6.2	3.1	7.5	7.5	1.7	1.7
November	4.0	4.6	7.8	3.1	4.2	4.8	5.9	2.9	7.6	7.4	1.3	1.4
December	3.8	4.3	6.5	3.1	4.0	4.7	5.8	2.6	7.0	7.0	1.5	1.4
2002												
January	3.9	4.4	6.2	3.1	4.2	5.0	6.0	2.9	7.0	7.0	1.5	1.6
February	3.9	4.4	6.6	3.1	4.2	4.8	5.8	2.8	7.1	7.1	1.6	1.5
March	3.6	4.0	5.9	2.8	3.9	4.6	5.8	2.7	6.8	6.7	1.4	1.4
April	3.9	4.4	6.9	2.9	4.0	4.7	5.6	2.9	7.0	7.0	1.6	1.6
May	3.9	4.4	6.5	3.1	4.1	4.9	6.6	2.8	6.7	6.7	1.4	1.4
June	3.8	4.2	6.3	2.9	4.1	4.8	5.5	2.4	6.9	6.7	1.5	1.5
July	4.1	4.6	7.3	3.1	4.1	4.8	6.9	2.8	7.6	7.1	1.6	1.5
August	3.8	4.2	5.6	3.0	4.1	5.0	5.7	2.7	6.8	6.6	1.4	1.4
September	3.8	4.3	6.6	2.9	4.1	4.9	6.0	2.6	6.6	6.7	1.5	1.4
October	3.7	4.2	6.6	3.0	4.0	4.7	5.8	2.7	6.0	6.2	1.6	1.6
November	3.8	4.2	6.1	2.9	4.1	4.8	6.1	2.6	6.6	6.5	1.6	1.6
December	3.9	4.5	6.7	3.0	4.0	4.7	6.5	2.8	6.7	6.7	1.4	1.4
2003												
January	3.8	4.3	6.7	3.0	4.0	4.7	5.7	2.9	6.9	6.8	1.6	1.5
February	3.8	4.3	6.0	3.0	4.1	5.3	5.7	2.6	6.8	6.7	1.5	1.4
March	3.6	3.9	6.1	2.7	3.9	4.7	5.1	2.7	6.6	6.4	1.6	1.5
April	3.7	4.1	6.1	3.0	3.5	4.2	5.9	2.4	6.7	6.6	1.5	1.5
May	3.6	4.1	6.4	2.6	3.8	4.5	5.1	2.8	6.9	6.7	1.5	1.4
June	3.7	4.2	6.3	2.8	4.0	4.6	5.5	2.9	6.5	6.5	1.4	1.4
July	3.6	4.1	6.1	3.0	3.9	4.3	5.3	2.8	6.2	6.2	1.5	1.4
August	3.7	4.1	6.7	2.6	3.8	4.4	5.4	2.8	6.6	6.4	1.5	1.5
September	3.7	4.1	6.6	2.6	3.8	4.4	5.1	2.8	6.6	6.5	1.5	1.5
October	3.8	4.3	6.0	2.7	4.4	5.1	5.4	2.7	6.6	6.6	1.4	1.3
November	3.6	4.1	6.5	2.7	4.0	4.6	5.1	2.7	6.7	6.5	1.5	1.4
December	3.8	4.3	6.1	2.7	4.2	4.9	5.3	2.6	7.0	7.1	1.5	1.5
2004												
January	3.7	4.1	6.3	2.7	4.1	4.9	5.5	2.7	6.7	6.7	1.9	1.7
February	3.7	4.1	6.6	2.7	4.1	4.9	4.5	2.8	6.7	6.5	1.5	1.4
March	3.8	4.2	6.6	2.8	4.2	4.9	5.7	2.7	6.9	6.9	1.5	1.5
April	3.8	4.3	5.9	2.7	4.3	5.1	5.5	2.6	6.7	6.6	1.3	1.4
May	3.6	4.1	5.9	2.6	4.1	4.7	5.2	2.6	6.7	6.8	1.4	1.3
June	3.8	4.2	6.6	2.7	4.0	4.4	5.6	2.6	6.7	6.7	1.5	1.5
July	3.8	4.2	5.8	2.7	4.3	5.1	5.3	2.6	7.0	6.9	1.8	1.8
August	3.8	4.3	5.8	2.8	4.2	4.9	5.6	2.7	7.1	7.0	1.3	1.4
September	3.8	4.2	5.9	2.9	4.0	4.7	5.3	2.8	7.0	6.5	1.5	1.6
October	3.8	4.2	6.1	2.7	4.3	5.0	4.9	2.4	7.1	7.0	1.5	1.5
November	3.9	4.4	6.3	2.8	4.5	5.3	5.6	2.8	6.8	6.8	1.5	1.5
December	3.9	4.4	6.1	2.7	4.4	5.4	5.9	2.7	6.7	6.6	1.6	1.5
2005												
January	4.0	4.5	7.3	2.8	4.4	5.0	5.9	2.8	7.5	7.4	1.5	1.5
February	3.9	4.3	6.4	2.5	4.2	5.0	5.9	2.9	6.5	6.5	1.5	1.5
March	3.9	4.4	5.9	2.7	4.4	5.6	6.0	3.0	6.8	6.8	1.5	1.5
April	3.8	4.3	5.9	2.7	4.1	4.9	5.8	2.9	6.0	6.1	1.5	1.5
May	3.9	4.4	6.4	2.6	4.4	5.1	5.8	2.7	6.8	6.7	1.4	1.4
June	3.8	4.3	5.9	2.7	4.3	5.0	5.8	2.7	7.1	7.0	1.5	1.4
July	3.7	4.2	5.5	2.8	4.2	5.1	5.8	2.6	6.9	7.0	1.4	1.3
August	3.9	4.4	6.5	2.8	4.3	5.2	6.0	2.8	6.8	7.0	1.5	1.5
September	4.1	4.6	6.6	3.0	4.4	5.3	5.7	2.8	7.7	7.4	1.5	1.5
October	3.8	4.2	6.3	2.7	4.2	4.9	5.1	2.7	7.0	7.1	1.5	1.6
November	3.7	4.1	5.7	2.7	4.1	4.5	4.7	2.7	7.1	7.2	1.5	1.5
December	3.8	4.2	6.0	2.5	4.3	4.8	5.1	2.8	6.9	6.9	1.6	1.5

[1]Total separations are the number of separations during the entire month.
[2]The total separations rate is the number of total separations during the entire month as a percent of total employment.
[4]Includes natural resources and mining, information, financial activities, and other services, not shown separately.
[5]Includes wholesale trade and transportation, warehousing, and utilities, not shown separately.
[6]Includes arts, entertainment, and recreation, not shown separately.
[7]Includes federal government, not shown separately.

Table 7-9. Separations Levels[1] and Rates,[2] by Industry, December 2000–September 2009—*Continued*

(Seasonally adjusted, levels in thousands, rates per 100.)

Year and month	Level[3]											
	Total[4]	Total private[4]	Construction	Manufacturing	Trade, transportation, and utilities[5]	Retail trade	Professional and business services	Education and health services	Leisure and hospitality[6]	Accommodation and food services	Government[7]	State and local government
2006												
January	4 735	4 449	423	367	1 070	776	883	425	910	787	309	260
February	5 228	4 885	412	379	1 146	812	921	453	962	847	340	288
March	5 117	4 751	453	419	1 095	794	864	459	926	792	352	292
April	5 121	4 757	428	364	1 141	836	886	494	825	732	346	291
May	5 610	5 238	492	429	1 198	851	1 093	573	908	762	377	308
June	5 333	4 941	417	398	1 167	837	932	510	909	781	371	312
July	5 349	5 041	450	428	1 148	796	965	544	885	754	359	293
August	5 143	4 764	404	408	1 148	771	922	487	879	757	344	276
September	5 276	4 910	408	387	1 104	776	1 010	458	873	757	357	279
October	5 285	4 945	438	387	1 099	756	996	506	896	774	331	289
November	5 399	5 046	481	398	1 107	770	1 006	489	981	841	350	293
December	5 223	4 884	429	405	1 050	762	959	508	956	815	338	290
2007												
January	4 986	4 682	408	398	1 064	745	939	489	925	783	325	277
February	5 221	4 863	428	425	1 067	741	973	487	920	787	364	289
March	5 280	4 919	381	408	1 114	757	964	499	922	780	361	276
April	5 275	4 905	417	396	1 077	739	964	482	935	800	348	275
May	5 295	4 908	414	415	1 112	784	944	510	905	777	384	297
June	5 177	4 825	407	412	1 088	736	839	518	927	798	341	271
July	5 273	4 837	440	402	1 040	711	948	485	920	790	458	366
August	5 230	4 853	433	424	1 057	744	941	504	905	789	346	276
September	5 147	4 820	417	418	1 062	747	925	458	869	738	323	240
October	5 156	4 840	401	405	1 088	754	955	484	902	763	305	267
November	5 128	4 803	411	407	1 083	732	945	520	906	747	320	277
December	4 984	4 652	410	363	1 055	740	850	477	918	784	334	294
2008												
January	4 920	4 625	418	371	1 050	725	918	515	894	758	307	260
February	5 088	4 789	410	372	1 060	731	924	534	932	788	293	258
March	5 020	4 717	443	363	1 035	722	936	529	878	747	294	268
April	5 152	4 825	461	393	1 090	741	924	506	884	763	300	277
May	4 933	4 641	428	360	973	672	908	502	916	766	296	268
June	4 963	4 674	451	369	1 031	692	928	495	823	714	295	269
July	4 847	4 588	425	332	1 058	728	891	508	841	712	299	273
August	4 888	4 587	436	348	1 031	699	871	505	857	708	290	268
September	4 852	4 553	412	371	1 046	684	809	488	830	714	294	280
October	4 910	4 607	440	404	1 034	680	906	507	794	670	294	265
November	4 863	4 571	472	384	1 030	680	909	466	773	673	282	258
December	4 958	4 673	452	419	1 041	664	898	498	755	647	278	251
2009												
January	4 949	4 686	524	476	1 049	645	866	494	763	650	277	267
February	4 833	4 555	463	424	920	590	951	498	731	635	271	251
March	4 712	4 434	463	401	1 001	646	778	466	751	649	265	251
April	4 641	4 362	437	390	982	678	839	462	716	612	255	243
May	4 356	4 066	411	367	951	601	771	419	684	596	288	250
June	4 306	3 939	355	352	816	549	698	489	696	594	340	272
July	4 430	4 147	444	329	874	578	738	500	713	594	298	274
August	4 284	3 976	342	313	850	567	728	509	704	593	293	271
September[8]	4 311	4 017	421	316	864	548	701	513	685	583	283	263

[1]Total separations are the number of separations during the entire month.
[2]The total separations rate is the number of total separations during the entire month as a percent of total employment.
[3]Detail will not necessarily add to totals because of the independent seasonal adjustment of the various series.
[4]Includes natural resources and mining, information, financial activities, and other services, not shown separately.
[5]Includes wholesale trade and transportation, warehousing, and utilities, not shown separately.
[6]Includes arts, entertainment, and recreation, not shown separately.
[7]Includes federal government, not shown separately.
[8]Preliminary.

Table 7-9. Separations Levels[1] and Rates,[2] by Industry, December 2000–September 2009—*Continued*

(Seasonally adjusted, levels in thousands, rates per 100.)

Year and month	Rate											
	Total[4]	Total private[4]	Construction	Manufacturing	Trade, transportation, and utilities[5]	Retail trade	Professional and business services	Education and health services	Leisure and hospitality[6]	Accommodation and food services	Government[7]	State and local government
2006												
January	3.5	3.9	5.6	2.6	4.1	5.1	5.1	2.4	7.0	7.1	1.4	1.4
February	3.9	4.3	5.4	2.7	4.4	5.3	5.3	2.6	7.4	7.6	1.6	1.5
March	3.8	4.2	5.9	2.9	4.2	5.2	5.0	2.6	7.1	7.1	1.6	1.5
April	3.8	4.2	5.5	2.6	4.4	5.4	5.1	2.8	6.3	6.6	1.6	1.5
May	4.1	4.6	6.4	3.0	4.6	5.6	6.2	3.2	7.0	6.8	1.7	1.6
June	3.9	4.3	5.4	2.8	4.4	5.5	5.3	2.9	7.0	7.0	1.7	1.6
July	3.9	4.4	5.8	3.0	4.4	5.2	5.5	3.1	6.7	6.7	1.6	1.5
August	3.8	4.2	5.2	2.9	4.4	5.0	5.2	2.7	6.7	6.8	1.6	1.4
September	3.9	4.3	5.3	2.7	4.2	5.1	5.7	2.6	6.6	6.7	1.6	1.4
October	3.9	4.3	5.7	2.7	4.2	4.9	5.6	2.8	6.8	6.9	1.5	1.5
November	3.9	4.4	6.3	2.8	4.2	5.0	5.7	2.7	7.4	7.4	1.6	1.5
December	3.8	4.2	5.6	2.9	4.0	5.0	5.4	2.8	7.2	7.2	1.5	1.5
2007												
January	3.6	4.1	5.3	2.8	4.0	4.8	5.3	2.7	6.9	6.9	1.5	1.4
February	3.8	4.2	5.6	3.0	4.0	4.8	5.4	2.7	6.9	6.9	1.6	1.5
March	3.8	4.3	4.9	2.9	4.2	4.9	5.4	2.7	6.9	6.8	1.6	1.4
April	3.8	4.3	5.4	2.8	4.0	4.8	5.4	2.6	7.0	7.0	1.6	1.4
May	3.8	4.3	5.4	3.0	4.2	5.0	5.3	2.8	6.7	6.8	1.7	1.5
June	3.8	4.2	5.3	3.0	4.1	4.7	4.7	2.8	6.9	7.0	1.5	1.4
July	3.8	4.2	5.8	2.9	3.9	4.6	5.3	2.6	6.9	6.9	2.1	1.9
August	3.8	4.2	5.7	3.1	4.0	4.8	5.2	2.7	6.7	6.9	1.6	1.4
September	3.7	4.2	5.5	3.0	4.0	4.8	5.2	2.5	6.5	6.4	1.4	1.2
October	3.7	4.2	5.3	2.9	4.1	4.9	5.3	2.6	6.7	6.6	1.4	1.4
November	3.7	4.2	5.4	3.0	4.0	4.7	5.2	2.8	6.7	6.5	1.4	1.4
December	3.6	4.0	5.4	2.6	3.9	4.8	4.7	2.6	6.8	6.8	1.5	1.5
2008												
January	3.6	4.0	5.6	2.7	3.9	4.7	5.1	2.8	6.6	6.6	1.4	1.3
February	3.7	4.1	5.5	2.7	4.0	4.7	5.1	2.9	6.9	6.8	1.3	1.3
March	3.6	4.1	6.0	2.7	3.9	4.7	5.2	2.8	6.5	6.5	1.3	1.4
April	3.7	4.2	6.3	2.9	4.1	4.8	5.1	2.7	6.5	6.6	1.3	1.4
May	3.6	4.0	5.9	2.7	3.7	4.4	5.1	2.7	6.8	6.7	1.3	1.4
June	3.6	4.1	6.2	2.7	3.9	4.5	5.2	2.6	6.1	6.2	1.3	1.4
July	3.5	4.0	5.9	2.5	4.0	4.7	5.0	2.7	6.2	6.2	1.3	1.4
August	3.6	4.0	6.1	2.6	3.9	4.6	4.9	2.7	6.4	6.2	1.3	1.4
September	3.5	4.0	5.8	2.8	4.0	4.5	4.6	2.6	6.2	6.2	1.3	1.4
October	3.6	4.0	6.2	3.1	4.0	4.5	5.1	2.7	5.9	5.9	1.3	1.3
November	3.6	4.0	6.8	2.9	4.0	4.5	5.2	2.4	5.8	5.9	1.3	1.3
December	3.7	4.1	6.6	3.2	4.0	4.4	5.2	2.6	5.7	5.7	1.2	1.3
2009												
January	3.7	4.2	7.8	3.8	4.1	4.3	5.0	2.6	5.7	5.7	1.2	1.3
February	3.6	4.1	7.0	3.4	3.6	3.9	5.6	2.6	5.5	5.6	1.2	1.3
March	3.5	4.0	7.2	3.3	3.9	4.3	4.6	2.4	5.7	5.8	1.2	1.3
April	3.5	4.0	6.9	3.2	3.9	4.6	5.0	2.4	5.4	5.4	1.1	1.2
May	3.3	3.7	6.5	3.1	3.8	4.1	4.6	2.2	5.2	5.3	1.3	1.3
June	3.3	3.6	5.7	3.0	3.2	3.7	4.2	2.5	5.3	5.3	1.5	1.4
July	3.4	3.8	7.2	2.8	3.5	3.9	4.4	2.6	5.4	5.3	1.3	1.4
August	3.3	3.7	5.6	2.7	3.4	3.8	4.4	2.6	5.3	5.3	1.3	1.4
September[8]	3.3	3.7	7.0	2.7	3.4	3.7	4.2	2.7	5.2	5.2	1.3	1.3

[1]Total separations are the number of separations during the entire month.
[2]The total separations rate is the number of total separations during the entire month as a percent of total employment.
[4]Includes natural resources and mining, information, financial activities, and other services, not shown separately.
[5]Includes wholesale trade and transportation, warehousing, and utilities, not shown separately.
[6]Includes arts, entertainment, and recreation, not shown separately.
[7]Includes federal government, not shown separately.
[8]Preliminary.

Table 7-10. Quits Levels[1] and Rates,[2] by Industry, December 2000–September 2009

(Seasonally adjusted, levels in thousands, rates per 100.)

Year and month	Level[3]											
	Total[4]	Total private[4]	Construction	Manufacturing	Trade, transportation, and utilities[5]	Retail trade	Professional and business services	Education and health services	Leisure and hospitality[6]	Accommodation and food services	Government[7]	State and local government
2000												
December	3 192	2 952	119	336	705	568	409	328	670	637	230	214
2001												
January	3 409	3 230	157	288	740	487	708	277	675	640	195	165
February	3 303	3 121	160	251	794	580	552	341	615	553	181	164
March	3 158	2 972	175	243	712	513	539	337	611	560	183	168
April	3 196	3 026	205	230	780	584	537	326	618	549	169	152
May	3 136	2 947	158	200	777	549	553	316	631	557	189	167
June	2 961	2 817	177	200	753	554	480	323	597	534	139	125
July	3 004	2 837	181	177	722	539	528	280	593	534	169	149
August	2 917	2 741	146	194	654	480	497	273	604	532	174	156
September	2 857	2 699	141	176	675	489	462	306	620	575	156	140
October	2 890	2 727	147	199	680	522	520	286	580	513	159	137
November	2 712	2 556	165	172	610	463	486	280	492	433	167	145
December	2 762	2 581	149	167	654	490	443	285	504	444	172	146
2002												
January	3 017	2 872	168	180	737	517	557	280	606	547	161	144
February	2 661	2 492	155	195	531	406	480	273	544	471	170	150
March	2 622	2 467	142	188	577	440	480	235	566	499	153	131
April	2 716	2 538	167	197	587	403	472	279	556	494	188	167
May	2 717	2 569	145	202	545	394	561	284	525	452	150	130
June	2 665	2 495	136	196	651	499	456	242	528	464	157	132
July	2 715	2 572	161	205	586	419	494	292	532	476	145	123
August	2 670	2 516	150	205	571	422	483	283	509	454	153	131
September	2 640	2 483	177	195	552	413	491	252	507	460	155	132
October	2 530	2 374	160	174	548	388	475	281	491	444	159	133
November	2 571	2 398	133	171	571	449	491	273	463	427	188	157
December	2 724	2 575	150	161	548	421	513	304	495	444	142	119
2003												
January	2 545	2 397	143	184	529	376	446	292	486	445	156	130
February	2 554	2 408	151	173	544	435	431	274	528	473	145	122
March	2 436	2 286	136	157	548	396	423	253	474	428	147	122
April	2 386	2 243	82	161	509	383	424	247	493	452	146	120
May	2 358	2 211	159	176	530	401	336	258	458	424	146	124
June	2 396	2 257	160	165	502	378	413	265	507	458	133	116
July	2 357	2 205	137	182	515	369	366	243	507	458	151	130
August	2 383	2 235	167	173	522	387	351	271	486	432	145	123
September	2 468	2 314	142	170	551	416	377	307	474	427	151	133
October	2 520	2 373	137	178	575	425	375	281	544	490	148	131
November	2 457	2 327	167	187	535	368	352	263	494	438	137	117
December	2 521	2 372	188	206	534	370	377	278	458	418	147	130
2004												
January	2 523	2 347	144	187	572	434	355	289	478	441	178	148
February	2 497	2 342	169	190	520	398	363	269	512	479	157	130
March	2 659	2 504	169	205	566	423	444	280	553	509	152	133
April	2 654	2 503	169	209	614	491	377	288	505	451	149	138
May	2 514	2 368	167	173	554	405	343	274	547	499	146	125
June	2 700	2 537	203	200	576	421	437	266	513	472	157	143
July	2 694	2 522	111	194	622	452	431	305	504	456	169	153
August	2 618	2 485	148	173	604	467	449	276	532	488	138	125
September	2 660	2 519	175	204	609	452	441	268	511	469	140	129
October	2 673	2 528	163	192	604	449	436	264	519	475	145	128
November	2 874	2 730	181	213	669	492	479	295	578	521	148	132
December	2 845	2 689	156	204	587	426	492	279	566	514	156	143
2005												
January	3 055	2 907	201	193	705	488	519	304	609	553	152	139
February	2 729	2 586	173	189	567	430	486	300	520	469	142	132
March	2 847	2 689	195	190	658	491	486	328	525	465	155	144
April	2 816	2 655	159	188	613	475	512	323	535	479	158	137
May	2 830	2 683	178	178	659	518	476	283	570	513	147	133
June	2 850	2 694	170	205	674	502	456	308	558	498	155	138
July	2 825	2 694	183	196	644	479	435	299	597	537	131	114
August	2 982	2 837	204	199	687	503	479	311	608	564	154	140
September	3 129	2 968	242	220	649	474	522	323	643	602	160	143
October	2 969	2 792	235	219	640	478	398	305	673	608	182	163
November	2 941	2 780	194	198	649	477	396	319	641	591	166	146
December	2 883	2 728	223	168	697	524	412	296	574	524	153	132

[1]Quits are the number of quits during the entire month.
[2]The quits rate is the number of quits during the entire month as a percent of total employment.
[3]Detail will not necessarily add to totals because of the independent seasonal adjustment of the various series.
[4]Includes natural resources and mining, information, financial activities, and other services, not shown separately.
[5]Includes wholesale trade and transportation, warehousing, and utilities, not shown separately.
[6]Includes arts, entertainment, and recreation, not shown separately.
[7]Includes federal government, not shown separately.

Table 7-10. Quits Levels[1] and Rates,[2] by Industry, December 2000–September 2009—*Continued*

(Seasonally adjusted, levels in thousands, rates per 100.)

Year and month	Rate											
	Total[4]	Total private[4]	Construc-tion	Manufac-turing	Trade, transpor-tation, and utilities[5]	Retail trade	Profes-sional and business services	Education and health services	Leisure and hospitality[6]	Accommo-dation and food services	Govern-ment[7]	State and local govern-ment
2000												
December	2.4	2.6	1.8	2.0	2.7	3.7	2.4	2.1	5.6	6.3	1.1	1.2
2001												
January	2.6	2.9	2.3	1.7	2.8	3.2	4.2	1.8	5.6	6.3	0.9	0.9
February	2.5	2.8	2.3	1.5	3.0	3.8	3.3	2.2	5.1	5.4	0.9	0.9
March	2.4	2.7	2.6	1.4	2.7	3.3	3.2	2.2	5.1	5.5	0.9	0.9
April	2.4	2.7	3.0	1.4	3.0	3.8	3.2	2.1	5.1	5.4	0.8	0.8
May	2.4	2.7	2.3	1.2	3.0	3.6	3.3	2.0	5.2	5.4	0.9	0.9
June	2.2	2.5	2.6	1.2	2.9	3.6	2.9	2.1	4.9	5.2	0.7	0.7
July	2.3	2.6	2.6	1.1	2.8	3.5	3.2	1.8	4.9	5.2	0.8	0.8
August	2.2	2.5	2.1	1.2	2.5	3.2	3.0	1.7	5.0	5.2	0.8	0.8
September	2.2	2.4	2.1	1.1	2.6	3.2	2.8	1.9	5.1	5.6	0.7	0.8
October	2.2	2.5	2.2	1.2	2.6	3.4	3.2	1.8	4.8	5.0	0.7	0.7
November	2.1	2.3	2.4	1.1	2.4	3.1	3.0	1.8	4.1	4.3	0.8	0.8
December	2.1	2.4	2.2	1.1	2.6	3.2	2.8	1.8	4.2	4.4	0.8	0.8
2002												
January	2.3	2.6	2.5	1.2	2.9	3.4	3.5	1.8	5.0	5.4	0.8	0.8
February	2.0	2.3	2.3	1.3	2.1	2.7	3.0	1.7	4.5	4.6	0.8	0.8
March	2.0	2.3	2.1	1.2	2.3	2.9	3.0	1.5	4.7	4.9	0.7	0.7
April	2.1	2.3	2.5	1.3	2.3	2.7	2.9	1.7	4.7	4.9	0.9	0.9
May	2.1	2.4	2.2	1.3	2.1	2.6	3.5	1.8	4.4	4.4	0.7	0.7
June	2.0	2.3	2.0	1.3	2.6	3.3	2.8	1.5	4.4	4.6	0.7	0.7
July	2.1	2.4	2.4	1.3	2.3	2.8	3.1	1.8	4.5	4.7	0.7	0.7
August	2.0	2.3	2.2	1.4	2.2	2.8	3.0	1.7	4.3	4.5	0.7	0.7
September	2.0	2.3	2.6	1.3	2.2	2.8	3.1	1.5	4.2	4.5	0.7	0.7
October	1.9	2.2	2.4	1.2	2.2	2.6	3.0	1.7	4.1	4.3	0.7	0.7
November	2.0	2.2	2.0	1.1	2.2	3.0	3.1	1.7	3.8	4.1	0.9	0.8
December	2.1	2.4	2.2	1.1	2.2	2.8	3.2	1.9	4.1	4.3	0.7	0.6
2003												
January	2.0	2.2	2.1	1.2	2.1	2.5	2.8	1.8	4.0	4.3	0.7	0.7
February	2.0	2.2	2.3	1.2	2.1	2.9	2.7	1.7	4.3	4.6	0.7	0.6
March	1.9	2.1	2.1	1.1	2.2	2.7	2.7	1.5	3.9	4.2	0.7	0.6
April	1.8	2.1	1.2	1.1	2.0	2.6	2.7	1.5	4.1	4.4	0.7	0.6
May	1.8	2.0	2.4	1.2	2.1	2.7	2.1	1.6	3.8	4.1	0.7	0.7
June	1.8	2.1	2.4	1.1	2.0	2.5	2.6	1.6	4.2	4.4	0.6	0.6
July	1.8	2.0	2.0	1.3	2.0	2.5	2.3	1.5	4.2	4.4	0.7	0.7
August	1.8	2.1	2.5	1.2	2.1	2.6	2.2	1.6	4.0	4.2	0.7	0.7
September	1.9	2.1	2.1	1.2	2.2	2.8	2.4	1.8	3.9	4.1	0.7	0.7
October	1.9	2.2	2.0	1.2	2.3	2.8	2.3	1.7	4.4	4.7	0.7	0.7
November	1.9	2.1	2.5	1.3	2.1	2.5	2.2	1.6	4.0	4.2	0.6	0.6
December	1.9	2.2	2.8	1.4	2.1	2.5	2.3	1.7	3.7	4.0	0.7	0.7
2004												
January	1.9	2.2	2.1	1.3	2.3	2.9	2.2	1.7	3.9	4.2	0.8	0.8
February	1.9	2.2	2.5	1.3	2.1	2.7	2.2	1.6	4.1	4.5	0.7	0.7
March	2.0	2.3	2.5	1.4	2.2	2.8	2.7	1.7	4.4	4.8	0.7	0.7
April	2.0	2.3	2.4	1.5	2.4	3.3	2.3	1.7	4.1	4.3	0.7	0.7
May	1.9	2.2	2.4	1.2	2.2	2.7	2.1	1.6	4.4	4.7	0.7	0.7
June	2.1	2.3	2.9	1.4	2.3	2.8	2.7	1.6	4.1	4.4	0.7	0.8
July	2.0	2.3	1.6	1.4	2.4	3.0	2.6	1.8	4.0	4.3	0.8	0.8
August	2.0	2.3	2.1	1.2	2.4	3.1	2.7	1.6	4.3	4.6	0.6	0.7
September	2.0	2.3	2.5	1.4	2.4	3.0	2.7	1.6	4.1	4.4	0.6	0.7
October	2.0	2.3	2.3	1.3	2.4	3.0	2.6	1.5	4.1	4.4	0.7	0.7
November	2.2	2.5	2.6	1.5	2.6	3.3	2.9	1.7	4.6	4.8	0.7	0.7
December	2.2	2.4	2.2	1.4	2.3	2.8	3.0	1.6	4.5	4.8	0.7	0.8
2005												
January	2.3	2.6	2.8	1.4	2.7	3.2	3.1	1.8	4.8	5.1	0.7	0.7
February	2.1	2.3	2.4	1.3	2.2	2.8	2.9	1.7	4.1	4.3	0.7	0.7
March	2.1	2.4	2.7	1.3	2.5	3.2	2.9	1.9	4.1	4.3	0.7	0.8
April	2.1	2.4	2.2	1.3	2.4	3.1	3.1	1.9	4.2	4.4	0.7	0.7
May	2.1	2.4	2.4	1.2	2.5	3.4	2.8	1.6	4.5	4.7	0.7	0.7
June	2.1	2.4	2.3	1.4	2.6	3.3	2.7	1.8	4.3	4.5	0.7	0.7
July	2.1	2.4	2.5	1.4	2.5	3.1	2.6	1.7	4.6	4.9	0.6	0.6
August	2.2	2.5	2.8	1.4	2.6	3.3	2.8	1.8	4.7	5.1	0.7	0.7
September	2.3	2.6	3.3	1.6	2.5	3.1	3.1	1.8	5.0	5.5	0.7	0.7
October	2.2	2.5	3.1	1.5	2.5	3.1	2.3	1.7	5.2	5.6	0.8	0.9
November	2.2	2.5	2.6	1.4	2.5	3.1	2.3	1.8	5.0	5.4	0.8	0.8
December	2.1	2.4	3.0	1.2	2.7	3.4	2.4	1.7	4.4	4.8	0.7	0.7

[1]Quits are the number of quits during the entire month.
[2]The quits rate is the number of quits during the entire month as a percent of total employment.
[4]Includes natural resources and mining, information, financial activities, and other services, not shown separately.
[5]Includes wholesale trade and transportation, warehousing, and utilities, not shown separately.
[6]Includes arts, entertainment, and recreation, not shown separately.
[7]Includes federal government, not shown separately.

Table 7-10. Quits Levels[1] and Rates,[2] by Industry, December 2000–September 2009—*Continued*

(Seasonally adjusted, levels in thousands, rates per 100.)

Year and month	Level[3]											
	Total[4]	Total private[4]	Construction	Manufacturing	Trade, transportation, and utilities[5]	Retail trade	Professional and business services	Education and health services	Leisure and hospitality[6]	Accommodation and food services	Government[7]	State and local government
2006												
January	2 913	2 768	206	198	657	487	429	267	664	593	145	123
February	3 059	2 885	196	203	693	521	460	307	660	608	174	152
March	3 047	2 876	201	202	699	526	491	295	649	589	168	143
April	2 803	2 631	209	191	691	518	471	297	534	483	171	145
May	3 067	2 879	205	225	699	515	488	334	620	571	183	157
June	3 105	2 917	211	197	657	482	499	340	689	629	184	151
July	3 052	2 877	186	227	680	511	478	333	594	552	174	147
August	3 035	2 855	166	212	713	486	485	333	609	564	186	155
September	3 018	2 842	161	184	671	497	555	303	609	574	173	137
October	2 987	2 822	172	208	635	468	542	334	592	543	168	145
November	3 161	2 990	165	232	719	519	549	321	636	575	171	145
December	3 166	2 990	162	239	662	487	563	345	667	614	173	150
2007												
January	3 060	2 891	166	228	649	465	542	295	629	583	165	143
February	3 050	2 884	150	218	677	491	528	330	638	582	164	139
March	3 068	2 887	161	223	672	473	507	318	634	581	182	152
April	2 927	2 759	152	215	651	478	493	310	644	596	166	143
May	3 047	2 863	163	219	703	510	477	340	606	559	179	150
June	2 836	2 667	129	213	665	479	427	306	639	587	166	141
July	2 943	2 755	187	195	592	425	505	319	645	590	187	157
August	2 955	2 811	176	221	608	450	476	324	645	582	157	133
September	2 649	2 484	145	190	610	442	463	273	478	432	162	135
October	2 871	2 714	156	200	618	454	495	297	626	571	159	143
November	2 811	2 646	159	180	563	402	478	328	629	577	165	151
December	2 877	2 725	158	197	658	494	403	299	647	582	148	134
2008												
January	2 926	2 770	151	206	643	474	443	319	598	531	151	134
February	2 871	2 717	175	194	608	427	485	312	614	556	151	136
March	2 731	2 595	142	190	588	418	456	322	596	552	132	124
April	2 820	2 668	161	187	595	416	464	321	625	576	150	142
May	2 650	2 510	142	165	570	395	481	268	617	560	138	129
June	2 682	2 548	153	166	571	400	487	299	585	532	138	130
July	2 550	2 415	152	147	556	397	473	295	565	510	135	127
August	2 453	2 322	151	146	541	397	361	285	529	487	139	131
September	2 454	2 319	128	147	580	414	368	290	514	467	134	133
October	2 436	2 305	107	143	548	377	477	294	516	476	132	122
November	2 201	2 076	109	122	489	352	349	251	469	437	122	117
December	2 114	1 984	92	87	518	379	297	256	461	435	130	121
2009												
January	2 063	1 945	85	105	469	360	326	248	443	412	105	100
February	1 911	1 831	87	105	372	323	310	258	431	399	115	110
March	1 856	1 749	102	81	444	344	278	249	433	402	107	106
April	1 777	1 678	74	80	385	271	272	228	430	392	99	96
May	1 788	1 682	84	86	398	296	281	249	396	351	107	97
June	1 787	1 680	70	93	391	299	257	264	429	378	111	99
July	1 778	1 673	68	82	415	295	265	235	411	372	107	101
August	1 779	1 680	67	85	407	309	269	249	413	374	106	97
September[8]	1 805	1 709	91	91	435	336	271	268	363	351	100	96

[1]Quits are the number of quits during the entire month.
[2]The quits rate is the number of quits during the entire month as a percent of total employment.
[3]Detail will not necessarily add to totals because of the independent seasonal adjustment of the various series.
[4]Includes natural resources and mining, information, financial activities, and other services, not shown separately.
[5]Includes wholesale trade and transportation, warehousing, and utilities, not shown separately.
[6]Includes arts, entertainment, and recreation, not shown separately.
[7]Includes federal government, not shown separately.
[8]Preliminary.

Table 7-10. Quits Levels[1] and Rates,[2] by Industry, December 2000–September 2009—*Continued*

(Seasonally adjusted, levels in thousands, rates per 100.)

Year and month	Rate											
	Total[4]	Total private[4]	Construction	Manufacturing	Trade, transportation, and utilities[5]	Retail trade	Professional and business services	Education and health services	Leisure and hospitality[6]	Accommodation and food services	Government[7]	State and local government
2006												
January	2.2	2.4	2.7	1.4	2.5	3.2	2.5	1.5	5.1	5.4	0.7	0.6
February	2.3	2.5	2.6	1.4	2.6	3.4	2.7	1.7	5.1	5.5	0.8	0.8
March	2.2	2.5	2.6	1.4	2.7	3.4	2.8	1.7	5.0	5.3	0.8	0.7
April	2.1	2.3	2.7	1.3	2.6	3.4	2.7	1.7	4.1	4.3	0.8	0.8
May	2.3	2.5	2.7	1.6	2.7	3.4	2.8	1.9	4.8	5.1	0.8	0.8
June	2.3	2.6	2.7	1.4	2.5	3.1	2.8	1.9	5.3	5.7	0.8	0.8
July	2.2	2.5	2.4	1.6	2.6	3.3	2.7	1.9	4.5	4.9	0.8	0.8
August	2.2	2.5	2.1	1.5	2.7	3.2	2.7	1.9	4.6	5.0	0.8	0.8
September	2.2	2.5	2.1	1.3	2.6	3.2	3.1	1.7	4.6	5.1	0.8	0.7
October	2.2	2.5	2.2	1.5	2.4	3.0	3.1	1.9	4.5	4.8	0.8	0.7
November	2.3	2.6	2.1	1.7	2.7	3.4	3.1	1.8	4.8	5.1	0.8	0.8
December	2.3	2.6	2.1	1.7	2.5	3.2	3.2	1.9	5.0	5.4	0.8	0.8
2007												
January	2.2	2.5	2.2	1.6	2.4	3.0	3.0	1.6	4.7	5.1	0.7	0.7
February	2.2	2.5	2.0	1.6	2.5	3.2	3.0	1.8	4.8	5.1	0.7	0.7
March	2.2	2.5	2.1	1.6	2.5	3.0	2.8	1.8	4.7	5.1	0.8	0.8
April	2.1	2.4	2.0	1.5	2.4	3.1	2.8	1.7	4.8	5.2	0.7	0.7
May	2.2	2.5	2.1	1.6	2.6	3.3	2.7	1.9	4.5	4.9	0.8	0.8
June	2.1	2.3	1.7	1.5	2.5	3.1	2.4	1.7	4.8	5.1	0.7	0.7
July	2.1	2.4	2.4	1.4	2.2	2.7	2.8	1.7	4.8	5.1	0.8	0.8
August	2.1	2.4	2.3	1.6	2.3	2.9	2.7	1.8	4.8	5.1	0.7	0.7
September	1.9	2.2	1.9	1.4	2.3	2.9	2.6	1.5	3.5	3.8	0.7	0.7
October	2.1	2.3	2.1	1.5	2.3	2.9	2.7	1.6	4.6	5.0	0.7	0.7
November	2.0	2.3	2.1	1.3	2.1	2.6	2.7	1.8	4.6	5.0	0.7	0.8
December	2.1	2.4	2.1	1.4	2.5	3.2	2.2	1.6	4.8	5.0	0.7	0.7
2008												
January	2.1	2.4	2.0	1.5	2.4	3.0	2.5	1.7	4.4	4.6	0.7	0.7
February	2.1	2.4	2.3	1.4	2.3	2.8	2.7	1.7	4.5	4.8	0.7	0.7
March	2.0	2.2	1.9	1.4	2.2	2.7	2.5	1.7	4.4	4.8	0.6	0.6
April	2.0	2.3	2.2	1.4	2.2	2.7	2.6	1.7	4.6	5.0	0.7	0.7
May	1.9	2.2	2.0	1.2	2.1	2.6	2.7	1.4	4.6	4.9	0.6	0.7
June	2.0	2.2	2.1	1.2	2.2	2.6	2.7	1.6	4.3	4.6	0.6	0.7
July	1.9	2.1	2.1	1.1	2.1	2.6	2.7	1.6	4.2	4.4	0.6	0.6
August	1.8	2.0	2.1	1.1	2.1	2.6	2.0	1.5	3.9	4.2	0.6	0.7
September	1.8	2.0	1.8	1.1	2.2	2.7	2.1	1.5	3.8	4.1	0.6	0.7
October	1.8	2.0	1.5	1.1	2.1	2.5	2.7	1.5	3.8	4.2	0.6	0.6
November	1.6	1.8	1.6	0.9	1.9	2.3	2.0	1.3	3.5	3.8	0.5	0.6
December	1.6	1.8	1.3	0.7	2.0	2.5	1.7	1.3	3.5	3.8	0.6	0.6
2009												
January	1.5	1.7	1.3	0.8	1.8	2.4	1.9	1.3	3.3	3.6	0.5	0.5
February	1.4	1.6	1.3	0.8	1.5	2.2	1.8	1.3	3.3	3.5	0.5	0.6
March	1.4	1.6	1.6	0.7	1.7	2.3	1.6	1.3	3.3	3.6	0.5	0.5
April	1.3	1.5	1.2	0.7	1.5	1.8	1.6	1.2	3.3	3.5	0.4	0.5
May	1.4	1.5	1.3	0.7	1.6	2.0	1.7	1.3	3.0	3.1	0.5	0.5
June	1.4	1.5	1.1	0.8	1.5	2.0	1.5	1.4	3.3	3.4	0.5	0.5
July	1.4	1.5	1.1	0.7	1.6	2.0	1.6	1.2	3.1	3.3	0.5	0.5
August	1.4	1.5	1.1	0.7	1.6	2.1	1.6	1.3	3.1	3.3	0.5	0.5
September[8]	1.4	1.6	1.5	0.8	1.7	2.3	1.6	1.4	2.8	3.1	0.4	0.5

[1]Quits are the number of quits during the entire month.
[2]The quits rate is the number of quits during the entire month as a percent of total employment.
[4]Includes natural resources and mining, information, financial activities, and other services, not shown separately.
[5]Includes wholesale trade and transportation, warehousing, and utilities, not shown separately.
[6]Includes arts, entertainment, and recreation, not shown separately.
[7]Includes federal government, not shown separately.
[8]Preliminary.

Table 7-11. Layoffs and Discharges Levels[1] and Rates,[2] by Industry, December 2000–September 2009

(Not seasonally adjusted, levels in thousands, rates per 100.)

Year and month	Level												
	Total	Total private	Mining and logging	Construc-tion	Manufac-turing	Durable goods	Non-durable goods	Trade, transpor-tation, and utilities	Whole-sale trade	Retail trade	Transpor-tation, ware-housing, and utilities	Infor-mation	Financial activities
2001	24 351	23 206	106	3 193	3 309	1 993	1 319	4 557	854	2 986	717	572	838
2002	23 325	22 123	106	3 118	2 689	1 653	1 038	4 537	810	2 992	735	537	951
2003	23 959	22 665	107	3 143	2 328	1 414	914	4 783	835	3 142	806	426	772
2004	23 387	22 012	82	2 944	1 997	1 215	781	4 807	789	3 072	947	390	787
2005	22 766	21 468	78	2 925	1 842	1 150	691	4 639	762	2 919	958	273	861
2006	21 433	20 069	74	2 623	1 814	1 019	796	4 181	646	2 853	682	257	869
2007	22 539	21 176	91	2 848	1 963	1 205	757	4 284	821	2 753	707	315	1 107
2008	24 370	23 146	117	3 347	2 217	1 413	801	4 691	973	2 907	811	365	1 100
2000													
December	2 135	2 054	23	362	209	110	99	444	91	316	37	23	30
2001													
January	3 185	3 084	11	372	379	254	125	926	135	685	107	86	191
February	1 411	1 361	4	272	201	120	81	233	64	150	19	37	45
March	1 886	1 843	7	248	234	132	103	330	36	264	30	21	51
April	1 872	1 812	5	165	322	211	112	301	73	175	54	61	64
May	1 587	1 495	5	202	255	147	108	312	46	211	54	38	38
June	1 780	1 621	9	205	287	153	134	302	43	206	53	45	38
July	1 949	1 856	9	191	298	166	132	372	100	222	49	43	54
August	1 859	1 658	8	231	224	140	84	267	51	173	43	41	41
September	2 171	2 064	7	261	223	127	96	349	63	227	59	39	83
October	2 482	2 355	11	329	350	231	119	390	108	221	61	63	99
November	2 097	2 048	13	359	258	157	101	365	71	195	99	62	70
December	2 072	2 009	17	358	278	155	124	410	64	257	89	36	64
2002													
January	2 920	2 804	11	347	400	247	153	686	85	505	97	131	194
February	1 596	1 549	6	255	195	107	88	398	69	263	66	23	53
March	1 428	1 386	11	200	189	132	57	276	59	162	55	32	41
April	1 860	1 796	13	213	243	151	92	339	57	225	57	59	63
May	1 593	1 502	8	214	182	107	75	366	81	249	36	32	70
June	1 722	1 569	5	223	196	116	80	257	47	153	57	38	84
July	2 209	2 060	15	287	216	128	88	334	90	199	45	39	77
August	1 872	1 723	8	209	189	133	56	319	51	210	58	37	78
September	1 978	1 810	6	244	188	119	69	353	63	229	61	25	71
October	2 098	2 011	7	326	249	161	89	368	50	270	48	42	92
November	1 837	1 764	6	276	193	116	78	335	86	195	53	49	65
December	2 212	2 149	10	324	249	136	113	506	72	332	102	30	63
2003													
January	3 132	3 014	18	404	352	217	135	757	102	575	81	94	156
February	1 572	1 519	9	220	179	109	70	352	44	275	33	32	41
March	1 474	1 417	8	216	184	111	73	283	45	192	46	36	61
April	1 931	1 853	8	265	261	144	117	296	65	182	49	25	45
May	1 595	1 498	5	197	136	78	57	313	95	171	47	25	47
June	1 905	1 755	8	184	196	122	74	362	48	233	81	41	47
July	2 021	1 887	8	226	223	123	100	372	95	199	78	32	106
August	2 076	1 898	12	289	149	106	44	359	62	202	95	25	44
September	1 979	1 820	3	285	148	93	56	290	91	155	44	16	68
October	2 214	2 126	7	310	186	103	83	446	91	284	71	32	60
November	1 798	1 702	5	274	152	107	44	353	41	258	54	33	41
December	2 262	2 176	16	273	162	101	61	600	56	416	127	35	56
2004													
January	3 028	2 879	12	363	266	152	114	769	98	543	128	63	110
February	1 511	1 466	10	245	136	79	57	399	65	283	51	29	33
March	1 565	1 514	5	221	150	94	56	303	55	179	69	39	56
April	1 855	1 797	6	191	167	90	77	348	95	201	52	29	51
May	1 497	1 413	5	170	131	65	66	353	61	202	90	35	35
June	1 733	1 575	4	189	133	89	44	290	55	166	69	40	55
July	1 940	1 759	6	246	167	102	65	368	69	230	69	24	55
August	2 085	1 938	7	249	192	131	60	324	73	170	82	20	98
September	2 014	1 812	4	195	152	99	53	302	50	188	64	38	68
October	2 058	1 950	7	277	192	115	77	349	67	214	69	35	91
November	1 846	1 756	8	279	156	103	53	377	60	237	80	17	66
December	2 255	2 153	8	319	155	96	59	625	41	459	124	21	69
2005													
January	3 023	2 914	12	459	270	176	93	713	95	503	114	57	173
February	1 559	1 507	6	250	112	73	40	376	50	266	60	12	65
March	1 634	1 585	5	174	150	86	64	308	40	217	51	23	59
April	1 797	1 728	7	222	184	129	55	343	81	197	65	20	94
May	1 576	1 472	4	205	132	89	43	358	84	175	99	20	57
June	1 804	1 657	4	189	128	80	48	320	46	198	77	16	28
July	1 883	1 736	6	186	154	99	55	358	62	228	68	26	59
August	1 984	1 804	6	252	145	96	49	323	48	222	53	18	51
September	2 002	1 832	8	223	141	81	60	370	33	258	78	19	66
October	1 908	1 816	8	258	148	93	54	348	73	204	71	19	95
November	1 617	1 544	4	235	142	71	71	321	74	168	80	24	53
December	1 979	1 873	8	272	136	77	59	501	76	283	142	19	61

[1]Layoffs and discharges are the number of layoffs and discharges during the entire month.
[2]The layoffs and discharges rate is the number of layoffs and discharges during the entire month as a percent of total employment.

Table 7-11. Layoffs and Discharges Levels[1] and Rates,[2] by Industry, December 2000–September 2009
—Continued

(Not seasonally adjusted, levels in thousands, rates per 100.)

Year and month	Finance and insurance	Real estate and rental and leasing	Profes- sional and business services	Education and health services	Educa- tional services	Health care and social assistance	Leisure and hospitality	Arts, enter- tainment, and recreation	Accommo- dation and food services	Other services	Govern- ment	Federal	State and local govern- ment
2001	539	301	4 850	1 538	264	1 274	3 552	964	2 590	686	1 146	113	1 032
2002	577	375	4 637	1 626	246	1 380	3 090	806	2 285	839	1 205	142	1 057
2003	422	348	4 923	1 732	359	1 372	3 407	966	2 442	1 043	1 294	160	1 134
2004	428	359	4 908	1 656	287	1 371	3 582	1 058	2 524	860	1 374	159	1 215
2005	473	389	5 080	1 679	299	1 381	3 231	904	2 328	857	1 297	161	1 139
2006	466	405	4 581	1 685	340	1 348	3 050	833	2 217	937	1 363	191	1 172
2007	605	500	4 744	1 737	387	1 350	3 174	910	2 262	914	1 364	225	1 137
2008	640	461	5 110	2 069	426	1 644	3 152	898	2 256	977	1 227	109	1 114
2000													
December	26	5	634	119	43	76	174	53	121	35	81	6	75
2001													
January	172	20	541	184	29	156	288	79	209	104	101	28	73
February	23	22	322	84	9	75	138	44	94	25	49	5	44
March	22	29	545	92	11	81	243	38	205	73	43	6	37
April	48	16	323	96	24	72	397	62	335	76	60	7	53
May	28	10	362	98	18	80	159	26	133	26	93	7	86
June	20	18	337	138	23	115	212	41	172	48	159	5	154
July	45	9	316	220	35	185	293	73	220	60	93	8	85
August	27	14	321	172	59	113	258	97	161	95	201	8	193
September	30	53	434	113	13	100	497	246	251	57	107	12	95
October	61	38	461	169	24	144	435	101	334	48	127	12	115
November	34	37	379	95	10	85	401	116	286	46	50	6	43
December	29	35	509	77	9	68	231	41	190	28	63	9	54
2002													
January	152	43	470	227	33	193	253	44	209	85	116	26	89
February	39	14	286	103	9	94	188	26	162	42	47	8	39
March	23	19	344	116	18	98	146	30	116	31	42	10	32
April	44	19	367	135	20	115	275	91	184	90	65	12	53
May	51	18	284	135	24	110	171	21	150	41	91	7	84
June	57	27	330	148	24	124	210	23	187	79	153	9	144
July	45	33	469	177	27	150	335	103	232	112	149	12	136
August	41	37	312	148	29	119	293	114	179	131	150	8	141
September	26	44	370	136	31	105	345	128	217	73	168	15	152
October	30	62	424	125	10	116	326	62	264	51	87	14	72
November	33	32	400	71	3	69	320	112	209	49	74	14	60
Docomber	36	27	581	105	18	87	228	52	176	55	63	7	55
2003													
January	89	67	547	199	25	173	362	83	279	124	118	26	92
February	32	9	343	98	13	86	177	46	131	66	53	7	46
March	33	28	283	103	9	94	202	54	148	42	57	9	49
April	27	18	454	113	20	93	312	115	196	74	78	10	68
May	28	19	302	166	41	124	266	79	187	41	98	9	88
June	23	24	385	201	61	140	223	33	191	109	150	11	139
July	51	55	390	229	63	166	196	33	163	105	134	11	123
August	21	22	405	190	56	134	297	97	201	128	178	11	167
September	36	32	377	112	17	96	403	167	236	117	159	13	147
October	36	24	485	135	22	112	367	103	264	99	88	21	67
November	23	17	392	102	15	87	295	102	193	55	96	27	68
December	23	33	560	84	17	67	307	54	253	83	85	5	80
2004													
January	62	48	673	187	26	162	356	75	282	80	149	27	121
February	23	10	259	110	13	97	196	65	131	49	45	9	36
March	27	29	385	111	19	92	206	42	164	38	51	6	45
April	28	23	484	135	14	121	308	89	219	79	58	7	51
May	22	13	315	134	28	106	182	50	132	53	83	9	75
June	26	29	375	163	48	115	279	49	230	46	158	21	137
July	34	21	368	135	25	110	322	61	261	68	181	12	169
August	61	37	375	170	34	137	336	124	212	167	147	10	137
September	32	36	360	171	35	136	436	230	206	85	202	12	190
October	47	44	354	107	9	98	498	136	361	40	108	14	94
November	38	28	387	109	16	93	250	81	169	108	90	8	82
December	28	41	573	124	20	104	213	56	157	47	102	24	78
2005													
January	113	60	580	199	22	177	342	69	272	110	108	14	94
February	24	41	323	117	10	107	188	39	149	58	52	8	44
March	35	24	437	137	14	123	234	29	205	58	49	7	42
April	64	31	428	156	23	133	223	60	163	49	69	12	57
May	34	23	265	155	45	111	191	48	143	84	104	10	94
June	19	9	455	148	29	119	320	58	262	48	148	18	130
July	35	24	509	143	32	111	237	31	206	58	147	13	134
August	40	11	438	164	24	140	252	88	164	156	180	15	165
September	24	42	363	128	35	93	435	237	199	79	170	18	153
October	42	53	429	121	18	103	324	91	234	66	92	9	84
November	18	35	364	92	11	81	270	95	175	39	73	10	64
December	25	36	489	119	36	83	215	59	156	52	105	27	78

[1]Layoffs and discharges are the number of layoffs and discharges during the entire month.
[2]The layoffs and discharges rate is the number of layoffs and discharges during the entire month as a percent of total employment.

Table 7-11. Layoffs and Discharges Levels[1] and Rates,[2] by Industry, December 2000–September 2009
—Continued

(Not seasonally adjusted, levels in thousands, rates per 100.)

Year and month	Rate												
	Total	Total private	Mining and logging	Construction	Manufacturing	Durable goods	Non-durable goods	Trade, transportation, and utilities	Wholesale trade	Retail trade	Transportation, warehousing, and utilities	Information	Financial activities
2001	18.5	21.0	17.5	46.8	20.1	19.3	21.6	17.5	14.8	19.6	14.4	15.8	10.7
2002	17.9	20.3	18.2	46.4	17.6	17.4	18.0	17.8	14.3	19.9	15.2	15.8	12.1
2003	18.4	20.9	18.7	46.7	16.0	15.8	16.5	18.9	14.9	21.1	16.9	13.4	9.7
2004	17.8	20.0	13.9	42.2	14.0	13.6	14.5	18.8	13.9	20.4	19.7	12.5	9.8
2005	17.0	19.2	12.4	39.9	12.9	12.8	13.1	17.9	13.2	19.1	19.5	8.9	10.6
2006	15.7	17.6	10.8	34.1	12.8	11.3	15.4	15.9	10.9	18.6	13.6	8.5	10.4
2007	16.4	18.4	12.6	37.3	14.1	13.7	14.9	16.1	13.6	17.7	13.9	10.4	13.3
2008	17.8	20.2	15.1	46.4	16.5	16.7	16.2	17.8	16.3	18.9	16.0	12.2	13.5
2000													
December	1.6	1.8	3.9	5.4	1.2	1.0	1.6	1.6	1.5	2.0	0.7	0.6	0.4
2001													
January	2.4	2.8	1.9	5.8	2.2	2.4	2.0	3.5	2.3	4.5	2.1	2.3	2.5
February	1.1	1.2	0.7	4.3	1.2	1.1	1.3	0.9	1.1	1.0	0.4	1.0	0.6
March	1.4	1.7	1.2	3.8	1.4	1.2	1.7	1.3	0.6	1.8	0.6	0.6	0.7
April	1.4	1.6	0.9	2.5	1.9	2.0	1.8	1.2	1.3	1.2	1.1	1.7	0.8
May	1.2	1.3	0.9	2.9	1.5	1.4	1.8	1.2	0.8	1.4	1.1	1.0	0.5
June	1.3	1.4	1.5	2.9	1.7	1.5	2.2	1.2	0.7	1.3	1.1	1.2	0.5
July	1.5	1.7	1.4	2.7	1.8	1.6	2.2	1.4	1.7	1.5	1.0	1.2	0.7
August	1.4	1.5	1.3	3.2	1.4	1.4	1.4	1.0	0.9	1.1	0.9	1.1	0.5
September	1.6	1.9	1.2	3.7	1.4	1.3	1.6	1.4	1.1	1.5	1.2	1.1	1.1
October	1.9	2.1	1.8	4.7	2.2	2.3	2.0	1.5	1.9	1.5	1.2	1.8	1.3
November	1.6	1.9	2.1	5.2	1.6	1.6	1.7	1.4	1.2	1.3	2.0	1.7	0.9
December	1.6	1.8	2.8	5.3	1.8	1.8	1.6	2.1	1.6	1.1	1.6	1.0	0.8
2002													
January	2.3	2.6	2.0	5.5	2.6	2.6	2.6	2.7	1.5	3.4	2.0	3.8	2.5
February	1.2	1.4	1.1	4.0	1.3	1.1	1.5	1.6	1.2	1.8	1.4	0.7	0.7
March	1.1	1.3	1.9	3.1	1.2	1.4	1.0	1.1	1.0	1.1	1.2	0.9	0.5
April	1.4	1.7	2.3	3.2	1.6	1.6	1.6	1.3	1.0	1.5	1.2	1.7	0.8
May	1.2	1.4	1.3	3.2	1.2	1.1	1.3	1.4	1.4	1.7	0.8	0.9	0.9
June	1.3	1.4	0.9	3.2	1.3	1.2	1.4	1.0	0.8	1.0	1.2	1.1	1.1
July	1.7	1.9	2.5	4.1	1.4	1.4	1.5	1.3	1.6	1.3	0.9	1.1	1.0
August	1.4	1.6	1.4	3.0	1.2	1.4	1.0	1.3	0.9	1.4	1.2	1.1	1.0
September	1.5	1.7	1.0	3.5	1.2	1.3	1.2	1.4	1.1	1.5	1.3	0.7	0.9
October	1.6	1.8	1.3	4.7	1.7	1.7	1.5	1.4	0.9	1.8	1.0	1.2	1.2
November	1.4	1.6	1.0	4.1	1.3	1.2	1.4	1.3	1.5	1.3	1.1	1.5	0.8
December	1.7	2.0	1.7	4.9	1.7	1.5	2.0	1.9	1.3	2.1	2.1	0.9	0.8
2003													
January	2.4	2.8	3.3	6.4	2.4	2.4	2.4	3.0	1.8	3.9	1.7	2.9	2.0
February	1.2	1.4	1.5	3.5	1.2	1.2	1.3	1.4	0.8	1.9	0.7	1.0	0.5
March	1.1	1.3	1.4	3.4	1.3	1.2	1.3	1.1	0.8	1.3	1.0	1.1	0.8
April	1.5	1.7	1.4	4.1	1.8	1.6	2.1	1.2	1.2	1.2	1.0	0.8	0.6
May	1.2	1.4	0.9	2.9	0.9	0.9	1.0	1.2	1.7	1.2	1.0	0.8	0.6
June	1.5	1.6	1.3	2.6	1.3	1.4	1.3	1.4	0.9	1.6	1.7	1.3	0.6
July	1.6	1.7	1.3	3.2	1.5	1.4	1.8	1.5	1.7	1.3	1.7	1.0	1.3
August	1.6	1.7	2.1	4.1	1.0	1.2	0.8	1.4	1.1	1.4	2.0	0.8	0.5
September	1.5	1.7	0.6	4.1	1.0	1.0	1.0	1.1	1.6	1.0	0.9	0.5	0.9
October	1.7	1.9	1.2	4.4	1.3	1.2	1.5	1.8	1.6	1.9	1.5	1.0	0.8
November	1.4	1.6	0.9	4.0	1.1	1.2	0.8	1.4	0.7	1.7	1.1	1.0	0.5
December	1.7	2.0	2.8	4.1	1.1	1.1	1.1	2.3	1.0	2.7	2.6	1.1	0.7
2004													
January	2.4	2.7	2.1	5.6	1.9	1.7	2.1	3.1	1.8	3.7	2.7	2.0	1.4
February	1.2	1.4	1.8	3.8	1.0	0.9	1.1	1.6	1.2	1.9	1.1	0.9	0.4
March	1.2	1.4	0.8	3.4	1.1	1.1	1.0	1.2	1.0	1.2	1.4	1.3	0.7
April	1.4	1.6	1.1	2.8	1.2	1.0	1.4	1.4	1.7	1.4	1.1	0.9	0.6
May	1.1	1.3	0.9	2.4	0.9	0.7	1.2	1.4	1.1	1.3	1.9	1.1	0.4
June	1.3	1.4	0.7	2.6	0.9	1.0	0.8	1.1	1.0	1.1	1.4	1.3	0.7
July	1.5	1.6	0.9	3.4	1.2	1.1	1.2	1.4	1.2	1.5	1.4	0.8	0.7
August	1.6	1.7	1.1	3.4	1.3	1.5	1.1	1.3	1.3	1.1	1.7	0.6	1.2
September	1.5	1.6	0.7	2.7	1.1	1.1	1.0	1.2	0.9	1.3	1.3	1.2	0.8
October	1.5	1.8	1.2	3.8	1.3	1.3	1.4	1.4	1.2	1.4	1.4	1.1	1.1
November	1.4	1.6	1.4	3.9	1.1	1.2	1.0	1.4	1.1	1.5	1.6	0.6	0.8
December	1.7	1.9	1.4	4.5	1.1	1.1	1.1	2.4	0.7	2.9	2.5	0.7	0.9
2005													
January	2.3	2.7	2.1	6.9	1.9	2.0	1.8	2.8	1.7	3.3	2.4	1.9	2.2
February	1.2	1.4	0.9	3.7	0.8	0.8	0.8	1.5	0.9	1.8	1.2	0.4	0.8
March	1.2	1.4	0.8	2.6	1.1	1.0	1.2	1.2	0.7	1.4	1.1	0.7	0.7
April	1.3	1.6	1.2	3.1	1.3	1.4	1.0	1.3	1.4	1.3	1.3	0.7	1.2
May	1.2	1.3	0.6	2.8	0.9	1.0	0.8	1.4	1.5	1.2	2.0	0.6	0.7
June	1.3	1.5	0.7	2.5	0.9	0.9	0.9	1.2	0.8	1.3	1.6	0.5	0.3
July	1.4	1.5	0.9	2.4	1.1	1.1	1.0	1.4	1.1	1.5	1.4	0.8	0.7
August	1.5	1.6	1.0	3.3	1.0	1.1	0.9	1.2	0.8	1.4	1.1	0.6	0.6
September	1.5	1.6	1.3	2.9	1.0	0.9	1.1	1.4	0.6	1.7	1.6	0.6	0.8
October	1.4	1.6	1.2	3.4	1.0	1.0	1.0	1.3	1.3	1.3	1.4	0.6	1.2
November	1.2	1.4	0.6	3.1	1.0	0.8	1.4	1.2	1.3	1.1	1.6	0.8	0.6
December	1.5	1.7	1.2	3.7	1.0	0.9	1.1	1.9	1.3	1.8	2.8	0.6	0.7

[1] Layoffs and discharges are the number of layoffs and discharges during the entire month.
[2] The layoffs and discharges rate is the number of layoffs and discharges during the entire month as a percent of total employment.

Table 7-11. Layoffs and Discharges Levels[1] and Rates,[2] by Industry, December 2000–September 2009
—Continued

(Not seasonally adjusted, levels in thousands, rates per 100.)

Year and month	Finance and insurance	Real estate and rental and leasing	Professional and business services	Education and health services	Educational services	Health care and social assistance	Leisure and hospitality	Arts, entertainment, and recreation	Accommodation and food services	Other services	Government	Federal	State and local government
2001	9.3	14.8	29.4	9.8	10.5	9.7	29.5	52.9	25.4	13.0	5.4	4.1	5.6
2002	9.9	18.4	29.0	10.0	9.3	10.2	25.8	45.2	22.4	15.6	5.6	5.1	5.6
2003	7.1	16.9	30.8	10.4	13.3	9.9	28.0	53.3	23.6	19.3	6.0	5.8	6.0
2004	7.2	17.2	29.9	9.8	10.4	9.7	28.7	57.2	23.7	15.9	6.4	5.8	6.4
2005	7.9	18.2	30.0	9.7	10.5	9.5	25.2	47.8	21.3	15.9	5.9	5.9	6.0
2006	7.6	18.6	26.1	9.5	11.7	9.0	23.3	43.2	19.8	17.2	6.2	7.0	6.1
2007	9.9	23.1	26.4	9.5	13.2	8.8	23.6	46.2	19.7	16.6	6.1	8.2	5.8
2008	10.6	21.6	28.7	11.0	14.0	10.4	23.4	45.6	19.6	17.7	5.5	3.9	5.6
2000													
December	0.5	0.2	3.8	0.8	1.7	0.6	1.5	3.3	1.2	0.7	0.4	0.2	0.4
2001													
January	3.0	1.0	3.3	1.2	1.2	1.2	2.5	5.0	2.1	2.0	0.5	1.0	0.4
February	0.4	1.1	2.0	0.5	0.3	0.6	1.2	2.8	1.0	0.5	0.2	0.2	0.2
March	0.4	1.4	3.3	0.6	0.4	0.6	2.1	2.3	2.1	1.4	0.2	0.2	0.2
April	0.8	0.8	1.9	0.6	0.9	0.6	3.3	3.5	3.3	1.5	0.3	0.2	0.3
May	0.5	0.5	2.2	0.6	0.7	0.6	1.3	1.3	1.3	0.5	0.4	0.3	0.5
June	0.3	0.9	2.0	0.9	1.0	0.9	1.7	1.9	1.6	0.9	0.8	0.2	0.8
July	0.8	0.4	1.9	1.4	1.6	1.4	2.3	3.4	2.1	1.1	0.5	0.3	0.5
August	0.5	0.7	1.9	1.1	2.7	0.9	2.0	4.6	1.5	1.8	1.0	0.3	1.1
September	0.5	2.6	2.6	0.7	0.5	0.8	4.1	13.0	2.4	1.1	0.5	0.4	0.5
October	1.0	1.9	2.8	1.1	0.9	1.1	3.6	5.6	3.3	0.9	0.6	0.4	0.6
November	0.6	1.8	2.3	0.6	0.4	0.6	3.4	7.0	2.8	0.9	0.2	0.2	0.2
December	0.5	1.7	3.2	0.5	0.3	0.5	2.0	2.5	1.9	0.5	0.3	0.3	0.3
2002													
January	2.6	2.1	3.0	1.4	1.3	1.4	2.2	2.7	2.1	1.6	0.5	1.0	0.5
February	0.7	0.7	1.8	0.6	0.3	0.7	1.6	1.6	1.6	0.8	0.2	0.3	0.2
March	0.4	0.9	2.2	0.7	0.7	0.7	1.3	1.8	1.2	0.6	0.2	0.3	0.2
April	0.8	0.9	2.3	0.8	0.7	0.9	2.3	5.3	1.8	1.7	0.3	0.4	0.3
May	0.9	0.9	1.8	0.8	0.9	0.8	1.4	1.2	1.5	0.8	0.4	0.2	0.4
June	1.0	1.3	2.0	0.9	1.0	0.9	1.7	1.2	1.8	1.5	0.7	0.3	0.8
July	0.8	1.6	2.9	1.1	1.1	1.1	2.7	5.0	2.2	2.1	0.7	0.4	0.8
August	0.7	1.8	1.9	0.9	1.2	0.9	2.3	5.7	1.7	2.4	0.7	0.3	0.8
September	0.5	2.2	2.3	0.8	1.2	0.8	2.8	6.9	2.1	1.4	0.8	0.6	0.8
October	0.5	3.0	2.6	0.8	0.3	0.8	2.7	3.6	2.6	1.0	0.4	0.5	0.4
November	0.6	1.6	2.5	0.4	0.1	0.5	2.7	6.7	2.1	0.9	0.3	0.5	0.3
December	0.6	1.3	3.7	0.6	0.6	0.6	1.9	3.1	1.7	1.0	0.3	0.3	0.3
2003													
January	1.5	3.4	3.5	1.2	1.0	1.3	3.1	5.1	2.8	2.3	0.5	0.9	0.5
February	0.5	0.5	2.2	0.6	0.4	0.6	1.5	2.8	1.3	1.2	0.2	0.3	0.2
March	0.6	1.4	1.8	0.6	0.3	0.7	1.7	3.2	1.5	0.8	0.3	0.3	0.3
April	0.5	0.9	2.9	0.7	0.7	0.7	2.6	6.6	1.9	1.4	0.4	0.3	0.4
May	0.5	0.9	1.9	1.0	1.5	0.9	2.2	4.2	1.8	0.7	0.4	0.3	0.5
June	0.4	1.1	2.4	1.2	2.4	1.0	1.8	1.6	1.8	2.0	0.7	0.4	0.7
July	0.8	2.6	2.4	1.4	2.6	1.2	1.5	1.6	1.5	1.9	0.7	0.4	0.7
August	0.4	1.1	2.5	1.2	2.4	1.0	2.3	4.7	1.9	2.4	0.9	0.4	0.9
September	0.6	1.5	2.3	0.7	0.6	0.7	3.3	8.9	2.2	2.2	0.7	0.5	0.8
October	0.6	1.2	3.0	0.8	0.8	0.8	3.0	5.9	2.5	1.8	0.4	0.7	0.4
November	0.4	0.8	2.4	0.6	0.5	0.6	2.5	6.1	1.9	1.0	0.4	1.0	0.4
December	0.4	1.6	3.5	0.5	0.6	0.5	2.6	3.2	2.4	1.5	0.4	0.2	0.4
2004													
January	1.0	2.4	4.3	1.1	1.0	1.2	3.0	4.6	2.8	1.5	0.7	1.0	0.6
February	0.4	0.5	1.6	0.7	0.4	0.7	1.7	4.0	1.3	0.9	0.2	0.3	0.2
March	0.5	1.4	2.4	0.7	0.7	0.6	1.7	2.5	1.6	0.7	0.2	0.2	0.2
April	0.5	1.1	3.0	0.8	0.5	0.9	2.5	4.9	2.1	1.5	0.3	0.3	0.3
May	0.4	0.6	1.9	0.8	1.0	0.7	1.4	2.6	1.2	1.0	0.4	0.3	0.4
June	0.4	1.4	2.3	1.0	1.9	0.8	2.1	2.3	2.1	0.8	0.7	0.8	0.7
July	0.6	1.0	2.2	0.8	1.0	0.8	2.5	2.9	2.4	1.2	0.9	0.4	1.0
August	1.0	1.7	2.3	1.0	1.4	1.0	2.6	5.9	1.9	3.1	0.7	0.4	0.8
September	0.5	1.7	2.2	1.0	1.3	1.0	3.4	11.9	1.9	1.6	0.9	0.4	1.0
October	0.8	2.1	2.1	0.6	0.3	0.7	4.0	7.5	3.4	0.7	0.5	0.5	0.5
November	0.6	1.3	2.3	0.6	0.6	0.6	2.0	4.7	1.6	2.0	0.4	0.3	0.4
December	0.5	2.0	3.5	0.7	0.7	0.7	1.7	3.3	1.5	0.9	0.5	0.9	0.4
2005													
January	1.9	2.9	3.6	1.2	0.8	1.2	2.8	4.2	2.6	2.1	0.5	0.5	0.5
February	0.4	2.0	2.0	0.7	0.3	0.7	1.5	2.3	1.4	1.1	0.2	0.3	0.2
March	0.6	1.2	2.6	0.8	0.5	0.9	1.9	1.7	1.9	1.1	0.2	0.3	0.2
April	1.1	1.5	2.6	0.9	0.8	0.9	1.8	3.3	1.5	0.9	0.3	0.4	0.3
May	0.6	1.1	1.6	0.9	1.5	0.8	1.5	2.4	1.3	1.6	0.5	0.4	0.5
June	0.3	0.4	2.7	0.9	1.1	0.8	2.4	2.7	2.3	0.9	0.7	0.7	0.7
July	0.6	1.1	3.0	0.8	1.3	0.8	1.8	1.4	1.8	1.1	0.7	0.5	0.8
August	0.7	0.5	2.5	1.0	1.0	1.0	1.9	4.0	1.4	2.9	0.9	0.6	0.9
September	0.4	2.0	2.1	0.7	1.2	0.6	3.3	11.9	1.8	1.5	0.8	0.6	0.8
October	0.7	2.5	2.5	0.7	0.6	0.7	2.5	4.9	2.1	1.2	0.4	0.3	0.4
November	0.3	1.6	2.1	0.5	0.4	0.5	2.1	5.4	1.6	0.7	0.3	0.3	0.3
December	0.4	1.7	2.8	0.7	1.2	0.6	1.7	3.4	1.4	1.0	0.5	1.0	0.4

[1] Layoffs and discharges are the number of layoffs and discharges during the entire month.
[2] The layoffs and discharges rate is the number of layoffs and discharges during the entire month as a percent of total employment.

Table 7-11. Layoffs and Discharges Levels[1] and Rates,[2] by Industry, December 2000–September 2009
—Continued

(Not seasonally adjusted, levels in thousands, rates per 100.)

Year and month	Level												
	Total	Total private	Mining and logging	Construc- tion	Manufac- turing	Durable goods	Non- durable goods	Trade, transpor- tation, and utilities	Whole- sale trade	Retail trade	Transpor- tation, ware- housing, and utilities	Infor- mation	Financial activities
2006													
January	2 379	2 269	8	323	204	100	104	649	55	498	96	22	112
February	1 391	1 341	6	179	114	61	53	312	46	233	32	17	61
March	1 319	1 259	7	177	164	77	87	222	35	151	36	14	69
April	1 770	1 698	10	149	162	71	92	315	51	237	27	33	83
May	1 635	1 518	3	168	140	83	57	317	48	209	60	13	51
June	1 601	1 408	2	127	133	72	62	339	48	238	53	14	55
July	1 889	1 722	4	211	152	94	58	351	102	191	58	25	81
August	1 752	1 612	5	210	150	91	59	305	49	198	58	19	79
September	1 865	1 677	10	205	154	97	57	302	55	185	62	16	61
October	2 031	1 934	6	264	159	95	63	344	67	200	77	29	75
November	1 814	1 733	6	316	137	89	48	287	46	186	56	23	62
December	1 987	1 898	7	294	145	89	56	438	44	327	67	32	80
2007													
January	2 513	2 404	14	341	227	139	88	601	70	419	112	77	132
February	1 404	1 355	6	233	147	93	54	281	36	207	37	24	61
March	1 476	1 425	4	158	141	90	50	258	49	154	54	17	98
April	1 853	1 789	6	229	156	97	59	307	67	181	60	21	106
May	1 506	1 385	5	169	130	77	53	297	55	196	46	21	69
June	1 775	1 621	4	215	136	89	47	284	75	162	46	21	59
July	1 943	1 692	7	200	181	111	70	361	91	208	61	34	105
August	1 943	1 767	9	236	158	95	63	335	62	220	53	28	101
September	2 130	1 988	7	256	170	106	64	341	69	229	44	18	97
October	2 091	2 006	9	264	196	118	77	384	87	232	64	21	115
November	1 907	1 842	10	265	179	111	68	392	67	245	80	14	76
December	1 998	1 902	10	282	142	79	64	443	93	300	50	19	88
2008													
January	2 701	2 589	17	386	229	154	75	636	130	418	88	53	179
February	1 483	1 448	9	200	135	77	58	315	55	219	41	15	55
March	1 543	1 489	6	229	122	77	45	270	57	169	44	29	67
April	1 829	1 773	10	235	202	127	74	336	89	188	59	22	92
May	1 605	1 497	4	205	143	89	54	284	48	193	43	14	60
June	1 826	1 667	6	220	155	96	59	349	75	211	63	30	74
July	2 031	1 878	7	228	153	107	46	403	61	250	92	23	125
August	2 227	2 071	6	255	168	121	46	369	66	232	71	16	106
September	2 015	1 861	6	268	176	113	63	349	71	206	72	29	73
October	2 295	2 208	12	353	253	157	96	403	93	239	71	54	93
November	2 184	2 115	16	379	212	126	85	414	85	251	78	38	81
December	2 631	2 550	18	389	269	169	100	563	143	331	89	42	95
2009													
January	3 715	3 571	23	583	513	351	162	814	254	430	131	97	293
February	2 021	1 969	15	314	267	183	85	400	86	242	73	33	109
March	2 029	1 970	23	285	274	202	73	368	82	204	83	40	115
April	2 469	2 398	19	323	314	236	78	494	106	316	71	42	110
May	1 838	1 702	14	249	216	147	70	374	106	206	62	23	75
June	1 931	1 710	11	229	190	126	64	314	68	174	72	39	90
July	2 476	2 297	25	366	197	109	87	384	81	216	87	55	139
August	2 277	2 063	11	274	181	102	79	322	79	178	64	22	111
September[3]	2 095	1 912	14	314	171	101	70	303	65	135	103	12	61

[1]Layoffs and discharges are the number of layoffs and discharges during the entire month.
[2]The layoffs and discharges rate is the number of layoffs and discharges during the entire month as a percent of total employment.
[3]Preliminary.

Table 7-11. Layoffs and Discharges Levels[1] and Rates,[2] by Industry, December 2000–September 2009 —Continued

(Not seasonally adjusted, levels in thousands, rates per 100.)

Year and month	Level												
	Finance and insurance	Real estate and rental and leasing	Professional and business services	Education and health services	Educational services	Health care and social assistance	Leisure and hospitality	Arts, entertainment, and recreation	Accommodation and food services	Other services	Government	Federal	State and local government
2006													
January	70	43	414	180	28	152	266	37	230	90	111	18	92
February	41	20	336	86	8	79	179	32	147	50	51	9	42
March	31	39	286	111	20	91	180	37	143	29	60	11	48
April	44	38	375	151	24	127	262	47	214	158	71	13	58
May	28	23	363	228	51	177	188	68	120	49	117	13	104
June	29	26	315	170	52	118	191	43	148	63	193	19	174
July	36	45	404	184	41	144	228	55	173	81	166	22	144
August	44	35	331	146	28	118	266	93	173	102	139	27	113
September	35	26	399	120	28	92	320	148	172	89	188	25	163
October	35	41	437	121	21	100	396	111	285	104	97	10	88
November	23	39	413	86	13	74	341	98	243	63	81	9	72
December	50	30	508	102	26	76	233	64	169	59	89	15	74
2007													
January	75	57	447	186	43	143	310	90	220	69	109	20	89
February	32	29	297	96	20	76	186	48	138	25	49	12	37
March	47	50	386	129	19	110	187	48	139	48	51	15	37
April	52	54	441	143	31	111	265	89	177	115	64	14	50
May	27	43	284	160	42	118	219	54	164	30	121	18	103
June	39	20	329	211	66	145	263	52	211	100	154	25	128
July	61	44	364	143	23	120	187	29	157	108	251	28	223
August	72	28	342	184	62	122	248	56	191	127	176	26	150
September	54	43	388	147	21	127	467	151	316	97	142	29	113
October	73	43	474	130	14	116	353	123	230	59	86	10	76
November	21	54	455	102	20	82	269	120	149	81	65	9	55
December	52	35	537	106	26	80	220	50	170	55	96	19	76
2008													
January	121	58	518	219	35	184	273	71	202	80	112	26	86
February	32	23	311	127	14	113	226	53	173	53	36	6	29
March	47	20	381	145	16	129	189	52	137	52	54	6	48
April	62	30	452	139	35	104	225	65	161	60	56	7	48
May	29	31	255	224	52	173	211	67	144	96	109	5	103
June	46	28	369	207	58	148	203	32	170	55	158	10	148
July	72	54	370	227	58	169	210	34	176	131	153	6	147
August	66	39	427	220	58	162	373	141	232	133	156	10	146
September	40	33	374	141	23	119	368	117	252	77	154	7	147
October	41	53	442	147	27	120	354	126	229	96	88	8	79
November	37	44	532	105	19	86	282	80	202	56	69	4	65
December	47	48	679	168	31	137	238	60	178	88	82	14	68
2009													
January	189	104	564	236	34	202	332	76	257	114	144	11	133
February	58	52	454	138	17	122	182	34	148	55	52	5	47
March	61	54	418	132	13	119	228	40	188	87	59	4	55
April	68	41	532	195	28	167	278	66	212	90	72	4	67
May	52	23	309	152	52	99	213	24	189	78	135	10	125
June	52	38	308	209	48	161	231	38	194	88	221	20	201
July	85	54	404	294	88	206	269	57	211	164	179	4	175
August	50	61	384	260	75	185	327	100	226	171	214	10	204
September[3]	26	36	345	184	30	155	361	144	217	146	183	11	172

[1] Layoffs and discharges are the number of layoffs and discharges during the entire month.
[2] The layoffs and discharges rate is the number of layoffs and discharges during the entire month as a percent of total employment.
[3] Preliminary.

Table 7-11. Layoffs and Discharges Levels[1] and Rates,[2] by Industry, December 2000–September 2009
—Continued

(Not seasonally adjusted, levels in thousands, rates per 100.)

Year and month	Rate												
	Total	Total private	Mining and logging	Construction	Manufacturing	Durable goods	Non-durable goods	Trade, transportation, and utilities	Wholesale trade	Retail trade	Transportation, warehousing, and utilities	Information	Financial activities
2006													
January	1.8	2.0	1.3	4.5	1.4	1.1	2.0	2.5	0.9	3.3	1.9	0.7	1.4
February	1.0	1.2	1.0	2.5	0.8	0.7	1.0	1.2	0.8	1.5	0.7	0.5	0.7
March	1.0	1.1	1.1	2.4	1.2	0.9	1.7	0.9	0.6	1.0	0.7	0.5	0.8
April	1.3	1.5	1.5	2.0	1.1	0.8	1.8	1.2	0.9	1.6	0.5	1.1	1.0
May	1.2	1.3	0.4	2.2	1.0	0.9	1.1	1.2	0.8	1.4	1.2	0.4	0.6
June	1.2	1.2	0.3	1.6	0.9	0.8	1.2	1.3	0.8	1.6	1.1	0.4	0.7
July	1.4	1.5	0.6	2.6	1.1	1.1	1.1	1.3	1.7	1.2	1.2	0.8	1.0
August	1.3	1.4	0.8	2.6	1.1	1.0	1.1	1.2	0.8	1.3	1.2	0.6	0.9
September	1.4	1.5	1.4	2.6	1.1	1.1	1.1	1.2	0.9	1.2	1.2	0.5	0.7
October	1.5	1.7	0.8	3.3	1.1	1.1	1.2	1.3	1.1	1.3	1.5	1.0	0.9
November	1.3	1.5	0.8	4.1	1.0	1.0	0.9	1.1	0.8	1.2	1.1	0.8	0.7
December	1.4	1.6	1.0	3.9	1.0	1.0	1.1	1.6	0.7	2.0	1.3	1.1	1.0
2007													
January	1.9	2.1	2.1	4.7	1.6	1.6	1.7	2.3	1.2	2.7	2.2	2.6	1.6
February	1.0	1.2	0.8	3.2	1.1	1.1	1.1	1.1	0.6	1.4	0.7	0.8	0.7
March	1.1	1.3	0.6	2.2	1.0	1.0	1.0	1.0	0.8	1.0	1.1	0.6	1.2
April	1.3	1.6	0.8	3.0	1.1	1.1	1.2	1.2	1.1	1.2	1.2	0.7	1.3
May	1.1	1.2	0.7	2.2	0.9	0.9	1.1	1.1	0.9	1.3	0.9	0.7	0.8
June	1.3	1.4	0.5	2.7	1.0	1.0	0.9	1.1	1.2	1.0	0.9	0.7	0.7
July	1.4	1.5	1.0	2.5	1.3	1.3	1.4	1.4	1.5	1.3	1.2	1.1	1.3
August	1.4	1.5	1.2	3.0	1.1	1.1	1.2	1.3	1.0	1.4	1.0	0.9	1.2
September	1.5	1.7	1.0	3.3	1.2	1.2	1.3	1.3	1.1	1.5	0.8	0.6	1.2
October	1.5	1.7	1.3	3.4	1.4	1.4	1.5	1.4	1.4	1.5	1.2	0.7	1.4
November	1.4	1.6	1.3	3.5	1.3	1.3	1.4	1.4	1.1	1.5	1.6	0.5	0.9
December	1.4	1.6	1.3	3.8	1.0	0.9	1.3	1.6	1.5	1.9	1.0	0.6	1.1
2008													
January	2.0	2.3	2.3	5.5	1.7	1.8	1.5	2.4	2.2	2.7	1.7	1.8	2.2
February	1.1	1.3	1.2	2.9	1.0	0.9	1.2	1.2	0.9	1.4	0.8	0.5	0.7
March	1.1	1.3	0.8	3.3	0.9	0.9	0.9	1.0	1.0	1.1	0.9	0.9	0.8
April	1.3	1.5	1.4	3.3	1.5	1.5	1.5	1.3	1.5	1.2	1.2	0.7	1.1
May	1.2	1.3	0.5	2.8	1.1	1.0	1.1	1.1	0.8	1.3	0.8	0.5	0.7
June	1.3	1.4	0.7	2.9	1.1	1.1	1.2	1.3	1.2	1.4	1.2	1.0	0.9
July	1.5	1.6	0.9	3.0	1.1	1.3	0.9	1.5	1.0	1.6	1.8	0.8	1.5
August	1.6	1.8	0.7	3.4	1.2	1.4	0.9	1.4	1.1	1.5	1.4	0.5	1.3
September	1.5	1.6	0.7	3.6	1.3	1.3	1.3	1.3	1.2	1.4	1.4	1.0	0.9
October	1.7	1.9	1.5	4.8	1.9	1.9	1.9	1.5	1.6	1.6	1.4	1.8	1.2
November	1.6	1.9	2.1	5.4	1.6	1.5	1.7	1.6	1.4	1.6	1.6	1.3	1.0
December	1.9	2.3	2.4	5.8	2.1	2.1	2.1	2.1	2.4	2.1	1.8	1.4	1.2
2009													
January	2.8	3.3	3.1	9.3	4.1	4.5	3.4	3.2	4.4	2.9	2.7	3.4	3.7
February	1.5	1.8	2.0	5.1	2.2	2.4	1.8	1.6	1.5	1.7	1.5	1.1	1.4
March	1.5	1.8	3.1	4.7	2.3	2.7	1.6	1.5	1.4	1.4	1.7	1.4	1.5
April	1.9	2.2	2.6	5.2	2.6	3.2	1.7	2.0	1.9	2.2	1.5	1.5	1.4
May	1.4	1.6	2.0	3.9	1.8	2.0	1.5	1.5	1.9	1.4	1.3	0.8	1.0
June	1.5	1.6	1.5	3.6	1.6	1.7	1.4	1.2	1.2	1.2	1.5	1.4	1.2
July	1.9	2.1	3.5	5.7	1.7	1.5	1.9	1.5	1.4	1.5	1.8	1.9	1.8
August	1.7	1.9	1.5	4.3	1.5	1.4	1.7	1.3	1.4	1.2	1.4	0.8	1.4
September[3]	1.6	1.8	1.9	5.0	1.4	1.4	1.5	1.2	1.2	0.9	2.2	0.4	0.8

[1]Layoffs and discharges are the number of layoffs and discharges during the entire month.
[2]The layoffs and discharges rate is the number of layoffs and discharges during the entire month as a percent of total employment.
[3]Preliminary.

Table 7-11. Layoffs and Discharges Levels[1] and Rates,[2] by Industry, December 2000–September 2009 —Continued

(Not seasonally adjusted, levels in thousands, rates per 100.)

Year and month	Rate												
	Finance and insurance	Real estate and rental and leasing	Professional and business services	Education and health services	Educational services	Health care and social assistance	Leisure and hospitality	Arts, entertainment, and recreation	Accommodation and food services	Other services	Government	Federal	State and local government
2006													
January	1.1	2.0	2.4	1.0	1.0	1.0	2.2	2.2	2.2	1.7	0.5	0.7	0.5
February	0.7	0.9	2.0	0.5	0.2	0.5	1.4	1.9	1.4	0.9	0.2	0.3	0.2
March	0.5	1.8	1.7	0.6	0.7	0.6	1.4	2.1	1.3	0.5	0.3	0.4	0.2
April	0.7	1.8	2.2	0.8	0.8	0.9	2.0	2.5	1.9	2.9	0.3	0.5	0.3
May	0.5	1.0	2.1	1.3	1.7	1.2	1.4	3.4	1.1	0.9	0.5	0.5	0.5
June	0.5	1.2	1.8	1.0	2.0	0.8	1.4	2.0	1.3	1.1	0.9	0.7	0.9
July	0.6	2.0	2.3	1.1	1.6	1.0	1.7	2.4	1.5	1.5	0.8	0.8	0.8
August	0.7	1.6	1.9	0.8	1.1	0.8	1.9	4.2	1.5	1.9	0.7	1.0	0.6
September	0.6	1.2	2.2	0.7	1.0	0.6	2.4	7.4	1.5	1.6	0.9	0.9	0.8
October	0.6	1.9	2.4	0.7	0.7	0.7	3.0	5.8	2.5	1.9	0.4	0.4	0.4
November	0.4	1.8	2.3	0.5	0.4	0.5	2.6	5.4	2.2	1.2	0.4	0.3	0.4
December	0.8	1.4	2.8	0.6	0.8	0.5	1.8	3.5	1.5	1.1	0.4	0.6	0.4
2007													
January	1.2	2.7	2.6	1.0	1.5	0.9	2.4	5.2	2.0	1.3	0.5	0.7	0.5
February	0.5	1.3	1.7	0.5	0.7	0.5	1.5	2.7	1.3	0.5	0.2	0.4	0.2
March	0.8	2.4	2.2	0.7	0.6	0.7	1.4	2.6	1.2	0.9	0.2	0.5	0.2
April	0.9	2.5	2.5	0.8	1.0	0.7	2.0	4.6	1.6	2.1	0.3	0.5	0.3
May	0.4	2.0	1.6	0.9	1.4	0.8	1.6	2.7	1.4	0.5	0.5	0.7	0.5
June	0.6	0.9	1.8	1.2	2.4	0.9	1.9	2.3	1.8	1.8	0.7	0.9	0.7
July	1.0	2.0	2.0	0.8	0.9	0.8	1.3	1.3	1.3	1.9	1.2	1.0	1.2
August	1.2	1.3	1.9	1.0	2.4	0.8	1.8	2.5	1.6	2.3	0.8	1.0	0.8
September	0.9	2.0	2.1	0.8	0.7	0.8	3.4	7.4	2.7	1.8	0.6	1.1	0.6
October	1.2	2.0	2.6	0.7	0.5	0.7	2.6	6.3	2.0	1.1	0.4	0.3	0.4
November	0.4	2.5	2.5	0.5	0.6	0.5	2.0	6.5	1.3	1.5	0.3	0.3	0.3
December	0.9	1.6	3.0	0.6	0.8	0.5	1.7	2.7	1.5	1.0	0.4	0.7	0.4
2008													
January	2.0	2.7	2.9	1.2	1.2	1.2	2.1	4.0	1.8	1.5	0.5	1.0	0.4
February	0.5	1.1	1.8	0.7	0.5	0.7	1.7	3.0	1.5	1.0	0.2	0.2	0.1
March	0.8	1.0	2.1	0.8	0.5	0.8	1.4	2.8	1.2	0.9	0.2	0.2	0.2
April	1.0	1.4	2.5	0.7	1.1	0.7	1.7	3.3	1.4	1.1	0.2	0.3	0.2
May	0.5	1.4	1.4	1.2	1.7	1.1	1.5	3.3	1.2	1.7	0.5	0.2	0.5
June	0.8	1.3	2.1	1.1	2.0	0.9	1.4	1.5	1.4	1.0	0.7	0.4	0.8
July	1.2	2.5	2.1	1.2	2.1	1.1	1.5	1.5	1.5	2.3	0.7	0.2	0.8
August	1.1	1.8	2.4	1.2	2.1	1.0	2.6	6.3	2.0	2.4	0.7	0.3	0.8
September	0.7	1.5	2.1	0.7	0.8	0.7	2.7	5.8	2.2	1.4	0.7	0.2	0.7
October	0.7	2.5	2.5	0.8	0.8	0.8	2.7	6.6	2.0	1.7	0.4	0.3	0.4
November	0.6	2.1	3.0	0.5	0.6	0.5	2.2	4.4	1.8	1.0	0.3	0.1	0.3
December	0.8	2.3	3.9	0.9	1.0	0.9	1.8	3.3	1.6	1.6	0.4	0.5	0.3
2009													
January	3.2	5.1	3.3	1.2	1.1	1.3	2.6	4.4	2.3	2.1	0.6	0.4	0.7
February	1.0	2.6	2.7	0.7	0.5	0.8	1.4	1.9	1.4	1.0	0.2	0.2	0.2
March	1.0	2.7	2.5	0.7	0.4	0.7	1.8	2.3	1.7	1.6	0.3	0.1	0.3
April	1.2	2.1	3.2	1.0	0.9	1.0	2.1	3.5	1.9	1.7	0.3	0.1	0.3
May	0.9	1.1	1.8	0.8	1.7	0.6	1.6	1.2	1.7	1.4	0.6	0.4	0.6
June	0.9	1.9	1.8	1.1	1.7	1.0	1.7	1.8	1.7	1.6	1.0	0.7	1.0
July	1.5	2.7	2.4	1.5	3.2	1.3	1.9	2.6	1.8	3.0	0.8	0.1	0.9
August	0.9	3.0	2.3	1.4	2.7	1.1	2.4	4.7	1.9	3.1	1.0	0.4	1.1
September[3]	0.5	1.8	2.1	1.0	1.0	1.0	2.7	7.3	1.9	2.7	0.8	0.4	0.9

[1]Layoffs and discharges are the number of layoffs and discharges during the entire month.
[2]The layoffs and discharges rate is the number of layoffs and discharges during the entire month as a percent of total employment.
[3]Preliminary.

Table 7-12. Other Separations Levels[1] and Rates,[2] by Industry, December 2000–September 2009

(Not seasonally adjusted, levels in thousands, rates per 100.)

Year and month	Level											
	Total[3]	Total private[3]	Construction	Manufacturing	Trade, transportation, and utilities[4]	Retail trade	Professional and business services	Education and health services	Leisure and hospitality[5]	Accommodation and food services	Government[6]	State and local government
2001	4 852	4 145	269	515	850	548	990	407	452	382	707	546
2002	4 708	3 901	215	494	898	544	965	407	368	333	809	661
2003	4 536	3 766	181	462	870	492	767	435	411	364	771	610
2004	4 425	3 636	231	349	951	550	668	385	407	368	791	609
2005	4 364	3 643	198	426	796	468	797	390	367	340	719	572
2006	4 870	4 123	355	429	1 105	668	851	423	326	280	745	542
2007	4 463	3 591	220	393	956	623	644	444	324	267	872	559
2008	3 969	3 319	233	332	974	658	568	454	322	278	647	538
2000												
December	347	296	23	47	86	35	46	28	30	20	51	41
2001												
January	642	540	33	68	155	120	66	46	67	61	102	54
February	270	234	8	33	69	50	17	28	37	35	36	27
March	343	307	16	51	53	33	88	31	30	27	36	27
April	462	402	29	47	89	60	82	36	30	23	60	49
May	318	263	17	36	62	36	75	21	27	22	55	47
June	480	401	17	46	35	18	172	49	30	30	79	71
July	492	400	40	44	61	32	88	29	56	48	92	79
August	443	387	40	60	53	31	104	44	42	23	56	44
September	368	306	21	29	67	45	72	35	36	30	62	53
October	385	338	22	44	95	52	67	33	40	32	47	35
November	271	235	17	22	49	32	49	27	22	18	36	27
December	378	332	9	35	62	39	110	28	35	33	46	33
2002												
January	635	530	20	72	118	74	146	51	35	31	106	79
February	300	253	10	37	66	34	62	27	19	18	47	35
March	324	279	16	34	38	21	79	33	30	29	44	35
April	421	368	24	40	67	43	91	47	38	36	53	40
May	316	256	11	39	54	30	75	26	26	23	60	50
June	381	285	7	37	66	39	69	28	42	38	96	88
July	499	402	7	47	113	83	101	37	37	34	97	83
August	367	299	23	39	94	62	60	30	25	24	68	57
September	400	340	18	30	92	56	76	39	34	26	60	47
October	366	297	19	46	62	29	63	37	29	26	70	60
November	303	263	17	40	68	40	46	25	25	23	41	29
December	396	329	43	33	60	33	97	27	28	25	67	58
2003												
January	745	624	29	71	163	88	121	72	64	61	121	82
February	292	249	11	44	84	54	36	19	20	19	43	33
March	331	278	11	36	53	31	82	41	38	37	53	40
April	381	324	14	49	58	22	78	34	33	30	58	43
May	333	265	10	28	60	37	54	35	30	28	68	53
June	367	283	22	27	66	36	53	42	27	26	84	74
July	428	345	19	40	81	47	90	35	26	25	83	75
August	357	291	9	42	45	27	71	25	45	26	67	57
September	364	301	8	29	89	54	48	35	31	28	63	54
October	356	310	16	42	66	37	46	32	33	27	45	34
November	268	232	19	25	53	31	43	24	41	37	36	26
December	314	264	13	29	52	28	45	41	23	20	50	39
2004												
January	649	502	46	47	110	61	48	57	60	57	147	83
February	258	213	12	25	46	25	37	37	19	18	46	37
March	300	256	11	29	89	56	55	18	17	15	44	35
April	346	303	13	31	85	38	57	27	34	33	43	34
May	344	281	9	31	66	48	57	39	39	35	64	50
June	401	296	11	31	87	48	75	31	21	18	104	95
July	428	332	18	31	85	57	68	28	38	34	96	82
August	378	313	15	26	94	47	52	40	50	48	65	56
September	359	309	30	29	61	32	50	33	39	31	50	40
October	380	330	46	20	99	56	57	30	20	16	50	35
November	265	232	8	16	62	45	48	22	44	39	34	23
December	317	269	12	33	67	37	64	23	26	24	48	39
2005												
January	581	479	12	51	101	53	59	53	60	54	101	73
February	311	262	10	29	63	39	77	25	20	19	49	37
March	283	233	7	28	72	55	46	15	19	19	50	39
April	343	290	16	35	72	37	53	27	23	20	53	37
May	339	287	12	33	48	26	79	41	34	32	52	44
June	336	230	21	25	56	32	42	35	21	20	106	92
July	362	286	10	47	63	40	41	39	20	18	76	62
August	372	312	26	42	58	35	66	39	38	36	60	50
September	319	263	18	33	67	35	66	31	16	13	56	40
October	351	312	27	33	60	37	88	32	26	24	38	32
November	302	272	27	32	49	27	57	19	23	22	30	25
December	465	417	12	38	87	52	123	34	67	63	48	41

[1]Other separations are the number of other separations during the entire month.
[2]The other separations rate is the number of other separations during the entire month as a percent of total employment.
[3]Includes natural resources and mining, information, financial activities, and other services, not shown separately.
[4]Includes wholesale trade and transportation, warehousing, and utilities, not shown separately.
[5]Includes arts, entertainment, and recreation, not shown separately.
[6]Includes federal government, not shown separately.

Table 7-12. Other Separations Levels[1] and Rates,[2] by Industry, December 2000–September 2009—*Continued*

(Not seasonally adjusted, levels in thousands, rates per 100.)

Year and month	Rate											
	Total[3]	Total private[3]	Construc-tion	Manufac-turing	Trade, transpor-tation, and utilities[4]	Retail trade	Profes-sional and business services	Education and health services	Leisure and hospitality[5]	Accommo-dation and food services	Govern-ment[6]	State and local govern-ment
2001	3.7	3.7	3.9	3.1	3.3	3.6	6.0	2.6	3.8	3.7	3.3	3.0
2002	3.6	3.6	3.2	3.2	3.5	3.6	6.0	2.5	3.1	3.3	3.8	3.5
2003	3.5	3.5	2.7	3.2	3.4	3.3	4.8	2.6	3.4	3.5	3.6	3.2
2004	3.4	3.3	3.3	2.4	3.7	3.7	4.1	2.3	3.3	3.5	3.7	3.2
2005	3.3	3.3	2.7	3.0	3.1	3.1	4.7	2.2	2.9	3.1	3.3	3.0
2006	3.6	3.6	4.6	3.0	4.2	4.4	4.8	2.4	2.5	2.5	3.4	2.8
2007	3.2	3.1	2.9	2.8	3.6	4.0	3.6	2.4	2.4	2.3	3.9	2.9
2008	2.9	2.9	3.2	2.5	3.7	4.3	3.2	2.4	2.4	2.4	2.9	2.7
2000												
December	0.3	0.3	0.3	0.3	0.3	0.2	0.3	0.2	0.3	0.2	0.2	0.2
2001												
January	0.5	0.5	0.5	0.4	0.6	0.8	0.4	0.3	0.6	0.6	0.5	0.3
February	0.2	0.2	0.1	0.2	0.3	0.3	0.1	0.2	0.3	0.4	0.2	0.1
March	0.3	0.3	0.2	0.3	0.2	0.2	0.5	0.2	0.3	0.3	0.2	0.1
April	0.3	0.4	0.4	0.3	0.3	0.4	0.5	0.2	0.3	0.2	0.3	0.3
May	0.2	0.2	0.2	0.2	0.2	0.2	0.5	0.1	0.2	0.2	0.3	0.3
June	0.4	0.4	0.2	0.3	0.1	0.1	1.0	0.3	0.2	0.3	0.4	0.4
July	0.4	0.4	0.6	0.3	0.2	0.2	0.5	0.2	0.4	0.5	0.5	0.5
August	0.3	0.3	0.6	0.4	0.2	0.2	0.6	0.3	0.3	0.2	0.3	0.3
September	0.3	0.3	0.3	0.2	0.3	0.3	0.4	0.2	0.3	0.3	0.3	0.3
October	0.3	0.3	0.3	0.3	0.4	0.3	0.4	0.2	0.3	0.3	0.2	0.2
November	0.2	0.2	0.3	0.1	0.2	0.2	0.3	0.2	0.2	0.2	0.2	0.1
December	0.3	0.3	0.1	0.2	0.2	0.2	0.7	0.2	0.3	0.3	0.2	0.2
2002												
January	0.5	0.5	0.3	0.5	0.5	0.5	0.9	0.3	0.3	0.3	0.5	0.4
February	0.2	0.2	0.2	0.2	0.3	0.2	0.4	0.2	0.2	0.2	0.2	0.2
March	0.2	0.3	0.2	0.2	0.2	0.1	0.5	0.2	0.3	0.3	0.2	0.2
April	0.3	0.3	0.4	0.3	0.3	0.3	0.6	0.3	0.3	0.4	0.2	0.2
May	0.2	0.2	0.2	0.3	0.2	0.2	0.5	0.2	0.2	0.2	0.3	0.3
June	0.3	0.3	0.1	0.2	0.3	0.3	0.4	0.2	0.3	0.4	0.4	0.5
July	0.4	0.4	0.1	0.3	0.4	0.6	0.6	0.2	0.3	0.3	0.5	0.5
August	0.3	0.3	0.3	0.3	0.4	0.4	0.4	0.2	0.2	0.2	0.3	0.3
September	0.3	0.3	0.3	0.2	0.2	0.4	0.5	0.2	0.3	0.3	0.3	0.3
October	0.3	0.3	0.3	0.3	0.2	0.2	0.4	0.2	0.2	0.3	0.3	0.3
November	0.2	0.2	0.2	0.3	0.3	0.3	0.3	0.1	0.2	0.2	0.2	0.2
December	0.3	0.3	0.7	0.2	0.2	0.2	0.6	0.2	0.2	0.2	0.3	0.3
2003												
January	0.6	0.6	0.5	0.5	0.6	0.6	0.8	0.4	0.6	0.6	0.6	0.4
February	0.2	0.2	0.2	0.3	0.3	0.4	0.2	0.1	0.2	0.2	0.2	0.2
March	0.3	0.3	0.2	0.2	0.2	0.2	0.5	0.2	0.3	0.4	0.2	0.2
April	0.3	0.3	0.2	0.3	0.2	0.2	0.5	0.2	0.3	0.3	0.3	0.2
May	0.3	0.2	0.1	0.2	0.2	0.2	0.3	0.2	0.2	0.3	0.3	0.3
June	0.3	0.3	0.3	0.2	0.3	0.2	0.3	0.3	0.2	0.2	0.4	0.4
July	0.3	0.3	0.3	0.3	0.3	0.3	0.6	0.2	0.2	0.2	0.4	0.4
August	0.3	0.3	0.1	0.3	0.2	0.2	0.4	0.2	0.4	0.2	0.3	0.3
September	0.3	0.3	0.1	0.2	0.4	0.4	0.3	0.2	0.3	0.3	0.3	0.3
October	0.3	0.3	0.2	0.2	0.3	0.3	0.3	0.2	0.3	0.3	0.2	0.2
November	0.2	0.2	0.3	0.2	0.2	0.2	0.3	0.1	0.3	0.4	0.2	0.1
December	0.2	0.2	0.2	0.2	0.2	0.2	0.3	0.2	0.2	0.2	0.2	0.2
2004												
January	0.5	0.5	0.7	0.3	0.4	0.4	0.3	0.3	0.5	0.6	0.7	0.4
February	0.2	0.2	0.2	0.2	0.2	0.2	0.2	0.2	0.2	0.2	0.2	0.2
March	0.2	0.2	0.2	0.2	0.4	0.4	0.3	0.1	0.1	0.1	0.2	0.2
April	0.3	0.3	0.2	0.2	0.3	0.3	0.3	0.2	0.3	0.3	0.2	0.2
May	0.3	0.3	0.1	0.2	0.3	0.3	0.3	0.2	0.3	0.3	0.3	0.3
June	0.3	0.3	0.2	0.2	0.3	0.3	0.5	0.2	0.2	0.2	0.5	0.5
July	0.3	0.3	0.2	0.2	0.3	0.4	0.4	0.2	0.3	0.3	0.5	0.5
August	0.3	0.3	0.2	0.2	0.4	0.3	0.3	0.2	0.4	0.4	0.3	0.3
September	0.3	0.3	0.4	0.2	0.2	0.2	0.3	0.2	0.3	0.3	0.2	0.2
October	0.3	0.3	0.6	0.1	0.4	0.4	0.3	0.2	0.2	0.1	0.2	0.2
November	0.2	0.2	0.1	0.1	0.2	0.3	0.3	0.1	0.4	0.4	0.2	0.1
December	0.2	0.2	0.2	0.2	0.3	0.2	0.4	0.1	0.2	0.2	0.2	0.2
2005												
January	0.4	0.4	0.2	0.4	0.4	0.4	0.4	0.3	0.5	0.5	0.5	0.4
February	0.2	0.2	0.2	0.2	0.2	0.3	0.5	0.1	0.2	0.2	0.2	0.2
March	0.2	0.2	0.1	0.2	0.3	0.4	0.3	0.1	0.2	0.2	0.2	0.2
April	0.3	0.3	0.2	0.2	0.3	0.2	0.3	0.2	0.2	0.2	0.2	0.2
May	0.3	0.3	0.2	0.2	0.2	0.2	0.5	0.2	0.3	0.3	0.2	0.2
June	0.2	0.2	0.3	0.2	0.2	0.2	0.2	0.2	0.2	0.2	0.5	0.5
July	0.3	0.3	0.1	0.3	0.2	0.3	0.2	0.2	0.2	0.1	0.4	0.3
August	0.3	0.3	0.3	0.3	0.2	0.2	0.4	0.2	0.3	0.3	0.3	0.3
September	0.2	0.2	0.2	0.2	0.3	0.2	0.4	0.2	0.1	0.1	0.3	0.2
October	0.3	0.3	0.4	0.2	0.2	0.2	0.5	0.2	0.2	0.2	0.2	0.2
November	0.2	0.2	0.4	0.2	0.2	0.2	0.3	0.1	0.2	0.2	0.1	0.1
December	0.3	0.4	0.2	0.3	0.3	0.3	0.7	0.2	0.5	0.6	0.2	0.2

[1]Other separations are the number of other separations during the entire month.
[2]The other separations rate is the number of other separations during the entire month as a percent of total employment.
[3]Includes natural resources and mining, information, financial activities, and other services, not shown separately.
[4]Includes wholesale trade and transportation, warehousing, and utilities, not shown separately.
[5]Includes arts, entertainment, and recreation, not shown separately.
[6]Includes federal government, not shown separately.

Table 7-12. Other Separations Levels[1] and Rates,[2] by Industry, December 2000–September 2009—*Continued*

(Not seasonally adjusted, levels in thousands, rates per 100.)

Year and month	Level											
	Total[3]	Total private[3]	Construction	Manufacturing	Trade, transportation, and utilities[4]	Retail trade	Professional and business services	Education and health services	Leisure and hospitality[5]	Accommodation and food services	Government[6]	State and local government
2006												
January	610	519	25	68	110	60	177	40	26	20	91	55
February	318	280	20	40	86	50	37	21	33	28	38	26
March	341	293	20	35	86	48	62	27	23	21	48	33
April	428	377	42	34	91	49	62	52	38	34	51	36
May	431	363	44	29	119	74	61	28	33	28	68	48
June	474	372	25	42	113	74	85	36	25	24	102	88
July	490	411	27	47	96	53	84	63	24	23	79	63
August	365	281	19	32	72	46	44	35	33	27	83	62
September	364	300	35	27	84	59	43	26	17	14	64	37
October	420	382	46	30	90	52	80	35	30	27	38	31
November	296	262	31	22	66	47	66	30	16	12	34	25
December	333	283	21	23	92	56	50	30	28	22	49	38
2007												
January	593	506	31	53	139	101	67	78	28	23	87	55
February	324	264	25	37	67	41	58	21	21	19	60	39
March	316	264	22	29	87	60	45	27	22	18	52	28
April	385	325	9	49	81	53	53	30	32	27	60	33
May	312	232	22	34	52	31	38	31	18	14	81	47
June	415	290	8	38	90	58	50	43	23	20	125	92
July	474	360	23	23	75	45	73	52	43	35	114	74
August	360	268	10	26	69	43	55	28	45	31	92	53
September	334	255	11	34	69	48	63	25	17	14	79	37
October	339	305	19	22	65	37	51	42	30	26	33	26
November	277	244	22	27	75	57	37	28	22	20	33	27
December	334	278	18	21	87	49	54	39	23	20	56	48
2008												
January	446	365	19	47	84	55	67	48	59	56	80	52
February	291	252	17	25	84	72	35	40	16	15	39	30
March	332	290	21	36	82	67	74	35	15	14	42	32
April	422	378	37	33	130	110	33	45	39	31	44	38
May	283	232	17	22	63	45	40	33	32	29	50	41
June	303	212	17	24	63	42	30	30	31	29	91	84
July	360	289	16	26	94	51	42	28	30	26	71	64
August	303	247	16	24	85	50	38	42	18	15	56	47
September	340	279	10	27	78	43	51	36	25	14	61	53
October	331	288	25	34	71	43	53	49	17	15	42	37
November	269	237	19	18	73	46	40	42	23	19	32	27
December	289	250	19	16	67	34	65	26	17	15	39	33
2009												
January	514	445	23	46	121	61	64	97	25	18	69	54
February	272	242	10	18	55	39	65	47	27	27	30	25
March	284	251	9	23	74	46	48	50	16	14	33	27
April	384	346	20	23	120	93	71	40	14	12	38	32
May	288	235	7	22	82	60	45	28	21	20	53	39
June	364	255	9	35	43	31	48	56	36	31	109	78
July	351	260	12	22	73	51	57	36	26	21	91	73
August	338	280	6	23	77	64	42	55	30	25	58	50
September[7]	309	256	7	17	84	47	48	41	31	28	53	44

[1]Other separations are the number of other separations during the entire month.
[2]The other separations rate is the number of other separations during the entire month as a percent of total employment.
[3]Includes natural resources and mining, information, financial activities, and other services, not shown separately.
[4]Includes wholesale trade and transportation, warehousing, and utilities, not shown separately.
[5]Includes arts, entertainment, and recreation, not shown separately.
[6]Includes federal government, not shown separately.
[7]Preliminary.

Table 7-12. Other Separations Levels[1] and Rates,[2] by Industry, December 2000–September 2009—Continued

(Not seasonally adjusted, levels in thousands, rates per 100.)

Year and month	Rate											
	Total[3]	Total private[3]	Construction	Manufacturing	Trade, transportation, and utilities[4]	Retail trade	Professional and business services	Education and health services	Leisure and hospitality[5]	Accommodation and food services	Government[6]	State and local government
2006												
January	0.5	0.5	0.3	0.5	0.4	0.4	1.0	0.2	0.2	0.2	0.4	0.3
February	0.2	0.3	0.3	0.3	0.3	0.3	0.2	0.1	0.3	0.3	0.2	0.1
March	0.3	0.3	0.3	0.3	0.3	0.3	0.4	0.2	0.2	0.2	0.2	0.2
April	0.3	0.3	0.6	0.2	0.4	0.3	0.4	0.3	0.3	0.3	0.2	0.2
May	0.3	0.3	0.6	0.2	0.5	0.5	0.4	0.2	0.2	0.2	0.3	0.2
June	0.3	0.3	0.3	0.3	0.4	0.5	0.5	0.2	0.2	0.2	0.5	0.5
July	0.4	0.4	0.3	0.3	0.4	0.3	0.5	0.4	0.2	0.2	0.4	0.3
August	0.3	0.2	0.2	0.2	0.3	0.3	0.2	0.2	0.2	0.2	0.4	0.3
September	0.3	0.3	0.4	0.2	0.3	0.4	0.2	0.1	0.1	0.1	0.3	0.2
October	0.3	0.3	0.6	0.2	0.3	0.3	0.4	0.2	0.2	0.2	0.2	0.2
November	0.2	0.2	0.4	0.2	0.2	0.3	0.4	0.2	0.1	0.1	0.2	0.1
December	0.2	0.2	0.3	0.2	0.3	0.4	0.3	0.2	0.2	0.2	0.2	0.2
2007												
January	0.4	0.4	0.4	0.4	0.5	0.7	0.4	0.4	0.2	0.2	0.4	0.3
February	0.2	0.2	0.3	0.3	0.3	0.3	0.3	0.1	0.2	0.2	0.3	0.2
March	0.2	0.2	0.3	0.2	0.3	0.4	0.3	0.1	0.2	0.2	0.2	0.1
April	0.3	0.3	0.1	0.4	0.3	0.3	0.3	0.2	0.2	0.2	0.3	0.2
May	0.2	0.2	0.3	0.2	0.2	0.2	0.2	0.2	0.1	0.1	0.4	0.2
June	0.3	0.2	0.1	0.3	0.3	0.4	0.3	0.2	0.2	0.2	0.6	0.5
July	0.3	0.3	0.3	0.2	0.3	0.3	0.4	0.3	0.3	0.3	0.5	0.4
August	0.3	0.2	0.1	0.2	0.3	0.3	0.3	0.2	0.3	0.3	0.4	0.3
September	0.2	0.2	0.1	0.2	0.3	0.3	0.3	0.1	0.1	0.1	0.4	0.2
October	0.2	0.3	0.2	0.2	0.2	0.2	0.3	0.2	0.2	0.2	0.1	0.1
November	0.2	0.2	0.3	0.2	0.3	0.4	0.2	0.2	0.2	0.2	0.1	0.1
December	0.2	0.2	0.2	0.2	0.3	0.3	0.3	0.2	0.2	0.2	0.2	0.2
2008												
January	0.3	0.3	0.3	0.3	0.3	0.4	0.4	0.3	0.5	0.5	0.4	0.3
February	0.2	0.2	0.2	0.2	0.3	0.5	0.2	0.2	0.1	0.1	0.2	0.2
March	0.2	0.3	0.3	0.3	0.3	0.4	0.4	0.2	0.1	0.1	0.2	0.2
April	0.3	0.3	0.5	0.2	0.5	0.7	0.2	0.2	0.3	0.3	0.2	0.2
May	0.2	0.2	0.2	0.2	0.2	0.3	0.2	0.2	0.2	0.3	0.2	0.2
June	0.2	0.2	0.2	0.2	0.2	0.3	0.2	0.2	0.2	0.2	0.4	0.4
July	0.3	0.2	0.2	0.2	0.4	0.3	0.2	0.2	0.2	0.2	0.3	0.3
August	0.2	0.2	0.2	0.2	0.3	0.3	0.2	0.2	0.1	0.1	0.3	0.3
September	0.2	0.2	0.1	0.2	0.3	0.3	0.3	0.2	0.2	0.1	0.3	0.3
October	0.2	0.3	0.3	0.3	0.3	0.3	0.3	0.3	0.1	0.1	0.2	0.2
November	0.2	0.2	0.3	0.1	0.3	0.3	0.2	0.2	0.2	0.2	0.1	0.1
December	0.2	0.2	0.3	0.1	0.3	0.2	0.4	0.1	0.1	0.1	0.2	0.2
2009												
January	0.4	0.4	0.4	0.4	0.5	0.4	0.4	0.5	0.2	0.2	0.3	0.3
February	0.2	0.2	0.2	0.1	0.2	0.3	0.4	0.2	0.2	0.2	0.1	0.1
March	0.2	0.2	0.2	0.2	0.3	0.3	0.3	0.3	0.1	0.1	0.1	0.1
April	0.3	0.3	0.3	0.2	0.5	0.6	0.4	0.2	0.1	0.1	0.2	0.2
May	0.2	0.2	0.1	0.2	0.3	0.4	0.3	0.1	0.2	0.2	0.2	0.2
June	0.3	0.2	0.1	0.3	0.2	0.2	0.3	0.3	0.3	0.3	0.5	0.4
July	0.3	0.2	0.2	0.2	0.3	0.3	0.3	0.2	0.2	0.2	0.4	0.4
August	0.3	0.3	0.1	0.2	0.3	0.4	0.3	0.3	0.2	0.2	0.3	0.3
September[7]	0.2	0.2	0.1	0.1	0.3	0.3	0.3	0.2	0.2	0.2	0.2	0.2

[1]Other separations are the number of other separations during the entire month.
[2]The other separations rate is the number of other separations during the entire month as a percent of total employment.
[3]Includes natural resources and mining, information, financial activities, and other services, not shown separately.
[4]Includes wholesale trade and transportation, warehousing, and utilities, not shown separately.
[5]Includes arts, entertainment, and recreation, not shown separately.
[6]Includes federal government, not shown separately.
[7]Preliminary.

Chapter Eight

LABOR-MANAGEMENT RELATIONS

LABOR-MANAGEMENT RELATIONS

HIGHLIGHTS

This chapter contains information on historical trends in union membership, earnings, and work stoppages.

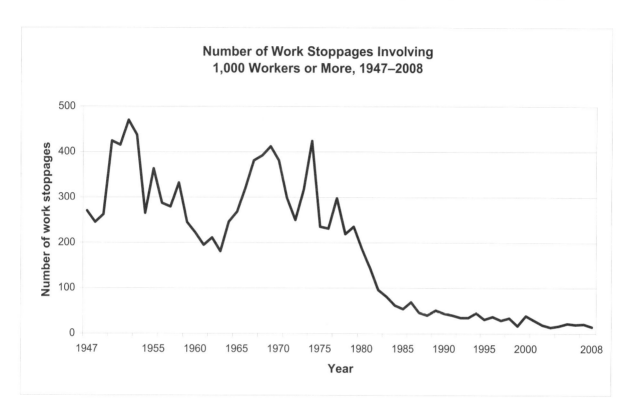

The number of work stoppages has declined dramatically since 1947 and has been gradually declining since the early 1980s. In 2008, there were only 15 work stoppages that involved 1,000 workers or more. In comparison, there were 187 work stoppages involving 1,000 workers or more in 1980, 44 work stoppages in 1990, and 39 work stoppages in 2000. (See Table 8-1.)

OTHER HIGHLIGHTS

- In 2008, the number of workers belonging to a union rose by 428,000 to 16.1 million. Union members accounted for 12.4 percent of employed wage and salary workers, an increase from 12.1 percent in 2007. In 1983, the first year for which comparable union data are available, the union membership rate was 20.1 percent. (See Table 8-5.)

- The median weekly earnings of union members was significantly higher than that of non-union members in both the private and public sector. In the private sector, the median weekly earnings of union members was 23.3 percent higher than that of non-union members, and in the public sector it was 20.5 percent higher than that of non-union members. (See Table 8-4)

- Education, training, and library occupations had the highest unionization rate among all occupations at 38.7 percent, followed by protective service occupations, at 35.4 percent. Government workers were nearly five times more likely to belong to a union than private sector employees. (See Table 8-3.)

- Among the five states reporting union membership rates below 5.0 percent in 2008, North Carolina posted the lowest rate (3.5 percent). Three states had union membership rates over 20.0 percent in 2008—New York (24.9 percent), Hawaii (24.3 percent), and Alaska (23.5 percent). (See Table 8-6.)

NOTES AND DEFINITIONS

WORK STOPPAGES

Collection and Coverage

Data on work stoppages measure the number and duration of major strikes or lockouts (involving 1,000 workers or more) during the year, the number of workers involved in these stoppages, and the amount of time lost due to these stoppages.

Information on work stoppages is obtained from reports issued by the Federal Mediation and Conciliation Service, state labor market information offices, Bureau of Labor Statistics (BLS) Strike Reports from the Office of Employment and Unemployment Statistics, and media sources such as the *Daily Labor Report* and the *Wall Street Journal*. One or both parties involved in the work stoppage (employer and/or union) is contacted to verify the duration of the stoppage and number of workers idled by the stoppage.

Concepts and Definitions

Major work stoppage includes both worker-initiated strikes and employer-initiated lockouts involving 1,000 workers or more. BLS does not distinguish between lockouts and strikes in its statistics.

Workers involved consists of workers directly involved in the stoppage. This category does not measure the indirect or secondary effect of stoppages on other establishments whose employees are idle from material shortages or lack of service.

Days of idleness is calculated by taking the number of workers involved in the strike or lockout and multiplying it by the number of days workers are off the job. The number of working days lost for every major work stoppage is based on a 5-day workweek (Monday through Friday), excluding federal holidays.

Sources of Additional Information

Additional information is available in BLS news release USDL 09-0150, "Major Work Stoppages in 2008" on the BLS Web site at <http://www.bls.gov/wsp/home.htm>.

UNION MEMBERSHIP

Collection and Coverage

The estimates of union membership are obtained from the Current Population Survey (CPS), which provides basic information on the labor force, employment, and unemployment. The survey is conducted monthly for the Bureau

of Labor Statistics by the U.S. Census Bureau from a scientifically selected national sample of about 60,000 households. The union membership and earnings data are tabulated from one-quarter of the CPS monthly sample and are limited to wage and salary workers. All self-employed workers are excluded. The data in these tables are annual averages.

Union membership data for 2008 are not strictly comparable with data for 2007 and earlier years because of the introduction of updated population controls with the release of January data. The effect of the revised population controls on the union membership estimates is unknown. However, the effect of the new controls on the monthly CPS estimates was to decrease the December 2007 employment level by 598,000 and the unemployment level by 40,000. The updated controls had little or no effect on unemployment rates and other ratios.

Concepts and Definitions

Union members are members of a labor union or an employee association similar to a union.

Represented by unions refers to union members, as well as to workers who have no union affiliation but whose jobs are covered by a union contract.

Usual weekly earnings represent earnings before taxes and other deductions and include any overtime pay, commissions, or tips usually received (at the main job in the case of multiple jobholders). Prior to 1994, respondents were asked how much they usually earned per week. Since January 1994, respondents have been asked to identify the easiest way for them to report earnings (hourly, weekly, biweekly, twice monthly, monthly, annually, other) and how much they usually earn in the reported time period. Earnings reported on a basis other than weekly are converted to a weekly equivalent. The term "usual" is as perceived by the respondent. If the respondent asks for a definition of "usual," interviewers are instructed to define the term as more than half of the weeks worked during the past 4 or 5 months.

Median earnings is the amount which divides a given earnings distribution into two equal groups, one having earnings above the median and the other having earnings below the median. The estimating procedure places each reported or calculated weekly earnings value into $50-wide intervals which are centered around multiples of $50. The actual value is estimated through the linear interpolation of the interval in which the median lies.

Wage and salary workers are workers who receive wages, salaries, commissions, tips, payment in kind, or piece rates. The group includes employees in both the private and public sectors, but, for the purposes of the union membership and earnings series, excludes all self-employed persons, regardless of whether or not their businesses are incorporated.

Full-time workers are workers who usually work 35 hours or more per week at their sole or principal job.

Part-time workers are workers who usually work fewer than 35 hours per week at their sole or principal job.

Hispanic or Latino ethnicity refers to persons who identified themselves in the enumeration process as being Spanish, Hispanic, or Latino. Persons whose ethnicity is identified as Hispanic or Latino may be of any race.

Sources of Additional Information

For additional information see BLS news release USDL 09-0095, "Union Members in 2008."

Table 8-1. Work Stoppages Involving 1,000 Workers or More, 1947–2008

(Number, percent.)

Year	Stoppages beginning during the year		Days idle during the year[1]	
	Number	Workers involved (thousands)[2]	Number (thousands)	Percent of estimated total working time[3]
1947	270	1 629	25 720	. . .
1948	245	1 435	26 127	0.22
1949	262	2 537	43 420	0.38
1950	424	1 698	30 390	0.26
1951	415	1 462	15 070	0.12
1952	470	2 746	48 820	0.38
1953	437	1 623	18 130	0.14
1954	265	1 075	16 630	0.13
1955	363	2 055	21 180	0.16
1956	287	1 370	26 840	0.20
1957	279	887	10 340	0.07
1958	332	1 587	17 900	0.13
1959	245	1 381	60 850	0.43
1960	222	896	13 260	0.09
1961	195	1 031	10 140	0.07
1962	211	793	11 760	0.08
1963	181	512	10 020	0.07
1964	246	1 183	16 220	0.11
1965	268	999	15 140	0.10
1966	321	1 300	16 000	0.10
1967	381	2 192	31 320	0.18
1968	392	1 855	35 367	0.20
1969	412	1 576	29 397	0.16
1970	381	2 468	52 761	0.29
1971	298	2 516	35 538	0.19
1972	250	975	16 764	0.09
1973	317	1 400	16 260	0.08
1974	424	1 796	31 809	0.16
1975	235	965	17 563	0.09
1976	231	1 519	23 962	0.12
1977	298	1 212	21 258	0.10
1978	219	1 006	23 774	0.11
1979	235	1 021	20 409	0.09
1980	187	795	20 844	0.09
1981	145	729	16 908	0.07
1982	96	656	9 061	0.04
1983	81	909	17 461	0.08
1984	62	376	8 499	0.04
1985	54	324	7 079	0.03
1986	69	533	11 861	0.05
1987	46	174	4 481	0.02
1988	40	118	4 381	0.02
1989	51	452	16 996	0.07
1990	44	185	5 926	0.02
1991	40	392	4 584	0.02
1992	35	364	3 989	0.01
1993	35	182	3 981	0.01
1994	45	322	5 021	0.02
1995	31	192	5 771	0.02
1996	37	273	4 889	0.02
1997	29	339	4 497	0.01
1998	34	387	5 116	0.02
1999	17	73	1 996	0.01
2000	39	394	20 419	0.06
2001	29	99	1 151	([4])
2002	19	46	660	([4])
2003	14	129	4 091	0.01
2004	17	171	3 344	0.01
2005	22	100	1 736	0.01
2006	20	70	2 688	0.01
2007	21	189	1 265	([4])
2008	15	72	1 954	0.01

[1]Days idle include all stoppages in effect during the reference period. For work stoppages that are still ongoing at the end of the calendar year, only those days of idleness during the calendar year are counted.
[2]Workers are counted more than once if involved in more than one stoppage during the reference period.
[3]Agricultural and government workers are included in the calculation of estimated working time; private household, forestry, and fishery workers are excluded.
[4]Less than 0.005 percent.
. . . = Not available.

Table 8-2. Union Affiliation of Employed Wage and Salary Workers, by Selected Characteristics, 2003–2008

(Numbers in thousands, percent.)

Characteristic	2003					2004					2005				
	Total employed	Member of union[1]		Represented by union[2]		Total employed	Member of union[1]		Represented by union[2]		Total employed	Member of union[1]		Represented by union[2]	
		Total	Percent of employed	Total	Percent of employed		Total	Percent of employed	Total	Percent of employed		Total	Percent of employed	Total	Percent of employed
SEX AND AGE															
Both Sexes, 16 Years and Over	122 358	15 776	12.9	17 448	14.3	123 554	15 472	12.5	17 087	13.8	125 889	15 685	12.5	17 223	13.7
16 to 24 years	18 904	966	5.1	1 124	5.9	19 109	890	4.7	1 019	5.3	19 283	878	4.6	1 019	5.3
25 years and over	103 454	14 810	14.3	16 324	15.8	104 444	14 581	14.0	16 069	15.4	106 606	14 808	13.9	16 204	15.2
25 to 34 years	28 179	3 097	11.0	3 455	12.3	28 202	2 982	10.6	3 316	11.8	28 450	3 044	10.7	3 368	11.8
35 to 44 years	30 714	4 308	14.0	4 717	15.4	30 470	4 173	13.7	4 590	15.1	30 654	4 211	13.7	4 579	14.9
45 to 54 years	27 567	4 848	17.6	5 307	19.3	28 039	4 771	17.0	5 233	18.7	28 714	4 731	16.5	5 158	18.0
55 to 64 years	13 633	2 300	16.9	2 547	18.7	14 239	2 390	16.8	2 617	18.4	15 158	2 496	16.5	2 732	18.0
65 years and over	3 361	258	7.7	297	8.8	3 495	264	7.5	314	9.0	3 631	325	8.9	366	10.1
Men, 16 Years and Over	63 236	9 044	14.3	9 848	15.6	64 145	8 878	13.8	9 638	15.0	65 466	8 870	13.5	9 597	14.7
16 to 24 years	9 683	595	6.1	685	7.1	9 835	557	5.7	627	6.4	9 860	523	5.3	603	6.1
25 years and over	53 553	8 450	15.8	9 163	17.1	54 310	8 321	15.3	9 010	16.6	55 606	8 347	15.0	8 994	16.2
25 to 34 years	15 263	1 826	12.0	2 005	13.1	15 391	1 722	11.2	1 873	12.2	15 559	1 754	11.3	1 915	12.3
35 to 44 years	16 080	2 535	15.8	2 735	17.0	16 035	2 449	15.3	2 658	16.6	16 196	2 422	15.0	2 582	15.9
45 to 54 years	13 723	2 684	19.6	2 891	21.1	14 026	2 699	19.2	2 903	20.7	14 421	2 658	18.4	2 849	19.8
55 to 64 years	6 776	1 271	18.8	1 377	20.3	7 117	1 309	18.4	1 414	19.9	7 606	1 346	17.7	1 458	19.2
65 years and over	1 710	133	7.8	155	9.0	1 741	142	8.2	163	9.4	1 824	167	9.1	190	10.4
Women, 16 Years and Over	59 122	6 732	11.4	7 601	12.9	59 408	6 593	11.1	7 450	12.5	60 423	6 815	11.3	7 626	12.6
16 to 24 years	9 221	371	4.0	439	4.8	9 274	333	3.6	391	4.2	9 423	354	3.8	417	4.4
25 years and over	49 901	6 360	12.7	7 161	14.4	50 134	6 260	12.5	7 058	14.1	51 000	6 461	12.7	7 210	14.1
25 to 34 years	12 916	1 270	9.8	1 451	11.2	12 811	1 261	9.8	1 443	11.3	12 891	1 290	10.0	1 454	11.3
35 to 44 years	14 634	1 773	12.1	1 982	13.5	14 435	1 725	11.9	1 931	13.4	14 457	1 790	12.4	1 997	13.8
45 to 54 years	13 844	2 163	15.6	2 416	17.5	14 014	2 072	14.8	2 330	16.6	14 293	2 073	14.5	2 309	16.2
55 to 64 years	6 857	1 029	15.0	1 170	17.1	7 122	1 081	15.2	1 203	16.9	7 552	1 150	15.2	1 274	16.9
65 years and over	1 651	125	7.6	142	8.6	1 753	121	6.9	151	8.6	1 806	158	8.8	176	9.8
RACE, HISPANIC ORIGIN, AND SEX															
White, 16 Years and Over[3]	100 589	12 535	12.5	13 849	13.8	101 340	12 381	12.2	13 657	13.5	102 967	12 520	12.2	13 755	13.4
Men	52 827	7 378	14.0	8 016	15.2	53 432	7 260	13.6	7 854	14.7	54 462	7 275	13.4	7 858	14.4
Women	47 762	5 157	10.8	5 834	12.2	47 908	5 121	10.7	5 803	12.1	48 505	5 245	10.8	5 897	12.2
Black, 16 Years and Over[3]	13 928	2 298	16.5	2 540	18.2	14 090	2 130	15.1	2 355	16.7	14 459	2 178	15.1	2 391	16.5
Men	6 302	1 153	18.3	1 249	19.8	6 409	1 085	16.9	1 185	18.5	6 603	1 062	16.1	1 166	17.7
Women	7 626	1 145	15.0	1 291	16.9	7 681	1 045	13.6	1 170	15.2	7 857	1 115	14.2	1 225	15.6
Asian, 16 Years and Over[3]	5 096	581	11.4	659	12.9	5 280	603	11.4	670	12.7	5 479	614	11.2	666	12.2
Men	2 699	296	11.0	346	12.8	2 815	328	11.7	371	13.2	2 881	314	10.9	337	11.7
Women	2 397	285	11.9	313	13.1	2 465	275	11.1	299	12.1	2 598	299	11.5	329	12.7
Hispanic, 16 Years and Over[4]	16 068	1 712	10.7	1 913	11.9	16 533	1 676	10.1	1 888	11.4	17 191	1 793	10.4	1 981	11.5
Men	9 567	1 050	11.0	1 160	12.1	9 857	1 016	10.3	1 130	11.5	10 324	1 093	10.6	1 185	11.5
Women	6 501	662	10.2	753	11.6	6 676	661	9.9	758	11.4	6 866	700	10.2	796	11.6
FULL- OR PART-TIME STATUS[5]															
Full-time workers	100 302	14 263	14.2	15 732	15.7	101 224	14 029	13.9	15 463	15.3	103 560	14 207	13.7	15 551	15.0
Part-time workers	21 809	1 479	6.8	1 679	7.7	22 047	1 406	6.4	1 587	7.2	22 052	1 441	6.5	1 630	7.4

Note: Beginning in January 2006, data reflect revised population controls used in the household survey.

[1] Data refer to members of a labor union or to an employee association similar to a union.

[2] Data refer to members of a labor union or to an employee association similar to a union, as well as to workers who report no union affiliation but whose jobs are covered by a union or an employee association contract.

[3] Beginning in 2003, persons who selected this race group only; persons who selected more than one race group are not included. Prior to 2003, persons who reported more than one race group were included in the group they identified as their main race. Additionally, estimates for the above race groups (White, Black, and Asian) do not sum to totals because data are not presented for all races.

[4] May be of any race.

[5] The distinction between full- and part-time workers is based on hours usually worked. Data will not sum to totals because full- or part-time status on the principal job is not identifiable for a small number of multiple job holders.

Table 8-2. Union Affiliation of Employed Wage and Salary Workers, by Selected Characteristics, 2003–2008
—*Continued*

(Numbers in thousands, percent.)

Characteristic	2006					2007					2008				
	Total employed	Member of union[1]		Represented by union[2]		Total employed	Member of union[1]		Represented by union[2]		Total employed	Member of union[1]		Represented by union[2]	
		Total	Percent of employed	Total	Percent of employed		Total	Percent of employed	Total	Percent of employed		Total	Percent of employed	Total	Percent of employed
SEX AND AGE															
Both Sexes, 16 Years and Over	128 237	15 359	12.0	16 860	13.1	129 767	15 670	12.1	17 243	13.3	129 377	16 098	12.4	17 761	13.7
16 to 24 years	19 538	857	4.4	978	5.0	19 395	939	4.8	1 068	5.5	18 705	930	5.0	1 062	5.7
25 years and over	108 699	14 502	13.3	15 883	14.6	110 372	14 731	13.3	16 176	14.7	110 672	15 168	13.7	16 699	15.1
25 to 34 years	28 805	2 899	10.1	3 195	11.1	29 409	3 050	10.4	3 358	11.4	29 276	3 120	10.7	3 443	11.8
35 to 44 years	30 526	3 997	13.1	4 356	14.3	30 296	3 972	13.1	4 362	14.4	29 708	3 993	13.4	4 365	14.7
45 to 54 years	29 401	4 710	16.0	5 131	17.5	29 731	4 664	15.7	5 087	17.1	29 787	4 767	16.0	5 228	17.6
55 to 64 years	16 095	2 568	16.0	2 832	17.6	16 752	2 691	16.1	2 967	17.7	17 430	2 887	16.6	3 209	18.4
65 years and over	3 872	328	8.5	370	9.5	4 183	355	8.5	402	9.6	4 471	401	9.0	454	10.2
Men, 16 Years and Over	66 811	8 657	13.0	9 360	14.0	67 468	8 767	13.0	9 494	14.1	66 846	8 938	13.4	9 724	14.5
16 to 24 years	10 130	543	5.4	608	6.0	9 959	551	5.5	627	6.3	9 537	555	5.8	617	6.5
25 years and over	56 682	8 114	14.3	8 752	15.4	57 509	8 217	14.3	8 867	15.4	57 309	8 383	14.6	9 107	15.9
25 to 34 years	15 677	1 650	10.5	1 793	11.4	15 994	1 736	10.9	1 884	11.8	15 780	1 750	11.1	1 909	12.1
35 to 44 years	16 159	2 309	14.3	2 488	15.4	16 070	2 318	14.4	2 501	15.6	15 653	2 307	14.7	2 491	15.9
45 to 54 years	14 867	2 617	17.6	2 807	18.9	15 040	2 578	17.1	2 745	18.3	14 988	2 608	17.4	2 812	18.8
55 to 64 years	7 990	1 370	17.1	1 474	18.4	8 286	1 403	16.9	1 532	18.5	8 657	1 525	17.6	1 682	19.4
65 years and over	1 989	167	8.4	190	9.6	2 119	181	8.5	205	9.7	2 230	193	8.7	213	9.6
Women, 16 Years and Over	61 426	6 702	10.9	7 501	12.2	62 299	6 903	11.1	7 749	12.4	62 532	7 160	11.4	8 036	12.9
16 to 24 years	9 408	315	3.3	370	3.9	9 436	388	4.1	441	4.7	9 168	374	4.1	445	4.8
25 years and over	52 018	6 388	12.3	7 131	13.7	52 863	6 514	12.3	7 308	13.8	53 364	6 785	12.7	7 592	14.2
25 to 34 years	13 127	1 249	9.5	1 401	10.7	13 416	1 313	9.8	1 474	11.0	13 496	1 370	10.1	1 534	11.4
35 to 44 years	14 368	1 687	11.7	1 867	13.0	14 226	1 653	11.6	1 861	13.1	14 055	1 685	12.0	1 874	13.3
45 to 54 years	14 534	2 093	14.4	2 325	16.0	14 691	2 086	14.2	2 341	15.9	14 799	2 159	14.6	2 416	16.3
55 to 64 years	8 106	1 198	14.8	1 358	16.8	8 466	1 288	15.2	1 435	17.0	8 773	1 363	15.5	1 527	17.4
65 years and over	1 883	160	8.5	180	9.5	2 065	174	8.4	197	9.5	2 241	208	9.3	241	10.7
RACE, HISPANIC ORIGIN, AND SEX															
White, 16 Years and Over[3]	104 668	12 259	11.7	13 424	12.8	105 515	12 487	11.8	13 715	13.0	105 052	12 863	12.2	14 222	13.5
Men	55 459	7 115	12.8	7 668	13.8	55 771	7 134	12.8	7 708	13.8	55 197	7 309	13.2	7 961	14.4
Women	49 209	5 144	10.5	5 756	11.7	49 743	5 352	10.8	6 007	12.1	49 855	5 555	11.1	6 261	12.6
Black, 16 Years and Over[3]	14 878	2 163	14.5	2 391	16.1	15 177	2 165	14.3	2 403	15.8	15 030	2 178	14.5	2 370	15.8
Men	6 788	1 056	15.6	1 158	17.1	6 945	1 097	15.8	1 205	17.3	6 809	1 081	15.9	1 159	17.0
Women	8 090	1 107	13.7	1 233	15.2	8 232	1 067	13.0	1 198	14.6	8 221	1 097	13.3	1 211	14.7
Asian, 16 Years and Over[3]	5 703	592	10.4	657	11.5	6 016	654	10.9	720	12.0	6 157	653	10.6	714	11.6
Men	3 015	286	9.5	316	10.5	3 168	324	10.2	348	11.0	3 216	310	9.6	339	10.6
Women	2 688	306	11.4	340	12.7	2 849	330	11.6	372	13.1	2 941	344	11.7	374	12.7
Hispanic, 16 Years and Over[4]	18 121	1 770	9.8	1 935	10.7	18 778	1 837	9.8	2 026	10.8	18 572	1 960	10.6	2 168	11.7
Men	10 842	1 064	9.8	1 144	10.6	11 163	1 108	9.9	1 208	10.8	10 998	1 204	11.0	1 317	12.0
Women	7 279	706	9.7	791	10.9	7 615	728	9.6	818	10.7	7 574	756	10.0	852	11.2
FULL- OR PART-TIME STATUS[5]															
Full-time workers	106 106	13 938	13.1	15 244	14.4	107 339	14 201	13.2	15 570	14.5	106 648	14 561	13.7	16 029	15.0
Part-time workers	21 863	1 382	6.3	1 573	7.2	22 172	1 437	6.5	1 635	7.4	22 497	1 505	6.7	1 697	7.5

Note: Beginning in January 2006, data reflect revised population controls used in the household survey.

[1]Data refer to members of a labor union or to an employee association similar to a union.
[2]Data refer to members of a labor union or to an employee association similar to a union, as well as to workers who report no union affiliation but whose jobs are covered by a union or an employee association contract.
[3]Beginning in 2003, persons who selected this race group only; persons who selected more than one race group are not included. Prior to 2003, persons who reported more than one race group were included in the group they identified as their main race. Additionally, estimates for the above race groups (White, Black, and Asian) do not sum to totals because data are not presented for all races.
[4]May be of any race.
[5]The distinction between full- and part-time workers is based on hours usually worked. Data will not sum to totals because full- or part-time status on the principal job is not identifiable for a small number of multiple job holders.

Table 8-3. Union Affiliation of Wage and Salary Workers, by Occupation and Industry, 2007–2008

(Thousands of people, percent.)

Occupation and industry	2007					2008				
	Total employed	Member of union[1]		Represented by union[2]		Total employed	Member of union[1]		Represented by union[2]	
		Total	Percent of employed	Total	Percent of employed		Total	Percent of employed	Total	Percent of employed
OCCUPATION										
Management, professional, and related	44 547	5 853	13.1	6 656	14.9	45 538	6 110	13.4	6 948	15.3
Management, business, and financial operations	17 003	849	5.0	1 020	6.0	17 326	866	5.0	1 039	6.0
Management	11 656	530	4.5	633	5.4	11 843	564	4.8	679	5.7
Business and financial operations	5 348	319	6.0	386	7.2	5 483	302	5.5	360	6.6
Professional and related	27 543	5 004	18.2	5 636	20.5	28 212	5 244	18.6	5 909	20.9
Computer and mathematical	3 252	157	4.8	188	5.8	3 488	170	4.9	210	6.0
Architecture and engineering	2 744	215	7.8	240	8.7	2 746	203	7.4	233	8.5
Life, physical, and social science	1 270	113	8.9	138	10.9	1 209	106	8.8	132	10.9
Community and social service	2 187	326	14.9	375	17.1	2 222	363	16.3	406	18.3
Legal	1 288	71	5.5	83	6.4	1 318	74	5.6	87	6.6
Education, training, and library	8 288	3 087	37.2	3 439	41.5	8 424	3 259	38.7	3 630	43.1
Arts, design, entertainment, sports, and media	1 955	152	7.8	182	9.3	1 994	141	7.1	167	8.4
Health care practitioner and technical	6 558	883	13.5	992	15.1	6 813	928	13.6	1 045	15.3
Services	21 784	2 481	11.4	2 692	12.4	22 114	2 624	11.9	2 831	12.8
Health care support	2 987	304	10.2	332	11.1	3 028	296	9.8	317	10.5
Protective service	3 025	1 066	35.2	1 127	37.2	3 023	1 069	35.4	1 122	37.1
Food preparation and serving related	7 500	325	4.3	371	4.9	7 694	401	5.2	444	5.8
Building and grounds cleaning and maintenance	4 642	497	10.7	549	11.8	4 648	534	11.5	592	12.7
Personal care and service	3 631	289	8.0	314	8.6	3 721	324	8.7	357	9.6
Sales and office	32 978	2 386	7.2	2 659	8.1	32 479	2 395	7.4	2 710	8.3
Sales and related	14 079	462	3.3	521	3.7	13 708	447	3.3	531	3.9
Office and administrative support	18 900	1 925	10.2	2 138	11.3	18 770	1 949	10.4	2 179	11.6
Natural resources, construction, and maintenance	13 325	2 252	16.9	2 363	17.7	12 444	2 208	17.7	2 303	18.5
Farming, fishing, and forestry	876	23	2.7	28	3.2	901	39	4.3	46	5.1
Construction and extraction	7 708	1 434	18.6	1 480	19.2	6 876	1 391	20.2	1 445	21.0
Installation, maintenance, and repair	4 742	794	16.8	855	18.0	4 668	778	16.7	812	17.4
Production, transportation, and material moving	17 133	2 699	15.8	2 874	16.8	16 802	2 760	16.4	2 968	17.7
Production	8 903	1 243	14.0	1 314	14.8	8 601	1 269	14.8	1 370	15.9
Transportation and material moving	8 231	1 456	17.7	1 560	19.0	8 202	1 491	18.2	1 599	19.5
INDUSTRY										
Private sector	108 714	8 114	7.5	8 870	8.2	108 073	8 265	7.6	9 084	8.4
Agriculture and related industries	1 046	16	1.5	19	1.8	1 057	30	2.8	35	3.4
Nonagricultural industries	107 668	8 098	7.5	8 851	8.2	107 016	8 236	7.7	9 049	8.5
Mining	705	66	9.3	72	10.2	776	54	6.9	61	7.9
Construction	8 561	1 193	13.9	1 232	14.4	7 652	1 195	15.6	1 241	16.2
Manufacturing	15 341	1 734	11.3	1 845	12.0	15 131	1 723	11.4	1 862	12.3
Durable goods	9 770	1 107	11.3	1 172	12.0	9 728	1 139	11.7	1 223	12.6
Nondurable goods	5 571	628	11.3	673	12.1	5 403	584	10.8	639	11.8
Wholesale and retail trade	18 896	990	5.2	1 075	5.7	18 622	976	5.2	1 096	5.9
Wholesale trade	3 951	205	5.2	224	5.7	3 635	194	5.3	214	5.9
Retail trade	14 945	785	5.3	851	5.7	14 987	782	5.2	881	5.9
Transportation and utilities	5 488	1 211	22.1	1 282	23.4	5 544	1 231	22.2	1 298	23.4
Transportation and warehousing	4 654	974	20.9	1 037	22.3	4 639	988	21.3	1 041	22.4
Utilities	834	237	28.4	245	29.4	906	243	26.9	257	28.3
Information[3]	3 211	389	12.1	420	13.1	3 056	388	12.7	420	13.7
Publishing, except Internet	850	62	7.3	65	7.7	717	52	7.2	62	8.7
Motion pictures and sound recording	309	35	11.5	39	12.5	337	38	11.4	39	11.7
Broadcasting, except Internet	588	51	8.7	62	10.6	561	53	9.5	59	10.6
Telecommunications	1 186	233	19.7	246	20.8	1 184	228	19.3	242	20.4
Financial activities	8 858	174	2.0	215	2.4	8 654	157	1.8	199	2.3
Finance and insurance	6 531	99	1.5	129	2.0	6 536	86	1.3	115	1.8
Finance	4 313	55	1.3	76	1.8	4 312	45	1.0	62	1.4
Insurance	2 218	45	2.0	53	2.4	2 224	41	1.9	53	2.4
Real estate and rental and leasing	2 327	74	3.2	86	3.7	2 118	71	3.3	84	4.0
Professional and business services	12 022	290	2.4	360	3.0	11 967	253	2.1	324	2.7
Professional and technical services	6 962	98	1.4	147	2.1	7 234	93	1.3	128	1.8
Management, administrative, and waste services	5 060	191	3.8	213	4.2	4 733	159	3.4	196	4.1
Education and health services	18 120	1 591	8.8	1 815	10.0	18 841	1 723	9.1	1 940	10.3
Education services	3 513	444	12.6	529	15.1	3 657	504	13.8	584	16.0
Health care and social assistance	14 607	1 147	7.9	1 286	8.8	15 184	1 219	8.0	1 356	8.9
Leisure and hospitality	10 956	302	2.8	354	3.2	11 187	361	3.2	408	3.6
Arts, entertainment, and recreation	1 966	122	6.2	138	7.0	2 044	131	6.4	150	7.3
Accommodation and food services	8 990	180	2.0	217	2.4	9 144	231	2.5	258	2.8
Accommodation	1 414	109	7.7	123	8.7	1 447	115	7.9	120	8.3
Food services and drinking places	7 575	70	0.9	94	1.2	7 696	116	1.5	138	1.8
Other services[3]	5 510	159	2.9	181	3.3	5 585	175	3.1	200	3.6
Other services, except private households	4 727	150	3.2	172	3.6	4 785	164	3.4	185	3.9
Public sector	21 053	7 557	35.9	8 373	39.8	21 305	7 832	36.8	8 676	40.7
Federal government	3 423	916	26.8	1 079	31.5	3 542	994	28.1	1 167	33.0
State government	6 384	1 943	30.4	2 168	34.0	6 176	1 955	31.6	2 167	35.1
Local government	11 246	4 698	41.8	5 126	45.6	11 586	4 884	42.2	5 342	46.1

Note: Updated population controls are introduced annually with the release of January data. Data refer to the sole or principal job of full- and part-time workers. Excluded are all self-employed workers, regardless of whether or not their businesses are incorporated.

[1]Data refer to members of a labor union or an employee association similar to a union.
[2]Data refer to members of a labor union or an employee association similar to a union, as well as to workers who report no union affiliation but whose jobs are covered by a union or an employee association contract.
[3]Includes other industries, not shown separately.

Table 8-4. Median Weekly Earnings of Full-Time Wage and Salary Workers, by Union Affiliation, Occupation, and Industry, 2007–2008

(Dollars.)

Occupation and industry	2007				2008			
	Total	Member of union[1]	Represented by union[2]	Non-union	Total	Member of union[1]	Represented by union[2]	Non-union
OCCUPATION								
Management, professional, and related	996	996	992	996	1 025	1 028	1 017	1 028
Management, business, and financial operations	1 080	1 066	1 072	1 081	1 128	1 113	1 120	1 129
Management	1 161	1 172	1 165	1 160	1 204	1 235	1 236	1 199
Business and financial operations	941	934	950	940	974	925	943	978
Professional and related	951	987	980	942	980	1 018	1 004	973
Computer and mathematical	1 229	1 188	1 204	1 231	1 242	1 149	1 139	1 248
Architecture and engineering	1 213	1 179	1 178	1 221	1 244	1 223	1 243	1 244
Life, physical, and social science	1 053	1 147	1 144	1 036	1 035	1 169	1 144	1 018
Community and social service	755	920	909	732	788	983	978	743
Legal	1 148	1 180	1 151	1 148	1 174	1 186	1 265	1 169
Education, training, and library	841	959	947	742	866	974	957	765
Arts, design, entertainment, sports, and media	829	1 000	1 009	807	882	1 110	1 098	858
Health care practitioner and technical	920	1 005	1 019	906	962	1 070	1 061	943
Services	454	666	654	421	475	691	679	440
Health care support	454	502	502	446	465	526	526	457
Protective service	719	954	946	610	748	990	983	620
Food preparation and serving related	385	502	495	379	402	502	496	398
Building and grounds cleaning and maintenance	422	551	543	407	431	596	593	412
Personal care and service	434	585	585	420	475	580	570	463
Sales and office	598	717	715	587	614	741	736	603
Sales and related	643	648	648	643	656	679	683	655
Office and administrative support	581	726	724	560	601	749	744	585
Natural resources, construction, and maintenance	670	973	961	617	702	990	984	647
Farming, fishing, and forestry	372	(³)	(³)	369	420	(³)	(³)	418
Construction and extraction	646	976	968	597	688	992	989	621
Installation, maintenance, and repair	749	975	962	709	774	1 002	994	729
Production, transportation, and material moving	577	759	753	540	594	777	770	560
Production	581	761	755	552	595	765	759	567
Transportation and material moving	570	757	750	523	593	789	779	550
INDUSTRY								
Private sector	666	818	813	651	694	838	829	680
Agriculture and related industries	412	(³)	(³)	411	444	(³)	(³)	446
Nonagricultural industries	670	819	814	654	698	840	831	683
Mining	969	960	950	975	1 007	1 024	1 032	1 003
Construction	673	1 000	993	624	712	1 014	1 012	668
Manufacturing	719	783	779	708	741	796	795	733
Durable goods	744	818	815	732	772	829	827	763
Nondurable goods	669	714	712	659	685	729	729	675
Wholesale and retail trade	587	639	632	584	603	643	638	601
Wholesale trade	720	756	753	717	741	775	763	739
Retail trade	538	608	601	532	564	598	596	561
Transportation and utilities	738	902	894	695	787	958	950	747
Transportation and warehousing	696	846	835	657	744	897	895	710
Utilities	994	1 056	1 052	954	1 061	1 161	1 142	1 010
Information[4]	891	1 000	994	867	898	1 011	1 001	871
Publishing, except Internet	881	931	933	877	856	(³)	979	846
Motion pictures and sound recording	889	(³)	(³)	797	883	(³)	(³)	800
Broadcasting, except Internet	786	(³)	(³)	770	806	(³)	944	794
Telecommunications	951	1 003	1 000	927	969	1 006	1 000	953
Financial activities	782	728	738	784	814	782	782	816
Finance and insurance	820	722	746	822	857	762	774	859
Finance	835	717	773	836	864	(³)	829	865
Insurance	795	(³)	(³)	799	846	(³)	(³)	849
Real estate and rental and leasing	691	739	718	690	703	789	783	696
Professional and business services	783	800	822	782	835	814	817	836
Professional and technical services	1 031	991	1 041	1 031	1 065	1 129	1 140	1 064
Management, administrative, and waste services	524	733	686	519	544	682	695	538
Education and health services	671	779	781	657	685	795	798	671
Education services	766	824	812	754	773	892	868	762
Health care and social assistance	644	752	762	632	661	756	768	652
Leisure and hospitality	440	580	572	431	470	584	575	462
Arts, entertainment, and recreation	587	633	634	581	590	651	638	586
Accommodation and food services	413	534	528	410	435	563	552	427
Accommodation	492	554	546	481	508	605	602	494
Food services and drinking places	399	476	490	398	417	497	491	416
Other services[4]	581	803	789	574	610	878	810	606
Other services, except private households	600	822	806	593	629	893	849	622
Public sector	816	901	896	749	842	923	918	766
Federal government	965	927	933	996	972	949	959	989
State government	772	865	856	731	812	900	889	753
Local government	787	907	899	688	814	925	917	719

Note: Updated population controls are introduced annually with the release of January data. Data refer to the sole or principal job of full- and part-time workers. Excluded are all self-employed workers, regardless of whether or not their businesses are incorporated.

[1]Data refer to members of a labor union or an employee association similar to a union.
[2]Data refer to members of a labor union or an employee association similar to a union, as well as to workers who report no union affiliation but whose jobs are covered by a union or an employee association contract.
[3]Data not shown where base is less than 50,000.
[4]Includes other industries, not shown separately.

Table 8-5. Union or Employee Association Members Among Wage and Salary Employees, 1977–2008

(Numbers in thousands, percent.)

Year	Total wage and salary employment	Union or employee association member	Union or association members as a percent of total wage and salary employment
1977	81 334	19 335	23.8
1978	84 968	19 548	23.0
1979	87 117	20 986	24.1
1980	87 480	20 095	23.0
1981	. . .	. . .	. . .
1982	. . .	. . .	. . .
1983[1]	88 290	17 717	20.1
1984	92 194	17 340	18.8
1985	94 521	16 996	18.0
1986	96 903	16 975	17.5
1987	99 303	16 913	17.0
1988	101 407	17 002	16.8
1989	103 480	16 980	16.4
1990	103 905	16 740	16.1
1991	102 786	16 568	16.1
1992	103 688	16 390	15.8
1993	105 087	16 598	15.8
1994[2]	107 989	16 748	15.5
1995	110 038	16 360	14.9
1996	111 960	16 269	14.5
1997	114 533	16 110	14.1
1998	116 730	16 211	13.9
1999	118 963	16 477	13.9
2000	120 786	16 258	13.5
2001	122 482	16 387	13.4
2002	121 826	16 145	13.3
2003	122 358	15 776	12.9
2004	123 554	15 472	12.5
2005	125 889	15 685	12.5
2006	128 237	15 359	12.0
2007	129 767	15 670	12.1
2008	129 377	16 098	12.4

Note: Beginning in January 2006, updated population controls are introduced annually with the release of January data.

[1]Annual average data beginning in 1983 are not directly comparable with the data for 1977–1980.
[2]Data beginning in 1994 are not strictly comparable with data for 1993 and earlier years because of the introduction of a major redesign of the Current Population Survey questionnaire and collection methodology and the introduction of 1990 census–based population controls.
. . . = Not available.

Table 8-6. Union Affiliation of Employed Wage and Salary Workers, by State, 2007–2008

(Numbers in thousands, percent.)

State	2007					2008				
	Total employed	Member of union[1]		Represented by union[2]		Total employed	Member of union[1]		Represented by union[2]	
		Total	Percent of employed	Total	Percent of employed		Total	Percent of employed	Total	Percent of employed
UNITED STATES	129 767	15 670	12.1	17 243	13.3	129 377	16 098	12.4	17 761	13.7
Alabama	1 895	180	9.5	201	10.6	1 858	181	9.8	199	10.7
Alaska	284	68	23.8	70	24.7	289	68	23.5	71	24.7
Arizona	2 619	230	8.8	255	9.7	2 579	227	8.8	254	9.8
Arkansas	1 154	62	5.4	75	6.5	1 158	68	5.9	85	7.3
California	14 856	2 474	16.7	2 650	17.8	14 889	2 740	18.4	2 909	19.5
Colorado	2 204	191	8.7	202	9.2	2 254	181	8.0	208	9.2
Connecticut	1 617	253	15.6	269	16.6	1 625	275	16.9	291	17.9
Delaware	396	47	12.0	50	12.8	391	52	13.4	57	14.7
District of Columbia	278	29	10.3	38	13.6	288	35	12.2	41	14.3
Florida	7 741	455	5.9	562	7.3	7 573	482	6.4	601	7.9
Georgia	4 181	186	4.4	226	5.4	4 084	151	3.7	189	4.6
Hawaii	556	130	23.4	135	24.2	562	136	24.3	143	25.5
Idaho	635	33	5.3	41	6.4	602	42	7.1	48	8.0
Illinois	5 802	842	14.5	884	15.2	5 662	939	16.6	993	17.5
Indiana	2 779	333	12.0	359	12.9	2 811	349	12.4	386	13.7
Iowa	1 417	149	10.5	185	13.1	1 437	153	10.6	187	13.0
Kansas	1 274	89	7.0	110	8.7	1 273	89	7.0	111	8.7
Kentucky	1 734	157	9.1	192	11.1	1 703	146	8.6	163	9.6
Louisiana	1 670	94	5.6	108	6.5	1 724	80	4.6	97	5.6
Maine	574	67	11.7	79	13.8	574	71	12.3	84	14.7
Maryland	2 598	335	12.9	376	14.5	2 610	329	12.6	380	14.5
Massachusetts	2 882	379	13.2	402	14.0	2 909	458	15.7	491	16.9
Michigan	4 193	819	19.5	865	20.6	4 089	771	18.8	801	19.6
Minnesota	2 460	400	16.3	419	17.0	2 430	392	16.1	412	17.0
Mississippi	1 068	72	6.7	95	8.9	1 089	57	5.3	79	7.3
Missouri	2 585	275	10.7	308	11.9	2 543	285	11.2	327	12.8
Montana	399	54	13.5	62	15.6	389	47	12.2	61	15.7
Nebraska	836	65	7.8	81	9.7	840	70	8.3	90	10.7
Nevada	1 177	182	15.4	208	17.7	1 192	199	16.7	217	18.2
New Hampshire	631	61	9.7	70	11.2	635	67	10.6	79	12.4
New Jersey	3 897	748	19.2	802	20.6	3 843	703	18.3	731	19.0
New Mexico	800	62	7.7	91	11.4	807	58	7.2	94	11.6
New York	8 150	2 055	25.2	2 146	26.3	8 165	2 029	24.9	2 170	26.6
North Carolina	3 771	114	3.0	147	3.9	3 799	132	3.5	189	5.0
North Dakota	303	19	6.4	23	7.6	308	19	6.1	25	8.2
Ohio	5 187	730	14.1	797	15.4	5 046	716	14.2	783	15.5
Oklahoma	1 456	103	7.1	124	8.5	1 529	102	6.6	127	8.3
Oregon	1 582	227	14.3	243	15.4	1 566	259	16.6	272	17.4
Pennsylvania	5 496	830	15.1	910	16.6	5 504	847	15.4	899	16.3
Rhode Island	497	75	15.0	78	15.8	471	78	16.5	82	17.4
South Carolina	1 873	78	4.1	111	5.9	1 792	70	3.9	105	5.8
South Dakota	354	23	6.5	27	7.7	369	18	5.0	24	6.4
Tennessee	2 596	138	5.3	166	6.4	2 534	139	5.5	166	6.6
Texas	9 899	463	4.7	566	5.7	9 991	449	4.5	559	5.6
Utah	1 153	67	5.8	78	6.8	1 178	68	5.8	84	7.1
Vermont	288	30	10.4	35	12.2	284	29	10.4	36	12.8
Virginia	3 502	129	3.7	167	4.8	3 597	146	4.1	178	5.0
Washington	2 874	579	20.2	616	21.4	2 912	578	19.8	626	21.5
West Virginia	724	97	13.3	107	14.7	736	101	13.8	112	15.3
Wisconsin	2 631	376	14.3	405	15.4	2 642	396	15.0	422	16.0
Wyoming	239	19	7.9	22	9.4	241	19	7.7	21	8.9

Note: Updated population controls are introduced annually with the release of January data. Data refer to the sole or principal job of full- and part-time workers. Excluded are all self-employed workers, regardless of whether or not their businesses are incorporated.

[1]Data refer to members of a labor union or an employee association similar to a union.
[2]Data refer to members of a labor union or an employee association similar to a union, as well as to workers who report no union affiliation but whose jobs are covered by a union or an employee association contract.

Chapter Nine

PRICES

PRICES

HIGHLIGHTS

This chapter examines the movement of prices, which is one of the most important indicators of the state of the economy. Several indexes are covered: the Producer Price Index (PPI), which gives information about prices received by producers; the Consumer Price Index (CPI), which gives information about prices paid by consumers; and the Import Price Index (MPI) and the Export Price Index (XPI), which give information about prices involved in various foreign trade, export, and import price indexes.

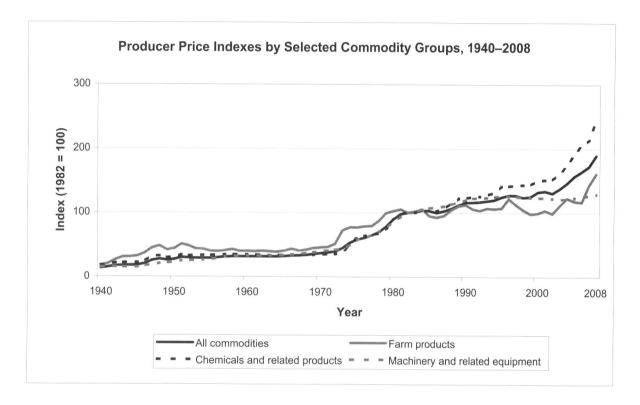

In 2008, the PPI for all commodities increased 9.8 percent after only increasing 4.8 percent in 2007. The PPI for farm products grew rapidly in 2008, increasing by 12.5 percent, and grew even faster for chemicals and related products, which increased by 14.3 percent. However, the PPI did not increase at a fast rate for every commodity. The PPI for machinery and equipment grew by only 1.9 percent in 2008, while the PPIs for hides, leather, and related products and lumber and wood products decreased. (See Table 9-2.)

OTHER HIGHLIGHTS

• In 2008, the PPI for consumer goods continued to increase faster than the PPI for capital equipment (7.3 percent compared to 2.9 percent). From 2000 to 2008, the PPI for consumer goods grew 34.8 percent, while the PPI for capital equipment only grew by 10.8 percent. (See Table 9-1.)

• The PPI for finished goods increased by 6.3 percent in 2008, compared to 3.9 percent in 2007. Since 2000, the PPI for finished goods increased by 28.3 percent. (See Table 9-1.)

• At the intermediate level, the PPI for processed fuels and lubricants increased at a much faster rate (18.6 percent) than the PPI for supplies (7.5 percent) or containers (6.4 percent). (See Table 9-1.)

NOTES AND DEFINITIONS

PRODUCER PRICE INDEX

Coverage

The Producer Price Index (PPI) measures average changes in prices received by domestic producers of goods and services. PPIs measure price change from the perspective of the seller. This contrasts with other measures, such as the Consumer Price Index (CPI). CPIs measure price change from the purchaser's perspective. Sellers' and purchasers' prices can differ due to government subsidies, sales and excise taxes, and distribution costs.

More than 9,000 PPIs for individual products and groups of products are released each month. PPIs are available for the products of virtually every industry in the mining and manufacturing sectors of the U.S. economy. New PPIs are gradually being introduced for the products of industries in the construction, trade, finance, and services sectors of the economy.

More than 100,000 price quotations per month are organized into three sets of PPIs: (1) stage-of-processing indexes, (2) commodity indexes, and (3) indexes for the net output of industries and their products. The stage-of-processing structure organizes products by class of buyer and degree of fabrication. The commodity structure organizes products by similarity of end use or material composition. The entire output of various industries is sampled to derive price indexes for the net output of industries and their products.

Within the stage-of-processing system, finished goods are commodities that will not undergo further processing and that are ready for sale to the final demand user— either an individual consumer or a business firm. Consumer foods include unprocessed foods, such as eggs and fresh vegetables, and processed foods, such as bakery products and meats. Other finished consumer goods include durable goods, such as automobiles, household furniture, and appliances; and nondurable goods, such as apparel and home heating oil. Capital equipment includes producer durable goods, such as heavy motor trucks, tractors, and machine tools.

The stage-of-processing category for intermediate materials, supplies, and components includes commodities that have been processed but require further processing, such as flour, cotton, yarn, steel mill products, and lumber. The intermediate goods category also encompasses physically complete nondurable goods purchased by business firms as inputs for their operations, such as diesel fuel, belts and belting, paper boxes, and fertilizers.

Crude materials for further processing are products entering the market for the first time that have not been manufactured or fabricated; these products will not be sold directly to consumers. Crude foodstuffs and feedstuffs includes items such as grains and livestock; examples of crude nonfood materials include raw cotton, crude petroleum, coal, hides and skins, and iron and steel scrap.

PPIs for the net output of industries and their products are grouped according to the North American Industry Classification System (NAICS). Prior to the release of January 2004, industry-based PPIs were published according to the Standard Industrial Classification (SIC) system. Industry price indexes are compatible with other economic time series organized by industry, such as data on employment, wages, and productivity.

Sources of Additional Information

For more information on the underlying concepts and methodology of the Producer Price Index, see Chapter 14 in the *BLS Handbook of Methods*, which is available on the BLS Web site at <http://www.bls.gov/opub/hom/>.

Table 9-1. Producer Price Indexes, by Stage of Processing, 1947–2008

(1982 = 100.)

Year	Crude materials for further processing				Intermediate materials, supplies, and components						Finished goods		
	Total	Foodstuffs and feedstuffs	Nonfood materials, except fuel	Fuel	Total	Materials and components for construction	Components for manufacturing	Processed fuels and lubricants	Containers	Supplies	Total	Consumer goods	Capital equipment
1947	31.7	45.1	24.0	7.5	23.3	22.5	21.3	14.4	23.4	28.5	26.4	28.6	19.8
1948	34.7	48.8	26.7	8.9	25.2	24.9	23.0	16.4	24.4	29.8	28.5	30.8	21.6
1949	30.1	40.5	24.3	8.8	24.2	24.9	23.4	14.9	24.5	28.0	27.7	29.4	22.7
1950	32.7	43.4	27.8	8.8	25.3	26.2	24.3	15.2	25.2	29.0	28.2	29.9	23.2
1951	37.6	50.2	32.0	9.0	28.4	28.7	27.6	15.9	29.6	32.6	30.8	32.7	25.5
1952	34.5	47.3	27.8	9.0	27.5	28.5	27.6	15.7	28.0	32.6	30.6	32.3	25.9
1953	31.9	42.3	26.6	9.3	27.7	29.0	28.1	15.8	28.0	31.0	30.3	31.7	26.3
1954	31.6	42.3	26.1	8.9	27.9	29.1	28.3	15.8	28.5	31.7	30.4	31.7	26.7
1955	30.4	38.4	27.5	8.9	28.4	30.3	29.5	15.8	28.9	31.2	30.5	31.5	27.4
1956	30.6	37.6	28.6	9.5	29.6	31.8	32.2	16.3	31.0	32.0	31.3	32.0	29.5
1957	31.2	39.2	28.2	10.1	30.3	32.0	33.5	17.2	32.4	32.3	32.5	32.9	31.3
1958	31.9	41.6	27.1	10.2	30.4	32.0	33.8	16.2	33.2	33.1	33.2	33.6	32.1
1959	31.1	38.8	28.1	10.4	30.8	32.9	34.2	16.2	33.0	33.5	33.1	33.3	32.7
1960	30.4	38.4	26.9	10.5	30.8	32.7	34.0	16.6	33.4	33.3	33.4	33.6	32.8
1961	30.2	37.9	27.2	10.5	30.6	32.2	33.7	16.8	33.2	33.7	33.4	33.6	32.9
1962	30.5	38.6	27.1	10.4	30.6	32.1	33.4	16.7	33.6	34.5	33.5	33.7	33.0
1963	29.9	37.5	26.7	10.5	30.7	32.2	33.4	16.6	33.2	35.0	33.4	33.5	33.1
1964	29.6	36.6	27.2	10.5	30.8	32.5	33.7	16.2	32.9	34.7	33.5	33.6	33.4
1965	31.1	39.2	27.7	10.6	31.2	32.8	34.2	16.5	33.5	35.0	34.1	34.2	33.8
1966	33.1	42.7	28.3	10.9	32.0	33.6	35.4	16.8	34.5	36.5	35.2	35.4	34.6
1967	31.3	40.3	26.5	11.3	32.2	34.0	36.5	16.9	35.0	36.8	35.6	35.6	35.8
1968	31.8	40.9	27.1	11.5	33.0	35.7	37.3	16.5	35.9	37.1	36.6	36.5	37.0
1969	33.9	44.1	28.4	12.0	34.1	37.7	38.5	16.6	37.2	37.8	38.0	37.9	38.3
1970	35.2	45.2	29.1	13.8	35.4	38.3	40.6	17.7	39.0	39.7	39.3	39.1	40.1
1971	36.0	46.1	29.4	15.7	36.8	40.8	41.9	19.5	40.8	40.8	40.5	40.2	41.7
1972	39.9	51.5	32.3	16.8	38.2	43.0	42.9	20.1	42.7	42.5	41.8	41.5	42.8
1973	54.5	72.6	42.9	18.6	42.4	46.5	44.3	22.2	45.2	51.7	45.6	46.0	44.2
1974	61.4	76.4	54.5	24.8	52.5	55.0	51.1	33.6	53.3	56.8	52.6	53.1	50.5
1975	61.6	77.4	50.0	30.6	58.0	60.1	57.8	39.4	60.0	61.8	58.2	58.2	58.2
1976	63.4	76.8	54.9	34.5	60.9	64.1	60.8	42.3	63.1	65.8	60.8	60.4	62.1
1977	65.5	77.5	56.3	42.0	64.9	69.3	64.5	47.7	65.9	69.3	64.7	64.3	66.1
1978	73.4	87.3	61.9	48.2	69.5	76.5	69.2	49.9	71.0	72.9	69.8	69.4	71.3
1979	85.9	100.0	75.5	57.3	78.4	84.2	75.8	61.6	79.4	80.2	77.6	77.5	77.5
1980	95.3	104.6	91.8	69.4	90.3	91.3	84.6	85.0	89.1	89.9	88.0	88.6	85.8
1981	103.0	103.9	109.8	84.8	98.6	97.9	94.7	100.6	96.7	96.9	96.1	96.6	94.6
1982	100.0	100.0	100.0	100.0	100.0	100.0	100.0	100.0	100.0	100.0	100.0	100.0	100.0
1983	101.3	101.8	98.8	105.1	100.6	102.8	102.4	95.4	100.4	101.8	101.6	101.3	102.8
1984	103.5	104.7	101.0	105.1	103.1	105.6	105.0	95.7	105.9	104.1	103.7	103.3	105.2
1985	95.8	94.8	94.3	102.7	102.7	107.3	106.4	92.8	109.0	104.4	104.7	103.8	107.5
1986	87.7	93.2	76.0	92.2	99.1	108.1	107.5	72.7	110.3	105.6	103.2	101.4	109.7
1987	93.7	96.2	88.5	84.1	101.5	109.8	108.8	73.3	114.5	107.7	105.4	103.6	111.7
1988	96.0	106.1	85.9	82.1	107.1	116.1	112.3	71.2	120.1	113.7	108.0	106.2	114.3
1989	103.1	111.2	95.8	85.3	112.0	121.3	116.4	76.4	125.4	118.1	113.6	112.1	118.8
1990	108.9	113.1	107.3	84.8	114.5	122.9	119.0	85.9	127.7	119.4	119.2	118.2	122.9
1991	101.2	105.5	97.5	82.9	114.4	124.5	121.0	85.3	128.1	121.4	121.7	120.5	126.7
1992	100.4	105.1	94.2	84.0	114.7	126.5	122.0	84.5	127.7	122.7	123.2	121.7	129.1
1993	102.4	108.4	94.1	87.1	116.2	132.0	123.0	84.7	126.4	125.0	124.7	123.0	131.4
1994	101.8	106.5	97.0	82.4	118.5	136.6	124.3	83.1	129.7	127.0	125.5	123.3	134.1
1995	102.7	105.8	105.8	72.1	124.9	142.1	126.5	84.2	148.8	132.1	127.9	125.6	136.7
1996	113.8	121.5	105.7	92.6	125.7	143.6	126.9	90.0	141.1	135.9	131.3	129.5	138.3
1997	111.1	112.2	103.5	101.3	125.6	146.5	126.4	89.3	136.0	135.9	131.8	130.2	138.2
1998	96.8	103.9	84.5	86.7	123.0	146.8	125.9	81.1	140.8	134.8	130.7	128.9	137.6
1999	98.2	98.7	91.1	91.2	123.2	148.9	125.7	84.6	142.5	134.2	133.0	132.0	137.6
2000	120.6	100.2	118.0	136.9	129.2	150.7	126.2	102.0	151.6	136.9	138.0	138.2	138.8
2001	121.0	106.1	101.5	151.4	129.7	150.6	126.4	104.5	153.1	138.7	140.7	141.5	139.7
2002	108.1	99.5	101.0	117.3	127.8	151.3	126.1	96.3	152.1	138.9	138.9	139.4	139.1
2003	135.3	113.5	116.9	185.7	133.7	153.6	125.9	112.6	153.7	141.5	143.3	145.3	139.5
2004	159.0	127.0	149.2	211.4	142.6	166.4	127.4	124.3	159.3	146.7	148.5	151.7	141.4
2005	182.2	122.7	176.7	279.7	154.0	176.6	129.9	150.0	167.1	151.9	155.7	160.4	144.6
2006	184.8	119.3	210.0	241.5	164.0	188.4	134.5	162.8	175.0	157.0	160.4	166.0	146.9
2007	207.1	146.7	238.7	236.8	170.7	192.5	136.3	173.9	180.3	161.7	166.6	173.5	149.5
2008	251.8	163.4	308.5	298.3	188.3	205.4	140.3	206.2	191.8	173.8	177.1	186.3	153.8

Table 9-2. Producer Price Indexes, by Commodity Group, 1913–2008

(1982 = 100.)

Year	All commodities	Farm products	Processed foods and feeds	Industrial commodities													
				Total	Textile products and apparel	Hides, leather, and related products	Fuels and related products and power	Chemicals and related products	Rubber and plastics products	Lumber and wood products	Pulp, paper, and allied products	Metals and metal products	Machinery and equipment	Furniture and household durables	Non-metallic mineral products	Transportation equipment	Miscellaneous products
1913	12.0	18.0	...	11.9	...	...	...	...	...	...	...	...	...	...	...	...	...
1914	11.8	17.9	...	11.3	...	...	...	...	...	...	...	...	...	...	...	...	...
1915	12.0	18.0	...	11.6	...	...	...	...	...	...	...	...	...	...	...	...	...
1916	14.7	21.3	...	15.0	...	...	...	...	...	...	...	...	...	...	...	...	...
1917	20.2	32.6	...	19.5	...	...	...	...	...	...	...	...	...	...	...	...	...
1918	22.6	37.4	...	21.1	...	...	...	...	...	...	...	...	...	...	...	...	...
1919	23.9	39.8	...	22.0	...	...	...	...	...	...	...	...	...	...	...	...	...
1920	26.6	38.0	...	27.4	...	...	...	...	...	...	...	...	...	...	...	...	...
1921	16.8	22.3	...	17.8	...	...	...	...	...	...	...	...	...	...	...	...	...
1922	16.7	23.7	...	17.4	...	...	...	...	...	...	...	...	...	...	...	...	...
1923	17.3	24.9	...	17.8	...	...	...	...	...	...	...	...	...	...	...	...	...
1924	16.9	25.2	...	17.0	...	...	...	...	...	...	...	...	...	...	...	...	...
1925	17.8	27.7	...	17.5	...	...	...	...	...	...	...	...	...	...	...	...	...
1926	17.2	25.3	...	17.0	...	17.1	10.3	...	47.1	9.3	...	13.7	...	28.6	16.4	...	...
1927	16.5	25.1	...	16.0	...	18.4	9.1	...	35.7	8.8	...	12.9	...	27.9	15.7	...	...
1928	16.7	26.7	...	15.8	...	20.7	8.7	...	28.3	8.5	...	12.9	...	27.2	16.2	...	...
1929	16.4	26.4	...	15.6	...	18.6	8.6	...	24.6	8.8	...	13.3	...	27.0	16.0	...	...
1930	14.9	22.4	...	14.5	...	17.1	8.1	...	21.5	8.0	...	12.0	...	26.5	15.9	...	...
1931	12.6	16.4	...	12.8	...	14.7	7.0	...	18.3	6.5	...	10.8	...	24.4	14.9	...	...
1932	11.2	12.2	...	11.9	...	12.5	7.3	...	15.9	5.6	...	9.9	...	21.5	13.9	...	...
1933	11.4	13.0	...	12.1	...	13.8	6.9	16.2	16.7	6.7	...	10.2	...	21.6	14.7	...	...
1934	12.9	16.5	...	13.3	...	14.8	7.6	17.0	19.5	7.8	...	11.2	...	23.4	15.7	...	...
1935	13.8	19.8	...	13.3	...	15.3	7.6	17.7	19.6	7.5	...	11.2	...	23.2	15.7	...	...
1936	13.9	20.4	...	13.5	...	16.3	7.9	17.8	21.1	7.9	...	11.4	...	23.6	15.8	...	...
1937	14.9	21.8	...	14.5	...	17.9	8.0	18.6	24.9	9.3	...	13.1	...	26.1	16.1	...	...
1938	13.5	17.3	...	13.9	...	15.8	7.9	17.7	24.4	8.5	...	12.6	...	25.5	15.6	...	...
1939	13.3	16.5	...	13.9	...	16.3	7.5	17.6	25.4	8.7	...	12.5	14.8	25.4	15.3	...	...
1940	13.5	17.1	...	14.1	...	17.2	7.4	17.9	23.7	9.6	...	12.5	14.9	26.0	15.3	...	...
1941	15.1	20.8	...	15.1	...	18.4	7.9	19.5	25.5	11.5	...	12.8	15.1	27.6	15.7	...	...
1942	17.0	26.7	...	16.2	...	20.1	8.1	21.7	29.7	12.5	...	13.0	15.4	29.9	16.3	...	...
1943	17.8	30.9	...	16.5	...	20.1	8.3	21.9	30.5	13.2	...	12.9	15.2	29.7	16.4	...	...
1944	17.9	31.2	...	16.7	...	19.9	8.6	22.2	30.1	14.3	...	12.9	15.1	30.5	16.7	...	...
1945	18.2	32.4	...	17.0	...	20.1	8.7	22.3	29.2	14.5	...	13.1	15.1	30.5	17.4	...	...
1946	20.8	37.5	...	18.6	...	23.3	9.3	24.1	29.3	16.6	...	14.7	16.6	32.4	18.5	...	...
1947	25.6	45.1	33.0	22.7	50.6	31.7	11.1	32.1	29.2	25.8	25.1	18.2	19.3	37.2	20.7	...	26.6
1948	27.7	48.5	35.3	24.6	52.8	32.1	13.1	32.8	30.2	29.5	26.2	20.7	20.9	39.4	22.4	...	27.7
1949	26.3	41.9	32.1	24.1	48.3	30.4	12.4	30.0	29.2	27.3	25.1	20.9	21.9	40.1	23.0	...	28.2
1950	27.3	44.0	33.2	25.0	50.2	32.9	12.6	30.4	35.6	31.4	25.7	22.0	22.6	40.9	23.5	...	28.6
1951	30.4	51.2	36.9	27.6	56.0	37.7	13.0	34.8	43.7	34.1	30.5	24.5	25.3	44.4	25.0	...	30.3
1952	29.6	48.4	36.4	26.9	50.5	30.5	13.0	33.0	39.6	33.2	29.7	24.5	25.3	43.5	25.0	...	30.2
1953	29.2	43.8	34.8	27.2	49.3	31.0	13.4	33.4	36.9	33.1	29.6	25.3	25.9	44.4	26.0	...	31.0
1954	29.3	43.2	35.4	27.2	48.2	29.5	13.2	33.8	37.5	32.5	29.6	25.5	26.3	44.9	26.6	...	31.3
1955	29.3	40.5	33.8	27.8	48.2	29.4	13.2	33.7	42.4	34.1	30.4	27.2	27.2	45.1	27.3	...	31.3
1956	30.3	40.0	33.8	29.1	48.2	31.2	13.6	33.9	43.0	34.6	32.4	29.6	29.3	46.3	28.5	...	31.7
1957	31.2	41.1	34.8	29.9	48.3	31.2	14.3	34.6	42.8	32.8	33.0	30.2	31.4	47.5	29.6	...	32.6
1958	31.6	42.9	36.5	30.0	47.4	31.6	13.7	34.9	42.8	32.5	33.4	30.0	32.1	47.9	29.9	...	33.3
1959	31.7	40.2	35.6	30.5	48.1	35.9	13.7	34.8	42.6	34.7	33.7	30.6	32.8	48.0	30.3	...	33.4
1960	31.7	40.1	35.6	30.5	48.6	34.6	13.9	34.8	42.7	33.5	34.0	30.6	33.0	47.8	30.4	...	33.6
1961	31.6	39.7	36.2	30.4	47.8	34.9	14.0	34.5	41.1	32.0	33.0	30.5	33.0	47.5	30.5	...	33.7
1962	31.7	40.4	36.5	30.4	48.2	35.3	14.0	33.9	39.9	32.2	33.4	30.2	33.0	47.2	30.5	...	33.9
1963	31.6	39.6	36.8	30.3	48.2	34.3	13.9	33.5	40.1	32.8	33.1	30.3	33.1	46.9	30.3	...	34.2
1964	31.6	39.0	36.7	30.5	48.5	34.4	13.5	33.6	39.6	33.5	33.0	31.1	33.3	47.1	30.4	...	34.4
1965	32.3	40.7	38.0	30.9	48.8	35.9	13.8	33.9	39.7	33.7	33.3	32.0	33.7	46.8	30.4	...	34.7
1966	33.3	43.7	40.2	31.5	48.9	39.4	14.1	34.0	40.5	35.2	34.2	32.8	34.7	47.4	30.7	...	35.3
1967	33.4	41.3	39.8	32.0	48.9	38.1	14.4	34.2	41.4	35.1	34.6	33.2	35.9	48.3	31.2	...	36.2
1968	34.2	42.3	40.6	32.8	50.7	39.3	14.3	34.1	42.8	39.8	35.0	34.0	37.0	49.7	32.4	...	37.0
1969	35.6	45.0	42.7	33.9	51.8	41.5	14.6	34.2	43.6	44.0	36.0	36.0	38.2	50.7	33.6	40.4	38.1
1970	36.9	45.8	44.6	35.2	52.4	42.0	15.3	35.0	44.9	39.9	37.5	38.7	40.0	51.9	35.3	41.9	39.8
1971	38.1	46.6	45.5	36.5	53.3	43.4	16.6	35.6	45.2	44.7	38.1	39.4	41.4	53.1	38.2	44.2	40.8
1972	39.8	51.6	48.0	37.8	55.5	50.0	17.1	35.6	45.3	50.7	39.3	40.9	42.3	53.8	39.4	45.5	41.5
1973	45.0	72.7	58.9	40.3	60.5	54.5	19.4	37.6	46.6	62.2	42.3	44.0	43.7	55.7	40.7	46.1	43.3
1974	53.5	77.4	68.0	49.2	68.0	55.2	30.1	50.2	56.4	64.5	52.5	57.0	50.0	61.8	47.8	50.3	48.1

. . . = Not available.

Table 9-2. Producer Price Indexes, by Commodity Group, 1913–2008—*Continued*

(1982 = 100.)

Year	All com-modities	Farm products	Processed foods and feeds	Industrial commodities													
				Total	Textile products and apparel	Hides, leather, and related products	Fuels and related products and power	Chemi-cals and related products	Rubber and plastics products	Lumber and wood products	Pulp, paper, and allied products	Metals and metal products	Machin-ery and equip-ment	Furniture and house-hold durables	Non-metallic mineral products	Trans-porta-tion equip-ment	Miscel-laneous products
1975	58.4	77.0	72.6	54.9	67.4	56.5	35.4	62.0	62.2	62.1	59.0	61.5	57.9	67.5	54.4	56.7	53.4
1976	61.1	78.8	70.8	58.4	72.4	63.9	38.3	64.0	66.0	72.2	62.1	65.0	61.3	70.3	58.2	60.5	55.6
1977	64.9	79.4	74.0	62.5	75.3	68.3	43.6	65.9	69.4	83.0	64.6	69.3	65.2	73.2	62.6	64.6	59.4
1978	69.9	87.7	80.6	67.0	78.1	76.1	46.5	68.0	72.4	96.9	67.7	75.3	70.3	77.5	69.6	69.5	66.7
1979	78.7	99.6	88.5	75.7	82.5	96.1	58.9	76.0	80.5	105.5	75.9	86.0	76.7	82.8	77.6	75.3	75.5
1980	89.8	102.9	95.9	88.0	89.7	94.7	82.8	89.0	90.1	101.5	86.3	95.0	86.0	90.7	88.4	82.9	93.6
1981	98.0	105.2	98.9	97.4	97.6	99.3	100.2	98.4	96.4	102.8	94.8	99.6	94.4	95.9	96.7	94.3	96.1
1982	100.0	100.0	100.0	100.0	100.0	100.0	100.0	100.0	100.0	100.0	100.0	100.0	100.0	100.0	100.0	100.0	100.0
1983	101.3	102.4	101.8	101.1	100.3	103.2	95.9	100.3	100.8	107.9	103.3	101.8	102.7	103.4	101.6	102.8	104.8
1984	103.7	105.5	105.4	103.3	102.7	109.0	94.8	102.9	102.3	108.0	110.3	104.8	105.1	105.7	105.4	105.2	107.0
1985	103.2	95.1	103.5	103.7	102.9	108.9	91.4	103.7	101.9	106.6	113.3	104.4	107.2	107.1	108.6	107.9	109.4
1986	100.2	92.9	105.4	100.0	103.2	113.0	69.8	102.6	101.9	107.2	116.1	103.2	108.8	108.2	110.0	110.5	111.6
1987	102.8	95.5	107.9	102.6	105.1	120.4	70.2	106.4	103.0	112.8	121.8	107.1	110.4	109.9	110.0	112.5	114.9
1988	106.9	104.9	112.7	106.3	109.2	131.4	66.7	116.3	109.3	118.9	130.4	118.7	113.2	113.1	111.2	114.3	120.2
1989	112.2	110.9	117.8	111.6	112.3	136.3	72.9	123.0	112.6	126.7	137.8	124.1	117.4	116.9	112.6	117.7	126.5
1990	116.3	112.2	121.9	115.8	115.0	141.7	82.3	123.6	113.6	129.7	141.2	122.9	120.7	119.2	114.7	121.5	134.2
1991	116.5	105.7	121.9	116.5	116.3	138.9	81.2	125.6	115.1	132.1	142.9	120.2	123.0	121.2	117.2	126.4	140.8
1992	117.2	103.6	122.1	117.4	117.8	140.4	80.4	125.9	115.1	146.6	145.2	119.2	123.4	122.2	117.3	130.4	145.3
1993	118.9	107.1	124.0	119.0	118.0	143.7	80.0	128.2	116.0	174.0	147.3	119.2	124.0	123.7	120.0	133.7	145.4
1994	120.4	106.3	125.5	120.7	118.3	148.5	77.8	132.1	117.6	180.0	152.5	124.8	125.1	126.1	124.2	137.2	141.9
1995	124.7	107.4	127.0	125.5	120.8	153.7	78.0	142.5	124.3	178.1	172.2	134.5	126.6	128.2	129.0	139.7	145.4
1996	127.7	122.4	133.3	127.3	122.4	150.5	85.8	142.1	123.8	176.1	168.7	131.0	126.5	130.4	131.0	141.7	147.7
1997	127.6	112.9	134.0	127.7	122.6	154.2	86.1	143.6	123.2	183.8	167.9	131.8	125.9	130.8	133.2	141.6	150.9
1998	124.4	104.6	131.6	124.8	122.9	148.0	75.3	143.9	122.6	179.1	171.7	127.8	124.9	131.3	135.4	141.2	156.0
1999	125.5	98.4	131.1	126.5	121.1	146.0	80.5	144.2	122.5	183.6	174.1	124.6	124.3	131.7	138.9	141.8	166.6
2000	132.7	99.5	133.1	134.8	121.4	151.5	103.5	151.0	125.5	178.2	183.7	128.1	124.0	132.6	142.5	143.8	170.8
2001	134.2	103.8	137.3	135.7	121.3	158.4	105.3	151.8	127.2	174.4	184.8	125.4	123.7	133.2	144.3	145.2	181.3
2002	131.1	99.0	136.2	132.4	119.9	157.6	93.2	151.9	126.8	173.3	185.9	125.9	122.9	133.5	146.2	144.6	182.4
2003	138.1	111.5	143.4	139.1	119.8	162.3	112.9	161.8	130.1	177.4	190.0	129.2	121.9	133.9	148.2	145.7	179.6
2004	146.7	123.3	151.2	147.6	121.0	164.5	126.9	174.4	133.8	195.6	195.7	149.6	122.1	135.1	153.2	148.6	183.2
2005	157.4	118.5	153.1	160.2	122.8	165.4	156.4	192.0	143.8	196.5	202.6	160.8	123.7	139.4	164.2	151.0	195.1
2006	164.7	117.0	153.8	168.8	124.5	168.4	166.7	205.8	153.8	194.4	209.8	181.6	126.2	142.6	179.9	152.6	205.6
2007	172.6	143.4	165.1	175.1	125.8	173.6	177.6	214.8	155.0	192.4	216.9	193.5	127.3	144.7	186.2	155.0	210.3
2008	189.6	161.3	180.5	192.3	128.9	173.1	214.6	245.5	165.9	191.3	226.8	213.0	129.7	148.9	197.1	158.6	216.6

Table 9-3. Producer Price Indexes for the Net Output of Selected Industries, 1998–2008

(December 2003 = 100, unless otherwise specified.)

Industry	1998	1999	2000	2001	2002	2003	2004	2005	2006	2007	2008
Agriculture, Forestry, Fishing, and Hunting											
Logging[1]	188.1	182.7	177.5	167.5	165.0	168.7	175.2	179.0	176.6	175.0	171.5
Mining											
Oil and gas extraction[2]	68.3	78.5	126.8	127.5	107.0	160.1	192.7	262.0	252.5	267.1	347.5
Mining (except oil and gas)	. . .	. . .	. . .	. . .	. . .	. . .	109.5	126.6	147.9	158.4	180.8
Coal mining [2]	89.5	87.3	84.8	91.3	93.9	94.4	104.1	118.2	126.9	130.6	162.2
Metal ore mining[3]	73.2	70.3	73.8	70.8	73.6	81.6	111.8	146.0	204.6	226.4	232.6
Iron ore mining[3]	94.5	94.0	93.9	95.2	94.2	95.0	97.2	115.7	131.2	127.5	141.0
Gold ore and silver ore mining[3]	61.1	58.2	57.0	55.2	62.6	72.6	82.6	89.5	121.3	138.8	143.9
Copper, nickel, lead, and zinc mining[4]	76.8	71.3	88.7	81.7	80.1	90.1	147.7	195.2	350.2	386.5	390.3
Other metal ore mining[2]	27.6	25.9	26.4	24.7	28.9	34.9	80.0	159.1	128.7	145.5	147.8
Nonmetallic mineral mining and quarrying[3]	132.2	134.0	137.0	141.0	143.5	146.4	151.2	161.3	176.0	191.1	217.6
Stone mining and quarrying[3]	138.8	142.1	147.3	152.2	156.1	160.2	166.1	176.7	192.7	210.2	224.7
Sand, gravel, clay, and refractory minerals mining	. . .	. . .	. . .	. . .	. . .	. . .	102.4	108.8	117.6	126.1	135.1
Other nonmetallic mineral mining and quarrying[3]	110.1	108.0	106.8	107.1	107.7	108.4	111.4	120.8	133.8	148.3	222.5
Mining support activities	. . .	. . .	. . .	. . .	. . .	. . .	104.8	133.9	172.0	170.9	174.0
Utilities	. . .	. . .	. . .	. . .	. . .	. . .	104.9	117.6	123.1	127.0	136.5
Electric power generation, transmission, and distribution	. . .	. . .	. . .	. . .	. . .	. . .	103.3	111.3	118.8	122.7	130.7
Electric power generation	. . .	. . .	. . .	. . .	. . .	. . .	105.2	121.6	128.0	132.0	145.5
Electric power transmission, control, and distribution	. . .	. . .	. . .	. . .	. . .	. . .	102.5	107.1	115.1	118.9	124.8
Natural gas distribution	. . .	. . .	. . .	. . .	. . .	. . .	107.3	126.6	129.3	129.0	142.9
Manufacturing											
Food[3]	126.3	126.3	128.5	132.8	132.0	137.4	144.3	146.1	146.8	158.6	173.8
Animal food	. . .	. . .	. . .	. . .	. . .	. . .	103.3	98.2	101.8	118.6	147.8
Grain and oilseed milling	. . .	. . .	. . .	. . .	. . .	. . .	103.1	99.8	104.7	121.2	157.4
Flour milling and malt	. . .	. . .	. . .	. . .	. . .	. . .	102.6	100.5	109.1	128.5	178.8
Starch and vegetable fats and oils	. . .	. . .	. . .	. . .	. . .	. . .	103.6	97.9	102.4	122.2	163.1
Breakfast cereal manufacturing	. . .	. . .	. . .	. . .	. . .	. . .	101.7	105.0	106.9	108.9	112.1
Sugar and confectionery product[3]	128.8	129.4	127.5	129.3	133.7	139.5	141.4	147.3	154.7	155.4	166.7
Sugar	. . .	. . .	. . .	. . .	. . .	. . .	99.7	105.6	123.4	111.1	114.4
Chocolate and confectionery from cacao beans	. . .	. . .	. . .	. . .	. . .	. . .	100.1	101.7	103.9	107.2	116.9
Confectionery from purchased chocolate	. . .	. . .	. . .	. . .	. . .	. . .	100.1	102.2	103.8	109.1	120.0
Non-chocolate confectionery	. . .	. . .	. . .	. . .	. . .	. . .	104.0	111.0	113.0	114.9	121.1
Fruit and vegetable preserving and specialty food[3]	130.1	131.7	132.1	133.3	135.2	136.6	139.2	141.7	144.5	147.6	156.5
Frozen food	. . .	. . .	. . .	. . .	. . .	. . .	101.6	103.9	107.7	108.9	113.5
Fruit and vegetable canning, pickling, and drying	. . .	. . .	. . .	. . .	. . .	. . .	100.5	104.0	107.3	112.5	120.5
Dairy product[3]	133.1	133.8	129.9	141.2	133.3	135.8	151.0	151.3	147.4	174.5	179.1
Dairy product (except frozen)	. . .	. . .	. . .	. . .	. . .	. . .	108.4	108.5	105.0	126.9	130.0
Ice cream and frozen dessert	. . .	. . .	. . .	. . .	. . .	. . .	103.3	104.7	106.9	110.6	114.8
Animal slaughtering and processing[3]	109.2	108.9	115.0	120.3	114.0	125.8	134.2	135.8	130.8	139.1	145.8
Seafood product preparation and packaging	. . .	. . .	. . .	. . .	. . .	. . .	102.4	106.2	107.0	112.8	123.6
Bakery and tortilla	. . .	. . .	. . .	. . .	. . .	. . .	100.8	102.6	105.3	109.8	123.5
Bread and bakery product	. . .	. . .	. . .	. . .	. . .	. . .	101.1	103.4	106.6	111.1	125.0
Cookie, cracker, and pasta	. . .	. . .	. . .	. . .	. . .	. . .	100.5	101.3	103.2	107.3	120.3
Tortilla	. . .	. . .	. . .	. . .	. . .	. . .	100.4	102.5	103.9	113.3	129.6
Other food	. . .	. . .	. . .	. . .	. . .	. . .	101.1	105.4	107.0	110.6	119.9
Snack food	. . .	. . .	. . .	. . .	. . .	. . .	101.4	108.4	108.5	109.5	119.2
Coffee and tea	. . .	. . .	. . .	. . .	. . .	. . .	101.7	115.1	117.3	124.3	135.4
Flavoring syrup and concentrate	. . .	. . .	. . .	. . .	. . .	. . .	101.0	103.1	106.5	109.1	113.4
Seasoning and dressing	. . .	. . .	. . .	. . .	. . .	. . .	101.1	101.3	102.7	106.7	116.2
All other food	. . .	. . .	. . .	. . .	. . .	. . .	100.4	100.8	103.1	108.2	118.5
Beverage and tobacco product	. . .	. . .	. . .	. . .	. . .	. . .	101.0	104.8	106.3	109.6	114.4
Beverage[3]	127.2	129.8	134.4	138.6	140.8	142.7	146.4	150.4	153.3	155.2	162.2
Soft drink and ice	. . .	. . .	. . .	. . .	. . .	. . .	102.1	104.1	106.8	109.3	114.5
Breweries	. . .	. . .	. . .	. . .	. . .	. . .	101.3	105.6	105.6	104.0	108.7
Wineries	. . .	. . .	. . .	. . .	. . .	. . .	100.7	104.2	109.8	112.0	114.6
Distilleries	. . .	. . .	. . .	. . .	. . .	. . .	100.1	100.6	101.9	106.5	113.7
Tobacco[3]	243.1	325.7	345.8	386.1	401.9	377.9	379.7	401.0	403.8	429.5	446.9
Tobacco stemming and redrying[5]	104.2	104.7	109.0	112.3	114.7	117.5	119.4	119.9	109.4	112.6	113.4
Tobacco product[6]	260.4	356.7	379.3	425.8	442.8	411.7	412.5	436.3	440.2	468.4	487.6
Textile mills	. . .	. . .	. . .	. . .	. . .	. . .	101.1	103.6	106.6	108.2	112.4
Fiber, yarn, and thread mills[3]	112.1	106.9	105.5	103.0	99.8	100.9	105.6	108.8	111.1	114.0	121.1
Fabric mills	. . .	. . .	. . .	. . .	. . .	. . .	101.0	103.0	105.8	106.2	109.7
Broadwoven fabric mills	. . .	. . .	. . .	. . .	. . .	. . .	101.1	103.2	106.7	108.1	111.7
Narrow fabric mills and schiffli mach embroidery[5]	123.8	124.3	125.3	126.2	126.0	125.1	126.2	129.3	131.1	132.5	134.6
Nonwoven fabric mills	. . .	. . .	. . .	. . .	. . .	. . .	101.5	105.6	108.1	108.2	112.8
Knit fabric mills	. . .	. . .	. . .	. . .	. . .	. . .	100.4	100.5	101.3	99.4	101.2
Textile and fabric finishing mills	. . .	. . .	. . .	. . .	. . .	. . .	99.9	102.8	106.5	109.5	113.4
Fabric coating mills	. . .	. . .	. . .	. . .	. . .	. . .	100.2	104.9	113.4	116.5	123.9
Textile product mills	. . .	. . .	. . .	. . .	. . .	. . .	101.4	105.3	108.4	109.6	112.4
Textile furnishings mills	. . .	. . .	. . .	. . .	. . .	. . .	101.1	105.1	108.6	110.0	112.0
Carpet and rug mills[3]	116.3	115.4	117.8	118.9	119.0	121.8	124.6	132.9	140.2	141.6	144.6
Curtain and linen mills	. . .	. . .	. . .	. . .	. . .	. . .	100.2	100.3	100.5	102.1	103.5
Other textile product mills	. . .	. . .	. . .	. . .	. . .	. . .	102.0	105.4	107.9	108.8	113.3
Textile bag and canvas mills	. . .	. . .	. . .	. . .	. . .	. . .	102.7	104.9	107.5	111.5	115.1
All other textile product mills	. . .	. . .	. . .	. . .	. . .	. . .	101.7	105.6	108.0	107.8	112.7

[1] December 1981 = 100.
[2] December 1985 = 100.
[3] December 1984 = 100.
[4] June 1988 = 100.
[5] June 1984 = 100.
[6] December 1982 = 100.
. . . = Not available.

Table 9-3. Producer Price Indexes for the Net Output of Selected Industries, 1998–2008—*Continued*

(December 2003 = 100, unless otherwise specified.)

Industry	1998	1999	2000	2001	2002	2003	2004	2005	2006	2007	2008
Manufacturing—*Continued*											
Apparel	...	...	...	...	...	...	100.0	100.0	100.5	101.5	102.4
Apparel knitting mills[3]	116.6	114.0	113.9	113.7	112.7	111.6	110.3	109.6	110.5	110.9	112.9
Cut and sew apparel	...	...	...	...	...	...	100.2	100.2	100.6	101.7	102.4
Cut and sew apparel contractors	...	...	...	...	...	...	100.2	103.0	105.3	105.9	106.3
Men's and boys' cut and sew apparel	...	...	...	...	...	...	99.9	98.4	98.0	98.2	99.2
Women's and girls' cut and sew apparel	...	...	...	...	...	...	100.4	100.8	101.0	102.2	102.6
Other cut and sew apparel	...	...	...	...	...	...	100.2	102.3	107.1	111.8	114.7
Accessories and other apparel	...	...	...	...	...	...	100.5	101.6	102.2	103.5	106.5
Leather and allied product[3]	137.1	136.5	137.9	141.3	141.1	142.8	143.6	144.5	146.6	149.7	153.5
Leather and hide tanning and finishing[7]	171.6	168.8	174.6	191.7	191.4	200.5	205.7	204.8	208.4	215.9	221.3
Footwear	...	...	...	...	...	...	100.1	101.1	102.2	103.3	106.3
Other leather and allied product	...	...	...	...	...	...	99.8	100.7	102.6	104.7	106.6
Wood product	...	...	...	...	...	...	106.7	108.6	108.5	107.0	107.4
Sawmills and wood preservation	...	...	...	...	...	...	110.5	110.7	107.9	103.8	99.3
Plywood, and engineered wood product	...	...	...	...	...	...	107.0	105.2	99.6	94.6	95.8
Other wood product	...	...	...	...	...	...	104.7	108.3	111.4	112.4	114.3
Millwork	...	...	...	...	...	...	104.8	105.4	106.7	107.3	107.5
Wood container and pallet	...	...	...	...	...	...	102.8	107.1	110.9	109.9	111.7
All other wood product	...	...	...	...	...	...	105.0	111.3	115.9	118.0	122.3
Paper	...	...	...	...	...	...	102.6	106.9	112.3	115.7	122.8
Pulp, paper, and paperboard mills	...	...	...	...	...	...	103.8	109.4	115.7	119.3	129.0
Pulp mills[6]	125.1	122.7	143.4	122.9	116.5	120.9	131.3	137.4	144.8	163.2	175.5
Paper mills[7]	144.5	139.7	148.8	150.5	144.1	145.7	151.1	161.0	168.1	170.8	184.6
Paperboard mills[6]	165.1	166.9	192.2	187.3	179.5	180.2	189.9	196.0	212.7	224.1	242.4
Converted paper product	...	...	...	...	...	...	101.9	105.5	110.5	113.9	119.4
Paper container[3]	141.1	144.1	157.1	158.9	157.0	157.3	161.5	167.1	177.1	182.9	192.3
Paper bag and coated and treated paper	...	...	...	...	...	...	101.7	105.8	110.4	113.3	117.8
Stationery product	...	...	...	...	...	...	101.7	106.8	110.5	114.7	120.2
Other converted paper product	...	...	...	...	...	...	97.0	98.7	100.0	102.8	107.9
Printing and related support activities	...	...	...	...	...	...	101.1	103.1	105.6	106.7	109.4
Printing	...	...	...	...	...	...	101.2	103.3	105.9	107.1	109.9
Printing support activities	...	...	...	...	...	...	100.4	100.0	100.4	100.9	101.2
Petroleum and coal product[3]	66.3	76.8	112.8	105.3	98.8	122.0	149.9	200.4	235.5	260.3	329.2
Petroleum refineries[8]	62.3	73.6	111.6	103.1	96.3	121.2	151.5	205.3	241.0	266.9	338.3
Asphalt paving, roofing, and saturated materials[3]	102.0	102.8	113.5	116.9	119.7	125.1	127.1	138.6	164.8	174.2	213.5
Other petroleum and coal product[3]	142.5	142.1	150.3	159.3	160.5	165.3	172.0	197.8	238.3	253.5	320.2
Chemical[3]	148.7	149.7	156.7	158.4	157.3	164.6	172.8	187.3	196.8	203.3	228.2
Basic chemical[3]	160.1	161.4	177.3	173.5	170.6	183.0	197.7	225.9	244.3	254.4	309.0
Petrochemical	...	...	...	...	...	...	120.7	151.0	164.7	168.5	212.6
Industrial gas	...	...	...	...	...	...	108.3	118.3	123.0	123.2	140.9
Synthetic dye and pigment	...	...	...	...	...	...	104.2	108.7	112.0	118.1	125.5
Other basic inorganic chemical	...	...	...	...	...	...	103.1	120.4	149.4	159.5	206.6
Other basic organic chemical	...	...	...	...	...	...	...	...	...	...	...
Resin, synthetic rubber, and artificial and synthetic fiber and filament[3]	115.9	115.4	128.0	126.2	119.7	131.0	145.5	169.4	175.2	174.6	193.0
Resin and synthetic rubber	...	...	...	...	...	...	115.1	136.5	141.2	140.4	156.3
Artificial and synthetic fiber and filament	...	...	...	...	...	...	101.2	107.8	111.1	110.6	113.7
Pesticide, fertilizer, and other agricultural chemical[3]	128.5	123.2	124.9	132.0	127.0	135.3	142.7	151.3	156.6	179.4	278.7
Fertilizer	...	...	...	...	...	...	107.3	118.1	123.5	151.8	277.5
Pesticide and other agricultural chemical	...	...	...	...	...	...	100.6	102.2	104.4	106.9	115.5
Pharmaceutical and medicine[3]	203.1	210.1	215.7	220.5	226.3	235.4	244.2	255.2	266.3	276.0	293.3
Paint, coating, and adhesive	...	...	...	...	...	...	101.9	108.8	116.9	121.5	129.8
Adhesive	...	...	...	...	...	...	100.5	106.4	114.8	119.0	127.4
Soap, cleaners, and toilet preparation[3]	128.7	130.3	132.5	134.2	134.2	134.9	136.9	140.5	144.6	147.2	153.0
Soap and cleaning compound	...	...	...	...	...	...	102.0	105.8	110.5	112.5	120.8
Toilet preparation	...	...	...	...	...	...	100.0	101.2	102.1	103.9	104.3
Other chemical product and preparation	...	...	...	...	...	...	101.6	108.6	114.2	118.0	126.5
Printing ink	...	...	...	...	...	...	100.0	103.0	107.2	114.2	123.5
Explosives[9]	...	...	...	...	...	...	...	...	...	103.1	113.1
All other chemical product and preparation	...	...	...	...	...	...	101.8	109.4	115.3	118.7	127.0
Plastics and rubber product[3]	122.1	122.2	124.6	125.9	125.5	128.4	131.7	141.2	149.7	150.6	161.3
Plastics product[10]	106.8	107.1	109.8	111.0	110.2	113.0	116.2	125.8	134.1	133.9	143.4
Unsupported plastics film, sheet, and bag	...	...	...	...	...	...	104.2	116.9	124.4	123.8	137.9
Plastics pipe, fitting, and unsupported shape	...	...	...	...	...	...	108.5	122.6	142.8	136.2	147.6
Laminated plastics plate, sheet, and shape	...	...	...	...	...	...	101.7	105.0	108.4	107.7	112.5
Polystyrene foam product	...	...	...	...	...	...	104.6	117.0	120.8	125.7	136.1
Foam product (except polystyrene)	...	...	...	...	...	...	100.2	110.0	136.6	132.5	140.0
Plastics bottle	...	...	...	...	...	...	103.1	114.8	119.5	118.3	126.8
Other plastics product	...	...	...	...	...	...	101.3	107.1	111.7	112.5	118.6
Rubber product	...	...	...	...	...	...	102.1	106.7	111.8	115.2	123.6
Tire[7]	102.0	100.4	100.4	101.5	102.7	105.6	110.5	116.9	123.8	128.6	140.2
Rubber and plastics hose and belting	...	...	...	...	...	...	102.3	107.4	111.0	113.6	120.1
Other rubber product	120.2	119.9	120.5	121.3	121.4	121.8	121.9	125.1	130.2	133.0	140.4
Nonmetallic mineral product[3]	129.3	132.6	134.7	136.0	137.1	138.0	142.7	152.0	163.4	166.8	170.9
Clay product and refractory	...	...	...	...	...	...	101.5	105.1	110.4	113.1	116.0
Pottery, ceramics, and plumbing fixture[3]	133.5	138.1	139.7	150.2	150.1	150.6	152.1	154.3	159.8	163.3	164.1
Clay building material and refractories	...	...	...	...	...	...	102.2	107.8	114.5	117.5	122.1
Glass and glass product	...	...	...	...	...	...	100.1	101.6	103.7	105.8	108.6

[3]December 1984 = 100.
[6]December 1982 = 100.
[7]June 1981 = 100.
[8]June 1985 = 100.
[9]December 2006 = 100.
[10]June 1993 = 100.
. . . = Not available.

Table 9-3. Producer Price Indexes for the Net Output of Selected Industries, 1998–2008—*Continued*

(December 2003 = 100, unless otherwise specified.)

Industry	1998	1999	2000	2001	2002	2003	2004	2005	2006	2007	2008
Manufacturing—*Continued*											
Cement and concrete product	. . .	. . .	. . .	. . .	. . .	. . .	104.2	114.8	126.6	131.9	136.4
Cement[11]	144.2	149.1	148.6	148.7	151.1	150.5	155.4	175.2	197.7	208.4	207.8
Ready-mix concrete	. . .	. . .	. . .	. . .	. . .	. . .	104.5	117.3	130.6	135.6	139.7
Concrete pipe, brick, and block	. . .	. . .	. . .	. . .	. . .	. . .	102.5	109.2	116.7	121.0	127.9
Other concrete products	. . .	. . .	. . .	. . .	. . .	. . .	104.7	111.3	121.0	126.6	132.2
Lime and gypsum product	. . .	. . .	. . .	. . .	. . .	. . .	110.0	124.5	145.1	128.1	119.4
Lime	. . .	. . .	. . .	. . .	. . .	. . .	103.5	112.4	121.8	129.1	136.5
Gypsum product	. . .	. . .	. . .	. . .	. . .	. . .	111.9	127.9	151.6	128.6	116.0
Other nonmetallic mineral product[3]	127.4	131.3	130.9	132.0	132.6	133.4	137.2	142.5	150.2	152.0	154.9
Abrasive product	. . .	. . .	. . .	. . .	. . .	. . .	100.2	103.1	107.2	110.4	118.1
All other nonmetallic mineral product	. . .	. . .	. . .	. . .	. . .	. . .	103.5	108.0	114.5	115.2	115.7
Primary metal[3]	120.9	115.8	119.8	116.1	116.2	118.4	142.8	156.3	179.3	190.5	211.9
Iron and steel mills and ferroalloy	. . .	. . .	. . .	. . .	. . .	. . .	127.7	136.7	150.9	160.8	189.7
Steel product from purchased steel	. . .	. . .	. . .	. . .	. . .	. . .	133.1	146.2	148.2	151.1	189.8
Iron/steel pipe and tube from purchased steel	. . .	. . .	. . .	. . .	. . .	. . .	147.9	160.1	164.1	168.1	206.6
Rolling and drawing of purchased steel	. . .	. . .	. . .	. . .	. . .	. . .	123.7	137.5	138.1	140.8	180.6
Alumina and aluminum production and processing	. . .	. . .	. . .	. . .	. . .	. . .	114.0	131.2	136.3	139.0	
Nonferrous (except aluminum) production and processing	. . .	. . .	. . .	. . .	. . .	. . .	113.6	137.6	202.8	223.0	218.6
Copper rolling, drawing, extruding, and alloying	. . .	. . .	. . .	. . .	. . .	. . .	118.2	138.9	222.0	232.8	232.9
Other nonferrous rolling, drawing, extruding, and alloying	. . .	. . .	. . .	. . .	. . .	. . .	110.3	136.2	181.2	206.0	195.8
Foundries	. . .	. . .	. . .	. . .	. . .	. . .	103.9	110.9	118.7	126.3	138.6
Ferrous metal foundries[3]	129.7	130.4	132.1	132.7	133.0	133.5	140.4	152.5	160.1	168.5	188.7
Nonferrous metal foundries[3]	132.7	131.6	133.5	134.1	134.4	135.6	140.0	145.0	160.4	173.2	185.6
Fabricated metal product[3]	128.7	129.1	130.3	131.0	131.7	132.9	141.3	149.5	155.7	162.3	174.4
Forging and stamping	. . .	. . .	. . .	. . .	. . .	. . .	107.0	113.3	116.8	120.9	130.8
Cutlery and handtool	. . .	. . .	. . .	. . .	. . .	. . .	105.5	108.9	111.8	115.8	
Architectural and structural metals	. . .	. . .	. . .	. . .	. . .	. . .	111.2	118.0	122.6	127.4	140.9
Plate work and fabricated structural product	. . .	. . .	. . .	. . .	. . .	. . .	115.2	124.2	128.9	135.2	155.4
Ornamental and architectural metal product	. . .	. . .	. . .	. . .	. . .	. . .	108.3	113.5	118.1	121.7	129.9
Boiler, tank, and shipping container	. . .	. . .	. . .	. . .	. . .	. . .	106.8	115.7	120.3	126.2	136.5
Power boiler and heat exchanger	. . .	. . .	. . .	. . .	. . .	. . .		124.2	132.4	136.9	147.3
Metal tank (heavy gauge)	. . .	. . .	. . .	. . .	. . .	. . .		120.8	125.6	132.3	143.2
Light gauge metal container[3]	102.3	100.7	101.0	100.8	102.7	105.4	110.4	117.5	121.0	127.1	137.8
Hardware	. . .	. . .	. . .	. . .	. . .	. . .	103.4	107.2	110.7	115.3	122.4
Spring and wire product	. . .	. . .	. . .	. . .	. . .	. . .	108.9	114.4	117.9	120.7	138.4
Machine shops; turned product; and screw, nut, and bolt	. . .	. . .	. . .	. . .	. . .	. . .	102.8	108.4	113.0	118.8	125.2
Machine shops	. . .	. . .	. . .	. . .	. . .	. . .	102.4	107.4	109.8	112.4	119.4
Turned product and screw, nut, and bolt[3]	122.7	121.8	122.9	122.8	123.4	123.6	128.4	136.6	147.1	161.2	167.9
Coating, engraving, heat treating, and other activity	. . .	. . .	. . .	. . .	. . .	. . .	102.0	104.2	110.6	115.5	119.5
Other fabricated metal product	. . .	. . .	. . .	. . .	. . .	. . .	103.8	109.8	115.7	121.5	128.4
Metal valve	. . .	. . .	. . .	. . .	. . .	. . .	103.0	109.8	118.1	126.6	132.8
All other fabricated metal product	. . .	. . .	. . .	. . .	. . .	. . .	104.5	109.9	113.7	117.1	124.7
Machinery	. . .	. . .	. . .	. . .	. . .	. . .	101.9	105.6	108.8	112.1	117.0
Agricultural, construction, and mining machinery	. . .	. . .	. . .	. . .	. . .	. . .	102.4	107.4	111.7	115.4	120.3
Agricultural implement	. . .	. . .	. . .	. . .	. . .	. . .	101.8	105.8	107.8	110.5	114.5
Construction machinery	. . .	. . .	. . .	. . .	. . .	. . .	102.9	107.7	112.5	115.8	119.4
Mining and oil and gas field machinery	. . .	. . .	. . .	. . .	. . .	. . .	102.7	110.6	119.5	127.3	137.9
Industrial machinery[3]	145.4	147.2	148.7	149.9	149.6	150.1	153.0	155.9	158.9	162.8	166.4
Sawmill and woodworking machinery	. . .	. . .	. . .	. . .	. . .	. . .	101.5	105.0	108.2	110.6	115.4
Plastics and rubber industry machinery	. . .	. . .	. . .	. . .	. . .	. . .	102.8	106.3	109.4	111.4	115.2
Other industrial machinery[3]	145.4	147.2	148.7	149.9	149.6	150.1	152.7	155.3	158.0	162.0	165.2
Commercial and service industry machinery	. . .	. . .	. . .	. . .	. . .	. . .	101.3	102.9	103.9	106.0	109.3
HVAC and commercial refrigeration equipment	. . .	. . .	. . .	. . .	. . .	. . .	101.9	108.0	112.1	117.8	123.0
Metalworking machinery	. . .	. . .	. . .	. . .	. . .	. . .	100.8	103.3	105.8	106.8	108.8
Turbine, and power transmission equipment[3]	133.9	135.7	136.6	137.7	138.9	139.1	140.8	143.2	148.0	152.6	162.9
Other general purpose machinery	. . .	. . .	. . .	. . .	. . .	. . .	103.0	107.6	111.2	115.0	121.4
Pump and compressor	. . .	. . .	. . .	. . .	. . .	. . .	102.2	108.4	112.6	117.9	123.6
Material handling equipment	. . .	. . .	. . .	. . .	. . .	. . .	104.6	110.6	114.4	118.2	125.3
All other general purpose machinery	. . .	. . .	. . .	. . .	. . .	. . .	102.5	105.7	108.7	112.0	118.1
Computer and electronic product	. . .	. . .	. . .	. . .	. . .	. . .	99.0	97.5	96.5	94.2	92.7
Computer and peripheral equipment[9]	191.7	172.8	162.2	153.1	139.5	123.9	115.4	107.8	102.1	94.5	86.4
Communications equipment[2]	115.0	113.0	110.4	108.6	105.0	101.7	98.4	97.0	95.9	95.8	97.1
Telephone apparatus	. . .	. . .	. . .	. . .	. . .	. . .	95.3	93.2	91.1	90.5	91.3
Radio/TV broadcast and wireless communication equipment	. . .	. . .	. . .	. . .	. . .	. . .	99.4	98.7	98.2	98.6	100.3
Other communications equipment	. . .	. . .	. . .	. . .	. . .	. . .	99.8	99.7	101.2	101.6	103.5
Audio and video equipment	. . .	. . .	. . .	. . .	. . .	. . .	98.1	95.6	93.7	90.9	89.3
Semiconductor and other electronic component[3]	91.9	90.1	88.8	86.4	84.9	81.1	78.3	76.5	75.1	70.2	66.3
Navigation, measuring, medical, and control instruments	. . .	. . .	. . .	. . .	. . .	. . .	100.6	101.9	103.5	104.9	106.5
Manufacturing and reproducing magnetic and optical media	. . .	. . .	. . .	. . .	. . .	. . .	98.0	97.0	95.5	92.2	93.8
Electrical equipment, appliance and component	. . .	. . .	. . .	. . .	. . .	. . .	103.2	108.0	116.6	122.2	127.8
Electric lighting equipment	. . .	. . .	. . .	. . .	. . .	. . .	100.8	103.5	105.9	108.2	110.9
Electric lamp bulb and part	. . .	. . .	. . .	. . .	. . .	. . .	98.1	100.2	98.6	98.8	99.6
Lighting fixture	. . .	. . .	. . .	. . .	. . .	. . .	101.7	104.6	108.2	111.2	114.3
Household appliance[3]	107.5	107.2	106.2	104.6	104.2	103.1	103.1	106.3	107.7	109.3	112.6
Small electrical appliance	. . .	. . .	. . .	. . .	. . .	. . .	99.9	101.8	103.0	105.3	106.0
Major appliance	. . .	. . .	. . .	. . .	. . .	. . .	100.6	104.2	105.6	106.8	110.8
Electrical equipment	. . .	. . .	. . .	. . .	. . .	. . .	101.9	107.2	113.7	120.6	127.3
Other electrical equipment and component	. . .	. . .	. . .	. . .	. . .	. . .	106.6	112.5	129.1	136.7	144.0
Battery	. . .	. . .	. . .	. . .	. . .	. . .	102.2	105.7	112.6	126.2	139.8
Communications and energy wire and cable	. . .	. . .	. . .	. . .	. . .	. . .	106.8	115.8	150.3	161.3	167.9
Wiring device	. . .	. . .	. . .	. . .	. . .	. . .	113.6	118.9	128.6	133.9	140.9
All other electrical equipment and component	. . .	. . .	. . .	. . .	. . .	. . .	101.7	105.4	109.3	110.3	114.0

[2]December 1985 = 100.
[3]December 1984 = 100.
[9]December 2006 = 100.
[11]June 1982 = 100.
. . . = Not available.

Table 9-3. Producer Price Indexes for the Net Output of Selected Industries, 1998–2008—*Continued*

(December 2003 = 100, unless otherwise specified.)

Industry	1998	1999	2000	2001	2002	2003	2004	2005	2006	2007	2008
Manufacturing—*Continued*											
Transportation equipment	. . .	. . .	. . .	. . .	. . .	. . .	100.9	102.5	103.2	104.9	107.3
Motor vehicle	. . .	. . .	. . .	. . .	. . .	. . .	99.4	98.7	96.1	96.6	98.0
Automobile and light truck motor vehicle	. . .	. . .	. . .	. . .	. . .	. . .	99.2	98.2	95.1	95.3	96.6
Motor vehicle body and trailer	. . .	. . .	. . .	. . .	. . .	. . .	104.0	109.7	113.7	117.2	121.5
Motor vehicle parts	. . .	. . .	. . .	. . .	. . .	. . .	101.4	102.7	104.8	106.8	108.8
Motor vehicle steering and suspension parts	. . .	. . .	. . .	. . .	. . .	. . .	101.8	105.1	106.3	105.0	106.5
Aerospace product and parts[8]	143.4	144.8	149.9	154.7	157.3	162.2	168.0	176.0	182.8	188.6	196.2
Railroad rolling stock[5]	127.6	128.2	128.6	128.3	127.7	129.0	135.8	150.5	158.4	165.6	169.3
Ship and boat building[3]	144.1	145.6	149.0	152.6	156.8	163.0	169.6	175.0	181.4	188.3	193.8
Other transportation equipment	. . .	. . .	. . .	. . .	. . .	. . .	101.1	103.6	104.8	106.3	106.4
Furniture and related product[3]	139.7	141.3	143.3	145.1	146.3	147.4	151.5	157.8	162.5	165.7	171.7
Household and institutional furniture and kitchen cabinet[3]	138.4	140.3	142.5	144.4	146.2	147.0	148.6	152.6	157.4	160.8	166.5
Wood kitchen cabinet and countertop	. . .	. . .	. . .	. . .	. . .	. . .	101.1	103.2	106.3	108.4	111.2
Household and institutional furniture	. . .	. . .	. . .	. . .	. . .	. . .	101.1	104.0	107.4	109.7	114.0
Office furniture (including fixtures)	. . .	. . .	. . .	. . .	. . .	. . .	105.1	111.5	113.8	116.7	121.2
Other furniture-related product	. . .	. . .	. . .	. . .	. . .	. . .	104.0	110.6	115.2	114.9	118.5
Mattress	. . .	. . .	. . .	. . .	. . .	. . .	105.6	115.0	120.6	119.2	123.9
Blind and shade	142.2	144.7	148.7	150.6	151.6	152.3	153.9	157.7	162.4	164.4	166.9
Miscellaneous	. . .	. . .	. . .	. . .	. . .	. . .	101.2	102.9	104.7	107.0	109.9
Medical equipment and supplies	. . .	. . .	. . .	. . .	. . .	. . .	101.3	102.5	103.8	105.1	107.4
Other miscellaneous[2]	129.7	130.3	130.9	132.4	133.3	133.9	135.2	138.4	142.0	146.5	151.1
Jewelry and silverware[2]	127.1	126.4	127.1	128.0	129.1	131.0	134.6	138.7	146.5	152.6	161.7
Sporting and athletic goods	. . .	. . .	. . .	. . .	. . .	. . .	101.3	102.0	103.6	107.6	106.2
Doll, toy, and game	. . .	. . .	. . .	. . .	. . .	. . .	100.3	101.7	102.7	104.9	107.9
Office supplies (except paper)[2]	130.9	132.0	132.0	131.4	132.8	132.9	133.1	135.8	136.2	139.0	141.1
Sign	. . .	. . .	. . .	. . .	. . .	. . .	100.9	104.6	106.9	109.1	111.2
All other miscellaneous	. . .	. . .	. . .	. . .	. . .	. . .	101.0	103.7	106.7	110.2	115.4
Wholesale Trade											
Merchant wholesalers, durable goods[12]	. . .	. . .	. . .	. . .	. . .	. . .	. . .	102.0	106.3	110.4	116.4
Merchant wholesalers, nondurable goods[13]	. . .	. . .	. . .	. . .	. . .	. . .	. . .	. . .	106.2	112.2	120.5
Wholesale trade agents and brokers[13]	. . .	. . .	. . .	. . .	. . .	. . .	. . .	. . .	102.4	105.5	110.4
Retail Trade											
Motor vehicle and parts dealers	. . .	. . .	. . .	. . .	. . .	. . .	103.5	106.9	112.8	115.5	118.0
Automobile dealers	. . .	. . .	. . .	. . .	. . .	. . .	102.9	105.4	110.8	113.2	113.8
New car dealers[14]	. . .	. . .	99.7	103.1	108.7	111.5	113.5	116.3	122.3	125.0	125.7
Recreational vehicle dealers[15]	. . .	. . .	. . .	98.8	112.2	109.7	121.4	133.6	133.8	142.4	143.5
Automotive parts, accessories, and tire stores[16]	. . .	. . .	. . .	. . .	100.9	104.2	109.4	115.1	124.3	128.2	142.0
Automotive parts and accessories stores	. . .	. . .	. . .	. . .	. . .	. . .	106.8	110.9	119.7	125.6	140.3
Tire dealers	. . .	. . .	. . .	. . .	. . .	. . .	102.0	110.7	119.3	117.5	128.1
Furniture and home furnishings stores	. . .	. . .	. . .	. . .	. . .	. . .	102.4	110.7	116.6	117.4	120.3
Furniture stores	. . .	. . .	. . .	. . .	. . .	. . .	100.8	108.0	111.0	110.6	113.7
Floor covering stores	. . .	. . .	. . .	. . .	. . .	. . .	104.6	114.4	124.3	127.0	129.8
Electronics and appliance stores	. . .	. . .	. . .	. . .	. . .	. . .	99.0	98.9	99.4	106.1	110.8
Appliance, TV, and other electronics stores	. . .	. . .	. . .	. . .	. . .	. . .	101.8	103.5	103.8	104.9	112.8
Computer and software stores	. . .	. . .	. . .	. . .	. . .	. . .	95.2	92.4	91.7	91.7	84.6
Camera and photographic supplies stores	. . .	. . .	. . .	. . .	. . .	. . .	88.6	82.0	95.5	91.3	86.7
Building material and garden equipment and supplies dealers	. . .	. . .	. . .	. . .	. . .	. . .	108.3	109.9	118.4	120.1	119.2
Building material and supplies dealers	. . .	. . .	. . .	. . .	. . .	. . .	108.7	109.9	119.8	122.4	121.0
Home centers	. . .	. . .	. . .	. . .	. . .	. . .	107.0	109.6	122.5	121.8	115.7
Paint and wallpaper stores	. . .	. . .	. . .	. . .	. . .	. . .	99.5	104.4	106.2	110.3	121.8
Hardware stores	. . .	. . .	. . .	. . .	. . .	. . .	103.1	108.2	112.3	114.3	114.3
Other building material dealers	. . .	. . .	. . .	. . .	. . .	. . .	111.4	110.8	121.3	128.9	130.6
Lawn and garden equipment and supplies stores	. . .	. . .	. . .	. . .	. . .	. . .	105.8	110.3	111.5	106.8	110.1
Nursery, garden, and farm supply stores	. . .	. . .	. . .	. . .	. . .	. . .	105.8	110.3	111.5	106.8	110.1
Food and beverage stores[14]	. . .	. . .	103.8	109.6	113.4	117.6	123.2	131.0	134.7	139.6	149.3
Grocery stores	. . .	. . .	. . .	. . .	. . .	. . .	103.5	110.7	114.0	117.9	126.1
Grocery (except convenience) stores	. . .	. . .	. . .	. . .	. . .	. . .	103.5	110.7	114.0	117.9	126.1
Specialty food stores	. . .	. . .	. . .	. . .	. . .	. . .	107.1	110.2	114.1	122.9	132.4
Beer, wine, and liquor stores[17]	. . .	. . .	. . .	102.9	103.5	106.9	110.7	111.0	111.3	113.2	120.6
Health and personal care stores	. . .	. . .	. . .	. . .	. . .	. . .	101.7	107.6	118.7	123.1	130.5
Pharmacies and drug stores[17]	. . .	. . .	. . .	102.4	112.4	116.6	119.8	127.9	142.0	148.5	158.7
Optical goods stores	. . .	. . .	. . .	. . .	. . .	. . .	99.8	100.1	101.5	103.0	104.8
Gasoline stations[15]	. . .	. . .	. . .	105.6	66.8	54.1	51.3	51.0	50.9	74.0	70.3
Gasoline stations with convenience stores	. . .	. . .	. . .	. . .	. . .	. . .	102.5	104.3	110.0	123.0	135.0
Other gasoline stations	. . .	. . .	. . .	. . .	. . .	. . .	132.8	118.1	84.2	216.2	151.4
Clothing and clothing accessories stores	. . .	. . .	. . .	. . .	. . .	. . .	100.5	103.3	105.4	107.0	110.7
Clothing stores	. . .	. . .	. . .	. . .	. . .	. . .	99.3	102.4	104.4	105.3	107.5
Men's clothing stores	. . .	. . .	. . .	. . .	. . .	. . .	100.2	102.1	98.9	99.8	98.3
Women's clothing stores	. . .	. . .	. . .	. . .	. . .	. . .	102.9	103.3	108.6	110.7	114.6
Family clothing stores	. . .	. . .	. . .	. . .	. . .	. . .	97.8	102.2	104.3	104.0	105.9
Shoe stores	. . .	. . .	. . .	. . .	. . .	. . .	103.9	105.0	105.7	109.7	114.0
Jewelry, luggage, and leather goods stores	. . .	. . .	. . .	. . .	. . .	. . .	101.8	104.9	108.7	110.9	120.4
Jewelry stores	. . .	. . .	. . .	. . .	. . .	. . .	101.8	104.8	108.6	110.8	120.7
Luggage and leather goods stores	. . .	. . .	. . .	. . .	. . .	. . .	101.4	106.5	111.0	113.5	116.8

[2]December 1985 = 100.
[3]December 1984 = 100.
[5]June 1984 = 100.
[8]June 1985 = 100.
[12]June 2004 = 100.
[13]June 2005 = 100.
[14]December 1999 = 100.
[15]June 2001 = 100.
[16]December 2001 = 100.
[17]June 2000 = 100.
. . . = Not available.

Table 9-3. Producer Price Indexes for the Net Output of Selected Industries, 1998–2008—*Continued*

(December 2003 = 100, unless otherwise specified.)

Industry	1998	1999	2000	2001	2002	2003	2004	2005	2006	2007	2008
Retail Trade—*Continued*											
Sporting goods, hobby, book, and music stores	...	...	...	...	...	...	96.6	96.6	98.4	103.4	111.6
Sporting goods, hobby, and musical instrument stores	...	...	...	...	...	...	97.8	99.0	102.5	107.7	119.5
Sporting goods stores	...	...	...	...	...	...	95.0	96.1	99.2	112.7	130.7
Hobby, toy, and game stores	...	...	...	...	...	...	100.5	101.7	105.7	101.9	108.5
Sewing, needlework, and piece goods stores	...	...	...	...	...	...	103.2	104.7	109.0	108.2	110.5
Book, periodical, and music stores	...	...	...	...	...	...	94.7	92.5	91.6	95.4	96.2
Bookstores and news dealers	...	...	...	...	...	...	95.0	92.0	94.2	97.1	98.0
Prerecorded tape, CD, and record stores	...	...	...	...	...	...	93.9	93.8	84.4	91.0	91.5
General merchandise stores	...	...	...	...	...	...	103.1	103.4	106.6	110.0	112.9
Department stores	...	...	...	...	...	...	105.4	105.1	105.6	111.4	117.8
Other general merchandise stores	...	...	...	...	...	...	97.7	99.5	108.9	110.0	107.9
Florists	...	...	...	...	...	...	100.2	100.2	102.8	107.3	108.6
Office supplies, stationery, and gift stores	...	...	...	...	...	...	99.7	101.7	104.3	107.8	112.0
Office supplies and stationery stores	...	...	...	...	...	...	100.4	102.9	107.1	113.6	119.4
Gift, novelty, and souvenir stores	...	...	...	...	...	...	98.7	100.0	100.1	101.2	104.0
Manufactured (mobile) home dealers	...	...	...	...	...	...	107.7	116.7	123.2	118.3	113.6
Nonstore retailers	...	...	...	...	...	...	107.5	119.8	118.9	129.2	144.1
Vending machine operators	...	...	...	...	...	...	101.5	104.4	105.7	106.4	110.6
Fuel dealers[17]	...	...	...	120.5	113.8	122.7	129.4	147.3	138.9	138.3	174.2
Transportation and Warehousing											
Air transportation[18]	124.5	130.8	147.7	157.2	157.8	162.1	162.3	171.0	180.4	183.7	203.8
Scheduled air transportation[19]	149.3	157.3	180.1	193.0	193.3	198.5	198.6	209.3	220.5	224.5	248.9
Nonscheduled air transportation[20]	99.2	102.2	107.3	112.7	114.7	117.8	119.9	126.7	136.8	148.5	165.8
Rail transportation[20]	101.7	101.3	102.6	104.5	106.6	108.8	113.4	125.2	135.9	140.9	157.3
Water transportation	...	...	...	...	...	...	101.3	106.4	111.1	113.5	127.0
Inland water transportation	...	...	...	...	...	...	103.2	119.3	144.1	146.7	172.0
Truck transportation	...	...	...	...	...	...	103.1	109.0	113.2	115.4	123.0
General freight trucking	...	...	...	...	...	...	105.2	111.5	115.3	119.6	130.2
General freight trucking, local	...	...	...	...	...	...	105.2	111.5	115.3	119.6	130.2
General freight trucking, long distance	...	...	...	...	...	...	103.2	109.7	113.8	115.9	122.2
Specialized freight trucking	...	...	...	...	...	...	102.3	107.0	111.4	113.1	122.1
Used household and office goods moving	...	...	...	...	...	...	102.6	106.0	107.8	108.8	112.2
Specialized freight (except used) trucking, local	...	...	...	...	...	...	102.7	107.1	112.3	114.2	126.7
Specialized freight (except used) trucking, long distance	...	...	...	...	...	...	101.7	107.5	112.8	114.8	123.6
Pipeline transportation of crude oil	...	...	...	...	...	...	103.9	113.3	122.0	125.4	137.1
Other pipeline transportation	...	...	...	...	...	...	101.4	105.2	108.2	115.0	121.6
Pipeline transportation of refined petroleum products	...	...	...	...	...	...	101.4	105.2	108.2	115.0	121.6
Transportation support activities	...	...	...	...	...	...	101.1	104.1	106.5	108.5	111.7
Air transportation support activities[20]	105.2	108.6	114.2	117.5	121.4	125.1	128.1	134.2	138.6	141.0	145.4
Airport operations	...	...	...	...	...	...	101.1	104.8	108.6	109.6	112.3
Other air transportation support activities	...	...	...	...	...	...	102.0	107.5	110.8	112.9	117.0
Water transportation support activities	...	...	...	...	...	...	101.0	103.5	107.7	112.7	117.3
Port and harbor operations	...	...	...	...	...	...	102.4	105.9	108.8	114.8	117.7
Marine cargo handling	...	...	...	...	...	...	100.5	102.2	105.1	109.0	110.7
Navigational services to shipping	...	...	...	...	...	...	101.5	105.7	113.9	120.6	133.8
Freight transportation arrangement[20]	97.7	97.3	98.3	98.2	97.5	97.9	98.9	99.1	98.8	100.2	102.5
Postal service[21]	132.3	135.3	135.2	143.4	150.2	155.0	155.0	155.0	164.7	171.9	178.9
Couriers and messengers	...	...	...	...	...	...	106.1	113.8	121.5	131.5	142.0
Couriers	...	...	...	...	...	...	106.6	115.0	123.2	133.5	144.4
Local messengers and local delivery	...	...	...	...	...	...	101.1	102.7	104.4	108.1	112.2
Warehousing and storage[9]	86.5	89.0	90.8	93.2	94.5	95.8	...	...	...	102.5	106.5
General warehousing and storage	...	...	...	...	...	...	100.3	101.5	103.8	107.3	111.9
Refrigerated warehousing and storage	...	...	...	...	...	...	100.5	101.0	102.4	104.0	106.7
Farm product warehousing and storage	...	...	...	...	...	...	100.2	101.5	103.8	104.0	108.7
Information											
Publishing industries, except Internet	...	...	...	...	...	...	101.5	104.1	106.2	108.1	110.6
Newspaper, book, and directory publishers	...	...	...	...	...	...	102.1	105.5	108.3	111.8	115.1
Newspaper publishers[22]	328.7	339.3	351.3	367.9	381.9	395.7	409.7	426.2	439.0	450.3	459.2
Periodical publishers[22]	276.9	284.9	292.6	305.9	320.4	332.4	339.1	347.6	354.4	369.5	383.1
Book publishers[3]	178.9	184.7	190.2	195.6	201.5	208.2	215.7	224.3	232.8	240.2	250.9
Directory and mailing list publishers	...	...	...	...	...	...	101.3	103.3	105.4	108.4	111.1
Other publishers	...	...	...	...	...	...	100.7	103.9	104.9	107.9	108.8
Software publishers	...	...	...	...	...	...	99.8	99.8	100.1	99.6	100.7
Broadcasting, except Internet	...	...	...	...	...	...	101.2	102.1	102.8	101.4	106.7
Radio and television broadcasting[15]	...	...	...	98.2	97.1	99.8	102.8	101.9	101.1	101.3	101.7
Radio broadcasting	...	...	...	...	...	...	102.7	106.3	105.8	104.3	103.7
Television broadcasting	...	...	...	...	...	...	100.5	97.3	96.3	97.3	98.0
Cable networks	...	...	...	...	...	...	101.4	104.3	106.7	103.6	111.9
Telecommunications	...	...	...	...	...	...	99.8	98.1	98.3	100.8	101.1
Wired telecommunications carriers[23]	...	...	96.4	93.6	89.9	88.1	86.3	85.8	86.6	89.3	90.7
Wireless telecommunications carriers	...	...	...	...	...	...	98.4	86.4	80.9	80.4	76.1
Cable and other program distribution	...	...	...	...	...	...	102.2	106.5	109.6	113.7	116.2
ISPs and Web search portals[12]	...	...	...	...	...	...	...	95.9	87.6	72.8	73.4
Data processing and related services	...	...	...	...	...	...	98.8	98.8	99.7	100.3	100.9

[3]December 1984 = 100.
[9]December 2006 = 100.
[12]June 2004 = 100.
[15]June 2001 = 100.
[17]June 2000 = 100.
[18]December 1992 = 100.
[19]December 1989 = 100.
[20]December 1996 = 100.
[21]June 1989 = 100.
[22]December 1979 = 100.
[23]June 1999 = 100.
. . . = Not available.

Table 9-3. Producer Price Indexes for the Net Output of Selected Industries, 1998–2008—*Continued*

(December 2003 = 100, unless otherwise specified.)

Industry	1998	1999	2000	2001	2002	2003	2004	2005	2006	2007	2008
Other Services											
Depository credit intermediation	...	...	...	...	...	...	102.5	105.0	111.2	112.8	102.6
Security, commodity contracts, and like activity	...	...	...	...	...	...	103.4	109.4	113.8	119.9	119.5
Security and commodity contracts, intermediation, and brokerage[17]	...	...	...	88.1	81.8	82.5	84.2	88.1	90.1	92.8	94.2
Investment banking and securities dealing	...	...	...	...	...	...	102.6	109.1	111.0	113.6	125.4
Securities brokerage	...	...	...	...	...	...	100.0	102.2	105.2	109.7	103.4
Portfolio management	...	...	...	...	...	...	108.1	117.8	124.8	137.1	131.2
Investment advice	...	...	...	...	...	...	102.0	104.8	119.4	129.7	133.4
Insurance carriers and related activities	...	...	...	...	...	...	101.9	104.5	106.3	107.7	110.1
Insurance carriers	...	...	...	...	...	...	101.9	104.5	106.4	107.7	110.2
Direct life/health/medical insurance carriers	...	...	...	...	...	...	102.2	105.1	107.6	109.5	112.6
Other direct insurance carriers[24]	...	100.7	101.9	104.3	108.7	115.0	118.7	121.0	121.7	122.1	123.6
Insurance agencies and brokerages	...	...	...	...	...	...	100.8	101.8	102.2	102.9	103.4
Lessors of nonresidential building (except miniwarehouse)	...	...	...	...	...	...	102.3	105.1	107.7	107.2	110.6
Lessors of miniwarehouse and self-storage units	...	...	...	...	...	...	102.0	105.6	109.2	110.6	113.4
Offices of real estate agents and brokers	...	...	...	...	...	...	101.8	108.1	110.9	110.8	106.5
Real estate property managers	...	...	...	...	...	...	100.9	102.2	102.9	103.8	108.1
Automotive equipment rental and leasing[15]	...	...	...	...	103.9	106.6	107.8	109.0	115.2	118.0	126.4
Passenger car rental and leasing	...	...	...	...	...	...	98.2	99.9	108.0	108.2	116.5
Truck, utility trailer, and RV rental and leasing	...	...	...	...	...	...	99.9	99.9	101.2	107.7	114.7
Legal services[20]	106.1	108.7	112.5	117.9	121.7	125.6	131.8	138.5	145.2	153.6	161.6
Offices of lawyers[20]	106.1	108.7	112.5	117.9	121.7	125.6	131.8	138.5	145.2	153.6	161.6
Architectural, engineering, and related services[20]	105.1	108.5	111.8	115.9	121.1	124.3	126.8	129.2	134.4	140.0	141.0
Architectural services	...	...	...	...	...	...	99.7	102.0	106.0	109.3	110.5
Engineering services	...	...	...	...	...	...	101.5	103.4	107.6	112.2	113.0
Management and technical consulting services[25]	...	...	...	...	...	...	...	...	...	102.8	105.7
Advertising agencies	...	...	...	...	...	...	100.1	101.4	104.1	105.0	106.0
Employment services[20]	103.2	105.2	107.3	108.2	108.9	111.4	113.9	116.3	119.2	121.7	123.2
Employment placement agencies	...	...	...	...	...	...	102.2	104.4	104.4	105.8	106.4
Temporary help services	...	...	...	...	...	...	101.7	104.0	106.9	109.4	110.7
Employee leasing services	...	...	...	...	...	...	101.3	102.9	105.4	107.6	109.0
Travel agencies	...	...	...	...	...	...	96.9	95.9	99.5	101.0	99.7
Janitorial services	...	...	...	...	...	...	100.9	101.9	103.7	106.0	109.1
Waste collection	...	...	...	...	...	...	101.3	102.5	104.5	107.6	112.4
Amusement and theme parks[25]	...	...	...	...	...	...	...	...	...	105.2	109.8
Accommodations[20]	108.1	112.7	116.2	121.3	121.3	122.0	125.2	131.9	136.7	142.9	146.0
Hotels (except casino hotels) and motels	...	...	...	...	...	...	103.5	110.0	114.1	119.8	124.2
Casino hotels	...	...	...	...	...	...	105.0	107.5	110.8	113.0	110.9
Health Care and Social Assistance											
Offices of physicians[20]	103.2	105.5	107.3	110.4	110.3	112.1	114.3	116.4	117.5	122.3	123.6
Medical and diagnostic laboratories	...	...	...	...	...	...	100.0	104.1	104.4	107.0	107.3
Home health care services[20]	106.2	107.1	111.1	114.0	116.6	117.0	119.8	121.1	121.8	124.0	126.1
Hospitals[18]	114.4	116.4	119.4	123.0	127.5	134.9	141.5	146.9	153.3	158.6	163.4
General medical and surgical hospitals	...	...	...	...	...	...	102.9	106.7	111.2	115.1	118.6
Psychiatric and substance abuse hospitals	...	...	...	...	...	...	101.1	103.7	106.2	110.0	113.4
Other specialty hospitals	...	...	...	...	...	...	103.8	109.6	122.8	126.7	128.4
Nursing care facilities	...	...	...	...	...	...	102.6	106.4	109.6	114.7	119.2
Residential mental retardation facilities	...	...	...	...	...	...	101.2	104.5	108.5	112.7	118.3

[15]June 2001 = 100.
[17]June 2000 = 100.
[18]December 1992 = 100.
[20]December 1996 = 100.
[24]December 1998 = 100.
[25]June 2006 = 100.
... = Not available.

CONSUMER PRICE INDEX

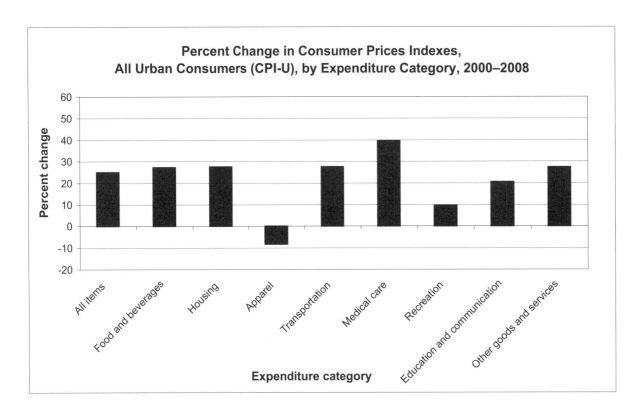

While the Consumer Price Index for all Urban Consumers (CPI-U) for all items increased by 25.0 percent from 2000 to 2008, the CPI-U for medical care increased by 39.6 percent. The CPI-U also increased rapidly for housing and transportation (27.5 percent for each) from 2000 to 2008. The CPI-U for apparel declined by 8.3 percent. (See Table 9-8.)

OTHER HIGHLIGHTS

- From 2007 to 2008, the CPI-U for all items rose 3.8 percent, while the CPI-U for energy commodities grew 18.0 percent. (See Tables 9-4 and 9-5.)

- Hospital and related services continued to be the fastest growing component of the medical care, increasing by 7.0 percent from 2007 to 2008, followed by medical care services (4.2 percent), professional services (3.4 percent), and medical care commodities (2.1 percent). (See Table 9-8.)

- Among the selected metropolitan statistical areas, the CPI-U for Pittsburgh, PA, grew the fastest from 2007 to 2008, rising 4.9 percent. In Detroit-Ann Arbor-Flint, MI, and St. Louis, MO-IL, the CPI-U rose much slower than average, increasing at 2.3 and 2.8 percent, respectively. (See Table 9-10.)

NOTES AND DEFINITIONS

CONSUMER PRICE INDEX

The Consumer Price Index (CPI) is a measure of the average change over time in the prices of consumer items—goods and services that people buy for day-to-day living. The CPI is a complex construct that combines economic theory with sampling and other statistical techniques and uses data from several surveys to produce a timely and precise measure of average price change for the consumption sector of the American economy.

The Bureau of Labor Statistics (BLS) publishes CPIs for two population groups: (1) the CPI for Urban Wage Earners and Clerical Workers (CPI-W), which covers households of wage earners and clerical workers that comprise approximately 32 percent of the total population and (2) the CPI for All Urban Consumers (CPI-U) and the Chained CPI for All Urban Consumers (C-CPI-U), which cover approximately 87 percent of the total population and include in addition to wage earners and clerical worker households, groups such as professional, managerial, and technical workers, the self-employed, short-term workers, the unemployed, and retirees and others not in the labor force. BLS began publishing the CPI-U in January 1978, but did not begin publishing the C-CPI-U until August 2002 with data beginning in January 2000. The CPI-W is much older than either the CPI-U or C-CPI-U.

The CPIs are based on prices of food, clothing, shelter, and fuels, transportation fares, charges for doctors' and dentists' services, drugs, and other goods and services that people buy for day-to-day living. Prices are collected each month in 87 urban areas across the country from about 4,000 housing units and approximately 25,000 retail establishments-department stores, supermarkets, hospitals, filling stations, and other types of stores and service establishments. All taxes directly associated with the purchase and use of items are included in the index. Prices of fuels and a few other items are obtained every month in all 87 locations. Prices of most other commodities and services are collected every month in the three largest geographic areas and every other month in other areas. Prices of most goods and services are obtained by personal visits or telephone calls from BLS trained representatives.

In calculating the index, price changes for the various items in each location are averaged together with weights, which represent their importance in the spending of the appropriate population group. Local data are then combined to obtain a U.S. city average. For the CPI-U and CPI-W separate indexes are also published by size of city, by region of the country, for cross-classifications of regions and population-size classes, and for 27 local areas. Area indexes do not measure differences in the level of prices among cities; they only measure the average change in prices for each area since the base period. For the C-CPI-U data are issued only at the national level. It is important to note that the CPI-U and CPI-W are considered final when released, but the C-CPI-U is issued in preliminary form and subject to two annual revisions. The prices used in the C-CPI-U are the same as those used to produce the CPI-U and the CPI-W, but the C-CPI-U uses a different formula and different weights to combine basic indexes.

The Consumer Price Index Research Series Using Current Methods (CPI-U-RS), shown in Table 9-11, provides estimates for the period since 1977 of what the CPI would have been had the most current methods been in effect. Each time there are new methods introduced into the CPI, the CPI-U-RS is revised from 1978 forward.

Sources of Additional Information

An extensive description of the methodology is available in the updated version of Chapter 17 in the *BLS Handbook of Methods*. Additional detailed data can be found in the *Consumer Price Index Detailed Report* and in special reports. These resources can be found on the BLS Web site at <http://www.bls.gov>.

Table 9-4. Consumer Price Indexes, All Urban Consumers (CPI-U): U.S. City Average, Major Groups, 1967–2008

(1982–1984 = 100, unless otherwise specified.)

Year	All items	Food and beverages	Housing	Apparel	Transportation	Medical care	Recreation[1]	Education and communication[1]	Other goods and services
1967	33.4	35.0	30.8	51.0	33.3	28.2	. . .	. . .	35.1
1968	34.8	36.2	32.0	53.7	34.3	29.9	. . .	. . .	36.9
1969	36.7	38.1	34.0	56.8	35.7	31.9	. . .	. . .	38.7
1970	38.8	40.1	36.4	59.2	37.5	34.0	. . .	. . .	40.9
1971	40.5	41.4	38.0	61.1	39.5	36.1	. . .	. . .	42.9
1972	41.8	43.1	39.4	62.3	39.9	37.3	. . .	. . .	44.7
1973	44.4	48.8	41.2	64.6	41.2	38.8	. . .	. . .	46.4
1974	49.3	55.5	45.8	69.4	45.8	42.4	. . .	. . .	49.8
1975	53.8	60.2	50.7	72.5	50.1	47.5	. . .	. . .	53.9
1976	56.9	62.1	53.8	75.2	55.1	52.0	. . .	. . .	57.0
1977	60.6	65.8	57.4	78.6	59.0	57.0	. . .	. . .	60.4
1978	65.2	72.2	62.4	81.4	61.7	61.8	. . .	. . .	64.3
1979	72.6	79.9	70.1	84.9	70.5	67.5	. . .	. . .	68.9
1980	82.4	86.7	81.1	90.9	83.1	74.9	. . .	. . .	75.2
1981	90.9	93.5	90.4	95.3	93.2	82.9	. . .	. . .	82.6
1982	96.5	97.3	96.9	97.8	97.0	92.5	. . .	. . .	91.1
1983	99.6	99.5	99.5	100.2	99.3	100.6	. . .	. . .	101.1
1984	103.9	103.2	103.6	102.1	103.7	106.8	. . .	. . .	107.9
1985	107.6	105.6	107.7	105.0	106.4	113.5	. . .	. . .	114.5
1986	109.6	109.1	110.9	105.9	102.3	122.0	. . .	. . .	121.4
1987	113.6	113.5	114.2	110.6	105.4	130.1	. . .	. . .	128.5
1988	118.3	118.2	118.5	115.4	108.7	138.6	. . .	. . .	137.0
1989	124.0	124.9	123.0	118.6	114.1	149.3	. . .	. . .	147.7
1990	130.7	132.1	128.5	124.1	120.5	162.8	. . .	. . .	159.0
1991	136.2	136.8	133.6	128.7	123.8	177.0	. . .	. . .	171.6
1992	140.3	138.7	137.5	131.9	126.5	190.1	. . .	. . .	183.3
1993	144.5	141.6	141.2	133.7	130.4	201.4	90.7	85.5	192.9
1994	148.2	144.9	144.8	133.4	134.3	211.0	92.7	88.8	198.5
1995	152.4	148.9	148.5	132.0	139.1	220.5	94.5	92.2	206.9
1996	156.9	153.7	152.8	131.7	143.0	228.2	97.4	95.3	215.4
1997	160.5	157.7	156.8	132.9	144.3	234.6	99.6	98.4	224.8
1998	163.0	161.1	160.4	133.0	141.6	242.1	101.1	100.3	237.7
1999	166.6	164.6	163.9	131.3	144.4	250.6	102.0	101.2	258.3
2000	172.2	168.4	169.6	129.6	153.3	260.8	103.3	102.5	271.1
2001	177.1	173.6	176.4	127.3	154.3	272.8	104.9	105.2	282.6
2002	179.9	176.8	180.3	124.0	152.9	285.6	106.2	107.9	293.2
2003	184.0	180.5	184.8	120.9	157.6	297.1	107.5	109.8	298.7
2004	188.9	186.6	189.5	120.4	163.1	310.1	108.6	111.6	304.7
2005	195.3	191.2	195.7	119.5	173.9	323.2	109.4	113.7	313.4
2006	201.6	195.7	203.2	119.5	180.9	336.2	110.9	116.8	321.7
2007	207.3	203.3	209.6	119.0	184.7	351.1	111.4	119.6	333.3
2008	215.3	214.2	216.3	118.9	195.5	364.1	113.3	123.6	345.4

[1]December 1997 = 100.
. . . = Not available.

Table 9-5. Consumer Price Indexes, All Urban Consumers (CPI-U): U.S. City Average, Commodity, Service, and Special Groups, 1967–2008

(1982–1984 = 100, unless otherwise specified.)

Year	All items less food	All items less shelter	All items less medical care	All items less energy	All items less food and energy	Commodities	Commodities less food and beverages	Commodities less food and energy	Energy commodities	Nondurables	Nondurables less food	Nondurables less food and apparel
1967	33.4	35.2	33.7	34.4	34.7	36.8	38.3	41.3	23.9	35.7	37.6	32.6
1968	34.9	36.7	35.1	35.9	36.3	38.1	39.7	42.9	24.4	37.1	39.1	33.7
1969	36.8	38.4	37.0	38.0	38.4	39.9	41.4	44.7	25.2	38.9	40.9	34.9
1970	39.0	40.3	39.2	40.3	40.8	41.7	43.1	46.7	25.6	40.8	42.5	36.3
1971	40.8	42.0	40.8	42.0	42.7	43.2	44.7	48.5	26.1	42.1	44.0	37.6
1972	42.0	43.3	42.1	43.4	44.0	44.5	45.8	49.7	26.4	43.5	45.0	38.6
1973	43.7	46.2	44.8	46.1	45.6	47.8	47.3	51.1	29.1	47.5	46.9	40.3
1974	48.0	51.4	49.8	50.6	49.4	53.5	52.4	55.0	40.4	54.0	52.9	46.9
1975	52.5	56.0	54.3	55.1	53.9	58.2	57.3	60.1	43.4	58.3	57.0	51.5
1976	56.0	59.3	57.2	58.2	57.4	60.7	60.2	63.2	45.4	60.5	59.5	54.1
1977	59.6	63.1	60.8	61.9	61.0	64.2	63.6	66.5	48.7	64.0	62.5	57.2
1978	63.9	67.4	65.4	66.7	65.5	68.8	67.3	70.5	51.0	68.6	65.5	60.4
1979	71.2	74.2	72.9	73.4	71.9	76.6	75.2	76.4	68.7	77.2	74.6	71.2
1980	81.5	82.9	82.8	81.9	80.8	86.0	85.7	83.5	95.2	87.6	88.4	87.1
1981	90.4	91.0	91.4	90.1	89.2	93.2	93.1	90.0	107.6	95.2	96.7	96.8
1982	96.3	96.2	96.8	96.1	95.8	97.0	96.9	95.3	102.9	97.8	98.3	98.2
1983	99.7	99.8	99.6	99.6	99.6	99.8	100.0	100.2	99.0	99.7	100.0	100.0
1984	104.0	103.9	103.7	104.3	104.6	103.2	103.1	104.4	98.1	102.5	101.7	101.8
1985	108.0	107.0	107.2	108.4	109.1	105.4	105.2	107.1	98.2	104.8	104.1	104.1
1986	109.8	108.0	108.8	112.6	113.5	104.4	101.4	108.6	77.2	103.5	98.5	96.9
1987	113.6	111.6	112.6	117.2	118.2	107.7	104.0	111.8	80.2	107.5	101.8	100.3
1988	118.3	115.9	117.0	122.3	123.4	111.5	107.3	115.8	80.8	111.8	105.8	104.0
1989	123.7	121.6	122.4	128.1	129.0	116.7	111.6	119.6	87.9	118.2	111.7	111.3
1990	130.3	128.2	128.8	134.7	135.5	122.8	117.0	123.6	101.2	126.0	119.9	120.9
1991	136.1	133.5	133.8	140.9	142.1	126.6	120.4	128.8	99.1	130.3	124.5	125.7
1992	140.8	137.3	137.5	145.4	147.3	129.1	123.2	132.5	98.3	132.8	127.6	128.9
1993	145.1	141.4	141.2	150.0	152.2	131.5	125.3	135.2	97.3	135.1	129.3	130.7
1994	149.0	144.8	144.7	154.1	156.5	133.8	126.9	137.1	97.6	136.8	129.7	131.6
1995	153.1	148.6	148.6	158.7	161.2	136.4	128.9	139.3	98.8	139.3	130.9	134.1
1996	157.5	152.8	152.8	163.1	165.6	139.9	131.5	141.3	105.7	143.5	134.5	139.5
1997	161.1	155.9	156.3	167.1	169.5	141.8	132.2	142.3	105.7	146.4	136.3	141.8
1998	163.4	157.2	158.6	170.9	173.4	141.9	130.5	143.2	92.1	146.9	134.6	139.2
1999	167.0	160.2	162.0	174.4	177.0	144.4	132.5	144.1	100.0	151.2	139.4	147.5
2000	173.0	165.7	167.3	178.6	181.3	149.2	137.7	144.9	129.5	158.2	149.1	162.9
2001	177.8	169.7	171.9	183.5	186.1	150.7	137.2	145.3	125.2	160.6	149.1	164.1
2002	180.5	170.8	174.3	187.7	190.5	149.7	134.2	143.7	117.1	161.1	147.4	163.3
2003	184.7	174.6	178.1	190.6	193.2	151.2	134.5	140.9	136.7	165.3	151.9	172.1
2004	189.4	179.3	182.7	194.4	196.6	154.7	136.7	139.6	161.2	172.2	159.3	183.8
2005	196.0	186.1	188.7	198.7	200.9	160.2	142.5	140.3	197.4	180.2	170.1	201.2
2006	202.7	191.9	194.7	203.7	205.9	164.0	145.9	140.6	223.0	186.7	178.2	213.9
2007	208.1	196.6	200.1	208.9	210.7	167.5	147.5	140.1	241.0	193.5	184.0	223.4
2008	215.5	205.5	207.8	214.8	215.6	174.8	153.0	140.2	284.4	205.9	197.3	244.4

Table 9-5. Consumer Price Indexes, All Urban Consumers (CPI-U): U.S. City Average, Commodity, Service, and Special Groups, 1967–2008—*Continued*

(1982–1984 = 100, unless otherwise specified.)

Year	Total services[1]	Rent of shelter[2]	Gas (piped) and electricity	Transportation services	Medical care services	Other services	Services less medical care	Energy	Services less energy
1967	28.8	. . .	. . .	32.6	26.0	36.0	29.3	23.8	29.3
1968	30.3	. . .	. . .	33.9	27.9	38.1	30.8	24.2	30.9
1969	32.4	. . .	. . .	36.3	30.2	40.0	32.9	24.8	33.2
1970	35.0	. . .	. . .	40.2	32.3	42.2	35.6	25.5	36.0
1971	37.0	. . .	. . .	43.4	34.7	44.4	37.5	26.5	38.0
1972	38.4	. . .	. . .	44.4	35.9	45.6	38.9	27.2	39.4
1973	40.1	. . .	. . .	44.7	37.5	47.7	40.6	29.4	41.1
1974	43.8	. . .	. . .	46.3	41.4	51.3	44.3	38.1	44.8
1975	48.0	. . .	. . .	49.8	46.6	55.1	48.3	42.1	48.8
1976	52.0	. . .	. . .	56.9	51.3	58.4	52.2	45.1	52.7
1977	56.0	. . .	. . .	61.5	56.4	62.1	55.9	49.4	56.5
1978	60.8	. . .	. . .	64.4	61.2	66.4	60.7	52.5	61.3
1979	67.5	. . .	. . .	69.5	67.2	71.9	67.5	65.7	68.2
1980	77.9	. . .	. . .	79.2	74.8	78.7	78.2	86.0	78.5
1981	88.1	. . .	. . .	88.6	82.8	86.1	88.7	97.7	88.7
1982	96.0	. . .	. . .	96.1	92.6	93.5	96.4	99.2	96.3
1983	99.4	102.7	. . .	99.1	100.7	100.0	99.2	99.9	99.2
1984	104.6	107.7	. . .	104.8	106.7	106.5	104.4	100.9	104.5
1985	109.9	113.9	. . .	110.0	113.2	113.0	109.6	101.6	110.2
1986	115.4	120.2	. . .	116.3	121.9	119.4	114.6	88.2	116.5
1987	120.2	125.9	. . .	121.9	130.0	125.7	119.1	88.6	122.0
1988	125.7	132.0	. . .	128.0	138.3	132.6	124.3	89.3	127.9
1989	131.9	138.0	. . .	135.6	148.9	140.9	130.1	94.3	134.4
1990	139.2	145.5	. . .	144.2	162.7	150.2	136.8	102.1	142.3
1991	146.3	152.1	. . .	151.2	177.1	159.8	143.3	102.5	149.8
1992	152.0	157.3	. . .	155.7	190.5	168.5	148.4	103.0	155.9
1993	157.9	162.0	. . .	162.9	202.9	177.0	153.6	104.2	161.9
1994	163.1	167.0	. . .	168.6	213.4	185.4	158.4	104.6	167.6
1995	168.7	172.4	. . .	175.9	224.2	193.3	163.5	105.2	173.7
1996	174.1	178.0	. . .	180.5	232.4	201.4	168.7	110.1	179.4
1997	179.4	183.4	. . .	185.0	239.1	209.6	173.9	111.5	185.0
1998	184.2	189.6	121.2	187.9	246.8	216.9	178.4	102.9	190.6
1999	188.8	195.0	120.9	190.7	255.1	223.1	182.7	106.6	195.7
2000	195.3	201.3	128.0	196.1	266.0	229.9	188.9	124.6	202.1
2001	203.4	208.9	142.4	201.9	278.8	238.0	196.6	129.3	209.6
2002	209.8	216.7	134.4	209.1	292.9	246.4	202.5	121.7	217.5
2003	216.5	221.9	145.0	216.3	306.0	254.4	208.7	136.5	223.8
2004	222.8	227.9	150.6	220.6	321.3	261.3	214.5	151.4	230.2
2005	230.1	233.7	166.5	225.7	336.7	268.4	221.2	177.1	236.6
2006	238.9	241.9	182.1	230.8	350.6	277.5	229.6	196.9	244.7
2007	246.8	250.8	186.3	233.7	369.3	285.6	236.8	207.7	253.1
2008	255.5	257.2	202.2	244.1	384.9	295.8	245.0	236.7	261.0

[1]Includes tenants, household insurance, water, sewer, trash, and household operations services, not shown separately.
[2]December 1982 = 100.
. . . = Not available.

Table 9-6. Consumer Price Indexes, All Urban Consumers (CPI-U): U.S. City Average, Selected Groups and Purchasing Power of the Consumer Dollar, 1913–2008

(1982–1984 = 100, unless otherwise specified.)

Year	All items	Food	Rent of primary residence	Owners' equivalent of primary residence[1]	Apparel	Purchasing power of the consumer dollar[2]
1913	9.9	10.0	21.0	. . .	14.9	10.08
1914	10.0	10.2	21.0	. . .	15.0	9.94
1915	10.1	10.0	21.1	. . .	15.3	9.84
1916	10.9	11.3	21.3	. . .	16.8	9.15
1917	12.8	14.5	21.2	. . .	20.2	7.79
1918	15.1	16.7	21.5	. . .	27.3	6.64
1919	17.3	18.6	23.3	. . .	36.2	5.78
1920	20.0	21.0	27.4	. . .	43.1	4.99
1921	17.9	15.9	31.5	. . .	33.2	5.59
1922	16.8	14.9	32.4	. . .	27.0	5.96
1923	17.1	15.4	33.2	. . .	27.1	5.86
1924	17.1	15.2	34.4	. . .	26.8	5.85
1925	17.5	16.5	34.6	. . .	26.3	5.70
1926	17.7	17.0	34.2	. . .	25.9	5.65
1927	17.4	16.4	33.7	. . .	25.3	5.76
1928	17.1	16.3	32.9	. . .	25.0	5.83
1929	17.1	16.5	32.1	. . .	24.7	5.83
1930	16.7	15.6	31.2	. . .	24.2	5.99
1931	15.2	12.9	29.6	. . .	22.0	6.56
1932	13.7	10.7	26.5	. . .	19.5	7.32
1933	13.0	10.4	22.9	. . .	18.8	7.71
1934	13.4	11.6	21.4	. . .	20.6	7.46
1935	13.7	12.4	21.4	. . .	20.8	7.28
1936	13.9	12.6	21.9	. . .	21.0	7.21
1937	14.4	13.1	22.9	. . .	22.0	6.96
1938	14.1	12.1	23.7	. . .	21.9	7.09
1939	13.9	11.8	23.7	. . .	21.6	7.20
1940	14.0	12.0	23.7	. . .	21.8	7.13
1941	14.7	13.1	24.2	. . .	22.8	6.79
1942	16.3	15.4	24.7	. . .	26.7	6.13
1943	17.3	17.1	24.7	. . .	27.8	5.78
1944	17.6	16.9	24.8	. . .	29.8	5.68
1945	18.0	17.3	24.8	. . .	31.4	5.55
1946	19.5	19.8	25.0	. . .	34.4	5.12
1947	22.3	24.1	25.8	. . .	39.9	4.47
1948	24.1	26.1	27.5	. . .	42.5	4.15
1949	23.8	25.0	28.7	. . .	40.8	4.19
1950	24.1	25.4	29.7	. . .	40.3	4.15
1951	26.0	28.2	30.9	. . .	43.9	3.85
1952	26.5	28.7	32.2	. . .	43.5	3.77
1953	26.7	28.3	33.9	. . .	43.1	3.74
1954	26.9	28.2	35.1	. . .	43.1	3.72
1955	26.8	27.8	35.6	. . .	42.9	3.73
1956	27.2	28.0	36.3	. . .	43.7	3.68
1957	28.1	28.9	37.0	. . .	44.5	3.55
1958	28.9	30.2	37.6	. . .	44.6	3.46
1959	29.1	29.7	38.2	. . .	45.0	3.43
1960	29.6	30.0	38.7	. . .	45.7	3.37
1961	29.9	30.4	39.2	. . .	46.1	3.34
1962	30.2	30.6	39.7	. . .	46.3	3.30
1963	30.6	31.1	40.1	. . .	46.9	3.27
1964	31.0	31.5	40.5	. . .	47.3	3.22
1965	31.5	32.2	40.9	. . .	47.8	3.17
1966	32.4	33.8	41.5	. . .	49.0	3.08
1967	33.4	34.1	42.2	. . .	51.0	2.99
1968	34.8	35.3	43.3	. . .	53.7	2.87
1969	36.7	37.1	44.7	. . .	56.8	2.73
1970	38.8	39.2	46.5	. . .	59.2	2.57
1971	40.5	40.4	48.7	. . .	61.1	2.47
1972	41.8	42.1	50.4	. . .	62.3	2.39
1973	44.4	48.2	52.5	. . .	64.6	2.25
1974	49.3	55.1	55.2	. . .	69.4	2.03
1975	53.8	59.8	58.0	. . .	72.5	1.86
1976	56.9	61.6	61.1	. . .	75.2	1.76
1977	60.6	65.5	64.8	. . .	78.6	1.65
1978	65.2	72.0	69.3	. . .	81.4	1.53
1979	72.6	79.9	74.3	. . .	84.9	1.38

[1]December 1982 = 100.
[2]Purchasing power in 1982–1984 = $1.00.
. . . = Not available.

Table 9-6. Consumer Price Indexes, All Urban Consumers (CPI-U): U.S. City Average, Selected Groups and Purchasing Power of the Consumer Dollar, 1913–2008—*Continued*

(1982–1984 = 100, unless otherwise specified.)

Year	All items	Food	Rent of primary residence	Owners' equivalent of primary residence[1]	Apparel	Purchasing power of the consumer dollar[2]
1980	82.4	86.8	80.9	. . .	90.9	1.22
1981	90.9	93.6	87.9	. . .	95.3	1.10
1982	96.5	97.4	94.6	. . .	97.8	1.04
1983	99.6	99.4	100.1	102.5	100.2	1.00
1984	103.9	103.2	105.3	107.3	102.1	0.96
1985	107.6	105.6	111.8	113.2	105.0	0.93
1986	109.6	109.0	118.3	119.4	105.9	0.91
1987	113.6	113.5	123.1	124.8	110.6	0.88
1988	118.3	118.2	127.8	131.1	115.4	0.85
1989	124.0	125.1	132.8	137.4	118.6	0.81
1990	130.7	132.4	138.4	144.8	124.1	0.77
1991	136.2	136.3	143.3	150.4	128.7	0.73
1992	140.3	137.9	146.9	155.5	131.9	0.71
1993	144.5	140.9	150.3	160.5	133.7	0.69
1994	148.2	144.3	154.0	165.8	133.4	0.68
1995	152.4	148.4	157.8	171.3	132.0	0.66
1996	156.9	153.3	162.0	176.8	131.7	0.64
1997	160.5	157.3	166.7	181.9	132.9	0.62
1998	163.0	160.7	172.1	187.8	133.0	0.61
1999	166.6	164.1	177.5	192.9	131.3	0.60
2000	172.2	167.8	183.9	198.7	129.6	0.58
2001	177.1	173.1	192.1	206.3	127.3	0.57
2002	179.9	176.2	199.7	214.7	124.0	0.56
2003	184.0	180.0	205.5	219.9	120.9	0.54
2004	188.9	186.2	211.0	224.9	120.4	0.53
2005	195.3	190.7	217.3	230.2	119.5	0.51
2006	201.6	195.2	225.1	238.2	119.5	0.50
2007	207.3	202.9	234.7	246.2	119.0	0.48
2008	215.3	214.1	243.3	252.4	118.9	0.47

[1]December 1982 = 100.
[2]Purchasing power in 1982–1984 = $1.00.
. . . = Not available.

Table 9-7. Consumer Price Indexes, Urban Wage Earners and Clerical Workers (CPI-W): U.S. City Average, Major Groups, 1913–2008

(1982–1984 = 100, unless otherwise specified.)

Year	All items	Food and beverages	Housing	Apparel	Transportation	Medical care	Recreation[1]	Education and communication[1]	Other goods and services
1913	10.0	. . .	. . .	15.0	. . .	. . .	. . .	. . .	. . .
1914	10.1	. . .	. . .	15.1	. . .	. . .	. . .	. . .	. . .
1915	10.2	. . .	. . .	15.4	. . .	. . .	. . .	. . .	. . .
1916	11.0	. . .	. . .	16.9	. . .	. . .	. . .	. . .	. . .
1917	12.9	. . .	. . .	20.3	. . .	. . .	. . .	. . .	. . .
1918	15.1	. . .	. . .	27.5	. . .	. . .	. . .	. . .	. . .
1919	17.4	. . .	. . .	36.4	. . .	. . .	. . .	. . .	. . .
1920	20.1	. . .	. . .	43.3	. . .	. . .	. . .	. . .	. . .
1921	18.0	. . .	. . .	33.4	. . .	. . .	. . .	. . .	. . .
1922	16.9	. . .	. . .	27.2	. . .	. . .	. . .	. . .	. . .
1923	17.2	. . .	. . .	27.2	. . .	. . .	. . .	. . .	. . .
1924	17.2	. . .	. . .	26.9	. . .	. . .	. . .	. . .	. . .
1925	17.6	. . .	. . .	26.4	. . .	. . .	. . .	. . .	. . .
1926	17.8	. . .	. . .	26.0	. . .	. . .	. . .	. . .	. . .
1927	17.5	. . .	. . .	25.5	. . .	. . .	. . .	. . .	. . .
1928	17.2	. . .	. . .	25.1	. . .	. . .	. . .	. . .	. . .
1929	17.2	. . .	. . .	24.8	. . .	. . .	. . .	. . .	. . .
1930	16.8	. . .	. . .	24.3	. . .	. . .	. . .	. . .	. . .
1931	15.3	. . .	. . .	22.1	. . .	. . .	. . .	. . .	. . .
1932	13.7	. . .	. . .	19.6	. . .	. . .	. . .	. . .	. . .
1933	13.0	. . .	. . .	18.9	. . .	. . .	. . .	. . .	. . .
1934	13.5	. . .	. . .	20.7	. . .	. . .	. . .	. . .	. . .
1935	13.8	. . .	. . .	20.9	14.1	10.2	. . .	. . .	. . .
1936	13.9	. . .	. . .	21.1	14.2	10.3	. . .	. . .	. . .
1937	14.4	. . .	. . .	22.1	14.5	10.4	. . .	. . .	. . .
1938	14.2	. . .	. . .	22.0	14.6	10.4	. . .	. . .	. . .
1939	14.0	. . .	. . .	21.7	14.2	10.4	. . .	. . .	. . .
1940	14.1	. . .	. . .	21.9	14.1	10.4	. . .	. . .	. . .
1941	14.8	. . .	. . .	23.0	14.6	10.5	. . .	. . .	. . .
1942	16.4	. . .	. . .	26.8	15.9	10.8	. . .	. . .	. . .
1943	17.4	. . .	. . .	28.0	15.8	11.3	. . .	. . .	. . .
1944	17.7	. . .	. . .	30.0	15.8	11.6	. . .	. . .	. . .
1945	18.1	. . .	. . .	31.5	15.8	11.9	. . .	. . .	. . .
1946	19.6	. . .	. . .	34.6	16.6	12.6	. . .	. . .	. . .
1947	22.5	. . .	. . .	40.1	18.4	13.6	. . .	. . .	. . .
1948	24.2	. . .	. . .	42.7	20.4	14.5	. . .	. . .	. . .
1949	24.0	. . .	. . .	41.0	22.0	14.9	. . .	. . .	. . .
1950	24.2	. . .	. . .	40.5	22.6	15.2	. . .	. . .	. . .
1951	26.1	. . .	. . .	44.1	24.0	15.9	. . .	. . .	. . .
1952	26.7	. . .	. . .	43.7	25.6	16.8	. . .	. . .	. . .
1953	26.9	. . .	. . .	43.3	26.3	17.4	. . .	. . .	. . .
1954	27.0	. . .	. . .	43.3	25.9	17.9	. . .	. . .	. . .
1955	26.9	. . .	. . .	43.1	25.6	18.3	. . .	. . .	. . .
1956	27.3	. . .	. . .	44.0	26.1	19.0	. . .	. . .	. . .
1957	28.3	. . .	. . .	44.7	27.6	19.8	. . .	. . .	. . .
1958	29.1	. . .	. . .	44.8	28.4	20.7	. . .	. . .	. . .
1959	29.3	. . .	. . .	45.2	29.6	21.6	. . .	. . .	. . .
1960	29.8	. . .	. . .	45.9	29.6	22.4	. . .	. . .	. . .
1961	30.1	. . .	. . .	46.3	30.0	23.0	. . .	. . .	. . .
1962	30.4	. . .	. . .	46.6	30.6	23.6	. . .	. . .	. . .
1963	30.8	. . .	. . .	47.1	30.8	24.2	. . .	. . .	. . .
1964	31.2	. . .	. . .	47.5	31.2	24.7	. . .	. . .	. . .
1965	31.7	. . .	. . .	48.0	31.7	25.3	. . .	. . .	. . .
1966	32.6	. . .	. . .	49.2	32.2	26.4	. . .	. . .	. . .
1967	33.6	35.0	31.1	51.2	33.1	28.3	. . .	. . .	35.4
1968	35.0	36.2	32.3	54.0	34.1	30.0	. . .	. . .	37.2
1969	36.9	38.0	34.3	57.1	35.5	32.1	. . .	. . .	39.1
1970	39.0	40.1	36.7	59.5	37.3	34.1	. . .	. . .	41.3
1971	40.7	41.3	38.3	61.4	39.2	36.3	. . .	. . .	43.3
1972	42.1	43.1	39.8	62.7	39.7	37.5	. . .	. . .	45.1
1973	44.7	48.8	41.5	65.0	41.0	39.0	. . .	. . .	46.9
1974	49.6	55.5	46.2	69.8	45.5	42.6	. . .	. . .	50.2
1975	54.1	60.2	51.1	72.9	49.8	47.7	. . .	. . .	54.4
1976	57.2	62.0	54.2	75.6	54.7	52.3	. . .	. . .	57.6
1977	60.9	65.7	57.9	79.0	58.6	57.3	. . .	. . .	60.9
1978	65.6	72.1	62.9	81.7	61.5	62.1	. . .	. . .	64.8
1979	73.1	79.9	70.7	85.2	70.4	68.0	. . .	. . .	69.4

[1]December 1997 = 100.
. . . = Not available.

Table 9-7. Consumer Price Indexes, Urban Wage Earners and Clerical Workers (CPI-W): U.S. City Average, Major Groups, 1913–2008—*Continued*

(1982–1984 = 100, unless otherwise specified.)

Year	All items	Food and beverages	Housing	Apparel	Transportation	Medical care	Recreation[1]	Education and communication[1]	Other goods and services
1980	82.9	86.9	81.7	90.9	82.9	75.6	. . .	. . .	75.6
1981	91.4	93.6	91.1	95.6	93.0	83.5	. . .	. . .	82.5
1982	96.9	97.3	97.7	97.8	97.0	92.5	. . .	. . .	90.9
1983	99.8	99.5	100.0	100.2	99.2	100.5	. . .	. . .	101.3
1984	103.3	103.2	102.2	102.0	103.8	106.9	. . .	. . .	107.9
1985	106.9	105.5	106.6	105.0	106.4	113.6	. . .	. . .	114.2
1986	108.6	108.9	109.7	105.8	101.7	122.0	. . .	. . .	120.9
1987	112.5	113.3	112.8	110.4	105.1	130.2	. . .	. . .	127.8
1988	117.0	117.9	116.8	114.9	108.3	139.0	. . .	. . .	136.5
1989	122.6	124.6	121.2	117.9	113.9	149.6	. . .	. . .	147.4
1990	129.0	131.8	126.4	123.1	120.1	162.7	. . .	. . .	158.9
1991	134.3	136.5	131.2	127.4	123.1	176.5	. . .	. . .	171.7
1992	138.2	138.3	135.0	130.7	125.8	189.6	. . .	. . .	183.3
1993	142.1	141.2	138.5	132.4	129.4	200.9	91.2	86.0	192.2
1994	145.6	144.4	142.0	132.2	133.4	210.4	93.0	89.1	196.4
1995	149.8	148.3	145.4	130.9	138.8	219.8	94.7	92.3	204.2
1996	154.1	153.2	149.6	130.9	142.8	227.6	97.5	95.4	212.2
1997	157.6	157.2	153.4	132.1	143.6	234.0	99.7	98.5	221.6
1998	159.7	160.4	156.7	131.6	140.5	241.4	100.9	100.4	236.1
1999	163.2	163.8	160.0	130.1	143.4	249.7	101.3	101.5	261.9
2000	168.9	167.7	165.4	128.3	152.8	259.9	102.4	102.7	276.5
2001	173.5	173.0	172.1	126.1	153.6	271.8	103.6	105.3	289.5
2002	175.9	176.1	175.7	123.1	151.8	284.6	104.6	107.6	302.0
2003	179.8	179.9	180.4	120.0	156.3	296.3	105.5	109.0	307.0
2004	184.5	186.2	185.0	120.0	161.5	309.5	106.3	110.0	312.6
2005	191.0	190.5	191.2	119.1	173.0	322.8	106.8	111.4	322.2
2006	197.1	194.9	198.5	119.1	180.3	335.7	108.2	113.9	330.9
2007	202.8	202.5	204.8	118.5	184.3	350.9	108.6	116.3	344.0
2008	211.1	213.5	211.8	118.7	195.7	364.2	110.1	119.8	357.9

[1]December 1997 = 100.
. . . = Not available.

Table 9-8. Consumer Price Indexes, All Urban Consumers (CPI-U): U.S. City Average, by Expenditure Category, 1990–2008

(1982–1984 = 100, unless otherwise specified.)

Expenditure category	1990	1991	1992	1993	1994	1995	1996	1997	1998
ALL ITEMS	130.7	136.2	140.3	144.5	148.2	152.4	156.9	160.5	163.0
Food and Beverages	132.1	136.8	138.7	141.6	144.9	148.9	153.7	157.7	161.1
Food	132.4	136.3	137.9	140.9	144.3	148.4	153.3	157.3	160.7
Food at home	132.3	135.8	136.8	140.1	144.1	148.8	154.3	158.1	161.1
Cereals and bakery product	140.0	145.8	151.5	156.6	163.0	167.5	174.0	177.6	181.1
Meats, poultry, fish, and eggs	130.0	132.6	130.9	135.5	137.2	138.8	144.8	148.5	147.3
Dairy and related product	126.5	125.1	128.5	129.4	131.7	132.8	142.1	145.5	150.8
Fruits and vegetables	149.0	155.8	155.4	159.0	165.0	177.7	183.9	187.5	198.2
Nonalcoholic beverages and beverage materials	113.5	114.1	114.3	114.6	123.2	131.7	128.6	133.4	133.0
Other food at home	123.4	127.3	128.8	130.5	135.6	140.8	142.9	147.3	150.8
Sugar and sweets	124.7	129.3	133.1	133.4	135.2	137.5	143.7	147.8	150.2
Fats and oils	126.3	131.7	129.8	130.0	133.5	137.3	140.5	141.7	146.9
Other food	131.2	137.1	140.1	143.7	147.5	151.1	156.2	161.2	165.5
Other miscellaneous food[1]	. . .	. . .	. . .	. . .	. . .	. . .	. . .	. . .	102.6
Food away from home	133.4	137.9	140.7	143.2	145.7	149.0	152.7	157.0	161.1
Other food away from home[1]	. . .	. . .	. . .	. . .	. . .	. . .	. . .	. . .	101.6
Alcoholic beverages	129.3	142.8	147.3	149.6	151.5	153.9	158.5	162.8	165.7
Housing	128.5	133.6	137.5	141.2	144.8	148.5	152.8	156.8	160.4
Shelter	140.0	146.3	151.2	155.7	160.5	165.7	171.0	176.3	182.1
Rent of primary residence	138.4	143.3	146.9	150.3	154.0	157.8	162.0	166.7	172.1
Lodging away from home[1]	. . .	. . .	. . .	. . .	. . .	. . .	. . .	. . .	109.0
Owners' equivalent rent of primary residence[2]	144.8	150.4	155.5	160.5	165.8	171.3	176.8	181.9	187.8
Tenants' and household insurance[1]	. . .	. . .	. . .	. . .	. . .	. . .	. . .	. . .	99.8
Fuels and utilities	111.6	115.3	117.8	121.3	122.8	123.7	127.5	130.8	128.5
Household energy	104.5	106.7	108.1	111.2	111.7	111.5	115.2	117.9	113.7
Fuel oil and other fuels	99.3	94.6	90.7	90.3	88.8	88.1	99.2	99.8	90.0
Gas (piped) and electricity	109.3	112.6	114.8	118.5	119.2	119.2	122.1	125.1	121.2
Water, sewer, and trash collection services[1]	. . .	. . .	. . .	. . .	. . .	. . .	. . .	. . .	101.6
Household furnishings and operations	113.3	116.0	118.0	119.3	121.0	123.0	124.7	125.4	126.6
Household operations[1]	. . .	. . .	. . .	. . .	. . .	. . .	. . .	. . .	101.5
Apparel	124.1	128.7	131.9	133.7	133.4	132.0	131.7	132.9	133.0
Men's and boys' apparel	120.4	124.2	126.5	127.5	126.4	126.2	127.7	130.1	131.8
Women's and girls' apparel	122.6	127.6	130.4	132.6	130.9	126.9	124.7	126.1	126.0
Infants' and toddlers' apparel	125.8	128.9	129.3	127.1	128.1	127.2	129.7	129.0	126.1
Footwear	117.4	120.9	125.0	125.9	126.0	125.4	126.6	127.6	128.0
Transportation	120.5	123.8	126.5	130.4	134.3	139.1	143.0	144.3	141.6
Private transportation	118.8	121.9	124.6	127.5	131.4	136.3	140.0	141.0	137.9
New and used motor vehicles[1]	. . .	. . .	. . .	91.8	95.5	99.4	101.0	100.5	100.1
New vehicles	121.4	126.0	129.2	132.7	137.6	141.0	143.7	144.3	143.4
Used cars and trucks	117.6	118.1	123.2	133.9	141.7	156.5	157.0	151.1	150.6
Motor fuel	101.2	99.4	99.0	98.0	98.5	100.0	106.3	106.2	92.2
Gasoline (all types)	101.0	99.2	99.0	97.7	98.2	99.8	105.9	105.8	91.6
Motor vehicle parts and equipment	100.9	102.2	103.1	101.6	101.4	102.1	102.2	101.9	101.1
Motor vehicle maintenance and repair	130.1	136.0	141.3	145.9	150.2	154.0	158.4	162.7	167.1
Public transportation	142.6	148.9	151.4	167.0	172.0	175.9	181.9	186.7	190.3
Medical Care	162.8	177.0	190.1	201.4	211.0	220.5	228.2	234.6	242.1
Medical care commodities	163.4	176.8	188.1	195.0	200.7	204.5	210.4	215.3	221.8
Medical care services	162.7	177.1	190.5	202.9	213.4	224.2	232.4	239.1	246.8
Professional services	156.1	165.7	175.8	184.7	192.5	201.0	208.3	215.4	222.2
Hospital and related services	178.0	196.1	214.0	231.9	245.6	257.8	269.5	278.4	287.5
Recreation[1]	. . .	. . .	. . .	90.7	92.7	94.5	97.4	99.6	101.1
Video and audio[1]	. . .	. . .	. . .	96.5	95.4	95.1	96.6	99.4	101.1
Education and Communication[1]	. . .	. . .	. . .	85.5	88.8	92.2	95.3	98.4	100.3
Education[1]	. . .	. . .	. . .	78.4	83.3	88.0	92.7	97.3	102.1
Educational books and supplies	171.3	180.3	190.3	197.6	205.5	214.4	226.9	238.4	250.8
Tuition, other school fees, and childcare	175.7	191.4	208.5	225.3	239.8	253.8	267.1	280.4	294.2
Communication[1]	. . .	. . .	. . .	96.7	97.6	98.8	99.6	100.3	98.7
Information and information processing[1]	. . .	. . .	. . .	97.7	98.6	98.7	99.5	100.4	98.5
Telephone services[1]	. . .	. . .	. . .	. . .	. . .	. . .	. . .	. . .	100.7
Information technology, hardware, and services[3]	93.5	88.6	83.7	78.8	72.0	63.8	57.2	50.1	39.9
Personal computers and peripheral equipment[1]	. . .	. . .	. . .	. . .	. . .	. . .	. . .	. . .	875.1
Other Goods and Services	159.0	171.6	183.3	192.9	198.5	206.9	215.4	224.8	237.7
Tobacco and smoking product	181.5	202.7	219.8	228.4	220.0	225.7	232.8	243.7	274.8
Personal care	130.4	134.9	138.3	141.5	144.6	147.1	150.1	152.7	156.7
Personal care product	128.2	132.8	136.5	139.0	141.5	143.1	144.3	144.2	148.3
Personal care services	132.8	137.0	140.0	144.0	147.9	151.5	156.6	162.4	166.0
Miscellaneous personal services	158.4	168.8	177.5	186.1	195.9	205.9	215.6	226.1	234.7

[1]December 1997 = 100.
[2]December 1982 = 100.
[3]December 1988 = 100.
. . . = Not available.

Table 9-8. Consumer Price Indexes, All Urban Consumers (CPI-U): U.S. City Average, by Expenditure Category, 1990–2008—*Continued*

(1982–1984 = 100, unless otherwise specified.)

Expenditure category	1999	2000	2001	2002	2003	2004	2005	2006	2007	2008
ALL ITEMS	166.6	172.2	177.1	179.9	184.0	188.9	195.3	201.6	207.3	215.3
Food and Beverages	164.6	168.4	173.6	176.8	180.5	186.6	191.2	195.7	203.3	214.2
Food	164.1	167.8	173.1	176.2	180.0	186.2	190.7	195.2	202.9	214.1
Food at home	164.2	167.9	173.4	175.6	179.4	186.2	189.8	193.1	201.2	214.1
Cereals and bakery product	185.0	188.3	193.8	198.0	202.8	206.0	209.0	212.8	222.1	244.9
Meats, poultry, fish, and eggs	147.9	154.5	161.3	162.1	169.3	181.7	184.7	186.6	195.6	204.7
Dairy and related product	159.6	160.7	167.1	168.1	167.9	180.2	182.4	181.4	194.8	210.4
Fruits and vegetables	203.1	204.6	212.2	220.9	225.9	232.7	241.4	252.9	262.6	278.9
Nonalcoholic beverages and beverage materials	134.3	137.8	139.2	139.2	139.8	140.4	144.4	147.4	153.4	160.0
Other food at home	153.5	155.6	159.6	160.8	162.6	164.9	167.0	169.6	173.3	184.2
Sugar and sweets	152.3	154.0	155.7	159.0	162.0	163.2	165.2	171.5	176.8	186.6
Fats and oils	148.3	147.4	155.7	155.4	157.4	167.8	167.7	168.0	172.9	196.8
Other food	168.9	172.2	176.0	177.1	178.8	179.7	182.5	185.0	188.2	198.1
Other miscellaneous food[1]	104.9	107.5	108.9	109.2	110.3	110.4	111.3	113.9	115.1	119.9
Food away from home	165.1	169.0	173.9	178.3	182.1	187.5	193.4	199.4	206.7	215.8
Other food away from home[1]	105.2	109.0	113.4	117.7	121.3	125.3	131.3	136.6	144.1	150.6
Alcoholic beverages	169.7	174.7	179.3	183.6	187.2	192.1	195.9	200.7	207.0	214.5
Housing	163.9	169.6	176.4	180.3	184.8	189.5	195.7	203.2	209.6	216.3
Shelter	187.3	193.4	200.6	208.1	213.1	218.8	224.4	232.1	240.6	246.7
Rent of primary residence	177.5	183.9	192.1	199.7	205.5	211.0	217.3	225.1	234.7	243.3
Lodging away from home[1]	112.3	117.5	118.6	118.3	119.3	125.9	130.3	136.0	142.8	143.7
Owners' equivalent rent of primary residence[2]	192.9	198.7	206.3	214.7	219.9	224.9	230.2	238.2	246.2	252.4
Tenants' and household insurance[1]	101.3	103.7	106.2	108.7	114.8	116.2	117.6	116.5	117.0	118.8
Fuels and utilities	128.8	137.9	150.2	143.6	154.5	161.9	179.0	194.7	200.6	220.0
Household energy	113.5	122.8	135.4	127.2	138.2	144.4	161.6	177.1	181.7	200.8
Fuel oil and other fuels	91.4	129.7	129.3	115.5	139.5	160.5	208.6	234.9	251.5	334.4
Gas (piped) and electricity	120.9	128.0	142.4	134.4	145.0	150.6	166.5	182.1	186.3	202.2
Water, sewer, and trash collection services[1]	104.0	106.5	109.6	113.0	117.2	124.0	130.3	136.8	143.7	152.1
Household furnishings and operations	126.7	128.2	129.1	128.3	126.1	125.5	126.1	127.0	126.9	127.8
Household operations[1]	104.5	110.5	115.6	119.0	121.8	125.0	130.3	136.6	140.6	147.5
Apparel	131.3	129.6	127.3	124.0	120.9	120.4	119.5	119.5	119.0	118.9
Men's and boys' apparel	131.1	129.7	125.7	121.7	118.0	117.5	116.1	114.1	112.4	113.0
Women's and girls' apparel	123.3	121.5	119.3	115.8	113.1	113.0	110.8	110.7	110.3	107.5
Infants' and toddlers' apparel	129.0	130.6	129.2	126.4	122.1	118.5	116.7	116.5	113.9	113.8
Footwear	125.7	123.8	123.0	121.4	119.6	119.3	122.6	123.5	122.4	124.2
Transportation	144.4	153.3	154.3	152.9	157.6	163.1	173.9	180.9	184.7	195.5
Private transportation	140.5	149.1	150.0	148.8	153.6	159.4	170.2	177.0	180.8	191.0
New and used motor vehicles[1]	100.1	100.8	101.3	99.2	96.5	94.2	95.6	95.6	94.3	93.3
New vehicles	142.9	142.8	142.1	140.0	137.9	137.1	137.9	137.6	136.3	134.2
Used cars and trucks	152.0	155.8	158.7	152.0	142.9	133.3	139.4	140.0	135.7	134.0
Motor fuel	100.7	129.3	124.7	116.6	135.8	160.4	195.7	221.0	239.1	279.7
Gasoline (all types)	100.1	128.6	124.0	116.0	135.1	159.7	194.7	219.9	238.0	277.5
Motor vehicle parts and equipment	100.5	101.5	104.8	106.9	107.8	108.7	111.9	117.3	121.6	128.7
Motor vehicle maintenance and repair	171.9	177.3	183.5	190.2	195.6	200.2	206.9	215.6	223.0	233.9
Public transportation	197.7	209.6	210.6	207.4	209.3	209.1	217.3	226.6	230.0	250.5
Medical Care	250.6	260.8	272.8	285.6	297.1	310.1	323.2	336.2	351.1	364.1
Medical care commodities	230.7	238.1	247.6	256.4	262.8	269.3	276.0	285.9	290.0	296.0
Medical care services	255.1	266.0	278.8	292.9	306.0	321.3	336.7	350.6	369.3	384.9
Professional services	229.2	237.7	246.5	253.9	261.2	271.5	281.7	289.3	300.8	311.0
Hospital and related services	299.5	317.3	338.3	367.8	394.8	417.9	439.9	468.1	498.9	534.0
Recreation[1]	102.0	103.3	104.9	106.2	107.5	108.6	109.4	110.9	111.4	113.3
Video and audio[1]	100.7	101.0	101.5	102.8	103.6	104.2	104.2	104.6	102.9	102.6
Education and Communication[1]	101.2	102.5	105.2	107.9	109.8	111.6	113.7	116.8	119.6	123.6
Education[1]	107.0	112.5	118.5	126.0	134.4	143.7	152.7	162.1	171.4	181.3
Educational books and supplies	261.7	279.9	295.9	317.6	335.4	351.0	365.6	388.9	420.4	450.2
Tuition, other school fees, and childcare	308.4	324.0	341.1	362.1	386.7	414.3	440.9	468.1	494.1	522.1
Communication[1]	96.0	93.6	93.3	92.3	89.7	86.7	84.7	84.1	83.4	84.2
Information and information processing[1]	95.5	92.8	92.3	90.8	87.8	84.6	82.6	81.7	80.7	81.4
Telephone services[1]	100.1	98.5	99.3	99.7	98.3	95.8	94.9	95.8	98.2	100.5
Information technology, hardware, and services[3]	30.5	25.9	21.3	18.3	16.1	14.8	13.6	12.5	10.6	10.1
Personal computers and peripheral equipment[1]	598.7	459.9	330.1	248.4	196.9	171.2	143.2	120.9	108.4	94.9
Other Goods and Services	258.3	271.1	282.6	293.2	298.7	304.7	313.4	321.7	333.3	345.4
Tobacco and smoking product	355.8	394.9	425.2	461.5	469.0	478.0	502.8	519.9	554.2	588.7
Personal care	161.1	165.6	170.5	174.7	178.0	181.7	185.6	190.2	195.6	201.3
Personal care product	151.8	153.7	155.1	154.7	153.5	153.9	154.4	155.8	158.3	159.3
Personal care services	171.4	178.1	184.3	188.4	193.2	197.6	203.9	209.7	216.6	223.7
Miscellaneous personal services	243.0	252.3	263.1	274.4	283.5	293.9	303.0	313.6	325.0	338.9

[1]December 1997 = 100.
[2]December 1982 = 100.
[3]December 1988 = 100.

Table 9-9. Relative Importance of Components in the Consumer Price Index: U.S. City Average, Selected Groups, December 1997–December 2008

(Percent distribution.)

Index and year	All items	Food and beverages	Housing	Apparel	Transportation	Medical care	Recreation	Education and communication	Other goods and services
ALL URBAN CONSUMERS (CPI-U)									
December 1997	100.0	16.3	39.6	4.9	17.6	5.6	6.1	5.5	4.3
December 1998	100.0	16.4	39.8	4.8	17.0	5.7	6.1	5.5	4.6
December 1999	100.0	16.3	39.6	4.7	17.5	5.8	6.0	5.4	4.7
December 2000	100.0	16.2	40.0	4.4	17.6	5.8	5.9	5.3	4.8
December 2001[1]	100.0	16.4	40.5	4.2	16.6	6.0	5.9	5.4	4.9
December 2001[2]	100.0	15.7	40.9	4.4	17.1	5.8	6.0	5.8	4.3
December 2002	100.0	15.6	40.9	4.2	17.3	6.0	5.9	5.8	4.4
December 2003	100.0	15.4	42.1	4.0	16.9	6.1	5.9	5.9	3.8
December 2004	100.0	15.3	42.0	3.8	17.4	6.1	5.7	5.8	3.8
December 2005	100.0	15.1	42.2	3.7	17.7	6.2	5.6	5.8	3.7
December 2006	100.0	15.0	42.7	3.7	17.2	6.3	5.6	6.0	3.5
December 2007	100.0	14.9	42.4	3.7	17.7	6.2	5.6	6.1	3.3
December 2008	100.0	15.8	43.4	3.7	15.3	6.4	5.7	6.3	3.4
URBAN WAGE EARNERS AND WORKERS (CPI-W)									
December 1997	100.0	17.9	36.5	5.3	19.8	4.6	6.0	5.4	4.5
December 1998	100.0	18.0	36.7	5.2	19.2	4.7	5.9	5.4	5.0
December 1999	100.0	17.9	36.5	5.0	19.7	4.7	5.8	5.3	5.1
December 2000	100.0	17.8	36.8	4.8	19.9	4.7	5.7	5.2	5.2
December 2001[1]	100.0	18.0	37.3	4.6	18.8	4.9	5.7	5.3	5.4
December 2001[2]	100.0	17.2	38.1	4.8	19.4	4.6	5.6	5.6	4.5
December 2002	100.0	17.1	38.1	4.6	19.7	4.7	5.6	5.6	4.6
December 2003	100.0	17.2	39.1	4.4	19.1	5.0	5.7	5.6	3.9
December 2004	100.0	17.0	39.0	4.2	19.8	5.0	5.5	5.5	3.9
December 2005	100.0	16.8	39.2	4.0	20.1	5.1	5.4	5.4	3.9
December 2006	100.0	16.5	40.5	4.0	19.5	5.2	5.0	5.6	3.7
December 2007	100.0	15.9	40.0	4.0	20.1	5.2	5.3	6.0	3.5
December 2008	100.0	16.9	41.3	4.0	17.1	5.4	5.5	6.2	3.7

[1]1993–1995 weights.
[2]1999–2000 weights.

Table 9-10. Consumer Price Indexes, All Urban Consumers (CPI-U), All Items: Selected Metropolitan Statistical Areas, Selected Years, 1965–2008

(1982–1984 = 100, unless otherwise specified.)

Area	1965	1970	1975	1980	1985	1986	1987	1988	1989	1990	1991	1992	1993	1994
NORTHEAST														
Boston-Brockton-Nashua, MA-NH-ME-CT	32.5	40.2	55.8	82.6	109.4	112.2	117.1	124.2	131.3	138.9	145.0	148.6	152.9	154.9
New York-Northern New Jersey-Long Island, NY-NJ-CT-PA	32.6	41.2	57.6	82.1	108.7	112.3	118.0	123.7	130.6	138.5	144.8	150.0	154.5	158.2
Philadelphia-Wilmington-Atlantic City, PA-NJ-DE-MD	32.8	40.8	56.8	83.6	108.8	111.5	116.8	122.4	128.3	135.8	142.2	146.6	150.2	154.6
Pittsburgh, PA	31.4	38.1	52.4	81.0	106.9	108.2	111.4	114.9	120.1	126.2	131.3	136.0	139.9	144.6
NORTH CENTRAL														
Chicago-Gary-Kenosha, IL-IN-WI	31.7	38.9	52.8	82.2	107.7	110.0	114.5	119.0	125.0	131.7	137.0	141.1	145.4	148.6
Cincinnati-Hamilton, OH-KY-IN	30.5	37.4	51.8	82.1	106.6	107.6	111.9	116.1	120.9	126.5	131.4	134.1	137.8	142.4
Cleveland-Akron, OH	29.6	37.2	50.2	78.9	107.8	109.4	112.7	116.7	122.7	129.0	134.2	136.8	140.3	144.4
Detroit-Ann Arbor-Flint, MI	31.2	39.5	53.9	85.3	106.8	108.3	111.7	116.1	122.3	128.6	133.1	135.9	139.6	144.0
Kansas City, MO-KS	32.2	39.0	53.2	83.6	107.7	108.7	113.1	117.4	121.6	126.0	131.2	134.3	138.1	141.3
Milwaukee-Racine, WI	31.0	37.5	50.8	81.4	107.0	107.4	111.5	115.9	120.8	126.2	132.2	137.1	142.1	147.0
Minneapolis-St. Paul, MN-WI	30.1	37.4	51.2	78.9	107.0	108.4	111.6	117.2	122.0	127.0	130.4	135.0	139.2	143.6
St. Louis, MO-IL	31.7	38.8	52.6	82.5	107.1	108.6	112.2	115.7	121.8	128.1	132.1	134.7	137.5	141.3
SOUTH														
Atlanta, GA	31.2	38.6	53.6	80.3	108.9	112.2	116.5	120.4	126.1	131.7	135.9	138.5	143.4	146.7
Dallas-Fort Worth, TX	29.9	37.6	50.4	81.5	108.2	109.9	112.9	116.1	119.5	125.1	130.8	133.9	137.3	141.2
Houston-Galveston-Brazoria, TX	29.6	36.4	51.4	82.7	104.9	103.9	106.5	109.5	114.1	120.6	125.1	129.1	133.4	137.9
Miami-Fort Lauderdale, FL	...	...	...	81.1	106.5	107.9	111.8	116.8	121.5	128.0	132.3	134.5	139.1	143.6
Tampa-St. Petersburg-Clearwater, FL[1]	...	...	...	...	...	...	100.0	103.7	107.2	111.7	116.4	119.2	124.0	126.5
Washington-Baltimore, DC-MD-VA-WV[2]	...	...	...	...	...	...	...	...	...	...	...	...	...	...
WEST														
Anchorage, AK	35.3	41.1	57.1	85.5	105.8	107.8	108.2	108.6	111.7	118.6	124.0	128.2	132.2	135.0
Denver-Boulder-Greeley, CO	28.8	34.5	48.4	78.4	107.1	107.9	110.8	113.7	115.8	120.9	125.6	130.3	135.8	141.8
Honolulu, HI	34.4	41.5	56.3	83.0	106.8	109.4	114.9	121.7	128.7	138.1	148.0	155.1	160.1	164.5
Los Angeles-Riverside-Orange County, CA	32.4	38.7	53.3	83.7	108.4	111.9	116.7	122.1	128.3	135.9	141.4	146.5	150.3	152.3
Phoenix-Mesa, AZ	...	...	...	...	...	...	...	...	...	...	...	...	...	...
Portland-Salem, OR-WA	32.3	38.7	53.5	87.2	106.7	108.2	110.9	114.7	120.4	127.4	133.9	139.8	144.7	148.9
San Diego, CA	28.2	34.1	47.6	79.4	110.4	113.5	117.5	123.4	130.6	138.4	143.4	147.4	150.6	154.5
San Francisco-Oakland-San Jose, CA	30.8	37.7	51.8	80.4	108.4	111.6	115.4	120.5	126.4	132.1	137.9	142.5	146.3	148.7
Seattle-Tacoma-Bremerton, WA	31.0	37.4	51.1	82.7	105.6	106.7	109.2	112.8	118.1	126.8	134.1	139.0	142.9	147.8

Area	1995	1996	1997	1998	1999	2000	2001	2002	2003	2004	2005	2006	2007	2008
NORTHEAST														
Boston-Brockton-Nashua, MA-NH-ME-CT	158.6	163.3	167.9	171.7	176.0	183.6	191.5	196.5	203.9	209.5	216.4	223.1	227.4	235.4
New York-Northern New Jersey-Long Island, NY-NJ-CT-PA	162.2	166.9	170.8	173.6	177.0	182.5	187.1	191.9	197.8	204.8	212.7	220.7	226.9	235.8
Philadelphia-Wilmington-Atlantic City, PA-NJ-DE-MD	158.7	162.8	166.5	168.2	171.9	176.5	181.3	184.9	188.8	196.5	204.2	212.1	216.7	224.1
Pittsburgh, PA	149.2	153.2	157.0	159.2	162.5	168.0	172.5	174.0	177.5	183.0	189.8	195.7	201.5	211.3
NORTH CENTRAL														
Chicago-Gary-Kenosha, IL-IN-WI	153.3	157.4	161.7	165.0	168.4	173.8	178.3	181.2	184.5	188.6	194.3	198.3	204.8	212.5
Cincinnati-Hamilton, OH-KY-IN	146.2	149.6	152.1	155.1	159.2	164.8	167.9	170.0	173.4	176.5	181.6	188.6	193.9	201.5
Cleveland-Akron, OH	147.9	152.0	156.1	159.8	162.5	168.0	172.9	173.3	176.2	181.6	187.9	191.1	196.0	203.0
Detroit-Ann Arbor-Flint, MI	148.6	152.5	156.3	159.8	163.9	169.8	174.4	178.9	182.5	185.4	190.8	196.6	200.1	204.7
Kansas City, MO-KS	145.3	151.6	155.8	157.8	160.1	166.6	172.2	174.0	177.0	180.7	185.3	190.1	194.5	201.2
Milwaukee-Racine, WI	151.0	154.7	157.7	160.3	163.7	168.6	171.7	174.0	177.7	180.2	185.2	189.9	194.1	203.0
Minneapolis-St. Paul, MN-WI	147.0	151.9	155.4	158.3	163.3	170.1	176.5	179.6	182.7	187.9	193.1	196.2	201.2	209.0
St. Louis, MO-IL	145.2	149.6	152.9	154.5	157.6	163.1	167.3	169.1	173.4	180.3	186.2	189.5	193.2	198.7
SOUTH														
Atlanta, GA	150.9	156.0	158.9	161.2	164.8	170.6	176.2	178.2	180.8	183.2	188.9	193.8	200.0	206.5
Dallas-Fort Worth, TX	144.9	148.8	151.4	153.6	158.0	164.7	170.4	172.7	176.2	178.7	184.7	190.1	193.2	201.8
Houston-Galveston-Brazoria, TX	139.8	142.7	145.4	146.8	148.7	154.2	158.8	159.2	163.7	169.5	175.6	180.6	183.8	190.0
Miami-Fort Lauderdale, FL	148.9	153.7	158.4	160.5	162.4	167.8	173.0	175.5	180.6	185.6	194.3	203.9	212.4	222.1
Tampa-St. Petersburg-Clearwater, FL[1]	129.7	131.6	134.0	137.5	140.6	145.7	148.8	153.9	158.1	162.0	168.5	175.2	184.3	190.1
Washington-Baltimore, DC-MD-VA-WV[2]	...	...	100.8	102.1	104.2	107.6	110.4	113.0	116.2	119.5	124.3	128.8	133.5	139.5
WEST														
Anchorage, AK	138.9	142.7	144.8	146.9	148.4	150.9	155.2	158.2	162.5	166.7	171.8	177.3	181.2	189.5
Denver-Boulder-Greeley, CO	147.9	153.1	158.1	161.9	166.6	173.2	181.3	184.8	186.8	187.0	190.9	197.7	202.0	209.9
Honolulu, HI	168.1	170.7	171.9	171.5	173.3	176.3	178.4	180.3	184.5	190.6	197.8	209.4	219.5	228.9
Los Angeles-Riverside-Orange County, CA	154.6	157.5	160.0	162.3	166.1	171.6	177.3	182.2	187.0	193.2	201.8	210.4	217.3	225.0
Phoenix-Mesa, AZ	...	...	...	...	...	...	101.2	103.3	105.2	108.3	111.5	115.3	119.3
Portland-Salem, OR-WA	153.2	158.6	164.0	167.1	172.6	178.0	182.4	183.8	186.3	191.1	196.0	201.1	208.6	215.4
San Diego, CA	156.8	160.9	163.7	166.9	172.8	182.8	191.2	197.9	205.3	212.8	220.6	228.1	233.3	242.3
San Francisco-Oakland-San Jose, CA	151.6	155.1	160.4	165.5	172.5	180.2	189.9	193.0	196.4	198.8	202.7	209.2	216.0	222.8
Seattle-Tacoma-Bremerton, WA	152.3	157.5	163.0	167.7	172.8	179.2	185.7	189.3	192.3	194.7	200.2	207.6	215.7	224.7

[1]1987 = 100.
[2]November 1996 = 100.
. . . = Not available.

Table 9-11. Consumer Price Index Research Series, Using Current Methods (CPI-U-RS), by Month and Annual Average, 1977–2008

(December 1977 = 100.)

Year	January	February	March	April	May	June	July	August	September	October	November	December	Annual average
1977	. . .	. . .	. . .	. . .	. . .	. . .	. . .	. . .	. . .	. . .	. . .	100.0	. . .
1978	100.5	101.1	101.8	102.7	103.6	104.6	105.0	105.5	106.1	106.7	107.3	107.9	104.4
1979	108.7	109.7	110.7	111.8	113.0	114.1	115.2	116.0	117.1	117.9	118.5	119.5	114.4
1980	120.9	122.4	123.8	124.8	125.8	126.7	127.6	128.6	130.0	130.8	131.5	132.4	127.1
1981	133.6	135.3	136.4	137.1	137.9	138.7	139.7	140.7	141.8	142.4	142.9	143.4	139.2
1982	144.2	144.7	144.9	145.1	146.1	147.5	148.5	148.8	149.5	150.2	150.5	150.7	147.6
1983	151.1	151.2	151.3	152.4	153.2	153.8	154.4	154.8	155.6	156.0	156.2	156.4	153.9
1984	157.3	158.0	158.4	159.1	159.5	160.0	160.5	161.1	161.9	162.3	162.3	162.4	160.2
1985	162.6	163.3	164.0	164.7	165.3	165.8	166.1	166.4	167.0	167.4	167.9	168.3	165.7
1986	168.8	168.3	167.5	167.1	167.7	168.5	168.5	168.7	169.7	169.7	169.8	169.9	168.7
1987	170.9	171.6	172.3	173.2	173.7	174.3	174.6	175.6	176.4	176.8	176.9	176.8	174.4
1988	177.3	177.6	178.3	179.2	179.8	180.5	181.1	181.9	183.0	183.5	183.6	183.7	180.8
1989	184.6	185.2	186.2	187.5	188.4	188.8	189.3	189.5	190.2	190.9	191.2	191.5	188.6
1990	193.3	194.2	195.2	195.5	195.8	196.9	197.6	199.3	200.9	202.1	202.3	202.4	198.0
1991	203.3	203.5	203.6	203.9	204.4	204.9	205.0	205.6	206.4	206.6	207.1	207.2	205.1
1992	207.5	208.1	209.0	209.3	209.6	210.1	210.4	211.0	211.6	212.2	212.5	212.3	210.3
1993	212.9	213.7	214.3	214.9	215.3	215.5	215.6	216.1	216.4	217.1	217.3	217.1	215.5
1994	217.4	218.0	218.8	219.0	219.2	219.9	220.4	221.1	221.5	221.6	221.9	221.8	220.1
1995	222.6	223.3	224.0	224.7	225.1	225.6	225.7	226.1	226.5	227.1	226.9	226.8	225.4
1996	227.9	228.7	229.8	230.6	231.2	231.3	231.7	232.0	232.7	233.4	233.8	233.8	231.4
1997	234.5	235.2	235.6	235.9	235.8	236.2	236.3	236.7	237.5	237.9	237.8	237.4	236.4
1998	237.8	238.2	238.6	239.1	239.4	239.6	239.8	240.2	240.5	241.0	241.0	240.7	239.7
1999	241.4	241.7	242.4	244.1	244.1	244.2	244.9	245.6	246.7	247.2	247.3	247.3	244.7
2000	248.0	249.4	251.4	251.6	251.8	253.2	253.7	253.8	255.1	255.5	255.7	255.5	252.9
2001	257.1	258.2	258.8	259.8	260.9	261.4	260.6	260.7	261.8	260.9	260.4	259.4	260.0
2002	260.1	261.1	262.5	264.0	264.0	264.2	264.5	265.3	265.8	266.3	266.3	265.7	264.2
2003	266.8	268.9	270.5	269.9	269.5	269.8	270.1	271.1	271.9	271.7	270.9	270.6	270.1
2004	272.0	273.5	275.2	276.1	277.6	278.5	278.2	278.3	278.8	280.4	280.5	279.5	277.4
2005	280.0	281.6	283.8	285.7	285.5	285.6	286.9	288.3	291.9	292.5	290.2	288.9	286.7
2006	291.2	291.8	293.5	295.9	297.3	297.9	298.8	299.5	298.0	296.4	295.9	296.4	296.1
2007	297.2	298.8	301.6	303.5	305.4	306.0	305.9	305.3	306.2	306.8	308.6	308.4	304.5
2008	310.0	310.9	313.6	315.5	318.1	321.3	323.0	321.7	321.3	318.0	311.9	308.7	316.2

. . . = Not available.

NOTES AND DEFINITIONS

IMPORT AND EXPORT PRICE INDEXES

Collection and Coverage

The International Price Program (IPP) at the Bureau of Labor Statistics (BLS) produces Import/Export Price Indexes (MXP) which contain data on changes in the prices of nonmilitary goods and services traded between the U.S. and the rest of the world.

The MXP are primarily used to deflate foreign trade statistics produced by the U.S. government. The MXP are also a valuable input into the processes of measuring inflation, formulating fiscal and monetary policy, forecasting future prices, conducting elasticity studies, measuring U.S. industrial competitiveness, analyzing exchange rates, negotiating trade contracts, and analyzing import prices by locality of origin. The IPP collects prices as close as possible to the first day of each reference month.

The formula used to calculate the MXP is a modified form of the Laspeyres index. A Laspeyres index uses fixed base period quantities to aggregate prices. This means that the quality of goods and services is fixed; new goods do not appear, and the prices of goods that disappear must be observable. Because these implications are not consistent with the actually workings of the economy, adjustments must be made to the index.

The merchandise item price indexes are classified by end use for the Bureau of Economic Analysis System, by industry according to the North American Industry Classification System (NAICS), and product category according to the Harmonized System (HS). While classification by end use and product category are self-explanatory, a couple of notes are in order for classifying items by industry. In the NAICS tables, for both imports and exports, items are classified by output industry, not input industry. As an example, NAICS import index 326 (plastics and rubber products) would include outputs such as manufactured plastic rather than inputs such as petroleum. The NAICS classification structure also matches the classification system used by the PPI to produce the NAICS primary products indexes.

The Import Price Indexes (MPI) are based on U.S. dollar prices paid by the U.S. importer. The prices are generally either "free on board" (f.o.b.) foreign port or "cost, insur-ance, and freight" (c.i.f.) U.S. port transaction prices, depending on the practices of the individual industry. The index for crude petroleum is calculated from data collected by the Department of Energy.

Prices used in the import indexes by locality of origin are a subset of the data collected for the Import Price Indexes. Beginning with January 2002, the indexes are defined by locality of origin using a nomenclature based upon the North American Industry Classification System (NAICS). Nonmanufactured goods are defined as NAICS 11 and 21, and manufactured goods are defined as NAICS 31–33.

The Export Price Indexes (XPI) are classified by end use, determined by BEA. The prices used are generally either "free alongside ship" (f.a.s.) factory or "free on board" (f.o.b.) transaction prices, depending on the practices of the individual industry. Prices used in the grain index, excluding rice, are obtained from the Department of Agriculture.

Starting in September 2008 the Import Air Passenger Fares Indexes represent changes in the average revenue per passenger received by foreign carriers from U.S. residents and are calculated from data obtained from an airline consulting service. These data include tickets sold by travel agencies and travel websites. Tickets sold directly by the airlines are excluded, as are frequent flyer tickets generally. Starting in January 2008 the Export Air Passenger Fares Indexes represent changes in the average revenue per passenger received by U.S. carriers from foreign residents and are calculated from data collected directly from airlines. These data include frequent flyer tickets and those sold by consolidators. Taxes and fees are included in the Import Air Passenger Fares Index and excluded from the Export Air Passenger Fares Index. The Air Freight Indexes are calculated from data collected directly from airlines. These data exclude mail and passenger baggage. The scope of the service being priced is the movement of freight from airport to airport only, and does not include any ground transportation or port service.

Sources of Additional Information

Concepts and methodology are described in Chapter 15 of the *BLS Handbook of Methods* and in monthly BLS press releases. These resources are available on the BLS Web site at <http://www.bls.gov>.

Table 9-12. U.S. Export Price Indexes for Selected Categories of Goods, by End Use, 1998–2008

(2000 = 100, unless otherwise indicated.)

Commodity	1998				1999				2000			
	March	June	September	December	March	June	September	December	March	June	September	December
ALL COMMODITIES	100.7	99.9	98.5	98.5	97.9	98.2	98.5	99.0	100.0	100.1	100.4	100.1
Foods, Feeds, and Beverages	109.3	107.8	101.9	105.5	101.1	102.9	101.4	99.5	100.8	100.8	98.7	101.2
Agricultural foods, feeds, and beverages excluding distilled beverages	111.6	110.1	102.5	106.5	100.6	101.6	101.5	99.3	100.9	100.9	98.6	101.5
Nonagricultural foods (fish, distilled beverages)	87.8	86.2	96.7	96.7	105.4	115.2	100.0	101.4	99.6	99.9	99.7	98.2
Industrial Supplies and Materials	96.2	95.2	92.6	91.6	91.1	92.1	94.2	96.5	100.1	100.2	101.7	100.0
Industrial supplies and materials, durable	100.8	99.7	97.6	96.6	96.2	96.1	96.2	98.6	100.7	99.9	100.4	99.5
Industrial supplies and materials, nondurable	93.5	92.5	89.8	88.7	88.1	89.7	93.0	95.3	99.8	100.4	102.4	100.2
Agricultural industrial supplies and materials	111.2	113.9	108.4	104.3	100.7	98.8	96.5	96.7	98.0	98.6	103.2	104.6
Nonagricultural industrial supplies and materials	95.2	94.0	91.6	90.8	90.5	91.6	94.1	96.5	100.3	100.3	101.6	99.7
Fuels and lubricants	74.1	72.4	66.7	66.6	66.3	71.6	80.3	86.4	103.1	97.3	111.3	104.9
Nonagricultural supplies and materials excluding fuels and building materials	98.4	97.2	95.2	94.3	93.8	94.3	96.0	97.9	99.8	100.8	100.2	98.8
Selected building materials	98.2	95.9	96.7	96.0	97.4	97.9	97.4	98.8	100.5	100.2	99.7	99.2
Capital Goods	102.5	101.6	101.1	101.0	100.8	100.4	100.0	99.9	99.9	99.9	100.0	100.2
Electrical generating equipment	102.1	101.4	101.0	100.3	99.9	99.8	99.1	99.3	99.6	100.0	100.7	100.5
Nonelectrical machinery	104.1	103.0	102.4	102.2	101.8	101.3	100.8	100.4	100.2	100.0	99.8	99.7
Transportation equipment excluding motor vehicles[1]	. . .	. . .	. . .	. . .	. . .	. . .	. . .	. . .	. . .	. . .	. . .	. . .
Automotive Vehicles, Parts, and Engines	98.1	98.2	98.2	98.6	98.8	99.0	99.1	99.6	99.9	99.9	100.3	100.1
Consumer Goods, Excluding Automotives	100.1	99.6	99.7	99.5	99.5	99.6	99.6	100.1	100.0	99.9	99.9	99.7
Nondurables, manufactured	100.0	99.7	99.7	99.5	99.8	99.8	99.8	100.6	100.1	99.8	99.8	99.6
Durables, manufactured	100.1	99.5	99.6	99.4	99.1	99.3	99.4	99.5	99.8	100.1	100.1	99.9
Agricultural Commodities	111.5	110.8	103.5	106.1	100.6	101.1	100.7	98.9	100.4	100.5	99.4	102.0
Nonagricultural Commodities	99.6	98.8	98.0	97.8	97.7	97.9	98.3	99.0	100.0	100.0	100.5	99.9

Commodity	2001				2002				2003			
	March	June	September	December	March	June	September	December	March	June	September	December
ALL COMMODITIES	100.0	99.4	99.0	97.6	97.6	98.0	98.8	98.6	99.7	99.5	99.8	100.8
Foods, Feeds, and Beverages	101.0	100.4	102.6	100.7	99.7	101.5	109.8	108.7	108.2	111.3	115.3	122.4
Agricultural foods, feeds, and beverages excluding distilled beverages	101.2	101.2	103.6	101.6	100.0	101.7	110.7	109.5	108.1	111.2	116.3	123.8
Nonagricultural foods (fish, distilled beverages)	99.4	92.6	92.9	92.1	98.3	100.7	101.3	102.3	110.0	113.1	106.5	108.5
Industrial Supplies and Materials	98.9	97.2	95.2	91.4	91.9	94.6	95.9	96.0	100.6	100.1	100.2	102.5
Industrial supplies and materials, durable	98.6	97.6	95.9	93.8	94.4	96.0	96.4	96.6	99.2	99.7	100.4	103.3
Industrial supplies and materials, nondurable	99.0	96.9	94.8	90.0	90.4	93.9	95.8	95.8	101.7	100.6	100.4	102.2
Agricultural industrial supplies and materials	101.7	99.3	96.8	93.3	93.6	95.8	98.4	101.9	104.8	104.4	107.3	117.5
Nonagricultural industrial supplies and materials	98.7	97.0	95.1	91.3	91.8	94.5	95.8	95.7	100.3	99.8	99.8	101.7
Fuels and lubricants	100.3	102.8	103.2	83.5	85.6	86.7	92.9	91.3	108.0	97.0	97.6	99.0
Nonagricultural supplies and materials excluding fuels and building materials	98.5	96.1	93.8	92.3	92.6	95.7	96.4	96.4	99.9	100.7	100.5	102.5
Selected building materials	97.5	97.0	95.5	94.2	94.2	94.2	96.2	96.2	96.4	96.3	98.4	99.5
Capital Goods	100.6	100.3	100.0	99.4	99.4	98.7	98.4	98.1	98.3	97.6	97.5	97.5
Electrical generating equipment	100.9	101.7	101.6	101.5	102.1	102.0	102.0	101.9	101.6	101.6	101.7	101.7
Nonelectrical machinery	99.7	99.1	98.6	97.7	97.5	96.6	96.0	95.4	95.6	94.5	94.3	94.1
Transportation equipment excluding motor vehicles[1]	. . .	. . .	. . .	100.0	100.9	100.8	101.7	102.5	103.5	104.0	105.1	105.7
Automotive Vehicles, Parts, and Engines	100.3	100.4	100.4	100.5	100.9	100.9	101.1	101.3	101.5	101.6	101.8	101.8
Consumer Goods, Excluding Automotives	99.6	99.4	99.7	99.9	99.1	99.1	99.3	99.3	99.4	99.6	99.4	99.9
Nondurables, manufactured	99.0	99.0	99.1	99.1	98.1	98.5	98.7	98.7	98.7	98.8	98.5	99.2
Durables, manufactured	100.2	100.0	100.4	100.5	99.7	99.4	99.6	99.6	99.7	100.1	100.1	100.3
Agricultural Commodities	101.3	100.9	102.5	100.2	98.9	100.7	108.6	108.2	107.5	110.0	114.7	122.7
Nonagricultural Commodities	99.9	99.3	98.6	97.4	97.5	97.8	98.0	97.8	99.1	98.7	98.6	99.1

[1]December 2001 = 100.
. . . = Not available.

Table 9-12. U.S. Export Price Indexes for Selected Categories of Goods, by End Use, 1998–2008—*Continued*

(2000 = 100, unless otherwise indicated.)

Commodity	2004				2005				2006			
	March	June	September	December	March	June	September	December	March	June	September	December
ALL COMMODITIES	103.0	103.4	103.8	104.8	106.4	106.7	107.5	107.7	108.8	111.2	111.7	112.5
Foods, Feeds, and Beverages	130.5	129.1	118.7	116.9	120.9	125.2	122.8	121.9	121.7	125.6	128.8	138.7
Agricultural foods, feeds, and beverages excluding distilled beverages	132.4	131.1	119.3	116.6	120.7	125.6	122.6	121.7	121.5	125.7	129.1	140.5
Nonagricultural foods (fish, distilled beverages)	112.1	110.7	113.0	118.4	121.8	120.1	123.6	123.6	123.2	125.0	126.0	123.5
Industrial Supplies and Materials	108.1	109.9	114.0	118.0	122.3	122.3	127.4	127.9	131.3	138.8	139.5	139.4
Industrial supplies and materials, durable	110.3	111.8	116.0	120.2	122.6	122.7	123.4	129.1	135.7	146.2	146.9	150.1
Industrial supplies and materials, nondurable	107.0	108.9	112.9	116.9	122.2	122.1	129.8	127.4	129.0	134.9	135.7	133.9
Agricultural industrial supplies and materials	117.2	110.7	109.4	109.5	115.6	115.8	116.4	117.4	116.8	117.3	118.1	123.9
Nonagricultural industrial supplies and materials	107.7	109.9	114.3	118.6	122.8	122.8	128.2	128.7	132.3	140.2	140.9	140.5
Fuels and lubricants	108.9	114.9	121.5	125.4	143.8	148.8	184.8	163.4	173.5	196.3	191.1	183.5
Nonagricultural supplies and materials excluding fuels and building materials	108.1	110.0	114.4	118.9	121.4	120.6	122.2	125.7	128.5	134.7	136.3	136.8
Selected building materials	102.3	103.4	104.0	104.4	105.3	106.2	105.7	106.5	108.5	109.8	110.0	111.5
Capital Goods	98.0	97.8	97.8	98.2	98.4	98.4	97.6	97.7	98.2	98.4	98.5	98.8
Electrical generating equipment	102.0	102.0	102.4	103.6	103.9	103.4	102.6	103.6	104.4	104.8	105.1	106.2
Nonelectrical machinery	94.5	94.1	93.9	93.9	93.9	93.7	92.7	92.5	92.7	92.7	92.6	92.6
Transportation equipment excluding motor vehicles[1]	106.6	107.2	108.3	109.5	111.1	111.8	112.6	113.8	116.0	117.1	117.7	119.1
Automotive Vehicles, Parts, and Engines	101.9	102.3	102.5	102.9	103.3	103.4	103.7	103.9	104.4	104.9	105.2	105.5
Consumer Goods, Excluding Automotives	100.2	100.4	101.0	101.2	101.6	101.5	101.9	101.9	102.3	103.5	104.0	104.0
Nondurables, manufactured	99.9	100.0	101.0	101.0	101.5	101.2	101.5	101.6	102.4	103.3	103.8	104.0
Durables, manufactured	100.1	100.7	100.9	101.1	101.5	101.5	101.8	101.5	101.3	102.4	103.1	102.8
Agricultural Commodities	129.7	127.4	117.6	115.4	119.9	123.9	121.5	121.0	120.7	124.1	127.1	137.3
Nonagricultural Commodities	100.9	101.5	102.8	104.1	105.4	105.4	106.5	106.8	108.0	110.3	110.6	110.7

Commodity	2007				2008			
	March	June	September	December	March	June	September	December
ALL COMMODITIES	114.7	116.0	116.7	119.3	123.8	126.1	124.9	115.8
Foods, Feeds, and Beverages	146.9	148.6	157.8	171.1	196.9	198.0	190.4	155.1
Agricultural foods, feeds, and beverages excluding distilled beverages	149.2	151.0	160.8	175.2	202.6	204.0	195.6	156.6
Nonagricultural foods (fish, distilled beverages)	128.0	128.5	133.0	136.1	148.3	146.1	145.5	143.5
Industrial Supplies and Materials	145.5	149.0	148.8	154.1	165.5	173.2	169.4	139.6
Industrial supplies and materials, durable	160.2	160.9	155.5	159.2	172.7	172.9	167.1	141.5
Industrial supplies and materials, nondurable	137.6	142.8	145.5	151.9	162.0	174.2	171.6	139.1
Agricultural industrial supplies and materials	127.3	128.7	140.0	144.7	159.3	158.0	157.4	126.1
Nonagricultural industrial supplies and materials	146.7	150.4	149.5	154.9	166.1	174.3	170.3	140.5
Fuels and lubricants	188.8	201.1	200.9	222.8	249.5	297.2	267.2	166.8
Nonagricultural supplies and materials excluding fuels and building materials	143.5	146.1	145.0	148.5	158.2	161.6	160.8	138.8
Selected building materials	112.7	113.9	114.4	113.7	114.2	113.8	115.4	115.1
Capital Goods	99.2	99.6	99.9	100.6	101.2	102.0	101.8	101.5
Electrical generating equipment	106.0	106.5	106.7	107.5	108.6	108.9	109.5	109.0
Nonelectrical machinery	92.8	92.9	93.1	93.6	93.7	94.2	93.9	93.3
Transportation equipment excluding motor vehicles[1]	121.1	122.3	123.4	125.0	128.1	130.3	130.7	131.5
Automotive Vehicles, Parts, and Engines	105.9	106.1	106.3	106.7	107.1	107.4	107.9	108.0
Consumer Goods, Excluding Automotives	104.8	105.8	106.2	107.3	108.0	108.2	109.3	109.0
Nondurables, manufactured	105.0	106.7	107.0	108.2	109.3	110.1	109.0	107.2
Durables, manufactured	103.4	103.7	104.2	105.2	105.4	105.2	108.7	109.7
Agricultural Commodities	145.0	146.7	156.8	169.3	194.3	195.2	188.3	150.8
Nonagricultural Commodities	112.6	113.8	113.8	115.7	118.8	121.2	120.4	113.2

[1]December 2001 = 100.

Table 9-13. U.S. Import Price Indexes for Selected Categories of Goods, by End Use, 1998–2008

(2000 = 100, unless otherwise indicated.)

Commodity	1998				1999				2000			
	March	June	September	December	March	June	September	December	March	June	September	December
ALL COMMODITIES	94.1	93.1	92.2	91.0	91.5	92.9	95.8	97.4	99.9	100.2	101.6	100.5
Foods, Feeds, and Beverages	105.4	105.9	104.0	103.7	101.5	102.2	100.7	103.4	101.0	99.4	98.9	99.3
Agricultural foods, feeds, and beverages, excluding distilled beverages	110.2	109.5	108.2	109.0	104.6	105.4	103.3	106.0	102.1	99.2	97.3	99.3
Nonagricultural foods (fish and distilled beverages)	95.4	98.5	95.3	92.9	95.0	95.7	95.4	97.9	98.5	99.7	102.3	99.2
Industrial Supplies and Materials	74.3	72.9	71.8	67.6	70.1	75.9	85.3	90.4	99.0	100.7	105.5	102.9
Fuels and lubricants	48.1	46.6	46.4	38.9	43.9	55.3	74.8	83.5	97.2	101.3	111.3	106.1
Paper and paper base stocks	93.7	93.9	91.9	90.5	90.1	88.4	90.1	93.4	95.5	100.0	103.2	104.5
Materials associated with nondurable supplies and materials	100.0	99.2	96.4	95.7	95.3	95.2	95.5	97.0	98.5	99.9	101.1	101.5
Selected building materials	99.8	95.2	99.7	98.2	103.0	109.0	108.3	106.1	107.1	100.3	94.3	94.7
Unfinished metals related to durable goods	90.1	89.1	85.2	83.2	83.3	84.6	86.0	90.9	102.7	100.7	101.5	99.5
Finished metals related to durable goods	102.7	101.3	101.4	100.3	99.8	99.7	99.2	100.0	100.6	100.5	100.3	99.4
Nonmetals related to durable goods	105.6	104.6	101.6	101.2	100.9	99.5	99.9	99.9	100.2	99.5	99.7	99.7
Industrial Supplies and Materials, Durable	96.2	94.4	93.0	91.5	92.4	94.1	94.6	96.7	102.9	100.4	99.6	98.5
Industrial Supplies and Materials, Excluding Fuels[1]	. . .	. . .	. . .	. . .	. . .	. . .	. . .	. . .	. . .	. . .	. . .	. . .
Industrial Supplies and Materials, Excluding Petroleum	94.2	93.0	91.1	90.2	89.9	90.9	92.6	94.8	98.9	99.9	101.0	105.4
Industrial Supplies and Materials, Nondurable, Excluding Petroleum	92.1	91.4	89.0	88.7	87.2	87.4	90.4	92.7	94.6	99.3	102.6	112.9
Capital Goods	107.5	105.8	104.4	104.5	103.5	102.1	101.4	101.0	100.5	100.0	99.7	98.9
Electric generating equipment	102.4	101.7	99.3	100.5	99.5	98.1	98.2	97.7	98.7	101.1	100.3	99.8
Nonelectrical machinery	109.1	107.1	105.7	105.6	104.5	103.0	102.1	101.6	100.9	99.9	99.5	98.6
Transportation equipment, excluding motor vehicles[1]	. . .	. . .	. . .	. . .	. . .	. . .	. . .	. . .	. . .	. . .	. . .	. . .
Automotive Parts and Accessories	99.1	98.7	97.8	97.8	97.8	98.2	98.5	99.1	99.4	100.9	100.3	100.0
Consumer Goods, Excluding Automotive	101.8	101.4	101.0	101.1	101.2	100.6	100.9	100.7	100.3	99.6	99.8	99.5
Nondurables, manufactured	100.9	100.9	100.8	100.8	101.0	100.4	100.8	100.6	100.3	99.6	99.8	99.6
Nonmanufactured consumer goods	98.3	98.9	97.8	97.3	99.2	98.2	100.1	100.0	100.3	98.2	99.8	99.0
All Imports, Excluding Fuels	. . .	. . .	. . .	. . .	. . .	. . .	. . .	. . .	. . .	. . .	. . .	. . .
All Imports, Excluding Petroleum	101.4	100.5	99.4	99.4	99.0	98.8	98.9	99.4	100.0	99.9	100.0	100.7

Commodity	2001				2002				2003			
	March	June	September	December	March	June	September	December	March	June	September	December
ALL COMMODITIES	98.3	97.6	95.9	91.4	92.8	94.1	95.5	95.2	99.1	96.2	96.2	97.5
Foods, Feeds, and Beverages	98.9	95.4	95.0	94.6	95.0	96.2	99.7	100.2	102.6	100.7	101.8	103.2
Agricultural foods, feeds, and beverages, excluding distilled beverages	101.0	97.0	97.8	98.3	99.5	101.3	105.4	106.0	109.6	107.1	108.3	110.9
Nonagricultural foods (fish and distilled beverages)	94.5	92.2	89.2	86.8	85.5	85.1	87.3	87.5	86.9	86.6	87.6	86.0
Industrial Supplies and Materials	96.0	95.5	91.0	77.6	84.9	89.8	95.2	94.6	109.7	98.2	98.9	103.6
Fuels and lubricants	91.1	90.9	86.1	61.6	76.4	85.8	96.2	94.7	125.2	100.3	99.4	107.2
Paper and paper base stocks	104.4	100.0	93.9	90.7	88.0	87.1	90.5	89.1	91.0	94.1	94.0	93.9
Materials associated with nondurable supplies and materials	102.8	100.3	97.9	96.2	95.9	97.1	99.4	100.1	104.2	103.0	102.5	104.4
Selected building materials	91.9	111.1	103.7	92.9	100.7	99.1	97.6	95.0	96.3	96.7	110.3	108.0
Unfinished metals related to durable goods	99.5	93.6	87.1	82.1	83.8	88.5	89.7	91.5	92.8	92.2	93.4	99.2
Finished metals related to durable goods	98.3	99.4	98.2	97.9	97.1	96.5	97.1	96.8	96.1	97.4	99.0	101.0
Nonmetals related to durable goods	101.6	100.6	100.4	99.0	97.2	96.7	96.9	97.1	97.9	98.2	97.5	98.2
Industrial Supplies and Materials, Durable	98.1	99.1	94.1	89.1	91.1	92.3	92.7	92.7	93.6	93.7	97.3	99.5
Industrial Supplies and Materials, Excluding Fuels[1]	. . .	. . .	. . .	100.0	101.0	102.1	103.4	103.6	105.8	105.7	107.9	110.1
Industrial Supplies and Materials, Excluding Petroleum	102.1	99.8	94.2	90.0	90.3	92.9	93.9	95.2	104.3	99.9	100.3	102.1
Industrial Supplies and Materials, Nondurable, Excluding Petroleum	106.4	100.7	94.2	90.9	89.3	93.4	95.2	98.1	117.1	107.2	103.8	105.0
Capital Goods	98.7	97.7	96.8	96.2	95.2	95.1	94.7	93.9	93.7	93.8	93.5	92.9
Electric generating equipment	102.1	101.8	101.4	100.6	95.5	95.1	95.7	94.9	95.5	96.6	95.8	96.8
Nonelectrical machinery	98.0	96.7	95.6	94.9	94.4	94.4	93.7	92.8	92.5	92.3	92.1	91.1
Transportation equipment, excluding motor vehicles[1]	. . .	. . .	. . .	100.0	100.5	100.4	101.0	101.0	101.6	102.0	102.2	102.8
Automotive Parts and Accessories	99.3	98.7	98.0	97.4	97.1	98.0	98.3	98.0	98.0	98.3	97.8	98.8
Consumer Goods, Excluding Automotive	99.8	99.3	99.1	98.7	98.2	98.1	98.1	98.0	97.9	98.1	97.9	98.1
Nondurables, manufactured	100.2	99.8	99.6	99.7	99.2	99.1	99.5	99.7	99.7	99.8	99.7	100.1
Nonmanufactured consumer goods	99.3	99.2	97.9	96.4	96.1	95.6	95.4	95.4	95.7	96.2	95.7	96.2
All Imports, Excluding Fuels	. . .	. . .	. . .	100.0	99.7	99.9	100.1	100.0	100.3	100.3	100.6	101.0
All Imports, Excluding Petroleum	100.0	98.9	97.3	96.2	95.8	96.2	96.4	96.5	98.1	97.3	97.3	97.7

[1]December 2001 = 100.
. . . = Not available.

Table 9-13. U.S. Import Price Indexes for Selected Categories of Goods, by End Use, 1998–2008—*Continued*

(2000 = 100, unless otherwise indicated.)

Commodity	2004				2005				2006			
	March	June	September	December	March	June	September	December	March	June	September	December
ALL COMMODITIES	100.2	101.7	104.1	104.0	107.8	109.2	114.4	112.3	112.7	117.3	116.2	115.1
Foods, Feeds, and Beverages	105.9	106.9	108.7	111.5	115.9	114.1	114.2	117.5	117.0	118.0	120.9	122.6
Agricultural foods, feeds, and beverages, excluding distilled beverages	113.0	114.3	116.4	120.7	125.7	123.5	122.6	127.2	125.4	126.8	130.4	133.7
Nonagricultural foods (fish and distilled beverages)	90.1	90.3	91.4	91.0	94.0	93.1	95.6	95.9	98.3	98.5	99.8	97.9
Industrial Supplies and Materials	112.7	119.3	128.5	126.4	139.8	145.5	167.2	158.6	160.4	178.1	172.2	166.6
Fuels and lubricants	120.2	130.9	146.2	141.0	165.6	178.0	222.1	202.4	201.5	230.2	216.3	204.3
Paper and paper base stocks	95.6	99.0	101.1	101.3	103.8	103.8	104.3	106.1	107.7	111.3	113.1	112.8
Materials associated with nondurable supplies and materials	105.4	106.0	108.0	109.8	113.0	113.5	117.3	117.8	119.3	120.6	121.8	123.0
Selected building materials	118.4	120.5	125.6	115.6	122.7	118.1	117.6	116.9	118.0	117.2	115.8	110.6
Unfinished metals related to durable goods	114.9	124.4	133.1	138.5	140.4	139.9	138.2	145.8	161.1	193.2	194.4	195.9
Finished metals related to durable goods	104.8	108.1	112.4	114.7	115.9	116.6	117.3	117.6	119.2	125.3	128.4	128.9
Nonmetals related to durable goods	99.3	98.7	98.8	99.7	100.8	100.9	100.7	100.5	100.8	101.1	101.3	101.7
Industrial Supplies and Materials, Durable	108.5	112.8	117.8	118.0	120.8	119.7	119.1	121.4	127.2	139.1	139.8	139.2
Industrial Supplies and Materials, Excluding Fuels[1]	116.5	119.8	124.1	124.8	128.0	127.5	128.5	130.3	134.9	143.7	144.7	144.7
Industrial Supplies and Materials, Excluding Petroleum	107.9	112.5	114.4	118.8	119.9	120.2	126.8	132.2	128.1	133.9	135.1	138.3
Industrial Supplies and Materials, Nondurable, Excluding Petroleum	107.1	112.0	110.2	119.7	118.7	120.7	135.4	144.3	128.3	126.7	128.5	136.3
Capital Goods	93.1	92.2	92.0	92.2	92.3	92.3	91.5	91.0	91.1	91.2	91.3	91.5
Electric generating equipment	97.8	97.0	97.4	98.0	98.8	98.8	99.0	99.3	100.1	102.1	102.7	103.0
Nonelectrical machinery	91.2	90.1	89.8	89.9	89.8	89.8	88.7	88.1	88.0	87.8	87.8	87.9
Transportation equipment, excluding motor vehicles[1]	103.5	104.0	103.9	104.5	105.6	106.0	106.4	106.1	107.0	107.9	108.3	109.1
Automotive Parts and Accessories	99.6	100.1	100.2	101.5	101.8	102.0	102.1	101.8	101.6	102.7	103.0	103.0
Consumer Goods, Excluding Automotive	98.7	98.5	98.4	99.0	99.9	99.9	99.7	99.6	99.6	99.8	100.5	101.0
Nondurables, manufactured	101.3	100.9	100.8	101.4	102.8	102.8	103.1	102.7	102.8	102.6	103.0	103.4
Nonmanufactured consumer goods	96.4	96.8	97.9	98.2	100.3	101.8	100.6	101.2	98.2	98.6	100.5	101.8
All Imports, Excluding Fuels	102.4	102.7	103.4	104.0	105.0	104.9	104.8	105.1	105.7	107.2	107.8	108.1
All Imports, Excluding Petroleum	99.1	99.7	100.1	101.3	102.0	102.0	102.8	103.7	103.0	104.2	104.8	105.7

Commodity	2007				2008			
	March	June	September	December	March	June	September	December
ALL COMMODITIES	115.9	120.0	121.8	127.3	133.5	145.5	137.8	114.5
Foods, Feeds, and Beverages	124.6	127.8	131.8	134.4	141.8	147.7	147.9	142.3
Agricultural foods, feeds, and beverages, excluding distilled beverages	135.1	139.5	144.4	148.3	157.3	165.1	165.1	159.4
Nonagricultural foods (fish and distilled beverages)	101.3	101.5	103.5	103.0	106.8	108.4	109.1	103.8
Industrial Supplies and Materials	169.8	185.6	190.7	211.3	234.5	283.0	248.9	150.4
Fuels and lubricants	209.6	238.2	250.0	290.3	329.0	423.7	346.3	153.9
Paper and paper base stocks	111.5	110.8	111.2	109.2	114.1	117.3	119.9	113.2
Materials associated with nondurable supplies and materials	124.0	125.4	128.2	135.3	147.8	152.9	162.4	148.5
Selected building materials	111.4	113.1	116.9	116.0	114.1	119.2	122.7	118.1
Unfinished metals related to durable goods	202.9	219.7	209.1	217.2	241.5	273.2	255.4	185.7
Finished metals related to durable goods	125.4	133.7	134.8	135.0	145.8	158.7	159.9	140.8
Nonmetals related to durable goods	101.8	101.6	102.5	103.8	105.2	107.6	111.4	109.0
Industrial Supplies and Materials, Durable	141.0	148.4	146.3	149.1	158.9	173.5	169.7	141.8
Industrial Supplies and Materials, Excluding Fuels[1]	146.2	151.6	151.2	155.4	166.8	178.8	179.5	155.1
Industrial Supplies and Materials, Excluding Petroleum	139.3	144.6	141.0	147.5	159.4	173.7	167.4	146.0
Industrial Supplies and Materials, Nondurable, Excluding Petroleum	136.3	139.1	133.6	144.5	159.3	173.0	163.5	150.8
Capital Goods	91.1	91.3	91.9	92.2	92.2	93.2	93.3	92.7
Electric generating equipment	104.3	105.7	106.5	107.9	109.3	112.0	112.9	111.4
Nonelectrical machinery	87.2	87.2	87.7	87.7	87.5	88.2	88.2	87.5
Transportation equipment, excluding motor vehicles[1]	110.1	111.0	113.4	114.7	115.3	117.7	118.2	120.2
Automotive Parts and Accessories	103.5	103.3	103.6	104.8	106.2	106.7	107.4	108.8
Consumer Goods, Excluding Automotive	101.3	101.4	102.1	102.6	104.0	104.9	105.1	104.4
Nondurables, manufactured	104.1	104.3	105.0	105.5	107.5	107.9	108.2	108.2
Nonmanufactured consumer goods	102.2	102.6	103.4	103.8	104.3	106.6	106.6	103.6
All Imports, Excluding Fuels	108.4	109.5	110.1	111.4	113.9	116.5	116.8	112.7
All Imports, Excluding Petroleum	105.9	107.1	107.1	108.9	111.6	114.9	114.0	109.9

[1]December 2001 = 100.

Table 9-14. U.S. Import Price Indexes for Selected Categories of Goods, by Locality of Origin, 1995–2008

(2000 = 100, unless otherwise indicated.)

Category and year	Percent of U.S. imports[1]	Month			
		March	June	September	December
INDUSTRIALIZED COUNTRIES[2]					
Total Goods	42.4				
1995		97.4	99.8	100.0	100.0
1996		99.7	98.8	99.3	99.4
1997		97.4	96.5	96.4	96.1
1998		94.6	94.0	93.3	93.8
1999		94.1	94.8	96.4	97.5
2000		99.5	100.1	100.9	101.4
2001		100.2	99.0	96.5	93.7
2002		94.3	95.7	96.9	96.7
2003		100.0	98.4	98.6	100.0
2004		103.4	104.7	106.3	107.5
2005		109.7	110.0	113.5	114.1
2006		113.5	117.4	117.0	116.4
2007		117.9	119.7	120.4	124.2
2008		130.9	139.6	135.1	119.1
Manufactured Goods	37.6				
1995		100.0	102.6	102.9	102.9
1996		102.1	101.1	101.4	100.7
1997		99.5	98.9	98.8	98.6
1998		97.8	97.5	96.7	97.3
1999		97.6	97.7	98.1	98.9
2000		100.2	99.9	100.2	99.8
2001		99.9	99.2	97.6	96.0
2002		95.6	96.3	96.9	96.7
2003		97.8	97.7	98.2	99.4
2004		102.1	102.8	104.0	104.6
2005		106.3	106.6	106.7	107.7
2006		109.0	111.8	111.8	111.1
2007		112.5	113.5	114.5	116.3
2008		120.1	124.3	124.2	115.7
Nonmanufactured Goods	4.4				
1995		66.3	67.6	65.2	66.0
1996		71.6	72.3	76.0	84.3
1997		73.3	68.9	69.4	68.5
1998		59.3	56.8	57.2	55.7
1999		56.9	65.1	78.7	83.2
2000		92.7	102.2	107.5	118.2
2001		103.9	97.2	85.2	69.9
2002		82.9	93.8	102.4	102.7
2003		134.3	113.7	108.9	112.4
2004		122.9	133.1	138.7	147.1
2005		156.7	158.0	203.0	199.2
2006		170.9	190.0	183.7	184.9
2007		185.6	197.9	195.4	228.2
2008		275.6	346.8	279.0	154.5
OTHER COUNTRIES					
Total Goods	57.6				
1995		97.5	98.7	97.4	97.6
1996		99.8	99.0	101.3	102.7
1997		100.6	99.4	98.7	96.6
1998		92.4	90.7	89.5	86.8
1999		87.7	90.3	94.5	96.9
2000		99.8	100.4	102.5	99.5
2001		97.0	96.6	95.0	88.6
2002		90.9	92.2	94.3	93.4
2003		96.7	93.1	93.3	94.1
2004		96.3	97.9	101.5	99.7
2005		105.0	107.0	112.1	109.5
2006		110.8	115.5	114.0	111.8
2007		113.1	118.0	121.1	127.5
2008		133.3	147.3	139.0	111.2

[1]Based on 2008 trade values.
[2]Includes Western Europe, Canada, Japan, Australia, New Zealand and South Africa.

Table 9-14. U.S. Import Price Indexes for Selected Categories of Goods, by Locality of Origin, 1995–2008
—Continued

(2000 = 100, unless otherwise indicated.)

Category and year	Percent of U.S. imports[1]	Month			
		March	June	September	December
Manufactured Goods	44.9				
1995		107.3	108.8	108.6	108.4
1996		108.9	108.4	107.9	108.6
1997		108.4	107.8	107.0	105.3
1998		103.5	102.2	100.6	99.6
1999		98.8	98.9	99.0	99.3
2000		99.8	99.7	100.3	100.2
2001		99.6	98.8	97.9	96.0
2002		95.6	95.9	96.2	95.8
2003		96.5	95.1	95.1	94.5
2004		95.2	96.2	97.2	97.1
2005		98.4	98.7	99.3	99.6
2006		99.4	101.2	101.2	100.7
2007		102.0	103.6	104.1	106.0
2008		107.8	111.8	111.3	103.4
Nonmanufactured Goods	12.4				
1995		69.5	70.3	66.1	67.3
1996		73.7	72.1	80.9	84.5
1997		75.8	72.6	72.2	68.8
1998		57.1	54.9	54.5	46.8
1999		53.0	63.6	80.3	89.2
2000		99.9	102.4	109.2	97.4
2001		88.9	89.7	86.1	65.3
2002		81.3	88.2	99.6	96.4
2003		113.3	98.0	98.8	106.5
2004		118.1	123.2	141.5	130.3
2005		158.0	169.5	199.8	181.3
2006		191.7	215.4	204.6	191.1
2007		192.4	220.6	241.6	279.0
2008		314.6	402.3	336.0	160.2
CANADA					
Total Goods	16.0				
1995		92.1	93.8	94.8	94.7
1996		94.3	93.5	93.8	95.1
1997		93.2	92.6	93.2	92.0
1998		90.1	89.7	89.3	88.7
1999		88.8	90.6	93.5	94.7
2000		97.2	99.8	102.4	105.6
2001		102.6	101.8	97.0	93.2
2002		96.1	97.8	99.6	99.2
2003		106.6	103.1	103.9	104.4
2004		110.0	112.3	114.4	116.6
2005		120.1	119.6	128.2	129.6
2006		125.4	130.6	129.7	129.2
2007		130.2	135.0	135.0	142.3
2008		152.0	171.2	160.1	129.8
Manufactured Goods	11.7				
1995		98.0	99.4	100.7	100.5
1996		99.0	98.0	97.7	97.4
1997		98.0	98.0	98.3	97.3
1998		96.7	96.6	96.3	95.5
1999		95.5	96.1	96.9	97.7
2000		98.8	98.9	101.3	101.8
2001		101.6	102.8	99.9	98.1
2002		99.1	98.7	99.5	98.9
2003		100.9	101.1	103.2	103.3
2004		107.4	108.2	110.3	110.7
2005		113.7	112.9	113.1	115.6
2006		117.2	120.0	119.9	118.7
2007		119.5	123.7	125.3	127.6
2008		128.8	137.5	138.7	126.8
Nonmanufactured Goods	4.0				
1995		61.7	64.4	63.9	64.8
1996		70.3	70.7	74.4	84.3
1997		69.9	66.6	68.1	66.4
1998		58.4	56.6	56.5	56.3
1999		56.5	64.2	76.8	79.9
2000		89.3	103.6	107.6	124.4
2001		108.1	97.9	83.1	69.8
2002		83.8	96.8	104.1	104.9
2003		143.1	119.0	111.5	114.0
2004		126.1	138.0	138.9	150.5
2005		157.9	159.8	210.8	207.4
2006		171.3	189.2	183.1	187.1
2007		187.8	195.9	187.7	222.3
2008		273.7	345.1	273.0	150.8

[1]Based on 2008 trade values.

Table 9-14. U.S. Import Price Indexes for Selected Categories of Goods, by Locality of Origin, 1995–2008
      —Continued

(2000 = 100, unless otherwise indicated.)

Category and year	Percent of U.S. imports[1]	Month			
		March	June	September	December
EUROPEAN UNION					
Total Goods	17.4				
1995		97.7	99.5	99.7	100.4
1996		101.3	101.0	101.7	101.9
1997		100.5	100.0	99.1	100.1
1998		98.9	98.8	98.7	99.4
1999		98.8	99.1	99.9	100.3
2000		100.8	100.1	100.0	98.9
2001		99.0	98.8	98.2	97.4
2002		97.4	99.2	101.0	100.9
2003		103.2	102.8	102.8	104.3
2004		107.4	108.5	110.0	111.6
2005		113.8	114.1	115.7	114.5
2006		117.7	120.4	120.5	119.6
2007		121.3	121.6	122.3	124.1
2008		129.7	133.9	131.5	124.3
Manufactured Goods	17.1				
1995		98.6	100.4	100.9	101.5
1996		102.3	101.8	102.4	102.3
1997		101.0	100.8	100.1	101.0
1998		100.4	100.6	100.5	101.5
1999		100.9	100.6	100.8	100.8
2000		100.8	99.9	99.6	98.6
2001		99.2	98.8	98.7	98.4
2002		98.1	99.9	101.5	101.4
2003		103.3	103.2	103.2	104.5
2004		107.4	108.4	109.3	110.9
2005		112.8	113.0	113.8	112.9
2006		116.0	118.0	118.4	118.0
2007		119.5	119.2	119.7	121.1
2008		126.5	130.1	128.2	121.8
Nonmanufactured Goods	0.2				
1995		72.8	74.5	71.2	73.0
1996		78.8	80.6	85.7	91.7
1997		89.3	82.2	76.5	78.4
1998		65.6	58.7	58.8	53.4
1999		53.6	66.6	81.3	88.7
2000		100.4	102.9	107.9	106.2
2001		96.0	99.5	89.1	75.7
2002		86.6	88.7	99.6	104.1
2003		118.8	106.7	111.5	118.8
2004		128.4	135.1	157.9	163.1
2005		177.1	177.5	209.7	191.1
2006		211.4	231.9	219.9	198.7
2007		205.2	234.6	274.9	304.8
2008		323.4	400.2	332.3	230.8
LATIN AMERICA					
Total Goods	17.8				
1998		84.3	83.9	83.0	80.4
1999		81.7	85.3	90.7	94.2
2000		98.9	100.9	103.5	99.5
2001		99.5	98.9	97.2	90.6
2002		94.0	96.2	100.0	98.9
2003		104.8	99.6	99.8	102.6
2004		106.3	108.6	114.7	113.1
2005		122.1	126.3	133.8	131.0
2006		134.0	142.8	140.2	136.4
2007		138.1	146.3	152.3	161.5
2008		171.6	193.9	181.7	135.4
Manufactured Goods	12.5				
1998		94.8	95.0	93.8	93.5
1999		92.0	93.6	94.6	96.0
2000		98.3	99.6	101.6	102.3
2001		104.2	103.5	102.5	101.4
2002		101.5	102.4	104.2	103.8
2003		108.2	103.6	104.4	105.8
2004		107.5	109.1	112.0	113.9
2005		117.1	118.6	120.1	122.2
2006		123.2	128.9	128.4	125.8
2007		127.4	131.4	132.5	134.3
2008		139.3	146.0	145.4	127.7

[1]Based on 2008 trade values.

Table 9-14. U.S. Import Price Indexes for Selected Categories of Goods, by Locality of Origin, 1995–2008 —Continued

(2000 = 100, unless otherwise indicated.)

Category and year	Percent of U.S. imports[1]	Month			
		March	June	September	December
Nonmanufactured Goods	5.2				
1998		60.8	59.7	59.4	51.9
1999		59.3	67.2	82.1	90.2
2000		100.2	103.5	107.8	93.6
2001		89.3	89.0	86.0	67.3
2002		83.5	90.7	103.0	99.3
2003		111.7	103.5	100.9	109.8
2004		121.1	125.9	144.6	130.1
2005		161.0	175.1	205.1	184.6
2006		195.5	217.2	205.7	197.1
2007		199.3	225.0	250.7	289.5
2008		320.9	409.2	348.3	181.5
CHINA					
Total Goods	16.9				
2004		99.5	99.7	99.6	99.0
2005		98.8	98.8	98.4	98.5
2006		97.9	97.4	97.4	97.3
2007		97.4	98.1	99.1	99.6
2008		101.1	102.8	103.7	102.4
JAPAN					
Total Goods	7.5				
1995		108.6	112.5	112.0	111.0
1996		110.1	108.4	107.8	106.5
1997		104.6	103.2	102.7	101.0
1998		99.8	98.2	96.8	98.0
1999		98.2	98.2	98.6	99.6
2000		99.6	100.0	99.9	99.9
2001		99.4	98.6	97.8	97.0
2002		95.6	95.4	95.0	94.6
2003		94.4	94.2	93.8	94.7
2004		95.2	95.1	95.3	95.9
2005		95.9	95.8	95.8	95.2
2006		94.6	94.7	94.4	94.1
2007		93.9	94.0	93.9	94.2
2008		94.6	95.1	94.9	96.0
ASIAN NEWLY INDUSTRIALIZED COUNTRIES[2]					
Total Goods	5.6				
1995		120.9	121.3	121.5	120.8
1996		120.6	119.6	118.1	117.3
1997		116.6	115.3	113.8	111.3
1998		108.7	105.2	103.0	102.0
1999		101.3	100.8	100.7	100.8
2000		100.6	99.9	100.0	99.3
2001		97.3	96.4	95.2	93.8
2002		93.3	92.6	92.5	91.3
2003		91.2	91.5	91.7	90.9
2004		90.3	90.6	91.0	90.6
2005		90.9	90.0	89.7	88.5
2006		88.8	89.2	89.3	89.1
2007		88.7	88.5	88.8	88.9
2008		89.2	91.1	93.2	89.2

[1]Based on 2008 trade values.
[2]Includes Western Europe, Canada, Japan, Australia, New Zealand and South Africa.

Table 9-15. U.S. International Price Indexes for Selected Transportation Services, 1995–2008

(2000 = 100.)

Category and year	March	June	September	December
AIR FREIGHT				
Import Air Freight				
1995	115.8	118.7	112.9	115.1
1996	113.7	112.2	112.0	110.6
1997	104.1	104.5	102.5	100.1
1998	93.0	94.2	92.8	100.2
1999	101.5	98.7	100.6	102.8
2000	100.7	100.1	100.2	99.0
2001	98.9	96.0	95.9	95.6
2002	96.7	99.7	101.2	106.9
2003	110.2	111.5	116.8	114.9
2004	117.1	117.5	120.0	126.8
2005	128.6	128.4	129.7	128.9
2006	129.7	135.2	133.1	131.2
2007	130.7	132.3	134.2	141.8
2008	144.4	158.7	157.1	138.5
Export Air Freight				
1996	. . .	. . .	. . .	112.9
1997	111.1	110.4	109.0	105.4
1998	107.1	106.6	108.0	109.2
1999	102.1	102.5	100.8	99.1
2000	99.1	100.8	100.8	99.4
2001	99.7	98.4	98.6	97.9
2002	95.5	97.9	98.3	95.2
2003	96.3	95.2	95.1	95.4
2004	97.1	99.1	100.3	106.1
2005	106.4	110.1	110.9	112.0
2006	113.6	115.9	117.9	116.7
2007	117.0	117.0	119.8	127.1
2008	132.0	140.8	144.3	135.0
Inbound Air Freight				
1995	113.6	116.5	111.0	111.7
1996	108.6	107.7	108.2	107.6
1997	101.3	101.8	100.3	97.9
1998	93.9	94.4	92.7	99.0
1999	99.6	97.6	99.5	102.8
2000	100.7	100.1	100.2	99.0
2001	97.9	95.1	94.9	95.1
2002	93.9	98.3	100.3	105.9
2003	108.8	109.4	112.5	112.9
2004	116.2	116.6	118.7	125.1
2005	126.3	125.6	127.5	124.6
2006	124.6	129.2	128.9	127.1
2007	126.6	127.3	129.6	138.1
2008	140.7	152.1	151.6	136.8
Outbound Air Freight				
1995	108.2	108.1	108.6	107.8
1996	107.3	107.6	107.0	107.3
1997	108.0	107.3	107.7	105.7
1998	105.2	103.8	103.7	103.0
1999	100.3	100.4	100.3	99.2
2000	99.2	100.3	100.2	100.2
2001	100.1	98.0	97.6	97.8
2002	95.9	98.4	97.3	95.4
2003	97.2	95.4	95.5	94.9
2004	96.1	99.0	100.7	104.7
2005	103.8	107.2	112.4	112.0
2006	113.5	117.2	116.9	113.8
2007	112.3	114.3	117.0	124.3
2008	128.9	143.7	147.0	130.4

. . . = Not available.

Table 9-15. U.S. International Price Indexes for Selected Transportation Services, 1995–2008—*Continued*

(2000 = 100.)

Category and year	March	June	September	December
AIR PASSENGER FARES				
Import Air Passenger Fares				
1995	80.2	88.1	86.4	82.6
1996	82.0	88.1	86.8	84.3
1997	84.7	95.5	94.0	88.0
1998	87.1	94.9	95.1	88.6
1999	87.5	98.9	99.5	89.7
2000	92.5	103.5	105.1	98.9
2001	101.1	112.8	116.4	105.7
2002	103.1	119.1	125.2	107.2
2003	108.6	122.3	125.9	107.0
2004	103.6	123.1	121.0	111.7
2005	110.0	128.1	124.0	116.3
2006	114.9	136.7	130.9	125.4
2007	122.9	144.6	140.2	135.3
2008	131.3	171.6	161.3	157.3
Export Air Passenger Fares				
1995	92.4	99.4	96.4	91.6
1996	93.0	94.4	97.7	94.7
1997	85.3	97.7	95.0	87.4
1998	89.5	90.2	90.6	93.1
1999	95.5	96.8	100.6	98.6
2000	98.1	101.5	102.6	97.7
2001	99.6	100.4	102.5	98.4
2002	97.5	103.2	108.1	103.2
2003	108.4	117.0	118.0	118.4
2004	123.2	123.8	130.1	134.0
2005	136.3	136.2	139.5	128.3
2006	130.8	139.3	142.4	137.3
2007	140.2	147.3	154.6	155.7
2008	156.4	171.4	171.9	164.6

Chapter Ten

INTERNATIONAL LABOR COMPARISONS

INTERNATIONAL LABOR COMPARISONS

HIGHLIGHTS

This chapter compares several summary statistics of labor force status, manufacturing productivity, and consumer prices for the United States with similar statistics for other countries. Different concepts and methodologies can make comparisons between countries difficult, but the Bureau of Labor Statistics (BLS) makes adjustments to reconcile as much of the data as possible.

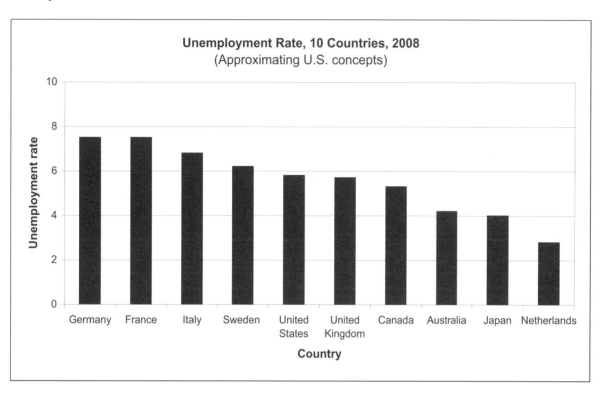

Western European countries continued to have the highest unemployment rates in 2008. Germany and France had the highest unemployment rate of the countries compared, each at 7.5 percent, followed by Italy (6.8 percent) and Sweden (6.2 percent). Although the unemployment rate was lower in the United States, it increased from 4.6 percent in 2007 to 5.8 percent in 2008. (See Table 10-1.)

OTHER HIGHLIGHTS

- In 2008, the unemployment rates for men ranged from 2.6 percent in the Netherlands to 7.5 percent in Germany, while the unemployment rates for women ranged from 3.0 in the Netherlands to 8.5 percent in Italy. (See Table 10-2.) The unemployment rates among youth also varied by country, ranging from 5.3 percent in the Netherlands to 21.5 percent in Italy. Youth are defined as 16- to 24-year-olds in the United States, Canada, France, Sweden, and the United Kingdom; otherwise, they are defined as 15- to 24-year-olds. (See Table 10-2 and 10-3.)

- Manufacturing labor productivity declined in 2008 in 11 of the 16 economies compared in Table 10-9. In countries where productivity increased, it increased at a much slower rate in 2008 than in 2007. In the Republic of Korea, labor productivity increased by 7.6 percent in 2007, but only increased by 1.3 percent in 2008. Likewise, in the United States, labor productivity only increased 1.3 percent in 2008, after increasing by 4.7 percent in 2007. (See Table 10-9.)

- Real Gross Domestic Product (GDP), stated in U.S. dollars, declined in 7 of the 16 countries compared in Table 10-13. The United States, which experienced a slight increase in real GDP, had the second highest real gross domestic product (GDP) per capita in 2008 ($43,250), exceeded only by Norway ($49,416). (See Table 10-13.)

NOTES AND DEFINITIONS

Collection and Coverage

From its inception, the Bureau of Labor Statistics (BLS) has conducted a program of research and statistical analysis that compares labor conditions in the United States with those in selected foreign countries. The principal comparative measures of the International Labor Comparisons (ILC) program (formerly called the Foreign Labor Statistics program) cover the labor force, employment, and unemployment; trends in labor productivity and unit labor costs in manufacturing; hourly compensation costs for manufacturing production workers, and consumer prices. All of the measures are based upon statistical data and other source materials from (a) the statistical agencies of the foreign countries studied; (b) international and supranational bodies such as the United Nations, the International Labour Office (ILO), the Organisation for Economic Co-operation and Development (OECD), and the Statistical Office of the European Communities (EUROSTAT), which attempt to obtain comparable country data; and (c) private agencies such as banks, industry associations, and research institutions.

International statistical comparisons should be made with caution, as the statistical concepts and methods in each country are primarily fashioned to meet domestic (rather than international) needs. Whenever possible, BLS adjusts the data to improve comparability.

Labor Force, Employment, and Unemployment

To compare unemployment across countries, BLS publishes monthly, quarterly, an annual unemployment rates for 10 countries that have been adjusted as closely as possible to U.S. concepts. The 10 countries are the United States, Canada, Australia, Japan, France, Germany, Italy, the Netherlands, Sweden, and the United Kingdom. BLS publishes additional annual labor force statistics on a civilian basis for the same 10 countries: working-age population, labor force, employment by major economic sector (agriculture, industry, manufacturing, and services), unemployment, employment-population ratios by sex, unemployment rates by age and sex, and women's share of the labor force.

Foreign country data are adjusted as closely as possible to the U.S. definitions. Primary areas of adjustment address conceptual differences in upper age limits and definitions of employment and unemployment, provided that reliable data are available to make these adjustments. Adjustments are made where applicable to include employed and unemployed persons above upper age limits; some European countries do not include persons older than age 64 in their labor force measures, because a large portion of this population has retired. Adjustments are made to exclude active duty military from employment figures, although a small number of career military may be included in some

European countries. Adjustments are made to exclude unpaid family workers who worked fewer than 15 hours per week from employment figures; U.S. concepts do not include them in employment; most foreign countries include all unpaid family workers regardless of the number of hours worked. Adjustments are made to include full-time students seeking work and available for work as unemployed when they are classified as not in the labor force.

Where possible, lower age limits are based on the age at which compulsory schooling ends in each country, rather than based on the U.S. standard of 16 years of age and over. Lower age limits have ranged between 13 and 16 over the years covered; currently, the lower age limits are either 15 or 16 in all 10 countries.

Some adjustments for comparability are not made because data are unavailable for adjustment purposes. For example, no adjustments to unemployment are usually made for deviations from U.S. concepts in the treatment of persons waiting to start a new job or passive job seekers. These conceptual differences have little impact on the measures. Furthermore, BLS studies have concluded that no adjustments should be made for persons on layoff who are counted as employed in some countries because of their strong job attachment as evidenced by, for example, payment of salary or the existence of a recall date. In the United States, persons on layoff have weaker job attachment and are classified as unemployed. Finally, employment data by economic sector are not fully comparable with U.S. definitions for some countries because all data required to make adjustments at the sector level are not available. Therefore, the sum of employment by sector may not equal total adjusted employment

Hourly Compensation Costs

Measures of hourly compensation costs are prepared by BLS to assess international differences in manufacturing employer labor costs. For several reasons, comparisons based on the more readily available average earnings statistics published by many countries can be misleading. National definitions of average earnings differ considerably; average earnings do not include all items of labor compensation, and the omitted items of compensation frequently represent a large proportion of total compensation. For many years, data on hourly compensation costs covered production workers only; recently, the series has been extended to cover all employees as well.

Hourly compensation costs include (1) hourly direct pay and (2) employer social insurance expenditures and other labor taxes. Hourly direct pay includes all payments made directly to the worker, before payroll deductions of any kind, consisting of pay for time worked and other direct pay. Social insurance expenditures and other labor taxes include employer expenditures for legally required insurance programs, contractual and private benefit plans, and other labor taxes. Other labor taxes refer to taxes on payrolls or employment (or reductions to reflect subsidies), even if they do not finance programs that directly benefit workers, because such taxes are regarded as labor costs.

Productivity and Unit Labor Costs

Time series indexes of manufacturing labor productivity (output per hour) and unit labor costs are constructed from three basic aggregate measures: Total real output, hours worked, and nominal compensation. Indexes for unit labor costs are prepared on a national currency basis and, using currency exchange rates, a U.S. dollar basis. With the additional collection of annual employment in manufacturing and the use of consumer price indexes, a total of 15 time series indexes are constructed.

The employment, hours, and compensation measures refer to employees (wage and salary workers) in Belgium and Taiwan and to all employed persons (employees plus the self-employed and unpaid family workers) in all other economies.

In general, the measures relate to total manufacturing as defined by the International Standard Industrial Classification (ISIC). However, the measures for France include parts of mining. Data for the United States are in accordance with the North American Industry Classification System (NAICS), except compensation data before 1987, which are based on SIC 1987. Canadian data are in accordance with NAICS 97 starting in 1961.

The data for the most recent years are based on the United Nations System of National Accounts 1993 (SNA 93). For earlier years, data were compiled according to previously used systems.

To obtain historical time series, BLS sometimes links together data series that were compiled according to different accounting systems by national statistical offices.

Consumer Price Index

The indexes and percent changes in this chapter are based upon national consumer price indexes as published by each country. They have not been adjusted for comparability.

National differences exist, for example, in population coverage, frequency of market basket weight changes, and treatment of homeowner costs. The data in these tables are not available in this form from the foreign statistical agencies.

The indexes in Table 10-11 are calculated by rebasing the official indexes of each country to the official U.S. base year. Because of the change in base year, the indexes may differ from the official indexes published by national statistical agencies.

Percent change in Table 10-12 is computed using the compound rate method. The figures may differ from official percent changes published by national statistical agencies because of rounding. In Sweden and Switzerland, the national statistical agencies calculate the official percent changes from more precise index values than those that they publish.

Real Gross Domestic Product per Capita and per Employed Person

Measures of gross domestic product (GDP), population, and employment are obtained from national statistical sources. While these data are generally comparable to one another, some differences remain in the countries' statistical methodologies, which may affect comparability. The GDP measures used for all countries come from their national accounts sources. For all countries, the most recent series use the 1993 United Nations System of National Accounts (SNA 93). However, some earlier series have been prepared using 1968 United Nations System of National Accounts (SNA 68). The U.S. GDP series is based on the system of national income and product accounts (NIPAs) estimated by the Bureau of Economic Analysis (BEA).

Sources of Additional Information

An extensive description of the methodology can be found in Chapter 12 in the *BLS Handbook of Methods*. For more information on international comparison of labor and manufacturing productivity, see BLS news release USDL 09-1271, "International Comparisons of Manufacturing Productivity and Unit Labor Costs Trends, 2008" on the BLS Web site at <http://www.bls.gov/fls/>.

Table 10-1. Employment Status of the Working-Age Population, Adjusted to U.S. Concepts, 10 Countries, 1970–2008

(Numbers in thousands, percent.)

Category and year	United States	Canada	Australia	Japan	France	Germany¹	Italy	Netherlands	Sweden	United Kingdom
Employed										
1970	78 678	7 919	5 388	50 150	20 270	26 107	19 083	. . .	3 850	. . .
1971	79 367	8 104	5 517	50 470	20 420	26 222	19 016	. . .	3 854	24 315
1972	82 153	8 344	5 601	50 590	20 540	26 289	18 710	. . .	3 856	24 385
1973	85 064	8 761	5 765	51 920	20 840	26 593	18 874	5 050	3 873	24 777
1974	86 794	9 125	5 891	51 710	21 030	26 247	19 284	5 100	3 956	24 849
1975	85 846	9 284	5 866	51 530	20 869	25 536	19 395	5 070	4 056	24 758
1976	88 752	9 652	5 946	52 030	21 041	25 396	19 504	5 100	4 082	24 611
1977	92 017	9 825	6 000	52 720	21 235	25 428	19 668	5 210	4 093	24 638
1978	96 048	10 124	6 038	53 370	21 326	25 647	19 725	5 260	4 109	24 774
1979	98 824	10 561	6 111	54 040	21 392	26 074	19 932	5 350	4 174	25 031
1980	99 303	10 872	6 284	54 600	21 443	26 486	20 195	5 520	4 226	24 917
1981	100 397	11 192	6 416	55 060	21 345	26 453	20 279	5 550	4 219	24 256
1982	99 526	10 847	6 415	55 620	21 390	26 149	20 246	5 520	4 213	23 781
1983	100 834	10 936	6 300	56 550	21 378	25 765	20 320	5 420	4 218	23 607
1984	105 005	11 211	6 494	56 870	21 199	25 826	20 392	5 490	4 249	24 115
1985	107 150	11 526	6 697	57 250	21 128	26 018	20 492	5 650	4 293	24 422
1986	109 597	11 873	6 984	57 740	21 244	26 383	20 614	5 740	4 326	24 578
1987	112 440	12 221	7 142	58 310	21 321	26 584	20 591	5 756	4 340	25 072
1988	114 968	12 591	7 413	59 300	21 521	26 799	20 868	5 917	4 410	25 905
1989	117 342	12 876	7 734	60 490	21 842	27 201	20 773	6 048	4 480	26 588
1990	118 793	12 964	7 877	61 710	22 075	27 952	21 080	6 251	4 513	26 713
1991	117 718	12 754	7 698	62 920	22 113	36 871	21 364	6 427	4 447	26 007
1992	118 492	12 643	7 660	63 630	22 000	36 390	21 233	6 559	4 265	25 388
1993	120 259	12 705	7 699	63 830	21 715	35 989	20 549	6 554	4 027	25 161
1994	123 060	12 975	7 942	63 860	21 746	35 756	20 176	6 614	3 990	25 374
1995	124 900	13 210	8 256	63 900	21 956	35 780	20 034	6 821	4 053	25 694
1996	126 708	13 338	8 364	64 200	22 037	35 637	20 124	6 966	4 014	25 941
1997	129 558	13 637	8 444	64 900	22 176	35 508	20 169	7 189	3 974	26 413
1998	131 463	13 973	8 618	64 450	22 597	36 059	20 370	7 408	4 036	26 684
1999	133 488	14 331	8 762	63 920	23 080	36 042	20 617	7 605	4 116	27 058
2000	136 891	14 681	8 989	63 790	23 689	36 236	20 973	7 813	4 230	27 375
2001	136 933	14 866	9 088	63 460	24 146	36 350	21 359	8 014	4 303	27 604
2002	136 485	15 223	9 271	62 650	24 316	36 018	21 666	8 114	4 311	27 815
2003	137 736	15 586	9 485	62 510	24 325	35 615	21 972	8 069	4 301	28 077
2004	139 252	15 861	9 662	62 640	24 346	35 604	22 124	8 052	4 279	28 380
2005	141 730	16 080	9 998	62 910	24 497	36 185	22 290	8 056	4 334	28 674
2006	144 427	16 393	10 255	63 210	24 737	36 978	22 721	8 205	4 416	28 928
2007	146 047	16 767	10 539	63 510	25 088	37 815	22 953	8 408	4 530	29 127
2008	145 362	17 025	10 777	63 250	25 474	38 480	23 137	8 537	4 582	29 343
Unemployed										
1970	4 093	476	91	590	530	140	640	. . .	59	. . .
1971	5 016	535	107	640	580	160	640	. . .	101	1 059
1972	4 882	553	150	730	610	190	740	. . .	107	1 116
1973	4 365	515	136	680	590	190	720	160	98	946
1974	5 156	514	162	730	630	420	620	190	80	949
1975	7 929	690	303	1 000	791	890	690	270	67	1 174
1976	7 406	716	298	1 080	891	890	790	290	66	1 414
1977	6 991	836	358	1 100	1 012	900	840	270	75	1 470
1978	6 202	898	405	1 240	1 060	870	850	280	94	1 453
1979	6 137	831	408	1 170	1 209	780	920	290	88	1 432
1980	7 637	854	409	1 140	1 303	770	920	350	86	1 833
1981	8 273	887	394	1 260	1 542	1 090	1 040	540	108	2 609
1982	10 678	1 298	495	1 360	1 687	1 560	1 160	630	137	2 875
1983	10 717	1 437	697	1 560	1 761	1 900	1 270	700	151	3 081
1984	8 539	1 377	641	1 610	2 068	1 970	1 280	710	136	3 241
1985	8 312	1 309	603	1 560	2 204	2 010	1 310	600	124	3 151
1986	8 237	1 216	601	1 670	2 228	1 860	1 680	640	117	3 161
1987	7 425	1 123	612	1 730	2 267	1 800	1 760	622	100	2 940
1988	6 701	999	558	1 550	2 189	1 810	1 790	609	86	2 445
1989	6 528	982	490	1 420	2 048	1 640	1 760	558	74	2 082
1990	7 047	1 083	563	1 340	1 991	1 460	1 590	516	84	2 053
1991	8 628	1 386	788	1 360	2 043	2 204	1 580	490	147	2 530
1992	9 613	1 507	897	1 420	2 278	2 615	1 680	478	261	2 821
1993	8 940	1 533	914	1 660	2 554	3 113	2 227	437	416	2 928
1994	7 996	1 372	829	1 920	2 721	3 318	2 421	492	426	2 675
1995	7 404	1 246	739	2 100	2 580	3 200	2 544	523	404	2 441
1996	7 236	1 285	751	2 250	2 738	3 505	2 555	489	441	2 301
1997	6 739	1 248	759	2 300	2 779	3 907	2 584	423	445	1 991
1998	6 210	1 162	721	2 790	2 680	3 693	2 634	337	368	1 791
1999	5 880	1 072	652	3 170	2 625	3 333	2 559	277	313	1 728
2000	5 692	956	602	3 200	2 262	3 065	2 388	239	260	1 587
2001	6 801	1 026	658	3 400	2 071	3 110	2 164	186	227	1 489
2002	8 378	1 143	630	3 590	2 132	3 396	2 062	231	234	1 528
2003	8 774	1 147	599	3 500	2 299	3 661	2 048	310	264	1 488
2004	8 149	1 093	551	3 130	2 412	4 107	1 960	387	300	1 423
2005	7 591	1 028	531	2 940	2 429	4 575	1 889	402	367	1 463
2006	7 001	958	516	2 750	2 432	4 272	1 673	336	336	1 670
2007	7 078	929	482	2 570	2 217	3 601	1 506	278	298	1 652
2008	8 924	962	477	2 650	2 067	3 140	1 692	243	305	1 783

¹Unified Germany from 1991 onward; data for previous years relate to the former West Germany.
. . . = Not available.

Table 10-1. Employment Status of the Working-Age Population, Adjusted to U.S. Concepts, 10 Countries, 1970–2008—*Continued*

(Numbers in thousands, percent.)

Category and year	United States	Canada	Australia	Japan	France	Germany[1]	Italy	Netherlands	Sweden	United Kingdom
Civilian Labor Force Participation Rate										
1970	60.4	57.8	62.1	64.5	57.5	56.9	49.0	. . .	64.0	. . .
1971	60.2	58.1	62.2	64.3	57.4	56.5	48.7	. . .	64.2	62.8
1972	60.4	58.6	62.3	63.8	57.2	56.2	47.7	. . .	64.1	62.9
1973	60.8	59.7	62.6	64.0	57.4	56.3	47.6	53.4	64.1	63.1
1974	61.3	60.5	63.0	63.1	57.4	55.7	47.7	53.5	64.8	63.1
1975	61.2	61.1	63.2	62.4	57.0	55.0	47.7	54.5	65.9	63.1
1976	61.6	62.5	62.7	62.4	57.2	54.6	48.0	54.1	66.0	63.0
1977	62.3	62.8	62.7	62.5	57.5	54.4	48.2	54.2	65.9	62.7
1978	63.2	63.7	61.9	62.8	57.4	54.4	47.8	54.0	66.1	62.6
1979	63.7	64.5	61.6	62.7	57.4	54.5	48.0	54.2	66.6	62.7
1980	63.8	65.0	62.1	62.6	57.2	54.7	48.1	55.4	66.9	62.8
1981	63.9	65.6	61.9	62.6	57.0	54.7	48.3	56.7	66.8	62.7
1982	64.0	64.9	61.7	62.7	57.0	54.6	47.7	56.6	66.8	61.9
1983	64.0	65.2	61.4	63.1	56.7	54.3	47.5	55.7	66.7	61.6
1984	64.4	65.5	61.5	62.7	56.5	54.4	47.3	55.7	66.6	62.7
1985	64.8	65.9	61.7	62.3	56.2	54.7	47.2	55.5	66.7	62.9
1986	65.3	66.4	62.8	62.1	56.1	54.9	47.8	56.0	67.0	62.9
1987	65.6	66.8	62.9	61.9	55.9	55.0	47.6	55.2	66.5	63.2
1988	65.9	67.1	63.3	61.9	55.7	55.1	47.4	55.9	67.0	63.8
1989	66.5	67.5	64.1	62.2	55.5	55.2	47.3	56.1	67.3	64.3
1990	66.5	67.4	64.7	62.6	55.5	55.4	47.2	57.0	67.4	64.3
1991	66.2	66.8	64.2	63.2	55.4	58.8	47.8	57.7	67.0	63.7
1992	66.4	65.9	63.9	63.4	55.3	58.1	47.5	58.3	65.8	62.9
1993	66.3	65.5	63.5	63.3	55.0	57.8	48.3	57.5	64.5	62.6
1994	66.6	65.2	63.9	63.1	55.1	57.4	47.6	58.0	63.7	62.4
1995	66.6	64.9	64.5	62.9	55.0	57.1	47.3	59.6	64.0	62.4
1996	66.8	64.8	64.6	63.0	55.2	57.1	47.3	60.2	63.9	62.4
1997	67.1	65.1	64.3	63.2	55.3	57.3	47.3	61.1	63.2	62.5
1998	67.1	65.4	64.3	62.8	55.6	57.7	47.7	61.8	62.8	62.4
1999	67.1	65.9	64.0	62.4	56.2	56.9	47.9	62.5	62.7	62.8
2000	67.1	66.0	64.4	62.0	56.3	56.7	48.1	63.4	63.7	62.8
2001	66.8	66.1	64.4	61.6	56.4	56.7	48.3	64.0	63.7	62.7
2002	66.6	67.1	64.3	60.8	56.4	56.4	48.5	64.7	63.9	62.9
2003	66.2	67.7	64.6	60.3	56.3	56.0	49.1	64.6	63.9	62.9
2004	66.0	67.7	64.6	60.0	56.2	56.4	49.1	64.8	63.6	63.0
2005	66.0	67.4	65.4	60.0	56.1	57.6	48.7	64.7	64.9	63.1
2006	66.2	67.4	65.8	60.0	56.3	58.2	48.9	65.1	65.0	63.5
2007	66.0	67.7	66.2	60.0	56.2	58.4	48.6	65.9	65.4	63.4
2008	66.0	67.9	66.6	59.8	56.3	58.6	49.0	66.3	65.2	63.6
Unemployment Rate										
1970	4.9	5.7	1.7	1.2	2.5	0.5	3.2	. . .	1.5	. . .
1971	5.9	6.2	1.9	1.3	2.8	0.6	3.3	. . .	2.6	4.2
1972	5.6	6.2	2.6	1.4	2.9	0.7	3.8	. . .	2.7	4.4
1973	4.9	5.6	2.3	1.3	2.8	0.7	3.7	3.1	2.5	3.7
1974	5.6	5.3	2.7	1.4	2.9	1.6	3.1	3.6	2.0	3.7
1975	8.5	6.9	4.9	1.9	3.7	3.4	3.4	5.1	1.6	4.5
1976	7.7	6.9	4.8	2.0	4.1	3.4	3.9	5.4	1.6	5.4
1977	7.1	7.8	5.6	2.0	4.5	3.4	4.1	4.9	1.8	5.6
1978	6.1	8.1	6.3	2.3	4.7	3.3	4.1	5.1	2.2	5.5
1979	5.8	7.3	6.3	2.1	5.3	2.9	4.4	5.1	2.1	5.4
1980	7.1	7.3	6.1	2.0	5.7	2.8	4.4	6.0	2.0	6.9
1981	7.6	7.3	5.8	2.2	6.7	4.0	4.9	8.9	2.5	9.7
1982	9.7	10.7	7.2	2.4	7.3	5.6	5.4	10.2	3.1	10.8
1983	9.6	11.6	10.0	2.7	7.6	6.9	5.9	11.4	3.5	11.5
1984	7.5	10.9	9.0	2.8	8.9	7.1	5.9	11.5	3.1	11.8
1985	7.2	10.2	8.3	2.7	9.4	7.2	6.0	9.6	2.8	11.4
1986	7.0	9.3	7.9	2.8	9.5	6.6	7.5	10.0	2.6	11.4
1987	6.2	8.4	7.9	2.9	9.6	6.3	7.9	9.8	2.3	10.5
1988	5.5	7.4	7.0	2.5	9.2	6.3	7.9	9.3	1.9	8.6
1989	5.3	7.1	6.0	2.3	8.6	5.7	7.8	8.4	1.6	7.3
1990	5.6	7.7	6.7	2.1	8.3	5.0	7.0	7.6	1.8	7.1
1991	6.8	9.8	9.3	2.1	8.5	5.6	6.9	7.1	3.2	8.9
1992	7.5	10.6	10.5	2.2	9.4	6.7	7.3	6.8	5.8	10.0
1993	6.9	10.8	10.6	2.5	10.5	8.0	9.8	6.3	9.4	10.4
1994	6.1	9.6	9.4	2.9	11.1	8.5	10.7	6.9	9.6	9.5
1995	5.6	8.6	8.2	3.2	10.5	8.2	11.3	7.1	9.1	8.7
1996	5.4	8.8	8.2	3.4	11.1	9.0	11.3	6.6	9.9	8.1
1997	4.9	8.4	8.3	3.4	11.1	9.9	11.4	5.6	10.1	7.0
1998	4.5	7.7	7.7	4.1	10.6	9.3	11.5	4.4	8.4	6.3
1999	4.2	7.0	6.9	4.7	10.2	8.5	11.0	3.5	7.1	6.0
2000	4.0	6.1	6.3	4.8	8.7	7.8	10.2	3.0	5.8	5.5
2001	4.7	6.5	6.8	5.1	7.9	7.9	9.2	2.3	5.0	5.1
2002	5.8	7.0	6.4	5.4	8.1	8.6	8.7	2.8	5.1	5.2
2003	6.0	6.9	5.9	5.3	8.6	9.3	8.5	3.7	5.8	5.0
2004	5.5	6.4	5.4	4.8	9.0	10.3	8.1	4.6	6.6	4.8
2005	5.1	6.0	5.0	4.5	9.0	11.2	7.8	4.8	7.8	4.9
2006	4.6	5.5	4.8	4.2	9.0	10.4	6.9	3.9	7.1	5.5
2007	4.6	5.3	4.4	3.9	8.1	8.7	6.2	3.2	6.2	5.4
2008	5.8	5.3	4.2	4.0	7.5	7.5	6.8	2.8	6.2	5.7

[1]Unified Germany from 1991 onward; data for previous years relate to the former West Germany.
. . . = Not available.

Table 10-2. Unemployment Rates by Sex and Country, Adjusted to U.S. Concepts, 10 Countries, 1970–2008

(Percent.)

Sex and year	United States	Canada	Australia	Japan	France	Germany¹	Italy	Netherlands	Sweden	United Kingdom
Men										
1970	4.4	5.6	1.1	1.2	1.5	0.5	2.5	. . .	1.4	. . .
1971	5.3	6.0	1.3	1.2	1.7	0.5	2.5	. . .	2.4	3.6
1972	5.0	5.8	1.9	1.5	1.8	0.7	2.9	. . .	2.5	3.9
1973	4.2	4.9	1.6	1.3	1.6	0.6	2.7	2.6	2.2	3.0
1974	4.9	4.8	1.9	1.4	1.8	1.5	2.3	2.8	1.7	3.0
1975	7.9	6.2	3.8	1.8	2.7	3.3	2.5	3.9	1.4	4.1
1976	7.1	6.3	3.9	2.2	2.9	3.0	2.7	4.1	1.3	5.2
1977	6.3	7.3	4.6	2.0	3.3	2.9	2.8	3.8	1.5	5.3
1978	5.3	7.5	5.4	2.2	3.5	2.7	2.8	3.6	2.1	5.1
1979	5.1	6.7	5.2	1.9	3.9	2.3	3.0	3.6	1.9	4.9
1980	6.9	6.9	5.1	1.7	4.0	2.3	2.9	4.2	1.7	6.7
1981	7.4	7.0	4.8	2.0	5.0	3.3	3.3	6.9	2.4	10.3
1982	9.9	11.1	6.4	2.1	5.6	5.0	3.8	8.6	3.0	11.6
1983	9.9	12.2	9.7	2.5	6.0	6.2	4.1	10.4	3.4	12.3
1984	7.4	11.1	8.7	2.5	7.4	6.2	4.2	10.4	3.0	12.0
1985	7.0	10.4	7.9	2.2	8.0	6.2	4.2	8.4	2.8	11.8
1986	6.9	9.4	7.6	2.4	8.0	5.5	5.2	7.9	2.6	11.8
1987	6.2	8.3	7.6	2.2	7.9	5.4	5.5	7.3	2.3	10.9
1988	5.5	7.2	6.6	2.0	7.4	5.3	5.5	7.3	1.9	8.9
1989	5.2	7.0	5.6	1.8	6.6	4.6	5.4	6.4	1.6	7.4
1990	5.7	7.9	6.6	1.7	6.5	4.2	4.8	5.6	1.9	7.4
1991	7.2	10.5	9.7	1.7	6.7	4.6	4.9	5.4	3.5	9.9
1992	7.9	11.6	11.2	1.8	7.7	5.5	5.3	5.4	6.8	11.8
1993	7.2	11.5	11.3	2.1	9.1	6.7	7.4	5.3	11.0	12.4
1994	6.2	10.2	9.8	2.3	9.8	7.3	8.4	6.1	11.0	11.3
1995	5.6	9.1	8.6	2.6	9.0	7.3	8.7	5.9	9.9	10.1
1996	5.4	9.2	8.5	2.8	9.7	8.4	8.8	5.3	10.4	9.5
1997	4.9	8.7	8.5	2.8	9.9	9.4	8.8	4.5	10.4	7.9
1998	4.4	8.1	8.0	3.5	9.3	8.9	8.9	3.5	8.7	7.0
1999	4.1	7.3	7.1	4.0	8.9	8.1	8.6	2.8	7.4	6.6
2000	3.9	6.3	6.5	4.1	7.4	7.6	7.9	2.3	6.2	6.0
2001	4.8	6.9	7.0	4.4	6.6	7.8	7.2	1.8	5.3	5.7
2002	5.9	7.5	6.5	4.7	7.2	8.8	6.8	2.5	5.6	5.8
2003	6.3	7.3	5.9	4.3	7.8	9.7	6.6	3.5	6.3	5.6
2004	5.6	6.8	5.3	3.9	8.2	10.6	6.5	4.4	6.9	5.2
2005	5.1	6.3	4.9	3.5	8.2	11.5	6.3	4.5	7.8	5.3
2006	4.6	5.8	4.7	3.3	8.2	10.5	5.5	3.6	6.9	5.8
2007	4.7	5.6	4.0	3.2	7.6	8.6	5.0	2.8	5.8	5.7
2008	6.1	5.8	4.0	3.4	7.0	7.5	5.6	2.6	5.8	6.2
Women										
1970	5.9	5.8	2.8	2.2	4.2	0.6	5.2	. . .	1.7	. . .
1971	6.9	6.6	3.1	3.0	4.6	0.8	5.2	. . .	2.8	5.1
1972	6.6	7.0	3.9	3.4	4.7	0.8	5.9	. . .	3.0	5.1
1973	6.0	6.7	3.6	2.6	4.6	0.9	6.2	4.3	2.8	4.8
1974	6.7	6.4	4.1	3.2	4.7	1.8	5.2	5.6	2.4	4.7
1975	9.3	8.1	7.0	3.9	5.1	3.5	5.8	8.2	2.0	5.1
1976	8.6	7.9	6.4	3.9	5.9	3.9	6.5	8.6	2.0	5.8
1977	8.2	8.8	7.5	4.3	6.5	4.3	6.8	7.6	2.2	6.2
1978	7.2	9.1	7.9	4.3	6.6	4.2	6.8	8.6	2.4	6.2
1979	6.8	8.3	8.2	4.1	7.4	3.9	7.3	8.8	2.3	6.2
1980	7.4	7.9	7.9	3.3	8.3	3.6	7.4	9.7	2.3	7.1
1981	7.9	7.8	7.4	3.5	9.2	4.8	8.1	12.9	2.7	8.8
1982	9.4	10.1	8.5	3.5	9.6	6.5	8.6	13.3	3.4	9.5
1983	9.2	10.8	10.4	3.7	9.8	7.9	9.4	13.9	3.5	10.5
1984	7.6	10.7	9.5	3.3	11.0	8.5	9.4	13.9	3.2	11.6
1985	7.4	10.0	8.8	3.0	11.3	8.6	9.4	11.9	2.9	11.0
1986	7.1	9.2	8.5	3.2	11.4	8.1	11.8	13.7	2.7	10.9
1987	6.2	8.6	8.3	3.2	11.8	7.8	12.0	13.7	2.3	10.0
1988	5.6	7.6	7.5	2.9	11.6	7.8	12.3	12.6	1.9	8.3
1989	5.4	7.1	6.5	2.7	11.0	7.2	12.1	11.6	1.7	7.1
1990	5.5	7.5	6.8	2.5	10.6	6.1	10.8	10.8	1.8	6.8
1991	6.4	9.0	8.7	2.5	10.7	7.0	10.4	9.6	2.9	7.5
1992	7.0	9.4	9.5	2.5	11.5	8.4	10.8	8.9	4.6	7.7
1993	6.6	9.9	9.7	3.0	12.2	9.6	13.8	7.7	7.6	7.9
1994	6.0	8.8	9.0	3.1	12.7	10.1	14.6	8.1	8.2	7.4
1995	5.6	8.0	7.7	3.4	12.3	9.4	15.4	8.8	8.1	6.9
1996	5.4	8.2	7.8	3.5	12.6	9.6	15.3	8.4	9.3	6.4
1997	5.0	8.0	7.9	3.7	12.6	10.6	15.4	7.0	9.7	5.9
1998	4.6	7.2	7.4	4.2	12.1	9.8	15.4	5.5	8.0	5.4
1999	4.3	6.6	6.7	4.5	11.7	8.9	14.8	4.5	6.7	5.2
2000	4.1	5.8	6.1	4.8	10.3	8.1	13.7	3.8	5.4	4.9
2001	4.7	6.0	6.4	4.8	9.4	7.9	12.2	2.8	4.7	4.5
2002	5.6	6.4	6.2	5.2	9.1	8.3	11.5	3.1	4.7	4.5
2003	5.7	6.4	6.0	4.9	9.6	8.8	11.4	3.9	5.2	4.4
2004	5.4	6.0	5.5	4.6	10.0	10.0	10.6	4.9	6.1	4.3
2005	5.1	5.6	5.2	4.1	10.0	10.9	10.1	5.1	7.5	4.4
2006	4.6	5.2	4.9	4.0	9.8	10.2	8.8	4.4	7.1	5.0
2007	4.5	4.8	4.8	4.2	8.7	8.8	7.9	3.7	6.4	5.0
2008	5.4	4.8	4.6	4.3	8.0	7.6	8.5	3.0	6.3	5.1

¹Unified Germany from 1991 onward; data for previous years relate to the former West Germany.
. . . = Not available.

Table 10-3. Unemployment Rates Among Youth, Adjusted to U.S. Concepts, 10 Countries, 1970–2008

(Percent.)

Year	United States	Canada	Australia	Japan	France	Germany[1]	Italy	Netherlands	Sweden	United Kingdom
1970	11.0	...	...	2.0	4.9	0.4	10.4	...	2.9	...
1971	12.7	...	...	2.1	5.5	0.6	10.3	...	5.1	...
1972	12.1	...	...	2.5	5.9	0.7	13.6	...	5.7	...
1973	10.5	...	...	2.3	5.8	0.8	13.2	3.8	5.3	...
1974	11.9	...	...	2.4	6.3	2.2	12.0	5.1	4.4	...
1975	16.1	...	...	3.1	7.9	4.7	13.2	8.2	3.7	...
1976	14.7	12.4	...	3.2	9.1	4.8	15.2	9.3	3.8	...
1977	13.6	13.8	...	3.6	10.6	5.0	14.9	8.9	4.5	...
1978	12.3	13.9	12.6	3.8	11.1	4.5	15.4	9.6	5.6	...
1979	11.8	12.6	13.0	3.7	12.8	3.6	16.0	10.2	5.1	...
1980	13.9	12.7	12.5	3.5	14.3	3.7	15.8	11.9	5.1	...
1981	14.9	12.6	11.4	4.0	16.8	5.7	17.3	16.8	6.4	...
1982	17.8	18.1	13.8	4.3	18.4	8.2	19.4	19.8	7.7	...
1983	17.2	19.1	18.3	4.6	19.3	9.6	20.9	20.9	8.1	...
1984	13.9	17.2	16.8	4.9	23.6	10.7	21.6	20.8	6.1	19.8
1985	13.6	15.9	15.2	4.8	24.0	10.0	22.2	17.4	5.9	18.0
1986	13.3	14.6	14.8	5.2	22.3	8.0	25.5	16.8	5.7	18.2
1987	12.2	13.0	14.6	5.3	21.2	7.4	25.8	15.2	5.3	15.4
1988	11.0	11.2	13.1	4.9	20.1	6.9	24.8	14.1	4.3	12.6
1989	10.9	10.5	10.8	4.5	17.7	5.5	23.9	12.5	4.0	10.1
1990	11.2	12.0	12.6	4.3	17.8	4.6	21.3	11.5	4.6	10.6
1991	13.4	15.4	17.0	4.4	18.9	5.5	21.2	10.7	8.0	14.3
1992	14.2	16.8	18.8	4.5	20.6	6.4	22.8	9.7	13.9	16.8
1993	13.4	16.7	18.2	5.1	24.4	7.8	27.8	9.9	23.5	18.0
1994	12.5	14.9	16.5	5.5	26.4	8.5	29.4	10.4	23.8	16.8
1995	12.1	13.9	14.8	6.1	24.6	8.4	30.6	12.9	20.2	15.8
1996	12.0	14.5	15.1	6.7	26.1	9.7	30.6	12.1	21.5	15.4
1997	11.3	15.5	15.7	6.7	26.9	10.6	30.4	9.5	21.1	14.2
1998	10.4	14.6	14.6	7.8	24.6	9.4	30.1	8.2	17.1	13.6
1999	9.9	13.4	13.3	9.2	24.5	8.8	29.0	7.1	14.6	13.0
2000	9.3	11.7	12.1	9.3	19.5	8.6	27.3	5.8	12.0	12.5
2001	10.6	11.9	13.5	9.7	18.1	8.4	24.4	4.6	12.0	12.0
2002	12.0	12.8	12.8	10.0	19.5	10.0	23.4	5.1	13.1	12.2
2003	12.4	12.8	12.0	10.3	17.5	10.8	24.0	6.4	14.0	12.4
2004	11.8	12.4	11.4	9.6	19.0	12.9	23.8	8.0	17.2	12.3
2005	11.3	11.3	10.6	8.8	19.4	15.5	24.2	8.3	22.2	13.0
2006	10.5	10.6	10.0	8.1	20.6	13.8	22.0	6.6	21.1	14.2
2007	10.5	10.1	9.4	7.8	18.2	11.9	20.6	6.0	18.7	14.4
2008	12.8	10.6	8.9	7.3	17.5	10.5	21.5	5.3	19.1	15.2

Note: Youth are defined as 16- to 24-year-olds in the United States, Canada, France, Sweden, and the United Kingdom; otherwise, they are defined as 15- to 24-year-olds.

[1]Unified Germany from 1991 onward; data for previous years relate to the former West Germany.
. . . = Not available.

Table 10-4. Employment-Population Ratios by Sex, Adjusted to U.S. Concepts, 10 Countries, 1970–2008

(Ratio.)

Sex and year	United States	Canada	Australia	Japan	France	Germany[1]	Italy	Netherlands	Sweden	United Kingdom
Total										
1970	57.4	54.5	61.1	63.8	56.1	56.6	47.4	. . .	63.1	. . .
1971	56.6	54.5	61.0	63.4	55.8	56.2	47.1	. . .	62.6	60.2
1972	57.0	54.9	60.6	62.9	55.6	55.8	45.9	. . .	62.4	60.1
1973	57.8	56.4	61.2	63.2	55.8	55.9	45.8	51.8	62.5	60.8
1974	57.8	57.3	61.3	62.2	55.8	54.8	46.2	51.6	63.6	60.7
1975	56.1	56.9	60.1	61.2	54.9	53.2	46.0	51.7	64.8	60.2
1976	56.8	58.2	59.7	61.1	54.9	52.8	46.1	51.2	64.9	59.5
1977	57.9	57.9	59.2	61.3	54.9	52.5	46.2	51.6	64.8	59.2
1978	59.3	58.5	58.0	61.3	54.7	52.6	45.9	51.3	64.6	59.1
1979	59.9	59.8	57.8	61.4	54.3	52.9	45.9	51.4	65.3	59.3
1980	59.2	60.3	58.3	61.3	53.9	53.1	46.0	52.1	65.6	58.5
1981	59.0	60.8	58.4	61.2	53.2	52.5	45.9	51.7	65.1	56.6
1982	57.8	58.0	57.3	61.2	52.8	51.6	45.1	50.8	64.7	55.2
1983	57.9	57.6	55.3	61.4	52.4	50.6	44.7	49.3	64.4	54.5
1984	59.5	58.3	56.0	61.0	51.5	50.5	44.5	49.3	64.5	55.3
1985	60.1	59.2	56.6	60.6	50.9	50.8	44.4	50.1	64.8	55.7
1986	60.7	60.2	57.8	60.4	50.8	51.3	44.2	50.3	65.2	55.7
1987	61.5	61.2	58.0	60.1	50.5	51.5	43.8	49.8	65.0	56.6
1988	62.3	62.2	58.9	60.4	50.5	51.6	43.7	50.7	65.7	58.3
1989	63.0	62.7	60.3	60.8	50.8	52.0	43.6	51.4	66.2	59.6
1990	62.8	62.2	60.4	61.3	50.9	52.6	43.9	52.7	66.1	59.8
1991	61.7	60.2	58.2	61.8	50.7	55.5	44.5	53.6	64.9	58.1
1992	61.5	58.9	57.2	62.0	50.1	54.2	44.0	54.3	62.0	56.6
1993	61.7	58.5	56.8	61.7	49.2	53.2	43.6	53.9	58.5	56.1
1994	62.5	59.0	57.8	61.3	49.0	52.6	42.5	54.0	57.5	56.4
1995	62.9	59.3	59.2	60.9	49.2	52.4	42.0	55.4	58.2	57.0
1996	63.2	59.1	59.3	60.9	49.1	52.0	42.0	56.2	57.6	57.3
1997	63.8	59.6	59.0	61.0	49.1	51.6	41.9	57.7	56.9	58.1
1998	64.1	60.4	59.3	60.2	49.7	52.3	42.2	59.1	57.6	58.5
1999	64.3	61.3	59.6	59.4	50.4	52.1	42.6	60.3	58.3	59.0
2000	64.4	62.0	60.3	59.0	51.4	52.2	43.2	61.5	60.1	59.4
2001	63.7	61.9	60.0	58.4	51.9	52.2	43.8	62.6	60.5	59.5
2002	62.7	62.4	60.2	57.5	51.8	51.5	44.3	62.9	60.6	59.6
2003	62.3	63.1	60.8	57.1	51.5	50.8	44.9	62.2	60.2	59.8
2004	62.3	63.3	61.1	57.1	51.1	50.6	45.1	61.8	59.5	60.0
2005	62.7	63.4	62.1	57.3	51.1	51.2	44.9	61.6	59.9	60.0
2006	63.1	63.6	62.6	57.5	51.2	52.2	45.5	62.5	60.4	60.1
2007	63.0	64.2	63.3	57.6	51.6	53.3	45.6	63.7	61.3	60.0
2008	62.2	64.2	63.8	57.4	52.1	54.2	45.6	64.5	61.1	59.9
Men										
1970	76.2	73.4	83.2	80.5	76.3	78.4	71.9	. . .	77.4	. . .
1971	74.9	72.7	82.7	80.9	75.3	77.1	71.6	. . .	76.2	80.1
1972	75.0	73.0	82.0	80.6	74.4	75.8	69.9	. . .	75.4	79.5
1973	75.5	74.3	81.8	80.8	74.3	75.3	69.3	77.3	75.1	79.9
1974	74.9	74.9	81.1	80.5	74.0	73.5	69.4	77.1	75.6	79.0
1975	71.7	73.5	79.1	79.5	72.3	70.9	68.8	76.9	76.0	77.9
1976	72.0	74.2	78.3	79.2	71.9	70.3	68.5	75.9	75.6	76.7
1977	72.8	73.3	77.3	78.7	71.4	69.9	67.5	75.7	74.5	75.9
1978	73.8	73.4	75.5	78.2	70.6	69.7	66.8	75.0	73.5	75.3
1979	73.8	74.3	75.3	78.2	69.8	69.8	66.3	74.3	73.7	75.0
1980	72.0	74.0	75.1	77.9	69.1	69.6	66.0	74.1	73.6	73.3
1981	71.3	73.9	75.1	77.8	67.6	68.5	65.6	72.2	72.0	70.1
1982	69.0	69.3	73.4	77.4	66.5	67.0	64.4	69.5	71.3	68.0
1983	68.8	68.3	70.1	77.1	65.3	65.8	63.5	67.4	70.4	66.7
1984	70.7	68.9	70.5	76.4	63.7	65.7	62.9	66.6	70.2	67.2
1985	70.9	69.4	70.6	75.9	62.5	65.8	62.5	67.6	70.5	67.1
1986	71.0	70.3	70.8	75.4	62.0	66.4	61.8	66.7	70.6	66.6
1987	71.5	71.0	70.3	74.9	61.4	66.2	60.9	64.8	69.7	67.2
1988	72.0	71.6	71.0	75.0	61.2	66.0	60.4	65.0	70.3	69.0
1989	72.5	71.8	72.1	75.0	61.4	65.9	59.9	65.7	70.9	70.2
1990	72.0	70.6	71.4	75.4	61.4	65.6	60.0	66.5	70.6	70.0
1991	70.4	67.6	68.2	75.8	60.7	67.9	60.6	66.8	69.2	67.3
1992	69.8	65.7	66.6	76.1	59.5	66.3	59.8	67.2	65.7	64.8
1993	70.0	65.3	66.0	75.9	57.8	64.7	58.8	65.5	61.6	63.7
1994	70.4	65.9	67.2	75.4	57.3	63.8	57.2	65.2	60.9	64.2
1995	70.8	66.1	68.2	75.0	57.4	63.1	56.2	66.7	62.0	64.7
1996	70.9	65.8	68.1	74.9	57.0	62.1	55.8	67.5	61.5	64.9
1997	71.3	66.4	67.7	74.9	56.8	61.3	55.5	68.5	61.0	65.9
1998	71.6	66.8	67.9	73.9	57.4	61.9	55.4	69.8	62.1	66.2
1999	71.6	67.6	68.2	73.0	58.1	60.7	55.5	70.4	62.5	66.6
2000	71.9	68.2	68.4	72.5	59.1	60.6	55.8	71.4	64.2	66.9
2001	70.9	67.7	67.6	71.5	59.6	60.2	56.0	72.0	64.4	66.9
2002	69.7	67.9	67.8	70.4	59.2	58.9	56.3	71.9	64.3	66.7
2003	68.9	68.3	68.1	69.9	58.3	57.5	56.9	70.6	63.7	66.9
2004	69.2	68.5	68.8	69.6	57.7	57.3	56.9	70.0	63.0	66.9
2005	69.6	68.6	69.4	69.7	57.5	57.9	56.8	69.2	63.8	66.8
2006	70.1	68.6	69.8	69.8	57.5	58.8	57.3	70.0	64.5	66.7
2007	69.8	68.8	70.3	70.0	57.7	59.9	57.3	70.9	65.5	66.7
2008	68.5	68.8	70.6	69.6	58.1	60.8	56.9	71.3	65.2	66.4

[1]Unified Germany from 1991 onward; data for previous years relate to the former West Germany.
. . . = Not available.

Table 10-4. Employment-Population Ratios by Sex, Adjusted to U.S. Concepts, 10 Countries, 1970–2008
—*Continued*

(Ratio.)

Sex and year	United States	Canada	Australia	Japan	France	Germany[1]	Italy	Netherlands	Sweden	United Kingdom
Women										
1970	40.8	36.1	39.3	48.2	38.1	38.1	25.0	. . .	49.1	. . .
1971	40.4	36.8	39.7	47.2	38.4	38.2	24.9	. . .	49.5	42.3
1972	41.0	37.4	39.6	46.2	38.7	38.6	24.1	. . .	50.0	42.6
1973	42.0	39.1	40.9	46.8	39.2	39.1	24.5	27.3	50.3	43.6
1974	42.6	40.2	41.7	45.1	39.4	38.7	25.1	27.1	52.0	44.2
1975	42.0	40.8	41.4	44.0	39.2	37.9	25.3	27.1	54.1	44.2
1976	43.2	42.6	41.5	44.1	39.7	37.8	25.8	27.3	54.7	44.0
1977	44.5	42.9	41.5	44.9	40.1	37.7	26.9	28.2	55.5	44.0
1978	46.4	44.0	41.0	45.5	40.4	37.9	26.9	28.4	56.1	44.4
1979	47.5	45.7	40.7	45.7	40.5	38.4	27.3	29.2	57.2	45.0
1980	47.7	46.9	41.9	45.7	40.4	38.9	27.9	31.0	58.0	45.1
1981	48.0	48.2	42.1	45.7	40.3	38.7	28.0	31.9	58.5	44.3
1982	47.7	47.0	41.5	45.9	40.6	38.1	27.7	32.8	58.4	43.5
1983	48.0	47.3	40.8	46.7	40.7	37.3	27.6	31.9	58.6	43.3
1984	49.5	48.2	41.8	46.5	40.6	37.3	27.6	32.7	59.1	44.4
1985	50.4	49.4	43.0	46.3	40.5	37.6	27.8	33.4	59.7	45.2
1986	51.4	50.5	45.1	46.2	40.7	38.0	28.1	34.7	60.1	45.8
1987	52.5	51.6	45.8	46.2	40.8	38.5	28.3	35.4	60.5	46.9
1988	53.4	53.0	47.0	46.6	40.9	39.0	28.3	37.0	61.2	48.5
1989	54.3	53.9	48.8	47.4	41.3	39.7	28.6	37.7	61.7	49.9
1990	54.3	54.1	49.5	48.0	41.5	40.9	29.2	39.4	61.8	50.3
1991	53.7	53.2	48.4	48.6	41.7	44.3	29.7	40.9	60.6	49.6
1992	53.8	52.4	48.0	48.7	41.7	43.4	29.7	41.9	58.4	49.1
1993	54.1	51.9	47.7	48.3	41.5	42.7	29.7	42.8	55.5	49.0
1994	55.3	52.4	48.8	48.0	41.6	42.3	29.2	43.3	54.3	49.3
1995	55.6	52.7	50.5	47.7	41.9	42.7	29.1	44.4	54.7	49.8
1996	56.0	52.6	50.6	47.7	42.0	42.8	29.4	45.3	53.9	50.3
1997	56.8	53.2	50.5	47.9	42.2	42.7	29.6	47.3	53.0	51.0
1998	57.1	54.3	51.0	47.4	42.8	43.5	30.1	48.7	53.3	51.4
1999	57.4	55.2	51.3	46.6	43.5	44.1	30.8	50.5	54.2	52.0
2000	57.5	56.0	52.5	46.4	44.4	44.4	31.6	52.0	56.1	52.5
2001	57.0	56.2	52.6	46.2	44.9	44.8	32.7	53.4	56.7	52.7
2002	56.3	57.1	52.9	45.4	45.2	44.7	33.3	54.3	57.1	53.0
2003	56.1	58.0	53.6	45.3	45.2	44.5	34.0	54.1	56.8	53.1
2004	56.0	58.3	53.7	45.5	45.2	44.3	34.2	54.0	56.1	53.4
2005	56.2	58.3	55.0	45.7	45.2	44.9	34.1	54.3	56.0	53.7
2006	56.6	58.9	55.7	46.0	45.6	46.0	34.7	55.2	56.4	53.8
2007	56.6	59.7	56.4	46.1	46.1	47.1	34.9	56.8	57.4	53.6
2008	56.2	59.8	57.1	46.0	46.7	48.0	35.3	57.8	57.1	53.8

[1]Unified Germany from 1991 onward; data for previous years relate to the former West Germany.
. . . = Not available.

Table 10-5. Women's Share of the Labor Force, Adjusted to U.S. Concepts, 10 Countries, 1970–2008

(Percent.)

Year	United States	Canada	Australia	Japan	France	Germany[1]	Italy	Netherlands	Sweden	United Kingdom
1970	38.1	33.6	32.8	38.9	36.6	36.5	28.2	. . .	39.6	. . .
1971	38.2	34.4	33.2	38.4	37.0	36.8	28.3	. . .	40.3	37.4
1972	38.5	34.9	33.4	37.9	37.4	37.3	28.1	. . .	40.8	37.6
1973	38.9	35.6	34.1	38.2	37.7	37.7	28.7	27.1	41.1	38.2
1974	39.4	36.1	34.8	37.4	38.0	38.0	29.1	27.2	41.9	38.7
1975	40.0	36.9	35.5	37.0	38.2	38.5	29.4	27.5	42.7	38.8
1976	40.5	37.4	35.6	37.1	38.8	38.8	30.2	28.0	43.1	38.9
1977	41.0	37.9	36.1	37.7	39.3	39.0	31.4	28.6	43.8	39.2
1978	41.7	38.6	36.3	38.1	39.8	39.2	31.5	29.2	44.4	39.6
1979	42.1	39.2	36.4	38.3	40.2	39.3	32.2	30.1	44.8	40.1
1980	42.5	39.8	37.1	38.4	40.6	39.5	32.7	31.5	45.3	40.4
1981	43.0	40.5	37.2	38.4	41.1	39.7	33.0	33.0	46.1	40.6
1982	43.3	40.9	37.3	38.7	41.6	39.8	33.2	34.1	46.4	40.7
1983	43.5	41.4	37.5	39.2	42.0	39.8	33.5	34.0	46.7	41.1
1984	43.8	41.9	38.0	39.3	42.6	39.9	33.7	34.8	47.0	41.8
1985	44.2	42.4	38.6	39.4	42.9	40.1	34.0	34.9	47.2	42.2
1986	44.5	42.7	39.6	39.5	43.2	40.2	34.9	36.7	47.3	42.7
1987	44.8	43.1	40.0	39.6	43.7	40.3	35.3	37.9	47.7	43.0
1988	45.0	43.6	40.5	39.8	43.9	40.7	35.6	38.7	47.8	43.2
1989	45.2	43.9	41.1	40.1	44.0	41.0	35.9	38.7	47.8	43.5
1990	45.2	44.2	41.6	40.3	44.1	41.5	36.2	39.5	47.8	43.7
1991	45.3	44.6	41.8	40.5	44.4	42.8	36.3	40.0	47.7	43.8
1992	45.4	44.7	41.9	40.5	44.9	42.8	36.7	40.2	47.7	44.0
1993	45.5	44.9	42.0	40.3	45.3	42.8	37.4	41.1	47.7	44.3
1994	46.0	44.9	42.4	40.4	45.6	42.9	37.6	41.3	47.6	44.5
1995	46.1	45.1	42.9	40.3	45.8	43.1	38.0	41.5	47.6	44.7
1996	46.2	45.1	43.0	40.4	45.9	43.3	38.4	41.8	47.7	44.9
1997	46.2	45.3	43.1	40.5	46.0	43.4	38.6	42.3	47.5	45.1
1998	46.3	45.5	43.3	40.5	46.1	43.5	39.1	42.4	47.2	45.3
1999	46.5	45.7	43.5	40.4	46.2	44.0	39.5	43.0	47.4	45.4
2000	46.5	45.9	44.0	40.5	46.2	44.3	39.8	43.3	47.5	45.6
2001	46.5	46.0	44.3	40.7	46.2	44.4	40.3	43.6	47.7	45.6
2002	46.5	46.2	44.4	40.7	46.2	44.7	40.5	44.0	47.8	45.7
2003	46.6	46.5	44.8	40.8	46.6	45.0	40.7	44.3	47.8	45.7
2004	46.4	46.6	44.6	41.1	46.8	45.1	40.7	44.5	47.8	45.8
2005	46.4	46.6	45.0	41.2	46.9	45.1	40.5	45.0	47.5	45.9
2006	46.3	46.9	45.2	41.3	47.1	45.4	40.6	45.2	47.5	46.0
2007	46.4	47.0	45.3	41.3	47.1	45.6	40.6	45.6	47.5	45.8
2008	46.5	47.0	45.4	41.4	47.2	45.7	41.1	45.8	47.4	45.8

[1]Unified Germany from 1991 onward; data for previous years relate to the former West Germany.
. . . = Not available.

Table 10-6. Percent of Employment in Agriculture, Adjusted to U.S. Concepts, 10 Countries, 1970–2008

(Percent.)

Year	United States	Canada	Australia	Japan	France	Germany[1]	Italy	Netherlands	Sweden	United Kingdom[2]
1970	4.5	7.6	8.1	16.9	13.5	8.5	20.1	. . .	8.2	. . .
1971	4.4	7.5	7.7	15.5	12.9	8.0	20.1	. . .	7.8	3.2
1972	4.4	6.9	7.9	14.4	12.1	7.6	19.0	. . .	7.5	3.0
1973	4.2	6.5	7.4	13.1	11.3	7.2	18.2	6.1	7.2	3.0
1974	4.2	6.3	7.0	12.6	10.8	6.9	17.4	6.0	6.7	2.8
1975	4.1	6.1	6.9	12.4	10.4	6.7	16.7	5.9	6.5	2.8
1976	3.9	5.7	6.6	11.9	9.9	6.2	16.4	5.7	6.2	2.8
1977	3.7	5.5	6.7	11.6	9.5	5.9	15.8	5.6	6.1	2.8
1978	3.7	5.2	6.4	11.4	9.2	5.7	15.4	5.6	6.1	2.8
1979	3.5	5.2	6.5	10.8	8.9	5.3	14.9	5.4	5.8	2.7
1980	3.6	5.0	6.5	10.1	8.6	5.2	14.2	5.2	5.6	2.6
1981	3.5	4.9	6.5	9.7	8.3	5.0	13.3	5.2	5.6	2.7
1982	3.6	5.0	6.5	9.4	8.0	4.9	12.4	5.3	5.6	2.7
1983	3.5	5.1	6.6	8.9	7.7	4.8	12.3	5.3	5.5	2.7
1984	3.3	4.9	6.2	8.5	7.5	4.7	11.7	5.2	5.2	2.6
1985	3.1	5.6	6.1	8.4	7.3	4.5	11.0	5.1	4.9	2.3
1986	3.1	4.7	6.1	8.1	7.0	4.3	10.7	5.0	4.7	2.2
1987	3.0	4.5	5.8	8.0	6.7	4.1	10.4	4.9	4.5	2.3
1988	2.9	4.4	5.8	7.6	6.4	3.9	9.8	4.7	4.4	2.3
1989	2.9	4.2	5.5	7.3	6.0	3.7	9.3	4.7	4.3	2.2
1990	2.9	4.2	5.6	6.9	5.7	3.5	8.9	4.6	3.9	2.1
1991	2.9	4.3	5.5	6.4	5.4	4.1	8.5	4.5	3.8	2.3
1992	2.9	4.2	5.3	6.1	5.2	3.8	8.2	4.0	3.8	2.2
1993	2.7	4.3	5.3	5.7	5.0	3.5	7.1	3.9	3.9	2.0
1994	2.9	4.2	5.1	5.6	4.8	3.3	6.9	4.0	3.9	2.1
1995	2.9	4.0	4.9	5.5	4.6	3.1	6.6	3.8	3.5	2.1
1996	2.8	4.0	5.0	5.3	4.5	3.0	6.2	3.9	3.3	1.9
1997	2.7	3.8	5.1	5.1	4.4	2.9	6.2	3.8	3.1	1.8
1998	2.7	3.8	4.9	5.0	4.3	2.8	5.9	3.3	2.9	1.7
1999	2.6	3.5	4.9	4.9	4.1	2.8	5.5	3.2	3.1	1.6
2000	1.8	3.3	4.9	4.8	3.9	2.6	5.3	3.2	2.9	1.5
2001	1.7	2.8	4.8	4.7	3.7	2.6	5.3	3.0	2.6	1.4
2002	1.7	2.8	4.4	4.5	3.6	2.5	5.0	3.0	2.5	1.3
2003	1.7	2.8	3.9	4.4	3.6	2.5	4.9	3.0	2.5	1.3
2004	1.6	2.6	3.7	4.3	3.6	2.4	4.5	3.1	2.5	1.3
2005	1.6	2.7	3.6	4.2	3.5	2.4	4.2	3.3	2.3	1.4
2006	1.5	2.6	3.4	4.1	3.4	2.3	4.3	3.3	2.2	1.4
2007	1.4	2.5	3.3	4.1	3.3	2.3	4.0	3.1	2.2	1.4
2008	1.5	2.3	3.3	4.0	. . .	2.3	3.9	2.8	2.2	1.5

Note: Agriculture includes agriculture, forestry, hunting, and fishing.

[1]Unified Germany from 1991 onward; data for previous years relate to the former West Germany.
[2]Sectoral employment is only partially adjusted to U.S. concepts prior to 1984.
. . . = Not available.

Table 10-7. Percent of Employment in Industry, Adjusted to U.S. Concepts, 10 Countries, 1970–2008

(Percent.)

Year	United States	Canada	Australia	Japan	France	Germany[1]	Italy	Netherlands	Sweden	United Kingdom[2]
1970	33.1	29.8	34.6	35.7	38.4	48.7	38.8	. . .	37.9	. . .
1971	31.7	29.4	34.3	35.9	38.5	47.7	39.0	. . .	37.1	42.0
1972	31.4	29.2	33.5	36.2	38.5	47.0	38.8	. . .	36.3	41.2
1973	32.0	29.5	33.4	37.0	38.7	46.8	38.4	35.1	36.3	40.9
1974	31.4	29.5	33.0	36.8	38.6	45.9	38.4	34.3	36.3	40.6
1975	29.5	28.1	31.5	35.6	37.8	44.5	38.3	33.2	35.8	39.0
1976	29.6	27.8	31.0	35.6	37.1	44.1	37.5	32.3	34.8	38.1
1977	29.7	27.4	30.4	35.1	36.6	43.8	37.6	32.1	33.7	38.0
1978	30.0	27.3	29.3	34.8	35.9	43.5	37.4	31.8	32.4	37.7
1979	30.2	27.5	29.0	34.7	35.2	43.3	37.0	31.0	31.9	37.3
1980	29.3	27.1	28.6	35.1	34.9	42.9	37.0	29.7	31.5	36.2
1981	28.9	26.8	28.3	35.1	34.0	42.2	36.5	28.4	30.6	34.3
1982	27.2	24.8	27.4	34.5	33.6	41.3	36.1	27.5	29.5	33.1
1983	26.8	24.1	25.9	34.4	32.8	40.6	35.1	27.3	29.1	32.0
1984	27.3	24.2	25.5	34.5	31.9	40.3	33.4	27.3	29.0	34.2
1985	26.9	24.0	24.8	34.6	31.0	40.1	32.6	26.6	29.0	33.8
1986	26.6	24.1	24.1	34.2	30.4	39.9	32.0	26.1	29.1	33.1
1987	26.0	24.1	23.9	33.5	29.8	39.5	31.5	26.3	28.7	31.9
1988	25.8	24.3	23.8	33.9	29.4	39.0	31.5	25.7	28.3	31.9
1989	25.6	24.3	24.2	34.1	29.2	38.9	31.5	25.9	28.4	31.8
1990	25.1	23.6	23.2	33.9	28.7	38.9	31.4	25.9	28.2	31.2
1991	24.2	22.0	22.0	34.2	28.3	39.8	31.4	25.1	27.2	31.4
1992	23.5	21.3	21.7	34.3	27.5	38.9	31.3	24.3	25.6	29.1
1993	23.0	20.7	21.8	33.9	26.4	37.8	33.3	24.0	24.5	28.4
1994	23.0	20.9	21.8	33.7	25.6	36.6	33.2	22.9	24.0	26.8
1995	23.0	21.2	21.4	33.1	25.4	35.3	33.0	22.8	25.0	26.6
1996	22.9	21.1	21.1	32.9	24.9	34.4	32.7	22.3	25.2	26.5
1997	23.0	21.4	20.8	32.8	24.4	33.9	32.4	22.3	25.0	26.2
1998	22.7	21.5	20.6	31.7	23.9	33.6	32.3	21.7	24.9	25.8
1999	22.2	21.7	20.2	31.3	23.5	33.2	32.1	21.6	24.3	25.1
2000	22.0	21.9	20.6	30.9	23.2	32.8	31.6	21.2	23.7	24.3
2001	21.3	21.7	19.8	30.1	23.1	32.3	31.4	21.1	23.2	23.9
2002	20.3	21.8	20.0	29.0	22.8	31.7	31.3	20.2	22.5	23.3
2003	20.0	21.5	19.9	28.5	22.5	31.0	31.4	19.6	22.0	22.5
2004	20.0	21.6	20.3	27.6	22.0	30.7	30.3	20.0	21.9	21.9
2005	19.8	21.3	20.1	27.1	21.7	29.1	30.4	20.0	21.4	21.6
2006	19.9	20.9	20.2	27.1	22.0	29.0	29.8	19.7	21.4	21.5
2007	19.8	20.5	20.2	27.0	21.8	29.1	29.9	19.6	21.1	21.5
2008	19.1	20.3	20.5	26.5	. . .	29.0	29.4	18.9	21.1	20.8

Note: Industry includes manufacturing, mining, and construction.

[1]Unified Germany from 1991 onward; data for previous years relate to the former West Germany.
[2]Sectoral employment is only partially adjusted to U.S. concepts prior to 1984.
. . . = Not available.

Table 10-8. Percent of Employment in Manufacturing, Adjusted to U.S. Concepts, 10 Countries, 1970–2008

(Percent.)

Year	United States	Canada	Australia	Japan	France	Germany[1]	Italy	Netherlands	Sweden	United Kingdom[2]
1970	26.4	22.3	24.4	27.4	27.5	39.5	27.7	. . .	27.7	. . .
1971	24.7	21.8	24.1	27.4	27.8	37.4	28.0	. . .	27.4	33.9
1972	24.3	21.8	23.5	27.3	28.0	36.9	27.9	. . .	27.2	32.9
1973	24.8	22.0	23.3	27.8	28.2	36.7	27.9	25.3	27.6	32.3
1974	24.2	21.7	22.9	27.6	28.3	36.5	28.1	25.1	28.4	32.4
1975	22.7	20.2	21.3	26.1	27.8	35.7	28.0	24.5	28.1	31.0
1976	22.8	19.2	21.2	25.8	27.3	35.2	27.7	23.6	27.0	30.2
1977	22.7	18.8	20.9	25.3	26.9	35.1	27.6	23.2	26.0	30.4
1978	22.7	18.9	19.9	24.8	26.4	34.8	27.3	22.7	25.0	30.1
1979	22.7	19.2	19.6	24.6	26.0	34.5	26.9	22.0	24.7	29.5
1980	22.1	19.1	19.4	25.0	25.6	34.0	26.9	21.3	24.3	28.3
1981	21.7	18.5	19.2	25.1	24.9	33.4	26.3	20.8	23.4	26.5
1982	20.4	17.2	18.6	24.7	24.7	32.8	25.8	20.1	22.5	25.5
1983	19.8	16.8	17.8	24.8	24.3	32.2	25.0	19.6	22.4	24.3
1984	20.0	17.1	17.3	25.2	23.8	32.1	23.9	19.6	22.5	25.1
1985	19.5	16.7	16.1	25.3	23.2	32.3	23.2	19.5	22.6	25.0
1986	19.1	16.9	15.5	24.9	22.7	32.3	22.9	19.4	22.8	24.8
1987	18.6	16.7	15.4	24.4	22.1	32.0	22.5	19.5	22.0	23.4
1988	18.5	16.6	15.3	24.5	21.6	31.6	22.6	18.8	21.7	23.6
1989	18.5	16.5	15.1	24.5	21.4	31.6	22.8	19.1	21.7	22.8
1990	18.0	15.8	14.4	24.3	21.0	31.6	22.6	19.1	21.0	22.4
1991	17.5	14.8	13.7	24.6	20.7	30.7	22.1	18.3	19.9	22.9
1992	17.0	14.3	13.7	24.6	20.1	29.5	22.0	18.1	18.9	21.4
1993	16.4	14.0	13.5	23.9	19.5	28.1	24.6	17.7	18.3	21.2
1994	16.4	14.0	13.5	23.4	18.9	26.6	24.7	16.7	18.2	19.1
1995	16.4	14.4	13.0	22.7	18.7	25.2	24.9	16.4	19.0	19.1
1996	16.2	14.4	12.8	22.5	18.5	24.3	24.6	15.9	19.3	19.2
1997	16.1	14.7	12.9	22.2	18.2	24.0	24.2	15.7	19.3	18.8
1998	15.8	15.0	12.3	21.4	17.9	24.1	24.3	15.2	19.1	18.4
1999	15.0	15.3	11.8	21.0	17.5	23.8	24.1	15.1	18.5	17.7
2000	14.4	15.3	12.0	20.7	17.3	23.9	23.6	14.8	18.0	16.9
2001	13.5	15.0	11.6	20.2	17.1	23.7	23.1	14.5	17.5	16.2
2002	12.6	15.0	11.5	19.1	16.7	23.6	23.0	13.8	16.7	15.7
2003	12.3	14.6	11.0	18.8	16.3	23.3	22.9	13.5	16.2	14.5
2004	11.8	14.4	10.9	18.3	15.9	23.1	21.9	13.7	16.0	13.7
2005	11.5	13.7	10.4	18.1	15.4	22.2	21.6	13.7	15.3	13.2
2006	11.3	12.9	10.0	18.3	15.0	22.0	21.2	13.3	15.0	12.9
2007	11.2	12.2	9.9	18.3	14.8	22.2	21.2	13.2	14.6	12.8
2008	10.9	11.6	9.8	18.0	. . .	22.1	20.8	12.4	14.3	12.0

[1]Unified Germany from 1991 onward; data for previous years relate to the former West Germany.
[2]Sectoral employment is only partially adjusted to U.S. concepts prior to 1984.
. . . = Not available.

Table 10-9. Indexes of Manufacturing Productivity and Related Measures, 16 Countries, 1950–2008

(2002 = 100.)

Category and year	United States	Canada	Australia	Japan	Korea, Republic of	Taiwan	Belgium	Denmark	France	Germany[1]	Italy	Netherlands	Norway	Spain	Sweden	United Kingdom
Output																
1950	18.3	13.6	...	2.2	...	...	...	22.9	17.2	13.8	7.7	14.1	35.3	...	15.9	44.7
1951	20.3	14.8	...	3.2	...	...	...	23.1	19.1	15.9	8.8	14.7	38.1	...	17.0	46.0
1952	21.0	15.4	...	3.4	...	...	...	22.0	18.4	18.0	9.2	14.7	37.2	...	16.5	43.7
1953	22.5	16.5	...	4.2	...	...	...	22.8	18.2	20.0	9.9	16.3	39.2	...	16.9	46.9
1954	20.9	16.1	...	4.6	...	...	...	24.7	19.7	22.4	10.9	17.8	41.7	...	17.6	49.3
1955	23.1	17.7	...	5.0	...	...	...	25.2	20.5	26.2	11.9	19.4	43.2	...	18.4	52.5
1956	23.0	19.3	...	6.2	...	...	...	25.5	22.0	28.3	12.8	20.9	45.7	...	19.4	52.4
1957	23.3	19.3	...	7.4	...	...	...	27.1	23.3	30.3	13.7	21.8	46.4	...	20.4	53.6
1958	21.4	18.9	...	7.2	...	...	...	28.2	23.6	31.9	14.0	21.8	45.8	...	20.8	53.1
1959	23.9	20.3	...	8.8	...	...	...	31.6	23.6	34.9	15.5	24.0	48.1	...	22.0	56.2
1960	23.9	20.7	...	11.0	...	...	26.5	34.9	25.4	39.6	17.5	26.7	52.2	...	23.7	60.7
1961	24.0	21.5	...	13.2	...	...	27.7	36.8	27.0	42.0	19.3	27.6	54.4	...	25.3	60.8
1962	26.2	24.2	...	14.3	...	...	29.8	40.0	29.1	44.0	21.4	29.0	54.8	...	27.2	61.0
1963	28.4	25.9	...	16.0	...	...	31.2	40.5	32.4	44.9	22.8	30.2	58.1	...	28.6	63.2
1964	30.4	28.3	...	18.6	...	...	34.1	45.2	34.4	48.8	23.1	33.1	62.3	22.4	31.1	68.9
1965	33.4	30.9	...	19.3	...	...	35.2	48.2	36.5	52.5	24.3	35.4	65.5	25.0	33.3	70.8
1966	36.3	32.9	...	21.8	...	...	37.2	49.2	39.4	53.3	26.5	37.3	69.4	27.4	34.2	72.1
1967	36.0	33.4	...	26.2	...	...	37.7	50.8	41.5	52.1	29.1	38.8	71.7	28.8	35.3	72.5
1968	38.0	35.5	...	30.2	...	...	40.3	55.6	43.8	57.5	31.9	42.5	73.4	31.1	37.1	78.1
1969	39.0	37.8	...	35.2	...	...	45.1	59.5	47.7	64.3	33.9	46.6	78.8	35.3	40.1	81.0
1970	36.8	36.9	...	40.1	3.0	8.6	49.7	62.0	51.4	67.6	36.6	48.2	82.4	37.9	41.6	81.3
1971	37.8	38.9	...	42.0	3.5	10.6	51.9	63.4	54.2	68.3	36.9	49.3	84.6	40.1	41.9	80.5
1972	41.2	42.2	...	45.8	4.1	12.9	55.8	67.1	55.1	70.4	39.4	51.4	88.6	45.9	42.1	82.1
1973	45.4	46.0	...	51.6	5.4	15.2	60.9	69.2	58.6	74.8	44.7	54.6	93.6	50.5	45.1	89.7
1974	43.4	47.7	...	50.3	6.3	14.4	63.3	69.6	61.4	74.1	48.8	57.3	96.8	53.3	47.6	88.6
1975	40.4	44.6	62.9	47.7	7.1	15.0	58.6	68.1	59.0	70.7	47.7	54.0	94.9	52.6	47.7	82.5
1976	44.7	48.3	64.6	51.8	8.9	18.5	63.0	69.9	62.8	76.1	55.1	57.2	94.4	54.4	47.7	84.0
1977	48.2	50.0	64.2	53.5	10.2	21.0	62.3	70.8	66.1	77.5	57.9	57.0	94.3	57.2	45.0	85.7
1978	50.6	53.7	65.2	55.0	12.4	25.5	64.1	70.5	67.3	79.0	60.3	58.1	92.5	58.5	43.8	86.2
1979	52.4	56.0	68.6	59.8	13.6	27.5	65.8	74.5	68.9	83.1	66.4	59.5	96.2	58.7	46.6	86.0
1980	49.6	55.2	70.3	61.9	13.4	30.2	67.5	77.3	69.5	81.3	71.1	59.3	95.1	58.8	46.8	78.5
1981	52.0	56.6	72.2	64.1	14.8	32.4	66.6	74.8	69.7	80.4	69.9	58.7	93.1	57.4	45.3	73.8
1982	48.2	50.3	70.4	65.8	15.8	33.1	69.4	76.9	70.6	77.7	68.9	58.0	92.7	57.0	45.4	73.7
1983	52.0	52.6	66.0	67.0	18.3	37.3	72.9	82.6	72.3	78.9	68.8	59.7	91.2	58.4	48.3	75.2
1984	56.7	59.6	69.7	70.5	21.4	42.7	75.2	85.9	72.4	81.2	71.1	63.6	95.7	58.5	52.1	77.9
1985	58.3	62.1	72.3	77.6	22.8	44.0	76.9	88.6	73.6	84.2	73.6	65.4	99.2	59.5	53.0	80.2
1986	58.2	62.3	72.2	77.3	27.4	51.4	76.9	90.2	73.5	85.5	75.4	67.8	98.8	61.0	53.5	81.3
1987	62.6	65.1	75.9	80.1	32.7	58.1	76.6	86.3	73.4	83.9	78.0	69.2	100.9	65.6	54.7	85.1
1988	66.2	69.4	81.4	86.5	36.6	59.7	80.5	84.7	76.6	86.6	83.4	71.1	96.2	68.7	56.3	91.4
1989	67.0	71.0	82.9	92.0	37.8	61.4	85.5	87.3	79.6	89.6	87.1	74.4	92.5	71.8	56.7	95.0
1990	66.2	68.7	81.5	98.9	41.3	60.5	87.2	85.5	81.5	94.5	88.2	77.0	91.4	73.7	56.1	94.9
1991	65.3	63.8	78.8	104.3	45.0	64.1	86.8	84.3	81.6	98.0	87.9	77.6	89.4	75.1	52.8	90.1
1992	67.5	64.4	78.2	102.3	46.9	66.5	86.3	84.1	80.7	95.8	87.7	78.3	89.9	74.9	50.6	90.0
1993	70.3	67.9	81.2	98.8	49.3	67.1	83.7	81.5	78.3	88.1	85.6	77.8	91.7	72.0	51.7	91.4
1994	75.7	73.1	85.4	97.5	54.9	71.1	87.5	90.3	80.9	90.9	91.4	82.0	94.1	73.2	59.7	95.6
1995	79.1	76.5	84.9	101.7	61.3	75.0	89.9	94.7	83.8	90.1	95.7	85.1	94.6	76.0	67.5	97.1
1996	82.1	77.5	87.6	105.6	65.3	78.9	90.2	90.3	83.6	88.2	95.2	86.3	98.4	77.9	69.7	97.9
1997	87.1	82.3	89.6	108.2	68.4	83.5	94.5	97.7	87.5	92.0	96.6	87.5	102.7	82.9	75.1	99.6
1998	92.9	86.5	92.1	102.5	63.0	86.1	96.1	98.5	91.7	93.1	97.5	90.5	101.9	87.9	81.3	100.3
1999	96.9	93.7	91.9	102.1	76.8	92.4	96.4	99.4	94.8	94.0	97.3	93.8	101.8	92.9	89.0	101.3
2000	103.0	103.2	96.3	107.4	89.8	99.2	100.7	102.9	99.1	100.4	101.4	100.1	101.3	97.0	96.3	103.6
2001	97.3	99.2	95.4	101.6	92.0	91.8	100.8	103.0	100.1	102.1	101.1	99.9	100.5	100.1	94.1	102.2
2002	100.0	100.0	100.0	100.0	100.0	100.0	100.0	100.0	100.0	100.0	100.0	100.0	100.0	100.0	100.0	100.0
2003	101.1	99.4	101.7	105.3	105.4	105.3	98.6	97.2	101.9	100.7	97.3	98.9	103.3	101.2	104.9	99.7
2004	106.8	101.4	101.8	111.4	115.9	115.6	102.2	98.8	102.8	104.3	98.0	102.3	109.2	101.9	114.5	101.9
2005	107.7	103.0	101.4	117.2	123.1	123.6	102.0	99.3	105.2	107.8	97.8	104.3	114.1	103.1	119.8	101.7
2006	113.6	102.6	100.5	121.3	133.0	132.5	104.9	103.4	104.9	115.6	101.1	107.9	117.5	105.0	129.2	103.4
2007	116.9	101.6	103.7	125.7	142.5	146.3	107.6	107.2	105.7	122.7	103.1	111.3	123.6	106.0	132.2	104.0
2008	113.7	95.9	105.4	121.4	146.9	144.7	107.1	105.2	103.2	123.5	98.4	110.6	127.3	103.8	127.6	101.0

[1]Unified Germany from 1991 onward; data for previous years relate to the former West Germany.
. . . = Not available.

Table 10-9. Indexes of Manufacturing Productivity and Related Measures, 16 Countries, 1950–2008
—Continued

(2002 = 100.)

Category and year	United States	Canada	Australia	Japan	Korea, Republic of	Taiwan	Belgium	Denmark	France	Germany¹	Italy	Nether- lands	Norway	Spain	Sweden	United Kingdom
Output Per Hour																
1950	19.5	18.7	...	3.9	...	...	...	15.4	10.4	9.9	9.2	9.0	22.5	...	11.0	20.8
1951	20.1	19.5	...	4.8	...	...	...	15.5	11.0	10.6	10.3	9.4	23.9	...	11.3	20.9
1952	20.5	20.0	...	5.1	...	...	...	15.4	10.9	11.6	10.7	9.6	23.6	...	11.3	20.1
1953	20.9	20.7	...	5.8	...	...	...	15.6	11.2	12.4	11.2	10.5	24.8	...	11.9	21.1
1954	21.3	21.6	...	6.2	...	...	...	16.3	11.9	13.1	11.8	11.0	26.0	...	11.9	21.7
1955	22.3	23.0	...	6.5	...	...	...	16.7	12.3	14.2	12.9	11.6	26.2	...	12.1	22.5
1956	21.8	24.0	...	7.2	...	...	...	17.2	13.1	14.8	13.6	12.3	28.0	...	12.8	22.5
1957	22.4	24.1	...	8.1	...	...	...	17.8	13.5	16.2	13.8	12.8	28.9	...	13.5	23.0
1958	22.5	24.9	...	7.6	...	...	...	18.5	13.8	17.2	14.1	13.1	29.3	...	14.1	23.5
1959	23.5	26.3	...	8.9	...	...	...	19.8	14.1	18.8	15.2	14.1	31.4	...	14.9	24.4
1960	23.7	27.2	...	10.5	...	...	13.7	20.4	14.8	20.6	16.1	14.9	33.7	...	15.4	25.5
1961	24.3	28.7	...	11.8	...	...	13.9	21.6	15.7	21.6	17.4	15.7	35.0	...	16.2	25.5
1962	25.5	31.1	...	12.5	...	...	14.6	22.7	16.6	23.1	19.3	16.3	34.9	...	17.4	26.1
1963	27.2	32.4	...	13.5	...	...	15.2	23.4	18.1	24.0	19.8	17.0	36.8	...	18.5	27.5
1964	28.5	33.9	...	15.3	...	...	16.2	25.3	18.7	26.2	20.0	18.5	38.8	...	20.1	29.3
1965	29.6	35.5	...	15.9	...	...	17.0	26.6	20.2	27.7	22.3	19.8	41.1	...	21.6	30.2
1966	30.2	36.3	...	17.4	...	...	18.2	27.9	21.7	28.9	24.2	21.1	42.9	...	22.5	31.2
1967	30.2	36.4	...	19.7	...	...	19.2	30.5	23.4	30.6	25.4	22.7	44.4	...	24.4	32.6
1968	31.4	38.4	...	22.1	...	...	20.9	33.9	25.5	33.2	27.4	25.5	47.1	...	26.6	35.2
1969	31.8	40.2	...	25.3	...	...	22.8	36.0	27.4	35.5	28.4	28.0	51.6	...	28.8	36.0
1970	31.9	39.9	...	28.4	...	...	25.2	38.3	29.0	36.7	30.3	29.3	53.1	...	29.5	36.7
1971	33.9	42.0	...	30.1	...	...	26.8	41.4	30.1	38.1	30.9	30.7	54.8	...	30.8	38.5
1972	35.4	44.1	...	33.0	...	...	29.9	44.1	31.1	40.5	33.4	33.5	57.6	...	32.3	40.7
1973	37.1	46.6	...	36.0	...	20.1	33.3	47.0	32.6	43.1	36.7	36.6	61.1	...	34.7	43.6
1974	36.2	48.1	...	36.9	...	19.6	35.0	48.6	34.4	44.6	40.2	39.7	63.4	...	36.2	44.3
1975	37.5	47.0	49.9	38.0	...	20.6	36.3	53.8	34.9	46.5	39.4	39.3	62.9	...	36.7	43.4
1976	39.5	51.1	53.0	40.3	...	22.5	40.0	55.1	36.3	49.8	45.4	43.2	64.3	...	37.3	45.3
1977	41.0	54.1	54.1	41.9	...	23.6	42.0	57.3	38.9	51.3	47.4	43.8	65.3	...	36.7	45.7
1978	41.4	55.8	55.4	43.6	...	26.6	44.5	58.4	40.6	53.1	49.3	45.9	66.5	...	37.7	46.3
1979	41.9	56.0	58.0	47.1	...	27.7	46.9	62.1	42.0	55.3	53.9	47.9	71.4	56.0	40.7	46.6
1980	41.6	55.2	59.0	47.9	...	29.3	49.9	66.1	42.9	54.5	56.8	48.0	70.1	57.9	41.3	46.3
1981	43.8	56.9	61.0	49.4	...	32.4	53.5	68.0	45.1	55.5	57.3	48.3	69.6	61.3	41.1	48.4
1982	44.2	57.0	63.3	51.2	...	33.1	56.1	69.8	48.5	55.5	57.4	48.9	72.5	63.6	41.9	50.9
1983	47.3	60.4	64.0	51.2	...	35.5	61.9	75.0	51.2	58.3	59.7	52.4	74.8	67.7	44.5	54.5
1984	48.5	67.0	67.6	52.3	...	36.4	64.9	75.1	53.1	60.2	64.9	57.8	79.5	71.2	47.5	57.0
1985	50.0	68.6	69.4	57.3	23.0	37.3	66.4	75.6	56.0	62.8	68.1	60.4	82.1	75.0	47.6	59.0
1986	50.7	66.5	69.1	57.5	24.9	41.0	67.0	74.1	56.8	63.2	69.4	62.3	80.8	74.6	48.8	61.3
1987	54.3	66.9	71.2	59.9	27.0	44.9	67.9	74.3	57.2	62.1	72.2	63.4	84.5	80.4	49.0	64.3
1988	55.7	68.1	72.9	62.8	28.8	46.6	70.2	76.0	60.0	64.5	75.4	64.8	83.6	81.6	48.9	67.9
1989	56.1	69.1	72.8	66.1	31.2	50.4	74.0	80.5	62.5	66.7	78.2	67.6	85.8	80.4	50.5	70.6
1990	56.9	70.7	74.1	70.9	34.6	53.6	73.9	79.3	63.6	69.8	78.1	68.3	87.8	80.0	50.9	72.8
1991	58.5	71.4	75.6	74.5	38.8	57.8	75.7	80.3	65.3	71.9	78.3	68.5	88.2	82.8	51.0	76.1
1992	60.8	74.6	75.8	75.3	41.9	59.7	76.4	80.5	66.4	73.1	81.6	69.7	89.3	86.0	52.8	80.7
1993	62.5	78.0	77.9	76.8	45.3	60.4	78.3	80.8	68.0	73.8	82.5	72.3	89.3	87.5	56.8	81.4
1994	65.8	82.4	80.0	78.2	49.4	62.8	82.3	90.8	72.4	79.3	89.8	79.0	89.2	90.2	62.7	83.5
1995	68.3	83.3	79.0	83.4	54.3	67.4	86.0	90.8	75.2	80.6	94.2	82.1	88.1	93.3	66.6	82.1
1996	71.0	83.0	81.3	87.2	59.7	72.5	87.3	87.8	75.5	82.9	94.6	83.9	90.8	92.2	68.8	81.4
1997	74.0	86.7	83.0	90.3	67.3	75.5	92.7	94.8	79.9	87.7	96.5	84.1	91.0	93.1	75.1	82.9
1998	79.1	90.9	87.0	91.2	75.0	79.1	93.9	94.3	84.1	88.1	95.2	86.6	88.7	94.7	79.6	83.7
1999	83.1	94.8	88.3	93.6	83.5	84.0	93.3	95.8	87.8	90.2	95.9	90.1	91.7	96.4	86.9	87.8
2000	89.5	100.5	93.6	98.5	90.6	88.3	96.8	99.2	94.0	96.5	100.9	96.6	94.6	97.4	92.8	93.7
2001	90.4	98.4	95.9	96.5	90.1	92.2	97.0	99.4	95.9	99.0	101.2	97.1	97.2	99.6	90.1	97.0
2002	100.0	100.0	100.0	100.0	100.0	100.0	100.0	100.0	100.0	100.0	100.0	100.0	100.0	100.0	100.0	100.0
2003	106.4	100.4	101.8	106.8	106.8	102.6	102.9	104.2	104.5	103.6	97.9	102.1	108.7	102.5	108.1	104.2
2004	112.9	101.6	103.1	114.3	117.8	107.1	108.1	110.2	107.3	107.5	99.3	109.0	115.1	104.4	119.7	110.8
2005	115.1	105.0	103.8	121.7	130.8	114.8	111.0	113.7	112.3	113.5	100.8	113.9	119.1	106.4	127.1	115.5
2006	120.5	107.3	104.8	122.9	146.8	122.5	115.1	119.0	114.9	123.1	102.6	118.2	116.7	108.5	139.0	119.8
2007	126.2	110.2	106.8	127.2	157.9	133.5	120.2	119.4	116.3	129.3	103.1	121.4	116.4	111.1	139.7	123.8
2008	127.8	107.3	105.9	127.0	159.9	132.8	120.8	114.1	115.4	129.2	99.6	119.7	117.2	110.1	134.6	124.2

¹Unified Germany from 1991 onward; data for previous years relate to the former West Germany.
. . . = Not available.

Table 10-9. Indexes of Manufacturing Productivity and Related Measures, 16 Countries, 1950–2008
—Continued

(2002 = 100.)

Category and year	United States	Canada	Australia	Japan	Korea, Republic of	Taiwan	Belgium	Denmark	France	Germany[1]	Italy	Nether-lands	Norway	Spain	Sweden	United Kingdom
Employment Index																
1950	91.7	68.5	. . .	48.9	. . .	. . .	. . .	110.6	126.4	98.3	72.8	118.9	116.2	. . .	124.8	190.5
1951	98.6	72.7	. . .	54.1	. . .	. . .	. . .	112.8	129.2	105.3	73.4	120.0	118.0	. . .	127.9	195.2
1952	100.0	74.5	. . .	55.1	. . .	. . .	. . .	108.4	127.3	108.2	73.7	117.1	117.3	. . .	125.9	194.6
1953	105.5	76.7	. . .	59.3	. . .	. . .	. . .	111.2	124.3	111.6	75.2	118.6	117.0	. . .	123.4	197.3
1954	98.1	73.3	. . .	61.3	. . .	. . .	. . .	115.2	124.4	116.9	77.9	124.1	119.1	. . .	128.5	199.9
1955	101.5	75.1	. . .	63.2	. . .	. . .	. . .	114.3	125.7	124.9	78.6	126.9	122.0	. . .	132.7	204.8
1956	103.7	78.2	. . .	68.3	. . .	. . .	. . .	113.5	127.9	131.2	81.2	129.3	120.9	. . .	133.7	206.1
1957	103.3	78.6	. . .	73.2	. . .	. . .	. . .	116.3	131.4	134.7	84.5	130.5	121.2	. . .	133.6	206.1
1958	95.9	74.6	. . .	77.0	. . .	. . .	. . .	117.6	132.0	135.7	85.6	127.8	117.7	. . .	132.5	202.7
1959	100.3	75.4	. . .	78.2	. . .	. . .	. . .	126.4	129.2	136.3	87.3	129.8	118.0	. . .	133.9	204.4
1960	101.0	74.7	. . .	82.9	. . .	. . .	156.3	136.6	130.4	141.4	91.3	134.8	119.1	. . .	141.0	213.2
1961	98.2	74.0	. . .	89.3	. . .	. . .	161.5	140.3	131.2	145.5	94.2	137.8	121.6	. . .	144.6	216.2
1962	101.4	76.4	. . .	93.9	. . .	. . .	165.1	143.9	132.4	146.1	97.2	140.4	123.0	. . .	145.5	214.2
1963	102.3	78.0	. . .	97.7	. . .	. . .	166.7	143.5	135.2	145.2	100.3	141.2	124.5	. . .	145.7	210.8
1964	103.9	81.5	. . .	100.6	. . .	. . .	171.5	147.0	137.7	145.2	100.6	142.9	125.5	. . .	147.7	214.0
1965	108.7	84.7	. . .	101.9	. . .	. . .	171.3	149.5	136.3	147.8	98.2	143.7	127.6	. . .	148.1	216.8
1966	115.7	89.1	. . .	104.9	. . .	. . .	171.1	148.1	136.9	146.2	97.6	142.8	129.4	. . .	146.3	217.4
1967	117.1	89.9	. . .	111.2	. . .	. . .	165.8	141.5	136.3	138.3	100.8	138.6	130.1	. . .	141.5	210.7
1968	119.1	90.7	. . .	115.0	. . .	. . .	163.1	142.1	133.8	139.4	102.2	137.7	128.7	. . .	139.2	208.7
1969	121.5	92.5	. . .	118.4	. . .	. . .	168.6	145.4	137.6	145.2	105.7	139.5	129.2	. . .	141.5	211.6
1970	116.7	91.9	. . .	121.2	. . .	. . .	173.1	146.2	141.0	148.6	109.1	140.2	132.1	. . .	143.8	211.2
1971	112.3	92.4	. . .	121.8	. . .	. . .	172.3	139.6	142.9	147.6	110.9	138.3	132.9	. . .	139.0	204.0
1972	115.6	95.1	. . .	121.8	. . .	. . .	169.9	142.0	144.7	144.9	110.3	133.8	134.2	. . .	136.9	199.2
1973	121.6	99.2	. . .	127.0	. . .	62.8	171.0	143.0	148.0	145.8	112.4	132.5	134.5	. . .	138.9	200.4
1974	121.1	100.0	. . .	125.7	. . .	63.6	173.6	137.8	149.9	142.3	116.3	132.6	135.9	. . .	141.9	201.1
1975	110.6	97.1	149.5	118.7	. . .	61.7	163.1	125.8	146.4	133.6	117.7	128.5	134.9	. . .	143.1	192.0
1976	114.7	96.4	145.4	118.1	. . .	69.3	156.5	125.3	146.0	130.6	118.2	124.2	134.8	. . .	142.6	185.8
1977	118.9	95.3	141.4	116.9	. . .	74.8	150.4	123.6	146.1	131.1	119.5	122.6	135.0	. . .	137.6	186.4
1978	123.9	98.2	139.5	115.3	. . .	81.2	144.1	122.1	144.7	130.8	119.8	120.4	132.3	. . .	133.7	185.7
1979	127.1	102.4	140.5	115.1	. . .	84.7	140.3	121.5	142.4	132.4	121.7	119.5	130.6	99.2	134.0	184.9
1980	122.5	102.6	141.2	117.3	. . .	87.5	137.4	118.6	140.5	133.6	123.4	118.3	130.7	96.9	133.9	176.0
1981	121.9	102.0	142.1	118.5	. . .	89.3	129.5	113.3	135.6	131.2	120.7	115.7	128.6	90.9	129.9	160.2
1982	113.6	91.4	136.9	118.0	. . .	89.4	125.8	112.1	133.3	127.3	118.5	111.7	124.1	86.5	125.2	150.9
1983	111.5	89.4	125.9	120.0	. . .	93.8	123.1	111.1	130.6	123.1	115.6	107.1	117.7	84.7	122.7	143.2
1984	117.2	91.4	124.7	122.5	. . .	104.0	121.8	115.8	126.5	122.5	110.9	105.0	116.5	82.6	123.3	140.8
1985	116.6	92.6	124.9	123.7	87.7	107.5	119.8	121.1	123.1	124.1	109.0	106.1	117.4	80.3	124.8	139.9
1986	114.8	95.8	125.4	123.1	95.4	112.3	118.7	124.3	120.7	126.0	108.3	107.1	118.6	81.7	124.8	137.0
1987	115.2	98.3	127.4	121.5	106.9	115.9	115.9	121.5	117.8	126.1	106.9	107.9	118.7	84.6	123.9	135.8
1988	117.2	102.0	131.3	124.1	114.9	116.2	115.7	117.1	116.2	125.9	108.4	107.8	113.4	86.3	126.1	137.2
1989	117.9	103.3	128.7	126.7	114.0	112.2	117.2	115.6	116.7	127.7	109.6	108.6	105.7	89.1	124.0	137.6
1990	116.1	98.7	121.8	128.7	113.8	105.0	118.2	115.7	117.0	131.2	110.8	111.4	102.2	92.1	119.9	134.1
1991	112.1	91.1	113.5	131.8	111.8	103.1	117.0	113.4	115.1	133.1	110.3	112.1	99.0	91.0	112.4	124.0
1992	110.2	87.5	107.4	132.1	109.2	103.5	115.2	110.4	111.2	123.2	106.4	111.4	97.3	88.1	102.3	116.7
1993	110.3	87.0	104.8	127.8	106.3	103.1	110.8	106.9	105.9	114.6	102.7	106.8	99.0	83.4	94.7	113.3
1994	111.7	88.9	109.0	123.6	107.6	104.9	106.5	105.7	102.8	108.7	101.1	102.9	101.4	81.8	94.8	113.8
1995	113.3	91.7	108.3	120.1	109.1	103.4	105.9	108.9	103.0	106.1	100.6	102.5	104.1	83.1	100.3	116.7
1996	113.2	93.2	104.8	118.5	107.3	101.5	104.4	107.9	102.0	103.2	99.4	101.3	105.7	85.2	100.2	118.2
1997	114.1	94.6	106.0	118.2	101.2	102.8	102.8	107.2	100.9	101.7	99.0	102.5	110.3	89.0	99.2	118.3
1998	115.1	95.3	106.0	113.2	87.1	103.1	103.0	106.5	100.8	102.1	100.7	103.4	112.0	92.6	101.3	117.9
1999	113.3	98.3	103.5	110.1	88.3	103.7	101.7	104.2	100.5	101.0	100.0	103.2	107.8	95.6	100.8	114.0
2000	113.0	102.2	102.2	108.0	96.3	106.0	102.9	102.7	101.4	101.9	99.4	102.9	105.0	98.0	101.3	109.9
2001	107.8	100.4	99.0	105.1	101.3	101.3	103.9	102.6	102.1	102.3	99.2	102.5	101.8	99.6	102.8	104.9
2002	100.0	100.0	100.0	100.0	100.0	100.0	100.0	100.0	100.0	100.0	100.0	100.0	100.0	100.0	100.0	100.0
2003	95.3	99.4	98.1	97.8	98.8	102.3	97.1	95.5	97.6	97.4	100.8	96.5	95.9	100.4	97.1	95.0
2004	94.0	99.1	98.7	95.7	99.6	106.1	95.1	91.4	94.2	95.9	99.8	93.5	92.6	101.5	92.7	91.0
2005	93.5	98.5	97.0	94.9	100.4	106.9	94.0	89.4	92.3	94.4	99.1	91.4	92.6	102.2	91.7	86.8
2006	93.0	95.9	95.8	96.4	99.7	108.2	92.9	89.2	90.6	93.7	100.0	90.9	97.3	102.0	91.0	85.3
2007	91.4	92.6	97.5	96.9	99.7	109.7	92.1	90.9	89.3	94.8	100.7	91.2	102.1	101.4	91.5	82.6
2008	88.2	90.2	99.0	95.2	99.4	110.6	91.8	92.4	87.9	96.3	99.5	91.7	104.7	100.9	91.0	80.2

[1]Unified Germany from 1991 onward; data for previous years relate to the former West Germany.
. . . = Not available.

Table 10-9. Indexes of Manufacturing Productivity and Related Measures, 16 Countries, 1950–2008
—Continued

(2002 = 100.)

Category and year	United States	Canada	Australia	Japan	Korea, Republic of	Taiwan	Belgium	Denmark	France	Germany¹	Italy	Nether-lands	Norway	Spain	Sweden	United Kingdom
Hourly Compensation Index, U.S. Currency Basis																
1950	6.1	6.0	...	0.5	...	...	...	1.7	1.8	1.1	2.0	1.4	1.6	...	2.4	2.2
1951	6.7	7.1	...	0.7	...	...	...	1.9	2.2	1.3	2.2	1.5	1.8	...	2.8	2.4
1952	7.1	8.4	...	0.8	...	...	...	2.1	2.8	1.4	2.4	1.6	2.0	...	3.3	2.6
1953	7.5	8.7	...	0.8	...	...	...	2.1	2.9	1.4	2.5	1.7	2.2	...	3.5	2.8
1954	7.8	9.3	...	0.9	...	...	...	2.2	3.1	1.5	2.6	1.9	2.3	...	3.6	2.9
1955	8.1	9.5	...	0.9	...	...	...	2.3	3.3	1.6	2.9	2.0	2.4	...	3.8	3.1
1956	8.6	10.0	...	1.0	...	...	...	2.5	3.8	1.8	3.1	2.2	2.6	...	4.1	3.4
1957	9.1	11.0	...	1.0	...	...	...	2.7	3.4	2.0	3.2	2.5	2.8	...	4.4	3.6
1958	9.6	11.4	...	1.1	...	...	...	2.8	4.0	2.2	3.4	2.6	3.0	...	4.7	3.9
1959	9.9	12.0	...	1.2	...	...	...	3.0	3.7	2.4	3.5	2.7	3.2	...	4.9	4.0
1960	10.3	12.5	...	1.3	...	...	3.6	3.2	4.0	2.7	3.8	2.9	3.4	...	5.3	4.2
1961	10.6	12.2	...	1.5	...	...	3.8	3.6	4.4	3.1	4.2	3.4	3.7	...	5.8	4.5
1962	11.0	12.0	...	1.7	...	...	4.0	3.9	4.8	3.6	4.9	3.7	4.1	...	6.5	4.7
1963	11.3	12.5	...	1.9	...	...	4.5	4.2	5.4	3.8	5.9	4.0	4.3	...	7.1	4.9
1964	11.8	13.0	...	2.1	...	...	5.1	4.6	5.8	4.1	6.2	4.7	4.6	...	7.8	5.2
1965	12.0	13.9	...	2.4	...	...	5.6	5.1	6.3	4.5	6.7	5.2	5.1	...	8.6	5.7
1966	12.6	15.0	...	2.7	...	...	6.2	5.8	6.7	4.9	7.1	5.8	5.6	...	9.4	6.2
1967	13.3	15.7	...	3.0	...	...	6.8	6.4	7.4	5.2	7.8	6.5	6.2	...	10.5	6.3
1968	14.3	16.8	...	3.5	...	...	7.2	6.5	8.3	5.6	8.3	7.2	6.9	...	11.3	5.9
1969	15.3	18.1	...	4.2	...	...	7.9	7.4	8.8	6.2	9.1	8.2	7.6	...	12.2	6.4
1970	16.4	19.8	...	5.0	...	...	9.0	8.4	9.1	7.8	11.1	9.2	8.4	...	13.7	7.4
1971	17.4	21.8	...	5.9	...	...	10.7	9.9	10.2	9.2	13.0	10.8	9.8	...	15.7	8.6
1972	18.3	23.9	...	7.8	...	...	13.9	11.7	12.5	11.1	15.1	13.5	11.7	...	18.8	10.2
1973	19.6	25.8	...	10.7	...	5.9	18.8	16.4	16.3	15.1	17.9	18.6	15.1	...	23.2	11.3
1974	21.8	30.8	...	13.0	...	8.7	23.0	19.9	17.9	17.6	20.9	23.1	18.5	...	26.8	13.0
1975	24.5	34.1	...	14.8	...	9.3	29.5	25.5	24.6	20.5	25.7	26.5	23.3	...	35.1	16.4
1976	26.5	40.7	...	16.0	...	10.4	32.5	27.2	24.6	21.5	25.2	28.7	25.8	...	39.1	15.5
1977	28.9	41.9	...	19.5	...	11.3	37.8	30.7	27.2	25.4	28.3	32.5	29.7	...	41.8	16.9
1978	31.2	41.8	...	26.8	...	13.1	46.1	37.0	33.6	31.6	33.5	39.7	33.0	...	45.7	21.7
1979	34.2	44.4	...	27.2	...	15.9	52.6	43.8	40.2	37.2	41.4	46.2	35.8	47.2	51.8	28.4
1980	38.2	48.8	...	27.9	...	19.5	58.7	45.7	46.3	40.7	46.9	48.2	40.0	50.7	58.5	37.9
1981	42.1	53.6	...	30.7	...	24.5	50.3	40.1	41.6	34.8	42.3	39.4	38.2	46.6	53.9	38.2
1982	45.9	59.8	...	28.5	...	25.2	42.8	37.8	40.7	34.3	41.5	39.0	37.8	44.7	46.6	36.3
1983	47.3	64.0	...	30.7	...	25.6	42.0	37.7	39.3	34.1	43.3	38.8	36.7	38.9	42.4	33.7
1984	48.9	64.7	...	31.6	...	27.6	40.4	35.7	37.7	32.1	43.4	36.9	35.9	39.0	42.7	32.0
1985	51.4	64.7	...	32.7	16.5	29.5	41.5	37.2	39.9	32.9	44.8	37.8	37.3	40.7	45.2	34.0
1986	53.8	64.7	...	48.2	17.6	34.9	56.6	50.8	54.1	46.3	61.2	53.4	47.2	54.2	59.0	41.8
1987	55.6	69.3	...	57.8	21.0	45.5	69.7	66.5	65.0	58.4	75.9	67.1	58.8	69.0	70.7	51.8
1988	57.5	78.1	...	66.8	29.3	54.4	72.0	71.8	67.9	62.2	81.2	69.2	64.5	76.5	77.5	60.1
1989	59.3	85.1	...	65.7	36.8	66.8	71.3	70.3	66.8	61.1	85.0	65.6	63.7	78.8	81.5	59.1
1990	62.1	92.0	88.6	66.8	41.7	75.1	88.1	87.3	81.8	76.4	104.8	79.2	74.7	101.9	98.3	72.0
1991	65.8	100.2	93.4	76.6	50.7	82.9	93.0	88.3	83.5	79.1	110.1	81.3	75.9	110.6	104.5	80.3
1992	68.9	99.5	90.2	84.3	55.6	94.4	101.7	95.7	93.7	92.0	118.0	91.2	81.4	127.0	113.6	80.4
1993	70.5	94.4	86.2	98.9	62.8	95.2	99.1	91.2	91.5	92.2	96.3	90.1	72.3	111.5	82.7	69.1
1994	72.2	91.7	93.9	109.5	72.0	99.7	103.2	96.4	97.0	98.4	99.1	96.1	74.9	110.1	85.7	72.2
1995	73.4	93.4	100.9	123.1	91.3	107.8	120.5	111.6	111.1	117.4	103.7	111.8	87.2	123.4	97.7	75.8
1996	74.6	95.5	111.6	107.3	102.0	110.9	116.7	112.2	110.4	117.0	115.5	108.4	89.1	124.3	112.0	74.7
1997	76.5	96.3	108.9	99.7	94.2	109.0	104.7	101.8	99.5	103.4	109.5	96.1	84.8	110.0	103.6	81.8
1998	81.2	94.5	95.9	94.4	69.4	97.0	104.9	103.1	99.2	103.4	105.5	98.5	84.2	108.7	103.4	89.0
1999	84.8	96.4	102.3	108.6	82.1	102.5	101.9	101.3	98.2	101.4	103.3	97.7	86.1	103.8	102.5	91.9
2000	91.3	99.6	96.3	113.9	94.2	107.8	89.9	89.2	89.6	92.4	91.9	88.8	80.6	91.3	96.0	91.4
2001	94.8	98.1	91.0	102.3	86.2	105.8	90.8	90.8	89.2	92.4	92.0	89.7	83.7	92.1	89.2	90.7
2002	100.0	100.0	100.0	100.0	100.0	100.0	100.0	100.0	100.0	100.0	100.0	100.0	100.0	100.0	100.0	100.0
2003	108.0	116.6	124.7	105.7	110.6	101.4	123.9	128.0	122.5	122.4	124.2	124.5	117.4	125.8	125.8	114.1
2004	108.9	130.0	148.1	114.3	131.6	105.7	139.7	146.0	138.9	135.3	141.2	142.6	127.3	143.0	142.0	133.7
2005	112.5	145.7	163.2	113.2	170.6	113.6	144.0	154.2	144.1	137.1	145.9	144.9	139.6	150.0	144.5	140.4
2006	114.7	160.4	172.1	106.1	201.6	115.7	150.5	163.2	151.1	144.0	150.2	150.3	148.8	158.0	150.6	149.3
2007	119.6	175.4	201.7	104.5	220.4	118.2	173.0	182.8	169.4	159.9	167.5	169.3	170.7	180.9	172.3	167.5
2008	123.2	180.4	210.6	121.2	190.2	124.7	191.3	202.2	187.3	176.1	184.6	187.8	187.3	203.7	182.1	159.0

¹Unified Germany from 1991 onward; data for previous years relate to the former West Germany.
. . . = Not available.

Table 10-9. Indexes of Manufacturing Productivity and Related Measures, 16 Countries, 1950–2008
—Continued

(2002 = 100.)

Category and year	United States	Canada	Australia	Japan	Korea, Republic of	Taiwan	Belgium	Denmark	France	Germany[1]	Italy	Nether-lands	Norway	Spain	Sweden	United Kingdom
Average Hours Index																
1950	102.2	106.4	. . .	118.6	. . .	. . .	. . .	134.4	130.8	141.5	114.9	131.4	134.9	. . .	116.0	112.6
1951	102.4	104.7	. . .	121.0	. . .	. . .	. . .	132.5	134.7	142.4	116.6	130.4	135.3	. . .	117.2	112.9
1952	102.5	103.3	. . .	122.0	. . .	. . .	. . .	132.4	132.5	143.6	116.1	130.7	134.5	. . .	116.2	112.0
1953	102.1	103.9	. . .	123.4	. . .	. . .	. . .	131.7	131.0	144.4	117.3	131.0	135.5	. . .	114.9	112.8
1954	100.3	102.0	. . .	122.1	. . .	. . .	. . .	132.0	132.5	146.8	118.7	131.0	134.9	. . .	115.3	113.7
1955	102.4	102.5	. . .	122.2	. . .	. . .	. . .	131.9	132.7	148.2	117.8	131.7	135.2	. . .	115.1	114.0
1956	101.7	103.2	. . .	125.6	. . .	. . .	. . .	130.8	131.2	146.0	116.5	131.1	134.9	. . .	113.3	113.0
1957	100.4	101.9	. . .	124.9	. . .	. . .	. . .	130.4	131.0	138.8	117.1	130.7	132.4	. . .	113.4	112.9
1958	99.1	101.9	. . .	124.2	. . .	. . .	. . .	129.7	129.7	136.5	116.0	130.7	133.1	. . .	111.7	111.6
1959	101.4	102.6	. . .	125.8	. . .	. . .	. . .	126.5	129.6	136.1	117.4	131.0	129.9	. . .	110.1	112.6
1960	100.2	101.8	. . .	126.9	. . .	. . .	123.4	125.2	131.8	136.1	119.1	133.0	130.0	. . .	108.9	111.7
1961	100.3	101.3	. . .	125.0	. . .	. . .	123.1	121.5	131.3	133.7	117.8	127.4	128.0	. . .	108.0	110.2
1962	101.4	102.0	. . .	122.4	. . .	. . .	123.4	122.5	132.3	130.3	114.1	126.6	127.6	. . .	107.2	109.1
1963	101.8	102.2	. . .	121.5	. . .	. . .	123.2	120.6	132.4	128.6	114.7	126.2	127.0	. . .	106.0	108.9
1964	102.4	102.7	. . .	120.8	. . .	. . .	122.8	121.6	133.1	128.5	114.7	125.0	127.8	. . .	104.8	109.8
1965	103.6	102.8	. . .	118.8	. . .	. . .	120.8	121.4	132.2	128.1	110.9	124.6	124.9	. . .	104.1	108.3
1966	103.9	102.0	. . .	119.4	. . .	. . .	119.9	119.1	132.5	126.4	112.1	123.9	125.2	. . .	103.9	106.4
1967	101.9	102.1	. . .	119.5	. . .	. . .	118.3	118.0	130.4	123.0	113.7	123.4	124.0	. . .	102.2	105.6
1968	101.8	101.9	. . .	119.2	. . .	. . .	118.4	115.4	128.7	124.5	113.7	121.1	121.1	. . .	100.1	106.5
1969	101.0	101.4	. . .	117.6	. . .	. . .	117.2	113.6	126.5	124.6	112.9	119.5	118.3	. . .	98.4	106.5
1970	98.9	100.7	. . .	116.4	. . .	. . .	114.0	110.5	125.7	124.0	110.9	117.3	117.4	. . .	98.2	104.8
1971	99.2	100.4	. . .	114.5	. . .	. . .	112.4	109.7	126.0	121.3	107.8	116.2	116.2	. . .	97.9	102.3
1972	100.8	100.5	. . .	113.8	. . .	. . .	109.8	107.1	122.4	120.1	107.0	114.5	114.5	. . .	95.3	101.4
1973	100.7	99.7	. . .	112.9	. . .	120.3	107.1	103.0	121.5	119.1	108.3	112.4	113.8	. . .	93.6	102.7
1974	98.8	99.0	. . .	108.2	. . .	115.6	104.4	103.9	119.1	116.7	104.5	108.8	112.3	. . .	92.7	99.4
1975	97.3	97.7	84.3	105.7	. . .	118.2	98.8	100.6	115.4	113.8	102.7	106.9	111.8	. . .	90.8	99.1
1976	98.5	98.0	83.7	108.8	. . .	119.0	100.6	101.1	118.6	117.1	102.7	106.6	108.9	. . .	89.8	99.9
1977	98.8	97.0	83.9	109.1	. . .	118.8	100.2	100.0	116.5	115.3	102.2	106.2	107.0	. . .	89.1	100.6
1978	98.9	98.0	84.4	109.5	. . .	118.0	100.0	99.0	114.7	113.8	101.9	105.1	105.1	. . .	86.8	100.2
1979	98.4	97.6	84.3	110.3	. . .	117.3	100.0	98.6	115.4	113.4	101.2	103.9	103.2	105.7	85.5	99.8
1980	97.5	97.4	84.4	110.2	. . .	117.6	98.4	98.7	115.2	111.8	101.4	104.5	103.8	104.9	84.6	96.5
1981	97.3	97.5	83.4	109.4	. . .	112.1	96.2	97.2	113.9	110.4	101.1	105.1	104.0	103.0	84.9	95.1
1982	96.0	96.5	81.3	109.0	. . .	111.8	98.3	98.3	109.2	109.8	101.3	106.2	103.1	103.5	86.4	96.0
1983	98.5	97.5	81.9	109.1	. . .	111.9	95.8	99.1	108.1	110.0	99.6	106.4	103.6	101.9	88.5	96.2
1984	99.9	97.4	82.7	110.1	. . .	113.0	95.2	98.8	107.8	110.0	98.8	104.8	103.3	99.4	88.9	97.0
1985	100.1	97.8	83.4	109.5	113.3	109.6	96.6	96.7	106.8	108.0	99.2	102.1	103.0	98.9	89.1	97.0
1986	99.9	97.8	83.3	109.2	115.3	111.5	96.7	98.0	107.3	107.4	100.2	101.6	103.1	100.0	87.9	96.8
1987	100.0	99.1	83.7	109.9	113.3	111.6	97.5	95.5	108.9	107.1	101.1	101.1	100.6	96.4	90.2	97.5
1988	101.3	99.9	85.1	111.0	110.6	110.2	99.1	95.2	110.0	106.7	102.1	101.8	101.4	97.5	91.3	98.0
1989	101.3	99.4	88.5	109.8	106.4	108.6	98.6	93.8	109.1	105.2	101.6	101.3	102.1	100.2	90.5	97.9
1990	100.3	98.5	90.3	108.5	104.7	107.6	99.8	93.2	109.6	103.1	101.9	101.2	101.8	100.0	91.9	97.2
1991	99.6	98.0	91.8	106.1	103.7	107.7	98.1	92.6	108.6	102.5	101.9	101.0	102.4	99.7	92.1	95.5
1992	100.8	98.7	96.0	102.8	102.5	107.7	98.0	94.5	109.3	106.3	101.1	100.9	103.5	98.9	93.8	95.6
1993	102.0	100.1	99.5	100.6	102.3	107.7	96.6	94.5	108.9	104.1	101.1	100.8	103.8	98.6	95.9	99.1
1994	103.1	99.9	97.9	100.9	103.3	108.0	99.7	94.1	108.7	105.3	100.6	100.9	104.0	99.2	100.4	100.6
1995	102.3	100.2	99.2	101.6	103.5	107.5	98.6	95.8	108.1	105.3	101.0	101.2	103.1	97.9	100.9	101.3
1996	102.2	100.2	102.7	102.1	101.9	107.3	99.0	95.4	108.5	103.1	101.2	101.6	102.5	99.1	101.2	101.8
1997	103.1	100.4	101.9	101.4	100.5	107.6	99.1	96.2	108.5	103.1	101.1	101.5	102.3	100.1	100.9	101.5
1998	102.0	100.0	100.0	99.3	96.5	105.6	99.3	98.1	108.1	103.6	101.7	101.1	102.6	100.2	101.0	101.6
1999	102.9	100.6	100.6	99.2	104.2	106.2	101.6	99.5	107.4	103.2	101.5	100.8	103.0	100.9	101.5	101.3
2000	101.9	100.5	100.6	100.9	103.0	106.0	101.1	101.0	104.0	102.1	101.1	100.7	102.0	101.7	102.5	100.6
2001	99.9	100.4	100.5	100.1	100.7	98.4	100.1	101.0	102.3	100.8	100.7	100.5	101.5	101.0	101.5	100.5
2002	100.0	100.0	100.0	100.0	100.0	100.0	100.0	100.0	100.0	100.0	100.0	100.0	100.0	100.0	100.0	100.0
2003	99.8	99.5	101.9	100.8	99.9	100.4	98.6	97.8	99.9	99.9	98.7	100.3	99.1	98.4	99.9	100.8
2004	100.7	100.8	100.1	101.9	98.8	101.7	99.4	98.1	101.7	101.2	98.9	100.4	102.5	96.2	103.2	101.1
2005	100.1	99.6	100.8	101.4	93.7	100.7	97.8	97.7	101.5	100.6	97.9	100.2	103.4	94.8	102.8	101.5
2006	101.4	99.7	100.0	102.3	90.8	99.9	98.0	97.4	100.8	100.3	98.6	100.4	103.5	94.9	102.2	101.1
2007	101.4	99.6	99.6	101.9	90.5	99.9	97.3	98.8	101.8	100.1	99.4	100.5	104.0	94.1	103.4	101.6
2008	100.9	99.1	100.6	100.5	92.5	98.5	96.5	99.8	101.7	99.2	99.4	100.8	103.8	93.5	104.1	101.4

[1]Unified Germany from 1991 onward; data for previous years relate to the former West Germany.
. . . = Not available.

Table 10-9. Indexes of Manufacturing Productivity and Related Measures, 16 Countries, 1950–2008
—Continued

(2002 = 100.)

Category and year	United States	Canada	Australia	Japan	Korea, Republic of	Taiwan	Belgium	Denmark	France	Germany¹	Italy	Nether-lands	Norway	Spain	Sweden	United Kingdom
Aggregate Hours Index																
1950	93.7	72.9	...	57.9	...	...	...	148.6	165.3	139.2	83.6	156.2	156.8	...	144.7	214.4
1951	101.0	76.2	...	65.5	...	...	...	149.5	174.0	149.9	85.6	156.5	159.6	...	149.9	220.4
1952	102.5	76.9	...	67.2	...	...	...	143.5	168.6	155.4	85.6	153.0	157.8	...	146.3	218.0
1953	107.7	79.7	...	73.2	...	...	...	146.4	162.9	161.2	88.2	155.4	158.5	...	141.8	222.6
1954	98.4	74.7	...	74.9	...	...	...	152.1	164.8	171.6	92.5	162.6	160.6	...	148.2	227.2
1955	104.0	76.9	...	77.2	...	...	...	150.8	166.8	185.1	92.6	167.2	165.0	...	152.8	233.5
1956	105.5	80.7	...	85.8	...	...	...	148.5	167.7	191.6	94.6	169.5	163.1	...	151.5	232.9
1957	103.8	80.0	...	91.5	...	...	...	151.7	172.1	187.0	99.0	170.5	160.6	...	151.5	232.7
1958	95.0	76.0	...	95.7	...	...	...	152.6	171.3	185.2	99.4	167.0	156.6	...	147.9	226.3
1959	101.6	77.3	...	98.3	...	...	...	159.9	167.5	185.6	102.5	170.2	153.3	...	147.3	230.1
1960	101.2	76.0	...	105.2	...	...	192.8	171.0	171.8	192.4	108.8	179.3	154.8	...	153.6	238.1
1961	98.5	75.0	...	111.6	...	...	198.7	170.6	172.3	194.6	111.0	175.7	155.7	...	156.2	238.2
1962	102.8	77.9	...	115.0	...	...	203.7	176.2	175.2	190.4	110.9	177.8	157.0	...	155.9	233.6
1963	104.1	79.7	...	118.7	...	...	205.4	173.1	179.0	186.7	115.0	178.1	158.1	...	154.5	229.7
1964	106.5	83.7	...	121.6	...	...	210.7	178.7	183.3	186.6	115.4	178.6	160.4	...	154.8	235.1
1965	112.6	87.1	...	121.1	...	...	207.0	181.5	180.2	189.3	108.9	179.1	159.3	...	154.2	234.8
1966	120.2	90.9	...	125.2	...	...	205.1	176.4	181.4	184.8	109.5	176.9	162.0	...	152.0	231.4
1967	119.3	91.8	...	132.9	...	...	196.2	166.9	177.7	170.2	114.6	171.0	161.3	...	144.7	222.5
1968	121.3	92.4	...	137.1	...	...	193.0	164.1	172.2	173.5	116.1	166.9	155.8	...	139.3	222.2
1969	122.7	93.9	...	139.3	...	...	197.6	165.1	174.1	181.0	119.3	166.6	152.8	...	139.3	225.2
1970	115.5	92.5	...	141.1	...	...	197.4	161.6	177.3	184.3	121.0	164.5	155.1	...	141.2	221.4
1971	111.4	92.8	...	139.4	...	...	193.6	153.1	180.2	179.1	119.6	160.7	154.5	...	136.1	208.8
1972	116.4	95.6	...	138.7	...	...	186.6	152.1	177.1	174.0	118.1	153.3	153.7	...	130.4	202.0
1973	122.4	98.9	...	143.3	...	75.5	183.2	147.3	179.8	173.6	121.8	148.9	153.1	...	130.1	205.8
1974	119.7	99.0	...	136.1	...	73.5	181.2	143.3	178.5	166.2	121.5	144.4	152.6	...	131.5	199.9
1975	107.6	94.9	126.1	125.5	...	72.9	161.2	126.5	169.0	152.0	120.9	137.4	150.8	...	129.9	190.2
1976	113.0	94.5	121.8	128.5	...	82.5	157.5	126.7	173.2	152.9	121.4	132.4	146.7	...	128.0	185.7
1977	117.5	92.5	118.7	127.6	...	88.8	150.6	123.6	170.2	151.2	122.1	130.2	144.5	...	122.6	187.6
1978	122.5	96.2	117.8	126.2	...	95.9	144.0	120.8	165.9	148.9	122.2	126.6	139.0	...	116.0	186.0
1979	125.0	99.9	118.4	126.9	...	99.4	140.3	119.9	164.3	150.1	123.1	124.1	134.8	104.8	114.6	184.5
1980	119.4	100.0	119.1	129.3	...	102.9	135.3	117.0	161.9	149.3	125.1	123.6	135.6	101.6	113.2	169.8
1981	118.6	99.4	118.5	129.7	...	100.1	124.5	110.0	154.4	144.9	122.0	121.5	133.8	93.6	110.2	152.4
1982	109.1	88.2	111.3	128.6	...	100.0	123.6	110.2	145.5	139.8	120.0	118.6	127.9	89.5	108.2	144.8
1983	109.9	87.1	103.1	130.8	...	104.9	117.9	110.1	141.2	135.3	115.1	113.9	121.9	86.3	108.6	137.9
1984	117.1	89.1	103.2	134.9	...	117.5	115.9	114.4	136.3	134.8	109.6	110.0	120.4	82.2	109.6	136.6
1985	116.7	90.6	104.1	135.5	99.3	117.7	115.7	117.2	131.5	134.0	108.1	108.3	120.9	79.4	111.2	135.8
1986	114.7	93.7	104.5	134.4	109.9	125.2	114.7	121.8	129.5	135.4	108.6	108.9	122.3	81.7	109.6	132.6
1987	115.2	97.4	106.7	133.6	121.1	129.3	112.9	116.1	128.3	135.1	108.0	109.1	119.4	81.6	111.7	132.4
1988	118.7	102.0	111.6	137.8	127.0	128.1	114.6	111.5	127.7	134.3	110.6	109.8	115.0	84.1	115.1	134.5
1989	119.4	102.7	113.8	139.2	121.4	121.9	115.5	108.5	127.3	134.3	111.4	110.1	107.8	89.3	112.3	134.7
1990	116.5	97.2	110.0	139.6	119.2	113.0	117.9	107.8	128.2	135.3	113.0	112.7	104.1	92.1	110.2	130.4
1991	111.6	89.3	104.2	139.9	116.0	111.0	114.7	105.0	125.0	136.4	112.3	113.2	101.4	90.7	103.5	118.4
1992	111.0	86.4	103.2	135.7	112.0	111.5	112.9	104.4	121.6	131.0	107.5	112.4	100.7	87.1	96.0	111.5
1993	112.5	87.1	104.3	128.6	108.8	111.0	107.0	101.0	115.2	119.3	103.8	107.7	102.8	82.2	90.9	112.2
1994	115.1	88.8	106.7	124.7	111.1	113.3	106.3	99.5	111.8	114.5	101.8	103.9	105.5	81.1	95.1	114.5
1995	115.9	91.8	107.4	122.0	113.0	111.2	104.5	104.3	111.3	111.7	101.6	103.7	107.3	81.4	101.3	118.2
1996	115.7	93.4	107.7	121.0	109.3	108.9	103.4	102.9	110.7	106.4	100.7	102.9	108.4	84.5	101.3	120.3
1997	117.7	94.9	108.0	119.9	101.7	110.6	101.9	103.1	109.4	104.9	100.1	104.0	112.8	89.0	100.1	120.1
1998	117.4	95.2	105.9	112.5	84.0	108.8	102.3	104.5	109.0	105.8	102.5	104.5	115.0	92.8	102.2	119.8
1999	116.6	98.9	104.1	109.1	92.0	110.1	103.4	103.7	108.0	104.2	101.5	104.1	111.0	96.4	102.4	115.4
2000	115.1	102.7	102.9	109.0	99.1	112.4	104.0	103.7	105.4	104.0	100.5	103.6	107.1	99.7	103.8	110.6
2001	107.6	100.8	99.5	105.3	102.0	99.6	104.0	103.7	104.4	103.1	99.9	103.0	103.4	100.5	104.3	105.4
2002	100.0	100.0	100.0	100.0	100.0	100.0	100.0	100.0	100.0	100.0	100.0	100.0	100.0	100.0	100.0	100.0
2003	95.1	99.0	99.9	98.6	98.7	102.7	95.8	93.3	97.5	97.3	99.4	96.8	95.1	98.8	97.0	95.7
2004	94.6	99.8	98.7	97.5	98.3	107.9	94.5	89.6	95.8	97.1	98.7	93.9	94.9	97.6	95.7	92.0
2005	93.6	98.1	97.7	96.3	94.1	107.7	91.9	87.3	93.7	95.0	97.0	91.6	95.8	96.8	94.2	88.1
2006	94.3	95.6	95.9	98.6	90.6	108.2	91.1	86.9	91.3	93.9	98.6	91.3	100.7	96.8	93.0	86.3
2007	92.6	92.2	97.1	98.8	90.2	109.6	89.5	89.8	90.8	94.9	100.0	91.7	106.2	95.4	94.6	84.0
2008	89.0	89.3	99.6	95.7	91.9	109.0	88.6	92.2	89.4	95.6	98.9	92.4	108.6	94.3	94.8	81.3

¹Unified Germany from 1991 onward; data for previous years relate to the former West Germany.
. . . = Not available.

Table 10-10. Hourly Compensation Costs in U.S. Dollars for Production Workers in Manufacturing, 32 Countries and Selected Areas, Selected Years, 1996–2007

(Dollars.)

Region and country	1996	1998	2000	2002	2004	2005	2006	2007
Americas								
United States	22.11	23.12	24.63	27.01	28.94	29.74	29.98	30.56
Argentina	7.32	7.87	8.05	2.98	4.47	5.45	6.57	7.98
Brazil	7.12	6.69	4.31	3.07	3.81	5.01	5.99	7.13
Canada	19.01	18.08	18.68	18.78	24.20	26.73	29.27	31.91
Mexico	2.32	2.37	2.89	3.44	3.34	3.57	3.72	3.91
Asia and Oceania								
Australia	19.86	17.82	17.12	17.94	27.45	29.44	30.48	34.75
Israel	11.34	12.21	12.77	12.34	13.56	13.88	14.25	15.92
Japan	23.93	20.83	25.34	21.75	25.59	25.56	24.32	23.95
Korea, Republic of	9.17	6.37	9.26	9.80	12.04	14.30	16.59	18.36
New Zealand	12.57	10.43	9.31	10.12	15.17	16.64	16.08	19.19
Philippines	1.27	0.92	0.90	0.90	0.97	1.06	1.21	1.37
Singapore	11.88	11.49	11.65	12.04	13.15	13.22	13.77	15.43
Taiwan	6.91	6.31	7.35	6.84	7.26	7.87	8.11	8.15
Europe								
Austria	31.45	28.06	24.57	26.34	35.65	36.91	38.26	43.17
Belgium	27.49	24.68	22.03	23.81	32.85	33.69	34.85	38.75
Czech Republic	3.42	3.54	3.39	4.60	6.55	7.28	8.14	9.67
Denmark	...	26.04	24.07	27.33	37.53	39.20	41.18	47.54
Finland	25.12	22.45	19.90	22.52	32.51	33.73	35.28	39.74
France	28.18	25.27	21.67	23.07	31.50	32.22	33.60	37.68
Germany	...	33.29	29.26	31.59	43.94	43.58	46.14	50.73
Hungary	3.70	3.68	3.56	5.05	7.50	8.16	8.41	10.49
Ireland	17.52	17.28	16.32	19.69	28.41	29.44	30.74	35.62
Italy	20.88	19.21	16.57	18.50	26.97	27.74	28.70	32.19
Netherlands	...	23.79	20.97	24.15	34.09	34.79	35.50	39.47
Norway	...	28.01	26.16	32.29	41.92	44.61	47.17	55.03
Poland	...	3.50	3.40	4.05	4.81	5.68	6.29	7.69
Portugal	5.81	5.73	5.42	6.40	8.96	9.30	9.38	10.29
Slovakia	...	2.92	2.62	3.27	5.23	5.85	6.62	8.49
Spain	15.30	13.94	12.24	13.77	19.83	20.59	21.66	24.55
Sweden	25.68	23.76	21.86	22.96	32.70	32.80	34.32	38.80
Switzerland	32.95	28.37	24.71	28.05	35.65	35.98	36.18	38.34
United Kingdom	16.48	19.94	20.11	22.37	30.05	31.27	32.50	36.66
Trade-Weighted Measures								
All 31 foreign economies	...	16.18	16.24	16.64	21.59	22.63	23.77	25.93
OECD[1]	...	17.22	17.31	17.83	23.31	24.41	25.63	27.96
Europe	...	24.22	21.79	24.08	33.27	33.86	35.32	39.41
Euro Area[2]	...	25.41	22.39	24.64	34.50	34.93	36.53	40.71
Eastern Europe[3]	...	3.44	3.32	4.33	5.99	6.73	7.33	9.01
East Asia ex-Japan[4]	...	6.99	8.47	8.61	9.85	10.95	12.04	13.12

[1]Organization for Economic Cooperation and Development.
[2]Euro Area refers to European Union member countries in this release that have adopted the Euro as the common currency as of January 1, 2009.
[3]Eastern Europe refers to the Czech Republic, Hungary, Poland, and Slovakia.
[4]East Asia ex-Japan includes the Republic of Korea, the Philippines, Singapore, and Taiwan.
. . . = Not available.

Table 10-11. Consumer Price Indexes, 16 Countries, 1950–2008

(1982–1984 = 100.)

Year	United States[2]	Canada[3]	Japan[4]	Australia[5]	Austria[6]	Bel- gium[7]	Den- mark[8]	France[9]	Ger- many[10]	Italy	Nether- lands[11]	Norway[12]	Spain[13]	Sweden	Switzer- land[14]	United Kingdom
Consumer Price Index[1]																
1950	24.1	21.6	. . .	12.6	. . .	24.0	12.2	11.2	34.0	. . .	21.0	13.5	5.5	13.4	33.2	9.8
1951	26.0	23.8	. . .	15.1	. . .	26.3	13.6	13.1	36.6	. . .	23.1	15.7	6.0	15.7	34.8	10.7
1952	26.5	24.5	. . .	17.7	. . .	26.5	13.9	14.7	37.3	. . .	23.1	17.1	5.9	16.8	35.7	11.7
1953	26.7	24.2	. . .	18.4	. . .	26.4	13.8	14.5	36.7	10.3	23.1	17.5	6.0	16.9	35.5	12.1
1954	26.9	24.4	. . .	18.6	. . .	26.9	14.1	14.4	36.8	10.6	24.0	18.2	6.1	17.0	35.7	12.3
1955	26.8	24.4	. . .	19.0	. . .	26.7	15.0	14.6	37.3	10.9	24.5	18.4	6.3	17.5	36.0	12.8
1956	27.2	24.7	. . .	20.1	. . .	27.4	15.8	14.9	38.4	11.2	24.9	19.1	6.7	18.4	36.6	13.5
1957	28.1	25.6	. . .	20.6	. . .	28.2	16.0	15.3	39.1	11.4	26.5	19.7	7.4	19.2	37.3	14.0
1958	28.9	26.3	. . .	20.9	31.6	28.6	16.2	17.6	40.0	11.7	27.0	20.6	8.4	20.0	38.0	14.4
1959	29.1	26.4	. . .	21.3	32.0	29.0	16.5	18.7	40.3	11.7	27.2	21.2	9.0	20.2	37.7	14.5
1960	29.6	26.8	. . .	22.1	32.6	29.0	16.9	19.4	40.9	11.9	27.9	21.2	9.1	21.0	38.3	14.6
1961	29.9	27.1	. . .	22.6	33.8	29.3	17.6	20.0	42.0	12.2	28.4	21.7	9.2	21.5	39.0	15.1
1962	30.2	27.5	. . .	22.6	35.3	29.8	18.8	21.0	43.1	12.7	28.9	22.8	9.7	22.5	40.7	15.8
1963	30.6	27.8	. . .	22.7	36.2	30.4	19.7	22.0	44.4	13.7	30.0	23.3	10.6	23.2	42.1	16.1
1964	31.0	28.3	. . .	23.2	37.6	31.7	20.5	22.7	45.5	14.5	31.7	24.6	11.3	23.9	43.4	16.6
1965	31.5	29.0	. . .	24.1	39.5	32.9	21.8	23.3	46.9	15.2	33.3	25.7	12.8	25.2	44.8	17.4
1966	32.4	30.2	. . .	24.9	40.3	34.3	23.3	23.9	48.5	15.5	35.3	26.6	13.6	26.8	47.0	18.1
1967	33.4	31.3	. . .	25.7	41.9	35.3	25.0	24.6	49.4	16.1	36.4	27.7	14.5	27.9	48.9	18.6
1968	34.8	32.5	. . .	26.4	43.1	36.3	27.0	25.7	50.2	16.3	37.7	28.8	15.2	28.5	50.1	19.4
1969	36.7	34.0	. . .	27.2	44.4	37.6	27.9	27.3	51.1	16.7	40.5	29.5	15.5	29.2	51.3	20.5
1970	38.8	35.1	38.4	28.2	46.4	39.1	29.7	28.8	52.9	17.5	42.3	32.6	16.4	31.3	53.2	21.8
1971	40.5	36.1	40.9	29.8	48.5	40.8	31.5	30.3	55.7	18.4	45.5	34.8	17.7	33.6	56.6	23.8
1972	41.8	37.8	42.9	31.7	51.6	43.0	33.6	32.2	58.7	19.4	49.1	37.2	19.2	35.6	60.4	25.5
1973	44.4	40.8	47.9	34.6	55.5	46.0	36.7	34.6	62.8	21.6	53.0	40.1	21.4	38.0	65.7	27.8
1974	49.3	45.3	59.0	39.9	60.8	51.8	42.3	39.3	67.2	25.7	58.1	43.8	24.8	41.7	72.1	32.3
1975	53.8	50.1	65.9	45.9	65.9	58.5	46.4	43.9	71.2	30.0	64.0	48.9	29.0	45.8	77.0	40.1
1976	56.9	53.7	72.2	52.0	70.8	63.8	50.5	48.2	74.2	35.1	69.6	53.4	34.1	50.6	78.3	46.8
1977	60.6	58.1	78.1	58.5	74.6	68.4	56.2	52.7	77.0	41.0	74.3	58.4	42.4	56.3	79.3	54.2
1978	65.2	63.2	81.4	63.1	77.3	71.4	61.8	57.5	79.1	46.0	77.3	63.1	50.8	62.0	80.1	58.7
1979	72.6	69.1	84.3	68.8	80.2	74.6	67.7	63.6	82.3	52.8	80.6	66.0	58.8	66.4	83.0	66.6
1980	82.4	76.0	91.0	75.8	85.2	79.6	76.1	72.3	86.8	64.0	85.8	73.3	67.9	75.5	86.4	78.5
1981	90.9	85.5	95.3	83.1	91.0	85.6	85.0	82.0	92.2	75.4	91.6	83.2	77.8	84.6	92.0	87.9
1982	96.5	94.9	98.1	92.5	96.0	93.1	93.6	91.6	97.1	87.8	97.1	92.6	89.0	91.9	97.1	95.4
1983	99.6	100.4	99.8	101.8	99.2	100.3	100.1	100.5	100.2	100.7	99.8	100.5	99.9	100.0	100.0	99.8
1984	103.9	104.7	102.1	105.8	104.8	106.6	106.3	107.9	102.7	111.5	103.1	106.9	111.1	108.1	102.9	104.8
1985	107.6	108.9	104.2	112.9	108.2	111.8	111.3	114.2	104.8	121.8	105.4	112.9	120.9	116.1	106.4	111.1
1986	109.6	113.4	104.8	123.2	110.0	113.3	115.4	117.2	104.7	129.0	105.6	120.9	131.6	121.0	107.2	114.9
1987	113.6	118.4	104.9	133.6	111.6	115.0	120.1	120.9	104.9	135.1	105.1	131.5	138.5	126.0	108.7	119.7
1988	118.3	123.0	105.6	143.3	113.7	116.4	125.5	124.2	106.2	141.9	105.8	140.2	145.2	133.4	110.7	125.6
1989	124.0	129.3	108.0	154.1	116.6	120.0	131.5	128.6	109.2	150.8	107.0	146.6	155.0	142.0	114.2	135.4
1990	130.7	135.5	111.3	165.3	120.4	124.1	135.0	133.0	112.1	160.5	109.6	152.6	165.4	156.7	120.5	148.2
1991	136.2	143.1	115.1	170.7	124.4	128.1	138.2	137.3	116.3	170.6	113.8	157.9	175.2	171.5	127.6	156.9
1992	140.3	145.2	117.0	172.4	129.4	131.2	141.1	140.5	122.3	179.6	118.1	161.6	185.6	175.6	132.6	162.7
1993	144.5	147.9	118.5	175.5	134.1	134.8	142.9	143.5	127.6	187.8	120.5	165.2	194.1	183.8	137.1	165.3
1994	148.2	148.1	119.2	178.8	138.1	138.0	145.7	145.8	131.2	195.5	123.8	167.6	203.3	187.8	138.3	169.3
1995	152.4	151.4	119.1	187.1	141.2	140.1	148.8	148.4	133.4	205.8	126.0	171.8	212.8	192.4	140.7	175.2
1996	156.9	153.6	119.2	192.0	143.8	142.9	151.9	151.3	135.3	214.0	128.7	173.8	220.3	193.5	141.8	179.4
1997	160.5	156.2	121.5	192.5	145.7	145.3	155.2	153.2	137.9	218.3	131.5	178.4	224.7	194.7	142.6	185.1
1998	163.0	157.8	122.2	194.1	147.0	146.6	158.1	154.3	139.3	222.6	134.1	182.4	228.8	194.2	142.6	191.4
1999	166.6	160.5	121.8	197.0	147.9	148.3	162.0	155.0	140.0	226.3	137.0	186.6	234.1	195.1	143.8	194.3
2000	172.2	164.9	120.9	205.8	151.4	152.1	166.8	157.7	142.0	232.1	140.2	192.4	242.1	196.9	145.9	200.1
2001	177.1	169.0	120.1	214.8	155.4	155.8	170.7	160.3	144.8	238.5	146.1	198.2	250.8	201.6	147.5	203.6
2002	179.9	172.8	119.0	221.2	158.2	158.4	174.8	163.4	146.9	244.5	150.9	200.8	259.7	206.0	148.4	207.0
2003	184.0	177.6	118.7	227.4	160.3	160.9	178.5	166.8	148.5	251.0	154.0	205.7	267.6	209.9	149.3	213.0
2004	188.9	180.9	118.7	232.7	163.6	164.3	180.5	170.3	150.9	256.6	156.0	206.6	275.7	210.7	150.5	219.4
2005	195.3	184.9	118.3	238.9	167.4	168.8	183.8	173.4	153.2	261.6	158.6	209.9	285.0	211.7	152.2	225.6
2006	201.6	188.5	118.7	247.4	169.9	171.9	187.3	176.2	155.7	267.1	160.4	214.7	295.0	214.5	153.9	232.8
2007	207.3	192.7	118.7	253.1	173.6	175.0	190.5	178.9	159.2	272.0	163.0	216.3	303.3	219.3	155.0	242.7
2008	215.3	197.2	120.3	264.1	179.1	182.9	197.0	183.9	163.3	281.1	167.1	224.5	315.6	226.8	158.8	252.4

[1]The figures may differ from official indexes published by national statistical agencies because of rounding.
[2]Urban wage earners and clerical workers prior to 1978 and all urban consumers from 1978 onward.
[3]All households from January 1995, all urban households from September 1978 to December 1994, and middle-income urban households prior to September 1978.
[4]Excluding imputed rent for owner-occupied households prior to 1970.
[5]Urban worker households prior to September 1998.
[6]Worker households prior to 1966.
[7]Excluding rent and several other services prior to 1976.
[8]Excluding rent prior to 1964.
[9]All households from 1991, urban worker households prior to 1991; worker households in Paris only prior to 1962.
[10]Unified Germany from 1991 onward; data for previous years relate to the former West Germany.
[11]Employee households from 2001, low-income employee households prior to 2001.
[12]Urban worker households prior to 1960.
[13]All family households from 1993, middle-income family households prior to 1993.
[14]Urban worker households prior to May 1993.
. . . = Not available.

Table 10-12. Consumer Price Indexes, Average Annual Percent Change, 16 Countries, 1950–2008

(Percent.)

Year	United States[2]	Canada[3]	Japan[4]	Australia[5]	Austria[6]	Belgium[7]	Denmark[8]	France[9]	Germany[10]	Italy	Netherlands[11]	Norway[12]	Spain[13]	Sweden	Switzerland[14]	United Kingdom
1950–2008	3.8	3.9	. . .	5.4	. . .	3.6	4.9	4.9	2.7	. . .	3.6	5.0	7.2	5.0	2.7	5.8
1960–2008	4.2	4.2	. . .	5.3	3.6	3.9	5.3	4.8	2.9	6.8	3.8	5.0	7.7	5.1	3.0	6.1
1970–2008	4.6	4.6	3.0	6.1	3.6	4.1	5.1	5.0	3.0	7.6	3.7	5.2	8.1	5.4	2.9	6.7
1980–2008	3.5	3.5	1.0	4.6	2.7	3.0	3.5	3.4	2.3	5.4	2.4	4.1	5.6	4.0	2.2	4.3
1990–2008	2.8	2.1	0.4	2.6	2.2	2.2	2.1	1.8	2.1	3.2	2.4	2.2	3.7	2.1	1.5	3.0
2000–2008	2.8	2.3	-0.1	3.2	2.1	2.3	2.1	1.9	1.8	2.4	2.2	1.9	3.4	1.8	1.1	2.9
1950–1955	2.1	2.4	. . .	8.6	. . .	2.2	4.3	5.4	1.9	. . .	3.0	6.4	2.8	5.4	1.6	5.5
1955–1960	2.0	1.9	. . .	3.1	. . .	1.7	2.3	5.8	1.9	1.9	2.7	2.8	7.6	3.7	1.2	2.6
1960–1965	1.3	1.6	. . .	1.8	3.9	2.5	5.3	3.7	2.8	4.9	3.6	4.0	7.0	3.7	3.2	3.5
1965–1970	4.3	3.9	. . .	3.2	3.3	3.5	6.4	4.3	2.4	3.0	4.9	4.9	5.1	4.4	3.5	4.6
1970–1975	6.8	7.4	11.4	10.3	7.3	8.4	9.3	8.8	6.1	11.3	8.6	8.4	12.1	8.0	7.7	13.0
1975–1980	8.9	8.7	6.7	10.6	5.3	6.4	10.4	10.5	4.0	16.3	6.0	8.4	18.6	10.5	2.3	14.4
1980–1985	5.5	7.4	2.8	8.3	4.9	7.0	7.9	9.6	3.8	13.7	4.2	9.0	12.2	9.0	4.3	7.2
1985–1990	4.0	4.5	1.3	7.9	2.2	2.1	3.9	3.1	1.4	5.7	0.8	6.2	6.5	6.2	2.5	5.9
1990–1995	3.1	2.2	1.4	2.5	3.2	2.4	2.0	2.2	3.5	5.1	2.8	2.4	5.2	4.2	3.1	3.4
1995–2000	2.5	1.7	0.3	1.9	1.4	1.7	2.3	1.2	1.3	2.4	2.2	2.3	2.6	0.5	0.7	2.7
2000–2005	2.5	2.3	-0.4	3.0	2.0	2.1	2.0	1.9	1.5	2.4	2.5	1.8	3.3	1.5	0.8	2.4
1970–1971	4.4	3.0	6.5	6.0	4.7	4.3	5.9	5.5	5.2	4.8	7.5	6.7	8.2	7.4	6.6	9.4
1971–1972	3.2	4.8	4.9	6.0	6.3	5.4	6.7	6.2	5.4	5.7	7.8	6.8	8.3	6.0	6.7	7.1
1972–1973	6.2	7.8	11.6	9.2	7.6	7.0	9.3	7.3	7.1	10.8	8.0	7.8	11.4	6.7	8.7	9.1
1973–1974	11.0	11.0	23.2	15.3	9.5	12.7	15.3	13.7	6.9	19.1	9.6	9.1	15.7	9.9	9.8	16.0
1974–1975	9.1	10.7	11.6	15.2	8.4	12.8	9.6	11.8	6.0	17.0	10.2	11.7	17.0	9.8	6.7	24.2
1975–1976	5.8	7.2	9.5	13.4	7.3	9.2	9.0	9.6	4.2	16.8	8.8	9.3	17.6	10.4	1.7	16.5
1976–1977	6.5	8.0	8.2	12.3	5.5	7.1	11.1	9.4	3.7	17.0	6.7	9.2	24.5	11.3	1.3	15.8
1977–1978	7.6	8.9	4.2	8.0	3.6	4.5	10.0	9.1	2.7	12.1	4.1	8.1	19.8	10.1	1.1	8.3
1978–1979	11.3	9.3	3.6	9.1	3.7	4.5	9.6	10.8	4.1	14.8	4.2	4.6	15.7	7.2	3.6	13.4
1979–1980	13.5	10.0	7.9	10.2	6.3	6.6	12.3	13.6	5.4	21.2	6.5	11.0	15.6	13.6	4.0	18.0
1980–1981	10.3	12.5	4.8	9.6	6.8	7.6	11.7	13.4	6.3	17.8	6.7	13.4	14.5	12.1	6.6	11.9
1981–1982	6.2	10.9	2.9	11.2	5.4	8.7	10.1	11.8	5.2	16.5	6.0	11.4	14.4	8.6	5.5	8.6
1982–1983	3.2	5.8	1.8	10.1	3.3	7.7	6.9	9.6	3.2	14.7	2.8	8.5	12.2	8.9	3.0	4.6
1983–1984	4.3	4.3	2.3	3.9	5.7	6.4	6.3	7.4	2.5	10.8	3.3	6.4	11.3	8.0	2.9	5.0
1984–1985	3.6	4.0	2.1	6.7	3.2	4.9	4.7	5.8	2.0	9.2	2.2	5.6	8.8	7.4	3.4	6.1
1985–1986	1.9	4.1	0.6	9.1	1.7	1.3	3.7	2.7	-0.1	5.9	0.2	7.1	8.8	4.2	0.7	3.4
1986–1987	3.6	4.4	0.1	8.5	1.4	1.6	4.0	3.1	0.2	4.7	-0.5	8.7	5.2	4.2	1.4	4.2
1987–1988	4.1	3.9	0.7	7.3	1.9	1.2	4.5	2.7	1.2	5.0	0.7	6.7	4.8	5.8	1.8	4.9
1988–1989	4.8	5.1	2.2	7.5	2.6	3.1	4.8	3.6	2.8	6.3	1.1	4.6	6.8	6.4	3.2	7.8
1989–1990	5.4	4.8	3.1	7.3	3.3	3.4	2.6	3.4	2.6	6.5	2.5	4.1	6.7	10.4	5.5	9.5
1990–1991	4.2	5.6	3.4	3.2	3.3	3.2	2.4	3.2	3.7	6.3	3.9	3.5	5.9	9.4	5.8	5.9
1991–1992	3.0	1.4	1.6	1.0	4.0	2.4	2.1	2.4	5.1	5.3	3.7	2.3	5.9	2.4	4.0	3.7
1992–1993	3.0	1.9	1.3	1.8	3.6	2.8	1.2	2.1	4.4	4.6	2.1	2.3	4.6	4.7	3.3	1.6
1993–1994	2.6	0.1	0.6	1.9	2.9	2.4	2.0	1.6	2.8	4.1	2.8	1.4	4.7	2.2	0.9	2.4
1994–1995	2.8	2.2	-0.1	4.6	2.2	1.5	2.1	1.8	1.8	5.3	1.8	2.5	4.7	2.5	1.8	3.5
1995–1996	3.0	1.5	0.1	2.6	1.9	2.1	2.1	2.0	1.4	4.0	2.1	1.2	3.6	0.5	0.8	2.4
1996–1997	2.3	1.7	1.9	0.3	1.3	1.6	2.2	1.2	1.9	2.0	2.2	2.6	2.0	0.7	0.5	3.1
1997–1998	1.6	1.0	0.6	0.9	0.9	0.9	1.8	0.7	1.0	2.0	2.0	2.2	1.8	-0.3	0.0	3.4
1998–1999	2.2	1.8	-0.3	1.5	0.6	1.1	2.5	0.5	0.6	1.7	2.2	2.3	2.3	0.5	0.9	1.5
1999–2000	3.4	2.7	-0.8	4.5	2.3	2.5	2.9	1.7	1.4	2.5	2.3	3.1	3.4	0.9	1.5	3.0
2000–2001	2.8	2.5	-0.7	4.4	2.7	2.5	2.4	1.7	1.9	2.7	4.2	3.0	3.6	2.4	1.0	1.8
2001–2002	1.6	2.2	-0.9	3.0	1.8	1.6	2.4	1.9	1.5	2.5	3.3	1.3	3.5	2.2	0.6	1.7
2002–2003	2.3	2.8	-0.3	2.8	1.4	1.6	2.1	2.1	1.0	2.7	2.1	2.5	3.0	1.9	0.6	2.9
2003–2004	2.7	1.8	0.0	2.3	2.1	2.1	1.2	2.1	1.7	2.2	1.2	0.4	3.0	0.4	0.8	3.0
2004–2005	3.4	2.2	-0.3	2.7	2.3	2.8	1.8	1.8	1.5	2.0	1.7	1.6	3.4	0.5	1.1	2.8
2005–2006	3.2	2.0	0.3	3.5	1.5	1.8	1.9	1.6	1.6	2.1	1.2	2.3	3.5	1.4	1.1	3.2
2006–2007	2.8	2.2	0.0	2.3	2.2	1.8	1.7	1.5	2.3	1.8	1.6	0.8	2.8	2.2	0.7	4.3
2007–2008	3.8	2.3	1.4	4.4	3.2	4.5	3.4	2.8	2.6	3.3	2.5	3.8	4.1	3.4	2.5	4.0

[1]The figures may differ from official indexes published by national statistical agencies because of rounding.
[2]Urban wage earners and clerical workers prior to 1978 and all urban consumers from 1978 onward.
[3]All households from January 1995, all urban households from September 1978 to December 1994, and middle-income urban households prior to September 1978.
[4]Excluding imputed rent for owner-occupied households prior to 1970.
[5]Urban worker households prior to September 1998.
[7]Excluding rent and several other services prior to 1976.
[8]Excluding rent prior to 1964.
[9]All households from 1991, urban worker households prior to 1991; worker households in Paris only prior to 1962.
[10]Unified Germany from 1991 onward; data for previous years relate to the former West Germany.
[11]Employee households from 2001, low-income employee households prior to 2001.
[12]Urban worker households prior to 1960.
[13]All family households from 1993, middle-income family households prior to 1993.
[14]Urban worker households prior to May 1993.
. . . = Not available.

Table 10-13. Real Gross Domestic Product (GDP) Per Capita, 16 Countries, 1960–2008

(2005 U.S. dollars.)

Year	United States	Canada	Australia	Japan	Korea, Republic of	Austria	Belgium	Denmark	France	Germany[1]	Italy	Nether-lands	Norway	Spain	Sweden	United Kingdom
1960	15 644	13 016	13 268	5 698	1 877	10 020	10 094	11 799	9 531	11 702	8 369	12 344	12 488	. . .	11 871	12 382
1961	15 749	13 158	12 853	6 375	1 929	10 495	10 561	12 409	9 899	12 082	8 996	12 534	13 149	. . .	12 487	12 566
1962	16 448	13 819	13 343	6 858	1 914	10 681	11 067	12 994	10 389	12 498	9 490	12 891	13 395	. . .	12 946	12 587
1963	16 922	14 284	13 864	7 385	2 032	11 045	11 462	12 951	10 855	12 726	9 949	13 135	13 798	. . .	13 561	13 046
1964	17 660	14 925	14 494	8 124	2 171	11 634	12 145	14 001	11 439	13 438	10 144	14 075	14 380	8 878	14 378	13 668
1965	18 560	15 590	14 899	8 409	2 238	11 889	12 463	14 558	11 885	14 001	10 387	14 619	15 023	9 332	14 786	13 880
1966	19 543	16 319	15 067	9 287	2 448	12 472	12 771	14 777	12 406	14 263	10 924	14 832	15 465	9 902	14 952	14 071
1967	19 818	16 496	15 817	10 197	2 533	12 752	13 192	15 478	12 915	14 186	11 623	15 442	16 292	10 209	15 338	14 335
1968	20 567	17 036	16 412	11 284	2 755	13 253	13 692	16 238	13 386	14 905	12 306	16 310	16 516	10 773	15 803	14 868
1969	20 994	17 639	17 171	12 484	3 066	14 036	14 561	17 205	14 232	15 866	12 983	17 220	17 117	11 596	16 478	15 109
1970	20 789	17 921	17 935	13 488	3 263	14 984	15 479	17 255	14 967	16 505	13 600	18 055	17 340	11 943	17 386	15 400
1971	21 218	18 117	17 815	13 889	3 463	15 680	16 011	17 682	15 601	16 834	13 783	18 603	18 193	12 333	17 431	15 640
1972	22 104	18 884	17 913	14 849	3 550	16 557	16 793	18 315	16 182	17 439	14 211	19 064	19 005	13 179	17 777	16 162
1973	23 155	19 953	18 443	15 820	3 908	17 270	17 731	18 105	16 889	18 180	15 121	19 940	19 718	14 049	18 449	17 287
1974	22 827	20 403	18 442	15 418	4 117	17 920	18 401	18 648	17 755	18 193	15 848	20 466	20 344	14 706	18 983	17 056
1975	22 563	20 474	18 625	15 701	4 290	17 903	18 078	18 367	17 501	18 031	15 425	20 291	21 249	14 652	19 391	16 953
1976	23 536	21 256	19 109	16 158	4 668	18 756	19 054	19 437	18 200	19 083	16 441	21 021	22 375	14 961	19 527	17 402
1977	24 376	21 736	19 225	16 710	5 055	19 687	19 123	19 757	18 762	19 667	16 791	21 422	23 203	15 174	19 146	17 824
1978	25 462	22 371	19 421	17 434	5 442	19 674	19 631	19 631	19 420	20 281	17 273	21 869	24 005	15 194	19 424	18 403
1979	25 978	22 993	20 013	18 237	5 723	20 783	20 035	20 888	20 019	21 127	18 250	22 158	24 966	15 089	20 127	18 876
1980	25 621	23 190	20 341	18 606	5 551	21 154	20 878	20 784	20 253	21 262	18 837	22 274	26 007	15 204	20 429	18 453
1981	26 005	23 708	20 859	19 015	5 802	21 070	20 807	20 611	20 325	21 243	18 973	21 946	26 319	15 097	20 364	18 200
1982	25 259	22 758	20 506	19 405	6 131	21 465	20 925	21 390	20 696	21 058	19 038	21 576	26 255	15 204	20 594	18 603
1983	26 163	23 146	20 136	19 584	6 693	22 134	20 992	21 975	20 831	21 504	19 253	21 936	27 180	15 400	20 957	19 269
1984	27 798	24 261	21 141	20 066	7 146	22 149	21 510	22 904	21 039	22 199	19 870	22 522	28 701	15 611	21 831	19 751
1985	28 690	25 190	22 063	20 956	7 557	22 682	21 858	23 817	21 293	22 705	20 420	22 999	30 147	15 915	22 274	20 409
1986	29 416	25 545	22 204	21 468	8 277	23 193	22 248	24 964	21 705	23 222	21 003	23 512	31 253	16 383	22 857	21 180
1987	30 139	26 281	22 831	22 177	9 106	23 490	22 742	24 998	22 125	23 561	21 671	23 807	31 660	17 250	23 568	22 099
1988	31 101	27 232	23 371	23 580	9 977	24 130	23 694	24 951	23 011	24 290	22 569	24 467	31 436	18 088	24 088	23 165
1989	31 899	27 446	24 039	24 735	10 545	24 920	24 474	25 084	23 829	24 922	23 316	25 400	31 619	18 925	24 591	23 627
1990	32 135	27 086	24 033	25 936	11 398	25 763	25 168	25 445	24 327	25 847	23 775	26 284	32 118	19 611	24 648	23 745
1991	31 657	26 205	23 465	26 699	12 345	26 358	25 534	25 707	24 453	26 804	24 116	26 709	32 957	20 064	24 207	23 332
1992	32 278	26 121	23 652	26 858	12 936	26 562	25 820	26 129	24 667	27 193	24 293	26 960	33 922	20 184	23 775	23 307
1993	32 713	26 438	24 344	26 844	13 590	26 443	25 472	26 014	24 338	26 781	24 062	27 107	34 660	19 914	23 151	23 771
1994	33 618	27 405	25 272	27 070	14 603	26 924	26 212	27 365	24 787	27 410	24 575	27 744	36 205	20 333	23 894	24 725
1995	34 055	27 884	25 875	27 534	15 782	27 565	26 754	28 071	25 222	27 847	25 269	28 462	37 525	20 845	24 714	25 406
1996	34 906	28 039	26 579	28 225	16 726	28 142	27 022	28 690	25 415	28 043	25 539	29 307	39 239	21 300	25 035	26 075
1997	36 042	28 935	27 390	28 600	17 341	28 708	27 904	29 482	25 894	28 495	26 003	30 402	41 132	22 066	25 636	26 868
1998	37 112	29 871	28 436	27 944	16 036	29 707	28 312	30 015	26 704	29 081	26 360	31 402	41 984	22 971	26 599	27 760
1999	38 323	31 267	29 391	27 862	17 433	30 640	29 212	30 683	27 463	29 645	26 742	32 652	42 542	23 868	27 799	28 622
2000	39 292	32 598	30 019	28 600	18 755	31 682	30 233	31 659	28 344	30 559	27 717	33 698	43 642	24 792	28 976	29 641
2001	39 187	32 824	30 221	28 565	19 331	31 725	30 368	31 771	28 663	30 881	28 203	34 088	44 286	25 282	29 204	30 254
2002	39 432	33 405	31 134	28 602	20 598	32 089	30 689	31 810	28 750	30 828	28 242	33 894	44 710	25 475	29 811	30 779
2003	40 050	33 708	31 658	28 959	21 070	32 202	30 865	31 849	28 860	30 747	28 018	33 849	44 899	25 848	30 268	31 522
2004	41 137	34 420	32 505	29 732	21 961	32 815	31 642	32 499	29 358	31 125	28 168	34 493	46 359	26 267	31 394	32 235
2005	41 961	35 075	32 964	30 312	22 783	33 528	32 049	33 199	29 692	31 380	28 144	35 111	47 306	26 754	32 300	32 684
2006	42 725	35 798	33 417	30 929	23 884	34 481	32 789	34 194	30 148	32 347	28 554	36 243	47 996	27 456	33 482	33 418
2007	43 170	36 377	34 119	31 652	25 021	35 396	33 446	34 608	30 667	33 184	28 789	37 415	48 991	28 010	34 086	34 209
2008	43 250	36 123	34 254	31 446	25 498	35 868	33 616	34 013	30 624	33 663	28 245	38 035	49 416	27 747	33 744	34 356

[1]Unified Germany from 1991 onward; data for previous years relate to the former West Germany.
. . . = Not available.

Table 10-14. Real Gross Domestic Product (GDP) Per Employed Person, 16 Countries, 1960–2008

(2005 U.S. dollars.)

Year	United States	Canada	Australia	Japan	Korea, Republic of	Austria	Belgium	Denmark	France	Germany[1]	Italy	Netherlands	Norway	Spain	Sweden	United Kingdom
1960	41 409	37 322	32 804	11 429	...	20 529	26 247	25 342	22 247	23 481	20 079	30 834	29 241	...	24 309	26 862
1961	42 356	37 918	32 527	12 616	...	21 501	27 349	26 446	23 358	24 231	21 589	31 272	30 614	...	25 484	27 202
1962	44 141	39 453	33 584	13 544	...	22 120	28 337	27 482	24 969	25 273	22 995	31 976	31 266	...	26 425	27 365
1963	45 439	40 605	34 583	14 610	7 324	23 181	29 363	27 273	26 341	25 922	24 695	32 587	32 318	...	27 695	28 479
1964	47 048	41 754	35 649	16 006	7 891	24 622	30 964	29 112	27 750	27 625	25 474	34 779	33 842	...	29 165	29 645
1965	48 869	42 844	36 206	16 656	7 919	25 497	31 943	29 961	29 023	28 940	26 965	36 313	35 315	...	30 072	30 005
1966	50 543	43 900	35 718	17 975	8 656	27 161	32 836	30 152	30 334	29 839	29 053	37 042	36 504	...	30 658	30 517
1967	50 615	43 809	37 243	19 564	8 848	28 442	34 259	31 852	31 762	30 749	30 755	39 126	38 559	...	32 031	31 633
1968	51 965	45 030	38 360	21 485	9 376	30 109	35 738	33 404	33 277	32 398	32 785	41 363	39 392	...	32 848	33 118
1969	52 282	45 854	39 979	23 821	10 417	32 058	37 471	34 893	35 149	34 282	35 036	43 452	40 808	...	33 857	33 806
1970	52 079	46 685	40 934	25 974	10 939	34 273	39 823	34 950	36 820	35 558	36 726	45 580	40 961	...	35 356	34 660
1971	53 621	47 439	41 570	26 924	11 449	35 633	40 996	36 052	38 587	36 497	37 381	47 266	42 903	29 451	35 760	35 413
1972	54 846	48 558	41 868	29 038	11 461	37 568	43 253	36 818	40 158	37 898	38 861	49 365	44 648	31 463	36 459	36 599
1973	56 155	49 424	42 532	30 677	12 180	38 861	45 407	37 731	42 220	39 275	41 049	52 030	46 318	33 068	37 764	38 638
1974	54 847	49 151	42 734	30 429	12 507	39 875	46 568	37 730	43 734	39 835	42 645	53 303	47 459	34 799	38 213	38 046
1975	55 360	49 141	43 784	31 448	12 945	40 026	46 548	37 767	43 693	40 422	41 721	53 717	49 027	35 695	38 431	37 962
1976	56 469	50 682	44 941	32 432	13 482	41 718	49 406	39 399	45 278	42 801	44 246	55 805	50 188	37 282	38 704	39 191
1977	57 033	51 544	44 986	33 455	14 367	43 281	49 841	40 279	46 512	43 956	45 240	56 033	50 855	38 590	38 010	40 093
1978	57 746	51 999	45 904	34 878	14 999	45 157	51 164	40 901	48 118	44 907	46 552	56 987	51 918	40 148	38 531	41 180
1979	57 949	51 729	47 002	36 417	15 793	45 157	51 782	42 114	49 565	46 029	48 783	57 136	53 435	41 094	39 436	41 862
1980	57 537	51 345	47 028	37 188	15 466	45 547	54 087	42 281	50 270	45 775	49 738	56 140	54 520	42 634	39 666	41 159
1981	58 333	51 640	47 982	37 989	16 021	45 661	54 948	42 604	50 928	45 869	50 198	55 395	54 663	43 623	39 523	41 688
1982	57 674	51 804	48 008	38 723	16 769	47 195	56 006	44 045	52 104	45 986	50 303	54 992	54 715	44 549	40 070	43 416
1983	59 503	52 832	48 649	38 760	18 414	48 913	56 759	45 209	52 890	47 470	50 727	57 184	56 947	45 496	40 702	45 320
1984	61 286	54 534	50 179	39 834	20 011	48 987	58 272	46 403	54 012	48 728	52 367	58 205	59 853	47 367	42 090	45 556
1985	62 557	55 541	51 480	41 633	20 600	50 044	58 906	47 156	55 139	49 349	53 327	58 060	61 356	48 969	42 573	46 611
1986	63 304	55 191	50 431	42 646	22 001	51 052	59 584	48 332	56 281	49 817	54 478	58 748	61 808	49 417	43 522	48 187
1987	63 812	55 924	51 503	44 090	23 175	51 770	60 641	48 256	57 244	50 190	56 088	59 826	61 654	49 774	44 670	49 412
1988	65 035	56 981	51 643	46 532	24 859	52 797	62 596	48 571	59 335	51 656	57 820	60 162	61 890	50 539	45 240	50 257
1989	66 009	57 187	51 798	48 283	25 491	54 116	63 768	49 067	60 783	52 760	59 374	61 550	64 338	51 126	45 828	50 114
1990	66 465	56 905	51 623	49 961	27 017	55 312	64 820	50 135	61 897	54 160	59 643	62 085	66 166	51 118	45 868	50 280
1991	66 975	56 705	52 222	50 606	28 661	56 451	65 938	51 087	62 458	55 511	59 445	61 961	68 903	51 797	46 044	50 921
1992	68 845	57 775	53 551	50 527	29 770	57 190	67 253	52 720	63 681	57 584	60 342	61 755	71 481	53 016	47 608	52 238
1993	69 748	58 847	55 409	50 461	31 227	57 671	67 109	53 508	63 923	57 889	61 457	62 604	72 956	54 002	49 202	53 916
1994	70 982	60 434	56 391	50 962	32 844	58 930	69 538	56 671	65 244	59 489	63 831	64 004	75 608	55 550	51 638	55 807
1995	71 756	61 045	56 250	51 890	34 861	60 537	70 645	57 515	66 039	60 477	65 766	64 109	77 170	56 016	52 834	56 842
1996	73 400	61 480	57 790	53 094	36 516	61 640	71 266	58 427	66 522	61 246	66 109	64 962	79 499	56 558	54 039	57 951
1997	75 059	62 767	59 657	53 554	37 564	62 496	73 105	59 293	67 713	62 409	67 137	65 651	81 399	57 081	56 088	58 829
1998	77 086	63 768	61 340	53 082	37 228	64 095	72 927	59 659	69 035	62 924	67 411	66 282	81 412	57 393	57 262	60 339
1999	79 326	65 618	63 099	53 747	40 051	65 249	74 460	60 605	69 902	63 332	67 664	67 566	82 301	58 014	58 662	61 580
2000	80 222	67 389	63 606	55 630	41 673	67 000	75 757	62 309	70 738	64 163	68 829	68 390	84 499	58 890	59 776	63 258
2001	80 777	67 755	64 216	56 157	42 438	66 866	75 273	62 062	70 791	64 674	68 693	67 943	85 879	59 155	59 163	64 289
2002	82 285	68 073	65 686	57 200	44 247	68 031	76 519	62 272	71 076	65 038	67 845	67 177	86 835	59 448	60 560	65 143
2003	83 520	67 757	66 089	58 199	45 549	68 624	77 241	63 258	71 758	65 517	66 832	67 785	88 629	59 421	62 078	66 337
2004	85 624	68 674	67 309	59 667	46 770	69 405	78 979	65 092	73 452	66 045	67 558	69 439	91 625	59 306	65 094	67 456
2005	86 641	69 676	67 058	60 591	47 985	70 362	79 411	65 968	74 431	66 605	67 612	70 825	93 000	59 065	67 063	68 163
2006	87 437	70 470	67 563	61 557	49 827	71 729	80 658	66 839	75 342	68 146	67 662	71 874	91 791	58 956	68 749	69 500
2007	88 238	70 746	68 328	62 763	51 741	72 618	81 419	66 144	76 063	68 644	67 875	72 582	90 905	59 242	69 002	71 130
2008	89 626	69 991	68 198	62 578	52 568	72 622	80 976	64 840	75 989	68 547	66 959	72 995	90 074	60 283	68 219	71 121

[1]Unified Germany from 1991 onward; data for previous years relate to the former West Germany.
. . . = Not available.

Table 10-15. Real Gross Domestic Product (GDP) Per Hour Worked, 16 Countries, 1970–2008

(2005 U.S. dollars.)

Year	United States	Canada	Australia	Japan	Korea, Republic of	Austria	Belgium	Denmark	France	Germany[1]	Italy	Nether-lands	Norway	Spain	Sweden	United Kingdom
1970	27.24	24.32	. . .	. . .	. . .	. . .	21.23	18.55	17.97	18.71	. . .	. . .	22.32	. . .	. . .	. . .
1971	28.28	24.94	. . .	. . .	. . .	. . .	21.97	19.44	18.86	19.50	. . .	. . .	23.66	. . .	. . .	19.50
1972	28.98	25.68	. . .	. . .	. . .	. . .	23.49	20.48	20.17	20.55	. . .	. . .	25.08	. . .	. . .	19.92
1973	29.70	26.19	. . .	. . .	. . .	. . .	25.05	21.51	21.38	21.65	. . .	. . .	26.23	. . .	. . .	20.93
1974	29.44	26.25	. . .	. . .	. . .	. . .	26.09	21.65	22.52	22.33	. . .	. . .	27.20	. . .	. . .	20.77
1975	30.25	26.47	. . .	. . .	. . .	. . .	26.21	22.55	22.83	23.17	. . .	. . .	28.37	. . .	. . .	21.07
1976	30.97	27.73	. . .	. . .	. . .	. . .	27.77	23.39	23.33	24.07	. . .	. . .	29.97	. . .	. . .	21.84
1977	31.29	28.30	. . .	. . .	. . .	. . .	28.43	24.25	24.46	25.13	. . .	. . .	31.04	21.01	. . .	22.22
1978	31.55	28.46	24.64	. . .	. . .	. . .	29.46	24.90	25.73	26.03	. . .	. . .	32.41	22.12	. . .	22.80
1979	31.69	28.36	25.35	. . .	. . .	. . .	30.11	25.75	26.54	26.88	. . .	. . .	33.82	23.27	. . .	23.21
1980	31.71	28.54	25.71	. . .	5.52	. . .	31.82	25.49	27.03	26.96	26.76	. . .	34.51	24.32	25.91	23.21
1981	32.44	28.71	26.10	. . .	5.75	. . .	32.77	26.11	27.66	27.26	26.91	. . .	34.81	25.27	25.96	24.00
1982	32.29	29.13	26.83	. . .	5.77	. . .	33.68	26.83	29.50	27.35	26.81	. . .	35.10	25.80	26.08	25.05
1983	33.16	29.76	27.35	. . .	6.39	. . .	34.01	27.60	30.24	28.27	27.04	. . .	36.66	26.83	26.33	26.24
1984	33.83	30.64	27.85	. . .	6.98	. . .	34.42	28.42	31.01	29.14	28.07	. . .	38.66	28.53	27.19	26.28
1985	34.44	30.97	28.69	. . .	7.19	. . .	34.69	29.13	32.30	29.99	28.64	. . .	39.78	29.81	27.43	26.85
1986	35.22	30.83	28.00	. . .	7.85	. . .	35.49	29.80	33.07	30.42	29.13	. . .	40.18	30.08	28.07	27.84
1987	35.45	31.05	28.34	. . .	8.04	. . .	36.44	30.40	33.39	30.77	29.68	. . .	40.81	31.20	28.63	28.46
1988	35.85	31.31	28.58	. . .	8.57	. . .	37.89	30.95	34.42	31.72	30.54	. . .	40.90	31.59	28.82	28.82
1989	36.12	31.52	28.69	. . .	8.99	. . .	38.79	31.62	35.58	32.87	31.63	. . .	42.59	31.79	29.02	28.67
1990	36.73	31.67	28.88	. . .	9.66	. . .	39.14	32.58	36.31	34.56	31.95	. . .	44.04	31.79	29.12	28.97
1991	37.20	31.98	29.17	. . .	10.32	. . .	40.73	33.31	36.86	35.86	31.97	. . .	45.93	32.38	29.48	29.77
1992	38.40	32.61	29.68	. . .	10.90	. . .	42.09	33.92	37.58	36.77	32.39	. . .	47.34	33.21	30.14	30.66
1993	38.53	32.73	30.93	. . .	11.40	. . .	43.18	34.41	38.01	37.35	32.99	. . .	48.41	34.02	30.81	31.70
1994	38.86	33.31	31.29	. . .	12.05	. . .	44.75	36.61	38.95	38.45	34.38	. . .	50.24	35.06	31.58	32.60
1995	38.88	33.83	31.25	. . .	12.77	32.71	44.71	37.34	40.01	39.43	35.38	42.25	51.87	35.19	32.21	33.14
1996	39.82	33.77	32.65	27.77	13.43	33.06	45.86	38.17	40.19	40.35	35.29	42.60	53.62	35.53	32.69	33.79
1997	40.42	34.80	33.21	28.44	14.05	33.30	46.65	38.40	41.07	41.37	36.03	43.36	55.09	35.63	33.83	34.33
1998	41.22	35.51	34.14	28.53	14.29	34.06	46.21	38.26	42.16	41.86	35.86	44.26	55.17	35.56	34.57	35.28
1999	42.23	36.46	35.21	29.16	15.28	34.71	47.10	38.63	42.87	42.46	36.08	45.26	55.84	35.60	35.24	36.18
2000	43.20	37.54	35.45	29.95	15.84	35.57	48.75	39.40	44.45	43.56	36.98	46.07	58.07	35.62	36.40	37.51
2001	44.06	37.95	36.81	30.55	16.19	35.38	47.73	39.11	44.85	44.35	37.27	46.38	60.09	35.87	36.56	38.07
2002	45.36	38.49	37.53	31.38	17.09	36.11	48.46	39.44	46.24	45.00	37.05	46.69	61.41	36.10	37.97	38.97
2003	46.74	38.63	37.59	31.92	17.84	36.26	49.04	40.12	46.82	45.53	36.61	47.32	63.37	36.41	39.25	39.91
2004	47.90	38.75	38.71	32.66	18.47	36.53	50.99	41.21	47.05	45.82	37.00	48.87	64.65	36.66	40.55	40.67
2005	48.56	39.54	38.34	33.41	19.18	37.33	50.74	41.78	47.76	46.45	37.17	49.83	65.49	36.97	41.78	40.99
2006	49.01	40.05	39.22	33.78	20.00	38.21	51.34	42.18	49.06	47.60	37.29	50.59	64.92	37.29	42.99	41.93
2007	49.67	40.34	40.32	34.65	21.13	39.01	51.99	41.36	48.99	47.89	37.25	51.02	64.14	37.95	42.73	42.85
2008	50.69	40.12	39.08	34.97	21.98	39.38	51.71	40.34	48.99	47.89	36.74	51.44	63.35	38.62	41.98	42.94

[1]Unified Germany from 1991 onward; data for previous years relate to the former West Germany.
. . . = Not available.

Table 10-16. Real Gross Domestic Product (GDP) Per Capita and Per Employed Person, Average Annual Percent Change, 16 Countries, Selected Years, 1979–2008

(Percent.)

Category and country	1979–2008	1979–1990	1990–1995	1995–2000	2000–2008	2002–2003	2003–2004	2004–2005	2005–2006	2006–2007	2007–2008
Real GDP Per Capita											
United States	1.8	2.0	1.2	2.9	1.2	1.6	2.7	2.0	1.8	1.0	0.2
Canada	1.6	1.5	0.6	3.2	1.3	0.9	2.1	1.9	2.1	1.6	-0.7
Australia	1.9	1.7	1.5	3.0	1.7	1.7	2.7	1.4	1.4	2.1	0.4
Japan	1.9	3.3	1.2	0.8	1.2	1.2	2.7	1.9	2.0	2.3	-0.7
Korea, Republic of	5.3	6.5	6.7	3.5	3.9	2.3	4.2	3.7	4.8	4.8	1.9
Austria	1.9	2.0	1.4	2.8	1.6	0.4	1.9	2.2	2.8	2.7	1.3
Belgium	1.8	2.1	1.2	2.5	1.3	0.6	2.5	1.3	2.3	2.0	0.5
Denmark	1.7	1.8	2.0	2.4	0.9	0.1	2.0	2.2	3.0	1.2	-1.7
France	1.5	1.8	0.7	2.4	1.0	0.4	1.7	1.1	1.5	1.7	-0.1
Germany[1]	1.6	1.9	1.5	1.9	1.2	-0.3	1.2	0.8	3.1	2.6	1.4
Italy	1.5	2.4	1.2	1.9	0.2	-0.8	0.5	-0.1	1.5	0.8	-1.9
Netherlands	1.9	1.6	1.6	3.4	1.5	-0.1	1.9	1.8	3.2	3.2	1.7
Norway	2.4	2.3	3.2	3.1	1.6	0.4	3.3	2.0	1.5	2.1	0.9
Spain	2.1	2.4	1.2	3.5	1.4	1.5	1.6	1.9	2.6	2.0	-0.9
Sweden	1.8	1.9	0.1	3.2	1.9	1.5	3.7	2.9	3.7	1.8	-1.0
United Kingdom	2.1	2.1	1.4	3.1	1.9	2.4	2.3	1.4	2.2	2.4	0.4
Real GDP Per Employed Person											
United States	1.5	1.3	1.5	2.3	1.4	1.5	2.5	1.2	0.9	0.9	1.6
Canada	1.1	0.9	1.4	2.0	0.5	-0.5	1.4	1.5	1.1	0.4	-1.1
Australia	1.3	0.9	1.7	2.5	0.9	0.6	1.8	-0.4	0.8	1.1	-0.2
Japan	1.9	2.9	0.8	1.4	1.5	1.7	2.5	1.5	1.6	2.0	-0.3
Korea, Republic of	4.2	5.0	5.2	3.6	2.9	2.9	2.7	2.6	3.8	3.8	1.6
Austria	1.7	1.9	1.8	2.0	1.0	0.9	1.1	1.4	1.9	1.2	0.0
Belgium	1.6	2.1	1.7	1.4	0.8	0.9	2.3	0.5	1.6	0.9	-0.5
Denmark	1.6	1.6	2.8	1.6	0.5	1.6	2.9	1.3	1.3	-1.0	-2.0
France	1.5	2.0	1.3	1.4	0.9	1.0	2.4	1.3	1.2	1.0	-0.1
Germany[1]	1.4	1.5	2.2	1.2	0.8	0.7	0.8	0.8	2.3	0.7	-0.1
Italy	1.1	1.8	2.0	0.9	-0.3	-1.5	1.1	0.1	0.1	0.3	-1.4
Netherlands	0.8	0.8	0.6	1.3	0.8	0.9	2.4	2.0	1.5	1.0	0.6
Norway	1.8	2.0	3.1	1.8	0.8	2.1	3.4	1.5	-1.3	-1.0	-0.9
Spain	1.3	2.0	1.8	1.0	0.3	0.0	-0.2	-0.4	-0.2	0.5	1.8
Sweden	1.9	1.4	2.9	2.5	1.7	2.5	4.9	3.0	2.5	0.4	-1.1
United Kingdom	1.8	1.7	2.5	2.2	1.5	1.8	1.7	1.0	2.0	2.3	0.0

[1]Data for Germany for years before 1991 pertain to the former West Germany.

Table 10-17. Real Gross Domestic Product (GDP) Per Hour Worked, Average Annual Percent Change, 16 Countries, Selected Years, 1979–2008

(Percent.)

Country	1979–2008	1979–1990	1990–1995	1995–2000	2000–2008	2002–2003	2003–2004	2004–2005	2005–2006	2006–2007	2007–2008
Real GDP Per Capita											
United States	1.6	1.4	1.1	2.1	2.0	3.0	2.5	1.4	0.9	1.3	2.1
Canada	1.2	1.0	1.3	2.1	0.8	0.4	0.3	2.0	1.3	0.7	-0.6
Australia	1.5	1.2	1.6	2.6	1.2	0.2	3.0	-1.0	2.3	2.8	-3.1
Japan	...	...	...	...	2.0	1.7	2.3	2.3	1.1	2.6	0.9
Korea, Republic of	...	...	5.7	4.4	4.2	4.4	3.5	3.9	4.3	5.6	4.0
Austria	...	...	...	1.7	1.3	0.4	0.7	2.2	2.4	2.1	0.9
Belgium	1.9	2.4	2.7	1.7	0.7	1.2	4.0	-0.5	1.2	1.3	-0.5
Denmark	1.6	2.2	2.8	1.1	0.3	1.7	2.7	1.4	0.9	-1.9	-2.5
France	2.1	2.9	2.0	2.1	1.2	1.3	0.5	1.5	2.7	-0.1	0.0
Germany[1]	2.0	2.3	2.7	2.0	1.2	1.2	0.6	1.4	2.5	0.6	0.0
Italy	...	...	2.1	0.9	-0.1	-1.2	1.1	0.5	0.3	-0.1	-1.4
Netherlands	...	...	...	1.8	1.4	1.4	3.3	2.0	1.5	0.9	0.8
Norway	2.2	2.4	3.3	2.3	1.1	3.2	2.0	1.3	-0.9	-1.2	-1.2
Spain	1.8	2.9	2.1	0.2	1.0	0.9	0.7	0.8	0.9	1.8	1.8
Sweden	...	...	2.0	2.5	1.8	3.4	3.3	3.1	2.9	-0.6	-1.8
United Kingdom	2.1	2.0	2.7	2.5	1.7	2.4	1.9	0.8	2.3	2.2	0.2

[1]Data for Germany for years before 1991 pertain to the former West Germany.

Chapter Eleven

CONSUMER EXPENDITURES

CONSUMER EXPENDITURES

HIGHLIGHTS

The principal objective of the Consumer Expenditure Survey (CE) is to collect information about the buying habits of American households. The survey breaks down expenditures for different demographic categories, such as income, age, family size, and geographic location. These data are used in a variety of government, business, and academic research projects and provide important weights for the periodic revisions of the Consumer Price Index (CPI).

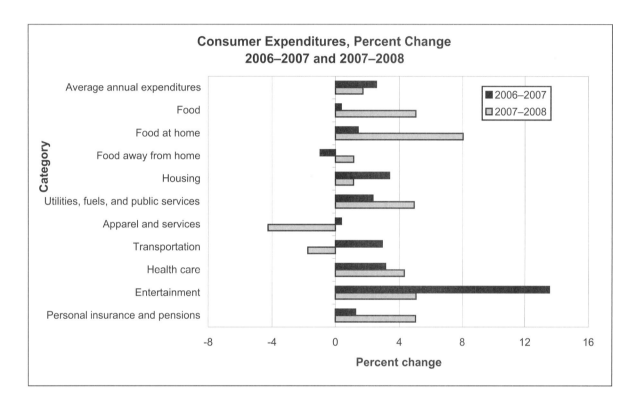

Increases in spending on food (5.1 percent), health care (4.3 percent), and housing (1.1 percent), along with a decline in spending on apparel and services (-4.3 percent) and transportation (-1.8 percent), contributed to an overall increase of 1.7 percent in 2008. Among the other major components, spending increased for entertainment (5.1 percent) and personal insurance and pensions (5.0 percent). (See Table 11-1.)

OTHER HIGHLIGHTS

• The increase in spending of 1.7 percent in 2008 was the smallest increase since the 0.3 percent rise in 2003. In 2007, expenditures rose 2.6 percent. (See Table 11-1.)

• According to educational attainment, average annual expenditures ranged from $29,903 for those will less than high school diploma to $79,198 for those with a master's, professional, or doctoral degree. (See Table 11-13.)

• Average annual expenditures were highest for those in the West ($55,453), followed by those in the Northeast ($54,918), the South ($47,846), and the Midwest ($46,823). (See Table 11-16.)

NOTES AND DEFINITIONS

Purpose, Collection, and Coverage

The buying habits of American consumers change over time because of changes in relative prices, real income, family size and composition, and other determinants of tastes and preferences. The introduction of new products into the marketplace and the emergence of new concepts in retailing also influence consumer buying habits. Data from the Consumer Expenditure Survey (CE), the only national survey that relates family expenditures to demographic characteristics, are of great importance to researchers. The survey data are also used to revise the Consumer Price Index market baskets and item samples.

Until the 1970s, the Bureau of Labor Statistics (BLS) conducted surveys of consumer expenditures approximately once every 10 years. The last such survey was conducted in 1972–1973. In late 1979, in a significant departure from previous methodology, BLS initiated a survey to be conducted on a continuous basis with rotating panels of respondents.

The current CE is similar to its 1972–1973 predecessor in that it consists of two separate components. Each component has its own questionnaire and sample: (1) the Interview Survey, in which an interviewer visits each consumer unit every three months for a twelve-month period; and (2) the Diary Survey, a record-keeping survey completed by other consumer units for two consecutive one-week periods. The Census Bureau, under contract to BLS, collects the data for both components of the survey. Beginning in 1999, the sample was increased from 5,000 to 7,500 households.

In 2003, the survey modified the questions on race and Hispanic origin to comply with the new standards for maintaining, collecting, and presenting federal data on race and ethnicity for federal statistical agencies. Beginning with the data collected in 2003, the CE tables use data collected from the new race and ethnicity questions. A number of new classifications were made with publication of the 2003 data.

Beginning with the publication of the 2004 tables, the CE has been implementing multiple imputations of income data. Prior to 2004, the CE only published income data collected from complete income reporters. The introduction of multiply imputed income data affects the published CE tables in several ways, because income data are now published for all consumer units (instead of for complete reporters only). The most obvious result of this change is seen on the tables showing expenditures categorized by income before taxes, including income by quintile. Starting with the 2004 data, columns describing income, expenditures, and characteristics for "total complete reporting" and "incomplete reporting of income" no longer appear in these tables, and the column entitled "all consumer units" appears on all income tables. Due to the implementation of income imputation, data for 2004 are not strictly comparable to those of prior years, especially for the income tables. Averages for demographic characteristics and annual expenditures will change due to differences between the incomplete and complete income reporters in these categories. Furthermore, certain expenditures (such as personal insurance and pensions) are computed using income data. As a result of imputation, average annual values for these expenditures may be substantially different in the 2004 CE tables than in tables for previous years. The regular flow of data resulting from this design substantially enhances the usefulness of the survey by providing more timely information on consumption patterns within different kinds of consumer units.

The *Interview Survey* is designed to collect data on the types of expenditures that respondents can be expected to recall after a period of three months or longer. These include relatively large expenditures (such as those for property, travel, automobiles, and major appliances) and expenditures that occur on a regular basis (such as those for rent, utilities, insurance premiums, and clothing). The interview also obtains "global estimates" for food and other selected items. The survey collects data for approximately 95 percent of total expenditures. Each sample household is interviewed once per quarter, for five consecutive quarters.

The *Diary Survey* is designed to collect data on expenditures for frequently purchased items that are more difficult to recall over longer periods of time. Respondents complete a diary of expenses for two consecutive 1-week periods. Expenditures for tobacco, drugs (including nonprescription drugs), and personal care supplies and services are also collected in the Diary Survey.

Participants in both surveys record dollar amounts for goods and services purchased during the reporting period, regardless of whether payment was made at the time of purchase. Excluded from both surveys are business-related expenditures and expenditures for which the family is reimbursed. Information is collected on demographic and family characteristics at the initial interview for each survey.

The tables in this chapter present integrated data from the Diary Survey and the Interview Survey and provide a complete accounting of consumer expenditures and income, which neither survey component is designed to do alone. Data for some expenditure items are only collected in one of the surveys. For example, the Diary Survey does not collect data for expenditures on overnight travel or information on reimbursements, while the Interview Survey records these purchases. Examples of expenditures for which reimbursements are netted out include those for medical care, auto repair, and construction, repairs, alterations, and maintenance of property.

For items unique to one survey or the other, the choice of which survey to use as the source of data is obvious. However, there is considerable overlap in coverage between the two surveys. Integrating the data thus presents the problem of determining the appropriate survey component. When data are available from both survey sources, the more reliable of the two (as determined by statistical methods) is selected. As a result, some items are selected from the Interview Survey and others are selected from the Diary Survey.

Data Included in This Book

Data for single characteristics are for calendar year 2008, and data for two cross-classified characteristics are for an average of calendar years 2007 and 2008. Income values from the survey are derived from "complete income reporters" only. Complete income reporters are defined as consumer units that provide values for at least one of the major sources of their income: wages and salaries, self-employment income, retirement income, dividends and interest, and welfare benefits. Some consumer units are defined as complete income reporters, even though they may not have provided a full accounting of all income from all sources.

Consumer units are classified by quintiles of income before taxes, age of reference person, size of consumer unit, region, composition of consumer unit, number of earners in consumer unit, housing tenure, race, type of area (urban or rural), and occupation.

Concepts and Definitions

A *consumer unit* comprises either (1) all members of a particular household related by blood, marriage, adoption, or other legal arrangements; (2) a person living alone, sharing a household with others, living as a roomer in a private home or lodging house or in permanent living quarters in a hotel or motel, but who is financially independent; or (3) two or more persons living together who pool their income to make joint expenditure decisions. Financial independence is determined by the three major expense categories: housing, food, and other living expenses. To be considered financially independent, at least two of the three major expense categories have to be provided by the respondent.

The terms "family," "household," and "consumer unit" are used interchangeably in descriptions of the CE.

An *earner* is a consumer unit member, 14 years of age or older, who reported having worked at least 1 week during the 12 months prior to the interview date.

The *education of reference person* refers to the number of years of formal education of the reference person, on the basis of the highest grade completed. If enrolled at time of the interview, the interviewer records the grade currently attended. Persons not reporting the extent of their education are classified under no school or not reported.

Housing tenure refers to the family's principal place of residence during the survey. "Owner" includes families living in their own homes, cooperatives or condominium apartments, or townhouses. "Renter" includes families paying rent, as well as families living rent-free in lieu of wages.

The *householder* or *reference person* is the first member of the consumer unit mentioned by the respondent as owner or renter of the premises at the time of the initial interview.

Quintiles of income before taxes refers to the ranking of complete income reporters in ascending order, according to the level of total before-tax income reported by the consumer unit. The ranking is then divided into five equal groups. Incomplete income reporters are not ranked and are shown separately.

Total expenditures include the transaction costs, including excise and sales taxes of goods and services acquired during the interview period. Estimates include expenditures for gifts and contributions and payments for pensions and personal insurance.

Sources of Additional Information

More extensive descriptions and tables can be found in an updated version of Chapter 16 in the *BLS Handbook of Methods* and in an anthology of articles relating to consumer expenditures. These resources can be found on the BLS Web site at <http://www.bls.gov>.

Table 11-1. Consumer Expenditures, Annual Average of All Consumer Units, 1997–2008

(Number, dollar, percent.)

Item	1997	1998	1999	2000	2001	2002	2003	2004	2005	2006	2007	2008
NUMBER OF CONSUMER UNITS (THOUSANDS)	105 576	107 182	108 465	109 367	110 339	112 108	115 356	116 282	117 356	118 843	120 171	120 770
CONSUMER UNIT CHARACTERISTICS												
Income Before Taxes	39 926	41 622	43 951	44 649	47 507	49 430	51 128	54 453	58 712	60 533	63 091	63 563
Age of Reference Person	47.7	47.6	47.9	48.2	48.1	48.1	48.0	48.5	48.6	49.0	48.8	49.1
Average Number in Consumer Unit												
All persons	2.5	2.5	2.5	2.5	2.5	2.5	2.5	2.5	2.5	3.0	2.5	2.5
Children under 18 years	0.7	0.7	0.7	0.7	0.7	0.7	0.6	0.6	0.6	1.0	0.6	0.6
Persons 65 years and over	0.3	0.3	0.3	0.3	0.3	0.3	0.3	0.3	0.3	0.0	0.3	0.3
Earners	1.3	1.3	1.3	1.4	1.4	1.4	1.3	1.3	1.3	1.0	1.3	1.3
Vehicles	2.0	2.0	1.9	1.9	1.9	2.0	1.9	1.9	2.0	2.0	1.9	2.0
Percent Homeowner	64	64	65	66	66	66	67	68	67	67	67	66
With mortgage	38	39	38	39	40	41	41	42	43	43	43	42
Without mortgage	26	26	27	27	26	26	26	25	25	24	23	24
AVERAGE ANNUAL EXPENDITURES	34 819	35 535	36 995	38 045	39 518	40 677	40 817	43 395	46 409	48 398	49 638	50 486
Food	4 801	4 810	5 031	5 158	5 321	5 375	5 340	5 781	5 931	6 111	6 133	6 443
Food at home	2 880	2 780	2 915	3 021	3 086	3 099	3 129	3 347	3 297	3 417	3 465	3 744
Cereals and bakery products	453	425	448	453	452	450	442	461	445	446	460	507
Meats, poultry, fish, and eggs	453	425	448	453	452	798	825	880	764	797	777	846
Dairy products	314	301	322	325	332	328	328	371	378	368	387	430
Fruits and vegetables	476	472	500	521	522	552	535	561	552	592	600	657
Other food at home	895	858	896	927	952	970	999	1 075	1 158	1 212	1 241	1 305
Food away from home	1 921	2 030	2 116	2 137	2 235	2 276	2 211	2 434	2 634	2 694	2 668	2 698
Alcoholic Beverages	309	309	318	372	349	376	391	459	426	497	457	444
Housing	11 272	11 713	12 057	12 319	13 011	13 283	13 432	13 918	15 167	16 366	16 920	17 109
Shelter	6 344	6 680	7 016	7 114	7 602	7 829	7 887	7 998	8 805	9 673	10 023	10 183
Owned dwellings	3 935	4 245	4 525	4 602	4 979	5 165	5 263	5 324	5 958	6 516	6 730	6 760
Rented dwellings	1 983	1 978	2 027	2 034	2 134	2 160	2 179	2 201	2 345	2 590	2 602	2 724
Other lodging	426	458	465	478	489	505	445	473	502	567	691	698
Utilities, fuels, and public services	2 412	2 405	2 377	2 489	2 767	2 684	2 811	2 927	3 183	3 397	3 477	3 649
Household operations	548	546	666	684	676	706	707	753	801	948	984	998
Housekeeping supplies	455	482	498	482	509	545	529	594	611	640	639	654
Household furnishings and equipment	1 512	1 601	1 499	1 549	1 458	1 518	1 497	1 646	1 767	1 708	1 797	1 624
Apparel and Services	1 729	1 674	1 743	1 856	1 743	1 749	1 640	1 816	1 886	1 874	1 881	1 801
Transportation	6 457	6 616	7 011	7 417	7 633	7 759	7 781	7 801	8 344	8 508	8 758	8 604
Vehicle purchases (net outlay)	2 736	2 964	3 305	3 418	3 579	3 665	3 732	3 397	3 544	3 421	3 244	2 755
Gasoline and motor oil	1 098	1 017	1 055	1 291	1 279	1 235	1 333	1 598	2 013	2 227	2 384	2 715
Other vehicle expenses	2 230	2 206	2 254	2 281	2 375	2 471	2 331	2 365	2 339	2 355	2 592	2 621
Public transportation	393	429	397	427	400	389	385	441	448	505	538	513
Health Care	1 841	1 903	1 959	2 066	2 182	2 350	2 416	2 574	2 664	2 766	2 853	2 976
Health insurance	881	913	923	983	1 061	1 168	1 252	1 332	1 361	1 465	1 545	1 653
Medical services	531	542	558	568	573	590	591	648	677	670	709	727
Drugs	320	346	370	416	449	487	467	480	521	514	481	482
Medical supplies	108	102	109	99	100	105	107	114	105	117	118	114
Entertainment	1 813	1 746	1 891	1 863	1 953	2 079	2 060	2 218	2 388	2 376	2 698	2 835
Personal Care Products and Services	528	401	408	564	465	526	527	581	541	585	588	616
Reading	164	161	159	146	141	139	127	130	126	117	118	116
Education	571	580	635	632	648	752	783	905	940	888	945	1 046
Tobacco Products and Smoking Supplies	264	273	300	319	308	320	290	288	319	327	323	317
Miscellaneous	847	860	867	776	750	792	606	690	808	846	808	840
Cash Contributions	1 001	1 109	1 181	1 192	1 258	1 277	1 370	1 408	1 663	1 869	1 821	1 737
Personal Insurance and Pensions	3 223	3 381	3 436	3 365	3 737	3 899	4 055	4 823	5 204	5 270	5 336	5 605
Life and other personal insurance	379	398	394	399	410	406	397	390	381	322	309	317
Pensions and Social Security	2 844	2 982	3 042	2 966	3 326	3 493	3 658	4 433	4 823	4 948	5 027	5 288

Table 11-2. Shares of Annual Average Consumer Expenditures and Characteristics of All Consumer Units, 1997–2008

(Number, dollar, percent.)

Item	1997	1998	1999	2000	2001	2002	2003	2004	2005	2006	2007	2008
NUMBER OF CONSUMER UNITS (THOUSANDS)	105 576	107 182	108 465	109 367	110 339	112 108	115 356	116 282	117 356	118 843	120 171	120 770
CONSUMER UNIT CHARACTERISTICS												
Income Before Taxes	39 926	41 622	43 951	44 649	47 507	49 430	51 128	54 453	58 712	60 533	63 091	63 563
Age of Reference Person	47.7	47.6	47.9	48.2	48.1	48.1	48.4	48.5	48.6	48.7	48.8	49.1
Average Number in Consumer Unit												
All persons	2.5	2.5	2.5	2.5	2.5	2.5	2.5	2.5	2.5	2.5	2.5	2.5
Children under 18 years	0.7	0.7	0.7	0.7	0.7	0.7	0.6	0.6	0.6	0.6	0.6	0.6
Persons 65 years and over	0.3	0.3	0.3	0.3	0.3	0.3	0.3	0.3	0.3	0.3	0.3	0.3
Earners	1.3	1.3	1.3	1.4	1.4	1.4	1.3	1.3	1.3	1.3	1.3	1.3
Vehicles	2.0	2.0	1.9	1.9	1.9	2.0	1.9	1.9	2.0	1.9	1.9	2.0
Percent Homeowner	64	64	65	66	66	66	67	68	67	67	67	66
With mortgage	38	39	38	39	40	41	41	42	43	43	43	42
Without mortgage	26	26	27	27	26	26	26	25	25	24	23	24
AVERAGE ANNUAL EXPENDITURES	34 819	35 535	36 995	38 045	39 518	40 677	40 817	43 395	46 409	48 398	49 638	50 486
Food	13.8	13.5	13.6	13.6	13.5	13.2	13.1	13.3	12.8	12.6	12.4	12.8
Food at home	8.3	7.8	7.9	7.9	7.8	7.6	7.7	7.7	7.1	7.1	7.0	7.4
Cereals and bakery products	1.3	1.2	1.2	1.2	1.1	1.1	1.1	1.1	1.0	0.9	0.9	1.0
Meats, poultry, fish, and eggs	2.1	2.0	2.0	2.1	2.1	2.0	2.0	2.0	1.6	1.6	1.6	1.7
Dairy products	0.9	0.8	0.9	0.9	0.8	0.8	0.8	0.9	0.8	0.8	0.8	0.9
Fruits and vegetables	1.4	1.3	1.4	1.4	1.3	1.4	1.3	1.3	1.2	1.2	1.2	1.3
Other food at home	2.6	2.4	2.4	2.4	2.4	2.4	2.4	2.5	2.5	2.5	2.5	2.6
Food away from home	5.5	5.7	5.7	5.6	5.7	5.6	5.4	5.6	5.7	5.6	5.4	5.3
Alcoholic Beverages	0.9	0.9	0.9	1.0	0.9	0.9	1.0	1.1	0.9	1.0	0.9	0.9
Housing	32.4	33.0	32.6	32.4	32.9	32.7	32.9	32.1	32.7	33.8	34.1	33.9
Shelter	18.2	18.8	19.0	18.7	19.2	19.2	19.3	18.4	19.0	20.0	20.2	20.2
Owned dwellings	11.3	11.9	12.2	12.1	12.6	12.7	12.9	12.3	12.8	13.5	13.6	13.4
Rented dwellings	5.7	5.6	5.5	5.3	5.4	5.3	5.3	5.1	5.1	5.4	5.2	5.4
Other lodging	1.2	1.3	1.3	1.3	1.2	1.2	1.1	1.1	1.1	1.2	1.4	1.4
Utilities, fuels, and public services	6.9	6.8	6.4	6.5	7.0	6.6	6.9	6.7	6.9	7.0	7.0	7.2
Household operations	1.6	1.5	1.8	1.8	1.7	1.7	1.7	1.7	1.7	2.0	2.0	2.0
Housekeeping supplies	1.3	1.4	1.3	1.3	1.3	1.3	1.3	1.4	1.3	1.3	1.3	1.3
Household furnishings and equipment	4.3	4.5	4.1	4.1	3.7	3.7	3.7	3.8	3.8	3.5	3.6	3.2
Apparel and Services	5.0	4.7	4.7	4.9	4.4	4.3	4.0	4.2	4.1	3.9	3.8	3.6
Transportation	18.5	18.6	19.0	19.5	19.3	19.1	19.1	18.0	18.0	17.6	17.6	17.0
Vehicle purchases (net outlay)	7.9	8.3	8.9	9.0	9.1	9.0	9.1	7.8	7.6	7.1	6.5	5.5
Gasoline and motor oil	3.2	2.9	2.9	3.4	3.2	3.0	3.3	3.7	4.3	4.6	4.8	5.4
Other vehicle expenses	6.4	6.2	6.1	6.0	6.0	6.1	5.7	5.5	5.0	4.9	5.2	5.2
Public transportation	1.1	1.2	1.1	1.1	1.0	1.0	0.9	1.0	1.0	1.0	1.1	1.0
Health Care	5.3	5.4	5.3	5.4	5.5	5.8	5.9	5.9	5.7	5.7	5.7	5.9
Health insurance	2.5	2.6	2.5	2.6	2.7	2.9	3.1	3.1	2.9	3.0	3.1	3.3
Medical services	1.5	1.5	1.5	1.5	1.4	1.5	1.4	1.5	1.5	1.4	1.4	1.4
Drugs	0.9	1.0	1.0	1.1	1.1	1.2	1.1	1.1	1.1	1.1	1.0	1.0
Medical supplies	0.3	0.3	0.3	0.3	0.3	0.3	0.3	0.3	0.2	0.2	0.2	0.2
Entertainment	5.2	4.9	5.1	4.9	4.9	5.1	5.0	5.1	5.1	4.9	5.4	5.6
Personal Care Products and Services	1.5	1.1	1.1	1.5	1.2	1.3	1.3	1.3	1.2	1.2	1.2	1.2
Reading	0.5	0.5	0.4	0.4	0.4	0.3	0.3	0.3	0.3	0.2	0.2	0.2
Education	1.6	1.6	1.7	1.7	1.6	1.8	1.9	2.1	2.0	1.8	1.9	2.1
Tobacco Products and Smoking Supplies	0.8	0.8	0.8	0.8	0.8	0.8	0.7	0.7	0.7	0.7	0.7	0.6
Miscellaneous	2.4	2.4	2.3	2.0	1.9	1.9	1.5	1.6	1.7	1.7	1.6	1.7
Cash Contributions	2.9	3.1	3.2	3.1	3.2	3.1	3.4	3.2	3.6	3.9	3.7	3.4
Personal Insurance and Pensions	9.3	9.5	9.3	8.8	9.5	9.6	9.9	11.1	11.2	10.9	10.8	11.1
Life and other personal insurance	1.1	1.1	1.1	1.0	1.0	1.0	1.0	0.9	0.8	0.7	0.6	0.6
Pensions and Social Security	8.2	8.4	8.2	7.8	8.4	8.6	9.0	10.2	10.4	10.2	10.1	10.5

Table 11-3. Consumer Expenditures, Averages by Income Before Taxes, 2008

(Number, dollar, percent.)

Item	All consumer units	Less than $5,000	$5,000 to $9,999	$10,000 to $14,999	$15,000 to $19,999	$20,000 to $29,999	$30,000 to $39,999	$40,000 to $49,999	$50,000 to $69,999	$70,000 and over
NUMBER OF CONSUMER UNITS (THOUSANDS)	120 770	4 463	5 340	7 883	7 625	14 700	12 198	11 287	18 287	38 987
CONSUMER UNIT CHARACTERISTICS										
Income Before Taxes	63 563	-1 092	8 003	12 662	17 461	24 896	34 708	44 733	59 319	128 930
Income After Taxes	61 774	-814	8 214	13 119	17 840	25 355	35 027	44 621	58 610	123 254
Age of Reference Person	49.1	41.9	48.9	56.2	55.6	52.5	49.4	47.9	47.0	47.1
Average Number in Consumer Unit										
All persons	2.5	1.7	1.6	1.7	1.8	2.1	2.3	2.5	2.7	3.1
Children under 18 years	0.6	0.4	0.3	0.4	0.4	0.5	0.6	0.6	0.7	0.8
Persons 65 years and over	0.3	0.2	0.3	0.5	0.5	0.5	0.4	0.3	0.2	0.2
Earners	1.3	0.5	0.4	0.5	0.6	0.9	1.1	1.3	1.6	1.9
Vehicles	2.0	0.9	0.8	1.0	1.2	1.5	1.7	1.9	2.2	2.7
Percent Distribution										
Male	47	46	39	31	40	42	44	47	49	54
Female	53	54	61	69	60	58	56	53	51	46
Percent Homeowner	66	29	29	42	50	56	60	64	73	88
With mortgage	42	14	9	11	15	22	30	40	51	70
Without mortgage	24	15	20	31	35	34	29	24	22	18
AVERAGE ANNUAL EXPENDITURES	50 486	23 036	19 125	21 120	25 536	30 367	35 778	40 527	50 465	83 700
Food	6 443	3 872	3 184	3 320	3 556	4 209	5 130	5 446	6 388	9 884
Food at home	3 744	2 493	2 166	2 286	2 474	2 751	3 243	3 338	3 762	5 253
Cereals and bakery products	507	355	281	330	343	361	425	437	508	720
Meats, poultry, fish, and eggs	846	557	537	532	540	669	791	794	848	1 133
Dairy products	430	292	253	261	310	299	379	371	417	612
Fruits and vegetables	657	437	391	391	421	492	570	556	662	929
Other food at home	1 305	853	704	771	860	930	1 079	1 181	1 327	1 859
Food away from home	2 698	1 379	1 018	1 035	1 081	1 458	1 887	2 108	2 626	4 631
Alcoholic Beverages	444	269	175	190	137	230	317	374	445	749
Housing	17 109	9 020	7 640	8 657	10 083	11 241	12 541	14 599	17 056	26 789
Shelter	10 183	5 908	4 595	4 879	5 874	6 502	7 266	8 590	10 062	16 171
Owned dwellings	6 700	2 424	1 323	1 593	2 267	2 984	3 673	5 080	6 789	12 788
Rented dwellings	2 724	3 203	3 147	3 135	3 453	3 258	3 292	3 183	2 759	1 858
Other lodging	698	280	125	151	153	260	301	328	514	1 525
Utilities, fuels, and public services	3 649	1 859	1 967	2 359	2 595	2 971	3 244	3 488	3 876	4 875
Household operations	998	259	234	374	483	505	541	620	940	1 878
Housekeeping supplies	654	309	280	420	388	443	515	533	630	1 007
Household furnishings and equipment	1 624	685	564	625	744	819	975	1 369	1 548	2 858
Apparel and Services	1 801	1 006	845	983	929	1 105	1 381	1 241	1 713	2 945
Transportation	8 604	3 088	2 931	2 987	4 457	5 591	6 436	7 225	9 359	13 805
Vehicle purchases (net outlay)	2 755	430	810	606	1 346	1 770	2 069	2 098	3 093	4 615
Gasoline and motor oil	2 715	1 225	1 090	1 179	1 464	1 922	2 310	2 620	3 033	3 967
Other vehicle expenses	2 621	1 131	755	1 006	1 494	1 688	1 803	2 248	2 841	4 192
Public transportation	513	303	277	196	153	211	254	259	393	1 031
Health Care	2 976	1 384	1 207	1 660	2 108	2 403	2 696	2 741	3 229	4 087
Health insurance	1 653	767	613	1 112	1 324	1 423	1 560	1 607	1 730	2 165
Medical services	727	301	271	282	313	448	557	565	857	1 153
Drugs	482	254	254	197	408	453	494	480	525	597
Medical supplies	114	61	69	68	62	79	85	89	117	173
Entertainment	2 835	1 393	917	961	1 169	1 629	1 874	2 122	2 936	4 875
Personal Care Products and Services	616	379	254	277	336	378	467	503	591	994
Reading	116	51	40	50	73	74	77	91	118	190
Education	1 046	1 059	839	489	286	316	406	495	613	2 171
Tobacco Products and Smoking Supplies	317	227	241	305	264	313	317	347	392	307
Miscellaneous	840	358	191	236	441	440	623	693	899	1 414
Cash Contributions	1 737	533	362	545	834	865	1 106	1 188	1 529	3 262
Personal Insurance and Pensions	5 605	397	299	461	865	1 573	2 406	3 462	5 197	12 228
Life and other personal insurance	317	94	47	98	83	142	181	211	282	625
Pensions and Social Security	5 288	303	252	363	782	1 431	2 226	3 251	4 915	11 603

Table 11-4. Consumer Expenditures, Averages by Higher Income Before Taxes, 2008

(Number, dollar, percent.)

Item	All consumer units	Less than $70,000	$70,000 to $79,000	$80,000 to $99,999	$100,000 and over	$100,000 to $119,000	$120,000 to $149,999	$150,000 and over
NUMBER OF CONSUMER UNITS (THOUSANDS)	120 770	81 783	7 354	10 017	21 615	7 136	5 777	8 702
CONSUMER UNIT CHARACTERISTICS								
Income Before Taxes	63 563	32 401	74 486	88 839	166 035	108 630	132 531	235 348
Income After Taxes	61 774	32 465	73 072	86 462	157 379	105 048	127 295	220 261
Age of Reference Person	49.1	50.0	46.1	46.9	47.5	46.8	47.2	48.3
Average Number in Consumer Unit								
All persons	2.5	2.2	2.9	3.0	3.2	3.1	3.3	3.2
Children under 18 years	0.6	0.5	0.8	0.8	0.8	0.8	0.9	0.8
Persons 65 years and over	0.3	0.4	0.2	0.2	0.2	0.2	0.1	0.2
Earners	1.3	1.0	1.8	1.9	2.0	2.0	2.1	2.1
Vehicles	2.0	1.6	2.5	2.6	2.8	2.8	2.9	2.9
Percent Distribution								
Male	47	43	53	52	55	53	56	57
Female	53	57	47	48	45	47	44	43
Percent Homeowner	66	56	82	84	92	89	93	93
With mortgage	42	29	62	65	75	74	76	74
Without mortgage	24	27	20	18	17	15	16	19
AVERAGE ANNUAL EXPENDITURES	50 486	34 687	58 742	67 180	100 065	77 586	91 590	124 678
Food	6 443	4 818	7 503	8 760	11 302	9 773	10 969	13 011
Food at home	3 744	3 033	4 312	5 062	5 690	5 390	5 755	5 940
Cereals and bakery products	507	407	593	718	766	743	782	778
Meats, poultry, fish, and eggs	846	711	952	1 092	1 220	1 183	1 194	1 279
Dairy products	430	344	484	601	664	627	680	690
Fruits and vegetables	657	529	735	878	1 025	946	991	1 132
Other food at home	1 305	1 043	1 548	1 773	2 015	1 891	2 107	2 061
Food away from home	2 698	1 784	3 191	3 698	5 611	4 383	5 214	7 071
Alcoholic Beverages	444	300	507	584	919	761	904	1 083
Housing	17 109	12 499	19 617	21 360	31 784	25 002	28 058	39 909
Shelter	10 183	7 328	11 633	12 396	19 465	15 095	16 754	24 848
Owned dwellings	6 760	3 887	8 824	9 567	15 629	12 179	13 792	19 679
Rented dwellings	2 724	3 137	2 194	2 087	1 638	1 587	1 400	1 838
Other lodging	698	304	615	742	2 198	1 330	1 562	3 332
Utilities, fuels, and public services	3 649	3 065	4 257	4 536	5 242	4 632	5 083	5 848
Household operations	998	578	1 097	1 367	2 381	1 487	2 033	3 345
Housekeeping supplies	654	488	728	898	1 165	1 147	1 097	1 238
Household furnishings and equipment	1 624	1 039	1 902	2 163	3 531	2 642	3 091	4 631
Apparel and Services	1 801	1 260	1 813	2 351	3 643	2 734	3 122	4 886
Transportation	8 604	6 127	10 449	12 227	15 674	13 424	15 720	17 486
Vehicle purchases (net outlay)	2 755	1 868	3 114	3 916	5 450	4 546	5 764	5 984
Gasoline and motor oil	2 715	2 118	3 528	3 770	4 208	3 954	4 237	4 396
Other vehicle expenses	2 621	1 875	3 296	3 932	4 612	4 106	4 568	5 048
Public transportation	513	266	512	608	1 404	818	1 151	2 058
Health Care	2 976	2 446	3 503	3 695	4 471	4 037	4 316	4 931
Health insurance	1 653	1 410	1 859	2 052	2 321	2 100	2 229	2 564
Medical services	727	524	996	949	1 301	1 151	1 276	1 437
Drugs	482	428	518	541	651	615	644	686
Medical supplies	114	86	130	153	198	171	167	244
Entertainment	2 835	1 866	3 261	3 982	5 869	4 306	6 363	6 835
Personal Care Products and Services	616	436	700	788	1 198	947	1 138	1 472
Reading	116	81	128	145	233	197	210	278
Education	1 046	509	808	1 179	3 096	1 662	1 934	5 044
Tobacco Products and Smoking Supplies	317	321	385	354	258	322	244	217
Miscellaneous	840	566	929	1 012	1 767	1 278	1 612	2 277
Cash Contributions	1 737	1 009	2 200	2 318	4 061	2 357	3 054	6 127
Personal Insurance and Pensions	5 605	2 448	6 939	8 425	15 791	10 785	13 945	21 120
Life and other personal insurance	317	170	366	402	816	503	686	1 160
Pensions and Social Security	5 288	2 278	6 573	8 023	14 974	10 282	13 259	19 961

Table 11-5. Consumer Expenditures, Averages by Quintiles of Income Before Taxes, 2008

(Number, dollar, percent.)

Item	All consumer units	Lowest 20 percent	Second 20 percent	Third 20 percent	Fourth 20 percent	Highest 20 percent
NUMBER OF CONSUMER UNITS (THOUSANDS)	120 770	24 122	24 143	24 172	24 157	24 177
CONSUMER UNIT CHARACTERISTICS						
Income Before Taxes	63 563	10 263	27 442	47 196	74 090	158 652
Income After Taxes	61 774	10 608	27 843	46 936	72 628	150 692
Age of Reference Person	49.1	51.6	51.6	47.9	46.9	47.4
Average Number in Consumer Unit						
All persons	2.5	1.7	2.2	2.6	2.8	3.2
Children under 18 years	0.6	0.4	0.5	0.7	0.7	0.8
Persons 65 years and over	0.3	0.4	0.5	0.3	0.2	0.2
Earners	1.3	0.5	0.9	1.4	1.7	2.0
Vehicles	2.0	1.0	1.5	2.0	2.4	2.8
Percent Distribution						
Male	47	38	43	47	51	55
Female	53	62	57	53	49	45
Percent Homeowner	66	39	56	67	79	91
With mortgage	42	12	24	42	59	74
Without mortgage	24	26	32	25	20	17
AVERAGE ANNUAL EXPENDITURES	50 486	22 304	31 751	42 659	58 632	97 003
Food	6 443	3 473	4 560	5 602	7 589	10 982
Food at home	3 744	2 369	2 929	3 436	4 340	5 645
Cereals and bakery products	507	330	380	461	598	764
Meats, poultry, fish, and eggs	846	542	715	809	956	1 209
Dairy products	430	280	329	386	489	664
Fruits and vegetables	657	409	524	583	753	1 015
Other food at home	1 305	808	982	1 196	1 543	1 994
Food away from home	2 698	1 103	1 631	2 167	3 249	5 336
Alcoholic Beverages	444	183	275	350	539	873
Housing	17 109	8 900	11 583	14 917	19 327	30 791
Shelter	10 183	5 287	6 743	8 743	11 307	18 820
Owned dwellings	6 760	1 856	3 169	5 346	8 318	15 098
Rented dwellings	2 724	3 259	3 311	3 045	2 352	1 657
Other lodging	698	173	263	351	637	2 066
Utilities, fuels, and public services	3 649	2 238	3 019	3 580	4 229	5 177
Household operations	998	351	510	692	1 142	2 291
Housekeeping supplies	654	373	454	553	759	1 132
Household furnishings and equipment	1 624	651	857	1 351	1 890	3 371
Apparel and Services	1 801	962	1 151	1 361	2 037	3 490
Transportation	8 604	3 430	5 657	7 834	10 469	15 614
Vehicle purchases (net outlay)	2 755	845	1 672	2 490	3 304	5 457
Gasoline and motor oil	2 715	1 243	2 019	2 704	3 418	4 186
Other vehicle expenses	2 621	1 122	1 740	2 340	3 263	4 636
Public transportation	513	220	226	300	483	1 335
Health Care	2 976	1 624	2 457	2 886	3 518	4 391
Health insurance	1 653	985	1 438	1 667	1 869	2 306
Medical services	727	296	476	625	980	1 255
Drugs	482	277	465	490	546	632
Medical supplies	114	65	78	103	123	198
Entertainment	2 835	1 082	1 716	2 422	3 276	5 673
Personal Care Products and Services	616	306	402	512	702	1 157
Reading	116	55	73	101	128	225
Education	1 046	625	361	498	843	2 899
Tobacco Products and Smoking Supplies	317	268	311	354	382	268
Miscellaneous	840	297	512	758	954	1 675
Cash Contributions	1 737	567	915	1 315	2 042	3 839
Personal Insurance and Pensions	5 605	532	1 778	3 748	6 825	15 126
Life and other personal insurance	317	83	146	236	350	767
Pensions and Social Security	5 288	449	1 632	3 512	6 475	14 358

Table 11-6. Consumer Expenditures, Averages by Occupation of Reference Person, 2008

(Number, dollar, percent.)

Item	Self-employed workers	Wage and salary earners						Retired	All others, including those not reporting
		Total wage and salary earners	Managers and professional workers	Technical sales and clerical workers	Service workers	Construction workers and mechanics	Operators, fabricators, and laborers		
NUMBER OF CONSUMER UNITS (THOUSANDS)	5 629	78 486	30 518	21 583	12 664	4 352	9 369	21 174	15 481
CONSUMER UNIT CHARACTERISTICS									
Income Before Taxes	89 675	73 261	101 521	61 308	48 020	60 607	48 739	34 585	44 534
Income After Taxes	88 184	70 775	96 592	60 008	47 685	59 296	48 021	34 445	43 914
Age of Reference Person	48.1	43.2	44.8	41.7	41.8	42.5	43.8	73.5	45.7
Average Number in Consumer Unit									
All persons	2.7	2.6	2.6	2.6	2.6	2.8	2.6	1.7	2.9
Children under 18 years	0.8	0.7	0.7	0.7	0.7	0.7	0.7	0.1	0.9
Persons 65 years and over	0.2	0.1	0.1	0.1	0.1	0.1	0.1	1.2	0.2
Earners	1.7	1.7	1.7	1.7	1.6	1.8	1.7	0.2	0.7
Vehicles	2.3	2.1	2.2	2.0	1.8	2.2	2.1	1.6	1.6
Percent Distribution									
Male	56	51	50	41	45	91	71	43	27
Female	44	49	50	59	55	9	29	57	73
Percent Homeowner	78	64	75	59	52	63	59	80	55
With mortgage	56	49	60	46	36	43	41	20	33
Without mortgage	22	15	15	13	16	20	18	60	21
AVERAGE ANNUAL EXPENDITURES	62 031	55 606	70 194	51 584	41 430	46 526	40 936	36 003	40 525
Food	7 420	6 949	8 050	6 931	5 555	6 374	5 624	4 806	5 909
Food at home	4 387	3 823	4 215	3 831	3 189	3 664	3 491	3 178	3 912
Cereals and bakery products	581	514	559	527	430	482	475	444	531
Meats, poultry, fish, and eggs	930	860	911	850	753	914	846	711	930
Dairy products	536	435	497	434	357	385	369	365	454
Fruits and vegetables	829	657	751	623	545	601	619	595	680
Other food at home	1 511	1 356	1 498	1 398	1 105	1 282	1 182	1 063	1 317
Food away from home	3 032	3 126	3 835	3 100	2 366	2 711	2 134	1 627	1 997
Alcoholic Beverages	546	512	602	544	422	429	309	274	319
Housing	19 872	18 585	23 471	17 081	14 543	15 490	13 072	12 828	14 517
Shelter	11 851	11 308	14 535	10 270	8 816	9 106	7 580	6 778	8 531
Owned dwellings	8 935	7 524	10 393	6 550	5 048	5 536	4 696	4 529	5 148
Rented dwellings	2 128	3 009	2 818	3 144	3 468	3 139	2 643	1 640	2 981
Other lodging	787	774	1 324	576	299	432	241	609	402
Utilities, fuels, and public services	4 074	3 765	4 177	3 565	3 417	3 800	3 337	3 299	3 387
Household operations	1 156	1 096	1 602	982	618	801	496	821	679
Housekeeping supplies	798	670	823	619	518	459	612	639	557
Household furnishings and equipment	1 994	1 745	2 335	1 643	1 174	1 324	1 047	1 291	1 362
Apparel and Services	1 838	2 046	2 647	1 784	1 705	1 520	1 442	1 042	1 636
Transportation	9 287	9 752	11 278	9 630	7 579	8 731	8 482	5 675	6 581
Vehicle purchases (net outlay)	2 466	3 242	3 800	3 274	2 387	2 617	2 795	1 604	1 964
Gasoline and motor oil	3 152	3 040	3 288	2 918	2 631	3 353	2 921	1 667	2 340
Other vehicle expenses	3 047	2 912	3 259	3 050	2 269	2 409	2 574	1 953	1 947
Public transportation	623	558	930	388	292	352	192	451	330
Health Care	3 894	2 619	3 331	2 437	1 910	2 049	1 946	4 571	2 268
Health insurance	2 074	1 412	1 756	1 356	1 043	1 027	1 103	2 771	1 193
Medical services	1 224	695	949	613	468	547	430	810	594
Drugs	516	404	478	372	332	396	343	830	386
Medical supplies	80	108	148	96	68	79	69	160	94
Entertainment	3 268	3 171	4 051	3 054	2 172	2 622	2 207	2 036	2 121
Personal Care Products and Services	652	669	875	650	495	419	403	520	472
Reading	135	114	169	101	65	63	56	145	79
Education	1 168	1 250	2 037	1 051	530	470	483	274	1 024
Tobacco Products and Smoking Supplies	284	338	245	354	381	532	454	172	419
Miscellaneous	1 117	920	1 150	865	751	848	564	594	667
Cash Contributions	2 599	1 682	2 296	1 351	1 139	1 490	1 265	1 953	1 405
Personal Insurance and Pensions	9 953	6 998	9 990	5 751	4 182	5 488	4 629	1 113	3 107
Life and other personal insurance	446	338	470	275	275	233	184	253	252
Pensions and Social Security	9 507	6 660	9 520	5 476	3 907	5 256	4 445	860	2 856

Table 11-7. Consumer Expenditures, Averages by Number of Earners, 2008

(Number, dollar, percent.)

Item	All consumer units	Single consumer		Consumer units of two or more persons			
		No earner	One earner	No earner	One earner	Two earners	Three or more earners
NUMBER OF CONSUMER UNITS (THOUSANDS)	120 770	13 365	21 699	10 762	25 011	40 395	9 540
CONSUMER UNIT CHARACTERISTICS							
Income Before Taxes	63 563	17 682	42 426	31 513	58 601	92 124	104 141
Income After Taxes	61 774	17 720	40 455	31 711	57 562	89 071	101 349
Age of Reference Person	49.1	69.0	42.4	65.3	47.5	43.3	46.4
Average Number in Consumer Unit							
All persons	2.5	1.0	1.0	2.3	3.0	3.1	4.4
Children under 18 years	0.6	X	X	0.3	1.0	0.9	1.0
Persons 65 years and over	0.3	0.7	0.1	1.2	0.3	0.1	0.1
Earners	1.3	X	1.0	X	1.0	2.0	3.3
Vehicles	2.0	0.9	1.2	1.8	1.9	2.5	3.2
Percent Distribution							
Male	47	34	54	50	39	51	47
Female	53	66	46	50	61	49	53
Percent Homeowner	66	58	44	77	67	75	80
With mortgage	42	13	30	19	44	59	63
Without mortgage	24	45	13	58	23	17	17
AVERAGE ANNUAL EXPENDITURES	50 486	21 824	35 202	37 908	50 348	66 344	73 159
Food	6 443	2 788	4 119	5 479	6 669	8 166	10 202
Food at home	3 744	1 923	2 006	3 788	4 213	4 500	5 812
Cereals and bakery products	507	274	255	511	581	603	806
Meats, poultry, fish, and eggs	846	410	428	874	989	1 004	1 341
Dairy products	430	230	237	439	477	522	621
Fruits and vegetables	657	365	364	686	747	772	978
Other food at home	1 305	643	722	1 278	1 419	1 599	2 066
Food away from home	2 698	865	2 113	1 691	2 456	3 665	4 390
Alcoholic Beverages	444	149	508	286	352	577	587
Housing	17 109	9 561	12 704	12 879	18 044	21 472	21 563
Shelter	10 183	5 574	8 704	6 609	10 521	12 770	12 196
Owned dwellings	6 760	2 647	4 326	4 432	7 084	9 308	9 049
Rented dwellings	2 724	2 716	3 950	1 488	2 752	2 501	2 216
Other lodging	698	211	428	689	685	961	931
Utilities, fuels, and public services	3 649	2 292	2 248	3 584	3 916	4 308	5 322
Household operations	998	635	434	766	1 085	1 452	895
Housekeeping supplies	654	346	348	712	745	759	1 042
Household furnishings and equipment	1 624	715	969	1 207	1 777	2 184	2 109
Apparel and Services	1 801	628	1 100	1 116	1 935	2 491	2 576
Transportation	8 604	2 564	5 591	6 793	7 960	11 744	14 416
Vehicle purchases (net outlay)	2 755	447	1 692	2 224	2 367	4 008	4 714
Gasoline and motor oil	2 715	835	1 723	1 966	2 739	3 594	4 663
Other vehicle expenses	2 621	1 070	1 799	2 088	2 375	3 465	4 397
Public transportation	513	212	378	515	479	676	642
Health Care	2 976	2 443	1 438	5 010	3 183	3 164	3 586
Health insurance	1 653	1 587	752	2 886	1 749	1 726	1 847
Medical services	727	381	391	980	780	860	984
Drugs	482	384	243	950	541	455	595
Medical supplies	114	91	51	194	113	123	160
Entertainment	2 835	1 134	1 972	2 122	2 746	3 963	3 477
Personal Care Products and Services	616	341	415	517	606	781	905
Reading	116	87	89	140	111	132	140
Education	1 046	333	768	313	887	1 442	2 244
Tobacco Products and Smoking Supplies	317	151	253	276	328	361	518
Miscellaneous	840	319	704	595	803	1 152	926
Cash Contributions	1 737	1 182	1 396	1 833	1 827	1 918	2 175
Personal Insurance and Pensions	5 605	144	4 144	550	4 896	8 981	9 843
Life and other personal insurance	317	104	111	258	391	429	477
Pensions and Social Security	5 288	[1]40	4 034	293	4 504	8 552	9 365

[1]Data are likely to have large sampling errors.
X = Not applicable.

Table 11-8. Consumer Expenditures, Averages by Size of Consumer Unit, 2008

(Number, dollar, percent.)

Item	All consumer units	One person	Two or more persons	Two persons	Three persons	Four persons	Five or more persons
NUMBER OF CONSUMER UNITS (THOUSANDS)	120 770	35 064	85 706	39 629	17 982	16 514	11 580
CONSUMER UNIT CHARACTERISTICS							
Income Before Taxes	63 563	32 994	76 068	68 168	77 032	87 390	85 464
Income After Taxes	61 774	31 789	74 041	65 755	74 618	85 501	85 156
Age of Reference Person	49.1	52.6	47.6	53.9	44.0	41.1	41.5
Average Number in Consumer Unit							
All persons	2.5	1.0	3.1	2.0	3.0	4.0	5.6
Children under 18 years	0.6	X	0.9	0.1	0.8	1.6	2.7
Persons 65 years and over	0.3	0.3	0.3	0.5	0.2	0.1	0.1
Earners	1.3	0.6	1.6	1.2	1.7	1.9	2.2
Vehicles	2.0	1.1	2.3	2.2	2.3	2.5	2.5
Percent Distribution							
Male	47	47	47	51	43	44	42
Female	53	53	53	49	57	56	58
Percent Homeowner	66	49	74	75	69	75	72
With mortgage	42	24	50	42	51	63	58
Without mortgage	24	25	24	34	18	12	14
AVERAGE ANNUAL EXPENDITURES	50 486	30 120	58 786	53 320	59 488	65 955	66 262
Food	6 443	3 620	7 581	6 276	7 598	9 172	9 805
Food at home	3 744	1 975	4 457	3 626	4 508	5 279	6 061
Cereals and bakery products	507	262	606	476	599	754	854
Meats, poultry, fish, and eggs	846	421	1 017	821	1 042	1 153	1 451
Dairy products	430	234	508	411	507	622	683
Fruits and vegetables	657	365	775	654	791	884	1 007
Other food at home	1 305	693	1 551	1 264	1 569	1 866	2 066
Food away from home	2 698	1 645	3 124	2 650	3 090	3 892	3 743
Alcoholic Beverages	444	374	473	527	439	429	402
Housing	17 109	11 507	19 396	17 330	19 660	22 266	21 961
Shelter	10 183	7 511	11 276	10 143	11 267	13 138	12 513
Owned dwellings	6 760	3 686	8 018	6 931	7 824	10 036	9 162
Rented dwellings	2 724	3 480	2 415	2 204	2 647	2 398	2 805
Other lodging	698	345	843	1 008	796	704	546
Utilities, fuels, and public services	3 649	2 265	4 216	3 798	4 214	4 635	5 050
Household operations	998	511	1 197	884	1 293	1 667	1 447
Housekeeping supplies	654	347	778	691	775	910	900
Household furnishings and equipment	1 624	873	1 930	1 815	2 111	1 916	2 050
Apparel and Services	1 801	922	2 156	1 710	2 376	2 494	2 847
Transportation	8 604	4 439	10 305	9 225	10 758	11 515	11 602
Vehicle purchases (net outlay)	2 755	1 217	3 384	2 987	3 849	3 538	3 800
Gasoline and motor oil	2 715	1 384	3 259	2 789	3 280	3 805	4 057
Other vehicle expenses	2 621	1 523	3 067	2 829	3 062	3 609	3 151
Public transportation	513	314	595	620	568	563	594
Health Care	2 976	1 821	3 448	3 972	2 944	3 039	3 022
Health insurance	1 653	1 070	1 892	2 204	1 615	1 700	1 527
Medical services	727	387	865	937	716	798	946
Drugs	482	296	558	689	482	412	432
Medical supplies	114	67	133	141	131	128	116
Entertainment	2 835	1 655	3 315	3 178	3 070	3 714	3 612
Personal Care Products and Services	616	388	708	638	733	805	777
Reading	116	88	128	144	123	115	98
Education	1 046	602	1 227	866	1 404	1 626	1 617
Tobacco Products and Smoking Supplies	317	214	359	326	421	350	385
Miscellaneous	840	558	955	955	1 005	946	888
Cash Contributions	1 737	1 314	1 909	2 079	1 873	1 603	1 821
Personal Insurance and Pensions	5 605	2 620	6 826	6 095	7 084	7 881	7 426
Life and other personal insurance	317	108	402	421	399	380	376
Pensions and Social Security	5 288	2 511	6 424	5 674	6 685	7 501	7 050

X = Not applicable.

Table 11-9. Consumer Expenditures, Averages by Composition of Consumer Unit, 2008

(Number, dollar, percent.)

Item		Husband and wife consumer units						One parent, at least one child under 18 years	Single person and other consumer units
	Total	Husband and wife only	Husband and wife with children				Other husband and wife consumer units		
			Total	Oldest child under 6 years	Oldest child 6 to 17 years	Oldest child 18 years or over			
NUMBER OF CONSUMER UNITS (THOUSANDS)	61 244	26 919	29 804	5 343	15 479	8 982	4 521	6 977	52 550
CONSUMER UNIT CHARACTERISTICS									
Income Before Taxes	85 829	75 312	94 697	81 190	97 616	97 702	89 986	37 100	41 125
Income After Taxes	83 274	72 457	92 159	79 792	94 644	95 233	89 100	37 645	39 920
Age of Reference Person	49.4	57.6	42.2	32.1	40.1	51.7	48.7	38.8	50.0
Average Number in Consumer Unit									
All persons	3.2	2.0	4.0	3.5	4.2	3.9	4.9	2.9	1.6
Children under 18 years	0.9	X	1.6	1.5	2.2	0.6	1.4	1.8	0.2
Persons 65 years and over	0.4	0.7	0.1	([1])	([1])	0.2	0.5	([1])	0.3
Earners	1.7	1.2	2.0	1.6	1.8	2.5	2.3	1.0	1.0
Vehicles	2.6	2.4	2.7	2.1	2.5	3.2	2.8	1.1	1.3
Percent Distribution									
Male	53	58	50	50	48	52	44	15	44
Female	47	42	50	50	52	48	56	85	56
Percent Homeowner	83	86	81	67	82	88	78	40	51
With mortgage	57	45	67	61	71	63	55	33	27
Without mortgage	26	41	14	6	11	25	23	8	24
AVERAGE ANNUAL EXPENDITURES	65 016	58 164	71 308	63 194	72 724	73 809	64 445	37 129	35 278
Food	8 255	6 772	9 478	7 512	9 856	10 043	9 105	5 162	4 480
Food at home	4 806	3 913	5 478	4 488	5 664	5 777	5 752	3 210	2 567
Cereals and bakery products	660	516	770	576	814	813	812	448	334
Meats, poultry, fish, and eggs	1 072	871	1 201	826	1 246	1 358	1 432	762	592
Dairy products	559	455	644	560	674	642	628	360	286
Fruits and vegetables	858	732	950	858	955	997	1 020	458	446
Other food at home	1 656	1 339	1 914	1 667	1 974	1 966	1 860	1 181	909
Food away from home	3 449	2 859	4 000	3 024	4 192	4 267	3 352	1 953	1 913
Alcoholic Beverages	500	550	465	424	444	528	428	193	411
Housing	20 974	18 256	23 369	24 705	24 087	21 345	21 385	14 892	12 891
Shelter	12 097	10 485	13 549	13 901	14 462	11 767	12 120	8 936	8 118
Owned dwellings	9 329	7 811	10 744	10 187	11 749	9 345	9 037	4 347	4 087
Rented dwellings	1 752	1 417	1 952	3 271	1 880	1 292	2 429	4 288	3 650
Other lodging	1 016	1 257	853	443	833	1 130	653	301	381
Utilities, fuels, and public services	4 465	4 025	4 754	3 869	4 818	5 172	5 172	3 313	2 744
Household operations	1 310	871	1 720	3 398	1 648	846	1 213	1 095	621
Housekeeping supplies	881	782	965	971	883	1 108	920	520	405
Household furnishings and equipment	2 222	2 092	2 380	2 567	2 276	2 452	1 960	1 028	1 003
Apparel and Services	2 280	1 696	2 838	2 472	2 973	2 834	2 088	1 855	1 232
Transportation	11 450	10 202	12 436	10 500	12 046	14 294	12 378	5 912	5 637
Vehicle purchases (net outlay)	3 723	3 272	4 056	3 655	3 954	4 470	4 218	1 883	1 742
Gasoline and motor oil	3 563	3 005	3 983	3 299	3 994	4 373	4 113	2 085	1 810
Other vehicle expenses	3 474	3 185	3 738	3 075	3 459	4 647	3 454	1 661	1 748
Public transportation	690	740	659	471	640	804	593	283	338
Health Care	3 984	4 725	3 407	2 593	3 366	3 964	3 374	1 530	1 992
Health insurance	2 185	2 641	1 824	1 512	1 766	2 109	1 850	798	1 147
Medical services	1 007	1 091	972	688	1 034	1 034	739	441	438
Drugs	641	831	467	304	417	652	651	215	332
Medical supplies	151	162	144	88	149	169	135	76	75
Entertainment	3 798	3 621	4 124	3 461	4 597	3 705	2 702	1 832	1 840
Personal Care Products and Services	786	710	868	692	857	998	703	533	427
Reading	147	166	134	100	134	155	113	57	88
Education	1 403	835	1 956	441	1 758	3 200	1 139	657	681
Tobacco Products and Smoking Supplies	327	300	318	230	301	402	542	245	314
Miscellaneous	1 004	951	1 034	809	1 024	1 186	1 120	629	675
Cash Contributions	2 282	2 578	2 094	1 367	2 119	2 481	1 762	741	1 233
Personal Insurance and Pensions	7 827	6 802	8 786	7 888	9 162	8 673	7 604	2 891	3 376
Life and other personal insurance	496	534	465	288	491	523	476	139	132
Pensions and Social Security	7 331	6 267	8 322	7 600	8 671	8 150	7 129	2 753	3 244

[1]Value less than or equal to 0.05.
X = Not applicable.

Table 11-10. Consumer Expenditures, Averages by Age of Reference Person, 2008

(Number, dollar, percent.)

Item	All consumer units	Under 25 years	25 to 34 years	35 to 44 years	45 to 54 years	55 to 64 years	65 years and over	65 to 74 years	75 years and over
NUMBER OF CONSUMER UNITS (THOUSANDS)	120 770	8 227	20 208	22 834	25 614	19 826	24 062	12 580	11 481
CONSUMER UNIT CHARACTERISTICS									
Income Before Taxes	63 563	28 127	59 878	77 582	81 844	71 653	39 341	45 232	32 886
Income After Taxes	61 774	27 907	58 809	75 677	78 537	69 009	38 841	44 402	32 747
Age of Reference Person	49.1	21.5	29.6	39.7	49.4	59.3	75.0	69.0	81.6
Average Number in Consumer Unit									
All persons	2.5	2.0	2.8	3.3	2.7	2.1	1.7	1.8	1.5
Children under 18 years	0.6	0.4	1.0	1.4	0.6	0.2	(¹)	0.1	(¹)
Persons 65 years and over	0.3	(¹)	(¹)	(¹)	(¹)	0.1	1.4	1.4	1.3
Earners	1.3	1.3	1.5	1.6	1.7	1.3	0.4	0.6	0.2
Vehicles	2.0	1.2	1.7	2.1	2.4	2.2	1.6	1.8	1.3
Percent Distribution									
Male	47	47	50	46	47	49	43	46	40
Female	53	53	50	54	53	51	57	54	60
Percent Homeowner	66	15	46	67	75	81	79	81	76
With mortgage	42	11	41	58	57	46	21	29	12
Without mortgage	24	4	6	9	19	35	58	52	64
AVERAGE ANNUAL EXPENDITURES	50 486	29 325	48 159	58 808	61 179	54 783	36 844	41 433	31 692
Food	6 443	4 447	6 229	7 849	7 696	6 357	4 692	5 338	3 935
Food at home	3 744	2 330	3 393	4 509	4 452	3 710	3 075	3 421	2 667
Cereals and bakery products	507	281	454	620	600	492	435	473	390
Meats, poultry, fish, and eggs	846	573	742	1 014	1 018	845	687	781	576
Dairy products	430	256	395	518	506	419	362	406	309
Fruits and vegetables	657	370	583	754	779	682	577	616	531
Other food at home	1 305	851	1 219	1 603	1 549	1 272	1 015	1 145	863
Food away from home	2 698	2 117	2 836	3 340	3 244	2 646	1 617	1 917	1 268
Alcoholic Beverages	444	448	491	462	505	525	251	343	144
Housing	17 109	9 975	17 318	20 649	19 562	17 611	12 993	13 845	12 035
Shelter	10 183	6 530	10 935	12 689	11 629	10 112	6 933	7 281	6 553
Owned dwellings	6 760	1 383	5 873	9 056	8 606	7 387	4 685	5 334	3 974
Rented dwellings	2 724	4 940	4 734	3 013	2 037	1 607	1 658	1 294	2 057
Other lodging	698	206	328	621	986	1 128	590	652	522
Utilities, fuels, and public services	3 649	1 875	3 152	4 130	4 247	3 974	3 314	3 538	3 067
Household operations	998	326	1 137	1 376	964	879	884	750	1 032
Housekeeping supplies	654	303	594	664	765	743	627	747	485
Household furnishings and equipment	1 624	942	1 499	1 789	1 956	1 894	1 235	1 529	898
Apparel and Services	1 801	1 351	1 965	2 235	2 228	1 622	1 092	1 381	755
Transportation	8 604	5 464	8 699	9 797	10 691	9 377	5 620	6 740	4 392
Vehicle purchases (net outlay)	2 755	1 988	3 149	3 122	3 351	2 999	1 502	1 920	1 044
Gasoline and motor oil	2 715	1 974	2 754	3 347	3 298	2 818	1 629	2 045	1 173
Other vehicle expenses	2 621	1 273	2 380	2 798	3 414	2 921	2 039	2 261	1 793
Public transportation	513	229	416	530	628	638	450	513	382
Health Care	2 976	682	1 737	2 499	2 930	3 825	4 605	4 779	4 413
Health insurance	1 653	389	983	1 341	1 523	1 945	2 844	2 901	2 783
Medical services	727	143	472	711	838	1 022	793	853	728
Drugs	482	117	215	349	432	714	821	880	756
Medical supplies	114	33	67	98	138	144	145	145	146
Entertainment	2 835	1 608	2 766	3 603	3 297	3 036	1 914	2 418	1 349
Personal Care Products and Services	616	370	547	728	736	630	512	559	456
Reading	116	48	79	102	124	157	142	152	132
Education	1 046	1 691	759	953	2 012	867	272	345	192
Tobacco Products and Smoking Supplies	317	251	298	354	437	354	161	227	88
Miscellaneous	840	280	726	862	957	1 316	588	659	507
Cash Contributions	1 737	427	1 036	1 550	2 152	2 163	2 156	2 033	2 291
Personal Insurance and Pensions	5 605	2 283	5 510	7 165	7 853	6 943	1 846	2 616	1 003
Life and other personal insurance	317	37	155	284	394	519	330	461	187
Pensions and Social Security	5 288	2 246	5 354	6 881	7 458	6 424	1 516	2 155	815

¹Value less than or equal to 0.05.

Table 11-11. Consumer Expenditures, Averages by Race of Reference Person, 2008

(Number, dollar, percent.)

Item	All consumer units	White, Asian, and other races			Black
		Total	White and other races	Asian	
NUMBER OF CONSUMER UNITS (THOUSANDS)	120 770	105 938	101 329	4 609	14 832
CONSUMER UNIT CHARACTERISTICS					
Income Before Taxes	63 563	66 340	65 905	75 917	43 722
Income After Taxes	61 774	64 335	63 916	73 528	43 482
Age of Reference Person	49.1	49.4	49.6	43.5	46.9
Average Number in Consumer Unit					
All persons	2.5	2.5	2.5	2.7	2.5
Children under 18 years	0.6	0.6	0.6	0.6	0.8
Persons 65 years and over	0.3	0.3	0.3	0.2	0.2
Earners	1.3	1.3	1.3	1.4	1.2
Vehicles	2.0	2.0	2.1	1.5	1.3
Percent Distribution					
Male	47	48	47	61	39
Female	53	52	53	39	61
Percent Homeowner	66	69	70	55	46
With mortgage	42	44	44	42	32
Without mortgage	24	26	26	13	14
AVERAGE ANNUAL EXPENDITURES	50 486	52 397	52 265	55 430	36 721
Food	6 443	6 693	6 676	7 089	4 594
Food at home	3 744	3 868	3 865	3 943	2 825
Cereals and bakery products	507	524	522	562	382
Meats, poultry, fish, and eggs	846	846	839	1 010	848
Dairy products	430	452	457	326	263
Fruits and vegetables	657	685	678	852	447
Other food at home	1 305	1 361	1 368	1 193	886
Food away from home	2 698	2 824	2 811	3 147	1 768
Alcoholic Beverages	444	476	484	300	205
Housing	17 109	17 574	17 456	20 138	13 770
Shelter	10 183	10 491	10 345	13 703	7 985
Owned dwellings	6 760	7 155	7 095	8 471	3 940
Rented dwellings	2 724	2 579	2 484	4 680	3 762
Other lodging	698	756	766	552	282
Utilities, fuels, and public services	3 649	3 656	3 674	3 275	3 598
Household operations	998	1 052	1 057	931	610
Housekeeping supplies	654	680	688	494	461
Household furnishings and equipment	1 624	1 694	1 693	1 735	1 116
Apparel and Services	1 801	1 776	1 767	1 997	1 983
Transportation	8 604	8 895	8 889	9 049	6 520
Vehicle purchases (net outlay)	2 755	2 865	2 885	2 414	1 969
Gasoline and motor oil	2 715	2 779	2 790	2 539	2 257
Other vehicle expenses	2 621	2 703	2 698	2 815	2 033
Public transportation	513	548	515	1 280	261
Health Care	2 976	3 169	3 211	2 233	1 595
Health insurance	1 653	1 743	1 757	1 425	1 015
Medical services	727	787	804	412	292
Drugs	482	514	524	298	252
Medical supplies	114	124	126	97	36
Entertainment	2 835	3 022	3 007	3 447	1 478
Personal Care Products and Services	616	628	630	584	528
Reading	116	126	127	90	47
Education	1 046	1 121	1 096	1 676	508
Tobacco Products and Smoking Supplies	317	330	337	166	223
Miscellaneous	840	878	884	736	565
Cash Contributions	1 737	1 816	1 845	1 165	1 171
Personal Insurance and Pensions	5 605	5 895	5 856	6 760	3 532
Life and other personal insurance	317	326	325	332	254
Pensions and Social Security	5 288	5 570	5 531	6 428	3 278

Table 11-12. Consumer Expenditures, Averages by Hispanic Origin of Reference Person, 2008

(Number, dollar, percent.)

Item	All consumer units	Hispanic[1]	Not Hispanic		
			Total	White, Asian, and other races	Black
NUMBER OF CONSUMER UNITS (THOUSANDS)	120 770	13 975	106 795	92 214	14 580
CONSUMER UNIT CHARACTERISTICS					
Income Before Taxes	63 563	49 317	65 427	68 842	43 826
Income After Taxes	61 774	48 955	63 451	66 590	43 600
Age of Reference Person	49.1	43.1	49.9	50.3	47.0
Average Number in Consumer Unit					
All persons	2.5	3.2	2.4	2.4	2.5
Children under 18 years	0.6	1.1	0.6	0.5	0.8
Persons 65 years and over	0.3	0.2	0.3	0.3	0.2
Earners	1.3	1.5	1.3	1.3	1.2
Vehicles	2.0	1.6	2.0	2.1	1.3
Percent Distribution					
Male	47	46	47	48	39
Female	53	54	53	52	61
Percent Homeowner	66	51	68	72	46
With mortgage	42	36	43	45	32
Without mortgage	24	15	25	27	15
AVERAGE ANNUAL EXPENDITURES	50 486	43 052	51 457	53 773	36 685
Food	6 443	6 596	6 423	6 706	4 566
Food at home	3 744	4 039	3 707	3 842	2 813
Cereals and bakery products	507	509	507	526	380
Meats, poultry, fish, and eggs	846	1 039	822	818	844
Dairy products	430	429	430	455	262
Fruits and vegetables	657	789	640	670	444
Other food at home	1 305	1 274	1 309	1 373	882
Food away from home	2 698	2 556	2 716	2 864	1 753
Alcoholic Beverages	444	297	463	502	208
Housing	17 109	15 582	17 307	17 868	13 743
Shelter	10 183	9 688	10 248	10 611	7 953
Owned dwellings	6 760	5 334	6 947	7 425	3 921
Rented dwellings	2 724	4 065	2 549	2 360	3 745
Other lodging	698	289	752	826	286
Utilities, fuels, and public services	3 649	3 457	3 674	3 685	3 610
Household operations	998	797	1 024	1 090	602
Housekeeping supplies	654	542	669	700	461
Household furnishings and equipment	1 624	1 098	1 692	1 782	1 117
Apparel and Services	1 801	2 119	1 760	1 728	1 973
Transportation	8 604	7 986	8 684	9 025	6 525
Vehicle purchases (net outlay)	2 755	2 554	2 781	2 911	1 961
Gasoline and motor oil	2 715	2 717	2 715	2 787	2 259
Other vehicle expenses	2 621	2 335	2 658	2 755	2 041
Public transportation	513	380	530	573	264
Health Care	2 976	1 571	3 160	3 406	1 596
Health insurance	1 653	816	1 763	1 881	1 013
Medical services	727	407	768	843	296
Drugs	482	274	509	550	250
Medical supplies	114	75	119	132	36
Entertainment	2 835	1 787	2 971	3 203	1 480
Personal Care Products and Services	616	545	625	641	520
Reading	116	38	126	139	48
Education	1 046	669	1 095	1 186	516
Tobacco Products and Smoking Supplies	317	143	339	357	225
Miscellaneous	840	586	873	921	567
Cash Contributions	1 737	1 010	1 832	1 935	1 178
Personal Insurance and Pensions	5 605	4 124	5 799	6 156	3 542
Life and other personal insurance	317	116	343	357	255
Pensions and Social Security	5 288	4 007	5 456	5 799	3 287

[1]May be of any race.

Table 11-13. Consumer Expenditures, Averages by Education of Reference Person, 2008

(Number, dollar, percent.)

Item	All consumer units	Less than a college graduate					College graduate or more		
		Total	Less than a high school graduate	High school graduate	High school graduate with some college	Associate's degree	Total	Bachelor's degree	Master's, professional, or doctoral degree
NUMBER OF CONSUMER UNITS (THOUSANDS)	120 770	85 845	17 600	30 761	26 386	11 097	34 925	22 428	12 498
CONSUMER UNIT CHARACTERISTICS									
Income Before Taxes	63 563	49 375	32 909	48 364	55 403	63 964	98 434	88 888	115 564
Income After Taxes	61 774	48 666	32 956	47 903	54 385	62 098	93 991	85 575	109 095
Age of Reference Person	49.1	49.6	54.1	51.4	45.0	48.2	47.8	46.5	50.2
Average Number in Consumer Unit									
All persons	2.5	2.5	2.6	2.5	2.4	2.5	2.5	2.5	2.4
Children under 18 years	0.6	0.6	0.7	0.6	0.6	0.7	0.6	0.6	0.6
Persons 65 years and over	0.3	0.3	0.5	0.4	0.2	0.2	0.2	0.2	0.3
Earners	1.3	1.3	1.1	1.3	1.3	1.4	1.4	1.5	1.4
Vehicles	2.0	1.9	1.5	2.0	1.9	2.2	2.1	2.1	2.1
Percent Distribution									
Male	47	45	45	45	46	42	51	51	52
Female	53	55	55	55	54	58	49	49	48
Percent Homeowner	66	62	53	66	59	70	78	75	81
With mortgage	42	36	23	37	39	48	57	56	59
Without mortgage	24	26	30	30	20	21	20	19	22
AVERAGE ANNUAL EXPENDITURES	50 486	42 205	29 903	40 850	47 205	53 385	70 858	66 221	79 198
Food	6 443	5 777	4 692	5 583	6 143	7 087	8 086	7 798	8 614
Food at home	3 744	3 526	3 195	3 486	3 567	4 045	4 284	4 192	4 456
Cereals and bakery products	507	477	433	480	475	540	581	571	599
Meats, poultry, fish, and eggs	846	833	837	839	794	905	880	878	884
Dairy products	430	398	355	386	404	488	507	493	531
Fruits and vegetables	657	595	553	573	605	699	810	780	865
Other food at home	1 305	1 223	1 016	1 208	1 290	1 413	1 507	1 469	1 577
Food away from home	2 698	2 251	1 498	2 097	2 576	3 042	3 802	3 606	4 159
Alcoholic Beverages	444	343	163	326	419	473	694	669	739
Housing	17 109	14 218	10 952	13 559	15 749	17 576	24 217	22 541	27 228
Shelter	10 183	8 197	6 125	7 627	9 354	10 314	15 065	14 037	16 910
Owned dwellings	6 760	5 015	2 989	4 691	5 835	7 180	11 050	10 247	12 491
Rented dwellings	2 724	2 779	3 007	2 543	2 976	2 600	2 592	2 624	2 532
Other lodging	698	403	129	393	543	534	1 424	1 166	1 887
Utilities, fuels, and public services	3 649	3 457	3 084	3 536	3 447	3 854	4 122	4 012	4 319
Household operations	998	701	365	681	840	955	1 727	1 458	2 211
Housekeeping supplies	654	584	572	546	598	680	828	784	911
Household furnishings and equipment	1 624	1 280	807	1 169	1 510	1 773	2 474	2 251	2 877
Apparel and Services	1 801	1 521	1 275	1 357	1 746	1 818	2 491	2 464	2 536
Transportation	8 604	7 712	5 293	7 735	8 341	9 954	10 795	10 260	11 763
Vehicle purchases (net outlay)	2 755	2 452	1 544	2 461	2 650	3 399	3 499	3 408	3 662
Gasoline and motor oil	2 715	2 585	2 020	2 620	2 703	3 099	3 035	3 014	3 073
Other vehicle expenses	2 621	2 381	1 545	2 402	2 622	3 038	3 211	3 018	3 564
Public transportation	513	295	184	253	366	417	1 050	820	1 463
Health Care	2 976	2 657	2 008	2 733	2 788	3 158	3 761	3 477	4 270
Health insurance	1 653	1 499	1 204	1 576	1 490	1 770	2 034	1 893	2 286
Medical services	727	605	359	576	721	796	1 026	933	1 193
Drugs	482	457	386	485	469	466	543	504	613
Medical supplies	114	96	58	95	109	126	158	147	178
Entertainment	2 835	2 272	1 318	2 129	2 700	3 146	4 220	4 048	4 530
Personal Care Products and Services	616	506	329	479	585	664	887	860	934
Reading	116	82	43	76	100	118	200	168	258
Education	1 046	602	146	419	1 013	853	2 137	1 889	2 582
Tobacco Products and Smoking Supplies	317	379	384	427	331	351	164	184	127
Miscellaneous	840	675	291	734	799	814	1 244	1 251	1 232
Cash Contributions	1 737	1 302	774	1 273	1 548	1 638	2 804	2 371	3 581
Personal Insurance and Pensions	5 605	4 159	2 234	4 020	4 943	5 736	9 159	8 242	10 805
Life and other personal insurance	317	244	142	237	271	358	496	456	569
Pensions and Social Security	5 288	3 915	2 091	3 782	4 671	5 378	8 663	7 787	10 236

Table 11-14. Consumer Expenditures, Averages by Housing Tenure and Type of Area, 2008

(Number, dollar, percent.)

Item	All consumer units	Housing tenure				Type of area			
		Homeowner			Renter	Urban			Rural
		Total	Homeowner with mortgage	Homeowner without mortgage		Total	Central city	Other urban	
NUMBER OF CONSUMER UNITS (THOUSANDS)	120 770	80 278	51 084	29 194	40 492	110 103	34 690	75 413	10 668
CONSUMER UNIT CHARACTERISTICS									
Income Before Taxes	63 563	76 973	88 957	56 003	36 976	64 788	55 651	68 991	50 917
Income After Taxes	61 774	74 566	86 233	54 150	36 412	62 934	53 965	67 059	49 797
Age of Reference Person	49.1	52.9	47.2	62.8	41.5	48.7	46.6	49.7	53.1
Average Number in Consumer Unit									
All persons	2.5	2.6	2.9	2.2	2.2	2.5	2.4	2.5	2.5
Children under 18 years	0.6	0.6	0.8	0.3	0.6	0.6	0.6	0.6	0.6
Persons 65 years and over	0.3	0.4	0.2	0.7	0.2	0.3	0.3	0.3	0.4
Earners	1.3	1.4	1.7	0.9	1.2	1.3	1.3	1.4	1.3
Vehicles	2.0	2.4	2.5	2.2	1.1	1.9	1.5	2.1	2.5
Percent Distribution									
Male	47	47	48	45	46	47	46	47	44
Female	53	53	52	55	54	53	54	53	56
Percent Homeowner	66	100	100	100	X	65	50	72	81
With mortgage	42	64	100	X	X	43	33	47	40
Without mortgage	24	36	X	100	X	22	17	25	42
AVERAGE ANNUAL EXPENDITURES	50 486	58 801	66 689	44 545	33 984	51 148	45 843	53 574	43 572
Food	6 443	7 196	7 757	5 983	4 942	6 522	6 218	6 657	5 566
Food at home	3 744	4 159	4 385	3 656	2 918	3 765	3 601	3 837	3 514
Cereals and bakery products	507	568	594	509	386	510	471	527	475
Meats, poultry, fish, and eggs	846	916	962	814	707	848	859	843	828
Dairy products	430	484	503	442	321	429	387	448	434
Fruits and vegetables	657	735	764	670	502	665	648	672	569
Other food at home	1 305	1 457	1 563	1 221	1 003	1 314	1 236	1 348	1 207
Food away from home	2 698	3 037	3 372	2 327	2 023	2 757	2 618	2 820	2 052
Alcoholic Beverages	444	483	543	353	366	463	500	448	233
Housing	17 109	19 442	23 382	12 525	12 479	17 571	16 144	18 223	12 336
Shelter	10 183	11 093	14 487	5 154	8 379	10 611	10 051	10 868	5 769
Owned dwellings	6 760	10 099	13 426	4 277	142	6 978	5 249	7 774	4 511
Rented dwellings	2 724	51	35	81	8 024	2 909	4 215	2 308	823
Other lodging	698	943	1 027	796	213	724	587	787	436
Utilities, fuels, and public services	3 649	4 323	4 569	3 892	2 314	3 640	3 216	3 835	3 741
Household operations	998	1 232	1 380	972	533	1 040	934	1 089	557
Housekeeping supplies	654	781	789	763	402	641	577	669	800
Household furnishings and equipment	1 624	2 013	2 156	1 744	852	1 639	1 365	1 762	1 468
Apparel and Services	1 801	1 993	2 196	1 574	1 417	1 847	1 865	1 840	1 298
Transportation	8 604	10 085	11 269	7 995	5 665	8 541	7 078	9 211	9 249
Vehicle purchases (net outlay)	2 755	3 201	3 647	2 420	1 870	2 700	2 215	2 922	3 325
Gasoline and motor oil	2 715	3 147	3 518	2 497	1 859	2 674	2 098	2 939	3 137
Other vehicle expenses	2 621	3 123	3 443	2 542	1 622	2 632	2 199	2 827	2 503
Public transportation	513	614	660	536	314	535	566	522	284
Health Care	2 976	3 753	3 489	4 220	1 435	2 938	2 405	3 182	3 371
Health insurance	1 653	2 071	1 854	2 450	826	1 637	1 316	1 784	1 824
Medical services	727	941	951	925	301	716	608	766	836
Drugs	482	598	546	694	252	471	389	508	599
Medical supplies	114	142	138	150	57	114	91	124	112
Entertainment	2 835	3 410	3 875	2 524	1 692	2 830	2 572	2 949	2 887
Personal Care Products and Services	616	716	782	586	416	629	591	647	474
Reading	116	143	143	142	64	118	111	121	101
Education	1 046	1 182	1 373	842	776	1 093	994	1 139	554
Tobacco Products and Smoking Supplies	317	291	299	277	367	300	263	317	488
Miscellaneous	840	997	1 065	876	528	847	756	889	756
Cash Contributions	1 737	2 157	1 981	2 465	904	1 749	1 477	1 874	1 612
Personal Insurance and Pensions	5 605	6 953	8 536	4 183	2 933	5 698	4 872	6 078	4 648
Life and other personal insurance	317	426	488	319	99	317	226	359	312
Pensions and Social Security	5 288	6 526	8 048	3 864	2 833	5 381	4 645	5 719	4 335

X = Not applicable.

Table 11-15. Consumer Expenditures, Averages by Population Size of Area of Residence, 2008

(Number, dollar, percent.)

Item	All consumer units	Outside urban area	Urban consumer units						
			Total	Less than 100,000	100,000 to 249,999	250,000 to 999,999	1,000,000 to 2,499,999	2,500,000 to 4,999,999	5,000,000 and over
NUMBER OF CONSUMER UNITS (THOUSANDS)	120 770	24 640	96 130	18 795	9 295	19 850	16 129	17 037	15 024
CONSUMER UNIT CHARACTERISTICS									
Income Before Taxes	63 563	59 912	64 498	49 076	60 996	60 035	66 941	74 849	77 494
Income After Taxes	61 774	58 507	62 611	48 346	59 780	58 414	64 348	71 720	75 558
Age of Reference Person	49.1	52.5	48.2	47.6	47.7	47.9	48.5	47.4	50.3
Average Number in Consumer Unit									
All persons	2.5	2.5	2.5	2.4	2.5	2.4	2.4	2.5	2.6
Children under 18 years	0.6	0.6	0.6	0.6	0.7	0.6	0.6	0.7	0.6
Persons 65 years and over	0.3	0.4	0.3	0.3	0.3	0.3	0.3	0.2	0.3
Earners	1.3	1.3	1.3	1.2	1.3	1.3	1.4	1.4	1.4
Vehicles	2.0	2.6	1.8	1.9	2.0	1.8	1.8	1.8	1.5
Percent Distribution									
Male	47	47	47	42	49	49	47	48	46
Female	53	53	53	58	51	51	53	52	54
Percent Homeowner	66	83	62	61	65	64	65	61	59
With mortgage	42	46	41	37	43	42	46	43	38
Without mortgage	24	37	21	24	22	22	18	19	20
AVERAGE ANNUAL EXPENDITURES	50 486	48 265	51 055	41 179	47 960	49 700	52 775	57 288	58 155
Food	6 443	5 928	6 574	5 616	6 045	6 724	6 794	7 090	7 047
Food at home	3 744	3 582	3 786	3 411	3 448	3 978	3 922	3 934	3 895
Cereals and bakery products	507	494	510	469	484	539	517	529	512
Meats, poultry, fish, and eggs	846	791	860	742	748	896	912	865	962
Dairy products	430	432	429	385	397	468	434	450	423
Fruits and vegetables	657	603	671	567	596	677	680	712	771
Other food at home	1 305	1 262	1 316	1 247	1 223	1 396	1 380	1 378	1 228
Food away from home	2 698	2 346	2 788	2 206	2 597	2 747	2 872	3 156	3 152
Alcoholic Beverages	444	332	473	352	518	441	485	602	475
Housing	17 109	14 754	17 712	13 316	15 881	16 155	18 133	20 688	22 586
Shelter	10 183	7 664	10 829	7 215	9 302	9 392	11 072	13 357	15 065
Owned dwellings	6 760	6 140	6 919	4 593	6 335	6 074	7 409	8 339	9 172
Rented dwellings	2 724	940	3 182	2 106	2 332	2 623	3 121	4 169	4 737
Other lodging	698	583	728	516	635	695	542	849	1 156
Utilities, fuels, and public services	3 649	3 845	3 599	3 360	3 544	3 411	3 632	3 778	3 943
Household operations	998	798	1 049	657	917	1 013	1 100	1 297	1 331
Housekeeping supplies	654	746	631	618	594	629	702	628	602
Household furnishings and equipment	1 624	1 702	1 605	1 465	1 524	1 710	1 627	1 628	1 645
Apparel and Services	1 801	1 439	1 893	1 509	1 649	1 762	2 190	1 908	2 342
Transportation	8 604	9 355	8 411	7 138	8 704	8 575	8 667	9 153	8 477
Vehicle purchases (net outlay)	2 755	3 072	2 673	2 225	3 160	3 088	2 812	2 640	2 275
Gasoline and motor oil	2 715	3 304	2 564	2 464	2 574	2 530	2 569	2 880	2 364
Other vehicle expenses	2 621	2 649	2 614	2 165	2 581	2 508	2 795	2 846	2 871
Public transportation	513	330	560	285	389	449	490	787	967
Health Care	2 976	3 420	2 862	2 661	2 770	3 129	2 854	2 767	2 935
Health insurance	1 653	1 918	1 586	1 477	1 526	1 705	1 621	1 549	1 605
Medical services	727	819	703	618	707	780	647	691	778
Drugs	482	561	462	477	428	513	453	417	456
Medical supplies	114	122	112	89	109	131	132	110	96
Entertainment	2 835	3 161	2 751	2 317	2 898	2 636	3 360	2 763	2 703
Personal Care Products and Services	616	536	636	505	548	644	665	718	719
Reading	116	112	117	97	109	136	113	124	119
Education	1 046	712	1 131	880	745	1 107	949	1 269	1 756
Tobacco Products and Smoking Supplies	317	455	281	352	358	271	288	216	225
Miscellaneous	840	895	825	712	615	723	954	1 008	892
Cash Contributions	1 737	1 924	1 688	1 510	1 520	1 993	1 415	2 040	1 508
Personal Insurance and Pensions	5 605	5 241	5 698	4 215	5 599	5 404	5 908	6 941	6 371
Life and other personal insurance	317	348	309	232	293	342	345	294	348
Pensions and Social Security	5 288	4 893	5 390	3 983	5 306	5 062	5 563	6 647	6 023

Table 11-16. Consumer Expenditures, Averages by Region of Residence, 2008

(Number, dollar, percent.)

Item	All consumer units	Region[1]			
		Northeast	South	Midwest	West
NUMBER OF CONSUMER UNITS (THOUSANDS)	120 770	22 348	27 786	43 696	26 941
CONSUMER UNIT CHARACTERISTICS					
Income Before Taxes	63 563	70 436	61 063	58 881	68 031
Income After Taxes	61 774	68 179	59 793	57 492	65 447
Age of Reference Person	49.1	51.0	48.6	49.2	47.7
Average Number in Consumer Unit					
All persons	2.5	2.4	2.4	2.5	2.6
Children under 18 years	0.6	0.6	0.6	0.6	0.7
Persons 65 years and over	0.3	0.3	0.3	0.3	0.3
Earners	1.3	1.3	1.3	1.3	1.4
Vehicles	2.0	1.7	2.1	1.9	2.0
Percent Distribution					
Male	47	45	48	46	49
Female	53	55	52	54	51
Percent Homeowner	66	65	68	68	63
With mortgage	42	41	43	41	44
Without mortgage	24	24	25	27	19
AVERAGE ANNUAL EXPENDITURES	50 486	54 918	47 846	46 823	55 453
Food	6 443	6 959	5 966	6 109	7 037
Food at home	3 744	4 021	3 528	3 494	4 140
Cereals and bakery products	507	579	483	472	528
Meats, poultry, fish, and eggs	846	920	750	843	888
Dairy products	430	461	421	392	473
Fruits and vegetables	657	725	591	580	792
Other food at home	1 305	1 336	1 283	1 207	1 459
Food away from home	2 698	2 938	2 438	2 615	2 897
Alcoholic Beverages	444	455	450	389	518
Housing	17 109	19 525	15 550	15 276	19 682
Shelter	10 183	12 023	8 923	8 479	12 721
Owned dwellings	6 760	7 889	6 282	5 643	8 130
Rented dwellings	2 724	3 068	2 000	2 297	3 880
Other lodging	698	1 066	641	539	711
Utilities, fuels, and public services	3 649	4 117	3 527	3 661	3 369
Household operations	998	1 177	863	911	1 128
Housekeeping supplies	654	665	678	646	635
Household furnishings and equipment	1 624	1 543	1 559	1 580	1 829
Apparel and Services	1 801	1 974	1 618	1 772	1 888
Transportation	8 604	8 898	8 418	8 482	8 745
Vehicle purchases (net outlay)	2 755	2 687	2 872	2 726	2 737
Gasoline and motor oil	2 715	2 386	2 664	2 937	2 679
Other vehicle expenses	2 621	3 059	2 472	2 488	2 623
Public transportation	513	765	410	331	706
Health Care	2 976	3 035	3 049	2 849	3 057
Health insurance	1 653	1 758	1 729	1 592	1 588
Medical services	727	693	717	655	881
Drugs	482	457	474	497	487
Medical supplies	114	127	128	106	101
Entertainment	2 835	2 960	2 758	2 512	3 333
Personal Care Products and Services	616	638	551	580	721
Reading	116	141	118	87	140
Education	1 046	1 585	1 029	797	1 019
Tobacco Products and Smoking Supplies	317	324	357	324	257
Miscellaneous	840	952	725	743	1 020
Cash Contributions	1 737	1 485	1 705	1 744	1 966
Personal Insurance and Pensions	5 605	5 987	5 552	5 158	6 067
Life and other personal insurance	317	384	306	321	265
Pensions and Social Security	5 288	5 602	5 246	4 837	5 803

[1]The states that comprise the Census regions are: Northeast—Connecticut, Maine, Massachusetts, New Hampshire, New Jersey, New York, Pennsylvania, Rhode Island, and Vermont; South—Alabama, Arkansas, Delaware, District of Columbia, Florida, Georgia, Kentucky, Louisiana, Maryland, Mississippi, North Carolina, Oklahoma, South Carolina, Tennessee, Texas, Virginia, and West Virginia; Midwest—Illinois, Indiana, Iowa, Kansas, Michigan, Minnesota, Missouri, Nebraska, North Dakota, Ohio, South Dakota, and Wisconsin; and West—Alaska, Arizona, California, Colorado, Hawaii, Idaho, Montana, Nevada, New Mexico, Oregon, Utah, Washington, and Wyoming.

Table 11-17. Consumer Expenditures, Averages for Single Men by Income Before Taxes, 2007–2008

(Number, dollar, percent.)

Item	All single men	Complete reporting of income						
		Less than $5,000	$5,000 to $9,999	$10,000 to $14,999	$15,000 to $19,999	$20,000 to $29,999	$30,000 to $39,999	$40,000 and over
NUMBER OF CONSUMER UNITS (THOUSANDS)	16 353	1 391	1 498	1 684	1 668	2 397	2 043	5 673
CONSUMER UNIT CHARACTERISTICS								
Income Before Taxes	36 962	113	7 992	12 590	17 366	24 730	34 276	72 782
Income After Taxes	35 196	84	7 886	12 584	17 267	24 220	33 465	68 265
Age of Reference Person	46.7	36.4	43.2	52.9	52.7	49.0	45.6	46.0
Average Number in Consumer Unit								
All persons	1.0	1.0	1.0	1.0	1.0	1.0	1.0	1.0
Persons 65 years and over	0.2	0.1	0.2	0.4	0.4	0.2	0.1	0.1
Earners	0.7	0.5	0.5	0.4	0.5	0.7	0.9	0.9
Vehicles	1.3	0.8	0.7	1.0	1.2	1.3	1.4	1.6
Percent Homeowner	45	22	17	32	41	43	48	62
With mortgage	25	9	5	8	9	18	28	46
Without mortgage	19	13	12	24	32	25	20	15
AVERAGE ANNUAL EXPENDITURES	30 981	17 563	16 376	18 225	19 972	24 903	28 850	47 887
Food	3 758	2 671	2 652	2 724	2 489	2 995	3 724	5 064
Food at home	1 817	1 338	1 627	1 679	1 416	1 661	1 866	2 104
Cereals and bakery products	235	193	213	239	198	210	219	270
Meats, poultry, fish, and eggs	411	317	384	382	286	373	448	467
Dairy products	204	146	166	193	187	196	210	227
Fruits and vegetables	310	191	287	285	225	291	337	355
Other food at home	658	491	577	580	520	591	652	785
Food away from home	1 941	1 333	1 025	1 045	1 073	1 334	1 858	2 960
Alcoholic Beverages	598	330	282	287	383	423	593	916
Housing	11 222	6 520	6 230	7 283	7 870	9 005	10 406	17 002
Shelter	7 518	4 637	3 987	4 742	5 116	5 918	6 867	11 599
Owned dwellings	3 625	1 331	704	1 218	1 411	2 137	2 949	7 197
Rented dwellings	3 577	3 125	3 211	3 390	3 588	3 637	3 677	3 776
Other lodging	316	181	[1]72	134	117	143	241	626
Utilities, fuels, and public services	2 118	1 170	1 175	1 595	1 911	2 073	2 295	2 769
Household operations	392	185	94	164	287	286	318	691
Housekeeping supplies	255	164	156	289	162	195	191	348
Household furnishings and equipment	940	364	819	492	394	533	736	1 595
Apparel and Services	824	633	582	591	245	682	817	1 179
Transportation	5 143	2 726	2 395	2 731	3 556	4 808	5 028	7 760
Vehicle purchases (net outlay)	1 634	867	679	[1]442	896	1 686	1 590	2 640
Gasoline and motor oil	1 608	922	913	972	1 241	1 570	1 719	2 234
Other vehicle expenses	1 582	789	707	1 139	1 167	1 365	1 459	2 335
Public transportation	318	148	96	177	252	188	261	551
Health Care	1 345	667	641	1 213	1 494	1 360	1 265	1 710
Health insurance	782	335	363	820	860	877	752	940
Medical services	285	169	127	133	286	211	252	446
Drugs	224	119	136	258	310	236	199	238
Medical supplies	52	[1]45	[1]15	2	38	35	61	87
Entertainment	1 628	852	799	863	961	1 414	1 650	2 500
Personal Care Products and Services	195	114	133	130	118	190	221	256
Reading	81	31	38	55	79	70	60	126
Education	742	1 826	1 493	817	417	548	258	607
Tobacco Products and Smoking Supplies	302	206	295	260	318	345	364	294
Miscellaneous	576	317	118	285	293	401	496	1 024
Cash Contributions	1 460	438	328	524	1 006	823	1 323	2 740
Personal Insurance and Pensions	3 106	232	390	460	743	1 840	2 644	6 710
Life and other personal insurance	141	[1]26	44	75	58	285	100	193
Pensions and Social Security	2 965	206	345	385	685	1 556	2 544	6 517

[1]Data are likely to have large sampling errors.

Table 11-18. Consumer Expenditures, Averages for Single Women by Income Before Taxes, 2007–2008

(Number, dollar, percent.)

Item	All single women	Complete reporting of income						
		Less than $5,000	$5,000 to $9,999	$10,000 to $14,999	$15,000 to $19,999	$20,000 to $29,999	$30,000 to $39,999	$40,000 and over
NUMBER OF CONSUMER UNITS (THOUSANDS)	19 049	1 554	2 250	3 214	2 436	3 132	2 207	4 256
CONSUMER UNIT CHARACTERISTICS								
Income Before Taxes	28 620	1 286	8 110	12 610	17 072	24 576	34 236	68 204
Income After Taxes	27 692	1 359	8 176	12 714	17 083	24 233	33 309	64 637
Age of Reference Person	57.5	45.4	56.5	67.3	65.6	60.4	52.2	50.9
Average Number in Consumer Unit								
All persons	1.0	1.0	1.0	1.0	1.0	1.0	1.0	1.0
Persons 65 years and over	0.4	0.3	0.4	0.7	0.6	0.5	0.3	0.2
Earners	0.5	0.4	0.3	0.2	0.4	0.6	0.8	0.9
Vehicles	0.9	0.5	0.5	0.7	0.9	1.1	1.1	1.2
Percent Homeowner	55	25	33	54	59	58	57	71
With mortgage	24	11	7	10	16	20	33	51
Without mortgage	31	14	26	44	43	38	24	20
AVERAGE ANNUAL EXPENDITURES	28 598	15 809	14 675	18 224	23 335	26 902	32 553	50 199
Food	3 226	2 344	2 057	2 485	2 602	2 986	3 578	4 908
Food at home	1 960	1 434	1 465	1 686	1 744	1 887	2 178	2 600
Cereals and bakery products	263	192	199	235	268	259	270	329
Meats, poultry, fish, and eggs	401	309	316	400	301	407	449	492
Dairy products	229	164	170	196	224	208	258	305
Fruits and vegetables	372	280	295	310	313	355	430	496
Other food at home	694	488	485	544	638	658	772	978
Food away from home	1 267	910	592	799	859	1 099	1 400	2 308
Alcoholic Beverages	231	184	83	107	104	143	261	522
Housing	11 528	6 791	6 464	7 859	10 309	11 021	12 865	19 011
Shelter	7 225	4 484	3 829	4 531	6 101	6 818	8 261	12 459
Owned dwellings	3 684	1 401	1 039	1 856	2 816	3 140	3 961	8 049
Rented dwellings	3 160	2 910	2 719	2 590	3 097	3 456	3 811	3 395
Other lodging	381	173	71	85	189	222	489	1 015
Utilities, fuels, and public services	2 336	1 343	1 657	2 149	2 390	2 396	2 585	2 993
Household operations	590	169	214	371	616	553	530	1 149
Housekeeping supplies	397	225	240	303	369	384	438	590
Household furnishings and equipment	981	570	523	504	832	869	1 049	1 820
Apparel and Services	1 053	762	514	687	755	782	1 158	1 974
Transportation	3 929	1 770	1 955	2 256	3 351	4 085	5 130	6 562
Vehicle purchases (net outlay)	1 104	[1]319	[1]675	741	[1]892	1 252	[1]1 282	1 812
Gasoline and motor oil	1 090	621	609	668	883	1 201	1 435	1 692
Other vehicle expenses	1 415	535	527	705	1 411	1 419	2 093	2 326
Public transportation	320	295	145	142	165	214	320	732
Health Care	2 200	920	1 101	1 975	2 620	2 575	2 416	2 785
Health insurance	1 246	556	609	1 384	1 658	1 512	1 241	1 300
Medical services	489	128	198	287	388	492	675	887
Drugs	385	204	255	237	505	475	423	472
Medical supplies	81	32	39	67	70	96	78	126
Entertainment	1 451	711	675	823	974	1 377	1 458	2 866
Personal Care Products and Services	531	331	253	305	433	485	590	964
Reading	102	50	41	70	94	106	96	182
Education	500	1 199	703	272	236	309	516	589
Tobacco Products and Smoking Supplies	148	126	168	139	103	196	172	128
Miscellaneous	518	161	190	236	288	464	540	1 192
Cash Contributions	1 100	271	249	702	897	997	1 323	2 228
Personal Insurance and Pensions	2 082	188	223	309	568	1 377	2 451	6 288
Life and other personal insurance	116	35	59	105	142	113	144	155
Pensions and Social Security	1 966	153	164	204	426	1 265	2 307	6 132

[1]Data are likely to have large sampling errors.

Table 11-19. Consumer Expenditures, Averages for Age Groups by Income Before Taxes: Reference Person Under 25 Years of Age, 2007–2008

(Number, dollar, percent.)

Item	Total	Complete reporting of income						
		Less than $5,000	$5,000 to $9,999	$10,000 to $14,999	$15,000 to $19,999	$20,000 to $29,999	$30,000 to $39,999	$40,000 and over
NUMBER OF CONSUMER UNITS (THOUSANDS)	8 188	1 339	1 187	846	780	1 058	830	2 147
CONSUMER UNIT CHARACTERISTICS								
Income Before Taxes	29 777	2 452	7 328	12 383	17 303	24 611	34 521	71 333
Income After Taxes	29 348	2 551	7 434	12 514	17 420	24 561	34 454	69 533
Age of Reference Person	21.5	20.4	20.9	21.3	21.7	21.9	21.9	22.3
Average Number in Consumer Unit								
All persons	2.0	1.2	1.4	1.6	1.9	2.1	2.3	2.8
Children under 18 years	0.4	0.1	0.2	0.3	0.5	0.5	0.6	0.5
Earners	1.3	0.7	0.9	1.0	1.2	1.4	1.6	2.0
Vehicles	1.2	0.5	0.6	0.9	1.1	1.3	1.5	1.9
Percent Distribution								
Male	47	50	48	47	45	46	45	48
Female	53	50	52	53	55	54	55	52
Percent Homeowner	15	3	2	3	7	14	21	37
With mortgage	11	([1])	1	2	4	7	17	27
Without mortgage	5	3	1	2	2	6	4	10
AVERAGE ANNUAL EXPENDITURES	29 386	13 396	17 907	19 238	23 084	27 849	34 643	49 715
Food	4 291	2 435	2 757	2 895	3 053	3 929	4 477	6 928
Food at home	2 297	1 115	1 422	1 718	1 689	2 196	2 545	3 597
Cereals and bakery products	277	145	173	220	219	246	313	428
Meats, poultry, fish, and eggs	532	240	314	431	300	586	564	825
Dairy products	247	139	148	177	207	236	288	367
Fruits and vegetables	355	168	190	251	274	334	372	586
Other food at home	887	423	596	639	689	794	1 008	1 391
Food away from home	1 994	1 320	1 336	1 178	1 364	1 734	1 932	3 331
Alcoholic Beverages	455	255	257	321	259	323	422	854
Housing	9 787	4 260	5 837	6 767	8 315	9 584	11 849	16 335
Shelter	6 376	3 091	4 031	4 688	5 702	5 992	7 634	10 334
Owned dwellings	1 390	171	201	[2]85	408	663	1 494	3 999
Rented dwellings	4 796	2 763	3 666	4 447	5 181	5 211	5 920	6 045
Other lodging	190	156	164	[2]155	[2]113	117	[2]220	290
Utilities, fuels, and public services	1 844	591	946	1 309	1 546	2 121	2 386	3 095
Household operations	344	91	182	160	230	298	472	679
Housekeeping supplies	290	152	114	180	178	301	305	499
Household furnishings and equipment	933	336	564	430	659	871	1 051	1 728
Apparel and Services	1 414	616	847	970	975	1 668	1 397	2 256
Transportation	5 586	1 798	2 875	3 494	4 708	5 147	7 954	9 793
Vehicle purchases (net outlay)	2 130	[2]550	1 247	1 205	2 004	1 518	3 786	3 673
Gasoline and motor oil	1 867	737	1 061	1 329	1 558	2 042	2 448	3 032
Other vehicle expenses	1 320	370	430	783	999	1 365	1 516	2 536
Public transportation	269	140	137	176	147	222	203	552
Health Care	741	143	239	314	498	882	987	1 474
Health insurance	393	53	93	121	238	421	523	872
Medical services	205	30	87	110	127	301	281	366
Drugs	110	47	41	69	102	122	151	178
Medical supplies	33	[2]13	[2]18	[2]14	[2]31	39	[2]32	59
Entertainment	1 527	735	833	960	1 261	1 609	1 766	2 534
Personal Care Products and Services	353	204	220	231	244	299	402	601
Reading	50	30	38	30	78	54	53	63
Education	1 738	2 505	3 149	1 870	1 584	1 448	1 009	913
Tobacco Products and Smoking Supplies	270	79	129	267	307	313	459	362
Miscellaneous	324	118	91	106	235	277	786	526
Cash Contributions	488	76	258	230	353	398	415	1 095
Personal Insurance and Pensions	2 361	143	377	784	1 213	1 918	2 666	5 981
Life and other personal insurance	38	[2]4	[2]3	[2]4	[2]29	[2]52	55	81
Pensions and Social Security	2 323	139	374	779	1 184	1 866	2 611	5 899

[1]Value less than or equal to 0.5.
[2]Data are likely to have large sampling errors.

Table 11-20. Consumer Expenditures, Averages for Age Groups by Income Before Taxes: Reference Person 25 to 34 Years of Age, 2007–2008

(Number, dollar, percent.)

Item	Total	Complete reporting of income								
		Less than $5,000	$5,000 to $9,999	$10,000 to $14,999	$15,000 to $19,999	$20,000 to $29,999	$30,000 to $39,999	$40,000 to $49,999	$50,000 to $69,999	$70,000 and over
NUMBER OF CONSUMER UNITS (THOUSANDS)	20 354	565	603	964	1 069	2 488	2 444	2 356	3 803	6 062
CONSUMER UNIT CHARACTERISTICS										
Income Before Taxes	58 558	-2 321	8 016	12 651	17 525	24 998	34 597	44 349	59 139	112 391
Income After Taxes	57 276	-1 889	8 502	13 689	18 245	25 400	34 717	44 043	57 999	108 329
Age of Reference Person	29.6	29.0	29.1	29.4	29.1	29.1	29.2	29.4	29.6	30.2
Average Number in Consumer Unit										
All persons	2.8	2.3	2.4	2.7	2.6	2.6	2.6	2.7	2.8	3.2
Children under 18 years	1.1	1.0	1.1	1.3	1.2	1.1	1.0	1.0	1.0	1.1
Persons 65 years and over	([1])	...	([1])	([1])	([1])	([1])	([1])	([1])	([1])	([1])
Earners	1.5	0.6	0.8	0.9	1.1	1.3	1.4	1.5	1.7	1.9
Vehicles	1.7	0.7	0.8	0.9	1.0	1.3	1.5	1.7	2.0	2.2
Percent Distribution										
Male	49	47	38	33	45	45	45	53	55	51
Female	51	53	62	67	55	55	55	47	45	49
Percent Homeowner	47	17	13	13	18	22	36	41	56	74
With mortgage	41	11	5	5	12	16	27	35	50	71
Without mortgage	6	6	8	8	7	6	9	6	6	3
AVERAGE ANNUAL EXPENDITURES	47 833	23 495	20 797	23 757	24 400	29 479	35 852	40 372	50 418	73 725
Food	6 114	4 039	3 700	4 192	3 956	4 196	5 113	5 500	6 171	8 327
Food at home	3 301	2 771	2 289	2 728	2 504	2 578	3 069	3 047	3 216	4 110
Cereals and bakery products	440	399	293	389	336	326	412	393	435	551
Meats, poultry, fish, and eggs	717	691	639	580	621	644	665	661	698	836
Dairy products	381	276	235	301	302	301	364	333	374	480
Fruits and vegetables	556	375	443	472	386	440	508	466	554	707
Other food at home	1 207	1 030	679	986	859	867	1 120	1 194	1 154	1 537
Food away from home	2 813	1 268	1 411	1 464	1 452	1 618	2 044	2 452	2 955	4 217
Alcoholic Beverages	503	[2]87	219	162	142	220	435	567	545	736
Housing	17 323	8 937	8 591	9 728	10 041	11 158	12 823	14 817	17 752	26 390
Shelter	10 734	6 071	5 672	5 712	6 333	6 982	8 091	9 466	10 780	16 317
Owned dwellings	5 929	1 466	888	751	949	1 454	2 633	4 132	6 260	12 206
Rented dwellings	4 509	4 508	4 633	4 869	5 359	5 438	5 322	5 155	4 244	3 496
Other lodging	296	[2]96	[2]151	[2]92	[2]25	90	137	179	276	615
Utilities, fuels, and public services	3 107	2 025	1 884	2 159	2 124	2 457	2 807	2 854	3 338	3 996
Household operations	1 156	171	287	501	444	513	607	701	1 164	2 221
Housekeeping supplies	558	248	302	444	340	374	424	470	499	828
Household furnishings and equipment	1 768	423	445	911	800	832	893	1 327	1 970	3 029
Apparel and Services	2 036	1 931	1 209	1 699	1 116	1 452	1 685	1 611	1 983	2 857
Transportation	8 883	3 857	3 472	3 605	4 636	6 064	6 999	7 125	10 124	13 276
Vehicle purchases (net outlay)	3 542	[2]1 193	[2]1 011	1 066	1 848	2 404	2 645	2 039	4 194	5 710
Gasoline and motor oil	2 599	1 107	1 231	1 477	1 622	1 918	2 324	2 699	2 861	3 412
Other vehicle expenses	2 336	1 377	1 048	862	993	1 543	1 801	2 110	2 710	3 396
Public transportation	406	180	182	200	174	199	229	276	359	758
Health Care	1 739	518	491	489	464	890	1 391	1 847	2 000	2 679
Health insurance	950	[2]220	262	222	237	474	792	959	1 196	1 429
Medical services	514	136	100	151	143	247	346	627	512	849
Drugs	209	64	113	76	60	133	205	190	225	305
Medical supplies	66	[2]98	[2]16	[2]40	[2]23	37	48	71	66	96
Entertainment	2 613	871	855	1 035	1 093	1 550	1 757	2 096	2 948	4 161
Personal Care Products and Services	530	405	271	371	282	309	426	414	498	818
Reading	75	32	32	37	34	40	49	75	76	122
Education	681	1 698	391	724	326	544	459	565	672	865
Tobacco Products and Smoking Supplies	315	320	418	273	303	323	337	354	384	242
Miscellaneous	657	226	183	244	267	231	572	592	723	1 066
Cash Contributions	1 031	328	348	421	515	587	816	911	1 031	1 670
Personal Insurance and Pensions	5 333	245	618	776	1 226	1 915	2 990	3 899	5 513	10 518
Life and other personal insurance	160	[2]34	[2]41	[2]40	37	58	82	110	139	329
Pensions and Social Security	5 174	211	577	735	1 189	1 857	2 909	3 789	5 374	10 189

[1]Value less than or equal to 0.05.
[2]Data are likely to have large sampling errors.
. . . = Not available.

Table 11-21. Consumer Expenditures, Averages for Age Groups by Income Before Taxes: Reference Person 35 to 44 Years of Age, 2007–2008

(Number, dollar, percent.)

Item	Total	Complete reporting of income								
		Less than $5,000	$5,000 to $9,999	$10,000 to $14,999	$15,000 to $19,999	$20,000 to $29,999	$30,000 to $39,999	$40,000 to $49,999	$50,000 to $69,999	$70,000 and over
NUMBER OF CONSUMER UNITS (THOUSANDS)	23 125	522	515	749	828	2 173	2 245	2 262	4 111	9 718
CONSUMER UNIT CHARACTERISTICS										
Income Before Taxes	77 055	-3 021	8 321	12 894	17 513	24 978	34 831	44 614	59 530	131 382
Income After Taxes	74 854	-3 274	8 522	13 409	17 906	25 563	35 292	44 500	58 904	126 128
Age of Reference Person	39.6	39.8	39.9	39.6	39.5	39.6	39.4	39.4	39.6	39.7
Average Number in Consumer Unit										
All persons	3.3	2.5	2.1	2.6	2.7	2.9	3.0	3.1	3.3	3.7
Children under 18 years	1.3	1.1	0.8	1.2	1.2	1.2	1.3	1.2	1.3	1.5
Persons 65 years and over	(^{1})	(^{1})	(^{1})	(^{1})	(^{1})	(^{1})	(^{1})	(^{1})	(^{1})	(^{1})
Earners	1.6	0.6	0.5	0.9	1.0	1.3	1.4	1.6	1.8	2.0
Vehicles	2.1	1.1	0.8	1.2	1.2	1.5	1.6	1.9	2.3	2.7
Percent Distribution										
Male	46	42	38	33	32	39	45	45	49	50
Female	54	58	62	67	68	61	55	55	51	50
Percent Homeowner	68	37	20	27	32	44	48	59	70	89
With mortgage	59	27	13	14	19	32	36	48	62	83
Without mortgage	9	10	7	14	13	12	13	11	8	6
AVERAGE ANNUAL EXPENDITURES	58 872	26 684	18 775	22 137	25 631	31 005	36 212	42 152	51 853	86 861
Food	7 619	4 128	2 929	3 683	4 314	4 665	5 542	6 129	6 991	10 454
Food at home	4 315	2 593	2 082	2 623	3 081	2 978	3 554	3 767	4 033	5 513
Cereals and bakery products	584	329	240	338	406	361	471	508	556	760
Meats, poultry, fish, and eggs	995	649	517	587	799	771	963	967	928	1 184
Dairy products	488	294	228	333	305	296	393	421	457	638
Fruits and vegetables	715	428	314	471	489	490	573	608	653	930
Other food at home	1 534	893	782	894	1 082	1 059	1 155	1 264	1 439	2 002
Food away from home	3 304	1 535	847	1 060	1 233	1 687	1 988	2 362	2 957	4 942
Alcoholic Beverages	466	315	^{2}123	79	185	229	320	216	443	706
Housing	20 802	11 732	8 468	9 707	10 340	12 067	13 523	15 544	17 878	29 801
Shelter	12 724	7 562	5 200	5 820	6 395	7 405	8 161	9 362	11 019	18 219
Owned dwellings	9 145	3 877	1 268	1 616	1 928	3 143	3 627	5 121	7 504	15 289
Rented dwellings	2 930	3 535	3 845	4 185	4 368	4 145	4 280	3 890	3 156	1 727
Other lodging	649	^{2}150	^{2}87	^{2}19	^{2}99	117	254	352	359	1 204
Utilities, fuels, and public services	4 028	2 494	2 148	2 568	2 534	3 039	3 263	3 662	3 944	4 968
Household operations	1 399	376	207	333	329	402	600	612	878	2 502
Housekeeping supplies	655	276	281	385	396	361	473	511	594	913
Household furnishings and equipment	1 996	1 024	632	601	686	860	1 026	1 396	1 444	3 199
Apparel and Services	2 286	1 364	725	700	921	1 260	1 471	1 488	1 776	3 495
Transportation	10 182	3 683	2 875	3 864	4 691	5 666	6 622	7 625	10 242	14 288
Vehicle purchases (net outlay)	3 659	^{2}657	^{2}555	^{2}1 243	1 360	1 834	2 273	2 563	3 887	5 254
Gasoline and motor oil	3 105	1 618	1 300	1 503	1 738	2 119	2 280	2 663	3 281	3 961
Other vehicle expenses	2 883	1 246	922	958	1 356	1 529	1 819	2 108	2 729	4 158
Public transportation	535	162	98	160	237	184	250	292	344	915
Health Care	2 406	1 292	755	775	961	1 133	1 500	1 873	2 376	3 434
Health insurance	1 304	725	244	484	565	571	812	1 112	1 263	1 858
Medical services	680	358	265	97	202	302	391	447	727	992
Drugs	326	155	203	175	164	200	234	251	303	444
Medical supplies	96	^{2}53	^{2}44	^{2}18	^{2}31	60	62	64	83	141
Entertainment	3 577	1 524	814	1 035	1 160	1 407	1 826	2 200	2 766	5 810
Personal Care Products and Services	694	338	226	245	316	358	420	513	599	1 029
Reading	105	37	31	33	29	47	46	65	81	170
Education	885	386	^{2}293	237	260	265	368	339	583	1 561
Tobacco Products and Smoking Supplies	366	371	430	472	450	411	415	431	427	285
Miscellaneous	853	229	190	175	454	440	466	582	896	1 237
Cash Contributions	1 560	717	587	395	399	543	831	1 244	1 341	2 408
Personal Insurance and Pensions	7 071	568	329	738	1 151	2 514	2 862	3 902	5 454	12 183
Life and other personal insurance	285	^{2}81	^{2}37	^{2}40	60	71	123	165	213	490
Pensions and Social Security	6 786	486	291	698	1 091	2 443	2 740	3 737	5 241	11 693

^{1}Value less than or equal to 0.05.
^{2}Data are likely to have large sampling errors.

Table 11-22. Consumer Expenditures, Averages for Age Groups by Income Before Taxes: Reference Person 45 to 54 Years of Age, 2007–2008

(Number, dollar, percent.)

Item		Complete reporting of income								
	Total	Less than $5,000	$5,000 to $9,999	$10,000 to $14,999	$15,000 to $19,999	$20,000 to $29,999	$30,000 to $39,999	$40,000 to $49,999	$50,000 to $69,999	$70,000 and over
NUMBER OF CONSUMER UNITS (THOUSANDS)	25 430	567	700	779	914	2 138	2 423	2 415	4 140	11 353
CONSUMER UNIT CHARACTERISTICS										
Income Before Taxes	81 207	-2 708	7 988	12 645	17 199	25 042	34 661	44 713	59 977	135 790
Income After Taxes	77 811	-2 759	7 985	12 961	17 404	25 047	34 325	44 046	58 293	128 977
Age of Reference Person	49.4	49.4	49.6	49.7	49.3	49.3	49.4	49.3	49.6	49.4
Average Number in Consumer Unit										
All persons	2.7	1.8	1.7	2.0	2.0	2.2	2.4	2.4	2.7	3.1
Children under 18 years	0.6	0.4	0.3	0.5	0.4	0.4	0.5	0.5	0.6	0.7
Persons 65 years and over	(1)	. . .	(1)	(1)	(1)	(1)	(1)	(1)	(1)	(1)
Earners	1.7	0.5	0.4	0.7	0.9	1.2	1.3	1.5	1.8	2.2
Vehicles	2.3	0.9	0.7	1.0	1.4	1.5	1.6	1.9	2.4	3.0
Percent Distribution										
Male	48	47	33	33	39	39	43	47	43	55
Female	52	53	67	67	61	61	57	53	57	45
Percent Homeowner	75	40	32	37	51	50	61	71	79	92
With mortgage	58	22	16	21	24	31	42	53	59	76
Without mortgage	18	18	16	16	27	19	19	18	20	16
AVERAGE ANNUAL EXPENDITURES	59 765	24 786	20 286	23 563	24 688	29 065	35 028	39 530	49 931	88 320
Food	7 441	4 279	3 503	4 158	3 529	4 170	4 688	5 560	6 274	10 458
Food at home	4 229	3 025	2 655	2 658	2 536	2 799	2 948	3 447	3 752	5 540
Cereals and bakery products	561	452	361	389	331	359	357	438	510	739
Meats, poultry, fish, and eggs	963	652	616	642	602	672	771	852	843	1 220
Dairy products	475	349	282	305	281	318	328	372	405	631
Fruits and vegetables	732	585	500	414	379	500	544	610	641	952
Other food at home	1 498	987	897	908	943	950	948	1 174	1 352	1 997
Food away from home	3 212	1 254	847	1 500	993	1 372	1 740	2 114	2 522	4 917
Alcoholic Beverages	502	304	239	169	356	242	271	425	393	722
Housing	19 379	9 922	8 630	9 664	10 349	11 166	12 887	14 279	16 199	27 099
Shelter	11 623	6 058	4 789	5 318	6 311	6 722	7 817	8 541	9 435	16 372
Owned dwellings	8 616	3 221	1 940	1 888	2 887	3 047	4 572	5 728	6 921	13 365
Rented dwellings	2 046	2 730	2 826	3 343	3 331	3 548	3 057	2 552	2 058	1 160
Other lodging	961	[2]107	[2]23	[2]87	[2]93	127	188	260	456	1 847
Utilities, fuels, and public services	4 151	2 509	2 379	2 797	2 824	2 967	3 302	3 580	4 022	5 114
Household operations	916	222	216	367	386	354	391	408	636	1 502
Housekeeping supplies	745	460	347	520	375	426	553	482	568	1 058
Household furnishings and equipment	1 945	673	899	662	452	696	824	1 269	1 538	3 053
Apparel and Services	2 209	1 463	1 339	1 389	752	976	1 184	1 362	1 748	3 288
Transportation	10 320	3 781	2 619	3 132	3 939	5 038	6 560	6 529	9 773	14 939
Vehicle purchases (net outlay)	3 288	[2]194	[2]948	[2]686	[2]980	1 331	1 837	1 706	3 304	4 959
Gasoline and motor oil	3 074	1 130	934	1 247	1 563	1 950	2 332	2 499	3 051	4 051
Other vehicle expenses	3 314	2 285	545	1 069	1 214	1 537	2 094	2 104	2 997	4 836
Public transportation	644	173	191	130	183	220	298	220	422	1 093
Health Care	2 861	1 283	1 168	789	1 325	1 685	1 896	2 239	2 814	3 890
Health insurance	1 455	708	392	688	620	801	1 038	1 139	1 479	1 949
Medical services	805	247	208	413	276	505	473	544	754	1 141
Drugs	464	218	273	-376	400	319	310	477	478	606
Medical supplies	137	[2]110	[2]295	64	[2]29	60	75	79	104	194
Entertainment	3 231	1 458	1 098	1 109	1 002	1 448	1 454	1 693	2 553	5 078
Personal Care Products and Services	711	289	236	246	247	349	379	513	578	1 065
Reading	131	65	32	33	42	45	51	70	107	208
Education	1 851	[2]102	[2]268	305	209	346	368	844	951	3 417
Tobacco Products and Smoking Supplies	413	498	428	573	427	474	403	383	485	366
Miscellaneous	982	181	290	817	771	369	1 047	593	780	1 355
Cash Contributions	2 062	536	178	392	657	755	873	1 099	1 378	3 437
Personal Insurance and Pensions	7 672	624	258	787	1 082	2 000	2 968	3 940	5 896	12 998
Life and other personal insurance	398	[2]62	63	150	89	127	148	218	265	669
Pensions and Social Security	7 274	562	195	637	993	1 874	2 820	3 722	5 631	12 330

[1]Value less than or equal to 0.05.
[2]Data are likely to have large sampling errors.
. . . = Not available.

Table 11-23. Consumer Expenditures, Averages for Age Groups by Income Before Taxes: Reference Person 55 to 64 Years of Age, 2007–2008

(Number, dollar, percent.)

Item		Complete reporting of income								
	Total	Less than $5,000	$5,000 to $9,999	$10,000 to $14,999	$15,000 to $19,999	$20,000 to $29,999	$30,000 to $39,999	$40,000 to $49,999	$50,000 to $69,999	$70,000 and over
NUMBER OF CONSUMER UNITS (THOUSANDS)	19 644	581	844	1 020	989	2 138	1 929	1 860	3 142	7 142
CONSUMER UNIT CHARACTERISTICS										
Income Before Taxes	71 353	-6 031	8 210	12 620	17 306	25 080	34 574	44 892	59 399	136 968
Income After Taxes	68 492	-6 248	8 263	12 703	17 048	25 094	34 272	43 848	57 592	130 228
Age of Reference Person	59.3	59.1	59.4	59.8	59.8	59.5	59.4	59.2	59.3	59.0
Average Number in Consumer Unit										
All persons	2.1	1.5	1.4	1.5	1.7	1.8	1.9	2.0	2.2	2.5
Children under 18 years	0.2	[1]0.1	[1]0.1	[1]0.1	0.2	0.1	0.2	0.2	0.2	0.2
Persons 65 years and over	0.1	...	...	0.1	0.2	0.1	0.2	0.1	0.1	0.1
Earners	1.3	0.4	0.3	0.5	0.7	0.9	1.1	1.3	1.5	1.9
Vehicles	2.2	1.4	1.0	1.3	1.5	1.7	1.9	2.1	2.4	2.8
Percent Distribution										
Male	49	52	37	39	47	39	42	49	50	57
Female	51	48	63	61	53	61	58	51	50	43
Percent Homeowner	81	60	49	58	62	74	75	83	86	94
With mortgage	46	30	19	20	23	34	36	44	54	62
Without mortgage	35	30	30	38	39	40	39	39	32	32
AVERAGE ANNUAL EXPENDITURES	54 287	29 879	18 043	21 477	27 819	30 444	34 027	40 943	51 253	86 173
Food	6 300	3 734	3 181	3 077	3 283	3 891	4 395	5 337	6 268	9 196
Food at home	3 586	2 589	2 522	2 170	2 230	2 580	2 639	3 263	3 757	4 731
Cereals and bakery products	474	379	324	323	307	352	332	417	493	624
Meats, poultry, fish, and eggs	803	576	672	527	446	610	625	781	851	1 013
Dairy products	402	330	254	241	293	275	290	347	403	543
Fruits and vegetables	662	466	485	359	387	453	485	584	691	894
Other food at home	1 246	837	787	720	796	890	906	1 133	1 319	1 657
Food away from home	2 714	1 145	660	907	1 054	1 311	1 755	2 074	2 511	4 466
Alcoholic Beverages	529	228	111	178	170	280	282	366	547	869
Housing	17 417	11 680	7 624	8 396	10 299	11 019	11 514	12 971	16 953	26 161
Shelter	9 944	7 318	4 283	4 634	5 698	6 312	6 365	7 115	9 713	15 066
Owned dwellings	7 226	4 271	1 839	2 117	2 789	4 062	3 976	5 163	7 266	11 793
Rented dwellings	1 574	2 456	2 309	2 296	2 541	1 913	2 127	1 489	1 486	987
Other lodging	1 144	590	[1]135	221	368	337	262	464	961	2 286
Utilities, fuels, and public services	3 865	2 433	2 277	2 503	2 928	3 028	3 308	3 528	3 950	4 944
Household operations	870	413	211	257	489	338	381	518	736	1 566
Housekeeping supplies	821	473	344	372	361	477	432	593	764	1 315
Household furnishings and equipment	1 918	1 044	509	630	823	864	1 029	1 217	1 789	3 270
Apparel and Services	1 752	858	570	551	639	889	1 462	1 204	1 635	2 798
Transportation	9 491	3 896	2 857	4 337	5 540	6 463	6 530	7 849	9 101	14 299
Vehicle purchases (net outlay)	3 172	[1]483	[1]425	[1]1 529	[1]1 879	2 406	1 902	2 208	2 925	5 061
Gasoline and motor oil	2 662	1 656	1 221	1 276	1 767	1 917	2 075	2 429	2 834	3 603
Other vehicle expenses	2 957	1 434	1 130	1 370	1 523	1 957	2 364	2 810	2 865	4 239
Public transportation	700	322	82	162	370	182	189	402	477	1 395
Health Care	3 652	2 466	1 214	1 842	2 615	2 550	2 779	3 430	3 910	4 947
Health insurance	1 849	1 376	568	1 001	1 340	1 419	1 455	1 798	1 872	2 468
Medical services	953	554	317	291	596	477	606	822	1 084	1 419
Drugs	694	487	320	490	575	567	645	682	732	837
Medical supplies	156	[1]50	[1]10	61	103	87	73	128	221	223
Entertainment	2 885	2 663	983	977	1 510	1 361	1 767	2 415	3 140	4 355
Personal Care Products and Services	631	432	225	223	281	327	417	473	595	1 004
Reading	154	80	40	53	69	71	81	122	153	252
Education	898	[1]829	[1]24	[1]141	[1]218	98	229	509	498	1 906
Tobacco Products and Smoking Supplies	353	253	306	376	347	358	373	377	437	315
Miscellaneous	1 201	794	226	264	760	604	530	792	1 159	2 024
Cash Contributions	2 452	972	366	518	1 112	723	1 037	1 583	1 594	4 783
Personal Insurance and Pensions	6 572	993	315	546	975	1 809	2 629	3 515	5 265	13 262
Life and other personal insurance	491	187	102	145	161	239	240	304	422	878
Pensions and Social Security	6 081	806	213	401	814	1 571	2 389	3 211	4 843	12 384

[1]Data are likely to have large sampling errors.

Table 11-24. Consumer Expenditures, Averages for Age Groups by Income Before Taxes: Reference Person 65 Years of Age and Over, 2007–2008

(Number, dollar, percent.)

Item	Total	Complete reporting of income								
		Less than $5,000	$5,000 to $9,999	$10,000 to $14,999	$15,000 to $19,999	$20,000 to $29,999	$30,000 to $39,999	$40,000 to $49,999	$50,000 to $69,999	$70,000 and over
NUMBER OF CONSUMER UNITS (THOUSANDS)	23 731	750	1 524	3 359	3 013	4 715	2 834	1 948	2 413	3 177
CONSUMER UNIT CHARACTERISTICS										
Income Before Taxes	39 816	472	8 442	12 716	17 401	24 715	34 993	44 823	59 050	123 093
Income After Taxes	39 008	40	8 529	12 805	17 535	24 662	34 730	44 309	58 354	118 049
Age of Reference Person	75.1	75.0	76.9	77.6	77.3	75.5	74.1	73.8	73.3	71.9
Average Number in Consumer Unit										
All persons	1.7	1.3	1.2	1.2	1.3	1.7	1.8	2.0	2.1	2.3
Children under 18 years	(^{1})	(^{1})	(^{1})	(^{1})	(^{1})	(^{1})	(^{1})	0.1	0.1	0.1
Persons 65 years and over	1.4	1.2	1.1	1.1	1.2	1.4	1.5	1.5	1.5	1.6
Earners	0.4	0.2	0.1	0.1	0.1	0.3	0.4	0.6	0.8	1.2
Vehicles	1.6	0.9	0.7	0.9	1.2	1.5	1.8	2.0	2.1	2.5
Percent Distribution										
Male	43	32	27	27	35	43	43	50	56	64
Female	57	68	73	73	65	57	57	50	44	36
Percent Homeowner	79	54	51	63	73	81	88	88	91	96
With mortgage	21	16	7	10	13	17	22	27	32	42
Without mortgage	58	38	45	53	60	65	66	61	58	53
AVERAGE ANNUAL EXPENDITURES	36 687	20 526	15 207	19 276	24 095	30 641	35 318	41 728	49 058	78 014
Food	4 604	3 144	2 068	2 782	2 895	4 023	4 860	5 005	6 053	8 595
Food at home	2 990	1 891	1 602	1 965	2 070	2 788	3 311	3 232	3 806	4 828
Cereals and bakery products	420	245	234	275	305	397	464	445	543	657
Meats, poultry, fish, and eggs	661	376	347	498	410	648	707	678	874	1 028
Dairy products	347	197	194	221	257	305	393	384	451	557
Fruits and vegetables	567	429	320	364	392	522	616	597	691	964
Other food at home	996	644	506	606	706	917	1 131	1 127	1 248	1 622
Food away from home	1 613	1 253	466	817	825	1 235	1 549	1 773	2 247	3 767
Alcoholic Beverages	268	^{2}92	38	154	74	222	221	244	327	787
Housing	12 698	8 600	7 154	8 068	9 621	11 040	11 763	14 002	16 278	23 742
Shelter	6 797	5 390	3 656	4 451	5 335	5 862	6 111	7 038	8 335	13 186
Owned dwellings	4 552	2 262	1 414	2 132	2 867	3 772	4 336	5 283	6 295	10 328
Rented dwellings	1 649	2 940	2 158	2 220	2 298	1 782	1 210	1 288	1 127	690
Other lodging	597	^{2}188	^{2}85	99	169	308	565	467	913	2 168
Utilities, fuels, and public services	3 217	2 277	2 004	2 344	2 654	3 031	3 364	3 619	3 804	4 929
Household operations	855	297	276	413	561	633	589	1 042	1 338	2 095
Housekeeping supplies	595	240	260	352	334	527	638	727	881	1 019
Household furnishings and equipment	1 235	395	957	508	736	989	1 061	1 575	1 920	2 514
Apparel and Services	1 066	549	301	608	744	713	953	962	1 633	2 565
Transportation	5 701	3 047	1 857	2 340	3 845	5 037	5 406	7 348	7 860	12 007
Vehicle purchases (net outlay)	1 736	^{2}518	^{2}288	^{2}457	1 360	1 556	1 601	2 088	2 493	4 025
Gasoline and motor oil	1 546	833	622	721	995	1 441	1 700	1 959	2 163	2 850
Other vehicle expenses	1 984	1 187	603	986	1 311	1 808	1 697	2 944	2 783	3 744
Public transportation	435	508	344	175	180	232	408	356	421	1 388
Health Care	4 618	2 548	1 999	2 619	3 421	4 514	5 413	5 536	6 360	7 145
Health insurance	2 808	1 521	1 339	1 801	2 277	2 818	3 353	3 378	3 557	3 963
Medical services	818	412	246	326	400	746	889	804	1 446	1 682
Drugs	840	525	359	435	669	823	985	1 130	1 162	1 193
Medical supplies	152	^{2}90	55	58	75	127	186	224	195	308
Entertainment	1 939	782	561	790	1 020	1 585	2 222	1 892	2 786	4 547
Personal Care Products and Services	520	219	220	267	361	438	547	571	714	1 050
Reading	143	69	47	78	101	119	136	172	209	288
Education	282	^{2}44	^{2}33	^{2}133	39	153	87	158	195	1 346
Tobacco Products and Smoking Supplies	168	112	120	127	152	178	216	168	202	182
Miscellaneous	629	393	220	271	379	496	597	995	867	1 303
Cash Contributions	2 218	677	416	858	1 005	1 267	1 896	3 080	2 844	6 728
Personal Insurance and Pensions	1 833	250	173	182	437	855	1 001	1 596	2 729	7 730
Life and other personal insurance	330	132	93	125	162	317	302	264	436	868
Pensions and Social Security	1 503	117	80	57	275	539	699	1 332	2 293	6 863

^{1}Value less than or equal to 0.05.
^{2}Data are likely to have large sampling errors.

Chapter Twelve

AMERICAN TIME USE SURVEY

AMERICAN TIME USE SURVEY

HIGHLIGHTS

This chapter presents data from the American Time Use Survey (ATUS). The survey was introduced in the sixth edition of the *Handbook of U.S. Labor Statistics*. Its purpose is to collect data on the activities people do during the day and the amount of time they spend on each one.

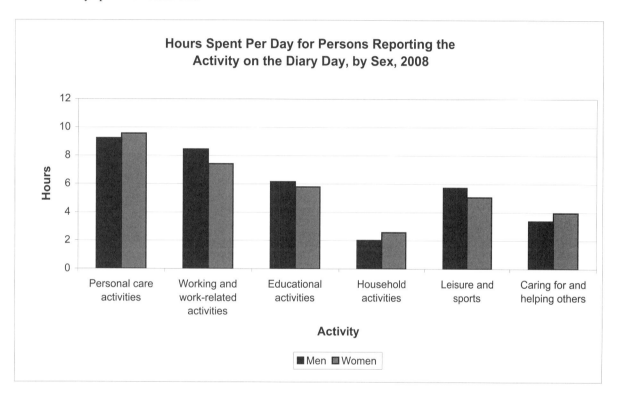

Hours Spent Per Day for Persons Reporting the Activity on the Diary Day, by Sex, 2008

In 2008, on days that they worked, men worked nearly one hour more than women. This difference partly reflects women's greater likelihood of working part-time. However, even among full-time workers (those usually working 35 hours or more per week), men worked longer than women—8.3 versus 7.7 hours. Men were also more likely than women to participate in sports, exercise, or recreation on any given day and on the days that they participated, men spent more time in these activities than women did—1.9 versus 1.3 hours. (See Tables 12-1 and 12-3.)

OTHER HIGHLIGHTS

- On an average day, 20 percent of men did housework—such as cleaning or doing laundry—compared with 50 percent of women. Thirty-eight percent of men did food preparation or cleanup compared with 65 percent of women. (See Table 12-1.)

- Adults age 75 and over spent 7.6 hours engaged in leisure activities on an average day—more than any other age group; 35- to 44-year-olds spent just over 4 hours engaged in leisure and sports activities—less than other age group. (See Table 12-2.)

- On the days that they worked, 35 percent of employed people age 25 and over with a bachelor's degree or higher did some work at home compared with only 9 percent of those with less than a high school diploma. (See Table 12-5.)

- Watching TV was the leisure activity that occupied the most time, accounting for about half of leisure time, on average, for both men and women. Socializing, such as visiting with friends or attending or hosting social events, was the next most common leisure activity, accounting for about three-quarters of an hour per day for both sexes. (See Table 12-1.)

NOTES AND DEFINITIONS

Survey Methodology

While the Bureau of Labor Statistics (BLS) has long produced statistics about the labor market, including information about employment, hours, and earnings, the American Time Use Survey (ATUS) marks the first time that a federal statistical agency has produced estimates on how Americans spend another critical resource—their time. Data collection for the ATUS began in January 2003. Sample cases for the survey are selected monthly, and interviews are conducted continuously throughout the year. In 2008, approximately 12,700 individuals were interviewed.

ATUS sample households are chosen from the households that have completed their eighth (final) interview for the Current Population Survey (CPS), the nation's monthly household labor force survey. (See Chapter 1 of this *Handbook* for a description of the CPS.) ATUS sample households are selected to ensure that estimates will be representative of the nation.

An individual age 15 years or older is randomly chosen from each sample household. This "designated person" takes part in a one-time telephone interview about his or her activities on the previous day (the "diary day").

All ATUS interviews are conducted using Computer Assisted Telephone Interviewing. Procedures are in place to collect information from the small number of households that did not provide a telephone number during the CPS interview.

Concepts and Definitions

Average day. The average day measure reflects an average distribution across all persons in the reference population and all days of the week. Average day measures for the entire population provide a mechanism for seeing the overall distribution of time allocation for society as a whole. The ATUS collects data about daily activities from all segments of the population age 15 and over, including persons who are employed and not employed. Many activities are not typically done on a daily basis, and some activities are only done by a subset of the population.

Average hours per day. The average number of hours spent in a 24-hour day (between 4 a.m. on the diary day and 4 a.m. on the interview day) doing a specified activity.

Average hours per day, population. The average number of hours per day spent on a particular activity is computed using all responses from the sample population, including those from respondents who did not do the particular activity on their diary day. These estimates reflect the total number of respondents engaged in an activity and the total amount of time they spent on the activity.

Average hours per day, persons reporting the activity on the diary day. The average number of hours per day spent on a particular activity is computed using responses only from those engaged in the particular activity on the diary day.

Diary day. The diary day is the day about which the designated person reports. For example, the diary day of a designated person interviewed on Tuesday would be Monday.

Earnings

Usual weekly earnings. Data represent the earnings of full-time wage and salary workers before taxes and other deductions and include any overtime pay, commissions, or tips usually received (at the main job in the case of multiple jobholders). Usual weekly earnings are only updated in ATUS for about a third of employed respondents—if the respondent changed jobs or employment status or if the CPS weekly earnings value was imputed. This means that the earnings information could be out of date because the CPS interview was done 2 to 5 months prior to the ATUS interview. Respondents are asked to identify the easiest way for them to report earnings (hourly, weekly, biweekly, twice monthly, annually, or other) and how much they usually earn in the reported time period. Earnings reported on a basis other than weekly are converted to a weekly equivalent. The term "usual" is as perceived by the respondent. If the respondent asks for a definition of usual, interviewers are instructed to define the term as more than half the weeks worked during the past 4 or 5 months.

Weekly earnings ranges. The ranges used represent approximately 25 percent of full-time wage and salary workers. For example, 25 percent of full-time wage and salary workers with one job only had weekly earnings of $500 or less. These dollar values vary from year to year.

Employment Status

Employed. All persons who, at any time during the seven days prior to the interview: 1) did any work at all as paid employees, worked in their own business professions, or on their own farms, or usually worked 15 hours or more an unpaid workers in family-operated enterprises; and 2) all those who were not working but had jobs or businesses from which they were temporarily absent due to illness, bad weather, vacation, childcare problems, labor-management disputes, maternity or paternity leave, job training, or other family or personal reasons, whether or not they were paid for the time off or were seeking other jobs.

Employed full time. Full-time workers are those who usually work 35 hours or more per week at all jobs combined.

Employed part time. Part-time workers are those who usually work fewer than 35 hours per week at all jobs combined.

Not employed. Persons are not employed if they do not meet the conditions for employment. Not employed workers include those classified as unemployed as well as those classified as not in the labor force (using CPS definitions).

The numbers of employed and not employed persons in this report do not correspond to published totals from the CPS. While the information on employment from the ATUS is useful for assessing work in the context of other daily activities, the employment data are not intended for analysis of current employment trends. Compared to the CPS and other estimates of employment, the ATUS estimates are based on a much smaller sample and are only available with a substantial lag.

Household children. Household children are children under 18 years of age who reside in the household of the ATUS respondent. The children may be related to the respondent (such as their own children, grandchildren, nieces, nephews, brothers, or sisters) or not related (such as foster children or children of roommates). For secondary childcare calculations, respondents are asked about care of household children under 13 years of age.

Primary activity. A primary activity is the main activity of a respondent at a specified time.

Secondary activities. A secondary (or simultaneous) activity is an activity done at the same time as a primary activity. With the exception of the care of children under age 13, information on secondary activities is not systematically collected in the ATUS.

Major Activity Category Definitions

Personal care activities. Personal care activities include sleeping, bathing, dressing, health-related self-care, and personal or private activities. Receiving unpaid personal care from others (for example, "my sister put polish on my nails") is also captured in this category.

Eating and drinking. All time spent eating or drinking (except when identified by the respondent as part of a work or volunteer activity), whether alone, with others, at home, at a place of purchase, in transit, or somewhere else, is classified in this category.

Household activities. Household activities are those done by respondents to maintain their households. These include housework, cooking, yard care, pet care, vehicle maintenance and repair, and home maintenance, repair, decoration, and renovation. Food preparation is always classified as a household activity. Household management and organizational activities—such as filling out paperwork, balancing a checkbook, or planning a party—are also included in this category.

Purchasing goods and services. This category includes the purchase of consumer goods as well as the purchase or use of professional and personal care services, household services, and government services. Most purchases and rentals

of consumer goods, regardless of mode or place of purchase or rental (in person, via telephone, over the Internet, at home, or in a store), are classified in this category. Time spent obtaining, receiving, and purchasing professional and personal care services provided by someone else is also classified in this category, which also includes time spent arranging for and purchasing household services provided by someone else.

Caring for and helping household members. Time spent doing activities to care for or help any child (under age 18) or adult in the household, regardless of relationship to the respondent or the physical or mental health status of the person being helped, is classified here. Caring for and helping activities for household children and adults are coded separately in subcategories.

Caring for and helping non-household members. Time spent caring for and helping any child or adult who is not part of the respondent's household, regardless of the relationship to the respondent or the physical or mental health status of the person being helped, is classified in this category.

Working and work-related activities. This category includes time spent working, doing activities as part of one's job, engaging in income-generating activities (not as part of one's job), and job search activities. "Working" includes hours spent doing the specific tasks required of one's main or other job, regardless of location or time of day. Travel time related to working and work-related activities includes time spent commuting to and from one's job, as well as time spent traveling for work-related activities, generating income, and job searching.

Educational activities. Educational activities include taking classes (including Internet and other distance-learning courses), doing research and homework, and taking care of administrative tasks, such as registering for classes or obtaining a school ID. For high school students, before- and after-school extracurricular activities (except sports) also are classified as educational activities.

Organizational, civic, and religious activities. This category captures time spent volunteering for or through an organization, performing civic obligations, and participating in religious and spiritual activities.

Leisure and sports. The leisure and sports category includes sports, exercise, and recreation; socializing and communicating; and other leisure activities, such as watching television, reading or attending entertainment events.

Telephone calls, mail, and e-mail. This category captures telephone communication and handling household or personal mail and e-mail. Telephone and Internet purchases are classified in purchasing goods and services.

Other activities, not elsewhere classified. This residual category includes security procedures related to traveling, traveling not associated with a specific activity category, ambiguous activities that could not be coded, or missing activities that were considered too private to report.

Sources of Additional Information

Additional information, including expanded definitions and estimation methodology, is available from BLS news release USDL 09-0704, "American Time Use Survey—2008 Results"; the June 2005 edition of the *Monthly Labor Review;* and the *ATUS User's Guide,* June 2008. All of these resources are available on the BLS Web site at <http://www.bls.gov/tus/>.

Table 12-1. Average Hours Per Day Spent in Primary Activities[1] for the Total Population and for Persons Reporting the Activity on the Diary Day, by Activity Category and Sex, 2007 and 2008 Annual Averages

(Hours, percent.)

Activity	Hours per day, total population			Percent of population reporting the activity on the diary day			Hours per day for persons reporting the activity on the diary day		
	Both sexes	Men	Women	Both sexes	Men	Women	Both sexes	Men	Women
2007									
All Activities[2]	24.00	24.00	24.00	X	X	X	X	X	X
Personal care activities	9.33	9.14	9.51	100.0	100.0	100.0	9.33	9.14	9.51
Sleeping	8.57	8.52	8.63	99.9	99.9	99.9	8.58	8.53	8.63
Eating and drinking	1.24	1.27	1.20	95.4	95.7	95.1	1.30	1.33	1.26
Household activities	1.84	1.43	2.22	74.4	65.6	82.7	2.47	2.18	2.69
Housework	0.64	0.29	0.97	36.2	19.7	51.7	1.76	1.46	1.87
Food preparation and cleanup	0.52	0.28	0.74	50.8	37.3	63.5	1.02	0.75	1.17
Lawn and garden care	0.21	0.30	0.12	10.3	12.9	7.9	2.00	2.32	1.51
Household management	0.14	0.12	0.16	18.2	15.2	21.0	0.78	0.82	0.75
Purchasing goods and services	0.78	0.63	0.92	44.3	40.1	48.2	1.77	1.58	1.92
Consumer goods purchases	0.39	0.31	0.48	40.6	37.2	43.8	0.97	0.83	1.09
Professional and personal care services	0.09	0.06	0.12	8.4	6.3	10.4	1.04	0.88	1.13
Caring for and helping household members	0.53	0.33	0.72	25.5	20.3	30.4	2.08	1.62	2.38
Caring for and helping household children	0.42	0.25	0.58	21.8	16.4	26.9	1.92	1.49	2.17
Caring for and helping non-household members	0.20	0.17	0.23	12.8	10.7	14.8	1.56	1.56	1.56
Caring for and helping non-household adults	0.07	0.07	0.07	8.0	7.2	8.8	0.87	0.95	0.81
Working and work-related activities	3.81	4.52	3.14	47.8	54.2	41.7	7.98	8.34	7.53
Working	3.47	4.09	2.89	45.9	51.9	40.2	7.56	7.87	7.18
Educational activities	0.43	0.41	0.44	7.9	7.6	8.2	5.42	5.39	5.44
Attending class	0.26	0.26	0.25	5.0	4.9	5.0	5.15	5.20	5.10
Homework and research	0.14	0.12	0.15	5.4	4.6	6.0	2.53	2.52	2.54
Organizational, civic, and religious activities	0.35	0.28	0.41	14.5	11.8	17.1	2.42	2.42	2.42
Religious and spiritual activities	0.15	0.11	0.18	8.9	6.9	10.8	1.66	0.64	1.67
Volunteering (organizational and civic activities)	0.16	0.13	0.18	7.1	6.0	8.2	2.22	2.21	2.23
Leisure and sports	5.11	5.48	4.76	95.8	96.0	95.6	5.33	5.71	4.98
Socializing and communicating	0.73	0.67	0.78	38.4	35.3	41.4	1.89	1.89	1.89
Watching television	2.62	2.88	2.38	79.5	81.4	77.7	3.30	3.54	3.07
Participating in sports, exercise, and recreation	0.32	0.42	0.22	18.5	21.4	15.7	1.71	1.96	1.39
Telephone calls, mail, and e-mail	0.19	0.13	0.24	24.4	19.1	29.3	0.76	0.66	0.82
Other activities n.e.c.	0.20	0.20	0.19	14.1	13.0	15.1	1.40	1.57	1.26
2008									
All Activities[2]	24.00	24.00	24.00	X	X	X	X	X	X
Personal care activities	9.39	9.22	9.55	100.0	100.0	100.0	9.39	9.23	9.55
Sleeping	8.60	8.56	8.64	99.9	99.9	99.9	8.61	8.57	8.64
Eating and drinking	1.23	1.28	1.18	96.0	96.5	95.6	1.28	1.33	1.23
Household activities	1.73	1.30	2.13	73.7	64.2	82.6	2.34	2.02	2.58
Housework	0.58	0.24	0.90	35.5	19.7	50.3	1.64	1.23	1.79
Food preparation and cleanup	0.52	0.30	0.73	52.3	38.4	65.3	1.00	0.78	1.12
Lawn and garden care	0.19	0.26	0.12	9.4	11.0	7.9	2.00	2.35	1.56
Household management	0.13	0.10	0.15	18.1	14.5	21.5	0.70	0.68	0.71
Purchasing goods and services	0.77	0.60	0.92	44.8	39.2	50.0	1.71	1.53	1.85
Consumer goods purchases	0.38	0.28	0.48	40.7	35.6	45.4	0.94	0.79	1.05
Professional and personal care services	0.08	0.06	0.11	8.9	6.7	11.0	0.92	0.84	0.97
Caring for and helping household members	0.53	0.36	0.70	26.1	20.7	31.2	2.04	1.72	2.24
Caring for and helping household children	0.42	0.27	0.55	22.4	17.2	27.2	1.86	1.59	2.01
Caring for and helping non-household members	0.23	0.18	0.27	13.3	11.0	15.6	1.69	1.66	1.72
Caring for and helping non-household adults	0.07	0.08	0.07	8.5	7.8	9.1	0.87	0.98	0.78
Working and work-related activities	3.73	4.52	2.99	46.7	53.5	40.3	7.99	8.44	7.42
Working	3.38	4.06	2.73	44.7	51.1	38.7	7.56	7.95	7.06
Educational activities	0.47	0.42	0.52	7.9	6.9	9.0	5.94	6.15	5.79
Attending class	0.27	0.27	0.27	5.2	5.0	5.3	5.22	5.37	5.09
Homework and research	0.16	0.12	0.20	5.8	4.6	7.0	2.72	2.49	2.87
Organizational, civic, and religious activities	0.33	0.30	0.37	14.6	12.4	16.7	2.29	2.42	2.20
Religious and spiritual activities	0.14	0.12	0.17	9.2	7.7	10.7	1.55	1.54	1.55
Volunteering (organizational and civic activities)	0.15	0.14	0.16	7.0	6.0	7.9	2.15	2.38	1.99
Leisure and sports	5.18	5.52	4.86	96.2	96.4	96.0	5.39	5.73	5.06
Socializing and communicating	0.71	0.66	0.76	38.9	36.1	41.6	1.83	1.83	1.82
Watching television	2.77	3.01	2.55	80.9	82.3	79.6	3.43	3.66	3.20
Participating in sports, exercise, and recreation	0.30	0.40	0.20	17.9	21.0	15.0	1.64	1.91	1.30
Telephone calls, mail, and e-mail	0.21	0.14	0.28	26.3	20.3	31.9	0.80	0.67	0.89
Other activities n.e.c.	0.20	0.17	0.24	14.6	12.6	16.5	1.39	1.32	1.44

Note: Data refer to respondents age 15 years and over, unless otherwise specified.

n.e.c. = Not elsewhere classified.

[1]A primary activity is designated by a respondent as his or her main activity. Other activities done simultaneously are not included.
[2]All major activity categories include related travel time.
X = Not applicable.

Table 12-2. Average Hours Per Day Spent in Primary Activities[1] for the Total Population, by Age, Sex, Race, Hispanic Origin, and Educational Attainment, 2008 Annual Averages

(Hours.)

Characteristic	Hours per day spent in primary activities[2]											
	Personal care activities	Eating and drinking	Household activities	Purchasing goods and services	Caring for and helping household members	Caring for and helping non-household members	Working and work-related activities	Educational activities	Organizational, civic, and religious activities	Leisure activities	Telephone calls, mail, and e-mail	Other activities n.e.c.
Both Sexes, 15 Years and Over	9.39	1.23	1.73	0.77	0.53	0.23	3.73	0.47	0.33	5.18	0.21	0.20
15 to 19 years	10.37	1.01	0.67	0.56	0.12	0.22	1.37	3.09	0.26	5.69	0.38	0.25
20 to 24 years	9.63	1.10	1.06	0.71	0.53	0.24	4.36	1.21	0.11	4.70	0.22	0.12
25 to 34 years	9.29	1.17	1.47	0.72	1.07	0.14	4.93	0.31	0.22	4.34	0.15	0.18
35 to 44 years	9.12	1.19	1.86	0.80	1.04	0.17	4.93	0.09	0.31	4.16	0.14	0.20
45 to 54 years	9.11	1.19	1.89	0.76	0.40	0.22	4.95	0.09	0.37	4.67	0.19	0.17
55 to 64 years	9.05	1.34	2.09	0.87	0.20	0.40	3.54	0.03	0.41	5.66	0.21	0.22
65 to 74 years	9.51	1.46	2.27	0.92	0.09	0.31	1.23	0.02	0.54	7.12	0.25	0.29
75 years and over	10.02	1.52	2.34	0.75	0.08	0.14	0.37	0.03	0.54	7.62	0.32	0.27
Men, 15 Years and Over	9.22	1.28	1.30	0.60	0.36	0.18	4.52	0.42	0.30	5.52	0.14	0.17
15 to 19 years	10.29	1.07	0.59	0.41	0.08	0.14	1.23	3.14	0.27	6.32	0.23	0.23
20 to 24 years	9.59	1.08	0.87	0.47	0.19	0.19	5.31	0.65	0.10	5.30	0.15	0.11
25 to 34 years	9.15	1.22	1.06	0.58	0.62	0.12	5.97	0.32	0.16	4.55	0.11	0.14
35 to 44 years	8.91	1.26	1.33	0.58	0.72	0.18	6.14	0.04	0.26	4.32	0.10	0.16
45 to 54 years	8.83	1.26	1.48	0.57	0.35	0.15	5.75	0.03	0.36	4.98	0.11	0.14
55 to 64 years	8.95	1.37	1.63	0.67	0.15	0.30	4.15	0.01	0.32	6.15	0.12	0.18
65 to 74 years	9.40	1.54	1.77	0.87	0.08	0.27	1.42	0.00	0.53	7.69	0.17	0.24
75 years and over	9.84	1.62	1.70	0.75	0.09	0.16	0.55	0.01	0.61	8.29	0.17	0.22
Women, 15 Years and Over	9.55	1.18	2.13	0.92	0.70	0.27	2.99	0.52	0.37	4.86	0.28	0.24
15 to 19 years	10.45	0.94	0.76	0.71	0.17	0.30	1.52	3.04	0.26	5.05	0.53	0.27
20 to 24 years	9.68	1.12	1.24	0.96	0.88	0.30	3.39	1.79	0.11	4.09	0.30	0.13
25 to 34 years	9.44	1.11	1.89	0.87	1.52	0.16	3.90	0.30	0.27	4.13	0.19	0.22
35 to 44 years	9.33	1.11	2.37	1.01	1.34	0.15	3.76	0.14	0.37	4.01	0.18	0.23
45 to 54 years	9.38	1.11	2.29	0.94	0.45	0.29	4.18	0.14	0.38	4.37	0.26	0.20
55 to 64 years	9.15	1.30	2.52	1.05	0.24	0.49	2.97	0.05	0.49	5.21	0.29	0.26
65 to 74 years	9.60	1.40	2.69	0.96	0.09	0.35	1.06	0.02	0.56	6.63	0.31	0.33
75 years and over	10.14	1.46	2.75	0.76	0.08	0.13	0.25	0.04	0.50	7.18	0.41	0.30
White, 15 Years and Over	9.33	1.27	1.80	0.77	0.54	0.23	3.77	0.45	0.31	5.13	0.20	0.21
Men	9.18	1.32	1.36	0.59	0.36	0.18	4.62	0.40	0.28	5.42	0.12	0.17
Women	9.49	1.22	2.22	0.94	0.71	0.28	2.95	0.50	0.34	4.84	0.27	0.24
Black, 15 Years and Over	9.80	0.89	1.31	0.72	0.44	0.23	3.26	0.49	0.51	5.87	0.27	0.20
Men	9.55	0.94	0.98	0.63	0.30	0.20	3.53	0.65	0.47	6.44	0.19	0.12
Women	10.01	0.85	1.58	0.80	0.56	0.26	3.03	0.36	0.54	5.40	0.34	0.27
Hispanic,[3] 15 Years and Over	9.69	1.14	1.76	0.80	0.72	0.18	3.93	0.64	0.23	4.60	0.12	0.18
Men	9.63	1.17	1.03	0.63	0.40	0.15	5.12	0.44	0.22	5.01	0.08	0.11
Women	9.75	1.11	2.55	0.98	1.06	0.20	2.67	0.85	0.24	4.16	0.16	0.26
Marital Status and Sex												
Married, spouse present	9.11	1.32	2.01	0.82	0.76	0.23	4.06	0.10	0.40	4.81	0.16	0.21
Men	8.92	1.39	1.50	0.65	0.55	0.18	4.94	0.06	0.38	5.17	0.10	0.17
Women	9.31	1.26	2.53	0.99	0.97	0.29	3.16	0.15	0.43	4.44	0.22	0.25
Other marital statuses	9.71	1.12	1.40	0.71	0.27	0.22	3.35	0.90	0.26	5.60	0.27	0.19
Men	9.61	1.15	1.05	0.54	0.12	0.19	3.98	0.88	0.20	5.96	0.18	0.16
Women	9.80	1.10	1.70	0.85	0.41	0.25	2.82	0.91	0.31	5.30	0.35	0.22
Educational Attainment, 25 Years and Over												
Less than a high school diploma	9.98	1.14	1.98	0.68	0.52	0.15	2.89	0.02	0.30	6.08	0.11	0.16
High school graduate, no college[4]	9.31	1.21	2.04	0.71	0.45	0.26	3.51	0.04	0.35	5.76	0.16	0.20
Some college or associate degree	9.19	1.25	1.90	0.86	0.57	0.26	3.91	0.21	0.36	5.04	0.23	0.21
Bachelor's degree and higher[5]	8.98	1.38	1.76	0.87	0.73	0.20	4.75	0.15	0.41	4.33	0.22	0.23

Note: Data refer to persons age 15 years and over, unless otherwise specified

n.e.c. = Not elsewhere classified.

[1]A primary activity is designated by a respondent as his or her main activity. Other activities done simultaneously are not included.
[2]All major activity categories include related travel time.
[3]May be of any race.
[4]Includes persons with a high school diploma or equivalent.
[5]Includes persons with bachelor's, master's, professional, and doctoral degrees.

Table 12-3. Average Hours Worked Per Day by Employed Persons on Weekdays and Weekends, by Selected Characteristics, 2008 Annual Averages

(Number, percent.)

Characteristic	Total employed (thousands)	Worked on an average day			Worked on an average weekday			Worked on an average Saturday, Sunday, or holiday[1]		
		Number (thousands)	Percent	Hours per day[2]	Number[3] (thousands)	Percent	Hours per day[2]	Number[4] (thousands)	Percent	Hours per day[2]
Both Sexes[5]	155 371	105 735	68.1	7.59	128 146	82.5	7.93	52 792	34.0	5.61
Full-time worker	121 122	87 297	72.1	8.05	107 129	88.4	8.44	41 090	33.9	5.69
Part-time worker	34 250	18 439	53.8	5.37	21 151	61.8	5.39	11 705	34.2	5.32
Men[5]	83 045	58 744	70.7	7.97	71 008	85.5	8.33	29 667	35.7	5.88
Full-time worker	71 006	52 368	73.8	8.27	63 652	89.6	8.65	25 257	35.6	5.95
Part-time worker	12 039	6 376	53.0	5.47	7 275	60.4	5.45	4 404	36.6	5.52
Women[5]	72 326	46 991	65.0	7.11	57 133	79.0	7.43	23 132	32.0	5.26
Full-time worker	50 115	34 928	69.7	7.73	43 458	86.7	8.13	15 892	31.7	5.28
Part-time worker	22 211	12 063	54.3	5.33	13 868	62.4	5.35	7 258	32.7	5.19
Multiple Job Holding Status										
Single job holder	140 936	93 810	66.6	7.57	114 733	81.4	7.90	44 289	31.4	5.51
Multiple job holder	14 436	11 925	82.6	7.73	13 423	93.0	8.17	8 451	58.5	6.13
Educational Attainment, 25 Years and Over										
Less than a high school diploma	11 659	7 955	68.2	8.17	9 724	83.4	8.31	2 939	25.2	6.80
High school graduate, no college[6]	36 749	24 843	67.6	7.86	31 339	85.3	8.07	10 699	29.1	6.53
Some college or associate degree	33 637	22 655	67.4	7.63	27 369	81.4	7.96	11 506	34.2	5.76
Bachelor's degree or higher[7]	48 938	35 669	72.9	7.42	43 317	88.5	7.99	17 643	36.1	4.07

Note: Data refer to persons age 15 years and over, unless otherwise specified.

[1]Holidays are New Year's Day, Easter, Memorial Day, the Fourth of July, Labor Day, Thanksgiving Day, and Christmas Day.
[2]Includes work at main and other job(s) and excludes travel related to work.
[3]Number was derived by multiplying the "total employed" by the percentage of employed persons who worked on an average weekday.
[4]Number was derived by multiplying the "total employed" by the percentage of employed persons who worked on an average Saturday, Sunday, or holiday.
[5]Includes workers whose hours vary.
[6]Includes persons with a high school diploma or equivalent.
[7]Includes persons with bachelor's, master's, professional, and doctoral degrees.

Table 12-4. Average Hours Worked Per Day at Main Job Only by Employed Persons on Weekdays and Weekend Days, by Selected Characteristics, 2008 Annual Averages

(Number, percent.)

Characteristic	Total employed (thousands)	Worked on an average day			Worked on an average weekday			Worked on an average Saturday, Sunday, or holiday[1]		
		Number (thousands)	Percent	Hours per day[2]	Number[3] (thousands)	Percent	Hours per day[2]	Number[4] (thousands)	Percent	Hours per day[2]
Class of Worker										
Wage and salary workers	143 898	96 088	66.8	7.58	117 859	81.9	7.89	44 639	31.0	5.64
Self-employed workers	11 170	7 773	69.6	6.43	9 062	81.1	6.81	4 706	42.1	4.70
Occupation										
Management, business, and financial operations	24 405	18 295	75.0	7.85	22 449	92.0	8.43	7 978	32.7	3.80
Professional and related	33 260	22 179	66.7	7.16	27 922	84.0	7.60	9 328	28.0	4.25
Services	26 974	16 622	61.6	6.84	18 734	69.4	6.89	11 075	41.1	6.62
Sales and related	16 961	11 991	70.7	7.59	13 408	79.1	7.99	8 388	49.5	5.96
Office and administrative support	19 613	11 751	59.9	7.18	15 902	81.1	7.32	3 748	19.1	6.03
Farming, fishing, and forestry	(5)	(5)	(5)	(5)	(5)	(5)	(5)	(5)	(5)	(5)
Construction and extraction	9 097	6 246	68.7	8.05	7 659	84.2	8.25	1 967	21.6	(5)
Installation, maintenance, and repair	4 610	3 274	71.0	8.38	4 099	88.9	8.59	1 267	27.5	(5)
Production	9 805	6 455	65.8	7.94	8 207	83.7	8.08	2 198	22.4	(5)
Transportation and material moving	9 346	6 338	67.8	8.19	7 724	82.7	8.45	3 401	36.4	6.95
Earnings of Full-Time Wage and Salary Earners[6]										
$0 to $480	25 926	17 273	66.6	8.06	21 274	82.1	8.24	8 232	31.8	7.03
$481 to $730	23 205	15 793	68.1	8.07	20 598	88.8	8.25	5 014	21.6	6.40
$731 to $1,150	24 531	17 091	69.7	7.91	21 246	86.6	8.36	7 544	30.8	5.00
$1,151 and higher	24 584	17 979	73.1	8.17	22 427	91.2	8.77	7 704	31.3	4.13

Note: Data refer to persons age 15 years and over, unless otherwise specified.

[1]Holidays are New Year's Day, Easter, Memorial Day, the Fourth of July, Labor Day, Thanksgiving Day, and Christmas Day.
[2]Includes work at main job only and excludes travel related to work.
[3]Number was derived by multiplying the "total employed" by the percentage of employed persons who worked on an average weekday.
[4]Number was derived by multiplying the "total employed" by the percentage of employed persons who worked on an average Saturday, Sunday, or holiday.
[5]Data not shown where base is less than 1.2 million.
[6]These values are based on usual weekly earnings. Each earnings range represents approximately 25 percent of full-time wage and salary workers.

Table 12-5. Average Hours Worked Per Day at All Jobs by Employed Persons at Workplaces or at Home, by Selected Characteristics, 2008 Annual Averages

(Number, percent.)

Characteristic	Total employed (thousands)	Employed persons who reported working on an average day[1]								
		Number (thousands)	Percent	Hours of work	Location of work[2]					
					Persons who reported working at their workplaces on an average day			Persons who reported working at home on an average day[3]		
					Number (thousands)	Percent	Hours of work at workplace	Number (thousands)	Percent	Hours of work at home
Full- and Part-Time Status and Sex										
Both sexes[4]	155 371	105 735	68.1	7.59	90 443	85.5	7.88	22 272	21.1	2.90
Full-time worker	121 122	87 297	72.1	8.05	75 647	86.7	8.31	18 232	20.9	3.01
Part-time worker	34 250	18 439	53.8	5.37	14 796	80.2	5.73	4 040	21.9	2.36
Men[4]	83 045	58 744	70.7	7.97	50 883	86.6	8.17	11 751	20.0	3.03
Full-time worker	71 006	52 368	73.8	8.27	45 700	87.3	8.44	10 522	20.1	3.13
Part-time worker	12 039	6 376	53.0	5.47	5 183	81.3	5.77	1 229	19.3	2.23
Women[4]	72 326	46 991	65.0	7.11	39 560	84.2	7.52	10 521	22.4	2.74
Full-time worker	50 115	34 928	69.7	7.73	29 947	85.7	8.10	7 710	22.1	2.86
Part-time worker	22 211	12 063	54.3	5.33	9 613	79.7	5.71	2 811	23.3	2.42
Multiple Job Holding Status										
Single job holder	140 936	93 810	66.6	7.57	81 323	86.7	7.86	18 025	19.2	2.88
Multiple job holder	14 436	11 925	82.6	7.73	9 120	76.5	8.13	4 247	35.6	2.95
Educational Attainment, 25 Years and Over										
Less than a high school diploma	11 659	7 955	68.2	8.17	7 238	91.0	8.34	680	8.6	([5])
High school graduate, no college[6]	36 749	24 843	67.6	7.86	22 113	89.0	8.03	3 203	12.9	3.49
Some college or associate degree	33 637	22 655	67.4	7.63	19 458	85.9	7.95	4 647	20.5	3.03
Bachelor's degree or higher[7]	48 938	35 669	72.9	7.42	28 008	78.5	7.90	12 604	35.3	2.70

Note: Data refer to persons age 15 years and over, unless otherwise specified.

[1]Includes work at main and other job(s) and excludes travel related to work.
[2]Respondents may have worked at more than one location.
[3]"Working at home" includes any time the respondent reported doing activities that were identified as "part of one's job"; this category is not restricted to persons whose usual workplace is their home.
[4]Includes workers whose hours vary.
[5]Data not shown where base is less than 1.2 million.
[6]Includes persons with a high school diploma or equivalent.
[7]Includes persons with bachelor's, master's, professional, and doctoral degrees.

Table 12-6. Average Hours Worked Per Day at Main Job Only by Employed Persons at Workplaces or at Home, by Selected Characteristics, 2008 Annual Averages

(Number, percent.)

Characteristic	Total employed (thousands)	Employed persons who reported working on an average day[1]								
		Number (thousands)	Percent	Hours of work	Location of work[2]					
					Persons who reported working at their workplaces on an average day			Persons who reported working at home on an average day[3]		
					Number (thousands)	Percent	Hours of work at workplace	Number (thousands)	Percent	Hours of work at home
Class of Worker										
Wage and salary worker	143 898	96 088	66.8	7.58	85 115	88.6	7.87	16 361	17.0	2.50
Self-employed worker	11 170	7 773	69.6	6.43	3 954	50.9	6.96	4 299	55.3	4.08
Occupation										
Management, business, and financial operations	24 405	18 295	75.0	7.85	14 311	78.2	8.33	5 459	29.8	3.18
Professional and related	33 260	22 179	66.7	7.16	17 575	79.2	7.72	7 129	32.1	2.54
Services	26 974	16 622	61.6	6.84	14 522	87.4	7.09	2 163	13.0	3.67
Sales and related	16 961	11 991	70.7	7.59	10 309	86.0	7.84	2 914	24.3	2.84
Office and administrative support	19 613	11 751	59.9	7.18	10 563	89.9	7.53	1 444	12.3	(4)
Farming, fishing, and forestry	(4)	(4)	(4)	(4)	(4)	(4)	(4)	(4)	(4)	(4)
Construction and extraction	9 097	6 246	68.7	8.05	6 003	96.1	8.19	343	5.5	(4)
Installation, maintenance, and repair	4 610	3 274	71.0	8.38	3 149	96.2	8.53	300	9.2	(4)
Production	9 805	6 455	65.8	7.94	6 106	94.6	8.21	358	5.5	(4)
Transportation and material moving	9 346	6 338	67.8	8.19	5 903	93.1	8.01	464	7.3	(4)
Earnings of Full-Time Wage and Salary Earners[5]										
$0 to $480	25 926	17 273	66.6	8.06	16 308	94.4	8.07	1 384	8.0	(4)
$481 to $730	23 205	15 793	68.1	8.07	15 098	95.6	8.20	1 187	7.5	1.77
$731 to $1,150	24 531	17 091	69.7	7.91	15 334	89.7	8.29	2 788	16.3	1.97
$1,151 and higher	24 584	17 979	73.1	8.17	14 990	83.4	8.59	5 559	30.9	2.46

Note: Data refer to persons age 15 years and over, unless otherwise specified.

[1]Includes work at main job only and excludes travel related to work.
[2]Respondents may have worked at more than one location.
[3]"Working at home" includes any time the respondent reported doing activities that were identified as "part of one's job"; this category is not restricted to persons whose usual workplace is their home.
[4]Data not shown where base is less than 1.2 million.
[5]These values are based on usual weekly earnings. Each earnings range covers approximately 25 percent of full-time wage and salary workers.

Table 12-7. Average Hours Per Day Spent by Persons Age 18 Years and Over Caring for Household Children Under 18 Years, by Sex of Respondent, Age of Youngest Household Child, and Day, 2004–2008 Combined Annual Averages

(Number.)

Activity	Hours per day caring for household children								
	Total			Weekdays			Weekends and holidays[1]		
	Both sexes	Men	Women	Both sexes	Men	Women	Both sexes	Men	Women
Persons in Households with Children Under 18 Years									
Caring for household children as a primary activity	1.32	0.84	1.73	1.41	0.82	1.91	1.11	0.88	1.31
Physical care	0.45	0.24	0.63	0.47	0.23	0.68	0.39	0.24	0.52
Education-related activities	0.10	0.06	0.13	0.13	0.08	0.17	0.03	0.02	0.04
Reading to/with children	0.04	0.02	0.05	0.04	0.02	0.05	0.03	0.02	0.04
Talking to/with children	0.05	0.03	0.07	0.06	0.03	0.08	0.03	0.02	0.05
Playing/doing hobbies with children	0.26	0.23	0.29	0.25	0.20	0.29	0.30	0.30	0.30
Looking after children	0.08	0.06	0.09	0.07	0.05	0.09	0.09	0.08	0.09
Attending children's events	0.06	0.05	0.07	0.05	0.04	0.06	0.08	0.07	0.09
Travel related to care of household children	0.17	0.11	0.23	0.21	0.12	0.28	0.09	0.07	0.10
Other childcare activities	0.11	0.05	0.16	0.14	0.06	0.20	0.06	0.05	0.07
Persons in Households with Youngest Child 6 to 17 Years									
Caring for household children as a primary activity	0.79	0.51	1.02	0.88	0.53	1.17	0.57	0.45	0.67
Physical care	0.15	0.08	0.22	0.18	0.09	0.25	0.10	0.06	0.13
Education-related activities	0.12	0.07	0.16	0.15	0.09	0.20	0.05	0.04	0.05
Reading to/with children	0.02	0.01	0.02	0.02	0.01	0.02	0.02	0.01	0.02
Talking to/with children	0.07	0.03	0.10	0.08	0.04	0.11	0.05	0.03	0.06
Playing/doing hobbies with children	0.06	0.07	0.05	0.05	0.07	0.04	0.08	0.09	0.07
Looking after children	0.04	0.03	0.06	0.04	0.03	0.06	0.05	0.04	0.06
Attending children's events	0.07	0.06	0.09	0.06	0.05	0.07	0.10	0.08	0.11
Travel related to care of household children	0.16	0.10	0.21	0.19	0.12	0.25	0.09	0.08	0.10
Other childcare activities	0.09	0.05	0.13	0.11	0.05	0.16	0.05	0.04	0.06
Persons in Households with Youngest Child Under 6 Years									
Caring for household children as a primary activity	1.95	1.24	2.55	2.05	1.18	2.77	1.74	1.38	2.03
Physical care	0.80	0.42	1.12	0.83	0.41	1.18	0.74	0.46	0.97
Education-related activities	0.07	0.05	0.10	0.10	0.06	0.13	0.02	0.01	0.03
Reading to/with children	0.06	0.04	0.08	0.07	0.04	0.09	0.05	0.04	0.07
Talking to/with children	0.03	0.02	0.04	0.04	0.02	0.05	0.02	0.02	0.03
Playing/doing hobbies with children	0.51	0.43	0.57	0.48	0.37	0.58	0.56	0.56	0.56
Looking after children	0.11	0.09	0.13	0.10	0.07	0.13	0.13	0.12	0.14
Attending children's events	0.04	0.03	0.05	0.03	0.02	0.04	0.05	0.05	0.05
Travel related to care of household children	0.19	0.11	0.25	0.23	0.12	0.31	0.09	0.07	0.10
Other childcare activities	0.14	0.06	0.21	0.17	0.07	0.25	0.08	0.05	0.10

Note: Universe includes respondents age 18 years and over living in households with children under 18 years of age, whether or not they provided childcare.

[1]Holidays are New Year's Day, Easter, Memorial Day, the Fourth of July, Labor Day, Thanksgiving Day, and Christmas Day. Data were not collected for Christmas Day in 2003, Thanksgiving Day from 2003 to 2005, and New Year's Day in 2007.

Table 12-8. Average Hours Per Day Spent in Primary Activities[1] by the Total Population Age 18 Years and Over, by Activity Category, Employment Status, Presence and Age of Household Children, and Sex, 2008 Annual Averages

(Number.)

Activity	Hours spent per day in primary activities								
	Household with children under 6 years			Household with children 6 to 17 years			Household with no children under 18 years		
	Both sexes	Men	Women	Both sexes	Men	Women	Both sexes	Men	Women
TOTAL									
All Activities[2]	24.00	24.00	24.00	24.00	24.00	24.00	24.00	24.00	24.00
Personal care activities	9.13	8.85	9.37	9.18	8.99	9.34	9.44	9.29	9.60
Sleeping	8.46	8.28	8.62	8.40	8.34	8.45	8.62	8.60	8.64
Eating and drinking	1.15	1.17	1.14	1.14	1.23	1.06	1.30	1.34	1.26
Household activities	1.84	1.20	2.38	1.87	1.30	2.34	1.76	1.41	2.11
Housework	0.68	0.23	1.07	0.67	0.25	1.02	0.56	0.25	0.85
Food preparation and cleanup	0.70	0.36	0.99	0.60	0.30	0.84	0.49	0.31	0.67
Lawn and garden care	0.11	0.14	0.08	0.16	0.26	0.08	0.23	0.31	0.16
Household management	0.10	0.09	0.11	0.13	0.09	0.17	0.14	0.11	0.17
Purchasing goods and services	0.71	0.54	0.85	0.78	0.54	0.98	0.81	0.66	0.95
Consumer goods purchases	0.38	0.29	0.46	0.40	0.27	0.52	0.39	0.30	0.47
Professional and personal care services	0.06	0.03	0.09	0.07	0.04	0.09	0.10	0.07	0.12
Caring for and helping household members	1.98	1.38	2.48	0.90	0.65	1.10	0.06	0.04	0.07
Caring for and helping household children	1.73	1.21	2.16	0.69	0.48	0.86	X	X	X
Caring for and helping non-household members	0.12	0.12	0.12	0.17	0.13	0.21	0.28	0.22	0.34
Caring for and helping non-household adults	0.05	0.08	0.03	0.07	0.05	0.08	0.09	0.09	0.08
Working and work-related activities	4.33	5.99	2.92	4.53	5.56	3.68	3.61	4.26	2.97
Working	3.90	5.36	2.68	4.12	5.02	3.37	3.28	3.84	2.72
Educational activities	0.20	0.13	0.26	0.32	0.25	0.38	0.25	0.16	0.33
Attending class	0.10	0.05	0.14	0.13	0.12	0.15	0.09	0.06	0.12
Homework and research	0.08	0.06	0.09	0.14	0.10	0.18	0.14	0.09	0.19
Organizational, civic, and religious activities	0.24	0.20	0.28	0.39	0.39	0.39	0.35	0.30	0.40
Religious and spiritual activities	0.13	0.10	0.16	0.15	0.15	0.15	0.15	0.12	0.18
Volunteering (organizational and civic activities)	0.08	0.07	0.08	0.19	0.19	0.19	0.16	0.14	0.18
Leisure and sports	3.97	4.16	3.80	4.35	4.69	4.07	5.72	6.02	5.43
Socializing and communicating	0.71	0.59	0.81	0.66	0.63	0.68	0.71	0.66	0.75
Watching television	2.21	2.43	2.02	2.37	2.55	2.22	3.14	3.40	2.88
Participating in sports, exercise, and recreation	0.19	0.24	0.15	0.28	0.35	0.21	0.27	0.36	0.18
Telephone calls, mail, and e-mail	0.13	0.07	0.17	0.19	0.09	0.27	0.23	0.15	0.30
Other activities n.e.c.	0.20	0.17	0.23	0.19	0.18	0.19	0.20	0.16	0.25
EMPLOYED									
All Activities[2]	24.00	24.00	24.00	24.00	24.00	24.00	24.00	24.00	24.00
Personal care activities	8.91	8.74	9.13	9.00	8.86	9.14	9.13	9.00	9.28
Sleeping	8.24	8.16	8.34	8.21	8.20	8.22	8.32	8.33	8.30
Eating and drinking	1.16	1.18	1.13	1.15	1.24	1.06	1.25	1.30	1.20
Household activities	1.46	1.14	1.86	1.66	1.20	2.10	1.43	1.17	1.74
Housework	0.47	0.21	0.80	0.58	0.23	0.92	0.44	0.23	0.69
Food preparation and cleanup	0.54	0.35	0.77	0.51	0.28	0.74	0.38	0.25	0.54
Lawn and garden care	0.10	0.15	0.04	0.15	0.23	0.07	0.17	0.22	0.11
Household management	0.10	0.08	0.11	0.13	0.09	0.17	0.12	0.10	0.15
Purchasing goods and services	0.63	0.53	0.76	0.72	0.55	0.89	0.76	0.60	0.94
Consumer goods purchases	0.33	0.27	0.40	0.38	0.27	0.48	0.37	0.28	0.47
Professional and personal care services	0.05	0.02	0.08	0.06	0.04	0.08	0.07	0.04	0.11
Caring for and helping household members	1.69	1.34	2.15	0.82	0.63	1.01	0.04	0.03	0.05
Caring for and helping household children	1.47	1.18	1.84	0.62	0.48	0.77	X	X	X
Caring for and helping non-household members	0.11	0.12	0.10	0.15	0.13	0.16	0.24	0.19	0.29
Caring for and helping non-household adults	0.06	0.08	0.03	0.05	0.05	0.06	0.08	0.08	0.08
Working and work-related activities	5.75	6.54	4.77	5.79	6.53	5.08	5.74	6.20	5.19
Working	5.27	5.94	4.44	5.33	5.98	4.69	5.25	5.64	4.79
Educational activities	0.17	0.12	0.22	0.21	0.15	0.27	0.27	0.14	0.42
Attending class	0.08	0.05	0.11	0.09	0.08	0.11	0.09	0.05	0.15
Homework and research	0.07	0.06	0.08	0.09	0.05	0.13	0.15	0.07	0.24
Organizational, civic, and religious activities	0.21	0.19	0.24	0.37	0.38	0.37	0.30	0.25	0.37
Religious and spiritual activities	0.11	0.10	0.13	0.14	0.16	0.13	0.12	0.10	0.14
Volunteering (organizational and civic activities)	0.07	0.08	0.07	0.18	0.17	0.19	0.15	0.12	0.19
Leisure and sports	3.63	3.87	3.34	3.82	4.10	3.54	4.51	4.84	4.13
Socializing and communicating	0.61	0.57	0.65	0.59	0.56	0.63	0.62	0.60	0.65
Watching television	2.00	2.19	1.76	2.05	2.22	1.88	2.40	2.64	2.11
Participating in sports, exercise, and recreation	0.20	0.24	0.16	0.27	0.32	0.21	0.28	0.36	0.19
Telephone calls, mail, and e-mail	0.09	0.06	0.12	0.16	0.09	0.23	0.18	0.14	0.23
Other activities n.e.c.	0.18	0.16	0.20	0.16	0.16	0.16	0.15	0.13	0.17

n.e.c. = Not elsewhere classified.

[1]A primary activity is designated by a respondent as his or her main activity. Other activities done simultaneously are not included.
[2]All major activity categories include related travel time.
X = Not applicable.

Table 12-8. Average Hours Per Day Spent in Primary Activities[1] by the Total Population Age 18 Years and Over, by Activity Category, Employment Status, Presence and Age of Household Children, and Sex, 2008 Annual Averages—*Continued*

(Number.)

Activity	Hours spent per day in primary activities								
	Household with children under 6 years			Household with children 6 to 17 years			Household with no children under 18 years		
	Both sexes	Men	Women	Both sexes	Men	Women	Both sexes	Men	Women
NOT EMPLOYED									
All Activities[2]	24.00	24.00	24.00	24.00	24.00	24.00	24.00	24.00	24.00
Personal care activities	9.75	9.88	9.72	9.81	9.71	9.86	9.95	9.88	10.01
Sleeping	9.10	9.32	9.05	9.06	9.10	9.04	9.11	9.17	9.07
Eating and drinking	1.14	1.10	1.15	1.10	1.15	1.08	1.37	1.43	1.33
Household activities	2.92	1.73	3.16	2.59	1.87	2.92	2.31	1.91	2.60
Housework	1.28	0.39	1.47	0.98	0.33	1.29	0.75	0.31	1.07
Food preparation and cleanup	1.18	0.46	1.33	0.88	0.42	1.10	0.67	0.44	0.85
Lawn and garden care	0.12	0.10	0.13	0.23	0.43	0.13	0.34	0.49	0.22
Household management	0.12	0.13	0.12	0.16	0.12	0.17	0.16	0.12	0.19
Purchasing goods and services	0.95	0.70	1.00	0.97	0.48	1.20	0.88	0.78	0.96
Consumer goods purchases	0.54	0.40	0.57	0.50	0.23	0.62	0.41	0.34	0.47
Professional and personal care services	0.10	0.11	0.10	0.11	0.04	0.14	0.14	0.14	0.14
Caring for and helping household members	2.78	1.77	2.99	1.16	0.75	1.35	0.09	0.06	0.10
Caring for and helping household children	2.45	1.54	2.64	0.91	0.51	1.09	X	X	X
Caring for and helping non-household members	0.15	0.16	0.15	0.27	0.14	0.33	0.34	0.26	0.40
Caring for and helping non-household adults	0.05	0.07	0.04	0.12	0.07	0.14	0.10	0.11	0.09
Working and work-related activities	0.29	1.02	0.13	0.24	0.48	0.13	0.11	0.15	0.08
Working	0.03	0.07	0.02	0.01	0.00	0.01	0.02	0.01	0.02
Educational activities	0.30	0.20	0.32	0.69	0.78	0.65	0.21	0.22	0.21
Attending class	0.16	0.06	0.18	0.28	0.35	0.25	0.07	0.08	0.07
Homework and research	0.10	0.12	0.09	0.32	0.34	0.32	0.12	0.12	0.13
Organizational, civic, and religious activities	0.32	0.22	0.34	0.45	0.46	0.45	0.43	0.43	0.44
Religious and spiritual activities	0.19	0.12	0.20	0.16	0.12	0.19	0.21	0.17	0.23
Volunteering (organizational and civic activities)	0.08	0.07	0.09	0.23	0.28	0.21	0.18	0.20	0.16
Leisure and sports	4.91	6.86	4.50	6.15	7.80	5.39	7.71	8.51	7.12
Socializing and communicating	1.02	0.83	1.05	0.89	1.04	0.82	0.84	0.77	0.89
Watching television	2.78	4.56	2.41	3.46	4.26	3.09	4.36	5.02	3.88
Participating in sports, exercise, and recreation	0.14	0.24	0.12	0.32	0.54	0.22	0.25	0.37	0.16
Telephone calls, mail, and e-mail	0.24	0.17	0.26	0.27	0.10	0.35	0.30	0.17	0.40
Other activities n.e.c.	0.27	0.20	0.29	0.29	0.29	0.29	0.30	0.22	0.36

n.e.c. = Not elsewhere classified.

[1]A primary activity is designated by a respondent as his or her main activity. Other activities done simultaneously are not included.
[2]All major activity categories include related travel time.
X = Not applicable.

Table 12-9. Average Hours Per Day Spent in Leisure and Sports Activities for the Total Population, by Selected Characteristics, 2008 Annual Averages

(Number.)

Characteristic	Total, all leisure and sports activities			Participating in sports, exercise, and recreation		Socializing and communicating		Watching TV	
	Total, all days	Weekdays	Weekends and holidays[1]	Weekdays	Weekends and holidays[1]	Weekdays	Weekends and holidays[1]	Weekdays	Weekends and holidays[1]
Sex									
Men	5.52	4.84	7.11	0.36	0.50	0.49	1.06	2.72	3.70
Women	4.86	4.42	5.88	0.19	0.21	0.59	1.17	2.39	2.90
Age									
Total, 15 years and over	5.18	4.62	6.48	0.27	0.35	0.54	1.12	2.55	3.29
15 to 19 years	5.69	5.04	7.15	0.73	0.64	0.73	1.39	1.92	2.69
20 to 24 years	4.70	3.91	6.59	0.26	0.56	0.67	1.35	1.86	3.01
25 to 34 years	4.34	3.69	5.93	0.22	0.31	0.51	1.38	2.04	2.76
35 to 44 years	4.16	3.52	5.66	0.21	0.35	0.43	1.08	2.01	2.96
45 to 54 years	4.67	4.11	5.97	0.22	0.31	0.41	0.97	2.59	3.18
55 to 64 years	5.66	5.20	6.76	0.22	0.27	0.59	0.98	3.02	3.86
65 to 74 years	7.12	6.87	7.70	0.29	0.32	0.62	0.98	3.96	4.12
75 years and over	7.62	7.46	7.98	0.20	0.11	0.57	0.78	4.05	4.54
Race and Hispanic Origin									
White	5.13	4.56	6.46	0.28	0.37	0.53	1.12	2.46	3.21
Black	5.87	5.42	6.92	0.26	0.28	0.63	1.10	3.36	4.10
Hispanic[2]	4.60	3.98	6.10	0.23	0.31	0.54	1.21	2.29	3.23
Employment Status									
Employed	4.22	3.51	5.88	0.24	0.36	0.44	1.07	1.92	2.95
Full-time workers	4.10	3.35	5.85	0.23	0.36	0.40	1.05	1.86	3.00
Part-time workers	4.63	4.07	6.00	0.28	0.37	0.59	1.16	2.10	2.74
Not employed	6.99	6.73	7.58	0.32	0.32	0.72	1.20	3.76	3.92
Earnings of Full-Time Wage and Salary Earners[3]									
$0 to $480	4.50	3.79	6.10	0.19	0.35	0.47	0.98	2.11	3.47
$481 to $730	4.43	3.61	6.25	0.19	0.33	0.54	1.30	1.93	3.36
$731 to $1,150	4.11	3.43	5.69	0.32	0.34	0.35	0.90	1.98	3.06
$1,151 and higher	3.79	2.94	5.76	0.21	0.46	0.32	0.96	1.64	2.58
Presence and Age of Children									
No household children under 18 years	5.73	5.21	6.95	0.28	0.32	0.56	1.08	2.88	3.63
Household children under 18 years	4.32	3.71	5.73	0.26	0.40	0.51	1.17	2.04	2.76
Children 13 to 17 years, none younger	4.75	4.13	6.15	0.26	0.48	0.56	1.08	2.09	2.90
Children 6 to 12 years, none younger	4.42	3.82	5.82	0.36	0.48	0.49	1.13	2.07	2.78
Youngest child under 6 years	4.01	3.41	5.42	0.18	0.29	0.49	1.24	2.00	2.66
Marital Status and Sex									
Married, spouse present	4.81	4.27	6.06	0.23	0.30	0.47	1.07	2.45	3.13
Men	5.17	4.59	6.54	0.30	0.41	0.38	0.99	2.76	3.55
Women	4.44	3.95	5.57	0.17	0.19	0.56	1.16	2.13	2.71
Other marital status	5.60	5.02	6.96	0.31	0.41	0.62	1.17	2.67	3.47
Men	5.96	5.16	7.83	0.43	0.62	0.62	1.16	2.67	3.89
Women	5.30	4.91	6.22	0.21	0.23	0.61	1.17	2.67	3.11
Educational Attainment, 25 Years and Over									
Less than a high school diploma	6.08	5.64	7.14	0.16	0.20	0.53	1.14	3.67	4.30
High school graduate, no college[4]	5.76	5.32	6.79	0.18	0.28	0.54	1.07	3.35	3.87
Some college or associate degree	5.04	4.58	6.16	0.23	0.25	0.51	1.01	2.53	3.25
Bachelor's degree or higher[5]	4.33	3.67	5.87	0.29	0.38	0.45	1.06	1.78	2.65

Note: Data refer to respondents age 15 years and over, unless otherwise specified.

[1]Holidays are New Year's Day, Easter, Memorial Day, the Fourth of July, Labor Day, Thanksgiving Day, and Christmas Day.
[2]May be of any race.
[3]These values are based on usual weekly earnings. Each earnings range covers approximately 25 percent of full-time wage and salary workers.
[4]Includes persons with a high school diploma or equivalent.
[5]Includes persons with bachelor's, master's, professional, and doctoral degrees.

Table 12-9. Average Hours Per Day Spent in Leisure and Sports Activities for the Total Population, by Selected Characteristics, 2008 Annual Averages—*Continued*

(Number.)

Characteristic	Reading		Relaxing/thinking		Playing games and computer use for leisure		Other leisure and sports activities, including travel[6]	
	Weekdays	Weekends and holidays[1]	Weekdays	Weekends and holidays[1]	Weekdays	Weekends and holidays[1]	Weekdays	Weekends and holidays[1]
Sex								
Men	0.27	0.32	0.28	0.26	0.33	0.55	0.39	0.72
Women	0.37	0.46	0.26	0.26	0.28	0.31	0.33	0.58
Age								
Total, 15 years and over	0.32	0.39	0.27	0.26	0.31	0.43	0.36	0.65
15 to 19 years	0.17	0.16	0.12	0.17	0.70	0.98	0.67	1.11
20 to 24 years	0.12	0.13	0.18	0.19	0.33	0.70	0.48	0.64
25 to 34 years	0.11	0.13	0.19	0.18	0.33	0.46	0.28	0.70
35 to 44 years	0.18	0.22	0.17	0.12	0.25	0.31	0.28	0.61
45 to 54 years	0.23	0.36	0.26	0.29	0.12	0.31	0.28	0.55
55 to 64 years	0.52	0.55	0.29	0.26	0.23	0.25	0.33	0.60
65 to 74 years	0.77	0.82	0.41	0.54	0.35	0.40	0.47	0.52
75 years and over	0.96	1.23	0.82	0.55	0.44	0.28	0.41	0.49
Race and Hispanic Origin								
White	0.36	0.42	0.24	0.24	0.31	0.43	0.37	0.67
Black	0.16	0.20	0.45	0.37	0.25	0.32	0.30	0.55
Hispanic[2]	0.11	0.18	0.33	0.30	0.22	0.29	0.25	0.59
Employment Status								
Employed	0.22	0.30	0.18	0.19	0.20	0.37	0.31	0.63
Full-time workers	0.19	0.28	0.18	0.19	0.18	0.34	0.30	0.63
Part-time workers	0.31	0.39	0.17	0.21	0.26	0.50	0.36	0.64
Not employed	0.52	0.56	0.44	0.39	0.51	0.52	0.46	0.67
Earnings of Full-Time Wage and Salary Earners[3]								
$0 to $480	0.18	0.17	0.29	0.19	0.19	0.42	0.37	0.52
$481 to $730	0.15	0.23	0.18	0.20	0.26	0.27	0.37	0.57
$731 to $1,150	0.17	0.28	0.17	0.21	0.14	0.33	0.29	0.58
$1,151 and higher	0.24	0.42	0.12	0.15	0.15	0.33	0.26	0.86
Presence and Age of Children								
No household children under 18 years	0.44	0.50	0.29	0.30	0.35	0.47	0.41	0.66
Household children under 18 years	0.14	0.22	0.23	0.20	0.24	0.35	0.29	0.63
Children 13 to 17 years, none younger	0.19	0.35	0.27	0.23	0.37	0.44	0.38	0.66
Children 6 to 12 years, none younger	0.16	0.22	0.22	0.15	0.22	0.38	0.30	0.67
Youngest child under 6 years	0.10	0.15	0.23	0.22	0.18	0.27	0.24	0.58
Marital Status and Sex								
Married, spouse present	0.34	0.42	0.28	0.25	0.20	0.32	0.31	0.57
Men	0.31	0.37	0.33	0.26	0.18	0.35	0.34	0.60
Women	0.36	0.46	0.23	0.24	0.22	0.28	0.27	0.53
Other marital status	0.31	0.36	0.26	0.27	0.42	0.55	0.43	0.73
Men	0.23	0.26	0.22	0.25	0.52	0.79	0.47	0.86
Women	0.38	0.45	0.30	0.29	0.34	0.35	0.40	0.62
Educational Attainment, 25 Years and Over								
Less than a high school diploma	0.15	0.24	0.65	0.57	0.19	0.20	0.27	0.49
High school graduate, no college[4]	0.36	0.39	0.32	0.33	0.26	0.33	0.30	0.53
Some college or associate degree	0.38	0.43	0.24	0.22	0.32	0.45	0.37	0.55
Bachelor's degree or higher[5]	0.43	0.59	0.17	0.16	0.24	0.30	0.31	0.74

Note: Data refer to respondents age 15 years and over, unless otherwise specified.

[1]Holidays are New Year's Day, Easter, Memorial Day, the Fourth of July, Labor Day, Thanksgiving Day, and Christmas Day.
[2]May be of any race.
[3]These values are based on usual weekly earnings. Each earnings range covers approximately 25 percent of full-time wage and salary workers.
[4]Includes persons with a high school diploma or equivalent.
[5]Includes persons with bachelor's, master's, professional, and doctoral degrees.
[6]Includes other leisure and sports activities, not elsewhere classified, and travel related to leisure and sports activities.

Chapter Thirteen

INCOME IN THE UNITED STATES
(CENSUS BUREAU)

INCOME IN THE UNITED STATES (CENSUS BUREAU)

HIGHLIGHTS

This chapter presents data on income and earnings in the United States collected by the Census Bureau. Income, as distinguished from earnings, includes income from pensions, investments, and other sources and is measured as real income in 2008 dollars.

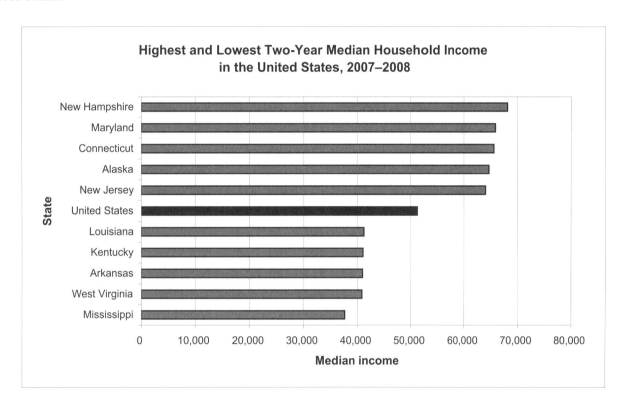

The two-year average median household income in the United States for 2007–2008 was $51,233, a 0.1 percent decline from the two-year median income of $51,283 in 2005–2006. New Hampshire had the highest two-year median income at $68,175, followed Maryland at $65,932 and Connecticut at $65,644. Mississippi had the lowest two-year median household income at $37,579 and was the only state to have a two-year median household income under $40,000. (See Table 13-5.)

OTHER HIGHLIGHTS:

- Real median household income fell between 2007 and 2008, and the decline was widespread. Median income fell for family and nonfamily households, native- and foreign-born households, households in three of the four regions, and households of each race category and those of Hispanic origin. These declines in income coincide with the recession that started in December 2007. (See Table 13-1)

- In 2008, real median income declined 5.6 percent for Hispanics, 4.4 percent for Asians, 3.3 percent for Whites, and 2.8 percent for Blacks. (See Table 13-1.)

- By region, the West had the highest median household income with $55,085 in 2008, while the South had the lowest at $45,590. The Northeast was the only region that experienced an increase in real median income in 2008. However, the increase was minimal—only 0.1 percent. (See Table 13-1.)

- Median family income ranged from $46,668 in Mississippi to $85,761 in New Jersey. (See Table 13-7.)

NOTES AND DEFINITIONS

Collection and Coverage

The data in tables 13-1 through 13-5 are from the Annual Social and Economic Supplement (ASEC) to the 2009 Current Population Survey (CPS). The CPS ASEC provides timely estimates of household income and individual earnings, as well as the distribution of that income. The population represented (the population universe) is the civilian noninstitutionalized population living in the United States. Members of the Armed Forces living off post or with their families on post are included if at least one civilian adult lives in the household. Most of the data from the CPS ASEC were collected in March (with some data collected in February and April), and the data were controlled to independent population estimates for March 2009. The estimates in these tables are based on responses from a sample of the population and may differ from actual values because of sampling variability or other factors. As a result, apparent differences between the estimates for two or more groups may not be statistically significant. All comparative statements have undergone statistical testing and are significant at the 90 percent confidence level unless otherwise noted.

For tables 13-6 and 13-7, the data are from the American Community Survey (ACS). The ACS is an annual survey that covers the same type of information that had been collected every 10 years from the decennial census long form questionnaire. The ACS eliminated the need for a separate long form in the 2010 Census. The CPS ASEC and ACS surveys differ in the length and detail of its questionnaire, the number of households interviewed, the methodology used to collect and process the data, and, consequently, in the income and poverty estimates produced.

The sample size of the ACS is much larger (approximately 3 million) compared to the sample size of the CPS ASEC (100,000). Although it is smaller, the CPS ASEC is a high quality source of information due to its detailed questionnaire and experienced interviewing staff. Another notable difference between the two surveys is that the ACS is a mandatory whereas the CPS ASEC is voluntary. More information on the differences between the two surveys is available on the Census Bureau Web site at <http://www.census.gov/hhes/www/income/definitions.html>.

Concepts and Definitions

The *Gini index of income inequality* (also known as the Gini ratio, Gini coefficient, or index of income concentration) is a statistical measure that summarizes the dispersion of income across an entire income distribution. Values range from 0 to 1. A Gini value of 1 indicates "perfect" inequality; that is, one household has all the income and the rest have none. A value of zero indicates "perfect" equality, a situation in which all households have equal income.

Equivalence-adjusted income inequality is another way to measure income inequality. Equivalence adjusted income takes into consideration the number of people living in the household and how these people share resources and take advantage of economies of scale. For example, the household-income-based distribution treats income of $30,000 for a single-person household and a family household similarly, while the equivalence-adjusted income of $30,000 for a single-person household would be more than twice the equivalence-adjusted income of $30,000 for a family household with two adults and two children. The equivalence adjustment used here is based on a three-parameter scale that reflects:

1. On average, children consume less than adults.
2. As family size increases, expenses do not increase at the same rate.
3. The increase in expenses is larger for a first child of a single-parent family than the first child of a two-adult family.

Additional Information

Additional information is available in the Census publication "Income, Poverty, and Health Insurance Coverage in the United States: 2008," on the Census Bureau Web site at <http://www.census.gov/hhes/www/income/income.html>.

Table 13-1. Income and Earnings Summary Measures, by Selected Characteristics, 2007 and 2008

(Numbers in thousands, dollars, percent; income in 2008 dollars.)

Characteristic	2007			2008			Percent change in real median income (2008 less 2007)	
	Number	Median income (dollars)		Number	Median income (dollars)		Estimate	90 percent confidence interval[1] (+/-)
		Estimate	90 percent confidence interval[1] (+/-)		Estimate	90 percent confidence interval[1] (+/-)		
Households								
All households	116 783	52163	239	117 181	50303	225	-3.6	0.50
Type of Household								
Family households	77 873	64755	335	78 850	62621	423	-3.3	0.67
Married-couple	58 370	75582	548	59 118	73010	540	-3.4	0.81
Female householder, no husband present	14 404	34652	612	14 480	33073	620	-4.6	1.98
Male householder, no wife present	5 100	51754	1 148	5 252	49186	1 092	-5.0	2.40
Nonfamily households	38 910	31335	270	38 331	30078	306	-4.0	1.03
Female householder	21 038	25227	413	20 637	25014	383	-0.8	1.79
Male householder	17 872	38180	430	17 694	36006	436	-5.7	1.26
Race[2] and Hispanic Origin of Householder								
White	95 112	54117	263	95 297	52312	250	-3.3	0.53
White, not Hispanic	82 765	57030	422	82 884	55530	370	-2.6	0.78
Black	14 551	35219	811	14 595	34218	725	-2.8	2.45
Asian	4 494	68643	2 366	4 573	65637	2 280	-4.4	3.77
Hispanic[3]	13 339	40165	888	13 425	37913	799	-5.6	1.94
Age of Householder								
Under 65 years	92 671	58718	313	92 346	56791	341	-3.3	0.63
15 to 24 years	6 554	33011	562	6 357	32270	617	-2.2	2.02
25 to 34 years	19 225	52976	487	19 302	51400	536	-3.0	1.09
35 to 44 years	22 448	64511	512	22 171	62954	944	-2.4	1.40
45 to 54 years	24 536	67992	746	24 633	64349	933	-5.4	1.40
55 to 64 years	19 909	59591	828	19 883	57265	875	-3.9	1.60
65 years and over	24 113	29393	389	24 834	29744	370	1.2	1.48
Nativity of Householder								
Native	101 104	52904	258	101 585	51056	245	-3.5	0.53
Foreign-born	15 680	45929	1 245	15 596	43493	1 022	-5.3	2.75
Naturalized citizen	7 469	54094	1 158	7 668	51524	949	-4.8	2.18
Not a citizen	8 211	39083	1 244	7 928	37951	1 056	-2.9	3.32
Region								
Northeast	21 351	54283	723	21 309	54346	1 105	0.1	2.01
Midwest	26 266	52209	490	26 282	50112	535	-4.0	1.10
South	43 062	47961	453	43 423	45590	446	-4.9	1.04
West	26 105	56218	837	26 166	55085	867	-2.0	1.71
Metropolitan Status								
Inside metropolitan statistical areas	97 591	53823	261	97 865	51853	245	-3.7	0.53
Inside principal cities	39 072	45904	615	39 065	44197	564	-3.7	1.44
Outside principal cities	58 520	59651	501	58 800	57904	579	-2.9	1.03
Outside metropolitan statistical areas[4]	19 192	42176	653	19 315	40785	663	-3.3	1.75
Earnings of Full-Time Year-Round Workers								
Men with earnings	62 984	46846	256	59 861	46367	239	-1.0	0.62
Women with earnings	45 613	36451	174	44 156	35745	174	-1.9	0.56
Per Capita Income[5]								
All races[2]	299 106	27834	164	301 483	26964	161	-3.1	0.68
White	239 399	29413	190	240 852	28502	186	-3.1	0.74
White, not Hispanic	196 768	32244	220	197 159	31313	217	-2.9	0.79
Black	37 775	19136	362	38 076	18406	327	-3.8	2.09
Asian	13 268	31050	936	13 315	30292	920	-2.4	3.49
Hispanic[3]	46 026	16203	282	47 485	15674	293	-3.3	1.83

[1]A 90-percent confidence interval is a measure of an estimate's variability. The larger the confidence interval in relation to the size of the estimate, the less reliable the estimate.
[2]Federal surveys now give respondents the option of reporting more than one race. Therefore, there are two basic ways of defining a race group. A group such as Asian may be defined as those who reported Asian and no other race (the race-alone or single-race concept) or as those who reported Asian regardless of whether they also reported another race (the race-alone-or-in-combination concept). This table shows data using the race-alone concept. The use of the single-race population does not imply that it is the preferred method of presenting or analyzing data; the Census Bureau uses a variety of approaches. Information on people who reported more than one race, such as White and American Indian and Alaska Native or Asian and Black or African American, is available from Census 2000 through American FactFinder. About 2.6 percent of respondents reported more than one race in Census 2000.
[3]May be of any race.
[4]The "outside metropolitan statistical areas" category includes both micropolitan statistical areas and territory outside of metropolitan and micropolitan statistical areas.
[5]The data shown in this section are per capita incomes and their respective confidence intervals. Per capita income is the mean income computed for every man, woman, and child in a particular group. It is derived by dividing the total income of a particular group by the total population in that group (excluding patients or inmates in institutional quarters).

Table 13-2. Households, by Total Money Income, Race, and Hispanic Origin of Householder, 1967–2008

(Numbers in thousands, percent, dollars; income in 2008 CPI-U-RS adjusted dollars.)

Race and Hispanic origin of householder and year	Number	Percent distribution										Median income (dollars)		Mean income (dollars)	
		Total	Under $5,000	$5,000 to $9,999	$10,000 to $14,999	$15,000 to $24,999	$25,000 to $34,999	$35,000 to $49,999	$50,000 to $74,999	$75,000 to $99,000	$100,000 and over	Value	Standard error	Value	Standard error
All Races															
1967[1]	60 813	100.0	3.7	7.3	6.7	12.1	13.7	19.9	22.2	8.3	6.1	40 261	147	45 029	147
1968	62 214	100.0	3.2	6.8	6.1	12.2	12.5	20.3	22.8	9.6	6.4	41 995	152	47 511	152
1969	63 401	100.0	3.0	6.7	6.1	11.6	11.9	19.1	23.4	10.5	7.6	43 557	161	49 554	156
1970	64 778	100.0	3.1	6.8	6.3	11.8	12.0	19.1	22.6	10.6	7.7	43 219	158	49 489	158
1971[2]	66 676	100.0	3.1	6.7	6.6	12.3	12.0	18.7	22.5	10.3	7.7	42 798	166	49 222	156
1972[3]	68 251	100.0	2.6	6.2	6.7	12.1	11.5	17.4	22.8	11.2	9.4	44 632	170	51 945	161
1973	69 859	100.0	2.4	5.6	6.8	12.2	11.3	16.9	22.7	11.8	10.2	45 533	173	52 658	160
1974[4,5]	71 163	100.0	2.2	5.7	7.0	12.5	11.8	18.2	22.0	11.4	9.3	44 091	169	51 561	161
1975[5]	72 867	100.0	2.3	5.9	7.6	12.9	12.3	17.3	22.3	11.0	8.5	42 936	175	50 137	156
1976[6]	74 142	100.0	2.2	5.8	7.3	13.0	12.2	16.5	22.4	11.5	9.2	43 649	162	51 342	158
1977	76 030	100.0	2.1	5.8	7.2	13.0	11.9	16.6	21.8	11.8	9.8	43 925	165	52 107	159
1978	77 330	100.0	2.1	5.6	6.9	12.8	11.5	16.1	21.8	12.2	10.9	45 625	185	53 699	206
1979[7]	80 776	100.0	2.2	5.7	6.9	12.3	12.0	15.7	22.0	12.1	11.1	45 498	216	54 047	205
1980	82 368	100.0	2.3	5.9	7.2	12.7	12.1	16.3	21.4	11.6	10.6	44 059	226	52 401	192
1981	83 527	100.0	2.5	5.9	7.3	13.1	12.5	16.1	20.9	11.2	10.5	43 328	227	51 762	189
1982	83 918	100.0	2.7	5.9	7.5	12.7	12.3	16.6	20.5	11.1	10.8	43 212	195	52 077	193
1983[8]	85 407	100.0	2.8	6.0	7.1	13.1	12.2	16.3	20.3	11.1	11.2	42 910	195	52 188	195
1984	86 789	100.0	2.5	5.7	7.1	12.7	11.9	16.3	19.8	11.9	12.1	44 242	201	54 208	199
1985[9]	88 458	100.0	2.6	5.8	6.9	12.3	11.6	16.0	20.1	11.9	12.8	45 069	244	55 466	219
1986	89 479	100.0	2.7	5.7	6.6	11.7	11.4	15.3	20.3	12.3	14.0	46 665	242	57 653	234
1987[10]	91 124	100.0	2.5	5.6	6.6	11.7	11.2	15.2	20.0	12.4	14.8	47 251	223	58 762	241
1988	92 830	100.0	2.3	5.6	6.5	11.6	11.4	15.0	20.0	12.4	15.2	47 614	233	59 492	266
1989	93 347	100.0	2.3	5.1	6.3	11.6	11.3	14.9	20.1	12.4	16.1	48 463	267	61 228	267
1990	94 312	100.0	2.4	5.5	6.0	11.8	11.1	15.7	19.9	12.3	15.1	47 818	244	59 731	252
1991	95 669	100.0	2.5	5.6	6.5	12.2	11.3	15.7	19.4	11.9	14.9	46 445	224	58 464	241
1992[11]	96 426	100.0	2.7	5.7	6.4	12.8	11.1	15.5	19.0	12.4	14.6	· 46 063	218	58 399	245
1993[12]	97 107	100.0	2.8	5.4	6.8	12.5	11.0	15.7	18.5	11.8	15.4	45 839	214	60 787	329
1994[13]	98 990	100.0	2.7	5.1	6.7	12.5	11.4	14.9	18.9	11.7	16.1	46 351	211	61 966	333
1995[14]	99 627	100.0	2.4	4.8	6.3	12.2	11.0	15.4	19.2	12.2	16.5	47 803	276	63 041	345
1996	101 018	100.0	2.4	5.0	6.2	12.4	11.2	14.6	18.7	12.6	17.1	48 499	245	64 392	361
1997	102 528	100.0	2.6	4.7	5.9	11.8	11.2	14.4	18.9	12.1	18.4	49 497	229	66 466	372
1998	103 874	100.0	2.6	4.4	5.6	11.3	10.8	14.3	18.8	12.6	19.6	51 295	303	68 404	369
1999[15]	106 434	100.0	2.3	4.0	5.5	11.3	10.9	14.0	18.4	12.7	20.9	52 587	246	70 731	367
2000[16]	108 209	100.0	2.4	4.0	5.3	10.9	10.7	14.3	18.4	13.0	21.0	52 500	165	71 436	281
2001	109 297	100.0	2.6	4.1	5.6	11.4	10.4	14.8	17.9	12.5	20.6	51 356	157	70 790	282
2002	111 278	100.0	2.8	4.3	5.8	11.4	10.6	14.5	17.9	12.5	20.2	50 756	166	69 238	260
2003	112 000	100.0	3.0	4.2	5.9	11.5	10.3	14.6	17.7	12.2	20.6	50 711	220	69 148	253
2004[17]	113 343	100.0	3.2	4.0	5.9	11.4	11.3	13.9	18.1	12.1	20.1	50 535	223	68 923	260
2005	114 384	100.0	3.1	4.2	5.7	11.5	10.8	14.1	18.0	12.2	20.4	51 093	171	69 862	264
2006	116 011	100.0	3.0	3.9	5.7	11.1	11.1	14.1	18.1	11.7	21.3	51 473	221	71 089	274
2007	116 783	100.0	2.9	4.1	5.8	11.3	10.5	14.0	18.0	12.0	21.4	52 163	145	70 207	245
2008	117 181	100.0	3.0	4.1	5.8	11.8	10.9	14.0	17.9	11.9	20.5	50 303	137	68 424	242
White[18]															
1967[1]	54 188	100.0	3.4	6.7	6.1	11.4	13.4	20.4	23.3	8.8	6.5	41 985	152	46 675	158
1968	55 394	100.0	2.9	6.2	5.7	11.4	12.2	20.8	23.9	10.2	6.8	43 726	163	49 220	163
1969	56 248	100.0	2.6	6.0	5.8	10.8	11.5	19.3	24.5	11.2	8.2	45 457	166	51 392	171
1970	57 575	100.0	2.8	6.3	5.8	11.2	11.6	19.4	23.6	11.1	8.2	45 015	173	51 220	168
1971[2]	59 463	100.0	2.7	6.1	6.1	11.7	11.7	19.0	23.5	10.9	8.3	44 766	171	51 004	166
1972[3]	60 618	100.0	2.3	5.5	6.1	11.3	11.2	17.7	23.8	11.8	10.2	46 822	180	53 966	175
1973	61 965	100.0	2.1	5.0	6.3	11.6	10.9	17.0	23.5	12.6	11.0	47 720	182	54 694	173
1974[4,5]	62 984	100.0	1.9	4.9	6.5	11.9	11.5	18.5	22.9	11.9	10.1	46 111	173	53 470	173
1975[5]	64 392	100.0	2.0	5.1	7.0	12.4	12.1	17.5	23.1	11.6	9.1	44 901	164	51 989	171
1976[6]	65 353	100.0	1.9	5.0	6.7	12.3	12.0	16.6	23.2	12.2	10.0	45 723	189	53 317	172
1977	66 934	100.0	1.9	5.0	6.7	12.3	11.7	16.8	22.6	12.5	10.5	46 190	194	54 142	175
1978	68 028	100.0	1.8	4.7	6.4	12.3	11.4	16.2	22.7	12.8	11.7	47 430	209	55 689	224
1979[7]	70 766	100.0	1.9	4.8	6.3	11.7	11.8	15.9	22.8	12.7	11.9	47 704	227	56 178	224

[1]Implementation of a new Curent Population Survey (CPS) Annual Social and Economic Supplements (ASEC) processing system.
[2]Introduction of 1970 census sample design and population controls.
[3]Full implementation of 1970 census–based sample design.
[4]Implementation of a new CPS ASEC processing system. Questionnaire expanded to ask 11 income questions.
[5]Some of these estimates were derived using Pareto interpolation and may differ from published data that were derived using linear interpolation.
[6]First-year medians were derived using both Pareto and linear interpolation. Before this year, all medians were derived using linear interpolation.
[7]Implementation of 1980 census population controls. Questionnaire expanded to show 27 possible values from a list of 51 possible sources of income.
[8]Implementation of Hispanic population weighting controls and introduction of 1980 census–based sample design.
[9]Recording of amounts for earnings from longest job increased to $299,999. Full implementation of 1980 census–based sample design.
[10]Implementation of a new CPS ASEC processing system.
[11]Implementation of 1990 census population controls.
[12]Data collection method changed from paper and pencil to computer-assisted interviewing. In addition, the 1994 ASEC was revised to allow for the coding of different income amounts on selected questionnaire items. Limits either increased or decreased in the following categories: earnings limits increased to $999,999, Social Security limits increased to $49,999, Supplemental Security Income and public assistance limits increased to $24,999, veterans' benefits limits increased to $99,999, and child support and alimony limits decreased to $49,999.
[13]Introduction of 1990 census sample design.
[14]Full implementation of 1990 census–based sample design and metropolitan definitions, 7,000 household sample reduction, and revised editing of responses on race.
[15]Implementation of the 2000 census–based population controls.
[16]Implementation of a 28,000 household sample expansion.
[17]Data revised to reflect a correction to the weights in the 2005 ASEC.
[18]For 2001 and earlier years, the CPS allowed respondents to report only one race group.

Table 13-2. Households, by Total Money Income, Race, and Hispanic Origin of Householder, 1967–2008
—Continued

(Numbers in thousands, percent, dollars; income in 2008 CPI-U-RS adjusted dollars.)

Race and Hispanic origin of householder and year	Number	Percent distribution										Median income (dollars)		Mean income (dollars)	
		Total	Under $5,000	$5,000 to $9,999	$10,000 to $14,999	$15,000 to $24,999	$25,000 to $34,999	$35,000 to $49,999	$50,000 to $74,999	$75,000 to $99,000	$100,000 and over	Value	Standard error	Value	Standard error
White[18]—Continued															
1980	71 872	100.0	1.9	5.0	6.6	12.1	11.9	16.6	22.3	12.2	11.4	46 482	239	54 515	209
1981	72 845	100.0	2.1	4.9	6.8	12.5	12.4	16.4	21.7	11.8	11.4	45 779	211	53 931	204
1982	73 182	100.0	2.3	4.9	7.0	12.1	12.2	16.9	21.2	11.7	11.7	45 238	206	54 223	212
1983[8]	74 376	100.0	2.3	5.0	6.5	12.6	12.1	16.7	21.1	11.7	12.1	44 999	203	54 354	212
1984	75 328	100.0	2.1	4.8	6.5	12.1	11.8	16.5	20.6	12.5	13.0	46 674	235	56 444	219
1985[9]	76 576	100.0	2.2	4.9	6.4	11.8	11.5	16.2	20.8	12.4	13.8	47 531	254	57 742	242
1986	77 284	100.0	2.2	4.7	6.3	11.2	11.3	15.4	21.0	12.9	15.0	49 061	238	60 054	257
1987[10]	78 519	100.0	2.0	4.6	6.1	11.1	11.1	15.4	20.9	13.1	15.7	49 783	250	61 273	265
1988	79 734	100.0	1.9	4.5	6.0	11.0	11.3	15.2	20.8	13.1	16.2	50 335	297	62 030	292
1989	80 163	100.0	1.8	4.1	5.8	11.2	11.1	15.1	20.8	13.0	17.1	50 978	248	63 778	295
1990	80 968	100.0	1.9	4.5	5.5	11.5	11.0	16.0	20.5	13.0	16.1	49 875	228	62 141	278
1991	81 675	100.0	1.9	4.5	5.9	11.9	11.2	15.9	20.0	12.5	16.0	48 670	236	60 932	265
1992[11]	81 795	100.0	2.1	4.6	6.0	12.3	10.9	15.8	19.6	13.1	15.7	48 428	235	61 036	272
1993[12]	82 387	100.0	2.2	4.6	6.2	12.1	10.8	15.9	19.3	12.5	16.5	48 362	282	63 511	367
1994[13]	83 737	100.0	2.2	4.1	6.3	12.0	11.4	15.1	19.4	12.2	17.3	48 885	274	64 697	376
1995[14]	84 511	100.0	1.9	4.0	5.9	11.8	10.8	15.5	19.6	12.7	17.6	50 174	262	65 553	380
1996	85 059	100.0	1.9	4.2	5.7	12.0	11.0	14.8	19.2	13.1	18.2	50 779	262	66 949	396
1997	86 106	100.0	2.1	4.0	5.4	11.5	11.0	14.4	19.3	12.6	19.7	52 128	330	69 422	423
1998	87 212	100.0	2.1	3.7	5.2	10.8	10.6	14.3	19.3	13.2	20.8	53 969	270	71 507	421
1999[15]	88 893	100.0	1.8	3.3	5.2	11.0	10.7	14.0	18.8	13.3	22.0	54 692	277	73 301	415
2000[16]	90 030	100.0	2.0	3.4	5.0	10.5	10.4	14.2	18.6	13.6	22.2	54 908	243	74 085	318
2001	90 682	100.0	2.1	3.5	5.3	11.1	10.1	14.8	18.2	13.1	21.8	54 140	254	73 592	316
White Alone[18]															
2002	91 645	100.0	2.2	3.6	5.5	11.0	10.4	14.3	18.4	13.1	21.5	53 960	219	72 008	293
2003	91 962	100.0	2.5	3.5	5.6	11.1	10.2	14.5	18.1	12.6	21.9	53 419	210	72 099	289
2004[17]	92 880	100.0	2.6	3.4	5.6	11.0	11.1	13.9	18.4	12.6	21.4	53 184	209	71 708	295
2005	93 588	100.0	2.5	3.5	5.3	11.1	10.7	14.3	18.3	12.8	21.6	53 550	234	72 749	301
2006	94 705	100.0	2.4	3.2	5.3	10.7	10.9	14.1	18.6	12.2	22.6	54 113	157	73 798	308
2007	95 112	100.0	2.3	3.4	5.4	11.0	10.3	13.9	18.3	12.5	22.7	54 117	160	73 033	278
2008	95 297	100.0	2.5	3.4	5.5	11.5	10.6	13.9	18.4	12.5	21.7	52 312	152	71 191	274
White, Not Hispanic[19]															
1972[3]	58 005	100.0	2.3	5.5	6.0	11.1	10.9	17.5	24.0	12.1	10.5	47 490	226	54 592	244
1973	59 236	100.0	2.1	5.0	6.3	11.4	10.6	16.9	23.7	12.8	11.3	48 140	225	55 305	234
1974[4,5]	60 164	100.0	1.9	4.9	6.4	11.6	11.3	18.4	23.1	12.2	10.4	46 505	228	54 073	236
1975[5]	61 533	100.0	2.0	5.0	6.9	12.2	12.0	17.4	23.4	11.9	9.4	45 240	240	52 626	255
1976[6]	62 365	100.0	1.9	4.9	6.5	12.1	11.9	16.6	23.4	12.5	10.3	46 656	272	54 002	241
1977	63 721	100.0	1.9	4.9	6.6	12.1	11.5	16.7	22.8	12.8	10.8	47 106	265	54 812	259
1978	64 836	100.0	1.8	4.7	6.3	12.1	11.2	16.1	22.8	13.0	12.0	48 323	254	56 347	242
1979[7]	67 203	100.0	1.9	4.8	6.2	11.5	11.6	15.8	23.0	13.0	12.3	48 375	268	56 828	249
1980	68 106	100.0	1.8	4.9	6.5	11.8	11.7	16.5	22.5	12.5	11.7	47 306	108	55 232	249
1981	68 996	100.0	2.1	4.8	6.6	12.3	12.2	16.3	21.9	12.1	11.7	46 440	236	54 610	227
1982	69 214	100.0	2.2	4.8	6.8	11.8	12.1	16.8	21.5	11.9	12.1	45 997	231	55 020	236
1983[8]	. . .	. . .	2.2	4.8	6.2	12.3	11.9	16.6	21.4	12.0	12.5	. . .	. . .	. . .	. . .
1984	70 586	100.0	2.0	4.5	6.3	11.8	11.6	16.5	20.9	12.8	13.5	47 643	264	57 425	257
1985[9]	71 540	100.0	2.1	4.7	6.2	11.4	11.4	16.2	21.1	12.8	14.3	48 600	248	58 866	267
1986	72 067	100.0	2.1	4.5	6.1	10.8	11.1	15.4	21.3	13.3	15.5	50 176	259	61 246	281
1987[10]	73 120	100.0	1.8	4.3	5.9	10.8	10.9	15.3	21.2	13.4	16.4	51 152	285	62 471	290
1988	74 067	100.0	1.7	4.2	5.8	10.7	11.1	15.1	21.1	13.4	16.9	51 722	304	63 296	297
1989	74 495	100.0	1.6	3.9	5.7	10.9	10.8	15.0	21.0	13.3	17.8	52 074	255	65 056	319
1990	75 035	100.0	1.8	4.3	5.3	11.1	10.9	15.9	20.7	13.4	16.8	51 015	238	63 518	287
1991	75 625	100.0	1.8	4.3	5.7	11.5	11.1	15.9	20.2	12.9	16.6	49 832	245	62 239	278
1992[11]	75 107	100.0	1.9	4.3	5.7	11.9	10.7	15.7	19.8	13.5	16.4	50 054	310	62 586	289
1993[12]	75 697	100.0	2.1	4.3	5.8	11.7	10.6	15.7	19.7	12.8	17.3	50 142	293	65 186	389
1994[13]	77 004	100.0	2.1	3.8	6.0	11.7	11.2	15.0	19.7	12.6	18.1	50 463	267	66 345	394

[3]Full implementation of 1970 census–based sample design.
[4]Implementation of a new CPS ASEC processing system. Questionnaire expanded to ask 11 income questions.
[5]Some of these estimates were derived using Pareto interpolation and may differ from published data that were derived using linear interpolation.
[6]First-year medians were derived using both Pareto and linear interpolation. Before this year, all medians were derived using linear interpolation.
[7]Implementation of 1980 census population controls. Questionnaire expanded to show 27 possible values from a list of 51 possible sources of income.
[8]Implementation of Hispanic population weighting controls and introduction of 1980 census–based sample design.
[9]Recording of amounts for earnings from longest job increased to $299,999. Full implementation of 1980 census–based sample design.
[10]Implementation of a new CPS ASEC processing system.
[11]Implementation of 1990 census population controls.
[12]Data collection method changed from paper and pencil to computer-assisted interviewing. In addition, the 1994 ASEC was revised to allow for the coding of different income amounts on selected questionnaire items. Limits either increased or decreased in the following categories: earnings limits increased to $999,999, Social Security limits increased to $49,999, Supplemental Security Income and public assistance limits increased to $24,999, veterans' benefits limits increased to $99,999, and child support and alimony limits decreased to $49,999.
[13]Introduction of 1990 census sample design.
[14]Full implementation of 1990 census–based sample design and metropolitan definitions, 7,000 household sample reduction, and revised editing of responses on race.
[15]Implementation of the 2000 census–based population controls.
[16]Implementation of a 28,000 household sample expansion.
[17]Data revised to reflect a correction to the weights in the 2005 ASEC.
[18]For 2001 and earlier years, the CPS allowed respondents to report only one race group.
[19]Beginning with the 2003 CPS, respondents were allowed to choose one or more races. White alone refers to people who reported White and did not report any other race category. The use of this single-race population does not imply that it is the preferred method of presenting or analyzing the data; the Census Bureau uses a variety of approaches. Information on people who reported more than one race, such as White and American Indian and Alaska Native or Asian and Black or African American, is available from Census 2000 through American FactFinder. About 2.6 percent of respondents reported more than one race in Census 2000.
. . . = Not available.

Table 13-2. Households, by Total Money Income, Race, and Hispanic Origin of Householder, 1967–2008
—Continued

(Numbers in thousands, percent, dollars; income in 2008 CPI-U-RS adjusted dollars.)

Race and Hispanic origin of householder and year	Number	Percent distribution										Median income (dollars)		Mean income (dollars)	
		Total	Under $5,000	$5,000 to $9,999	$10,000 to $14,999	$15,000 to $24,999	$25,000 to $34,999	$35,000 to $49,999	$50,000 to $74,999	$75,000 to $99,000	$100,000 and over	Value	Standard error	Value	Standard error
White, Not Hispanic[19]—Continued															
1995[14]	76 932	100.0	1.7	3.6	5.5	11.3	10.5	15.4	20.1	13.2	18.6	52 155	272	67 691	405
1996	77 240	100.0	1.7	3.8	5.5	11.4	10.7	14.7	19.5	13.6	19.2	53 001	363	68 974	. . .
1997	77 936	100.0	1.9	3.6	5.1	11.1	10.6	14.2	19.4	13.2	20.9	54 274	284	71 647	. . .
2000[16]	78 577	100.0	1.9	3.4	5.0	10.3	10.2	14.0	19.6	13.7	22.0	55 983	322	73 797	451
1999[15]	79 819	100.0	1.7	3.1	4.9	10.5	10.3	13.7	18.9	13.6	23.2	57 059	361	75 705	448
2000[16]	80 527	100.0	1.9	3.3	4.9	10.0	10.1	13.9	18.5	13.9	23.5	57 042	229	76 339	343
2001	80 818	100.0	2.0	3.4	5.1	10.6	9.8	14.3	18.3	13.4	23.1	56 314	234	75 942	344
White Alone, Not Hispanic[19]															
2002	81 166	100.0	2.1	3.5	5.3	10.5	9.9	13.9	18.4	13.6	22.8	56 131	220	74 341	316
2003	81 148	100.0	2.3	3.3	5.4	10.5	9.8	14.1	18.2	13.1	23.3	55 931	270	74 791	317
2004[17]	81 628	100.0	2.4	3.2	5.4	10.5	10.6	13.5	18.5	13.0	22.8	55 751	255	74 386	324
2005	82 003	100.0	2.3	3.3	5.1	10.5	10.2	13.8	18.4	13.2	23.1	56 009	190	75 662	334
2006	82 675	100.0	2.3	3.0	5.0	10.2	10.5	13.7	18.6	12.6	24.1	55 982	201	76 615	339
2007	82 765	100.0	2.1	3.2	5.2	10.5	9.8	13.5	18.3	12.9	24.4	57 030	256	75 994	306
2008	82 884	100.0	2.2	3.2	5.2	11.0	10.0	13.5	18.6	13.0	23.2	55 530	225	74 102	303
Black[18]															
1967[1]	5 728	100.0	6.8	13.2	12.4	19.2	16.9	14.4	12.0	3.1	2.1	24 377	406	29 292	327
1968	5 870	100.0	6.1	12.6	10.3	20.1	15.5	16.5	12.9	4.1	1.9	25 784	374	31 403	331
1969	6 053	100.0	6.0	12.2	9.7	18.8	15.6	17.4	13.8	4.4	2.1	27 477	405	32 710	348
1970	6 180	100.0	6.3	12.4	10.2	17.5	15.5	16.5	14.0	5.3	2.4	27 399	376	33 456	361
1971[2]	6 578	100.0	6.0	12.3	11.6	18.1	14.8	16.3	13.8	5.1	2.1	26 443	393	32 767	337
1972[3]	6 809	100.0	5.2	12.0	11.8	17.9	14.5	15.4	14.7	5.8	2.6	27 330	410	34 524	368
1973	7 040	100.0	4.8	11.2	11.5	17.9	14.9	15.7	15.7	5.2	3.3	28 090	437	34 882	347
1974[4,5]	7 263	100.0	4.3	12.6	11.1	18.1	14.7	16.5	14.3	6.2	2.3	27 422	331	34 105	303
1975[5]	7 489	100.0	4.5	13.1	12.5	17.3	13.5	16.2	15.2	5.3	2.5	26 955	397	33 647	298
1976[6]	7 776	100.0	4.0	12.0	12.6	18.4	13.7	15.2	15.6	5.8	2.8	27 188	337	34 737	310
1977	7 977	100.0	3.7	12.8	11.1	19.5	14.0	15.2	14.5	5.6	3.5	27 257	366	34 924	311
1978	8 066	100.0	4.0	13.0	11.5	17.2	12.9	15.5	14.8	7.2	3.9	28 503	603	36 427	476
1979[7]	8 586	100.0	4.6	12.6	11.6	17.5	13.8	14.2	15.2	6.8	3.7	28 007	511	35 937	442
1980	8 847	100.0	5.1	13.9	11.6	17.7	13.6	14.2	14.1	6.4	3.5	26 779	505	34 755	428
1981	8 961	100.0	5.6	13.8	12.1	18.0	13.2	14.1	13.9	5.9	3.4	25 689	432	33 746	409
1982	8 916	100.0	6.0	14.0	11.6	17.3	13.2	14.5	14.9	5.6	2.9	25 639	411	33 734	422
1983[8]	9 236	100.0	6.5	14.0	11.6	16.8	13.6	13.8	13.9	6.1	3.7	25 536	479	33 964	419
1984	9 480	100.0	5.6	13.8	11.2	17.5	13.3	14.4	13.1	6.7	4.5	26 589	511	35 461	436
1985[9]	9 797	100.0	5.6	13.3	10.8	16.5	13.3	14.2	14.8	6.8	4.8	28 279	550	36 896	479
1986	9 922	100.0	6.6	13.6	9.8	15.8	12.6	14.3	14.8	6.9	5.6	28 265	555	37 922	515
1987[10]	10 192	100.0	5.8	13.9	10.7	15.3	12.6	15.0	13.9	6.9	5.9	28 414	544	38 366	528
1988	10 561	100.0	5.2	13.9	10.8	15.7	12.3	13.8	13.9	7.7	6.6	28 694	598	39 310	574
1989	10 486	100.0	5.8	12.9	9.5	14.8	13.0	14.0	15.8	7.1	7.1	30 317	617	40 229	547
1990	10 671	100.0	6.2	13.2	9.6	15.0	12.3	14.4	15.3	7.4	6.5	29 825	680	39 627	535
1991	11 083	100.0	6.7	13.1	10.6	15.3	11.5	14.5	15.3	6.9	6.1	28 995	609	38 608	504
1992[11]	11 269	100.0	6.7	13.6	10.0	16.1	12.1	14.0	14.4	7.2	5.8	28 199	576	38 266	519
1993[12]	11 281	100.0	6.8	11.9	11.3	15.6	12.4	15.1	13.4	6.9	6.6	28 660	566	39 953	663
1994[13]	11 655	100.0	5.8	12.1	9.7	16.2	12.1	13.5	15.0	8.0	7.6	30 208	562	42 034	603
1995[14]	11 577	100.0	5.5	10.8	9.5	15.6	12.8	14.9	15.8	7.9	7.2	31 414	536	42 646	729
1996	12 109	100.0	5.6	10.4	9.5	16.0	12.3	14.5	15.2	8.7	7.8	32 087	631	44 355	866
1997	12 474	100.0	5.5	9.8	9.0	14.7	13.5	14.6	16.3	8.6	7.9	33 506	576	44 090	633
1998	12 579	100.0	5.8	9.9	8.7	15.2	12.8	14.2	15.5	8.5	9.4	33 442	524	45 034	602
1999[15]	12 838	100.0	4.7	8.9	8.3	14.5	12.7	14.1	16.4	8.9	11.6	36 065	672	49 700	713
2000[16]	13 174	100.0	4.9	8.2	7.3	14.3	13.0	15.2	17.6	9.0	10.5	37 093	491	48 984	496
2001	13 315	100.0	5.6	8.4	8.0	14.4	12.9	15.4	16.2	9.1	9.9	35 840	422	47 732	503

[1]Implementation of a new Curent Population Survey (CPS) Annual Social and Economic Supplements (ASEC) processing system.
[2]Introduction of 1970 census sample design and population controls.
[3]Full implementation of 1970 census–based sample design.
[4]Implementation of a new CPS ASEC processing system. Questionnaire expanded to ask 11 income questions.
[5]Some of these estimates were derived using Pareto interpolation and may differ from published data that were derived using linear interpolation.
[6]First-year medians were derived using both Pareto and linear interpolation. Before this year, all medians were derived using linear interpolation.
[7]Implementation of 1980 census population controls. Questionnaire expanded to show 27 possible values from a list of 51 possible sources of income.
[8]Implementation of Hispanic population weighting controls and introduction of 1980 census–based sample design.
[9]Recording of amounts for earnings from longest job increased to $299,999. Full implementation of 1980 census–based sample design.
[10]Implementation of a new CPS ASEC processing system.
[11]Implementation of 1990 census population controls.
[12]Data collection method changed from paper and pencil to computer-assisted interviewing. In addition, the 1994 ASEC was revised to allow for the coding of different income amounts on selected questionnaire items. Limits either increased or decreased in the following categories: earnings limits increased to $999,999, Social Security limits increased to $49,999, Supplemental Security Income and public assistance limits increased to $24,999, veterans' benefits limits increased to $99,999, and child support and alimony limits decreased to $49,999.
[13]Introduction of 1990 census sample design.
[14]Full implementation of 1990 census–based sample design and metropolitan definitions, 7,000 household sample reduction, and revised editing of responses on race.
[15]Implementation of the 2000 census–based population controls.
[16]Implementation of a 28,000 household sample expansion.
[17]Data revised to reflect a correction to the weights in the 2005 ASEC.
[18]For 2001 and earlier years, the CPS allowed respondents to report only one race group.
[19]Beginning with the 2003 CPS, respondents were allowed to choose one or more races. White alone refers to people who reported White and did not report any other race category. The use of this single-race population does not imply that it is the preferred method of presenting or analyzing the data; the Census Bureau uses a variety of approaches. Information on people who reported more than one race, such as White and American Indian and Alaska Native or Asian and Black or African American, is available from Census 2000 through American FactFinder. About 2.6 percent of respondents reported more than one race in Census 2000.
. . . = Not available.

Table 13-2. Households, by Total Money Income, Race, and Hispanic Origin of Householder, 1967–2008
—Continued

(Numbers in thousands, percent, dollars; income in 2008 CPI-U-RS adjusted dollars.)

Race and Hispanic origin of householder and year	Number	Percent distribution										Median income (dollars)		Mean income (dollars)	
		Total	Under $5,000	$5,000 to $9,999	$10,000 to $14,999	$15,000 to $24,999	$25,000 to $34,999	$35,000 to $49,999	$50,000 to $74,999	$75,000 to $99,000	$100,000 and over	Value	Standard error	Value	Standard error
Black Alone[20]															
2002	13 465	100.0	6.0	8.7	8.5	14.9	12.4	15.8	15.0	8.7	10.1	34 739	468	47 886	553
2003	13 629	100.0	6.3	8.7	8.5	14.8	11.9	15.5	15.7	8.5	10.0	34 705	452	46 980	503
2004[17]	13 809	100.0	7.0	8.2	8.9	14.2	13.3	14.9	15.7	8.5	9.3	34 304	357	46 316	502
2005	14 002	100.0	6.2	9.1	8.5	15.5	12.2	14.6	15.8	8.3	9.7	34 033	332	46 822	508
2006	14 354	100.0	6.4	8.1	8.8	14.6	13.3	14.4	15.8	8.2	10.3	34 139	257	48 190	596
2007	14 551	100.0	6.1	8.7	8.7	14.1	12.5	14.6	16.2	8.6	10.6	35 219	493	48 423	540
2008	14 595	100.0	6.0	8.6	8.4	14.5	13.4	15.6	15.4	8.2	10.0	34 218	441	46 533	498
Black Alone or in Combination															
2002	13 778	100.0	6.0	8.6	8.5	14.8	12.4	15.8	15.0	8.7	10.2	34 920	460	48 273	563
2003	13 969	100.0	6.2	8.6	8.6	14.8	12.0	15.4	15.7	8.6	10.1	34 756	437	47 197	500
2004[17]	14 151	100.0	7.0	8.2	8.8	14.1	13.2	14.9	15.8	8.5	9.4	34 464	316	46 460	494
2005	14 399	100.0	6.2	9.0	8.5	15.6	12.2	14.5	15.8	8.4	9.8	34 139	325	47 123	513
2006	14 709	100.0	6.4	8.1	8.8	14.5	13.3	14.4	15.9	8.3	10.5	34 313	254	48 581	596
2007	14 976	100.0	6.1	8.6	8.7	14.0	12.3	14.7	16.2	8.6	10.8	35 401	483	48 630	532
2008	15 056	100.0	6.0	8.5	8.3	14.5	13.4	15.6	15.4	8.2	10.1	34 345	439	46 679	488
Asian and Pacific Islander[18]															
1987[10]	. . .	100.0	4.3	3.0	4.7	12.2	9.0	11.3	18.8	12.9	23.8	58 428	2 172	. . .	. . .
1988	1 913	100.0	2.4	4.2	3.9	11.5	8.1	13.7	20.0	12.1	24.0	56 432	2 319	70 552	2 107
1989	1 988	100.0	2.8	2.0	5.4	8.3	8.8	13.3	19.8	15.6	23.9	60 527	1 636	75 244	2 190
1990	1 958	100.0	3.8	2.7	4.2	9.5	8.2	12.5	20.6	14.0	24.6	61 403	1 819	74 119	2 098
1991	2 094	100.0	3.3	3.9	4.4	8.7	10.5	14.6	17.9	14.1	22.6	56 193	1 813	71 346	2 103
1992[11]	2 262	100.0	3.7	3.2	4.8	10.3	8.9	13.0	20.8	12.4	22.8	56 836	1 640	70 442	1 937
1993[12]	2 233	100.0	4.4	4.1	6.0	9.6	9.8	13.1	15.3	14.0	23.7	56 266	2 767	73 722	2 968
1994[13]	2 040	100.0	3.9	3.2	4.8	10.2	8.2	13.5	19.0	13.5	23.7	58 157	2 204	75 512	2 691
1995[14]	2 777	100.0	4.4	2.3	5.9	9.8	7.3	14.1	19.8	13.4	23.0	56 975	1 429	77 476	3 126
1996	2 998	100.0	3.4	3.8	5.0	9.2	8.5	12.1	19.0	12.9	26.2	59 135	2 119	77 269	2 771
1997	3 125	100.0	3.9	3.4	4.2	8.4	8.6	12.5	19.1	13.6	26.4	60 523	1 683	78 769	2 441
1998	3 308	100.0	4.2	2.9	3.6	8.7	8.8	13.2	17.6	13.6	27.5	61 521	1 712	79 423	2 294
1999[15]	3 742	100.0	3.7	2.7	4.6	7.1	7.8	13.2	17.1	13.5	30.3	65 850	2 321	87 077	2 207
2000[16]	3 963	100.0	3.2	2.3	3.6	7.1	8.0	11.7	17.0	15.0	32.1	69 713	1 189	91 018	1 889
2001	4 071	100.0	4.0	2.4	3.9	8.0	8.5	12.9	17.4	12.6	30.3	65 228	1 557	88 973	2 100
Asian Alone[21]															
2002	3 917	100.0	4.0	2.4	3.8	8.7	8.2	13.2	18.1	12.7	28.9	62 984	1 102	83 834	1 635
2003	4 040	100.0	4.7	4.1	4.3	9.3	5.3	12.2	16.6	14.0	29.5	65 206	1 281	81 916	1 450
2004[17]	4 123	100.0	3.5	2.9	3.7	8.1	8.2	11.0	19.3	12.6	30.5	65 547	1 393	87 219	1 687
2005	4 273	100.0	4.1	3.0	4.1	7.9	7.2	10.3	18.6	13.0	31.9	67 380	785	88 337	1 558
2006	4 454	100.0	3.4	2.8	3.9	7.1	8.4	11.3	17.0	13.2	32.8	68 599	1 788	94 287	2 029
2007	4 494	100.0	3.6	2.8	3.9	8.1	7.4	11.4	17.1	13.1	32.8	68 643	1 438	88 285	1 558
2008	4 573	100.0	4.5	2.5	4.8	8.6	7.6	11.8	15.7	12.3	32.3	65 637	1 386	86 185	1 503
Asian Alone or in Combination															
2002	4 079	100.0	4.0	2.5	3.9	8.6	8.2	13.2	18.3	12.8	28.6	62 576	947	83 150	1 581
2003	4 235	100.0	4.5	4.1	4.4	9.3	5.5	12.1	16.7	14.1	29.1	64 694	1 442	81 259	1 398
2004[17]	4 346	100.0	3.5	3.0	3.7	8.1	8.2	11.1	19.3	12.8	30.2	65 484	1 320	86 779	1 638
2005	4 500	100.0	4.1	2.9	4.1	7.8	7.2	10.6	18.4	13.1	31.8	67 330	804	88 228	1 540
2006	4 664	100.0	3.3	2.8	3.9	7.0	8.3	11.6	17.2	13.3	32.6	68 238	1 727	93 470	1 956
2007	4 715	100.0	3.6	2.7	3.9	8.0	7.4	11.6	17.2	13.1	32.5	68 407	1 439	87 810	1 502
2008	4 805	100.0	4.3	2.5	4.8	8.7	7.6	11.9	15.6	12.4	32.1	65 567	1 413	86 323	1 487

[10]Implementation of a new CPS ASEC processing system.
[11]Implementation of 1990 census population controls.
[12]Data collection method changed from paper and pencil to computer-assisted interviewing. In addition, the 1994 ASEC was revised to allow for the coding of different income amounts on selected questionnaire items. Limits either increased or decreased in the following categories: earnings limits increased to $999,999, Social Security limits increased to $49,999, Supplemental Security Income and public assistance limits increased to $24,999, veterans' benefits limits increased to $99,999, and child support and alimony limits decreased to $49,999.
[13]Introduction of 1990 census sample design.
[14]Full implementation of 1990 census–based sample design and metropolitan definitions, 7,000 household sample reduction, and revised editing of responses on race.
[15]Implementation of the 2000 census–based population controls.
[16]Implementation of a 28,000 household sample expansion.
[17]Data revised to reflect a correction to the weights in the 2005 ASEC.
[18]For 2001 and earlier years, the CPS allowed respondents to report only one race group.
[20]Black alone refers to persons who reported Black and did not report any other race category.
[21]Asian alone refers to persons who reported Asian and did not report any other race category.
. . . = Not available.

Table 13-2. Households, by Total Money Income, Race, and Hispanic Origin of Householder, 1967–2008
—Continued

(Numbers in thousands, percent, dollars; income in 2008 CPI-U-RS adjusted dollars.)

Race and Hispanic origin of householder and year	Number	Percent distribution										Median income (dollars)		Mean income (dollars)	
		Total	Under $5,000	$5,000 to $9,999	$10,000 to $14,999	$15,000 to $24,999	$25,000 to $34,999	$35,000 to $49,999	$50,000 to $74,999	$75,000 to $99,000	$100,000 and over	Value	Standard error	Value	Standard error
Hispanic[22]															
1972	2 655	100.0	2.5	5.3	9.0	17.9	16.4	21.3	18.1	6.0	3.6	35 334	690	40 614	690
1973	2 722	100.0	2.9	5.5	7.4	17.1	17.4	18.8	20.7	6.7	3.7	35 276	801	40 985	667
1974	2 897	100.0	2.3	6.1	8.8	18.3	14.8	20.0	19.3	6.6	3.9	35 069	768	40 626	662
1975	2 948	100.0	2.9	8.0	9.4	18.2	15.6	18.7	18.4	5.7	3.1	32 257	713	38 293	680
1976	3 081	100.0	2.7	7.9	10.2	17.5	15.5	17.5	18.5	6.8	3.3	32 924	702	38 907	633
1977	3 304	100.0	2.8	6.2	9.5	16.7	16.0	19.1	18.8	6.5	4.4	34 458	605	40 666	628
1978	3 291	100.0	2.8	6.0	9.2	16.3	15.2	18.4	19.7	7.8	4.8	35 748	866	42 227	854
1979	3 684	100.0	2.8	6.5	8.5	15.6	15.4	18.2	19.0	8.1	6.0	36 048	1 039	43 616	876
1980	3 906	100.0	3.6	7.6	8.7	17.1	15.0	17.8	17.4	7.9	5.1	33 961	920	41 482	826
1981	3 980	100.0	3.3	6.9	9.3	16.8	14.6	17.9	17.8	8.2	5.2	34 755	952	41 735	797
1982	4 085	100.0	3.8	7.6	11.2	16.7	14.5	17.3	16.4	7.8	4.7	32 515	859	40 129	814
1983	4 326	100.0	4.1	8.2	10.8	16.1	14.8	17.8	16.2	7.0	5.0	32 680	828	39 795	764
1984	4 883	100.0	4.1	8.6	9.4	16.0	13.8	17.0	17.1	8.6	5.6	33 539	841	41 704	813
1985	5 213	100.0	3.6	8.3	9.6	17.6	13.3	16.6	16.9	7.7	6.3	33 328	779	41 644	677
1986	5 418	100.0	4.1	8.0	8.9	16.4	13.9	16.1	17.4	8.0	7.3	34 398	896	43 434	714
1987	5 642	100.0	4.0	8.6	8.7	15.6	13.5	16.6	17.1	8.7	7.3	35 058	761	44 939	832
1988	5 910	100.0	3.8	8.8	8.2	15.3	13.9	16.3	17.5	8.6	7.6	35 606	902	45 459	964
1989	5 933	100.0	3.8	7.4	8.0	14.4	14.4	16.1	17.8	9.7	8.4	36 752	713	46 930	806
1990	6 220	100.0	3.4	7.7	8.5	16.4	12.9	17.5	18.2	7.9	7.4	35 660	731	44 670	736
1991	6 379	100.0	3.6	7.6	8.9	16.6	13.5	16.8	17.3	7.9	7.7	34 982	728	44 512	712
1992	7 153	100.0	3.8	8.0	8.9	17.2	13.5	16.9	16.5	8.3	6.9	33 976	702	43 336	681
1993	7 362	100.0	3.6	7.9	10.1	16.6	13.6	17.9	15.0	8.1	7.3	33 580	675	44 446	935
1994	7 735	100.0	3.7	8.3	10.3	16.1	13.8	15.8	16.4	7.6	8.1	33 647	625	45 371	1 132
1995	7 939	100.0	4.1	8.2	9.8	17.0	14.3	16.6	14.9	8.0	6.9	32 069	699	43 770	982
1996	8 225	100.0	3.5	8.1	8.0	17.7	14.7	15.3	16.3	8.2	8.1	34 033	660	46 467	1 075
1997	8 590	100.0	3.7	8.0	8.3	15.3	14.4	15.9	17.5	7.8	9.2	35 617	635	47 996	968
1998	9 060	100.0	4.0	6.5	7.8	15.0	13.9	17.0	17.0	8.9	9.9	37 371	720	50 497	1 074
1999	9 579	100.0	3.1	4.9	7.1	15.3	14.1	16.8	17.9	10.1	10.8	39 730	578	52 192	927
2000	10 034	100.0	2.9	4.9	5.9	14.7	13.1	17.4	19.0	10.8	11.3	41 470	598	54 986	791
2001	10 499	100.0	3.5	4.6	6.8	14.9	12.9	17.9	17.5	10.5	11.4	40 820	518	53 977	682
2002	11 339	100.0	3.8	5.0	6.4	14.9	14.0	17.0	18.1	9.6	11.2	39 618	577	53 722	718
2003	11 693	100.0	4.1	4.8	6.6	15.5	13.5	17.9	17.1	9.4	11.1	38 629	537	52 058	576
2004	12 178	100.0	4.1	5.1	6.8	14.7	14.9	16.2	18.2	9.1	11.0	39 064	547	52 294	639
2005	12 519	100.0	3.7	5.4	6.5	15.2	14.0	17.1	17.9	9.3	11.1	39 668	394	51 988	523
2006	12 973	100.0	3.4	5.1	6.9	14.5	13.4	17.1	18.1	9.4	12.1	40 346	539	54 008	619
2007	13 339	100.0	3.5	5.1	6.9	14.6	13.8	16.4	18.3	10.1	11.2	40 165	540	52 781	556
2008	13 425	100.0	4.0	5.3	7.5	14.6	14.5	16.4	16.9	9.2	11.7	37 913	486	51 572	534

[22]Because Hispanics may be of any race, data in this report for Hispanics overlap with data for racial groups. Hispanic origin was reported by 12.7 percent of White householders who reported only one race, 3.1 percent of Black householders who reported only one race, and 1.4 percent of Asian householders who reported only one race. Data users should exercise caution when interpreting aggregate results for the Hispanic population and for race groups, because these populations consist of many distinct groups that differ in socioeconomic characteristics, culture, and recentness of immigration. Data were first collected for Hispanics in 1972.

Table 13-3. Change in Real Median Household Income During Recessions, 1969 to 2008

(Percent.)

Recessions[1]	Income years	Percent change in real median income
December 1969 to November 1970	1969 to 1971	-1.7
November 1973 to March 1975	1973 to 1975	-5.7
January 1980 to July 1980 and July 1981 to November 1982	1978 to 1983	-6.0
July 1990 to March 1991	1989 to 1991[2]	-3.9
March 2001 to November 2001	1999 to 2002	-3.5
December 2007, trough not yet defined	2007 to 2008	-3.6

[1]Recessions are determined by the National Bureau of Economic Research, a private research organization.
[2]For comparablity purposes, the 1989 median household income used in this calculation ($48,319 in 2008 dollars), is based on data that reflect the implementation of the 1990 decennial census poulation controls.

Table 13-4. Income Distribution Measures Using Money Income and Equivalence-Adjusted Income 2007 and 2008

(Percent distribution.)

Measure	2007				2008				Percent change, 2008 less 2007			
	Money income		Equivalence-adjusted income		Money income		Equivalence-adjusted income		Money income		Equivalence-adjusted income	
	Estimate	90 percent confidence interval[1] (+/-)	Estimate	90 perecnt confidence interval[1] (+/-)	Estimate	90 percent confidence interval[1] (+/-)	Estimate	90 percent confidence interval[1] (+/-)	Estimate	90 percent confidence interval[1] (+/-)	Estimate	90 percent confidence interval[1] (+/-)
Shares of Aggregate Income by Percentile												
Lowest quintile	3.4	0.04	3.7	0.03	3.4	0.04	3.6	0.03	0.0	1.27	-2.7	1.00
Second quintile	8.7	0.10	9.6	0.07	8.6	0.09	9.4	0.07	-1.1	1.23	-2.1	0.87
Middle quintile	14.8	0.16	15.3	0.12	14.7	0.16	15.1	0.11	-0.7	1.23	-1.3	0.85
Fourth quintile	23.4	0.25	22.9	0.17	23.3	0.25	22.9	0.17	-0.4	1.24	0.0	0.85
Highest quintile	49.7	0.54	48.5	0.35	50.0	0.54	49.0	0.36	0.6	1.06	1.0	0.84
Top 5 percent	21.2	0.48	21.1	0.31	21.5	0.49	21.4	0.31	1.4	2.63	1.4	1.70
Summary Measures												
Gini index of income inequality	0.463	0.005	0.445	0.003	0.466	0.005	0.451	0.003	0.600	1.100	1.300	0.720

[1]A 90-percent confidence interval is a measure of an estimate's variability. The larger the confidence interval in relation to the size of the estimate, the less reliable the estimate.

Table 13-5. Two-Year-Average[1] Median Household Income by State, 2005 to 2008

(Income in 2008 dollars, percent.)

| State | 2-year-average | | | | Change in median income (2007–2008 average less 2005–2006 average) | |
| | 2005–2006 | | 2007–2008 | | | |
	Median money income	90 percent confidence interval[2]	Median money income	90 percent confidence interval[2]	Dollars	Percent change
UNITED STATES	51 283	266	51 233	191	-50	-0.1
Alabama	40 751	1 642	44 155	2 119	3 405	8.4
Alaska	60 945	2 072	64 701	2 684	3 756	6.2
Arizona	49 863	1 847	47 972	1 866	-1 891	-3.8
Arkansas	40 001	1 557	40 974	1 755	973	2.4
California	58 078	852	57 445	998	-633	-1.1
Colorado	57 559	2 061	62 217	2 033	4 658	8.1
Connecticut	64 662	2 787	65 644	3 274	983	1.5
Delaware	56 252	2 074	53 695	2 485	-2 558	-4.5
District of Columbia	50 695	2 840	54 162	1 983	3 467	6.8
Florida	48 095	1 063	46 206	988	-1 890	-3.9
Georgia	51 673	1 508	48 369	1 543	-3 304	-6.4
Hawaii	65 146	2 043	64 002	2 515	-1 145	-1.8
Idaho	49 036	1 881	49 247	2 048	211	0.4
Illinois	52 677	1 579	53 889	1 570	1 212	2.3
Indiana	47 647	1 712	47 898	1 682	252	0.5
Iowa	51 339	2 075	50 465	1 895	-875	-1.7
Kansas	47 498	1 642	49 119	2 230	1 621	3.4
Kentucky	41 320	1 429	41 058	1 414	-262	-0.6
Louisiana	40 016	1 995	41 232	1 679	1 216	3.0
Maine	48 592	2 370	48 481	1 951	-111	-0.2
Maryland	67 364	2 256	65 932	2 361	-1 433	-2.1
Massachusetts	60 434	2 811	60 515	2 714	81	0.1
Michigan	51 305	1 379	50 528	1 348	-777	-1.5
Minnesota	59 910	1 806	57 607	2 303	-2 303	-3.8
Mississippi	36 674	2 109	37 579	1 230	905	2.5
Missouri	47 507	1 759	46 906	1 549	-602	-1.3
Montana	42 524	1 391	44 116	2 384	1 592	3.7
Nebraska	52 134	2 154	50 896	1 817	-1 238	-2.4
Nevada	54 500	2 169	55 440	2 774	940	1.7
New Hampshire	64 512	2 596	68 175	3 513	3 663	5.7
New Jersey	71 284	3 115	64 070	2 601	-7 214	-10.1
New Mexico	42 850	2 188	44 081	1 969	1 231	2.9
New York	51 763	1 332	50 643	1 112	-1 120	-2.2
North Carolina	44 441	1 310	44 058	1 330	-384	-0.9
North Dakota	45 184	1 925	49 325	1 702	4 142	9.2
Ohio	48 884	1 256	48 960	1 341	77	0.2
Oklahoma	41 497	2 233	45 494	1 671	3 998	9.6
Oregon	49 495	2 044	51 947	1 881	2 452	5.0
Pennsylvania	51 416	1 183	50 850	1 067	-566	-1.1
Rhode Island	55 980	2 406	54 767	2 927	-1 213	-2.2
South Carolina	43 338	1 870	44 034	1 862	696	1.6
South Dakota	48 051	2 207	49 901	1 304	1 850	3.9
Tennessee	43 458	1 452	41 240	1 602	-2 218	-5.1
Texas	45 966	932	47 157	947	1 191	2.6
Utah	59 395	2 183	59 062	1 890	-333	-0.6
Vermont	55 716	1 890	49 959	1 659	-5 757	-10.3
Virginia	59 126	2 040	61 710	1 936	2 584	4.4
Washington	57 148	1 679	58 472	2 586	1 324	2.3
West Virginia	40 611	1 679	40 851	1 652	240	0.6
Wisconsin	52 223	1 705	52 224	1 310	1	0.0
Wyoming	49 777	2 209	51 977	2 024	2 200	4.4

[1]The 2-year-average median is the sum of two inflation-adjusted single-year medians divided by 2.
[2]A 90-percent confidence interval is a measure of an estimate's variability. The larger the confidence interval in relation to the size of the estimate, the less reliable the estimate.

Table 13-6. Median Family Income in the Past Twelve Months, by the Number of Earners and State, 2008

(Income in 2008 inflation-adjusted dollars.)

State	Total	No earners	1 earner	2 earners	3 or more earners
UNITED STATES	63 366	30 914	43 253	79 462	97 969
Alabama	54 270	25 394	38 415	71 349	90 657
Alaska	79 541	42 041	52 130	90 617	114 142
Arizona	60 547	36 756	42 628	77 750	93 215
Arkansas	47 648	26 333	33 531	63 384	80 730
California	70 029	31 178	48 140	89 164	101 837
Colorado	70 164	36 804	47 253	83 919	99 283
Connecticut	85 344	36 819	58 529	102 185	119 413
Delaware	68 745	41 780	46 414	85 987	108 799
District of Columbia	66 722	15 962	42 270	116 442	104 229
Florida	57 455	35 982	41 226	73 975	91 025
Georgia	60 268	25 934	40 691	77 451	92 727
Hawaii	78 659	39 567	55 418	88 319	113 173
Idaho	54 695	36 382	39 625	64 739	82 018
Illinois	68 958	31 763	46 105	84 101	102 407
Indiana	59 380	30 433	40 828	73 635	91 309
Iowa	61 663	33 733	40 061	72 522	88 522
Kansas	62 462	35 076	41 357	74 953	90 179
Kentucky	51 729	23 993	37 584	70 031	89 485
Louisiana	53 963	23 567	37 464	74 019	94 051
Maine	57 719	27 897	38 812	71 809	87 704
Maryland	84 415	38 895	55 238	101 371	115 789
Massachusetts	81 569	29 827	53 505	98 887	115 622
Michigan	60 615	33 196	43 611	76 942	95 313
Minnesota	71 817	36 713	45 262	83 215	100 697
Mississippi	46 668	19 473	32 068	66 469	81 074
Missouri	58 088	30 654	39 645	72 054	91 931
Montana	56 820	31 938	40 122	66 996	87 613
Nebraska	62 067	32 371	40 352	71 437	89 335
Nevada	64 910	36 008	46 316	78 317	95 949
New Hampshire	76 710	31 460	51 515	88 656	108 896
New Jersey	85 761	36 310	60 026	101 923	124 344
New Mexico	52 172	28 999	36 773	71 357	85 521
New York	67 877	27 891	46 485	87 498	107 946
North Carolina	56 588	28 029	38 794	72 296	86 578
North Dakota	61 109	29 284	36 884	72 664	91 204
Ohio	60 061	30 543	41 873	75 070	93 661
Oklahoma	53 862	28 647	39 068	68 656	81 089
Oregon	61 190	34 469	42 495	74 346	89 402
Pennsylvania	63 316	29 800	44 555	78 899	100 436
Rhode Island	71 992	30 231	45 222	88 736	108 803
South Carolina	55 664	28 157	39 191	73 065	89 087
South Dakota	60 104	31 112	36 844	68 389	85 777
Tennessee	53 799	26 815	37 732	69 008	85 728
Texas	58 765	27 087	38 940	75 978	88 225
Utah	65 226	37 872	50 568	68 498	98 539
Vermont	63 438	31 853	41 742	74 384	91 842
Virginia	73 192	34 477	48 362	89 379	106 667
Washington	70 498	39 245	51 344	84 611	100 202
West Virginia	49 082	26 488	39 275	65 985	84 652
Wisconsin	65 622	34 472	42 356	76 651	96 731
Wyoming	66 504	31 096	44 161	77 765	109 547

Table 13-7. Median Family Income in the Past Twelve Months, by Size of Family and State, 2008

(Income in 2008 inflation-adjusted dollars.)

State	Total	2-person families	3-person families	4-person families	5-person families	6-person families	7-or-more-person families
UNITED STATES	63 366	56 538	64 779	75 782	71 765	66 922	68 146
Alabama	54 270	48 075	55 631	65 311	62 431	57 482	49 656
Alaska	79 541	74 073	77 544	85 422	89 221	94 893	81 200
Arizona	60 547	56 894	62 066	69 452	63 472	57 657	56 663
Arkansas	47 648	44 415	48 721	57 905	49 443	51 465	44 501
California	70 029	64 878	70 890	79 477	68 073	67 499	74 290
Colorado	70 164	64 985	69 977	81 644	73 105	74 100	74 289
Connecticut	85 344	72 586	86 643	102 124	108 055	89 435	89 260
Delaware	68 745	60 953	70 075	88 725	78 364	86 105	69 190
District of Columbia	66 722	68 892	69 294	60 418	82 458	30 253	51 720
Florida	57 455	52 259	58 574	69 009	66 248	63 759	66 941
Georgia	60 268	55 258	61 104	68 502	63 364	64 654	59 212
Hawaii	78 659	67 199	77 539	91 483	86 463	89 544	117 593
Idaho	54 695	51 474	52 765	62 051	58 400	57 479	61 398
Illinois	68 958	60 052	71 329	81 465	76 898	70 010	76 118
Indiana	59 380	52 554	59 650	70 873	69 530	65 006	64 880
Iowa	61 663	55 284	64 372	72 961	71 070	64 788	55 270
Kansas	62 462	57 767	63 438	72 610	70 213	60 738	62 020
Kentucky	51 729	45 653	54 683	64 459	57 596	60 480	60 663
Louisiana	53 963	48 287	53 461	66 256	62 991	59 281	54 074
Maine	57 719	50 912	62 076	70 374	66 259	72 620	62 269
Maryland	84 415	73 061	85 455	101 803	94 750	95 544	97 272
Massachusetts	81 569	69 451	82 591	99 648	96 141	104 012	106 985
Michigan	60 615	52 620	61 737	74 824	73 576	64 639	57 733
Minnesota	71 817	62 384	75 073	86 637	83 506	84 013	66 475
Mississippi	46 668	42 758	46 685	58 518	51 038	44 196	44 760
Missouri	58 088	51 568	60 371	71 059	67 664	67 079	62 052
Montana	56 820	52 497	58 636	65 827	63 701	63 582	59 479
Nebraska	62 067	56 861	63 702	72 542	70 402	70 199	65 345
Nevada	64 910	60 449	67 052	71 104	70 660	61 087	81 426
New Hampshire	76 710	64 204	79 668	93 926	91 560	97 314	90 152
New Jersey	85 761	72 000	86 070	103 261	100 126	100 992	98 415
New Mexico	52 172	50 637	50 630	55 561	60 951	56 930	61 156
New York	67 877	58 109	69 421	82 457	80 515	77 393	78 728
North Carolina	56 588	52 194	56 930	67 295	62 396	57 644	51 448
North Dakota	61 109	54 662	62 635	75 140	73 505	63 750	49 328
Ohio	60 061	52 216	61 772	73 301	71 930	69 136	68 978
Oklahoma	53 862	50 891	54 522	62 037	58 603	55 680	50 884
Oregon	61 190	56 019	62 832	72 667	67 164	62 927	69 807
Pennsylvania	63 316	53 763	67 757	77 867	76 179	71 453	67 571
Rhode Island	71 992	62 806	76 846	87 002	77 853	84 644	74 797
South Carolina	55 664	51 374	55 296	65 655	64 046	60 504	54 201
South Dakota	60 104	54 331	63 153	70 182	66 960	60 732	59 306
Tennessee	53 799	49 110	54 014	64 228	63 052	55 590	56 194
Texas	58 765	55 859	59 222	66 381	58 607	54 391	55 052
Utah	65 226	56 932	61 905	69 990	71 190	80 574	79 855
Vermont	63 438	56 858	65 326	74 163	73 579	77 288	51 141
Virginia	73 192	65 122	74 151	85 939	85 590	75 200	86 963
Washington	70 498	64 158	72 533	82 716	73 804	67 489	72 990
West Virginia	49 082	43 224	51 836	58 479	60 418	58 353	45 281
Wisconsin	65 622	57 405	68 123	80 530	76 261	68 438	61 223
Wyoming	66 504	59 830	65 820	76 964	82 446	68 660	86 135

Chapter Fourteen

OCCUPATIONAL SAFETY AND HEALTH

OCCUPATIONAL SAFETY AND HEALTH

HIGHLIGHTS

This chapter includes data on work-related illnesses and injuries and fatal work injuries from the Injuries, Illnesses, and Fatalities (IIF) program. Data are classified by industry and selected worker characteristics.

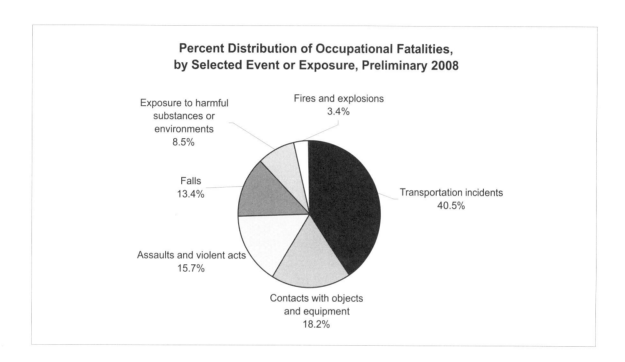

Percent Distribution of Occupational Fatalities, by Selected Event or Exposure, Preliminary 2008

A total of 5,071 fatal occupational injuries were recorded in the United States in 2008, down from 5,657 in 2007. The rate of fatal injuries was 3.6 per 100,000 full-time equivalent workers, down from 4.0 in 2007. Transportation incidents, which continued to account for more of the fatalities than any other event, fell 13 percent from 2007 to 2008. (See Table 14-4.)

OTHER HIGHLIGHTS

- The rate of nonfatal occupational injuries and illnesses declined to 3.9 cases per 100 equivalent full-time workers in 2008, down from 4.2 cases in 2007. Air transportation workers and couriers had the highest rate at 8.7 per 100 equivalent full-time workers, followed by nursing and residential care facilities at 8.4 per 100 equivalent full-time workers. (See Table 14-1.)

- Men accounted for 63.9 percent of all nonfatal occupation injuries and illnesses involving days away from work. (See Table 14-2.)

- Truck drivers who drove tractor trailers or a similar type of vehicle had the highest median number of days away from work at 17, followed by industrial machinery mechanics (15 days), electricians (13 days), and truck drivers who drove light or delivery type vehicles (13 days). (See Table 14-3.)

- While the total number of workplace fatalities declined, the number of fatalities among workers in the agriculture, forestry, fishing, and hunting industry sector rose 11 percent in 2008 after declining in 2007. Fatalities of workers in crop production led the increase, rising 18 percent. (See Table 14-5.)

NOTES AND DEFINITIONS

Collection and Coverage

The Injuries, Illnesses, and Fatalities (IIF) program at the Bureau of Labor Statistics (BLS) provides annual reports on the number of workplace injuries, illnesses, and fatalities. BLS has reported annually on the number of work-related injuries, illnesses, and fatalities since the early 1970s after the Occupational Safety and Health Act of 1970 was passed.

Nonfatal Occupational Injuries and Illnesses

The Survey of Occupational Injuries and Illnesses is a federal-state program in which employer's reports are collected annually from about 176,000 private industry establishments and processed by state agencies cooperating with the BLS. Summary information on the number of injuries and illnesses is copied by these employers directly from their recordkeeping logs to the survey questionnaire. The questionnaire also asks for the number of employee hours worked (needed in the calculation of incidence rates) as well as its average employment (needed to verify the unit's employment-size class).

Occupational injury and illness data for coal, metal, and nonmetal mining and for railroad activities were provided by the Department of Labor's Mine Safety and Health Administration and the Department of Transportation's Federal Railroad Administration. The survey excludes all work-related fatalities as well as nonfatal work injuries and illnesses to the self employed; to workers on farms with 10 or fewer employees; to private household workers; and, nationally, to federal, state, and local government workers.

Injuries and illnesses logged by employers conform with definitions and recordkeeping guidelines set by the Occupational Safety and Health Administration, U.S. Department of Labor. Under those guidelines, nonfatal cases are recordable if they are occupational illnesses or if they are occupational injuries which involve lost worktime, medical treatment other than first aid, restriction of work or motion, loss of consciousness, or transfer to another job. Employers keep counts of injuries separate from illnesses and also identify for each whether a case involved any days away from work or days of restricted work activity, or both, beyond the day of injury or onset of illness.

Occupational injuries, such as sprains, cuts, and fractures, account for the vast majority of all cases that employers log and report to the BLS survey. Occupational illnesses are new cases recognized, diagnosed, and reported during the year. Overwhelmingly, those reported are easier to directly relate to workplace activity (e.g., contact dermatitis or carpal tunnel syndrome) than are long-term latent illnesses, such as cancers. The latter illnesses are believed to be under recorded and, thus, understated in the BLS survey.

Concepts and Definitions

Days away from work are cases that involve days away from work, days of restricted work activity, or both.

The data are presented in the form of *incidence rates*, defined as the number of injuries and illnesses or cases of days away from work per 100 full-time employees. The formula is (N/EH) x 200,000, where N = number of injuries and illnesses or days away from work, EH = total hours worked by all employees during the calendar year, and 200,000 represents the base for 100 full-time equivalent workers (working 40 hours per week, 50 weeks per year).

Median days away from work is a measure used to summarize the varying lengths of absences from work among the cases with days away from work. The median is the point at which half of the cases involved more days away from work and half involved less days away from work.

Occupational illness is an abnormal condition or disorder (other than one resulting from an occupational injury) caused by exposure to environmental factors associated with employment. It includes acute and chronic illnesses and diseases that may have been caused by inhalation, absorption, ingestion, or direct contact. Long-term latent illnesses can be difficult to relate to the workplace and are believed to be understated in this survey.

Occupational injury is any injury—such as a cut, fracture, sprain, or amputation—that results from a work accident or from exposure to an incident in the work environment

Fatal Occupational Injuries

The Bureau of Labor Statistics (BLS) Census of Fatal Occupational Injuries (CFOI) produces comprehensive, accurate, and timely counts of fatal work injuries. CFOI is a federal-state cooperative program that has been implemented in all 50 states and the District of Columbia since 1992. To compile counts that are as complete as possible, the census uses multiple sources to identify, verify, and profile fatal worker injuries. Information about each workplace fatality—occupation and other worker characteristics, equipment involved, and circumstances of the event—is obtained by cross referencing the source records, such as death certificates, workers' compensation reports, and federal and state agency administrative reports. To ensure that fatalities are work-related, cases are substantiated with two or more independent source documents, or a source document and a follow-up questionnaire.

Data compiled by the CFOI program are issued annually for the preceding calendar year. These data are used by safety and health policy analysts and researchers to help prevent fatal work injuries by:

- Informing workers of life threatening hazards associated with various jobs;
- Promoting safer work practices through enhanced job safety training;
- Assessing and improving workplace safety standards; and
- Identifying new areas of safety research.

The National Safety Council has adopted the Census of Fatal Occupational Injuries figure, beginning with the 1992 data year, as the authoritative count for work related deaths in the United States.

Sources of Additional Information

For more extensive definitions and description of collection methods see BLS news release USDL 09-1302, "Workplace Injuries and Illnesses in 2008," for injuries and illnesses; USDL 09-0979, "National Census of Fatal Occupational Injuries in 2008," available on the BLS Web site at <http://www.bls.gov/iif/>.

Table 14-1. Incidence Rates[1] of Nonfatal Occupational Injuries and Illnesses, by Selected Industries and Case Types, 2008

(Number, rate per 100 full-time workers.)

Industry[2]	NAICS code[3]	2008 average annual employment (thousands)[4]	Total recordable cases	Cases with days away from work, job transfer, or restriction			Other recordable cases
				Total	Cases with days away from work[5]	Cases with job transfer or restriction	
PRIVATE INDUSTRY[6]		115 353	3.9	2.0	1.1	0.9	1.9
Goods-Producing[6]		23 012	4.9	2.6	1.4	1.2	2.2
Natural resources and mining[6,7]		1 679	4.1	2.5	1.6	0.9	1.7
Agriculture, forestry, fishing, and hunting[6]	11	992	5.3	2.9	1.8	1.1	2.3
Crop production[6]	111	419	5.3	3.0	1.7	1.3	2.3
Animal production	112	161	6.9	3.5	2.5	1.0	3.3
Forestry and logging	113	64	4.0	2.7	2.3	0.4	1.3
Fishing, hunting and trapping	114	9	3.5	2.3	2.2	. . .	1.2
Support activities for agriculture and forestry	115	338	4.4	2.5	1.4	1.1	1.9
Mining[7]	21	688	2.9	2.0	1.3	0.7	1.0
Oil and gas extraction	211	154	1.4	0.7	0.4	0.4	0.6
Mining (except oil and gas)[8]	212	224	3.5	2.4	1.7	0.6	1.2
Support activities for mining	213	310	3.2	2.2	1.4	0.9	0.9
Construction	23	7 597	4.7	2.5	1.7	0.7	2.2
Construction of buildings	236	1 793	4.0	2.1	1.5	0.6	1.9
Heavy and civil engineering construction	237	1 002	4.2	2.2	1.4	0.8	1.9
Specialty trade contractors	238	4 801	5.1	2.7	1.9	0.8	2.4
Manufacturing	31-33	13 735	5.0	2.7	1.2	1.5	2.3
Food	311	1 490	6.2	4.0	1.4	2.6	2.2
Beverage and tobacco product	312	202	6.8	4.7	2.0	2.7	2.1
Textile mills	313	161	3.6	2.0	0.8	1.1	1.6
Textile product mills	314	147	4.1	2.3	0.9	1.3	1.9
Apparel	315	220	2.6	1.2	0.6	0.5	1.4
Leather and allied product	316	35	5.8	3.2	1.4	1.8	2.5
Wood product	321	490	7.2	3.8	2.0	1.8	3.4
Paper	322	450	3.7	2.0	1.0	1.0	1.7
Printing and related support activities	323	613	3.2	1.8	0.9	0.8	1.5
Petroleum and coal products	324	117	1.9	1.0	0.4	0.6	0.8
Chemical manufacturing	325	882	2.7	1.6	0.8	0.9	1.1
Plastics and rubber products	326	749	5.7	3.2	1.4	1.8	2.5
Nonmetallic mineral product	327	492	5.9	3.5	1.7	1.9	2.4
Primary metal	331	451	7.2	4.1	1.8	2.3	3.1
Fabricated metal product	332	1 560	6.8	3.2	1.6	1.6	3.6
Machinery	333	1 171	5.6	2.6	1.2	1.4	3.0
Computer and electronic product	334	1 265	1.8	0.9	0.4	0.5	0.9
Electrical equipment, appliance, and component	335	430	4.1	2.2	0.9	1.3	1.9
Transportation equipment	336	1 658	6.0	3.1	1.3	1.9	2.9
Furniture and related product	337	507	5.8	3.2	1.4	1.8	2.6
Miscellaneous	339	646	3.6	1.8	0.8	0.9	1.8
Service-Providing		92 341	3.6	1.8	1.1	0.8	1.8
Trade, transportation, and utilities[9]		26 759	4.4	2.6	1.4	1.1	1.9
Wholesale trade	42	6 084	3.7	2.2	1.2	1.0	1.5
Merchant wholesalers, durable goods	423	3 128	3.6	2.0	1.1	0.8	1.6
Merchant wholesalers, nondurable goods	424	2 087	4.7	3.1	1.6	1.5	1.6
Wholesale electronic markets and agents and brokers	425	868	1.9	1.0	0.6	0.4	0.8
Retail trade	44-45	15 762	4.4	2.3	1.2	1.1	2.0
Motor vehicle and parts dealers	441	1 911	4.2	1.7	1.1	0.6	2.4
Furniture and home furnishings stores	442	560	4.1	2.3	1.5	0.9	1.7
Electronics and appliance stores	443	567	2.0	1.1	0.7	0.4	0.9
Building material and garden equipment and supplies dealers	444	1 294	5.8	3.5	1.5	2.1	2.3
Food and beverage stores	445	2 910	5.7	3.2	1.7	1.5	2.4
Health and personal care stores	446	1 056	2.2	0.8	0.5	0.3	1.3
Gasoline stations	447	869	3.4	1.5	0.9	0.6	1.9
Clothing and clothing accessories stores	448	1 526	2.4	0.8	0.6	0.2	1.6
Sporting goods, hobby, book, and music stores	451	664	3.4	1.2	0.6	0.5	2.3
General merchandise stores	452	3 086	5.7	3.4	1.5	1.9	2.3
Miscellaneous store retailers	453	876	3.2	1.7	0.9	0.7	1.6
Nonstore retailers	454	444	3.3	2.0	0.9	1.1	1.3

Note: Components may not sum to totals because of rounding.

[1] The incidence rates represent the number of injuries and illnesses per 100 full-time workers and were calculated as: (N/EH) x 200,000 (where N = number of injuries and illnesses; EH = total hours worked by all employees during the calendar year; 200,000 = base for 100 equivalent full-time workers working 40 hours per week, 50 weeks per year).
[2] Totals include data for industries not shown separately.
[3] North American Industry Classification System—United States, 2002.
[4] Employment is expressed as an average annual value and is derived primarily from the Bureau of Labor Statistics's (BLS) Quarterly Census of Employment and Wages (QCEW) program.
[5] Days away from work cases include those that result in days away from work with or without job transfer or restriction.
[6] Excludes farms with fewer than 11 employees.
[7] Data for mining include establishments not governed by the Department of Labor's Mine Safety and Health Administration (MSHA) rules and reporting, such as those in oil and gas extraction and related support activities. Data for mining operators in coal, metal, and nonmetal mining are provided to BLS by MSHA. Independent mining contractors are excluded from the coal, metal, and nonmetal mining industries. These data do not reflect the changes the Occupational Safety and Health Administration (OSHA) made to its record-keeping requirements effective January 1, 2002; thus, estimates for these industries are not comparable to estimates in other industries.
[8] Data for mining operators in this industry are provided to BLS by MSHA. Independent mining contractors are excluded. These data do not reflect the changes OSHA made to its record-keeping requirements effective January 1, 2002; thus, estimates for these industries are not comparable to estimates in other industries.
[9] Data for employers in rail transportation are provided to BLS by the Department of Transportation's Federal Railroad Administration (FRA).
. . . = Not available.

Table 14-1. Incidence Rates[1] of Nonfatal Occupational Injuries and Illnesses, by Selected Industries and Case Types, 2008—*Continued*

(Number, rate per 100 full-time workers.)

Industry[2]	NAICS code[3]	2008 average annual employment (thousands)[4]	Total recordable cases	Cases with days away from work, job transfer, or restriction			Other recordable cases
				Total	Cases with days away from work[5]	Cases with job transfer or restriction	
Service-Providing—*Continued*							
Transportation and warehousing	48-49	4 352	5.7	3.9	2.5	1.4	1.8
Air transportation	481	499	8.7	6.8	4.7	2.1	1.9
Rail transportation[9]	482	. . .	2.2	1.6	1.4	0.2	0.6
Water transportation	483	66	3.0	1.7	1.2	0.5	1.3
Truck transportation	484	1 438	5.2	3.3	2.5	0.9	1.8
Transit and ground passenger transportation	485	414	5.2	3.1	2.3	0.8	2.1
Pipeline transportation	486	40	1.6	0.9	0.5	0.3	0.8
Scenic and sightseeing transportation	487	30	3.6	1.8	1.4	0.4	1.8
Support activities for transportation	488	597	4.0	2.6	1.6	0.9	1.5
Couriers and messengers	492	581	8.7	5.9	3.2	2.6	2.9
Warehousing and storage	493	681	6.8	4.8	2.0	2.9	2.0
Utilities	22	561	3.5	1.9	1.1	0.8	1.6
Information	51	2 904	2.0	1.1	0.7	0.4	0.9
Publishing industries (except Internet)	511	898	1.6	0.8	0.5	0.3	0.8
Motion picture and sound recording industries	512	388	2.6	0.9	0.6	0.3	1.7
Broadcasting (except Internet)	515	333	1.9	1.0	0.6	0.4	0.9
Telecommunications	517	847	2.6	1.7	1.1	0.6	0.9
Internet service providers, Web search portals, and data processing services	518	346	1.0	0.5	0.3	0.1	0.6
Other information services	519	54	1.9	1.2	0.9	0.4	0.7
Financial activities		8 133	1.5	0.7	0.5	0.2	0.8
Finance and insurance	52	6 012	0.9	0.3	0.2	0.1	0.6
Monetary authorities—central bank	521	22	1.3	0.6	0.4	0.2	0.7
Credit intermediation and related activities	522	2 827	1.1	0.4	0.3	0.1	0.7
Securities, commodity contracts, and other financial investments and related activities	523	884	. . .	0.1	0.1	([10])	0.2
Insurance carriers and related activities	524	2 183	0.9	0.3	0.2	0.1	0.6
Funds, trusts, and other financial vehicles	525	96	0.6	0.3	0.2	0.1	0.3
Real estate and rental and leasing	53	2 120	3.1	1.8	1.2	0.6	1.4
Real estate	531	1 457	2.7	1.5	1.1	0.4	1.2
Rental and leasing services	532	635	4.1	2.4	1.4	1.0	1.8
Lessors of nonfinancial intangible assets (except copyrighted works)	533	28	0.6	0.2	0.2	. . .	0.4
Professional and business services		18 141	1.9	1.0	0.6	0.3	0.9
Professional, scientific, and technical services	54	7 946	1.1	0.5	0.3	0.2	0.7
Management of companies and enterprises	55	1 912	1.6	0.7	0.4	0.3	0.9
Administrative and support and waste management and remediation services	56	8 284	3.1	1.8	1.2	0.6	1.4
Administrative and support services		7 922	2.9	1.6	1.1	0.6	1.3
Waste management and remediation services	562	362	5.5	3.2	2.0	1.2	2.4
Education and health services		17 914	5.0	2.3	1.3	1.0	2.7
Education services	61	2 376	2.3	1.0	0.7	0.3	1.4
Health care and social assistance	62	15 538	5.4	2.5	1.4	1.1	2.9
Ambulatory health care services	621	5 643	2.7	1.0	0.7	0.3	1.8
Hospitals	622	4 549	7.6	3.0	1.7	1.3	4.6
Nursing and residential care facilities		2 993	8.4	5.0	2.5	2.5	3.4
Social assistance	624	2 354	3.5	1.8	1.3	0.6	1.7
Leisure and hospitality		13 835	4.2	1.6	1.0	0.7	2.6
Arts, entertainment, and recreation	71	2 129	5.1	2.4	1.2	1.1	2.7
Performing arts, spectator sports, and related industries	711	422	6.1	2.7	1.3	1.4	3.4
Museums, historical sites, and similar institutions	712	131	4.7	2.3	1.2	1.1	2.4
Amusement, gambling, and recreation industries	713	1 576	4.9	2.3	1.2	1.1	2.6
Accommodation and food services	72	11 706	4.1	1.5	0.9	0.6	2.6
Accommodation	721	1 938	5.6	2.8	1.5	1.3	2.9
Food services and drinking places	722	9 768	3.7	1.2	0.8	0.4	2.5
Other services		4 655	3.1	1.5	1.0	0.5	1.6
Other services, except public administration	81	4 655	3.1	1.5	1.0	0.5	1.6
Repair and maintenance	811	1 264	3.8	1.9	1.4	0.5	1.9
Personal and laundry services	812	1 346	2.8	1.5	0.8	0.7	1.4
Religious, grantmaking, civic, professional, and similar organizations	813	1 362	2.4	1.0	0.7	0.3	1.4

Note: Components may not sum to totals because of rounding.

[1]The incidence rates represent the number of injuries and illnesses per 100 full-time workers and were calculated as: (N/EH) x 200,000 (where N = number of injuries and illnesses; EH = total hours worked by all employees during the calendar year; 200,000 = base for 100 equivalent full-time workers working 40 hours per week, 50 weeks per year).
[2]Totals include data for industries not shown separately.
[3]North American Industry Classification System—United States, 2002.
[4]Employment is expressed as an average annual value and is derived primarily from the Bureau of Labor Statistics's (BLS) Quarterly Census of Employment and Wages (QCEW) program.
[5]Days away from work cases include those that result in days away from work with or without job transfer or restriction.
[9]Data for employers in rail transportation are provided to BLS by the Department of Transportation's Federal Railroad Administration (FRA).
[10]Data too small to be displayed.
. . . = Not available.

Table 14-2. Number of Nonfatal Occupational Injuries and Illnesses Involving Days Away from Work,[1] by Selected Worker Characteristics and Private Industry, 2008

(Number.)

Characteristic	Total private[2]	Goods-producing[2]			
		All goods-producing	Natural resources and mining[3]	Construction	Manufacturing
TOTAL CASES	1 078 140	311 890	26 710	120 240	164 940
Sex					
Men	688 790	269 780	23 760	117 240	128 780
Women	384 930	41 820	2 820	2 980	36 020
Age[4]					
14 to 15 years	130	20	. . .	. . .	. . .
16 to 19 years	31 010	6 370	840	2 410	3 110
20 to 24 years	107 880	31 530	3 780	13 540	14 210
25 to 34 years	239 580	77 440	7 690	35 940	33 800
35 to 44 years	251 490	77 350	5 530	31 260	40 560
45 to 54 years	261 030	74 630	5 350	25 090	44 190
55 to 64 years	142 840	35 540	2 630	9 710	23 200
65 years and over	28 420	5 230	420	1 010	3 800
Length of Service with Employer					
Less than 3 months	117 130	38 170	5 340	17 350	15 480
3 to 11 months	218 510	60 690	6 640	26 590	27 460
1 to 5 years	388 160	111 660	8 720	46 380	56 560
More than 5 years	338 320	98 240	5 550	28 840	63 860
Race and Hispanic Origin					
White only	464 500	159 960	8 600	66 810	84 550
Black only	83 970	18 040	410	4 850	12 770
Hispanic only[5]	145 870	59 550	9 110	25 360	25 090
Asian only	15 090	3 690	100	560	3 040
Native Hawaiian or Pacific Islander only	2 920	690	40	310	350
American Indian or Alaskan Native only	4 230	1 430	180	650	610
Hispanic[5] and other race	930	350	70	150	130
Multiple races	760	220	. . .	70	130
Not reported	359 870	67 980	8 200	21 480	38 300

Characteristic	Service-providing							
	All service-providing	Trade, transportation, and utilities[6]	Information	Financial activities	Professional and business services	Education and health services	Leisure and hospitality	Other services
TOTAL CASES	766 250	328 220	18 070	35 010	85 540	182 750	86 190	30 470
Sex								
Men	419 010	229 630	12 980	19 480	56 080	36 650	42 040	22 160
Women	343 100	95 070	5 090	15 530	29 040	145 980	44 110	8 280
Age[4]								
14 to 15 years	110	40	. . .	. . .	. . .	. . .	50	. . .
16 to 19 years	24 640	10 780	320	490	1 660	2 770	7 800	820
20 to 24 years	76 360	34 510	900	2 820	8 910	15 670	10 500	3 050
25 to 34 years	162 150	66 800	3 670	7 050	19 920	36 710	19 840	8 160
35 to 44 years	174 150	74 590	5 340	7 730	20 800	40 830	17 930	6 920
45 to 54 years	186 400	80 690	4 560	10 080	18 580	48 450	16 870	7 160
55 to 64 years	107 300	45 650	2 360	4 990	11 090	30 230	9 410	3 570
65 years and over	23 190	10 710	430	1 670	1 890	5 800	2 160	510
Length of Service with Employer								
Less than 3 months	78 970	31 650	1 020	3 750	11 670	14 130	13 570	3 180
3 to 11 months	157 820	63 680	2 240	7 520	20 470	35 610	21 930	6 370
1 to 5 years	276 510	116 670	4 760	12 480	29 900	69 800	31 960	10 940
More than 5 years	240 070	109 010	9 540	11 100	21 630	61 370	17 590	9 840
Race and Hispanic Origin								
White only	304 540	127 830	5 580	14 580	32 360	76 690	30 830	16 680
Black only	65 930	18 800	870	2 810	7 830	26 560	7 270	1 790
Hispanic only[5]	86 320	31 810	810	5 310	16 860	14 730	12 850	3 960
Asian only	11 400	2 720	160	330	1 200	3 450	3 170	360
Native Hawaiian or Pacific Islander only	2 230	780	60	110	240	540	470	30
American Indian or Alaskan Native only	2 800	1 040	50	180	120	690	680	50
Hispanic[5] and other race	580	60	. . .	. . .	30	60	420	. . .
Multiple races	550	190	. . .	. . .	. . .	150	170	. . .
Not reported	291 890	144 990	10 530	11 690	26 910	59 880	30 330	7 570

Note: Components may not sum to totals because of rounding.

[1]Days away from work cases include those that result in days away from work with or without restricted work activity.
[2]Excludes farms with fewer than 11 employees.
[3]Data for mining include establishments not governed by the Department of Labor's Mine Safety and Health Administration (MSHA) rules and reporting, such as those in oil and gas extraction and related support activities. Data for mining operators in coal, metal, and nonmetal mining are provided to the Bureau of Labor Statistics (BLS) by MSHA. Independent mining contractors are excluded from the coal, metal, and nonmetal mining industries. These data do not reflect the changes the Occupational Safety and Health Administration (OSHA) made to its record-keeping requirements effective January 1, 2002; thus, estimates for these industries are not comparable to estimates in other industries.
[4]Data are not shown separately for injured workers under 14 years of age; these workers accounted for fewer than 50 cases.
[5]May be of any race.
[6]Data for employers in rail transportation are provided to BLS by the Department of Transportation's Federal Railroad Administration (FRA).
. . . = Not available.

Table 14-3. Number and Percent Distribution of Nonfatal Occupational Injuries and Illnesses Involving Days Away from Work[1] by Selected Occupation and Number of Days Away from Work, Private Industry, 2008

(Number, percent.)

Occupation	Total number of cases	Percent of days away from work cases involving:								Median days away from work
		Total	1 day	2 days	3 to 5 days	6 to 10 days	11 to 20 days	21 to 30 days	31 days or more	
TOTAL	1 078 140	100.0	14.9	11.0	17.8	11.9	11.7	6.8	26.0	8
Labor and freight, stock, and material movers, hand	79 590	100.0	15.4	10.2	18.1	11.3	11.7	7.2	26.1	8
Truck drivers, heavy and tractor-trailer	57 700	100.0	9.0	6.8	14.8	11.6	11.2	7.2	39.4	17
Nursing aides, orderlies, and attendants	44 610	100.0	15.3	13.9	22.7	14.7	10.3	5.3	17.9	5
Construction laborers	31 310	100.0	13.8	9.5	16.9	13.2	11.9	6.6	28.0	9
Retail salespersons	28 900	100.0	12.5	11.1	19.8	12.5	11.3	6.9	25.8	8
Janitors and cleaners, except maids and housekeeping cleaners	28 110	100.0	15.4	11.1	18.7	12.8	11.7	6.0	24.4	7
Truck drivers, light or delivery services	28 040	100.0	9.2	8.1	16.0	12.5	11.5	7.3	35.3	13
Maintenance and repair workers, general	20 800	100.0	15.6	13.7	16.6	9.6	11.3	6.0	27.1	7
Registered nurses	19 070	100.0	15.8	11.7	22.3	12.3	11.2	6.3	20.2	6
Maids and housekeeping cleaners	18 650	100.0	13.7	10.9	22.2	12.9	10.5	6.8	23.1	7
Carpenters	18 160	100.0	14.0	11.2	15.5	10.8	10.0	5.9	32.5	10
Stock clerks and order fillers	18 020	100.0	16.4	11.5	19.0	13.3	10.4	6.6	23.0	7
First line supervisors/mangers of retail sales workers	15 310	100.0	10.1	13.1	20.1	12.5	8.6	6.5	29.3	7
Automotive service technicians and mechanics	14 440	100.0	20.8	15.3	15.4	12.0	7.3	10.1	19.1	5
Landscaping and groundskeeping workers	13 500	100.0	11.9	8.4	17.9	13.8	13.3	10.9	23.8	10
Cashiers	12 360	100.0	14.5	12.5	18.2	14.1	14.8	5.7	20.1	7
Combined food preparation and serving workers, including fast food	12 280	100.0	16.5	14.9	20.1	8.3	16.6	5.0	18.5	5
Welders, cutters, solderers, and brazers	10 870	100.0	18.8	13.2	16.3	9.2	10.1	6.9	25.5	6
Electricians	10 320	100.0	17.7	8.0	14.9	6.9	10.5	8.0	33.7	13
Customer service representatives	10 120	100.0	17.6	8.8	15.0	10.5	14.9	5.5	27.7	9
Plumbers, pipefitters, and steamfitters	9 230	100.0	16.0	9.6	18.9	8.9	14.2	6.5	26.0	10
Cooks, restaurant	9 160	100.0	17.2	11.9	24.0	17.0	16.5	4.0	9.3	5
Security guards	8 270	100.0	13.4	10.5	16.2	10.9	16.9	6.3	25.9	10
Home health aides	8 120	100.0	8.1	8.1	17.7	15.3	10.6	8.5	31.8	11
Food preparation workers	8 000	100.0	22.4	11.6	19.6	13.4	15.0	3.8	14.2	5
Waiters and waitresses	7 970	100.0	20.6	9.5	14.1	13.3	10.3	10.5	21.7	7
Industrial machinery mechanics	7 820	100.0	13.0	10.4	11.0	8.4	12.1	13.9	31.1	15

Note: Percentages may not sum to 100 because of rounding.

[1]Days away from work cases include those that result in days away from work with or without restricted work activity.

Table 14-4. Fatal Occupational Injuries, by Selected Worker Characteristics and Selected Event or Exposure, Preliminary 2008

(Number, percent.)

Characteristic	Fatalities		Selected event or exposure[1] (percent of total for characteristic category)			
	Number	Percent	Highway[2]	Homicides	Falls	Struck by object
TOTAL	5 071	100	23	10	13	10
Employee Status						
Wage and salary workers[3]	4 071	80	25	9	14	9
Self-employed[4]	1 000	20	12	14	11	15
Sex						
Men	4 703	93	22	9	14	11
Women	368	7	28	26	11	3
Age[5]						
Under 16 years	11	([6])	. . .	. . .	. . .	. . .
16 to 17 years	23	([6])	30	13	. . .	. . .
18 to 19 years	63	1	25	16	8	8
20 to 24 years	339	7	20	9	11	11
25 to 34 years	840	17	24	12	10	11
35 to 44 years	1 084	21	24	12	12	9
45 to 54 years	1 257	25	23	9	14	9
55 to 64 years	887	17	25	8	15	11
65 years and over	559	11	17	7	21	12
Race and Hispanic Origin						
White	3 560	70	23	7	13	11
Black	514	10	28	23	7	8
Hispanic[7]	774	15	18	11	20	10
American Indian or Alaskan Native	30	1	40	. . .	. . .	10
Asian	131	3	12	35	11	5
Native Hawaiian or Pacific Islander	6	([6])	50	. . .	. . .	. . .
Multiple races	6	([6])	. . .	. . .	. . .	. . .
Other or not reported	50	1	20	16	8	. . .

Note: Totals for 2008 are preliminary. Totals for major categories may include subcategories not shown separately. Components may not sum to totals because of rounding.

[1]The figure shown is the percentage of the total fatalities for that demographic group.
[2]"Highway" includes deaths to vehicle occupants resulting from traffic incidents that occur on the public roadway, shoulder, or surrounding area. It excludes incidents occurring entirely off the roadway, such as in parking lots or on farms; incidents involving trains; and deaths of pedestrians or other non-passengers.
[3]May include volunteers and other workers receiving compensation.
[4]Includes self-employed workers, owners of unincorporated businesses and farms, paid and unpaid family workers, and members of partnerships; may also include owners of incorporated businesses.
[5]There were eight fatalities for which there was insufficient information to determine the age of the decedent.
[6]Less than or equal to 0.5 percent.
[7]May be of any race.
. . . = Not available.

Table 14-5. Fatal Occupational Injuries, by Occupation and Selected Event or Exposure, Preliminary 2008

(Number, percent.)

Occupation[1]	Fatalities		Selected event or exposure (percent of total for characteristic category)[2]			
	Number	Percent	Highway[3]	Homicide	Falls	Struck by object
TOTAL	5 071	100	23	10	13	10
Management	538	11	10	9	10	14
Top executives	28	1	11	21	...	...
Operations specialties managers	23	(⁴)	22	17	...	...
Other management	480	9	9	8	10	15
Business and financial operations	24	(⁴)	46	...	12	...
Computer and mathematical	7	(⁴)	...	...	...	...
Architecture and engineering	39	1	49	...	18	...
Engineers	29	1	41	...	24	...
Life, physical, and social science	22	(⁴)	18	...	...	...
Community and social services	31	1	52	13	13	...
Legal	15	(⁴)	33	20	...	...
Education, training, and library	25	(⁴)	28	...	...	...
Arts, design, entertainment, sports, and media	55	1	16	22	13	...
Entertainers and performers, sports and related workers	28	1	...	...	14	...
Health care practitioners and technical	60	1	10	8	5	...
Health diagnosing and treating practitioners	36	1	11	8	...	...
Health technologists and technicians	23	(⁴)	...	...	13	...
Health care support	18	(⁴)	44	...	...	...
Protective service	300	6	27	31	5	3
Fire fighting and prevention workers	44	1	25	...	...	...
Law enforcement workers	144	3	38	33	3	2
Other protective service workers	81	2	5	46	7	...
Food preparation and serving related	65	1	8	54	9	...
Supervisors, food preparation and serving workers	24	(⁴)	12	62	...	...
Building and grounds cleaning and maintenance	227	4	12	6	23	15
Building cleaning and pest control workers	64	1	20	17	31	...
Grounds maintenance workers	128	3	9	...	20	20
Personal care and service	53	1	13	25	9	...
Sales and related	266	5	17	49	6	6
Supervisors, sales workers	124	2	8	52	6	9
Retail sales workers	90	2	8	58	6	6
Sales representatives, services	12	(⁴)	42	33	...	...
Sales representatives, wholesale and manufacturing	16	(⁴)	94	...	...	...
Office and administrative support	88	2	35	27	15	...
Material recording, scheduling, dispatching, and distributing workers	39	1	64	8	10	...
Farming, fishing, and forestry	274	5	11	3	2	27
Agricultural workers	133	3	19	4	4	8
Fishing and hunting workers	50	1	...	...	...	...
Forest, conservation, and logging workers	82	2	...	...	...	73
Construction and extraction	966	19	10	1	32	12
Supervisors, construction and extraction workers	108	2	14	3	24	15
Construction trades workers	720	14	9	1	37	10
Extraction workers	81	2	14	...	9	25
Installation, maintenance, and repair	345	7	11	3	19	17
Vehicle and mobile equipment mechanics, installers, and repairers	110	2	11	3	5	30
Other installation, maintenance, and repair	187	4	11	3	25	11
Production	261	5	3	6	10	12
Supervisors, production workers	34	1	...	9	...	9
Metal workers and plastic workers	102	2	3	6	13	15
Transportation and material moving	1 330	26	47	6	6	7
Air transportation workers	91	2	...	...	...	...
Motor vehicle operators	908	18	66	6	4	6
Water transportation workers	35	1	...	...	...	11
Material moving workers	248	5	9	6	12	14
Military	53	1	8	...	6	...

Note: Totals for 2007 are preliminary. Totals for major categories may include subcategories not shown separately. Components may not sum to totals because of rounding. There were three fatalities for which there was insufficient information to determine a specific occupation classification.

[1]Based on the 2000 Standard Occupational Classification (SOC) system.
[2]The figure shown is the percentage of total fatalities for that occupation group.
[3]"Highway" includes deaths to vehicle occupants resulting from traffic incidents that occur on the public roadway, shoulder, or surrounding area. It excludes incidents occurring entirely off the roadway, such as in parking lots or on farms; incidents involving trains; and deaths of pedestrians or other non-passengers.
[4]Less than or equal to 0.5 percent.
... = Not available.

INDEX